Taxation in the Republic of Ireland

2011

Taxation in the Republic of Ireland

2011

Amanda-Jayne Comyn
Barrister-at-Law, AITI, TEP

from an original text by
Eric L Harvey FCA AITI

Bloomsbury Professional

Published by
Bloomsbury Professional
Maxwelton House
41–43 Boltro Road
Haywards Heath
West Sussex
RH16 1BJ

Bloomsbury Professional
Fitzwilliam Business Centre
26 Upper Pembroke Street
Dublin 2

ISBN 978 1 84766 689 5

British Library Cataloguing-in-Publication Data
A catalogue record for this book is available from the British Library

Typeset by Marie Armah-Kwantreng, Dublin, Ireland
Printed in Great Britain by
CPI William Clowes, Beccles NR34 7TL

About This Book

The Finance Act 2011 has seen modifications across all heads of tax. This book reflects the adjustments to the tax system brought about by each section of the Finance Act as they apply to each tax head. An overview of the main changes is as follows:

*   adjustments to standard rate tax bands and personal tax credits;
*   introduction of the new Universal Social Charge together with the abolition of PRSI and Levies;
*   changes to tax based property shelters;
*   changes to pension legislation including: new maximum draw downs, minimum amounts that have to be transferred to AMRFs and maximum contributions to personal pensions;
*   changes to BES and Seed Capital Schemes including the simplification and extension of same;
*   changes to RCT including a reduced rate of 20%;
*   adjustment to the conditions attaching to the start-up company relief;
*   changes to the R&D credit system;
*   abolition of all stamp duty property related reliefs;
*   CAT reduction of tax free thresholds;
*   anti-avoidance legislation with particular focus on trusts.

The second Finance Act in 2011, Finance (No 2) Act 2011 gives effect to the taxation measures announced in the Jobs Initiative on 10 May. There were a small but important number of changes to the tax code. The changes introduced were as follows:

*   section 1 makes three amendments to the Taxes Consolidation Act 1997, s 766B, primarily for the purpose of enhancing the flexibility for accounting for the R&D tax credit on an 'above-the-line' basis.
*   section 2 relates to Air Travel Tax and amends the Finance (No 2) Act 2008, s 55 to empower the Minister for Finance to appoint, by order, a day on or after which passenger departures would not be subject to the tax.
*   section 3 amends the Value-Added Tax Consolidation Act 2010 to provide for a second reduced VAT rate of 9%, in respect of certain goods and services, for the period 1 July 2011 to 31 December 2013. The amendment provides that the 9% rate will apply mainly to restaurant and catering services, hotel and holiday accommodation, admissions to cinemas, theatres, certain musical performances, museums and art gallery exhibitions, fairgrounds or amusement park services, the use of sporting facilities, hairdressing services, printed matter such as brochures, maps, programmes, leaflets, catalogues, magazines and newspapers.
*   section 4 provides for the levy on pension schemes announced in the Jobs Initiative. It inserts a the Stamp Duties Consolidation Act 1999, s 125B which imposes an annual stamp duty of 0.6% on the market value of assets under

management in pension schemes approved by the Revenue Commissioners under Irish tax legislation.

The Finance (No 3) Bill 2011 proposes to introduce the necessary amendments to the tax legislation required following the Civil Partnership and Certain Rights and Obligations of Cohabitants Act 2010 (the 'Civil Partnership Act'). The effect of the Civil Partnership Act was to grant rights to civil partners similar to married couples. The Act also provides a mechanism for financially dependent cohabitees to apply to court for redress following the breakdown of a cohabiting relationship or on the death of the cohabitee ('the Redress Scheme').

The measures in the Bill effectively provides civil partners and their children with the same tax reliefs and exemptions which a married couple and their children enjoy.

There are several minor provisions where civil partners are not on an equal footing to married couples, however these are likely to be an oversight in the drafting of the Bill and will, most likely, be rectified prior to the enactment of the legislation.

The tax status of cohabiting couples has remained largely unchanged save in relation to the introduction of a number of exemptions for payments and transfers of property ordered by a court under the Redress Scheme. However if a transfer does not arise under this scheme, ie a couple voluntarily agree to transfer property between themselves rather than going to court, such a transfer will be liable to gift or inheritance tax in full and the new exemptions will not apply. Similarly, there has been no provision made for inheritances between cohabitees. As it stands, regardless of the provisions of a cohabitee's will, a cohabitee may only receive tax relief on any inheritance from their former cohabitee if they apply to court under the Redress Scheme. Therefore, where cohabiting couples are considering making provision for one another, either during their lifetime or as part of their succession planning, the most tax-efficient manner of doing so will be to apply to the courts under the Redress Scheme.

The Finance (No 3) Bill does not affect the normal taxing procedures. In the next edition of this book, there will be a chapter dedicated to setting out the changes once this Bill is enacted. The enactment of this Bill is not expected until later this year.

This edition could not have happened without the patience and assistance provided by Amy Hayes at Bloomsbury Professional.

Please note that this book is intended as a general guide to taxation law and practice in Ireland.

The author does not accept any responsibility for any loss or damage to any person by reason of reliance upon the contents of this publication nor for any loss or damage suffered by any person acting or refraining from acting as a result of the material in this publication.

Professional advice should always be sought before acting on any topic covered in this publication.

Contents

The following subjects are in the same alphabetical order in the book.

Abbreviations and References

References throughout the book are to legislation of the Republic of Ireland and numbered sections and schedules are from the Taxes Consolidation Act 1997 unless otherwise stated.

ABBREVIATIONS

ACT	=	Advance Corporation Tax.
Art	=	Article.
CAT, CATA	=	Capital Acquisitions Tax (Act 1976).
CATCA	=	Capital Acquisitions Tax Consolidation Act 2003.
CGT, CGTA 1975	=	Capital Gains Tax (Act 1975).
CGT(A)A 1978	=	Capital Gains Tax (Amendment) Act 1978.
CT, CTA 1976	=	Corporation Tax (Act 1976).
DTR	=	Double taxation relief.
EC	=	European Communities.
EEC	=	European Economic Community.
EU	=	European Union.
FA	=	Finance Act.
F(MP)A 1968	=	Finance (Miscellaneous Provisions) Act 1968.
F(Mines)A 1974	=	Finance (Taxation of Profits of Certain Mines) Act 1974.
FY	=	Financial year.
HC	=	High Court.
IT, ITA 1967	=	Income Tax (Act 1967).
KB(I)	=	King's Bench Division of the High Court of Justice in Ireland.
NI	=	Northern Ireland.
PRSI	=	Pay-Related Social Insurance.
q.v.	=	quod vide (= which see).
RI	=	Republic of Ireland.
RPT	=	Residential Property Tax.
s	=	section.
SC	=	Supreme Court.
Sch	=	Schedule.
Sec	=	Section of the Taxes Consolidation Act 1997.
Sp C	=	Special Commissioners.
TCA	=	Taxes Consolidation Act 1997.
UK	=	United Kingdom (including Northern Ireland).
VAT, VATA	=	Value-Added Tax (Act 1972).

VAT(A)A	=	Value-Added Tax (Amendment) Act 1978.
VATCA	=	Value-Added Tax Consolidation Act 2010

LAW REPORTS

All ER	=	All England Law Reports (LexisNexis UK, Halsbury House, 35 Chancery Lane, London WC2A 1EL).
ATC	=	Annotated Tax Cases (Sweet & Maxwell Group, 100 Avenue Road, London NW3 3PF).
ILRM	=	Irish Law Reports Monthly (Thomson Round Hall, 43 Fitzwilliam Place, Dublin 2).
IR	=	Irish Reports (Incorporated Council of Law Reporting for Ireland, 3rd Floor Aras U' Dhalaigh, Inns Quay, Dublin 7).
ITC	=	Irish Tax Cases (Postal trade section, 4–5 Harcourt Road, Dublin 2).
ITR	=	Irish Tax Reports (Bloomsbury Professional, Fitzwilliam Business Centre, 26 Upper Pembroke St, Dublin 2).
SSCD	=	Simon's Special Commissioners' Decisions (LexisNexis UK, as above).
TC	=	Official Reports of UK Tax Cases (HMSO, PO Box 29, Norwich NR3 1GN).
TL	=	Tax Case Leaflets (as for ITC above).

1 Administration and General

1.1 The Republic adopted UK tax law (with a few modifications) up to, and including, the *FA 1922* and so the two tax codes are broadly similar but with substantial divergences arising in subsequent Finance Acts. The *Income Tax Act 1967* consolidated the legislation relating to income tax and surtax. Surtax was abolished from 6 April 1974 onwards [*FA 1974, s 10*] and replaced by higher rates of tax in a new unified tax system, see **2.2** 'Allowances, credits and rates'. Companies were charged to corporation tax under the *Corporation Tax Act 1976*; before that Act they were charged to income tax and corporation profits tax. Value-added tax was enacted in 1972, wealth tax and capital gains tax in 1975, and capital acquisitions tax in 1976. Wealth tax was suspended from 5 April 1978 onwards. Youth employment and income levies were introduced from 1982/83 and 1983/84 respectively, the latter ceasing after 1985/86 apart from a brief reappearance in 1993/94. Advance corporation tax applied to most distributions after 8 February 1983 and before 6 April 1999, from which date a dividend withholding tax is introduced. Residential property tax was first imposed in respect of property value on 5 April 1983 and abolished after 5 April 1996. Farm Tax was introduced by the *Farm Tax Act 1985* with effect from 6 October 1986, and its proposed repeal was announced in the 1987 Budget Statement, making the tax applicable for one year only. The income tax, corporation tax and capital gains tax legislation was consolidated in the *TCA 1997*, generally from 6 April 1997. The capital acquisitions tax legislation was consolidated in the *CATCA 2003*. All legislation, regulations, etc can be obtained from Government Publications, Sun Alliance House, Molesworth Street, Dublin 2 or by mail order from Postal trade section, 51 St Stephen's Green, Dublin 2 (tel 01 6476000).

Details of the Revenue On-line Service ('ROS') are available on the Revenue website (see below) and are continually covered in the Revenue Tax Briefing (see also below).

The Revenue website is at www.revenue.ie. It includes *inter alia* an index of the Precedents upon which the Revenue draw in making decisions (www.revenue.ie/services/foi/precednt/topics.htm) and detailed Notes for Guidance on the *Taxes Consolidation Act 1997* (www.revenue.ie/publications/legisltn/itca_03htm), *Finance Acts* and the *CATCA 2003* (www.revenue.ie/pdf/catnfg7.pdf), giving a section-by-section analysis of the provisions of those Acts.

The Revenue publish a quarterly Revenue Tax Briefing containing articles on current tax issues and other information, including an annual Supplement containing a comprehensive list of Revenue publications, including Statements of Practice and information leaflets, and a wide range of Tables and reference charts. These are available on the Revenue's website (as above). The Revenue's Forms and Leaflets Service may be contacted on Dublin 1890 306 706.

For how and when the Revenue switched to use of euro, see Revenue Tax Briefing Issue 46 pp 18–21. The conversion rate is €1 = £0.787564.

1.2 UK High Court decisions before 1923/24 are part of the law adopted by the Republic but subsequent UK cases are not binding on RI Courts although regard is had to them in matters of interpretation where the law is similar.

1.3 As from 1969/70 the former Schs A and B were abolished [*FA 1969, s 65 and Sch 5*] and assessments to income tax are now made under three Schs, C, D and E. [*TCA 1997, ss 17, 18, 19*] Sch D is dealt with under five Cases, I, II, III, IV and V (V replacing Sch A). [*TCA 1997, s 18(2)*] Sch F was added from 6 April 1976. [*TCA 1997, s 20; CTA 1976, s 83*]

1.4 The administration of the Income Tax Acts is in the charge of the Revenue Commissioners [*TCA 1997, s 849*] who are appointed by the Government and form a branch of the Department of Finance. Their address is The Revenue Commissioners, Dublin Castle, Dublin 2. Appeal Commissioners are appointed by the Minister for Finance to hear appeals [*TCA 1997, s 850*] and Inspectors of Taxes, appointed by the Revenue Commissioners, are responsible for making assessments (with a few exceptions) [*TCA 1997, ss 852, 918, 919*] and may grant allowances etc. [*TCA 1997, s 920*] Collection of tax is by the Collector-General and his nominated officers. [*TCA 1997, s 851*]

1.5 Revenue assignments are currently as follows.

Information, Communications, Technology and Logistics	Liam Ryan
Investigations and Prosecutions	Denis Graham
Revenue Solicitor	Marie-Claire Maney
Collector-General	Gerry Harrahill
Customs & Accountant General	Willie Farrell
Border Midlands West Region	Joe Howley
Dublin Region	Niall Cody
East South-East Region	Gerry Howard
Large Cases	Frank Mullen
South-West Region	Tony Buckley

1.6 For general guidance on enquiries, see the Revenue Commissioners' publication 'Guidelines for Practitioners on making enquiries to Revenue Offices' which does, however, note that the enquiry system is not 'a vehicle for debate on arguable issues, advance rulings or assistance in relation to tax planning'. See Revenue Tax Briefing Issue 48 pp 11–14 for guidelines on seeking opinions on tax consequences of certain complex or unusual transactions and Issue 54 p 16.

1.7 The Exchequer financial year (and local authorities' financial year) was changed to the calendar year by *The Exchequer and Local Financial Years Act 1974*. There was a transitional period from 1 April 1974 to 31 December 1974 and 1975 was the first full calendar year for Budget purposes. For tax purposes the year of assessment was changed to the calendar year by *FA 2001, s 77* from 2002, with a short transitional tax year 2001 from 6 April 2001 to 31 December 2001. Previously, years of assessment ran from 6 April to 5 April.

1.8 The Revenue Commissioners may disclose information to authorised persons (as specified) for the purpose of establishing the entitlement of a claimant to relief under the *Rates on Agricultural Land (Relief) Acts 1939–1978* and any subsequent enactment. [*TCA 1997, s 1092*]. Power to disclose information in matters concerning pay-related social welfare benefits is conferred by the *Social Welfare (Pay-related Benefit) Act 1973, s 12*. Information may also be disclosed to the Ombudsman for the purposes of any investigation under the *Ombudsman Act 1980*. [*TCA 1997, s 1093*] The Revenue Commissioners are also required to compile a quarterly list of tax defaulters, for publication in *Iris Oifigiúil*, to be publicised or reproduced as they consider appropriate. *FA 2011, s 76* provides that where the taxpayer agrees the amount of a settlement but does not pay this amount, the settlement amount is to be published regardless. Both conditions must be fulfilled before settlement details can be published.

It also provides that where, in a Revenue audit or investigation, a taxpayer does not agree a settlement amount involving tax, interest and penalties, but:

(i)   liability to tax is determined by the Appeal Commissioners or the Courts

(ii)   a tax geared penalty is determined by the Courts,

these amounts whether paid or not may also be published.

The lists include all persons upon whom a fine, etc was imposed by a court during the year for a tax offence, or with whom a negotiated settlement (including, from 23 March 2000, a settlement in the full amount) in respect of tax, interest and penalties forgone was reached in the year in lieu of initiation of proceedings for such a fine, etc or (from 23 March 2000) following the initiation of such proceedings. Settlements following complete voluntary disclosure, or for a sum not exceeding €12,700/£10,000, or (from 25 March 2002) where the fine, penalty etc did not exceed 15 per cent of the tax, are excluded. For liabilities arising from 1 January 2005, the limit is increased to €30,000 and is to be increased by ministerial order every five years by reference to the Consumer Price Index The list may include such details of the defaults as the Commissioners think fit. The list is extended to customs duties from 25 March 2002. [*TCA 1997, s 1086; FA 1983, s 23; FA 1997, s 158; FA 2000, s 162; FA 2002, s 126; FA 2005, s 143*]

For income, capital gains and corporation tax purposes, the Revenue Commissioners may make use of, or produce in evidence, all documents and information to which they have lawfully had access for the purposes of the *Taxes Acts*. [*TCA 1997, s 872(2)*]

Double Taxation Treaties generally provide for exchange of information between Revenue authorities. In addition, for the purposes of prevention or detection of tax evasion, a statutory framework is in place from 1 January 2003 for exchange of information with territories with which RI does not have a double tax treaty. Since 25 March 2004, the legislation is extended to include gift and inheritance tax and other taxes of a similar nature. [*TCA 1997, s 912A; FA 2003, s 38; FA 2004, s 82*] Provision is made for exchange of information relating to payments of interest to residents of EU Member States through the implementation of Council Directive 2003/48/EC of 3 June 2003 on taxation of savings income in the form of interest payments and related matters with effect from 1 July 2005. [*TCA 1997, s 898B–898R; FA 2004, s 90; SI 286/05*]

1.9 Any records which a person is obliged to keep, to issue or to produce for inspection for any tax purposes may be dealt with by any electronic, etc process conforming to the requirements of the Revenue Commissioners, and the requirements in evidence are appropriately adjusted. The Revenue is similarly empowered to carry out its functions by electronic, etc means. [*TCA 1997, s s887, 928, 967; FA 2001, ss 232, 236(a)(ii)*] There are appropriate inspection powers relating to computer documents and records. [*TCA 1997, s 912*] For the Revenue's requirements on electronic storage, see Revenue Tax Briefing Issue 46 pp 24, 25. The Revenue are permitted to copy (including electronically) records (eg taxpayer returns) and destroy the originals without prejudicing their evidential value (see *s 1096B; FA 2002, s 135*).

1.10 The *Finance Act 1992* introduced considerably increased powers of entry and inspection for the Revenue Commissioners in relation to the full range of tax liabilities, with increased penalties for non-compliance (see now *ss 903–906* as amended). See Revenue Tax Briefing Issue 49 pp 6–13 regarding the Revenue code of conduct for audits. An updated Code of Practice has come into force as of 1 October 2010. In situations where an audit was ongoing but not settled before this date, the taxpayer has the option of which Code of Practice they wish to settle under. The Revenue Commissioners have issued a detailed booklet on the new Code of Practice which is available on their website www.revenue,ie.

1.11 See *TCA 1997, s 910* (as amended) for Revenue Commissioners' powers to obtain information regarding payments by or on behalf of Ministers.

1.12 Relevant offences. A 'relevant person' in relation to a company who, having regard to information obtained in the course of assisting or advising the company in relation to its accounts or tax returns, etc, becomes aware that the company has committed or is committing one or more material 'relevant offences', is obliged without undue delay to notify the company in writing of particulars of the offence(s) and to request the company, within six months, either to rectify the matter or to notify the appropriate officer (as designated by the Revenue Commissioners, see below) of the offence(s). Unless satisfied that such action has been taken by the company, the 'relevant person' must cease to assist or advise the company (except in relation to legal proceedings extant or pending at a time six months after the original notification to the company), and must not do so again until three years after the original notification (or, if earlier, when satisfied that the required action has been taken by the company).

An auditor ceasing to act by virtue of the above is required to give the company written notification of his or her resignation and to send a copy of that notification to the appropriate officer (as above).

A 'relevant person' is liable to a penalty of up to £5,000/€6,345 and two years' imprisonment for failure to comply with the above, or for knowingly or wilfully making an incorrect notification of a 'relevant offence'. Proceedings in relation to such failures may be commenced at any time within six years from the date the original notification to the company was (or should have been) given. It is, however, a good defence against failure to comply to show that awareness that a 'relevant offence' had been committed arose from assisting or advising the company in preparing for litigation in the ordinary course of professional engagement.

The taking of any action required by these provisions cannot be regarded as a contravention of any duty or give rise to any liability or action in any Court.

The name of the officer of the Revenue Commissioners to whom copies of notices should be sent is published in *Iris Oifigiúil*.

A *'relevant person'* is an auditor (as defined), or a person who assists or advises the company for reward in the preparation or delivery of any document which he or she knows is, or is likely, to be used for tax purposes (but excluding PAYE employees of the company). *'Relevant offence'* is defined to include a wide range of knowing or wilful failures in relation to taxes, duties, levies or charges under the care and management of the Revenue Commissioners, including the making of incorrect returns, failure to make returns, false relief claims and falsification of documents. [*TCA 1997, s 1079*]

1.13 Tax clearance certificates. Application may be made to the Collector-General for a tax clearance certificate (valid for a specified period) stating that the holder is in compliance with all obligations imposed under the *Tax Acts*, the *Capital Gains Tax Acts* and the *Value-Added Tax Act 1972* in relation to payment of tax, interest or penalties and the delivery of returns. Such a certificate is required as a condition for the award of certain public sector contracts, but may be applied for any purpose (subject to minor exclusions). It may, with the applicant's consent, be published electronically (eg on the Revenue's website). [*TCA 1997, s 1095; FA 2002, s 127(b)*]

See also *s 1094* (as amended by *FA 1999, s 212; FA 2000, s 163; FA 2001, s 234; FA 2002, s 127(a)*) as regards clearance certificates in relation to certain licences, and *FA 1998, s 132* as regards clearance certificates for criminal legal aid work.

1.14 Authorised officers. Since 1 July 1998, a system of identity cards is introduced for officers of the Revenue Commissioners authorised, nominated or appointed to exercise or perform any statutory functions. The cards are evidence of the relevant authorisation. [*TCA 1997, s 858; SI 212/98*]

1.15 Interest on repayments. Since 1 November 2003, interest (without deduction of tax) is paid on repayments of tax at a rate of 0.011 per cent per day from the day after the end of the year of assessment or chargeable period or date of payment of the tax (whichever is later) where the repayment is due to a mistaken assumption by the Revenue in the application of the law. Otherwise interest is paid from six months after the repayment claim is made, if the repayment has not been made by that date. A de minimis limit of €10 applies to interest payments. Interest payments are disregarded in computing income or profit. No interest is due where the offset provisions apply. For time limits within which claims must be made see **10.1** 'Claims'. For the position prior to 1 November 2003 and preliminary tax paid prior to that date, see **28.11** 'Self-assessment'. [*TCA 1997, s 865A; FA 2003, s 17; SI 508/03*]

OFFSET AND APPROPRIATION OF TAX

[*TCA 1997, ss 1006A, 1006B; FA 2000, s 164; FA 2001, s 239; FA 2002, s 125*]

1.16 With effect from 23 March 2000, the Revenue Commissioners are given wide powers:

(*a*) to set repayments (including interest) against outstanding liabilities (including interest) across the range of taxes, duties and charges;

(*b*) to appropriate payments in respect of which the taxpayer has provided no, or imprecise, accounting instructions against any outstanding liabilities under the *Tax Acts*, the *Capital Gains Tax Acts* or the *Value-Added Tax Acts*; and

(*c*) to withhold repayments (without interest) pending delivery of returns.

RI has now implemented the EC Directives on mutual assistance between Member States on the provision of information in respect of, and the recovery in the State of, claims made by other Member States in respect of debts due to that State from certain levies, duties, taxes and other matters. [*SI 462/02*]

Regulations specify the order of priority of liabilities, including amounts due to other Member States. See *SI 471/02*. The provisions are *inter alia* aimed at facilitating the introduction of consolidated billing by the Revenue. For the practical operational arrangements in respect of amounts due in RI, see Revenue Tax Briefing Issue 45 pp 10, 11.

REVIEW PROCEDURES

1.17 For the handling of internal reviews of the Revenue's handling of taxpayers' affairs, see Statement of Practice SP–GEN/2/99, May 1999.

TAXPAYER CONFIDENTIALITY

1.18 Up to *FA 2011* there has been no specific legislation protecting the confidentiality of taxpayer's information. This is now addressed in *FA 2011*, which provides that all taxpayer information held by the Revenue Commissioners is confidential and may only be disclosed in accordance with that section or other legislation. Any Revenue official who knowingly breaches the legislation will be guilty of an offence and liable to a fine of up to €10,000.

[*FA 2011, s 77*]

2 Allowances, Credits and Rates – for Income Tax

Headings in this section are:

2.1 In the following pages of this section, all rates and allowances or tax credits for 2000/01 onwards are shown, and where a rate in force for 2000/01 commenced in an earlier year that earlier year is shown also. Changes are shown for and from the year in which they commenced with the current rates etc in bold type. A separate **six-year summary** appears inside the front cover.

Since 1 January 2002, the year of assessment (or 'tax year') for both income tax and capital gains tax coincides with the calendar year and is so described. Before 6 April 2001, years of assessment ran from 6 April to 5 April (eg the year of assessment 2000/01 ran from 6 April 2000 to 5 April 2001), and there is a transitional short tax year 2001 from 6 April 2001 to 31 December 2001. [*TCA 1997, ss 2(1), 5(1), 14(2); FA 2001, s 77(1)*]

Since 25 March 2005, PAYE taxpayers are empowered to make claims for reliefs or tax repayments by electronic means including telephone. The treatment of such claims is subject to terms and conditions laid down by Revenue. All records in support of the claim must be retained for six years from the end of the year of assessment to which the claim relates. Revenue may enquire into a claim if notice of the intention to do so is given within four years from the end of the year of assessment in which the claim or any amendment to the claim is made. [*TCA 1997, s 864A, 886A; FA 2005, ss 23, 25*]

Total Income is the income from all sources as estimated in accordance with the *Income Tax Acts.* [*TCA 1997, s 3(1)*] It consists of earned and unearned income less charges, losses, etc, and less certain maintenance payments (see **23.3** 'Married persons') and other specified deductions (see eg **12.9** 'Corporation tax' and **21.7** 'Investment in corporate trades').

Taxable Income is Total Income less personal allowances (but see below) and items treated as such (see **2.23**(*b*)(*c*), **2.28**, **2.30** and **2.41** below). For 1999/2000 onwards, certain personal allowances are given by way of a reduction in income tax liability and not as a deduction from total income. This applies to most allowances for 2000/01 and to all from 2001 onwards, and they are thereafter designated tax credits instead of allowances. [*TCA 1997, s 458 as amended*]

INCOME TAX LEVY FOR 2009 AND 2010 (ABOLISHED FROM 1 JANUARY 2011)

2.2 *FA 2010, s 2* abolished the income tax levy with effect for the 2011 year of assessment and for subsequent years of assessment. The income levy together with PRSI and the health levy have been replaced in their entirety with a 'Universal Social Charge'. (See below and 41 'Health Contributions and Universal Social Charge' for more details.)

The income levy was introduced under the provisions of *Finance (No 2) Act 2008* which inserted a new *Pt 18A* into the *Taxes Consolidation Act 1997*. The purpose of this section was to introduce an income tax levy effective from 1 January 2009.

A levy was imposed, on an individualised basis to PAYE or payroll workers, of 1 per cent on income up to and including €100,001, a charge of 2 per cent for income in excess of €100,001 but not greater than €250,120 and a charge of 3 per cent thereafter. The rate of the levy was changed for income earned from 1 May 2009 and applied to each tax year thereafter up to 31 December 2010. The levy was as follows:

- 2%: Income up to €75,036 pa;

- 4%: Income between €75,037 and €174,980 pa;

- 6%: Income in excess of €174,980 pa.

The levy applied to self employed individuals was:
The 2009 annual rates and thresholds of the Income Levy were as follows:

- 1.67%: Income up to €75,036 per annum.

- 3%: Income between €75,037 and €100,100 per annum.

- 3.33%: Income between €100,101 and €174,980 per annum.

- 4.67%: Income between €174,981 and €250,120 per annum.

- 5%: Income in excess of €250,120 per annum.

The levy applied to all income in a similar manner to the Taxes Consolidation Act but was applied before granting relief for pension contributions or deductions for capital allowances. Social welfare payments and a number of similar type payments made by other Departments, as well as similar payments from other states were excluded.

There was an age-related exemption for persons aged over 65 years who had a gross income of less than €20,000 with a provision for double that limit for a married couple.

An exemption threshold applied of €15,028 so as to exclude those on low incomes. Where the age-related or low income thresholds were exceeded, the levy was payable on all income.

FA 2010, s 3 made a number of technical amendments to the income levy *TCA 1997, s 531B* was re-written for the purposes of clarity. In addition to this, certain tax agreements (under *s 825(1)(a)(ii)(II)*) were placed on the same footing as Double Tax Agreements with respect to the income levy. Cross Border Relief under *s 825* was extended to the income levy. Finally, relief from the income levy for 2010was provided for certain capital expenditure incurred in meeting the requirements of the EU Nitrates Directive.

UNIVERSAL SOCIAL CHARGE

2.3 *FA 2011, s 3* has introduced a new Universal Social Charge effective as of 1 January 2011. This Universal Social Charge replaces the income levy and the health levy. The Universal Social Charge will be applied on an individualised basis, a charge of 2 per cent on income up to and including €10,036, a charge of 4 per cent for income in excess of €10,036 but not greater than €16,016 and a charge of 7 per cent thereafter. The charge will apply to all income in a similar manner to the Tax Acts, but including certain income which is statutorily exempt from income tax. The charge will be applied before granting relief for pension contributions. There will be an age-related exemption to the 7 per cent rate for persons aged over 70 years.

An exemption threshold of 4,004 will apply so as to exclude those on very low incomes. Where this threshold is exceeded, the Universal Social Charge will be payable on all income.

Rate	Employed	Self Employed
0%	14,004	4,004
2%	10,036	10,036
4%	10,037–16,016	10,037–16,016
7%	Over 16,016	16,017–100,000
10%		Over 100,000

THE UNIFIED TAX SYSTEM FOR 1974/75 ONWARDS

2.4 On 6 April 1974 a unified system of income tax on individuals replaced the previous dual structure of income tax and surtax (now abolished). A single graduated tax comprising reduced, standard and higher rates became applicable to all income, whether earned or unearned.

RATES OF TAX FOR 2011

[TCA 1997, s 15; FA 2001, s 3; FA 2002, s 2; FA 2005, s 2; FA 2006, s 2, FA 2007, s 2, FA 2008, s 2, s 2 FA 2009, s 2]

2.5 For 2011 two separate graduated scales of tax apply as follows:

(*a*)   For a husband whose wife's income (if any) is treated as his own (or *vice versa*) (see **23.1** 'Married persons'):

Taxable Incomes	On Taxable Income	Rate	Equal to tax of
€	€		€
Standard Rate			
First 41,800	0–41,800	20%	8,360
Higher Rate			
Above 41,800	41,800 upwards	41%	

(*b*)   In any other case:

Taxable Incomes	On Taxable Income	Rate	Equal to tax of
€	€		€
Standard Rate			
First 32,800	0–32,800	20%	6,560
Higher Rate			
Above 32,800	32,800 upwards	41%	

As regards (*a*) above, where both spouses are in receipt of income which is chargeable on the husband (or on the wife) the standard rate band is extended by the lesser of €23,800 and the lesser of the two incomes (after any deduction specifically attributable to such income and after deducting any 'relevant interest' (see **13.9** 'Deduction of tax at source')), ie to a maximum of €65,600. Income chargeable under PAYE (see **34.11** 'Sch E') is correspondingly adjusted.

As regards (*b*) above, for a widow(er) or single parent entitled to the single parent allowance under *s 462* (see **2.20** below), the standard rate band is increased to €36,800.

These rates apply to any individual charged to income tax unless he is acting in a fiduciary or representative capacity. Standard rate applies to annual payments etc, see **13** 'Deduction of tax at source'.

For the purpose of ascertaining the total amount of income which is to be charged at the rates shown above, any income which has suffered (or is deemed to have suffered) tax at source is included at the gross amount. A credit is then given for the tax suffered in order to determine the net amount of tax payable. Such taxed income shall be regarded as income chargeable under Sch D, Case IV. [*TCA 1997, s 59*]

RATES OF TAX FOR 2000/01 TO 2010

[*TCA 1997, s 15; FA 1999, s 3; FA 2000, s 3(a); FA 2001, s 3, FA 2002, s 2; FA 2003, s 2; FA 2005, s 2*]

2.6 For 2009 and 2010 two separate graduated scales of tax apply as follows:

(*a*) For a husband whose wife's income (if any) is treated as his own (or *vice versa*) (see **23.1** 'Married persons'):

Taxable Incomes	On Taxable Income	Rate	Equal to tax of
€	€		€
Standard Rate			
First 45,400	0–45,400	20%	9,080
Higher Rate			
Above 45,400	45,400 upwards	41%	

(*b*) In any other case:

Taxable Incomes	On Taxable Income	Rate	Equal to tax of
€	€		€
Standard Rate			
First 36,400	0–36,400	20%	7,280
Higher Rate			
Above 36,400	36,400 upwards	41%	

As regards (*a*) above, where both spouses are in receipt of income which is chargeable on the husband (or on the wife) the standard rate band is extended by the lesser of €26,400 and the lesser of the two incomes (after any deduction specifically attributable to such income and after deducting any 'relevant interest' (see **13.9** 'Deduction of tax at source')), ie to a maximum of €72,800. Income chargeable under PAYE (see **34.11** 'Sch E') is correspondingly adjusted.

As regards (*b*) above, for a widow(er) or single parent entitled to the single parent allowance under *s 462* (see **2.20** below), the standard rate band is increased to €40,400.

These rates apply to any individual charged to income tax unless he is acting in a fiduciary or representative capacity. Standard rate applies to annual payments etc, see **13** 'Deduction of tax at source'.

For the purpose of ascertaining the total amount of income which is to be charged at the rates shown above, any income which has suffered (or is deemed to have suffered) tax at source is included at the gross amount. A credit is then given for the tax suffered in order to determine the net amount of tax payable. Such taxed income shall be regarded as income chargeable under Sch D, Case IV. [*TCA 1997, s 59*]

For 2008 two separate graduated scales of tax apply as follows:

(*a*)   For a husband whose wife's income (if any) is treated as his own (or *vice versa*) (see **23.1** 'Married persons'):

Taxable Incomes	On Taxable Income	Rate	Equal to tax of
€	€		€
Standard Rate			
First 44,400	0–44,400	20%	8,880
Higher Rate			
Above 44,400	44,400 upwards	41%	

(*b*)   In any other case:

Taxable Incomes	On Taxable Income	Rate	Equal to tax of
€	€		€
Standard Rate			
First 35,400	0–35,400	20%	7,080
Higher Rate			
Above 35,400	35,400 upwards	41%	

For 2007 two separate graduated scales of tax apply as follows:

(*a*)   For a husband whose wife's income (if any) is treated as his own (or *vice versa*) (see **23.1** 'Married persons'):

Taxable Incomes	On Taxable Income	Rate	Equal to tax of
€	€		€
Standard Rate			
First 43,000	0–43,000	20%	8,600
Higher Rate			
Above 43,000	43,000 upwards	41%	

(*b*)   In any other case:

Taxable Incomes	On Taxable Income	Rate	Equal to tax of
€	€		€
Standard Rate			
First 34,000	0–34,000	20%	6,800
Higher Rate			
Above 34,000	34,000 upwards	41%	

As regards (*a*) above, where both spouses are in receipt of income which is chargeable on the husband (or on the wife) the standard rate band is extended by the lesser of

€25,000 and the lesser of the two incomes (after any deduction specifically attributable to such income and after deducting any 'relevant interest' (see **13.9** 'Deduction of tax at source')), ie to a maximum of €68,000. Income chargeable under PAYE (see **34.11** 'Sch E') is correspondingly adjusted.

As regards (*b*) above, for a widow(er) or single parent entitled to the single parent allowance under *s 462* (see **2.20** below), the standard rate band is increased by €6,000 to €38,000.

These rates apply to any individual charged to income tax unless he is acting in a fiduciary or representative capacity. Standard rate applies to annual payments etc, see **13** 'Deduction of tax at source'.

For the purpose of ascertaining the total amount of income which is to be charged at the rates shown above, any income which has suffered (or is deemed to have suffered) tax at source is included at the gross amount. A credit is then given for the tax suffered in order to determine the net amount of tax payable. Such taxed income shall be regarded as income chargeable under Sch D, Case IV. [*TCA 1997, s 59*]

For 2006 two separate graduated scales of tax apply as follows:

(*a*) For a husband whose wife's income (if any) is treated as his own (or *vice versa*) (see **23.1** 'Married persons'):

Taxable Incomes €	On Taxable Income €	Rate	Equal to tax of €
Standard Rate			
First 41,000	0–41,000	20%	8,200
Higher Rate			
Above 41,000	41,000 upwards	42%	

(*b*) In any other case:

Taxable Incomes €	On Taxable Income €	Rate	Equal to tax of €
Standard Rate			
First 32,000	0–32,000	20%	6,400
Higher Rate			
Above 32,000	32,000 upwards	42%	

As regards (*a*) above, where both spouses are in receipt of income which is chargeable on the husband (or on the wife) the standard rate band is extended by the lesser of €23,000 and the lesser of the two incomes (after any deduction specifically attributable to such income and after deducting any 'relevant interest' (see **13.9** 'Deduction of tax at source')), ie to a maximum of €64,000. Income chargeable under PAYE (see **34.11** 'Sch E') is correspondingly adjusted.

As regards (*b*) above, for a widow(er) or single parent entitled to the single parent allowance under *s 462* (see **2.20** below), the standard rate band is increased by €4,000 to €36,000.

These rates apply to any individual charged to income tax unless he is acting in a fiduciary or representative capacity. Standard rate applies to annual payments etc, see **13** 'Deduction of tax at source'.

For the purpose of ascertaining the total amount of income which is to be charged at the rates shown above, any income which has suffered (or is deemed to have suffered) tax at source is included at the gross amount. A credit is then given for the tax suffered in order to determine the net amount of tax payable. Such taxed income shall be regarded as income chargeable under Sch D, Case IV. [*TCA 1997, s 59*]

For 2005 two separate graduated scales of tax apply as follows:

(*a*)   For a husband whose wife's income (if any) is treated as his own (or *vice versa*) (see **23.1** 'Married persons'):

Taxable Incomes	On Taxable Income	Rate	Equal to tax of
€	€		€
Standard Rate			
First 38,400	0–38,400	20%	7,680
Higher Rate			
Above 38,400	38,400 upwards	42%	

(*b*)   In any other case:

Taxable Incomes	On Taxable Income	Rate	Equal to tax of
€	€		€
Standard Rate			
First 29,400	0–29,400	20%	5,880
Higher Rate			
Above 29,400	29,400 upwards	42%	

As regards (*a*) above, where both spouses are in receipt of income which is chargeable on the husband (or on the wife) the standard rate band is extended by the lesser of €20,400 and the lesser of the two incomes (after any deduction specifically attributable to such income and after deducting any 'relevant interest' (see **13.9** 'Deduction of tax at source')), ie to a maximum of €58,800. Income chargeable under PAYE (see **34.11** 'Sch E') is correspondingly adjusted.

As regards (*b*) above, for a widow(er) or single parent entitled to the single parent allowance under *s 462* (see **2.20** below), the standard rate band is increased by €4,000 to €33,400.

These rates apply to any individual charged to income tax unless he is acting in a fiduciary or representative capacity. Standard rate applies to annual payments etc, see **13** 'Deduction of tax at source'.

From 2002 to 2004 two separate graduated scales of tax apply as follows:

(*a*)   For a husband whose wife's income (if any) is treated as his own (or *vice versa*) (see **23.1** 'Married persons'):

Taxable Incomes	On Taxable Income	Rate	Equal to tax of
€	€		€
Standard Rate			
First 37,000	0–37,000	20%	7,400
Higher Rate			
Above 37,000	37,001 upwards	42%	

(*b*)   In any other case:

	On		Equal to
Taxable Incomes	Taxable Income	Rate	tax of
€	€		€
Standard Rate			
First 28,000	0–28,000	20%	5,600
Higher Rate			
Above 28,000	28,001 upwards	42%	

As regards (*a*) above, where both spouses are in receipt of income which is chargeable on the husband (or on the wife) the standard rate band is extended by the lesser of €19,000 and the lesser of the two incomes (after any deduction specifically attributable to such income and after deducting any 'relevant interest' (see **13.9** 'Deduction of tax at source')), ie to a maximum of €56,000. Income chargeable under PAYE (see **34.11** 'Sch E') is correspondingly adjusted.

As regards (*b*) above, for a widow(er) or single parent entitled to the single parent allowance under *s 462* (see **2.20** below), the standard rate band is increased by €4,000 to €32,000.

For the short tax year 2001 two separate graduated scales of tax apply as follows:

(*a*)   For a husband whose wife's income (if any) is treated as his own (or *vice versa*) (see **23.1** 'Married persons'):

Taxable Incomes	On Taxable Income	Rate	Equal to tax of
£	£		£
Standard Rate			
First 21,460	0–21,460	20%	4,292
Higher Rate			
Above 21,460	21,461 upwards	42%	

(*b*)   In any other case:

Taxable Incomes	On Taxable Income	Rate	Equal to tax of
£	£		£
Standard Rate			
First 14,800	0–14,800	20%	2,960
Higher Rate			
Above 14,800	14,801 upwards	42%	

As regards (*a*) above, where both spouses are in receipt of income which is chargeable on the husband (or on the wife) the standard rate band is extended by the lesser of £8,140 and the lesser of the two incomes (after any deduction specifically attributable to such income and after deducting any 'relevant interest' (see **13.9** 'Deduction of tax at source'), ie to a maximum of £29,600. Income chargeable under PAYE (see **34.11** 'Sch E') is correspondingly adjusted.

As regards (*b*) above, for a widow(er) or single parent entitled to the single parent allowance under *s 462* (see **2.19** below), the standard rate band is increased by £2,331 to £17,131.

For 2000/01 two separate graduated scales of tax apply as follows:

(*a*)   For a husband whose wife's income (if any) is treated as his own (or *vice versa*) (see **23.1** 'Married persons'):

Taxable Incomes £	On Taxable Income £	Rate	Equal to tax of £
Standard Rate			
First 28,000	0–28,000	22%	6,160
Higher Rate			
Above 28,000	28,001 upwards	44%	

(*b*)   In any other case:

Taxable Incomes £	On Taxable Income £	Rate	Equal to tax of £
Standard Rate			
First 17,000	0–17,000	22%	3,740
Higher Rate			
Above 17,000	17,001 upwards	44%	

As regards (*a*) above, where both spouses are in receipt of income which is chargeable on the husband (or on the wife) the standard rate band is extended by the lesser of £6,000 and the lesser of the two incomes (after any deduction specifically attributable to such income), ie to a maximum of £34,000. Income chargeable under PAYE (see **34.11** 'Sch E') is correspondingly adjusted.

As regards (*b*) above, for a widow(er) or single parent entitled to the single parent allowance under *s 462* (see **2.20** below), the standard rate band is increased by £3,150 to £20,150.

STANDARD RATE

2.7 [*TCA 1997, s 15; FA 1999, s 3; FA 2000, s 3(a); FA 2001, s 3(b)(c); FA 2002, s 2(b)*]

For	2000/01	22%
From	**2001**	**20%**

AGE ALLOWANCE/TAX CREDIT

[*TCA 1997, s 464; FA 2000, s 8(a); FA 2001, Sch 1 para 1(j); FA 2002, s 3, Sch 1 para 1(e); FA 2006, s 3*]

2.8 From **2000/01 onwards**, a relief may be claimed in addition to those under **2.12** to **2.14** below (and is similarly given by means of a reduction in income tax liability) if a person (or a spouse whose income is treated as his or hers, and who is living with him or her) is aged 65 or over at any time in the year of assessment. The available tax credit for **2001 onwards** is:

		Single	Married
For	2001	£119	£238
From	2002	€205	€410
For	2006	€250	€500
For	2007	€275	€550
For	2008	€325	€650
For	2009/2010	€325	€650
For	2011	€245	€490

For 2000/01 only, the relief is in effect given in the same way by reference to amounts of £176 and £352 respectively.

A person may also be entitled to the age exemption under **2.9** below.

AGE EXEMPTION

[*TCA 1997, ss 187(2)(3), 188; FA 1999, s 2; FA 2000, s 2, Sch 1 para 3; FA 2001, s 4; FA 2002, s 4, FA 2003, s 2; FA 2004, s 2; FA 2005, s 4; FA 2006, s 4*]

2.9 A person receiving the age allowance or tax credit (see above) may claim exemption from income tax if their total income does not exceed a *specified amount*, as follows:

		Single	Married
		£	£
For	2000/01	7,500	15,000
For	2001	6,290	12,580
		€	€
For	2002	13,000	26,000
For	2003	15,000	30,000
For	2004	15,500	31,000
For	2005	16,500	33,000
For	2006	17,000	34,000
For	2007	19,000	38,000
For	2008	20,000	40,000
For	2009	20,000	40,000
For	2010	20,000	40,000
For	**2011**	**18,000**	**36,000**

The specified amounts are increased as for low income exemption (see **2.11** below) where there are 'qualifying children'.

Marginal relief applies to limit income tax payable (disregarding, for 2001 onwards, any interest relief under *s 244* (see **20.3** 'Interest payable')) in appropriate cases. The limit is **40 per cent** of the excess over the appropriate exemption limit, up to a total income of twice that exemption limit. 'Total income' for this purpose includes that arising outside RI and not chargeable to tax.

LOW INCOME EXEMPTION

[*TCA 1997, ss 187, 188(1); FA 1999, s 2; FA 2001, Sch 1 para 1(d), 2(a)*]

2.10 Up to 31 December 2007 a complete exemption from income tax was granted to individuals whose total income (including that arising outside RI and not chargeable to tax) did not exceed a *specified amount*. This amount depended on whether the individual was entitled to the married allowance or not. The specified amounts were as follows:

		Single	Married
		£	£
From	1998/99	4,100	8,200
For	2001	3,034	6,068
		€	€
From	**2002**	**5,210**	**10,420**

The specified amounts were increased by the following amounts in respect of (*a*) the first 'qualifying child' (see **2.20** below) living at any time in the year of assessment and the second such child, and (*b*) the third and subsequent such children.

		(a)	(b)
From	1995/96	£450	£650
For	2001	£333	£481
From	**2002**	**€575**	**€830**

Only one increase was allowed in respect of a child, and, where appropriate, the increase was apportioned by reference to expenditure on maintenance.

Marginal relief applied to limit income tax payable (disregarding, for 2001 onwards, any interest relief under *s 244* (see **20.3** 'Interest payable')) to **40 per cent** of the excess of income over the specified amount, up to a total income of twice the specified amount. 'Total income' for this purpose included that arising outside RI and not chargeable to tax.

The exemption was available to non-RI residents (see **38.205** 'Tax cases').

Finance Act 2008 provided for the cessation of the general exemption limits provided for under *s 187* and the associated system of marginal relief with effect from 1 January 2008. The relevant section also provided for the amendment of a number of other sections in *TCA 1997* consequent on the cessation of *s 187*.

Section 188 was also amended to increase the income tax exemption limits for those aged 65 years and over. The new limits are €20,000 for single people and €40,000 for married couples. The Finance Act substituted the provisions relating to the increase in the *specified amount* where there is a 'qualifying child' into *s 188*. The same provisions apply and are as follows:

The amounts provided for under the amended *s 188* (ie €20,000 for single persons and €40,000 for married couples) are increased by the following amounts in respect of

(a) the first 'qualifying child' (see **2.20** below) living at any time in the year of assessment and the second such child, and (b) the third and subsequent such children.

		(a)	(b)
From	2008	€575	€830
From	**2009**	**€575**	**€830**

Only one increase is allowed in respect of a child, and, where appropriate, the increase is apportioned by reference to expenditure on maintenance.

SINGLE ALLOWANCE/TAX CREDIT

[*TCA 1997, s 461; FA 1999, s 4; FA 2000, s 4; FA 2001, 2(1), Sch 1 para 1(f); FA 2002, s 3, Sch 1 para 1(a); FA 2005, s 3, Sch 1; FA 2006, s 3*]

2.11 (Unmarried, separated or divorced person, or each of husband and wife electing to be treated as a single person)

From 1999/2000 onwards, relief is given by means of a reduction in the claimant's income tax liability (excluding any liability in respect of tax deducted from payments made under *s 16(2)*). The reduction is the smaller of a percentage of the relief amount equal to the standard rate of tax for the year of assessment (see **2.7** above) and what would otherwise be the claimant's total income tax liability.

For	2000/01	£4,700

For **2001 onwards**, the relief is expressed as an available tax credit, and the reduction is the smaller of the available tax credit and what would otherwise be the claimant's total income tax liability.

For	2001	£814
From	2002	€1,520
For	2005	€1,580
For	2006	€1,630
For	2007	€1,760
For	2008	€1,830
For	2009	€1,830
For	2010	€1,830
For	**2011**	**€1,650**

WIDOW(ER) ALLOWANCE/TAX CREDIT

[*TCA 1997, ss 461, 461A; FA 1999, s 4; FA 2000, s 5(a); FA 2001, s 2(1), Sch 1 para 1(f)(g); FA 2002, s 3, Sch 1 para 1(a)(b); FA 2005, s 3, Sch 1; FA 2006 s 3*]

2.12 From 1999/2000, for a widow or widower not entitled to the married relief (see **2.14** below) whose spouse dies in the year of assessment, relief equal to the married relief (see **2.14** below) is given by way of a reduction in income tax liability (from 2001, as an available tax credit). Where neither the married nor the year of bereavement relief applies, the single personal relief (see **2.12** above) is available in the normal way, and there is an additional relief as follows:

(*a*)　For 2000/01 only, the additional allowance is £1,000, and relief is given by way of a reduction in income tax liability at the standard rate only in the same way as applies to the single personal relief;

(*b*)　For **2001 onwards**, the additional relief is expressed as an available tax credit in the same way as applies to the single personal relief. The tax credit available is as follows:

For	2001	£148
From	2002	€300
For	2005	€400
For	2006	€500
For	2007	€550
For	2008	€600
For	2009	€600
For	2010	€600
For	**2011**	**€540**

As regards (*a*) and (*b*) above, the additional relief is not available where there is an entitlement to the single parent relief (for which see **2.20** below).

MARRIED ALLOWANCE/TAX CREDIT

[*TCA 1997, s 461; FA 2000, s 4; FA 2001, s 2(1), Sch 1 para 1(f); FA 2002, s 3, Sch 1 para 1(a); FA 2005, s 3, Sch 1; FA 2006, s 3*]

2.13 (Due to a married man whose wife is living with him, or who is not living with him but is wholly or mainly maintained by him without his being entitled to a tax deduction for the maintenance payments. A wife maintaining her separated husband may similarly claim the relief. See **23.1** 'Married persons' for the circumstances in which the wife, rather than the husband, receives the relief.)

A husband and wife may, if either spouse so wishes, be treated as two single people for income tax purposes, each then qualifying for the single personal relief (see **2.11** above). No married relief will then be due. [*TCA 1997, s 1016*] See also **23.1** 'Married persons' as regards the year of marriage.

For 1999/2000 onwards, relief is given by means of a reduction in the claimant's income tax liability (excluding any liability in respect of tax deducted from payments made under *s 16(2)*). The reduction is the smaller of a percentage of the relief amount equal to the standard rate of tax for the year of assessment (see **2.7** above) and what would otherwise be the claimant's total income tax liability.

For	2000/01	£9,400

For **2001 onwards**, the relief is expressed as an available tax credit, and the reduction is the smaller of the available tax credit and what would otherwise be the claimant's total income tax liability.

For	2001	£1,628
From	2002	€3,040
For	2005	€3,160
For	2006	€3,260
For	2007	€3,520
For	2008	€3,660
For	2009	€3,660
For	2010	€3,660
For	**2011**	**€3,300**

EMPLOYEE ALLOWANCE/TAX CREDIT

[TCA 1997, s 472; FA 1999, s 7; FA 2001, s 2(1), Sch 1 para 1(o), 2(k); FA 2002, s 3, Sch 1 para 1(j); FA 2003, s 3; FA 2004, s 3; FA 2005, s 3, Sch 1; FA 2006, s 3]

2.14 A special relief may be given to any individual whose total income includes emoluments subject to the PAYE system (ie *Pt 42, Ch IV*). Emoluments paid by an individual to spouse or child, by a partnership to partner's spouse or child, or by body corporate etc to a 'proprietary director' (beneficial owner or controller of over 15 per cent of ordinary share capital) or spouse or child of such director, are not eligible for the relief, *except that* this does not apply to exclude emoluments paid to a child (unless a proprietary director in his/her own right) who meets certain requirements as an employed contributor under the *Social Welfare Acts*, provided that:

(*a*) the emoluments paid in the year exceed a specified limit;

(*b*) the child is required to, and does, devote substantially the whole of his/her time throughout the year to the duties of the employment; and

(*c*) the PAYE regulations, in so far as they apply, have been complied with in the year in relation to the emoluments.

The specified limit in (*a*) above is £3,600 for 2000/01 and earlier years, £2,664 for 2001 and €4,572 for 2002 and subsequent years.

For **2001 onwards**, the relief is expressed as an available tax credit. The claimant's total income tax liability (excluding any liability in respect of tax deducted from payments made under *s 16(2)*) is reduced by the smaller of the available tax credit and what would otherwise be the claimant's total income tax liability. The available tax credit is the lesser of a percentage of the emoluments equal to the standard rate of tax for the year of assessment (see **2.7** above) and a specified amount as follows:

For	2001	£296
For	2002	€660
For	2003	€800
For	2004	€1,040

For	2005	€1,270
For	2006	€1,490
For	2007	€1,760
For	2008	€1,830
For	2009	€1,830
For	2010	€1,830
For	**2011**	**€1,650**

For 2000/01, the relief is in effect given in the same way, the reduction in tax being up to £220, but expressed in terms of standard rate relief on an amount of £1,000. In any case where both a husband's and his wife's income are to be treated as the husband's for income tax purposes, relief up to the full amount may be allowed in respect of each spouse's emoluments.

The relief is also available in respect of emoluments of an individual's overseas office or employment, where the emoluments are chargeable in the country in which they arise under a system similar to the PAYE system and are also chargeable in full to tax under Sch D in RI, and where they would, if the office etc was held in RI by an RI resident, qualify for the relief as above.

Finance Act 2010, s 8 amends *s 997A* to ensure that, in the case of a proprietary director, the credit for PAYE tax remitted cannot exceed the PAYE tax actually deducted from his or her directorship emoluments.

LONG-TERM UNEMPLOYED

[*TCA 1997, s 472A; FA 1999, s 35; FA 2001, Sch 5*]

2.15 A 'qualifying individual' may claim a special deduction in relation to each of the three years of assessment commencing with the year of assessment in which a 'qualifying employment' commences or, on election, the following year. The deduction is made from so much of total income as is attributable to emoluments (restricted in the same way as for the employee relief, see **2.15** above) from the 'qualifying employment', up to the following amounts.

First year	€3,810/£3,000
Second year	€2,540/£2,000
Third year	€1,270/£1,000

Where for all or part of any of those years a 'qualifying child' is resident with the 'qualifying individual', the deduction for each such year is increased as follows:

First year	€1,270/£1,000
Second year	€850/£666
Third year	€425/£334

Only one such increase is allowed for any 'qualifying child', the additional deduction being divided where appropriate amongst those 'qualifying individuals' who maintain the child, either in proportion to the maintenance or in such manner as they jointly notify to the inspector. Maintenance deductible for tax purposes is disregarded for these purposes.

On a cessation of the 'qualifying employment' within the three years, any unused balance of the available deductions may be carried forward to the next, but only the next, 'qualifying employment'.

No deduction is available where the 'qualifying individual', or the employer, receives (or has received) in respect of the 'qualifying employment' any grant or subsidy funded wholly or mainly, directly or indirectly, by the State or by a statutory board or public or local authority.

From 1999/00, a *'qualifying individual'* is an individual who has not previously qualified who commences a 'qualifying employment', and who either:

(*a*)   immediately prior to commencement of the employment had been unemployed throughout the preceding twelve months, and receiving, in respect of that period of unemployment, unemployment benefit or assistance or one-parent family payment in respect of a continuous period of unemployment (within *Social Welfare Consolidation Act 1993, s 120(3)*) of not less than 312 days (disregarding Sundays); or

(*b*)   falls into any separate category approved for the purpose by the Minister for Social, Community and Family Affairs (which applies to people in receipt of Disability Allowance or Blind Person's Pension for at least twelve months).

For the purposes of (*a*) above, time spent on certain activities, programmes or courses for the unemployed may be treated as periods of unemployment, and related payments as unemployment payments.

A *'qualifying employment'* is an employment within Sch E commencing after 6 April 1998, of at least 30 hours duration per week, and capable of lasting at least twelve months. It does not include an employment:

(i)   from which the previous holder was unfairly dismissed;

(ii)   by an employer who has, in the 26 weeks prior to commencement, reduced his workforce by way of redundancy; or

(iii)   in respect of which more than 75 per cent of the emoluments arise from commissions.

A *'qualifying child'* is defined as for the single parent relief under **2.20** below.

Finance Act 2007, s 10 amends *s 126* by indefinitely extending the period the special exemption from taxation that applies to unemployment benefit payable to systematic short-time workers.

SEAFARER ALLOWANCE

[*TCA 1997, s 472B; FA 1999, s 15; FA 2001, s 30; SI 48/99; SI 126/03*]

2.16   Since 17 February 1999, an RI-resident 'qualifying individual', absent from RI at the end of at least a specified number of days in a year of assessment for the purposes of performing the duties of a 'qualifying employment', may claim a deduction up to a specified amount from so much of his or her taxable income as is attributable to income, profits or gains from the 'qualifying employment'. The specified number of days and amount are as follows:

	Days	Amount
1998/99 to 2000/01	169	£5,000
2001	119	£3,700
2002 onwards	**161**	**€6,350**

Where such relief is claimed, no relief is available under *s 823* (see **27.3** 'Residents and non-residents').

Subject to the exclusions referred to below, a *'qualifying employment'* is an office or employment (within Sch D or Sch E) the duties of which are performed wholly on a passenger or cargo ship (but not a fishing vessel) registered in an EC Member State on a voyage beginning or ending in a port outside RI (which includes mobile or fixed maritime rigs, etc). Incidental duties not performed on the ship on such a voyage are disregarded for this purpose. A *'qualifying individual'* is the holder of a qualifying employment who has entered into articles of agreement with the master of that ship.

There are exclusions for employments with any board, authority, etc established in RI by or under statute, or the emoluments of which are paid out of the State revenue, or where the income from the employment is taxable on the remittance basis (see **31.2** 'Sch D, Case III') or the split year residence rules of *s 822* (see **27.1** 'Residents and non-residents') apply.

For a general article explaining these provisions, see Revenue Tax Briefing Issue 36 pp 18, 19.

EMPLOYED PERSON TAKING CARE OF INCAPACITATED INDIVIDUAL

[*TCA 1997, s 467; FA 1999, s 9; FA 2000, Sch 1 para 4; FA 2001, s 7; FA 2002, s 5; FA 2006, s 5*]

2.17 Relief by means of a deduction from total income is available for **1999/2000 onwards** where the taxpayer or a relative of the taxpayer (including a relation by marriage and a person in respect of whom the taxpayer is or was the legal guardian) is, throughout the year of assessment, totally physically or mentally incapacitated, and the taxpayer (or, where the wife's income is, by election, treated as income of the husband, the taxpayer's spouse) has employed a person to take care of the incapacitated individual. *FA 2008, s 9* provides that relief may be granted in the first year in which the individual or the relative of the individual becomes permanently incapacitated. This is merely legislating for what is already Revenue practice. The carer may be employed through an agency. The amount of the deduction is the lesser of a specified amount in respect of each such incapacitated individual and the cost of employing the carer(s) in the year. Where more than one taxpayer is entitled to a deduction under this provision in respect of the same incapacitated individual, the aggregate deductions may not exceed the specified amount and the relief is apportioned in proportion to the costs actually borne. The specified amount is:

From	1999/2000	£8,500
For	2001	£7,400

From	2002	€30,000
For	2007	€50,000
For	2008	€50,000
For	2009	€50,000
For	2010	€50,000
For	**2011**	**€50,000**

HOME CARER'S ALLOWANCE/TAX CREDIT

[TCA 1997, s 466A; FA 2000, s 12; FA 2001, s 2(1), Sch 1 para 1(m), 2(i); FA 2002, s 3, Sch 1 para 1(h)]

2.18 From 2000/01 onwards, where for any year of assessment an individual is a 'qualifying claimant', the individual's income tax liability (excluding any liability in respect of tax deducted from payments made under *s 16(2)*) may be reduced. For **2001 onwards**, the relief is expressed as an available tax credit. The claimant's total income tax liability (excluding any liability in respect of tax deducted from payments made under *s 16(2)*) is reduced by the smaller of the available tax credit and what would otherwise be the claimant's total income tax liability. The available tax credit is:

For	2001	£444
From	2002	€770
Until	2007	€770
From	2008 – 2010	€900
For	**2011**	**€810**

For 2000/01 only, the relief is in effect given in the same way, the reduction in tax being up to £660, but expressed in terms of standard rate relief on an amount of up to £3,000.

Only one reduction is available to any 'qualifying claimant' for a year of assessment, and only one reduction is available in respect of a 'dependant person'. See below as regards restriction of relief by reference to the carer's income.

A *'qualifying claimant'* for a year of assessment is an individual whose spouse's income is treated as his or her own (see **23.1** 'Married persons') and who, or whose spouse, (the *'carer spouse'*) cares for one or more 'dependent persons' during the year. A *'dependent person'* is a person (other than the claimant's spouse) who resides (or is treated as residing, see below) with the claimant and is either:

(*a*)   a child in respect of whom the claimant (or spouse) receives child benefit under *Social Welfare (Consolidation) Act 1993, Pt IV* at any time during the year of assessment; or

(*b*)   an individual either aged 65 or over at any time during the year of assessment or permanently mentally or physically incapacitated.

The residence requirement is treated as satisfied where the dependant is a relative (including by marriage) of the claimant or spouse, or a person in respect of whom the claimant or spouse is or was the legal guardian, and lives in close proximity to the claimant (ie on the same or adjacent property or within two kilometres) with a direct system of communications between their residences.

Where in any year of assessment the carer spouse's income (in his or her own right) exceeds a total income limit (disregarding any carer's allowance under *Social Welfare (Consolidation) Act 1993, Pt III Ch 10* or carer's benefit under *Pt II, Ch 11A of that Act*), the available tax credit is reduced by one-half of that excess. (For 2000/01 only, the figure of £3,000 by reference to which relief is granted is instead reduced by three times that excess.) A reduction (or greater reduction) is nonetheless available for a year of assessment where the claimant was entitled to a reduction for the preceding year of assessment (other than by virtue of this exception), although the reduction for the current year may not then exceed that for the preceding year. The income limit is as follows:

For	2000/01	£4,000
For	2001	£2,960
From	**2002**	**€5,080**

Where relief is granted for a year of assessment under this provision, the increased standard rate band available to certain married couples (see **2.6** above) is not available unless the claimant elects (by written notice) to receive the benefit of the increased standard rate band instead of relief under this provision.

For an article on these provisions, see Revenue Tax Briefing Issue 39 pp 10, 11.

CHILD ALLOWANCE/TAX CREDIT

[*TCA 1997, ss 465, 467(4); FA 1999, s 6(a); FA 2000, s 9(a); FA 2001, s 2(1), Sch 1 para 1(k); FA 2002, s 3, Sch 1 para 1(f); FA 2005, s 3, Sch 1; FA 2006, s 3*]

2.19 The relief is available only in respect of incapacitated children, and is not available where relief is given under **2.17** above. (For additional relief for a single parent, see **2.20** below.) It is available in respect of any child permanently incapacitated by mental or physical infirmity from maintaining him- or herself (or, if under age 18 , whose infirmity is such that he or she would be so incapacitated if over 18) who became so incapacitated before age 21 or while in full-time education or training (eg apprentice or articled clerk). The taxpayer may claim for each child of his or her own or for any child of which he or she has the custody and which he or she maintains at his or her own expense (subject to restrictions to prevent double relief). Where two or more individuals are entitled to the relief in respect of a child, it is apportioned according to the amount expended by each on maintenance (and see **23.3** 'Married persons').

See **2.20** below as regards the meaning of 'child'.

For **2001 onwards**, the relief is expressed as an available tax credit. The claimant's total income tax liability (excluding any liability in respect of tax deducted from payments made under *s 16(2)*) is reduced by the smaller of the available tax credit and what would otherwise be the claimant's total income tax liability. The available tax credit is:

For	2001	£238
From	2002	€500
For	2005	€1,000
For	2006	€1,500
For	2007	€3,000

For	2008	€3,000
For	2009	€3,000
For	2010	€3,660
For	**2011**	**€3,300**

For 2000/01 only, the relief is in effect given in the same way, the reduction in tax being up to £352, but is expressed in terms of standard rate relief on an amount of £1,600.

For 2000/01 and earlier years, the relief amount (for 2000/01 the £1,600 amount) is reduced by £1 for every £1 of the child's income (excluding scholarships, bursaries, etc) over £2,100, and, if the child is over 18 (16) at the beginning of the year of assessment, is limited to the amount expended by the claimant on maintaining the child.

SINGLE PARENT ALLOWANCE/TAX CREDIT

[*TCA 1997, ss 462, 462A, 463; FA 1999, s 5; FA 2000, ss 6, 7; FA 2001, s 2(1), Sch 1 para 1(h)(i); FA 2002, s 3, Sch 1 para 1(c)(d); FA 2005, s 3, Sch 1; FA 2006, s 3*]

2.20 Applies to a widow(er) or other person not entitled to the married relief, or to the relief to a widow(er) in the year of bereavement, who during the year has a 'qualifying child' resident with him/her.

For **2001 onwards**, the relief is expressed as an available tax credit. The claimant's total income tax liability (excluding any liability in respect of tax deducted from payments made under *s 16(2)*) is reduced by the smaller of the available tax credit and what would otherwise be the claimant's total income tax liability. The available tax credit is as follows:

For	2001	£814
From	2002	€1,520
For	2005	€1,580
For	2006	€1,630
For	2007	€1,760
For	2008	€1,830
From	2009	€1,830
For	**2011**	**€1,650**

For 2000/01 only, relief is given by reference to a specified amount of £4,700 and is similarly given by means of a reduction in the claimant's income tax liability. The reduction is the smaller of a percentage of the specified amount equal to the standard rate of tax for the year of assessment (see **2.7** above) and what would otherwise be the claimant's total income tax liability.

A '*qualifying child*' is a child under 18 at the beginning of (or born in) the year of assessment, or over 18 at that time but either in full-time education or permanently incapacitated by reason of physical or mental infirmity from maintaining himself (having been so incapacitated before age 21 or while still in full-time education). The child must be the child of the claimant, or in the custody of the claimant and maintained at the claimant's expense for at least part of the year of assessment.

'*Child*' includes a stepchild and a child adopted under the *Adoption Acts* or equivalent foreign law. The *Status of Children Act 1987, s 3* applies in that:

(*a*)   relationships between persons are to be determined without regard to whether the parents of any person are or have been married to each other, unless the contrary intention appears; and

(*b*)   an adopted person shall, for the purposes of (*a*) above, be deemed from the date of adoption to be the child of the adopter or adopters, and not the child of any other person(s).

This applies for the purposes of the *Tax Acts* generally. See also **7.4** 'Capital acquisitions tax', **9.4** 'Capital gains tax', and **23.1** 'Married persons'. [*TCA 1997, ss 6, 8*]

Only one reduction, deduction or credit is available per claimant. The relief is not available to either spouse where the wife is living with the husband, and it is not available in the case of a man and woman living together as man and wife.

Limitation by reference to income of child. For 1999/2000 and 2000/01, the specified amount by reference to which the reduction of income tax liability is calculated is reduced or extinguished by any amount by which the child's own income (excluding scholarships, bursaries, etc) exceeds £720. There is no income limitation for 2001 and subsequent years.

Special relief for widowed parent following death of spouse. An individual whose spouse died in any of the five preceding years of assessment, and who has not remarried before the commencement of the year of assessment and has a 'qualifying child' (see above) resident with him/her for the whole or part of that year, is entitled to a special relief. For **2001 onwards**, the relief is expressed as an available tax credit. The claimant's total income tax liability (excluding any liability in respect of tax deducted from payments made under *s 16(2)*) is reduced by the smaller of the available tax credit and what would otherwise be the claimant's total income tax liability.

For **2011** the available tax credit is as follows:

First year after year of bereavement	€3,600
Second year after bereavement	€3.150
Third year after bereavement	€2,700
Fourth year after bereavement	€2,250
Fifth year after bereavement	€1,850

For **2009 and 2010**, the available tax credit is as follows:

First year after year of bereavement	€4,000
Second year after bereavement	€3,500
Third year after bereavement	€3,000
Fourth year after bereavement	€2,500
Fifth year after bereavement	€2,000

For **2008**, the available tax credit is as follows:

First year after year of bereavement	€4,000
Second year after bereavement	€3,500

Third year after bereavement	€3,000
Fourth year after bereavement	€2,500
Fifth year after bereavement	€2,000

For **2007**, the available tax credit is as follows:

First year after year of bereavement	€3,750
Second year after year of bereavement	€3,250
Third year after year of bereavement	€2,750
Fourth year after year of bereavement	€2,250
Fifth year after year of bereavement	€1,750

For **2006**, the available tax credit is as follows:

First year after year of bereavement	€3,100
Second year after year of bereavement	€2,600
Third year after year of bereavement	€2,100
Fourth year after year of bereavement	€1,600
Fifth year after year of bereavement	€1,100

For **2005**, the available tax credit is as follows:

First year after year of bereavement	€2,800
Second year after year of bereavement	€2,300
Third year after year of bereavement	€1,800
Fourth year after year of bereavement	€1,300
Fifth year after year of bereavement	€800

Prior to **2005**, the tax credit is:

First year after year of bereavement	€2,600/£2,000
Second year after year of bereavement	€2,100/£1,600
Third year after year of bereavement	€1,600/£1,200
Fourth year after year of bereavement	€1,100/£800
Fifth year after year of bereavement	€600/£400

For **2000/01** only, the relief is in effect given in the same way by reference to amounts of £2,200, £1,760, £1,320, £880 and £440 respectively.

The relief is, however, **not available** for any year of assessment in the case of a man and woman living together as man and wife. Only one allowance is available per claimant.

DEPENDENT RELATIVE ALLOWANCE/TAX CREDIT

[*TCA 1997, s 466; FA 2000, s 10(a); FA 2001, s 2(1) Sch 1 para 1(l), 2(h); FA 2002, s 3, Sch 1 para 1(g); FA 2006, s 3*]

2.21 Relief is available for:

(*a*) each relative incapacitated by old age or infirmity, or widowed mother, mother-in-law or father, if maintained by claimant; and (*b*)   any son or daughter resident with and maintained by the claimant, whose services the claimant is compelled to depend on because of his own old age or infirmity.

The relief is not available where child relief (see **2.19** above) or incapacitated individual relief (see **2.17** above) is claimed in respect of the same person. [*TCA 1997, s 465(2)(b) as inserted by FA 2001, Sch 1 para 1(k) (previously s 465(3)(c)); TCA 1997, s 467(4)*]

For **2001 onwards**, the relief is available where the income of the dependent relative does not exceed an income limit (which is the sum of a specified amount and the maximum contributory old age pension plus living alone allowance payable to a single person over 80 without dependants who is ordinarily resident on an island). It is expressed as an available tax credit. The claimant's total income tax liability (excluding any liability in respect of tax deducted from payments made under *s 16(2)*) is reduced by the smaller of the available tax credit and what would otherwise be the claimant's total income tax liability. The income limit and available tax credit are as follows:

		Income limit	Credit
For	2001	£4,989	£33
For	2002	€9,332	€60
For	2003	€9,852	€60
For	2004	€10,372	€60
For	2005	€10,997	€60
For	2006	€11,913	€80
For	2007	€11,913	€80
For	2008	€11,913	€80
For	2009	€11,913	€80
For	2010	€11,913	€80
For	**2011**	**€11,913**	**€70**

For 2000/01, the relief is given by means of a reduction of the claimant's income tax liability (excluding any liability in respect of tax deducted from payments made under *s 16(2)*). The reduction is the smaller of a percentage of the relief amount (see below) equal to the standard rate of tax for the year of assessment (see **2.6** above) and what would otherwise be the claimant's total income tax liability. For earlier years, the relief is given by means of a deduction from total income. Where income of the relative exceeds the limit below, the relief amount is reduced by £1 for each £1 of excess. The income limit is the sum of the maximum contributory old age pension plus living alone allowance payable to a single person over 80 without dependants. Where the income of the dependant relative exceeds €13,837 then there is no tax credit available.

		Amount	Income limit
For	2000/01	£220	£5,536
For	2009/2010		€13,837

BLIND PERSON ALLOWANCE/TAX CREDIT

[*TCA 1997, s 468; FA 1999, s 8; FA 2000, s 11(a); FA 2001, s 2(1), Sch 1 para 1(n); FA 2002, s 3, Sch 1 para 1(i); FA 2005, s 3, Sch 1; FA 2006, s 3*]

2.22 Claimable where the taxpayer (or, in the case of a taxpayer whose spouse's income is treated as his or her own (see **23.1** 'Married persons'), the taxpayer's spouse) is blind (as defined) for any part of a year of assessment. If both spouses are blind, double relief is given (as shown below).

For **2001 onwards**, the relief is expressed as an available tax credit. The claimant's total income tax liability (excluding any liability in respect of tax deducted from payments made under *s 16(2)*) is reduced by the smaller of the available tax credit and what would otherwise be the claimant's total income tax liability. The available tax credit is:

		Blind person	Both spouses blind
For	2001	£444	£888
From	2002	€800	€1,600
For	2005	€1,000	€2,000
For	2006	€1,500	€3,000
For	2007	€1.760	€3,250
For	2008	€1,830	€3,660
For	2009	€1,830	€3,660
For	2010	€1,830	€3,660
For	**2011**	**€1,650**	**€3,300**

For **2000/01** only, the relief is in effect given in the same way, the reduction in tax being up to £660/£1,320, but is expressed in terms of standard rate relief on an amount of £3,000/£6,000.

It is understood that, by concession, an additional allowance of €825/£650 (for 2001 only £481) is available as a deduction from total income in respect of a guide dog.

HEALTH EXPENSES

2.23

(*a*) **Health insurance**. [*TCA 1997, s 470; FA 2001, s 19; FA 2004, s 11; FA 2010, s 20*] Relief is given for payments to authorised insurers (for a list of which see Revenue Tax Briefing Issue 44 Supplement p 33) for insurance covering medical, surgical, nursing, hospital etc fees re sickness or accident to self, spouse or dependants (premiums being apportioned as necessary where the expenses covered are only partly allowable). Since 6 April 2001, the allowable expenses are extended to correspond to those for which relief is available under *s 469* (see (*b*) below) when met directly. The Table to *s 470B* has been amended which relates to the age-related tax credit in respect of health insurance premiums paid by individuals over the age of 50. *FA 2011, s 9* abolishes the credit for persons between the ages of 50–59 and increases the age related credit for persons aged 60 and over where the contract is entered into or renewed on or after 1st January 2011. The age-related tax credit in the case of persons insured over the age of 60 was increased for contracts entered into on or after 1 January 2010 and was again increased for contracts entered into on or after 1st January 2011. For those aged between 60–69 the credit was increased from €500 (pre-2010) to €525 (2010) to €625 (2011 and subsequent years) and for those aged between 70–79 the credit is increased from €950 (pre-2010) to €975 (2010) to €1,275 (2011 and subsequent years) and for those between 80–89 from €1,175 (pre-2010) to €1,250 (2010) to €1,725 (2011 and subsequent years). [*FA 2010, s 20, FA 2011, s 9*] **Since 1 January 2004**, relief for premiums for non-routine dental treatment provided by those who provide only dental insurance is also included. Relief is given at the standard rate only and for 2001 and subsequent tax years it is given by deduction of standard rate tax from premiums (or the allowable part thereof), the insurer recovering the tax deducted from the Revenue Commissioners (subject to regulations, see *SI 129/01*). See Revenue Tax Briefing Issue 43 pp 23, 24 for the working of the deduction scheme. For 2000/01 and earlier years, relief is given by a reduction in income tax liability (and is limited to that liability) and by reference to premiums paid in the preceding tax year, and for 2001 only relief may be given both for premiums paid in 2000/01 (by reduction of income tax liability) and for those paid in 2001 (by deduction). Relief for premiums paid in 2001 onwards is not clawed back from non-taxpayers. The Revenue Commissioners have appropriate powers of inspection to audit repayment claims by insurers (see *s 904E; FA 2001, s 22(1)*);

(*b*) **Costs**. [*TCA 1997, s 469; FA 1999, s 6(b); FA 2000, Sch 1 para 5; FA 2001, s 8, Sch 2 para 22; FA 2002, s 9*] An allowance is given (by tax repayment) for the cost (not recoverable by insurance or compensation etc) of certain medical, hospital etc fees, drugs etc in respect of self, spouse, dependants (including, from 2002 onwards, all relatives), housekeeper, so far as they exceed €125/£100 per individual or €250/£200 per family in any year without maximum. (For 2001 only, the figures are £74 and £148 respectively.) For procedures and guidelines in relation to *s 469* claims, see Revenue Tax Briefing Issue 17 p 5, Issue 33 pp 10–17, Issue 41 pp 30, 33, Issue 43 pp 15,16 and Issue 46 p 23.

Finance Act 2007, s 9 amends *s 469*. This section abolishes the requirement that there be a defined relationship between the taxpayer and the person on behalf of which the relief is claimed. The second amendment abolishes the two tier *de minimis* limits of €125 and €250 that currently exist so that the full amount of qualifying health expenses paid will qualify for tax relief;

Finance Act 2007, s 9 amends *469*. This section abolishes the requirement that there be a defined relationship between the taxpayer and the person on behalf of which the relief is claimed. The second amendment abolishes the two tier *de minimis* limits of €125 and €250 that currently exist so that the full amount of qualifying health expenses paid will qualify for tax relief;

Finance (No 2) Act 2008, amends *469*. This section provides that income tax relief in respect of expenditure incurred in the provision of health care will be granted at the standard rate of tax from 1 January 2009 with the exception of expenditure incurred in respect of nursing home expenses. These will continue to be allowed at the marginal rate for 2009;

(*c*)   **Permanent health benefit schemes**. [*TCA 1997, s 471*] An individual who makes a claim is entitled to a deduction for any premiums etc paid by him to a *bona fide* permanent health benefit scheme approved by the Revenue Commissioners (or in a standard form approved by them), up to a **maximum of ten per cent of his total income for the tax year**. Relief is also given where the premiums etc are paid by the employer so as to be a taxable benefit in kind;

(*d*)   **Long-term care insurance.** [*TCA 1997, s 470A; FA 2001, s 20; FA 2002, s 138, Sch 6; SI 130/01*] *Finance Act 2010, s 6* has abolished relief under *s 470A* as of from 1 January 2010. Since 6 April 2001, relief similar to that under (*a*) above is available for premiums paid by an RI-resident individual to a 'qualifying insurer' under an approved 'qualifying long-term care policy' (both of which terms are extensively defined) under which the beneficiary is the individual or a spouse, child or relative of the individual (or a relative of the spouse). The individual must, on entering into the policy, furnish the qualifying insurer with a signed declaration in prescribed form, including an undertaking to inform the insurer should the individual become non-resident. Relief is given by deduction of standard rate tax from the premiums, the insurer recovering the tax deducted from the Revenue Commissioners (subject to regulations). Relief is not clawed back from non-taxpayers. The Revenue Commissioners have appropriate powers of inspection to audit repayment claims by insurers (see *s 904G; FA 2001, s 22(4)*).

Benefits paid to an individual under such a permanent health benefit scheme are chargeable under Sch E (**34.1**).

RETIREMENT ANNUITIES

[*TCA 1997, ss 783–787; FA 1999, s 19; FA 2000, s 23; FA 2001, s 18; FA 2002, s 10; FA 2005, s 19; FA 2006, s 14*]

2.24 An individual may deduct from his 'net relevant earnings' (see below) chargeable to tax in a year of assessment any qualifying premium paid by him under an annuity contract (approved by the Revenue Commissioners) which (except as below) precludes:

(*a*)   any payment during the life of the individual other than an annuity commencing not earlier than age 60 nor later than age 75 (70 for contracts entered into before 6 April 1999), up to one-quarter of the value of which may be commuted for a lump sum at commencement of the annuity but capped at €1,250,000 from 7 December 2005; and

(*b*)   any payment after his death other than an annuity (not greater than the original annuity) to the surviving spouse or, if no annuity becomes payable either to the individual or spouse, the return of premiums paid, with reasonable interest or bonuses out of profits.

Prior to 1 January 2005, the contract must be with a person carrying on a life annuity business in RI. Since then, the contract may also be with an insurance undertaking authorised to transact business in RI.

From 2002 onwards, contributions may continue to be made to such a contract (or a contract commenced) after the source of relevant earnings has ceased. No immediate tax relief is available in respect of such contributions, but they may be carried forward indefinitely until such time (if any) as a source of relevant earnings is acquired against which they may be set under the rules described below.

Any payment on or after 1 January 2002 of an annuity under (*a*) or (*b*) above is chargeable under Sch E and subject to PAYE.

Payment of a lump sum (or the aggregate lump sums) under (a) above is tax-free up to 25 per cent of the maximum allowable pension fund (see below). Any excess is subject to income tax at the marginal rate. The maximum tax-free lump sum is currently set at €200,000 (with effect from 1 January 2011). The maximum tax-free lump sum up to 31 December 2010 was €1,250,000. Amounts received in excess of the €200,000 will be taxed at the standard rate (currently 20%) up to €575,000 ie on the next €375,000, with the balance being taxed at the individual's marginal rate of tax. [*FA 2011, s 19*] Prior to 7 December 2005, the tax-free amount was unlimited. The restriction does not apply to death-in-service benefit.

Contracts must offer an alternative option, exercisable at or before the time the annuity would otherwise have become payable, for the transfer either to the individual or to an approved retirement fund of the value of the annuity (net of any lump sum in commutation as under (*a*) above) reduced by €63,500/£50,000 (or to nil if the value of the annuity is less than €63,500/£50,000). Where the individual has previously exercised such an option in relation to another contract, any earlier such restriction is set against the €63,500/£50,000 restriction to be applied. The €63,500/£50,000 (or lesser) restriction does not apply if the individual has other pensions or annuities guaranteed for life totalling at least €12,700/£10,000 pa. This minimum guaranteed income has been increased to €18,000 with effect from 1 January 2011. Should this requirement not be met, the amount to be placed in an AMRF is to be increased from €63,500 to approximately €120,000. Both income and set-aside amounts are multiples of the maximum annual (Contributory) State Pension. Some transitional measures will apply. The amount by which the transfer to the individual or the approved retirement fund is required to be restricted must either be applied to the purchase of an immediate annuity or transferred to an approved minimum retirement fund. If the individual opts for an amount to be transferred to himself, that amount is treated as income of the individual chargeable to Sch E tax under PAYE (in full at the higher rate unless the Revenue Commissioners have directed otherwise). (Before 6 April 2000, the charge was under Sch D, Case IV.) Transfers to an approved retirement fund or an approved minimum retirement fund are free of tax. See further below as regards approved retirement funds and approved minimum retirement funds. Schemes approved before 6 April 1999 may be altered to allow for such an option, which, in the case of pensions which became payable after 1 December 1998 and before 6 April 1999, must then be exercised within six months of the pension having become payable.

The Revenue Commissioners may conditionally approve contracts with other specified provisions.

Finance Act 2007 inserts *s 772A* into *Pt 30, Ch 1* with the aim of simplifying the Revenue's approval process in relation to certain occupational pension scheme 'Products' in line with current approval of retirement annuity contracts and PRSAs. The effect of the new section was that Revenue can in certain circumstances approve generic retirement benefits product and provides for retirement benefit schemes established under such a product to be treated as approved schemes for tax purposes.

Finance Act 2010, s 16 has introduced a requirement for the delivery of certain information by electronic delivery in relation to Small Self-Administered Pension Schemes. In addition, *Sch 23* has been amended so that administrators of Small Self-Administered Pension Schemes who are already obliged to deliver annual scheme accounts to the Revenue Commissioners, to deliver those accounts by such electronic means as are required or approved by the Commissioners. This new obligation will apply in respect of schemes with account years ending on or after 1 January 2011. A condition of the approval is that the combined employer and employee contributions to such schemes in any tax year may not exceed the maximum aged related tax relievable contributions that may be made by an employee to a retirement scheme at present (as set out below).

[*TCA 1997, ss 784, 786; FA 1999, s 19; FA 2000, s 23(1)(c); FA 2001, s 18(a); FA 2002, s 10(1)(b)(2); FA 2010, s 16*]

See generally Revenue Booklet IT 14.

Contracts for dependants or for life assurance. The Commissioners may approve a contract under which:

(i) the main benefit is an annuity for a spouse or one or more dependants of an individual; or

(ii) the sole benefit is a lump sum, on death before age 75 (70 for contracts approved before 6 April 1999), payable to the personal representatives.

Conditions are laid down, which must be met by contracts falling within (ii) above, but the Commissioners may approve a contract under (i) above even if it does not meet the conditions. Any payment on or after 1 January 2002 of an annuity within (i) above is chargeable under Sch E and subject to PAYE. [*TCA 1997, ss 784(7), 785; FA 1999, s 19(1)(b)(iv); FA 2001, s 18(a)*]

Contributions to approved trust schemes providing similar benefits as above are treated as qualifying premiums. [*TCA 1997, ss 784(4), 785(5)*]

Total premiums deductible are limited to the percentage of 'net relevant earnings' set out in the table below:

Aged 30–39	20%
Aged 40–49	25%
Aged 50–54	30%
Aged 55–59	35%
Aged over 60	40%
Specified Individual	30%
All other cases	15%

The appropriate age category applies if that age is reached at any time in the year of assessment. The 'net relevant earnings' taken into account for this purpose may not exceed €115,000 for 2011 (€150,000 from 2009 to 2010) (€254,000/£200,000 from 1

January 2002 to 31 December 2008) (for 2001 only, £148,000) (or such other amount as the Minister for Finance may specify by order). It should be noted that the reduced figure for 2011 applies to contributions made in relation to a 2010 income tax liability but made in the 2011 tax year. From 2007, this sum is to be indexed annually in line with an earnings factor. A *'specified individual'* is an individual whose relevant earnings derive wholly or mainly from an occupation or profession specified in *Sch 23A*. These currently comprise athletes, badminton players, boxers, cyclists, footballers, golfers, jockeys, motor racing drivers, rugby players, squash players, swimmers and tennis players, but the list may be extended or restricted by regulation by the Minister for Finance. Prior to 2006, the upper limit was 30 per cent for individuals over 50. Within the limits, qualifying premiums under *s 785* (see above) were, before 6 April 2001, restricted to five per cent and were deducted before any other premiums. Subject to the Revenue making the necessary regulations, payment of premiums in respect of ordinary annual contributions will be subject to the net pay arrangements (see **2.26** 'Personal retirement savings accounts'). These regulations are effective from 1 January 2004. Since 1 January 2004, employers are required to return details of contributions made in respect of employees. [*TCA 1997, ss 787(2A)(6)(8)(9), 897A, Sch 23A; ITA 1967, s 236(1)–(1B); FA 1996, s 13(a); FA 1999, s 19(1)(b)(c); FA 2001, s 18(c), Sch 2 para 41; FA 2003, s 14; FA 2004, s 86; FA 2006, s 14, FA 2011, s 19*]

If qualifying premiums up to the maximum limit cannot be fully allowed because of an insufficiency of 'net relevant earnings', the disallowed part may be carried forward until it can be allowed within the limits for a later year. [*TCA 1997, s 787(10)*]

Where a qualifying premium is paid after the end of a year of assessment, but before the filing return date for the year (see **28.11** 'Returns'), an election may be made, before that date (a time limit which is strictly applied), to treat the premium as if it had been paid in the earlier year of assessment. [*TCA 1997, s 787(7); FA 1998, s 46*]

Relevant Earnings comprise income:

(i)   from non-pensionable employments etc;

(ii)   from property attached to such employment forming part of the emoluments; or

(iii)   chargeable under Sch D as immediately derived from a trade, profession etc carried on personally or as an active partner;

but not including remuneration from any investment company to a person controlling more than 15 per cent of its ordinary share capital, nor the relevant earnings of the individual's wife. [*TCA 1997, s 783(3)*]

Net Relevant Earnings are relevant earnings, as above, less deductions for tax purposes:

(*a*)   in respect of payments; or

(*b*)   in respect of losses or of capital allowances relating to activities, profits from which would be relevant earnings.

Net relevant earnings are capped at €150,000 from 1st January 2009. Where such deductions may be treated as made out of either relevant earnings or other income, then so far as possible, deductions under (*b*) are treated as made from relevant earnings but if treated in any year as made from income other than relevant earnings the net relevant earnings for the next year are treated as reduced to that extent with any balance being carried forward to the third year, and so on. [*TCA 1997, s 787(1)–(5)*]

Deemed Payment. Since 2 February 2006, the use of assets of an occupational scheme for certain transactions is deemed to be a pension payment under the scheme and subject to tax. The transactions are those which would be regarded as giving rise to a transfer out of the fund if undertaken in an approved retirement fund (see below) ie where the assets of the fund are used to make a loan to, or as security for a loan to, the individual or a connected person or are used to acquire property from the individual or a connected person, or assets of the fund are sold to the individual or a connected person. Assets used by the fund in the acquisition of a holiday home or residence for use by, and used by, the individual or a connected person are treated as no longer being assets of the fund, as are any funds used in the improvement or repair of the property and funds used in the purchase of shares in a close company (see **12.7** 'Corporation Tax') of which the individual is a participator. A company that would be a close company if resident in the State is deemed a close company for this purpose. Fund assets that are treated as a pension paid under the scheme are no longer regarded as assets of the scheme. Likewise property assets acquired with such fund assets are not regarded as assets of the scheme.

Maximum fund value Since 7 December 2005 a ceiling is placed on the total capital value of pension benefits that an individual can draw in his lifetime from tax relieved pension products where the benefits first come into payment on or after that date. The ceiling or 'standard fund threshold' was currently set at €5,400,000 up to the tax year 2011. The current ceiling is set at €2,300,000. An application may be made to Revenue before 7 June 2011 for a higher threshold (personal fund threshold) if the value of the individual's crystallised pension rights on or after 7 December 2005 together with their uncrystallised pension rights as at 7 December 2010 exceed the €2.3m threshold. A personal fund threshold certified by Revenue prior to 7 December 2010 continues to apply. [FA 2011, s 19] Where on 7 December 2005 an individual had a fund to which he was not yet entitled and the value of which exceeded €5,000,000, that higher figure ('personal fund threshold') applies to that individual subject to notification to Revenue. Both thresholds will be indexed from 2007 in line with an earnings factor. *Finance (No 2) Act 2008* amended the formula relating to the determination of the standard and personal fund thresholds contained in *s 787O(1)*. The amendment provided the Minister of Finance with discretion as to whether those thresholds should be indexed in line with an earnings adjustment factor in future years. It also amended, for the same reason, the formula in *s 790A(2)* relating to the determination of the annual earnings limit for tax relieved pension contributions. The amendments ensure that where no indexation is provided for, the thresholds and the annual earnings limit will remain at the previous year's amounts. The annual earnings limit for tax relieved pension contributions as of from 2009 has been set at €150,000. [*F(No 2)A 2008, s 16*] When an individual becomes entitled to receive a benefit under a pension scheme – a benefit crystallisation event (BCE) – a capital value is placed on the benefits that crystallise and the value is tested against the individuals' fund threshold. For defined benefit schemes, a factor of 20 must be used unless the pension scheme administrator can justify otherwise. Where the capital value of a BCE on its own or when added to previous BCEs exceeds the threshold of the individual, the excess is subject to an up-front income tax charge of 42 per cent payable by the administrator in the first instance although liability is joint and several with the individual. *Finance Act 2007* reduced the higher rate of income tax from 42 per cent to 41 per cent, therefore the chargeable excess where the capital value of the pension benefit received by an individual exceeds the standard fund threshold or personal fund threshold will be liable to tax at a rate of 41 per cent rather than 42 per cent. This is effective from 1 January 2007. The charge is without prejudice to any other income tax charge that might arise on the fund balance as and when benefits are taken from the scheme by way of pension, annuity, taxable cash lump sum or distribution from an ARF or AMRF. Where an annual benefit increases by the greater of five per cent or the consumer price index plus two per cent, the value of the individual's total pension entitlements are retested against the maximum threshold. Since 7 December 2005 to 31 March 2006, responsibility for accounting and paying any tax liability rests with the individual entitled to the benefits giving rise to the charge with certain reporting requirements being imposed on pension fund administrators where the capital value of a BCE made in the period is substantial. Provisions have been introduced to deal with fund/benefit valuations, BCE occurrences and commutation of entitlements to discharge tax liabilities etc.

The legislation introduced by *FA 2006* did not deal with the implications of Pension Adjustment Orders. This deficit is dealt with in *FA 2007, s 17* which amended *Pt 30, Ch 2C*. Where a couple are separating or divorcing the Courts are empowered under the *Family Law Act 1995* and the *Family Law (Divorce) Act 1996* to treat a pension as an asset of the couple and make an order over the division of same by way of a Pension Adjustment Order. The amendment provided that where there is a Pension Adjustment Order in place over a pension fund the calculation of the amount crystallised on a benefit crystallisation event should be determined as if the Pension Adjustment Order has not been made.

As such, any benefit arising under the Pension Adjustment Order is deemed to be a benefit arising to the individual for the purposes of determining whether the individuals standard fund threshold or personal fund threshold has been exceeded.

General Practitioners. Special arrangements apply to doctors who participate in the General Medical Services Superannuation Plan and also make retirement annuity payments.

Approved retirement funds and approved minimum retirement funds. Transfers may be made to approved retirement funds from retirement annuity contracts (see above) and from retirement benefit schemes, in the latter case only in relation to members who are 'proprietary directors' (broadly those controlling more than five per cent (before 6 April 2000, 20 per cent) of the voting rights in a company), and part of any such transfer may be required to be to an approved minimum retirement fund. With effect from 6 April 2000, transfers may be made to such funds from additional voluntary contributions made to retirement benefit schemes. See above as regards the conditions concerning such transfers from retirement annuity contracts (which are similar to those applicable in the case of proprietary directors). Transfers into both approved retirement funds and approved minimum retirement funds, and between approved funds, are free from tax, and the assets of a fund are in the beneficial ownership of the individual who elected for the transfer. In relation to funds created **on or after 6 April 2000**, income and gains arising in the fund are exempt from income and capital gains tax. For funds established before that date, they are chargeable on the individual who is the beneficial owner, and fund managers are required to keep appropriate records and make the necessary notifications. An annuity purchased with funds in an approved retirement fund or approved minimum retirement fund is not a 'purchased life annuity' within *s 788* (see **13.7** 'Deduction of tax at source').

Approved retirement funds. The individual may make transfers out of the fund at any time. **Since 6 April 2000**, such transfers are treated as income subject to Sch E tax under PAYE (in full at the higher rate unless the Revenue Commissioners direct otherwise). **Since 6 February 2003**, a transfer is treated as made out of the fund where the assets of the fund are used to make a loan to or as security for a loan to the individual or a connected person or are used to acquire property from the individual or a connected person or assets of the fund are sold to the individual or a connected person. Assets used by the fund in the acquisition of a holiday home or residence for use by, and used by, the individual or a connected person are treated as transfers, as are any funds used in the improvement or repair of the property and funds used in the purchase of shares in a close company (see **12.7** 'Close companies') of which the individual is a participator. A company that would be a close company if resident in the State is deemed a close company for this purpose. The amount of the deemed transfer is the value of the fund assets used in the acquisition or disposal. Since 2 February 2006, the acquisition of property for use in connection with any business of an ARF holder or a connected person is treated as a transfer out of the fund. Where the transfer follows the death of the individual, it is treated as the individual's income for the year of assessment of death, subject to PAYE as above, unless the transfer is to an approved retirement fund for the spouse or to or for the sole benefit of children of the individual under 21 at the date of death, in which case it is free of income tax. In the case of a transfer to a child aged 21 or over, or, in the case of a transfer to a spouse's fund, on a subsequent transfer on the spouse's death (other than to a child under 21), the fund manager is required to deduct tax at the standard rate of income tax in force at the time of the distribution, such deductions being treated as if made under PAYE, and the transfer attracts no further liability. Fund managers neither trading through a fixed place of business nor resident in RI must have an RI-resident appointee to discharge their responsibilities, including accounting for any tax deducted under PAYE as above, and where there are insufficient funds to meet such liabilities, there is provision for recovery from the individual entitled to the fund assets (or from the individual's estate).

For funds established before 6 April 2000, transfers are free of tax to the extent that they are out of income and gains. Where a transfer exceeds the accumulated income and gains (net of any earlier transfers), other than in the case of certain transfers on death (see below), the excess is chargeable as income under Sch D, Case IV. Where the transfer follows the death of the individual, the excess is treated as the individual's income for the year of assessment of death, on which the fund manager must account for higher rate tax, unless the transfer is to an approved retirement fund for the spouse or to or for the sole benefit of children of the individual under 21 at the date of death, in which case it is free of tax. In the case of a transfer to a spouse's fund, on a subsequent transfer on the spouse's death (other than to a child under 21) the fund manager must account for tax at 25 per cent rather than the higher rate, and the transfer attracts no further tax liability.

From 2007, a distribution of one per cent of the funds will be deemed to have been made during the year. This figure increases to two per cent for 2008 and three per cent for 2009 to 31 Decembe r2010 and fice per cent from 1 January 2011 and beyond.. The deemed distribution applies to funds created on or after 6 April 2000 where the ARF holder is 60 years or older for the whole tax year. Any deemed distribution is reduced by any actual distributions made in the year. The deemed distribution is regarded as a distribution made in January of the year following the year in respect of which the ARF assets are valued. Where an ARF holder has more than one fund managed by different fund managers, he may nominate the manager to operate the new provisions.

Finance Act 2007 extended the period in which a qualifying fund manager must account for any tax due on a notional distribution from an ARF. The notional distribution which is calculated as a percentage of the value of the assets in the ARF as of 31 December each year, will now be regarded as a distribution made not later than February in the year following the year in which the assets of the ARF are valued.

It has been clarified that the notional distribution from an ARF is to be calculated for the year of assessment 2010 and subsequent years at the rate of 5 per cent of the assets in the ARF at 31 December each year. A number of amendments have been made to *Ch 2C* and associated *Sch 23B* which deal with the lifetime limit on tax relieved pension funds. The changes ensure that where an individual with a PSRA decides at the point of taking pension benefits, to leave the funds in a PSRA rather than opting to transfer them to an ARF, then the act of leaving the funds in the PRSA will itself constitute a benefit crystallisation event for the purposes of the legislation. [*FA 2010, s 15*]

Approved minimum retirement funds. The individual may make transfers out of income and gains arising in the fund at any time. **Since 6 April 2000**, such transfers are dealt with in the same way as transfers out of approved retirement funds (as above). For funds established before that date, they are free of tax. No transfers may be made out of such funds other than of accumulated income and gains until the individual reaches 75 or dies, at which time the fund becomes an approved retirement fund and is treated as above. The above provisions relating to deemed transfers for approved retirement funds also apply.

As regards conditions applicable to approved retirement funds and approved minimum retirement funds, see *ss 784B, 784D*.

[*TCA 1997, ss 772(3A), 784A–784E; FA 1999, s 19; FA 2000, s 23; FA 2001, s 18(a), Sch 1 para 1(p); FA 2003, s 14; FA 2005, s 21; FA 2006, s 14*]

As regards approved funds generally, see Revenue Booklet IT 14 and Revenue Tax Briefing Issue 41 p 23.

PERSONAL RETIREMENT SAVINGS ACCOUNTS ('PRSAS')

[*TCA 1997, ss 787A–789; FA 2003, s 14; FA 2005, s 21; FA 2006, s 14*]

2.25 An individual may deduct from his 'net relevant earnings' (see below) chargeable to tax in a year of assessment, contributions paid by him under a contract (approved by the Revenue Commissioners) which provides that:

(*a*)　Any annuity payable or other assets made available to the PRSA contributor must not be payable or made available before age 60 or after age 75. An annuity must be a life annuity and must not be capable of commutation or assignment;

(*b*)　During the life of the PRSA contributor, assets are not made available otherwise than by way of (i) an annuity to the PRSA contributor, (ii) a tax-free lump sum, (iii) a payment subject to marginal rate income tax, (iv) a transfer to an Approved Retirement Fund (see **2.24** above), or (v) assets made available to the PRSA contributor where the PRSA provider retains such assets as would be required to be transferred to an Approved Minimum Retirement Fund (see **2.24** above) if the Approved Retirement Fund option were exercised; and

(c)   on death of the PRSA contributor no sums are payable other than an annuity to the surviving spouse (which cannot be greater than that payable to the PRSA contributor) or, where no annuity has become payable, a transfer of the PRSA assets to the estate of the PRSA contributor.

The contract must be with a person carrying on business in RI as a PRSA provider or RI-resident agent or (from 1 January 2005) with a person that has entered into a contract with the Revenue Commissioners for the discharge of all duties imposed under the legislation.

Finance (No 2) Act 2011, s 4 provides for a stamp duty levy on pension schemes as of from 19 May 2011. The section also introduces consequential changes to certain provisions of the *Taxes Consolidation Act 1997* relating to the approval conditions that apply to pension scheme providers located outside the State that seek to provide retirement benefits in the State. Under the existing legislation, such providers are required, unless they have a fiscal representative in the State, to enter into a contract with the Revenue Commissioners to the effect that all duties and obligations imposed by the pensions tax legislation will be discharged. These duties and obligations are now extended to include the levy.

Total premiums deductible are the greater of €1,525 (save for members of occupational pension schemes) or **20 per cent** of 'net relevant earnings' in the case of an individual aged at least 30 but not 40 or more at any time in the year of assessment, to **25 per cent** of 'net relevant earnings' in the case of an individual aged at least 40 but not 50 or more at any time in the year of assessment, to **30 per cent** of 'net relevant earnings' in the case of an individual aged at least 50 but not 55 or more at any time in the year of assessment, to 35 per cent of 'net relevant earnings' in the case of an individual aged at least 55 but not more than 60 at any time in the year of assessment, to 40 per cent of 'net relevant earnings' in the case of an individual aged at least 60 at any time in the year of assessment or to **15 per cent** of 'net relevant earnings' in any other case.

Relevant Earnings comprise income:

(i)   from employments etc;

(ii)   from property attached to such employment forming part of the emoluments; or

(iii)   chargeable under Sch D as immediately derived from a trade, profession etc carried on personally or as an active partner;

but not including remuneration from any investment company to a person controlling more than 15 per cent of its ordinary share capital, nor the relevant earnings of the individual's wife. [*TCA 1997, s 787B*]

Net Relevant Earnings are relevant earnings, as above, less deductions for tax purposes:

(a)   in respect of payments; or

(b)   in respect of losses or of capital allowances relating to activities, profits from which would be relevant earnings.

Where such deductions may be treated as made out of either relevant earnings or other income, then so far as possible, deductions under (*b*) are treated as made from relevant earnings but if treated in any year as made from income other than relevant earnings the net relevant earnings for the next year are treated as reduced to that extent, with any balance being carried forward to the third year, and so on. [*TCA 1997, s 787B*]

The maximum 'net relevant earnings' relievable in any one year is €254,000, to be indexed annually from 2007 in accordance with an earnings index. Contributions to a PRSA and a retirement annuity contract (see **2.24** above) are aggregated when calculating the maximum tax relief. Employees who are members of occupational pension schemes (other than solely for death in service benefit) may only use a PRSA as a vehicle for making additional voluntary contributions – 'additional voluntary PRSA contributions'. The percentage limits as applied to RAC premiums apply also to additional voluntary PRSA contributions. Contributions by the PRSA contributor to the occupational pension scheme are aggregated with additional voluntary PRSA contributions in determining the extent of relief to be given in the year of assessment.

Employer contributions made on behalf of an employee are a benefit in kind but are treated as contributions made by the employee for tax relief purposes. Where contributions are deducted from an employee's emoluments, relief is given under the 'net pay' arrangements, ie PAYE/PRSI is computed on the 'net-of-contribution' remuneration for the year in which the deduction is made. Employers are required to file information relating to employer and employee contributions. Penalties apply for failure to comply. [*TCA 1997, s 897A; FA 2004, s 86*]

The Revenue Commissioners have discretion to approve a PRSA product that satisfies the above conditions but also makes provision for early payment of an annuity or the making available of PRSA assets in certain circumstances or the payment of an annuity for a term certain and the assignment of that annuity in the event of the death of the PRSA contributor.

If contributions up to the maximum limit cannot be fully allowed because of an insufficiency of 'net relevant earnings', the disallowed part may be carried forward until it can be allowed within the limits for a later year.

Where a qualifying premium is paid after the end of a year of assessment, but before the filing return date for the year (see **28.11** 'Returns'), an election may be made before that date to treat the contribution as if it had been paid in the earlier year of assessment provided that the payment has not been made under the net pay arrangement.

Any payment of an annuity to the PRSA contributor or spouse, or payment of another sum (other than a tax-free lump sum) to the PRSA contributor, is chargeable under Sch E and subject to PAYE.

On retirement, the PRSA contributor may receive a tax-free lump sum of 25 per cent of the fund. The balance may be transferred to an approved retirement fund, subject to the approved minimum retirement fund requirements (see **2.25** above), or may remain in the PRSA fund for the benefit of the PRSA contributor. Where the individual leaves the funds in the PRSA, the act of leaving them in the PRSA will be deemed to constitute a 'benefit crystallisation event' for the purposes of the legislation. [*FA 2010, s 15*] The deemed distributions provisions relating to assets made available for the use of the contributor apply in a similar manner to those for approved retirement funds.

Transfers of funds from a retirement annuity contract to a PRSA are permitted. Transfers of funds from an occupational pension scheme to a PRSA are permitted where the contributor is a member of the occupational pension scheme for 15 years or less. The value of AVC contributions may be transferred without restriction. A refund from an occupational pension scheme may be transferred to a PRSA without application of the 20 per cent withholding tax charge ordinarily applicable to refunds.

Where the PRSA contributor dies before retirement, the PRSA fund may pass to his estate, free of income tax. Where the contributor dies after benefits have commenced, the assets in the PRSA fund are treated in the same manner as assets in an approved retirement fund.

The income and capital gains arising from investment of PRSA contributions are exempt from tax.

Maximum fund value The limitations that apply to retirement annuities apply also to a PRSA (see **2.24** above).

See generally Revenue Tax Briefing Issue 47 pp 29, 30 and Issue 50 pp 18, 19 and Revenue guidance note 'A Guide to Personal Retirement Savings Accounts [PRSAs]'.

PENSIONS – INCENTIVE TAX CREDITS

[*TCA 1997, s 848V–848AG*; *FA 2006, s 42*; Revenue e-Brief 20/2006]

2.26 From 2006, investment by an individual of funds matured from a special savings incentive account 'SSIA' (see **16.33**) in a retirement benefits scheme, annuity contract or PRSA attracts an incentive tax credit. The maximum investment credit is 25 per cent of the sum invested, subject to a maximum credit of €2,500 and is paid into the scheme by Revenue. Revenue will also pay into the scheme a part of the exit tax payable on maturity of the SSIA. The part of the exit tax payable is proportionate to the amount of the SSIA invested in the pension product. To avail of the scheme, the gross income of the individual in the year of assessment immediately prior to the year in which the account matures must not exceed €50,000. While the legislation requires that that income must be taxable entirely at the standard rate (or, if married, would be taxed at the standard rate if separate assessment had applied for the year), Revenue e-brief 20/2006 states that this requirement need not be met. Gross income includes exempt income and is before any deductions for losses, allowances, tax incentive reliefs etc and (save in the case of a trade), capital allowances. The individual must, within 3 months of maturity of the SSIA, provide a maturity statement to his pension fund administrator, subscribe all or part of the SSIA fund to the scheme, make a declaration as required by Revenue and not reduce any contribution that he is required to make to the scheme for the year. The declaration provides that the individual will not claim relief for his investment, or for €7,500 of that investment, if the investment exceeds that figure. [*FA 2006, ss 41, 42; SI 243/06*]

OVERSEAS PENSION PLANS – MIGRANT WORKERS

[*TCA 1997, ss 787M–787N*; *790A-B*; *Sch 23*; *FA 2005, s 21*; *FA 2006, s 14*; *SI 570/05*]

2.27 Since 1 January 2005, provision is made for a migrant worker to receive tax relief on pension contributions made to an overseas pension plan of which he was already a member prior to commencing employment in RI. Certain certification procedures and information provisions must be observed. The pension contribution is treated for tax purposes as a payment to an occupational pension scheme or retirement annuity contract. The remuneration limit of €254,000 applies. This figure is to be indexed annually from 2007. As required by the EU Pensions Directive, from 23 September 2005, investment income arising from contributions made to a scheme established in RI for the benefit of 'European members' of a 'European undertaking' as defined will be exempt from income tax as will underwriting commissions applied for the purposes of the scheme. The maximum fund value applicable to retirement annuities applies also (see **2.25** above).

ALLOWANCE TO OWNER-OCCUPIERS – URBAN RENEWAL, QUALIFYING ISLANDS ETC

2.28 Relief against total income may be claimed by an individual in respect of 'qualifying expenditure' attributable to work carried out in the period 1 August 1994 to 31 July 1997 inclusive (the *'qualifying period'*). The relief is available for the year of assessment in which the 'qualifying premises' is first in use as a dwelling after the incurring of the expenditure, and for any of the following nine years of assessment in which the 'qualifying premises' in respect of which the expenditure is incurred is the only or main residence of the individual. The amount of the relief is:

(*a*) where the 'qualifying expenditure' is on construction of the 'qualifying premises', **five per cent** of that expenditure;

(*b*) where the 'qualifying expenditure' is on 'refurbishment' of the 'qualifying premises', **ten per cent** of that expenditure.

The qualifying period may be extended to 31 July 1998 where the relevant local authority certifies (before 1 October 1997) that at least 15 per cent of the total cost had been incurred before 31 July 1997. This may be **further extended** to 31 December 1998 in certain cases involving delays outside the direct control of the person incurring the expenditure (**and further extended** to 30 April 1999 in certain cases where substantial expenditure had been incurred by 31 December 1998).

Where one of the ten years for which relief is available as above is the short tax year 2001, the amount of the relief for that year is restricted to 3.7 per cent (where (*a*) applies) or 7.4 per cent (where (*b*) applies), and relief is extended to the eleventh year, for which it is restricted to 1.3 per cent/2.6 per cent.

'Qualifying expenditure' is expenditure incurred by an individual on the construction or 'refurbishment' of a 'qualifying premises' which is first used, after the incurring of that expenditure, as the individual's only or main residence, net of any grants etc from the State or any statutory board or public or local authority. It includes expenditure on the development of the land (including gardens, access, etc), in particular demolition, groundworks, landscaping, walls, mains supplies and outhouses, etc for use by the occupants of the house. Expenditure borne by two or more persons is apportioned between or amongst them in the proportion in which they actually bore the expenditure. In practice, an appropriate proportion of expenditure incurred by an owner-occupier on purchasing property from a builder/developer qualifies for relief. See Revenue Tax Briefing Issue 29 p 6.

'*Refurbishment*' of a building means either or both of:

(i)   the carrying out of any works of construction, reconstruction, repair or renewal; and

(ii)   the provision or improvement of water, sewerage or heating facilities;

certified by the Minister for the Environment and Local Government, in a certificate of reasonable cost relating to any house contained in the building, as necessary to ensure the suitability as a dwelling of any house in the building, regardless of whether or not the number of houses in the building, or the shape or size of any such house, is altered in the course of the refurbishment. In practice, the Revenue accept that 'refurbishment' expenditure also includes expenditure on conversion. See Revenue Tax Briefing Issue 29 p 10.

'*Qualifying premises*' means a house (which includes any building or part of a building suitable for use as a dwelling, and land or outbuildings appurtenant thereto or usually enjoyed therewith) used solely as a dwelling:

(A)   the site of which is wholly within a designated area, or which fronts onto a designated street, so designated for the purpose by the Minister for Finance, which designation may specify a shorter period within the qualifying period referred to above;

(B)   of floor area not less than 30 sq metres or more than 125 sq metres (90 sq metres for expenditure incurred before 12 April 1995, except in the case of refurbishment expenditure) in the case of a self-contained flat or maisonette in a building of two or more storeys, or of not less than 35 sq metres or more than 125 sq metres in any other case;

(C)   in respect of which, if it is not a new house (within *Housing (Miscellaneous Provisions) Act 1979, s 4*), there is in force a 'certificate of reasonable cost', granted by the Minister for the Environment and Local Government, in which the construction or refurbishment cost specified is not less than that actually incurred;

(D)   complying with such conditions as to construction or improvement standards and service provision as the Minister may lay down under *Housing (Miscellaneous Provisions) Act 1979, s 4 or s 5*;

(E)   open to inspection by persons authorised in writing by the Minister at all reasonable times; and

(F)   which (or the development of which it is part) must comply with guidelines issued by the Minister concerning:

(i)   design, construction and refurbishment of the houses,

(ii)   total floor area and dimensions of rooms,

(iii)   provisions of ancillary facilities, and

(iv)   the 'balance' between the houses, the development and the location.

Where the qualifying premises front onto a designated street, relief under these provisions is available only in respect of refurbishment expenditure.

A house occupied by a person connected (within *s 10*) with the person claiming the deduction is excluded unless the lease is on arm's length terms.

An appeal lies to the Appeal Commissioners on any question arising under these provisions as it would in relation to an assessment to tax.

There is provision against double relief where relief is given under these provisions.

[*TCA 1997, ss 339, 340, 349, 350, 350A, 372AU; FA 1998, s 24; FA 1999, s 44(a)(b); FA 2001, Sch 2 para 20; FA 2002, s 24(3), Sch 2 para 1*]

Jointly-owned property. Where property is purchased in their joint names by married couples, relief may concessionally be granted, if so claimed, to the spouse who incurred the expenditure and, where the purchase was funded by borrowings, to the spouse who makes the repayments. The irrevocable agreement of both spouses to this treatment is required, together with an irrevocable undertaking from the spouse to whom relief is given to accept any balancing charge which may arise. See Revenue Tax Briefing Issue 37 p 9.

See below as regards continuing reliefs for urban renewal expenditure in the Temple Bar or Custom House Docks Areas of Dublin, and earlier reliefs for such expenditure in certain other areas. Where those earlier reliefs apply to certain expenditure incurred on or after 1 August 1994 as if it had been incurred before that date, the above provisions do not apply to such expenditure. [*TCA 1997, Sch 32 para 12; FA 1986, s 44(1)(g); FA 1994, s 35(1)(c)(iv)*] See also **8.10** 'Capital allowances', **30.25** 'Sch D, Cases I and II' and **33.11** 'Sch D, Case V'.

Expenditure on certain islands. Provisions similar to those described above in relation to qualifying premises in 'designated areas' apply to construction and refurbishment expenditure incurred between **1 August 1996 and 31 July 1999** inclusive on a dwelling the site of which is on a 'designated island' (see **33.13** 'Sch D, Case V'), with the following differences:

(I)   the requirement in (F) above that certain Ministerial guidelines must be complied with does not apply; and

(II)   both construction and refurbishment expenditure attract five per cent relief (ie the ten per cent refurbishment relief in (*b*) above is reduced to five per cent).

The qualifying period is extended to 31 December 1999 where the relevant local authority has certified (before 1 November 1999) that at least 15 per cent of the total cost had been incurred before 1 August 1999.

[*TCA 1997, ss 360, 364, 365, 372AU; FA 1999, s 46; FA 2000, s 43; FA 2001, Sch 2 para 21; FA 2002, s 24(3), Sch 2 para 1*]

Qualifying rural areas. Provisions similar to those described above in relation to qualifying premises in 'designated areas' apply to construction and refurbishment expenditure incurred between **6 April 1999 and 31 December 2004** (extended to **31 December 2006** subject to certain conditions being satisfied) inclusive on a dwelling the site of which is wholly within a 'qualifying rural area' (see **33.14** 'Sch D, Case V'). The differences are that the permitted floor area in (B) above is a minimum of 38 sq metres and a maximum of 210 sq metres, and the requirement in (F) above that certain Ministerial guidelines must be complied with does not apply. Since 1 July 1999 the deduction may be made from total income of either spouse where one spouse is treated as entitled to the income of both spouses (unless separate assessment applies, see **23.2** 'Married persons'). The period in which expenditure must be incurred is extended to **31 July 2008** provided that the conditions relating to the 31 December 2006 extension have been satisfied and at least 15 per cent of the construction or refurbishment cost is incurred by 31 December 2006. For expenditure incurred during 2007, relief is restricted to 75 per cent of expenditure incurred. For expenditure incurred in the period from 1 January 2008 to 31 July 2008, relief is restricted to 50 per cent of expenditure incurred.

[*TCA 1997, ss 372RA, 372S, 372AK–372AM, 372AQ–372AT, 372AV; FA 1999, s 47(1)(a)(f)(g); FA 2000, s 45; FA 2001, Sch 2 para 20; FA 2002, s 24, Sch 2 para 1; FA 2004, s 26; FA 2006, s 25*]

Park and ride facilities. Provisions similar to those described above in relation to qualifying premises in 'designated areas' apply to expenditure in a '*qualifying period*' **1 July 1999 to 31 December 2004** inclusive on the construction, but not the refurbishment, of a '*qualifying premises*', defined as above except that the requirement in (A) is that the site of the house is wholly within the site of a 'qualifying park and ride facility' (see **8.10** 'Capital allowances'), and that the house is certified as complying with the relevant guidelines relating to such facilities, the requirement in (B) is that the total floor area is not less than 38 sq metres and not more than 125 sq metres, and (F) does not apply. The qualifying period is extended to **31 December 2006** where a valid application for full planning permission has been made and acknowledged as received by 31 December 2004 (or 10 March 2002 in the case of permission sought under the *Local Government (Planning and Development) Regulations 1994*) or, where planning permission is not required, a detailed plan of the construction or refurbishment work is prepared, a binding written contract relating to that work is in existence and work to the value of five per cent of the development costs has been carried out by 31 December 2004. The period in which expenditure must be incurred is extended to **31 July 2008** provided that the conditions relating to the 31 December 2006 extension have been satisfied and at least 15 per cent of the construction or refurbishment cost is incurred by 31 December 2006. For expenditure incurred during 2007, relief is restricted to 75 per cent of expenditure incurred. For expenditure incurred in the period from 1 January 2008 to 31 July 2008, relief is restricted to 50 per cent of expenditure incurred.

A person is entitled to a deduction for capital expenditure under this provision only insofar as that expenditure, when aggregated with:

(i)   other expenditure, incurred at the same park and ride facility, in respect of which a deduction would, disregarding this restriction, be made under this provision; and

(ii)   expenditure, incurred at the same park and ride facility, in respect of which there is provision for a deduction under *s 372X* or *s 372AP* (rented residential accommodation, see **33.11** 'Sch D, Case V');

does not exceed one-half of the total expenditure incurred at that facility for which a deduction or allowance may be made under this provision, or *s 372V* or *s 372W* (see **8.10** 'Capital allowances'), or *s 372X* or *s 372AP* (see **33.11** 'Sch D, Case V'), disregarding this restriction and the similar restrictions applicable under *s 372W* and *s 372X* or *s 372AP*. The local authority must have issued a certificate that it is satisfied that this requirement has been met.

The deduction may be made from total income of either spouse where one spouse is treated as entitled to the income of both spouses (unless separate assessment applies, see **23.2** 'Married persons').

[*TCA 1997, ss 372U, 372Y, 372Z, 372AK–372AM, 372AQ–372AT, 372AV; FA 1999, s 70(1); FA 2000, s 46; FA 2001, Sch 2 para 21; FA 2002, ss 23(1)(e), 24, Sch 2 paras 1, 2; FA 2003, s 26; FA 2004, s 26; FA 2006, s 25*]

See also **8.10** 'Capital allowances', **33.11** 'Sch D, Case V'.

Integrated area plans and 'living over the shop' scheme. Provisions similar to those described above in relation to qualifying premises in 'designated areas' apply to construction, conversion or refurbishment expenditure on qualifying premises in 'qualifying areas' incurred between **1 August 1998 and 31 December 2002** inclusive (extended to **31 December 2006** where the relevant local authority or company authorised by that authority certifies (before 1 October 2003, on application made before 1 August 2003) that at least 15 per cent of the total cost had been incurred before 1 July 2003). The period in which expenditure must be incurred is extended to **31 July 2008** provided that the conditions relating to the 31 December 2006 extension have been satisfied and at least 15 per cent of the construction or refurbishment cost is incurred by 31 December 2006. For expenditure incurred during 2007, relief is restricted to 75 per cent of expenditure incurred. For expenditure incurred in the period from 1 January 2008 to 31 July 2008, relief is restricted to 50 per cent of expenditure incurred. A '*qualifying area*' is an area, within an area to which an Integrated Area Plan (under *Urban Renewal Act 1998, Pt II*) applies, which is so designated for one or all of construction, refurbishment or conversion by order by the Minister for Finance (now a 'qualifying urban area'), and the construction or refurbishment must be certified by the local authority concerned (or company authorised by such authority) as being consistent with the objectives of the Plan. Each designation order must specify a qualifying period within that referred to above. The Minister has power to amend or revoke an order. In relation to such expenditure, the condition in (B) above is amended to restrict relief in all cases to houses of floor area not less than 38 sq metres or more than 125 sq metres. Where part of a building is outside a qualifying area, relief is determined by floor area apportionment. Since 1 July 1999 the deduction may be made from total income of either spouse where one spouse is treated as entitled to the income of both spouses (unless separate assessment applies, see **23.2** 'Married persons').

These provisions are extended under the 'Living over the Shop Scheme' to expenditure on the refurbishment or 'necessary construction' of qualifying premises consisting of a house fronting on to a 'qualifying street' (or comprised in a building (or part) which does so) incurred between **6 April 2001 and 31 December 2004** inclusive (or in any shorter period within that period which may be specified in the order designating a particular street as a 'qualifying street', see below). The period is extended to **31 December 2006** where a valid application for full planning permission has been made and acknowledged as received by 31 December 2004 (or 10 March 2002 in the case of permission sought under the *Local Government (Planning and Development) Regulations 1994*) or, where planning permission is not required, a detailed plan of the construction or refurbishment work is prepared, a binding written contract relating to that work is in existence and work to the value of five per cent of the development costs has been carried out by 31 December 2004. The period in which expenditure must be incurred is extended to **31 July 2008** provided that the conditions relating to the 31 December 2006 extension have been satisfied and at least 15 per cent of the construction or refurbishment cost is incurred by 31 December 2006. For expenditure incurred during 2007, relief is restricted to 75 per cent of expenditure incurred. For expenditure incurred in the period from 1 January 2008 to 31 July 2008, relief is restricted to 50 per cent of expenditure incurred. The annual allowance for such expenditure is **ten per cent** whether it is refurbishment or construction expenditure. The house must be comprised in the upper floor(s) of an 'existing' or 'replacement building' the ground floor of which is in use for commercial purposes (or is temporarily vacant but subsequently so used), and the allowance is dependant on the corporation of the borough in whose area the house is situated certifying in writing that the refurbishment or construction is consistent with the aims, objectives and criteria for the Scheme as outlined in circular UR 43A of 13 September 2000 (as amended). For these purposes the following definitions apply. A *'qualifying street'* (within *s 372BA*) is a street (or part) in the city of Cork, Dublin, Galway, Limerick or Waterford which is so designated by order by the Minister for Finance. 'Street' for this purpose includes a road, square, quay or lane. An *'existing building'* is a building which existed on 13 September 2000, and *'necessary construction'* in relation to such a building means construction of either (*a*) an extension which increases the floor area by not more than 30 per cent and which is necessary to facilitate access or to provide essential facilities, or (*b*) an additional storey or storeys necessary for the restoration or enhancement of the streetscape, or (*c*) a *'replacement building'*, ie a building or structure (or part) constructed to replace an existing building where either (i) a demolition notice or order on the existing building (or part) was given or made after 12 September 2000 and before 31 March 2001 and the replacement building is consistent with the character and size of the existing building, or (ii) demolition of the existing building (being a single storey building) was required for structural reasons to facilitate the construction of an additional storey or storeys necessary for the restoration or enhancement of the streetscape.

[*TCA 1997, ss 372A, 372B, 372BA, 372I, 372J, 372K, 372AK–372AM, 372AQ– 372AT, 372AV; FA 1998, s 76; Urban Renewal Act 1998, s 11; FA 2000, s 44; FA 2001, s 60, Sch 2 para 20; FA 2002, ss 23(1)(b)(c), 24, Sch 2 paras 1, 3; FA 2003, ss 26, 27, 30; FA 2004, s 26; FA 2006, s 25; SI 642/04*]

See also **8.10** 'Capital allowances', **33.11** 'Sch D, Case V' and, as regards integrated area plans, **30.25** 'Sch D, Cases I and II'.

Town renewal schemes. Provisions similar to those described above in relation to qualifying premises in 'designated areas' apply to construction, conversion or refurbishment expenditure on qualifying premises in 'qualifying areas' incurred between **1 April 2000** and **31 December 2004** inclusive. The qualifying period is extended to **31 December 2006** where a valid application for full planning permission has been made and acknowledged as received by 31 December 2004 (or 10 March 2002 in the case of permission sought under the *Local Government (Planning and Development) Regulations 1994*) or, where planning permission is not required, a detailed plan of the construction or refurbishment work is prepared, a binding written contract relating to that work is in existence and work to the value of five per cent of the development costs has been carried out by 31 December 2004. The period in which expenditure must be incurred was extended to **31 July 2008** provided that the conditions relating to the 31 December 2006 extension have been satisfied and at least 15 per cent of the construction or refurbishment cost is incurred by 31 December 2006. For expenditure incurred during 2007, relief is restricted to 75 per cent of expenditure incurred. For expenditure incurred in the period from 1 January 2008 to 31 July 2008, relief is restricted to 50 per cent of expenditure incurred. A *'qualifying area'* is an area, within an area to which a Town Renewal Plan (under the relevant legislation) relates which is so designated by order by the Minister for Finance (now a 'qualifying town area'), and such orders may designate different classes of premises for relief and may apply to any or all of construction, conversion and refurbishment expenditure. In relation to refurbishment expenditure, relief is extended to include expenditure on certain work on the facade of a building. Each designation order must specify a qualifying period within that referred to above. In relation to such expenditure, the condition in (B) above is amended to restrict relief in all cases to houses of floor area not less than 38 sq metres or more than 125 sq metres (210 sq metres in the case of refurbishment expenditure incurred after 5 April 2001 and conversion expenditure from 1 January 2002), and in (C) above a 'certificate of compliance' granted by the Minister may instead be required in certain cases. In relation to refurbishment expenditure, relief is extended to include expenditure on certain work on the facade of a building. The Minister is empowered to amend or revoke a designation order. Where part of a building is outside a qualifying area, relief is determined by floor area apportionment. [*TCA 1997, ss 372AA, 372AB, 372AH, 372AI, 372AJ, 372AK–372AM, 372AQ–372AT, 372AV; FA 2000, s 89; FA 2001, s 80, Sch 2 para 20; FA 2002, s 24, Sch 2 para 1; FA 2003, ss 26, 29, 30; FA 2004, s 26; FA 2006, s 25*] See also **8.10** 'Capital allowances', **33.11** 'Sch D, Case III'.

For an article on Town Renewal Relief, including a list of towns recommended for designation, see Revenue Tax Briefing Issue 42 pp 24–27.

Expenditure incurred in the Temple Bar or Custom House Docks Areas of Dublin. Relief against total income of a year may be claimed by an individual in respect of 'qualifying expenditure' on an owner-occupied dwelling the site of which is wholly in the Custom House Docks Area (as specified in *Sch 5* or as extended by order of the Minister for Finance under *s 322(2)*, see *SI 466/99*) or the Temple Bar Area of Dublin. The relief given to the person incurring the expenditure is **five per cent (ten per cent** in the case of refurbishment expenditure in the Temple Bar Area and, after 26 January 1994, in the Custom House Docks Area) of the amount of the 'qualifying expenditure' in the year of assessment in which the expenditure is incurred and in any or all of the following nine consecutive years of assessment in which the dwelling continues to be that person's only or main residence. Where one of the ten years for which relief is available is the short tax year 2001, the amount of the relief for that year is restricted to **3.7 per cent (7.4 per cent)**, and relief is extended to the eleventh year, for which it is restricted to **1.3 per cent (2.6 per cent)**.

'*Qualifying expenditure*' is the net amount of expenditure incurred by the individual (after deducting any grants, etc), in the period commencing 6 April 1988 in relation to expenditure in the Custom House Docks Area and 6 April 1991 in the Temple Bar Area and ending on **5 April 1999** (31 December 1999 in certain cases where substantial expenditure had been incurred by 5 April 1999) in the Temple Bar Area and **31 December 1999** in the Custom House Docks Area, on the 'construction or refurbishment' of 'qualifying premises' which are first used, after the expenditure is incurred, by the individual as his only or main residence. Expenditure on the refurbishment of buildings existing on 1 January 1991 in the Temple Bar Area is deemed to include the lesser of the cost of acquisition of the building (excluding land) and the value of the building at 1 January 1991, provided that the actual expenditure incurred is at least equal to that lesser amount.

Expenditure in the Temple Bar Area qualifies for relief only if the building is approved by Temple Bar Renewal Ltd.

'*Qualifying premises*' means residential premises which would qualify for relief as described under **33.4** or **33.5** 'Sch D, Case V' if the conditions as to letting were satisfied, and expenditure is within the meaning of 'construction or refurbishment' if it would be so for those purposes. For expenditure incurred after 25 January 1994 on the refurbishment of flats and maisonettes in the Custom House Docks and Temple Bar Areas, the maximum permissible floor area is increased from 90 to 125 square metres, and from 12 April 1995 this applies also in relation to construction expenditure.

For the purposes of granting the relief, expenditure is treated as incurred on the earliest date on which the premises were in use as a dwelling after it was actually incurred. Expenditure incurred by more than one person is apportioned on a just and reasonable basis by the inspector, subject to revision on appeal by the Appeal Commissioners or Circuit Court. Appeals are generally to the Appeal Commissioners and are dealt with in the same way as appeals against assessments (see **4** 'Appeals').

[*TCA 1997, ss 322, 328, 329, 330, 337, 338, 372AU, Sch 5, Sch 6, Sch 32 para 11; FA 1986, ss 41, 44, Sch 4 as amended; FA 1991, ss 54, 55, Sch 2 as amended; Urban Renewal Act 1998, s 20(1)(a) (2); FA 1999, ss 42, 43; SI 465/99; FA 2001, Sch 2 para 20; FA 2002, s 24(3), Sch 2 para 1*]

See also **33.4, 33.5** 'Sch D, Case V'.

RELIEF FOR TRADE UNION SUBSCRIPTIONS

[*TCA 1997, s 472C; FA 2001, s 11; FA 2004, s 4; FA 2006, s 6, FA 2008, s 10, FA 2011, s 12*]

2.29 With effect from the tax year 2011 and subsequent tax years, relief for trade union subscriptions is abolished. *[FA 2011, s 12]* With effect from 6 April 2001, where an individual is a member of a 'trade union' at any time in a year of assessment, the individual (or the individual's spouse where the spouse's income is treated as that of the individual (see **23.1** 'Married persons')) may claim relief by way of a reduction of his or her liability to income tax (except insofar as required to cover charges, see **13.1** 'Deduction of tax at source') by the lesser of:

(*a*)   an amount equal to standard rate tax (see **2.7** above) on a 'specified amount'; and

(*b*)   the amount required to reduce that liability to nil.

The '*specified amount*' is:

For	2001	£74
From	2002	€130
From	2004	€200
For	2006	€300
For	2008	€350
For	2009	€350
From	**2010**	**€350**

The Trade Union Subscription is fixed at a flat rate of €350 as of from 2009. Full entitlement to the credit is available in 2009 and 2010 regardless of the amount of the subscription paid. Relief under this provision is given in priority to other personal allowances and reliefs. It is normally given in the year of assessment by reference to which it arises, but the relief in respect of 2001 is instead given in 2002 (in addition to the relief for that year), unless there is insufficient liability in 2002 for the full amount of both reliefs to be given, in which case the unallowed portion of the 2001 relief is carried back to 2001 (subject to the usual limitation to the amount required to reduce the income tax liability to nil).

A '*trade union*' is any body either holding a negotiation licence under the *Trade Union Act 1941* or excepted under *s 6 of that Act*, and certain Garda and defence force representative bodies. Membership of a second or further trade unions in a year of assessment is disregarded for the purposes of relief.

Employers and trade unions must, when requested by the Revenue Commissioners, supply the following information (so far as it is in their possession), in an approved electronic format unless the Commissioners otherwise direct, in relation to employees/ members entitled to the relief:

(i)   their name and address and Personal Public Service Number;

(ii)   the name of the trade union; and

(iii)   the name and address of the employer.

Finance Act 2007, s 9 amended *s 472C* by providing that employers are now permitted to share employees PPS numbers with trade unions in certain circumstances to enable trade unions make returns to Revenue of their members who qualify for the Trade Union Subscription Tax Credit.

The information may only be used by the Revenue Commissioners for the purposes of facilitating the granting of relief under this provision, *s 872* (see **1.8** 'Administration and General') being disapplied for this purpose.

RENT ALLOWANCE

[*TCA 1997, s 473; FA 2000, s 13; FA 2001, s 9; FA 2005, s 6; FA 2006, s 7*]

2.30 An individual may claim relief for rent paid in respect of premises which are his only or main residence. Any relief given is in *substitution* for any other relief to which the **claimant** might be entitled in respect of the payments.

For **2000/01 onwards**, the relief is given by means of a reduction of the claimant's income tax liability (excluding any liability in respect of tax deducted from payments made under *s 16(2)*). The reduction is the smallest of:

(*a*)   a percentage of the aggregate rent payments qualifying for relief for the year of assessment equal to the standard rate of tax for that year (see **2.6** above);

(*b*)   a similar percentage of the 'specified limit' for the year of assessment; and

(*c*)   what would otherwise be the claimant's total income tax liability.

Finance Act 2011, s 14 provides for a phased withdrawal of this relief over a seven year period for tenants who on 7 December 2010 were paying qualifying rent under a qualifying tenancy. The section provides for a gradual reduction of the relief with the relief completely withdrawn by 2018. The relief is abolished for new tenancies entered into on or after 7 December 2010.

The '*specified limit*' is as follows (*a*) in the case of a married person whose spouse's income is treated as his or her own (see **23.1** 'Married persons'), (*b*) in the case of a widow(er) or (*c*) in any other case, with the higher figures applicable where at any time during the year of assessment the claimant was 55 years of age or more.

		(*a*)		(*b*)		(*c*)	
		under 55	55 or over	under 55	55 or over	under 55	55 or over
For	2000/01	£1,500	£4,000	£1,125	£3,000	£750	£2,000
For	2001	£1,480	£2,960	£1,480	£2,960	£740	£1,480
From	2002	€2,540	€5,080	€2,540	€5,080	€1,270	€2,540
For	2005	€3,000	€6,000	€3,000	€6,000	€1,500	€3,000
For	2006	€3,300	€6,600	€3,300	€6,600	€1,650	€3,300
For	2007	€3,600	€7,200	€3,600	€7,200	€1,800	€3,600
For	2008	€4,000	€8,000	€4,000	€8,000	€2,000	€4,000
For	2009	€4,000	€8,000	€4,000	€8,000	€2,000	€4,000
For	2010	€4,000	€8,000	€4,000	€8,000	€2,000	€4,000
For	2011	€640	€1,280	€640	€1,280	€320	€640
For	2012	€480	€960	€480	€960	€240	€480
For	2013	€400	€720	€400	€720	€200	€400
For	2014	€320	€640	€320	€640	€160	€320
For	2015	€240	€480	€240	€480	€120	€240
For	2016	€160	€320	€160	€320	€80	€160
For	2017	€80	€160	€80	€160	€40	€80
For	**2018**	**€0**	**€0**	**€0**	**€0**	**€0**	**€0**

Where the claimant is a married person whose spouse's income is treated as his or her own (see **23.1** 'Married persons'), payments made by the claimant's spouse which would otherwise have qualified for relief are treated as having been made by the claimant.

The rent, including certain periodical payments in the nature of rent, must be for the bare right to use, occupy and enjoy a building (or part) and grounds, and must not be reimbursed to, or the subject of a subsidy enjoyed by, the person paying it. It must be payable under a tenancy (including a contract, licence or agreement), which must not be for a freehold estate or interest or for a definite period of 50 years or more (ignoring any statutory extension), and under which:

(i)   the rent must not be payable to certain public authorities; and

(ii)   no part of the rent may be treated as (part) consideration for a greater interest in the premises (or in any other property).

There are provisions for apportionment of composite payments by the inspector (subject to the usual appeal rights), and for time apportionment of rent for periods falling in more than one year of assessment. The Revenue Commissioners may make regulations as required to bring the scheme of allowance into effect.

For 1999/2000, relief is similarly available to claimants aged 55 or more at any time in the year of assessment, but is given by means of a deduction from total income of the aggregate payments qualifying for relief, subject to a maximum deduction of £2,000 for a married person whose spouse's income is treated as his or her own (see **23.1** 'Married persons'), of £1,500 for a widow(er) or of £1,000 in any other case. For claimants aged under 55 at the end of the year of assessment, relief is given by a reduction in income tax liability in the same way as it is given for 2000/01 onwards, but by reference to 'specified limits' of £1,000 for a married person whose spouse's income is treated as his or her own (see **23.1** 'Married persons'), £750 for a widow(er) or £500 in any other case.

Claims must be accompanied by details (in a form prescribed by the Revenue Commissioners) of the claimant, the person(s) entitled to the rent (including their tax reference number), the premises concerned, and the tenancy agreement, and by a receipt or acknowledgement in respect of the rent for which relief is claimed. On a request by the claimant, such a receipt, etc must be provided within seven days by the person(s) entitled to the rent. The receipt, etc must be in writing and contain the names and addresses of the claimant and of the person(s) entitled to the rent (and the tax reference number of the latter) and details of the amount and period of the rent paid.

The inspector may, however, waive the requirement for details of the person(s) entitled to the rent if he is satisfied that the claimant is unable to supply them. He may also waive the requirement for a receipt, etc if satisfactory proof is produced of the rent paid and of the name and address of the payee. Any decision by the inspector is subject to the usual appeal rights as if the claim were an appeal against an assessment.

RELIEF FOR DONATIONS TO APPROVED BODIES

[*TCA 1997, s 848A, Sch 26A; FA 2001, s 45; FA 2003, ss 21, 22; FA 2005, s 38; FA 2006, ss 20, 23; FA 2010, s 24*]

2.31 For 2001 onwards, relief is given in respect of any 'relevant donation' made in a year of assessment. A '*relevant donation*' is a donation to an 'approved body' within *Sch 26A* (for which see Revenue Tax Briefing Issue 44 p 16). Certain amendments have been made to the definition of Charities to bring Irish tax law in line with certain provisions of EU Treaties [*FA 2010, s 24*]. The donation must meet the following conditions.

(*a*)   It is not subject to a condition as to repayment;

(*b*)   Neither the donor nor any connected person (within *s 10*) receives a benefit directly or indirectly in consequence of making the donation;

(*c*)   It is not conditional on or associated with, or part of an arrangement involving, the acquisition of property by the approved body, otherwise than by way of gift, from the donor or a connected person (within *s 10*);

(*d*)   The donor must be RI-resident in the year of assessment in which the donation is made. If the donor is not a chargeable person within *s 951* for the year of assessment (ie in most cases all their income is dealt with under PAYE, see **28.11** 'Returns'), he or she must have given an 'appropriate certificate' (form CHY2 Cert, see Revenue Tax Briefing Issue 44 p 19) in relation to the donation to the approved body, and have paid the tax referred to in that certificate (and not be entitled to claim a repayment of that tax or any part of it). An '*appropriate certificate*' requires the donor's PPSN number and the following:

(i)   a statement that the donation satisfies these requirements,

(ii)   a statement that the donor has paid or will pay to the Revenue Commissioners income tax of an amount equal to tax at the standard or higher rate (or a mixture thereof), as the case may be, on the grossed-up amount of the donation, being neither tax the donor may charge against any other person or deduct, satisfy or retain out of any payments the donor is liable to make to any other person, nor tax deducted under the DIRT scheme (see **13.9** 'Deduction of tax at source'), and

(iii)   a statement specifying how much of the grossed-up amount in (ii) above has been or will be liable to income tax at the standard rate and how much at the higher rate.

In submitting the repayment claim referred to below, the approved body must give to the Revenue Commissioners the details contained in appropriate certificates, in approved form (by electronic means unless the Revenue Commissioners are satisfied that the approved body does not have the necessary facilities to do so) and accompanied by a declaration to the effect that the details (or written claim) are (is) correct and complete;

(*e*)   The donation must take the form of the payment of a sum or sums (or from 2006, a donation of quoted securities) to an approved body amounting in aggregate to at least **€250** (for 2001 only, **£148**) in the year of assessment.

For donations made **from 6 February 2003**, relief is restricted to ten per cent of total income where the donor is an employee of the approved body or a member of the approved body or an associated body. [*FA 2003, s 21*]

Where the relevant donation is made by an individual who is a chargeable person within *s 951* for the year of assessment in which it is made (ie broadly those whose tax is not fully dealt with under PAYE, see **28.11** 'Returns'), the amount of the donation is deducted from or set off against any income chargeable to tax for that year (but not for the purpose of determining relevant earnings within *s 787*, see **2.23** 'Allowances, credits and rates'), and the individual's total income (or, where appropriate, that of the spouse) is reduced accordingly. The relief must be claimed in the return for the year.

Where the relevant donation is made by an individual who is *not* a chargeable person within *s 951* for the year of assessment in which it is made (ie broadly those whose tax affairs are fully dealt with under PAYE, see **28.11** 'Returns'), the approved body is treated as if the grossed-up amount of the donation (as in (*d*)(ii) above) were an annual payment received under deduction of tax in the amounts and at the rates specified in the appropriate certificate, with the usual provisions for claims to repayment of the tax treated as deducted applying. If, however, the total amount of the tax referred to in (*d*)(ii) above is not paid by the donor, the repayment is limited to the amount of tax actually paid.

This relief replaces the separate reliefs for gifts etc described at **2.37–2.40** below, **17.5, 17.29** 'Exempt organisations' and **36.2**(A) 'Settlements'.

From 2007, the quantum of relief available to a high earning individual in any one year may be limited, see **2.45** 'Limitation on Investment Relief'. [*FA 2006, s 17*]

See **12.9** 'Corporation tax' for the associated relief for companies.

RELIEF FOR DONATIONS TO APPROVED SPORTS BODIES

[*TCA 1997, s 847A; FA 2002, s 41*]

2.32 Since 1 May 2002, relief is (except as below) given in respect of any 'relevant donation' made in a year of assessment. A '*relevant donation*' is a donation which meets the following conditions:

(*a*)   It is made to a sports body which has both a valid tax clearance certificate (which may be obtained from the Collector-General) and a certificate from the Revenue stating their opinion that it is within *s 235* (see **17.2** 'Exempt organisations') (and which is not excluded from exemption under that section by notice given by the Revenue);

(*b*)   It is made for the sole purpose of funding a project in respect of which the Minister for Tourism, Sport and Recreation has, on the application of the sports body, given (and not revoked) the appropriate certificate, and is or will be applied for that purpose. (It is a condition for certification that the aggregate cost of the project must not be, or be estimated to be, over €40,000,000.) 'Project' for this purpose means one or more of:

  (i)   the purchase, construction or refurbishment of a building or structure (or part) to be used for sporting or recreation activities provided by the body,

  (ii)   the purchase of land to be used in the provision of sporting or recreation facilities by the body,

  (iii) the purchase of permanently based non-personal equipment for use by the body in such provision,

  (iv)   the improvement of the playing pitches, surfaces or facilities of the body, and

  (v)   the repayment of (or payment of interest on) money borrowed by the body after 30 April 2002 for any of the purposes in (i) to (iv) above;

(*c*)   It is not otherwise deductible in computing profits or gains of a trade or profession;

(*d*)   It is not a relevant donation within *s 848A* (see **2.32** above);

(*e*)   It is not subject to a condition as to repayment;

(*f*)   Neither the donor nor any connected person (within *s 10*) receives a benefit directly or indirectly in consequence of making the donation (including, in particular, a right to membership of the sports body or to use its facilities);

(*g*)   It is not conditional on or associated with, or part of an arrangement involving, the acquisition of property by the sports body, otherwise than by way of gift, from the donor or a connected person (within *s 10*);

(*h*)   The donor must be RI-resident in the year of assessment in which the donation is made. If the donor is not a chargeable person within *s 951* for the year of assessment (ie in most cases all their income is dealt with under PAYE, see **28.11** 'Returns'), he or she must have given an 'appropriate certificate' (in such form as the Revenue Commissioners may prescribe) in relation to the donation to the sports body, and have paid the tax referred to in that certificate (and not be entitled to claim a repayment of that tax or any part of it). An *'appropriate certificate'* must contain the donor's PPSN number and the following:

(i)   a statement that the donation satisfies these requirements,

(ii)   a statement that the donor has paid or will pay to the Revenue Commissioners income tax of an amount equal to tax at the standard or higher rate (or a mixture thereof), as the case may be, on the grossed-up amount of the donation, being neither tax the donor may charge against any other person or deduct, satisfy or retain out of any payments the donor is liable to make to any other person, nor tax deducted under the DIRT scheme (see **13.9** 'Deduction of tax at source'), and

(iii)   a statement specifying how much of the grossed-up amount in (ii) above has been or will be liable to income tax at the standard rate and how much at the higher rate.

In submitting the repayment claim referred to below, the sports body must give to the Revenue Commissioners the details contained in appropriate certificates, in approved form (by electronic means unless the Revenue Commissioners are satisfied that the sports body does not have the necessary facilities to do so) and accompanied by a declaration to the effect that the details (or written claim) are (is) correct and complete;

(*i*)   The donation must take the form of the payment by the individual of a sum or sums of money to the sports body amounting in aggregate to at least €250 in the year of assessment.

No relief is available for a donation for a project within (*b*) above made at a time when the aggregate donations made at and before that time for the project exceed the €40,000,000 limit referred to. Every sports body within (*a*) above may be required to make a return containing particulars of the aggregate amount of relevant donations received in respect of each project within (*b*) above.

Where the relevant donation is made by an individual who is a chargeable person within *s 951* for the year of assessment in which it is made (ie broadly those whose tax is not fully dealt with under PAYE, see **28.11** 'Returns'), the amount of the donation is deducted from or set off against any income chargeable to tax for that year (but not for the purpose of determining relevant earnings within *s 787*, see **2.25** 'Allowances, credits and rates'), and the individual's total income (or, where appropriate, that of the spouse) is reduced accordingly. The relief must be claimed in the return for the year.

Where the relevant donation is made by an individual who is *not* a chargeable person within *s 951* for the year of assessment in which it is made (ie broadly those whose tax affairs are fully dealt with under PAYE, see **28.11** 'Returns'), the sports body is treated as if the grossed-up amount of the donation (as in (*h*)(ii) above) were an annual payment received under deduction of tax in the amounts and at the rates specified in the appropriate certificate, with the usual provisions for claims to repayment of the tax treated as deducted applying. If, however, the total amount of the tax referred to in (*h*)(ii) above is not paid by the donor, the repayment is limited to the amount actually paid.

Except in the case of a donation from an individual donor who is *not* a chargeable person within *s 951* (or for which relief is not available because the €40,000,000 limit has been exceeded), the sports body must give to the donor a signed receipt for each relevant donation, containing prescribed information and confirmation of the status and details of the donation.

Where relief has been granted under these provisions in respect of a relevant donation, and is for any reason found not to have been due (eg because it was not used for an approved project), exemption will not be available under *s 235* (see **17.2** 'Exempt organisations') for the amount of the donation.

Since *FA 2007*, the quantum of relief available to a high earning individual in any one year is limited, see **2.45** 'Limitation on Income Tax Relief for High Earners'. [*FA 2006, s 17*]

See **12.9** 'Corporation tax' for the associated relief for companies.

RELIEF FOR FEES PAID TO COLLEGES OR FOR PART-TIME THIRD LEVEL EDUCATION AND FOR POSTGRADUATE COURSE FEES (2000/01 AND EARLIER YEARS)

2.33 Private colleges. For 1996/97 to 2000/01 inclusive (after which see **2.35** below), an individual may claim relief for 'qualifying fees' proved to have been paid in respect of an 'approved course' for the academic year commencing after 31 July in the year of assessment. Relief is given by a reduction of liability to income tax for the year of assessment (except insofar as required to cover charges, see **13.1** 'Deduction of tax at source') by the lesser of:

(*a*)   an amount equal to standard rate tax (see **2.7** above) on the fees so paid; and

(*b*)   the amount required to reduce that liability to nil.

Finance Act 2011, s 15 amends the tax credit available on fees paid for certain third level fees. From 1 January 2011, the first €2,000 of the fee is disregarded for fees paid in respect of full time courses. The first €1,000 of the fee will be disregarded for fees paid in respect of part time courses.

The fees may be paid on the taxpayer's own behalf or on behalf of a spouse or child of the taxpayer or a person whose legal guardian the taxpayer is. Where the taxpayer is a married person whose spouse's income is treated as his or her own (see **23.1** 'Married persons'), then (unless separate assessment is claimed, see **23.2** 'Married persons') fees paid by the spouse are treated as having been paid by the taxpayer.

'*Qualifying fees*' are tuition fees approved by the Minister for Education for this purpose for the course and for the academic year in question, and an '*approved course*' is a full time undergraduate course of study, lasting at least two academic years, which is approved for this purpose by the Minister for Education, and in an RI college so approved. The Minister for Education is required, before 1 July in each year of assessment, to furnish the Revenue Commissioners with full details of approved colleges, courses and fees. Approval of a course or college may be withdrawn by notice to the college, with effect from the following year of assessment (such notice also to be published in the *Iris Oifigiúil*).

Claims to relief will only be admitted where a return in prescribed form of total income for the year of assessment is made, and relief is denied to the extent that a sum is received in respect of, or by reference to, the fees by way of grant, scholarship or otherwise.

[*TCA 1997, s 474; FA 2000, s 21(1)(b); FA 2001, s 29(2)*]

Publicly funded EU colleges. A similar relief applied **for 1999/2000 and 2000/01** (after which see **2.35** below) for 'qualifying fees' in respect of a *'qualifying course'*, ie a full-time undergraduate course of study, lasting at least two academic years, in a university or similar institution in an EU State (other than RI) maintained or assisted by grants from public funds of any EU State (a *'qualifying college'*). Courses in medicine, dentistry, veterinary medicine or teacher training were excluded. *'Qualifying fees'* were so much of the tuition fees for the course as is determined by the Minister for Education and Science to qualify in relation to the class of course concerned. A claim for relief under this section must be accompanied by a statement in writing by the college that it is a qualifying college and giving details of the course, its duration and the fees paid in respect of the course. [*TCA 1997, s 474A; FA 1999, s 26; FA 2000, s 21(1)(c); FA 2001, s 29(2)*]

Part-time third level education. **For 1996/97 to 2000/01 inclusive** (after which see **2.35** below), an individual without a certificate, diploma or degree in respect of an undergraduate course of study of at least two years duration (disregarding, from 6 April 1997, certain intermediate certificates or diplomas) may have claimed relief in the same way as above for tuition fees paid on his or her own behalf for the academic year commencing after 31 July in the year of assessment in respect of a part-time undergraduate course of at least two academic years duration in an 'approved college'. Since 6 April 1997, the definition is extended to include overseas colleges in the EU providing distance learning in RI to a required standard. Since 6 April 2000, relief is extended to fees paid on behalf of a spouse or child of the taxpayer or a person whose legal guardian the taxpayer is, and where the taxpayer is a married person whose spouse's income is treated as his or her own (see **23.1** 'Married persons'), then (unless separate assessment is claimed, see **23.2** 'Married persons') fees paid by the spouse are treated as having been paid by the taxpayer. For this purpose an *'approved college'* is a private college approved as above or a publicly funded third level institution. Since 6 April 1997, the spouse of a qualifying individual may claim the relief where the fees are paid by either of them and the wife's income is, by election, treated as that of the husband (see **23.1** 'Married persons'). Private college courses and fees must be approved as above, and restrictions on admission of claims apply as above [*TCA 1997, s 475; FA 2000, s 21(1)(d); FA 2001, s 29(2)*].

Postgraduate course fees. **For 2000/01 only** (after which see **2.35** below), an individual may have claimed claim relief in the same way as above for 'qualifying fees' proved to have been paid in respect of an 'approved course' for the academic year commencing after 31 July in the year of assessment. An *'approved course'* is a postgraduate course of study, lasting at least one but not more than four academic years, leading to a postgraduate award based on a thesis or the results of an examination, in a 'qualifying college' or (subject to certain further safeguards) in an *'approved college'*, ie an RI college or institution approved for the purpose by the Minister. A *'qualifying college'* is any university or similar institution of higher education in the EU (excluding RI), including one providing distance education, which is maintained or assisted by recurrent EU public funding. *'Qualifying fees'* are tuition fees relating to the approved course for the academic year in question, the qualifying proportion of which, in the case of courses at qualifying colleges, is determined by the Minister. In the case of courses at approved colleges, Ministerial approval of the amount of fees which qualify is required in certain cases. The Minister is required, before 1 July in each year of assessment, to furnish the Revenue Commissioners with full details of approved colleges, courses and fees. Ministerial approval of a course or college may be withdrawn by notice to the college, with effect from the following year of assessment (such notice also to be published in the *Iris Oifigiúil*). Claims to relief for fees paid to a qualifying college must be accompanied by a written statement by the college confirming the college's qualifying status and giving details of the course, its duration and the fees. Relief is denied to the extent that a sum is received in respect of, or by reference to, the fees by way of grant, scholarship or otherwise. [*TCA 1997, s 475A; FA 2000, s 21(1)(a); FA 2001, s 29(2)*]

RELIEF FOR FEES PAID FOR THIRD LEVEL EDUCATION AND FOR POSTGRADUATE COURSES (2001 ONWARDS)

[*TCA 1997, s 473A; FA 2001, s 29(1)*]

2.34 For 2001 onwards, the reliefs described at **2.33** above are amalgamated, with the removal of some of the restrictions on the specific reliefs in relation to repeat years, multiple courses and prior qualification. In particular, the exclusion of certain courses in medicine, dentistry, veterinary medicine and teacher training is removed. The relief is also extended to certain courses at private colleges in other Member States and at non-EU institutions.

Under *TCA 1997, s 473A*, an individual may claim relief for 'qualifying fees' proved to have been paid in respect of an 'approved course' for the academic year commencing after 31 July in the year of assessment. Relief is given by way of a reduction of liability to income tax for the year of assessment (except insofar as required to cover charges, see **13.1** 'Deduction of tax at source') by the lesser of:

(i)   an amount equal to standard rate tax (see **2.7** above) on the fees so paid; and

(ii)   the amount required to reduce that liability to nil.

The fees may be paid on the taxpayer's own behalf or on behalf of a spouse or child of the taxpayer or a person whose legal guardian the taxpayer is. *FA 2007* amends *473A* by abolishing the requirement that the be a relationship between the taxpayer and the person on behalf of whom the relevant fees are paid. This amendment took effect from 1 January 2007. Where the taxpayer is a married person whose spouse's income is treated as his or her own (see **23.1** 'Married persons'), then (unless separate assessment is claimed, see **23.2** 'Married persons') fees paid by the spouse are treated as having been paid by the taxpayer.

An 'approved college' is:

(*a*)   a college or institution of higher education in RI which either:

    (i)   provides courses to which a scheme approved by the Minister for Education and Science applies, or

    (ii)   operates in accordance with a code of standards laid down and approved by the Minister; or

(*b*)   any university or similar higher education institution in another EU Member State, either publicly maintained or duly accredited in the Member State in which it is situated;

(c)   a college or institution in another EU Member State, providing distance education in RI, which either:

    (i)   provides courses to which a scheme approved by the Minister applies, or

    (ii)   operates in accordance with a code of standards laid down and approved by the Minister; or

(d)   any university or similar higher education institution in a non-EU country, either publicly maintained or duly accredited in the country in which it is situated.

An 'approved course' is:

(1)   a full or part-time undergraduate course of at least two academic years' duration provided by a college within (a), (b) or (c) above and which, in the case of a college within (a)(ii) or (c)(ii), has received Ministerial approval; or

(2)   a postgraduate course, at an approved college, for holders of degrees or equivalent qualifications, lasting at least one but not more than four academic years, leading to a postgraduate award based on a thesis and/or the results of an examination. Where the college is within (a)(ii) above, Ministerial approval of the course is required.

The Minister is required, before 1 July in each year of assessment, to furnish the Revenue Commissioners with full details of approved colleges, courses and fees. Ministerial approval of a college or course may be withdrawn, with effect from the following year of assessment, by notice to the college (such notice also to be published in *Iris Oifigiúil*).

'Qualifying fees' are the course tuition fees approved for this purpose by the Minister.

Claims to relief for fees paid to an approved college must be accompanied by a written statement by the college confirming its qualifying status and giving details of the course, its duration and the fees. Relief is denied to the extent that a sum is received in respect of, or by reference to, the fees by way of grant, scholarship or otherwise.

RELIEF FOR FEES PAID FOR TRAINING COURSES

[*TCA 1997, s 476; FA 2000, s 21(1)(e)*]

2.35 An individual may claim relief for 'qualifying fees' proved to have been paid on his or her own behalf in respect of an approved course of training. For the year of assessment in which a certificate of competence has been awarded in respect of that course, relief is given by a reduction of liability to income tax (except insofar as required to cover charges, see **13.1** 'Deduction of tax at source') by the lesser of:

(a)   an amount equal to standard rate tax (see **2.7** above) on the fees so paid; and

(b)   the amount required to reduce that liability to nil.

Since 6 April 2000, relief is extended to fees paid on behalf of a spouse or child of the taxpayer or a person whose legal guardian the taxpayer is, and where the taxpayer is a married person whose spouse's income is treated as his or her own (see **23.1** 'Married persons'), then (unless separate assessment is claimed, see **23.2** 'Married persons') fees paid by the spouse are treated as having been paid by the taxpayer.

'*Qualifying fees*' are tuition fees for an approved course, subject to a minimum of €315/£250, to the extent that they do not exceed €1,270/£1,000. The course, and the person providing it, must both be approved for this purpose by An Foras Áiseanna Saothair, and such approval may be withdrawn by written notice to the provider. It must be a course of study or training (other than a postgraduate course) of less than two years duration leading to the award of a certificate of competence, and must be confined to such aspects of information technology, or such foreign languages, as are approved by the Minister for Enterprise and Employment for the purpose.

The spouse of the individual may claim the relief where the fees are paid by either of them and the wife's income is, by election, treated as that of the husband (see **23.1** 'Married persons'). Relief is, however, only given in respect of an individual for a year of assessment in respect of one approved course, and is denied to the extent that any sum is received in respect of, or by reference to, the fees by way of grant, scholarship or otherwise.

Relief under these provisions is in substitution for, and not in addition to, any other relief under the *Taxes Acts*.

ALLOWANCE FOR SERVICE CHARGES

[*TCA 1997, s 477; FA 2001, s 10; FA 2002, s 6; FA 2006, s 8; FA 2010, s 12*]

2.36 An individual may claim relief for local authority or similar service charges for which he or she was liable for the financial year to 31 December immediately prior to the year of assessment, provided that they were paid on time and in full. Relief is given by a reduction of liability to income tax for the year of assessment (except insofar as required to cover charges, see **13.1** 'Deduction of tax at source') by the lesser of:

(*a*) from **2006** an amount equal to standard rate tax (see **2.7** above) on the charges so paid but limited to standard rate tax on €400 or, for 2006 only, the fixed annual charge, if greater (limited, for 2001 and earlier years, to standard rate tax on **€195/£150**); and

(*b*) the amount required to reduce that liability to nil.

The ceiling limit of €400 was not increased by *FA 2007, 2008* or *(No 2) 2008* or *2010*. *FA 2010, s 12* provides for the abolishment of relief for service charges for the tax year 2011 and subsequent tax years. Full relief will apply in respect of service charges due for 2010 and actually paid for.

Any relief under these provisions is in substitution for, and not in addition to, any other deduction to which the individual might be entitled in respect of the payment.

Where the taxpayer is a married man whose wife's income is, by election, treated as his, he may claim relief for payments made by his wife. Where the service charges are paid on behalf of the claimant by an individual residing on a full-time basis in the premises to which they relate, the claimant may disclaim the relief in favour of that individual.

The service charges for which relief may be claimed are charges under certain *Acts* for the provision by or on behalf of a local authority (ie a council of a county or urban district, or a corporation of a county or other borough), of domestic water supply, domestic refuse collection or disposal or domestic sewage disposal facilities.

Domestic refuse collection and disposal services provided by a person or body other than a local authority are deemed to be provided by the local authority where the provider has notified the local authority of the provision of its service and provided such information as the local authority may request.

There are provisions for relief in respect of payments by members of group water supply schemes.

An individual wishing to claim relief under these provisions must, when requested by the Revenue Commissioners, provide certain details regarding the service provider and charge.

Prior to 2006, an individual wishing to claim relief under these provisions must furnish to the local authority to which charges are paid his Revenue and Social Insurance ('RSI') Number. If the conditions (as above) have been met in relation to the financial year in which he has so furnished his RSI number (and any arrears for earlier years have been paid in accordance with guidelines issued by the Department of the Environment), the local authority will then include the claimant in the return it is required to provide to the Revenue Commissioners for these purposes. Where, exceptionally, a valid claimant is not included in the return, the local authority must supply the claimant with a certificate, which must accompany the claim. In the case of refuse collection or disposal services provided and charged for by a person or body of persons other than the local authority where specified information is provided, and the service provider gives the claimant the appropriate certificate, a claim (accompanied by the certificate) may be made as if a payment had been made to the local authority for the service. Where such services, whether provided by the local authority or by some other such person or body, are charged for other than by way of a specified annual charge, relief (if not otherwise available) may be claimed as if a payment of **€195/£150** (before 2001, £50) had been made for the services. Where a service charge applies in respect of services other than domestic refuse collection and disposal, these further reliefs are available only where the claimant qualifies for relief in respect of such service charge.

RELIEF FOR GIFTS FOR EDUCATION IN THE ARTS [*TCA 1997, s 484*] AND TO COSPÓIR

[FA 1986, s 8; FA 1997, Sch 9 Pt II]

2.37 Relief against total income of a year may be claimed in respect of gifts before 6 April 2001, to certain approved educational bodies, totalling £100 or more in the year, to the extent that they do not total more than £10,000 in the year, gifts in all cases being taken as net of any consideration received as a result of making the gift. The gift(s) must not be deductible in computing profits or gains, nor income dispositions within *s 792*, and must be for the purpose of assisting the recipient body to promote the advancement in RI of an 'approved subject' and applied by the body for that purpose.

Where the donor is a wife whose income is, by election, treated as that of her husband, the deduction is made from her own income, her husband's total income being adjusted accordingly.

The Minister for Finance may give, and withdraw, his approval for this purpose to or from any RI body or institution which:

(*a*)   provides in RI any course with an entry requirement related to the results of the Leaving Certificate Examination, a matriculation examination of a recognised RI university or an equivalent non-RI examination; or

(*b*)   is permanently established solely for the advancement wholly or mainly in RI of one or more 'approved subjects', contributes to such advancement nationally or regionally, and is barred from distributing its assets or profits to its members.

For a list of approved bodies see Revenue Tax Briefing Issue 44 Supplement pp 38–40.

'*Approved subject*' means the practice of architecture, art and design, music and musical composition, theatre or film arts, or any other subject approved for the purpose by the Minister for Finance.

See **12.9** 'Corporation tax' for the associated relief for companies.

For gifts after 5 April 2001, see **2.32** above.

RELIEF FOR GIFTS TO THIRD LEVEL INSTITUTIONS

[*TCA 1997, s 485; FA 1999, s 36; FA 2000, s 50*]

2.38 For 1997/98 to 2000/01 relief against total income may be claimed (in the return under *s 951* (see **28.11** 'Returns') where relevant) in respect of a 'relevant gift' or gifts totalling £250 (for 1999/2000 and earlier years, £1,000) or more made in the year of assessment. The amount or value of any consideration received as a result of making the gift is deducted from the amount of the gift.

For 2000/01 only, any gifts unrelieved in the year of assessment of the gift due to an insufficiency of total income may be carried forward for up to three years.

A '*relevant gift*' is a gift of money made to a third level institution (or to an R1 fund-raising body for such an institution) for the sole purpose of funding a project certificated for this purpose by the Minister for Education on application by the institution. Since 6 April 1999 the relief is extended to all institutions of higher education (within *Higher Education Authority Act 1971, s 1*) and associated RI fund-raising bodies, and from 6 April 2000 it is further extended to gifts to development funds certificated by the Minister which are established by approved institutions to enable them to carry out projects. The money must be applied for that purpose, and the gift(s) must not otherwise be deductible in computing profits or gains of a trade or profession, nor income dispositions within *s 792*, nor within *s 484* (relief for gifts for education in the arts, see **2.37** above). The project must consist of the undertaking of research, the acquisition of equipment, the provision of facilities designed to increase student numbers in areas of skills needs, (in certain institutions) infrastructural development, or (from 6 April 2000) any other project approved by the Minister. Certification of a project or a development fund is subject to conditions specified therein (including a condition as to the amount or percentage of the cost of a project to be met by relevant gifts), which conditions may be amended, added to or revoked by written notice to the institution. Certification may be revoked, from the date written notice is given to the institution, where there is a failure to comply with any such condition.

Where the donor is an individual whose income is, by election, treated as that of his or her spouse, the deduction is made from the individual's own income, the spouse's total income being adjusted accordingly.

An institution in receipt of a relevant gift must give a signed receipt containing prescribed information confirming the status and details of the gift. The institution must, when required by notice, make a return to the Minister giving particulars of relevant gifts received for each approved project or development fund.

Ministerial functions may, from 6 April 2000, be delegated to the Higher Education Authority.

See **12.9** 'Corporation tax' for the associated relief for companies.

For gifts after 5 April 2001, see **2.32** above.

RELIEF FOR GIFTS TO DESIGNATED SCHOOLS

[*TCA 1997, s 485A; FA 1998, s 17*]

2.39 For 1998/99 to 2000/01 (from 2001 see **2.32** above), an individual may claim relief for a 'relevant gift' made in a year of assessment by a reduction of liability to income tax for that year (except insofar as required to cover charges, see **13.1** 'Deduction of tax at source') by the lesser of:

(*a*)   an amount equal to standard rate tax (see **2.7** above) on the net amount of the gift (ie after deducting the amount or value of any consideration received as a result of making the gift); and

(*b*)   the amount required to reduce that liability to nil.

No relief is available for a year of assessment where the total net amount of the 'relevant gifts' made by the individual in the year is £250 or less, or to the extent that it exceeds **£1,000**. Where the taxpayer is a married man whose wife's income is, by election, treated as his, he may claim relief for gifts made by his wife, but the £250 and £1,000 limits apply separately to such gifts.

Claims to relief are made in the return under *s 951* (see **28.11** 'Returns') where such a return is required.

A '*relevant gift*' is a gift of money for the sole purpose of funding the activities of a 'designated school' or schools, which is or will be applied for that purpose, and which is made either to the school itself (or to a person with control, management or trusteeship functions) or to an 'approved body'. It must not otherwise be deductible in computing profits or gains of a trade or profession, nor an income disposition within *s 792* (see **36.2** 'Settlements'), nor within *s 484* (relief for gifts for education in the arts, see **2.37** above). A '*designated school*' is a primary or post-primary school in receipt of grants by the Minister for Education and Science in excess of the normal capitation grants because a substantial proportion of the students are socially or economically disadvantaged. An '*approved body*' is a body of patrons, trustees, owners or governors of the school or schools in question, established solely to raise funds for the benefit of a named designated school or schools, and approved for this purpose by the Minister.

Designated schools and approved bodies must, when required to do so by notice, make a return to the Minister of aggregate relevant gifts received and, in the case of approved bodies, of the disposal of such gifts. They must also give a signed receipt for each such gift, containing prescribed information and confirming the status and details of the gift.

See also **12.9** 'Corporation tax'.

RELIEF FOR GIFTS TO THE SCIENTIFIC AND TECHNOLOGICAL EDUCATION (INVESTMENT) FUND ('STEIF')

[*TCA 1997, s 485B; FA 1999, s 37*]

2.40 For 1998/99 to 2000/01 (from 2001 see **2.32** above) relief against total income may be claimed (in the return under *s 951* (see **28.11** 'Returns') where relevant) in respect of a 'relevant gift' or gifts totalling £1,000 or more. The amount or value of any consideration received as a result of making the gift is deducted from the amount of the gift.

A *'relevant gift'* is a gift of money made to STEIF which is or will be applied by STEIF solely for the purposes for which the fund was established, and which is not otherwise deductible in computing profits or gains of a trade or profession, nor an income disposition within *s 792*, nor within *s 484* (relief for gifts for education in the arts, see **2.37** above).

Where the donor is a wife whose income is, by election, treated as that of her husband, the deduction is made from her own income, her husband's total income being adjusted accordingly.

STEIF must give a receipt containing prescribed information confirming the status and details of the gift and must, when required by notice, make a return to the Minister giving particulars of the aggregate amount of relevant gifts received in the period specified in the notice and of the disposal of those gifts.

See **12.9** 'Corporation tax') for the associated relief for companies.

RELIEF ON RETIREMENT OF SPORTSPERSONS

[*TCA 1997, s 480A; FA 2002, s 12*]

2.41 For cessations in **2002 and subsequent years,** a special relief applies to individuals who have engaged in a 'specified occupation', or who have carried on a 'specified profession', and who prove to the satisfaction of the Revenue Commissioners that they have permanently ceased to be engaged in the specified occupation (or to carry on the specified profession) in a year in which they are RI-resident. The occupations or professions concerned are those specified in *Sch 23A* for the purposes of retirement annuity contracts (see **2.24** above), all of which involve participation in sport.

For up to ten of the years of assessment from 1990/91 up to and including the year of cessation during which the individual was RI-resident, they may claim a deduction from their total income of an amount equal to **40 per cent** of receipts (before expenses) for the basis period for each year of assessment which arose wholly and exclusively from the specified occupation or profession. The receipts must have derived directly from actual participation in the sport concerned. They thus include:

(*a*)   in the case of an employment, all emoluments paid to the individual by the employer as a direct consequence of the individual's participation in the sport concerned; and (*b*)   in the case of a profession, all match or performance fees, prize moneys and appearance moneys paid to the individual as a direct consequence of such participation;

but exclude:

(i)   sponsorship moneys; and

(ii)   receipts for participation in advertisements, promotions, videos or television or radio programmes, for personal appearances or interviews, newspaper or magazine articles, or for the right to use the individual's image or name for promotional purposes.

The claim must be made in the return (see **28.11** 'Returns') for the year of cessation, and relief is given by repayment (without interest). The relief cannot create or augment a loss. It does not affect net relevant earnings for the year(s) concerned (see **2.24** above).

If the individual subsequently recommences the occupation or profession, relief is withdrawn by assessment (under Sch D, Case IV (**32**)), which may be made at any time, for the year(s) for which it was given.

SPECIAL RATE OF TAX ON RESIDENTIAL LAND TRANSACTIONS

[*TCA 1997, s 644A; FA 2000, s 52; FA 2004, s 83*]

2.42 A special **20 per cent** (up to 31 December 2008) rate of income tax applies to profits or gains arising after 30 November 1999 from dealing in or developing 'residential development land' in a business consisting of or including dealing in or developing land which is, or is treated as, a trade or part trade within Sch D. This rate has been increased to 25 per cent as of from 1 January 2009. It also applies to capital gains chargeable under Sch D, Case IV (see **3.9**(ii) 'Anti-avoidance legislation') arising from the disposal of 'residential development land'. Since 2009, such income has been taxed under normal income tax rules. [*FA 2009, s 6*]

The section also inserts a new *s 644AA* which introduces new rules for the treatment of certain trading losses arising from a trade of dealing in residential development land where if profits had been earned the profits would have qualified for the **20 per cent** incentive rate of income tax.

Under normal income tax rules, a loss sustained in a trade may be set sideways against the person's other income in the year in which the loss arises or may be carried forward for set-off against the income from the trade in subsequent tax years. In the case of losses sustained in a trade of dealing in residential development land, this could lead to a mismatch in that such losses (sustained in a trade in which if profits had been made would have been taxed at 20 per cent) could be set against the person's other income taxable at the higher **41 per cent** rate. The new section provides that such losses must first be converted into a tax credit, valued at 20 per cent of the loss, and then allows the tax credit to be set sideways in the year the loss is sustained against tax payable on the person's other income. Any unused part of the tax credit may be carried forward and set-off against tax on the income from the trade in subsequent years. Where dealing in residential development land is part of a larger trade, any carried forward tax credit may be set against tax on the income from the larger trade.

As respects a claim for the sideways set-off of losses arising in a trade of dealing in residential development land against a property developer's other income, the new rules apply where such a claim has not been made to and received by Revenue before 7 April 2009.

As respects the carry forward of such losses within the trade, the new rules apply unless the carry forward claim by the property developer is made to and received by Revenue before that date. For the purposes of the new rules, where a trade comprises partly of dealing in residential development land and partly of other activities the new section requires each part to be treated as a separate trade.

Finally, where a claim for terminal loss relief (ie on the permanent cessation of a trade) has not been made to and received by Revenue before 7 April 2009, the new section restricts the relief so that any part of the terminal loss that relates to a loss sustained, before 1 January 2009, in a trade of dealing in residential development land is 'ring-fenced' and can only be set against income arising in that trade, or in that part of a trade, in prior years.

Profits or gains attributable to 'construction operations' on the land are excluded, and where part of a trade is within these provisions it is treated as a separate trade. Any necessary apportionments are made on a just and reasonable basis.

Where the special rate applies, the profits or gains so chargeable are excluded from total income and no offset is allowed for personal allowances or credits, etc (see **2.8** *et seq.* above). The taxpayer may, however, elect for the special rate not to apply for a year of assessment, by written notice to the inspector by the specified return date (see **28.11** 'Returns'). There is no PRSI or health contribution charge (see **37.2** 'Social welfare system', **41.1** 'Youth employment levy and health contributions') on profits or gains brought into charge under these provisions (see Revenue Tax Briefing Issue 45 p 11).

'Residential development land' means land:

(*a*)   disposed of to a housing authority (within *Housing (Miscellaneous Provisions) Act 1992, s 23*), the National Building Agency Limited or an approved body under *Housing (Miscellaneous Provisions) Act 1992, s 6* and specified in the appropriate written certificate as being required for the purposes of the *Housing Acts 1996 to 1998*;

(*b*)   in respect of which permission for residential development (including any necessary ancillary development) has been granted (and has not ceased to exist) under *Local Government (Planning and Development) Acts 1963 to 1999* or the *Planning and Development Act 2000*; or

(*c*)   which is, in accordance with a development objective (in the planning authority development plan), for use solely or primarily for residential purposes.

'*Construction operations*' are as under *s 530* (see **13.8** 'Deduction of tax at source') but excluding the demolition or dismantling of any building or structure on the land, the construction or demolition of any roadworks, water mains, wells, sewers or land drainage installations forming part of the land, and any other operations preparatory to residential development on the land other than the laying of the foundations.

See also **12.2** 'Corporation tax' for the application of a similar 20 per cent rate for corporation tax purposes.

For an article, including computational examples, on the application of these provisions, see Revenue Tax Briefing Issue 40 pp 1–5.

INVESTMENT RELIEFS

2.43 See **12.24** 'Corporation tax' as regards availability to individuals of relief for investment in film production, **21** 'Investment in corporate trades' generally, and **34.5** 'Sch E' as regards employee relief for new share subscriptions.

RELIEF FOR INVESTMENT IN ENERGY EFFICIENCY OF RESIDENTIAL PREMISES IN THE STATE

2.44 *Finance Act 2011, s 13* introduces a new *TCA 1997, s 477A* which provides for relief from income tax at the standard rate on expenditure incurred by individuals who are not the landlord of the property concerned, on works carried out to improve the energy efficiency of residential premises situated in the State. A list of qualifying works will be maintained by the Sustainable Energy Authority of Ireland. Relief will be available for qualifying expenditure up to €10,000 for single persons and €15,000 for married couples who are jointly assessed. The Authority shall not issue a certificate of payment in any case where the aggregate of all qualifying expenditure included on certificates of payment previously issued for the year of assessment concerned exceeds €150,000,000. The relief will come into operation on the issuing of a Commencement Order by the Minister for Finance.

LIMITATION ON INCOME TAX RELIEF FOR HIGH EARNERS

2.45 From 2007, the quantum of certain investment-type and other reliefs available for use by high-income earning individuals is limited in any one year. The restriction applies to 'specified reliefs' – broadly income to which stallion, greyhound, woodland, patent royalty and artist exemptions apply, property-based tax incentives, the Business Expansion Scheme, film relief, interest relief in respect of investment in companies and partnerships and donations by individuals within the Self Assessment system to certain sporting, charitable and other bodies and applies also to the carry forward of unutilised 'specified reliefs'. The effect of this restriction on the use of specified reliefs ensures that a high income earner pays tax at the standard rate ie an effective rate of 20 per cent. *FA 2010, s 23* has increased this effective rate from 20 per cent to 30 per cent for individuals who are fully subject to the restriction on the use of certain reliefs for the tax year 2010 onwards. This 30 per cent rate will apply at income levels in excess of €400,000 and above with a graduated application of the restriction between income levels of €125,000 and €400,000. Relief in respect of the 'specified reliefs' is, in effect, limited to the greater of €250,000 or 50 per cent of the adjusted income of the taxpayer for the year of assessment. A tapering restriction applies to adjusted income between €250,000 and €500,000. The limitation applies only where the adjusted income of the individual exceeds €250,000. Adjusted income is taxable income excluding interest subject to DIRT (and certain foreign source deposit interest income treated in the same way as interest subject to DIRT) and income in respect of residential land taxed at the 20 per cent rate (this rate has been increased to 25 per cent as of 1 January 2009) and before any deduction for 'specified reliefs'. Where the limitation applies, the total amount of the 'specified reliefs' less the greater of €250,000 or 50 per cent of the adjusted income is added back to the individual's taxable income to give an increased taxable income amount for the year which is taxable at the normal income tax rates. Where the 'specified reliefs' are limited in a tax year, any unutilised relief is carried forward for relief in subsequent years. The limitation does not apply to capital allowances on plant and machinery or to normal business expenses. It does not impact on the tax life or the tax written down value of a building. The availability of relief under a double taxation agreement is unaffected. The provisions of the Tax Acts relating to assessment and collection of tax apply to amounts due under the provision. [*FA 2006, s 17*]

Finance Act 2007, s 18 amended *Ch 2A* as introduced by *FA 2006*. This section introduced new provisions to ensure that the restriction operates as intended by correcting various references and modifying some of the terminology used in various provisions of the overall measure.

Section 485 has been introduced to deal with interaction of the restriction with the taxation of married couples who are jointly or separately assessed. The section ensures that each individual is treated as single persons when determining the level of relief to which each individual is entitled. In addition where one of both of the spouses has an income below the €250,000 threshold the restriction of the relief will not be applied. The actual application of the restriction requires that certain reliefs are being claimed. The restriction will not apply where these reliefs are not being claimed regardless of the level of the person's income.

The restriction of specified reliefs applies from 1 January 2007. A new schedule was introduced by *FA 2007* which set out reliefs carried forward from 2006 and prior periods. The carry forward reliefs dealt with in *Sch 2A* relate to capital allowances and loss reliefs under *ss 304, 382, 305 and 384*. The Schedule sets out the basis for apportioning between restricted and unrestricted reliefs carried forward under the aforementioned sections. The Schedule involves looking back at the reliefs claimed in 2006 and the previous three tax years. There is a formula provided to determine the restricted portion of the reliefs and it is as follows:

$$RF = SR/TR$$

RF= relief forward

SR and TR are defined separately for the relevant sections.

In addition to the changes outlined above, additional categories of income have been included in the definition of 'ring-fenced' income:

(*a*)   payments and income, in respect of certain foreign life policies, which are taxed at 23 per cent; and

(*b*)   payments and income, in respect of certain offshore funds, which are taxed at 23 per cent.

Section 485FB ensures that any individual who is subject to the restriction is a chargeable person for the purposes of *Pt 41*. This means that any such individuals are within the self assessment system and will be required to file a tax return and are under the tax payment rules.

A further amendment requires that a statement be supplied to the Revenue by those affected by the restriction setting out the following:

(i)   calculation of taxable income before and after the restriction;

(ii)   tax due after the restriction; and

(iii)   specified reliefs used in a year and included in the aggregate of the specified reliefs.

This statement will be submitted at the same time as and together with the individual's tax return, In the event that spouses are on joint assessment or separate assessment each spouse will have to return such a statement which will then be combined on one form.

SIMPLIFYING THE GRANTING OF RELIEFS

2.46 *Finance Act 2007, s 9* inserted a new section (*s 894A*) which states that the Revenue, on a voluntary basis or upon request can get information from third parties relating to expenditure by taxpayers that qualifies for tax relief. This information can be used by Revenue only for the purposes of granting tax relief and for no other purpose. Where, on the basis of the information obtained, the Revenue are satisfied as to the entitlement of a taxpayer to the relief, then they may grant the relief, then they may grant the relief to the taxpayer without the need for a formal claim. The provisions outlined above in relation to trade union subscriptions is an example of how this amendment will work in practice.

3 Anti-Avoidance Legislation

Cross-references. See **30.27** 'Sch D, Cases I and II' for certain 'Bond Washing' and 'Dividend Stripping' transactions; **8.2** 'Capital allowances'; **9.8**; 'Capital gains tax'; **38.134** 'Tax cases'; and generally under **12** 'Corporation tax'.

TRANSACTIONS TO AVOID LIABILITY TO TAX

[*TCA 1997, ss 811; 811A*]

3.1 A general anti-avoidance provision applies as respects any 'tax avoidance transaction' any part of which is undertaken or arranged after 24 January 1989, and which (apart from this provision) gives rise to a reduction, avoidance or deferral of tax arising by virtue of any other transaction carried out wholly on or after a date which could not fall before 25 January 1989, or a refund, repayment or increased repayment of tax which would otherwise first become payable on a date which could not fall earlier than that date. The provision applies to any tax, levy or charge under the care and management of the Revenue Commissioners, and any interest, penalty etc thereon.

A transaction (as widely defined) is a '*tax avoidance transaction*' if, having regard to the results of the transaction, its use in achieving those results, and any other means by which the results (or part) could have been achieved, the Revenue Commissioners form the opinion that (apart from these provisions) it gives rise to a 'tax advantage' and was not undertaken or arranged primarily for any other purpose. Excluded is any case in which the Revenue Commissioners are satisfied that either:

(*a*)   although some other transaction giving rise to greater tax liability could have achieved the same purpose(s), the transaction was undertaken or arranged by a person with a view to realising profits in his business activities, and not primarily to give rise to a tax advantage; or

(*b*)   it was undertaken or arranged for the purpose of obtaining a relief, allowance or abatement under any provision *of the Acts* and would not result in a misuse or abuse of the provision having regard to its purpose.

A '*tax advantage*' is a reduction, avoidance or deferral of any charge or assessment to tax, or a refund or repayment of tax, or increase therein, whether current, potential or prospective, arising out of a transaction, including a transaction where another transaction would not have been undertaken or arranged to achieve the intended results. The Revenue Commissioners are to take into account the form and substance of the transaction and of any other related or connected transactions, and the final outcome and result of all such transactions.

Having formed the opinion that a transaction is a tax avoidance transaction, the Revenue Commissioners are required to calculate the tax advantage from the transaction and the tax consequences, to withdraw or deny that advantage, that would flow from the decision that the transaction fell within these provisions (and any adjustment they consider necessary to afford relief from double taxation), and to notify those details to any person whose tax advantage it is proposed to cancel, or to whom relief from double taxation would be given. Appeal may be made (within 30 days) to the Appeal Commissioners, but only on the grounds that the transaction is not an avoidance transaction, or that the tax advantage (or relief) is incorrectly calculated, or that the tax consequences would not be just or reasonable. The appeal proceeds in like manner to an appeal against an income tax assessment (other than the restriction as to grounds), and appeals against the same opinion may (at the request of the appellants) be heard together. The Appeal Commissioners may accept, reject or amend a notice where the appeal is on the ground that the transaction is not a tax avoidance transaction, and they may confirm or adjust the tax advantage or tax consequences or relief in the notice if the appeal is on those grounds. The Revenue Commissioners may amend, add to or withdraw a notice by further notice, which is treated as a new notice under these provisions, but not so as to set aside or alter any matter which has become final and conclusive on appeal made with regard to that matter.

Requirements as to confidentiality are waived in relation to the giving of notice under these provisions, or in relation to appeals against such notices. Any Revenue officer may be nominated to carry out the functions of the Revenue Commissioners under this provision. There was no provision for such a delegation under *s 811A*. This has now been corrected by the *Finance (No 2) Act 2008*.

Where the Revenue Commissioners' opinion (subject to any amendments) becomes final and conclusive (ie if there is no timely appeal, if the appeal is determined without the notice being cancelled or, from 2 February 2006, when settled by agreement between the taxpayer and Revenue where the transaction is undertaken or the tax adjustment arises on or after that date), all such adjustments may be made as are just and reasonable, and are specified in the notice, to withdraw or deny the tax advantage. These include the allowance or disallowance of deductions etc, the allocation or denial of deductions, losses, reliefs, exemptions etc, and the recharacterisation of the nature of payments etc, and the granting of relief from any resulting double taxation. There is no further right of appeal against such adjustments.

Part 33, which deals with certain anti-avoidance provisions has been amended by *FA 2010, s 149*. The amendment inserts a new *Ch 3* into that Part which places new mandatory disclosure obligations on promoters of certain tax related transactions to give details of those transactions to the Revenue Commissioners shortly after they are first marketed or made available for use. The legislation was subject to a commencement order and regulations being issued. The legislation has come into effect from 17 January 2011 with the first reports being made by 17 April 2011 with the Finance Act confirming these commencement dates. [*FA 2011, s 73*] In certain limited circumstances, the users of such transactions are required to provide the information ie where the promoter is offshore, where the promoter claims legal professional privilege or where they have entered into a transaction not involving a promoter. The new mandatory disclosure rules apply to transactions that have as a main benefit the obtaining of a tax advantage and that match certain features set out in the legislation.

Provision of the required information on transactions by promoters or users under the mandatory disclosure rules will be on a non-prejudicial basis. There will be no presumption or inference that a transaction disclosed under the rules is a tax avoidance transaction. Equally, the fact that a transaction may not come within the disclosure requirements cannot be regarded as an indicator that the transaction is not a tax avoidance transaction. The information on transactions will have to be provided within tight timescales and penalties will apply where a person fails to meet their obligations in that regard. Under the legislation the courts are given significant flexibility as to the level of penalty to apply. *FA 2011, s 72* provides that these details to not have to be disclosed to the Revenue Commissioners where the promoters are satisfied at the time that the details would have to be disclosed that the transaction had not been undertaken by that person. The time periods within which a disclosure has to be made, the information to be provided and the manner in which it is to be provided, along with further details of the classes of transaction that are intended to fall within the disclosure regime will be set out in regulations. While the new mandatory disclosure rules apply as on and from the date of passing of the Finance Act (3 April 2010), actual compliance with the rules can commence only after the various regulations are made. The commencement date of *FA 2010, s 149* (3 April 2010) is now changed to 17 January 2011 so as to align it with that of the Regulations giving effect to Chapter 3 of Part 33.

Since 31 March 2006 any tax due to Revenue on foot of a finding that a transaction is a tax avoidance transaction is subject to the 10 per cent surcharge due on late submission of returns (see **25.4** Payment of Tax). This surcharge has been increased from 10 per cent to 20 per cent. [*FA 2008, s 140*] The surcharge and interest due on payment or repayment of the tax by the taxpayer can be avoided through filing a protective notification of the transaction with Revenue within 90 days of the transaction commencing (or 2 May 2006, if later). A protective notification must contain full details of the transaction and full reference to tax law and how it is considered to apply to the transaction. The time period within which Revenue must form an opinion that a transaction is a tax avoidance transaction under *s 811* will be limited, where a full protective notification is made, to a period of two years from the date of the notification. The expression of doubt procedure is not regarded as a protective notification. The procedure does not involve or imply any doubt on the part of the taxpayer. It is a provision of information to Revenue to protect against the possibility of surcharge or interest. The procedure applies to transactions commenced after 2 February 2006 and to transactions implemented before that date but having the effect of reducing liabilities or creating tax repayments after that date. [*FA 2006, s 126*] See Revenue Guidance Note on Protective Notifications. A further amendment was introduced to encourage the use of the protective notification procedure. This amendment is in the case of any appeal against a Revenue opinion that a transaction is a tax avoidance transaction in circumstances where a full protective notification has not been made, the Appeal Commissioners and, in turn, the Courts will be required to determine the appeal on the basis of whether there were grounds on which the transaction specified in the Revenue notice of opinion could reasonably be considered to be a tax avoidance transaction. [*FA 2008, s 140*]

SCHEMES TO AVOID LIABILITY UNDER SCH F

[*TCA 1997, s 817; FA 2005, s 39; FA 2006, s 24*]

3.2 An anti-avoidance provision applies where a shareholder disposes of shares in a close company (see **12.7** 'Corporation tax') and, following the disposal or the carrying out of a scheme or arrangement of which it is a part, the interest of the shareholder in any trade or business (the '*specified business*') carried on by the company at the time of the disposal is not significantly reduced, whether or not the company continues to carry it on. Since 1 March 2005, the interest of a shareholder includes those of persons connected with him and the provision applies to a disposal of a holding company by a shareholder without a significant reduction in the entire business by that shareholder or connected persons. Since that date, an interest is not significantly reduced if the shareholder is entitled to any shares at the discretion of trustees and those shares were acquired from the shareholder (either directly or indirectly) with financial assistance (directly or indirectly) from a company controlled by the shareholder or connected persons. Since 1 March 2005, the section applies also to a gain attributable to a prior transfer of value to the company from another company controlled by the same person or connected persons.

Finance Act 2011, s 28 amends this to include companies within the meaning of *TCA 1997, s 432* and is effective for disposals after 26 January 2011. In addition the section provides that the holding of money by a company shall be deemed to be a business carried on by the company, regardless of how that money was contributed to, or acquired by, the company. Essentially the changes mean that the holding of money by a company shall now come within the definition of a 'trade or business' for the purposes of the provision and the definition of control required in order to come within the parameters of the provision will now be determined in line with the definitions set out in the close company legislation.The question of whether an interest is 'not significantly reduced' is determined by reference to beneficial ownership of, or entitlement to, ordinary share capital, or profits or assets available for distribution to equity holders, at any time after the disposal as compared with any time before the disposal.

A disposal of shares for this purpose includes a part disposal and a deemed disposal for CGT purposes, and certain arrangements which result in shares in another close company being issued to shareholders in respect of or in proportion to their holdings in the close company, but with those shares being either retained or cancelled, are nonetheless treated as a disposal (or part disposal) of those shares in exchange for the new shares.

Unless it is shown to the satisfaction of the inspector (or, on appeal, the Appeal Commissioners or Circuit Court judge) that the disposal was made for *bona fide* commercial reasons and not as part of a scheme or arrangement a purpose of which was the avoidance of tax, the proceeds of the disposal in money or money's worth or, if less, the excess of those proceeds over any new consideration given for the issue of the shares (and not previously taken into account under this provision), is treated as a distribution (see **12.10** 'Corporation tax') made at the time of the disposal. The amount so treated at any time may not exceed the aggregate of 'capital receipts' (ie amounts received in money or money's worth (other than the company's shares) and not, apart from this provision, chargeable to income tax) received by the shareholder in respect of the disposal or as part of a scheme or arrangement of which the disposal is part. Capital receipts received after the time of the disposal continue to result in deemed distributions at the time of the disposal. Interest on unpaid tax (see **25.4** 'Payment of tax') runs in respect of the distribution as if it were due and payable from the day on which the shareholder received the capital receipt. A tax credit was available in respect of the distribution only to the extent that ACT (see **12.26** 'Corporation tax') had been accounted for (or would have been but for being set off against distributions received).

Since 21 February 2006, the section also applies to any scheme to avoid income tax under Sch F through the extraction of money or money's worth from the company for the benefit of the shareholders without paying a dividend or making a distribution. [*FA 2006, s 24*]

LOAN TRANSACTIONS

[*TCA 1997, s 813*]

3.3 A new section (*s 591A*) has been introduced. Where, with reference to lending money or giving credit (or varying the terms of a loan or credit):

(*a*) a transaction provides for the payment of any annuity, or other annual payment, the payment is treated for all tax purposes (including CT) as if it were interest;

(*b*) a transaction provides for the subsequent repurchase or reacquisition by the former owner of any securities or other income-producing property transferred, the former owner is assessable under Sch D, Case IV on any income arising from the property before repayment of the loan etc;

(*c*) a transaction provides for a person to assign, surrender, waive or forgo income on property (without a sale or transfer), he is assessable under Sch D, Case IV on the amount of that income (without prejudice to the liability of any other person);

(*d*) credit is given for the purchase price of property and, during the subsistence of the debt, the purchaser's rights to income from the property are suspended or restricted, he is treated as if he had surrendered that income under (*c*) above.

CERTIFICATES OF DEPOSIT ETC

[*TCA 1997, s 814*]

3.4 Gains, not otherwise chargeable to tax, arising from the disposal of certificates of deposit and assignable deposits (as defined) are chargeable to tax under Sch D, Case IV on so much of the gain as is time-apportionable to the period from 3 April 1974 to disposal date. There is a right to set off losses against other Case IV income, including interest on the certificate.

BOND WASHING

[*TCA 1997, s 815; FA 1984, s 29; FA 1993, s 21; FA 1994, s 26*]

3.5 This provision applies (subject to certain exceptions) on the sale or transfer of 'securities' other than company shares, including Government and other securities exempt from capital gains tax (see **9.7(*f*)** 'Capital gains tax') and any stocks, bonds and obligations of any Government, municipal corporation, company or other body corporate, whether or not creating or evidencing a charge on assets.

If interest in respect of such a security is receivable otherwise than by the owner, interest is deemed to have accrued on a day-to-day basis during his whole period of ownership, and he is chargeable under Sch D, Case IV on interest so accrued up to the date of contract for the sale, etc (or the date of payment of consideration for the sale, etc if later), less any interest in respect of which he is otherwise chargeable to tax. If there are arrangements under which the owner agrees to buy back or reacquire the security (or to buy or acquire similar securities), or acquires an option (subsequently exercised) to do so, the charge under these provisions is on the interest deemed to accrue up to the next interest payment date after the sale, etc. On any subsequent resale, etc, the charge does not apply to interest treated as accruing before that payment date.

The exceptions are:

(*a*)   where the security has been held by the vendor for a continuous period of at least two years up to the date of contract for the sale, etc (or the date of payment of the consideration if later);

(*b*)   where the sale proceeds are taken into account under Sch D, Case I in the vendor's trade of dealing in securities;

(*c*)   where the sale or transfer is between spouses at a time when the wife is treated as living with her husband (see **23.1** 'Married persons');

(*d*)   where interest on the security is treated as a distribution (see **12.10** 'Corporation tax'); and

(*e*)   where the owner is an 'undertaking for collective investment' (see **12.22** 'Corporation tax'), and any gain or loss on the sale or transfer is a chargeable gain or an allowable loss.

For the purposes of (*a*) above:

(i)   the personal representatives of a deceased person, during administration of the estate, and the deceased are treated as the same person; and

(ii)   a husband and wife to whom (*c*) above applies are treated as the same person.

Identification. Securities disposed of are identified with securities of the same class (ie where they entitle the owner to the same rights against the same person as to capital and interest, and the same remedies for enforcement of those rights) acquired later before those acquired earlier.

Information. The inspector has wide powers to require such particulars as he considers necessary for the purposes of these provisions from the issuer of a security (or his agent) and from the owner of a security.

See also **30.27** 'Sch D, Cases I and II' for earlier provisions relating to share dealers, etc.

SHARES ISSUED IN LIEU OF CASH DIVIDENDS

[*TCA 1997, s 816; FA 1998, s 43*]

3.6 Where shares, stock, etc issued by a company are received as an alternative to a cash dividend, the cash amount forgone is treated as follows:

(i)   where the company is resident outside RI, it is treated as income received from securities and possessions outside RI and assessed and charged under Sch D, Case III (**31**);

(ii)   where the company is an RI-resident company any class of whose shares is listed on a stock exchange or quoted on the Developing Companies or Exploration Securities Markets or similar, it is treated as a distribution by the company (see **12.10** 'Corporation tax');

(iii)   where the company is any other RI-resident company, it is treated as profits or gains chargeable only under Sch D, Case IV (**32**).

Previously, quoted companies within (ii) above were excluded from these provisions, so that only (i) and (iii) above applied.

TRANSFER OF ASSETS ABROAD

3.7 Liability of transferor. Where an individual resident or ordinarily resident in RI has the power to enjoy (as widely defined), either forthwith or in the future, any income of a non-resident or non-domiciled person which arises as a result of a transfer of assets (or of any associated operation) *at any time*, then the income shall be deemed to be income of the resident individual for all tax purposes. Similarly if such an individual receives, or is entitled to receive, any capital sum by way of loan or repayment of a loan, or other non-income payment not for full consideration, which is in any way connected with the transfer (or any associated operation), the income arising to the non-resident or non-domiciled person as a result of the transfer is deemed to be the income of the resident individual. This applies also to sums received by a third person at the individual's direction or by the individual's assignment of the right to receive it. In either case, the provisions are disapplied where the individual shows that the transfer (together with any associated operations) was made for genuine business reasons and not for tax-avoidance purposes. New amendments have been introduced so that the individual must show to the satisfaction of the Revenue Commissioners that it would not be reasonable to conclude that both the transfer and any associated operations were not for the purpose of avoiding tax or where all genuine commercial transactions. A transaction is a genuine commercial transaction only where it is effected in the course of a trade or business, or with a view to setting up and commencing a trade or a business. In addition, the subjective intentions and purposes of any person who designed, effected or provided advice in relation to the transaction can be taken into consideration in determining their purpose. New provisions have also been introduced which allow the Revenue to apportion an exemption from Irish income tax on a just and reasonable basis where, due to the circumstances since the making of the transfer, the income is attributable to both exempt and non-exempt transactions, taking into account the old rules and the new rules. [*FA 2007, s 44*]

For income arising after 11 February 1998 (regardless of when the transfer of assets etc took place), it is made clear by *FA 1998, s 12* that these provisions apply:

(*a*)   regardless of whether or not the individual concerned was resident or ordinarily resident in RI when the transfer took place; and

(*b*)   where the purpose of the transfer is the avoidance of any form of direct taxation, and not just income tax.

Also after that date, an individual not of RI domicile is not chargeable under these provisions if he would not have been chargeable to income tax on the income had it in fact been his income.

The tax chargeable under these provisions will be under Sch D, Case IV for the year in which the benefit is received with the same deductions and reliefs as if the income had actually been received. There are provisions against a double charge on the same income or benefit. Certain provisions which exempt from tax the income of non-residents (eg on government securities payable to non-residents) will not apply. The Revenue have power to obtain information. See **38.218**, **38.219** 'Tax cases'.

[*TCA 1997, ss 806–810; FA 1998, s 12; FA 1999, s 60*].

Liability of non-transferor. Where, as a result of a transfer of assets (or of any associated operations), income becomes payable to a person resident or domiciled outside RI, and an individual resident or ordinarily resident in RI who is not liable as the transferor (as above) or otherwise receives a benefit provided out of those assets, the following provisions apply to benefits received and 'relevant income' arising after 10 February 1999, irrespective of when the transfer etc took place, unless the individual can show that the transfer (together with any associated operations) was made for genuine business reasons and not for tax avoidance purposes. The value of the benefit, up to the amount of 'relevant income' of years of assessment up to and including the year in which received, is treated as income of the resident or ordinarily resident individual for that year chargeable under Sch D, Case IV. Any excess benefit is carried forward against 'relevant income' of subsequent years and taxed accordingly.

Relief from double taxation is given where a benefit in the form of a capital payment has given rise to a chargeable gain under *s 579A* or *s 579F* (see **9.17** 'Capital gains tax').

'*Relevant income*' of a year of assessment is any income arising in that year to a non-resident or non-domiciled person and which by virtue of the transfer or associated operations can directly or indirectly be used to provide a benefit for the resident or ordinarily resident individual or to enable a benefit to be provided for him.

An individual domiciled outside RI is not taxable on a benefit not received in RI in respect of any relevant income on which, had he received it, he would, because of his domicile, not have been taxable. *s 72* (see **31.2** 'Sch D, Case III') applies for this purpose as if the benefit were income arising from possessions outside RI.

The provisions described above (in relation to the liability of transferors) concerning disapplication of non-resident exemptions and information powers apply equally to these provisions.

[*TCA 1997, s 807A; FA 1999, s 60(c)*]

TRANSACTIONS IN LAND

3.8

(i) **Extension of charge under Sch D, Case I** [*TCA 1997, ss 640, 641*].

Profits from dealing in or developing land otherwise not within Sch D are charged to tax under Case I if they would be so charged if all disposals were of a full interest in land acquired in the course of business by the disponer. The computation of such profits varies from normal Case I rules in several respects:

(*a*) Any consideration other than rent (or premiums treated as rent – see **33.6** 'Sch D, Case V') for the disposal of an interest in land is treated as a trading receipt;

(*b*) Any consideration for the granting of development rights in land (other than easement rights chargeable under Sch D, Case V (**33**)) is treated as a trading receipt;

(*c*) Any interest in land held as trading stock remains so until the trade ceases;

(*d*)   Any interest in land acquired other than for money or money's worth, or otherwise than as trading stock, is treated as acquired at market value at the time of becoming trading stock;

(*e*)   No deduction is allowed in respect of any payment for the surrender of a right to an annuity or other annual payment, subject to the exception of certain annuities, etc arising under a will or liability incurred for consideration, or the payment for which is chargeable to income or corporation tax on the payee;

(*f*)   A trader's expenditure in acquiring an interest in land subject to an annuity, etc is adjusted where a sum (not chargeable to income or corporation tax on the payee) is payable for the forfeiture or surrender of the right to the annuity, etc by some other person (other than in the course of a land dealing or development trade carried on by that other person). The expenditure is reduced to that payable if the right had not been forfeited or surrendered, the balance of the trader's expenditure being treated as payable by him for the forfeiture, etc of the right. All necessary apportionments and valuations are made by the inspector, or, on appeal, the Appeal Commissioners.

(ii)   **Charge under Sch D, Case IV** [*TCA 1997, ss 643–645*].

Where:

(*a*)   Land (or any property deriving its value from land) is acquired with the sole or main object of realising a gain from disposing of it;

(*b*)   Land is held as trading stock; or

(*c*)   Land is developed with the sole or main object of realising a gain from disposing of it when developed;

any capital gain from disposal of the land or any part of it (ie any amount not otherwise includible in any computation of income for tax purposes) which is realised (for himself or for any other person) by the person acquiring, holding or developing it (or by any connected person, as defined by *s 10*, or a person party to, or concerned in, any arrangement or scheme to realise the gain indirectly or by a series of transactions) is, subject as below, treated for all tax purposes as income of the person realising the gain (or the person who transmitted to him, directly or indirectly, the opportunity of making that gain) assessable, under Sch D, Case IV, for the chargeable period in which the gain is realised.

These provisions apply to a person, whether RI-resident or not, if all or any part of the land in question is in RI.

'*Land*' includes buildings, and any estate or interest in land or buildings.

'*Property deriving its value from land*' includes any shareholding in a company, partnership interest, or interest in settled property, deriving its value, directly or indirectly, from land, and any option, consent or embargo affecting the disposition of land. But see 'Exemptions' below.

Land is '*disposed of*' for the above purpose if, by any one or more transactions or by any arrangement or scheme (whether concerning the land or any property deriving its value therefrom), the property in, or control over, the land is effectively disposed of. Any number of transactions may be treated as a single arrangement or scheme if they have, or there is evidence of, a common purpose. See also under 'General' below.

Exemptions

(i)   An individual's gain made from the *sale, etc, of his residence* exempted from capital gains tax under *s 604* or which would be so exempt but for *s 604(14)* (acquired for purpose of making a gain);

(ii)   A gain on the sale of *shares in a company holding land as trading stock* (or a company owning, directly or indirectly, 90 per cent of the ordinary share capital of such a company) *provided that* the company disposes of the land by normal trade and makes all possible profit from it, and the share sale is not part of an arrangement or scheme to realise a land gain indirectly;

(iii)   (If the liability arises solely under (*c*) above). Any part of the gain fairly attributable to a *period before the intention was made* to develop the land.

Gains are to be computed 'as is just and reasonable in the circumstances', allowance being given only for expenses attributable to the land disposed of, and the following may be taken into account:

(A)   if a leasehold interest is disposed of out of an interest in land, the Sch D, Case I treatment in such a case of a person dealing in land;

(B)   any adjustments under *ss 99(2), 100(4)* for tax on lease premiums.

Where the computation of a gain in respect of the development of land (as under (*c*) above) is made on the footing that the land or property was appropriated as trading stock that land, etc, is also to be treated for purposes of capital gains tax (under *s 596*) as having been transferred to stock.

Where, under these provisions, tax is assessed on, and paid by, a person other than the one who actually realised the gain, the person paying the tax may recover it from the other party (for which purpose the Revenue will, on request, supply a certificate of income in respect of which tax has been paid).

General. There are provisions to prevent avoidance by the use of indirect means to transfer any property or right, or enhance or diminish its value, eg, by sales at less, or more, than full consideration, assigning share capital or rights in a company or partnership or an interest in settled property, disposal on the winding-up of any company, partnership or trust.

For ascertaining whether, and to what extent, the value of any property or right is derived from any other property or right, value may be traced through any number of companies, partnerships or trusts to its shareholders, etc, 'in such manner as is just and reasonable'.

The inspector may require, under penalty, any person to supply him with any particulars thought necessary, including particulars of:

(I)   transactions, etc, in which he acts, or acted, on behalf of others;

(II) transactions, etc which in the opinion of the inspector should be investigated; and

(III) what part, if any, he has taken, or is taking, in specified transactions, etc (under this heading a *solicitor* who has merely acted as professional adviser is not compelled to do more than state that he acted and give his client's name and address.)

(iii) Miscellaneous

(*a*) There are provisions for adjustment of sale price to market value in the case of certain transfers other than at market value between connected persons (as defined by *s 10*) [*TCA 1997, s 642*];

(*b*) The tax payable under these provisions may be postponed in certain circumstances [*TCA 1997, s 646*].

ANNUAL PAYMENTS FOR NON-TAXABLE CONSIDERATION

[*TCA 1997, s 242*]

3.9 This provision applies to a payment which is an annuity or other annual payment chargeable under Sch D, Case III, not being interest, an annuity granted in the ordinary course of a business of granting annuities, or a payment to an individual for surrender, assignment or release of an interest in settled property in favour of a person with a subsequent interest. Where such a payment is made under a liability incurred for a consideration in money or money's worth, which is not wholly brought into account for income or corporation tax purposes in computing the income of the payer, then the payment is not made under deduction of tax (see **13.1** 'Deduction of tax at source'), is not allowed as a deduction in computing the income of the payer, and is not a charge on income for corporation tax purposes (see **12.9** 'Corporation tax').

ARRANGEMENTS FOR REDUCING VALUE OF COMPANY SHARES

[*FA 1989, s 90; FA 1993, ss 126, 127*]

3.10 See generally **7** 'Capital acquisitions tax'.

The following anti-avoidance arrangements have effect as respects a gift or inheritance taken as a result of arrangements made after 24 January 1989:

(*a*) Where a person has an absolute interest in possession in shares in a private company (within *CATCA 2003, s 27(2); CATA 1976, s 16(2)*), and as a result of any arrangement the market value of those shares, or of any property representing them, is reduced, then for CAT purposes a 'specified amount' is treated as a benefit taken, immediately after the making of the arrangement, from that person, as disponer, by the beneficial owners of the shares whose market value is increased as a result of the arrangement or, if the shares are held in trust without any ascertainable beneficial owners, by the disponer in relation to that trust as if he were the beneficial owner. The 'specified amount' is apportioned according to the increase in value of the shares held.

The '*specified amount*' is the difference between the market value of the shares immediately before the arrangement was made (calculated under *CATCA 2003, s 27* as if each share were in a company controlled by a donee or successor) and that of the shares (or property) immediately after the arrangement was made (calculated under *CATCA 2003, s 26*), and is situate where the company is incorporated. For these purposes, *CATCA 2003, s 27* has effect as if:

(i)   references to the donee or successor were references to the disponer of the specified amount;

(ii)   the relevant time in relation to control of a company were the time immediately before the arrangement came into effect; and

(iii)   the shares were, immediately before the arrangement came into effect, the absolute property of the disponer of the specified amount.

(*b*)   Where an interest in property is limited by the disposition creating it to cease on an event (including a death and the expiry of a specified period), and immediately before the making of an arrangement the property includes shares in a private company, and the arrangement reduces the value of those shares (or of property representing them), then:

(i)   where the interest is an interest in possession, the property under the disposition is treated as including a 'specified amount' (as in (*a*) above);

(ii)   where the interest is not an interest in possession, (i) above applies as if it were; and

(iii)   the event on which the interest was to cease is, to the extent of the specified amount, treated as having happened immediately before the arrangement was made.

(*c*)   Where shares in a private company are subject to a discretionary trust, under or in consequence of a disposition, immediately before the making of an arrangement which reduces the value of the shares (or of property representing them), then for CAT purposes the specified amount is treated as a benefit taken, immediately after the making of the arrangement, by the beneficial owners of the shares whose market value is increased as a result of the arrangement or, if the shares are held in trust without any ascertainable beneficial owners, by the disponer in relation to that trust as if he were the beneficial owner. The specified amount is apportioned according to the increase in value of the shares held.

(*a*), (*b*) and (*c*) above do not prejudice any charge in respect of any gift or inheritance under any disposition on or after the making of the arrangement in question comprising shares in a company (or property representing such shares). Where shares held in trust under a disposition by any disponer are shares whose value is increased as a result of such arrangements as are referred to in (*a*), (*b*) or (*c*) above, any gift or inheritance taken under the disposition on or after the making of the arrangement and comprising those shares (or property representing them) is deemed to be taken from that disponer.

Where under (*a*) or (*c*) above the specified amount is treated as a benefit taken by the disponer in relation to a trust, the trustee of that trust shall, and the disponer shall not, be a person primarily accountable for the payment of tax in respect thereof. The tax, interest and expenses may be raised by the person accountable for the tax in respect of a specified amount by the sale or mortgage of, or of a terminable charge on, the shares whose value is increased as a result of the arrangement, whether or not those shares are vested in him. The tax remains a charge on the shares whose value is increased as a result of the arrangement.

Where shares in a company have been redeemed immediately after, and as a result of, an arrangement made after 5 May 1993, the redeemed shares are, for the purposes of (*a*), (*b*) or (*c*) above, and unless they are actually represented by property, deemed thereon to be represented by property with a market value of nil.

For the purposes of the special tax on discretionary trusts (see **7.14** 'Capital acquisitions tax'), the increase in value of shares subject to such a trust immediately after the arrangement is made (as above) is treated as property.

RESTRICTION ON SET-OFF OF PRE-ENTRY LOSSES WHERE A COMPANY JOINS A GROUP

[*TCA 1997, s 626A, Sch 18A; FA 1999, ss 56, 57; FA 2001, s 40*]

3.11 Special anti-avoidance provisions apply to any 'pre-entry losses' of a company which has become a member of a group (the '*relevant group*') on or after 1 March 1999. Since 1 January 2006 the provisions apply to a Societas Europaea (SE) and a European Cooperative Society (SCE) [*FA 2006, s 60*]. A '*pre-entry loss*' means any allowable loss which accrued to the company at a time before it became a member of the relevant group, in so far as it had not been allowed as a deduction from chargeable gains accruing to the company before that time, or the 'pre-entry proportion' (see below) of any allowable loss accruing to it on the disposal of any 'pre-entry asset'. A '*pre-entry asset*', in relation to any disposal, means any asset that was held, at the time immediately before it became a member of the relevant group, by any company (whether or not the one which makes the disposal). (Since 15 February 2001, the provisions are extended to include situations where assets of companies resident in other EU Member States become chargeable assets for RI capital gains tax purposes.) However, except as below, an asset is not a pre-entry asset if the company which held the asset at the time it became a member of the relevant group is not the company which makes the disposal and since that time the asset has been disposed of otherwise than on the no gain/no loss basis of *s 617* (see **12.15** 'Corporation tax'), unless the company making the disposal retains an interest in or over the asset. [*TCA 1997, Sch 18A para 1(1)–(4); FA 2001, s 40*] Certain spreading provisions relating to life assurance companies and collective investment schemes are disregarded in determining whether a loss accrued before a company became a member of a group. [*TCA 1997, Sch 18A para 1(9)*]

An asset (the '*second asset*') which derives its value wholly or partly from another asset (the '*first asset*') acquired or held by a company at any time is treated as the same asset if it is held subsequently by the same company, or by any company which is or has been a member of the same group of companies as that company (eg a freehold derived from a leasehold where the lessee acquires the reversion). Where this treatment applies, whether under this provision or otherwise, the second asset is treated as a pre-entry asset in relation to a company if the first asset would have been. [*TCA 1997, Sch 18A para 1(8)*]

The '*pre-entry proportion*' of an allowable loss accruing on the disposal of a pre-entry asset is the smaller of the allowable loss which would have accrued if the asset had been disposed of at market value at the 'relevant time' and the allowable loss accruing on the actual disposal. [*TCA 1997, Sch 18A para 2*] The '*relevant time*' is the time when the company by reference to which the asset is a pre-entry asset became a member of the relevant group. Where a company has become a member of the relevant group more than once, an asset is a pre-entry asset in relation to that company if it would be a pre-entry asset in relation to that company in respect of any of the entries into the group, but in these circumstances any reference to the time when a company became a member of the relevant group is a reference to the last time the company entered the group. [*TCA 1997, Sch 18A para 1(5)*]

Where the principal company of a group (the '*first group*') has at any time become a member of another group (the '*second group*') so that the two groups are treated as the same under *s 616(3)* (see **12.15** 'Corporation tax'), and the second group, together (in pursuance of *s 616(3)*) with the first group, is the relevant group, then, except in the following circumstances, the members of the first group are treated for the purposes of *Sch 18A* as having become members of the relevant group at that time, and not (by virtue of *s 616(3)*) at the times when they became members of the first group. The circumstances referred to are where:

(i)   the persons who immediately before the time when the principal company of the first group became a member of the second group owned the shares comprised in the issued share capital of the principal company of the first group are the same as the persons who, immediately after that time, owned the shares comprised in the issued share capital of the principal company of the relevant group; and

(ii)   the company which is the principal company of the relevant group immediately after that time was not the principal company of any group immediately before that time, and immediately after that time had assets consisting entirely, or almost entirely, of shares comprised in the issued share capital of the principal company of the first group.

[*TCA 1997, Sch 18A para 1(6)(7)*]

A pre-entry loss that accrued to a company before it became a member of the relevant group is deductible from a chargeable gain accruing to that company only if the gain is one accruing:

(*a*)   on a disposal made by that company before the date on which it became a member of the relevant group (the '*entry date*') and in the accounting period in which that date falls;

(*b*)   on the disposal of an asset which was held by that company immediately before the entry date; or

(*c*)   on the disposal of any asset which:

   (i)   was acquired by that company on or after the entry date from a person who was not a member of the relevant group at the time of the acquisition, and

   (ii)   since its acquisition from that person has not been used or held for any purposes other than those of a trade which was being carried on by that company at the time immediately before the entry date and which continued to be carried on by that company until the disposal.

The pre-entry proportion of an allowable loss accruing to any company on the disposal of a pre-entry asset is deductible from a chargeable gain accruing to that company only if:

(1)   the gain is one accruing on a disposal made, before the entry date and in the accounting period in which that date falls, by that company and that company is the one (the '*initial company*') by reference to which the asset on the disposal of which the loss accrues is a pre-entry asset;

(2)   the pre-entry asset and the asset on the disposal of which the gain accrues were each held by the same company at a time immediately before it became a member of the relevant group; or

(3)   the gain is one accruing on the disposal of an asset which:

(i)   was acquired by the initial company (whether before or after it became a member of the relevant group) from a person who, at the time of the acquisition, was not a member of that group, and

(ii)   since its acquisition from that person has not been used or held for any purposes other than those of a trade which was being carried on, immediately before it became a member of the relevant group, by the initial company and which continued to be carried on by the initial company until the disposal.

Where two or more companies become members of the relevant group at the same time and those companies (referred to below as the 'co-joiners') were all members of the same group of companies immediately before they became members of the relevant group, then:

(A)   an asset is treated for the purposes of (*b*) above as held, immediately before it became a member of the relevant group, by the company to which the pre-entry loss in question accrued if that company is one of the co-joiners and the asset was in fact so held by another co-joiner;

(B)   two or more assets are treated for the purposes of (2) above as assets held by the same company immediately before it became a member of the relevant group wherever they would be so treated if all the co-joiners were treated as a single company; and

(C)   the acquisition of an asset is treated for the purposes of (*c*) and (3) above as an acquisition by the company to which the pre-entry loss in question accrued if that company is one of the co-joiners and the asset was in fact acquired (whether before or after they became members of the relevant group) by another of the co-joiners.

If, however, (i) within any period of three years, a company becomes a member of a group of companies and there is (either earlier or later in that period, or at the same time) a 'major change in the nature or conduct of a trade' carried on by that company, or (ii) at any time after the scale of the activities in a trade carried on by a company has become small or negligible, and before any considerable revival of the trade, that company becomes a member of a group of companies, then the trade carried on before that change, or which has become small or negligible, is disregarded for the purposes of (*c*) and (3) above in relation to any time before the company became a member of the group in question. A '*major change in the nature or conduct of a trade*' includes a reference to a major change in the type of property dealt in, or services or facilities provided, in the trade, or a major change in customers, markets or outlets of the trade. This applies even if the change is the result of a gradual process which began outside the three-year period concerned. Where the operation of this provision depends on circumstances or events at a time after the company becomes a member of any group of companies (but not more than three years after), an assessment to give effect to the provisions may be made within six years from that time or the latest such time.

[*TCA 1997, Sch 18A para 4, 5*]

Where:

(I)   a company which is a member of a group of companies becomes at any time a member of another group of companies as the result of a disposal of shares in or other securities of that company or any other company; and

(II)   that disposal is a no gain/no loss disposal under any provision of the *Taxes Acts*,

Schedule 18A has effect in relation to the losses that accrued to that company before that time and the assets held by that company at that time as if any time when it was a member of the first group were included in the period during which it is treated as having been a member of the second group. [*TCA 1997, Sch 18A para 5*]

TREATMENT OF CERTAIN INTEREST PAID OR RECEIVED

3.12 Interest paid or received on or after 29 February 2000 is subject to additional anti-avoidance provisions:

(i)   Tax relief under *Pt 8* (*ss 237–267*) is denied for interest paid by any person under a transaction where a scheme has been effected or arrangements made such that the sole or main benefit expected to accrue to that person from the transaction is the obtaining of a reduction in tax liability by means of that relief. Where group relief is claimed for interest treated as a charge on income (see **12.15** 'Groups of companies'), the benefit to the claimant and surrendering companies taken together is taken into account for this purpose; [*TCA 1997, s 817A; FA 2000, s 73*]

(ii)   Where a person receives interest in a chargeable period or its basis period, and the interest would otherwise be taken into account in computing the person's Sch D income not for that chargeable period but for a subsequent chargeable period or periods (ie where it accrues in the later period(s)), it is instead taken into account in computing that person's Sch D income for the period in which it is received and not for the later period(s). For these purposes, where two basis periods overlap or coincide or one falls within the other, the common period is deemed to fall in the first period only, and any gap between basis periods is deemed to fall within the first; [*TCA 1997, s 817B; FA 2000, s 73*]

(iii) For accounting periods or years of assessment ending on or after 6 February 2003, where interest paid by a person to a connected person is a trading expense of the payer but not a trading receipt of the connected person, the interest is not deductible as a trading expense by the payer until it has been accounted for as income of the connected person for tax purposes. A company that is not RI tax resident and not directly or indirectly under the control of an RI resident person is excluded from the application of this provision. For the purposes of determining control, intermediate holding companies are ignored. [*TCA 1997, s 817C; FA 2003, s 44; FA 2004, s 32*]

CAPITAL GAINS TAX ON DISPOSAL OF SHARES IN A COMPANY

3.13 A new section (*s 591A*) has been included. The new section prevents a scheme involving the avoidance of capital gains tax on certain disposals of shares in a company. The avoidance can arise where, instead of a payment being made for the disposal of the shares, an abnormal dividend is paid to a company. A dividend received by a company is exempt from tax where it is from a company that is resident in the State whereas an amount received for the disposal of shares would be subject to capital gains tax.

The new section provides that, where an abnormal dividend is paid to a company in connection with the disposal of shares in a company, the amount of the dividend is to be treated for tax purposes as proceeds for the disposal of the shares rather than a dividend. [*FA 2008, s 51*]

TRANSFER PRICING LEGISLATION

3.14 A new *Pt 35A* will be inserted to introduce transfer pricing rules that apply the arm's length principle to trading transactions between associated persons. In simple terms the legislation effectively replaces any overstated expenses or understated receipts with market value figures. The new rules will apply to both domestic and cross border transactions. 'Arm's length' is to be construed in accordance with the OECD Transfer Pricing Guidelines. If an expense incurred by a trader in dealings with an associated person is greater than the 'arm's length' amount, or a sale by a trader to an associated person is at less than the 'arm's length' price, the trader's profits will be understated for Irish tax purposes. The transfer pricing rules will reverse this understatement of profits so that the full 'arm's length' profits will be taxed. No specific transfer pricing penalties are included within the legislation so the standard interest and penalty provisions should apply.

Small and medium enterprises are excluded from these transfer pricing rules (ie enterprises with less than 250 employees and either a turnover of less than €50m or assets of less than €43m on a group basis). Persons involved in transactions which are within the scope of the transfer pricing legislation are required to have records available that demonstrate compliance with the legislation. The legislation commences in 1 January 2011 in respect of transactions, the terms of which are agreed on or after 1 July 2010. [*FA 2010, s 42*]

4 Appeals

[*TCA 1997 Pt 40*]

Cross-references. See **7.12** 'Capital acquisitions tax' for appeals relating to that tax, **28.11** 'Returns' regarding the self-assessment provisions and **38.2–38.20** 'Tax cases' for relevant case law.

4.1 Appeals on all tax matters are made to the Appeal Commissioners (subject, on application by the taxpayer within ten days of their determination to a complete rehearing, fact and law, by a Circuit Judge) and thence to the High Court (law only) by transmission of a Stated Case. Cases may be continued to the Supreme Court. [*TCA 1997, ss 933, 941, 949*] One Commissioner may hear and determine an appeal [*TCA 1997, s 933(5)*] and issue a precept. [*TCA 1997, s 935(3)*] A barrister, solicitor, accountant or member of the Institute of Taxation, or any other person at the Commissioners' discretion, may represent taxpayer before Commissioners or Circuit Judge. [*TCA 1997, ss 934, 942(4)*] Appeals to the Circuit Court are held *in camera*. [*TCA 1997, s 942(9)*] The Commissioners may publish their decisions, suitably anonymised. [*TCA 1997, s 944A; FA 1998, s 134*] Decisions are now published on the appeal commissioners' website (www.appealcommissioners.ie). See **38.4–38.20** 'Tax cases' regarding admission of appeals and procedures generally.

4.2 Appeals against assessments and most other appeals must be made within 30 days. The Supreme Court decision in 2005 in *Harris v Quigley & Another* [2005] IESC 79 has led to a number of changes to the income tax appeal provisions. As a result of this decision new legislation was enacted that provides that where a determination of the Appeal Commissioners is to be reheard by a Circuit Court judge or a case is to be stated for the opinion of the High Court, the inspector will not be obliged to amend the assessment under appeal until the appeal process has been fully completed. As a result tax will be neither collected nor repaid by the Revenue Commissioners on the basis of an Appeal Commissioners determination. [*FA 2007, s 20*]. The inspector must then notify the appellant of the time and place of the hearing of the appeal unless an agreement has been reached with the appellant or the appellant has withdrawn the appeal (see **4.3** below). The inspector may also refrain from giving such notice, or withdraw a notice already given, if the inspector considers that the appeal may be settled by agreement. Failure to attend the hearing of an appeal against an assessment results in assessment being treated as if no appeal was made. Such appeals will be dismissed if no adjournment application is made to the Appeal Commissioners, or any such application is refused, and the required return or evidence in support of the appeal has not been made. The Appeal Commissioners may not refuse an adjournment application within nine months of the earlier of the date of the making of the assessment and the end of the year of assessment to which the assessment relates. They may determine the appeal if they are satisfied that sufficient information has been provided to enable them to do so. [*TCA 1997, s 933*] See further below. A late appeal may be accepted by the inspector if there is reasonable cause for the delay, but if the application is made 12 months or more after the date of the notice of assessment, it may only be accepted if at the time of the appeal the necessary returns, etc have been submitted to enable the appeal to be settled by agreement *and* the tax charged by the assessment, together with any interest due thereon, paid. A refusal to accept a late appeal application may be referred to the Appeal Commissioners on application to the inspector within 15 days of notification of the refusal and their consideration of the application is subject to similar conditions. A late appeal application will not be entertained as long as certain recovery proceedings are incomplete. [*TCA 1997, s 933(7)(9)*]

An inspector who considers that an appellant was not entitled to make an appeal may, by written notice to the appellant, refuse to accept the appeal. The appellant may appeal against such refusal within 15 days of the notice, and the Appeal Commissioners may then allow or refuse to allow the appeal to proceed, or arrange a hearing to determine the matter. Also in relation to such assessments, the appellant's agreement must be sought to the withdrawal of an appeal which has been listed for hearing, and the appellant also has the right to apply to the Appeal Commissioners (in writing) for a direction to the inspector to list an appeal for hearing, which they must give if satisfied that the appeal is likely to be determined at the first hearing. Also, the grounds on which the Appeal Commissioners may dismiss an appeal are expanded to cover cases of failure by the appellant to supply information required by the Appeal Commissioners. [*TCA 1997, s 933(1)(2)(6)*]

See also **28.11** 'Returns' regarding self-assessment.

4.3 The taxpayer and the inspector may reach an agreement to settle the appeal, but the inspector cannot oppose withdrawal of the appeal by the taxpayer, and the assessment then has effect as if no appeal had been made. [*TCA 1997, s 933(3)*]

4.4 Appeals on question of domicile, residence etc are to the Appeal Commissioners with a time limit of two months in certain cases. [*TCA 1997, ss 35(3)(4), 63(3)(4), 71(5)(6)*] See *TCA 1997, s 1004(5)* regarding unremittable income. See also **38.93** 'Tax cases' as regards jurisdiction.

5 Assessment Bases

5.1 The taxes dealt with in this book and their bases of assessment are as follows but see the further details in the other sections of the book under the headings shown in the first column below.

Assessed Under	Source Chargeable	Basis on which Assessed
Income Tax		
Sch C	Government stocks etc. taxed at source.	Actual interest etc paid in tax year.
Sch D, Case I	Trades, etc.	Profits on usual annual
Sch D, Case II	Professions.	Account ending in tax year.
Sch D, Case III	Interest, discounts, annuities, annual payments, income from foreign securities (except charged under Sch C) and foreign possessions.	Amount arising in tax year.
Sch D, Case IV	Sundry income not included in any other Case or Schedule.	Usually on actual income of tax year.
Sch D, Case V	Rents or easements.	Amount arising in tax year.
Sch E	Office, employment or pension.	Actual income of tax year.
Sch F	Dividends and distributions, plus tax credits, from companies resident in RI.	Actual dividends etc payable in tax year.
Capital Acquisitions Tax	Gifts and inheritances.	Value received.
Capital Gains Tax	Chargeable gains.	Gains on disposals in tax year.
Corporation Tax	Profits of company.	Profits of actual accounting period.
Value-Added Tax	Import of certain goods; supply of certain goods and services.	Value of imports; consideration receivable for goods and services.

6 Assessments to Income Tax

For assessments to other taxes, see under relevant sections of this book. See **28.11** 'Returns' as regards assessments under self-assessing procedures.

6.1 Assessments are made by inspectors (with minor exceptions) and notices of assessment must state the time limit for making appeals. [*TCA 1997, s 918*] Estimated assessments may be made in absence of satisfactory information. [*TCA 1997, s 922*] See **38.2**, **38.3** 'Tax cases' as regards additional assessments.

Where income is assessable and payable on the actual year basis (eg RI dividends, ground rents etc) the inspector shall estimate such income and any deductible charges (eg mortgage interest), for assessment purposes, and in computing the tax payable shall estimate any tax to be credited. Adjustments of these estimates are made automatically, without notice of appeal being given, provided the taxpayer notifies the inspector of the correct figures within one year after the end of the year of assessment. [*TCA 1997, s 926*]

6.2 The time limit for making assessments (except in cases of fraud or neglect) is four years (ten years prior to 1 January 2005) after the year of assessment [*TCA 1997, s 924(2)(b), 865A(5)(f); FA 2003, s 17)*] except assessments on personal representatives for which the time limit is two years after the end of year in which grant of representation or additional affidavit is lodged for estate duty or CAT, unless the grant etc was made or lodged in the year of death, when the time limit is three years. [*TCA 1997, s 1048*]

6.3 Income, profits etc are assessed to income tax under four Schs, C, D, E and F [*TCA 1997, ss 17–20*] with Sch D divided into five Cases [*TCA 1997, s 18(2)*].

7 Capital Acquisitions Tax

See also **3.11** 'Anti-avoidance legislation'.

7.1 The *Capital Acquisitions Tax Act 1976* (*CATA 1976*) became law on 31 March 1976. It introduced two complementary taxes, a gift tax on gifts taken on or after 28 February 1974 and an inheritance tax on inheritances taken on or after 1 April 1975. Certain transactions occurring on or after 28 February 1969 are relevant in determining the rate of tax on a gift or inheritance. The person chiefly accountable for payment of the tax is the recipient of the gift/inheritance (donee/successor).

FA 2000 introduced a radical change to the basis on which a charge to capital acquisitions tax ('CAT') will arise. Prior to 1 December 1999, such a charge arose only if the disponer was domiciled in RI or, in the case of a non-RI domiciled disponer, if the property was situated in RI. Gifts or inheritances of RI-situated property will remain within the charge to CAT regardless of the domicile or residence of the disponer or the beneficiary, but from 1 December 1999 a charge to CAT may arise on gifts and inheritances of foreign-situated assets if either the disponer or the beneficiary is resident or ordinarily resident in RI. Non-RI domiciled disponers or beneficiaries will only be within the charge to CAT on foreign-situated assets from 1 December 2004, and then only if they were RI-resident for the five consecutive tax years immediately preceding the tax year in which the date of the gift or inheritance falls and resident or ordinarily resident in RI in the tax year in which the date of the gift or inheritance falls.

Since 1 January 1999, taxpayers may conduct their CAT affairs in Euro (Statement of Practice CAT/01/99).

The legislation in relation to Capital Acquisitions Tax was consolidated in the *Capital Acquisitions Tax Consolidation Act 2003 (CATCA 2003)* which became law on 21 February 2003. See detailed Notes for Guidance at www.revenue.ie/publications/legisltn/legislat_d.htm. The provisions of the legislation are summarised below.

GIFT TAX

7.2 A gift will be deemed to be taken (by a donee) where, under or in consequence of any disposition, he becomes beneficially entitled in possession, otherwise than on a death, to any benefit otherwise than for full consideration in money or money's worth paid by him. Where the benefit is in a property which consists wholly or partly of private company shares (see **7.8** below), the 'full consideration' exclusion does not apply after 23 February 1993 where the consideration, being in relation to a disposition, could not reasonably be regarded as representing full consideration to the disponer for making the disposition, taking into account the disponer's position prior to the disposition. [*CATCA 2003, ss 4, 5(1); CATA 1976, ss 4, 5(1); FA 1993, s 121; FA 1994, s 147*]

A gift taken **on or after 1 December 1999** bears tax on its taxable value (see **7.9** below) after aggregation with the taxable value of all gifts and inheritances taken on or after 5 December 1991 (for gifts taken before 5 December 2001, all those taken on or after 2 December 1988) which have the same 'group threshold' (see **7.4** below).

[*CATCA 2003, Sch 2 Pt 1 para 3; CATA 1976, Sch 2 para 3; FA 2000, s 145; FA 2002, s 121*] A gift taken on or after 2 December 1998 and before 1 December 1999 bears tax on its taxable value at a rate determined by aggregating that taxable value with the taxable value of all taxable gifts and inheritances taken previously on or after 2 December 1988. For gifts taken on or after 26 March 1984 and before 2 December 1998, such aggregation applied from 2 June 1982. For gifts taken after 1 June 1982 and before 26 March 1984, earlier gifts and inheritances were aggregated only where the same Table (see **7.4** below) applied. The rate applicable to a gift completed after 27 February 1974 and before 2 June 1982 was determined by aggregating the taxable gift with the value of all relevant gifts from the same disponer since 28 February 1969 and of all taxable inheritances taken after 31 March 1975. [*CATA 1976, s 9, Sch 2 para 3; FA 1982, s 102; FA 1984, s 111; FA 1999, s 201*]

Where the disponer died before 1 April 1975, gift tax was not payable [*CATA 1976, s 6(3) as originally enacted*]. Where the disponer dies within two years of a gift made after 31 March 1975, inheritance tax is payable. [*CATCA 2003, s 3; CATA 1976, s 3*]

'**The date of the gift**' is the date on which the donee becomes beneficially entitled in possession [*CATCA 2003, s 2; CATA 1976, s 2*] but see *CATCA 2003, s 5(6); CATA 1976, s 5(6)* as amended by *FA 1982, s 99* as regards certain gifts under contract or agreement. See also **38.212** 'Tax cases'.

INHERITANCE TAX

7.3 An inheritance will be deemed to be taken (by a successor) where, under or in consequence of any disposition, he becomes beneficially entitled in possession on a death to any benefit otherwise than for full consideration in money or money's worth paid by him. Where the benefit is in a property which consists wholly or partly of private company shares (see **7.8** below), the 'full consideration' exclusion does not apply after 23 February 1993 where the consideration, being in relation to a disposition, could not reasonably be regarded as representing full consideration to the disponer for making the disposition, taking into account the disponer's position prior to the disposition. [*CATCA 2003, s 10(1); CATA 1976, s 11(1); FA 1993, s 123; FA 1994, s 148*]

'On a death' means:

(*a*)   (i)   on a person's death or at a time ascertainable only by reference to a death,

    (ii)   under a will or intestacy, or under the *Succession Act 1965, Pt IX or s 56*, or

    (iii)   in consequence of the failure by a person to exercise a right or power where that person was immediately before his death capable of exercising such right or power,

    (when 'the date of the inheritance' is the date of the death);

(*b*)   under a gift made on or after 1 April 1975 where the disponer dies within two years of the gift (when 'the date of the inheritance' is the date of the gift); or

(*c*)   on any further change in the interests under a trust after the cesser of an intervening life interest (when 'the date of the inheritance' is the date of the change).

[*CATCA 2003, ss 2(1), 3; CATA 1976, ss 2(1), 3*]

See, however, *CATCA 2003, s 5(6)*; *CATA 1976, s 5(6)* as amended by *FA 1982, s 99* as regards the date of certain inheritances under contract or agreement.

An inheritance taken **on or after 1 December 1999** bears tax on its taxable value (see **7.9** below) after aggregation with the taxable value of all gifts and inheritances taken on or after 5 December 1991 (for inheritances taken before 5 December 2001, all those taken on or after 2 December 1988) which have the same 'group threshold' (see **7.4** below). [*CATCA 2003, Sch 2 Pt 1 para 3; CATA 1976, Sch 2 para 3; FA 2000, s 145; FA 2002, s 121*] An inheritance taken on or after 2 December 1998 and before 1 December 1999 is aggregated with all previous taxable gifts and inheritances taken on or after 2 December 1988. For inheritances taken on or after 2 June 1982 and before 2 December 1998, aggregation applies from 2 June 1982 (but excluding gifts or inheritances to which the same Table (see **7.4** below) did not apply for gifts taken before 26 March 1984). A taxable inheritance taken before 2 June 1982 was aggregated with all previous taxable inheritances from the same disponer and with all relevant gifts (see **7.2** above) since 28 February 1969 from the same disponer. [*CATA 1976, Sch 2 para 3; FA 1982, s 102; FA 1984, s 111; FA 1999, s 201*]

Surviving joint tenant(s) will take an inheritance of the share of a deceased joint tenant which accrues on his death. [*CATCA 2003, s 13; CATA 1976, s 14*]

Disclaimer of an inheritance is not itself a gift; nor is waiver or abandonment of a claim to an inheritance. Liability to tax on the inheritance or claim will disappear unless any consideration in money or money's worth is received for the disclaimer, waiver or abandonment (in which case tax is payable on that consideration as though it was the inheritance from the disponer). [*CATCA 2003, s 12; CATA 1976, s 13*]

RATES OF TAX

7.4 For gifts and inheritances taken after 25 March 1984, a single table applies to all gifts and inheritances, but with different thresholds according to the relationship between disponer and donee/successor. The taxable value of the gift or inheritance is added to the sum of the taxable values of certain earlier gifts or inheritances (see **7.2, 7.3** above) and the tax chargeable is the excess of the tax on the aggregate over that on the earlier gifts or inheritances.

Gifts and inheritances taken **on or after 1 December 1999** are aggregated by reference to the applicable 'group threshold'. All gifts and inheritances within the same group threshold which are taken by a donee or successor on the same day are treated as one, the tax computed being apportioned rateably according to the taxable values. The rate of tax up to the 'threshold amount' is nil, the balance being chargeable at **20 per cent**. *Finance (No 2) Act 2008* increased the rate of tax to **22 per cent** and this rate applies to gifts or inheritances taken on or after 20 November 2008. [*F(No)A 2008, s 90*] For gifts or inheritances taken on or after 8 April 2009, the **rate of CAT is 25 per cent**.

The '*group thresholds*' for the tax year 2010 are:

€414,799   where the donee or successor is the child, or minor child of a deceased child, of the disponer, or, in relation to an inheritance taken on the death of the disponer, the parent of the disponer where the interest taken is not a limited interest.

€41,481   where the donee or successor is a lineal ancestor or descendant (other than a child, or minor child of a deceased child), brother or sister, or child of a brother or sister, of the disponer.

€20,740   where the donee or successor (not being a spouse of the disponer, for which see **7.5(*m*)** below) does not stand to the disponer in any of the above relationships.

The '*threshold amounts*' are the group thresholds indexed, after 31 December 2000, by reference to the consumer price index for the immediately preceding year. The figures applicable for subsequent years are accordingly:

2001	£316,800	£31,680	£15,840
2002	€422,148	€42,215	€21,108
2003	€441,198	€44,120	€22,060
2004	€456,438	€45,644	€22,822
2005	€466,725	€46,673	€23,336
2006	€478,155	€47,815	€23,908
2007	€496,824	€49,682	€24,841
2008	€521,208	€52,121	€26,060
2009 (to 7 April 2009)	€542,544	€54,254	€27,127
From 8 April 2009 to 31 December 2009	€434,000	€43,400	€21,700
From 1 January 2010 to 7 December 2010	€414,799	€41,481	€20,740
From 8 December 2010 to 31 December 2010	€332,084	€33,208	€16,604
From 1 January 2011	**€332,084**	**€33,208**	**€16,604**

For gifts and inheritances taken after 25 March 1984 and **before 1 December 1999**, all relevant gifts and inheritances are aggregated (see **7.2**, **7.3** above), and the rate of tax determined by reference to the following table. For inheritances, the taxable value is charged at the rate so determined, for gifts at 75 per cent of that rate. The tax is, however, limited to the amount which would be chargeable if the threshold applicable to the aggregate applied also in determining the tax on the earlier relevant gifts and inheritances.

The table is as follows for benefits taken on or after 11 April 1994 and before 1 December 1999:

Portion of Value	Rate of Tax	Portion of Value	Rate of Tax
(£)	(%)	(£)	(%)
The threshold amount	Nil	The next £30,000	30
The next £10,000	20	The balance	40

For gifts etc taken before 11 April 1994 but after 29 January 1991, the 30 per cent band was £40,000 and there was an additional £50,000 band taxable at 35 per cent. For gifts etc taken before 30 January 1991, there were additional £50,000 bands taxable at 40 per cent and 45 per cent, the balance being taxable at 55 per cent.

Prior to 1 December 1999, the 'threshold amount' is the greatest of the 'revised class thresholds' that apply in relation to all of the taxable gifts and inheritances included in the aggregate figure. A 'revised class threshold' is the lesser of the 'class threshold' applying to a gift or inheritance and the total of the taxable values of all taxable gifts and inheritances included in the aggregate and to which that 'class threshold' applies, with a minimum of the smallest of the 'class thresholds' that apply in relation to all of the taxable gifts and inheritances included in the aggregate. The 'class thresholds' are, for gifts and inheritances taken after 31 December 1989, indexed by reference to the consumer price index for the immediately preceding year. The base figures (which apply to gifts and inheritances taken before 1 January 1990) are:

£150,000   where the donee or successor is the spouse (but see **7.5** below re exemption), child, or minor child of a deceased child, of the disponer, or, in relation to an inheritance taken on the death of the disponer, the parent of the disponer where the interest taken is not a limited interest.

£20,000   where the donee or successor is a lineal ancestor or descendant (other than a child, or minor child of a deceased child), brother or sister, or child of a brother or sister, of the disponer.

£10,000   where the donee or successor does not stand to the disponer in any of those relationships.

The figures applicable for subsequent years up to 30 November 1999 are accordingly:

1990	£156,000	£20,800	£10,400
1991	£161,400	£21,520	£10,760
1992	£166,350	£22,180	£11,090
1993	£171,750	£22,900	£11,450
1994	£174,000	£23,200	£11,600
1995	£178,200	£23,760	£11,880
1996	£182,550	£24,340	£12,170
1997	£185,550	£24,740	£12,370
1998	£188,400	£25,120	£12,560
1999	£192,900	£25,720	£12,860

For gifts and inheritances taken before 26 March 1984, different tables apply according to the relationship between disponer and donee/successor. The taxable gift or inheritance is added as the 'top slice' to the aggregate of earlier relevant gifts or inheritances (see

7.2, **7.3** above), and, if an inheritance, taxed at the rate in the appropriate table, if a **gift, at 75 per cent** of such rate. The tables are as follows: I

Table I

Where the donee or successor is the spouse, child, or minor child of a deceased child, of the disponer.

Value (£)	Rate of Tax (%)
0–150,000	Nil
150,000–200,000	25
200,000–250,000	30
250,000–300,000	35
300,000–350,000	40
350,000–400,000	45
400,000 and over	50

TABLE II

Where the donee or successor is a lineal ancestor or a lineal descendant (other than a child) of the disponer.

Value taken after 31 March 1978	Rate of Tax	Value taken before 1 April 1978
(£)	(%)	(£)
0–30,000	Nil	0–15,000
30,000–33,000	5	15,000–18,000
33,000–38,000	7	18,000–23,000
38,000–48,000	10	23,000–33,000
48,000–58,000	13	33,000–43,000
58,000–68,000	16	43,000–53,000
68,000–78,000	19	53,000–63,000
78,000–88,000	22	63,000–73,000
88,000–103,000	25	73,000–88,000
103,000–118,000	28	88,000–103,000
118,000–133,000	31	103,000–118,000
133,000–148,000	34	118,000–133,000
148,000–163,000	37	133,000–148,000
163,000–178,000	40	148,000–163,000
178,000–193,000	43	163,000–178,000
193,000–208,000	46	178,000–193,000
208,000–223,000	49	193,000–208,000
223,000 and over	50	208,000 and over

TABLE III

Where the donee or successor is a brother or a sister, or a child of a brother, or of a sister, of the disponer.

Value taken after 31 March 1978	Rate of Tax	Value taken before 1 April 1978
(£)	(%)	(£)
0–20,000	Nil	0–10,000
20,000–23,000	10	10,000–13,000

Where the donee or successor is a brother or a sister, or a child of a brother, or of a sister, of the disponer.

Value taken after 31 March 1978	Rate of Tax	Value taken before 1 April 1978
(£)	(%)	(£)
23,000–28,000	12	13,000–18,000
28,000–38,000	15	18,000–28,000
38,000–48,000	19	28,000–38,000
48,000–58,000	23	38,000–48,000
58,000–68,000	27	48,000–58,000
68,000–78,000	31	58,000–68,000
78,000–93,000	35	68,000–83,000
93,000–108,000	40	83,000–98,000
108,000–123,000	45	98,000–113,000
123,000 and over	50	113,000 and over

TABLE IV

Where the relationship between donee/successor and disponer is not one referred to in Table I, II or III.

Value taken after 31 March 1978	Rate of Tax	Value taken before 1 April 1978
(£)	(%)	(£)
0–10,000	Nil	0–5,000
10,000–13,000	20	5,000–8,000
13,000–18,000	22	8,000–13,000
18,000–28,000	25	13,000–23,000
28,000–38,000	30	23,000–33,000

38,000–48,000	35	33,000–43,000
48,000–58,000	40	43,000–53,000
58,000–68,000	45	53,000–63,000
68,000–83,000	50	63,000–78,000
83,000–98,000	55	78,000–93,000
98,000 and over	60	93,000 and over

[*CATA 1976, Sch 2*; *FA 1978, s 41, Sch 3*; *FA 1984, s 111*; *FA 1990, s 128*; *FA 1991, ss 115, 116*; *FA 1994, ss 142, 145*; *FA 1997, s 136*; *FA 2000, ss 145, 153*]

Notes:

(i)   A widow(er) whose relationship to the disponer is not as close as that of his/her deceased spouse is attributed with the deceased spouse's relationship to the disponer;

(ii)   A nephew or niece of the disponer is treated as a child of his in relation to tax on gifts or inheritances taken (other than under a discretionary trust) after 30 April 1989 provided that the property comprised in the gift etc is either:

(*a*)   business assets used in connection with the trade, business or profession of the disponer, or

(*b*)   shares in a private trading company (see **7.8** below) controlled by the disponer (being also a director) throughout the 'relevant period',

and, throughout the 'relevant period', the nephew or niece has worked substantially on a full-time basis for the disponer in his trade etc (where (*a*) applies) or for the company in its trade etc (where (*b*) applies). For this purpose 'full-time' means more than 24 hours per week worked at a place where the trade etc is carried on (15 hours if it is carried on only by the disponer and spouse and the nephew or niece). '*Relevant period*' means the five years (excluding, in relation to work, reasonable periods of annual or sick leave) ending on the date of the disposition, or on the subsequent coming to an end of certain interests in possession of the disponer in the property comprised in the disposition. For gifts or inheritances taken before 1 May 1989, a similar simplified provision applies but without reference to the coming to an end of an interest in possession of the disponer. See **38.28** 'Tax cases';

(iii)   Where a person receives a gift or inheritance from a grandparent, following the cesser of his parent's limited interest in possession, under a disposition made before 1 April 1975 in consideration of his parents' marriage, he is treated as the grandparent's child in computing the tax payable on the gift or inheritance. This provision was introduced by *FA 1981* with retrospective effect and is now contained in *CATCA 2003, Sch 2 Pt 1 para 8*. Any consequential repayment of tax will not carry interest, notwithstanding *CATCA 2003, s 57; CATA 1976, s 46* (see **7.12** below). See **7.10** below for the payment of interest;

(iv) 'Child' includes stepchild and adopted child. *Finance Act 2007* included foster children in the definition of 'child'. For gifts and inheritances taken after 13 January 1988, the *Status of Children Act 1987, s 3* applies in that:

    (*a*)   relationships between persons are to be determined without regard to whether the parents of any person are or have been married to each other, unless the contrary intention appears, and

    (*b*)   an adopted person shall, for the purposes of (*a*), be deemed from the date of the adoption to be the child of the adopter or adopters, and not the child of any other person or persons.

For gifts and inheritances taken after 5 December 2000, and on a claim being made in that behalf, it also includes a foster child, ie a child who, throughout periods together comprising at least 5 years in the 18 years following the child's birth, has resided with the disponer and been under the care of, and maintained by, the disponer at the disponer's own expense. Such a claim cannot be based on the uncorroborated testimony of a single witness. The requirement to establish such a five-year period does not apply in the case of an inheritance taken from a foster parent where the fostering was formal under the appropriate child care regulations.

For gifts and inheritances taken on or after 30 March 2001, 'child' for these purposes also includes the relationship of an adopted child to its natural parent.

    [*CATCA 2003, s 2, Schs 1, 2; CATA 1976, ss 2, 59D, 59E, Schs 1, 2; FA 1978, s 41, Sch 3; FA 1981, s 46; FA 1989, s 83; FA 1992, s 223; FA 1993, s 130; TCA 1997, s 8; FA 2001, ss 221, 222*]

EXEMPTIONS

7.5

(*a*)   Small gifts. The first €3,000 (€1,270/£1,000 for periods ending before 1 January 2003 and £500 for periods ending before 1 January 1999) of taxable value taken from any one disponer during any year to 31 December is exempt. Additionally, the first £250 of aggregable value was, before 26 March 1984, ignored in computing tax; [*CATCA 2003, s 69; CATA 1976, s 53; FA 1978, s 44; FA 1984, s 110(2); FA 1999, s 204*]

(*b*)   Gifts or inheritances received by charities and applied for public or charitable purposes (which, for gifts, etc before 9 July 1987, had to be in RI or NI) are exempt, as are gifts so applied by such charities; [*CATCA 2003, s 76; CATA 1976, s 54; FA 1984, s 110(3); FA 1987, s 50; FA 2000, s 143*]

(*c*)   House or garden in RI of national, scientific, historic or artistic interest, provided reasonable viewing facilities have been allowed to the public for three years immediately preceding the date of the gift/inheritance, and continue to be allowed. The property must not be held for trading purposes and the exemption is lost on a sale or breach of conditions as under (*d*) below.

For viewing facilities to be 'reasonable' requires opening of at least a substantial part of the property to the public for at least 60 days in each year, including at least 40 days between 1 May and 30 September inclusive (90 and 60 days respectively for 1996 and earlier years), of which, for 2001 and subsequent years, at least ten must be Saturdays or Sundays, subject to any necessary temporary closure for repairs, etc. Adequate notice of opening must be given to the public, and any charge must be reasonable. For 1997 onwards, Bord Fáilte Éireann must, by 1 January in the year (1 July for 1997 only), be provided with full details of opening times and charges, etc. [*CATCA 2003, s 77; CATA 1976, s 55; FA 1978, s 39; FA 1984, s 110(4); FA 1995, s 160; FA 1997, s 137; FA 2000, ss 144, 146; SI 28/87*] See also (*t*) below;

(*d*) Objects of national, scientific, historic or artistic interest, not held for trading, provided they remain in RI and there are reasonable viewing facilities, and provided they are not sold (other than to a museum, university, etc in the State) within six years after the valuation date, and before the death of the donee or successor (for gifts or inheritances taken before 12 April 1995, before they form part of the property comprised in a subsequent gift or inheritance). The exemption also ceases if the conditions are breached after the valuation date and before:

   (i)   the sale of the object,

   (ii)   the death of the donee or successor, and

   (iii) the object's again forming part of the property comprised in a gift or inheritance (other, from 10 February 2000, than an inheritance arising under *FA 1986, s 103 (now CATCA 2003, s 20)*, see **7.14** below) in respect of which an absolute interest is taken by a person other than the spouse of the donee or successor (for gifts or inheritances taken before 12 April 1995, before it again forms part of the property comprised in a gift or inheritance).

Also exempt is a work of art normally kept outside RI which is comprised in an inheritance taken after 25 January 2001 in relation to which neither the disponer nor the successor is RI-resident or ordinarily resident, to the extent that the Commissioners are satisfied that it was brought into RI solely for public exhibition, cleaning or restoration;

[*CATCA 2003, s 77; CATA 1976, s 55; FA 1995, s 160; FA 2000, s 144; FA 2001, s 218*] See also (t) below.

(*e*) Payments by employer to employee by way of retirement gratuity, redundancy payment or pension (this may not apply if the employer is a relative of or a company controlled by the employee). But benefits under a superannuation scheme taken by persons other than the employee himself will be deemed to be taken from the employee, as disponer;[*CATCA 2003, s 80; CATA 1976, s 56*]

(*f*) Securities (and units of a unit trust scheme holding only such securities) received by donee/successor neither domiciled nor ordinarily resident in RI, the income from which is exempt from tax when owned by such a person, if:

   (i)   (unless the disponer was neither domiciled nor ordinarily resident in RI at the date of the disposition (as defined, ie date of death or of act of disposition by disponer) or the securities or units were owned by the disponer or subject to the disposition before 26 March 1997 and the disponer was neither domiciled nor ordinarily resident in RI at the date of the gift/inheritance)) the disponer was beneficial owner for fifteen years prior to the gift/inheritance (six years for gifts/inheritances taken before 24 February 2003 or where the securities were acquired before that date and three years for gifts/inheritances taken before 15 February 2001 or where the securities were acquired before that date), and

(ii) the securities were comprised in the gift/inheritance at both the date thereof and the valuation date;

[*CATCA 2003, s 81; FA 2003, s 150; CATA 1976, s 57; FA 1978, s 40; FA 1984, s 110(5); FA 1991, s 121; FA 1997, s 135; FA 2001, s 219*]

(g) Bona fide betting receipts or prizes; [*CATCA 2003, s 82(1); CATA 1976, s 58(1)*]

(h) Compensation or damages received by a person for a wrong or injury suffered by him or in respect of a fatal accident; [*CATCA 2003, s 82(1); CATA 1976, s 58(1)*]

(i) Certain payments in a bankruptcy situation; [*CATCA 2003, s 82(1); CATA 1976, s 58(1)*]

(j) Reasonable payments representing normal expenditure during the donor's lifetime for the support, maintenance or education of a spouse or child. Since 23 March 2000, this is extended to payments which would have been of such a nature during the disponer's lifetime which are received by a minor child for support, maintenance or education, where both parents are dead; [*CATCA 2003, s 82(2), (4); CATA 1976, s 58(2)(4); FA 2000, s 152*]

(k) Gifts or inheritances taken by a disponer under his own disposition, and gifts between associated companies (as defined); [*CATCA 2003, s 83; CATA 1976, s 59*]

(l) An inheritance taken by the spouse of the disponer after 29 January 1985, and a gift taken by the spouse of the disponer after 30 January 1990. [*CATCA 2003, ss 70, 71; FA 1985, s 59; FA 1990, s 127*] It is understood that the inheritance tax exemption extends to an appointment made after that date under a discretionary trust to the surviving spouse of the disponer.

Exemption also applies to a gift or inheritance taken by a spouse following dissolution of the marriage by virtue or in consequence of certain orders under *Family Law Act 1995* or *Family Law (Divorce) Act 1996, Pt III* or (from 10 February 2000) analogous foreign orders; [*Family Law Act 1995, s 51; Family Law (Divorce) Act 1996, s 34; CATCA 2003, s 88; FA 1997, s 142; FA 2000, s 149*]

(m) With effect from 30 May 1985, an inheritance consisting of an interest in an insurance policy:

(i) which is in a form approved by the Commissioners,

(ii) annual premiums on which are paid by the insured during his life, and

(iii) which is expressly effected under *CATCA 2003, s 72 (FA 1985, s 60)* for the purpose of paying 'relevant tax',

to the extent that the proceeds are applied in paying the 'relevant tax'. Any part of the proceeds not so applied is deemed to be taken on the day immediately after the later of the date of death of the insured and the latest date (if any) on which an inheritance is taken in respect of which 'relevant tax' is payable.

'*Relevant tax*' means inheritance tax payable in respect of an inheritance (excluding interests in qualifying insurance policies) taken on (or not later than one year after) the death of the insured under a disposition made by the insured. Since 30 May 1990, it also includes inheritance tax payable in respect of an inheritance taken under a disposition made by the spouse of the insured, taken on the date of death of the insured or only in the event of the insured not surviving the spouse by a period of up to 31 days, where the proceeds of the policy are payable either on the death of the survivor of the spouses (or on their simultaneous death), or on the contingency of the insured surviving the spouse. Since 29 May 1991, it also includes inheritance tax payable in respect of an inheritance taken under a disposition made by the spouse of the insured where the inheritance is taken on the date of death of the insured (and from 28 March 1996 this is widened to include any inheritance tax payable in respect of an inheritance taken on the date of death of the insured). In respect of policies of insurance taken out on or after 3 February 2005, the definition of 'relevant tax' includes approved retirement fund tax. 'Approved retirement fund tax' means tax which a qualifying fund manager is obliged to deduct in accordance with s *784A(4)(c)* of TCA 1997. That is to say, the income tax charge that arises in certain situations where an approved retirement fund passes on death.

With effect from 24 May 1989, relief is extended to policies effected by spouses, the proceeds of which are payable on the death of the survivor of the spouses, or on their simultaneous death.

An insurance policy within (*q*) below is within these provisions where the proceeds become payable on the death of the insured, provided that it would have been within these provisions if expressed to be so.

[*CATCA 2003, s 72; FA 1985, s 60; FA 1989, s 84; FA 1990, s 130; FA 1991, s 118; FA 1996, s 124*]

See Statement of Practice SP–CAT/2/91, issued by the Revenue Commissioners in June 1991, for examples of this relief and for the Revenue requirements for approval of policies;

(*n*) With effect from 24 May 1989, units in certain collective investment undertakings (see **12.22** 'Corporation tax') comprised in a gift or inheritance at the date of the gift etc and at the valuation date (see **7.7** below), where, at the date of the disposition, either the disponer is neither domiciled nor ordinarily resident in RI or the proper law of the disposition is not that of RI, and, at the date of the gift etc, the donee or successor is neither domiciled nor ordinarily resident in RI. For gifts or inheritances taken after 31 March 2000, the exemption is extended to units of investment undertakings within s *739B* (see **12.22** 'Corporation tax'), and the 'non-RI proper law' alternative to the requirement that the disponer is neither domiciled nor ordinarily resident in RI does not apply. The exemption has been extended to include units in collective investment schemes. [*FA 2010, s 144*] The latter applies to units of specified collective investment undertakings from

15 February 2001, but only where the units were acquired by the disponer on or after that date or became subject to the disposition on or after that date without having been in the disponer's beneficial ownership. [*CATCA 2003, s 75; FA 1989, s 85; FA 2001, s 224; FA 2005, s 134*] The exemption applies to units of a common contractual fund comprised in a gift or inheritance taken on or after [25 March 2005]; [*FA 2005, s 134; FA 2005, s 44*]

(*o*) Where an inheritance taken after 2 December 1997 and before 1 December 1999 consisted, at the date of the inheritance and at the valuation date, of a dwelling-house (or part), and was taken by a person who, at the date of the inheritance, was a lineal ancestor or descendant (other than a child or minor child of a deceased child), brother or sister, or child of a brother or sister, of the disponer, who had resided continuously with the disponer in the house (or in a house it replaced) for the period of ten years immediately preceding the date of the inheritance (five years in the case of a brother or sister aged at least 55 at that date), and who was not beneficially entitled in possession to any other dwelling-house (or part), the estimated market value of the house (or part) is reduced by the lesser of £150,000 and 80 per cent. This does not apply if the house was agricultural property and the successor was a farmer (see **7.9** below). For earlier inheritances, the reduction applied only to inheritances taken by a brother or sister of the disponer aged at least 55 at the date of the inheritance, and the reduction in market value was the lesser of £80,000 and 60 per cent (for inheritances taken before 10 May 1997, £60,000 and 60 per cent, for inheritances taken before 11 April 1994, £50,000 and 50 per cent). [*FA 1991, s 117; FA 1994, s 144; FA 1997, s 138; FA 1998, s 126; FA 2000, s 153*] See now **7.5**(*x*) below;

(*p*) With effect from 29 May 1991, the proceeds of an insurance policy:

(i) which is in a form approved by the Commissioners,

(ii) in respect of which annual premiums are paid by the insured,

(iii) the proceeds of which are payable on the 'appointed date', and

(iv) which is expressly effected for the purpose of paying 'relevant tax',

are, to the extent used to pay 'relevant tax', exempt from tax and not taken into account in computing tax. Subject to (*b*) and (*m*) above, an *inter vivos* disposition of the proceeds (or part) of such an insurance policy (other than in paying 'relevant tax') is not exempt from tax.

'*Relevant tax*' means gift or inheritance tax payable in connection with an *inter vivos* disposition made by the insured within one year after the 'appointed date', excluding such tax payable on an appointment out of an *inter vivos* discretionary trust set up by the insured.

The '*appointed date*' is a date occurring not earlier than eight years after the date on which the insurance policy is effected, or an earlier date on which the proceeds of a policy become payable either on the critical illness or on the death of the insured.

The 'insured' for these purposes may comprise an individual and spouse, together or separately, in the case of a joint insurance.

An insurance policy within (*n*) above is within these provisions where the proceeds are used to pay relevant tax (as above) arising under an *inter vivos* disposition made by the insured within one year after the appointed date.

[*CATCA 2003, s 73; FA 1991, s 119*]

See Statement of Practice SP–CAT/2/91, issued by the Revenue Commissioners in June 1991, for Revenue requirements for approval of such policies;

(*q*) Policies issued after 30 November 1992 to non-residents by life assurance companies operating in the International Financial Services Centre in Dublin are exempt from gift and inheritance tax provided that the donee or successor is neither domiciled nor ordinarily resident in RI at the date of the gift or inheritance, and that, at the date of the disposition, either the disporer is neither resident nor ordinarily resident in RI or the proper law of the disposition is not that of RI. The exemption is extended to all policies issued by life assurance companies for policies issued on or after 1 January 2001. The 'non-RI proper law' alternative to the requirement that the disporer is neither domiciled nor ordinarily resident in RI does not apply for gifts or inheritances taken on or after 15 February 2001, but only where the policy was acquired by the disporer on or after that date or became subject to the disposition on or after that date without having been in the disporer's beneficial ownership; [*CATCA 2003, s 74; FA 1993, s 133; FA 2001, s 226; FA 2002, s 122*]

(*r*) With effect from 12 April 1995, an inheritance taken by a parent from a child on the death of the child if the child had, within the preceding five years, taken a non-exempt gift or inheritance from a parent or parents; [*CATCA 2003, s 79; FA 1995, s 165*]

(*s*) A gift or inheritance taken after 11 April 1995 consisting in whole or part of shares in a private company (within *CATCA 2003, s 27; CATA 1976, s 16*) which (after the taking of the gift or inheritance) is, on the date of the gift or inheritance, controlled (within *CATCA 2003, s 27; CATA 1976, s 16*) by the donee or successor, to the extent that the value of the shares at the valuation date is attributable to 'relevant heritage property'. That property must have been in the beneficial ownership of the company (or a subsidiary within Companies Act 1963, s 155) on 12 April 1995.

'Relevant heritage property' is property to which *CATCA 2003, s 77; CATA 1976, s 55* applies (see (*c*)(*d*) above).

There are provisions for dealing with shares which are also relevant business property (see **7.9** below), and for the withdrawal of the exemption where either the shares or the relevant heritage property are sold (other than to a museum, university, etc within the State) within six years after the valuation date and before the death of the donee or successor, or the conditions referred to in (*d*) above are breached such that the exemption in (*c*) or (*d*) above would cease to apply;

[*CATCA 2003, s 78; FA 1995, s 166*]

(*t*) With effect from 28 March 1996, a gift or inheritance taken and applied (or to be applied) exclusively for the purpose of discharging medical expenses (including connected maintenance costs) of an individual permanently physically or mentally incapacitated; [*CATCA 2003, s 84; CATA 1976, s 59A; FA 1996, s 123*]

(*u*)   With effect from 6 April 1997, the receipt by an incapacitated individual of funds from a qualifying trust (see **16.18** 'Exempt income and special savings schemes') or of the income therefrom; [*CATCA 2003, s 82(3); CATA 1976, s 58(3); FA 1999, s 205*]

(*v*)   With effect from 25 March 1999, any part of a 'retirement fund' comprised in an inheritance. The value of any such part is not taken into account in computing tax where the disposition under which the inheritance is taken is the will or intestacy of the disponer and the successor is a child of the disponer who was 21 years of age or over at the date of the disposition. '*Retirement fund*' is an approved retirement fund or approved minimum retirement fund (see **2.23** 'Allowances, credits and rates') wholly comprised of property representing accrued rights of the disponer (or of a predeceased spouse) under an annuity contract or approved retirement benefits scheme (see **2.23** 'Allowances, credits and rates'), accumulations of income thereof or property representing those accumulations; [*CATCA 2003, s 85; CATA 1976, s 59B; FA 1999, s 206*]

(*w*)   With effect from 1 December 1999, a 'dwelling-house' comprised in a gift or inheritance taken by a donee or successor (or transferee within *CATCA 2003, s 32(2); CATA 1976, s 23(1)*, see **7.15** below) who:

(i)   has continuously occupied as his or her only or main residence either the dwelling-house itself throughout the three years up to the date of the gift, etc, or the dwelling-house and other property it replaced for three years out of the four years up to the date of the gift, etc,

(ii)   is not, at the date of the gift, etc beneficially entitled to, or to any interest in, any other dwelling-house, and

(iii)   (if he or she is under the age of 55 at the date of the gift, etc) continues to occupy the dwelling-house as his or her only or main residence throughout the period of six years from the date of the gift, etc (disregarding any periods of absence while working in an office or employment all the duties of which were performed outside RI).

A '*dwelling-house*' is a building (or part) used (or suitable for use) as a dwelling together with its curtilage up to one acre (or, if the curtilage exceeds one acre, that part of the curtilage which, if the remainder were separately occupied, would be the most suitable for occupation and enjoyment with the dwelling-house).

If the dwelling-house is sold or disposed of in whole or part within six years of the date of the gift, etc, and (unless the donee or successor was aged 55 or older at the date of the gift, etc) before the death of the donee or successor, the exemption ceases to apply unless the sale, etc occurs in consequence of the donee or successor requiring long-term medical care in a hospital, nursing home or convalescent home. The exemption also ceases if, within six years of the date of the gift, etc, and before the dwelling-house is sold or disposed of and before the death of the donee or successor, (iii) above ceases to be satisfied other than in consequence either of the donee or successor requiring such long-term care or of the employer of the donee or successor requiring him or her to reside elsewhere.

(iii) above is treated as satisfied where the dwelling-house is, within the six-year period, replaced by another dwelling-house, and the original and replacement dwelling-house (and any further replacement dwelling-house) are continuously occupied as the donee or successor's only or main residence for periods totalling at least six years out of the seven years commencing on the date of the gift, etc (disregarding certain periods of absence as under (iii) above). In these circumstances, the clawback of relief on disposal does not apply, but (except where the donee or successor was of age 55 or over at the date of the gift, etc) the exemption is restricted to that which would have applied if the replacement(s) had taken place immediately before the date of the gift, etc.

Finance Act 2007 introduced a number of restrictions on the operation of this relief as the Revenue was of the opinion that the relief was being abused. The restrictions only apply where the dwelling house is the subject of a gift. Firstly, any period of occupancy by the recipient of a gift of a dwelling house where the recipient resided in the house with the disponer (ie the disponer's principal private residence) will be disregarded for the purposes of the relief unless the person making the gift was compelled, by reason of old age of infirmity, to depend on the services of the recipient for that period.

Secondly, there is now a requirement that the dwelling house must be owned by the disponer for the three-year period prior to the gift, thus ruling out gifts of dwelling houses from bodies which are not disponers for CAT purposes (eg discretionary trusts or companies).

Finally, where replacement property is the subject of a gift, the period of occupancy of the replaced property by the recipient will only be taken into account where either the replaced property or the dwelling house which is the subject of the gift was also owned by the disponer prior to the date of the gift. These restrictions are effective in respect of gifts made on or after 20 February 2007.

[*CATCA 2003, s 86; CATA 1976, s 59C; FA 2000, s 151; FA 2001, s 220*]

See also **7.5**(*p*) above.

MEANING OF 'GIFT' AND 'INHERITANCE'

7.6 A gift or inheritance is deemed to consist of the whole or a proportionate part of the property in which the benefit is taken or on which it is or can be charged or secured. A gift or inheritance of a periodic payment which cannot be charged or secured is deemed to consist of a sum which would if invested on the date of the gift/inheritance in specified RI Government securities give an annual yield equal to the periodic payment. [*CATCA 2003, ss 5(2)(5), 10(2); CATA 1976, ss 5(2)(5), 11(2)*]

For gifts or inheritances taken on or after 1 December 1999 (except in the case of a gift or inheritance taken under a disposition made before that date, to which the earlier rules described below apply), '*taxable gift*' and '*taxable inheritance*' mean the whole property, wherever situate, where:

(*a*)   (except in the case of a successor in relation to the special charge on discretionary trusts (see **7.14** below) or probate tax (see **7.18** below)) the donee or successor is RI-resident or ordinarily resident in the year of assessment in which the gift is made or the inheritance taken; or

(*b*)   (except in the case of a gift taken under a discretionary trust) the disponer is RI-resident or ordinarily resident in the year of assessment in which the disposition under which the gift or inheritance is taken was made;

(*c*)   (in the case of a gift taken under a discretionary trust) the disponer is RI-resident or ordinarily resident in the year of assessment in which the disposition under which the gift is taken was made, or in which the gift was taken, or (if the disponer died before the gift was taken) in which the disponer died.

In any other case, it consists of so much of the property of which the gift consists, or which was to be appropriated to the inheritance or out of which property was to be so appropriated (but excluding any property which was not applicable to satisfy the inheritance), as is situate in RI at the date of the gift or inheritance, including rights to proceeds of sale of property to the extent that the property is unsold and situate in RI. A person not domiciled in RI on a particular date will only be treated as resident or ordinarily resident in RI on that date from 1 December 2004, and then only where that person had been RI-resident for the immediately preceding five years of assessment *and* is either resident or ordinarily resident in RI on that date.

For gifts or inheritances taken before 1 December 1999 (and on or after that date in the case of a gift or inheritance taken under a disposition made before that date), the above rules apply by reference to domicile rather than residence and ordinary residence, except that (*a*) above does not apply. There is an anti-avoidance provision to ensure that a person of RI domicile but who is not RI-resident or ordinarily resident cannot artificially change the locality of assets situate in RI by transferring them into a foreign, family-controlled company (within *CATCA 2003, s 27; CATA 1976, s 16*), by treating an appropriate proportion of the market value of the shares as being a sum situate in RI (see *CATCA 2003, ss 6(5), 11(5); CATA 1976, ss 6(4), 12(4)* introduced by *FA 2000, ss 137, 138*). *FA 2006, ss 113 and 114,* ensure that the market value of shares in a foreign, family-controlled company (within *CATCA 2003, s 27; CATA 1976, s 16*) which is attributable, directly or indirectly, to property situate in RI is deemed to be a sum situate in RI.

[*CATCA 2003, ss 2(6), 6, 11; CATA 1976, ss 2(5A), 6, 12; FA 1993, ss 122, 124; FA 2000, ss 137–139*]

The general case law applies as regards the situation of assets, broadly as follows in the specific instances referred to.

(i)   land – where it is physically situated;

(ii)   speciality debt – where the instrument is held;

(iii)   simple contract debt – where the debtor resides;

(iv)   judgment debt – where the judgment is recorded;

(v)   tangible movable property – where it is located;

(vi)   bank balances – where the account branch is located;

(vii)   trademark – where it is registered or used;

(viii)   currency – where it is situated;

(ix)   registered securities – where the principal register is kept;

(x)   goodwill – where the business to which it attaches is carried on;

(xi)   business assets – where the business is carried on.

Double taxation treaties (see Double tax relief – capital transfers) may, however, make special provision.

VALUATION DATE

7.7

(*a*)   For a **taxable gift**, the valuation date will be the date of the gift;

(*b*)   For a **taxable inheritance**, the valuation date will be:

    (i)   where the inheritance is taken as a *donatio mortis causa* or by reason of failure to exercise a power of revocation, the date of death,

    (ii)   where a gift becomes an inheritance because disponer dies within two years, the date of the gift,

    (iii)   for other inheritances, the earliest date of the following: earliest date on which the personal representative or any other person is entitled to retain the subject matter of the inheritance for the benefit of the successor; the date on which it is so retained; or the date of delivery, payment or other satisfaction of the subject matter to the successor.

[*CATCA 2003, s 30; CATA 1976, s 21*]

Where an inheritance is received in parts, each part will be treated as a separate inheritance. The Commissioners may determine valuation dates, subject to appeal. [*CATCA 2003, s 30(5)(6)(8)(9); CATA 1976, s 21(5)(6)(8)(9)*]

MARKET VALUE

7.8 Market value of any property will be the price, in the Commissioners' opinion, it would fetch if sold in the open market on the date it is to be valued, in circumstances which would obtain the best price for the vendor. The Commissioners may have property valued at their expense. In valuing unquoted shares it shall be assumed that all the relevant information which might be required by a prudent purchaser is available to him. [*CATCA 2003, s 26; CATA 1976, s 15*]

For gifts or inheritances taken after 23 February 1993, the market value of shares in a private company (as defined) which is controlled by the donee or successor shall be ascertained as if it formed an apportioned part of the market value of a 'group of shares', the apportionment, as between shares of the same class, being by reference to nominal amount, and as between shares of different classes, having due regard to the attached rights. The '*group of shares*' to be considered is the aggregate of those of the donee or successor, of relatives, nominees and nominees of relatives of the donee or successor, and of trustees of settlements whose objects include the donee or successor or such relatives. There are further detailed rules relating to certain private company holdings of shares.

Previously, private trading companies and private non-trading companies (as defined) controlled by the donee or successor were dealt with differently. The market value of shares in the former was ascertained as if each was part of a holding giving control, that of shares in the latter as if the company had been voluntarily wound up and all the assets realised and payment made on each share. See **38.29** 'Tax cases'.

[*CATCA 2003, s 27; CATA 1976, ss 16, 17; FA 1993, ss 125, 134; FA 1996, s 121*]

TAXABLE VALUE

7.9 The market value will be reduced by any debts or other liabilities to which the gift or inheritance is subject. The balance is the *incumbrance-free value* from which is deducted any *bona fide* consideration in money or money's worth by the donee or successor to give the taxable value. No deduction is allowed for specified items, including contingent liabilities (unless subsequently paid, when a claim may be made for adjustment of the tax), reimbursable amounts (unless reimbursement not obtained), liabilities created by the donee or successor, tax etc chargeable on the gift or inheritance, and any liability on exempt property. Foreign debts will be deducted primarily from foreign property. [*CATCA 2003, s 28; CATA 1976, s 18; FA 2001, s 216*] Where the disponer and donee/successor are related, the grant to the disponer of an annuity for life is not consideration for the gift or inheritance. [*CATCA 2003, ss 5(4), 10(2); CATA 1976, ss 5(4), 11(2)*] Where a gift or inheritance is taken free of tax, the taxable value includes the tax chargeable on the gift etc, but, for a gift etc taken after 17 July 1982, not tax chargeable on such tax. [*CATCA 2003, s 87; FA 1982, s 98*]

For events happening after 29 January 1985 which give rise to both gift or inheritance tax and capital gains tax, the capital gains tax is *not* deducted in arriving at taxable value. See **7.17** below for relief against the gift/inheritance tax liability. [*CATCA 2003, s 104; FA 1985, s 63*]

For a limited interest in property the incumbrance-free value will be reduced according to the age and sex of the donee or successor or the period of time for which the interest is to last. Rules and tables for calculating the reduction are set out in *CATCA 2003, Sch 1; CATA 1976, Sch 1*. Any consideration will be deducted from the reduced value. [*CATCA 2003, s 28(4); CATA 1976, s 18(4)*]

For agricultural property (ie agricultural land, woodlands, farmhouses, buildings and, after 10 April 1994, farm machinery, livestock and bloodstock) in RI *taken by a farmer* (as defined, see *CATCA 2003, s 89(1); CATA 1976, s 19(1)* as amended by *FA 2000, s 140(1)(a)*) as donee or successor, the market value is reduced to give the 'agricultural value', from which debts, liabilities and any consideration will be deducted in the proportion the agricultural value bears to the market value. *Finance (No 2) Act 2008* has amended the definition of *'agricultural property'* so that relief applies to agricultural land in a Member State of the European Union. This amendment applies to gifts or inheritances on or after 20 November 2008. [*F(No 2)A 2008, s 89*] The definition has been further amended by the provisions of *FA 2007, s 117* which provides that in order to meet the *farmer test,* the value of an 'off-farm' principal private residence which is a non-qualifying asset, is now to be determined after taking the borrowings on such a residence into account. The net result will be the taxable value. *FA 2006, s 118,* provides that, in the case of gifts and inheritances taken on or after 1 January 2005, the Single Farm Payment Entitlement will be treated as agricultural property.

For gifts or inheritances taken after 22 January 1997, market value is reduced by **90 per cent** to give agricultural value.

For gifts or inheritances taken after 22 January 1996 and before 23 January 1997, market value is reduced by 75 per cent to give agricultural value, except that in the case of gifts of agricultural property other than farm machinery, livestock and bloodstock it is reduced by 80 per cent up to market value £300,000 plus 50 per cent of the excess over £300,000 if this produces a greater reduction overall than 75 per cent.

As regards earlier gifts or inheritances, for farm machinery, livestock and bloodstock, the reduction is 50 per cent for gifts or inheritances taken after 7 February 1995 and before 23 January 1996, 25 per cent for those taken after 10 April 1994 and before 8 February 1995. For gifts of other agricultural property, the reduction is 50 per cent plus the lesser of 30 per cent and £90,000 (ie 80 per cent up to £300,000 plus 50 per cent on the excess) for gifts taken after 7 February 1995 and before 23 January 1996, 30 per cent plus the lesser of 50 per cent and £150,000 (ie 80 per cent up to £300,000 plus 30 per cent on the excess) for those taken after 10 April 1994 and before 8 February 1995. For inheritances of other agricultural property, the reduction is 50 per cent plus the lesser of 15 per cent and £45,000 (ie 65 per cent up to £300,000 plus 50 per cent on the excess) for inheritances taken after 7 February 1995 and before 23 January 1996, 30 per cent plus the lesser of 35 per cent and £105,000 (ie 65 per cent up to £300,000 plus 30 per cent on the excess) for those taken after 10 April 1994 and before 8 February 1995. The limit of £90,000 (£150,000) or £45,000 (£105,000) applies to the aggregate of all taxable gifts taken after 27 February 1969 and all taxable inheritances taken after 31 March 1975 which consist in whole or part of agricultural property (other than farm machinery, livestock and bloodstock) and which are taken by the same person from the same disponer. For earlier gifts and inheritances, the market value of all agricultural property (other than farm machinery, livestock and bloodstock) is reduced by a specified percentage subject to a specified limit, the amount of the specified limit again applying to the aggregate of taxable gifts and inheritances as above. For gifts, the specified percentage and limit are 75 per cent and £250,000 respectively from 17 June 1993 to 10 April 1994. Otherwise, for gifts and inheritances the specified percentage is 55 per cent from 30 January 1991 to 10 April 1994, previously 50 per cent, and the limit is £200,000 from 1 April 1982 to 10 April 1994, £150,000 from 1 April 1980 to 31 March 1982, previously £100,000.

These special reliefs are clawed back if the property (for gifts etc taken after 10 April 1994, excluding crops, trees or underwood, but including replacement agricultural property) is sold by the donee/successor, or compulsorily acquired, in his lifetime and within six years (ten years where the sale, etc occurred before 10 February 2000 *unless* the gift or inheritance was taken before 23 January 1996) of the date of the gift/ inheritance, without being replaced within a year (within four years in relation to compulsory acquisitions made after 5 December 2000, increased to six years on or after 25 March 2002) by further agricultural property. *FA 2005, s 126*, clarifies that for disposals or compulsory acquisitions on or after 3 February 2005, where only a portion of the disposal proceeds is reinvested in agricultural property within a year of disposal or 6 years of compulsory acquisition, a clawback of agricultural relief will arise on the portion of proceeds not so reinvested. *FA 2011, s 68* ensures that the relevant clawback period applicable to the relief will commence on the date of the gift or inheritance. Where the proceeds are used to acquire agricultural property which has been transferred by the donee or successor to his or her spouse, that property will not constitute 'other agricultural property' for the purposes of *CATCA 2003, s 89(4)*. This amendment applies to transfers from a spouse to his or her spouse on or after 4 February 2010. [*FA 2010, s 146*] *FA 2005, s 126* provides the following formula for calculating the market value of the non-agricultural property:

$$V1 \times \frac{N}{V2}$$

where:

V1   is the market value of all of the agricultural property on the valuation date;

V2   is the market value of the agricultural property immediately before the disposal or compulsory acquisition; and

N   is the amount of proceeds from the disposal or compulsory acquisition that was not expended in replacing the agricultural property disposed of (for this purpose, the proceeds include non-cash consideration).

Where, however, the event giving rise to the clawback occurs more than six years after the date of the gift or inheritance, the clawback only reduces the relief to that which would have been given under the rules applicable immediately before 23 January 1996. For gifts or inheritances taken on or after 2 June 1995, there is also a clawback of relief if the donee or successor is non-RI resident for any of the three years of assessment immediately following that in which the valuation date of the property concerned falls. [*CATCA 2003, s 89; CATA 1976, s 19; FA 1980, s 83; FA 1982, s 100; FA 1991, s 114; FA 1993, s 128; FA 1994, s 141; FA 1995, s 158; FA 1996, s 122; FA 1997, s 134; FA 2000, s 140; FA 2001, s 217; FA 2002, s 116*]

FA 2006, s 118, ensures that relief granted in respect of the development value of 'development land' will be clawed back where such property is disposed of in the period commencing six years after the date of the gift or inheritance and ending 10 years after that date. The clawback will be based on the value of the property on the valuation date of the gift or inheritance.

For '**relevant business property**', the taxable value of gifts and inheritances taken after 22 January 1997 is reduced by **90 per cent** (for those taken after 22 January 1996 and before 23 January 1997, 75 per cent; for those taken after 7 February 1995 and before 23 January 1996, 50 per cent). For gifts or inheritances taken after 10 April 1994 and before 8 February 1995, the reduction is 50 per cent in respect of the first £250,000 acquired by a donee or successor and 25 per cent in respect of the balance. The £250,000 limit applies to the aggregate of all such property taken after 10 April 1994 and before 8 February 1995 by the same donee or successor. The reduction does not apply in relation to discretionary trust tax or probate tax (see **7.14**, **7.18** below respectively). [*CATCA 2003, ss 91, 92; FA 1994, ss 125, 126; FA 1995, s 161; FA 1996, s 125; FA 1997, s 139*] For these purposes, donee or successor includes a transferee within *CATCA 2003, s 32(2); CATA 1976, s 23(1)* (see **7.15** below). [*CATCA 2003, s 90(4); FA 1994, s 124(4); FA 2001, s 227*]

Subject as below, '*relevant business property*' means any of the following:

(*a*)   Property consisting of a business, or an interest in a business, carried on for gain;

(*b*)   'Unquoted' shares or securities (ie shares or securities not quoted on a recognised stock exchange) in or of a company (not within (*c*) below) which on the valuation date (alone or with others in the beneficial ownership of the donee or successor) give control of more than 25 per cent of the votes on all matters affecting the company as a whole;

(c)   Unquoted shares or securities in or of a company which on the valuation date (and after the gift or inheritance is taken) is controlled by the donee or successor within *CATCA 2003, s 27; CATA 1976, s 16* (ie control by the donee or successor together with certain relatives, trustees etc). For gifts or inheritances taken before 28 March 1996, the shares or securities had also (alone or with others in the beneficial ownership of the donee or successor) to represent ten per cent or more of the nominal value of the company's share capital and securities.

(d)   Unquoted shares or securities in or of a company which do not fall within (b) or (c) above and which on the valuation date (alone or with others in the beneficial ownership of the donee or successor) represent ten per cent or more of the nominal value of the company's share capital and securities, *provided that* the donee or successor has devoted substantially the whole of his time to the service, in a managerial or technical capacity, of the company (or of a fellow group company or companies) throughout the five years prior to the date of the gift or inheritance;

(e)   Any land, building, machinery or plant which, immediately before the gift or inheritance, was used wholly or mainly for business purposes by a company of which the disponer then had voting control or by a partnership of which the disponer was then a partner (but see below for certain exclusions). For gifts or inheritances taken after 25 March 1997, 'disponer' for this purpose includes a person in whom the land, etc is vested for a beneficial interest in possession immediately before the gift or inheritance, and where shares, etc are vested in trustees, the voting power is attributed to the person beneficially entitled in possession thereto (unless no individual is so entitled);

(f)   Quoted shares in or securities of a company which would be within (b), (c) or (d) above if they were unquoted, *provided that* they, or other shares or securities represented by them, were in the beneficial ownership of the disponer immediately before the disposition and were unquoted at the date of commencement of that beneficial ownership or (if later) at 23 May 1994.

A business or interest in a business or shares in or securities of a company are *not* relevant business property if the business carried on consists wholly or mainly of dealing in currencies, securities, stocks or shares, land or buildings, or making or holding investments (but not so as to exclude holding companies of one or more companies whose business is not in any of those categories or shares or securities whose value is wholly or mainly attributable, directly or indirectly, to businesses that do not fall within any of those categories). As regards (e) above, there is a similar exclusion unless the disponer's interest in the business is, or the shares etc in the company are, relevant business property in relation to the gift or inheritance or a simultaneous gift or inheritance taken by the same donee or successor.

For gifts or inheritances taken before 15 February 2001, there were additional requirements as regards (b), (c) and (d) above that the company concerned be incorporated in RI, and as regards (e) above that the land, etc be situated in RI. Also, a business or interest in a business, or shares in or securities of a company, were *not* relevant business property if, on the date of the gift or inheritance, the business (or the business carried on by the company) was carried on wholly or mainly outside RI (in the case of a holding company, considering for this purpose the businesses carried on by the holding company and its subsidiaries as a whole).

[*CATCA 2003, s 93; FA 1994, s 127; FA 1996, s 126; FA 1997, s 140; FA 2001, s 228; FA 2004, s 78*]

Property is not relevant business property unless it was in the beneficial ownership of the disponer or spouse for a period of two years (in the case of an inheritance taken on the death of the disponer) or five years (in any other case) immediately prior to the date of the gift or inheritance. [*CATCA 2003, s 94; FA 1994, s 128*] Where property is replaced by other property, these requirements are satisfied by ownership for two out of the three, or five out of the six, years immediately prior to the date of the gift or inheritance, but not so as to increase the amount of the relief above what it would have been without such replacement(s). [*CATCA 2003, s 95; FA 1994, s 129*] Property acquired on a death is deemed to have been beneficially owned by the successor from the date of death. [*CATCA 2003, s 96; FA 1994, s 130*] There are provisions dealing with successive benefits within the two-year period. [*CATCA 2003, s 97; FA 1994, s 131*]

Valuation. The value of a business or of an interest in a business is the market value of the net business assets (including goodwill), disregarding (in the case of an interest in a business) any assets or liabilities other than those by reference to which the value of the entire business would be ascertained. Company shares or securities are valued excluding any group company whose business consists of dealing in currencies, etc (see above) (unless that business consists in holding land or buildings for fellow group companies not carrying on such business), and there is a similar exclusion for the value of companies in a group whose shares or securities are quoted, except in certain cases where they were previously unquoted. [*CATCA 2003, ss 98, 99; FA 1994, ss 132, 133*]

Excepted assets. The part of the taxable value of a gift or inheritance attributable to relevant business property excludes that attributable to 'excepted assets' and 'excluded property'. For gifts or inheritances taken before 10 February 2000, agricultural property (see above) is also excluded, but for gifts or inheritances taken after 11 April 1995 not if it was in the beneficial ownership of a company, and not an 'excepted asset' or 'excluded property'. An *'excepted asset'* is broadly an asset which was not used wholly or mainly for the purposes of the business (disregarding use for a business consisting of dealing in currencies, etc (see above) or, for gifts or inheritances taken before 10 February 2000 and where the business is not carried on by a company, for farming) throughout the two years prior to the date of the gift or inheritance (or for the period of ownership if shorter). Special rules apply in relation to use of land, buildings, machinery or plant within (*e*) above. Parts of land and buildings may be considered separately for these purposes. *'Excluded property'* is broadly a business (or interest in a business) owned by a company whose shares are relevant business property (or by a fellow group member of such a holding company), unless that business (or interest) would itself qualify as relevant business property if included in the gift or inheritance and owned by the disponer at all times when it was in the ownership of the company (or a fellow group member). [*CATCA 2003, s 100; FA 1994, s 134; FA 1995, s 162; FA 1998, s 128; FA 2000, s 148*]

Withdrawal of relief. There are provisions for the clawback of relief broadly where, within a period of six years from the date of the gift or inheritance, the property would not be relevant business property on a gift of such property at any time within that period, and where relevant business property is sold, redeemed or compulsorily acquired within that period without being replaced by qualifying property (in each case with a saving where the situation is restored within one year). *FA 2011, s 68* ensures that the relevant clawback period applicable to the relief will commence on the date of the gift or inheritance. Land, buildings, machinery or plant within (*e*) above (and replacements thereof) continue to be relevant business property for these purposes for so long as they are used for the business concerned. *FA 2005, s 127* clarifies that a partial clawback of the relief will arise where relevant business property has been replaced by other property and the market value of the relevant business property is greater than the market value of the replacement property. This change applies to replacements of property on or after 3 February 2005. Relief is not withdrawn where the donee or successor dies before the event which would otherwise cause the withdrawal (although this does not apply for gifts or inheritances taken before 12 April 1995). Where the event giving rise to the withdrawal of relief occurred before 10 February 2000, the withdrawal period is six years from the valuation date (or, for gifts or inheritances taken before 12 April 1995, the period until the property concerned is the subject of a subsequent gift or inheritance, if shorter), and for gifts or inheritances taken after 22 January 1996, there is additionally a clawback of four-ninths of the relief (one-third for gifts or inheritances taken before 23 January 1997) where the conditions described above occur after the six year time limit but before the expiry of ten years after the valuation date. [*CATCA 2003, s 101; FA 1994, s 135; FA 1995, s 163; FA 1996, s 127; FA 1997, s 141; FA 2000, s 148*]

FA 2006, s 118, ensures that the relief granted in respect of the development value of 'development land' will be clawed back where such property is disposed of in the period commencing six years after the date of the gift or inheritance and ending 10 years after that date. The clawback will be based on the value of the property on the valuation date of the gift or inheritance.

Avoidance of double relief. For gifts or inheritances taken on or after 10 February 2000, to the extent that agricultural property relief has been obtained (see above), business property relief is not available. [*CATCA 2003, s 102; FA 1994, s 135A; FA 2000, s 148*]

RETURNS AND ASSESSMENTS

7.10 The person primarily accountable for tax is the donee or successor. The following are also accountable: (*a*) the disponer (if a gift, or an inheritance taken before the disponer's death) and (*b*) every trustee, guardian, committee, agent (if agent previously notified in writing) or other person with care of any of the property or income, other than a person who is or derives title from a *bona fide* purchaser or mortgagee for full consideration in money or money's worth. The persons in (*b*) are only accountable for an amount of tax equal to the value of the property or income actually held by them. [*CATCA 2003, s 45; CATA 1976, s 35; FA 1980, s 84; FA 1989, s 81*]

Any person primarily liable for the tax must, within four months of the valuation date (see **7.7** above), or of the date of the notice requiring a return:

(*a*)   render a return of every taxable gift or inheritance, with its estimated market value on the valuation date and particulars relevant to assessment of the tax thereon;

(*b*)   assess the tax (and interest) which ought to be charged at that date; and

(*c*)   pay the tax, with the return, to the Accountant-General of the Commissioners.

Since 1 October 2003 a doubt may be expressed in relation to any matter to be included in the return. No interest charge will arise under *CATCA 2003, s 51(2)* in respect of any additional liability arising as a result of the doubt being determined by the Revenue, provided that the doubt is genuine. [*FA 2003, s 146(1)(c); SI 466/03*]

Since 1 December 1999, a return is only required in relation to a benefit taken if the current benefit together with any prior benefits after 1 December 1988 within the same group threshold (see **7.4** above) exceeds 80 per cent of the group threshold amount. Previously a return was required if the current and prior benefits after 1 June 1982 exceeded 80 per cent of the tax-free threshold. In either case the Commissioners may give written notice requiring a return. Since 1 October 2003, an accountable person is required to retain records for six years from the valuation date or the date of filing of returns if these are not filed by the due date. [*FA 2003, s 146(1)(b); SI 466/03*]

Instalment payment and payment by certain Government securities (see **7.12** below) continue to be available. The above procedure applies to the charge under *CATCA 2003, s 15 (FA 1984, s 106)* (see **7.14** below), and to any other gift or inheritance where the aggregate taxable value since 5 December 1991 (for gifts or inheritances taken before 5 December 2001, since 2 December 1988, for those taken before 2 December 1998, since 2 June 1982) exceeds 80 per cent of the relevant threshold (see **7.4** above), or where a return is required by notice. Any of the persons accountable for the tax by virtue of *CATCA 2003, s 45 (CATA 1976, s 35)* (see above) may be required, within not less than 30 days of being given notice, to make the return as above.

The Commissioners may also, by written notice, require any person to deliver (within not less than 30 days) a return giving details of any taxable gifts or inheritances taken during the period specified in the notice, including a nil return.

The Commissioners have powers to call for such particulars and evidence as they consider may be relevant to assessment of the tax, and may authorise a person to inspect any property comprised in the gift or inheritance and any relevant books, records etc. They may also require an additional return if they consider that a return is materially defective, and any accountable person becoming aware of a defect in a return he has delivered must, within three months, deliver an additional return. Since 1 January 2005 any enquiries, inspections and amendments to assessments must be made within four years of the date of receipt of the return, save in the case of fraud or neglect. [*FA 2003, s 145; SI 515/03*]

Where a return by an accountable person substantially underestimates the value of any property comprised in a gift or inheritance, the tax attributable to that property is subject to a surcharge as follows, the surcharge (subject to the usual appeal provisions) being treated as tax for the purposes of interest and collection.

Estimated value as % of ascertained value	*Surcharge*
Under 40%	30%
At least 40% but under 50%	20%
At least 50% but under 67%	10%

A return is also required from the *disponer* (within four months of the valuation date, see **7.7** above) giving all relevant particulars (including an estimate of the market value of the property comprised in the gift) in relation to gifts (but not inheritances) taken after 10 February 1999 where either:

(i)   the taxable value of the gift exceeds 80 per cent of the relevant threshold (see **7.4** above), or causes the aggregate taxable value of gifts and inheritances taken by the donee from the disponer since 5 December 1991 (for gifts or inheritances taken before 5 December 2001, since 2 December 1988) to exceed that limit; or

(ii)   the aggregate taxable value of gifts and inheritance taken by the donee from the disponer since 5 December 1991 (for gifts or inheritances taken before 5 December 2001, since 2 December 1988) prior to the gift already exceeded that limit.

See also **7.14** below as regards returns required from disponers in relation to discretionary trusts.

[*FA 2003, ss 145, 146; CATCA 2003, ss 46, 53; CATA 1976, s 36 as inserted by FA 1989, s 74; FA 1989, s 79; FA 1999, s 200; FA 2000, s 141; FA 2002, s 117*]

A return for these purposes must be made on a form provided by the Commissioners or in a form approved by them, and may be delivered by approved electronic etc means. Since 29 September 2003, returns may be filed electronically. [*CATCA 2003, s 47; CATA 1976, s 37; FA 1989, s 82; SI 443/03*]

The information required for the Revenue affidavit for probate is extended to cover details of the property subject to inheritances and of the successors thereunder. [*CATCA 2003, s 48; CATA 1976, s 38*]

Assessments may still be made by the Commissioners according to the return submitted or, if the returns are inadequate, to the best of their knowledge, information and belief. [*CATCA 2003, s 49; CATA 1976, s 39; FA 1989, s 75*]

FINANCE ACT 2010 – ADMINISTRATION CHANGES

7.11 The main changes made were as follows:

•   It removed the requirement for Revenue to certify the Inland Revenue affidavit before probate or letters of administration is/are issued by the Probate Office.

•   It provided for the future deployment of a platform that will allow the electronic filing of an Inland Revenue affidavit simultaneously to Revenue and the Probate Office.

•   It removed secondary accountability (ie where certain persons such as personal representatives of a deceased person were liable to pay CAT if a beneficiary of a gift or an inheritance did not pay the tax) and CAT being a charge on property for 12 years after the date of the gift or inheritance.

•   It provided for the appointment of an Irish-resident agent who will be responsible for paying inheritance tax where the personal representatives and one or more of the beneficiaries are non-resident. The person so appointed will be entitled to deduct a sufficient amount from the property comprised in the deceased person's estate in order to discharge the beneficiary's inheritance tax liability.

•   It provided that the payment of CAT and the filing of a return are brought into line with other self-assessment taxes. The due date for paying CAT and filing a return, where the valuation date arises in the period from 1 January to 31 August, will be on or before 31 October in that year. Where the valuation date arises in the period from 1 September to 31 December, the pay and file date will be on or before the 31 October in the following year. Interest will run on outstanding tax from 1 November in the relevant year.

- It introduced a surcharge similar to the one that already applies to other self-assessed taxes.

- It provided for the electronic filing of a return in the case where reliefs or exemptions (other than the exemption for small gifts) are being claimed by a beneficiary of a gift or an inheritance.

- It provided for an increase in the threshold requirement for Revenue to issue a clearance certificate in the case of deposit accounts held jointly in the name of the deceased person and another or others from €31,750 to €50,000. The abolition of secondary accountability and 12-year CAT charge applies retrospectively.

The changes in relation to the Inland Revenue affidavit, the payment of CAT and the filing of a return and interest on outstanding tax will come into effect on a date that will be specified in an Order made by the Revenue Commissioners. The other changes apply since the date of the passing of the *Finance Act 2010* (3 April 2010).

   [*FA 2010, s 147*]

PAYMENT AND INTEREST

7.12 The pay and file dates for CAT have been brought forward from 31 October to 30 September. This will mean that any CAT arising in relation to any gifts or inheritances received between 1 September 2010 and 31 August 2011 must be returned and the tax paid by 30 September 2011. [*FA 2011, s 70*] The amendment also makes consequential changes to the provisions relating to the time when interest is charged on tax which is paid after the due date and the surcharge for late returns. This amendment applies to returns delivered and tax paid on or after 21 January 2011.Previously tax was be due on the valuation date from accountable persons, as defined. Interest will be chargeable unless payment is made by the due date. As respects any unpaid tax or, as the case may be, any tax that has not been paid before 1 April 2005, *FA 2005, s 145,* provides that interest will be payable by reference to a daily rate for all periods of delay, whether before or after 1 April 2005. The rates of interest applicable for each period of delay are set out hereunder

Period	Percentage
31 March 1976 to 31 July 1978	0.0492%
1 August 1978 to 31 March 1998	0.0410%
1 April 1998 to 31 March 2005	0.0322%
1 April 2005 to date of payment	0.0273%

If payment is made within 30 days after an assessment, no interest accrues for that period. Where the tax is self-assessed (see **7.10** above), interest is not payable on tax paid within four months of the valuation date, and any conditional or incorrect amount of tax paid is treated as a payment on account. With effect from 11 February 1999 (1

December 1999 in certain cases), where a CAT relief is clawed back, interest generally arises only from the date of the event giving rise to the clawback. [*CATCA 2003, s 51; FA 1989, s 76; FA 1999, s 202; FA 2002, s 118; FA 2005, s 145*]. *Finance Act 2007, s 115* confirms that this is the case of a clawback of agricultural relief or business property relief. The section legislates the position that interest will only be charged from the date of the disposal of the property rather than the valuation date as was applied previously.

Except to the extent that the property of which a taxable gift or inheritance consists is personal property in which the donee or successor takes an absolute interest, payment may be made by five equal annual instalments (with interest as above on unpaid balances) commencing twelve months after the valuation date. All unpaid instalments become due on the sale or compulsory acquisition of the property of which the gift or inheritance consists (unless the interest of the donee or successor is a limited interest), but no instalments will be payable which, were the tax payable by instalments, would have been due after the death of a donee or successor with a life interest. In relation to gifts and inheritances taken after 7 February 1995 (but not an inheritance taken by a 'relevant trust' (see **7.18** below) or a discretionary trust (see **7.14** below)), to the extent that the tax is attributable to agricultural property (see **7.9** above) or 'relevant business property', the exclusion of tax in respect of personal property in which the donee or successor takes an absolute interest does not apply, and the interest rate on the unpaid balance is 0.0307 per cent per day or part of a day for the period from 8 February 1995 to 31 March 1998, 0.0241 per cent per day or part of a day for the period from 1 April 1998 to 31 March 2005 and 0.0204 per cent per day or part of a day from 1 April 2005 to the date of payment (variable by regulations) rather than as above (although the higher rate continues to apply on overdue instalments); also, the instalment facility is not withdrawn (as above) on the sale or compulsory acquisition of the property provided that it is replaced by other agricultural property within one year. '*Relevant business property*' is as in **7.9** above, but excluding quoted shares in or securities of a company and disregarding the minimum period of ownership requirements and certain exclusions in relation to 'excepted assets'. [*FA 2003, s 148; CATCA 2003, ss 54, 55; CATA 1976, s 43; FA 1995, s 164; FA 1996, s 129; FA 2005, s 145*]

Payment of inheritance tax (but not gift tax or discretionary trust tax, see **7.14** below) may be made by transfer of certain Government securities at par value (adjusted for outstanding interest accrued on a day to day basis). [*CATCA 2003, s 56; FA 1954, s 22; CATA 1976, s 45*]

Interest up to 30 April 1991 (and any penalties incurred, see **7.17** below) are waived where gift or inheritance tax in respect of a gift, etc taken before 31 January 1991 was due and payable by a donee or successor before 1 October 1991, and between 30 January 1991 and 30 September 1991 inclusive, a return was delivered and the tax assessed under *CATCA 2003, s 46 (CATA 1976, s 36)* (self-assessment, see **7.10** above) or *CATCA 2003, s 21 (FA 1986, s 104)* (discretionary trusts, see **7.14** below), and the tax was paid before 1 October 1991. Instalment payments and payments on account otherwise applicable against interest liability are applied towards discharge of the tax (but without repayment of any excess). The waiver does not apply where any other gift or inheritance tax is outstanding after 30 September 1991, or where any capital gains tax liability (including any interest and penalties) in respect of the disposal of the property comprised in the gift, etc remains unpaid at the time the gift or inheritance tax is paid. Interest on additional tax following the revaluation of property included in a self-assessed return delivered after 29 January 1991 is not waived. Fines, penalties and interest imposed by a court may not be waived. [*FA 1991, s 120*]

Tax overpaid will be refunded with tax-free interest at 0.0161 per cent per day or part (before 1 September 2002, at 0.5 per cent per month or part). Since 1 November 2003 tax repayments carry interest at a rate of 0.011 per cent per day from six months after the repayment claim is made, unless paid before that date. Where the repayment is due to a mistaken assumption in the operation of the law on the part of the Commissioners, interest is payable from the date of payment of the tax. Since 31 October 2003 repayment claims must be made within four years of the later of the valuation date or the date on which the tax is paid. This time limit now applies to overpayments of probate tax. [*FA 2010, s 143*] This time limit does not apply to claims made by 31 December 2004 in respect of repayments arising on or before 28 March 2003. The Commissioners may postpone or remit tax. The four year time limit for claiming repayments of tax overpaid will run from the date of payment of tax, where that tax has been paid within the four months after the valuation date. Where the tax has not been paid within the four month period, the four year time limit will run from the valuation date of the gift or inheritance. This amendment takes effect for gifts or inheritances on or after 31 January 2008 [*FA 2008, s 127*]. Tax on a gift which becomes an inheritance by death of disponer within two years will be set off against the inheritance tax. [*FA 2003, s 145; CATCA 2003, ss 52, 57, 59; CATA 1976, ss 42, 44, 46; FA 1986, s 109; SI 176/90; FA 1998, s 133(4)(6); FA 2002, s 129(3)(b); SI 515/03*]

Tax will be a charge on the property (not money or negotiable instruments) comprised in the gift or inheritance in priority to any charge or interest created by the donee/successor (except as against a *bona fide* purchaser or mortgagee for full consideration in money or money's worth without notice), but the charge will not preclude sale or exchange of settled property (in which case the charge will apply to the proceeds of sale or substituted property). [*CATCA 2003, s 60; CATA 1976, s 47*]

The Revenue Commissioners must give a receipt for payment of capital acquisitions tax. They may also be required to provide a certificate of tax paid in respect of property comprised in a taxable gift or inheritance and in certain other circumstances. [*CATCA 2003, s 61; CATA 1976, s 48; FA 1984, s 113; FA 2000, s 142*]

Subject to the self-certification provision referred to below, applications for the registration of title to land based on possession will not be granted without the production of a clearance certificate from the Revenue Commissioners confirming that, in the 'relevant period', any liabilities to gift or inheritance tax (including probate tax) charged on the land (and not charged prior to the date ownership was last registered) have been or will (within a reasonable time) be discharged. The *'relevant period'* is generally the period from 28 February 1974 to the date as of which the registration was made, but a certificate ending at an earlier date is deemed to satisfy these conditions if the Registrar has no reason to believe that a death relevant to the application occurred in the intervening period. Where the owner of the property (if any) at the date of the application was registered as such after 28 February 1974, the relevant period begins on the date of that registration. With effect from 15 May 1996, this requirement is relaxed by an alternative provision for self-certification (in prescribed form) by the solicitor for the applicant for registration. This applies where the solicitor is satisfied that either the area occupied by the property does not exceed five hectares and its market value does not exceed €19,050/£15,000, or its market value does not exceed €127,000/£100,000 where the applicant is a statutory authority, and that the property concerned is not part of a larger holding exceeding these limits. The latter restriction does not apply where the area does not exceed 500 sq metres and the market value does not exceed €2,540/ £2,000, provided the application is not part of a series of related transactions covering a single property exceeding those limits.

CATCA 2003, s 62 provides that title to property cannot be registered unless a Revenue Certificate is produced by the person who makes the application to have the property registered to the effect that a charge to gift tax or inheritance tax does not arise in respect of that property. This section is now amended to reflect the position in the *Registration of Deeds and Title Act 2006* and applies to applications to register property made on or after 6 November 2006. [*CATCA 2003, s 62; FA 1994, s 146; FA 1996, s 128, FA 2008, s 128*]

APPEALS

7.13 Appeals in relation to value of real property will be made to the Land Values Reference Committee under provisions of *F(1909–10)A 1910, s 33*. Appeals in other cases must be made within 30 days after date of assessment, and the provisions relating to income tax appeals generally apply (see **4** 'Appeals'). [*CATCA 2003, ss 66, 67; CATA 1976, ss 51, 52; FA 1995, s 159; FA 1998, s 134(3); FA 1999, s 203; FA 2002, s 119*]

Appeals may be made against any assessment or written decision of the Commissioners relevant to tax. Certain other decisions of the Commissioners are specifically appealable. [*CATCA 2003, ss 30(9), 67, 80(4); CATA 1976, ss 21(9), 52, 56(3)*]

For gifts and inheritances taken after 11 February 1998, no appeal under *CATCA 2003, ss 66 or 67 (CATA 1976, s 51 or s 52)* may be made until the return and payment as under *CATCA 2003, s 46(2) (CATA 1976, s 36(2))* (see **7.10** above) relating to the gift or inheritance in question have been made as if the appellant were the person primarily accountable for the tax. [*CATCA 2003, s 68; CATA 1976, s 52A; FA 1998, s 129*]

SPECIAL CHARGE ON DISCRETIONARY TRUSTS

7.14 Initial charge. New and existing discretionary trusts on or after 25 January 1984 are to be treated as becoming beneficially entitled in possession to property subject to the trust on the latest of:

(*a*)   the date the property became subject to the trust;

(*b*)   the date of death of the disponer; and

(*c*)   the date on which there ceases to be a 'principal object' (if any) of the trust under 21 (25 in relation to property becoming subject to the trust before 31 January 1993);

and as taking an inheritance on that latest date accordingly as if the trust and its trustees were a person. A 'principal object' of the trust is a spouse or child of the disponer (and, if such a child predeceases the disponer, any children of such a child) for whose benefit trust income or capital (or part) may be applied.

As regards (*c*) above, all property subject to a discretionary trust on 31 January 1993 is treated as becoming subject to the trust on that date.

Where property would be charged to tax more than once under the same disposition, tax is charged only on the earliest occasion it became so chargeable. [*CATCA 2003, s 15; FA 1984, s 106; FA 1985, s 64; FA 1992, s 224*]

An interest in expectancy or in a life assurance policy is not property for this purpose until respectively it ceases to be in expectancy or matures. [*CATCA 2003, ss 2(1), 15; FA 1984, ss 105, 106*]

The tax payable on a charge under these provisions is **6 per cent** (for inheritances taken before 11 April 1994, 3 per cent) of the taxable value (see **7.9** above) of the inheritance. However, the increase in the charge (from 3 per cent to 6 per cent) is refunded if, within five years of the death of the disponer or, in the case of trusts with principal objects, within five years of the youngest reaching 21 years of age, all property within the relevant trusts has been transferred absolutely to the beneficiaries.

Finance Act 2007 made an amendment to *CATCA 2003, s 18* and results directly out of a High Court decision in the previous year. The amendment provides that the reduced rate of tax (ie 3 per cent) applies where all the assets are appointed absolutely to one or more of the beneficiaries of a discretionary trust created under a deceased person's will within a period of five years after the date when the assets were transferred by the executors to the trustees of the discretionary trust, where none of the principal objects (ie the disponer's spouse, his or her children and certain grandchildren) of the trust was under the age of 21 years on the relevant date. The amendment applies in respect of inheritances deemed to be taken on or after 1 February 2007.

This applies equally as respects an inheritance deemed to be taken by a discretionary trust after 25 January 2001 on the death of a life tenant, the five-year period in such cases commencing on the date of death of the life tenant concerned. [*CATCA 2003, s 18; FA 1984, s 109; FA 1994, s 143; FA 2001, s 229*] See in particular **7.10** above as regards returns and payment of the tax.

Discretionary trusts created for the following purposes are, however, exempt from the above charge:

(i)   public or charitable purposes in RI or in Northern RI;

(ii)   the purposes of any retirement benefits scheme established under any enactment, or of certain other such schemes but excluding, after 4 April 1990, certain schemes relating to matters other than service in particular offices or employments;

(iii)   the purposes of a registered unit trust scheme;

(iv)   for the benefit of one or more named individuals incapable of managing their affairs through age, improvidence, or physical, mental or legal incapacity; or

(v)   for the upkeep of heritage property within **7.5**(*c*) above;

as are also such a trust in respect of property subject to the trust which, on termination, is gifted or bequeathed to the State, and an inheritance consisting of free use of property, etc which would otherwise be chargeable by virtue of *CATCA 2003, s 40; CATA 1976, s 31* (see **7.15** below). [*CATCA 2003, s 17; FA 1984, s 108; FA 1985, s 65; FA 1990, s 129*]

Appropriate modifications are applied to *CATA 1976* for the purposes of the above charge. [*CATCA 2003, s 16; FA 1984, s 107; FA 1989, s 78; FA 1993, s 131*]

Annual charge. Subject to the same exceptions and exemptions [*CATCA 2003, ss 20, 22; FA 1986, ss 103, 105*], a charge is levied on 5 April (the '*chargeable date*') in every calendar year in which property is on that date subject to a discretionary trust in relation to which the disponer is dead and none of the principal objects, if any, is under 21 (25 in relation to 5 April 1993 and earlier chargeable dates), as if the trust and trustees were a person taking an inheritance on that date. Property previously subject to the discretionary trust which is not subject to the trust on the chargeable date only because of the existence of an interest in possession which is revocable, or which is limited to cease other than on the death of the person entitled to the interest in possession or the expiry of a period certain of five years or more from the date of appointment of the interest, is treated as being subject to the trust. The charge does not arise where an initial charge as above arises on the same property, or on property representing it, on, or within one year prior to, the chargeable date. [*CATCA 2003, ss 19, 20; FA 1986, ss 102, 103; FA 1992, s 225*]

FA 2006, s 116, has changed the chargeable date from 5 April to 31 December for years 2007 and subsequent years. For the year 2006, there will be two chargeable dates (ie 5 April and 31 December), but the tax chargeable for the chargeable date arising on 31 December 2006 will be 73.97 per cent of the tax due on that date.

The tax payable on a charge under these provisions is **1 per cent** of the taxable value (see **7.9** above) of the inheritance. [*CATCA 2003, s 23; FA 1986, s 106*] The valuation date is the chargeable date, except that for the first charge under these provisions following an initial charge as above, the valuation date is the same as that for the initial charge. *Finance Act 2007, s 114* amends *CATCA 2003, s 21* to delete provisions that are redundant as a result of the High Court decision in relation to when the **1 per cent** levy arises in respect of a discretionary trust. The **1 per cent** charge used be applied during the administration of an estate. However, as a consequence of the High Court decision, the position is such that the **1 per cent** charge arises from the date the executors finalise the administration of the estate and transfer the property to the trustees of the discretionary trust. This provision has effect from 1 February 2007. A trustee at or after the date of the inheritance is required to make appropriate returns within four months after the valuation date, and to assess and pay the due tax to the Accountant-General of the Commissioners. A penalty of the lesser of £1,000/€1,265 and twice the tax payable may be imposed for failure to comply. Since 1 October 2003, where the trustee fails to comply with the requirement to deliver a return otherwise than by reason of fraud, the penalty imposed is the lesser of €1,265 and the difference between the tax paid and the tax that would have been payable if the return had been delivered and had been correct. [*CATCA 2003, ss 21, 25; FA 1986, ss 104, 108; FA 1993, s 132; FA 2006, s 117; SI 466/ 03*]

There are provisions enabling the market value of real property and unquoted shares agreed for one chargeable date to apply, subject to limitations, to the following two chargeable dates. [*CATCA 2003, s 24; FA 1986, s 107*]

FA 2006, s 116, provides that the market value of property agreed with Revenue in respect of the valuation date 5 April 2006 will be treated as the market value of that property for the valuation date in respect of the valuation date 31 December 2006.

Returns. Where property becomes subject to a discretionary trust after 10 February 1999 in consequence of a disposition by a person living and domiciled in RI, the disponer must, within four months, make a return giving details of the terms of the trust and the names and addresses of the trustees and the objects of the trust, together with an estimate of the market value at the date of the disposition of the property becoming

subject to the trust. [*CATCA 2003, s 46(15); CATA 1976, s 36(15); FA 1999, s 200*]
FA 2006, s 117, provides that the requirement to deliver a return applies to a person resident or ordinarily resident in RI.

OTHER PROVISIONS

7.15 Distributions from discretionary trusts will be taxed, as and when made, as an inheritance if the creation of the trust related to a death, and as a gift otherwise. [*CATCA 2003, s 31; CATA 1976, s 22*]

Joint tenants are treated for tax purposes as tenants in common in equal shares. [*CATCA 2003, ss 7, 13(2); CATA 1976, ss 7, 14(2)*]

Powers of appointment. Where the disposition is an exercise of, or failure to exercise, a general power of appointment the disponer is the holder of the power. In the case of a special power of appointment the disposition is the disposition creating the power and the disponer the creator of the power. [*CATCA 2003, s 36; CATA 1976, s 27*] A general power of appointment is deemed to exist in certain situations (eg in a tenant in tail in possession). [*CATCA 2003, s 2(2); CATA 1976, s 2(2)*]

Enlargement of a limited interest into an absolute interest (eg by receiving a reversion) is taxed on the taxable value of the absolute interest minus the value [*CATCA 2003, Sch 1; CATA 1976, Sch 1*] of the unexpired balance of the limited interest unless both interests are taken under the same disposition. [*CATCA 2003, s 35; CATA 1976, s 26*]

Free use of property, free loans etc will be taxed annually as a gift or inheritance of the value of the free facility for the year. [*CATCA 2003, s 40; CATA 1976, s 31*]

Gift terminable on contingency is treated as an absolute interest unless and until the contingency occurs (when it is reassessed as a limited interest for a term certain) [*CATCA 2003, s 29; CATA 1976, s 20*], but a **gift subject to a power of revocation by the disponer** is deemed not to render the donee beneficially entitled until the power ceases to be exercisable. [*CATCA 2003, s 39; CATA 1976, s 30*] See also **38.212** 'Tax cases'.

Gift-splitting will be ineffective because where a disposition enlarges the value of property already held by the donee/successor (but acquired by him since 28 February 1969) and derived from the same disponer, the difference between (*a*) the value of the original property and the newly received property taken as a unit and (*b*) the sum of their values taken separately is a deemed gift or inheritance. [*CATCA 2003, s 38; CATA 1976, s 29*]

Life assurance policy is deemed an interest in possession only when the policy matures or is surrendered or to the extent of any payment in whole or partial discharge. [*CATCA 2003, s 41; CATA 1976, s 32*]

Double aggregation and double charge: trust property. Property in respect of which tax is chargeable more than once on the same event, in relation to a gift or inheritance taken after 1 June 1982, is not to be included more than once in relation to that event in any aggregate referred to at **7.4** above, or in relation to the apportionment of tax due in respect of gifts or inheritances taken on the same day. [*CATCA 2003, s 103; FA 1985, s 61*]

With effect from the introduction of capital acquisitions tax, where tax is charged more than once in respect of the same property on the same event, the net tax which is earlier in priority is deducted against the tax later in priority. Again, no repayment interest supplement is payable. [*CATCA 2003, s 105; FA 1985, s 62*]

Other provisions include: dealings with or settlement of future interests [*CATCA 2003, ss 32, 34, 111; CATA 1976, ss 23, 25, 64*], release of limited interest [*CATCA 2003, s 33; CATA 1976, s 24*], cesser of liabilities [*CATCA 2003, s 37; CATA 1976, s 28*], connected successive dispositions [*CATCA 2003, s 8; CATA 1976, s 8*] and where *Succession Act 1965, s 98* applies [*CATCA 2003, s 42; CATA 1976, s 33*].

COMPANIES

7.16 Dispositions by or to a private company are treated as if the beneficial owners of shares and of certain entitlements in the company are the disponers, donees or successors, in proportion to the value of their interests in the company [*CATCA 2003, s 43; CATA 1976, s 34; FA 1993, s 129*].

A company resolution affecting company shares which benefits the estate of shareholder A at the expense of that of shareholder B is a deemed disposition by B if he could have prevented the resolution [*CATCA 2003, s 2(3); CATA 1976, s 2(3)*].

MISCELLANEOUS

7.17 Joint accounts (not current accounts) containing more than €31,750/£25,000 (for deaths before 26 January 2001, £5,000) are frozen if one of the holders dies, and no payments out are allowed without the Commissioners' consent [*CATCA 2003, s 109; CATA 1976, s 61; FA 2001, s 223*]. This does not apply where the holder who died was then the spouse of the other [*CATCA 2003, s 109(7); FA 1986, s 110*].

Capital gains tax. Where an event gives rise to both gift or inheritance tax liability and capital gains tax liability, the capital gains tax paid is credited against the gift or inheritance tax liability in respect of that event. The credit given is to be confined to the lesser amount of these two taxes attributable to each asset, or to a part of each asset, which is property charged with both taxes on the same event. Any necessary apportionment of reliefs or expenditure is made on a just and reasonable basis by the Commissioners (or, on appeal, by the Appeal Commissioners). [*CATCA 2003, s 104; FA 1985, s 63; FA 1988, s 66*]

FA 2006, s 119, provides that the credit granted will be withdrawn to the extent that the asset is disposed of within two years after the date of the gift or inheritance. *FA 2011, s 68* ensures that the relevant clawback period applicable to the relief will commence on the date of the gift or inheritance.

Double tax relief. Foreign tax on a gift/inheritance taken under a disposition on the happening of an event is allowed as a credit against gift tax/inheritance tax on the same event. There is power to make double tax agreements and arrangements regarding the exchange of information for the purpose of prevention and detection of tax evasion. A new amendment ensures that a Treaty entered into under s 106 of the Act will have the force of law only after the Government has made an Order that has been approved by the Dáil and legislation has been enacted by the Oireachtas inserting a reference to the Order into the Table which is being inserted into *CATCA 2003, s 106* by this amendment. [*CATCA 2003, ss 106, 107(2); CATA 1976, ss 66, 67(2); FA 1977, s 54(3), Sch 2; FA 2004, s 79; FA 2008, s 129*] See **14** 'Double tax relief – capital transfers' for the agreement with the United Kingdom.

Regulations may be made by the Commissioners as they think necessary [*CATCA 2003, s 116; CATA 1976, s 71*].

Penalties apply for failure to comply with *CATCA 2003, s 46 (CATA 1976, s 36)* (see **7.10** above) and for the delivery of incorrect returns or statements etc [*CATCA 2003, s 58; FA 2003, s 146(1)(d); CATA 1976, s 63; FA 1989, s 77; SI 466/03*]. See **7.12** above for the waiver of certain penalties.

PROBATE TAX

7.18 Where, under or in consequence of any disposition, property becomes subject to a 'relevant trust' on a death after 17 June 1993 and **before 6 December 2000**, the trust is deemed on the date of death to become beneficially entitled in possession to an absolute interest in that property and to take an inheritance accordingly as if the trust and the trustees were together a person for *CATA 1976* purposes (the date of death being the date of the inheritance). This is without prejudice to any charge to tax in respect of any inheritance, affecting the same property (or part) taken under the same disposition, by an object of the relevant trust or by a discretionary trust by virtue of *FA 1984, s 106(1)* (see **7.14** above) (any such inheritance being deemed to be taken after the deemed inheritance (except for the purposes of the exemptions under *CATA 1976, s 55(3)(4)*, see **7.5**(*d*) above)). A '*relevant trust*' is any trust under which, by virtue of *Succession Act 1965, s 10(3)*, the executors hold the estate of the deceased as trustees for the persons by law entitled thereto. It also includes certain trusts deemed to be created where a deceased estate vests in the President of the High Court under *s 13 of that Act. Sections 10 and 13* are both deemed to apply irrespective of the domicile of the deceased or the locality of the estate. [*FA 1993, ss 109, 110; FA 1994, s 137; FA 2001, s 225*]

Effectively, the tax applies to the property in an estate passing on the death of a person under his will or intestacy. It does not apply to eg joint property passing on a death by survivorship. If the deceased was domiciled in RI, all his assets, no matter where situate, come within the charge unless specifically exempted; otherwise, only RI assets come within the charge.

The provisions of *CATA 1976* apply appropriately adapted in relation to the above charge, so that from 1 December 1999, if the deceased was resident or ordinarily resident in RI at the time of death, all assets, no matter where situated, come within the charge, and assets situated in RI remain within the charge regardless of the residence of the deceased. In particular, the market value of agricultural property is reduced by 30 per cent, and the penalties under *CATA 1976, s 63* (see **7.17** above) are reduced by 80 per cent. [*FA 1993, s 111; FA 1994, s 138*] In relation to the exemption at **7.5**(*r*) above, the requirement that the successor is not domiciled or ordinarily resident in RI does not apply. [*FA 1993, s 119*]

Exemptions. The following property attracts exemption from probate tax:

(*a*)   certain rights to receive benefits under superannuation and other retirement schemes;

(*b*)   property willed for public or charitable purposes which is, or will be, applied for such purposes;

(*c*)   the dwelling-house (including grounds up to one acre and normal furniture and household effects) where (subject to various conditions and limits) it is occupied by a dependent child or relative by whom it is taken under the will etc. (For deaths before 24 May 1994, the dwelling-house was also exempt where the deceased was survived by a spouse, but see now below as regards general surviving spouse reliefs.)

[*FA 1993, s 112; FA 1994, s 139*]

Rate of tax. Tax is charged at the rate of **2 per cent** on the taxable value of the taxable inheritance under these provisions. No tax is payable where the taxable value does not exceed the 'relevant threshold'. For deaths on or after 1 December 1999 and before 6 December 2000, the *'relevant threshold'* is £40,000.

For deaths before 1 December 1999, the *'relevant threshold'* for each year is as follows:

1993	£10,000
1994	£10,150
1995	£10,390
1996	£10,650
1997	£10,820
1998	£10,980
1999	£11,250

Where the taxable value exceeds the relevant threshold, the tax is limited to the excess [*FA 1993, s 113; FA 2000, s 147*].

Quick succession relief applies where the spouse of the deceased dies within one year, or within five years if the surviving spouse is survived by a dependent child [*FA 1993, s 114*].

Incidence of tax. Property representing any share in the deceased's estate (so far as not exempt or not chargeable) bears its due proportion of the tax. Disputes may be determined, on application by any interested person, in the High Court or, if the amount in dispute is less than £15,000, the Circuit Court. [*FA 1993, s 115*]

Surviving or divorced spouse. Tax on property which, at the date of death of the deceased, represents the absolute share of the surviving spouse of the deceased in the estate is abated to nil. Except in the case of certain limited interests (see below), where property represents the shares of both the spouse and other person(s) in the estate, the tax borne by the property is abated in the proportion that the value of the spouse's interest (disregarding any interest in expectancy) bears to the total value of the property. Where a limited interest passes to the surviving spouse, the tax is not abated but does not become due and payable until the limited interest comes to an end. Certain other persons and trustees with an interest in the property on the cessation of the limited interest, or in whose care that property (or income therefrom) is placed at that time, are then accountable for the tax, which is a charge on the property.

Any tax borne by the dwelling-house where the spouse survives the deceased (ie where it is not, or not fully, comprised in the spouse's share in the estate and not within the exemption at (*c*) above) does not become due and payable until the date of death of the spouse. Certain other persons and trustees in whom property comprised in the original will etc is vested at or after the date of the spouse's death, and persons who took an inheritance thereunder including the dwelling-house (or part) or property representing it, are then accountable for the tax.

These provisions apply to a spouse in whose favour an order under *Family Law Act 1995, s 25* or *Family Law (Divorce) Act 1996, s 18* or (from 10 February 2000) an analogous foreign order has been made as they apply to a surviving spouse, by reference to property the subject of the order instead of the share in the estate.

[*FA 1993, s 115A; FA 1994, s 140; Family Law Act 1995, s 53; Family Law (Divorce) Act 1996, s 36; FA 1997, s 143; FA 2000, s 150*]

Payment and postponement of tax. The person applying for probate or letters of administration of the estate is required to make an assessment in prescribed form of the tax arising on the death, including any interest payable (as below), and to deliver it, with the Inland Revenue Affidavit, to the Commissioners, accompanied by payment of that tax (and interest). Where there are insufficient liquid assets in the estate to meet the tax, payment may be postponed as the Commissioners think fit. [*FA 1993, ss 116, 118*]

Interest on tax. The tax is due and payable on the valuation date (see **7.7** above), in effect the date of death, and simple interest runs from nine months after that date until payment at the rate of 0.0273 per cent per day or part of a day. The interest may not, however, exceed the amount of the tax. Where a payment on foot of the tax was made before the end of that nine-month period, it is discounted at the same rate for the part of the nine-month period remaining. Any repayment under *CATA 1976, s 46* (see **7.12** above) is made without regard to such discount. [*FA 1993, s 117; FA 1998, s 127; FA 2005, s 145*]

Abolition. Probate tax is **abolished** in respect of deaths occurring **on or after 6 December 2000** [*FA 2001, s 225*].

DOUBLE TAX RELIEF

7.19 *Finance Act 2008* amended *CATCA 2003, s 106* which provides for the making of arrangements for relief from double taxation and the exchange of information for the purposes of preventing and detecting tax evasion. The position up to then had been that a Treaty had the force of law once the Government made an Order that it had entered into the Treaty and that Order had been approved by the Dáil. The amendment provided that a Treaty entered into will only have the force of law after the Government has made an Order that has been approved by the Dáil and legislation has been enacted by the Oireachtas inserting a reference to the Order into the Table which is being inserted into s 106 by this amendment. This amendment has effect from 31 January 2008.

8 Capital Allowances

Cross-references. See also **18.5** 'Farming'; **22.4** 'Losses' for allowances on significant building; **24.2** and **24.6** 'Mines' for capital allowances applicable to mining; **30** 'Sch D, Cases I and II' **30.20** for patents, **30.24** for scientific research and **30.28** for staff recruitment.

Note: The *Corporation Tax Act 1976* replaced or amended much of the earlier legislation in order to adapt it for both corporation tax and income tax. See also **12.9** 'Corporation tax'. All the relevant legislation is now contained in the *Taxes Consolidation Act 1997*.

8.1 Capital allowances include the allowances mentioned in this section and in the cross-references above. [*TCA 1997, s 2(1)*] They are generally a deduction from the profits of trades etc (for corporation tax purposes, they are treated as trading expenses). [*TCA 1997, ss 304(2), 307(2)*] Where income tax profits are insufficient, excess allowances are carried forward [*TCA 1997, s 304(4); FA 2000, s 40(c)*] or may create or augment a loss (see **22** 'Losses'). [*TCA 1997, ss 392, 393*] Apportionment of consideration (including exchanges etc) is made where a lump sum relates to various assets [*TCA 1997, s 311*], subject to a right of appeal. [*TCA 1997, s 314*]

In respect of qualifying hospitals, mental health centres, childcare facilities and the Mid-Shannon Corridor tourism scheme, persons connected with property developers are excluded from claiming capital allowances. [*FA 2008, s 29*]

Lessors. Allowances to lessors are made by discharge or repayment of tax, primarily against income from the letting. [*TCA 1997, ss 278, 300*]

For income tax purposes, excess allowances are either carried forward against future income from the letting or (except as below), on an election within two years after the end of the year of assessment, set against other income of the year of assessment. [*TCA 1997, s 305(1); FA 2000, s 40(d)*] For capital expenditure incurred by lessors on or after 3 December 1997, set-off of industrial buildings allowances (including the special renewal reliefs under **8.10–8.12** below) against other income is restricted as follows (subject to transitional provisions for certain projects either commenced, or for which planning permission had been sought and obligations entered into, before that date or approved for grant assistance by an industrial development agency):

(*a*)   for such expenditure on buildings etc, other than hotels etc within **8.5**(ii) below (for which see (*b*) below) and holiday apartments and other self-catering accommodation in qualifying resort areas (for which full ring-fencing already applies, see **8.11**(*b*) below), set-off against other income for a year of assessment is restricted to €31,750 (£18,500 for 2001, previously £25,000);

(*b*)   for hotels etc within **8.5**(ii) below (but subject to the exclusions listed below), no set-off against other income is permissible. The exclusions are:

   (i)   holiday cottages,

   (ii)   buildings etc (other than holiday camps) in Cavan, Donegal, Leitrim, Mayo, Monaghan, Roscommon or Sligo (unless within a qualifying resort area, see **8.11** below) meeting a standard specified by the Minister for Tourism, Sport and Recreation.

As regards both (*a*) and (*b*) above, similar restrictions apply to inactive partners in partnership businesses for which such allowances are available.

For purchases by individuals of second-hand industrial or deemed industrial buildings, third level educational and childcare facilities from 1 January 2003, the capital allowances on the building may only be set against surplus income from the building where (i) a company was entitled to claim capital allowances on the building on or after 1 January 2003, (ii) the tax life of the building in respect of that work has not expired, and (iii) the individual is taxable under Case V (rental income – see **33** 'Sch D, Case V') on the income from the building. Anti-avoidance measures relating to the use of intermediary vehicles to circumvent this provision are effective from 19 March 2003 (see **20.3** 'Personal interest relief') [*TCA 1997, s 250A; FA 2004, s 22*].

[*TCA 1997, ss 409A, 409B, 409E; FA 1998, s 30; Urban Renewal Act 1998, s 20(1)(c); FA 1999, s 49(a); FA 2000, s 38; FA 2001, s 62(1)(c); FA 2003, s 13*]

Plant in leased buildings. For an article on the manner in which wear and tear allowances are granted in respect of plant in a leased building situated in RI, see Revenue Tax Briefing Issue 42 pp 28, 29.

For company lessors, see **12.9** 'Corporation tax'.

8.2 Anti-avoidance provisions apply to sales of assets:

(*a*) between persons under common control or where one party controls the other; or

(*b*) where sole or main benefit was obtaining capital allowances.

Generally, market value will apply and, for machinery and plant, no initial allowance is claimable by the buyer unless the sale is in ordinary course of seller's business. However, if only (*a*) applies, the parties may elect (provided no allowance or charge accrues to a non-resident) to substitute for market value the written down value, if lower, and any subsequent balancing charge will be made on the buyer as if he had always been the owner. [*TCA 1997, s 312*]

BASIS PERIODS

8.3 Initial allowances and balancing allowances and charges are made in the year of assessment related to the basis period in which the expenditure or sale etc occurred and wear and tear and writing-down allowances are given on assets in use at the end of that period. [*TCA 1997, ss 271(2), 272(2), 274(1), 283(2), 284(1), 288(1)*]

The basis periods for capital allowances follow the appropriate rules of assessment ie under Sch D, normally the current year with provisions for commencement and cessation; under Sch E, the year of assessment; and for corporation tax, the accounting period.

Where:

(*a*) basis periods overlap, the period common to both falls into the first period;

(*b*) there is an interval between basis periods, it forms part of second period, *unless* the business is discontinued or treated as discontinued in second period, in which case the interval is part of the first period.

[*TCA 1997, s 306*]

DREDGING

[*TCA 1997, ss 302, 303*]

8.4 Rates from 1960/61 onwards on capital expenditure incurred after 29 September 1956 are as follows:

(*a*)   **initial allowance** – ten per cent;

(*b*)   **writing-down allowance** – two per cent pa for 50 years subject to restriction on total of initial and writing-down allowances to amount of capital expenditure.

INDUSTRIAL BUILDINGS

[*TCA 1997, Pt 9, Ch 1*]

8.5 Allowances are on capital outlay on construction or refurbishment of a building for use in a trade (or part of a trade):

(i)   carried on in a mill, factory etc, or dock etc (including expenditure on a laboratory mainly concerned with mineral analysis in connection with mineral, including oil and gas, exploration and extraction);

(ii)   of hotel keeping (including use as holiday cottages (but see below for termination) and as a holiday camp and for expenditure incurred from 3 February 2005, guest houses and holiday hostels registered under the Tourist Traffic Acts). For expenditure incurred from 3 February 2005, subject to transitional arrangements (see below) a hotel must be registered under the Tourist Traffic Acts and for expenditure incurred from 25 March 2005, a holiday camp must be registered in a register of holiday camps maintained under the *Tourist Traffic Acts 1939 to 2003*;

(iii) of market gardening;

(iv)   of intensive production of livestock or eggs, other than in the course of farming as defined by *s 654*;

(v)   (for expenditure incurred after 23 April 1992) consisting of the operation or management of an airport, where the building, etc is an airport runway or apron used solely or mainly by aircraft carrying passengers or cargo for hire or reward;

(vi)   (for expenditure incurred after 2 December 1997) consisting of the operation or management of a registered nursing home under *Health (Nursing Homes) Act 1990, s 4* (and expenditure incurred in the five years commencing 25 March 2002 on adjacent 'qualifying residential units' (within *s 268(3A)* as amended by *FA 2004, s 23*) for the aged or infirm, and not wholly or partly met by grant assistance, will qualify for allowances under this heading). The definition for 'qualifying residential unit' is outlined. The qualifying period for this relief has been extended 31 July 2008 to 30 April 2010. The tax life and holding period of residential units for balancing allowance and balancing charge purposes is increased from 15 years to 20 years. The level at which capital expenditure may qualify is capped at 75 per cent for companies and at 50 per cent for individuals. [*FA 2007, s 28*]

In addition to this, the Health Service Executive (HSE) must certify, after first letting, that a residential unit meets the relevant conditions in the legislation. As part of this certification process, information in relation to the investment in the unit has to be provided to the HSE. The information to be provided is as follows:

(I)   the amount of capital expenditure incurred on the construction or refurbishment of the house,

(II)   the number and nature of the investors that are investing in the house,

(III)   the amount invested by each investor,

(IV)   the investors in the residential units certified by the HSE must, on an annual basis, submit a report to the HSE indicating occupancy levels in the residential units,

(V)   the report must also confirm that the units continue to meet the relevant conditions required under the certification provided by the HSE, [*FA 2008, s 28*]

        (see Revenue Tax Briefing Issue 50 pp 5, 6);

(vii)   (for expenditure incurred on or after 27 March 1998 or, in the case of Aer Rianta, the date of transfer of ownership of airport assets to the company) consisting of the operation or management of an airport (and not within (v) above);

(viii) (for expenditure incurred after 1 December 1998) consisting of the operation or management of a convalescent home satisfying certain conditions under the *Health (Nursing Homes) Act 1990*;

(ix)   (for expenditure incurred on or after 15 May 2002 or 28 March 2003 (depending on the nature of the facility) consisting of the operation or management by a charitable body or trust of a private hospital, provided that certain conditions are met (and mental health facilities from a date to be appointed (see *s 268(1A)(2A); FA 2003, s 24; FA 2004, s 24; FA 2006, s 36*); or

(x)   (for expenditure incurred from 15 May 2002 to 31 December 2006 or 31 July 2008 consisting of the operation or management of a sports injuries clinic, provided that certain conditions are met (see *s 268(1B)(2B); FA 2004, s 24; FA 2006, s 28*);

including expenditure on recreational facilities for employees and on site preparation, but excluding expenditure on dwellings (other than holiday cottages within (ii) and qualifying residential units within (vi)), retail shops, offices, etc, land acquisition, plant or machinery (although site preparation costs for installation are allowable), and certain other expenditure attracting other allowances. From 2007, the quantum of allowance available to a high earning individual in any one year may be limited, see **2.45** 'Limitation on Income Tax Relief for High Earners'. [*FA 2006, s 17*]

[*TCA 1997, ss 268, 270; FA 1998, ss 20(a), 22(a); FA 1999, s 48(a); FA 2000, s 36; FA 2001, s 64(1)(a); FA 2002, ss 32, 34; FA 2004, s 25; FA 2005, s 34*]

There is to be a general restriction on the amount of capital expenditure incurred on the construction or refurbishment of certain industrial buildings that qualifies for capital allowances. The restriction applies in the case of hotels, holiday camps, holiday cottages, sports injuries clinics and qualifying residential units associated with registered nursing homes. The restriction operates by providing that only 75 per cent of the capital expenditure attributable to the year 2007 and 50 per cent of the capital expenditure attributable to the period 1 January 2008 to 31 July 2008 qualifies for relief. In the case of qualifying residential units, the 75 per cent restriction for 2007 applies only from 25 March 2007. While, in general, expenditure is treated as incurred on the date on which it becomes due and payable, in deciding for the purposes of the 75 per cent or 50 per cent restrictions whether or not expenditure is incurred in a period, only the amount of expenditure that is attributable to work carried out in the period is taken into account. [*TCA 1997, ss 270, 316*; *FA 2006 s 26*]

Similarly, for expenditure in respect of hotels and holiday cottages to which the extension dates of 31 December 2006 or 31 July 2008 (see below) apply, the expenditure must be attributable to work actually carried out by those dates. [*TCA 1997, s 316; FA 2004, s 25*]

Expenditure incurred **after 22 April 1996** on a building, etc outside RI is excluded, unless it is being, or is to be, constructed for use for a trade the profits or gains from which are taxable in RI and it can be shown that a written contract for acquisition of the site, or a written agreement for an option to acquire it, was made before 24 April 1996, that a written contract for construction was entered into before 2 July 1996, and that construction had commenced before 2 July 1996 and is completed before 30 September 1998. [*TCA 1997, s 268(5); FA 1998, s 19*]

Holiday cottages For construction expenditure incurred **after 3 December 2002**, holiday cottages are no longer to be treated as in use for the purposes of hotel keeping. The termination date is extended to 31 December 2006 for construction or refurbishment expenditure incurred by that date where (to the extent that it is required) a valid planning application for full planning permission is made to the planning authority under the *Planning and Development Regulations 2001* to *2002* by 31 December 2004 and acknowledged by the authority as having been received by that date or has been made under the *Local Government (Planning and Development) Regulations 1994* by 10 March 2002 and acknowledged as having been received by that date. Where the development is an exempted development for planning purposes, the extension date applies where, by 31 December 2004, a detailed plan in relation to the development is prepared, a binding written contract in respect of the expenditure is entered into and work to the value of five per cent of the development cost is carried out. Subject to any conditions which the Minister for Finance may specify in regulations, where the conditions for the extension of the termination date to 31 December 2006 are met, the termination date is further extended to 31 July 2008 where a written binding contract is in place by 31 July 2006 and a local authority certificate issues before 31 March 2007 certifying that 15 per cent of construction expenditure has been incurred by 31 December 2006 and detailing the amount of expenditure incurred by 31 December 2006 and the projected expenditure in the period from 1 January 2007 to 31 July 2008. The amount of expenditure which is taken into account for the period from 1 January 2007 to 31 July 2008 for the purposes of qualifying for capital allowances cannot exceed the projected expenditure as certified by the local authority. This restriction applies before the application of the 75 per cent and 50 per cent restrictions (see below) and where expenditure for the period 1 January 2007 to 31 July 2008 is to be reduced for such purposes, the reduction is to take place in relation to the period 1 January 2008 to 31 July 2008 first. [*FA 2003, s 25; FA 2004, s 25; FA 2006, ss 26, 27*]

Allowances for expenditure incurred after 23 April 1992 on holiday cottages may only be set against income from the lettings (or from the trade for which the cottages are used), unless either (i) the expenditure was incurred before 6 April 1993 and, before 24 April 1992, either the construction work was contracted for or a contract for the lease or purchase of the land entered into and planning permission applied for, or (ii) the cottage was comprised in premises first registered after 5 April 2001 and, prior to registration, qualified for capital allowances under *s 353*, as a qualifying tourism facility in a qualifying resort area (see **8.11**(*b*) below), which allowances were, by virtue of the exceptions in **8.11**(i) and (ii) below, not subject to ring-fencing. [*TCA 1997, s 405; FA 2001, s 62(1)(a)*]

Hotels. For expenditure incurred **after 19 March 2001**, no allowances are available for expenditure on hotels which has been, or is to be, met, directly or indirectly, by grant assistance. Where capital expenditure is incurred on a hotel on construction or refurbishment work commenced after 5 April 2001, allowances are only available where the National Tourism Development Authority (previously, Bord Fáilte Éireann) has given the appropriate certificate in relation to the expenditure. A new *s 268(12A)* was inserted by *Finance (No 2) Act 2008*. This section provided that where there is a requirement to obtain approval from the European Commission for capital allowances for certain hotel projects, the relevant hotel projects do not lose capital allowances because of delays in receiving that approval. If, and when, the approval is received, the capital allowances will apply from the date the building was first used as a hotel following construction or refurbishment. The Commission may impose a ceiling on the amount of expenditure that can qualify for allowances. Where this happens, the amendment also provides that the adjusted expenditure approved by the European Commission will replace the expenditure that would otherwise have qualified for capital allowances. [*TCA 1997, s 268(11),(12),(12A); FA 2001, s 81; FA 2002, s 22; FA 2006, s 127, Sch 2; F(No 2)A 2008, s 22*]

For expenditure incurred from 3 February 2005 on a hotel, the hotel must (subject to transitional provisions) be registered under the Tourist Traffic Acts. The transitional provisions apply to capital expenditure incurred by 31 July 2006 where (to the extent that it is required) a valid planning application for full planning permission is made to the planning authority under the *Planning and Development Regulations 2001 to 2002* by 31 December 2004 and acknowledged by the authority as having been received by that date or has been made under the *Local Government (Planning and Development) Regulations 1994* by 10 March 2002 and acknowledged as having been received by that date. Where the development is an exempted development for planning purposes, the extension date applies where, by 31 December 2004, a detailed plan in relation to the development is prepared, a binding written contract in respect of the expenditure is entered into and work to the value of five per cent of the development cost is carried out. [*FA 2005, s 34*]

Buildings, etc bought *unused* (or, provided that no allowances have previously been claimed, within one year after first use) attract allowances on the cost of construction or the purchase price, whichever is the lesser. *Finance (No 2) Act 2008, s 19* has increased this one year time limit to two years and applies to sales taking place on or after 14 October 2008. If bought from a person who constructed the building as part of his trading activities, the allowance is on the purchase price. Allowances are reduced to the appropriate percentages (see above) for construction expenditure incurred in the period from 1 January 2007 to 31 July 2008. Expenditure on the land and certain other items (eg stamp duty and professional fees) which do not attract industrial buildings allowances are excluded from the cost of construction and, proportionately, from the purchase price. [*TCA 1997, s 279; FA 2006, s 26*]

Part of a building may qualify for allowance where the conditions are met in respect of that part. Where not more than one-tenth of the expenditure on a building relates to parts which do not qualify, the whole of the expenditure qualifies for allowance. [*TCA 1997, ss 268(8), 320(2)*] See also **38.43**, **38.44** 'Tax cases'.

Provision is made for the apportionment of construction expenditure where an industrial building or structure forms part of a building, or part or the whole of a building which is part of a single development consisting of a number of buildings. [*TCA 1997, s 270(3)*]

A building in temporary disuse after use as an industrial building continues to be treated as an industrial building. Where the trade for which it was in use, or the relevant interest, comes to an end during such disuse, allowances are made by way of discharge or repayment of tax and charges are made under Sch D, Case IV (or, where appropriate, allowances and charges are made in charging income under Sch D, Case V). [*TCA 1997, s 280*]

Where any such building is let for use in a trade (or, for expenditure incurred after 28 January 1981, to the Industrial Development Authority, the Shannon Free Airport Development Company Ltd, or Údarás na Gaeltachta, and then under a sub-lease for use in a trade), allowances are similarly available. [*TCA 1997, s 271(1)(2)*]

Allowances are also available on expenditure incurred before 1 April 1991 on the construction of car parks of three or more storeys for general public use. [*TCA 1997, Sch 32 para 9; FA 1981, s 25; FA 1988, s 49*]

Persons holding interests under certain '*property investment schemes*', which provide facilities for the public to share in the profits arising from industrial buildings, etc, are entitled to set their industrial buildings allowances in respect of those interests only against income arising from the interests, and not (where excess allowances arise) against their general income. [*TCA 1997, s 408*]

Room ownership schemes. Anti-avoidance provisions are introduced with effect from 26 March 1997 (subject to transitional provisions) denying industrial buildings allowances in respect of hotel investments by hotel partnerships involving room ownership schemes. [*TCA 1997, s 409*]

Educational institutions. For the period **from 1 July 1997 to 31 December 2006)**, certain expenditure on the construction of buildings for letting to third level educational institutions attracts industrial buildings annual allowances at a special 15 per cent rate (and machinery or plant wear and tear allowances (see **8.6**(*b*) below) may also be available as if the institution was carrying on a trade). No allowances are available unless the Minister for Finance issues a certificate (see below) and no such certificate may be issued unless an application for such certification was made by 31 December 2004 at the latest. Subject to those conditions being satisfied the termination date is further extended to 31 July 2008 where 15 per cent of construction expenditure has been incurred by 31 December 2006. For expenditure incurred during 2007, relief is restricted to 75 per cent of expenditure incurred. For expenditure incurred in the period from 1 January 2008 to 31 July 2008, relief is restricted to 50 per cent of expenditure incurred. In deciding for the purposes of the 75 per cent or 50 per cent restrictions whether or not expenditure is incurred in a period, only the amount of expenditure that is attributable to work carried out in the period is taken into account.

Appropriate certification by the Minister is required for the granting of such allowances, which are dependent on the institution obtaining outside finance of at least one-half of the cost of the construction. The approval powers may be delegated to An tÚdarás, the Higher Education Authority. Only expenditure incurred in respect of work actually carried out during the qualifying period is relieved. **From 2007**, the quantum of relief available to a high earning individual in any one year may be limited, see **2.45** 'Limitation on Income Tax Relief for High Earners'. [*TCA 1997, ss 270, 316, 843; FA 1998, s 44; FA 1999, s 51; FA 2001, s 76; FA 2002, s 35; FA 2004, s 27; FA 2005 s 33b; FA 2006, ss 17, 26, 34*]

Buildings used for childcare purposes. With effect from 2 December 1998, certain expenditure on the construction, conversion or refurbishment of buildings (excluding dwelling houses or parts thereof) for use for the purposes of providing a pre-school service, or such a service combined with a day-care or other service to cater for other children, attracts industrial buildings allowances. The scheme has a termination date of 30 September 2010 unless certain qualifying conditions are met, in which case the termination date can be extended. The qualifying conditions will depend on work carried out and planning permission requirements. Where there is no planning permission required the termination date is 31 March 2011 so long as at least 30 per cent of the construction, conversion or expenditure has been incurred before 30 September 2010. Where planning permission is required, the termination date is 31 March 2011 once a valid application for planning permission is submitted on or before that date and is acknowledged by the relevant planning authority. [*FA 2010, s 26*] For expenditure incurred on or after 1 December 1999:

(*a*)   relief may be obtained for 100 per cent of the expenditure, either by way of an initial 100 per cent allowance or by free depreciation annual allowances; but

(*b*)   allowances are not available where a person whose trade consists wholly or mainly of constructing or refurbishing buildings or structures for sale, or a person connected (within *s 10*) with such a person, incurred the expenditure.

For expenditure incurred before that date, annual allowances were available at a special 15 per cent rate.

A balancing allowance or charge will not arise on a sale etc of a building which, in the case of construction expenditure, is first used on or after 1 February 2007 and, in the case of conversion or refurbishment expenditure, which subsequent to the incurring of that expenditure is first used on or after 1 February 2007, where the sale etc of the building takes place more than 15 years after such first use. [*FA 2006, s 38*]

The premises must meet the requirements of the *Child Care (Pre-School Services) Regulations 1996 (SI 398/96)*. [*TCA 1997, s 843A; FA 1999, s 49(b); FA 2000, s 63*] **From 2007**, the quantum of relief available to a high earning individual in any one year may be limited, see **2.45** 'Limitation on Income Tax Relief for High Earners'. [*FA 2006, s 17*]

Second-hand buildings. For purchases by individuals of second-hand industrial or deemed industrial buildings, third level educational and childcare facilities from 1 January 2003, the capital allowances on the building may only be set against surplus income from the building where (i) a company was entitled to claim capital allowances on the building on or after 1 January 2003, (ii) the tax life of the building in respect of that work has not expired, and (iii) the individual is taxable under Case V (rental income – see **33** 'Sch D, Case V') on the income from the building. [*TCA 1997, s 409E; FA 2003, s 13*]

(*a*)　　**Initial Allowances** (generally abolished after 31 March 1992 but see below) may be claimed in the chargeable period, or its basis period, in which expenditure (net of grants etc) is incurred or, where let, in the chargeable period, or its basis period, in which the tenancy begins. [*TCA 1997, ss 271(1)(2), 317*]

Basic Allowance	10%	
The **increased allowances** are as follows		
Mill, factory etc or dock etc		
Since 14 December 1961	20%	
From 16 January 1975 to **31 March 1996** (but see below)	50%	*
Multi-storey car parks		
From 29 January 1981 to 31 March 1991 (and see **8.10** below)	50%	
Market gardening		
From 6 April 1974 to 31 March 1992	20%	
Livestock production		
From 6 April 1974 to 31 March 1992	20%	

[*ITA 1967, ss 254(2)(2A), 254(2B); FA 1990, s 74(b)*]

* Initial allowances up to 50 per cent continue to be available from 1 April 1992 to 31 December 1995 (or 31 December 1996) for expenditure to which 100 per cent increased writing down allowances continue to be available after 31 March 1988 (see **8.5**(*b*) below). They are further extended to 5 April 1999 in relation to the Temple Bar area (see **8.10** below) and to 24 January 1999 in relation to the Custom House Docks Area and Shannon Airport (see **8.5**(*b*)(i) below).

Initial allowances as above also continue to be available for expenditure incurred:

(i)　　up to 31 December 1997 (31 December 2002 where the company was included on a list of those entitled to 'Section 84A loans', see **12.10**(ii) 'Corporation tax'), extended to 30 June 1998 in certain cases, for a project approved after 31 December 1988 and before 1 January 1991 for grant assistance by the Industrial Development Authority, the Shannon Free Airport Development Co Ltd or Údarás na Gaeltachta, or

(ii)　　up to 31 December 1995 on certain tourist accommodation registered within six months of completion with the National Tourism Development Authority (previously, Bord Fáilte Éireann), provided that a binding contract for the building was entered into before 31 December 1990;

[*TCA 1997, ss 271(3)(4), 331, 368; FA 1988, s 51(4); FA 1990, s 81; FA 1995, ss 26, 27; FA 1996, s 27; FA 1997, ss 52–54; FA 1988, s 21(a); FA 2006, s 127, Sch 2*] (*b*) **Writing-down allowances**

These are available to the person entitled to the 'relevant interest' in an industrial building or structure on which allowable capital expenditure has been incurred after 29 September 1956. An allowance may be claimed annually while the building or structure remains in use as specified, and where a building qualifying as a hotel is converted for use as a qualifying nursing home this change of use is in effect disregarded. See below for the percentages applicable to the expenditure (net of any grants, etc) and periods when available. The total allowances claimed must not exceed 100 per cent of the expenditure. Following the sale of an industrial building or structure, the residue of expenditure is relieved over the remainder of the original period during which writing-down allowances were to be given. [*TCA 1997, s 272; FA 1998, ss 18(b), 22(b)*] No allowance is generally available for a chargeable period for which an initial allowance (see (*a*) above) is made (but see **8.10** below as regards certain urban renewal relief allowances).**From 2007**, the relief available in any year may be limited, see **2.45** 'Limitation on Income Tax Relief for High Earners'. [*TCA 1997, s 271(5)*]

Basic allowance –	2% pa for 50 years

It is increased to **four per cent pa for 25 years** for expenditure from 16 January 1975. Other **increased allowances** are as follows:

Mill, factory etc or dock etc

Expenditure from 2 February 1978

„	to 31 March 1988	up to 100% pa*
„	from 1 April 1988 to 31 March 1989	up to 75% pa*
„	from 1 April 1989 to 31 March 1991	up to 50% pa*
„	from 1 April 1991 to 31 March 1992	up to 25% pa*

Hotels etc

Expenditure after 31 December 1959 (ceases for holiday cottages in respect of expenditure incurred from (a) 4 December 2002 (b) 1 January 2007 or (c) 1 August 2008**)		10% pa for 10 years
Expenditure (not holiday cottages)	from 27 January 1994 to (a) 3 December 2002 (b) 31 December 2006 or (c) 31 July 2008**	15% pa for 7 years
Expenditure (not holiday cottages)	From (a) 4 December 2002 (b) 1 January 2007 or (c) 1 August 2008**	4% pa for 25 years
Expenditure from 3 February 2005 on holiday hostels and guest houses		4% pa for 25 years

Market gardening – expenditure after 5 April 1964

Expenditure from 6 April 1966	10% pa for 10 years

Livestock production – expenditure after 5 April 1971

Expenditure from 6 April 1974	10% pa for 10 years

Nursing homes and convalescent facilities

Expenditure from 3 December 1997 (nursing homes), 2 December 1998 (convalescent facilities), 15 May 2002 (qualifying hospitals) or a date to be appointed (mental health facilities)	15% pa for 7 years
Sports Injuries Clinics (expenditure from 15 May 2002 to (a) 31 December 2006 or (b) 31 July 2008 ***)	15% pa for 7 years

Finance Act 2009 made amendments to *s 268*. The amendments provide that certain schemes that were previously open-ended in relation to incurring qualifying expenditure for capital allowances purposes now have a termination date of 31 December 2009, unless certain qualifying criteria are met, in which case the termination date for qualifying expenditure on pipeline projects is extended. Subsection (9) of that section outlines the dates within which such qualifying expenditure must be incurred.

Termination dates beyond 31 December 2009 will only apply where certain qualifying conditions are met by that date. The qualifying conditions depend on the type of work to be carried out and whether or not the work requires planning permission. Where the work to be carried out does not require planning permission, the termination date is 30 June 2010 so long as at least 30 per cent of the construction or refurbishment costs has been incurred on or before 31 December 2009. Where planning permission is required in relation to the work to be carried out, the qualifying condition for a termination date beyond 31 December 2009 is that a valid application for full planning permission be submitted on or before that date, and be acknowledged by the relevant planning authority. In such cases, the termination date for qualifying expenditure is 30 June 2011 in the case of registered nursing homes, convalescent homes and mental health centres and 31 December 2013 in the case of qualifying hospitals.

The amendment to *s 316* ensures that, in relation to these types of facilities, the normal rule about capital expenditure being incurred when it is payable is disregarded and, instead, expenditure is treated as incurred when it is properly attributable to construction or refurbishment work that has actually been carried out:

> The four per cent rate applies to airport buildings etc in use for a trade within (vii) above for expenditure incurred from 27 March 1998 but, in the case of Aer Rianta, for expenditure incurred from 1 January 1999, the date of transfer of ownership of airport assets to the company. Also, in the case of Aer Rianta in relation to buildings etc in existence on 1 January 1999 (not being machinery or plant), four per cent writing-down allowances apply by reference to deemed expenditure on the commencement date of the original construction expenditure reduced by notional writing-down allowances for the period up to that date.

> *Only available where the person incurring the expenditure actually occupies the building. There is an additional requirement in the case of hotels that the premises must be registered with the National Tourism Development Authority (previously Bord Fáilte Éireann). The 100 per cent increased allowance continues to be available after 31 March 1988 on expenditure:

> (i)   relating to certain activities in Shannon Airport or the Custom House Docks Area (see **12.18** 'Corporation tax'),

> (ii)   relating to certain other qualifying premises (see **8.10** below),

(iii)   incurred before 31 December 1995 for a project approved by an industrial development agency before 1 January 1986,

(iv)   incurred before 31 December 1996 for a project approved by an industrial development agency after 31 December 1985 but before 1 January 1989, or

(v)   incurred before 31 December 1995 under a binding contract entered into before 28 January 1988.

For other expenditure incurred after 31 March 1988, increased allowances are not available for chargeable periods ending after 5 April 1999 or where an initial allowance has been made (see (*a*) above).

50 per cent allowances continue to be available after 31 March 1991 for expenditure incurred:

(i)   up to 31 December 1997 (or 31 December 2002 where the company was included on a list of those entitled to 'Section 84A loans' – see **12.10**(ii) 'Corporation tax'), extended to 30 June 1998 in certain cases, for a project approved after 31 December 1988 and before 1 January 1991 for grant assistance by the Industrial Development Authority, the Shannon Free Airport Development Co Ltd or Údarás na Gaeltachta, or

(ii)   up to 31 December 1995 on certain tourist accommodation registered within six months of completion with the National Tourism Development Authority (previously Bord Fáilte Éireann), provided that a binding contract for the provision of the building was entered into before 31 December 1990.

[*TCA 1997, ss 272(3)(3A), 273; FA 1998, ss 18(b), 21(a), 22(b); FA 1999, s 48(b); FA 2001, s 64(1)(b); FA 2003, s 25; FA 2006, s 127, Sch 2*]

No initial allowance is available for expenditure incurred after 5 April 1989 for a chargeable period for which accelerated writing-down allowances are claimed or for any subsequent chargeable period. [*TCA 1997, s 273(8)*]

In the case of an industrial building outside the scope of *s 272* above which is used by the owner for business purposes, five-twelfths of the rateable valuation may be deducted from profits. [*TCA 1997, s 85*]

**31 December 2006 applies to construction or refurbishment expenditure incurred by that date, where (to the extent required) a valid planning application for full planning permission under the *Planning and Development Regulations 2001 to 2002* is made to the planning authority by 31 December 2004 and acknowledged by the authority as having been received by that date or (to the extent required) a valid planning application under the *Local Government (Planning and Development) Regulations 1994* was made by 10 March 2002 and acknowledged by the authority as having been received by that date or the development is one to which a valid application for a certificate under *Dublin Docklands Development Act 1997, s 25(7)(a)(ii)* is made to the Authority by 31 December 2004 and acknowledged as received by the Authority by that date. Where the development is an exempted development for planning purposes, the later date applies where, by 31 December 2004, a detailed plan in relation to the development is prepared, a binding written contract in respect of the expenditure is entered into and work to the value of five per cent of the development cost is carried out. [*FA 2003, s 25; FA 2004, s 25*]

31 July 2008 applies to construction or refurbishment expenditure incurred by that date, subject to any conditions which the Minister for Finance may specify in regulations, where the conditions for the extension to 31 December 2006 (see above) are met, where a written binding contract is in place by 31 July 2006 and a local authority certificate issues before 31 March 2007 certifying that 15 per cent of construction expenditure has been incurred before 31 December 2006 and detailing the amount of expenditure incurred by 31 December 2006 and the projected expenditure in the period from 1 January 2007 to 31 July 2008. As already indicated, the expenditure on which allowances are available in the case of hotels, holiday camps, holiday cottages, sports injuries clinics and qualifying residential units associated with registered nursing homes for the period from 1 January 2007 to 31 July 2008 is restricted. For expenditure incurred during 2007, relief is restricted to 75 per cent of expenditure incurred. For expenditure incurred in the period from 1 January 2008 to 31 July 2008, relief is restricted to 50 per cent of expenditure incurred. The amount of expenditure which is taken into account for the period from 1 January 2007 to 31 July 2008 for the purposes of qualifying for capital allowances in the case of hotels, holiday camps and holiday cottages cannot exceed the projected expenditure as certified by the local authority. This restriction applies before the application of the 75 per cent and 50 per cent restrictions and where expenditure for the period 1 January 2007 to 31 July 2008 is to be reduced for such purposes, the reduction is to take place in relation to the period 1 January 2008 to 31 July 2008 first. [*FA 2006, ss 26, 27*]

*** The termination date is extended to 31 July 2008 where at least 15 per cent of construction or refurbishment cost is incurred by 31 December 2006. As previously indicated, for expenditure incurred during 2007, relief is restricted to 75 per cent of expenditure incurred, while for expenditure incurred in the period from 1 January 2008 to 31 July 2008, relief is restricted to 50 per cent of expenditure incurred; [*FA 2006, ss 26, 28*]

(*c*) **Balancing allowances or charges** may apply on sale, etc of buildings which have at any time attracted industrial buildings allowances. Any consideration, other than rent or a premium to be treated or partly treated as rent, received by the person entitled to the relevant interest in the building in respect of an interest subject to that relevant interest, also gives rise to a balancing adjustment (although no balancing allowance is available where an inferior interest in a building is disposed of after 4 March 2001). Balancing adjustments do not apply where the event, which would otherwise give rise to an adjustment, occurs **after** the end of the writing-down period for the building or after a specified period in some cases. The extent of the period (commonly called the 'tax life') depends on the type of building involved and the time when the expenditure on its construction or refurbishment was incurred. The tax life runs from, in the case of construction expenditure, the time when the building was first used and, in the case of refurbishment expenditure, the time when the building was first used subsequent to the incurring of that expenditure. The tax life of mills, factories, mineral laboratories and dock undertakings is 25 years from first use (or, where the expenditure was incurred before 16 January 1975, 50 years from first use). The tax life of market garden buildings, buildings used for the intensive production of cattle, etc, holiday cottages and sports injuries clinics is 10 years from first use. For private hospitals, nursing homes (including associated residential units for the aged or infirm), convalescent homes and childcare facilities the tax life is 15 years from first use, or 10 years from first use where first use is before 1 February 2007. For mental health centres the tax life is 15 years from first use, while for buildings used for third-level education it is 7 years from first use. In the case of an airport runway or an airport apron, the tax life is 25 years from first use or, in the case of Aer Rianta and airport runways and aprons existing on 1 January 1999, 25 years from 1 January, 1999. For other categories of airport buildings the tax life is 25 years after the building was first used in the case of new expenditure. For airport buildings existing on 1 January 1999 in the case of Aer Rianta, and in existence on 27 March 1998 in the case of other airport operators, the tax life is 25 years after 1 January 1999 or 27 March 1998, as appropriate.

In the case of holiday hostels and guest houses, the tax life is 25 years from first use. For hotels and holiday camps the tax life is 10 years from first use where the capital expenditure was incurred before 27 January 1994, 7 years from first use where the capital expenditure was incurred on or after 27 January 1994, and 25 years from first use where the capital expenditure is incurred on or after 4 December 2002 [or, subject to transitional arrangements, on or after 31 December 2006 or 31 July 2008]. The increase in the tax life of hotels and holiday camps to 25 years will not apply as respects capital expenditure incurred on the construction or refurbishment of a building by 31 December 2006, where (to the extent required) a valid planning application for full planning permission under the *Planning and Development Regulations 2001 to 2002* is made to the planning authority by 31 December 2004 and acknowledged by the authority as having been received by that date or (to the extent required) a valid planning application under the *Local Government (Planning and Development) Regulations 1994* was made by 10 March 2002 and acknowledged by the authority as having been received by that date, or the development is one to which a valid application for a certificate under *Dublin Docklands Development Act 1997, s 25(7)(a)(ii)* is made to the Authority by 31 December 2004 and acknowledged as received by the Authority by that date. Where the development is an exempted development for planning purposes, the 31 December 2006 date applies where, by 31 December 2004, a detailed plan in relation to the development is prepared, a binding written contract in respect of the expenditure is entered into and work to the value of five per cent of the development cost is carried out.

For hotels and holiday camps, further transitional arrangements apply in that, subject to any conditions which the Minister for Finance may specify in regulations, where the conditions for the extension to 31 December 2006 (see above) are met, the increase in the tax life to 25 years will not apply as respects capital expenditure incurred on construction or refurbishment by 31 July 2008, where a written binding contract is in place by 31 July 2006 and a local authority certificate issues before 31 March 2007 certifying that 15 per cent of construction expenditure has been incurred by 31 December 2006 and detailing the amount of expenditure incurred by 31 December 2006 and the projected expenditure in the period from 1 January 2007 to 31 July 2008. [*FA 2006, s 27*]

A balancing charge arises on certain buildings first used (or first used after refurbishment) on or after 1 January 2006 that subsequently cease to be used for their original purpose. The buildings ('relevant facilities') concerned are registered nursing homes, qualifying residential units, convalescent homes, qualifying private hospitals, qualifying mental health centres and certain childcare facilities. A balancing charge arises unless another 'relevant facility' is commenced in the building within six months of the cessation. [*FA 2006, s 39*] From 2007, the quantum of balancing allowance relieved in any one year may be limited, see **2.45** 'Limitation on Income Tax Relief for High Earners'. [*TCA 1997, ss 274, 276; FA 1998, ss 20(c), 22(c); FA 1999, s 48(c); FA 2001, ss 54, 64(1)(c); FA 2003, s 25, FA 2004, s 25; FA 2006, ss 17, 35–39*] See *TCA 1997, s 275* for restriction of balancing allowances on sales between connected persons.

It is understood that, by concession, balancing charges arising after cessation of a trade may be offset by unused trading losses and capital allowances in that trade.

Finance Act 2011, s 23 has introduced various changes to the availability of accelerated capital allowances as an offset against income and also the ability to carry forward unused allowances indefinitely. A new *TCA 1997, Pt 12, Ch 4A* which is deals with loss relief and capital allowances. Two separate changes are introduced with effect from a date to be specified by order of the Minister for Finance which cannot be earlier than 60 days after the publication of the impact assessment into this issue as mentioned in the Budget 2011). This date is called the relevant day. The first change narrows the range of income to which the allowances may apply, while the second curtails the ability of a person to carry-forward unused allowances beyond certain deadlines. These measures only apply to accelerated capital allowances arising under the various area and property-based tax incentive schemes and only to persons who are passive investors in the relevant businesses. (ie urban and renewal property reliefs.)

[*TCA 1997, ss 323, 331, 332, 341, 342, 343, 344, 352, 353, 372C, 372D, 372M, 372N, 372V, 372W, 372AC or 372AD*]

MACHINERY AND PLANT (INCLUDING SHIPS)

8.6 For the meaning of 'plant', see **38.35–38.42** 'Tax cases'. With effect from 23 May 1994, where a right to use or deal with computer software is acquired for trade purposes, then for capital allowance purposes the right and the software are regarded as machinery or plant provided for trade purposes and belonging to the person entitled to the right. Similarly computer software acquired for trade purposes (or, from 6 April 1994, for the purposes of a profession, employment or office) which would not otherwise constitute machinery or plant is treated as such. [*TCA 1997, ss 291, 301*] In respect of machinery and plant provided for use after 5 April 1996, capital expenditure is incurred on the day on which it becomes due and payable, and does not include any expenditure deductible in computing trading profits or gains. [*TCA 1997, s 316*]

See **8.18** in relation to the new scheme of capital allowances on the acquisition of intangible assets by companies:

(*a*) **Initial Allowances (generally abolished after 31 March 1992** [*ITA 1967, s 251*] but see below) may be claimed in the chargeable period or its basis period in which the capital expenditure was incurred on new machinery etc (not cars, lorries etc but including used and secondhand ships) for trades or professions. [*TCA 1997, s 283*] Initial allowances and 'free depreciation' allowances (see (*b*) below) cannot be claimed on the same expenditure. [*TCA 1997, s 285(8)*]

Basic allowance — 20%

This applies to expenditure between 6 April 1956 and 13 December 1961.
The **increased allowances** are as follows

From 14 December 1961	–	40%
From 1 April 1967	–	50%
From 1 April 1968	–	60%
From 1 April 1971 to 31 March 1988	–	100%
From 1 April 1988 to 31 March 1989	–	75%
From 1 April 1989 to 31 March 1991	–	50%
From 1 April 1991 to 31 March 1992	–	25%

The 100 per cent increased allowance continues to be available after 31 March 1988 on expenditure:

(i) relating to certain activities in Shannon Airport or the Custom House Docks Area (see **12.18** 'Corporation tax'),

(ii) relating to certain other qualifying premises (see **8.10** below),

(iii) incurred before 31 December 1995 for a project approved by an industrial development agency before 1 January 1986,

(iv) incurred before 31 December 1996 for a project approved by an industrial development agency after 31 December 1985 but before 1 January 1989,

(v) incurred before 31 December 1995 under a binding contract entered into before 28 January 1988, or

(vi) in a hotel-keeping trade where a binding contract for the provision of the building was entered into after 27 January 1988 and before 1 June 1988.

[*TCA 1997, s 283(3)(4); FA 1988, s 51; FA 1990, s 80; FA 1993, s 33; FA 1995, s 26; FA 1996, s 43*]

50 per cent increased allowances continue to be available after 31 March 1991 on expenditure:

(1) incurred up to 31 December 1997 (31 December 2002 where the company was included on a list of those entitled to 'Section 84A loans'

(see **12.10(ii)** 'Corporation tax')), extended to 30 June 1998 in certain cases, for a project approved after 31 December 1988 and before 1 January 1991 for grant assistance by the Industrial Development Authority, the Shannon Free Airport Development Co Ltd or Údarás na Gaeltachta, or

(2)   incurred up to 31 December 1995 on certain tourist accommodation registered within six months of completion with the National Tourism Development Authority (previously Bord Fáilte Éireann), provided that a binding contract for the provision of the building was entered into before 31 December 1990;

[*TCA 1997, s 283(3)(5); FA 1978, s 25; FA 1990, s 81; FA 1995, s 27; FA 1998, s 21(b); FA 2006, s 127, Sch 2*]

(*b*) **Wear and Tear Allowances**

Machinery and plant (new or used) provided for use after 31 March 1992 attracts a fixed annual wear and tear allowance on a straight-line basis for any chargeable period at the end of which the machinery, etc, is in use for trade purposes, provided that it has not been used other than for trade purposes. Allowances cannot in total exceed cost.

For expenditure incurred **from 4 December 2002 (or 1 February 2003** where transitional measures apply), except in the case of taxis and hire-cars or whitefish fishing boats (see below), the allowance is 12.5 per cent. Transitional measures apply where a written contract relating to the expenditure was entered into before 4 December 2002.

For expenditure incurred **from 1 January 2001 to 31 December 2002 (or 31 January 2003** where the above transitional measures apply), except in the case of taxis and hire-cars or whitefish fishing boats (see below), the allowance is 20 per cent.

For expenditure before 1 January 2001 (except in the case of cars, lorries, taxis and hire-cars or whitefish fishing boats, see below), the allowance is 15 per cent. For any chargeable period ending after 31 December 2001, however, an election may be made to bring within the regime for 1 January 2001 to 31 December 2002 (or 31 January 2003) all pre-1 January 2001 expenditure (other than on whitefish fishing boats), and all expenditure within those dates on taxis and hire-cars, for which an allowance is due for that period. 20 per cent straight-line allowances will then be available on the tax written-down value (ie the expenditure incurred less any allowances previously given). The election is irrevocable and must be included in the appropriate return for the first chargeable period or year of assessment to which it is to apply.

The allowance is proportionately reduced for chargeable or basis periods of less than twelve months. No allowance may be claimed for a chargeable period for which an initial allowance is made. No allowance may be claimed for expenditure on the construction of an industrial building or structure (or deemed industrial building or structure) (see **8.5** above).

Before 1 April 1992

New machinery etc (other than cars, lorries and ships)	–	10%, 121/2% and 25% pa on a reducing balance basis according to the nature of the asset.
Used and older assets	–	Various rates as for earlier periods.

No allowance may be claimed for expenditure incurred after 31 March 1989 for a chargeable period for which an initial allowance (see (*a*) above) is made unless the expenditure qualifies for the continuation of 100 per cent increased allowances (see below and (*a*) above).

For chargeable periods ending on or after 6 April 1996, such machinery and plant is brought within the 15 per cent straight-line allowances applicable to all machinery and plant provided for use after 31 March 1992 (but with the exceptions to those allowances for cars and lorries), by reference to written-down value at the end of the preceding chargeable period.

[*TCA 1997, ss 283(6), 284; ITA 1967, s 241; FA 1989, s 13; FA 1990, s 70; FA 1992, s 26; FA 1996, Sch 5 para 1(12)(a); FA 1997, Sch 9 para 1(16); FA 2001, s 53, Sch 2 para 19; FA 2002, s 31(1); FA 2003, s 23*]

See **8.5** above as regards certain machinery and plant provided for use in third level educational institutions.

Free depreciation

These accelerated allowances are generally abolished after 31 March 1992 and for chargeable periods ending after 5 April 1999 (but see below). [*TCA 1997, s 285(1)–(3)*]

Free depreciation applies to new machinery etc (other than cars and lorries but including ships) provided for use as follows:

From 1 April 1971 to 31 March 1988	–	up to 100%*
From 1 April 1988 to 31 March 1989	–	up to 75%
From 1 April 1989 to 31 March 1991	–	up to 50%
From 1 April 1991 to 31 March 1992	–	up to 25%

*The 100 per cent or 50 per cent allowance will continue to be available for expenditure for which a 100 per cent or 50 per cent initial allowance would have continued to be available (see (*a*) above). [*TCA 1997, s 285; FA 1998, s 21(b)*]

Free depreciation is also claimable, where available, on (for chargeable periods ending before 6 April 1999) new machinery (other than cars, lorries etc) purchased before 1 April 1971 but after 31 March 1967 for use in 'designated area' (as defined). [*TCA 1997, s 285(1)*]

Free depreciation and initial allowances (see (*a*) above) may not be claimed on the same expenditure. [*TCA 1997, s 283(6)*]

Cars and lorries. For expenditure incurred on or after 1 January 2001, cars and lorries are subject to the normal wear and tear allowances described above (ie annual allowances of 12.5 per cent or 20 per cent on a straight line basis, not in total exceeding cost). For expenditure incurred before 1 January 2001 (and subject to the election referred to above to bring all such expenditure within the new regime), they are rated at 20 per cent pa on a reducing balance basis. There is, however, a continuing restriction on the cost of passenger vehicles that may be taken into account for allowance purposes. The restricted figure of €23,000 was increased to €24,000 for cars bought on or after 1 January 2007 and up to 30 June 2008. The restricted capital cost that applies as of 1 July 2008 depends on which Group the car falls within. Cars are grouped by reference to carbon emissions. Group 1 contains categories A, B and C with Co2 emissions up to and including 155g/km. The allowable expenditure is €24,000 regardless of the cost of the car. Group 2 contains categories D and E with Co2 emissions from 156g/kg up to and including 190g/km. The allowable expenditure is 50 per cent of the relevant specified limit (ie €24,000) or 50 per cent of the actual cost of the car. Group 3 contains categories F and G with Co2 emissions that exceed 190g/km. There is no entitlement to wear and tear allowances for this group. Allowances for expenditure incurred in an accounting period ending after 31 December 2005, or in a basis period for 2006 or a later year of assessment, on new or second-hand vehicles costing over €23,000 are restricted as if the actual cost was €23,000. For accounting periods ending after 31 December 2002 and before 1 January 2006 and basis periods for 2002 to 2005, the figure is €22,000. For accounting periods ending after 31 December 2000 and basis periods ending after that date for 2000/01 or 2001, the figure is £17,000. For new vehicles, the limit was £16,500 for earlier expenditure incurred after 30 November 1999, £16,000 from 2 December 1998 to 30 November 1999, £15,500 from 3 December 1997 to 1 December 1998, £15,000 from 23 January 1997 to 2 December 1997, £14,000 from 9 February 1995 to 22 January 1997, £13,000 from 27 January 1994 to 8 February 1995, £10,000 from 30 January 1992 to 26 January 1994, £7,000 from 26 January 1989 to 29 January 1992, £6,000 from 28 January 1988 to 25 January 1989, £4,000 from 6 April 1986 to 27 January 1988, previously £3,500. The increases from £16,000 to £16,500, from £15,500 to £16,000, from £15,000 to £15,500, from £14,000 to £15,000, from £13,000 to £14,000 and from £10,000 to £13,000 apply only to new vehicles registered on or after 1 December 1999, 2 December 1998, 3 December 1997, 23 January 1997, 9 February 1995 and 27 January 1994 respectively. For second-hand cars as at each of those dates, the limit remained at £10,000. For all dates on which an increase applied other than 23 January 1997, 3 December 1997, 2 December 1998 and 1 December 1999, the increase did not apply in relation to expenditure incurred in the twelve months following each of those dates under a contract entered into before the date. Similar restrictions apply for renewal allowances, hire purchase and hiring charges. [*TCA 1997, ss 284(2), 373–380; FA 1998, s 29(a); FA 1999, s 53(a); FA 2000, s 35(a); FA 2001, s 61(1)(a); FA 2002, s 28(1)(a); FA 2006, s 21*]

The Euro equivalents of the various limits above are as follows:

| £17,000 | €21,585.55 |
| £16,500 | €20,950.68 |

£16,000	€20,315.81
£15,500	€19,680.94
£15,000	€19,046.07
£14,000	€17,776.33
£13,000	€16,506.60
£10,000	€12,697.38
£7,000	€8,888.17
£6,000	€7,618.43
£4,000	€5,078.95
£3,500	€4,444.08

Taxis and hire-cars. Subject to the election referred to above, the wear and tear allowance is increased from 20 per cent to 40 per cent pa for taxis and for cars let on short-term hire, ie on self-drive hire under agreements of eight weeks or less (with provisions to prevent consecutive lets to the same or connected persons). The conditions as to use must be satisfied for at least 75 per cent of the time for which the vehicle is in use or available for use (although the qualifying usage may drop to 50 per cent or more for a chargeable period provided that the 75 per cent level was satisfied in either the immediately preceding or in the immediately succeeding chargeable period). [*TCA 1997, s 286*]

Taxi licences. Expenditure incurred before 22 November 2000 on the acquisition of a taxi licence (or wheelchair accessible taxi licence), by an individual carrying on a carriage trade in the vehicle to which the licence relates, is deemed to have been incurred on 21 November 1997 (or the date the trade commenced if later) and attracts wear and tear allowances at the general 20 per cent rate referred to above but with effect from the date the expenditure is treated as having been incurred. There is restricted relief for expenditure on licences for vehicles used partly for a carriage trade and partly for letting, and special provision is made in relation to certain inherited licences. [*TCA 1997, s 286A; FA 2001, s 51*]

Whitefish fishing boats. The wear and tear allowance for registered sea fishing boats, for expenditure in the six years commencing on 4 September 1998, is increased to:

(i)   50 per cent of the capital expenditure (including on renewal, improvement or reinstatement) in the first chargeable or basis period at the end of which the boat belongs to the claimant and is in use for the purposes of his trade, and

(ii)   either (*a*) 15 per cent of the balance of that expenditure after deducting that part relieved under (i) above in each of the next six years, and ten per cent thereof in the following year, or (*b*) for expenditure incurred on or after 24 March 2004, 20 per cent of that balance in each of the next five years, allowances for chargeable or basis periods of less than one year being correspondingly reduced. The expenditure must be certified by Bord Iascaigh Mhara as capital expenditure incurred for the purposes of fleet renewal in the polyvalent and beam trawl segments of the fishing fleet. [*TCA 1997, s 284(3A); FA 1998, s 23(a); FA 2001, s 52, Sch 2 para 19; SI 321/98; SI 124/04*]

As regards both (*a*) and (*b*), expenditure incurred after 28 January 1986 is for allowance purposes taken as net of any grants, etc received, unless the terms of the agreement for the grant, etc were finally approved on or before 29 January 1986 or were under negotiation on that date and are finally approved before 1 January 1987. Allowances for actual expenditure by a company carrying on a food processing trade on food processing machinery or plant for use only in that trade are, however, given without taking account of any grant, etc received; [*TCA 1997, s 317*]

(*c*) **Investment Allowances** were also available (and not deductible in calculating initial or wear and tear allowances or free depreciation) on *new* machinery etc (not cars and lorries) for use in a 'designated area' (as defined in the *Industrial Development Act 1969*). The allowance was calculated on the cost less any grant, etc received, and was withdrawn if the asset was sold without being used for the trade, etc or within two years of first being so used.

From 1 April 1971 to 31 December 1980 – 20 per cent

[*FA 1971, ss 22–26; CTA 1976, Sch 1 paras 57–60; FA 1977, s 37; FA 1979, s 24*]

New ships purchased from 6 April 1957 to 23 July 1973 attracted an investment allowance of ten per cent. This was withdrawn if the ship was not used in trade or sold within five years of commencement of use. [*ITA 1967, ss 246–250; FA 1973, s 8; FA 1975, s 8; CTA 1976, Sch 1 paras 11–14; FA 1977, s 38; FA 1978, s 23*]

See also **38.41**'Tax cases';

(*d*) **Balancing allowances or charges** arise on sale or cessation of use, etc [*TCA 1997, s 288 et seq*] For special provisions relating to computer software, see *TCA 1997, s 288(1)(d), (3A), (4)(c); FA 2000, s 41*.

With effect from 1 January 2002, however, no balancing charge will be made where the proceeds of disposal, etc are less than €2,000, provided that the disposal is not to a connected person (within *TCA 1997, s 10*). [*TCA 1997, s 288(3B); FA 2002, s 31(2)*]

An election may be made to deduct a balancing charge on old machinery from the cost of new machinery replacing it. [*TCA 1997, s 290*]

A new section has been introduced [*TCA 1997, s 308A*] to provide that the transfer of trade assets in the course of a merger will not give rise to a balancing charge. The company acquiring the trade will be entitled to claim the same capital allowances as the company from which the trade was transferred. This provision ensures that Irish tax legislation accords with the provisions of the *EU Mergers Directive (Council Directive 2009/133/EC of 19 October 2009)*. [*FA 2010, s 51*]

A balancing charge arising on compensation for the decommissioning of a fishing vessel may be spread over a period of five years in line with the European Communities initiative concerning compensation for the decommissioning of fishing vessels. [*FA 2008, s 30*]

If any grant, etc is received in respect of wear and tear, for the purpose of determining a balancing allowance or charge a wear and tear allowance is treated as having been made in the chargeable period of the disposal, etc to the extent that the grant has not already been deducted from the expenditure. [*TCA 1997, s 297*] It is, however, understood that in practice the Revenue will not apply this so as to reduce a written-down value on disposal, etc below zero.

Where the proceeds, etc consist of payments under the EC scheme for decommissioning fishing vessels, any balancing charge is spread equally over three successive years commencing with the year of disposal. [*TCA 1997, s 288(6)*]

LEASING OF MACHINERY OR PLANT

8.7 For accounting periods ending on or after 4 February 2004, the tax treatment of short-term finance leases (not exceeding eight years) for company lessors may follow the accounting treatment (the interest element of the payment is taxed and no capital allowances are available) if the company lessor so claims. This treatment applies only in respect of assets having a useful predictable life of no more than eight years and the expenditure for which is incurred in the accounting period for which a claim for the application of the section is made. A claim must be made by the return filing date for that accounting period. Where no claim is made, the provisions relating to a separate trade of leasing apply as set out below. Amendments have been made to *s 299* and *s 80A* so as to:

(i)   eliminate any tax mismatch between the amount treated as income by the lessor and the amount deducted as an expense by the lessee, and

(ii)   to ensure that only one party to a lease can claim the benefit of capital allowances.

The section provides that lessees can only claim capital allowances where the lessor has made a claim under *s 80A* and also aligns the tax treatment of such lessors with the lessees to whom they lease the assets. *s 80A* has also been amended so as to enable a lessor company, engaged in the leasing of short-life assets by way of an operating lease, to elect to be taxed on the accounting profit from those leases. Where a lessor elects for this treatment, the new provisions will apply to operating leases of short-life assets which are in excess of a threshold amount. Where the lessor is a member of a group, this threshold amount is calculated on a group basis and represents the total value of all short-life assets let on an operating lease which are owned by the group at the end of the accounting period preceding the accounting period for which the election will apply.

FA 2011, s 27 has abolished, with effect from 1 January 2011, the 20 per cent investment allowance in respect of mineral exploration expenditure provided for under *TCA 1997, s 677* and the 20 per cent allowance for capital expenditure on new machinery and plant provided for under *TCA 1997, s 678* for the purposes of a trade of working a qualifying mine. *[FA 2011, s 27]*

[*TCA 1997, s 80A; FA 2004, s 35, FA 2010, s 52*]

Separate trade of leasing. Where machinery or plant or a film is, after 24 January 1984, provided for a trade of leasing, relief for capital allowances thereon (see **8.6** above) is restricted as below, unless the expenditure on its provision (or the cost of making the film) is either:

(i)   met wholly or partly, directly or indirectly, by the Industrial Development Authority, the Irish Film Board, the Shannon Free Airport Development Company Limited or Údarás na Gaeltachta;

(ii)   incurred under an obligation entered into before 25 January 1984; or

(iii)   incurred under an obligation entered into before 1 March 1984, pursuant to negotiations in progress before 26 January 1984.

The exclusion at (i) ceases to apply to expenditure on machinery or plant, other than a film, provided for leasing after 12 May 1986, unless it is under an obligation entered into either before 13 May 1986, or before 1 September 1986 pursuant to negotiations in progress before 13 May 1986. However, for expenditure incurred on the provision of machinery or plant (other than a film) for leasing after 12 May 1986 (and not under an obligation entered into before 13 May 1986, or before 1 September 1986 pursuant to negotiations in progress before 13 May 1986), a further exclusion from the restriction applies where the terms of the lease (provided that it is not between connected persons, as specially defined) include an undertaking that, during a period of at least three years following first use of the machinery or plant by the lessee, it will be used only for the purposes of a 'specified trade' carried on in RI by the lessee or his successor and, where it is provided for leasing after 3 March 1998, will not be used for any other trade, or business or activity other than the lessor's trade, except a 'specified trade' carried on by the lessor. A *'specified trade'* means a trade at least 75 per cent of whose turnover during the period of restriction under the undertaking derives from a trade consisting (or treated as consisting) of the manufacture of goods (see **12.18** 'Corporation tax'). There are provisions to correct the situation where it appears to the inspector (or, on appeal, to the Appeal Commissioners) that the undertaking has not been fulfilled.

Where a trade ceased to be a specified trade by virtue of the exclusions from manufacturing companies' relief in *FA 1990, s 41(1)* or *FA 1994, s 48(1)* (see **12.18** 'Corporation tax'), it is treated as continuing to be a specified trade in relation to expenditure incurred before 20 April 1990 or 11 April 1994 respectively under an obligation entered into before 20 April 1990.

For accounting periods ending **after 30 December 1993**, the exclusion is extended to expenditure on machinery or plant provided for leasing by a lessor in the course of 'relevant trading operations' within *s 445* or *s 446* (ie certain operations within Shannon Airport or the Custom House Docks Area attracting manufacturing companies' relief, see **12.18** 'Corporation tax'), *provided that* no initial or accelerated capital allowances (see **8.6**(*a*)(*b*) above) have been or will be made in respect of the expenditure.

For these purposes, 'leasing' includes letting on hire any item of machinery or plant and letting on charter a ship or aircraft (other than ship charters as part of trade activities of ship-operating companies), and the leasing part of a mixed trade is treated as a separate trade, with any appropriate apportionment. For accounting periods ending from

1 January 2006, where the activities of a company (or the group of which it is a member) consist wholly or mainly of pure leasing activities, the definition of leasing is extended to include asset financing, provision of leasing expertise, profits on disposal of leased assets and ancillary activities provided that these activities in conjunction with the leasing of plant and machinery comprise not less than 90 per cent of the company's activities. [*FA 2006, s 68*]

In respect of companies whose activities include the leasing of plant and machinery but who are not carrying on sufficient activities to be regarded as carrying on a trade, the provisions of *s 402* have been extended to apply to such companies. The provision enables such companies to compute their capital allowances and losses in their functional currency thereby eliminating potential inaccuracies arising from foreign exchange gains/losses. [*FA 2010, s 53*]

Any excess of such 'restricted' allowances over income from leasing may not be set against other income. Where a trade (including a deemed separate trade, see above) of leasing is carried on, losses attributable to 'restricted' allowances may only reduce profits or gains of the same trade, and may not be relieved in any other way. Profits arising from short-term leases for which an election is made under *s 80A* cannot be relieved by these allowances. For accounting periods ending from **3 February 2005**, losses may be surrendered by way of group relief to a group company carrying on a separate leasing trade. [*FA 2005, s 45*]

Section 80A has also been amended so as to enable a lessor company, engaged in the leasing of short-life assets by way of an operating lease, to elect to be taxed on the accounting profit from those leases. Where a lessor elects for this treatment, the new provisions will apply to operating leases of short-life assets which are in excess of a threshold amount. Where the lessor is a member of a group, this threshold amount is calculated on a group basis and represents the total value of all short-life assets let on an operating lease which are owned by the group at the end of the accounting period preceding the accounting period for which the election will apply. [*FA 2010, s 48*]

For income tax purposes, 'restricted' allowances, rather than other capital allowances, are set against any balancing charges, with only the balance being included in the loss claim. Where the loss claim exceeds the individual's income, he may specify the manner in which the loss relieved is to be attributed as between trading losses, 'restricted' allowances and other capital allowances.

For corporation tax purposes, a loss is similarly treated as attributable to 'restricted' allowances only in so far as it cannot be attributed to any other source. Equivalent restrictions apply to non-trading lessors.

Sea fishing boats. Temporary relief is available where enhanced wear and tear allowances are given for such boats for expenditure in the period of six years from 4 September 1998 (see **8.6**(*b*) above). The above restrictions do not apply to allowances for any such expenditure incurred in the first two years of that period, or to allowances for such expenditure by a company lessor in the remainder of the period.

[*TCA 1997, s 403; FA 1998, ss 23(b), 31; FA 1999, s 52; FA 2001, s 52(2); SI 124/ 04; FA 2005, s 45*]

Further restrictions – 'relevant leases'. Where, in the course of a trade, a person provides machinery or plant under a 'relevant lease', the letting is treated as a separate leasing trade (the '*specified leasing trade*') distinct from all other activities. The restrictions on relief for allowances described above in relation to the separate trade of leasing under *s 403* then apply to allowances in the specified leasing trade. This applies with effect **on and from 23 December 1993**, except that a lease is not a 'relevant lease' if a binding written contract for the letting was concluded before that day, or if the lease was written in the course of 'relevant trading operations' within *s 445* or *s 446* (see **12.18** 'Corporation tax'), or in certain other cases where the value of the asset(s) concerned does not exceed €63,500/£50,000. The detailed definition of a '*relevant lease*' is contained in *s 404(1)(b)*, but broadly it is any lease where there is an uneven spread of taxable lease payments involving a deferral of payments. Provided that lease payments are broadly on an even basis throughout the period during which 90 per cent (in certain cases, 95 per cent) of the original value of the leased machinery or plant is recovered, the lease is not a '*relevant lease*'. Seasonal factors in the case of leased agricultural machinery or plant are discounted, and there are special arrangements where expenditure is incurred on leased machinery or plant provided for certain new projects and attracting grant aid, and for which accelerated 50 per cent allowances are available under *s 283(5)* (see **8.6**(*a*) above). For accounting periods ending from 1 January 2006 leases that breach the 90 per cent rule due to exchange rate fluctuations only are not '*relevant leases*'. Also, provision is made for the set-off in certain circumstances of losses and capital allowances of long-term leases against the income of other long-term leases, against the leasing trade income of the company and against the leasing trade income of group companies. [*FA 2006, s 68*]

Anti-avoidance. Where, after 11 April 1994, either the terms of a machinery or plant lease entered into before that date are altered, or a machinery or plant lease is terminated and a further agreement for a lease of the machinery or plant entered into by the same or connected persons, and as a result lease payments after any given time are greater than they would otherwise have been, then unless the termination or change can be shown to have been effected for *bona fide* commercial reasons, the lease (including the terminated lease) is a relevant lease. There are arrangements for the withdrawal of any relief given which would not have been given if the lease was a relevant lease. Similarly, where a person who owned machinery or plant before 11 April 1994 disposes of it on or after that date to another person, and at or about that time the machinery or plant is leased back by that person to the original owner (or by or to connected persons), then unless the machinery or plant is new and unused, or the lease meets certain other conditions, the lease is a relevant lease.

[*TCA 1997, s 404; FA 1998, Sch 2 para 6; FA 2003, s 39; FA 2005, Sch 6(1)(g)*]

RESIDENTIAL BUILDINGS

8.8 See **33.4**, **33.5** 'Sch D, Case V' for relief on expenditure on certain such premises.

ROADS, BRIDGES, ETC

[*TCA 1997, Sch 32 para 10; FA 1981, s 26; FA 1984, s 39; FA 1989, s 17*]

8.9 Where, under an agreement with a road authority, capital expenditure (including interest where agreement was entered into after 5 April 1987) is incurred after 28 January 1981 and before 1 April 1992 (1 April 1989 where agreement was entered into before 6 April 1987) on the construction of toll roads, bridges, etc, 50 per cent of the expenditure may be set against income arising under such agreements in the same chargeable (or basis) period. Any balance of the allowable expenditure unrelieved may be carried forward without time limit against such income. In relation to expenditure incurred under agreements entered into after 5 April 1987, relief is available only against income arising under the agreement by virtue of which the expenditure was incurred, but all prior expenditure is treated as incurred in the chargeable period in which such income first arises, and further relief is available at the rate of ten per cent of the expenditure in each of the next five chargeable periods in which such income arises.

The expenditure must not be the subject of any other tax relief or allowance.

URBAN RENEWAL RELIEFS

8.10 From 2007, available relief under the schemes detailed below may be limited for high income earners, see **2.45** 'Limitation on Income Tax Relief for High Earners'. [*FA 2006, s 17*]

Expenditure incurred in the period 1 August 1994 to 31 July 1997 inclusive (or as extended). Enhanced industrial buildings allowances (see **8.5** above) are available for capital expenditure attributable to work carried out in the period 1 August 1994 to 31 July 1997 inclusive (the '*qualifying period*') on the construction or 'refurbishment' of a building or structure used for the purposes of a trade carried on in a mill, factory or other similar premises, where the site of the building, etc is wholly within a designated area, or the building, etc fronts onto a designated street etc (or part). Such areas and streets, etc are designated by the Minister for Finance, which designation may specify a shorter period within that referred to above. For such expenditure, an initial allowance of **25 per cent** or (in the case of expenditure by the occupier of the building, etc) annual writing-down allowances of up to **50 per cent** may be claimed. In the case of a building, etc fronting on a designated street, the enhanced allowances apply only to capital expenditure on the 'refurbishment' of buildings, etc existing on 1 August 1994, and are restricted to relief of expenditure up to the amount (if any) of expenditure on the existing building, etc which attracts relief under *s 347* or *s 348* or (as refurbishment expenditure) under *s 349* (reliefs for certain expenditure on residential accommodation, see **33.11** 'Sch D, Case V', **2.27** 'Allowances, credits and rates'). The balance of the expenditure may continue to attract the normal four per cent annual allowance.

The qualifying period may be extended to 31 July 1998 where the relevant local authority certified (before 1 October 1997) that at least 15 per cent of the total cost had been incurred before 31 July 1997, and this may be further extended to 31 December 1998 in certain cases involving delays outside the direct control of the person incurring the expenditure.

With effect from 12 April 1995, no balancing charge will be made in relation to a building, etc attracting allowances as above, where the event which would otherwise give rise to a charge occurs more than 13 years after first use (or, where relevant, after the incurring of the refurbishment expenditure).

'*Refurbishment*' means any construction, reconstruction, repair, renewal or maintenance work in the course of repair or restoration.

Industrial buildings allowances are also available in respect of capital expenditure attributable to work carried out in the qualifying period on the construction or refurbishment of '*qualifying premises*', ie premises within designated areas or fronting on designated streets, etc, which are not industrial buildings or structures, but which are used for trade or professional purposes or let on *bona fide* arm's length commercial terms. Any part of such premises in use as, or as part of, a dwelling-house is excluded, as is any part of premises, any part of the site of which is within the county boroughs of Dublin, Cork, Limerick, Galway or Waterford, in use as, or as part of, an office (except that use as an office is disregarded where the construction or refurbishment expenditure in the qualifying period on the part so used amounts to one-tenth or less of the total such expenditure on the premises). The allowances otherwise available (and any related balancing charges) are reduced by **one-half** in all cases, the total allowances being limited to 50 per cent of the qualifying expenditure. The allowances that may be claimed, after such reduction, are an initial **25 per cent** and annual allowances of **two per cent** or (in the case of expenditure by the occupier of the building, etc) accelerated annual allowances of up to **50 per cent**. The restrictions applicable to expenditure on industrial buildings or structures fronting on designated streets (see above) apply equally to expenditure on qualifying premises, but to the extent that refurbishment expenditure on the commercial element of the building exceeds the expenditure on the residential element, the capital allowances will be denied. No balancing charge (see **8.5**(*c*) above) will be made in respect of qualifying premises by reason of any event occurring more than 13 years after the premises were first used or, in the case of refurbishment expenditure, after that expenditure was incurred.

There is provision against double relief where relief is given under these provisions.

[*TCA 1997, ss 339–342, 350A; FA 1998, s 24(1)*; *FA 2006, s 17*]

See below as regards continuing allowances for urban renewal expenditure in the Docklands, Temple Bar or Custom House Docks Areas of Dublin, and earlier allowances for urban renewal expenditure in certain other areas. Where those earlier allowances apply to certain expenditure incurred on or after 1 August 1994 as if it had been incurred before that date, the above provisions do not apply to such expenditure. [*FA 1986, s 42(9); FA 1994, s 35(1)(a)(ii)*] See also **2.27** 'Allowances, credits and rates', **30.24** 'Sch D, Cases I and II' and **33.11** 'Sch D, Case V'.

Finance (No 2) Act 2008, s 21 inserts a new *Pt 11D*. The new Part introduces a scheme to facilitate the removal and relocation of certain facilities which may hinder the regeneration of urban docklands. The scheme arises from the [*EU Seveso II Directive (96/82/EC)* which seeks to protect public safety near locations where potentially dangerous activities are undertaken.

The relief given by way of accelerated capital allowances and 'additional relocation allowances' covers the removal costs relating to an increase in capacity are not allowable. The provisions will come into operation by the way of a commencement order to be made by the Minister for Finance following clearance by the European Commission from a State-aid perspective.

Jointly-owned property. Where property is purchased in their joint names by married couples, relief may concessionally be granted, if so claimed, to the spouse who incurred the expenditure and, where the purchase was funded by borrowings, to the spouse who makes the repayments. The irrevocable agreement of both spouses to this treatment is required, together with an irrevocable undertaking from the spouse to whom relief is given to accept any balancing charge which may arise. See Revenue Tax Briefing Issue 37 p 9.

Integrated qualifying area plans and 'living over the shop' scheme. Provisions similar to those described above in relation to buildings in designated areas also apply to construction or refurbishment expenditure on buildings in 'qualifying areas' incurred between **1 August 1998 and 31 December 2002** inclusive (extended to **31 December 2004** where the relevant local authority or company authorised by the authority certifies (before 1 October 2003 on application made before 1 August 2003) that at least 15 per cent of the total cost had been incurred before 1 July 2003). A *'qualifying area'* is an area, within an area to which an Integrated Area Plan (within *Urban Renewal Act 1998, Pt II*) applies, which is so designated by order by the Minister for Finance (now a 'qualifying urban area'), and the construction or refurbishment must be certified by the local authority concerned (or company authorised by such authority) as being consistent with the objectives of the Plan. Each designation order must specify a qualifying period within that referred to above. Also, in relation to reliefs for 'qualifying premises', the order must specify whether they are to apply to:

(*a*)   offices;

(*b*)   multi-storey car parks;

(*c*)   any other buildings etc on which the office element of the expenditure does not exceed ten per cent of the total expenditure in the qualifying period; or

(*d*)   the facade of a building at (*a*) or (*c*);

or to any combination of (*a*), (*b*), (*c*) or (d) and whether they are to apply to construction or refurbishment or both. The Minister may amend or revoke any order.

In relation to refurbishment expenditure, there is a further requirement that the expenditure is at least ten per cent of the market value of the building, etc immediately before the expenditure was incurred.

Since 1 July 1999, allowances are not available for expenditure incurred by a person whose trade consists wholly or mainly of constructing or refurbishing buildings or structures for sale, or by a person connected (within *s 10*) with such a person. They also cease to be available where the building, etc concerned is in use for the purposes of a trade or activity carried on by the person entitled to the relevant interest in the building (ie the owner-occupier):

(i)   in the agriculture sector, including the production, processing and marketing of agricultural products;

(ii)   in the coal, fishing or motor vehicle industries; or

(iii)   in the transport, steel, shipbuilding, synthetic fibres or financial services sectors;

or, **up to 31 December 2002,** was provided for the purposes of a project the regional aid for which is limited under EC Commission rules. For expenditure incurred **from 1 January 2003** and provided for a project that is subject to the notification requirements of a Multisectoral framework on regional aid for large investment projects, allowances are available only if EC Commission approval has been obtained.

Allowances are, however, extended to parts of buildings. Allowances available are 50 per cent initial allowances and four per cent annual allowances or (for owner-occupiers) up to 50 per cent free depreciation annual allowances.

No allowances are available under these provisions for expenditure incurred after 5 April 2001 any part of which has been or is to be met, directly or indirectly, by grant assistance.

These provisions are extended under the 'Living over the Shop Scheme' to expenditure on the construction or refurbishment of qualifying premises fronting on to a 'qualifying street' incurred between **6 April 2001 and 31 December 2004** inclusive (or in any shorter qualifying period within that period which may be specified in the order designating a particular street as a 'qualifying street', see below).

Qualifying premises in use as offices, or for the provision of mail order or financial services, or other than for the retailing of goods or the provision of services only in RI, are excluded. The qualifying premises must be comprised in the ground floor of an 'existing' or 'replacement building', and apart from the capital expenditure incurred in the qualifying period on the construction or refurbishment of the qualifying premises, expenditure must be incurred on the upper floor(s) of the 'existing' or 'replacement building' which attracts (or would if claimed attract) one of the other reliefs under the Scheme (see **2.27** 'Allowances, credits and rates', **33.11** 'Sch D, Case V'). Relief is in any event limited to the total amount of expenditure which attracts (or would attract) those other reliefs. The allowance is dependant on the corporation of the borough in whose area the premises are situated certifying in writing that the construction or refurbishment is consistent with the aims, objectives and criteria for the Scheme as outlined in circular UR 43A of 13 September 2000 (as amended). For these purposes the following definitions apply. A '*qualifying street*' (within *s 372BA*) is a street (or part) in the county borough of Cork, Dublin, Galway, Limerick or Waterford which is so designated by order by the Minister for Finance. 'Street' for this purpose includes a road, square, quay or lane. An '*existing building*' is a building which existed on 13 September 2000, and a '*replacement building*' is a building or structure (or part) constructed to replace an existing building where either (i) a demolition notice or order on the existing building (or part) was given or made after 12 September 2000 and before 31 March 2001 and the replacement building is consistent with the character and size of the existing building, or (ii) demolition of the existing building (being a single storey building) was required for structural reasons to facilitate the construction of an additional storey or storeys necessary for the restoration or enhancement of the streetscape.

The termination date for the scheme of capital allowances for both qualifying areas and qualifying streets under the living over the shop scheme **is extended to 31 July 2006** where, in the case of the qualifying areas scheme, 15 per cent of project costs (including site costs) were incurred by 30 June 2003 and the relevant local authority certified this fact by 30 September 2003 and, in the case of the living over the shop scheme, where a valid application for full planning permission has been made and acknowledged as received by 31 December 2004 (or 10 March 2002 in the case of permission sought under the *Local Government (Planning and Development) Regulations 1994*) or, where planning permission is not required, a detailed plan of the construction or refurbishment work is prepared, a binding written contract relating to that work is in existence and work to the value of five per cent of the development costs has been carried out by 31 December 2004. The termination date for both schemes **is further extended to 31 December 2006**, where the conditions for the extension to 31 July 2006 are satisfied and subject to any conditions which the Minister for Finance may impose by regulations, **to 31 July 2008** where those conditions are met, a binding written contract is in place by 31 July 2006 and a local authority certificate issues by 31 March 2007 certifying that 15 per cent of construction expenditure has been incurred by

31 December 2006 and detailing the amount of expenditure incurred by 31 December 2006 and the projected expenditure in the period from 1 January 2007 to 31 July 2008. For expenditure incurred during 2007, relief is restricted to 75 per cent of expenditure incurred. For expenditure incurred in the period from 1 January 2008 to 31 July 2008, relief is restricted to 50 per cent of expenditure incurred. Moreover, the amount of projected expenditure for the period 1 January 2007 to 31 July 2008, as certified by the local authority, will apply as a cap on the expenditure for that period which may be taken into account in calculating capital allowances, and this cap will apply before the application of the 75 per cent and 50 per cent restrictions. [*FA 2006, ss 26, 30*]

[*TCA 1997, ss 372A–372D, 372J, 372K; FA 1998, s 76; Urban Renewal Act 1998, ss 11, 19(a)(b); FA 2000, s 44; FA 2001, s 60; FA 2002, ss 23(1)(b)(c), 26, Sch 2 paras 2, 3; FA 2003, ss 26, 27; FA 2004, s 26; FA 2006, s 17*]

See also **2.27** 'Allowances, credits and rates', **2.45** 'Limitation on Income Tax Relief for High Earners', **33.11** 'Sch D, Case V' and, as regards integrated area plans, **30.24** 'Sch D, Cases I and II'.

Town renewal schemes. Provisions similar to those described above in relation to buildings in designated areas also apply to construction or refurbishment expenditure on industrial and commercial buildings in 'qualifying areas' incurred between **6 April 2001** and **31 December 2004** inclusive. The qualifying period is **extended to 31 July 2006** where a valid application for full planning permission has been made and acknowledged as received by 31 December 2004 (or 10 March 2002 in the case of permission sought under the *Local Government (Planning and Development) Regulations 1994*) or, where planning permission is not required, a detailed plan of the construction or refurbishment work is prepared, a binding written contract relating to that work is in existence and work to the value of five per cent of the development costs has been carried out by 31 December 2004.

The termination date for the scheme **is further extended to 31 December 2006**, where the conditions for the extension to 31 July 2006 are satisfied and, subject to any conditions which the Minister for Finance may impose by regulations, **to 31 July 2008** where those conditions are met, a binding written contract is in place by 31 July 2006 and a local authority certificate issues by 31 March 2007 certifying that 15 per cent of construction expenditure has been incurred by 31 December 2006 and detailing the amount of expenditure incurred by 31 December 2006 and the projected expenditure in the period from 1 January 2007 to 31 July 2008. For expenditure incurred during 2007, relief is restricted to 75 per cent of expenditure incurred. For expenditure incurred in the period from 1 January 2008 to 31 July 2008, relief is restricted to 50 per cent of expenditure incurred. Moreover, the amount of projected expenditure for the period 1 January 2007 to 31 July 2008, as certified by the local authority, will apply as a cap on the expenditure for that period which may be taken into account in calculating capital allowances, and this cap will apply before the application of the 75 per cent and 50 per cent restrictions. [*FA 2006, ss 26, 30*]

A '*qualifying area*' is an area, within an area to which a Town Renewal Plan (under the relevant legislation) relates which is so designated by order by the Minister for Finance (now a 'qualifying town area'). An order may be amended or revoked. For industrial and commercial buildings the order may designate the area for construction or refurbishment of a building. In relation to refurbishment expenditure, relief is extended to include expenditure on certain work on the facade of a building. An order may designate different classes of premises for relief. Each designation order must specify a qualifying period within that referred to above. Also, in relation to reliefs for 'qualifying premises', the order must specify whether they are to apply to any or all of (*a*) offices, (*b*) the facades of offices, (*c*) any other buildings etc on which the office element of the expenditure does not exceed ten per cent of the total expenditure in the qualifying period, and (*d*) the facade of such buildings. In relation to such expenditure, allowances in all cases available are 50 per cent initial allowances and four per cent annual allowances or (for owner-occupiers) up to 50 per cent free depreciation annual allowances. Allowances are not, however, available for expenditure incurred by a person whose trade consists wholly or mainly of constructing or refurbishing buildings or structures for sale, or by a person connected (within *s 10*) with such a person. They are also not available where the building, etc concerned is in use for the purposes of a trade or activity carried on by the person entitled to the relevant interest in the building (ie the owner-occupier):

(i)   in the agriculture sector, including the production, processing and marketing of agricultural products;

(ii)   in the coal, fishing or motor vehicle industries; or

(iii)   in the transport, steel, shipbuilding, synthetic fibres or financial services sectors;

or (**until 31 December 2002**) was provided for the purposes of a project the regional aid for which is limited under EC Commission rules. For expenditure incurred **from 1 January 2003**, and provided for a project that is subject to the notification requirements of a Multisectoral framework on regional aid for large investment projects allowances are available only if EC Commission approval has been obtained. For expenditure incurred after 5 April 2001, allowances are not available:

(*a*)   where any part of the expenditure has been, or is to be, met, directly or indirectly, by grant assistance; and

(*b*)   unless the relevant interest is held by a small or medium-sized enterprise ('SME') within the EC Regulations or, from 1 January 2005, a micro, small or medium-sized enterprise.

[*TCA 1997, ss 372AA–372AD, 372AJ; FA 2000, s 89; FA 2001, s 80; FA 2002, ss 26, 27, Sch 2 para 2; FA 2003, ss 26, 29; FA 2004, s 26; FA 2005, s 35; FA 2006, s 17*] See also **2.27** 'Allowances, credits and rates', **2.45** 'Limitation on Income Tax Relief for High Earners', **33.11** 'Sch D, Case V'.

For an article on Town Renewal Relief, including a list of towns recommended for designation, see Revenue Tax Briefing Issue 42 pp 24–27.

Enterprise areas. Industrial buildings allowances (see **8.5** above) are available on the special basis described below for all capital expenditure incurred in the 'qualifying period' on the construction or refurbishment of a 'qualifying building' as if it were an industrial building or structure. A '*qualifying building*' is a building or structure the site of which is wholly within an 'enterprise area' and in use for 'qualifying trading operations' carried on by a 'qualifying company', but excluding any part in use as, or as part of, a dwelling-house. Enterprise areas are either:

(*a*)   areas specified by order by the Minister for Finance (areas at East Wall and Macken Street/Grand Canal Street in Dublin, Westside in Galway and Blackpool in Cork), in relation to which the '*qualifying period*' is 1 August 1994 to 31 July

1997 inclusive (extended to 31 July 1998 where the relevant local authority certified (before 1 October 1997) that at least 15 per cent of the total cost had been incurred before 31 July 1997, and further extended to 31 December 1998 in certain cases involving delays outside the direct control of the person incurring the expenditure);

(*b*) those areas described in *Sch 7* (at Cherry Orchard/Gallanstown, Finglas and Rosslare Harbour), in relation to which the '*qualifying period*' is 1 July 1997 to 31 December 1999 inclusive (extended to 31 December 2000 where the relevant local authority certified (before 31 May 2000) that at least 50 per cent of the total cost had been incurred before 1 January 2000); or

(*c*) areas adjacent to Cork, Donegal, Galway, Kerry, Knock, Sligo or Waterford Airports which, on application by a 'qualifying company' intending to carry on 'qualifying trading operations' in such an area, are so designated by order by the Minister for Finance, in relation to which the order must specify a '*qualifying period*' which must start on or after 1 August 1994 and end on or before 31 December 1999 (extended to 31 December 2000 where the relevant local authority certified (before 31 May 2000) that at least 50 per cent of the total cost had been incurred before 1 January 2000).

As regards construction or refurbishment expenditure within (*c*) above, allowances are not available where a person whose trade consists wholly or mainly of constructing or refurbishing buildings or structures for sale, or a person connected (within *s 10*) with such a person, incurred the expenditure.

'*Qualifying trading operations*' means the manufacture of goods within *Pt 14* (see **12.18** 'Corporation tax'), the rendering of internationally traded services in the course of a service industry within *Industrial Development Act 1986* or, from a day to be appointed, the rendering of certain airport-related freight or logistical services. A '*qualifying company*' is a company approved for financial assistance under a scheme administered by Forfás, Forbairt, the Industrial Development Agency (Ireland) or (from 6 April 1998) Údarás na Gaeltachta, or which is engaged in certain airport-related freight or logistical services (as above), and to which a certificate for these purposes has been given by the Minister for Enterprise, Trade and Employment. Such a certificate may be conditional, may not be given unless the Minister is satisfied that the carrying on of the qualifying trading operations in the enterprise area will contribute to the balanced development of the area, and may be revoked (in particular if the company fails to comply with a notice requiring it to desist from activities having an adverse effect on the use or development of the area or otherwise inimical to its balanced development).

The allowances available are an initial allowance of 25 per cent (increased to 50 per cent from 1 January 1998 for areas within (*c*) above) or (where the person incurring the expenditure also occupies the building) free depreciation of up to 50 per cent, together with annual allowances of four per cent to a total of 100 per cent. Only expenditure attributable to work actually carried out during the qualifying period (as above) is treated as having been incurred in that period. No balancing charge will be made by reason of any event in relation to a qualifying building occurring more than 13 years after first use (or, where relevant, after the incurring of refurbishment expenditure).

There is provision against double relief where relief is given under these provisions.

[*TCA 1997, ss 339, 340, 343, 350A, Sch 7; FA 1998, s 24; FA 1999, s 44(c); FA 2000, s 42; FA 2006, s 17*]

Multi-storey car parks. Expenditure incurred in the period from 1 July 1995 to 30 June 1998 inclusive (the '*qualifying period*') on the construction or refurbishment of a public multi-storey car park certified by the local authority to be developed in accordance with criteria laid down by the Minister for the Environment and Local Government attracts industrial buildings allowances (see **8.5** above) at enhanced rates. In the case of refurbishment, the expenditure incurred in the qualifying period must amount to at least 20 per cent of the car park's market value immediately before the incurring of the expenditure. Expenditure is treated as incurred in the qualifying period only if it is properly attributable to work actually carried out in that period.

The qualifying period is extended to 30 September 1999 where at least 15 per cent of the total construction expenditure is certified before 30 September 1998 by the relevant local authority (under the relevant guidelines) to have been incurred before 1 July 1998, and to **31 July 2006** where 15 per cent of the total costs are so certified (before 1 January 2004) to have been incurred before 1 October 2003 and the car park is outside Cork and Dublin. The termination date in relation to car parks outside of Cork and Dublin **is extended to 31 December 2006**, where the conditions for the extension to 31 July 2006 are satisfied, and **to 31 July 2008** where those conditions are met and at least 15 per cent of the construction or refurbishment costs has been incurred by 31 December 2006. For expenditure incurred during 2007, relief is restricted to 75 per cent of expenditure incurred. For expenditure incurred in the period from 1 January 2008 to 31 July 2008, relief is restricted to 50 per cent of expenditure incurred. [*FA 2006, ss 26, 29*] The allowances available are either an initial allowance of 50 per cent and four per cent annual allowances or (only in the case of owner-occupied buildings) free depreciation annual allowances, in either case to a maximum total allowance of 100 per cent. For expenditure incurred on or before 31 July 1998, these allowances are halved, and this continues to apply after that date if a 'qualifying lease' within *s 345* (see **30.24** 'Sch D, Cases I and II') is granted in respect of the premises concerned. No balancing charge will be made by reason of any event in relation to a qualifying car park occurring more than 13 years after first use (or, where relevant, after the incurring of refurbishment expenditure).

There is provision against double relief where relief is given under these provisions.

[*TCA 1997, ss 344, 350A; FA 1998, s 26; FA 1999, s 44(d); FA 2000, s 42; FA 2001, s 59; FA 2002, s 23(1)(a); FA 2004, s 26; FA 2006, s 17*]

Park and ride facilities. Provisions similar to those applicable to multi-storey car parks (as above) apply to expenditure on the construction or refurbishment of a 'qualifying park and ride facility' in a '*qualifying period*' **1 July 1999 to 31 December 2004** inclusive. The qualifying period is extended to **31 July 2006** where a valid application for full planning permission has been made and acknowledged as received by 31 December 2004 (or 10 March 2002 in the case of permission sought under the *Local Government (Planning and Development) Regulations 1994*) or, where planning permission is not required, a detailed plan of the construction or refurbishment work is prepared, a binding written contract relating to that work is in existence and work to the value of five per cent of the development costs has been carried out by 31 December 2004. The termination date for the scheme **is further extended to 31 December 2006**, where the conditions for the extension to 31 July 2006 are satisfied and **to 31 July 2008**

where those conditions are met, and at least 15 per cent of the construction or refurbishment costs has been incurred by 31 December 2006. For expenditure incurred during 2007, relief is restricted to 75 per cent of expenditure incurred. For expenditure incurred in the period from 1 January 2008 to 31 July 2008, relief is restricted to 50 per cent of expenditure incurred. [*FA 2006, ss 26, 32*]

'*Park and ride facility*' means a building or structure in use to enable members of the general public to park mechanically propelled road vehicles for an appropriate charge and continue their journey by bus or train, and adjacent areas on which certain commercial or residential premises (see **30.24** 'Sch D, Cases I and II', **33.11** 'Sch D, Case V') are constructed. A '*qualifying park and ride facility*' is such a facility which the local authority in whose area the facility is situated certifies as complying with the relevant guidelines issued by the Minister for the Environment and Local Government. Those guidelines may include requirements as to the location, number of parking spaces, transport services, hours of operation and charges in relation to the facility, and other related matters. The differences are:

(*a*)   refurbishment expenditure must be not less than ten per cent of the market value of the facility before the expenditure is incurred, instead of 20 per cent;

(*b*)   the allowances are those which generally apply to multi-storey car parks after 31 July 1998, ie without the halving of the allowances applicable on or before that date.

Special provision is made from 6 April 2001 for the situation where a facility is first brought into use before the local authority is able to certify it, due to a delay in the provision of the related train service. In these circumstances, application of the industrial buildings allowance provisions commences on certification being given instead of on first use of the facility. If, however, the delay exceeds five years, no allowances are available.

Since 7 February 2002, allowances are not available where a person whose trade consists wholly or mainly of constructing or refurbishing buildings or structures for sale, or a person connected (within *s 10*) with such a person, incurred the expenditure.

[*TCA 1997, ss 372U, 372V; FA 1999, s 70(1); FA 2001, s 58(a); FA 2002, s 23, Sch 2 para 2; FA 2003, s 26; FA 2006, s 17*]

Similar allowances are given for expenditure in the same qualifying period on the construction or refurbishment of '*qualifying premises*', ie a building or structure the site of which is wholly within the site of a qualifying park and ride facility, and which is similarly certified as complying with the relevant guidelines, which is not an industrial building or structure, but which is used for trade or professional purposes or let on *bona fide* arm's length commercial terms. Any part in use as, or as part of, a dwelling-house is excluded. Since 6 April 2001, where the building or structure is in use for trade or professional purposes, that use must be for the retailing of goods or the provision of services only within RI and must not be as offices or for the provision of mail order or financial services, and the provision for deferral of allowances on the park and ride facility itself, where certification is delayed, applies equally to these ancillary allowances.

However, an allowance for expenditure under this provision will be given only insofar as that expenditure, when aggregated with:

(i)   other expenditure, incurred at the same park and ride facility, in respect of which an allowance would, disregarding this restriction, be made under this provision; and

(ii)   expenditure, incurred at the same park and ride facility, in respect of which there is provision for a deduction under *s 372X* or *s 372AP* (rented residential accommodation, see **33.11** 'Sch D, Case V') or *s 372Y* or *s 372AR* (owner occupiers, see **2.27** 'Allowances, credits and rates');

does not exceed one-half of the total expenditure incurred at that facility for which a deduction or allowance may be made under this provision, *s 372V* (see above), *s 372X* or *s 372AP* (see **33.11** 'Sch D, Case V') or *s 372Y* or *s 372AR* (see **2.27** 'Allowances, credits and rates'), disregarding this restriction and the similar restrictions applicable under *s 372X* or *s 372AP* and *s 372Y* or *s 372AR*. The local authority must have issued a certificate that it is satisfied that this requirement has been met.

[*TCA 1997, ss 372U, 372W; FA 1999, s 70(1); FA 2001, s 58(b); FA 2002, s 23, Sch 2 para 2; FA 2004, s 26; FA 2006, s 17*]

See also **2.27** 'Allowances, credits and rates', **33.11** 'Sch D, Case V'.

Expenditure incurred (or treated as incurred) before 1 August 1994 or in the **Temple Bar** or **Custom House Docks Areas** of Dublin. Industrial buildings allowances and charges are given or made in respect of capital expenditure incurred in the 'qualifying period' on construction of 'qualifying premises' as if the premises were an 'industrial building or structure' in use for a trade carried on in a mill, factory, etc (see **8.5** above), whether or not any such trading activity is carried on in the premises.

Relief is similarly available for expenditure on the refurbishment of buildings existing on 1 January 1991 within the Temple Bar Area (see (iii) below), and for this purpose expenditure is deemed to include the lesser of the cost of acquisition of the building (excluding land) and the value of the building at 1 January 1991, provided that the actual expenditure incurred is at least equal to the lesser of those amounts.

'*Qualifying premises*' means a building or structure the site of which is wholly within a 'designated area', which is not otherwise an 'industrial building or structure', and which is either in use for the purposes of a trade or profession or, whether or not so used, is let on *bona fide* arm's length commercial terms. Any building or structure in use as, or as part of, a dwelling house is excluded (but see **33.4** 'Sch D, Case V'). Buildings in the Temple Bar Area (see (iii) below) may fall within this definition whether or not they are otherwise 'industrial buildings or structures'.

A '*designated area*' is either:

(i)   the Custom House Docks Area of Dublin (as specified in *Sch 5* or as extended by order of the Minister for Finance under *s 322(2)*, see *SI 466/99*);

(ii)   certain areas of Dublin, Athlone, Castlebar, Cork, Dundalk, Kilkenny, Letterkenny, Limerick, Tralee, Tullamore, Sligo, Wexford, Waterford or Galway (as specified in *FA 1986, Sch 4 Pts III–VII*); or

(iii)   the Temple Bar Area (as specified in *Sch 6*).

See also *SIs 92, 287, 314/88*.

Expenditure in the Temple Bar Area qualifies for relief only if approved by Temple Bar Renewal Ltd.

In relation to premises in a designated area within (i) above, the '*qualifying period*' is the period of eleven years from 25 January 1988 to **31 December 1999** inclusive, extended to **30 June 2000** in the case of construction expenditure on a qualifying premises at least 51 per cent of the total of which is incurred before 1 January 2000. For designated areas within (ii) above, it is the period commencing on 23 October 1985 and ending on **31 July 1994** (and where at least 15 per cent of the total construction expenditure on qualifying premises was certified before 24 February 1994 by the relevant local authority (under the relevant guidelines) to have been incurred before 26 January 1994, further such expenditure incurred between 1 August and 31 December 1994 inclusive is treated as having been incurred in the qualifying period), and for the area within (iii) above, it is the period commencing on 6 April 1991 and ending on **5 April 1999** (31 December 1999 in certain cases where substantial expenditure had been incurred by 5 April 1999).

The normal rules for industrial buildings allowances apply (see **8.5** above) subject to the following amendments:

(A)   The allowances and charges apply for expenditure incurred up to the end of the qualifying period (see above);

(B)   The allowances and charges are reduced by one-half where the designated area is an area of Dublin not falling within (i) or (iii) above, and for construction expenditure where it is within (iii) above (and the allowances and charges are for this purpose computed as if this provision does not apply before the reduced allowance is given or charge made, but not so as to result in a balancing charge in excess of the allowances given);

(C)   Where the premises are in a designated area within (i) above, and the expenditure is incurred after 24 January 1998, the maximum enhanced annual allowance which may be claimed is 54 per cent, and no initial allowance is available for a period for which an enhanced annual allowance is claimed. This provision is, however, abolished from 5 January 2000;

(D)   Allowances for capital expenditure on multi-storey car parks which would otherwise be given under *FA 1981, s 25 or Sch 32 para 9* (see **8.5** above) are instead given under the current provisions, unless the allowances would thereby be reduced under (B) above;

(E)   The prohibition on the granting of a writing-down allowance for a chargeable period for which an initial allowance is made does not apply;

(F)   Since 6 May 1993, the period after first use (or after refurbishment) after the end of which no balancing charge may arise is reduced to 13 years (instead of 25 years) (see **8.5**(*c*) above).

The inspector determines the amount of expenditure on qualifying premises which is properly attributable to work on construction of the premises actually carried out during the qualifying period, subject to revision on appeal by the Appeal Commissioners or by the Circuit Court.

See also **8.5**(*a*)–(*b*) above as regards continuation of enhanced initial allowances and free depreciation for Temple Bar industrial buildings, etc (now in *s 331*).

[*TCA 1997, ss 322, 323, 330, 331, Sch 5, Sch 6, Sch 32 para 11; FA 1986, ss 41, 42, Sch 4; FA 1988, s 51; FA 1990, s 80; FA 1991, s 22(2); FA 1992, ss 29, 30; FA 1993, s 30(1)(a); FA 1994, ss 35(1)(a), 36; FA 1995, ss 32(1)(a)(b), 33; Urban Renewal Act 1998, s 20; FA 1999, ss 42, 43; SI 465/99; FA 2006, s 17]*

Mid-Shannon Corridor Tourism Infrastructure Investment Scheme. This is a new pilot scheme for tourism facilities in the mid-Shannon area. The scheme is aimed at encouraging the development of new tourism infrastructure or the refurbishment of existing tourism infrastructure, in that area. The list of qualifying areas is included in a new *Sch 8B*. The qualifying period for the scheme has been extended from two to four years so that the latest date for submission of applications is now 31 May 2012. To cater for any projects that may avail of the new date for the submission of applications for approval in principle, the period within which expenditure must be incurred for capital allowances purposes is also being extended by two years and will now end on 31 May 2015.

These new dates will come into operation by way of a commencement order to be made by the Minister for Finance following clearance from the EU Commission from a State-aid perspective [*FA 2010, s 27*]. As of 1 March 2011, the commencement order has yet to be made.

Relief will be available by way of accelerated capital allowances over seven years for qualifying construction and refurbishment expenditure incurred in the qualifying period. In the case of refurbishment the qualifying expenditure must exceed **20 per cent** of the market value of the property before work commences. In areas which are not in the BMW region only **80 per cent** of construction and refurbishment expenditure will qualify for relief. The nature of the tourism infrastructure buildings and structures which may qualify under the scheme will be set out in guidelines to be issued by the Minister for Arts, Sport and Tourism in consultation with the Minister for Finance. While relief will be available over seven years there will be a 15-year holding period in order to avoid a clawback of allowances given. Existing restrictions on the sideways set-off of excess capital allowances against non-rental income for passive investors will apply as will the restriction on the use of specified reliefs by high-income individuals which is effective from 1 January 2007.

Projects wishing to avail of relief must get approval in advance (for which an application must be made within one year of the commencement of the scheme) and also must get formal certification after completion. This approval and certification will be given by a special board established for the purposes of the scheme and will be carried out in accordance with the guidelines to be issued by the Minister for Arts, Sport and Tourism, in consultation with the Minister for Finance. Certain buildings such as those that facilitate gaming or gambling are specifically excluded from the scheme, as are licensed premises (but not restaurants). Accommodation facilities that are provided as part of a qualifying project may qualify for relief to the extent that expenditure on such facilities does not exceed **50 per cent** of the overall expenditure on the project or such lower percentage as may be specified in the guidelines for the type of project involved. This is subject to the over-riding condition that qualifying expenditure on accommodation facilities may not exceed qualifying expenditure on non-accommodation facilities. The scheme will be notified to the EU Commission under the new regional aid block exemption guidelines. [*FA 2007, s 29*] Qualifying expenditure under the scheme must comply with the European Commission's Regional Aid Guidelines and the State Aid Map for Ireland for the period 2007–2013 and that relief under the scheme cannot be availed of by beneficiaries that are subject to an outstanding recovery order following a previous decision of the Commission of the European Communities declaring aid in favour of that undertaking to be illegal and incompatible with the common market. [*FA 2008, s 27*]

QUALIFYING RESORT AREA RELIEFS

8.11 Special allowances are available for capital expenditure incurred in the '*qualifying period*' **1 July 1995 to 30 June 1998** inclusive on the construction or 'refurbishment' of certain buildings or structures wholly within a '*qualifying resort area*' ie a part of Achill, Arklow, Ballybunion, Bettystown, Bundoran, Clogherhead, Clonakilty, Courtown, Enniscrone, Kilkee, Lahinch, Laytown, Mosney, Salthill, Tramore, Westport or Youghal described in *Sch 8*. The allowances are given as industrial buildings allowances consisting of an initial allowance of **50 per cent** and annual allowances of **five per cent**, with free depreciation annual allowances of up to **75 per cent** where no initial allowance is claimed (up to a total of **100 per cent** allowances). They are, however, dependent, in the case of 'refurbishment' expenditure, on the total amount of such expenditure incurred in the qualifying period being not less than **20 per cent** of the market value of the building or structure (excluding land) immediately before the expenditure is incurred. Expenditure is treated as incurred in the qualifying period only if it is properly attributable to work actually carried out in that period.

The qualifying period is extended to **30 June 1999** where at least 15 per cent of the total expenditure is certified on or before 30 September 1998 by the relevant local authority (under the relevant guidelines) to have been incurred before 1 July 1998, and to **31 December 1999** where at least 50 per cent is so certified on or before 30 September 1999 to have been incurred before 1 July 1999.

'*Refurbishment*' for these purposes means any work of construction, reconstruction, repair or renewal, including the provision or improvement of water, sewerage or heating facilities, carried out in the course of repair or restoration, or maintenance in the nature of repair or restoration.

The allowances are given for:

(*a*)   industrial buildings or structures consisting of hotels, holiday camps or registered holiday cottages within **8.5**(ii) above (displacing the allowances otherwise available); and

(*b*)   buildings or structures which are not industrial buildings or structures within **8.5** above, and which are in use for the purposes of the operation of one or more 'qualifying tourism facilities', but excluding any part of a building, etc in use as, or as part of, a dwelling-house unless it is itself registered or listed as a 'qualifying tourism facility'.

This scheme of capital allowances at four per cent per annum is extended to include buildings and structures which are comprised in, and are in use as part of, premises which are included in the register for camping and caravan sites. This extension applies to expenditure incurred on or after 1 January 2008. [*FA 2008, s 28*] For the timing of claims for allowances under (*b*) above, see Revenue Tax Briefing Issue 43 p 38.

'*Qualifying tourism facilities*' are tourist accommodation facilities registered by the National Tourism Development Authority (prior to 2006, Bord Fáilte Éireann) under

Tourist Traffic Act 1939, Pt III or listed under *Tourist Traffic Act 1957, s 9*, and other facilities approved for the purpose by the Minister for Tourism, Sport and Recreation.

Allowances under (*a*) above are restricted to set-off against income from the lettings (or from the trade for which the cottage is used), and losses arising from the allowances are similarly restricted (see **8.5** above), and this applies equally to allowances under (*b*) above *except* where either:

(i)   before 5 April 1996, a binding contract for the acquisition or construction was entered into, or an application for planning permission for the construction received by the relevant authority, or a written opinion issued by the Revenue Commissioners that an allowance for the expenditure would not be restricted by virtue of *s 408* (see **8.5** above); or

(ii)   before 5 April 1996 expenditure was incurred on the acquisition of the land on which the construction or refurbishment is to take place by the person who incurred the construction or refurbishment expenditure, or a binding written contract entered into for its acquisition, and it can be proved to the satisfaction of the Revenue Commissioners that a detailed plan had been prepared, and detailed discussions with the planning authority had taken place (supported by an affidavit by the authority), after 7 February 1995 and before 5 April 1996.

As regards buildings, etc within (*b*) above which are registered or listed tourism accommodation facilities, their ceasing to be so registered or listed is treated as an event giving rise to a balancing charge, with sale, etc moneys equal to the aggregate of the residue of expenditure incurred on the construction or refurbishment immediately before that event and the allowances given (as above) in relation to that expenditure (so that all the allowances are in effect clawed back). However, no such balancing charge, nor such a charge by reason of any other event, will be made by reason of any event occurring more than eleven years after first use of the building, etc (or, where relevant, after the incurring of the refurbishment expenditure).

[*TCA 1997, ss 351–353, 355, Sch 8; FA 1998, s 27; FA 1999, s 45; FA 2006, ss 17, 127, Sch 2*]

See also **2.45** 'Limitation on Income Tax Relief for High Earners', **30.24** 'Sch D, Cases I and II' and **33.12** 'Sch D, Case V'.

QUALIFYING RURAL AREA RELIEFS

8.12 Industrial buildings, etc. Special allowances are available for capital expenditure incurred in the '*qualifying period*' commencing on 1 July 1999 and ending on **31 December 2004** on the construction or 'refurbishment' of buildings which are, or are to be, industrial buildings or structures within 8.5(i) above (docks being included from 6 April 1999) within a 'qualifying rural area'. The period is extended to **31 December 2006** where a valid application for full planning permission has been made and acknowledged as received by 31 December 2004 (or 10 March 2002 in the case of permission sought under the *Local Government (Planning and Development) Regulations 1994*) or, where planning permission is not required, a detailed plan of the construction or refurbishment work is prepared, a binding written contract relating to that work is in existence and work to the value of five per cent of the development costs has been carried out by 31 December 2004. Subject to any conditions which the

Minister for Finance may impose by regulations, the termination date is extended to 31 July 2008 where the above conditions are satisfied, a written binding contract is in place by 31 July 2006 and a local authority certificate issues by 31 March 2007 certifying that 15 per cent of construction expenditure has been incurred by 31 December 2006 and detailing the amount of expenditure incurred by 31 December 2006 and the projected expenditure in the period from 1 January 2007 to 31 July 2008. For expenditure incurred during 2007, relief is restricted to 75 per cent of expenditure incurred. For expenditure incurred in the period from 1 January 2008 to 31 July 2008, relief is restricted to 50 per cent of expenditure incurred. Moreover, the amount of projected expenditure for the period 1 January 2007 to 31 July 2008, as certified by the local authority, will apply as a cap on the expenditure for that period which may be taken into account in calculating capital allowances and this cap will apply before the application of the 75 per cent and 50 per cent restrictions. [*FA 2006, ss 26, 31*]

The enhanced allowances are an initial industrial building allowance of **50 per cent** with free depreciation annual allowances of up to **50 per cent** in aggregate where no initial allowance is claimed. They are, however, dependent, in the case of 'refurbishment' expenditure, on the total amount of such expenditure incurred in the qualifying period being not less than ten per cent of the market value of the building, etc (excluding land) immediately before the expenditure is incurred. No balancing charge (see **8.5**(*c*) above) arises in respect of a building, etc to which these provisions apply by reason of any event occurring more than 13 years after the premises were first used or, in the case of 'refurbishment' expenditure, after that expenditure was incurred. Expenditure is treated as incurred in the qualifying period only if it is properly attributable to work actually carried out in that period.

A '*qualifying rural area*' is an area of Cavan, Leitrim, Longford, Roscommon or Sligo specified in *Sch 8A* as inserted by *FA 1998, s 77(b)*.

'*Refurbishment*' for these purposes means any work of construction, reconstruction, repair or renewal, including the provision or improvement of water, sewerage or heating facilities, carried out in the course of repair or restoration, or maintenance in the nature of repair or restoration.

These provisions do not, however, apply to any building or structure in use for the purposes of a trade (or activity treated as a trade) where the number of individuals employed or engaged in carrying on the trade or activity is 250 or more or, from 1 July 1999, where the trade is carried on by the person entitled to the relevant interest in the building (ie the owner-occupier) and is in any of the following sectors: agriculture (including production, processing and marketing of agricultural products); transport; steel; ship-building; synthetic fibres; or financial services, or in the coal industry, the fishing industry or the motor vehicle industry. Also from 1 July 1999, allowances are not available where a person whose trade consists wholly or mainly of constructing or refurbishing buildings or structures for sale, or a person connected (within *s 10*) with such a person, incurred the expenditure. **Since 1 January 2003**, capital allowances will not be available on any expenditure incurred on large projects falling within the notification requirements of the European Commission Multisectoral framework on regional aid for large investment projects unless approval is obtained from the European Commission.

There is also provision against double relief where relief is given under any of the above provisions, and no allowances are available for expenditure incurred after 5 April

2001 any part of which has been or is to be met, directly or indirectly, by grant assistance.

[*TCA 1997, ss 372L, 372M, 372T; FA 1998, s 77; FA 1999, s 47(1)(b); FA 2000, s 45; FA 2001, s 59(1)(b)(v); FA 2002, ss 23(1)(d), 26, Sch 2 para 2; SI 206/99/; FA 2003, s 28; FA 2004, s 26; FA 2006, s 17; SI 642/05*]

Other commercial buildings. Industrial buildings allowances are also given for capital expenditure in the 'qualifying period' (as above) on the construction or refurbishment of 'qualifying premises' (expenditure being treated as incurred in the qualifying period only if it is properly attributable to work actually carried out in that period). '*Qualifying premises*' means a building or structure in a 'qualifying rural area' (as above) which is not an industrial building or structure within **8.5** above but which is either:

(*a*)   in use for the purposes of a trade or profession, or of a local authority approved scheme amongst whose objects is the provision of sewerage facilities, water supplies or public roads; or

(*b*)   whether or not so used, let on *bona fide* commercial terms for arm's length consideration;

but excluding any part of a building, etc in use as or as part of a dwelling house.

'Refurbishment' is defined as above.

The normal allowances (see **8.5** above) are for this purpose increased to an initial allowance of 50 per cent and unrestricted free depreciation annual allowances. However, before 1 July 1999, any allowance or charge under the normal provisions as so adjusted is halved, so that in effect an initial allowance of 25 per cent is available and free depreciation annual allowances of 50 per cent in aggregate allowed where no initial allowance is claimed, with two per cent annual allowances otherwise available. Since 1 July 1999, the total of annual allowances may not exceed 50 per cent of the qualifying expenditure.

The allowances are dependent, in the case of 'refurbishment' expenditure, on the total amount of such expenditure incurred in the qualifying period being not less than ten per cent of the market value of the building, etc (excluding land) immediately before the expenditure is incurred.

No balancing charge (see **8.5**(*c*) above) arises in respect of qualifying premises by reason of any event occurring more than 13 years after the premises were first used or, in the case of 'refurbishment' expenditure, after that expenditure was incurred.

These provisions do not, however, apply to any building or structure in use for the purposes of a trade (or activity treated as a trade) where the number of individuals employed or engaged in carrying on the trade or activity is 250 or more or, from 1 July 1999, where the trade is carried on by the person entitled to the relevant interest in the building (ie the owner-occupier) and is in any of the following sectors: agriculture (including production, processing and marketing of agricultural products); transport; steel; ship-building; synthetic fibres; or financial services, or in the coal industry, the fishing industry or the motor vehicle industry. Also from 1 July 1999, allowances are not available where a person whose trade consists wholly or mainly of constructing or refurbishing buildings or structures for sale, or a person connected (within *s 10*) with such a person, incurred the expenditure.

There is also provision against double relief where relief is given under any of the above provisions, and no allowances are available for expenditure incurred after 5 April 2001 any part of which has been or is to be met, directly or indirectly, by grant assistance from any source.

[*TCA 1997, ss 372L, 372N, 372T; FA 1998, s 77; Urban Renewal Act 1998, s 19(c); FA 2000, s 45; FA 2001, s 59(1)(b)(v); FA 2006, s 17*]

RESTRICTION ON URBAN AND RENEWAL RELIEFS

8.13 *Finance Act 2011, s 23* introduced restrictions on property based reliefs.

Section 23 relief

8.14 In summary the changes are as follows: for chargeable periods on or after the date to be specified by order of the Minister for Finance it is proposed that such reliefs will be restricted to income from that property itself. In addition, after a 10-year holding period, any unused relief will be lost. If the property is sold within this period or on or after the relevant day the new owner will not get s 23 relief and the seller continues to be subject to a claw back of relief already given which would be in the form of additional rental income subject to tax at marginal income tax rates in the case of an individual investor. Where any properties, to which the relief applies are not let under a qualifying lease by six months after the relevant day, the holding period will commence on that day. This will have the effect of shortening the period over which the relief can be claimed.

Accelerated capital allowances

8.15 The section provides that with effect from the next tax year commencing on or after the relevant day, where an individual becomes entitled to any capital allowances, including any balancing allowances, in respect of a building or structure for use in a trade, those allowances may only be set against the income of that trade. The allowances may not be used against income of another trade of that individual or against any other form of income. This restriction applies to capital allowances arising in a particular tax year as well as to those carried forward from a previous tax year. In addition, for any chargeable period commencing on or after the relevant day, where a person is in receipt of rental income from such a property, any capital allowances, to which that person is entitled may only be set-off against the rental income from the property itself.

Under the various property and area-based tax incentive schemes, the period over which capital allowances can be claimed may be seven or 10 years and in some cases greater than 10 years but less than 25 years.

The changes, introduced by the section, are for the seven and 10 year schemes, any unused capital allowances carried-forward to the respective 7th or 10th chargeable periods after the chargeable period in which they were first claimed, are lost. This applies where these chargeable periods have yet to be reached and those where they have already ended. In the former case, any unused amount carried forward beyond that period are lost. In the latter case, any unused amount carried forward into the next chargeable period commencing on or after the relevant day is also lost. Where the capital allowance is given over a period greater than 10 years, this period is reduced to seven chargeable periods, including the chargeable period in which the allowance was first claimed. The consequences of this are as follows; in circumstances where this seventh chargeable period ended before the relevant day, any capital allowances, which have yet to be given will be lost, and; where the seventh chargeable period has not yet ended as of the relevant day, the amount of capital allowances yet to be given is reduced by 20 per cent and given evenly over the balance of the seven chargeable periods; and in all cases, any capital allowances, carried forward beyond the end of the seventh chargeable period and into any subsequent chargeable period commencing on or after the relevant day are lost.

[*FA 2011, ss 23 and 24*]

See also **2.45** 'Limitation on Income Tax Relief for High Earners' and **33.14** 'Sch D, Case V'.

MISCELLANEOUS MATTERS

8.16 The total of annual wear and tear allowances and initial allowances must not exceed the cost of the asset. [*TCA 1997, s 283(7)*]

Expenditure on effluent treatment and water supply. Capital expenditure by a taxpayer for the purposes of treatment of trade effluent can qualify for capital allowances if it meets the normal conditions for such allowances. An equivalent relief is available for contributions to capital expenditure by a local authority on an effluent control scheme. If the contribution is for the purposes of his trade and the local authority expenditure is for provision of an asset for an approved scheme for treating trade effluent, then the taxpayer is entitled to capital allowances as though his contribution was expenditure by himself on such an asset. For expenditure incurred by the local authority after 14 February 2001, only writing-down and wear and tear allowances are available in respect of contributions (wear and tear allowances being at the rates of 12.5 per cent and 20 per cent referred to in **8.6**(*b*) above), but allowances are extended to contributions to expenditure on assets to be used for the supply of water under a written agreement between the contributor and the local authority. [*TCA 1997, s 310; FA 2001, s 50; FA 2003, s 23*]

Film production, etc expenditure. It is understood that film production expenses can qualify for capital allowances, provided that the master negative is retained by the production company and has an anticipated life of at least two years. Similar considerations apply to eg master copies of records and tapes. From 2007, the quantum of relief available to a high earning individual in any one year may be limited, see **2.45** 'Limitation on Income Tax Relief for High Earners'. [*FA 2006, s 17*]

Value-added tax claimable as a refund or deduction under *VATA ss 12, 20(3)* (see **39.12, 39.18** 'Value added tax') is disregarded in any claim to capital allowances or where chargeable on any disposal proceeds. [*TCA 1997, s 319*]

8.17 Energy Efficient Equipment. A new section was introduced which provides for accelerated capital allowances in respect of expenditure by companies on energy efficient equipment bought for the purposes of the trade. The scheme, which will run for a trial period of three years, will apply to new equipment in designated classes of technology. Equipment eligible under the scheme will be published in a list established by the Minister for Communications, Energy and Natural Resources (with the approval of the Minister for Finance) and maintained by the Sustainable Energy Authority of Ireland.

The main features of the new scheme are as follows:

— capital allowances of 100 per cent will be available in the first year in which the expenditure is incurred on the equipment covered by the scheme;

— to qualify, the equipment that is purchased must meet certain energy-efficiency criteria (laid down by the Minister for Communications, Energy and Natural Resources) and be specified on a list of approved products;

— energy-efficient equipment on the list will fall into one of three classes of technology and expenditure must be above a certain minimum amount to qualify for the increased allowance. The technology classes (and minimum expenditure amounts) are: motors and drives (€1,000), lighting (€3,000) and building energy management systems (€5,000);

— the list will be established, and may be amended, by order of the Minister for Communications, Energy and Natural Resources. Sustainable Energy Ireland (SEI) will be responsible for maintaining the list;

— The scheme will be confined to new energy-efficient equipment purchased by companies, and it will not apply to equipment that is leased, let or hired. It will run up to 31 December 2010.

The *Finance (No 2) Act 2008* amended the operation of this section to increase the number of classes of qualifying equipment from three to seven. The number of classes has been increased from seven to ten. [*FA 2010, s 40*] The scheme provides for 100 per cent capital allowances in the year of purchase on expenditure incurred by companies on qualifying equipment bought for the purposes of the trade. The new categories are:

— Information and Communications Technology;

— Heating and Electricity Provision;

— Process and Heating, Ventilation and Air-Conditioning (HVAC) Control Systems; and

— Electric and Alternative Fuel Vehicles.

These four additional categories are included in an amended *Sch 4A* and the amendments will come into effect from a date to be specified in a commencement order to be made by the Minister for Finance. The commencement order (*SI 399/2009*) was made on 9 October 2008. [*F(No 2)A 2008, s 37*]

The section provides that where accelerated capital allowances are provided for under the scheme for Electric and Alternative Fuel Vehicles, the value of the vehicle will be based on the lower of the actual cost of the vehicle or the €24,000 upper limit applying to low emission vehicles under *Pt 11C*. It also provides that accelerated allowances under the scheme for energy efficient equipment in *s 285A* will not apply where an allowance is claimed using emission based limited provided for under *s 380L (Pt 11C)*.

This scheme has been further extended for another three years to 31 December 2014. [*FA 2011, s 38*]

Specialist Palliative Care Units. This new scheme of capital allowances for capital expenditure incurred on the construction and refurbishment of qualifying specialist palliative care units was introduced in *FA 2008*. The scheme has similar terms, conditions and exclusions to those which apply in the case of qualifying private hospitals and qualifying mental health centres. For expenditure to qualify, the development of a facility must have pre-approval from the Health Service Executive (HSE), with the consent of the Minister for Health and Children, as being in line with national development plans and needs assessments for palliative care facilities. Among other requirements, a qualifying facility must have a minimum of 20 in-patient palliative care beds. *Finance (No 2) Act 2008, s 20* amended the definition of qualifying specialist palliative care units so that the required number of beds has been reduced from 20 to 8. The HSE must also certify, on an annual basis for 15 years from first use, that a facility has satisfied the terms and conditions in the legislation. A claw-back of the allowances will apply if a facility is sold or ceases to be used for the purposes of palliative care during this 15-year period. Relief for eligible capital expenditure incurred will be available at the rate of 15 per cent per annum in the first six years with ten per cent in year seven. Eligible expenditure is net of any grants or other financial assistance received towards development costs. The restriction on the use of tax reliefs by high income individuals applies to investors who avail of capital allowances under the scheme. Approval from a State-aid perspective is required from the EU Commission. Therefore, the scheme is subject to a commencement order which will be made when that approval has been obtained. [*FA 2008, s 26*] The date on which capital expenditure on qualifying units can qualify for capital allowances is being changed from the date on which *FA 2008, s 26* comes into operation – which will happen by way of a commencement order when approval of the scheme from a State-Aid perspective is obtained from the EU Commission – to the date of the passing of the *Finance Act 2008* (ie 13 March 2008).

CAPITAL ALLOWANCES ON INTANGIBLE ASSETS

8.18 *Finance Act 2009, s 13* introduced a new *Pt 9, Ch 2, s 291A*. The scheme provides for capital allowances against taxable income on capital expenditure incurred by companies on the provision of intangible assets for the purposes of a trade. The scheme applies to intangible assets which are recognised as such under generally accepted accounting practice and which are included in the specified categories listed in the new section.

Allowances provided under the scheme will reflect the standard accounting treatment of intangible assets and will be based on the amount charged to the profit and loss account of the company for the accounting period in respect of the amortisation or depreciation of the specified intangible asset. However, companies can opt instead for a fixed write-down period of 15 years at a rate of 7 per cent per annum and 2 per cent in the final year.

There will be no claw-back of allowances where an intangible asset is disposed of more than 15 years after the beginning of the accounting period in which the asset was first provided, provided that the disposal does not result in a connected company claiming allowances in respect of capital expenditure on the asset.

Activities which consist of the managing, developing or exploiting of a specified intangible asset and carried on by a company as part of a trade are to be treated as a separate trade (referred to as a 'relevant trade') and income from such activity is to be assessed separately. In addition, the aggregate amount of any allowances and related interest expense in an accounting period shall not exceed 80 per cent of the trading income from the relevant trade for that period excluding such allowances and/or interest. However, any excess allowances and/or interest expense shall be available for carry forward for offset against trading income of the relevant trade for succeeding accounting periods. Provision has also been made for a corresponding restriction on the amount of interest relief which may be claimed (under *s 247*) by an investing company providing funds to a company to acquire a specified intangible asset.

Expenditure on the provision of specified intangible assets will not qualify under the scheme where relief for such expenditure is otherwise available under the Taxes Consolidation Act. The scheme shall not apply to capital expenditure on specified intangible assets to the extent that this expenditure is in excess of an arm's length amount payable between independent parties and provision is made to enable the Revenue Commissioners to consult with an expert in this regard. Relief is also not available in respect of any expenditure incurred as part of a tax avoidance arrangement.

In the case of transfers of specified intangible assets between group companies, the acquiring company will be able to claim capital allowances on the assets acquired where both it and the transferring company jointly elect to opt out of the existing capital gains tax group relief provisions (under *TCA 1967, s 617*).

The allowances currently available for capital expenditure on the provision of computer software (under *s 291*) are being retained and the new scheme does not therefore apply to computer software. As patent rights and know-how are being included in the new scheme, the existing reliefs for capital expenditure on patent rights (*s 755*) and know-how (*s 768*) are being discontinued for companies, but with provision for companies to opt for these reliefs for a further two-year period.

The scheme applies to expenditure incurred by a company after 7 May 2009.

Finance Act 2010, s 43 amends the provisions relating to capital expenditure on intangible assets to provide for an amended definition of computer software. The amended definition of computer software provides for relief in relation to 'end-use' type software only. Computer software acquired for the purposes of its commercial exploitation by companies will be treated as expenditure on a specified intangible asset within the meaning of *s 291A* and relief for such expenditure will, accordingly, be available under this section.

To accommodate companies with planned investments, the amendment provides for a transition period of two years during which a company may elect to claim relief under *s 291* in respect of capital expenditure on computer software acquired for commercial exploitation.

The list of specified assets covered under the scheme is expanded to include applications for the grant or registration of patents, copyright and other intangible assets together with a broader definition of know-how.

A further amendment will ensure that relief will be available for capital expenditure prior to the commencement of the trade on the provision of specified intangible assets.

The last amendment relates to a technical amendment to clarify the activities, involving the use of the specified intangible assets, that constitute a separate trade for the purposes of determining the trading income of the relevant trade against which the capital allowances may be offset.

The new amendments by *FA 2010* take effect in relation to expenditure by companies after 4 February 2010.

9 Capital Gains Tax

9.1 The *Capital Gains Tax Act 1975* was enacted on 5 August 1975 and introduced capital gains tax (CGT) for years of assessment commencing on or after 6 April 1974. Substantial changes were made by the *Capital Gains Tax (Amendment) Act 1978*, under which, *inter alia*, allowable expenditure was increased by reference to the increase in the consumer price index since the expenditure was incurred (see **9.9** below). The enactments relating to CGT are consolidated in the *Taxes Consolidation Act 1997*, mainly in *Pts 19–21*. They continue to be referred to as the *Capital Gains Tax Acts* (see *s 1(2)*).

BASIS OF CHARGE

9.2 CGT is charged for a year of assessment (see **2.1** 'Allowances, credits and rates') in respect of chargeable gains accruing to a person in the year on any disposal or deemed disposal of assets. [*TCA 1997, s 28(1)(2); FA 2003, s 69*]

Persons chargeable are those resident or ordinarily resident in RI during the tax year, and anyone else who disposes of land or minerals or mineral rights in RI, or exploration or exploitation rights over the RI continental shelf, or unquoted shares or securities deriving their value from any of the assets mentioned above, or assets in RI used in a trade carried on by him in RI. For accounting periods ending from 1 March 2005, overseas assets of a life assurance business used or held for the purposes of the company's branch or agency in RI are also chargeable. **Since 6 February 2003**, receipts in respect of non-competition agreements that are not otherwise taxable are subject to capital gains tax. Persons resident or ordinarily resident in RI but not RI domiciled are chargeable, as respects assets outside RI and UK, on remittances to RI. (Losses on such overseas disposals are not allowed.) See also **27.5** 'Residents and non-residents' as regards non-residents' agents.

Since 20 November 2008 the remittance basis of taxation will apply to gains arising to all non-Irish domiciled persons in respect of non-Irish situated assets. *Section 29(4)* is amended to provide that any gain arising on the disposal of assets situated outside the State and the United Kingdom to a person who is resident or ordinarily resident, but not domiciled, in the State will be based on the actual amount received in the State. [*TCA 1997, s 29; FA 2003, s 70; FA 2005, s 41; F(No 2)A 2008, s 41*]

Since 24 February 2003, disposals by an individual of all or part of shares, or rights to acquire shares, in a company ('relevant assets') during a period of non-RI tax residence are subject to capital gains tax where (i) the period of non-RI tax residence is no more than five tax years, (ii) the individual was domiciled in the State at any time during the year prior to non-residence, (iii) the individual would have been subject to capital gains tax on any gain on a disposal of the relevant assets on each day of that year, (iv) the individual was beneficially entitled to the shares on the last day of the year in which RI tax residence ceased, (v) the shares or rights had a value of at least five per cent of the issued share capital of the company or more than €500,000 on that last day, and (vi) the disposal is made during the period of non-residence and would be taxable in RI if the individual was tax resident at the time. See also **9.4** below. [*FA 2003, s 69*]

Amount chargeable is the total of taxpayer's chargeable gains in the *actual year of assessment* after deduction of allowable losses for that year and, so far as not already deducted, in any previous year from 6 April 1974. [*TCA 1997, s 31*]

RATES

9.3 The rate of capital gains tax is **25 per cent** for disposals on or after 8 April 2009 (**20 per cent** on all disposals prior to this date) other than (see **9.16** below) certain disposals of interests in offshore funds (see **32.15** 'Sch D, Case IV') and disposals of foreign life assurance policies (see **9.7**(*g*) below)). **Since 15 October 2008** the rate of capital gains tax is increased to **22 per cent** on all disposals on or after this date other than (see **9.16** below) certain disposals of interests in offshore funds (see **32.15** 'Sch D, Case IV') and disposals of foreign life assurance policies (see **9.7**(*g*) below)) [*TCA 1997, ss 28(3); 649A; F(No 2)A 2008, s 43*]

ADMINISTRATION, RETURNS AND ASSESSMENT

9.4 The capital gains tax provisions relating to administration, assessment, returns, collection of tax and appeals are broadly similar to those which apply for income tax purposes. For the self-assessment provisions applicable for 1990/91 and subsequent years of assessment, see **28.12** 'Returns'. Proper books and records must be kept to enable true returns to be made, subject to a penalty up to £1,200/€1,520. [*TCA 1997, s 886*]

Returns may additionally be required from issuing houses etc; stockbrokers; auctioneers or persons dealing with tangible movable property; nominee shareholders; parties to a settlement; and by various persons in relation to non-resident companies or trusts. [*TCA 1997, ss 913–917C; FA 1999, s 92*]

Assessment of married persons. Gains of a wife living with her husband are assessed on the husband, and rules on returns and collection apply accordingly, unless either spouse claims separate assessment. Such a claim remains in force until withdrawn by notice. Allowable losses (see **9.10** below) not exhausted against gains of one spouse may be transferred to the other, unless there is separate assessment. [*TCA 1997, ss 913(8), 1028, 1029; FA 2001, Sch 2 para 59*]

Children. The *Status of Children Act 1987, s 3* applies in that:

(*a*)   relationships between persons are to be determined without regard to whether the parents of any person are or have been married to each other, unless the contrary intention appears; and

(*b*)   an adopted person shall, for the purposes of (*a*), be deemed from the date of the adoption to be the child of the adopter or adopters, and not the child of any other person or persons.
[*TCA 1997, s 8*]

Assessment, where tax unpaid, on donees, beneficiaries or shareholders. Where CGT payable on a gift is not paid by the donor, the donee may be assessed for the same amount of tax. He may recover the tax from the donor or, if the donor is dead, from his personal representatives, as a debt. A beneficiary absolutely entitled against the settlement trustees (or so entitled but for age or disability etc) who receives from the trustees an asset, or the proceeds of sale of an asset, on the previous disposal of which CGT has become due from the trustees but has been unpaid for six months or more, may be assessed in the name of the trustees. A person connected with an RI resident company who receives a capital distribution (other than a reduction of capital) in respect of shares in the company may be assessed in the company's name for CGT due but unpaid for six months or more in respect of a chargeable gain to which the distribution relates. He may recover the tax from the company. In all the above cases the assessment must be made *within two years* of the date on which the tax originally became payable. [*TCA 1997, ss 574(2), 977, 978*]

Assessment on liquidators, receivers, etc Disposals by a company liquidator or by a person entitled to an asset by way of security, or to the benefit of a charge or encumbrance on an asset, or by a person appointed to enforce or give effect to the security, etc (an *'accountable person'*) are generally treated as being disposals by the debtor or company owning the asset subject to the charge, etc [*TCA 1997, ss 78(8), 537, 570, 571(1)*]. See **38.46** 'Tax cases'. Any 'referable CGT' or 'referable corporation tax' (see below) attributable to the disposal is assessable on and recoverable from the accountable person out of the disposal proceeds, and is treated as a necessary disbursement out of those proceeds. The CGT or corporation tax liability of the owner of the asset is correspondingly reduced for the year of assessment or accounting period of the disposal, but the owner's chargeable gains are otherwise unaffected.

The assessment is made under Sch D, Case IV for the year of assessment of the disposal on an amount such that income tax at the standard rate thereon equals the referable CGT or corporation tax to be brought into charge (see below).

'Referable CGT' generally means the amount of CGT assessable on the debtor (apart from these provisions) in respect of disposals such as are referred to above (*'referable gains'*) reliefs and deductions being apportioned rateably. In cases where there are other gains in the year of assessment, the usual order of allowance of reliefs and deductions applies where tax would be chargeable at more than one rate or would be chargeable on both 'relevant disposals' (ie disposals of development land – see **9.16** below) and other disposals. Otherwise a proportion A/B of the liability on all gains in the year (apart from these provisions) is attributed to the referable gains, where:

A   is the CGT liability which would arise (apart from these provisions) if the referable gains were the debtor's only chargeable gains for the year, ignoring any deductions or reliefs, and

B   is the CGT liability which would arise (apart from these provisions) on all the owner's chargeable gains for the year, ignoring any deductions or reliefs.

'Referable corporation tax' is similarly broadly the CGT which would be assessable on the company (apart from these provisions) in respect of the referable gains if companies were chargeable to CGT under the normal CGT provisions, except that the corporation tax chargeable on referable gains (apart from these provisions) is generally substituted if less. There are similarly provisions determining the tax attributable to referable gains where there are gains other than referable gains and 'relevant disposals' (see above).

[*TCA 1997, s 571*]

Gains arising to temporary non-residents. Where a temporary non-resident (see **9.2** above) makes a relevant disposal, the individual is treated as having disposed of and immediately reacquired the assets at market value on the last day of the year of departure. The date for payment of the tax and submission of a return is determined as if the disposal occurred in the year of return. Credit is available for foreign tax paid in respect of the disposal in a tax treaty country. [*FA 2003, s 69*]

PAYMENT OF TAX

9.5 See also **28.12** 'Returns' as regards self-assessment.

Since 2003, CGT is payable by 31 October in the year of disposal for disposals before 1 October in the year and by 31 January following that year for disposals made from 1 October to 31 December. [*FA 2003, s 42*] For disposals on or after 1 January 2009, there are two periods for payment purposes. The first period is 1 January to 30 November and the second period is 1 December to 31 December. For disposals in the first period, CGT is payable on 15 December and for disposals in the second period, CGT is payable on 31 January of the following year. [*FA 2009*] For 2001 and 2002, CGT was payable on 31 October following the year of assessment. Prior to 2001, it was payable on 1 November following the year of assessment. Where consideration for a chargeable disposal is paid in instalments over a period beginning on or after the date of the disposal and exceeding 18 months, CGT may be allowed to be paid in instalments in cases of hardship. [*TCA 1997, ss 979, 981*] The chargeable gain on a disposal by a person neither resident nor ordinarily resident in RI at the time of disposal may, however, be assessed and charged before the end of the year of assessment of the disposal, and the tax is then payable within three months of the date of disposal or, if later, two months after the date of the assessment. [*TCA 1997, s 1042*]

Unremittable gains. Chargeable gains, included in an assessment, accruing on a disposal of assets outside RI may be disregarded by the Revenue Commissioners if they are satisfied that legislation or executive action of the foreign state prevents the gains being remitted to RI. [*TCA 1997, s 1005*]

Deduction of tax on certain disposals. A person by or through whom consideration exceeding €500,000 (£300,000/€381,000 for disposals after 22 March 2000 and before 1 January 2002, £150,000 for disposals after 26 March 1998 and before 23 March 2000) is payable on the disposal of land, minerals or mineral rights in RI, or of exploration or exploitation rights over the RI continental shelf, or of unquoted shares deriving their value from any of the foregoing (or of unquoted shares exchanged for such shares), or of goodwill of an RI trade, must deduct and account for an amount of CGT equal to *15 per cent of the consideration* unless the vendor produces to him a *clearance certificate*. On application by a vendor (or from 28 March 2003, his agent), an inspector of taxes must issue a clearance certificate (Form CG 50A), with a copy to the purchaser, if satisfied that the vendor is resident in RI or that CGT is not payable or has already been paid. For disposals on or after 23 March 2000, if the asset concerned is land on which a 'new house' (as defined) has been, or is in the course of being, built, certain other certification may be presented instead of a clearance certificate to avoid a deduction being made. Broadly the vendor may produce a valid certificate of authorisation (form C2) within *s 531* (see **13.8** 'Deduction of tax at source'), a valid tax clearance certificate within *s 1094* or *s 1095* (see **1.13** 'Administration and general') or (where none of those has been issued to the vendor) a special certificate for which application may be made to the Collector-General in the same way as if it were a tax clearance certificate. [*TCA 1997, s 980; CGTA 1975, Sch 4 para 11; FA 1995, s 76(a)(b); FA 1996, s 59(a); FA 1998, s 74; FA 2000, s 87; FA 2002, s 63; FA 2003, s 71*] See Revenue Tax Briefing Issue 35 pp 22–24 for procedure for obtaining forms CG 50A. See also **38.41**, **38.46** 'Tax cases'.

Where no clearance certificate or alternative certification (as above) is produced but the consideration is of a kind preventing the deduction being made, the purchaser must, within seven days of the disposal, notify particulars to the Revenue Commissioners and pay to the Collector-General an amount of capital gains tax equal to 15 per cent of the market value of the consideration, estimated to the best of the purchaser's knowledge and belief. This does not apply where the provisions of *s 978*, enabling tax chargeable on a disposal by way of gift to be assessed and charged on the donee (see **9.4** above), apply. An assessment is not required, but may be made if the tax is not paid within seven days of the disposal. The purchaser may recover an amount equal to tax so paid from the vendor as a simple contract debt in any competent court (unless a certificate is subsequently produced, in which case the tax will be repaid). Since 25 March 2005, credit is given to the vendor for the tax paid provided that proof of payment to the purchaser is forthcoming and the 15 per cent payment is received by Revenue. Prior to that date, this treatment was applied in practice. These provisions apply *mutatis mutandis* to joint purchasers. [*TCA 1997, s 980(9); CGTA 1975, Sch 4 para 11(7); FA 1995, s 76(c); FA 2000, s 87(1)(d); FA 2005, s 56*] A disposal by virtue of a capital sum being derived from assets (see **9.6**(*c*) below) is for the above purposes treated as the acquisition of the assets for that sum (whether in money or in money's worth) by the person paying the capital sum. This does not apply to the payment of insurance claims in respect of property damage. [*TCA 1997, s 980(11)*]

Since 25 March 2005, the certification requirements do not apply to certain bodies that are exempt from capital gains tax (see **9.7** (k)). [*FA 2005, s 56*]

See **25.3** 'Payment of tax', as regards interest on unpaid and overpaid tax.

DISPOSAL OF ASSETS

9.6 Assets comprise all forms of property, whether or not in RI, including options, debts, and other incorporeal property, and property created by its owner or otherwise arising without being acquired. Certain assets are exempt, see **9.7** below. [*TCA 1997, s 532*] For the **location** of certain assets, see *s 533*.

'**Disposal**' is not defined but it is regarded as meaning any transfer of ownership rights. The following are specifically stated to be disposals:

(*a*)   a gift [*TCA 1997, s 547(1)(a)*];

(*b*)   the grant (and in certain cases abandonment) of an option (including an option for a lease) (and see **9.15** below) [*TCA 1997, s 540*];

(*c*)   satisfaction of a debt or part (including a debt on a 'security'), although on a disposal by the original creditor only the disposal of a debt on a 'security' is chargeable. A '*security*' for this purpose includes any loan stock or similar security (other than certain Government etc securities (see **9.7**(*f*) below)) and certain company debentures (see *s 541(7)*) [*TCA 1997, s 541*];

(*d*)   the conversion of a foreign currency denominated bank account into euros on the day of introduction of the euro gives rise to a deemed market value disposal and reacquisition on the day preceding that day. Any gain is, however, assessed and charged only as funds are withdrawn from the account, subject to special rules for assurance companies and collective investment undertakings (see **12.16**, **12.22** 'Corporation tax') [*TCA 1997, s 541A; FA 1998, Sch 2 para 9; FA 1999, s 87*];

(*e*)   receipt by the owner of an asset of a capital sum by way of compensation (including insurance moneys) for damage, loss or depreciation of the asset or by way of payment for use or for waiver of rights (see also **9.7**(*n*)) [*TCA 1997, s 535(2)*] (and see **38.42** 'Tax cases');

(*f*)   receipt of or entitlement to a capital distribution on shares (deemed to be a part disposal of the shares), also receipt of any sum, except new shares, on a reorganisation of capital, conversion of securities, etc [*TCA 1997, ss 583–587*].

Part disposal occurs where any rights over the asset remain undisposed of, including where an interest is created by disposal (eg grant of a lease by the freeholder). [*TCA 1997, s 534*]

   The time of disposal if there is a contract is the date when the contract is made, or, if conditional, when the condition is satisfied (see **38.51** 'Tax cases'). A hire-purchase or similar transaction is a disposal at the time when the use and enjoyment of the assets begin (with adjustment of tax if ownership never passes). Where land is compulsorily acquired, disposal occurs on the date when the compensation is initially determined or, if earlier, the date of the authority's entry onto the land. Where, however, land used for farming is compulsorily purchased from a farmer for a road scheme, any chargeable gain is deemed to accrue when the consideration is received. For disposals on or after the 4 February 2010, the date of disposal where all land is subject to a compulsory purchase order is now the date the consideration is received. [*FA 2010, s 56*]

   [*TCA 1997, ss 539, 542; FA 2002, s 62; FA 2010, s 56*] See also Revenue Tax Briefing Issue 36 pp 14, 15.

   Death of owner is not a disposal, nor is any deed of family arrangement made within two years of death (or longer if Revenue Commissioners allow). [*TCA 1997, s 573*]

   Conveyance or transfer of an asset by way of security is not a disposal. Subsequent disposal under enforcement powers by a mortgagee or receiver is deemed to be a disposal by the owner/mortgagor. [*TCA 1997, s 537*] See also **9.4** above.

EXEMPTIONS AND RELIEFS

9.7

(*a*)   **Gains not exceeding €1,270/£1,000 (for 2001 only, £740) for an individual** in a year of assessment are exempt (gains are net after deduction of losses including losses brought forward from earlier years). If total gains exceed the exempt limit only the excess is chargeable. As regards married couples, each spouse is entitled to the full exemption. The exemption does not apply in cases of retirement relief (see (*q*) below). Where in a tax year an individual is chargeable to CGT at more than one rate (see **9.3** above), relief is allowed first against gains charged at the highest rate; [*TCA 1997, ss 601, 1028(4); FA 1998, s 75; FA 2001, Sch 2 para 34*]

(*b*)   **Any disposal of tangible movable property for €2,540/£2,000 or less** by an individual is exempt, with marginal relief limiting tax on disposals over €2,540/£2,000 to one-half of the excess. Any loss arising is restricted by the consideration being deemed to be €2,540/£2,000 if in fact it is less. The exemption does not apply to commodities sold by a dealer on a terminal market, to disposals of any kind of currency or to wasting assets. Splitting a set of assets is ineffective if the disposals are to the same person, or persons connected; [*TCA 1997, s 602*]

(*c*)   **Death** is not a disposal of property of which the deceased was competent to dispose. Personal representatives and legatees or persons succeeding on intestacy are deemed to have acquired such property at market value on the date of death. Deeds of family arrangement made within two years of death (or longer if the Revenue Commissioners allow) also do not constitute disposals; [*TCA 1997, s 573*]

(*d*)   **Transfers between husband and wife** who are living together are treated as disposals on a no gain/no loss basis, but on a subsequent disposal by the donee spouse the gain is computed on the basis of the acquisition by the donor spouse. These rules do not apply where the asset transferred is trading stock of either spouse. [*TCA 1997, s 1028*] The same rules apply to transfers inter-spouse by virtue or in consequence of a deed of separation or certain orders made (or treated as made or analogous to orders made) under *Family Law Act 1995*. [*TCA 1997, s 1030; FA 2000, s 88*] **Since 7 December 2005**, these rules do not apply to transfers of assets where the acquiring spouse would not be liable to RI capital gains tax if the asset was disposed of by that spouse in the year in which it is acquired; [*FA 2006, s 75*]

(*e*)   **Transfers between divorced persons** by virtue or in consequence of an order under *Family Law (Divorce) Act 1996, Pt III* are treated in the same way as transfers between husband and wife (see (*d*) above); [*TCA 1997, s 1031; FA 2006, s 75*]

(*f*)   **Exempt assets:** RI currency [*TCA 1997, s 532(b)*]; Government and other securities, as specified, and savings certificates, and unconditional futures contracts relating to such securities etc which require delivery (unless closed out); [*TCA 1997, s 607; FA 2001, s 241; FA 2003, s 43*]

(*g*)   **Life assurance policies and deferred annuity contracts** are exempt for the original beneficial owner and any subsequent owner who did not give consideration in money or money's worth (excluding certain policies, contracts or reinsurance contracts with foreign insurers issued or made after 19 May 1993, to which a capital gains tax rate of 40 per cent applies, and from 20 March 2001 this applies to gains arising after that date on pre-20 May 1993 policies, etc). Also excluded from the exemption are certain policies or contracts entered into or acquired without consideration for investment purposes by companies after 10 April 1994, for which special charging provisions apply (see **9.12** below). [*TCA

1997, ss 593–595; CGTA 1975, s 20A; FA 1995, s 68; FA 1997, s 74; FA 1998, s 65; FA 2001, s 66] See also **28.4** 'Returns';

(*h*)   **Private residence** (including additional grounds up to one acre) of an individual which has been the only or main residence throughout the period of ownership, except part or all of the last twelve months of ownership. Absences for periods of employment abroad do not break continuity of occupation, nor do absences not exceeding four years in all due to requirements of employer (and similar treatment applies in practice to periods of absence due to a spouse's employment, see Revenue Tax Briefing Issue 12 p 4). Apportionment of gain applies where the owner was only resident for part of the time. A married couple can have only one main residence, but occupation as only or main residence by a separated spouse prior to transfer of the property to that spouse as part of the financial settlement will, by concession, count as occupation by the transferor up to the date of disposal. The exemption applies equally to disposal by a trustee of settled property occupied by a beneficiary, and, in practice, to disposals by personal representatives where the residence is occupied as only or main residence before and after the death of the deceased by beneficiaries entitled to the proceeds of disposal under the will or intestacy. It does not apply to disposals wholly or mainly with the object of gain.

An additional similar relief is available for a gain on a dwelling-house and grounds which had been provided by the taxpayer rent-free and without consideration as the sole residence for his widowed mother, mother-in-law or father, or for any other relative incapacitated by old age or infirmity (only one such house being eligible).

Such relief will not in practice be denied where the dependent relative makes payments in respect of the property, provided that no net income is receivable by the individual entitled to the relief.

Where a property otherwise qualifying for private residence exemption would, apart from that exemption, give rise to a development land gain (see **9.16** below), then the exemption is restricted as below, the part of the gain not exempt being subject to the development land gains charge.

The part of the gain continuing to attract exemption is the excess of current use value (see **9.16** below) on disposal over:

(i)   if the property was held on 6 April 1974, the current use value on that date, or

(ii)   if the property was not held on 6 April 1974, the lesser of current use value on the date of acquisition and the cost of acquisition, plus the incidental costs of acquisition reduced, if appropriate, to the proportion that current use value represents of cost of acquisition at the date of acquisition,

in either case after inflation indexing, if applicable (see **9.9** below), less the proportion of incidental costs of disposal corresponding to the ratio of current use value on disposal to disposal consideration.

The restriction does not, however, apply where the total consideration in the year of assessment for disposals which would otherwise be subject to the restriction does not exceed €19,050/£15,000 (for 2001 only, £11,100);

[*TCA 1997, s 604; FA 2001, Sch 2 para 35*]

(*i*) **Tangible movable wasting assets** (see **9.12** below) are exempt, except to the extent that capital allowances were or could have been claimed because of use in a trade or profession. The exemption does not apply to commodities sold by a dealer on a terminal market; [*TCA 1997, s 603*]

(*j*) **Exempt bodies:** local authorities; trade unions and friendly societies exempt from income tax; Central Bank of Ireland; National Treasury Management Agency; the Health Service Executive; vocational education committees; committees of agriculture; the National Tourism Development Authority (previously, Bord Fáilte Éireann) and certain regional tourism authorities; Eolas; Forbairt; Forfás; Industrial Development Agency (Ireland); Industrial Development Authority; Shannon Free Airport Development Co Ltd; Údarás na Gaeltachta; Irish Horseracing Authority; Irish Thoroughbred Marketing Limited; Tote Ireland Ltd; bodies designated under *Securitisation (Proceeds of Certain Mortgages) Act 1995, s 4(1)*; Dublin Docklands Development Authority; National Rehabilitation Board; The National Pensions Reserve Fund Commission; Tourism Ireland Limited; an approved body within *s 235(1)* to the extent that its income is exempt from income or corporation tax; any body established by statute to promote games or sport and any company wholly owned by that body where the gain is applied solely for that purpose. Exemption similarly applies to disposals by the Dublin or Cork District Milk Boards, Dairysan Ltd or Glenlee (Cork) Ltd to the Interim Board established under *SI 408/94*, and to disposals by the Interim Board. Since 2004, exemption applies to gains accruing to the trustees of special trusts set up under *s 189A.* and from 2 February 2006, to The Courts Service and The Irish Auditing and Accounting Supervisory Authority. *Finance Act 2008* extended the bodies to which the exemption from CGT by virtue of *s 610* applies to include the Commission for Communications Regulation (Comreg) and the Digital Hub Development Agency. References to local authorities under *Sch 15* has been amended to those defined under Local Government Act 2001, s 2(1). [*TCA 1997, s 610, Sch 15; FA 1999, s 93; National Pensions Reserve Fund Act 2000; FA 2003, s 72; FA 2004, s 17; FA 2005, s 57; FA 2006, s 74; FA 2006, s 127, Sch 2*] See **17.10** 'Exempt organisations' as regards European Economic Interest Groupings and **17.2, 17.28** for limitations in respect of disposals by trade unions and sporting organisations from 2 February 2006. *Finance Act 2007* amended *Sch 15* for the purposes of *s 610* to provide that the exemption from capital gains tax applies provided that the full consideration received for the disposal and not just the gain are reinvested for the purpose of the body concerned. Any assets acquired by the new Pharmaceutical Society of Ireland of Ireland from the old Society under the Pharmacy Act 2007 will be charged to capital gains tax on a disposal of such assets by the new Society as if they had been owned by that body from the date they were acquired by the old Society. The amendment applies in relation to any disposals on or after 20 November 2008. *Section 611* is amended so that the public bodies qualifying for exemption are the national cultural institutions which are funded by way of a grant or grant-in-aid or funded directly by the Department of Arts, Sport and Tourism; [*TCA 1997, s 611A; F(No 2)A 2008, s 44; FA 2010, s 61* and *63*]

(*k*) **Charities** are exempt on gains applied for charitable purposes; [*TCA 1997, s 609(1)*]

(*l*) **Superannuation and similar funds** approved for income tax purposes are exempt. [*TCA 1997, s 608; FA 2005, s 58*] There is no charge to CGT on a disposal by a person of his rights to any payments from such a fund; [*TCA 1997, s 613(3)(a)*]

(*m*) **Miscellaneous exemptions:** instalment savings scheme bonuses; prize bond winnings; betting, lottery or sweepstake winnings; gains on a disposal of any debt (see **38.47–38.49** 'Tax cases') by the original creditor other than a debt on a non-exempt security (see **9.6**(*c*) above); [*TCA 1997, ss 541, 613(1)(2)*]

(*n*) **Compensation, or damages, for personal injury or professional injury** is exempt. [*TCA 1997, s 613(1)(c)*]. Capital sums received as compensation or insurance money on damage or destruction of an asset (not a wasting asset) are not chargeable if applied in restoring or replacing it (but the gain otherwise chargeable is, on a later disposal, deducted in the former case from allowable expenditure, before application of the inflation multiplier, if applicable (see **9.9** below), and in the latter from the cost of acquiring the replacement); [*TCA 1997, ss 536, 556(8)(9)*]

(*o*) **Settlements, trusts etc** Disposals of any interest under a settlement (including a life interest or annuity) are exempt for the original beneficial owner and any other person not giving consideration in money or money's worth or whose consideration was another such interest (but see **9.13** below for deemed disposals under settlements). As respects disposals on or after 11 February 1999, this exemption does not generally apply to a settlement if:

(i) the trustees are neither resident nor ordinarily resident in RI,

(ii) there has been a time when the trustees were neither resident nor ordinarily resident in RI, or fell to be regarded under double tax arrangements as resident outside RI, or

(iii) the property comprised in the settlement is or includes property derived from a settlement to which (ii) above applies.

See also **9.17** below.

A disposal of any annuity not granted by an insurance company or of annual payments under an unsecured covenant is also exempt;

[*TCA 1997, s 613(3)(4); FA 1999, s 90*]

(*p*) **Disposals to the State, charities or certain national or public bodies** by way of gift or not by arm's length bargain are treated as made on a no gain/no loss basis unless income or corporation tax relief is claimed under *s 848A*; [*TCA 1997, s 611; FA 2006, s 20*] (*q*) **Retirement relief:**

    (i)   *General.* There is relief for total consideration received up to €500,000 (€476,250/£375,000 from 2 December 1999 to 31 December 2002) on disposals by an individual aged 55 years or over of chargeable business assets (including goodwill, excluding shares etc held as investments) used for his (or his family or holding company's (as follows)) business or farm, or of shares or securities of his 'family company' or of a company which is a member of a trading group of which the holding company is his 'family company'. *Finance Act 2007* amended *s 598* to increase the ceiling for the relief from €500,000 to €750,000. (For concessional relief in the case of an individual aged over 54 years and suffering severe or chronic ill health, see Revenue e-Brief 14/2005.)

           FA 2008, s 54 introduced a '*bona fide*' test to retirement relief. The section provides that unless it is shown that the disposal is made for *bona fide* commercial reasons and does not form part of any arrangement or scheme of which the main purpose or one of the main purposes is the avoidance of liability to tax, relief will not be given.

           Disposals of land owned and used for farming for at least ten years ending with the transfer of an interest in the land under the Schemes of Early Retirement From Farming also qualify for relief (this includes disposals of leased land from 27 November 2000), and for disposals on or after 1 January 2002, this applies also to land, machinery or plant owned by the individual for a period of at least ten years prior to the disposal and used throughout that period by the family or holding company (provided also that the land, etc is disposed of at the same time, and to the same person, as the shares or securities in that company), and to land compulsorily purchased for a road scheme which had been let by the individual at any time in the period of five years prior to the disposal and which, immediately before that letting, had been owned and used for farming by the individual for at least the preceding ten years. *Finance Act 2008* amended *Pt 19, Ch 6* to give effect to a proposal in the Budget statement to grant relief to farming partnerships on the dissolution of such partnerships. The amendment provides that the asset being disposed of must have been owned and used by the farming partnership for ten years prior to the dissolution of the partnership. Where one of the partners acquired their interest in the partnership by way of an inheritance, the ten-year period will include the period of ownership of the disponer. The relief operates such that a gain will not be treated as accruing in respect of a relevant partnership asset and that asset will be treated as having been acquired at the same time and for the same consideration as it was originally acquired by the partner who disposed of the asset. This amendment will be effective from the date of the passing of the Act and will cease to be effective on 31 December 2013.

           Finance Act 2007, s 52 also extended the relief to include, in certain circumstances, disposals of land that has been let prior to its disposal,

The amendment provides that the land must have been let for a period not exceeding ten years ending with the date of the disposal and that it must have been owned and used for farming by the individual making the disposal for a period of not less than ten years prior to the letting of same. The disposal must also be to a child.

The final change to retirement relief and farming is provided under *Finance Act 2007* and the amendment provides that where a parent is disposing of land used for the purposes of farming to his or her child and the consideration for the disposal consists of other land, the parent acquiring this other land will be treated as having acquired this other land at the date and for the consideration that the child originally acquired it and he or she will be deemed to have farmed that land for the same period that the child farmed it.

Since 1 January 2005 the EU Single Farm Payment Entitlement is an asset for the purposes of the relief provided that the farmer meets the ownership and usage criteria in respect of the land disposed of at the same time. The relief applies also where the land is co-owned by a husband and wife but only one of the co-owners is a partner in a milk production partnership provided that certain usage and certification criteria are met. [*FA 2006, s 70*]

The relief for disposals of shares in family companies (and holding companies) is in the proportion that the value of its chargeable business assets (or those of the trading group) bears to that of its total chargeable assets. Relief may similarly be available where shares in the family company are treated as disposed of in consideration of a capital distribution by the company, insofar as the distribution does *not* consist of chargeable business assets (and see Revenue Tax Briefing Issue 26 pp 15, 16 for concessionary treatment where a company's chargeable business assets are sold as a preliminary to liquidation, so that a disproportionate part of the company's assets at the date of disposal are chargeable non-business assets).

Finance Act 2008 gave effect to the proposal in the Budget statement regarding the decommissioning of fishing vessels. Relief is being granted under *s 598* in respect of compensation payments made under the scheme for the decommissioning of fishing vessels implemented by the Minister for Agriculture, Fisheries and Food in accordance with *Council Regulation (EC) No 1198/2006* of 27 July 2006. The amendment provides that in order for the relief to apply the person who received the compensation payment must have owned and used the fishing vessel for the period of six years prior to the receipt of payment and must have been at least 45 years of age at that time.

Marginal relief applies to limit CGT to one-half of any excess consideration over €500,000 (€750,000 *FA 2007*). Except for tangible movable property, the chargeable business assets must have been owned for at least the ten years prior to the disposal and must have been chargeable business assets throughout that period, and shares in the family or subsidiary company must similarly have been owned for at least ten years and only qualify if the individual has been a working director for ten years, and a full-time working director for five years. A period of ownership by a spouse is treated as that of the individual. The period immediately prior to the death of a spouse throughout which the deceased was a full-time working director is treated as a period throughout which the spouse was a full-time working director. Provision is made to accommodate assets to which the provisions of *ss 597* and *600* have applied. For disposals from 6 February 2003, a period of use by a deceased spouse is treated as that of the individual and a period as director of a company to which the reconstruction or amalgamation provisions of *ss 586* and *587* have applied is treated as a period as director of the company. Separate disposals by an individual are aggregated. [*TCA 1997, s 598; CGTA 1975, s 26; FA 1995, s 71; FA 1996, s 60; FA 1998, s 72; FA 2000, s 85; FA 2002, s 59; FA 2003, s 68*]

(ii) *Disposals within the family.* Similar relief is available without limit where the whole or part of the individual's qualifying assets are disposed of to his children (including nephews and nieces who have helped full-time in the business for the previous five years). *Finance Act 2007* amended *s 599* to ensure that a child of a deceased child qualifies as a child for the purposes of this section. If the child etc later disposes of any of the assets within six years (ten years where the original disposal was before 6 April 1995), he is taxable on the retiring person's gain as well as on any gain he himself makes. Since 31 March 2006, this relief is extended to a foster child who has lived with and was under the care of the individual for at least five years prior to reaching the age of 18 and that fact is corroborated by more than one witness. [*TCA 1997, s 599; CGTA 1975, s 27; FA 1995, s 72; FA 2006, s 71*]

(iii) *Premiums for retiring farmers* paid under *European Communities (Retirement of Farmers) Regulations 1974 (SI 116/74)* are not counted as part of the consideration for any retirement disposal. This relief is independent of (i) and (ii) above; [*TCA 1997, s 612*]

(iv) A disposal whereby a company redeems, repays or purchases its own shares which is not treated as a distribution for the purposes of *Pt 6, Ch 2* is treated as a disposal coming within the remit of retirement relief. Any such disposals will be taken into account in determining the €750,000 ceiling on the relief. This applies to disposals on or after 4 February 2010. [*FA 2010, s 58*]

(*r*) **Replacement of business assets – 'rollover' relief. Prior to 4 December 2002,** gains arising on disposals of assets used solely for a trade etc, from which the consideration is entirely spent on acquiring new assets solely for use in the trade etc are (on a claim by the taxpayer) treated as not accruing until the new assets (or subsequent new assets similarly acquired) cease to be used in the trade etc. This deferment also applies, but only to a proportion of the gain, where all of the consideration, save a part not exceeding the gain, is spent on replacement. It is understood that, in practice, relief is generally available where the expenditure to which the proceeds of disposal of the existing asset is applied to enhance the value of, or to acquire a further interest in, assets already in use for trade purposes, and may also be available where the new asset is not immediately used for trade purposes. Assets qualifying are plant and machinery, goodwill (except where the receipt would be a trade profit), land and buildings, and financial assets of certain sporting bodies (see below). The new assets must be acquired within twelve months before or three years after the disposal of the old assets. The relief is also available to public authorities, trade associations, non-profit-making bodies, bodies promoting sports etc, professional persons and employees, farmers and persons managing woodlands. In the case of 'assets of an authorised racecourse' and 'assets of an authorised greyhound race track' (see *s 652(3)(a), (3A)(a)* and **9.16** below), the deferred gain accrues on the assets ceasing to be such assets. For disposals **from 4 December 2002**, this relief ceases to apply save where the new assets are acquired or an unconditional contract for acquisition is entered into before that date and the old assets are disposed of by 31 December 2003. [*TCA 1997, ss 597, 652(3)(3A); FA 1998, ss 71, 73; FA 2003, s 67*] See **38.50** 'Tax cases';

(*s*)   **Replacement of land etc compulsorily acquired.** There is relief similar to that in (*r*) above where land (with certain related assets) is disposed of to the State, local authority etc, under the exercise of compulsory purchase powers or following formal notice of intention to exercise such powers, and where the whole of the compensation or consideration received is applied in acquiring other assets of the same kind provided that the disposal is **prior to 4 December 2002** or the acquisition of other assets is prior to that date or after that date under unconditional contract entered into before that date and the disposal of the old assets is made by 31 December 2003. The replacement assets are identified with the original assets and no disposal is regarded as having occurred. The two kinds of assets are:

(i)   land and buildings, excluding trade assets within (ii) and houses entitled to relief under (*g*) above as principal private residences,

(ii)   trade assets consisting of land and buildings used and occupied solely for the purposes of the trade, plant and machinery, and goodwill (a trade of dealing in or developing land or of providing landlord's services etc is excluded if a profit on sale would be a trading profit).

The replacement assets must be acquired within twelve months before or three years after the disposal. If part of the compensation is not applied in acquiring the replacement assets there is a part disposal of the original assets; if money additional to the compensation is spent on acquiring the replacement assets, there is an acquisition of a proportionate part of those assets.

For disposals on or after 1 January 2002, (ii) above is extended to include land compulsorily purchased for a road scheme which had been let at any time in the period of five years prior to the disposal and which, immediately before that letting, had been owned and used for farming by the individual for at least the preceding ten years.

See **9.16** below for denial of this relief for disposals of development land (except in the case of compulsory purchase for road schemes and certain disposals by sports clubs), [*TCA 1997, s 605; FA 2002, s 61; FA 2003, s 67*]

(*t*) **Reinvestment relief.** If an individual (the '*reinvestor*') makes a 'material disposal' after 5 May 1993 **and before 4 December 2002** of shares or securities in a company and, within three years, applies the consideration for the disposal in making a 'qualifying investment', he may claim to be treated for capital gains tax purposes as if the chargeable gain on the disposal did not accrue until he disposes of the qualifying investment. If the disposal of the qualifying investment itself attracts relief under these provisions, the gain on the original disposal may be further deferred until a disposal occurs which is not within these provisions. Any necessary apportionment of overall consideration for these purposes is made on a just and reasonable basis.

If only part of the disposal consideration is reinvested as above, and the part not so reinvested is less than the gain accruing on the disposal, the reinvestor may claim a reduction in the gain on the material disposal to the amount of the consideration not so reinvested, the balance of the gain being deferred until disposal of the qualifying investment.

When the deferred gain is brought into charge, inflation indexing (see **9.9** below) is on the basis of the actual date of the material disposal.

Relief is denied unless the acquisition of the qualifying investment was made for *bona fide* commercial reasons and not wholly or partly for the purposes of realising a gain from its disposal.

A claim may be made after the relevant disposal and acquisition where all the conditions have been or will be satisfied, but relief is withdrawn where in the event the claimant is not entitled to the relief. A return of the relevant information in relation to such withdrawal is required with the return under *s 951* (see **28.12** 'Returns').

Relief is withdrawn for the year of assessment relating to the event giving rise to the failure to meet the requisite conditions, by the bringing into charge of the deferred chargeable gain, adjusted in respect of unused losses and annual exemption of the year of the material disposal and notional interest during the period of deferral.

A disposal of shares in or securities of a company is a '*material disposal*' if throughout the three years preceding the disposal (or throughout the period from commencement of trading by the company to the disposal, if shorter):

(i) the company has been a '*trading company*' or a '*holding company*' (ie its business has consisted wholly or mainly of the carrying on of trade(s) or, professions, or of the holding of shares in or securities of 51 per cent trading, etc subsidiaries), and

(ii) the reinvestor has been a full- or part-time employee or director (within *s 250*, see **20.3**(*c*)(ii) 'Interest payable') of the company or of companies which are members of the same group of trading companies.

An individual acquires a '*qualifying investment*' if he acquires '*eligible shares*' (ie new ordinary shares which, for five years after issue, carry no present or future preferential rights to dividends, or to assets on a winding up, or to be redeemed) in a 'qualifying company' and:

(A) he holds at least five per cent of the ordinary share capital at any time in the period from acquisition of the shares to the date one year after the material disposal (the 'initial period'),

(B) he holds at least 15 per cent of the ordinary share capital at any time in the initial period and the following two years (the 'specified period'),

(C) the company is not the company whose shares were the subject of the material disposal, nor a member of the same trading group as that company,

(D) the individual becomes a full-time employee or director of the company at any time in the initial period, and continues as such until the end of the specified period (or until the company commences to be wound up, or to be dissolved without being wound up), and

(E) the company uses the money raised through the share issue within the specified period to enable it, or enlarge its capacity, to undertake 'qualifying trading operations'.

An individual who would qualify for deferral under these provisions but for failing to satisfy either or both of (A) and (D) above may claim relief, provided that he was a full-time employee or director of the qualifying company throughout a period of two years beginning in the specified period, and that the tax on the disposal of the original holding has been paid in full. Relief is given by way of repayment of capital gains tax (which does not carry interest) to restore the position if deferral had applied. The chargeable gain on the disposal of the original holding is then treated as not accruing until the qualifying investment (or a further such investment, as above) is disposed of.

A company incorporated in RI is a '*qualifying company*' if:

(I) throughout the specified period, it is resident only in RI, is not listed on a stock exchange or quoted on an unlisted securities market, and exists wholly for the purpose of carrying on one or more 'qualifying trades' wholly or mainly in RI, and

(II) it is not, at any time in the specified period, under the control of another company (together with any connected persons within *s 10*), or a 51 per cent subsidiary (within *s 9*) of another company.

Since 6 April 1994, a '*qualifying trade*' is a trade (or, for disposals after 5 April 1995, a profession) which, throughout the specified period, is conducted on a commercial basis and with a view to the realisation of profits, and which consists (as regards at least 75 per cent of its trading, etc receipts in the specified period) of '*qualifying trading operations*', ie operations other than dealing in shares, securities, land, currencies, futures or traded options. Before 6 April 1994, the definition of '*qualifying trade*' for the purposes of the business expansion scheme (see **21.6** 'Investment in corporate trades') applied also for these purposes.

With effect from 6 April 1997, a company does not cease to be a qualifying company solely by virtue of its becoming quoted on the Developing Companies Market during the specified period.

A company ceases to be a qualifying company if, at any time in the specified period, a resolution is passed, or an order made, for the winding up of the company, or the company is dissolved without being wound up, unless the winding up or dissolution is for *bona fide* commercial reasons and is not part of a tax avoidance scheme and any net assets are distributed to members within three years from the commencement of the winding up or dissolution; [*TCA 1997, s 591; FA 1993, s 27; FA 1994, s 65; FA 1995, s 74; FA 1996, s 62; FA 2003, s 67*]

(*u*) **Works of art loaned for public display.** A disposal of any picture, print, book, manuscript, sculpture, piece of jewellery or work of art, after it has been loaned to an approved RI gallery or museum or (from 2 February 2006) the Irish Heritage Trust and placed on public display for at least ten years (six years prior to 2 February 2006), is treated as made at no gain or loss for CGT purposes, provided that its market value was €31,740/£25,000 or more (in the opinion of the Revenue Commissioners) at the time it was loaned. [*TCA 1997, s 606; FA 2006, s 73*] *Finance (No 2) Act 2008* reduced this relief from 100 per cent of the market value of the heritage items or heritage property to 80 per cent of the market value. The restriction applies on or after 1 January 2009. [*F(No 2)A 2008, s 87*] See, however, **34.3** 'Sch E – emoluments' as regards certain art objects loaned by companies to directors or employees;

(*v*) **Replacement of qualifying premises.** Where, on a disposal by a person **after 4 January 2001** of premises which were 'qualifying premises' throughout the period of ownership by that person, the consideration for the disposal is entirely spent on acquiring 'replacement premises', any chargeable gain on the disposal is treated as not accruing until the 'replacement premises' (or subsequent further 'replacement premises' similarly acquired) are disposed of or cease to be 'replacement premises' provided that the disposal is **prior to 4 December 2002** or the acquisition of 'replacement premises' is (or an unconditional contract for acquisition entered into) prior to that date and the old assets are disposed of by 31 December 2003. Proportionate relief is given where the premises were 'qualifying premises' for only part of the period of ownership. Where all the consideration other than an amount which is less than the gain on the disposal is applied to the acquisition of 'replacement premises', then (on a claim) deferment applies to the excess of the gain over the amount not so applied (or to a corresponding proportion of the chargeable gain where the gain is not fully chargeable). The 'replacement premises' (or further such premises) must be acquired (or an unconditional contract for the acquisition entered into) within the period from one year before to three years after the original disposal (subject to such extension of that period as the Revenue Commissioners may by written notice allow), and in the case of an unconditional contract the relief may be given on a provisional basis without waiting for the 'replacement premises' to be acquired. Relief is denied where the 'replacement premises' were acquired wholly or partly for the purpose of realising a gain from their disposal. Any necessary apportionments are made in a just and reasonable manner.

'*Qualifying premises*' in relation to a person means a building (or part), or an interest therein, in which there is not less than three separate dwellings (for disposals on or after 1 January 2002, one or more separate dwellings) and in respect of which the person is entitled to a rent or to receipts from any easement and all the requirements of regulations as to standards for rented houses, rent books and registration are complied with. '*Replacement premises*' are such premises, with at least the same number of separate dwellings (and not less than three), which the person acquires with the consideration from the disposal of qualifying premises;

[*TCA 1997, s 600A; FA 2001, s 92; FA 2002, s 60*]

(*w*) **Disposal of site to child.** No chargeable gain accrues on a disposal **after 5 December 2000** of land with a market value not exceeding **€254,000/£200,000** by a parent to his or her child to enable the child to construct a dwelling house on the land for occupation as the child's only or main residence. *Finance Act 2007* amended *s 603A* to restrict the size of the site transferred to the child. The amendment provides that the site must not exceed one acre excluding the part of the site on which the dwelling house will be constructed. The corresponding relief from stamp duty is also amended to reflect this new size restriction. The amendment is effective in respect of transfers on or after 7 February 2007.

Finance Act 2008 further amended *s 603A* to increase the cap of the market value of the site transferring from €254,000 to €500,000. Again, the corresponding stamp duty relief was amended to reflect the same. Where the child subsequently disposes of all or part of the land other than to his or her spouse, and the land disposed of does not contain a dwelling house constructed by the child since he or she acquired it and occupied as his or her only or main residence for at least three years, the chargeable gain which would have accrued on the disposal of the land (or part) to the child is treated as accruing to the child at the time of the original disposal. Only one disposal to a particular child may qualify for this relief, unless the chargeable gain originally exempted is brought into charge on the child in full (as above). Since 31 March 2006, this relief is extended to a foster child who has lived with and was under the care of the individual for at least five years prior to reaching the age of 18 and that fact is corroborated by more than one witness; [*TCA 1997, s 603A; FA 2001, s 93; FA 2006, s 72*]

(*x*) **Disposals of shares in subsidiary companies. Since 2 February 2004** a participation exemption is available to RI based holding companies for disposals in qualifying subsidiaries. For the exemption to apply, the subsidiary company (the investee) must be resident in a Member State of the EU (including RI) or a country with which RI has a double taxation agreement. The investee must exist wholly or mainly for the purposes of carrying on a trade or the collective business of the vendor company (the investor), its ten per cent qualifying subsidiaries, the investee (or, if the investee is not a ten per cent qualifying subsidiary, all of the investee's ten per cent qualifying subsidiaries), must consist wholly or mainly of the carrying on of a trade or trades. The investor must hold the investee company for a minimum period of 12 months ending in the previous 24 months. A five per cent shareholding test must be met and the disposal must occur while the investor is a parent company of the investee or within 2 years of that time. Shareholdings of companies within a 51 per cent group may be consolidated to satisfy the requisite shareholding and shareholding value tests. The exemption is extended to assets related to shares in the investee ie options over shares, securities convertible into shares etc in the investee provided that at the time of disposal either the investor or its collective 51 per cent group held shares in the investee which, if they were disposed of at the same time, would be eligible for exemption. Excluded from the exemption are disposals deemed to take place at no gain/no loss, gains that are already non-chargeable, disposals of shares in a life business fund and disposals of shares that derive the greater part of their value from land or mineral rights in RI. Since 2 February 2006, a deemed disposal arising on the cessation by a company of RI tax residence is also excluded. Where the investor transfers shares to a purchaser on the basis that it will buy the shares back at a future date, the investor is deemed to retain ownership of the shares during the intervening period. The same principle applies with a stock lending agreement. Where the investor acquires the shares in the investee in a share reorganisation, the relevant dates on the original shares may be included in determining eligibility for the exemption. An investor cannot make a negligible value claim under *s 538* in respect of shares to which the exemption would otherwise apply.

(*y*) *Finance Act 2010, s 25* has introduced certain provisions inserted by the *National Asset Management Agency Act 2009*. The provisions amend *ss 644AB and 649B* which concern the circumstances in which a special 80 per cent tax rates is to be applied to 'windfall' profits or gains from certain land disposals. The amendment provides for an exemption from the 80 per cent tax rate for disposals of small sites. For the purposes of the exemption, a small site is one that does not exceed 0.4047 hectares (one acre) in size and whose market value at the time of disposal does not exceed €250,000.

Sections 644AB and *649B*, as introduced, only deal with decisions to rezone land from one type of permitted land use to another. In certain circumstances, planning authorities may decide to grant planning permission for developments that contravene, in a significant way, the Development Plan for a particular area. As with rezoning decisions, such decisions may have the effect of increasing the market value of land. The amendment therefore subjects any profits or gains that are attributable to a 'material contravention' decision by a planning authority to the 80 per cent tax rate.

The exemption for small sites will apply in respect of disposals taking place on or after 30 October 2009. A later date of 4 February 2010 (publication date of Finance Bill) will apply to land disposals taking place following a 'material contravention' decision that is made on or after that date.

[*TCA 1997, s 626B, Sch 25A; FA 2004, s 42; SI 55/04; FA 2005, s 54; FA 2006, s 64; FA 2010, s 25*]

COMPUTATION OF GAINS AND LOSSES

[*TCA 1997, s 545*]

9.8 The gain or loss on disposal is the consideration for the disposal *less*:

(*a*)   consideration for its acquisition or, if asset created etc, expenditure in producing it;

(*b*)   incidental costs of acquisition (ie advertising, valuation costs, legal fees and expenses including stamp duty, etc);

(*c*)   expenditure on enhancing value of asset and costs incurred in establishing or defending title;

(*d*)   incidental costs of disposal (as for (*b*) above).

[*TCA 1997, s 552*]

More detailed rules on allowable deductions are given below. Deductions under (*a*)–(*c*) are inflation indexed to 31 December 2002 for acquisitions prior to that date, see **9.9** below.

Consideration on disposal is not defined but it is regarded as meaning any benefit in money or money's worth, excluding any amount chargeable or otherwise taken into account for income tax (except balancing charges and capitalised value of income payments such as rent). [*TCA 1997, s 551*] The consideration is deemed to be the *market value* of the asset where part of the consideration cannot be valued or where disposal is not by way of arm's length bargain (including gifts). [*TCA 1997, ss 547(4), 548*]

Consideration for acquisition is not defined but it is regarded as meaning money and/or money's worth given, again excluding amounts taken into account for income tax. The exclusion does not apply to outlay on assets subject to capital or renewals allowance, or on construction or refurbishment expenditure allowed as a deduction from rental income (see **33.4**, **33.5** 'Sch D, Case V'), unless a capital loss would arise, in which case such expenditure is excluded to the extent that a net allowance has been given in respect of it. [*TCA 1997, ss 329(11), 554, 555*] The consideration is deemed to be the *market value* of the asset where part of the consideration cannot be valued (including assets given for loss of office, diminution of emoluments, or services past or future), where acquisition is not by way of arm's length bargain (including gifts), and where a company distributes assets in respect of its shares (but this does not apply where there is no corresponding disposal of the asset and either there is no consideration in money or money's worth or the consideration is less than the market value of the asset). Property acquired after 11 February 1998 on a waiver by the State of its property rights on a dissolution in favour of shareholders is treated as acquired for the amount of the agreed payment for the waiver. [*TCA 1997, ss 547(1)(1A)(3), 548; FA 1998, s 68*]

Where, however, a company allots shares, in a bargain not at arm's length, to a connected person (as defined by *s 10*), the consideration given by that person for those shares is deemed to be the lesser of the actual consideration and the excess of the market value of his shares in the company immediately after the allotment over that (if any) immediately before the allotment. For this purpose shares includes stock, debentures, and any other interests in the company, and options in relation to such shares. [*TCA 1997, s 547(2)*] Interest is not an allowable deduction unless it is charged to capital by a company and is in respect of money borrowed to finance expenditure, allowable for capital gains tax purposes, on construction work. [*TCA 1997, s 552(3)*]

Where personal representatives, legatees etc dispose of an asset devolving on death, the acquisition consideration is deemed to be the asset's market value on the date of death. [*TCA 1997, s 573(2)*]

Appropriations to and from trading stock. Assets appropriated to trading stock on which, if they had then been sold at market value, a chargeable gain or allowable loss would have accrued, are treated as having been disposed of at market value on appropriation. If the trade profits are chargeable under Sch D, Case I, an election may be made for the deemed disposal provision not to apply, and instead for the market value at the time of appropriation to be reduced, in computing trade profits for income tax purposes, by the amount of the chargeable gain (or increased by the amount of the allowable loss) which would otherwise have arisen. No election is available where an allowable loss would have accrued on the appropriated asset. [*TCA 1997, s 596(1)(3)*]

On an asset ceasing to be trading stock (whether by appropriation for another purpose or by retention following cessation), it is treated as having been acquired at that time for a consideration equal to the value brought into the trade accounts in respect of it for income tax purposes. [*TCA 1997, s 596(2)*]

Acquisition deemed to be that of former owner. Where a married person has received an asset from spouse on a no gain/no loss basis (see **9.7** (*d*) above) and later disposes of it, he/she is deemed to have acquired it in the circumstances in which the spouse acquired it. [*TCA 1997, s 1028(7)*]

Part disposals. Except for any sums wholly attributable to the part disposed of, allowable deductions under (*a*)–(*c*) above are apportioned in the proportion the consideration received bears to that consideration plus the market value of the parts or rights undisposed of. [*TCA 1997, s 557*]

Bonus and rights issues. Shares acquired under such issues are treated as acquired at the same time as the shares in respect of which they were acquired, with any payment being treated as enhancement expenditure (see (*c*) above). See Revenue Tax Briefing Issue 40 pp 17–20.

Expenditure in a foreign currency is converted into RI currency at the arm's length exchange rate applicable when the expenditure was incurred. [*TCA 1997, s 552(1A); FA 1998, Sch 2 para 10*] Before this provision was enacted, a similar position applied based on case law.

INFLATION INDEXING OF ALLOWABLE DEDUCTIONS

9.9 Any item of deductible expenditure (including acquisition costs, if appropriate, but excluding incidental disposal costs) incurred more than twelve months before the date of disposal is multiplied by a figure reflecting the rate of inflation up to 31 December 2002 (but see **9.11** below as regards assets held on 6 April 1974). For disposals **from 1 January 2003**, no inflation increase will apply for the ownership period after 31 December 2002. The increase is not available to create or increase a loss (or gain) and if it would turn a gain into a loss (or *vice versa*) the disposal is deemed to have been on a no gain/no loss basis (see also **9.11** below for example of operation of these provisions). [*TCA 1997, s 556*] The appropriate multiplier by reference to year of disposal and year expenditure incurred is shown in the table below. [*TCA 1997, s 556(5); CGT(A)A 1978 s 3(4) and annual Capital Gains Tax (Multipliers) Regulations; FA 2003, s 65*]

LOSSES

9.10 Losses are computed in the same way as gains, and if a gain on the disposal would not have been chargeable then a loss is not allowable. Allowable losses are set-off against gains in the same year and any amount remaining is carried forward to gains in later years. Losses brought forward from earlier years must be applied first against current year gains, and before applying the annual exemption. Losses arising in the year of assessment of taxpayer's death which are not deducted in that year may be carried back successively against gains of the three preceding years. [*TCA 1997, ss 31, 546, 573(2)*]

Where in a tax year a person is chargeable (on capital gains) at more than one rate (see **9.3** above), losses are allowed first against gains chargeable at the highest rate [*TCA 1997, s 546(6)*], subject to the special rules relating to certain disposals of development land (see **9.16** below).

The entire loss or extinction of an asset is, with exceptions, deemed to be a disposal, so as to allow the loss to be claimed; as is the occasion of an asset's value becoming negligible (if the inspector is satisfied). Where a building is destroyed the loss is reduced by any increase in value of the adjacent land. Special provisions apply where the State waives its property rights on dissolution of a company in favour of shareholders. [*TCA 1997, s 538; FA 1998, s 67*]

CAPITAL GAINS TAX MULTIPLIERS											
Multipliers for disposals in the period ended											
Year in which expenditure incurred	5.4.93	5.4.94	5.4.95	5.4.96	5.4.97	5.4.98	5.4.99	5.4.00	5.4.01	31.12.01	31.12.02	31.12.03 et seq
1974/75	5.552	5.656	5.754	5.899	6.017	6.112	6.215	6.312	6.582	6.930	7.180	7.528
1975/76	4.484	4.568	4.647	4.764	4.860	4.936	5.020	5.099	5.316	5.597	5.799	6.080
1976/77	3.863	3.935	4.003	4.104	4.187	4.253	4.325	4.393	4.680	4.822	4.996	5.238
1977/78	3.312	3.373	3.432	3.518	3.589	3.646	3.707	3.766	3.926	4.133	4.283	4.490
1978/79	3.059	3.117	3.171	3.250	3.316	3.368	3.425	3.479	3.627	3.819	3.956	4.148
1979/80	2.760	2.812	2.861	2.933	2.992	3.039	3.090	3.139	3.272	3.445	3.570	3.742
1980/81	2.390	2.434	2.477	2.539	2.590	2.631	2.675	2.718	2.833	2.983	3.091	3.240
1981/82	1.975	2.012	2.047	2.099	2.141	2.174	2.211	2.246	2.342	2.465	2.554	2.678
1982/83	1.662	1.693	1.722	1.765	1.801	1.829	1.860	1.890	1.970	2.074	2.149	2.253
1983/84	1.478	1.505	1.531	1.570	1.601	1.627	1.654	1.680	1.752	1.844	1.911	2.003
1984/85	1.341	1.366	1.390	1.425	1.454	1.477	1.502	1.525	1.590	1.674	1.735	1.819
1985/86	1.263	1.287	1.309	1.342	1.369	1.390	1.414	1.436	1.497	1.577	1.633	1.713

1986/87	1.208	1.230	1.252	1.283	1.309	1.330	1.352	1.373	1.432	1.507	1.562	1.637
1987/88	1.168	1.190	1.210	1.241	1.266	1.285	1.307	1.328	1.384	1.457	1.510	1.583
1988/89	1.146	1.167	1.187	1.217	1.242	1.261	1.282	1.303	1.358	1.430	1.481	1.553
1989/90	1.109	1.130	1.149	1.178	1.202	1.221	1.241	1.261	1.314	1.384	1.434	1.503
1990/91	1.064	1.084	1.102	1.130	1.153	1.171	1.191	1.210	1.261	1.328	1.376	1.442
1991/92	1.037*	1.656	1.075	1.102	1.124	1.142	1.161	1.179	1.229	1.294	1.341	1.406
1992/93		1.019*	1.037	1.063	1.084	1.101	1.120	1.138	1.185	1.249	1.294	1.356
1993/94			1.018*	1.043	1.064	1.081	1.099	1.117	1.164	1.226	1.270	1.331
1994/95				1.026*	1.046	1.063	1.081	1.098	1.144	1.205	1.248	1.309
1995/96					1.021*	1.037	1.054	1.071	1.116	1.175	1.218	1.277
1996/97						1.016*	1.033	1.050	1.094	1.152	1.194	1.251
1997/98							1.016*	1.033	1.077	1.134	1.175	1.232
1998/99								1.016*	1.059	1.115	1.156	1.212
1999/00									1.043*	1.098	1.138	1.193
2000/01										1.053*	1.091	1.144
2001											1.037*	1.087
2002												1.049*
2003 and subsequent												1.000

*Does not apply to expenditure within twelve months of disposal

ASSETS HELD ON 6 APRIL 1974

9.11 For assets held on 6 April 1974, the acquisition cost is market value on that date, and this market value is increased by the appropriate inflation index multiplier for 1974/75 as described in **9.9** above. If the indexed amount produces a higher gain or loss than the actual monetary gain or loss (without time apportionment) then the actual gain or loss is taken. If the indexed amount turns an actual monetary gain into a loss (or *vice versa*), the disposal is deemed to produce neither a gain nor a loss.

Thus, the inflation indexing is not available to create or increase an allowable loss (nor to create or increase a chargeable gain). [*TCA 1997, s 556(3)(4)*] The following examples illustrate this.

Example 1 – **Indexed 1974 value greater than cost:**

			€
Cost 1970			5,000
Market value at 6.4.74		€6,000	
Indexed at sale in 2006			
	6,000 × 7.528		45,168
(a)	Sale proceeds in 2006		48,000
	Actual gain (48,000 – 5,000)		43,000
	Indexed gain (48,000 – 45,168)		2,832
	The lower (indexed) gain of £2,832 is taken.		
(b)	Sale proceeds in 2006		10,000
	Actual gain (10,000 – 5,000)		5,000

	Indexed loss (10,000 – 45,168)		(35,168)

Actual gain as compared with an indexed loss, so no gain/no loss results.

(*c*)	Sale proceeds in 2006		4,000
	Actual loss (4,000 – 5,000)		(1,000)
	Indexed loss (4,000 – 45,168)		(41,168)

The lower (actual) loss of €1,000 is taken.

Example 2 – **Indexed 1974 value lower than cost:**

			€
Cost 1972			20,000
Market value at 6.4.74		€2,500	
Indexed at sale in 2006			
	2,500 × 7.528		18,820
(*a*)	Sale proceeds in 2006		21,000
	Actual gain (21,000 – 20,000)		1,000
	Indexed gain (21,000 – 18,820)		2,180

The lower (actual) gain of €1,000 is taken.

(*b*)	Sale proceeds in 2006		19,000
	Actual loss (19,000 – 20,000)		(1,000)
	Indexed gain (19,000 – 18,820)		180

Actual loss as compared with an indexed gain, so no gain/no loss results.

(*c*)	Sale proceeds in 2006		10,000
	Actual loss (10,000 – 20,000)		(10,000)
	Indexed loss (10,000 – 18,820)		(8,820)

The lower (indexed) loss of €8,820 is taken.

SPECIAL RULES FOR ASSETS

9.12 Shares and securities. A 'first in/first out' rule applies to shares and securities of the same class. For disposals before 6 April 1978, shares and securities of the same class were pooled (except those held on 6 April 1974, to which 'first in/first out' applied in any case). Calls on shares or debentures, more than twelve months after their allotment, and expenditure on rights issues are deemed incurred when the consideration is given for the purposes of inflation indexing. [*TCA 1997, ss 580(1)–(3), 582, 584(4)*] Shares and securities held on 6 April 1978, from which disposals were made prior to that date, are identified by assuming that holdings originally acquired on different dates formed distinct parts of the pool and that each part, and the deductible expenditure attributable to it, is reduced proportionately by the pre-6 April 1978 disposals. Shares disposed of within four weeks after acquisition of shares of the same class are partly or wholly identified with the newly acquired shares. Where shares are acquired within four weeks after disposal of shares of the same class at a loss, the loss is only allowable against subsequent gains on the shares newly acquired. [*TCA 1997, ss 580(5), 581*]

Commodity futures and other assets not individually identifiable are subject to the same provisions as shares and securities. [*TCA 1997, s 580(4)*]

Wasting assets are assets, excluding freehold land, which have a predictable life (for tangible movables, useful life for its original purpose) not exceeding 50 years. *Plant and machinery* are deemed to have a life of less than 50 years. A life interest in settled property is a wasting asset when the actuarial life expectancy of the life tenant is 50 years or less. Deductible expenditure on a wasting asset, except any expenditure qualifying for capital allowances, is written off at a uniform rate over the remaining life of the asset (except as regards any residual or scrap value). [*TCA 1997, ss 560, 561*]

Leases of land are only wasting assets where the duration remaining is 50 years or less, but allowable expenditure is written off, not uniformly as above, but at a progressive rate laid down. Special provisions apply to premiums and sub-leases. [*TCA 1997, s 566, Sch 14*]

Life assurance policies etc: investment by companies. Special provisions apply for the computation of the chargeable gain on the disposal (see *s 593(3)(4)*) by a company of, or of an interest in, a policy of life assurance, or a deferred annuity contract on the life of any person, entered into, or acquired without consideration, after 10 April 1994 (not being a foreign policy etc within *s 594(1)(c)(ii)*). Policies entered into or acquired on or before that date are treated as entered into or acquired after that date where there are certain variations after that date.

Transitional provisions treat as having been made before 11 April 1994, and hence as excluded from these provisions, any contract entered into before 23 April 1994, where a broker's receipt was issued before 11 April 1994, and any policy taken out before 30 June 1994 as part of an endowment package in respect of a property which the company had contracted to acquire before 11 April 1994.

Unless the disposal results directly from the death, disablement or disease of a person (or one of a class of persons) specified in the policy, the exemption under **9.7**(*g*) above does not apply, and the gain is treated as the net amount of a gain from the gross amount of which corporation tax has been deducted at the standard rate of income tax. The gross amount of the gain is brought into charge for the accounting period of the disposal, the corporation tax treated as deducted being set off against corporation tax for the period, any excess being repaid to the company. These provisions do not apply to the computation of allowable losses on such policies, etc. [*TCA 1997, s 595*]

SETTLEMENTS AND TRUSTS

9.13 **'Settled property'** means any property held in trust, but not property held in trust for a person absolutely entitled to it as against the trustees (or who would be absolutely entitled but for being an infant or under a disability). [*TCA 1997, ss 5(1), 567(1)*]

Disposals by the trustees of assets constituting settled property attract CGT payable by the trustees out of trust moneys. Where the beneficiary is absolutely entitled (or would be but for infancy etc) to assets, disposals of those assets by the trustees are regarded as disposals by the beneficiary, who is assessed accordingly. Any allowable loss on that part of settled property which has not already been deducted can then be claimed by the beneficiary. The ending of the trust by transferring the assets to a beneficiary absolutely entitled is not a chargeable disposal. [*TCA 1997, ss 567(1)(2), 574, 576*]

Deemed disposals

(*a*) A gift in settlement (revocable or irrevocable) is deemed to be a disposal by the donor, even where the donor is a beneficiary and/or a trustee. (If the trust is for charitable purposes only the gift will be regarded as made on a no gain/no loss basis, see **9.7**(*q*) above);

(*b*) Termination (by death) of a life interest or annuity, without the relevant property ceasing to be settled property, is deemed to be a disposal of that property by the trustees (with reacquisition by them at market value), excluding assets comprised in an inheritance taken on death but exempt under *CATCA 2003, s 77* (see **7.5**(*c*) 'Capital acquisitions tax') (although the chargeable gain which would otherwise accrue is deemed to accrue to the trustees if and when that exemption subsequently ceases to apply);

(*c*) The occasion of a person becoming absolutely entitled to settled property (or absolutely entitled but for infancy etc) is deemed to be a disposal, by the trustees, of that property (which ceases to be settled property) with reacquisition at market value. Where the absolute entitlement arises by the termination of a life interest (not an annuity) by death, the gain is *exempt* and the reacquisition is at market value at the date of death. Where it arises on the relinquishment of a life interest, and the holder of that interest would have been entitled to retirement relief (see **9.7**(*r*) above) had he owned the property absolutely since commencement of the life interest, the trustees are given a corresponding relief on the deemed disposal;

(*d*) Property held on charitable trusts which ceases to be held on those trusts is deemed to be disposed of by the trustees with reacquisition by them at market value, with a corresponding charge, and where the property represents proceeds of earlier disposals, gains made up to ten years previously are brought into charge.

[*TCA 1997, ss 575–578, 609; FA 1998, s 69*]

UNIT TRUSTS

9.14 Unit trusts which are collective investment undertakings are subject to a special tax regime (see **12.22** 'Corporation tax'). Otherwise, they are chargeable to CGT unless all the units are held by exempt persons (eg charities) and (from 1 January 2001) the unit trust is not (and is not deemed to be) an authorised unit trust. Receipt of a capital distribution by a unit holder is treated as a part disposal by him of the holding in consideration of the distribution and is charged to CGT accordingly. [*TCA 1997, s 731; CGTA 1975, s 31; FA 1994, s 64; FA 2001, s 71*] There is exemption for gains from disposals of units of an assurance linked unit trust by the assurance company which administers the trust, so long as the units do not at any stage become the property of the policy owner. [*TCA 1997, s 731(6)*]

Finance Act 2010, s 31 inserts a new *Pt 27, Ch 5*. This sets out the tax treatment of a relevant UCITS. It ensures that an investment undertaking formed under the law of a Member State other than Ireland will not be liable to tax in Ireland by reason only of having a management company that is authorised under Irish law. A relevant UCITS is defined as an undertaking for collective investment in transferable securities that is subject to the EU UCITS Directive, formed under the laws of an EU Member State other than Ireland, whose management company is authorised as a management company under Irish regulations, and which would not be liable to tax in Ireland if its management company were not authorised under Irish regulations.

The section provides that a relevant UCITS is not chargeable to tax in Ireland in respect of its relevant profits. It also provides that unit holders in a relevant UCITS are to be treated in the same manner as unit holders in an offshore fund.

Finance Act 2010, s 30 introduces an annual declaration and reporting arrangement in respect of unit trusts. The requirements are as follows:

(i)   where the trustees, or any persons acting on behalf of the trustees, of each unit trust are satisfied as to the capital gains tax-exempt status of all its unit holders, they are required to make an annual declaration to that effect;

(ii)   an annual electronic statement must be made to the Revenue Commissioners specifying certain details in respect of each unit holder and stating whether the above declaration has, or has not, been made for that year. If that statement is not made, or is incorrect or incomplete, the trustees of the unit trust shall be liable to a penalty of €3,000.

The amendment is to apply for the year of assessment 2010 and subsequent years.

SPECIAL PROVISIONS

9.15 Transactions in company shares or securities. Receipt of a capital (ie not income) distribution by a person in respect of shares held by him is a part disposal of the shares except as follows. Subject to certain conditions, a new holding of shares and securities issued to a person in place of other shares or securities held by him will be treated as the same asset as the original holding, with no disposal regarded as having occurred, on a reorganisation of share capital or reduction of share capital (not paying off redeemable shares) or a conversion of securities. This applies also to certain unit trust reorganisations or reductions. These provisions do not apply to a conversion of securities or to a new holding of securities issued on or after **4 December 2002** in place of other shares and securities, unless a binding written agreement was in place before that date or the other company is quoted on a recognised stock exchange and its board of directors had, before that date, made a public announcement that they had agreed the terms of a recommended offer for the entire issued shares (or shares to be issued) of the company, or the company amalgamation provisions below apply.

Similar rules apply on an amalgamation by exchange of shares or a scheme of reconstruction or amalgamation provided that it can be shown that the exchange, etc was for *bona fide* commercial reasons and not part of any scheme or arrangement a main purpose of which was the avoidance of tax. These rules do not apply to the issue on or after **4 December 2002** of securities in the exchange unless a binding written agreement was in place before that date or a letter issued from the Revenue before that date confirming that the scheme is a scheme of reconstruction or the recipient is a member of the same group of companies (companies with a 75 per cent relationship resident in the EEA) as the issuing company for two years, commencing one year before the issue of the securities. On a transfer by an individual of an entire business as a going concern to a company, in return for shares, the net chargeable gains on the business assets are deferred by being apportioned among the shares and, on subsequent disposal of shares, this amount is deducted from the costs of acquisition of the shares, provided, in relation to transfers after 23 April 1992, that they are for *bona fide* commercial reasons and not part of any scheme or arrangement a main purpose of which was the avoidance of tax. [*TCA 1997, ss 583–587, 600; FA 2003, s 66*] See also Revenue Tax Briefing Issue 48 pp 15–17.

For the application of this relief to partitions of family trading companies, see Revenue Tax Briefing Issue 44 pp 34, 35.

The rules relating to company reorganisations (as above) apply equally where a company has no share capital, by reference to members' interest in the company as if they were shares. [*TCA 1997, s 587(3)*] Where this applies to an arrangement involving an assurance company carrying on mutual life business (eg on the demutualisation of such a company), any rights conferred on members to acquire shares in a successor company are treated as options (see below) granted for no consideration and having no value at the time of grant. Any shares issued under the arrangement are treated as having been acquired for, and having a value at the time of issue equal to, any consideration given by the member (other than consideration provided out of company assets or derived from the member's shares or other rights in the company), or if no such consideration is given, nil consideration. Where the shares issued in the successor company are settled on trustees on terms providing for their onward transfer to members of the assurance company for no new consideration, the members are in effect treated as having acquired the shares directly on issue. Since 1 January 2006, Revenue must be provided with certain information relating to rights conferred on members to acquire shares. [*TCA 1997, s 588; FA 2006, s 76*]

See also **30.27** 'Sch D, Cases I and II'.

Options. The grant of an option is a disposal of an asset (the option) but if the option is exercised then the grant of the option is treated as part of the larger transactions, so that the consideration for (or cost of) the option is aggregated with the consideration for (or cost of) its exercise in selling (or buying) the substantive asset. A *forfeited deposit* of purchase money is treated in the same way as a payment for an option which is not exercised. Most options are wasting assets, ceasing to exist when the rights to exercise them end. However, in the case of quoted or traded options, and options to acquire assets for use in a trade, abandonment of the option is a disposal thereof, and on the transfer or abandonment of the option the wasting asset provisions do not apply. The abandonment of an option is similarly treated as a disposal in any other case, but not so as to give rise to an allowable loss. [*TCA 1997, s 540*] See also **38.42** 'Tax cases'.

Company ceasing to be RI-resident. Where a company (other than an 'excluded company') ceases to be resident (other than by ceasing to exist) at any time (the '*relevant time*'), it is deemed to have disposed of all its assets (except as below) immediately before that time, and immediately to have reacquired them, at market value. Rollover relief (see **9.7**(*s*) above) does not apply where the new assets are acquired after the relevant time unless the new assets are excepted from these provisions. The excepted assets are RI-situated assets (including certain exploration or exploitation rights or assets) which are used by the company after the relevant time for a trade it carries on in RI through a branch or agency, or so used or held for the purposes of such a branch or agency. A company is an *'excluded company'* if at least 90 per cent of its issued share capital is held by a 'foreign company' or companies (or by a person or persons directly or indirectly controlled by such a company or companies). A *'foreign company'* is a non-RI resident company under the control of residents of a territory with which a double tax agreement is in force (see **15.2** 'Double tax relief – income and capital gains') and not under the control of RI residents. 'Control' is broadly as under *CTA s 102* (see **12.7** 'Corporation tax'). For company residence generally, see **11.3** 'Companies'.

Where, immediately after the relevant time, at least 75 per cent of the company's ordinary share capital is owned directly by an RI-resident company (the *'principal company'*), the companies may jointly elect (within two years after the relevant time) for postponement of the aggregate chargeable gains (less allowable losses) accruing on the deemed disposal of the company's *'foreign assets'* (ie assets situated outside RI immediately after the relevant time and used for a trade it carries on outside RI). The gain so postponed is brought into charge on the principal company in two ways:

(a)   if any of the foreign assets, chargeable gains on which are an element in the postponed gain, is disposed of within ten years after the relevant time (and (b) below has not previously applied), a corresponding proportion of the postponed gain is brought into charge;

(b)   if, at any time within ten years after the relevant time, the principal company either ceases to be RI-resident or ceases directly to own at least 75 per cent of the company's ordinary share capital, the whole postponed gain (less any part previously brought into charge under (a) above) is brought into charge at that time (immediately before that time where it ceases to be RI-resident).

There is, however, provision for allowable losses (or any part thereof) which the subsidiary company has not set against its chargeable gains to be deducted from the chargeable gains accruing to the principal company under (a) or (b) above, on joint election by the companies within two years of the gains so accruing.

Tax under the above provisions which is not paid within six months of the due date may be recovered from fellow group members of the company to which the chargeable gains accrued, or from certain directors of that company or of a company controlling it.

[*TCA 1997, ss 627–629; FA 1998, Sch 3 para 5; FA 2001, ss 38(1)(k), 78(2)(b); FA 2002, s 36(e)*; *FA 2006, s 60*]

Anti-avoidance provisions deal with transactions between connected persons, disposals in a series of transactions, and transfers at undervalue by a close company. *s 549* is amended by the *Finance (No 2) Act 2008* to prevent the avoidance of capital gains tax by the use of arrangement entered into by 'connected persons' within the meaning of *s 10*. The amendment counters an avoidance scheme which purports to generate artificial capital losses for offset against actual chargeable gains. The amendment applies to disposals made on or after 20 November 2008. *Finance Act 2010* has introduced further anti-avoidance measures to prevent the use of losses where there was no real economic loss. The measures target aggressive capital gains tax avoidance schemes which generate artificial losses on futures contracts. Capital allowances are disallowed where they arise from arrangements whose main purpose or one of whose main purposes was to secure a tax advantage. Profits and losses arising on gilt futures contracts are now calculated on the market price of the underlying gilt. [*TCA 1997, ss 10, 549, 550, 589; F(No 2)A 2008, s 42; FA 2010, s 59 and 60*]

Pre-entry losses. See **3.12** 'Anti-avoidance' for provisions restricting relief for allowable losses on a company becoming a member of a group.

Partnerships. It is understood that the UK Revenue Statement of Practice of 17 January 1975 'Partnerships' is acknowledged by the Revenue Commissioners to be a guide to the treatment of capital gains tax on partnerships. However, its application to any individual case may be considered on its merits. For an outline of the UK practice, see Tolley's Capital Gains Tax under Partnerships.

DEVELOPMENT LAND GAINS

[*TCA 1997, ss 648–653; FA 1998, ss 65, 73; F(No 2)A 1998, s 3; FA 1999, s 91; FA 2000, s 86; FA 2001, ss 94, 95, Sch 2 para 36; FA 2004, s 83*]

9.16 Disposals of '*development land*' are called '*relevant disposals*' and are subject to special rules.

Development land is land in RI the consideration for the disposal of which, or the market value of which at the time of disposal, exceeds the '*current use value*' of the land at the time of disposal. It also includes unquoted shares deriving their value (or the greater part thereof) directly or indirectly from such land.

Current use value of land is the market value on the assumption that it can never be developed (excluding certain minor development and certain development by a local authority or statutory undertaker).

The **rate** of capital gains tax on chargeable gains on relevant disposals is 20 per cent for disposals after 30 November 1999:

Inflation indexing of allowable expenditure in computing the chargeable gain on a relevant disposal (see **9.9** above) applies only to an amount limited to the '*current use value*' (see above) of the land at the date of acquisition and to the proportion of incidental acquisition costs referable to that value; or, if the land was held at 6 April 1974, to the current use value at that date.

'Rollover relief' (see **9.7**(*s*)(*t*) above) is not available in respect of consideration for a relevant disposal, except that:

(i)   such relief is available in respect of certain disposals by sports clubs;

(ii)   relief under **9.7**(*s*) above is not denied where either:

(*a*)   the relevant local authority certifies, on the basis of guidelines issued by the Minister for the Environment, that the land disposed of is subject to a use which is inconsistent with the protection and improvement of the amenities of the general area within which the land is situated or is otherwise damaging to the local environment,

(*b*)   both old and new assets are 'assets of an authorised racecourse' (within *s 652(3)(a)*), and in the case of the old assets have been so throughout the five years ending at the time of the disposal,

(c)   both old and new assets are 'assets of an authorised greyhound race track' (within *s 652(3A)(a)*), and in the case of the old assets have been so throughout the five years ending at the time of the disposal, or

(d)   the disposal was effected by an order made under *Dublin Docklands Development Authority Act 1997, s 28(1)*; and

(iii)   relief under **9.7**(*t*) is not denied where the land involved is acquired by the authority for the purposes of road building or widening. For relevant disposals after 5 December 2000 to which that relief accordingly applies, the period during which the replacement asset(s) must be acquired is extended to from two years before to eight years after the disposal of the original asset(s). Previously, the relief applied only where the land in question was farmland.

Losses from disposals *other than* relevant disposals may not be set against chargeable gains on relevant disposals. Losses on relevant disposals may be set against such gains, and are then not available for relief as allowable losses for the purposes of corporation tax on chargeable gains.

For individuals, these provisions apply only where the total consideration for relevant disposals in the year of assessment exceeds **€19,050/£15,000** (for 2001 only, £11,100).

Companies are liable to capital gains tax on chargeable gains on relevant disposals under these provisions, and not to corporation tax on the chargeable gains, so that trading or other losses may not be set against such gains. Corporation tax provisions relating to groups of companies are applied to capital gains tax for this purpose, with appropriate modifications. See also **12.13** 'Corporation tax' as regards restrictions on certain distributions out of gains on such disposals, and **12.25** 'Corporation tax' as regards changes following implementation of EEC Directive 90/434/EEC.

OVERSEAS MATTERS

9.17 Non-resident companies. A person resident or ordinarily resident in RI (and, if an individual, of RI domicile) who holds shares in a non-resident close company is chargeable on a proportion of the net gains accruing to the company in a year of assessment equal to the proportion of company assets to which he would be entitled on a liquidation. This does not apply to gains on currency or certain debts or trading assets, to gains distributed within two years, or to gains chargeable under *s 29(3)* (see **9.2** above) or *s 25(2)(b)* (see **12.19** 'Corporation tax'). Any tax so charged is an allowable deduction on any subsequent disposal of the shares. Where the shareholder is itself a non-resident close company, a further sub-apportionment may be made. The charge includes all participators (see **12.7** 'Corporation tax') or deemed participators in the company, provided that no apportionment applies where the participation is five per cent or less, and the relief for distributions within two years is given by set off against liability in respect of the distribution instead of by deduction. *Section 590* does not apply to chargeable gains made by trading companies. For disposals on or after 4 February 2010, this has been extended to cases where the gain is made by a non-trading company and to gains on certain intangible assets as defined in *s 291A*. [*TCA 1997, s 590; FA 1999, s 89; FA 2001, s 39; FA 2010, s 57*]

Offshore trusts. Since 1999/2000 certain deemed gains of trustees who are neither resident nor ordinarily resident in RI throughout a year of assessment are attributed as chargeable gains accruing to beneficiaries who receive capital payments (as widely defined) from the trustees, in proportion to (but not exceeding) the capital payments received. This applies where the settlor either does not have an 'interest in the settlement' (as widely defined for this purpose) at any time in the year of assessment, or he or she was not domiciled, resident or ordinarily resident in RI in that year of assessment or when he or she made the settlement. The gains concerned are the chargeable gains which would have arisen to the trustees had they been resident and ordinarily resident in RI. A charge to tax on such attributed chargeable gains arises, however, only where the beneficiary is, at any time in the year of assessment, domiciled in RI. In relation to any year of assessment, gains of earlier years not already treated as chargeable gains accruing to beneficiaries are available for attribution, and earlier capital payments not already treated as having given rise to a chargeable gain under these provisions are similarly taken into account. Payment of a liability under these provisions by the trustees is not treated as a payment to the beneficiary. A charge under these provisions displaces any charge under *s 579* (see below). [*TCA 1997, s 579A; FA 1999, s 88; FA 2002, s 47*] A capital payment received by a beneficiary in a period consisting of a year or years of assessment for which *s 579A does not* apply in relation to the settlement (a *'resident period'*), and not made in anticipation of a disposal by the trustees in a subsequent period consisting of a year or years of assessment to which it *does* apply (a *'non-resident period'*), is disregarded for the purposes of *s 579A* during the non-resident period. Where, however, a resident period follows a non-resident period, and in the last year of the non-resident period there remains a balance of trust gains which have not been treated as chargeable gains under *s 579A*, that section continues to apply in relation to capital payments received by beneficiaries in the resident period until the trust gains are exhausted. [*TCA 1997, s 579F; FA 1999, s 88*]

Where *s 579A* (as above) does not apply, a beneficiary either resident or ordinarily resident in RI, and domiciled in RI, in a year of assessment is (except as follows) chargeable on a proportion of gains accruing to a settlement the trustees of which are neither resident nor ordinarily resident in RI in that year, and which would have been chargeable on the trustees had they been domiciled and either resident or ordinarily resident in RI in that year, *provided that* the settlor was RI domiciled and resident or ordinarily resident either at the time of the settlement or when the gains arose. There is provision for the manner in which the apportionment between beneficiaries is to be made. For trust disposals on or after 7 March 2002, if the settlor is resident or ordinarily resident in RI at the time of the disposal, the gains are treated as arising to the settlor rather than the beneficiary. [*TCA 1997, ss 579, 579A(2)(b); FA 2002, s 47(1)(a)(f)*]

Trustees becoming neither resident nor ordinarily resident in RI at any time are deemed to have disposed, immediately before that time, of all assets representing settled property of the trust at market value at that time, and immediately to have reacquired them at that value. Certain RI assets continuing to be used for an RI trade carried on by the trustees are excluded, as are certain assets specified in double tax arrangements (see below). The application of rollover relief (see **9.7**(*s*) above) is restricted in these circumstances. [*TCA 1997, s 579B; FA 1999, s 88*] The assets to which *s 579B* applies are restricted where it applies as a result of the death of a trustee, and within six months the trustees become resident and ordinarily resident in RI, or where it applies within six months of the trustees having become resident and ordinarily resident in RI as a result of the death of a trustee. [*TCA 1997, s 579C; FA 1999, s 88*] A secondary liability for tax due under *s 579B* applies to any person who ceased to be a trustee in the twelve months prior to the migration unless the trustee can show that when they ceased to be a trustee there was no proposal for the migration. [*TCA 1997, s 579D; FA 1999, s 88; FA 2001, s 78(2)(b)*]

There are supplementary provisions to ensure that, where the disposal of an interest under a settlement is not within the exemption in **9.7**(*p*) above because the trustees are neither resident nor ordinarily resident in RI at the time of the disposal, the interest is treated as having been acquired at market value at the time the trustees ceased to be resident or ordinarily resident. These also make special provision where, before the trustees became neither resident nor ordinarily resident, they became treated as resident outside RI under double tax arrangements, so that *s 579E* applied (see below). If this occurred before the interest was acquired, then no relief is available. If it occurred after the interest was acquired but before the trustees became neither resident nor ordinarily resident, then the market value acquisition is deemed to have been at the time the trustees became treated as resident outside RI. [*TCA 1997, s 613A; FA 1999, s 90(1)(b)*]

Trustees ceasing to be liable to RI tax. Provisions similar to *s 579B* (as above) apply where trustees, while continuing to be resident and ordinarily resident in RI fall to be regarded under any double tax arrangements as resident in a territory outside RI and as not liable to RI tax on gains on disposals of trust assets specified in the arrangements. [*TCA 1997, s 579E; FA 1999, s 88*]

Double tax relief. The same power to make arrangements exists as for income tax. [*TCA 1997, s 828*] See **15** 'Double tax relief – income and capital gains'.

Offshore Income Gains. *Finance Act 2007* extends the scope of *s 746* which applies various anti avoidance provisions to chargeable gains where the disposal was made abroad for the benefit of a person resident in the State. A recent appeal case found that the provision only applies to a person who is ordinarily resident in the State. The amendment provides the following:

Where an offshore gain is:

(i)   made by a person who is not resident or domiciled in the State; and

(ii)   a resident or ordinarily resident of the State has the power to enjoy such gains;

then it will be treated as income of the person who has the power to enjoy it and will be subject to the offshore funds regime. The amendment is effective on or after 1 February 2007.

Withholding Tax. *s 980* provides for a deduction of withholding tax of 15 per cent of the sales proceeds where there is a disposal of a specified asset which exceeds €500,000. Specified assets are defined in *s 980*. *Finance Act 2007, s 56* amended this section to extend the period in which this tax must be paid and account given to the Revenue to within 30 days of making the deduction.

10 Claims

10.1 Time limit for a claim to repayment of tax is generally four years after the end of the year of assessment to which it relates for years of assessment (or chargeable periods in the case of companies) ending on or after 1 January 2003 and for any claims made on or after 1 January 2005 in respect of earlier years. Previously, the time limit was ten years. Provision is made for appeal. Prior to 3 February 2005, claims had to be accompanied by a return of income. From that date, certain claims for repayment by PAYE taxpayers do not require the filing of a return. [*TCA 1997, s 865; FA 2003, s 17; SI 508/03; FA 2005, s 24*]

10.2 Interest on repayment of tax. Since 1 November 2003, interest (without deduction of tax) is paid on repayments of tax at a rate of 0.011 per cent per day from the day after the end of the year of assessment or chargeable period or date of payment of tax (whichever is later) where the repayment is due to a mistaken assumption by the Revenue in the application of the law. Otherwise interest is paid from six months after the repayment claim is made, if the repayment has not been made by that date. Transitional measures apply to repayments of preliminary tax paid prior to 1 November 2003 (see **28.11** 'Self-assessment'). A de minimis limit of €10 applies to interest payments. Interest payments are disregarded in computing income or profit. No interest is due where the offset provisions apply. See **1.16** 'Offset and appropriation of tax'. [*TCA 1997, s 865A; FA 2003, s 17; SI 508/03*]

10.3 Claims by a contingent beneficiary in respect of income accumulated, up to 5 April 1973 only, under a trust must be made within six years after end of tax year in which contingency happens [*TCA 1997, Sch 32 para 21*] and claims for credit in respect of foreign tax are also limited to six years. [*TCA 1997, Sch 24 para 12*]

10.4 Relief for **double assessment** of the same amount is claimable under *s 929*.

10.5 Since 1 January 2005, relief for **'error or mistake'** in returns etc may be claimed in respect of an assessment within four years after the end of the year of assessment to which it relates. [*TCA 1997, s 865*] Previously a claim could be made within six years under the provisions of *s 930*. That section has now been deleted. [*FA 2003, s 17; SI 508/03*]

11 Companies

11.1 Under the *Corporation Tax Acts*, companies are liable to Corporation tax (**12**) on their profits. Previously companies were liable on their profits to both income tax (at the standard rate) and corporation profits tax.

11.2 Dividends. Since 6 April 1999, dividends are paid under deduction of dividend withholding tax with certain exceptions (see **13.12** 'Dividend withholding tax').

11.3 Residence. A company incorporated in RI is regarded for tax purposes as RI-resident, from the date of incorporation where it is incorporated after 10 February 1999, otherwise from 1 October 1999. This does not apply to a 'relevant company' which either carries on a trade in RI or is related to a company which carries on a trade in RI. It is also over-ridden where the company is treated under any double tax arrangements (see **15.2** 'Double tax relief – income and capital gains') as resident in the other state and not RI-resident.

A *'relevant company'* is a company:

(a)   under the direct or indirect control (as specially defined) of a person or persons resident for tax purposes in a 'relevant territory' (ie another EU Member State or a territory with whom double tax arrangements are in force under *s 826* (see **15.2** 'Double tax relief – income and capital gains') and not so controlled by a person or persons not so resident; or

(b)   which is, or is 'related' to, a company the principal class of whose shares is substantially and regularly traded on one or more recognised stock exchange in a relevant territory.

Companies are *'related'* for this purpose if one is a 50 per cent subsidiary of the other (ie if at least 50 per cent of its ordinary share capital is owned directly or indirectly by the other) or both are 50 per cent subsidiaries of a third company.

[*TCA 1997, s 23A; FA 1999, s 82; FA 2000, s 77*]

Where these provisions do not apply, company residence is determined according to case law principles, by reference to the place where effective management and control is exercised (which is usually the place where directors' meetings are held).

Since 1 January 2006, a Societas Europaea (SE) and a European Cooperative Society (SCE) with a registered office in RI do not cease to be RI-resident merely because the registered office is transferred out of RI. [*TCA 1997, s 23B; FA 2006, s 60*]

11.4 New companies – particulars to be supplied. Any company which is incorporated in RI, or which commences to carry on a trade, profession or business in RI, is required to deliver certain written particulars to the Revenue Commissioners within 30 days of its commencing to carry on a trade etc (wherever carried on), or of there being a material change in particulars previously supplied, or of an inspector giving notice requiring such particulars. The particulars required are, in every case:

(i)   the name and registered office address;

(ii)   the address of the principal place of business;

(iii)   the name and address of the secretary;

(iv)   the date of commencement, nature, and accounting date of the trade etc;

(v)   such other information as the Revenue Commissioners consider necessary for tax purposes;

and in the case of a company incorporated, but not resident, in RI:

(vi)   the territory in which it is resident for tax purposes;

(vii)   where the residence rule described in **11.3** above does not apply by virtue of the company being a relevant company which either carries on, or is related to a company which carries on, a trade in RI, the name and address of the company which carries on that trade; and

(viii) where the residence rule described in **11.3** above does not apply by virtue of the company being treated under double tax arrangements as resident in the other State and not RI-resident:

    (*a*)   if the company is controlled (within *s 432*) by another company the principal class of whose shares is substantially and regularly traded on one or more than one recognised stock exchange in a '*relevant territory*' (ie another EU Member State or a territory with which double taxation arrangements are in force) or territories, the name and registered office address of the other company,

    (*b*)   in any other case, the name and address of the individuals who are the ultimate beneficial owners (as defined) of the company,

and in the case of a company neither incorporated nor resident in RI, but carrying on a trade etc in RI;

(ix)   the address of the company's principal place of business in RI;

(x)   the name and address of the agent, manager, factor or other representative of the company; and

(xi)   the date of commencement of the company's trade etc in RI.

These requirements apply from 11 February 1999 in the case of companies incorporated on or after that date, otherwise from 1 October 1999. The Revenue Commissioners may notify the registrar of companies where a company fails to deliver the required particulars.

[*TCA 1997, s 882; FA 1999, s 83; FA 2000, s 78*]

12 Corporation Tax

Headings in this section are:

COMMENCEMENT OF CORPORATION TAX

12.1 Corporation tax ('CT') was introduced by the *Corporation Tax Act 1976*, the enactments relating to CT being consolidated in the *Taxes Consolidation Act 1997*, although continuing to be referred to as the *Corporation Tax Acts* (see *s 1(2)*). The rules for corporation tax apply generally from 1 April 1974 but exclude any income which was used as the basis of an income tax assessment for 1975/76 or any earlier year.

A company came within the charge to CT at different times according to the source of income involved. A company came within the charge to CT:

(*a*)   from the end of any 1975/76 income tax basis period ending before 6 April 1976, or the end of a 1974/75 basis period (if later); or

(*b*)   on 6 April 1976, if not charged to income tax for 1975/76 or if the 1975/76 income tax assessment was based on actual profits for that year.
   [*CTA 1976, s 173*]

If not liable as above, an RI company came within the scope of CT (for purposes of accounting periods, see **12.3** below) on 6 April 1976 or, if not then operative, when it commenced business or first made a chargeable gain or an allowable loss. [*CTA 1976, s 9(4)(6); TCA 1997, s 27(4)(6)*]

'Company' means any body corporate (including a trustee savings bank) but excluding the Health Service Executive (formerly health boards), European Economic

Interest Groupings, vocational education committees, agriculture committees and local authorities. [*TCA 1997, s 4(1); FA 2005, Sch 6(1)(a)*]

Income tax (except on any income received by a company in a fiduciary or representative capacity), corporation profits tax and capital gains tax ceased to be chargeable when CT became chargeable. [*CTA 1976, ss 1, 174*] Many provisions of the *Income Tax Acts* and the *Capital Gains Tax Acts* relating to the computation of income and chargeable gains are adopted for CT purposes.

SCHEME AND RATES OF TAX

12.2 A company is chargeable to CT on its profits wherever arising (other than profits accruing to it in fiduciary or representative capacity) for each financial year, ie year ending 31 December (and see **12.3** below). [*TCA 1997, s 26*] See **12.26** below as regards set-off of advance corporation tax.

Profits of a company comprise its **income** (computed by normal IT principles under each Schedule and then aggregated) and its **chargeable gains** (computed under CGT rules and then specifically reduced, see below). [*TCA 1997, ss 4(1), 76, 78*]

For a general article on corporation tax computations, see Revenue Tax Briefing Issue 40 pp 6–9.

The rates of tax are (by reference to financial year = FY)

	1998	FY 1999	FY 2000	FY 2001	FY 2002	From 2003
Standard rate	32%	28%	24%	20%	16%	12.5%
[*TCA 1997, s 21(1); FA 1997, s 59; FA 1998, s 55; FA 1999, s 71*]						
Reduced rate	25%	25%	12.5%	12.5%	12.5%	-
[*TCA 1997, ss 22(1)(a), 22A(2)(a); CTA 1976, s 28A; FA 1996, s 44; FA 1997, s 60; FA 1998, s 56; FA 2000, s 76*]						
Higher rate (see below)	–	–	25%	25%	25%	25%
[*TCA 1997, s 21A; FA 1999, s 73*]						
Residential land (see below)	–	–	20%	20%	20%	20%
[*TCA 1997, s 644B; FA 2000, s 52*]						
Manufacturing companies rate (see **12.18** below)	10%	10%	10%	10%	10%	10%
[*TCA 1997, s 448(2); FA 1980, s 41; FA 1990, Sch 2 Pt II; FA 1995, Sch 4 Pt II; FA 1997, Sch 6 Pt II; FA 1999, Sch 1 para 1*]						

* for periods to 31 March and from 1 April respectively.

See **12.28** below for the 12.5 per cent rate tonnage tax regime.

The full rate is reduced to **12.5 per cent** for financial year 2003 onwards. The effective manufacturing companies rate remains at **ten per cent** throughout. [*TCA 1997, ss 21(1), 22(1)(a), 448(2); FA 1999, ss 71, 72, Sch 1 para 1*]

A special rate of **12.5 per cent** applies for financial years 2001 to 2006 to profits from 'qualifying shipping activities' of companies carrying on 'qualifying shipping trades' (see **12.18** below). [*TCA 1997, s 21(1A); FA 2001, s 82(1)(a)*]

For financial year 2000 and subsequent years, a **higher rate** of **25 per cent** applies on income chargeable under Sch D, Case iii (**31**), Case IV (**32**) or Case V (**33**). The higher rate also applies to income of an 'excepted trade' (after deducting any charges paid wholly and exclusively for the purposes of the trade). An '*excepted trade*' is a trade (or part of a trade) consisting only of one or more of:

(*a*)   'working minerals' (as defined);

(*b*)   'petroleum activities' (as defined); or

(*c*)   dealing in or developing land other than 'qualifying land' (ie fully developed land, see *s 21A(1)*), but excluding any part consisting of 'construction operations'. (See also below as regards the special rate applicable to residential development land dealing.)

'*Construction operations*' are as under *s 530* (see **13.8** 'Deduction of tax at source'), but for financial year 2000 only and only in the case of residential development land dealing exclude the demolition or dismantling of any building or structure on the land, the construction or demolition of any roadworks, water mains, wells, sewers or land drainage installations forming part of the land, and any other operations preparatory to residential development on the land other than the laying of the foundations. This latter exclusion ensures that income from such operations is taxed at the 20 per cent **(25% as of 1 January 2009)** rate for that year (see below) and at the (lower) full rate of corporation tax thereafter.

Appropriate apportionments are made on a just and reasonable basis where only part of a trade (which is treated as a separate trade) is within (*a*), (*b*) or (*c*) above.

The higher rate does **not** apply to profits consisting of income from the sale of goods within the manufacturing companies relief (see **12.18** below) or of income arising in a trade of non-life insurance, reinsurance or (insofar as the income is attributable to shareholders) life business. [*TCA 1997, s 21A; FA 1999, s 73; FA 2000, s 75*]

Standard rate applies to a company's total profits except insofar as the reduced or higher rate applies (and subject to the manufacturing companies relief, see **12.18** below). [*TCA 1997, s 21(1)*]

Reduced rate. For financial year 2000 to 2002 inclusive the reduced rate of 12.5 per cent applies (subject as below) where the income does not exceed a certain level, with marginal relief where the income does not greatly exceed that level. For financial year 2003 onwards, the reduced rate ceases to be effective due to the reduction in the full rate to 12.5 per cent. Accounting periods straddling 31 December 2002 are accordingly treated as split into two accounting periods, the first ending on, and the second beginning immediately after, that date. The reduced rates do not apply where the ten per cent manufacturing companies rate (see **12.18** below) or the 25 per cent higher (or 20 per cent **(25% as of 1 January 2009)** development land) rate (see above) applies. Appropriate apportionments are made on a just and reasonable basis where part of a trade consists of excepted operations within the higher rate regime (as above), that part and the other part of the trade being treated as separate trades.

Subject as below, a reduced rate of **12.5 per cent** applies to profits other those arising in respect of chargeable gains (see below) where 'net relevant trading income' does not exceed the 'lower relevant maximum amount'. Where the 'net relevant trading income' exceeds the 'lower relevant maximum amount' but does not exceed the 'upper relevant maximum amount' the corporation tax otherwise chargeable is reduced by 23 per cent of the excess of the 'upper relevant maximum amount' over the 'net relevant trading income' for financial year 2000, by 30 per cent of that excess for financial year 2001, and by 14 per cent of that excess for financial year 2002. Accounting periods straddling 31 December in any year are treated as split into two accounting periods, the first ending on, and the second beginning immediately after, that date. The company's return under *s 951* (see **28.11** 'Returns') must contain a statement specifying the relief to be given under these provisions (and an amount so specified may not be altered) and the number of 'associated companies' (see below) for the accounting period.

The *'net relevant trading income'* is the trading income (other than any chargeable under Sch D, Case III or reduced by a trading loss brought forward, see **12.17**(*c*) below), net of any charges or trading losses of the period (disregarding income, charges or losses of an 'excepted trade (see above) or a trade within the manufacturing companies relief (see **12.18** below)). The *'lower'* and *'upper relevant maximum amounts'*, which are proportionately reduced where the accounting period is less than twelve months, are as follows.

	Lower	Upper
Financial year 2000	£50,000	£75,000
Financial year 2001	£200,000	£250,000
Financial year 2002	€254,000	€317,500

Where there are associated companies (as below), the lower and upper relevant maximum amounts are divided by one plus the number of any associated companies in the accounting period. However, where a company and all its associated companies have coterminous accounting periods, they may by written notice elect to apportion amongst them the relief which would be available as above if all the companies were a single company (with no associated companies) with an accounting period beginning on the earliest date on which any of the companies' accounting periods begins. A copy of the election must be delivered with the return under *s 951* (as above). The manner of the apportionment must be specified in the election (although none of them may be allocated an amount greater than that to which it would have been entitled had it had no associated companies). Where a company and all its associated companies do not have coterminous accounting periods, such an election may be made for any period common to the accounting periods of all the companies (a *'relevant period'*) as if the relevant period were an accounting period. The relief so calculated for all the relevant periods falling within an accounting period (and that calculated for the remaining part(s), if any, of the accounting period, treating each such part as a separate accounting period) are then aggregated for each of the companies (again with the restriction that none of them may be allocated an amount greater than that to which it would have been entitled had it had no associated companies). Associated companies with no net relevant trading income in the period (or in any part of the period during which the companies are associated) are disregarded, but otherwise associated companies are taken into account even if associated for part only of the accounting period, and companies associated with the same company in different parts of that company's accounting period will both be taken into account. Companies are for these purposes *'associated'* where one controls the other (within *s 432*) or they are under common control (and see **38.73** 'Tax cases').

[*TCA 1997, ss 22, 22A; FA 1998, s 56; FA 1999, s 72; FA 2000, s 76; FA 2001, s 83*]

Residential land. For accounting periods ending after 31 December 1999 (periods straddling that date being treated as two separate accounting periods, ending on and beginning immediately after that date) in which a company carries on an 'excepted trade' within *s 21A* (see above) which consists of or includes dealing in land which, at the time of disposal, is 'residential development land' (see **2.42** 'Allowances, credits and rates'), the corporation tax referable to income from such dealing is reduced by one-fifth, ie to **20 per cent**. This rate has been increased to **25 per cent** from 1 January 2009. This applies also where a charge arises under Sch D, Case IV (see **3.9**(ii) 'Anti-avoidance legislation') on capital gains arising from the disposal of residential development land. Special provision is made for determining the proportion of corporation tax to be so reduced by reference to the proportion of amounts receivable by the company which arise from such transactions (but excluding amounts attributable to 'construction operations', see **2.42** 'Allowances, credits and rates'), and for a similar apportionment of the corporation tax chargeable at 25 per cent under *s 21A*.

Finance Act 2009 also inserted a new *s 644C*. This section restricts the allowance of losses on residential land incurred before 1 January 2009 and carried forward to accounting periods beginning on or after that date to allowance on a value basis. This is to ensure that the effect of the tax treatment of trading losses is commensurate with the effect of the increase in the tax rate on trading income from 20 per cent to 25 per cent. The section also restricts to relief on a value basis any losses on residential development land activity which are set-off against income chargeable to tax at 25 per cent or which are carried back for set-off against similar income of an immediately preceding accounting period of the same duration, where the claim is made on or after Budget Day (7 April 2009). Finally, the section restricts terminal losses incurred in a trade, to the extent that those losses relate to dealing in residential land incurred before 31 December 2008, to relieving income of the trade charged at the effective rate of 20 per cent applying to trading profits from such dealing in land, where the claim for terminal loss relief is made on or after Budget Day.

For financial year 2000 only (with accounting periods straddling 31 December 2000 again being treated as two separate accounting periods ending on and beginning immediately after that date), the company may claim to have corporation tax attributable to dealing in fully developed land included under the above provisions. (For subsequent financial years, the full rate of corporation tax otherwise applicable to profits or gains from dealing in fully developed land (see above) will in any event be less than 20 per cent.) [*TCA 1997, s 644B; FA 2000, s 52*]

See **2.40** 'Allowances and rates' for corresponding income tax provisions.

For an article, including computational examples, on the application of these provisions, see Revenue Tax Briefing Issue 40 pp 1–5.

Corporation tax on chargeable gains is calculated on an amount of chargeable gains so as to result in CT payable equalling the capital gains tax which would be payable on the same chargeable gains if capital gains tax applied to companies. The allowable losses which may be set against gains are those accruing in the accounting period and unallowed losses of earlier accounting periods while the company was within the charge to CT. Where parts of an accounting period fall in two successive FYs (or deemed FYs, see below) for which different rates of CT apply, a time-weighted average rate of CT is used in determining the appropriate amount of chargeable gains to be taken into account.

Chargeable gains on certain disposals of development land are excluded, companies being directly liable for capital gains tax on such gains (see **9.16** 'Capital gains tax'). [*TCA 1997, s 78; CTA 1976, s 13; FA 1995, Sch 4 para 1; FA 1997, Sch 6 Pt I(1); FA 1998, Sch 6 para 2*]

ACCOUNTING PERIODS

12.3 While CT is charged on profits in a financial year (ie ending 31 December), assessments are made by reference to accounting periods. When an accounting period does not coincide with the financial year the profits for that accounting period are apportioned between financial years on a time basis. [*TCA 1997, s 26(3)*]

[*TCA 1997, s 26(4); FA 1995, Sch 4 para 1; FA 1997, Sch 6 Pt I(1); FA 1998, Sch 6 para 1*]

An accounting period **begins** when the company first comes within the charge to CT, or when an accounting period ends and the company is still within the charge to CT. An accounting period lasts twelve months or otherwise **ends** on:

(i)   the date to which a company makes up its accounts (so that for any company which makes up its accounts annually, subsequent accounting periods will coincide with its year of account);

(ii)   the company beginning or ceasing a trade within the charge to CT;

(iii)   the company beginning or ceasing to be resident in RI;

(iv)   the company ceasing to be within the charge to CT.
        [*TCA 1997, s 27(2)(3)*]

'Within the charge to CT' has an extended meaning so that every company resident in RI, whether or not assessable to CT, falls within the provisions relating to accounting periods on 6 April 1976 or (if later) the date when it starts to carry on business. [*TCA 1997, s 27(4); CTA s 9(4)*]

Where a company carries on several trades and makes up separate accounts for each using different accounting dates, the Commissioners may determine to which of those accounting dates (i) above applies. [*TCA 1997, s 27(5)*] If the beginning or end of any accounting period is uncertain an inspector may make an assessment for such period not exceeding twelve months as appears to him appropriate. [*TCA 1997, s 27(8)*]

ADMINISTRATION

12.4 CT is administered by the Revenue Commissioners [*TCA 1997, s 849*] and the same administrative provisions in general apply as under the Income Tax Acts. See **1** 'Administration and general'.

An election made by a company under IT rules will continue in effect under CT, if appropriate. [*CTA 1976, s 172*]

RETURNS AND ASSESSMENT

12.5 Self-assessing procedures. See **28.11** 'Returns' as regards procedures for returns, payment of preliminary tax and assessment, which apply to accounting periods ending after 30 September 1989.

Returns of profits and of distributions received from RI-resident companies and of surplus ACT (see **12.26** below), of certain payments from which income tax is to be deducted (see **12.20** below), of the amounts of certain tax credits (prior to their abolition) recoverable from the company and of such further particulars as may be prescribed by the notice must be made when required by notice from an inspector or officer of the Commissioners, and there are powers to demand information and production of books, accounts, documents, etc where a company fails to deliver a required return, or the inspector is not satisfied with a return. [*TCA 1997, ss 160(6), 884; FA 1999, s 210; FA 2000, Sch 2*] See **12.26** below as regards advance corporation tax returns and **13.12** 'Deduction of tax at source' as regards dividend withholding tax.

Every company which starts trading or carrying on a profession or business (in RI in the case of non-resident companies) must deliver particulars within 30 days and a company chargeable to CT which has not made a return of its profits must give notice to the inspector within one year of the end of the accounting period. Special provisions apply to RI incorporated but non-resident companies. Penalties apply for non-compliance. [*TCA 1997, ss 882, 883, 1073–1075*]

Assessments are made by an inspector, and if the company is not resident in RI may be made on any agent, manager or representative of the company. Estimated assessments may be made in the absence of satisfactory information. In the absence of fraud or neglect no assessment may be made more than ten years (four years from 1 January 2005) after the accounting period to which it relates. [*TCA 1997, s 919; FA 2003, s 17; SI 508/03*]

Assessment – special rules for capital gains. A person connected with a company resident in RI may be assessed to unpaid CT in respect of a chargeable gain accruing to the company on a disposal of assets (see **9.6**, **9.8** 'Capital gains tax') to the extent to which the gain was passed on to the connected person by a capital distribution (not being a reduction of capital) which also constituted a disposal of assets. Any person so assessed may reclaim the amount from the company. [*TCA 1997, s 614*]

On a transfer of the whole or part of a business for no consideration (other than the assumption of liabilities of the business) from one RI company to another in the course of a company reconstruction or amalgamation, the transferor company is treated as having made neither gain nor loss and the transferee is treated as having acquired the assets in the way in which the transferor company originally acquired them. With effect for disposals after 14 February 2001, this treatment is extended to companies resident in other EU Member States (or, from 1 January 2002, other EEA States with which double tax arrangements are in force) and carrying on trade in RI through a branch or agency of which the asset in question is a chargeable asset for RI capital gains tax purposes. [*TCA 1997, s 615; FA 2001, s 38(1)(a); FA 2002, s 36(a)*] For the application of this relief to partitions of family trading companies, see Revenue Tax Briefing Issue 44 pp 34, 35.

Interest on a loan for construction work which enhances the value of an asset (see **9.8** 'Capital gains tax') is allowable if charged to capital [*TCA 1997, s 553*] From 2 February 2004, certain RI holding companies can avail of a participation exemption for disposals in qualifying subsidiaries. See **9.7**(y) 'Capital gains tax'.

APPEALS AND PAYMENT OF TAX

12.6 Appeals are governed by *Pt 40* in the same way as those provisions apply for IT (see **4** 'Appeals').

Payment of CT. See **28.11** 'Returns'. Broadly, for accounting periods ending before 1 January 2002, preliminary tax is due within six months of the end of the accounting period (or by the 28th day of the sixth month if earlier). For accounting periods ending after 31 December 2005, the due date is to be moved to 31 days before the end of the accounting period (or by the 21st day of that month if earlier), being payable in varying proportions on the old and new dates during the transition (ie accounting periods ending after 31 December 2001 and before 1 January 2006 (see **28.11** 'Returns'). Any further tax assessed is due on the return filing date (due within one month of the date of the assessment for periods ending on or before 31 December 2002), except that it is due by the preliminary tax due date where either the assessment is made before that date or the preliminary tax has not been paid in full by the due date or falls short of certain requirements as to its amount in relation to the final liability. [*TCA 1997, s 958(1)–(4) as amended*]

Interest on unpaid tax is chargeable generally as for income tax (see **25.3** 'Payment of tax'). [*TCA 1997, ss 1080–1082*]

See **12.26** below as regards advance corporation tax and **13.12** 'Deduction of tax' at source as regards dividend withholding tax.

Profits from land dealing or development. Payment may be postponed in respect of profits attributable to a right to obtain a lease-back of the property sold. [*TCA 1997, s 647*]

CLOSE COMPANIES

12.7 A close company is a company:

(*a*)   which is under the control of:

    (i)   five or fewer participators, or

    (ii)   participators who are directors; or

(*b*)   more than half of whose distributable income would, on a full distribution, be paid directly or indirectly to five or fewer participators or to participators who are directors.

The following are not close companies:

(i)   a company not resident in RI;

(ii)   a registered industrial and provident society, or building society;

(iii)   a company controlled by the State;

(iv)   from 1 January 2003, a company controlled by or on behalf of an EC Member State or by the government of a country with which RI has a double tax treaty and which is not otherwise a close company;

(v)   a company controlled by one or more non-close companies, where one of the five or fewer participators necessary to its being treated as close is also a non-close company (non-resident companies being treated as close for this purpose if they would be so if RI-resident);

(vi)   a company in relation to which:

(A)   shares (not carrying a fixed rate of dividend) representing 35 per cent or more of the voting power are unconditionally and beneficially held by the public (as defined), and some of those shares have been quoted and dealt with on a recognised stock exchange within the preceding twelve months, and

(B)   the total voting power held by the principal members does not exceed 85 per cent (a principal member being a person whose shareholding exceeds five per cent in voting power and is one of the top five in voting power);

(vii)   a company which cannot be a close company except by including, as having control, persons with rights to distribution of assets on a winding up or in other circumstances and which would not be a close company if the rights of such persons excluded those of loan creditors who are non-close companies.
[*TCA 1997, ss 430, 431; FA 2003, s 63*]

Control means control (whether direct or indirect) of the company's affairs, or possession of the greater part of the share capital or voting power or entitlement to the greater part of the company's whole income or (on a winding up, etc) assets. [*TCA 1997, s 432(2)–(6)*] *Participator* means a person with a share or interest in the company's income or capital, and includes a shareholder, loan creditor, and a person entitled to secure that income or assets will be applied to his own benefit. *Director* includes both a manager and a beneficial owner of 20 per cent of the company's ordinary share capital. [*TCA 1997, s 433*]

Surcharge on undistributed income. There is an additional charge to corporation tax for each accounting period in which certain distributable income exceeds the distributions of a close company for the period by more than €635/£500 (with marginal relief for amounts slightly over that limit). Where the accumulated undistributed income at the end of the period (together with certain capital appropriations) is less than the excess, the lower amount is substituted for the excess. The limit is reduced for accounting periods of less than twelve months and where there are associated companies. The rate of surcharge is **20 per cent** of the excess, and the surcharge is treated as corporation tax chargeable for the earliest accounting period which ends at least twelve months after the end of the accounting period in respect of which the surcharge is made. If there is no such accounting period so ending, it is chargeable for the accounting period in respect of which the surcharge is made.

Section 434 has been amended to allow a company making a distribution and the company receiving it to jointly elect that the distribution will not be treated as a distribution for the purposes of *s 440*. This amendment allows an Irish resident holding company and an Irish resident company that pays a dividend to the holding company to elect that the dividend be afforded the same treatment as dividends received from a non-resident subsidiary. If such an election is made, the dividend received will be treated as not being a distribution received by the holding company and as not being a distribution made by the subsidiary. [*FA 2008, s 44*]

The distributions for an accounting period are all dividends declared in respect of the period and paid or payable during or within 18 months after the end of the period, together with all other distributions made in the accounting period.

[*TCA 1997, ss 434(2)(3), 440*]

For accounting periods ending after 13 March 2001, the distributable income by reference to the excess of which the surcharge applies is the '*distributable estate and investment income*' (or, in the case of a 'trading company', 92.5 per cent of that income), ie the 'estate and investment income' after deducting the amount of corporation tax which would be payable if computed on the basis of that income. The '*estate and investment income*' of a period is the amount by which the sum of:

(*a*) the franked investment income of the period (excluding certain distributions, see *s 434(1)*); and

(*b*) the sum determined by applying to the income of the company the fraction A/B where 'A' is the sum of estate income and investment income and 'B' is total income before deduction of current year losses and certain charges;

exceeds the aggregate of allowable charges on income (excluding any paid for the purposes of an excepted trade within *s 21A*, see **12.2** above) and allowable management expenses of the period. From the date on which *s 626B* becomes operative, no close company surcharge will apply to dividends and other distributions received by a close company which, broadly, at the time of receipt of the dividend or distribution, satisfies the conditions contained in *s 626B* for exemption from capital gains tax arising on the sale of shares in that subsidiary. A '*trading company*' is one which exists wholly or mainly for the purpose of carrying on a trade or whose income does not consist wholly or mainly of investment income or estate income. [*TCA 1997, ss 434(1)(5)(5A), 440(1)*; *FA 2001, s 91*; *FA 2003, s 163*; *FA 2004, s 36*; *FA 2006, s 127, Sch 2*]

For accounting periods ending before 14 March 2001, the distributable income by reference to the excess of which the surcharge applies is the aggregate of the company's '*distributable investment income*' and its '*distributable estate income*' (those terms being as defined in *s 434(5)*), those incomes being reduced by five per cent and 7.5 per cent respectively in the case of a trading company. There was no additional tax credit (prior to their abolition) in respect of the surcharge if income surcharged was later distributed. The distribution carried the normal tax credit only. [*TCA 1997, s 440(1)(5)*; *FA 2000, Sch 2*]

Service companies. In the case of a close company which is a '*service company*' (ie broadly a company whose business consists of or includes the carrying on of a profession or employment or the provision of certain related services, see *s 441(1)–(3)*), a similar surcharge arises, subject to similar conditions, on the excess of the distributable estate and investment income (as above) and 50 per cent of the 'distributable trading income' over distributions for the period. The surcharge is at the rate of **15 per cent**, except that a 20 per cent rate applies to so much of the excess as is not greater than the excess of the distributable estate and investment income over the distributions for the period. The trading company deduction applies equally to service companies. For accounting periods ending before 14 March 2001, the excess brought into surcharge was the excess over distributions of the aggregate of (i) 50 per cent of 'distributable income' and (ii) 50 per cent of 'distributable investment income' and 'distributable estate income' (all those terms being as defined in *s 434(1)(5)*), and the 20 per cent rate applied by reference to the excess of the amount in (ii) over distributions for the period. [*TCA 1997, s 441; FA 2001, s 91*] See **38.58** 'Tax cases'.

Distribution is given an extended meaning for close companies. It includes expenses (valued in the same way as benefits in kind) incurred by the company in providing participators or their associates with accommodation, entertainment, facilities, etc where such provision is *not* a taxable benefit in kind (see **34.3** 'Sch E'). [*TCA 1997, s 436*] Loan interest, exceeding a prescribed limit, paid to a director with a 'material interest' (broadly, more than five per cent of the ordinary share capital), or to such a director's associate, is also a distribution. [*TCA 1997, s 437*]

Loans to participators. A close company whose business does not include the making of loans is charged to IT on any loan or advance to a participator or associate of a participator who is an individual or which is a company acting in a fiduciary or representative capacity or a company not resident (for the purposes of corporation tax or similar tax) in a Member State of the EC (prior to 6 February 2003, not resident in RI). The tax payable is an amount equal to IT at the standard rate on the grossed-up equivalent of the loan. *Loan* includes any debt (except normal credit for normal supply of business goods or services), but a loan of £15,000/€19,050 or less to a borrower who works full-time for the company and does not have a material interest (see above) is exempt. All tax paid will be repaid on repayment of the loan. [*TCA 1997, s 438; FA 2003, s 45*] With effect from 6 February 2003, loans by companies controlled by a close company (or which come under the control of the close company some time after the making of the loan) are deemed to be loans made by the close company, unless it can be shown that there is no connection between the acquisition of the company and the making of the loan or the making of the loan and the provision of the funds to facilitate the loan. [*FA 2003, s 45*] Any interest charged due to late payment of the tax is not, however, repaid. [*TCA 1997, s 240(5)*] On the release or writing off of such a loan the amount of the loan received by the debtor is treated as income from which standard rate IT has already been deducted but the tax credit attributed is not repayable. [*TCA 1997, s 439*] For loans, etc made after 22 May 1983, the exclusion at (ii) above of industrial and provident societies from being close companies does not apply for this purpose. [*TCA 1997, s 438(8)*]

Finance Act 2011, s 29 has introduced further anti-avoidance legislation in respect of close companies. A new *TCA 1997, s 436A* is designed to counter attempts to extract funds from close companies on a tax-free basis through the use of settlements.

The section inserts a new new *TCA 1997, s 436A* provides that amounts settled by a close company on or after 21 January 2011 in connection with *relevant* settlements will be treated as a distribution to the trustees of the settlement. The section also contains a provision to ensure that where on or after 21 January 2011 an individual who is or was a member of a close company, or a relative of such an individual, receives an amount in money or money's worth out of assets comprised in a relevant settlement, the amount received (net of any consideration given) will be treated as annual profits or gains of the individual, or relative, chargeable to income tax under Case IV of Schedule D in the year of assessment in which it is received.

COMPUTATION OF PROFITS

12.8 Total profits. The figures for income and capital gains (as reduced) are added to give a company's total profits. From this figure may be deducted:

(i)   losses (see **12.17** below);

(ii)   charges on income (see **12.9** below);

(iii)   management expenses (see **12.9** below);

(iv)   group relief (see **12.15** below).

Income. In general, a company's income is computed for CT purposes in the same way as under income tax law, as though accounting periods were years of assessment. Thus, income from each source still falls to be computed under the Schedule and Case appropriate to that particular source, except that (*a*) income of any particular period is computed by reference to that period and no other (except for apportionment between accounting periods), and (*b*) income of a trade under Sch D, Case III is computed according to Sch D, Case I rules. [*TCA 1997, ss 76, 77(5)*] However, *s 71* (see **31.2** 'Sch D, Case III') does not apply. [*TCA 1997, s 76(7)*]

See **38.142** 'Tax cases' and Revenue Tax Briefing Issue 44 pp 36, 37 as regards circumstances in which deposit interest may be treated as a trading receipt.

Capital allowances and balancing charges (see **12.9** below) are applicable only in computing *income*.

Distributions received by a company (see **12.7** above and **12.10** below) are not taken into account in computing income. [*TCA 1997, s 129*] See **12.12** below as regards exemption of certain dividends from foreign subsidiaries.

Special rules for income [*TCA 1997, s 77(2)(4)(6)*]

(i)   beginning or ceasing to be within the charge to CT in respect of a trade is treated as the commencement or cessation of the trade (except where the trade is not regarded under tax law as permanently discontinued);

(ii)   income from letting rights to work minerals in RI – deduction is allowed, subject to restrictions, for management expenses, etc;

(iii)   foreign tax paid on income from foreign property is normally deductible against that income.

Chargeable gains and allowable losses are computed in the same way as under the *Capital Gains Tax Acts*, as though accounting periods were years of assessment, before being reduced (see **12.2** above). Provisions relating to CGT which can only apply to individuals do not apply under CT, in particular the reduced rates for periods of ownership exceeding three years, but in general references to income tax are read as referring to corporation tax. [*TCA 1997, s 78*] For the charge on gains on certain life policies, etc, see **9.12** 'Capital gains tax'.

Foreign currency considerations. *Exchange gains and losses*. The amount of any gain or loss, realised or unrealised, attributable to money held or payable for trade purposes, or to a related currency hedging contract, which results from an exchange rate change (or from the introduction of the euro) and which is properly credited or debited to the profit and loss account, is brought into account in computing trading income. Exchange gains and losses on such currency hedging contracts and on money held for trade purposes are correspondingly not chargeable gains or allowable losses (except in the case of certain companies carrying on exempt life assurance business). The 'profit and loss account' is the account of the company (or of the branch or agency business of a non-resident company) certified by the auditor as presenting a true and fair view of the profit or loss of the company (or business) in question. Gains or losses on currency contracts hedging risks relating to RI corporation tax liabilities are similarly neither chargeable gains nor allowable losses (thus matching the treatment of gains and losses in relation to the liabilities themselves) to the extent that they do not exceed the loss or gain relating to the liability concerned. [*TCA 1997, s 79; FA 1998, Sch 2 para 1*] See Revenue practice note at www.revenue.ie/services/foi/s16 2001/pt 14.pdf. For the considerations which applied prior to these specific provisions, see **38.158, 38.159** 'Tax cases'. For accounting periods ending on or after 6 February 2003, where the functional currency of the company is the Euro provision is made for the matching of the foreign currency asset with a foreign currency liability for acquisitions of share capital in foreign trading companies or holding companies of trading companies where the acquiror owns 25 per cent or more of the foreign company and the appropriate election is made within three weeks of acquisition of the foreign currency asset. The provision deals with the tax treatment on disposal only [*TCA 1997, s 79A; FA 2003, s 37*]. Since 1 January 2006 similar treatment applies to the matching of a foreign currency trading asset with redeemable share capital denominated in the same currency. This provision has no percentage holding requirement. [*TCA 1997, s 79B; FA 2006, s 61*]. This section was amended to ensure that unrealised foreign currency movements on the share capital can be taken into account for tax purposes over the period of the loan on a 'mark to market' basis. The second amendment provides that tax neutrality provided for under *s 79B*, which currently assumes a euro functional currency is also available to a company whose functional currency is other than the euro. [*FA 2007, s 49*]

Capital allowances. Allowances to be made in taxing a trade for expenditure becoming payable after that date are computed in the 'functional currency' of the company, and given effect as a trading expense or receipt in computing the trading income or loss in that currency. Where there is a change in functional currency, any earlier expenditure, and allowances in respect of that expenditure, are converted into the new functional currency by reference to the exchange rate on the day the expenditure was incurred. The *'functional currency'* is the currency of the primary economic environment in which the company operates, or, in the case of a non-resident company, in which the company carries on trading activities in RI, *except that* where the profit and loss account (as above) for a period of account has been prepared in the currency of RI, that is the functional currency for that period. The currency of the primary economic environment is determined with reference to the currency in which revenues and expenses are primarily generated and the company primarily borrows and lends (in relation to the RI trading activities in the case of a non-resident company). A change resulting from introduction of the euro is not treated as a change in currency for these purposes. [*TCA 1997, s 402(1)(2); FA 1998, Sch 2 para 5*]

Trading losses. For the purposes of loss set-offs, trading losses are computed in the 'functional currency' (as above) of the company, and are converted to the currency of RI by reference to the rate of exchange used to convert the trading income for the accounting period in which the loss is to be set off (or which would be used if there were such income). Where there is a change in functional currency, any loss incurred, and any set off referable to such a loss, which was previously computed by reference to the earlier functional currency is converted into the new functional currency by reference to the average exchange rate for the accounting period in which the loss was incurred. [*TCA 1997, s 402(1)(3)*]

DEDUCTIONS

12.9 Capital allowances and balancing charges apply to companies, with suitable modifications, as under the corresponding income tax provisions, for which see **8** 'Capital allowances' and the cross-references therein. The legislation refers to 'chargeable periods' which are the accounting periods of companies (and years of assessment for individuals, etc).

Allowances and charges relating to a trade are treated respectively as trading expenses and receipts. Initial allowances may be disclaimed by notice in writing within two years of end of accounting period. Allowances available primarily against a specified class of income are deducted as far as possible from income of that class. Where there is an insufficiency of income for that accounting period the balance may, on a claim, be dealt with as a loss as in **12.17** below (but restricted to one-half of the maximum claim where the return for the period is late, see **28.11** 'Returns'). [*TCA 1997, ss 307, 308, 1085(2)*]

Where a company takes over the business of another company which ceases to trade and at least a three-fourths interest in the trade remains in the same hands, there is no cessation or commencement of trading for the purposes of capital allowances. [*TCA 1997, s 400*]

Charges on income. Certain annual payments may be deductible from overall profits (and see below). These 'charges on income' include annuities and other annual payments, royalties and long lease rents but not distributions by the company nor any sum deductible in computing overall profits.

FA 2011, s 35 amends *TCA 1997, Sch 24, para 4(5)* to make it clear that a company is not permitted to allocate relevant trading charges on income as it sees fit in the computation of the credit due to it in respect of foreign tax paid on its income. The provision is to make clear that a company is not permitted to allocate relevant trade charges as it sees fit in the computation of the credit due to it in respect of foreign tax paid on its income. This is to have affect for accounting periods for which a return is made by the company on or after 7 December 2010 and for any other accounting periods where a DTR claim is made on or after 7 December 2010.

Interest payments within *s 247(2)* (see **20.3**(*c*)(i) 'Interest payable') may be charges on income. [*TCA 1997, s 243(7)–(9)*]

New provisions have been introduced by the *FA 2011, s 37* in relation to the deductibility of interest. Interest relief for companies on loans applied in lending to or acquiring shares in other companies. The main changes are as follows:

- In order for the interest on a loan to qualify for relief as a charge on income the borrowed money must be used wholly and exclusively by the ultimate recipient of the money, for the purposes of a trade, the purposes of property rental or for acquiring trading or property rental companies.

- The company qualifying for interest relief must have a material interest (broadly more than 5%) in the company that ultimately uses the borrowed money and these companies must have a common director. Previously it was sufficient to have the material interest in any connected company

•   Relief due may be restricted where investment money is lent to another company which is not within the charge to Irish corporation tax. Where a company which uses the money is a foreign company interest relief for the investor company will be given up to the amount that interest income is received by the investor company from the foreign investee company. Any balance of interest paid is capped at the amount paid less interest arising to the foreign company in respect of the loan. The intention of this provision is to restrict interest relief to the extent that the return is not taxable in Ireland

Similar restriction is provided where the loan is ultimately used by a company connected with the investee so that interest relating to monies used for the purpose of a trade will be relieved at the 12.5 per cent rate of corporation tax on trading income, rather than 25% as heretofore.

These provisions above are effective for loans made on or after 21 January 2011 other than such loan made in accordance with a binding written agreement made before that date. *[FA 2011, s 37].*

Payments must be charged to income not capital, and (unless short-term transactions within *s 792(1)(b)(ii)(iii))* must be under a liability incurred for valuable and sufficient consideration and, if the payer is non-resident, incurred wholly and exclusively for the purposes of a trade it carried on in RI through a branch or agency. *[TCA 1997, s 243(6)]*

Generally, payments to non-residents must be made under deduction of standard rate income tax (unless the Revenue Commissioners authorise the company to do otherwise. For accounting periods ending from 3 February 2005, deduction of tax is not required on interest payable to a bank, building society, stockbroker or discount house carrying on business in any member state of the EU and payments made under the provisions of *s 267I* (see **13.4**) are not excluded. *[FA 2005, s 49]* Since 10 February 2000, deduction is not required where it is interest falling within *s 246(3)(b) or (h)* (see **20.1**(i)(vii) 'Interest payable') or, from 30 March 2001, within *s 263(3)(a)* (see **20.1**(i) 'Interest payable') or *s 64(2)* (quoted Eurobond interest)) which the company accounts for, unless the payment is made out of income from securities and possessions outside RI brought into charge to tax under Sch D, Case III (**31**), or, from 6 February 2003, is interest falling within *s 246(3)(cc) or (ccc)*. *Finance (No 2) Act 2008* amended *s 198* to extend the exemption for non-residents from income tax in respect of interest received from Irish resident persons where the company or person receiving the interest is a tax resident of another EU State or a country with which Ireland has entered into a double tax treaty. The amendment extended this exemption to interest payments on the wholesale debt instruments to which *s 246A* applies. The exemption is also extended to discounts on securities which were issued in the course of a trade or business by a company or investment undertaking where the company or person receiving the discount is a tax resident of another EU State or country with which Ireland has a double tax treaty. *[TCA 1997, ss 246A; 243(5); FA 2000, s 65; FA 2001, s 37; FA 2003, s 48; F(No2)A 2008, s 23]*

For accounting periods ending after 5 March 2001, trade charges are not set against total profits, but (subject to special provisions in *s 454* in relation to charges for the purposes of activities within the manufacturing companies relief, see **12.18** below) may be set against any income from other trades (or from certain insurance trades which are excepted trades but are not subject to the special 25 per cent rate). Relief for any charges of an accounting period not so relieved (and not relieved under *s 454*) may be claimed by way of a deduction from corporation tax chargeable for the accounting period (subject to certain reservations) at the rate of corporation tax applicable to the associated income. Charges carried forward as trading losses (see **12.17**(*c*) below) are correspondingly reduced. Claims must be made within two years of the end of the accounting period in which the loss is incurred. Accounting periods are split as necessary for these purposes. These provisions do not apply to charges incurred for the purposes of an 'excepted trade' (see **12.2** above). [*TCA 1997, ss 243A, 243B; FA 2001, s 90; FA 2002, ss 54, 55; FA 2003, s 59; FA 2006, s 127, Sch 2*] See also Revenue Tax Briefing Issue 51 pp 14–15.

Management expenses of an RI *investment company* (excluding sums deductible from income under Sch D, Case V) are deductible from total profits in so far as they exceed the amount of any income (excluding franked investment income) derived from sources not charged to tax. For these purposes, allowances under *ss 109, 518(2), 519(2)* or *774* (see **16.20** 'Exempt income and special savings schemes', **30.23**, **30.26** 'Sch D, Cases I and II', **17.26** 'Exempt organisations') are included as management expenses, but see **30.10** 'Sch D, cases I and II' as regards business entertainment. 'Investment company' includes a savings bank. See also **38.229** 'Tax cases' regarding the definition of 'investment company'.

Where the management expenses, plus any charges on income paid wholly and exclusively for the purposes of the company's business, exceed the amount of profits from which they are deductible, the excess may be:

(*a*) carried forward to the succeeding accounting period and applied as though it had arisen in that succeeding accounting period; or

(*b*) on a written claim within two years, set off against any franked investment income in the accounting period, enabling the company to claim repayment of the tax credit (but this relief is not available for any amount carried forward from a previous year under (*a*) above).

[*TCA 1997, s 83*]

See **38.62** 'Tax cases'.

Approved profit sharing schemes. See **34.7** 'Sch E' as regards deduction of scheme contributions.

Investment in renewable energy generation. For an accounting period in which a company makes a 'relevant investment', it may claim a deduction from its total profits of the amount of that investment. Any unrelieved excess is carried forward and treated as a 'relevant investment' made in the next accounting period. The investment must be made during the '*qualifying period*' of seven years beginning 18 March 1999 and ending on 31 December 2006, and there is a limit of **€12,700,000/£10,000,000** on the aggregate 'relevant investments' by the company and any connected companies (within *s 10*) for which relief may be obtained in any twelve-month period ending on the day before an anniversary of that day. Where the limit is exceeded, the inspector or, on appeal, the Appeal Commissioners apportion the relief on a just and reasonable basis.

A '*relevant investment*' is a sum of money paid by a company on its own behalf directly to a 'qualifying company' for new ordinary shares in that company which, for five years from the date of issue, carry no present or future preferential rights to dividends, to assets on a winding-up or to be redeemed. A '*qualifying company*' is a company incorporated and resident in RI (and not resident elsewhere), which exists solely for the purpose of undertaking a renewable energy project (in one or more of solar power, windpower, hydropower and biomass), certificated for this purpose by the Minister for Public Enterprise (see below). The money must be paid to the qualifying company to enable it to undertake that project, and must be used within two years of receipt for that purpose. Any sum paid subject to repayment terms is excluded.

Relief is denied for a relevant investment in a qualifying company where the aggregate of that and earlier (or simultaneous) relevant investments in the company exceeds the lesser of 50 per cent of the capital cost of the project (net of land costs and contributions by the State or any other person) and £7,500,000/€9,525,000.

For the granting (and revocation) of a Ministerial certificate relating to a renewable energy project, see *s 486B(2)*. The certificate may impose conditions, which may be added to, amended or revoked.

A claim to relief may be allowed at any time after the payment is made to the qualifying company if it will be a relevant investment if used for the purposes specified above within two years, and provided that all the other conditions are or will be satisfied. It will be withdrawn if, by reason of any subsequent event or failure (including a failure by the qualifying company to comply with conditions imposed on its certification by the Minister), the company is not entitled to the relief allowed. Relief is similarly withdrawn (or not allowed) to the extent (if any) that the company disposes of the qualifying company shares within five years of the payment.

Where relief is so claimed, no other relief may be obtained for the payments in question (but see below as regards capital gains tax).

Claims must be accompanied by a certificate in specified form (form REG 3) issued by the qualifying company that the conditions for relief are or will be satisfied in relation to the qualifying company and the renewable energy project. Such a certificate may only be issued with the authority of an authorised officer of the Revenue Commissioners, to whom must be furnished:

(*a*)   a copy of the Ministerial certification of the project (and of any additions, amendments or revocations to the conditions for that certification);

(*b*)   a statement in specified form to the effect that the relief conditions are or will be satisfied, containing any information reasonably required by the Revenue Commissioners, and a declaration that it is correct to the best of the company's knowledge and belief; and

(*c*)   such other information as the Revenue Commissioners may reasonably require.

The issue of a certificate by the qualifying company without due authorisation, or the issue of a certificate, or making of a statement under (*b*) above, which, due to fraud or neglect, is false or misleading in a material respect, renders the qualifying company liable to a penalty not exceeding £500/€630 or (in the case of fraud) £1,000/€1,265. Any relief to which such a certificate or statement relates will be denied or withdrawn.

Anti-avoidance. There is a general prohibition on relief under these provisions for a relevant investment made by a company unless:

(i)   the relevant investment is made at the risk of the company and for *bona fide* commercial reasons and not as part of a scheme or arrangement a main purpose of which is the avoidance of tax; and

(ii)   neither the company nor any connected person (within *s 10*) receives any direct or indirect payment or benefit from the qualifying company, other than an arm's length payment for goods or services or a payment from the proceeds of exploiting the project to which the company is entitled under the terms of the investment.

Withdrawal of relief. Relief is withdrawn where required by a Sch D, Case IV assessment for the accounting period for which the relief was given.

Capital gains tax. Where shares in respect of which entitlement to relief arises as above are disposed of by the company five years or more after their acquisition by the company, the acquisition cost for capital gains tax purposes is determined without regard to the relief, except that any allowable loss is reduced or eliminated by the amount of the relief. [*TCA 1997, s 486B; FA 1998, s 62; FA 2002, s 43; FA 2004, s 39; SI 645/04*]

Research and development activities. Since 1 January 2004, a special relief relating to certain expenditure on such activities may be claimed by a '*qualified company*', ie a company which:

(*a*)   carries on a trade or is a 51 per cent subsidiary of such a company or a 51 per cent subsidiary of a holding company whose business consists wholly or mainly of holding stocks, shares or securities in one or more such company;

(*b*)   carries out research and development activities; and

(*c*)   maintains a record of expenditure incurred by it in those activities.

'*Research and development activities*' means systematic, investigative or experimental activities in a field of science or technology being one or more of the following:

(i)   basic research;

(ii)   applied research;

(iii)   experimental development;

and must also seek to achieve scientific or technological advancement, and involve the resolution of scientific or technological uncertainty. Activities may be included or excluded by regulations drawn up by the Minister for Enterprise, Trade and Employment (see *SI 434/04*).

Where a qualified company is entitled to a deduction (whether from income or by way of capital allowance) in respect of the expenditure it may also claim a credit of 20 per cent of qualifying incremental expenditure against its corporation tax liability for the relevant period. Unused credit may be carried forward indefinitely. Relief must be claimed in the company's annual return. In the case of an RI resident company, the expenditure is disqualified if the company is entitled to a deduction in respect of that expenditure in any other jurisdiction.

Two new sub-ss (4A) and (4B) have been inserted to *s 766* under the *Finance (No 2) Act 2008*. Where a company has a corporation tax liability in the accounting period preceding the accounting period in which the R&D expenditure giving rise to the tax credit applies, sub-s (4A) allows that company, where it has not fully utilised the amount of the credit, to use the excess to reduce the corporation tax of the preceding accounting period. Under *s 766(4)* any remaining excess can be carried forward indefinitely for use against future corporation tax liabilities. Alternatively, where a credit has not been fully utilised against corporation tax in the first accounting period and due to insufficient or no corporation tax liability in the preceding accounting period an excess still remains, a company may claim under sub-s (4B) to have any remaining excess paid to them by the Revenue Commissioners.

It is provided under the section that any payment by the Revenue Commissioners under the sub-s (4B) will not be income for the company for any tax purpose.

Section 766(4) allows a company which cannot fully utilise the tax credit in the accounting period in which it arises to carry that unused amount forward indefinitely for use against future corporation tax liabilities. This options still remains, but a company cannot carry forward any excess which has been used to reduce the corporation tax liability of the preceding accounting period by virtue of a claim under sub-s (4A) or any amount that has been paid to the company by virtue of new sub-s (4B).

The payment of any excess tax credit claimed under the new sub-s (4B) will be dealt with as follows (subject to *s 766B* which imposes a limit on the amount that can be paid):

1. A first payment of 33% of the excess shall be paid not earlier than the date on which the corporation tax return, in respect of the accounting period in which the R&D expenditure giving rise to the tax credit was incurred, is due.

2. Any remaining excess will then be used to reduce the corporation tax for the accounting period following the accounting period in which the entitlement arises. If there is any further remaining excess, the Revenue Commissioners will pay a second instalment equal to 50 per cent of that remaining amount. The second payment will not be paid earlier than 12 months after the date referred to above.

3. Where any excess remains. It will be used to reduce the corporation tax for the second accounting period following the accounting period in which the entitlement to the credit arises. If any excess still remains, the Revenue Commissioners will pay a third instalment equal to that remaining amount. The third payment will be made not earlier than 24 months after the date referred to above.

A time limit is imposed under *s 766(5)* on companies making a claim under the section. Such claims must be made within 12 months from the end of the accounting period in which the expenditure on R&D giving rise to the entitlement to the credit was incurred. This amendment applies to claims on or after 1 January 2009.The section also provides that any payment made by the Revenue Commissioners will be subject to *TCA 1997, s 1006A*. This will ensure that where the company has not complied with its obligation to deliver any return or pay any liability, the payment will be withheld or offset as the case may be.

The definition of 'threshold amount' has been amended so that eligible expenditure incurred by the company in carrying on research and development activities commencing before 2014, which is incremental to the expenditure that was incurred in the base year of 2003, may now be eligible for the 20 per cent tax credit. The relief has been increased from 20 per cent to 25 per cent of qualifying expenditure. The definition of 'threshold amount' has been amended to provide for the base year to remain as 2003 for all future accounting periods. [*F(No 2)A 2008, s 34*] In addition to this from 1 January 2007, expenditure incurred by companies on subcontracting research and development activities to unconnected parties may qualify for the tax credit to a limit of ten per cent of qualifying research and development expenditure in any one year. This is in addition to the current position which allows for an amount of up to five per cent of qualifying expenditure incurred and paid to universities of institutes of higher education [*FA 2007, s 46*].

'*Expenditure on research and development*' is certain capital and non-capital expenditure incurred by a company in respect of research and development activities which it carries on in the EEA and excludes expenditure on buildings or structures (but see below) and tax exempt royalties paid either to a connected person or where the royalties are regarded as excessive. The definition of 'expenditure on research and development' to clarify that where a company incurs expenditure on the provision of a 'specified intangible asset' within the meaning of *TCA 1997, s 291A*, such expenditure shall not constitute expenditure on machinery or plant for the purpose of the R&D tax credit. *[FA 2011, s 41]* .

For qualifying R & D expenditure (other than on buildings/structures), the relief is limited to the excess expenditure over an amount incurred in the appropriate base year. For 2004, 2005 and 2006, the base year is 2003. For subsequent years, the base year is the year that is three years prior to the year in question. For example, the base year for 2008 is 2005. A change has been made to the rolling base year such that the future position is as follows:

(i)   as respects accounting periods commencing before 2014, the base year is 2003;

(ii)   as respects later accounting periods, the base year is a corresponding year ending ten years before the end of the year of claim (eg for 2014 the base year will be 2004) [*FA 2008, s 50*].

The definition of '*threshold amount*' has been amended to provide for the base year to remain as 2003 for all future accounting periods. [*F(No 2)A 2008, s 34*]

No relief is available where relief in any form can be obtained by the qualifying company in another state or to the extent that expenditure is grant-aided. Revenue have published a note stating that expenditure may be treated as incurred on either (1) the date the plant and machinery is first brought into use for the purposes of a trade or (2) the date the expenditure becomes payable (subject to clawback if not brought into use for the purposes of a trade within two years of becoming payable). For accounting periods ending on or after 2 February 2006, relief is available on an apportionment basis where the machinery or plant are not used wholly and exclusively for research and development activities. Apportionment is on a just and reasonable basis with provision for revision if this apportionment ceases to be just and reasonable. From the same date, Revenue are empowered to consult with experts regarding expenditure incurred on research and development activities subject to the taxpayer company not demonstrating that a release of information would be prejudicial to its business.

Groups of companies. Companies that are members of a group of companies may elect how to share the tax credit among the members. Broadly, two companies are members of a group if one is a 51 per cent subsidiary of the other or both are 51 per cent subsidiaries of a third company. Where the accounting periods of the companies do not coincide, provision is made to establish the relevant year for the group.

Finance Act 2010, s 54 amends the definition of 'research and development centre' so that a company which is a member of a group that carries on R&D activities in different research and development centres in separate geographical locations, is required to keep records of expenditure incurred in respect of activities in each location. The definition is also amended such that where a group of companies carrying out R&D activities in different research and development centres in separate geographical locations (not less than 20kms apart) and subsequently ceases to use one of those centres for the purposes of a trade, the expenditure on R&D activities in respect of that centre may be excluded in the calculation of the 'threshold amount' used as the base to calculate the incremental R&D expenditure.

Where the research and development centre that has been closed down is subsequently used for the purposes of a trade by a company which is a member of the group, the aggregate amount by which the 'threshold amount' was reduced for each accounting period, in respect of that research and development centre, will be charged to tax under Case IV of Sch D. This claw-back will also apply where the R&D activities, which were carried on in that centre in the four years before the centre ceased to be used for the purposes of a trade, are subsequently carried on by any group company. In addition, a similar claw-back will apply if, within a period of 10 years commencing on the date that centre ceased to be so used, no company which is a member of the group remains within the charge to corporation tax.

Payments to universities. Where a sum is paid to a university for the carrying out of research and development in a relevant member state, that sum is included in expenditure on research and development to the extent that it does not exceed five per cent of that expenditure. [*TCA 1997, s 766; FA 2004, s 33; FA 2006, s 66; SI 425/04*]

Buildings. Where a company incurs expenditure on the construction or refurbishment of a building or structure which is to be used by it for research and development purposes and which expenditure qualifies for capital allowances in RI but does not entitle the qualifying company to relief in any other jurisdiction, a tax credit of 20 per cent of the expenditure is allowed over a four-year period as a credit against the company's corporation tax liability. Unused credit may be carried forward indefinitely. [*TCA 1997, s 766A; FA 2004, s 33; FA 2006, s 66*]

Finance (No 2) Act 2008 introduced three new definitions and amended the definition of *'relevant expenditure'*.

The amendment to the definition of relevant expenditure removes the requirement that the expenditure must be incurred on a building or structure that is to be used wholly or exclusively for the carrying on of R&D activities by the company. The amendment provides that the expenditure must be incurred on a *'qualifying building'*. This will enable companies who intend to build or refurbish such buildings or structures for both R&D and other activities to claim a tax credit in respect of a portion of the expenditure provided the building is a qualifying building. A *'qualifying building'* is defined as a building or structure, a minimum of 35 per cent of the use of which is attributable to the R&D activities carried on by the company for a defined four year period.

Where a company commences to trade, a claim in respect of expenditure incurred on R&D activities before commencement, will qualify for relief once that claim is made within twelve months from the end of the accounting period beginning at the date the company first carried on a trade. The amount of the credit due is the amount, which the company would have been entitled to claim, if it had been trading when the expenditure was incurred. [*FA 2010, s 50*]

The corporation tax of the company for the accounting period in which the relevant expenditure was incurred may be reduced by 25 per cent of the specified relevant expenditure. This replaces the current provisions whereby the credit is used to reduce the corporation tax of a company over a four year period.

The claw back provisions in *s 766A(3)* now apply if within a period of 10 years commencing at the beginning of the accounting period in which the relevant expenditure was incurred, the building or structure is sold or ceases to be used by the company for the purpose of R&D or for the purpose of the same trade that was carried on by the company at the beginning of four years. The amount to be charged to tax under Case IV Sch D in respect of the clawback in relation to that expenditure, is four times the aggregate amount by which the corporation tax of the company or another company was reduced, together with the amount of any payments made by the Revenue Commissioners. The payments referred to are now provided for in the new sub-s (4B).

The clawback also applies where the R&D activities which were carried out in a research and development centre the four years before the centre ceased to be used for the purposes of a trade are subsequently carried on by any group company. The clawback will also apply if, within a ten years commencing on the date that centre ceased to be so used, no company which is a member of the group remains within the charge to corporation tax.

There are two more new subsections inserted by *Finance (No 2) Act 2008*. These two new subsections are inserted into *s 766A* and are sub-ss (4A) and (4B) and operate in the exact same manner as *s 766(4A), (4B)*.

Section 766A(5) is amended to impose a time limit on companies making a claim under *s 766A*. Such claims should be made within 12 months from the end of the accounting period in which the relevant expenditure giving rise to the tax credit was incurred. This amendment applies to claims made under *s 766A* on or after 1 January 2009.

Section 766A(6) requires that an apportionment used to calculate *'specified relevant expenditure'* or to determine if a building is a qualifying building, must satisfy an Inspector of Taxes as being just and reasonable. In addition, it provides that if at any time such apportionment is no longer considered to be just and reasonable, any necessary adjustments will be made, which may result in an assessment or repayment.

New sub-ss (7) and (8) ensure that any excess tax credit paid by Revenue under *s 766A(4B)* will not be income of the company for any tax purposes and any such payments will be subject to *s 1006A*. This will ensure that where the company has not complied with its obligation to deliver any return or pay any liability, the payment will be withheld or offset as the case may be.

These provisions all come into operation by way of a commencement order to be made by the Minister for Finance following clearance by the European Commission of certain aspects of the amendments from a State-aid perspective.

A new *Pt 29, s 766B* was inserted by the *Finance (No 2) Act 2008*. The section places a limit on the amounts that can be paid to a company under *ss 766(4B) and 766A(4B)*. The limit imposed is the greater of (i) the corporation tax payable by the company for accounting periods ending in the 10 years prior to the period for which the company can make a claim under *ss 766(4A) and 766A(4A)* and (ii) the payroll liabilities for the period in which the expenditure giving rise to the claim under the *ss 766(4B) and 766A(4B)*, is incurred.

Where an amount payable by the Revenue Commissioners under *ss 766(4B) or 766A(4B)* is restricted by virtue of *s 766B*, any amount unused, by virtue of the restriction, can be carried forward indefinitely and used to reduce the corporation tax arising in future accounting periods.

Finance (No 2) Act 2011, s 1 has introduced a number of changes to s 766B which allows for greater flexibility for accounting for the R&D credit on an 'above the line' basis. The section firstly amends the definition of 'payroll liabilities' to include any amounts the company is required to remit to the Collector-General in respect of the Income Levy, Parking Levy and Universal Social Charge. Secondly it introduces a new definition of 'relevant payroll period', being a period which comprises the accounting period in which the R&D expenditure was incurred and the period immediately preceding and equal in length to that accounting period. Lastly, the section amends the limit on payable credits, provided for in *TCA 1997, s 766B*, subject to certain conditions.

For details of relief applying prior to 31 May 1999, see 2005 and previous editions. **Transmission capacity rights.** Since 28 March 2003, a new scheme of capital allowances is introduced for capital expenditure incurred by companies on or after 1 April 2000 for the purchase of capacity rights (or licences in respect of such rights), ie the right to use wired, radio or optical transmission paths for the transfer of voice, data or information. **Since 6 February 2003**, expenditure does not include payments incurred on or after that date for a licence or permission granted on or after that date under the *Wireless Telegraphy Acts 1926 to 1988* or the *Postal and Telecommunications Services Act 1983*. The allowances may only be given in taxing a trade for the purposes of which the rights were used, or by discharge or repayment of tax against income from capacity rights. Allowances are given for qualifying expenditure on a straight-line basis over seven years (or over the period for which the rights are purchased if longer) commencing with the start of the accounting period in which the expenditure was incurred or, if later, in which the trade for which the rights were purchased was commenced. The normal balancing adjustment provisions apply on a subsequent sale or disposal of the rights or on the rights coming to an end or ceasing altogether to be used. Anti-avoidance measures prevent entitlement to allowances through inter-group sale where the vendor was not entitled to allowances in respect of the rights. [*TCA 1997, ss 769A–769F; FA 2000, s 64; FA 2003, s 20*]

From accounting periods ending after 3 February 2004, a company lessor may claim to have the tax treatment of the income from the short-term leasing of assets computed on the basis of normal accounting practice – the lease interest income only is taxable and no claim to capital allowances arises. Where such a claim is made, no annual allowance is available. See **8.7** 'Capital allowances'. [*TCA 1997, s 80A; FA 2004, s 35*]

Relief for donations to approved bodies. Since 6 April 2001, relief is given in respect of any 'relevant donation' made by a company in an accounting period. A '*relevant donation*' is a donation to an 'approved body' within *Sch 26A* (for which see Revenue Tax Briefing Issue 44 p 16) which meets the following conditions:

(*a*)   it is not subject to a condition as to repayment;

(*b*)   neither the donor nor any connected person (within *s 10*) receives a benefit directly or indirectly in consequence of making the donation;

(*c*)   it is not conditional on or associated with, or part of an arrangement involving, the acquisition of property by the approved body, otherwise than by way of gift, from the donor or a connected person (within *s 10*);

(*d*)   it would not otherwise be deductible in computing profits or gains of a trade or profession or as a management expense;

(*e*)   the donation must take the form of the payment of a sum or sums (or, from 2006, a donation of quoted securities) to an approved body amounting in aggregate to at least **€250/£200** in the accounting period (reduced *pro rata* for accounting periods of less than twelve months).

The company may claim relief for a relevant donation made in an accounting period as a trading expense or as a management expense (as above), as appropriate. The claim must be made in the return for the period required by *s 951* (see **28.11** 'Returns').

This relief replaces the separate reliefs for gifts etc described below and at **30.33** 'Sch D, cases I and II'.

[*TCA 1997, s 848A, Sch 26A*; *FA 2001, s 45*; *FA 2006, ss 20, 23*]

See **2.30** 'Allowances, credits and rates' for the associated relief for individuals.

Relief for donations to approved sports bodies. Since 1 May 2002, relief is given in respect of any 'relevant donation' made by a company in an accounting period. A '*relevant donation*' is a donation which meets the following conditions:

(*a*)   it is made to a sports body which has both a valid tax clearance certificate (which may be obtained from the Collector-General) and a certificate from the Revenue stating their opinion that it is within *s 235* (see **17.2** 'Exempt organisations') (and which is not excluded from exemption under that section by notice given by the Revenue);

(*b*)   it is made for the sole purpose of funding a project in respect of which the Minister for Tourism, Sport and Recreation has, on the application of the sports body, given (and not revoked) the necessary certificate, and is or will be applied for that purpose. (It is a condition for certification that the aggregate cost of the project must not be, or be estimated to be, over €40,000,000.) 'Project' for this purpose means one or more of:

    (i)   the purchase, construction or refurbishment of a building or structure (or part) to be used for sporting or recreation activities provided by the body,

    (ii)   the purchase of land to be used in the provision of sporting or recreation facilities by the body,

    (iii)   the purchase of permanently based non-personal equipment for use by the body in such provision,

    (iv)   the improvement of the playing pitches, surfaces or facilities of the body, and

    (v)   the repayment of (or payment of interest on) money borrowed by the body after 30 April 2002 for any of the purposes in (i) to (iv) above;

(*c*)   it is not otherwise deductible in computing profits or gains of a trade or profession or as a management expense;

(*d*)   it is not a relevant donation within *s 848A* (see **2.30** above);

(*e*)   it is not subject to a condition as to repayment;

(*f*)   neither the donor nor any connected person (within *s 10*) receives a benefit directly or indirectly in consequence of making the donation;

(*g*)   it is not conditional on or associated with, or part of an arrangement involving, the acquisition of property by the sports body, otherwise than by way of gift, from the donor or a connected person (within *s 10*);

(*h*)   the donation must take the form of the payment by the company of a sum or sums of money to the sports body amounting in aggregate to at least €250 in the accounting period (reduced *pro rata* for accounting periods of less than 12 months).

No relief is available for a donation for a project within (*b*) above made at a time when the aggregate donations made at and before that time for the project exceed the €40,000,000 limit referred to. Every sports body within (*a*) above may be required to make a return containing particulars of the aggregate amount of relevant donations received in respect of each project within (*b*) above.

Except in the case of a donation for which relief is not available because the €40,000,000 limit has been exceeded, the sports body must give to the donor company a signed receipt for each relevant donation, containing prescribed information and confirmation of the status and details of the donation.

The company may claim relief for a relevant donation made in an accounting period as a trading expense or as a management expense (as above), as appropriate. The claim must be made in the return for the period required by *s 951* (see **28.11** 'Returns').

Where relief has been granted under these provisions in respect of a relevant donation, and is for any reason found not to have been due (eg because it was not used for an approved project), exemption will not be available under *s 235* (see **17.2** 'Exempt organisations') for the amount of the donation.

[*TCA 1997, s 847A*; *FA 2002, s 41*]

See **2.30** 'Allowances, credits and rates' for the associated relief for individuals.

Relief for gifts, etc before 6 April 2001. The following reliefs are replaced from 6 April 2001 by the consolidated relief for donations to approved bodies described above.

Charitable donations. A 'qualifying donation' to an 'eligible charity' made by a company after 5 April 1998 may be relieved by deduction as a trading expense or as a management expense of an investment company. Relief must be claimed with the return required under *s 951* (see **28.11** 'Returns') for the accounting period in which the payment is made. As regards aggregate donations to any one 'eligible charity' in an accounting period, no relief is available where the aggregate does not exceed £250, or to the extent that it exceeds £10,000. There is an overall limit on relief for all 'qualifying donations' in an accounting period of the lesser of £50,000 and ten per cent of the company's profits (before the relief). The £10,000 and £50,000 limits are proportionately reduced where the accounting period is less than twelve months.

A '*qualifying donation*' must be in money, not repayable, not an income disposition within *s 792* (see **36.2** 'Settlements'), and not conditional on or associated with or part of an arrangement involving the acquisition by the charity (other than by way of gift) of property from the donor company or a connected person (within *s 10*). Neither the company nor a connected person may receive any benefit in consequence of the donation, and the payment must not otherwise be deductible as a trading or management expense.

An '*eligible charity*' is any RI body holding the appropriate authorisation from the Revenue Commissioners, such authorisation having effect for a specified period not exceeding five years unless withdrawn by written notice. Broadly the body is required to demonstrate to the satisfaction of the Revenue Commissioners that it is a charity which has been granted relief under *s 207* (see **17.5** 'Exempt organisations') for at least the previous three years, and to comply with any conditions imposed for the purposes of the current relief. It must publish such information as the Minister for Finance may reasonably require, including audited accounts for its most recent accounting period. The Revenue Commissioners may give the name and address of the charity to any person. For a list of eligible charities, see Revenue Tax Briefing Issue 36 Supplement pp 34–38.

[*TCA 1997, s 486A; FA 1998, s 61*]

Gifts to The Enterprise Trust Limited. A gift made by a company to the Trust (or to any approved successor body) and applied solely for the objects set out in its memorandum of association, and which is neither (apart from this provision) deductible for trade purposes nor income within *s 792* (see **36.2** 'Settlements'), may, on a claim in the return under *s 951* (see **28.11** 'Returns'), be allowed as a trading deduction or as a management expense (see above) as appropriate. Any direct or indirect consideration received by the company as a result of making the gift is deducted from the amount of the gift to be allowed. Relief is dependent on a minimum contribution in excess of £500 in aggregate in an accounting period. There is a limit of £5,000,000 on total gifts received by the Trust which may obtain relief in each of the calendar years 1999 to 2002 inclusive, and the Trust must notify the company within 30 days of the making of the gift if relief is thereby denied. [*TCA 1997, s 88; FA 1998, s 63; FA 1999, s 75*]

Gifts to First Step. A gift made by a company to First Step Ltd after 31 May 1993 and before 1 January 2003 and applied solely for the objects for which First Step was incorporated, and which is neither a trade or professional deduction for corporation tax purposes nor income within *s 792* (see **36.2** 'Settlements'), may, on a claim, be treated as a loss incurred in a separate trade carried on in the accounting period in which the gift was made. Any direct or indirect consideration received by the company as a result of making the gift is deducted from the amount of the gift for this purpose. Relief is limited to total gifts by the company to First Step Ltd of £100,000 in any accounting period, and is dependent upon a minimum contribution in excess of £500 in an accounting period (each amount being proportionately reduced for accounting periods of less than twelve months). There is also a limit on total gifts received by First Step Ltd which may obtain relief (£1,500,000 in each of the years to 31 May 1994, 1995, 1996, 1997, 1998, 1999, 2000, 2001 and 2002, and £875,000 in the seven months to 31 December 2002), and First Step must notify the company within 30 days of the making of the gift if relief is thereby denied. [*TCA 1997, s 486; FA 1999, s 80*]

Gifts to third level institutions for approved projects. The relief for individuals making such gifts (see **2.38** 'Allowances, credits and rates') applies to gifts made by companies subject to the same conditions, the £250 (or £1,000) minimum applying by reference to an accounting period of the company instead of a year of assessment. Relief is given by treating the net gifts made in an accounting period as a loss incurred in a separate trade carried on in that period. Gifts for which relief cannot be so obtained may be carried forward and so treated in subsequent accounting periods up to and including the last accounting period ending not more than three years after the end of the accounting period in which the gift was made. [*TCA 1997, s 485; FA 1999, s 36; FA 2000, s 50*]

Gifts to designated schools. The relief for individuals making such gifts (see **2.39** 'Allowances, credits and rates') applies to gifts made by companies. The same conditions apply, except that relief is given for gifts in an accounting period to a particular school or approved body only if the aggregate gifts exceed £250, and only to the extent that the aggregate does not exceed £10,000, subject to an overall limit for the accounting period of the lesser of £50,000 and ten per cent of the company's profits (before the relief). The £10,000 and £50,000 limits are proportionately reduced where the accounting period is less than twelve months. Relief is given by deduction as a trading expense or as a management expense of an investment company. [*TCA 1997, s 485A; FA 1998, s 17*]

Gifts to the Scientific and Technological Education (Investment) Fund ('STEIF'). The relief for individuals making such gifts (see **2.40** 'Allowances, credits and rates') applies to gifts made by companies subject to the same conditions, the £1,000 minimum applying by reference to an accounting period of the company instead of a year of assessment. Relief is given by treating the net gifts made in an accounting period as a loss incurred in a separate trade carried on in that period. [*TCA 1997, s 485B; FA 1999, s 37*]

Gifts to The Foundation for Investing in Communities Limited. A gift made by a company to the Foundation (or any approved subsidiary) after 31 July 2000 and applied solely for the objects set out in its memorandum of association, and which is neither (apart from this provision) deductible for trade purposes nor income within *s 792* (see **36.2** 'Settlements'), may, on a claim in the return under *s 951* (see **28.11** 'Returns'), be allowed as a trading deduction or as a management expense (see above) as appropriate. Any direct or indirect consideration received by the company as a result of making the gift is deducted from the amount of the gift to be allowed. Relief is dependent on a minimum contribution in excess of £500 in aggregate in an accounting period (reduced *pro rata* for accounting periods of less than twelve months). There is also an overall limit of £5,000,000 on total gifts received by the Foundation which may obtain relief, and the Foundation must notify the company within 30 days of the making of the gift if relief is thereby denied. [*TCA 1997, s 87A; FA 2001, s 84*]

Deduction for Consideration on Acquisition of Shares. The Finance Act 2005 provided that a deduction would not be given in relation to computing taxable trading income of a company for consideration that consists of shares in the company or a connected company or a right to receive such shares. Provided certain conditions are met, a deduction is given for consideration incurred by the company on the arm's length acquisition of shares or payment to a connected company for the issue or transfer of shares in relation to share based consideration given by a company to employees. This is being extended to give a deduction for certain payments in respect of the right to receive shares. [*FA 2007, s 37*]

DISTRIBUTIONS

12.10 See **13.12** 'Deduction of tax at source' for dividend withholding tax applicable in respect of distributions.

In general, CT is not chargeable on dividends or other distributions by a company resident in RI, nor are they taken into account in computing CT. [*TCA 1997, s 129*] Distributions by RI-resident companies carry an exemption for 'qualifying non-resident persons' (including certain non-resident parent companies) from income tax and the income is not available to cover charges. The definition of a '*qualifying non-resident person*' is the same as that used for the purposes of the dividend withholding tax (see **13.12** 'Deduction of tax at source'), except that the requirement for a declaration under *Sch 2A* does not apply. Also, from 6 April 2000, the liability of individuals neither resident nor ordinarily resident in RI, but who are not qualifying non-resident persons, in respect of distributions by RI-resident companies is limited to the standard rate of tax, thus in effect being met by the dividend withholding tax.

[*TCA 1997, ss 136, 153; CTA 1976, s 88; FA 1990, s 36, Sch 1; FA 1995, s 45, Sch 2; FA 1997, s 37, Sch 2; FA 1998, s 51, Sch 5 para 1; FA 1999, s 28; FA 2000, s 31, Sch 2*]

Distribution does not include distributions made in respect of share capital in winding up, but does include:

(*a*)   any dividend, including a capital dividend;

(*b*)   any distribution out of assets in respect of shares in the company except a repayment of capital (see below) or an amount equal to any 'new consideration' (see below);

(*c*)   any amount met out of assets, otherwise than for new consideration, in respect of the redemption of any security issued by the company;

(*d*)   any interest or other distribution out of assets in respect of securities either:

    (i)   issued other than for new consideration in respect of shares in or securities of the company,

    (ii)   convertible into shares in, or carrying the right to receive shares in or securities of, the company, being neither quoted securities nor issued on comparable terms,

    (iii)   the interest on which:

        (I)   varies with the issuing company's results (which, from 15 February 2001, does not include a reduction in the event of the company's results improving or an increase in the event of their deteriorating), or

        (II)   (and to the extent that it) is at more than a reasonable commercial rate,

    (iv)   from 6 February 2003, held by a non EC-resident company (previously non RI-resident) of which the issuing company is a 75 per cent subsidiary, or where both are 75 per cent subsidiaries of another company which, if RI-resident, owns less than 90 per cent of the issuing company's share capital (but see below for election out of this treatment), or

(v)   'connected with' shares of the issuing company (ie it is necessary or advantageous for the holder of the securities to hold a proportionate number of those shares);

(*e*)   a transfer of assets or liabilities by a company to its members, or to a company by its members (except certain dealings with subsidiaries), to the extent that it exceeds the value of any new consideration;

(*f*)   an issue of bonus shares following a repayment of share capital (as defined) on or after 27 November 1975, except where the share capital repaid consisted of certain fully paid-up preference shares;

(*g*)   certain distributions made to members of an employee share ownership trust having an associated approved profit-sharing scheme.

[*TCA 1997, ss 130, 131; FA 1999, s 79; FA 2001, s 85; FA 2002, s 39; FA 2003, s 61; FA 2005, s 18*]

As regards interest etc within (*d*)(iv) above, see Revenue Tax Briefing Issue 45 p 9 for deduction of tax from such payments.

Repayment of share capital for the purposes of (*b*) and (*f*) above has a restricted meaning where share capital has been issued (after 26 November 1975) as paid up otherwise than for new consideration, and any amount so paid up is not a distribution. Subsequent distributions in respect of that share capital are only repayments of share capital to the extent that their total value exceeds that amount. [*TCA 1997, s 132*]

Non-close companies are excluded from (*f*) above and from *s 132* (see preceding paragraph) where:

(I)   the issue and repayment are separated by ten years or more; and

(II)   the issue (under (*f*)) or repayment (under *s 132*) relate to non-redeemable share capital.

[*TCA 1997, ss 131(4), 132(5)*]

New consideration means consideration not provided directly or indirectly out of the assets of the company, and must in addition consist of money or value received or certain other types of consideration as specified. [*TCA 1997, s 135*]

'*Section 84A loans*'. Interest, etc on a security within (*d*)(ii), (iii)(I) or (v) above (a '*relevant security*') paid by the borrower to another company within the charge to corporation tax is not treated as a distribution unless either:

(A)   the lender's ordinary trading activities include lending on relevant securities, and the borrower uses the loan in a 'specified trade' carried on in RI, of which the interest would, were it not a distribution, be treated as a trading expense; or

(B)   it exceeds a reasonable commercial return for the use of the principal, in which case only the excess is to be treated as a distribution.

A '*specified trade*' is a trade consisting as to at least 75 per cent (by reference to turnover) of the manufacture of goods or of activities which would, on a claim, be treated as such for the manufacturing companies relief (but not by virtue of a certificate under *s 445*) (see **12.18** below) or, in the case of a 75 per cent subsidiary of an agricultural or fishery society, either or both of the manufacture of goods and the wholesale sale of agricultural products or fish respectively. The use referred to in (A) above must be in the activities which qualify the trade as a specified trade.

Where a trade otherwise ceased to be a specified trade by virtue of the exclusions from manufacturing companies' relief in *FA 1990, s 41(1)* or *FA 1994, s 48(1)* (see **12.18** below), it is treated as continuing to be a specified trade in relation to interest on any principal advanced before 20 April 1990 or 11 April 1994 respectively.

(A) above does not apply to allow interest to be treated as a distribution to the extent that loans by the lender to the borrower on relevant securities held directly or indirectly by the lender exceed ten per cent of such loans (if any) on 12 April 1989.

After 30 January 1990, there is a ceiling on new loans interest on which may be treated as a distribution by virtue of (A) above. Broadly, the limit is 75 per cent (reduced to 40 per cent after 30 December 1991) of such loans outstanding on 12 April 1989 (which may be reduced if the loans outstanding fall below this limit), although there is a limited provision for further loans in certain specified exceptional cases. Otherwise, the only new loans which will qualify for this treatment, subject to a global limit, are those relating to certain new manufacturing projects.

In all cases, distribution treatment under these provisions is restricted to a seven-year period after the date on which the principal was advanced (or, in the case of principal advanced before 11 April 1994, to the period ending 11 April 2001).

Where the loan is denominated in a foreign currency, interest for a period beginning after 29 January 1991 which is computed on the basis of a rate in excess of 80 per cent of three month DIBOR or EIOR is not treated as a distribution in the hands of the recipient company. This does not apply where the principal was advanced:

(i)   before 30 January 1991 under an agreement made before that date, and the rate exceeded the 80 per cent limit on that date (but subject to further restriction after 19 December 1991 if the currency in which the loan was denominated on 30 January 1991 is changed);

(ii)   after 29 January 1991 for the purposes of certain trades specified in lists prepared by the Industrial Development Authority (broadly certain new manufacturing projects) (but subject to further restriction after 19 December 1991 where the rate exceeds that approved by the Minister for Finance in relation to such loans, or where the currency in which the loan was denominated when it was advanced is changed);

(iii)   after 17 April 1991, and the 80 per cent limit was exceeded only because the loan was denominated in sterling; or

(iv)   to a non-manufacturing company carrying on trading operations within *s 445* (see **12.18** below) in the Customs-free airport.

For these purposes the extension (after 5 May 1993) of a repayment period is treated as a repayment and further advance of the principal in question on the date on which it would otherwise have fallen to be repaid.

[*TCA 1997, s 133; CTA 1976, s 84A* as inserted by *FA 1989, s 21; FA 1990, s 41(4); FA 1994, ss 48(3), 50; FA 1998, Sch 2 para 4*]

The operation of (*d*)(iv) above may, on election, be excluded where a company providing certain financial services within a certificate issued by the Minister for Finance (see **12.18**(viii) below) (or which could be so certified if carried on in the Custom House Docks Area rather than Shannon airport) would, but for that provision, be able to deduct the interest as a trading expense in computing income from operations covered by that certificate, and where the interest is payable to a company resident in a territory with which arrangements under *s 826* (see **15.2** 'Double tax relief – income and capital gains') have been made. The election must be submitted with the company's return of profits for the accounting period for which the interest is payable. Since 6 April 2001, this relief is extended to interest paid by any RI-resident company in the ordinary course of a trade carried on by it, and the range of qualifying recipient companies is extended to include all companies resident in other EU Member States. Also from that date (enacting previous Revenue practices), payments by those companies to which the relief previously applied, or by banks carrying on *bona fide* banking business in RI, are, on election (as above), within the relief regardless of the non-RI territory in which the recipient company is resident, provided in both cases that the interest represents no more than a reasonable commercial return. [*TCA 1997, ss 452, 452A, 845A; FA 1998, Sch 3 para 4; FA 2001, ss 87, 88*]

See **12.7** above for extended meaning of distribution for close companies and see also **12.26** as regards ACT on certain distributions within (*d*) above.

Foreign currency transactions. Where the lender in relation to a security within (*d*)(ii), (iii)(I) or (v) above denominated in a foreign currency is a company whose ordinary trading activities include money-lending, and the interest (treated as a distribution) is computed on the basis of a rate which at any time in an accounting period exceeds 80 per cent of three-month DIBOR or EIOR (or comparable rate), then any profit or loss arising to the borrower from any foreign exchange transaction in connection with the loan is treated as a trading profit or loss of the accounting period. See, however, **12.18**(xvi) below as regards application of manufacturing companies relief to such exchange gains. [*TCA 1997, s 80; FA 1998, Sch 2 para 2*]

Foreign source finance. Similar earlier provisions, which applied to interest etc paid up to 31 December 1991, continue to have effect where the principal secured by the relevant security has been advanced out of money subscribed for foreign-owned share capital of the lender. Under the earlier provisions, interest etc on a relevant security is not treated as a distribution unless either:

(i)   the lender's ordinary trading activities include moneylending, and the interest, if not treated as a distribution, would be treated as a trading expense of a trade (other than a qualifying shipping trade within *s 407* (see **12.18** below)) carried on in RI in the accounting period of payment consisting of at least 75 per cent (by reference to turnover) of:

(*a*)   the manufacture of goods (including trades defined as such under **12.18** below), or

(*b*)   a service undertaking in respect of which an employment grant was made by the Industrial Development Authority under the *Industrial Development (No 2) Act 1981, s 2* (but see below),

or, in the case of a 75 per cent subsidiary of an agricultural or fishery society, either or both of the manufacture of goods and wholesale sales of agricultural products or fish respectively; or

(ii)   it exceeds a reasonable commercial return for the use of the principal, in which case only the excess is to be treated as a distribution.

The exclusion at (i)(*b*) above does not apply unless the obligation to pay the interest, etc arose under a binding written contract either entered into before 13 May 1986, or entered into before 1 September 1986 pursuant to negotiations in the course of which preliminary commitments or agreements had been entered into before 14 May 1986. [*TCA 1997, s 134; CTA 1976, s 84A as originally inserted by FA 1984, s 41*]

Company purchasing own shares – trading or holding companies. *Part IX of the Companies Act 1990* permits a company to purchase its own shares, subject to various requirements. Following introduction of the provisions now contained in *ss 173–186*, when certain conditions are satisfied, the purchase, repayment or redemption by a company of its own shares is not to be treated as a distribution, and the vendor will be liable to capital gains tax rather than income tax on the payment received. This may also apply to certain purchases by subsidiary companies of shares of the parent company. Except as further specified below in relation to quoted companies, the conditions to be satisfied are broadly as follows:

(i) The company must be either a trading company or a holding company, the main business of which is to hold shares in one or more 51 per cent subsidiaries in a 'trading group'. A *'trading group'* is a holding company plus one or more subsidiary companies whose business, taken together, consists wholly or mainly of the carrying on of a trade or trades. 'Trade' does not include dealing in shares, securities, land, futures or options;

(ii) Neither the company's shares nor those of a company of which it is a 51 per cent subsidiary may be quoted on a stock exchange list or dealt in on an unlisted securities market;

(iii) Either (*a*) or (*b*) as follows is satisfied:

    (*a*)   (I)   the purchase etc must be made wholly or mainly for the benefit of the trade of the company or any of its 51 per cent subsidiaries,

            (II)   the purchase etc must not form part of a scheme a main purpose of which is to enable the shareholder to participate in the profits of the company or any of its 51 per cent subsidiaries without receiving a dividend, and

            (III)   the conditions relating to the shareholder detailed at (iv)–(xi) below must be satisfied where applicable. *Finance Act 2010, s 34* has added further conditions which are at (xii) and (xiii) below.

    (*b*)   The person to whom the payment is made must apply the whole, or substantially the whole, of the payment (less any sum applied in discharging a liability to capital gains tax, if any, in respect of the purchase etc) to discharging:

            (I)   within four months of the valuation date (as defined in *CATA 1976, s 21*: see **7.7** 'Capital acquisitions tax') of a taxable inheritance of the company's shares, an inheritance tax liability in respect of that inheritance, or

            (II)   within one week of the purchase etc, a debt incurred by him for the purpose of discharging the inheritance tax liability in (I) above,

    and he could not have otherwise discharged that liability without undue hardship;

(iv) The vendor of the shares must be resident and (except in the case of a corporate vendor) ordinarily resident (see **27.1** 'Residents and non-residents') in RI for the chargeable period in which the purchase etc is made. Where the shares are held through a nominee, the nominee must also be so resident and ordinarily resident. The residence etc of a personal representative is for these purposes the same as the residence etc of the deceased immediately before his death. The residence etc of trustees is determined in accordance with *s 574*;

(v)   Except as below, the vendor must have owned the shares for at least the five years ending on the day of the purchase etc. If during that period the shares were transferred to the vendor by a person who was then his spouse living with him, any period during which the spouse owned the shares shall be treated as an ownership period of the vendor, provided that the transferor either is still the vendor's spouse living with him or is deceased at the time of purchase etc

If the vendor acquired the shares under a will or intestacy, or as a personal representative, ownership by the deceased person (and, in the former case, by his personal representative) count as ownership by the vendor, and the qualifying period is reduced to three years.

For purchases etc after 14 February 2001, if the shares were appropriated to the vendor under an approved profit-sharing scheme (see **34.6** 'Sch E'), and were not excess or unauthorised shares under the scheme, the qualifying period is reduced to three years.

Where identification of different holdings of shares of the same class is necessary, earlier acquisitions are taken into account before later ones, and previous disposals identified with later acquisitions before earlier ones, for this purpose. The time of acquisition of shares acquired through a reorganisation of share capital or securities etc is that determined under *ss 584–587* or *600*, except where the vendor is treated under *s 584(4)* as giving consideration, other than the old holding, for the acquisition of the shares;

(vi)   The vendor's shareholding must be 'substantially reduced' by the purchase etc. A shareholding is '*substantially reduced*' if and only if the proportion of the company's issued share capital held by him immediately after the purchase does not exceed 75 per cent of that immediately before the purchase. It is not regarded as so reduced if the share of the profits available for distribution to which the vendor would be entitled (beneficially, except in the case of trustees or personal representatives) immediately after the purchase etc is greater than 75 per cent of his entitlement immediately before the purchase etc;

(vii)   If, immediately after the purchase etc, any shares in the company are owned by an 'associate' of the vendor, the combined interests of the vendor and his associate(s) must satisfy the 'substantial reduction' condition at (vi) above.

'*Associate*' includes spouse and minor children, and a broad range of relationships whereby an individual or company may be able to influence the actions of another;

(viii) If the company making the purchase etc is, immediately before the purchase etc, a member of a 'group of companies', and, immediately after the purchase etc, either:

(*a*)   the vendor owns shares in other group member(s), or

(b)   he still owns shares in the company making the purchase etc *and* had immediately before the purchase etc, owned shares in other group member(s),

then the 'substantial reduction' condition at (vi) above must be satisfied in relation to his interest in the group as a whole, taken as the average of his proportionate holdings of the issued share capital of the company purchasing the shares and of all other group members in which he holds shares immediately before or after the purchase etc.

A '*group of companies*' for this purpose is a company which has one or more 51 per cent subsidiaries, but is not itself a 51 per cent subsidiary of any other company, together with those subsidiaries.

Where the whole or a significant part of the business carried on by an unquoted company (the 'successor company') was previously carried on by the company purchasing the shares (or a member of the same group), then, unless the successor company first carried on the business more than three years before the purchase etc, the successor company and any company of which it is a 51 per cent subsidiary are treated as being members of the same group as the company purchasing etc the shares;

(ix)   Where an associate (see (vii) above) of the vendor owns shares in any company in the same group (see (viii) above) as the company purchasing the shares immediately before the purchase etc, the combined interests of vendor and associate(s) must satisfy the 'substantial reduction' condition at (vi) above;

(x)   The vendor must not, immediately after the purchase etc, be 'connected with' the company purchasing the shares or any other company in the same group (see (viii) above).

The vendor is so '*connected with*' a company if, together with his associates (see (vii) above), he directly or indirectly possesses or is (or will be) entitled to acquire:

(a)   more than 30 per cent of its issued ordinary share capital, or its loan capital (ie any debt incurred by the company for money borrowed or capital assets acquired) and issued share capital, or its voting power, or

(b)   more than 30 per cent of its assets available for distribution to the company's equity holders (to be determined in accordance with *ss 413, 415*, modified as appropriate),

or if he has control of it;

(xi)   The purchase etc must not be part of a scheme or arrangement which is designed or likely to result in the vendor or any associate of his acquiring interests in the company such that, if he had those interests immediately after the purchase etc, any of the conditions in (vi) to (x) above could not have been satisfied. Any transaction occurring within one year of the purchase etc is deemed to be part of a scheme of which the purchase etc is also a part;

(xii)   The share buy-back must not be part of a scheme or arrangement the main purpose or one of the main purposes of which is to enable the owner of the shares to participate in the profits of the company or of any of its 51 per cent subsidiaries without receiving a dividend.

(xiii) Quoted companies are required to notify the Revenue Commissioners of any share buy-backs undertaken in an accounting period indicating whether the buy-back is to be treated as not being a distribution and to include such notification in the company's annual corporation tax return or such other form as may be prescribed by the Revenue Commissioners.

[*FA 2010, s 34*]

As regards condition (iii)(*a*)(I) above, the Revenue Commissioners would regard a buy-back as benefiting a trade where, for example, it is to resolve a disagreement between shareholders over management of the company, which could reasonably be expected to adversely affect the running of the trade, by removing the dissenting shareholder. It would not be satisfied where the sole or main purpose was to benefit the shareholder or to benefit an investment activity of the company. In general, it is unlikely that the condition will be satisfied unless the entire shareholding in question is acquired, apart possibly from a small holding retained by a retiring director for sentimental reasons or to avoid a negative impact on the business by remaining involved for a specified period. The Revenue Commissioners will offer an opinion on whether a particular transaction is for the benefit of the trade if supplied with all the relevant details. (Revenue Tax Briefing Issue 25 pp 9, 10).

Where any of the conditions in (vi) to (x) above are not satisfied in relation to the vendor, they will nevertheless be treated as satisfied where the vendor proposed or agreed to the purchase etc in order that the conditions in (vii) or (ix) above regarding the substantial reduction of the combined interests of a vendor and his associate(s) could be satisfied in respect of a purchase etc of shares owned by such an associate, to the extent that that result is produced by virtue of the purchase etc.

[*TCA 1997, ss 173, 176–181, 185, 186; FA 2001, s 35*]

Non-distribution treatment applies to *all* payments by *quoted companies* (ie companies any of whose shares are listed on a stock exchange or dealt in on an unlisted securities market) (and to fellow group members), on the redemption, repayment or purchase of its own shares. [*TCA 1997, ss 173(1), 175*]

When a company makes a payment which it treats as being not a distribution by virtue of these provisions, it must make a return in prescribed form to the inspector within nine months from the end of the accounting period in which it makes the payment. Alternatively, the inspector may by notice in writing require the company to make a return at an earlier time within the period (which is not to be less than 30 days) specified in the notice. [*TCA 1997, s 182*]

Any costs incurred by the company in buying back its own shares are not allowed as a deduction for tax purposes. [*FA 2008, s 48*]

Where a company makes a payment which it treats as being within the above provisions, any person connected with the company who knows of a scheme or arrangement within (xi) above which affects the payment shall within 60 days after he first knows of the payment and the scheme, give a notice to the inspector containing details of that scheme.

If the inspector has reason to believe that a payment etc treated by the company as being within the above provisions may form part of a scheme within (xi) above, he may require the company or any person connected with it (see (x) above) to furnish him, within not less than 60 days, with a written declaration as to whether, according to information reasonably obtainable, any such scheme or arrangement exists or has existed, and with such other information reasonably required by him as the company or person can reasonably obtain.

Any person receiving a payment etc treated as falling within the above provisions, or on whose behalf such a payment etc is received, may be required to notify the inspector as to whether he received the payment on his own or another's behalf and, in the latter case, to supply the other person's name and address.

The penalty provisions of *ss 1052–1054* apply to returns required as above.

[*TCA 1997, s 183*]

Dealers in securities. Where a company purchases its own shares (or those of a company of which it is a subsidiary) from a dealer (ie a person on whom the price received would normally be included in Sch D, Case I or II profits), then:

(*a*)   the purchase price is brought into account on the dealer under Sch D, Case I or II;

(*b*)   tax is not chargeable under Sch F, and (prior to the general abolition of tax credits from 6 April 1999) no tax credit is available; and

(*c*)   the normal corporation tax exemption for RI company distributions does not apply.

This does not, however, apply in relation to the redemption of fixed-rate preference shares (as defined), or certain other preference shares issued before 18 April 1991, which were issued to and continuously held by the person from whom they are redeemed. [*TCA 1997, s 174; FA 2000, Sch 2*]

Treasury shares (within *Companies Act 1990, s 209*) are for tax purposes treated as cancelled when purchased by the issuing company. Cancellation gives rise to neither chargeable gain nor allowable loss for CGT purposes. [*TCA 1997, s 184*]

Reciprocal arrangements between companies to make distributions to each other's members to avoid the above provisions will be ineffective. [*TCA 1997, s 135(3)*]

Shares with assured income or capital return. Special restrictions apply to distributions in respect of shares where an agreement, arrangement or understanding exists to eliminate the risk that the owner of the shares, or a connected person (within *s 10*), might at a particular time be unable to realise a particular amount, or might not receive a particular level of distributions, in respect of the shares. Where any person receives a distribution in respect of such shares, and the distribution would otherwise come within the special provisions relating to Shannon or export sales relief (see below), stallion or greyhound stud fees and commercial woodlands (see **30.1** 'Sch D, cases I and II') or patent royalties (see below), then those provisions do not apply to the distribution and the distribution is taxable under Sch D, Case IV (**32**). See also **21.5** 'Investment in corporate trades' for restriction of relief in respect of such shares.

These restrictions do not apply to such distributions received by non-residents, or by companies owned by non-residents which would otherwise only have been chargeable to corporation tax in respect of such distributions. This does not, however, affect the liability of any other RI resident. [*TCA 1997, s 155; FA 2000, Sch 2*]

Bonus issue stripping. No distribution falling within (*c*), (*d*) or (*f*) in the extended definition of 'distribution' above or disqualified from being a repayment of share capital by *s 132* will rank as franked investment income (see below) except insofar as it represents a normal return on the kind of investment held by the recipient. [*TCA 1997, s 137; FA 2000, Sch 2(b)*]

Patent royalties. Distributions (or parts) made out of exempt patent income (see **16.15** 'Exempt income and special savings schemes') are, except as further described below, also exempt in the hands of recipients (and successor distributions may similarly be exempt). In order to be exempt, the royalty payment must be tax deductible and made for *bona fide* commercial reasons and not as part of any tax avoidance arrangement. The recipient must be liable to tax in respect of the royalty in its country of residence or the country in which the permanent establishment is situated. [*FA 2010, s 55*] A distribution received by any person which is made other than in respect of 'eligible shares' is exempt only to the extent that the income out of which it is made is referable to a patent devised etc by the person receiving the distribution. '*Eligible shares*' are fully paid ordinary share capital carrying no present or future preferential rights to dividends or assets, or to be redeemed, and not subject to any different treatment from other shares of the same class.

Distributions out of income arising after 27 March 1996. A further restriction is placed on such distributions which would otherwise be exempt solely because the activities for the purposes of which the royalties etc were paid were treated as the manufacture of goods for manufacturing companies relief purposes (see **16.15**(*b*) 'Exempt income and special savings schemes'). Such distributions are exempt only to the extent that they do not exceed an amount determined by reference to certain research and development expenditure in RI (including all such expenditure for an accounting period in which at least 75 per cent was incurred in RI), on an extended group basis where appropriate, in each of the current and the two preceding accounting periods. Since 2 February 2006 the patent must also be an invention patented for bona fide commercial reasons and not primarily for tax avoidance reasons. From the same date a similar limitation applies to distributions made by a company in receipt of patent royalties from an unconnected person with whom it also has a franchising, licensing or other similar agreement. No restriction applies, however, where the Revenue Commissioners determine that a patent involves radical innovation and was not registered primarily to obtain tax exemption.

The restriction on the application of the general relief for patent income of individuals to the deviser (or joint deviser) of the patent (see **16.15** 'Exempt income and special savings schemes') applies equally to distributions received by individuals.

[*TCA 1997, s 141; CTA 1976, s 170; FA 1996, s 32(2)(3); FA 2000, Sch 2; FA 2006, s 55*]

See, however, above as regards certain shares carrying an assured return.

For an article setting out these provisions, see Revenue Tax Briefing Issue 38 pp 18–20.

DOUBLE TAXATION RELIEF

12.11 The present rules and agreements under IT are adopted for CT, and for that purpose are extended to cover capital gains subject to CT. [*TCA 1997, ss 826, 827, Sch 24; FA 1998, s 60*] See also **15.2** to **15.15** 'Double tax relief – income and capital gains'.

There are a number of provisions in the Taxes Acts that grant preferential treatment for payments to and from treaty countries. These typically deal with granting exemption from Irish tax on payments by Irish companies to non-resident recipients of dividends and interest and favourable tax treatments of such payments when received by Irish companies from foreign sources. There is also capital gains tax exemption for gains from disposals of foreign company shares. The requirement is that there be a tax treaty in force with the relevant foreign country. There can be a delay in bringing the treaties into force because of ratification procedures in either country. Given the possibility of delay, the treaty requirement is being relaxed to mere signing of the treaty, ie once a treaty has been signed with the country, companies dealing with that country can avail of these domestic provisions.

The amount of corporation tax against which foreign tax on income or gains may be credited is limited to corporation tax on the income or gains computed on a turnover basis from 1 January 2006. Previously credit was computed, broadly, by reference to the amount of the income or gains as measured for the purposes of RI tax, with all necessary apportionments being made, and taking account of special rates of corporation tax (eg manufacturing companies relief, see **12.18** below) where relevant. No corporation tax is attributable to certain income or gains taken out of charge by the allocation of deductions. [*TCA 1997, Sch 24 para 4; FA 2000, s 71; FA 2002, s 57(a); FA 2006, s 63*] Since 1 January 2006 provision is made for the pooling of foreign tax credits where the income concerned is interest income from an associate company in a tax treaty country. Also from 1 January 2006 a mechanism is introduced to calculate the underlying tax credit attaching to a dividend received from a foreign company that is a member of a group taxed on a consolidated basis. The formula introduced which calculates the amount of doubly taxed trading income that arises from a payment from which foreign tax is paid deducted, does not apply to foreign branch profits. A further amendment to the legislation provides that credit relief will also be available when the profits of the first company become profits of the second company other than by way of dividend, such as, for example, where there is a merger of companies. The relief will be limited, where appropriate, to the amount that would have been due had the profits been transferred instead of by way of dividend, and will not apply where the profits transfer as a result of a tax avoidance scheme. [*FA 2008, s 49*] Previously, the credit was agreed on a case by case basis with Revenue. [*FA 2006, s 63*]

Distribution by non-resident company to RI-resident parent – Implementation of Council Directive No 90/435/EEC of 23 July 1990 (as amended by Council Directive No 2003/123/EC of 22 December 2003. Where an RI-resident company receives from a non-resident 'subsidiary' a distribution (other than in a winding-up) chargeable to RI corporation tax, credit is allowed against that corporation tax (so far as not otherwise allowed) for withholding taxes charged on the distribution by other EEC Member States, and for so much of other Member States' taxes, not chargeable in respect of the distribution but borne by the subsidiary and attributable to profits represented by the distribution, as exceeds any tax credit in respect of the distribution repayable to the parent. Since 1 January 2004, credit against RI tax will also be allowed in respect of tax paid under the laws of an EU Member State by third and lower tier subsidiaries in respect of distributions received by the RI resident company, subject to a five per cent control of voting power test being met at each tier. The normal foreign dividend payment arrangements under *ss 60–64* do not apply to such distributions. The provisions of *Sch 24* apply as if the relief were under a double taxation agreement.

The above relief is confined to situations where credit for withholding and foreign taxes would not otherwise be allowed. As such credit may be obtained under a tax treaty or under the unilateral relief provisions allowing credit for third party taxes (see **15.15** 'Double tax relief – income and capital gains'), the relief is likely to be confined to situations where dividends are received from a non-treaty partner.

In the context of distributions by a non-resident subsidiary to an RI resident company, 'subsidiary' means a non-resident company at least five per cent (25 per cent prior to 1 January 2004) of whose share capital is owned by an RI resident company (a parent company) or a parent resident in a double taxation agreement jurisdiction (25 per cent otherwise), but a double taxation agreement may apply the test by reference to voting rights, and may impose a condition that the relationship exists for an uninterrupted two-year period.

[*TCA 1997, s 831*; *FA 1999, s 29*; *FA 2000, s 33*; *FA 1999, s 81*; *FA 2004, s 34*; *FA 2006, s 127, Sch 2*]

Dividend Withholding Tax. The requirement to withhold basic rate tax on distributions (see **13.12** 'Deduction of tax at source'), introduced for RI-resident company distributions made on or after 6 April 1999, does not apply to a distribution made to a non-RI resident parent by an RI-resident 'subsidiary'. Since 6 April 2000, this exemption is extended to distributions by unlimited companies within *Companies Act 1963, s 5(2)(c)* as unlimited companies were not provided for in the exemption under the 1990 directive. Since 1 January 2004, reference to unlimited companies is removed from *s 831* as they are provided for in the directive of 2003. The exemption does not apply if the majority of the voting rights in the parent company are controlled by persons other than persons resident for tax purposes in a 'relevant territory' (within *s 172A*, see **13.12** 'Deduction of tax at source') *unless* it is shown that the parent company exists for *bona fide* commercial reasons and does not form part of any arrangement or scheme a main purpose of which is avoidance of income tax (including dividend withholding tax), corporation tax or capital gains tax. Since 1 July 2005, the exemption is extended to parent companies tax resident in Switzerland. For this purpose, 'parent' means a company controlling 25 per cent of the voting power of a company resident in RI. [*FA 2005, s 47*]

For company residence generally, see **11.3** 'Companies'.

EXEMPTIONS AND RELIEFS

12.12 Income tax exemptions and reliefs apply to corporation tax as they apply to income tax. [*TCA 1997, s 76(6)*] Consequently, such provisions noted elsewhere in this book also apply to corporation tax.

National Co-operative Farm Relief Services Ltd. Grants to, and transfers of monies to members by, National Co-operative Farm Relief Services Ltd under the agreement with the Minister for Agriculture, Food and Forestry dated 4 July 1991 for support of farm relief services, or under the agreement dated 16 May 1995 for support of agricultural services development, are disregarded for corporation tax purposes. [*TCA 1997, s 221*]

This relief does not apply to any grant, payment, transfer or transmission of moneys referred to in sub-s (2) which is made on or after 1 January 2011. [*FA 2011, s 39*]

Foreign branch profits. Until 31 December 2010, profits or gains or losses from the carrying on of 'qualified foreign trading activities' are disregarded for corporation tax purposes, and gains on disposal of assets (other than land and minerals in RI and related assets) used wholly and exclusively for the trade consisting of those activities are not chargeable gains. Charges, management expenses, etc incurred for the purposes of that trade may not be relieved against any other profits. *Finance Act 2010, s 47* permits unused credits in respect of foreign tax on branch profits to be carried forward and credited against corporation tax in succeeding accounting periods. Excess losses of a foreign branch can now be carried forward. These losses may be set against profits of the branch arising after 1 January 2011 which is the date the exemption under *s 847* ceases to have effect. The foreign branch profits that become subject to Irish corporation tax will match the profits subject to tax in the foreign jurisdiction. [*FA 2010, s 48*]

'*Qualified foreign trading activities*' are trading activities carried on by a 'qualified company' through a branch or agency outside RI in a territory specified in the certificate given by the Minister for Finance certifying that the company is a 'qualified company', and a '*qualified company*' is an RI-resident company to which the Minister gave such a certificate before 15 February 2001 which has not been revoked. The conditions for the issue of such a certificate are broadly that the Minister must be satisfied that an investment plan submitted by the company will, before a date specified in the plan and agreed by the Minister, result in the company or an associated company (as defined for this purpose) making a substantial permanent capital investment in RI to create substantial new employment in trading operations in RI, the maintenance of which will depend on the carrying on of qualified foreign trading activities. There are provisions for the drawing up of guidelines relating to these requirements, and for the granting and revocation of certification.

Where the qualified foreign trading activities are carried on as part of a trade, those activities are treated as constituting a separate trade. There are provisions for the necessary attributions and apportionments on an arm's length basis for this purpose. [*TCA 1997, s 847; FA 2001, s 89; FA 2004, s 89, Sch 3(z); FA 2010, ss 47 and 48*]

Dividends from foreign subsidiaries. Certain dividends received by an RI resident company from a 51 per cent subsidiary resident in a territory with which arrangements under *s 826* (see **15.2** 'Double tax relief – income and capital gains') are in force are exempted from corporation tax. The dividends must be applied within the period from one year before to two years after receipt in RI, although this period may be extended at the Revenue Commissioners' discretion. They must be applied for the purposes of a plan certified by the Minister for Finance as being directed towards the creation or maintenance of employment in trading operations carried on or to be carried on in RI, and must be specified in a certificate given before 15 February 2001 as qualifying for relief. Details of plans and of the dividends concerned must be submitted to the Minister, and relief may be withdrawn or denied where dividends are not applied within the time limits referred to above. Plans may be submitted up to one year after implementation if there is reasonable cause for their being submitted after implementation. Claims for relief where a certificate has been given are to be submitted with the company's return of profits for the period in which the dividends are received in RI. [*TCA 1997, s 222; FA 1998, Sch 3 para 6; FA 2001, s 86*]

A number of changes have been made to the taxation of foreign dividends received by companies within the charge to Irish tax from companies that are resident for tax purposes in EU Member States or in countries with which Ireland has a tax treaty. Such dividends that are paid out of trading profits will in future be chargeable to tax here at the 12.5 per cent rate of corporation tax instead of at the 25 per cent rate. Where dividends do not qualify to be charged at the 12.5 per cent rate, they will continue to be charged at the 25 per cent rate. Where a dividend is paid partly out of trading profits and partly out of other profits, the part of the dividend that is paid out of trading profits of the dividend paying company will be taxable at the 12.5 per cent rate.

The 12.5 per cent rate has been extended in the case of foreign dividends to include dividends paid out of underlying trading profits of a company resident in a non-treaty country in cases where the company is owned directly or indirectly by a publicly-quoted company. [*FA 2010, s 50*]

This section also simplifies the rules for identifying the underlying profits out of which dividends are paid for the purposes of determining the rate of tax to be applied to those dividends. In addition to this, the section exempts from corporation tax foreign dividends received by portfolio investor companies where the dividends form part of the trading income of the company.

Trading profits of such foreign companies will be allowed to pass up through tiers of companies by way of dividend payments so that, when ultimately paid to a company within the charge to corporation tax in the State, that company will be taxed on the dividends received by it at the 12.5 per cent rate.

The full amount of a foreign dividend received by a company will be chargeable at the 12.5 per cent rate where certain conditions are met, notwithstanding that a part of the dividend may not be paid out of trading profits. The conditions are:

(*a*)   That 75 per cent or more of the dividend-paying company's profits must be trading profits, either trading profits of that company or dividends received by it out of trading profits of lower tier companies that are resident in EU Member States or in countries with which Ireland has a double tax treaty;

(*b*)   That an asset condition must be satisfied on a consolidated basis by the company that receives the dividend and all of its subsidiaries. The aggregate value of the trading assets of those companies must not be less than 75 per cent of the aggregate value of all of their assets.

Companies that are portfolio investors and that receive a dividend from a company resident in an EU Member State or a country with which Ireland has a double tax treaty will be taxed on the dividends at the 12.5 per cent rate. A portfolio investor in a company is an investor with a holding of not more than five per cent in the company. [*FA 2008, s 43*]

For reliefs generally, see paras **12.2**, **12.11**, **12.15**, **12.16**, **12.22** and **Chapters 16** and **17** below.

FRANKED INVESTMENT INCOME

12.13 *Franked investment income* means the distributions received by a company resident in RI from another such company, and consists of the distributions plus (for distributions made before 6 April 1999) the total tax credit thereon. Similarly, *franked* *payment* means the amount of a distribution made by a company resident in RI plus any tax credit thereon. [*TCA 1997, s 156; FA 1998, Sch 5 para 8*] Tax credits are abolished after 5 April 1999. [*TCA 1997, s 136(1); FA 1998, Sch 5 para 1; FA 2000, Sch 2*]

Finance Act 2010, s 49 has introduced a new anti-avoidance provision relating to the exemption for franked investment income. A new section [*s 129A*] has been inserted which denies exemption to dividends received by an Irish resident company from its subsidiary where the profits out of which the dividend is paid were earned when the subsidiary was resident outside the State. Such dividends are to be treated in the same manner as a dividend received from a foreign company. This provision applies where the paying company became resident in the State in the ten year period before the payment of the dividend.

See **12.26** below as regards use of such payments before 6 April 1999 to frank distributions otherwise giving rise to liability to ACT.

Where the total profits of a company for an accounting period are insufficient to exhaust all or any of its:

(i)   trading losses;

(ii)   charges on income;

(iii)   capital allowances deductible against total profits (ie exceeding the income of the specified class, see **12.9** above);

for that period, and the company has franked investment income in which tax credits are comprised (see above), the company may claim to have the remaining balance of those deductions set off against all or part of its franked investment income for the period and claim repayment of the tax credit (but see **12.26** below as regards restrictions on repayment of tax credit). Such a claim must be made within two years after the end of the accounting period of the loss etc. [*TCA 1997, s 157; FA 1998, Sch 5 para 9*] An investment company can additionally claim repayment of the tax credit by setting off its excess management expenses (see **12.9** above) against its franked investment income. [*TCA 1997, s 83(5)*]

See **38.60** 'Tax cases' as regards date of receipt of dividend for these purposes.

A company may subsequently claim (within two years after the end of an accounting period) to carry forward a deduction which has already been set off against franked investment income and instead have it set off against profits of the accounting period. In such a case the company will be charged under Sch D, Case IV for an amount of income tax equal to the amount of repaid tax credit. The liability is, for the purposes of charge, assessment, collection and recovery, treated as a corporation tax liability. [*TCA 1997, s 157(5)–(7)*]

Losses carried forward and terminal losses carried back (see **12.17** below) of certain financial concerns may similarly be set off against franked investment income in which tax credits are comprised for an accounting period which would be trading income but for having been taxed under other provisions, insofar as such losses exceed the profits available for set-off in that period. [*TCA 1997, s 158; FA 1998, Sch 5 para 10*]

GENERALLY ACCEPTED ACCOUNTING STANDARDS

[*TCA 1997, ss 76A, 76B, Sch 17A*; *FA 2005, s 48*; *FA 2006, s 61*]

12.14 For accounting periods commencing from 1 January 2005, all EU companies listed on a stock exchange are required to prepare their consolidated financial statements for the group in accordance with a common set of accounting standards called International Financial Reporting Standards ('IFRS') instead of the RI generally accepted accounting practice ('GAAP'). Individual accounts of companies may be prepared in accordance with IFRS. Once a company moves to IFRS, it is required to use IFRS for the future except in exceptional circumstances.

For accounting periods beginning from 1 January 2005, the profits or gains of a trade are computed, for RI tax purposes, in accordance with GAAP, subject to any adjustment required or authorised by law. For this purpose, GAAP includes accounts prepared in accordance with IFRS. Certain capitalised expenditure is allowed as a deduction in arriving at taxable profit, including interest costs, patent royalties and research and development expenditure. Capitalised labour costs associated with an asset will be taken into account in computing capital allowances for that asset. Unrealised gains and losses associated with financial assets or liabilities where movements in fair value are recognised in the profit and loss account are now taken into account for corporation tax purposes. Provision is made to ensure that tax relief is not given twice in respect of the same item as a result of the application of IFRS or that a move to IFRS should result in double taxation. Finally, where the changeover to IFRS results in adjustments to the closing figures in previous accounts, these adjustments are taxed or allowed over five years starting with the year in which the accounts are prepared under IFRS rules. A company can elect to be taxed for all accounting periods based on generally accepted accounting practice as it applied prior to 1 January 2005. The election must be made by the return filing date and is irrevocable. See 'Revenue Guidance Note on Section 48 Finance Act 2005'.

GROUPS

12.15 Definition of subsidiary. Whether a company is a 51 per cent or 75 per cent or 90 per cent subsidiary is determined by reference to beneficial ownership, direct or indirect, of the company's ordinary share capital. Indirect ownership through a chain of companies is traced as follows:

Where A Company holds ordinary shares in B Company which holds ordinary shares in C Company which in turn holds ordinary shares in X Company, the interest of A Company in X Company equals:

$$\frac{\text{Holding of A Co in B Co}}{\substack{\text{Total ordinary share} \\ \text{capital of B Co}}} \times \frac{\text{Holding of B Co in C Co}}{\substack{\text{Total ordinary share} \\ \text{capital of C Co}}} \times \frac{\text{Holding of C Co in X Co}}{\substack{\text{Total ordinary share} \\ \text{capital of X Co}}}$$

For a 75 per cent or 90 per cent subsidiary the shareholding of the parent must be at least 75 per cent or 90 per cent; for a 51 per cent subsidiary the shareholding must exceed 50 per cent. [*TCA 1997, s 9*]

Group relief. Any relief for corporation tax losses etc available to a company (the surrendering company) may be transferred to another company (the claimant company) where:

(*a*)   Both companies are RI-resident (for accounting periods ending after 30 June 1998, EU-resident, ie resident for corporation tax (or similar) purposes in an EU Member State, or, from 1 January 2002, resident in an EEA State with which double tax arrangements are in force) An amendment has been made following the decision of the European Court of Justice on foreign losses. This amendment gives relief to Irish companies in respect of their trading losses incurred by their non-Irish subsidiary companies that are resident in EU Member States and EEA states with which Ireland has a double tax treaty. Anti-avoidance provisions disallow losses where arrangements are entered into primarily to secure an amount that would qualify for the new group relief. [*FA 2007, s 411*]; and

(*b*)   Both are members of the same group of companies (ie one is a 75 per cent subsidiary of the other or both are 75 per cent subsidiaries of a third), or, *where the surrendering company is not a member of such a group* (other than as a 90 per cent subsidiary of a holding company as under (i) below), the surrendering company is:

    (i)   a trading company which is owned by a consortium, or which is a 90 per cent subsidiary of a holding company which is owned by a consortium, or

    (ii)   a holding company which is owned by a consortium;

and the claimant company is a member of that consortium.

Any payment made by the claimant company to the surrendering company for group relief, not exceeding that relief, is disregarded for tax purposes.

[*TCA 1997, s 411; FA 1999, s 78; FA 2002, s 37(b)*]

Holding company means a company whose sole or main business is the holding of shares or securities of trading companies which are its 90 per cent subsidiaries. A company is *owned by a consortium* if 75 per cent of its ordinary share capital (100 per cent before 6 April 2000) is owned *directly* and beneficially by five or fewer companies. [*TCA 1997, s 411(1)(a); FA 2000, s 79*]

Any shareholding in a company not resident in RI (for accounting periods ending after 30 June 1998, not EU-resident and, from 1 January 2002, not resident in an EEA State with which double tax arrangements are in force) is ignored, as is any shareholding a profit on sale of which would fall to be treated as a trading receipt. [*TCA 1997, s 411(1)(c); FA 1999, s 78; FA 2002, s 37(b)*]

To qualify as a 75 per cent or 90 per cent subsidiary under group relief the following conditions must be fulfilled in addition to the general definition above. Broadly, the parent company must be entitled to 75 per cent/90 per cent of the profits of the subsidiary available for distribution to equity holders and to 75 per cent/90 per cent of the assets which would be available for distribution to equity holders if the subsidiary were at that moment wound up. [*TCA 1997, ss 412–419*]

Subject to restrictions in the case of overseas trades, life assurance companies and farming and market gardening losses:

(i)   any corporation tax trading loss of a surrendering company; or

(ii)   any excess of its capital allowances, or charges on income, or (if an investment company) management expenses, over its profits (computed without deduction of any such allowances etc) in an accounting period;

may be deducted from the total profits of the claimant company (ignoring any subsequent reliefs carried back) in its corresponding accounting period. Where the claimant company is a member of a consortium, it is only entitled to such fraction of the relief as reflects the proportion of its holding in the surrendering company. [*TCA 1997, ss 420–422; FA 2001, s 65; FA 2006, s 127, Sch 2*] Where companies join or leave a group or consortium, relief is restricted by reference to the period during which both claimant and surrendering companies were members. [*TCA 1997, s 423*]

Claims must be made within two years of the end of the accounting period of the surrendering company, and be with the written consent of the surrendering company and (if appropriate) of the other members of the consortium. [*TCA 1997, s 429*] Two or more companies may claim in respect of the same relief of a surrendering company but the total relief cannot exceed what would have been available to a single claimant company. [*TCA 1997, ss 411(4), 428*] A claim for an accounting period ending after 31 March 1992 is restricted to one-half of the maximum claim where either the claimant company or the surrendering company has failed to submit its return for the period to which the claim relates by the required date (see **28.11** 'Returns'). [*TCA 1997, s 1085(2)*]

Ringfencing of losses and charges. For accounting periods ending after 5 March 2001, there are special provisions in effect restricting relief for trading losses and charges to relief against income chargeable at the same rate as that applicable to the trade in which the losses, etc were incurred. There is also, however, provision for relief for such losses, etc in excess of such income to be obtained by a reduction of the corporation tax chargeable equivalent to the applicable rate of corporation tax (eg ten per cent where the losses, etc relate to manufacturing income, see **12.18** below) on the amount of the excess. For claims made from 6 February 2003 the surrendering company must have exhausted all possible claims for off-set of losses. For accounting periods ending from 6 February 2003, losses are restricted to one-half of the maximum claim where the return for the period is late. These provisions do not apply to losses, etc incurred in an 'excepted trade' (see **12.2** above). Since 4 February 2004, group relief under the value basis cannot be used to shelter corporation tax arising to a life assurance company in respect of policy holders' profits. [*TCA 1997, ss 420A, 420B; FA 2001, s 90; FA 2002, ss 54, 55; FA 2003, s 59; FA 2004, s 38; FA 2006, s 127, Sch 2*] See also Revenue Tax Briefing Issue 51 pp 14–15.

Anti-avoidance provisions deal with limited or diminishing entitlement of equity holders [*TCA 1997, ss 416, 417*], and with transfer of a surrendering company between groups [*TCA 1997, s 424*], capital allowances in respect of machinery and plant for leasing [*TCA 1997, s 425*], and shares of a company in a partnership. [*TCA 1997, s 426*] An inspector has power to require information in respect of these three latter situations. [*TCA 1997, s 427*]

See also **12.26** below as regards surrender of advance corporation tax.

Intra-Group Borrowings to Finance Assets. The ability of a company to claim interest relief on intra group borrowings for investment in shares in other group companies was closed off in 2006. It was still possible to claim interest relief on intra group borrowings to purchase assets from other group companies.

FA 2011, s 35 seeks to deny a tax deduction where a company borrows from another group company and uses the fund to purchase assets (apart from trading stock or qualifying intangible assets) from another connected company. There is an exclusion for funding of leased assets in certain circumstances. Where such assets are purchased as part of an acquisition of a trade previously carried on by a company not within the charge to corporation tax, relief is given up to the amount of the taxable trading profits or gains of the acquired trade. An exception will be made where the assets acquired generated an income that was not within the charge to tax prior to their acquisition. In such a case, interest relief will be granted up to the amount of income generated by those assets. .Anti avoidance is included to counteract avoidance of the rules by using arrangements such as back to back loans with third parties.

The restriction will not apply to an interest expense payable where the sole business of the lending company is the on-lending of money which that company has borrowed from unconnected persons.

Interaction with manufacturing companies relief. For accounting periods to which the manufacturing companies relief applies (see **12.18** below), group or consortium relief for losses or charges on income attributable to the sale of goods by a company within the scheme of relief is restricted to set-off against similar income of other group or consortium members, as reduced by certain charges on income and losses under *ss 454, 455(3)*. For this purpose an accounting period straddling the final relief date is deemed to consist of two separate accounting periods, one ending on that date and the other commencing on the following day. Where relief for such losses etc is allowed, it acts to reduce income before terminal loss relief but after relief for other trading losses.

The restriction on relief does not apply to losses etc in a trade referable to capital allowances for certain commercial buildings in use by financial services companies operating in the Custom House Docks Area (see **12.18**(viii) below).

Where relief is surrendered under the above provision, it is set against the income from the sale of goods, which would otherwise give rise to manufacturing companies relief in the hands of the claimant company. The amount surrendered may not exceed the claimant company's income from the sale of goods.

For accounting periods ending after 5 March 2001, these provisions are revised to allow for the interaction with the prohibition of relief for charges and losses incurred in trades other than 'excepted trades' subject to the 25 per cent corporation tax rate (see **12.2** above) against income from such excepted trades. They are in any event repealed for 2003 and subsequent years. [*TCA 1997, s 456; FA 1999, s 74(f); FA 2001, s 90*]

Payments without deducting tax. Certain payments (chiefly charges on income) made between two RI resident companies (extended to EU resident companies and companies resident in an EEA country with which RI has a double taxation treaty for accounting periods ending from 1 March 2005) must be made without deduction of tax where:

(a) one is a 51 per cent subsidiary of the other or both are 51 per cent subsidiaries of a third RI-resident (for accounting periods ending after 30 June 1998, EU-resident or, from 1 January 2002, resident in an EEA State with which double tax arrangements are in force) company; or

(b) the payer company is a trading or holding company owned by a consortium of which the payee company is a member.

Holding company has the same meaning as above, and the same rules apply for disregarding shares held in non-resident (for accounting periods ending after 30 June 1998, not EU-resident or, from 1 January 2002, resident in an EEA State with which double tax arrangements are in force) companies or held for the purposes of a trade; but here a company is *owned by a consortium* if three-fourths or more of its ordinary share capital is beneficially owned by five or fewer RI-resident (for accounting periods ending after 30 June 1998, EU-resident or, from 1 January 2002, resident in an EEA State with which double tax arrangements are in force) companies none of which owns less than one-twentieth of the share capital.

[*TCA 1997, s 410; FA 1999, s 78; FA 2002, s 37(a); FA 2005, s 52*]

See also **12.26** below as regards dividends payable without accounting for advance corporation tax.

Deferment of tax on capital gains. A transfer of assets between companies in a group will be treated as being for a consideration such that no loss or gain accrues to the transferor company. This relief will not apply where the disposal consists of satisfying a debt or redeeming shares, or is a disposal of an interest in shares on a capital distribution. [*TCA 1997, s 617; FA 2001, s 38(1)(c)*] The relief applies to companies resident in RI or, for disposals after 14 February 2001, companies resident in another EU Member State (or, from 1 January 2002, in an EEA State with which double tax arrangements are in force) and carrying on trade in RI through a branch or agency of which the asset in question is a chargeable asset for RI capital gains tax purposes. 'Group' is defined in similar terms as for the purposes of group loss relief (see above), ie by reference to the extended 75 per cent requirement and taking into account companies resident in the EU or tax treaty countries. The relief is carried over where the principal company itself becomes a 75 per cent subsidiary thus enlarging the group. Since 1 January 2006 these provisions apply where the principal company in the group becomes (a) a newly formed Societas Europaea (SE) through merger, (b) becomes a subsidiary of a holding SE, (c) is transformed into an SE or (d) becomes a European Cooperative Society (SCE) in the course of a merger. [*TCA 1997, s 616; FA 1999, s 56(1)(a); FA 2001, s 38(1)(b); FA 2002, s 36(b); FA 2006, s 60*]

Further provisions clarify the situation as regards appropriations to and from stock in trade in the course of such transfers, provide for aggregation of capital allowances for the purpose of restricting an ultimate loss, and treat as one for the purposes of 'roll-over' relief all businesses carried on by the group. [*TCA 1997, ss 618, 619(1), 620; FA 2001, s 38(1)(d)(e)(f)*] Ownership of an asset by another group member prior to an intra-group transfer is treated as ownership by the transferee company in determining period of ownership for inflation indexing (see **9.9** 'Capital gains tax') but not to such transfers of development land (see **9.16** 'Capital gains tax'). [*TCA 1997, s 619(2)*] There is a deemed market value disposal and reacquisition in certain cases where an asset acquired by a company in a transaction to which *s 615, s 617* or *s 620* (see **12.5** and above) applies ceases to be a chargeable asset for RI capital gains tax purposes. [*TCA 1997, s 620A; FA 2001, s 38(1)(g)*]

There is a retrospective charge to corporation tax where the company in possession of an asset leaves the group within ten years of acquiring the asset under a relieved transaction. A 'deemed disposal and re-acquisition' provision renders the difference between (*a*) the no loss/no gain consideration under the relief, and (*b*) the market value of the asset on the date the company acquired it, a chargeable gain by the company for the accounting period in which it acquired the asset. This retrospective charge does not apply where the company left the group as part of a genuine commercial merger, but is subject to various anti-avoidance provisions. [*TCA 1997, ss 623, 624; FA 2001, s 38(1)(i)(j); FA 2002, s 36(d)*] Further anti-avoidance provisions deal with sales of shares of subsidiaries, losses manufactured by intra-group transfers at an undervalue or by share dealing or share cancellation, and losses caused by dividend stripping. [*TCA 1997, ss 621, 622, 625; FA 2001, s 38(1)(h); FA 2002, s 36(c)*] Following the change to the definition of 'group' from 11 February 1999, there are transitional provisions to prevent a charge arising under either *s 623* or *s 625* because a company leaves a group solely as a consequence of the revised definition. [*TCA 1997, ss 623A, 625A; FA 1999, s 56(1)(d)(e)*]

Pre-entry losses. See **3.12** 'Anti-avoidance' for provisions restricting relief for allowable losses on a company becoming a member of a group.

LIFE ASSURANCE COMPANIES

12.16 *Sections 706–730K, Sch 32 para 24* (as amended) contain detailed provisions for the taxation of assurance companies (within *Insurance Act 1936, s 3*), including relief for management expenses similar to that in **12.9** above. For these purposes, life assurance business is split between pension business (including from 1 January 2003, personal retirement savings account contracts [*FA 2003, s 54*] see **2.23** 'Allowances, credits and rates'), general annuity business, and other life assurance business. For accounting periods ending prior to 1 January 2003, special investment business was also a separate business. From that date, it is combined with other life assurance business. [*FA 2003, s 52*] A new regime is introduced by *FA 2000*, for both domestic and IFSC assurance companies, and there are accompanying provisions for the application of tax on payments in respect of, and on certain other events in relation to, a life assurance policy of a person resident or ordinarily resident in RI. Since 31 March 2006 a policy/ unit is deemed to mature every 8 years (or 12 years in certain circumstances) from inception to prevent constant deferral of tax payment on maturity. On ultimate maturity, credit is given for any tax paid on these deemed maturity dates and any overpayment is repaid. [*FA 2006, ss 48, 49, 50, 51, 54*] Prior to *FA 2000*, major changes were introduced from 1 January 1993, involving a reduction in the rate of tax generally applicable to the standard rate of income tax (see **2.5** 'Allowances, credits and rates') and a widening of the tax base, including taxation of certain unrealised gains (subject to spreading, generally over seven years, but phased in by the year 2000). *Finance (No 2) Act 2008, s 25* increases the rate of tax applying to life assurance policies and investment funds by three percentage points with effect from 1 January 2009. *Finance Act 2011, s 31* has increased the rate of tax by a further two percentage points. The amendment applies to the rates of exit tax and on domestic life assurance policies and investment undertakings under the gross roll up scheme introduced in the *Finance Act 2000*. It also increases the rates of tax that apply to profits and gains on life assurance policies and investment funds in other EU Member States, EEA States and OECD countries with which Ireland has a double taxation agreements. A similar increase is being applied to the rate of tax applying to a personal portfolio life policy or to an investment held in a personal investment undertaking. Since 1 January 2001, a new regime is introduced for the taxation of holders of certain foreign life assurance policies. Since 26 September 2001, special arrangements apply for the taxation of personal portfolio life policies. See **9.2** 'Capital Gains Tax' for taxation of gains on overseas assets of a life assurance company.

Certain changes were introduced in relation to an assurance company has established a branch in an EU or EEA Member State. *Section 730D(2A)* provides that a gain shall not arise on the happening of a chargeable event under the gross roll-up regime in relation to the life policy where the assurance company has established a branch in an EU or EEA Member State and has received written approval from the Revenue Commissioners that exit tax will not apply. This has been extended to situations where the life assurance company carries on business on a freedom of services basis (as provided for in the *EC (Life Assurance) Framework Regulations 1994 (SI No 360 of 1994), reg 50*), or under equivalent arrangement in an EEA Member State and the policy holder resides in an EU or EEA Member State other than Ireland. Written approval is required from the Revenue Commissioners. [*FA 2008, s 38*]

For general articles on the taxation of life assurance companies, see Revenue Tax Briefing Issue 41 pp 19–21, Issue 43 pp 9–11.

LOSSES

12.17 Relief for a loss (computed generally in the same way as income) incurred during an accounting period may be claimed:

(*a*)   by **set-off** against profits of any kind in that accounting period (but see further below) [*TCA 1997, s 396(2)*];

(*b*)   except for trades within Sch D, Case III, by **carry-back** against profits of any kind in a previous accounting period ending within a period immediately preceding, and of the same length as, the accounting period of the loss (with time apportionment of income etc of accounting periods partly within that period) [*TCA 1997, s 396(2)–(4)*];

(*c*)   by **carry-forward** against trading income from the same trade in succeeding accounting periods (charges on income, relating wholly and exclusively to a trade, which are unrelieved for the accounting period (see **12.9** above) may create or augment a loss for this purpose) [*TCA 1997, s 396(1); FA 2002, s 54(1)(b)(i)*];

(*d*)   if a **terminal loss,** ie any loss in a trade incurred in an accounting period wholly or partly falling within the twelve months prior to cessation of that trade, by carry-back against trading income of any accounting period falling wholly or partly (and if partly, by apportionment) in the three years preceding the twelve months [*TCA 1997, s 397*];

(*e*)   by **carry-forward against income of the same trade in a successor company** where the successor company takes over the business of the predecessor company which ceases to trade and at least a three-fourths interest in the trade remains in the same hands [*TCA 1997, s 400*];

(*f*)   if a Sch D, Case IV transaction, by carry-forward against later income of such transactions [*TCA 1997, s 399(1)*];

(*g*)   if a Sch D, Case V transaction, by carry-back against the income of such transactions in the preceding accounting period, and carry-forward of any remaining balance against subsequent such transactions [*TCA 1997, s 399(2)*];

(*h*)   by set-off against **surplus franked investment income,** see **12.13** above;

(*j*)   by way of **group relief,** see **12.15** above.

Claims under (*a*), (*b*) and (*g*) must be made within two years, and are restricted to one-half of the maximum claim where the return for the period is late (see **28.11** 'Returns'). [*TCA 1997, ss 396(9), 399(4), 1085(2)*] Relief under (*d*) is precluded in a situation to which (*e*) applies. [*TCA 1997, s 400(7)*]

Farming losses are subject to the same conditions as for income tax under *s 622*, see **18.6**(*d*) 'Farming'. [*TCA 1997, s 663*]

Financial concerns operating in RI through a branch or agency are subject to restriction of loss relief arising from holdings of exempt government securities issued under *s 43* (see **19.2** 'Government and other public loans') and certain other exempt securities issued under the authority of the Minister for Finance. [*TCA 1997, s 398*]

'Loss buying' – if there is a change in the ownership of a company and either (i) a major change in the nature or conduct of a trade occurs or has occurred within three years or (ii) at the time of the change of ownership the company's scale of activities is small, carry-forward relief under (*c*) for losses incurred before the change of ownership will be disallowed. [*TCA 1997, s 401*] See **38.74** 'Tax cases'.

Expenditure on 'significant buildings' may attract relief as if it were a trading loss. See **22.4** 'Losses'.

Limited partnership losses. See **22.5** 'Losses'.

'Ring-fencing' of losses. For accounting periods ending after 5 March 2001, trading losses are not relieved against total profits, but (subject to special provisions in relation to losses in activities within the manufacturing companies relief (see *s 455*), which applied also to earlier accounting periods, see **12.18** below) may be set against any income from other trades (or from certain insurance trades which are excepted trades but are not subject to the special 25 per cent rate) for the current or earlier periods (as under (*c*) above) as appropriate. Relief for any losses (other than certain losses of leasing trades) of an accounting period not so relieved (and not relieved under *s 455*) may be claimed by way of a deduction from corporation tax chargeable (subject to certain reservations) for the current or such earlier accounting periods at the rate of corporation tax applicable to the accounting period (eg at ten per cent where *s 455* applies). Trading losses carried forward (see (*c*) above) are correspondingly reduced (with provision for the displacement of non-trade charges, management expenses, etc where appropriate). Accounting periods are split as necessary for these purposes. These provisions do not apply to losses incurred in an 'excepted trade' (see **12.2** above). Claims must be made within two years of the end of the accounting period in which the losses arise and (for accounting periods ending from 6 February 2003) are restricted to one-half of the maximum claim where the return for the period is late. For claims made from 6 February 2003, all possible claims for off-set of losses must have been made before a claim for relief on a value basis may be made. Since 4 February 2004, relief for losses on a value basis cannot be used by life assurance companies to shelter corporation tax arising on policy holders' profits. [*TCA 1997, ss 396A, 396B; FA 2001, s 90; FA 2002, ss 54, 55; FA 2003, s 59; FA 2004, s 37; FA 2006, s 127, Sch 2*] See also Revenue Tax Briefing Issue 51 pp 14–15.

MANUFACTURING COMPANIES RELIEF

12.18 For all accounting periods (or parts) falling within the period **1 January 1981 to 31 December 2010** (31 December 2000 in relation to the special categories listed at (vi) and (vii) below), any company engaging in a trade which includes the manufacture and sale of 'goods' (as defined below) may claim relief from part of its CT liability. For trades (other than 'specified trades') set up and commenced after 22 July 1998, the relief period ends on 31 December 2002. A *'specified trade'* is a trade consisting of or including trading operations specified in a grant agreement between the company and an industrial development agency (as defined), on foot of an approval of grant assistance for the company made by the agency before 1 August 1998, but excluding such part of the trade as consists of certain expansion operations commenced after 22 July 1998 which would not fall within the terms of the grant agreement (such a part of a trade being treated as a separate trade for relief purposes, with income and expenses being apportioned on a just and reasonable basis). A company succeeding to a trade (or part trade) after 23 July 1998 inherits the reliefs which would have been available to the predecessor company.

'*Goods*' means goods manufactured (see **38.63–38.69** 'Tax cases') by the claimant company within RI. The provision within RI of services to another person consisting of the subjection of commodities or materials belonging to that person to a process of manufacturing is treated as being the manufacture of 'goods'. (The inspector may require information in support of such a claim.) Where goods are manufactured within RI by one company and sold by another, and either one company is a 90 per cent subsidiary of the other or both are 90 per cent subsidiaries of a third, the goods sold by the selling company are deemed to have been manufactured by it. Goods sold, directly or ultimately, to any intervention agency under EC regulations are excluded from this definition of 'goods', as are goods sold by retail by the claimant company. The 90 per cent subsidiary test must also be satisfied in relation to distributions of profits and of assets in a winding-up (see *ss 412–417*).

[*TCA 1997, ss 442, 443(1)(5)(7)(21)(22); FA 1999, s 74(a)*]

The following are also classed as the manufacture of goods for the purposes of this relief:

(i)   the production of fish on a fish farm within RI [*TCA 1997, s 443(2)*];

(ii)   (for accounting periods beginning before 1 June 1994) the cultivation of mushrooms within RI [*FA 1980, s 39(1A); FA 1994, s 48*];

(iii)   the repairing of ships within RI [*TCA 1997, s 443(8)*];

(iv)   the rendering within RI of design and planning services in connection with engineering works executed outside the EC [*TCA 1997, s 443(9)*];

(v)   the rendering of data processing or software development services (and related technical or consultancy services) where the work was carried out in RI in a service undertaking in respect of which an employment grant was made under *Industrial Development Act 1986, s 25* (previously *Industrial Development (No 2) Act 1981, s 2*) or *Industrial Development Act 1993, s 12(2)*, or in respect of which certain grants or financial assistance were made available by the Shannon Free Airport Development Co Ltd or Údarás na Gaeltachta [*TCA 1997, s 443(10)*];

(vi)   the carrying on of 'qualifying shipping activities' in the course of a 'qualifying shipping trade' [*TCA 1997, s 443(11)*];

(vii) the wholesale sale of export goods by a 'Special Trading House', ie a company whose trade consists solely of the carrying out of such sales [*TCA 1997, s 443(12)*];

(viii) (from a date to be specified in the relevant certificate) the provision by a company (the 'qualified company') of certain financial services in the Custom House Docks Area (as described in *Sch 5 para 2*, subject to extension by Order) in respect of which the Minister for Finance has given (and not revoked) a certificate for this purpose, which remains in force until 31 December 2005 (31 December 2002 in the case of operations approved by the Minister after 31 July 1998 for carry on in the Area). The circumstances in which the Minister may give (or revoke) such a certificate are laid down in detail, but are broadly designed to contribute to the development of the Custom House Docks Area as an International Financial Services Centre ('IFSC'). A certificate may be granted where operations are temporarily carried on outside the Area for reasons beyond the control of the company concerned. A limit of ten per cent is also placed on the rate of tax applying to income or chargeable gains from investments held abroad relating to certain foreign life assurance or unit trust business covered by such a certificate. Certain extensions of the classes of business within these provisions are introduced by *FA 2000, s 80*, to ensure continuity of such treatment for IFSC companies following other changes in the taxation of such companies. [*TCA 1997, ss 446, 451; FA 1998, Sch 2 para 8; FA 1999, s 74(c); FA 2000, ss 80, 83(1)(b)*];

(ix)   cultivating plants in RI by the process of micro-propagation or plant cloning [*TCA 1997, s 443(3)*];

(x)   repair or maintenance of aircraft within RI (other than in Shannon Airport, see below) [*TCA 1997, s 443(13)*];

(xi)   film production on a commercial basis primarily for public exhibition or for training or documentary purposes, on which at least 75 per cent of production work is carried out in RI [*TCA 1997, s 443(14)*] (and see **38.71** 'Tax cases');

(xii) meat processing within RI (in an establishment approved and inspected under *SI 284/87*) and fish processing within RI [*TCA 1997, s 443(4)*], but without prejudice to the exclusion of goods sold into intervention (see above) [*TCA 1997, s 443(7)(b)*], although this does *not* exclude the provision of processing services in relation to meat owned by the Intervention Agency [*TCA 1997, s 443(7)(c)*];

(xiii) the manufacture or repair of computer equipment or of sub-assemblies by the company which manufactured them (or by a connected company within *s 10*) [*TCA 1997, s 443(15)*];

(xiv) the sale by wholesale by certain agricultural and fishery societies of goods purchased from their members, which are themselves entitled to the manufacturing companies relief in respect of those goods (or would be but for the prohibition of sales into intervention) [*TCA 1997, s 443(16)*];

(xv) the sale by certain agricultural societies of milk purchased from their members and sold to certain milk product manufacturing companies certified for the purpose by the Minister for Agriculture. [*TCA 1997, s 443(17)*];

(xvi) exchange gains in respect of certain loans, which are deemed to be trading profits or gains (see **12.10** above) [*TCA 1997, s 443(18)*]);

(xvii) newspaper production (including the provision of related advertising services) [*TCA 1997, s 443(19)*] (and see now **38.70** 'Tax cases' and below).

As regards (viii) above, see also **12.10** above, **16.8** 'Exempt income and special savings schemes' as regards certain interest exemptions and **20.1**(vi) 'Interest payable' as regards deduction of tax from interest payments.

It is understood that the activities at (x) and (xii) above have always been regarded as qualifying for relief, despite the enacted commencement dates referred to.

The inspector may require information in support of a claim under (iii)–(viii), (x), (xi) or (xiii)–(xvii) above. [*TCA 1997, s 443(22)*]

The following are specifically excluded from being treated as the manufacture of goods for the purposes of relief:

(A) processes applied to any produce, product or material acquired in bulk to prepare it for sale or distribution;

(B) application of methods of preservation, pasteurisation or maturation etc to foodstuffs (but see **38.64** 'Tax cases');

(C) preparation of food or drink for human consumption shortly after preparation;

(D) improvements or alterations to articles or materials which do not change their character;

(E) repair, refurbishment, restoration etc of any articles or materials;

and relief is similarly denied (subject to (xvii) above) in respect of receipts from the rendering of advertising services by companies producing newspapers, magazines etc.

Relief is also denied where the manufacturing process is not carried out by the company claiming relief (subject to the exception referred to above in the case of 90 per cent subsidiaries).

[*TCA 1997, s 443(6)(20)*]

A '*qualifying shipping trade*' consists of the carrying on of '*qualifying shipping activities*', ie the carriage of passengers or cargo for reward (and provision of certain ancillary services) in a 'qualifying ship', the letting out on charter of such a ship for such purposes where the operation of the ship remains under the company's direction and control, the subjection of fish to a manufacturing process aboard such a ship, or the transport of supplies or personnel or provision of services to offshore installations. A '*qualifying ship*' is an RI registered, self-propelled, sea-going vessel of not less than 100 tons gross tonnage at least 51 per cent owned by RI residents, but excluding fishing vessels (other than factory ships, as indicated above), tugs (other than certain deep-sea tugs), platforms and other vessels not normally used for qualifying shipping activities. It also includes certain ships leased without crew from non-residents.

Where qualifying shipping activities are carried on before 1 January 2011 as part of a trade, they are treated as constituting a separate trade (except for the purposes of the commencement and cessation provisions and the carry-forward of trading losses). Capital allowances for a qualifying ship are available only in the separate trade, unless the ship is let on charter other than as described in (vi) above, in which case they are available against income from such letting. (Such letting is, however, brought within the restriction on allowances for leased plant and machinery under *s 403* (see **8.7** 'Capital allowances') notwithstanding the general exclusion of ship-operating companies (except in certain cases where a certificate issued by the Minister for the Marine is produced to the Revenue Commissioners).) Similarly, losses in the separate trade may only be set against other profits or surrendered as group relief (see **12.15** above) to the extent that the income against which they are set is from qualifying shipping activities. The separate trade is not excluded from the operation of the capital allowance leasing restrictions in *s 403* (see **8.7** 'Capital allowances') or the '*Section 84* loans' restrictions in *ss 133, 134* (see **12.10** above) despite its being brought within the manufacturing companies relief.

[*TCA 1997, ss 133(1)(d), 134(1)(d), 407; FA 2001, s 82(1)(b); FA 2003, s 40; FA 2006, s 58*]

It is understood that, in practice, the Revenue accept that magnetic tapes and discs etc representing software or data processing input are 'goods' for these purposes.

In addition, the Minister for Finance may issue a certificate with the effect that certain trading operations carried on within Shannon airport are similarly treated as the manufacture of goods. Such operations must consist of the repair or maintenance of aircraft or operations contributing (in the opinion of the Minister) to the use or development of the airport, or be ancillary to such operations or to the manufacture of goods as defined apart from this specific provision.

Specifically excluded are operations consisting of:

(*a*)   the rendering of services to passengers or in connection with the movement of aircraft or cargo;

(*b*)   the operation of a scheduled air transport service;

(*c*)   retail selling (other than certain mail order operations); or

(*d*)   the sale of fuel or other aircraft stores.

Such a certificate may be conditional, and may be revoked where any conditions are not met or where the trade ceases to be carried on within Shannon airport or by agreement. It is otherwise valid until 31 December 2005 (31 December 2002 in the case of operations approved by the Minister after 31 May 1998 for carry on in the airport).

The inspector may again require information in support of a claim under this provision. [*TCA 1997, s 445; FA 1998, Sch 2 para 7; FA 1999, s 74(b); FA 2000, s 83(1)(a)*] See also **16.7** 'Exempt income and special savings schemes' for exemption of certain interest paid in the course of such operations, and **20.1**(vi) 'Interest payable' as regards deduction of tax from interest payments.

It is understood that, for new projects, the Revenue Commissioners are prepared, on receipt of satisfactory detail, to give an opinion on whether the process described is likely to qualify for relief.

Apportionment on a time basis applies where an accounting period falls only partly within the date limits for relief. [*TCA 1997, s 442(2)*]

Basis of relief is a reduction of that part of the liability to CT (ignoring certain reliefs and surcharges and amounts treated as CT) referable to income from the sale of 'goods'. The reduction is 7/12ths, one-half and 3/8ths for periods falling in financial years 2000 to 2002 respectively, and to one-fifth for periods falling in financial year

2003 and subsequent financial years. (See **12.3** above for apportionment of profits to actual or deemed financial years.) The corporation tax to which the reduction is applied is adjusted to eliminate that chargeable at the reduced or higher rate (see **12.2** above). The effective rate is thus ten per cent. The CT thus relieved is that attributable to the company's income for the relevant period (ie profits chargeable to CT less that part attributable to chargeable gains without deduction of any amounts which may be set against profits or gains of more than one description), less that chargeable at the reduced or higher rate, reduced in the proportion that the income from the sale of 'goods' bears to total income. The income from the sale of 'goods' as a proportion of the income from the sale of both 'goods' and other merchandise is determined by the amounts receivable (excluding any duty or VAT) in respect of each category. If the trade has income other than from the sale of 'goods' and merchandise, the proportion of total income attributable to such sales is such as appears just and reasonable to the inspector (or the Commissioners on appeal). [*TCA 1997, ss 448(1)–(5), 457; FA 1998, Sch 6 para 3; FA 1999, Sch 1 para 1; FA 2000, s 83(1)(d)(i); FA 2005, ss 52, 53*]

For accounting periods beginning on or before 1 April 2000, there are provisions by which a smaller reduction in the rate of corporation tax may be applied in any particular case where a company qualifying for the relief is wholly or partly owned by a non-RI resident company or companies (or is itself non-resident and trades in RI through a branch or agency) and its operations contribute, or will do so, to the development of an International Financial Services Centre or Customs-free Airport (within *ss 445, 446* respectively, see above). [*TCA 1997, s 448(7); FA 2000, s 83(1)(d)(ii)(2)*] This is intended to deal with the situation where, due to anti-avoidance legislation in a foreign jurisdiction (eg Germany) a higher overall tax rate would otherwise apply.

Credit for foreign tax. Where the RI treaty system does not provide for double taxation relief, a measure of unilateral credit is available against foreign taxes paid on profits derived from sales of computer software or services or from Shannon Airport activities qualifying for manufacturing companies relief. The *'relevant foreign tax'* is foreign tax (which must correspond to income or corporation tax) deducted from the amount receivable and not repaid to the company, and not relieved by deduction under double tax arrangements.

Finance Act 2011, s 35 amends *Taxes Consolidation Act 1997, Sch 24, para 4(5)* to make it clear that a company is not permitted to allocate relevant trading charges on income as it sees fit in the computation of the credit due to it in respect of foreign tax paid on its income.

Unilateral credit relief has been extended in respect of royalty flows from persons resident in non-treaty countries to all trading companies. [*FA 2010, ss 45, 46*]

The corporation tax attributable to an amount receivable is ten per cent of the company's income attributable to that amount, reduced by the 'relevant foreign tax' (correspondingly increased where reduced manufacturing relief applies). Income from the sale of goods is increased by the 'relevant foreign tax' and is then reduced for this purpose in the proportion which the amount in question bears to the total amount receivable from the sale of goods in the period, the total income from the sale of goods being determined as in relation to the basis of relief (see above). [*TCA 1997, s 449; FA 1980, s 39C; FA 1995, s 63; FA 1998, s 59; FA 2000, s 83(1)(e); FA 2003, s 60(1)*]

Certain companies carrying on 'stand alone' non-banking financial trades which qualify as 'relevant trading operations' within *ss 445, 446* (see above) may elect to receive enhanced relief for foreign withholding tax deducted under double taxation agreements from interest payments from 'related' companies. In the case of *s 445*, the operations must be such as could be certified for the purposes of *s 446* if they were carried out in the Custom House Docks Area (ie broadly the provision of international financial services). Companies which are, or are '25 per cent subsidiaries' of, 'credit institutions' are excluded. Broadly, where an election is made for an accounting period (before the 'specified return date' for the period, see **28.11** 'Returns'), such foreign tax may be deducted from corporation tax attributable to income other than that which suffered the foreign tax, subject to a maximum additional credit in aggregate of 35 per cent of the corporation tax which would otherwise be payable on income attributable to interest received (whether or not from 'related companies') subject to double taxation agreements. [*TCA 1997, s 450*]

Restrictions on relief for charges on income and losses. For accounting periods to which the relief applies (and subject as below), relief for charges paid for the purposes of the sale of goods within the manufacturing companies relief, and for losses arising from such sales, is restricted. An accounting period straddling the final relief date is for these purposes split into two accounting periods, so that the restrictions apply to the deemed accounting period ending on that date.

Charges on income (see **12.9** above) are allowed as a deduction from total profits only to the extent that they do not exceed income (net of losses carried back) from the sale of goods within the relief in the period. A technical amendment is made to *s 448* to ensure that there is no question as to the existence of the ring fence for deductions relating to the manufacturing trade [*F(No 2)A 2008, s 32*].

Losses (see **12.17** above) are only allowed against other income of an accounting period to which the relief applies to the extent that that income arises from the sale of goods within the relief, and relief against income of earlier accounting periods (see **12.6**(*b*) above) is similarly restricted. These restrictions do not, however, apply to the extent that a loss is attributable to plant and machinery or industrial buildings allowances in respect of expenditure incurred before 31 March 1995 on a project approved by the Industrial Development Authority in the two years to 31 December 1988 (see **8.5**, **8.6** 'Capital allowances'), provided that one-half of the expenditure was incurred or contracted for before 1 April 1992, or to certain urban renewal relief capital allowances (see **8.10** 'Capital allowances') relating to the provision of financial services in the Custom House Docks Area. See *s 455(5)* for the effect of loss reliefs on the income taken into account in the computation of the manufacturing companies relief. For accounting periods ending after 5 March 2001, these provisions are revised to incorporate the restriction on relief of charges on income and trading losses arising other than in 'excepted trades' (see **12.2** above) against profits from such trades chargeable at the 25 per cent rate of corporation tax.

[*TCA 1997, ss 454, 455; CTA 1976, s 16A; FA 1999, s 74(d)(e); FA 2001, s 90*]

These provisions cease to apply from 1 January 2003.

Claims to relief must be made before the assessment for the period of claim becomes final and conclusive. [*TCA 1997, s 448(6)*]

Mining and construction operations income is excluded from relief. Also, where part or all of the minerals etc obtained are not sold but used in a combined trade which includes the manufacture of 'goods', such part of the income as appears just and reasonable to the inspector (or to the Commissioners on appeal) is treated as income from mining operations and excluded from relief. Similarly, where part of the amount receivable from the sale of 'goods' is consideration for carrying out construction operations, a 'just and reasonable' part of the income is excluded from relief. [*TCA 1997, s 444*]

Associated persons. An anti-avoidance section prevents tax avoidance by transactions between associated persons at artificial prices, the test of association being by reference to 'control' within the meaning of *s 11*. An inspector may require information for this purpose. [*TCA 1997, s 453*]

Distributions. For details on the complex provisions relating to the tax credit attached to distributions made before 6 April 1999 where manufacturing companies relief has been claimed see previous editions.

Group relief. See **12.15** above for the restriction on group relief of losses arising to companies within the manufacturing companies relief scheme.

NON-RESIDENTS

12.19 See **11.3** 'Companies' as regards company residence.

A **non-resident company** which carries on a trade in RI through a branch or agency is chargeable to CT on:

(*a*)   its trading income arising directly, or indirectly through the branch or agency (excluding distributions received from resident companies); and

(*b*)   such capital gains as would be chargeable in the hands of non-residents under the *Corporation Tax Acts* on the disposal of any assets used, held or acquired for the purposes of the branch or agency.

[*TCA 1997, s 25(1)(2)*] See **38.59** 'Tax cases'.

Non-resident companies remain liable to IT or CGT on income or chargeable gains arising in RI which is not or are not chargeable to CT. [*TCA 1997, s 21(2)(3)*] Where a non-resident company is chargeable to CT for one source of income and to IT for another, the capital allowances and balancing charges relating to particular income shall have effect in respect of the particular tax. [*TCA 1997, s 309*]

Non-resident banks, insurance companies and investment companies carrying on business in RI are charged to CT on foreign interest and dividends received by them in respect of their RI business. (Such sums are normally exempt, see **29.2** 'Sch C'; see also **12.11** above.) Certain reliefs are restricted. [*TCA 1997, s 845*]

Distributions. Non-resident companies meeting the definition of 'qualifying non-resident persons' (including certain non-resident parent companies) are entitled to an exemption from income tax on distributions by RI-resident companies. The income is accordingly not available to cover charges (see **13.1** 'Deduction of tax at source'). In certain circumstances, interest paid by a company to a non-resident 75 per cent parent or associated company will not be treated as a distribution of its profits and will therefore be a deductible trading expense. In certain cases double taxation can sometimes arise where the interest is disallowed as a trading expense under the distribution rule and is also taxed in the hands of a recipient as interest. Subject to the conditions of the section being met, a company paying yearly interest to a non-resident 75 per cent parent or associated company may treat such yearly interest as a deductible trading expense. [*FA 2007, s 50*] The definition of a '*qualifying non-resident person*' is the same as that used for the purposes of the dividend withholding tax (see **13.12** 'Deduction of tax at source'), except that the requirement for a declaration under *Sch 2A* does not apply. Also, from 6 April 2000, the liability of individuals neither resident nor ordinarily resident in RI, but who are not qualifying non-resident persons, in respect of distributions by RI-resident companies is limited to the standard rate of tax, thus in effect being met by the dividend withholding tax. [*TCA 1997, s 153; FA 1998, Sch 5 para 1; FA 1999, s 28; FA 2000, s 31*]

PAYMENTS – DEDUCTION OF TAX

12.20 All annual payments made by a resident company are deemed not to have been made out of profits brought into charge to tax and accordingly the company is obliged under *s 238* to deduct standard rate IT from the payment (even if made to another resident company) and account separately to the Revenue for the tax. [*TCA 1997, s 24(1)*] Where such a payment is received by a company the tax so deducted will be set against the company's liability to CT, and may be reclaimed if there is no CT liability. [*TCA 1997, s 24(2)*] The IT deducted may also be set off against the company's liability to IT deducted from payments it has itself made. [*TCA 1997, s 239(7)*]

A return of every payment from which a company has been obliged to deduct income tax, including any deemed payment in respect of a loan by a close company to a participator (see **12.7** above), must be made within nine months of the end of the accounting period in which the payment was made, and the tax becomes due and payable without assessment at the same time as any preliminary tax for the period (see **28.11** 'Returns'). The (net) income tax payable is treated for the purposes of charge, assessment, collection and recovery (and interest and penalties) as corporation tax payable for the accounting period, but without prejudice to the right to repayment as if it were income tax where appropriate. Returns of payments not made in an accounting period are required within six months after the date of the payment, and the income tax is due at the time by which the return must be made. Any assessment is treated as an income tax assessment for the year of assessment in which the payment was made. [*TCA 1997, s 239*] The normal income tax provisions relating to assessments, appeals, payment and interest apply. [*TCA 1997, s 240; FA 2002, s 129(1)(a)*]

A non-resident company within the charge to corporation tax must make a return of payments made in an accounting period from which it is required to deduct income tax under *s 238*. The income tax required to be deducted is treated as corporation tax chargeable for the accounting period for the purposes of charge, assessment, collection and recovery from the company, and of interest and penalties. [*TCA 1997, s 241*]

Charges on income. An annual payment may be deductible for CT purposes as a charge on income, see **12.9** above.

PETROLEUM TAXATION

12.21 There are special provisions, contained in *ss 684–697*, for the taxation of petroleum activities of exploration, exploitation, or the acquisition, enjoyment or exploitation of petroleum rights. Broadly, such activities are ring-fenced, and a special reduced rate of corporation tax applies for accounting periods ending prior to 3 February

2005. There are also provisions dealing specifically with reliefs for development, exploration and abandonment expenditure and for petroleum valuations. [*FA 2005, s 55*]

Profit Resource Rent Tax. This tax was introduced in 2008 by the insertion of a new chapter, *Pt 24, Ch 3*. The new chapter gives effect to the Government decision of 30 July 2007 that a Profit Resource Rent Tax will apply in the case of a petroleum lease entered into following on from an exploration licence awarded by the Minister for Communications, Energy and Natural Resources after 1 January 2007. The new tax will apply when profits exceed a certain threshold and applies in addition to the current 25 per cent rate of corporation tax that applies to profits from petroleum activities.

A key feature of the new tax is that it is based on the profit ratio of a petroleum field, which is defined as the rate of profits (net of 25 per cent corporation tax) for the field, divided by the accumulated level of capital investment in the field. Different rates of Profit Resource Rent Tax will apply, depending on the ratio, as follows:

Profit Ratio	Profit Resource Rent Tax Rate
4.5 or more	15%
3 or more and less than 4.5	10%
1.5 or more and less than 3	5%
Less than 1.5	Nil

The new chapter has the following sections:

Section 696B, which is the interpretation and application section, contains the following key definitions:

— taxable field, which is an area covered by a petroleum lease awarded on foot of an exploration licence awarded after 1 January 2007;

— cumulative field profits, which is the numerator in the profit ratio equation. For any accounting period of a company, this figure will be the sum of net profits (as defined) of the company in relation to a taxable field from 1 January 2007 up to the end of that accounting period; and

— cumulative field expenditure, which is the denominator in the profit ratio equation. For any accounting period of a company, this figure will be the sum of the capital expenditure (as defined) incurred by a company in relation to a taxable field from 1 January 2007 up to the end of that accounting period.

Section 696B also provides for the 'ring-fencing' of petroleum activities in respect of each taxable field, to ensure, for example, that a company cannot offset losses from any other activities against profits of a taxable field.

Section 696C contains the core rules about what the tax is and what it is being charged on. This section provides that the Profit Resource Rent Tax is an additional duty of corporation tax which applies when the profit ratio, calculated for an accounting period of a company in respect of a taxable field, is greater than or equal to 1.5. The rates of tax are graduated, as set out above.

Section 696D contains provisions in relation to groups of companies and provides, inter alia, for a situation where capital expenditure incurred by one company can be deemed to have been incurred by another company for the purposes of determining the cumulative expenditure, where one company is a subsidiary of the other or both are subsidiaries of a third company.

Section 696E provides for the submission of returns by companies in respect of the new licences granted on or after 1 January 2007. The returns will be submitted with the annual corporation tax return.

Section 696F contains the collection and general provisions in respect of the new tax. The normal corporation tax provisions for assessment, appeals, collection and recovery also apply to the Profit Resource Rent Tax. Interest charges will also apply in the case of late payment of the tax. [*FA 2008, s 45*]

SPECIAL BODIES

12.22 Industrial and provident societies. Any share or loan interest paid by a society registered under the *Industrial and Provident Societies Acts 1893–1978* is not subject to deduction of tax if paid to an RI resident (chargeable instead under Sch D, Case III) and is not a distribution. This applies equally to credit unions (see **17.8** 'Exempt organisations') from 6 April 1999. [*TCA 1997, s 700; FA 2000, s 32*]

Any discount, rebate, dividend or bonus granted by a society to members or others in respect of transactions with the society is deductible as an expense so long as the discount etc was based on the magnitude of the transaction and not on any share or interest in the capital of the society. Share or loan interest ranks as a deductible expense if wholly and exclusively for the purposes of a trade. [*TCA 1997, s 699(1)*]

Every society must make a return on or before 31 January each year (before 2002, 1 May) showing the name and address of every person to whom it has paid share or loan interest of £70/€90 (for 2001 only, £52) or more in the previous year of assessment and showing the amount actually paid. If such a return is not duly made, the society is precluded from relief under *s 97(2)(e)* (see **33.2** 'Sch D, Case V') or *s 699(1)* (see above) or *s 243* (charges on income) for that year of assessment. [*TCA 1997, s 700(3); FA 2001, Sch 2 para 39*]

In computing shareholdings for the purpose of group relief for trading losses, etc, or for group capital gains (see **12.15** above), any share capital of a registered industrial and provident society is treated as ordinary share capital. [*TCA 1997, ss 411(1)(b), 616(1)(d)*]

Agricultural and fishery co-operatives. Transfers by agricultural and fishery co-operatives of shares in subsidiary companies are granted certain tax exemptions, provided that the shares are distributed in proportion to the members' shares held in the co-operative before the transfer, that a corresponding proportion of each member's shares in the co-operative is cancelled following the transfer, that there is no other consideration for the transfer or cancellation, and that the transfer is effected for *bona fide* commercial reasons and does not form part of a scheme or arrangement a main purpose of which is the avoidance of corporation tax or capital gains tax. Where these conditions are met:

(*a*)   the transfer is not treated as a distribution (see **12.10** above);

(*b*)   the transfer is treated as being at no gain/no loss to the society for chargeable gains purposes;

(*c*)   the cancellation of each member's shares in the co-operative is not treated as a disposal for capital gains tax purposes; and

(d)   the shares transferred to a member are treated for capital gains tax purposes as acquired at the same time and for the same consideration as the member's cancelled shares in the co-operative. [*TCA 1997, s 701*]

See **12.12** above as regards exemption of certain grants.

Bank levy. There are special provisions for a bank or banking group which is liable to pay the bank levy under *FA 1992, s 200* to set off a part of the levy against its corporation tax liability. [*TCA 1997, s 487*]

Building societies: change of status. Where a building society converts into a company under *Building Societies Act 1989, Pt XI*, the following special provisions apply.

Capital allowances. The conversion does not give rise to any balancing adjustments, and the successor company stands in the shoes of the society as regards subsequent allowances and charges.

Financial assets. Financial assets constituting trading stock are valued at cost on the conversion for the purposes of *s 89* (trading stock of discontinued trade, see **30.31** 'Sch D, cases I and II'). The vesting in the successor company of financial assets, profits on whose disposal would be chargeable under Sch D, Case I, does not constitute a disposal, and the profit on disposal of those assets by the successor company is calculated by reference to the cost to the society.

Capital gains: assets vested in successor company. The conversion does not constitute a disposal for capital gains purposes, and all actions by the society in relation to such assets are treated as actions of the company for all subsequent capital gains matters.

Capital gains tax: shares etc in successor company. Any right to acquire shares in the successor company on favourable terms conferred on a member of the society is treated as an option acquired for no consideration and having, at the time of grant, no value (see **9.15** 'Capital gains tax').

Shares issued to members are treated as acquired for the new consideration (if any) given and as having a value equal to that acquisition cost at the time of acquisition. Where the shares are issued to trustees as settled property on terms providing for their transfer to members for no consideration, they are treated as acquired by the trustees for no consideration, the member's interest in the shares is treated as acquired for no consideration and as having no value, and when the member becomes absolutely entitled to the shares (or would do so but for a legal disability), the shares are treated as disposed of and reacquired by the trustees at no gain/no loss. Since 1 January 2006, Revenue must be provided with certain information relating to the share issue to members. [*FA 2006, s 77*]

Groups of companies. In relation to groups of companies (see **12.15** above), 'company' includes a building society incorporated under the *Building Societies Act 1989*, or deemed to be incorporated under *s 124(2)* of that Act. [*TCA 1997, s 703, Sch 16*]

Collective investment undertakings. A new regime for the taxation of 'investment undertakings' (as defined) is introduced by *FA 2000*. It applies to existing 'specified collective investment undertakings' (see below) **from 1 April 2000**, to all investment undertakings first issuing units on or after that date from the date of first issue, and to unit trusts becoming investment undertakings from the date of change. Other existing investment undertakings (ie broadly domestic ones) continue to be taxed as previously (see below). Broadly, under the new arrangements, no tax is paid annually on the profits of the undertaking. Instead, on the happening of a 'chargeable event' in relation to an investment undertaking (and subject to a number of exclusions, see below), a gain is treated as arising to the undertaking. *Finance (No 2) Act 2008, s 27* increased the rate of tax applying to life assurance policies and investment funds by three percentage points with effect from 1 January 2009. The amendment applies to the rates of exit tax and on domestic life assurance policies and investment undertakings under the gross roll up scheme introduced in the *Finance Act 2000*. It also increased the rates of tax that apply to profits and gains on life assurance policies and investment funds in other EU Member States, EEA States and OECD countries with which Ireland has a double taxation agreements. A similar increase was also applied to the rate of tax applying to a personal portfolio life policy or to an investment held in a personal investment undertaking. The undertaking is obliged to make a return of, and account to the Collector-General for, income tax on the amount of the gain so arising (including a nil return), and is entitled to deduct that tax from the payment to the unit holder (or to cancel units of the unit holder where appropriate). *Finance Act 2010, s 30* introduces an annual declaration and reporting arrangement in respect of unit trusts. The requirements are as follows:

(i)   where the trustees, or any persons acting on behalf of the trustees, of each unit trust are satisfied as to the capital gains tax-exempt status of all its unit holders, they are required to make an annual declaration to that effect.

(ii)   an annual electronic statement must be made to the Revenue Commissioners specifying certain details in respect of each unit holder and stating whether the above declaration has, or has not, been made for that year.

If that statement is not made, or is incorrect or incomplete, the trustees of the unit trust shall be liable to a penalty of €3,000. The amendment is to apply for the year of assessment 2010 and subsequent years.

The Revenue Commissioners have appropriate inspection powers in relation such returns (see *s 904D* introduced by *FA 2000, s 68(b)*).

A '*chargeable event*' is broadly:

(*a*)   the making of a distribution (made at intervals not exceeding a year) to the unit holder (other than on the cancellation, redemption or repurchase of units);

(*b*)   the making of any other payment to the unit holder (whether or not on the cancellation, redemption or repurchase of units) and (before 15 February 2001) other than on the death of the unit holder;

(*c*)   the transfer of units by a unit holder (and (before 15 February 2001) other than on the death of the unit holder); or

(*d*)   (effective for the appropriation or cancellation of a unit from 4 February 2004), the appropriation or cancellation of units to meet any tax payable in respect of a transfer of units by a unitholder.

The definition of '*chargeable event*' has expanded by including a definition for '*relevant period*' into *Pt 27, Ch 1A*. [*FA 2006, s 50*] The term 'relevant period' is defined as a period of eight years beginning with the acquisition of that unit by a unit holder and each subsequent eight years beginning immediately after the preceding relevant period.

This section also provides that a chargeable event will occur on the ending of a relevant period following the acquisition of the units of the investment undertaking.

New changes provide that the investment undertaking can make an irrevocable election in relation to a deemed disposal (as introduced by *FA 2006*) only, to value the units at the 30 June or 31 December prior to the date of the chargeable event rather than the date of the chargeable event itself. The second change provides that where the percentage of value of the chargeable units in an investment undertaking does not exceed 15 per cent of the value of the total units and the investment undertaking so elects, the amount of any excess tax arising, on a deemed disposal only, will be repaid to the unit holder by the Revenue Commissioners, rather than by the investment undertaking, on receipt of a claim by the unit holder. The third change introduced a De Minimis limit whereby the investment undertaking will not, in respect of a deemed disposal only, have to deduct the exit tax from the unit holder and account for it to the Revenue Commissioners where the value of the number of chargeable units in the investment undertaking is less than ten per pent of the value of the total units and the investment undertaking has made an election to report annually to the Revenue Commissioners certain details for each unit holder. Instead the unit holder will be required to return the gain directly to the Revenue Commissioners and to account for the appropriate tax. The final change extends the exemption from exit tax on the cancellation of units where it is part of a scheme of reconstruction or amalgamation of investment undertakings to also include exchanges of units in a sub-fund or sub-funds, of one umbrella fund for those in another umbrella fund. This exemption is given on condition that the exchange is effected for bona fide commercial reasons and not primarily for the avoiding of a liability to taxation. [*FA 2008*]

Finance Act 2007 sought to remove any uncertainty around the tax treatment of foreign investment structures. The amendments provides that the gross roll-up regime which was available to offshore funds in the EU/ECC and OECD countries will not apply to foreign entitles unless they are either:

(i)   an undertaking for collective investment undertaking formed under the law of an offshore state, similar in all material respects to an Investment Limited Partnership, and that holds a certificate of authorisation from the relevant foreign authority;

(ii)   a regulated fund authorised under the UCITS directive (as amended);

(iii)   a company formed under the law of an offshore state similar in all material respects to an authorised investment company within the meaning of *CA 1990, Pt XIII* and that holds an authorisation issued by the authorities of that state providing for the orderly regulation of such companies; or

(iv)   a unit trust scheme the trustees of which are not resident in the State which is similar in all material respects to an authorised unit trust scheme within the meaning of the *Unit Trust Act 1990* and that holds an authorisation issued by the authorities of that offshore state.

As a result of these amendments, the following regime is in fact the regime which applies to offshore funds going forward.

(A)   The definition of offshore fund remains as currently defined by law;

(B)   The gross roll-up regime which previously applied to EC/EEC and OECD resident funds will now only apply to regulated funds as defined above;

(C)   The gross roll-up regime is grandfathered for investors who have invested in EC/EEC and OECD offshore funds prior to 20 February 2007, provided their interest in those funds would not have qualified as a personal portfolio investment undertaking (PPIU) had the fund been regulated. Broadly, where an investor or a person connected with an investor has influence over the assets that are put into a regulated fund, the fund may be regarded as a PPIU (see below). The 20%/23% tax rates will therefore continue to apply for interests held in such retail funds where an investor has a purely passive interest;

(D)   Existing investors in unregulated funds which previously qualified for the gross roll-up regime will suffer marginal tax rates on the income distribution on or after 20 February 2007 where the interest in the fund would qualify as a PPIU if the fund were regulated. Capital gains from such funds would be taxed at 20 per cent. Investors who invest in unregulated EC/EEC or OECD offshore funds on or after 20 February 2007 will also be subject to this tax treatment;

(E)   The PPIU provisions which provide for a 43 per cent tax rate on income distributions and disposals in certain specified circumstances will only apply to regulated funds that qualify for the gross roll-up regime, The 43 per cent tax rate will apply from 20 February 2007 to any income distributions or capital gains arising from that date in respect of an interest in a fund which qualifies as a PPIU;

(F)   Exemption from exit tax for non-resident unit holders who make non-resident declarations to the investment undertaking, *FA 2010, s 27* reduces the administrative burden in the case of such undertakings. The section allows the exemption to apply where appropriate equivalent measures have been put in place by the investment undertaking to ensure that unit holders in the undertaking are not resident or ordinarily resident in the State and the undertaking has received approval from the Revenue Commissioners. Approval may be given as respects any unit holder or class of unit holders, and subject to such conditions as the Revenue Commissioners consider necessary to satisfy themselves about the equivalent measures. The Revenue Commissioners can withdraw approval where the undertaking has failed to comply with the conditions.

There is also a chargeable event on 31 December 2000 in respect of all unit holders at that date where the undertaking either commenced on or after 1 April 2000 or was an IFSC fund on 31 March 2000. Certain exchanges of units in sub-funds or (from 15 February 2001) for other units in the undertaking (which, from 15 February 2001, must be at arm's length) are excluded, as are transactions relating to units held in recognised clearing systems and certain transfers between spouses or former spouses. The amount of the gain treated as arising is the amount of the payment in (*a*) or (*b*) above except where it is for the cancellation, redemption or repurchase of units. In the latter case, and on any other chargeable event, special provision is made for determining the amount of the gain. The rate of tax to be applied is the standard rate (see **2.5** 'Allowances, credits and rates') where (*a*) above applies, the standard rate plus three per cent where (*b*) or (*c*) applies and 40 per cent in the case of the deemed chargeable event on 31 December 2000.

The main exclusions are where the investment undertaking is in possession of the appropriate declaration from a unit holder which is a pension scheme, life assurance company, other investment undertaking, special investment scheme, unit trust, charitable body, a PRSA administrator and (from 1 January 2003) an RI resident company in the case of a money market fund and a credit union. Since 1 January 2003, investment by the Courts Service is excluded – the Courts Service must account for any exit tax due on the allocation of payments to beneficial owners but (from 1 January 2005) no tax arises on a change in fund manager [*FA 2003, s 53; FA 2005, s 40*] There is also an exclusion where the unit holder is in possession of the appropriate declaration from a unit holder which is non-RI resident or (not being a company) non-RI ordinarily resident, provided that certain other validating conditions are satisfied. Since 1 January 2002 this is extended to certain RI-resident entities. Other exclusions apply in relation to certain chargeable events before 1 January 2001 in the case of specified collective investment undertakings, to certain intermediary unit holders and on certain amalgamations. Payments to non-RI resident companies and non-RI resident and ordinarily resident individuals are excluded from income tax and (from 31 March 2006) capital gains tax.

As respects the unit holder, where not a company, payments received in respect of units in money or money's worth are not included in total income unless tax was not deducted from the payment (or the units are held in a recognised clearing system), in which case it is chargeable under Sch D, Case IV (in the case of a payment for cancellation, redemption, repurchase or transfer of units, after deducting the consideration given for the units). A distribution to a company unit holder from which tax has been deducted and which would otherwise be income chargeable to corporation tax is treated as the net amount of an annual payment chargeable under Sch D, Case IV from which standard rate tax has been deducted. If tax has not been deducted (or the units are held in a recognised clearing system), the payment is chargeable under Sch D, Case IV. Special provision is made for other payments to companies. No repayment of tax deducted may be made to any person other than a company within the charge to corporation tax (except in rectifying certain errors or in relation to exemptions under *ss 189, 189A* or *192* (see **16.19**, **16.18** and **16.26** 'Exempt income and special savings schemes' respectively)). Special rules apply to deemed 31 December 2000 chargeable events and to units denominated in a foreign currency. Since 25 March 2005, the provisions of *s 1078* (see **28.2**) relating to revenue offences and sanctions apply.

See below for Common Contractual Funds.

[*TCA 1997, ss 739B–739G, Sch 2B; FA 2000, s 58; FA 2001, ss 74, 75; FA 2002, ss 44, 45; FA 2003, ss 52, 56; FA 2004, s 29; FA 2005, ss 44, 142; FA 2006, ss 46, 47, 52, 53*]

Before 1 April 2000 (and continuing for undertakings other than 'specified collective investment undertakings' which commenced before that date), a special taxation regime applied **from 6 April 1994** (**25 May 1993** if business was not commenced before that date, **6 April 1998** in the case of 'designated' and 'guaranteed undertakings for collective investment') to '*undertakings for collective investment*', ie those set up and authorised under the *European Communities (Undertakings for Collective Investment in Transferable Securities) Regulations 1989 (SI 78/89)*, schemes which are, or are deemed to be, authorised unit trust schemes within the meaning of the

Unit Trusts Act 1990 (other than unit trusts within *s 731(5)(a)*, see **9.14** 'Capital gains tax', and special investment schemes within *s 737*, see **16.31** 'Exempt income and special savings schemes'), and any authorised investment company, within the meaning of *Companies Act 1990, Pt XIII*, which has been designated in that authorisation as being able to raise capital by promoting the sale of its shares to the public, but excluding any 'offshore fund' (see **32.8** 'Sch D, case IV') and 'specified collective investment undertakings' (see below). For those categories of collective investment undertaking excluded from these provisions (as above), the earlier provisions described below continue to apply.

Broadly, the income and a measure of gains of such undertakings are taxable at a rate equivalent to the standard rate of income tax. *Non-company unitholders* are not entitled to any credit for or repayment of tax paid by the undertaking, but have no further liability as regards any payments received from the undertaking in respect of the units, and no capital gains tax liability on the disposal of units acquired after 5 April 1994 (or 5 April 1988 where applicable). As regards any units held on 5 April 1994 (or 5 April 1998), a chargeable gain or allowable loss arises on disposal by a non-company unitholder by reference to the market value of the units on that date (with inflation indexing and exemption under *s 731* (see **9.14** 'Capital gains tax') as if disposed of on that date), unless:

(*a*)   a smaller gain or a smaller loss accrued by reference to the actual disposal, in which case the normal rules apply by reference to the actual disposal; or

(*b*)   (in the case of a gain) a loss accrued by reference to the actual disposal or (in the case of a loss) a gain accrued by reference to the actual disposal, in which case the disposal is treated as giving rise to neither a gain nor a loss.

For *company unitholders*, any payment received from the undertaking in respect of units is treated as the net amount of an annual payment, chargeable under Sch D, Case IV, from which income tax has been deducted at the standard rate. Any chargeable gain accruing on the disposal of units after 5 April 1994 (or 5 April 1998 where applicable) is similarly treated as the net amount of a gain from the gross amount of which capital gains tax has been deducted at the standard rate of income tax. The gross amount of the gain is brought into charge for the accounting period of the disposal, the capital gains tax treated as deducted being set off against corporation tax for the period, any excess being repaid to the company. As regards any units held on 5 April 1994 (or 5 April 1998), the above provisions apply only to that part of the chargeable gain which would have accrued had the units been disposed of at market value on 5 April 1994 (or 5 April 1998). These provisions do not apply to the computation of allowable losses. Special provisions apply in relation to financial traders such as banks and insurance companies.

For all unitholders, where the units were acquired in a no gain/no loss transaction, ownership is treated as having included that of the previous owner(s) prior to such transactions. The capital gains tax provisions relating to units held on 5 April 1994 (or 5 April 1998) do not apply in the case of units in undertakings which commenced business after 25 May 1993.

As regards the determination of the profits of an undertaking for collective investment which are liable to standard rate tax as above, the following specific provisions apply:

(i)   distributions (including the attached tax credit) received by the undertaking are taxable, the tax credit being available against its taxation liabilities, any excess being repayable;

(ii)   the capital gains tax exemption of government securities (see **9.7**(*f*) 'Capital gains tax') does not generally apply;

(iii)   assets (other than securities within (ii) above) are treated as disposed of and reacquired at market value at the end of each chargeable period, the resultant net gain or loss being spread over that period and subsequent chargeable periods, at the rate of one-seventh per twelve months chargeable period (the whole remaining balance being chargeable if the undertaking ceases business before the whole gain or loss has been charged or allowed, and any excess of the allowable loss on an actual disposal of an asset over the allowable loss had there been no deemed acquisition(s) and disposal(s) of the asset similarly being spread over seven years);

(iv)   if the undertaking was carrying on business on 25 May 1993, it is treated as having acquired its assets at market value on 5 April 1994 (or 5 April 1998 where applicable);

(v)   inflation indexing (see **9.9** 'Capital gains tax') does not apply to disposals;

(vi)   net allowable losses for a chargeable period are set against income arising in that period, any excess being carried forward; and

(vii)   on a disposal of securities after 27 March 1996, the acquisition cost in the CGT computation is reduced by the amount of any interest accruing after the disposal and receivable in the following chargeable or basis period, and that amount is carried forward to the following chargeable period as a loss on the disposal.

Since 6 April 2000, provision is made for a collective investment undertaking to exchange its assets for units in another undertaking without a chargeable gain arising. The units are treated as acquired at the capital gains tax base cost of the assets they replaced.

A '*designated undertaking for collective investment*' is a collective investment undertaking 80 per cent of whose assets (in terms of consideration given), on 25 May 1993, were land or unquoted RI securities. A '*guaranteed undertaking for collective investment*' is such an undertaking all of the issued units of which, on 25 May 1993, carried a right to a single payment of a fixed amount plus an amount (which may be nil) related to a stock exchange index or indices. The references to 5 April 1988 in relation to designated and guaranteed undertakings may be amended to an earlier 5 April (1994 or later) where, in the case of a designated undertaking, the 80 per cent limit ceases to be exceeded in the preceding year, and in the case of a guaranteed undertaking, a payment is made to unitholders in the preceding year other than in cancellation of the units.

Section 732 (see **9.14** 'Capital gains tax') has no effect in relation to undertakings for collective investment, and the provisions in *s 805* and *s 440* (see **36.1** 'Settlements' and **12.7** above respectively) for surcharges on undistributed income do not apply. 'Relevant payments' out of 'relevant profits' (as defined under the earlier legislation, see below), and payments for the cancellation, redemption or repurchase of units are similarly not treated as distributions (see **12.10** above). [*TCA 1997, ss 734(7)–(9), 738–739A; Sch 32 para 25; FA 1998, s 49; FA 1999, s 64; FA 2000, s 57(b)(c), Sch 2*]

Before **6 April 1994** (or **25 May 1993** or **6 April 1998** as appropriate, see above), a separate tax regime is applicable to collective investment undertakings (defined broadly as above, see *s 734(1)(a)*). This regime continues to apply after 5 April 1994 in the case of those collective investment undertakings excluded from the provisions generally applicable after that date (see above), and may also from a specified date apply to certain property investment limited partnerships of non-RI residents (subject to their authorisation by the Central Bank).

Where this applies, the '*relevant profits*' (ie 'relevant income' and 'relevant gains') are not chargeable to tax on the undertaking, but are chargeable in the hands of any unit holder to whom a '*relevant payment*' is made (ie a payment by virtue of rights as a unit holder, other than in respect of the cancellation, redemption or repurchase of a unit) out of those profits, and who would have been taxable in RI on those profits if they had been received direct. Income is treated as arising at the time of the payment and is chargeable under Sch D, Case IV, and gains are treated as capital distributions made by a unit trust (see **9.14** 'Capital gains tax').

As originally enacted, the unit trust schemes within these provisions were registered schemes within the meaning of the *Unit Trusts Act 1972*, but this was subsequently amended to refer to schemes which are, or are deemed to be, authorised schemes (whose authorisation has not been revoked) within the meaning of the *Unit Trusts Act 1990*. Also within the provisions is any authorised investment company (whose authorisation has not been revoked), within the meaning of *Companies Act 1990, Pt XIII*, which has been (and continues to be) designated in that authorisation as being able to raise capital by promoting the sale of its shares to the public.

Certain unit trust schemes which require, or have required, any or all participators to effect a policy of assurance upon human life (but without the units in respect of which the requirement applied becoming the property of the owner of the policy) are not collective investment undertakings for these purposes. Such schemes are, however, treated as collective investment undertakings with effect from 1 April 1992 where, not later than 1 November 1992, the trustees paid one-half of the capital gains tax which would have been chargeable if they had disposed of all scheme assets at market value on 31 March 1992, and notified the Revenue Commissioners accordingly. Unit holders are treated for capital gains tax purposes as having acquired their units on 31 March 1992.

Certain limited companies wholly owned by specified collective investment undertakings (as above), or by the trustees thereof, to enable them to invest in certain financial instruments, are themselves specified collective investment undertakings.

In relation to collective investment undertakings, *s 732* (see **9.14** 'Capital gains tax') has no effect, and the provisions in *s 805* and *s 440* (see **36.1** 'Settlements' and **12.7** above respectively) for surcharges on undistributed income do not apply. Relevant payments out of relevant profits, and payments for cancellation, redemption or repurchase of units, are similarly not treated as distributions (see **12.10** above).

Section 1034 is not to apply to treat a non-resident as taxable in the name of an agent in RI in respect of a relevant payment out of relevant profits.

'*Relevant income*' is income, profits or gains which in the hands of an RI resident individual would be taxable as income, and '*relevant gains*' are gains which would similarly constitute chargeable gains in the hands of an RI resident.

Undertakings other than specified collective investment undertakings (see above) are required to deduct and to account to the Revenue for (as to which see *Sch 18*) the 'appropriate tax' in respect of any relevant payment made out of profits to an RI-resident unit holder, and of any undistributed income at the end of an accounting period from which tax has not previously been deducted. The '*appropriate tax*' is tax at the standard rate of income tax at the time of the payment or at the end of the accounting period, as appropriate, less an allowance for any tax previously deducted from undistributed income out of which a relevant payment is made, and for tax deducted under any other provision of the Taxes Acts from profits out of which a relevant payment is made or from undistributed income. The unit holder receiving a relevant payment from which appropriate tax has been deducted (or out of relevant profits from which such tax has been deducted) is liable (as above) on the sum of the actual payment and the appropriate tax deducted therefrom, and is entitled to a credit for the appropriate tax and to repayment where the credit exceeds his liability to tax in respect of the relevant payment (eg where he is in fact not RI resident at the time of the payment). Any necessary apportionment of the appropriate tax is made on a just and reasonable basis by the inspector (or, on appeal, by the Appeal Commissioners).

[*TCA 1997, ss 734–736, Sch 18; FA 1989, s 18, Sch 1; FA 1990, s 35; FA 1991, s 19; FA 1992, s 36; FA 1998, s 42; FA 1999, s 85(c)*]

PPIU – Personal Portfolio Investment Undertaking. *Finance Act 2007* introduced a new provision dealing with the taxation of PPIU's. The new provisions introduce an anti-avoidance provision in respect of regulated onshore funds (investment undertakings) and regulated offshore funds which operate as personal portfolio investment vehicles for individual investors. The legislation proposes an application of a 20 per cent surcharge in respect of income and gains arising from such investments, which effectively increases the rate of tax to 43 per cent. This is similar to the approach adopted for the personal portfolio life policies in the Finance Act 2002.

The surcharge applies to a PPIU which is defined broadly as a regulated offshore or onshore fund where, under the terms of the fund, the assets or property are or may be selected or influenced by the investor or a person connected with or acting on behalf of the investor, This is also extended to include situations where the investor has the option or the right to exercise such selection powers or can appoint an investor adviser.

A fund is not a PPIU if:

(i)   the property selected is or was available to the public;

(ii)   the opportunity to select the property was widely marketed by the fund to the public;

(iii)   the fund does not subject any person to any more burdensome or different treatment to that of any other investor, and

(iv)   where the terms of the investment opportunity set out the capital requirement as identified in marketing publications and 50 per cent or more of the property available for selection is land, then any one investor can hold a maximum of 1 per cent of the fund.

General. There are information requirements relating to RI resident holders of units in collective investment undertakings, which must be satisfied by any intermediary for an undertaking which markets its units in RI but is situated in another member state. [*TCA 1997, ss 893, 894, 896, 899; FA 2001, s 232*] See also Statement of Practice SP–IT/1/92 and **28.13** 'Returns'.

Common contractual funds. Prior to 2005, RI legislation provided for a common contractual fund formed under the EU UCITS Directive [*TCA 1997, s 739C*] Since 2005, provision is made for other forms of common contractual fund. Essentially these are 'pooling' funds. The legislation provides that the funds are tax transparent for institutional investors and are exempt from deposit interest retention tax. Profits and gains are treated as arising or accruing to the unit holders in proportion to the value of the units they hold. Certain reporting requirements are imposed. From 2006, a reconstruction or amalgamation of funds is not a taxable event. [*TCA 1997, s 739I; FA 2005, s 44; FA 2006, s 45*]

Company carrying on a mutual business or not carrying on business. The provisions relating to tax credit, etc will not apply to any distribution by such a company unless it is made out of profits charged to CT or out of franked investment income. [*TCA 1997, s 844*]

Partnerships involving companies. As under IT, partners are assessed individually (see **30.6** 'Sch D, cases I and II'). There are provisions for apportionment of accounting periods and the relevant amount of any capital allowance or balancing charge which would be applicable under IT rules is transformed into a trading expense or receipt, respectively, for CT purposes. [*TCA 1997, s 1009*]

Amendments were made to the current position regarding the taxation of partnerships under *s 1008* to prevent the use of its provisions for anti avoidance purposes. The tax adjusted profits of a partnership must, for tax purposes, be apportioned fully between the partners each year with the profits so apportioned being taxable in the hands of the partners at marginal tax rates. [*FA 2007, s 30*]

Securitisation of assets. As originally enacted, the legislation relating to the securitisation of assets provided that a company carrying on only a business of managing mortgage loans, acquired at arm's length from companies whose trade consisted of or included the making of such loans, was treated as carrying on a trade within Case I of Sch D, with appropriate deductions in respect of bad and doubtful debts. Purely ancillary activities did not preclude this treatment, which was also extended to 'qualified companies' within *s 446* (see **12.18**(viii) above – broadly providers of financial services in the International Financial Services Centre in the Custom House Docks area of Dublin) carrying on a business of managing certain assets of non-RI residents, such as loans, leases, trade or consumer receivables and other debts (provided also that the assets were not created or acquired and are not held in connection with an RI branch or agency trade) and which, prior to introduction of the euro, had to be denominated in a foreign currency. [*TCA 1997, s 110 as originally enacted; FA 1998, Sch 2 para 3*]

With effect **from 6 February 2003**, the above provisions are replaced for interest paid or arrangements entered into from that date. These new provisions apply to RI-resident companies carrying on in RI a business of holding or managing (or both the holding and managing of) 'qualifying assets' (a 'qualifying company') and carrying on no other RI activities other than those ancillary to that business, and in relation to which the market value of all 'qualifying assets' held or managed at any one time is not less than €10,000,000 on the day on which the assets are first acquired or held. The company must have notified the Revenue of its intention to be a qualifying company. The provisions do not apply to a company if any transaction is carried out by the company otherwise than at arm's length (save for interest payments described below). '*Qualifying assets*' are broadly financial assets.

Included in *Finance Act 2011, s 40* is an extension to the definition of qualifying assets which can be acquired by a *s 110* company to include (a) commodities and (b) plant and machinery which is subject to lease and (c) an extension of the application of the section to additional carbon offsets (which were previously limited to greenhouse gas emissions allowances). This amendment applies from 21 January 2011.

Additional changes were introduced in the Act which restrict the ability of a *s 110* company to deduct interest on Profit Participating Loans in certain situations. A tax deduction will only be available for interest payments on PPL's made to:

(*a*)   Irish resident persons;

(*b*)   a pension fund, government body or other specifically tax exempt person resident in a treaty country, provided certain conditions are met;

(*c*)   a non-resident in a treaty country which generally applies tax on foreign source income, provided a deduction is not available by reference to the amount of interest received; and

(*d*)   under a quoted eurobond or a wholesale debt instrument, provided certain conditions are met.

There have been similar restrictions introduced for total return swap payments. This structure is now restricted so that a deduction will not now be available for payments made under a return agreement as defined in the legislation. This includes swaps and other arrangements where the return is dependent on the results of the *s 110* company's business or any part of that business.

Both of these amendments include grandfathering provisions so that they only apply to arrangements made after 21 January 2011. This should extend to most existing *s 110* companies so that they should not be impacted by these proposed provisions unless they issue new securities or swap agreements. *[FA 2011, s 40]*

Business activities carried out by qualifying companies are treated as trade activities within Sch D, Case III but computed on Sch D, Case I principles, with appropriate deductions (and charges) in respect of bad and doubtful debts (and recoveries). Losses arising in any accounting period may be carried forward and set against losses of a subsequent period provided that the company continues to be a qualifying company. There is no provision for these losses to be surrendered within a group.

Payment of interest based on profits or at a greater than commercial rate is not treated as a distribution under *s 130(2)(d)(iii)* (see **12.10** 'Corporation tax') unless the interest is paid under a tax reduction scheme out of assets acquired from the recipient of the interest. *[FA 2003, s 48]*

For the period **from 6 April 1999 to 5 February 2003**, the original provisions of *s 110* were replaced by provisions to broadly similar effect ('revised provisions') and continue to apply to arrangements entered into during that period. These revised provisions (as below) apply to '*qualifying companies*', ie RI-resident companies carrying on in RI a business of management of 'qualifying assets', and carrying on no other RI activities other than those ancillary to that business, and in relation to which the market value of all 'qualifying assets' acquired from any one '*original lender*' (ie any government, public or local authority, company or other body corporate) is not less than €12,690,000 throughout the three months following the first acquisition of such assets from that lender. They do not apply to a company if any transaction is carried out by the company otherwise than at arm's length (except as below). In the case of a company which is a 'qualified company' within *s 446* (as above), a *'qualifying asset'* is an asset of a non-RI resident original lender, acquired directly or indirectly from the original lender, consisting of, or of an interest in or a contractual right to, any loan, lease, trade or consumer receivable or other debt or receivable whether secured or unsecured, but excluding any asset created, acquired or held by or in connection with a branch or agency through which the original lender carries on a trade in RI. In the case of any other company, a *'qualifying asset'* is an asset of an original lender, acquired directly or indirectly from the original lender, consisting of, or of an interest in, any financial asset (within *s 496(4)(a)*).

Business activities carried out by qualified companies are treated as trade activities within Sch D, Case I, with appropriate deductions (and charges) in respect of bad and doubtful debts (and recoveries). Profits from business activities carried out by any other qualifying companies are treated as annual profits or gains chargeable under Sch D, Case III (**31**), but computed on Sch D, Case I principles, with appropriate deductions (and charges) in respect of bad and doubtful debts (and recoveries) provided, in the case of deductions, that they would have been deductible as an expense of the trade of the original lender (being a company or other body corporate) if proved or estimated to be bad before being acquired by the qualifying company.

With effect from 10 February 2000 to 5 February 2003, any interest or other distribution paid by a qualifying company to an original lender (or to a company which is a 75 per cent subsidiary of the original lender, or of which the original lender is a 75 per cent subsidiary, or which is a fellow 75 per cent subsidiary with the original lender of such a parent company) in respect of a security falling within *s 130(2)(d)(iii)* (see **12.10**(*d*)(iii) above) is not a distribution by virtue of that section unless more than 25 per cent of the market value of all qualifying assets acquired by the qualifying company from the original lender (or other company as above) at the time of acquisition of the qualifying assets is represented by such securities. The carrying out of a non-arm's length transaction which gave rise to interest etc to which this provision applies (and which is not within the exception) does not prevent the company being a qualifying company (as above).

[*TCA 1997, s 110; FA 1999, s 32; FA 2000, s 82*]

Trustee savings banks: amalgamations. Where any assets or liabilities of a trustee savings bank are transferred (or deemed to be transferred) to another under *Trustee Savings Banks Act 1989, Pt IV*, those banks are treated for tax purposes as the same person. [*TCA 1997, s 704*]

Trustee savings banks: reorganisation into companies. Special provisions apply on the reorganisation of one or more trustee savings banks into a company (whether controlled by the Minister for Finance or not), or of a company within *sub-para (i)* of the *Trustee Savings Banks Act 1989, s 57(3)(c)* (company controlled by the Minister) into a company within *sub-para (ii)* of that subsection (company not so controlled).

Capital allowances. The transfer does not give rise to any balancing adjustment, and the successor stands in the shoes of the trustee savings bank as regards subsequent allowances and charges, except that no carry-forward is permitted of allowances unused by the trustee savings bank.

Trading losses incurred by a company controlled by the Minister may not be carried forward for set off against profits of a company not so controlled.

Financial assets. Financial assets constituting trading stock are valued at cost on the reorganisation for the purposes of *s 89* (trading stock of discontinued trade, see **30.31** 'Sch D, Cases I and II'). The acquisition by the successor company of any assets, profits on whose disposal would be chargeable under Sch D, Case I, does not constitute a disposal, and the profit on disposal of those assets by the successor company is calculated by reference to the original cost to the bank.

Capital gains. The disposal of an asset by the bank to the successor company in the course of the reorganisation is treated as being at no gain/no loss, and on any subsequent disposal the successor is treated as if the original acquisition were the successor's acquisition. Unused allowable losses may be transferred to the successor. For rollover relief purposes (see **9.7**(*s*) 'Capital gains tax') the bank and the successor are treated as if they were the same person, and in relation to any debt transferred to the successor, for capital gains tax purposes (see **9.7**(*n*) 'Capital gains tax') the successor is treated as the original creditor.

[*TCA 1997, s 705, Sch 17*]

INVESTMENT IN FILMS

12.23 A new scheme of reliefs is introduced **from 23 January 1996**, replacing those previously applicable. The previous rules continue to apply to investments made before that date and to investments made by 31 March 1996 where certain requirements are satisfied (for details of which see 2002 edition and earlier) .

Investments after 22 January 1996 (and not within the transitional provisions described above). An 'allowable investor company' which makes a 'relevant investment' in a 'qualifying company' on its own behalf during the 'qualifying period' commencing on 23 January 1996 and ending on **31 December 2008** may claim a 'relevant deduction' from its total profits for the accounting period in which the investment is made of 80 per cent of the 'relevant investment'. The relief was extended for four years until 31 December 2012. [*FA 2008*] This change was subject to a Ministerial Order (made on 13 September 2008). The relief has again been extended to 31 December 2015. The provision is subject to a Ministerial Order. [*FA 2011, s 32*] The overall ceiling on qualifying expenditure for any one film is increased from €35,000,000 to €50,000,000. [*FA 2008, s 32*] The relevant deduction has been decreased from 100 per cent to 80 per cent. This reduction was subject to a Ministerial Order. The order in relation to the extension of the relief and the aforementioned reduction was made on 13 September 2008. [*F(No 2)A 2008, s 28*] The relevant deduction has again been amended in *FA 2010, s 38*. The amendments to sub-ss (3) and (8) provide for all investors to carry forward 100 per cent of the amount of any unused relevant deduction to the following accounting period or, year of assessment, as the case may be. This is consistent with the amount of the relevant deduction to be allowed being increased from 80 per cent to 100 per cent of the relevant investment. Where the 'relevant deduction' exceeds those profits, 125 per cent of the excess is carried forward and treated as a *'relevant investment'* made in the following accounting period.

There are three limitations on the aggregate relief which may be obtained by the company and any 'connected companies' (within *s 10*) in any period of twelve months ending on an anniversary of 22 January 1996 and in the period 23 January 1999 to 5 April 2000:

(a)   an overall limitation on the aggregate of investments for which relief may be obtained of €10,160,000/£8,000,000 (all necessary apportionments being made by the inspector or, on appeal, the Appeal Commissioners);

(b)   relief for investments in any one 'qualifying company' may not exceed €3,810,000/£3,000,000; and

(c)   no more than €3,810,000/£3,000,000 may be invested to enable qualifying companies to produce films the total production cost of which (or of each of which) exceeds €5,080,000/£4,000,000.

The limit in (a) was €7,618,428.47/£6,000,000 in the year to 22 January 1997. It was reduced by any amount paid in that year and relieved under the old rules under the transitional provisions described above. The limit in (b) was €2,539,476.16/£2,000,000 for investments made before 26 March 1997, the €3,810,000/£3,000,000 limit in (c) similarly having been set at €2,539,476.16/£2,000,000 in the year commencing 23 January 1996.

An '*allowable investor company*' is any company not connected with the 'qualifying company'. A '*qualifying company*' is a company which exists solely for the purposes of producing and distributing a single 'qualifying film'. Since 6 April 2000, it is required to be either resident and incorporated in RI or carrying on a trade in RI through a branch or agency (the requirement before that date being that it be incorporated and resident in RI and not resident elsewhere). Companies with names including the words 'Ireland', 'Irish', 'Éireann', 'Éire' or 'National' are excluded with effect from 29 April 1997.

A '*qualifying film*' is a film produced on a commercial basis for theatrical or television distribution (excluding advertising programmes or commercials) certificated for the purpose by the Minister for Arts, Culture and the Gaeltacht. The conditions for such certification (which take account of the contribution of the film to the development of the film industry in RI and to cultural enhancement) include requirements:

(a)   that a minimum percentage of production work is carried out in RI (normally 75 per cent, but may be as low as ten per cent).This requirement ceased to apply from 1 January 2005;

(b)   that the proportion of total production costs met by 'relevant investments' does not exceed a permitted maximum. Since 20 July 2000 this is 66 per cent where those costs do not exceed €5,080,000/£4,000,000, reducing to 55 per cent where they exceed €6,350,000/£5,000,000, but with a limit on the costs met by 'relevant investments' of €15,000,000 from 1 January 2005 (€10,480,000/ £8,250,000 previously). Increased limits of 80 per cent of costs and a maximum cost of €35,000,000 will apply from a date to be appointed. [*FA 2006, s 18*] The overall ceiling of expenditure for any one film has been increased from €35,000,000 to €50,000,000. [*FA 2008, s 32* – this change was subject to a commencement order of the Minister for Finance after clearance with the European Commission which was made on 13th September 2008] Prior to 20 July 2000, the limits are 60 per cent, 50 per cent and £7,500,000 instead of 66 per cent, 55 per cent and £8,250,000, and where the percentage of production work carried out in RI is less than 50, the limit is a similar percentage of 'relevant investments'. Also prior to 20 July 2000, the percentage limits and the £7,500,000 maximum are increased by ten per cent where either (i) principal photography commences between 1 October and the following 31 January and continues to completion without unreasonable delay, or (ii) post-production work is to be carried out wholly or mainly in RI, and the £7,500,000 (£8,250,000) maximum is doubled where at least one-half of the production cost met by 'relevant investments' is met by allowable investor companies; and

(c)   that the Minister is notified in writing of the commencement of principal photography (or of animation or model work).

Such conditions may be amended, revoked or added to by written notice to the qualifying company, and failure to comply with a condition will result in the withdrawal of relief (see below) and may lead to revocation of the certificate.

A certificate will not be issued where production had commenced before certification was applied for.

Since 1 January 2005, certification is by the Revenue Commissioners following the issue of authorisation by the Minister for Arts, Sport and Tourism. Application is made in the first instance to the Revenue Commissioners who, following the issuing of authorisation from the Minister and examination of the company's proposal, may issue a certificate stating that the film is a qualifying film. The conditions attaching to the certificate include those specified in the authorisation from the Minister, including the level of employment in RI; a condition in relation to the minimum amount of money to be expended directly on employment and the provision of certain services and a condition that the total cost of the film will not exceed the specified percentage. Detailed regulations are to be made by the Revenue Commissioners with the consent of the Minister covering the administration of the relief. The Revenue Commissioners may refuse to issue a certificate where they believe that:

(i)   the budget or any part of the proposed expenditure is inflated;

(ii)   there is no commercial benefit from setting up the company; or

(iii)   the company will not meet the qualifying conditions.

A company is not a qualifying company unless:

(i)   it notifies the Revenue Commissioners in writing of when principal photography commences;

(ii)   save in limited circumstances, the financial arrangements that it enters into are with resident persons registered or operating in EU member states or in countries with which RI has a double tax agreement;

(iii)   it provides evidence to vouch all expenditure if requested;

(iv)   it notifies the Revenue Commissioners in writing of the date of completion of production and provides a copy of the film and a compliance report to them within the period specified in the regulations.

The Revenue Commissioners may amend or revoke a condition or add a condition into a certificate and may consult with any person as they consider necessary to carry out their functions. From 2006, any function of the Revenue Commissioners may be delegated to an authorised officer. [*FA 2004, s 28; FA 2005, s 36; FA 2006, s 18; FA 2010, s 38*]

A '*relevant investment*' is a sum of money paid directly to the qualifying company for shares in the company to enable it to produce a film for which the Minister (the Revenue Commissioners, since 1 January 2005) has given notice that a certificate (as above) has been duly applied for, and which is so used within two years of receipt. There must be no agreement for repayment of the sum, except in the event of a refusal of certification by the Minister (or Revenue Commissioners). The investment must be made for *bona fide* commercial reasons and not as part of a tax avoidance scheme, must be used in the production of a qualifying film, and must be made at the risk of the allowable investor company (and neither that company nor any person connected with it may be entitled to receive any payment or benefit from the qualifying company other than an arm's length payment for goods or services or a payment out of the proceeds of exploiting the film under the terms of the investment).

A claim to relief must be accompanied by a certificate (form FILM 3) from the qualifying company in prescribed form, and may be allowed once the sum which will, if the conditions are fulfilled, be a 'relevant investment' has been paid and principal photography (or animation or model work) has commenced. The company certificate requires authorisation by the Revenue Commissioners (form FILM 2), and there are information and penalty provisions in this regard.

Relief is withdrawn if any subsequent event or failure invalidates the claim, by a Sch D, Case IV assessment (at any time) for the accounting period for which the relief was given.

Where relief is or would, on a claim, be given under these provisions, no other tax relief is given for the sum representing the 'relevant investment'. If, however, the 'relevant investment' is made by way of subscription for new ordinary shares in the qualifying company, and the shares are held for at least one year, then the allowable cost for capital gains tax purposes on a subsequent disposal is determined disregarding the relief under these provisions, except that any resulting loss is restricted to the excess of the sum of 20 per cent of the 'relevant investments' and any other allowable deductions over the consideration received for the disposal.

Investments by individuals. A similar relief applies to investments by a '*qualifying individual*', ie an individual not connected with the qualifying company. A 'relevant deduction' may be made from the individual's total income in respect of 'relevant investments' (as above) in the period from 23 January 1996 to 31 December 2008, up to a maximum of (increased to €50,000 but subject to a Ministerial Order [*F(No 2)A 2008, s 28*]) €31,750/£25,000 (for 2001 only, £18,500) of investments in any year of assessment (reduced, for 1995/96, by any sums paid in that year but relieved under the old rules under the transitional provisions described above). The deduction is 80 per cent of such investments. Investments totalling less than €250/£200 (for 2001 only, £148) in a '*qualifying company'* in a year of assessment are excluded (although investments by a spouse whose income is, by election, treated as that of the individual are treated as made by the individual). Where the €31,750/£25,000 limit is exceeded, or where the 'relevant deduction' exceeds total income for a year of assessment, 125 per cent of the 'relevant deduction' which would otherwise have been available is carried forward and treated as a 'relevant investment' made in the following year and, if then unrelieved, in succeeding years of assessment. No amount may, however, be carried forward to a year after 2004. Such brought-forward amounts are relieved in priority to current year investments, those in respect of earlier years being relieved in priority to those in respect of more recent years. Other conditions, etc apply broadly as for investments by allowable investor companies (as above). [*TCA 1997, s 481, Sch 32 para 22(1)(6)–(8)*; *FA 1998, s 32*; *FA 1999, s 61*; *FA 2000, s 48*; *FA 2001, Sch 2 para 23*; *FA 2002, Sch 6 para 3(k)*; *FA 2003, s 58*; *FA 2004, s 28*; *FA 2005, s 36*; *FA 2006, s 18*]

TAX CREDIT

12.244 Tax credits are abolished after 5 April 1999. [*TCA 1997, s 136(1)*; *FA 1998, Sch 5 para 1*; *FA 2000, Sch 2*]

See **13.12** 'Deduction of tax at source' as regards dividend withholding tax applicable from that date.

TRANSFERS OF ASSETS – EC DIRECTIVE 2005/19 AMENDING EEC DIRECTIVE 90/434/EEC

12.25 *Sections 630–638* give effect to certain elements of the 'Mergers Directive' (90/434/EEC) as amended which were not already covered by RI legislation. These relate in the main to transfers of assets where trades are transferred in exchange for shares. Since 1 January 2006, the provisions apply to a European public limited liability company (Societas Europaea or SE) and to a European Cooperative Society (SCE). [*FA 2006, s 60*]

Transfers of assets generally. Where a company transfers the whole or part of a trade carried on in RI to another company in return for securities of the transferee, then:

(i)   the transferee takes over the capital allowances position of the transferor, no balancing allowances or charges arising on the transfer;

(ii)   the transferee takes over the chargeable gains position of the transferor, the transfer giving rise to no disposal for this purpose; and

(iii)   if the transferee disposes of the assets acquired within six years, the allowable deductions on the disposal are reduced by the appropriate proportion of the net chargeable gains which would have arisen on the transferor but for (ii) above.

(i)–(iii) above do not, however, apply if:

(*a*)   immediately after the transfer, the assets are not used by the transferee in an RI trade, or the transferee would not be chargeable in respect of any gains were it to dispose of any of the assets, or any of the assets are exempt from RI tax on disposal under a double taxation agreement; or

(*b*)   the transferor and transferee jointly so elect (by the due date for the return for the transferor's accounting period of the transfer, see **28.11** 'Returns').

[*TCA 1997, s 631*]

Transfer of asset to parent company. Where an asset in use for an RI trade is transferred to a company owning the whole of the transferor's capital, and the transfer would not otherwise fall within *s 617* (transfers within a group, see **12.15** above), then *ss 617–619* have effect as if the companies were RI-resident, provided that the asset is, immediately after the transfer, used in an RI trade, and that *s 631* (see above) does not apply. The exclusions from *s 631* described at (*a*) and (*b*) above apply also for these purposes. [*TCA 1997, s 632*] An anti-avoidance provision is being introduced to prevent the deferral of capital gains tax by the use of the gross-roll-up regime. The section provides that the capital gains tax deferral rules do not apply where assets are transferred into companies which are set up under *CA 1990, Pt XIII* and which are covered by the grossroll-up taxation regime. [*FA 2008, s 42*]

Transfer of development land. Where a company disposes of development land (see **9.16** 'Capital gains tax') to another company, *s 631* (see above) does not apply to the disposal, and *s 615* (reconstructions and amalgamations, see **12.5** above) would apply had the disposal not been of development land, then the disposal is treated as being at no gain/no loss, the acquiring company taking over the chargeable gains position of the disposing company. [*TCA 1997, s 633*]

Credit for tax. Where an RI-resident company transfers the whole or part of a trade carried on through a branch or agency in another Member State to a non-resident company, including all the assets used in the trade, and the consideration for the transfer consists wholly or partly of securities of the transferee company, then foreign tax which would have been payable on the transfer but for the Directives, or for domestic legislation deferring a charge to tax on gains in the case of such a transfer, is treated as tax payable for the purposes of double tax relief. [*TCA 1997, s 634*]

Anti-avoidance. *ss 631–634* (see above) do not have effect as respects a transfer unless it can be shown that the transfer was effected for *bona fide* commercial reasons and not as part of a scheme or arrangement a main purpose of which was the avoidance of income tax, corporation tax or capital gains tax. [*TCA 1997, s 635*]

Returns are required by the transferor company of transfers within *ss 631–634* (above), within nine months of the end of the accounting period of the transfer. [*TCA 1997, s 636*]

There are also provisions for such further relief to be given as the Revenue Commissioners consider just and reasonable in implementation of the Directive [*TCA 1997, s 637*], and for adjudication on any necessary apportionments. [*TCA 1997, s 638*]

ADVANCE CORPORATION TAX

12.26 Advance corporation tax is abolished for distributions made after 5 April 1999. [*TCA 1997, s 159; FA 1998, Sch 5 para 11*] Provision remains for set-off of 'surplus advance corporation tax' against a company's corporation tax liability on income for a period. 'Surplus advance corporation tax' is tax paid by a company in respect of distributions made prior to 6 April 1999 and neither repaid to it nor set against its corporation tax liability for a preceding accounting period. Broadly, income is defined as profit net of chargeable gains and before deductions for charges on income, expenses of management and other sums deductible from profits. [*TCA 1997, s 845B; FA 2003, s 41*]

TONNAGE TAX

12.27 Since 28 March 2003, certain shipping companies may elect for their shipping trade profits to be calculated by reference to the tonnage of the ships used in the trade and to be charged to corporation tax at a flat 12.5 per cent rate under a 'tonnage tax' regime. For details of the new regime, see *ss 697A–697Q, Sch 18B; FA 2002, s 53; FA 2003, s 62* and *FA 2006, s 67*.

TAX RELIEF FOR START UP COMPANIES

12.28 A new relief for start up companies is introduced in respect of companies that commencing to trade in 2009. This relief has been extended to companies that commence to trade in 2010. [*FA 2010, s 44*] This exemption has been extended for companies starting up in 2011. It applies for companies with an accounting period on or after 1 January 2011, [*FA 2011, s 34*] The exemption is granted in respect of the profits of a new trade and chargeable gains on the disposal of any assets used for the purposes of a new trade.

The exemption is granted by reducing the total corporation tax (including that amount referable to chargeable gains) relating to the trade to nil.

The relief has been amended so that the value of the relief will be linked to the amount of Employers' PRSI paid by a company in an accounting period, taking account of the Employer Job (PRSI) Incentive Scheme, subject to a maximum of €5,000 per employee and an overall limit of €40,000. If the amount of qualifying Employers' PRSI paid by a company in an accounting period is lower than the reduction in corporation tax otherwise applicable, relief will be based on this lower amount. The purpose of this change is to better target the relief at companies generating employment. This section is effective for accounting periods ending after 1 January 2011.

Prior to *FA 2011*, full relief was granted where the total amount of corporation tax payable by a company for an accounting period did not exceed €40,000. Marginal relief was granted where the total amount of corporation tax payable by a new company for an accounting period amounted to between €40,000 and €60,000. There was no relief where the corporation tax payable is €60,000 or more.

The exemption is available for a period of three years from the commencement of the new trade and separate exemptions are available for each new trade. However the relief will cease if part of the trade is transferred to a connected person. A company that takes over an existing trade or part of a trade, which was carried on in the State by another person, will not qualify in respect of the income the trade taken over. Service companies within *s 441* will not qualify and trades liable to corporation tax at the 25 per cent rate are excluded.

Finance Act 2011, s 34 introduced one final change to the relief such that the section now excludes a trade set up by a new company, the activities of which, if carried on a by an associated company of the new company, would form part of an existing trade carried on by that associated company.

It is proposed that this relief should comply with the EU *de mininis* aid Regulation which imposes a ceiling for State-aid under which assistance to a single recipient is deemed to have negligible impact on trade and competition and consequently does not require formal notification to the European Commission. The ceiling for aid under the *de minimis* rules is lower for the road transport sector than for other sectors and this is reflected in the legislation. While formal notification of this measure is not considered necessary, the section will not come into effect until discussions are held with the European Commission to ensure that the requirements of the *de minimis* Regulation are met. [*F(No 2)A 2008, s 31*]

NATIONAL ASSET MANAGEMENT AGENCY

12.29 *Finance Act 2010, s 25* has introduced certain provisions inserted by the *National Asset Management Agency Act 2009*. The provisions amend *ss 644AB* and *649B* which concern the circumstances in which a special 80 per cent tax rates is to be applied to "windfall" profits or gains from certain land disposals.

Section 644AB contains the income tax and corporation tax provisions and *s 649B* contains the capital gains tax provisions. The amendment changes both sections in the same way.

The amendment provides for an exemption from the 80 per cent tax rate for disposals of small sites. For the purposes of the exemption, a small site is one that does not exceed 0.4047 hectares (one acre) in size and whose market value at the time of disposal does not exceed €250,000.

Sections 644AB and *649B*, as introduced, only deal with decisions to rezone land from one type of permitted land use to another. In certain circumstances, planning authorities may decide to grant planning permission for developments that contravene, in a significant way, the Development Plan for a particular area. As with rezoning decisions, such decisions may have the effect of increasing the market value of land. The amendment therefore subjects any profits or gains that are attributable to a 'material contravention' decision by a planning authority to the 80 per cent tax rate.

The exemption for small sites will apply in respect of disposals taking place on or after 30 October 2009. A later date of 4 February 2010 (publication date of Finance Bill) will apply to land disposals taking place following a 'material contravention' decision that is made on or after that date.

13 Deduction of Tax at Source

13.1 Any annuity or other annual payment (except annual interest, rents chargeable on the recipient under Sch D, Case V (**33**), and certain maintenance payments, see **23.3** 'Married persons'). In relation to such payments and subject to **13.4** below in relation to payments between associated companies in the EU:

(*a*)   if payable wholly out of taxed income, no relief is given for the payment but the payer is entitled when making the payment to deduct and retain a sum representing standard rate tax from it [*TCA 1997, s 237*];

(*b*)   if not payable wholly out of taxed income, the payer *must* deduct standard rate tax and account to the Revenue for tax on so much of the payment as was made out of untaxed income [*TCA 1997, s 238*].

Where a payment, due in a year in which it could have been paid wholly or partly out of taxed income, is paid in a later year otherwise than out of taxed income, it is understood that an allowance is, by concession, made, in fixing the amount payable under (*b*) above, for the tax the payer would have been entitled to deduct under (*a*) above if the payment had been made on the due date.

See, however, **3.10** 'Anti-avoidance legislation'.

All deductions will be made at the standard rate in force when the payment becomes due where (*a*) above applies or at the time of payment where (*b*) above applies. [*TCA 1997, ss 237(1)(b), 238(2)*].

Annuities and annual payments by the National Treasury Management Agency and the National Development Finance Agency are paid without deduction of tax. [*TCA 1997, s 230(2); FA 2003, s 43*].

13.2 Annual interest. All interest is paid without deducting tax except interest paid by a company (unless a bank etc, see **20.1** 'Interest payable') or to a non-resident (save as noted at **13.4** below and **20.1** 'Interest payable'), in which cases deduction *must* be made and the *s 238* rules apply [*TCA 1997, s 246*], and interest paid by certain deposit-takers (see **13.8** below). In practice, deduction under *s 246* is not required where payments under £100 are made of penalty interest under *Prompt Payment of Accounts Act 1997* (see Revenue Tax Briefing Issue 31 p 13). There are special provisions for interest on quoted Eurobonds. [*TCA 1997, s 64*]. See also **38.240** 'Tax cases'.

13.3 Patent royalties. Payments for user of patent rights are governed by the provisions in **13.1** above. [*TCA 1997, ss 237(2), 238(2)*].

13.4 Interest and royalty payments – Implementation of *Council Directive 2003/49/ EC (3 June 2003)* **as amended.** Since 1 January 2004, withholding tax does not apply to certain payments of interest and royalties (including lease payments) and the recipient is not subject to income or corporation tax in RI on these payments. The payment must be bona fide and not for tax avoidance purposes and must be between companies that are associated for a minimum period of two years. Two companies are associated if one has at least 25 per cent voting control of the other or at least 25 per cent voting power of both companies is controlled by a third company. All companies must be resident in a Member State of the EU or, from 1 July 2005, resident in Switzerland (and not treated as resident in a non-EU member state under a Swiss double tax agreement) or be a permanent establishment in Switzerland. Interest paid by an RI resident company qualifies for the exemption. Interest paid by an RI branch of an EU resident company to a qualifying associated company qualifies for the exemption if the interest is paid for the purposes of an RI trade or rental activity. Payments made by an RI company to a branch of a company situate in a Member State also qualify for exemption where the receiving company is tax resident in another Member State and the associated company requirements are satisfied. The exemption does not apply in the following circumstances:

(i)   to penalty charges for late payment;

(ii)   interest paid on a debt that has no provision for capital repayment or where repayment falls due after 50 years;

(iii)   to royalties paid at greater than market value – in respect of the excess only;

(iv)   where the property giving rise to the entitlement to payment is held through a permanent establishment based in either RI or a non-EU Member State.

Greece, Portugal, the Czech Republic, Latvia, Lithuania, Poland and Slovakia will continue to apply withholding taxes on interest and royalties and Spain will continue to apply withholding tax on royalties during the transitional period. Provision is made for credit to be given on such withholding tax against domestic liabilities.

Reporting requirements operate from 1 July 2005 or such later date as directed by ministerial order. (see **20.4**) [*TCA 1997, s 267G–267K; FA 2004, s 41 and Sch 1; SI 644/ 04; FA 2005, s 50; 144; FA 2006, s 127, Sch 2*]

13.5 Tax under-deducted because of a change in the standard rate may:

(*a*)   in the case of interest, dividends etc payable by an agent, be charged on the recipient under Sch D, Case IV; or

(*b*)   in the case of annual payments, etc by persons entitled to deduct at source, be deducted from the next payment or, if no next payment, recovered as a debt due.

The above does not apply to a distribution by a company. [*TCA 1997, s 1087*]

13.6 Dividends. See **13.12** below as regards dividend withholding tax applicable from 6 April 1999. Dividend warrants, etc must show the tax related to the payment. [*TCA 1997, s 152; FA 1998, Sch 5 para 7; FA 2000, Sch 2*]

13.7 Purchased life annuities. The capital element in such annuities (as defined) is not treated as income (except where, for other tax purposes, a lump sum payment has to be taken into account in computing profits or losses). [*TCA 1997, ss 788, 789; FA 1999, s 20*]

13.8 Contractors in the construction industry or forestry or meat processing must deduct tax at 35 per cent from payments to sub-contractors, and account for the deductions monthly to the Revenue (including nil returns where appropriate), unless the sub-contractor produces a certificate (form C2) from the Revenue Commissioners enabling him to be exempted from such deduction. *Finance Act 2011, s 20* provides for a streamlined and modernised RCT system. A new online electronic RCT system has been introduced. A Principal will now have to apply online to Revenue to ascertain how much RCT, if any, should be deducted from payments to contractors engaged to carry out relevant operations. The rate will be communicated to both the Principal and the contractor.

The RCT withholding rate applicable going forward will depend on each contractor's own tax status.

(*a*) subcontractors who satisfy the current criteria for a C2 card will qualify for the 0% rate;

(*b*) a standard 20% RCT rate will apply to subcontractors who are registered for tax with an established compliance record;

(*c*) the 35% rate will remain and apply to subcontractors who are not registered with Revenue or where there is a history of non-compliance. The 35% rate also applies where a principal fails to apply for advance clearance.

Interim repayments to subcontractors will be replaced by an offset system as opposed to obtaining periodic repayments. The commencement of this new scheme is subject to a Ministerial Order.

There is provision for a reduced return/payment frequency on the part of principal contractors [*FA 2010, s 26*]. The provisions also extend the powers of the Revenue Commissioners to (i) require principals to submit additional information on the return form and (ii) allow the issuing of C2s to cover two tax years. The definition of construction payments has been extended to include the installation in or any or on any building of systems of telecommunications. The list of principal contractors who are obliged to operate RCT is extended to include any person carrying on a business involving the development of land and a board or body established under royal charter. [*FA 2007, s 35*] Since 7 March 2006 these provisions apply to operations carried on in RI irrespective of (a) the place of execution of the contract, (b) where payments under the contract are made and (c) whether or not the principal and sub-contractor are non-resident in RI or not liable to RI tax on the operations. Returns may be filed electronically from 14 April 2003. In certain cases where payment is made into a specified bank account, only details of form C2 have to be provided to the contractor. Before issuing an exemption certificate the Commissioners must be satisfied that the sub-contractor has permanent premises with proper equipment, stock and other facilities to carry out construction work (as defined) and has a satisfactory record of dealing with his tax affairs, etc. This requirement extends to connected persons in certain circumstances. The 'connected persons' rule is amended to provide that a person connected with a company engaged in a construction, land development, meat processing or forestry processing business must operate RCT in payments made by that person to a subcontractor in the performance of a relevant contract. The amendment is primarily aimed at companies obliged to operate RCT because they are connected with a company engaged in the business of land development or construction. In future, those companies will not have to operate RCT where they engage a subcontractor solely to carry out work on their own business premises provided they are not themselves engaged in the land development or construction business. The amendment also ensures that a person, not engaged in the business of land development or construction, who is connected with a company in the meat or forestry processing areas, does not have to operate RCT where that person engages a subcontractor solely to carry out construction operations in relation to a private dwelling or their own business premises. [*FA 2008, s 35*] Since 2 February 2006 Revenue must also be satisfied that the sub-contractor will continue to have a satisfactory record in dealing with his tax affairs in the future. Revenue may make regulations relating to administrative procedures. The enabling provision which allows regulations to be made governing various aspects of RCT has been amended to allow Revenue to exclude a principal and subcontractor from the requirement to make an RCT1 declaration where one of them comes within a class or classes of persons to be specified in the regulations. [*FA 2008, s 35*] There is an appeal procedure where a certificate is refused or cancelled. Penalties apply to cases of fraud or evasion. Interest on arrears of tax deducted and payable to the Revenue is at **0.0322 per cent** per day or part (before 1 September 2002, at **1 per cent** per month or part) and is payable gross and *not* deductible. Since 1 January 2003, failure to make a return may result in additional interest charges. [*SI 761/04*] See Revenue Tax Briefing Issue 51 pp 11, 12 and Issue 58 pp 1, 3.

As regards contracts entered into with gangs or groups of sub-contractors, the contractor is obliged to take into account the tax status of each member of the gang or group in determining the appropriate deduction.

Regulations (*The Income Tax (Relevant Contracts) Regulations 2000 (SI 71/00)* as amended) require contractors and sub-contractors, before entering into a contract, to make a declaration in a specified form (Form RCT 1) that, having regard to guidelines published by the Revenue Commissioners, they have satisfied themselves that in their opinion the contract they propose to enter into is not a contract of employment (without prejudice to whether it is in fact such a contract). They may also require sub-contractors to supply to contractors the necessary information and particulars, and that declarations be kept and made available for inspection.

A number of amendments are being made to meet commitments contained in *Towards 2016 (the Ten-Year Framework Social Partnership Agreement 2006–2015)* in relation to the strengthening of the RCT system. The specific changes are:

(i)   an enabling provision is included to allow the Revenue Commissioners to make provision for the increased monitoring of RCT1 declarations by requiring such declarations to be delivered to them in certain circumstances;

(ii)   the existing fixed penalties applying for failing to comply with regulations requiring the making of an RCT1 declaration are being extended to include a failure to comply with regulations requiring the delivery of an RCT1 declaration to the Revenue Commissioners.

Penalties of up to €1,265/£1,000 may be imposed for a wide range of infringements of the requirements of the deduction scheme, and for offences committed or penalties incurred proceedings may be instituted up to ten years after commission of the offence. Since 25 March 2005, the provisions of *s 1078* (see **28.2**) relating to revenue offences and sanctions apply.

The tax deducted from the sub-contractor may be set against his liability to income tax, corporation tax, capital gains tax, VAT, PAYE, Social Welfare pay-related contributions, health contributions and employment and training levies; and any excess may be repaid. Since 31 March 2006 repayment claims are subject to a four-year time limit.

Since 2 February 2006, the previous practice of Revenue of applying a limit on payments to certain sub-contractors on foot of a form C2 is put on a statutory basis.

[*TCA 1997, ss 530, 531, 1078; FA 1998, ss 37, 133(1)(6); FA 1999, s 18; FA 2001, s 28, Sch 2 para 31, 32; FA 2002, ss 51, 129(1)(b); FA 2003, s 33; FA 2004, s 20; FA 2005, s 142; FA 2006, ss 43, 44*].

The Revenue Commissioners have powers of entry and inspection similar to those which apply in relation to PAYE. [*TCA 1997, s 904*].

See **38.57** 'Tax cases'.

For certification procedures generally, see Revenue Tax Briefing Issue 37 pp 8, 9 and, in relation to certificates issued in the short tax year 2001, Issue 43 p 35.

DEPOSIT INTEREST RETENTION TAX ('DIRT')

13.9 Payments of '*relevant interest*', ie (subject to special rules for special term accounts) interest in respect of a 'relevant deposit', are, from 6 April 2000, made under deduction of tax at one of three rates:

(1)   in the case of interest on special savings accounts or special term accounts (see below):

27 per cent from 1 January 2011, 25 per cent from 8 April 2009, 23 per cent from 1 January 2009, 20 per cent pre-1 January 2009;

(2)   in the case of interest on a 'relevant deposit' made on or after 23 March 2000 *other than* one either:

(i)   within (1) above,

(ii)   where the interest is payable at least annually, or

(iii)   which is a 'specified deposit' within *s 260* (see below),

at a rate 3 per cent higher than the standard rate of tax (see **2.5** 'Allowances, credits and rates') in force at the time of payment; or

(3)   in the case of interest on any other 'relevant deposit', at that standard rate.

Finance (No 2) Act 2008, s 24 increased the rate of DIRT by three percentage points with effect from 1 January 2009. The section also provides for a number of consequential amendments to *Pt 8* to cater for the increase in rates. (But see **13.4** above relating to payments by companies to associated companies resident in the EU.)

Previously, tax was deducted at the standard rate except in the case of 'special savings accounts', see below, where the deduction was at the rate of 20 per cent. The provisions of *s 246* (see **20.1** 'Interest payable') regarding deduction of tax cease to apply to such payments. A 'relevant deposit taker' must treat every deposit as a 'relevant deposit' unless satisfied that it is not so, but once satisfied that a deposit is not a 'relevant deposit' it may continue so to treat it unless and until it comes into possession of information reasonably indicative that the deposit is, or may be, a 'relevant deposit'.

A '*relevant deposit taker*' is any of:

(*a*)   the holder of a licence under *Central Bank Act 1971, s 9* or EEC equivalent;

(*b*)   a building society under the *Building Societies Acts* or EEC equivalent;

(*c*)   a trustee savings bank under the *Trustee Savings Bank Acts*;

(*d*)   the Post Office Savings Bank;

(*e*)   (from 1 January 2002) a credit union.

A '*relevant deposit*' is any deposit (as widely defined) held by a relevant deposit taker other than a deposit:

(i)   made by a relevant deposit taker, the Central Bank of Ireland, Icarom plc, the Investor Compensation Company Ltd, the National Pension Reserve Fund Commission (or the State acting through it), the National Development Finance Agency or the National Treasury Management Agency (or the State acting through it), by whom the interest on the deposit is beneficially owned;

(ii)   which is a debt on a security issued by the relevant deposit taker and is listed on a stock exchange;

(iii)   which, where the relevant deposit taker is resident in RI, is held at a branch outside RI;

(iv)   which, where the relevant deposit taker is not resident in RI, is not held at a branch in RI;

(v)   denominated in a foreign currency (but this exclusion does not apply to deposits made by individuals after 31 May 1991, unless additional to deposits made on or before that date with the same deposit taker and denominated in the same currency, and ceases to apply to any deposit made after 31 December 1992);

(vi)   in respect of which no person beneficially entitled to the interest is resident in RI, provided that the appropriate declaration (see *s 263*) has been made to the relevant deposit taker;

(vii)   which is made by, and the interest on which is beneficially owned by, a company which is or will be within the charge to corporation tax in respect of the interest, or a 'pension scheme', which has made the declaration as under *s 265* (or its predecessor) to the deposit taker;

(viii)   the interest on which is exempt under *s 207(1)(b)* (charitable exemption), provided that the appropriate declaration (see *s 266*) has been made to the relevant deposit taker;

(ix)   held by a qualifying approved retirement fund manager as such (see **2.24** 'Allowances, credits and rates'); or

(x)   from 13 June 2003, certain wholesale debt instruments (see **20.1** 'Deduction of tax').

Interest (and any terminal bonus) in respect of a certified contractual savings scheme (SAYE scheme, see **16.8**(iv) 'Exempt income and special savings schemes') is treated for this purpose as not being paid in respect of a relevant deposit where it otherwise would be.

A '*pension scheme*' for the purposes of (vii) above is an exempt approved scheme under *s 774* (see **17.26** 'Exempt organisations') or a retirement annuity contract or trust scheme under *ss 784, 785* (see **2.24** 'Allowances, credits and rates', **17.29** 'Exempt organisations').

As regards (vii) and (viii) above, with effect from 25 March 2002 the requirement for a declaration within *s 265* or *s 266* was replaced by a requirement to provide the deposit taker with the depositor's tax reference number or, in the case of a pension scheme for which there is no such number or a charity, with the number assigned by the Revenue to the employer to which the pension scheme related or the charity (CHY) number, and the deposit taker is required to include all such numbers in the return required under *s 891* (see **28.4** 'Returns'). A new sub-s (1A) is inserted into *s 256* which provides that deposit interest can be paid to the deposit taker with deduction of DIRT where, at any time of the year of assessment, the individual beneficially entitled to the interest or his or her spouse is 65 years of age or over and their total income does not exceed the relevant income tax exemption limit. The individual concerned is required to make a declaration to that effect to the relevant deposit taker. This has also been extended to certain other persons where the individual beneficially entitled to the interest or his or her spouse is permanently incapacitated or where the persons entitled to the interest are trustees of a special trust for permanently incapacitated individuals who are exempt from tax under *s 189A(2)*. [*FA 2007, s 34*]

'Interest' for these purposes includes any amount paid in consideration of the making of a deposit (including dividends or other distributions in respect of shares in a building society but excluding certain redemption bonuses on ACC Bonus Bonds), and any sum paid to a relevant deposit taker on terms under which it will be repaid on demand or at an agreed time or in agreed circumstances is a deposit. As respects deposits after 5 April 2001, it also includes amounts in excess of the amount deposited which are dependent on changes in any financial index. Interest credited is treated as paid. [*TCA 1997, ss 256, 257, 265, 266, 519C(3), 784A(6); FA 1986, ss 31, 32; FA 1995, ss 11(1), 167; FA 1998, s 131; FA 1999, ss 68(a), 76(1)(b); FA 2000, ss 23(1)(d)(iii), 28(1); FA 2001, s 55(a); FA 2002, s 20; National Pensions Reserve Fund Act 2000, s 30(c); FA 2003, s 40*]

The relevant deposit taker must, if requested, supply a statement to any person beneficially entitled to '*relevant interest*' (ie interest paid on a relevant deposit) of the interest paid and the tax deducted on any date. [*TCA 1997, s 262*]

The financial institution is required to issue a statement of the amount of DIRT tax deducted from an interest payment automatically rather than on request. [*FA 2010, s 33*]

The relevant deposit taker is required to obtain the tax reference number of a person making a specified deposit. [*FA 2010, s 33*]

Penalty provisions apply for failure to comply with the above requirements. [*TCA 1997, Sch 29*]

The Revenue Commissioners have powers of inspection in relation to the records of relevant deposit-takers, and are required to report the results to the Committee of Public Accounts. [*TCA 1997, ss 904A, 904B; FA 1999, s 207; FA 2000, s 68; FA 2003, s 46*]

Bogus non-resident accounts. Following the discovery that interest on a large number of accounts for which exemption had been claimed under (vi) above was in fact in the beneficial ownership of persons resident in RI, the DIRT (plus interest and penalties) was recovered from the financial institutions concerned. Under Revenue Statement of Practice SP–GEN 1/01, the beneficial owners concerned were given until 15 November 2001 to make full disclosure and payment of all liabilities relating to such accounts (the 'underlying tax'). The consequences of failure to disclose and pay by that date are set out in s 5 of the Statement of Practice. See Revenue Tax Briefing Issue 49 pp 3–5 and Issue 51 p 7.

Special term accounts are 'medium' or 'long term accounts' in which relevant deposits made by individuals aged 16 or over are held and which meet the various conditions in *s 264A*. '*Medium*' and '*long term accounts*' are accounts with relevant deposit-takers any deposits in which are required to be held for at least three or five years respectively. *s 264A* requires *inter alia* that the account is not a foreign currency account and is not 'connected' (as defined) with any other account of all or part of any of any other account. Deposits may not exceed £500/€635 per month apart from the initial deposit, which may consist of the transfer relevant deposits held with the same deposit-taker, and a single deposit not exceeding £6,000/€7,620 which may be made at any time. Interest added to the account is not treated as a deposit for this purpose, and may be withdrawn without restriction within twelve months of being credited. Otherwise, the three or five year holding period may be breached only on the death of the holder (or of one of joint holders), except that one withdrawal is permitted by a holder aged 60 or over provided that the account was opened before he or she attained that age. An individual may hold only one account (whether sole or joint), except that a married person may have a joint account with the spouse as well as a sole account, and may not simultaneously hold a special term share account with a credit union (see below). A signed declaration by the account holder to the deposit-taker is required, confirming that the various conditions (as above) are met and that any breach of those conditions will be notified to the deposit-taker. A return under *s 264B* must be made by the deposit-taker to the Revenue of all special term accounts.

The first €480 (for 2001, £278) of interest on a medium term special term account, and the first €635 (for 2001, £370) of interest on a long term special term account, is excluded from being relevant interest (and the holder may elect to change a medium term account to a long term account, the higher limit then applying from the following year of assessment). Such interest is exempt from income tax and excluded from total income for income tax purposes. To the extent that the interest is relevant interest, and accordingly suffers the 20 per cent deduction, no further liability to income tax arises in respect of the interest. Where an account ceases to be a special term account, all interest (including past interest) becomes relevant interest, past interest being treated for this purpose as having been paid on the date of the change. The special arrangements described above for relevant interest on special term accounts do not apply to interest (or past interest) which accordingly becomes relevant interest. Where past interest has already been withdrawn, the appropriate tax which would have been deducted is deducted from the relevant deposit.

[*TCA 1997, ss 256(1), 261A, 264A, 264B; FA 2001, s 57; FA 2002, s 21(a)(b)(c)*]

Credit union dividends. Where a member so elects, shares in a credit union may, by agreement with the union, be held in a special share account, to which the DIRT scheme applies as if the shares were a relevant deposit and the dividends relevant interest. An individual member may further elect that the special share account be a medium or long term special share account, the conditions for which, and the taxation of dividends on which, are as for special term accounts (see above). [*TCA 1997, ss 267A–267F; FA 2001, s 57; FA 2002, s 21(d)(e)(f)*]

Special savings accounts are accounts not denominated in a foreign currency opened by an individual after 1 January 1993 and before 6 April 2001 in which a relevant deposit is made and which satisfies the conditions of *s 264*, including the making of a declaration as required under that section to the deposit taker. A deduction rate of 20 per cent applies to interest on such accounts, and no further liability to income tax arises in respect of such interest. The conditions of *s 264* are broadly as follows:

(*a*)   the individual must be of full age and beneficially entitled to the interest;

(*b*)   no withdrawals may be made within three months of opening the account;

(*c*)   withdrawals must be subject to 30 days notice;

(*d*)   the balance in the account must not exceed £50,000/€63,500;

(*e*)   there must be no agreements or arrangements affecting the interest rate for periods in excess of 24 months;

(*f*)   except for married couples, joint accounts are excluded;

(*g*)   only one account may be owned by an individual, except that married couples may have two single or two joint accounts;

(*h*)   the account must not be 'connected with' another account, ie neither account must have been opened or be operated in any respect by reference to the existence of the other;

(*i*)   all moneys held in the account must be subject to the same terms;

(*j*)   interest must not directly or indirectly be linked to, or determined by, the performance of stocks, shares, debentures or securities.

[*TCA 1997, ss 256(1), 264; FA 1986, s 37A; FA 1995, s 11(1); FA 2001, s 48(a)(iv)*]

It is understood that a transfer between branches of a bank will be disregarded in determining whether the account satisfies the above conditions.

See also **16.30** 'Exempt income and special savings schemes' as regards restrictions on this and other investments.

Liability to account for tax retained. The relevant deposit taker must, within 15 days from the end of each year of assessment, make a return to the Collector-General of the relevant interest paid in the year and of the tax retained, and pay over the tax retained. An assessment is not required, but may be raised where the tax is not paid over by the due date.

Finance Act 2010, s 33 provides for accelerated payments of DIRT tax by financial institutions to the Exchequer. This amendment will only take effect on the signing of a Ministerial Order.

The relevant deposit taker must also make a payment on account of the year-end liability by 20 October in each year of assessment, at least equal to the liability which would arise at the year end on the amount of relevant interest accrued (on a day-to-day basis) in the period from the first day of the year of assessment to 5 October in that year inclusive. If the payment on account exceeds the full liability, the excess is carried forward against future liability under these provisions. Again an assessment is not required but may be raised where necessary.

For 2001 and subsequent years of assessment, interest on relevant deposits is treated as accruing from day to day, and any interest so accrued which is unpaid on 31 December in a year of assessment is treated as relevant interest paid on that date, retention tax being accounted for accordingly. This does not apply if the interest cannot be determined until the date of payment, notwithstanding that the terms under which the deposit was made are fully complied with. When accrued interest on which tax is so accounted for is actually paid, a credit is given in the year of assessment of payment for the tax accounted for on accrual (relief being given against an earlier liability to account for tax before a later one).

Where the amount of retention tax paid for a year of assessment represents tax on less than a full year's accrued interest (for 2001 only, a full 270 days' accrued interest), the relevant deposit taker must make up the short-fall at the October payment date in the following year of assessment. In effect, a payment on that date will represent retention tax on a year's (or 270 days') accrued interest less the excess of the payment made in the first month of the previous year of assessment over the payment on account for that year. Credit will be given, where appropriate, against future payments.

There are provisions for the raising of assessments where no return is made or where the inspector is dissatisfied with a return, and for the adjustments necessary where an incorrect return is made. Interest at the rate of 1.25 per cent per month will arise where tax is paid late.

The normal income tax rules generally apply in relation to assessments, appeals, collection and recovery. [*TCA 1997, ss 258, 259; FA 2001, Sch 2 para 16, 17*]

Interest payable at intervals greater than one year. Where interest in respect of a 'specified deposit' made after 27 March 1996 is payable at intervals greater than one year, then unless the amount of the interest cannot be determined until the date of payment (notwithstanding that the deposit terms are fully complied with), the deposit taker is required to account for tax under these provisions on an annual basis. The interest is deemed to accrue from day to day, and to be relevant interest paid in the year of assessment in which it so accrues to the extent that it is not paid in that year. Tax so accounted for is set against the liability to account for tax when the interest is actually paid. There is, however, an exemption in certain cases where a payment on account is made (as above) of an appropriate amount. A '*specified deposit*' is a relevant deposit other than (i) a deposit held in a special savings scheme (see **16.29** 'Exempt income and special savings schemes') or (ii) a deposit made before 8 June 1996 under arrangements which were, or were being put, in place before 28 March 1996 in respect of which the interest is to any extent linked to or determined by changes in a financial index. [*TCA 1997, s 260; FA 2001, Sch 2 para 18*]

Taxation of relevant interest. Except as detailed below, tax retained out of relevant interest may not be repaid to any person who is not a company within the charge to corporation tax in respect of the payment. The gross amount is regarded as income chargeable under Sch D, Case IV and credit is given for the tax deducted. In the case of individual investors, where tax is deducted at the standard rate the standard rate band is extended by the gross amount chargeable for the year, and where tax is deducted at 3 per cent higher than the standard rate (see (3) above) the gross amount is chargeable at that higher rate, so that in either case no further liability arises. Except for the purposes of repayment claims by the sick and elderly (see below), the 'specified amount' for the age and low income exemptions (see **2.7**, **2.8** 'Allowances, credits and tax rates') is similarly increased by the amount of the grossed-up payment. Marginal relief in relation to those exemptions is calculated by reference to the tax payable after credit for DIRT, and the marginal relief limit of twice the specified amount is increased by the amount of the deposit interest.

Where a deposit not previously within these provisions becomes a relevant deposit, it is treated for Sch D, Case III (**31**) purposes as a separate source of income which ceases immediately before it comes within these provisions. Similarly where a deposit ceases to be a relevant deposit, it is treated for Sch D, Case III purposes as a separate source of income commencing immediately thereafter.

The exemption for small amounts of interest from the Post Office Savings Bank and certain other banks (see **16.7** 'Exempt income and special savings schemes') does not apply to interest paid in respect of relevant deposits.

[*TCA 1997, s 261; FA 1986, s 35; FA 1992, s 22; FA 2000, s 28(2)*]

Special rules apply to 'special savings accounts' (see above).

Repayments of retained tax may be made to a charity exempt under *s 207(1)* from income or corporation tax or to a qualifying trust exempt from income tax under *s 189A(2)* (see **16.18** 'Exempt income and special savings schemes'), where exemption may not have been agreed at the time of payment, and, on a claim not earlier than the end of the year to which the claim relates, to an individual who, or whose spouse, was aged 65 years or more at some time in the year, and to an individual who, or whose spouse, was, at the end of that year, permanently mentally or physically incapacitated from maintaining himself or herself. [*TCA 1997, s 267; FA 1999, s 12(b)*]

DEPOSIT INTEREST PAID BY EU LENDING INSTITUTIONS

13.10 Since 1 January 2005, interest received by RI resident individuals from lending institutions situate in other EU countries is subject to income tax at the standard rate and taxed under Case IV of Sch D provided that this tax is paid by the return filing date for the relevant year of assessment. Previously, the applicable rate was the marginal tax rate of the individual, taxed under Case III of Sch D. [*TCA 1997, s 267M; FA 2005, s 20*]

PAYMENTS FOR PROFESSIONAL SERVICES

13.11 Deduction of tax at the standard rate (see **2.5** 'Allowances, credits and rates') must be made from payments in respect of 'professional services' made to individuals, partnerships and companies by 'accountable persons'. Deductions are made from amounts *net* of VAT. **Since 25 March 2005**, payments made by an 'accountable person' to another 'accountable person' that is tax exempt are excluded as are payments made by an 'accountable person' to charities that are tax exempt (see **17.5** exempt organisations). [*TCA 1997, s 520; FA 2005, s 15*]

Where the 'accountable person' is an authorised insurer (see (*t*) below), payments to a medical practitioner in discharge of an insurance claim in respect of certain medical expenses are brought within the scheme. For this purpose, provision is made for payment direct to the practitioner by the insurer in relation to amounts so claimed, and regulations may be made to give full effect to these provisions.

The procedure applies generally for fees and similar payments, but does not apply to payments already covered by PAYE or the construction industry scheme established by *ss 530, 531* (see **13.8** above). Payments to non-residents come within the scope of the scheme, but it is understood that recipients in countries with which RI has a double taxation agreement will be entitled to receive a full refund if the income is not chargeable to RI tax. The procedure also applies to payments made on foot of *SI 388/02 European Communities (Late Payment in Commercial Transactions) Regulations 2002*. See Revenue Tax Briefing Issue 52 p 25.

Fees represented by the payments still have to be taken into account in calculating the profits or gains of the recipient for tax purposes. The tax deducted at source is, however, available for set-off, and provision is made for interim refunds to alleviate hardship, where a substantial proportion of fees is paid out to meet the expenses of the business.

The list of '*accountable persons*', includes:

(*a*)   A Minister of the Government;

(*b*)   A local authority within the meaning of *s 2(2) of the Local Government Act 1941*, and includes a body established under the *Local Government Services (Corporate Bodies) Act 1971*;

(*c*)   A health board;

(*d*)   The General Medical Services (Payments) Board established under the *General Medical Services (Payments) Board (Establishment) Order 1972 (SI 184/72)*;

(*e*)   The Attorney General;

(*f*)   The Director of Public Prosecutions;

(*g*)   The Revenue Commissioners;

(*h*)   The Commissioners of Public Works in Ireland;

(*i*)   The Legal Aid Board;

(*j*)   A vocational education committee or a technical college;

(*k*)   A harbour authority;

(*l*)   An Foras Áiseanna Saothair;

(*m*)   Údarás na Gaeltachta;

(*n*)   The Industrial Development Agency (Ireland);

(*o*)   Shannon Free Airport Development Company Limited;

(*p*)   The National Tourism Development Authority;

(*q*)   An institution of higher education within the meaning of the *Higher Education Authority Act 1971*;

(*r*)   Certain voluntary public or joint board hospitals;

(*s*)   An authorised insurer within *s 470* (for a list of which see Revenue Tax Briefing Issue 44 Supplement p 33).

The list includes the commercial State bodies and a number of non-commercial State bodies, and can be extended by Regulation. The full list is contained in *Sch 13 as amended*, but the Minister for Finance may further add to or delete from that list by Regulation (but without retrospective effect). The list has been amended to take account of the addition of seven new bodies, the change of the names of two bodies on the current list and the removal of two bodies from the up to date list. [*FA 2008*]

'*Professional services*' include:

(i)   services of a medical, dental, pharmaceutical, optical, aural or veterinary nature;

(ii)   services of an architectural, engineering, quantity surveying or surveying nature, and related services;

(iii)   services of accountancy, auditing or finance and services of financial, economic, marketing, advertising or other consultancies;

(iv)   services of a solicitor or barrister and other legal services;

(v)   geological services; and

(vi)   training services provided on behalf of An Foras Áiseanna Saothair.

Information and deduction forms. Recipients of professional fees must supply to the relevant accountable person:

(A)   in the case of a person resident in RI or a person having a permanent establishment or fixed base in RI:

(i)   details of their income tax or corporation tax number, and

(ii)   where relevant, their value-added tax registration number; or

(B)   in any other case, details of their country of residence and tax reference in that country.

Where that information has been supplied, the accountable person making a payment must give the recipient, in a form prescribed by the Revenue Commissioners (Form F45), particulars of:

(1)   name and address of recipient;

(2)   recipient's tax reference;

(3)   amount of gross payment;

(4)   amount of tax deducted; and

(5)   date of payment.

Accounting for tax deducted. Returns of all payments covered by the deduction scheme made in each income tax month, together with the tax deducted, must be submitted by the accountable person within 14 days (before 1 January 2002, 10 days) of the end of each income tax month. Nil returns are also required. The provisions relating to assessment, collection and recovery of relevant contracts tax (see **13.8** 'Contractors in the construction industry') are applied. [*FA 2003, s 10*] Revenue have powers of entry and inspection. [*FA 2003, s 159*]

Credit for tax borne. Credit is given for tax deducted:

(*a*)   in an accounting period of a company, for allowance against corporation tax for that period; or

(*b*)   in the basis period for a year of assessment in the case of an individual or partnership, for allowance against income tax for that year of assessment.

Where there is an interval between credit or basis periods or basis periods overlap, the common period or interval is deemed to be part of the second period only (except that where a twelve-month period of account ending between 1 January 2002 and 5 April 2002 inclusive is the basis period for both 2001 and 2002 (see **30.3** 'Sch D, Cases I and II'), it is deemed to be the basis period for 2001 only). The tax deduction form supplied by the accountable person (see above) must be produced in order to claim credit, with any necessary apportionment being made where the form refers to more than one person. Tax suffered cannot be set off more than once, or allowed both as a tax credit and as the basis for an interim refund (see below). Any excess of tax deducted over the corporation or income tax liability for a period may be repaid.

Interim refunds of tax suffered by deduction under these provisions in an accounting or basis period may be claimed in certain cases.

Ongoing businesses. Conditions for interim refund are that:

(i)   the accounts of the immediately preceding accounting or basis period must have been finalised, agreed and the tax thereon paid; and

(ii)   the claim must be supported by the appropriate tax deduction forms.

The amount of the interim refund will be the excess of the tax deducted and vouched as in (ii) above (less any previously refunded) over the tax liability referred to in (i) above, *less* any VAT, PAYE, or PRSI due but unpaid. Where the claim relates to the basis period for either 2001 or 2002, the tax liability referred to in (i) above is for this purpose reduced by 26 per cent (for 2001 claims) or increased by 35 per cent (for 2002 claims).

Commencing businesses. Where an interim refund is claimed for the first accounts period of a business, condition (ii) above applies as for ongoing businesses, but there are special provisions to determine the amount to be refunded. The inspector will, for that first period, determine tax at the standard rate on the figure resulting from the formula:

$$E \times \frac{A}{B} \times \frac{C}{P}$$

where   A   =   estimated payments for professional services of the period from which tax has been deducted at source

          B   =   estimated total income for the period

E   =   estimated allowable business expenditure during the period

P   =   estimated number of months and fractions of months in the period in respect of which the refund is made

C   =   estimated number of months and fractions of months in the period in respect of which the refund claim is made.

The resulting figure is compared with tax actually deducted (and not previously refunded) and the refund made is the lesser of the two figures.

Particular hardship. In cases of particular hardship, the Revenue Commissioners are enabled to waive any of the conditions and to authorise the inspector to make such refund as they consider to be just and reasonable. See Statement of Practice SP IT/3/90 for the circumstances in which such refund would be made and the basis of calculation of the refund. [*TCA 1997, ss 520–529, Sch 13; FA 1992, Sch 2 as amended; FA 1999, s 17; FA 2000, s 20; FA 2001, s 14, Sch 2 paras 28–30; FA 2003, s 10; FA 2004, s 5; FA 2005, s 13*]

DIVIDEND WITHHOLDING TAX

13.12 Since 6 April 1999, any RI-resident company making a 'relevant distribution' to a 'specified person' is, except as below, required to deduct an amount representing income tax at the standard rate (see **2.5** 'Allowances, credits and rates'). A '*relevant distribution*' is any distribution or deemed distribution within *ss 130–135* (see **12.10** 'Corporation tax'), *ss 436, 437* (certain payments by close companies, see **12.7** 'Corporation tax') or *s 816(2)(b)* (stock dividends made by quoted companies, see **3.7**(ii) 'Anti-avoidance legislation'), unless made to a Government Minister as such or the National Pension Reserve Fund Commission, and any unquoted company stock dividend within *s 816(2)(c)* giving rise to a charge under **32** 'Sch D, Case IV' (see **3.7**(iii) 'Anti-avoidance legislation'). A '*specified person*' is the person to whom the relevant distribution is made, whether or not that person is beneficially entitled to it. Distributions by collective investment undertakings (see **12.22** 'Corporation tax') are excluded, as are certain distributions to non-resident parent companies within *s 831* (see **12.11** 'Corporation tax') or out of certain exempt income or profits or disregarded income within *ss 140, 141* or *142* (see **12.10** 'Corporation tax').

The company must treat every relevant distribution to a specified person as within these provisions unless it is satisfied that one of the exemptions (see below) applies, in which case it may treat subsequent distributions to the specified person as not within these provisions until such time as it is in possession of information which can reasonably be taken to indicate that a distribution to that person is or may be within these provisions.

The company must retain all declarations (and accompanying certificates) and notifications (other than by the Revenue Commissioners) given to the company under *Sch 2A* (see below) for six years or, if longer, until three years after it has ceased to pay distributions to the person who made the declaration or gave the notification, and must make them available to the Revenue Commissioners when required to do so by written notice.

Finance Act 2010, s 29 removes the requirement for non-resident companies receiving dividends from Irish resident companies to provide a tax residence and/or auditor's certificate in order to obtain exemption from DWT at source. A self assessment system will now apply whereby a non-resident company will provide a declaration and certain information to the dividend paying company or intermediary to claim exemption from DWT, The declaration will extend to a period of sic years after which the new declaration must be provided for a DWT exemption to apply.

The amount of a non-cash relevant distribution is, in the case of a stock dividend, the amount of the deemed distribution or the amount chargeable under **32** 'Sch D, Case IV' (see **3.7**(ii)(iii) 'Anti-avoidance legislation'), and in any other case an amount equal to the value of the distribution (in any case disregarding the withholding tax). In the case of stock dividends, the withholding tax requirement is replaced by a requirement for the company to withhold additional stock to limit the value received by the recipient to the net amount which would have been received if the distribution had been in cash, and the company is required to account to the Collector-General (see below) for dividend withholding tax equal to that which would have been deducted but for this special provision. In the case of other non-cash distributions, the withholding tax requirement is replaced by a requirement that the company account to the Collector-General (see below) for dividend withholding tax equal to that which would have been deducted but for this special provision, and the company is entitled to recover a sum equal to that amount from the specified person (as a simple contract debt).

Computations of profits or gains are not affected by the deduction of dividend withholding tax, the full amount of relevant distributions being taken into account. See below as regards credit for, or repayment of, the tax withheld.

[*TCA 1997, ss 172A, 172B; FA 1999, s 27(a); FA 2000, ss 30(1)(b), 59*]

Exemptions. There are a number of exemptions from the dividend withholding requirement.

Excluded persons. The requirement does not apply to a distribution to an '*excluded person*', ie where the person beneficially entitled to the distribution is:

(*a*)   an RI-resident company;

(*b*)   an exempt approved pension scheme within *s 774* (see **17.26** 'Exempt organisations') or a retirement annuity contract or trust scheme within *ss 784, 785* (see **2.24** 'Allowances, credits and rates');

(*c*)   a qualifying employee share ownership trust within *Sch 12* (see **30.26**(*b*) 'Sch D, Cases I and II');

(*d*)   a collective investment undertaking (other than an offshore fund within *s 743*, see **32.5** 'Sch D, Case IV') within *ss 734, 738* or *739B* (see **12.22** 'Corporation tax');

(*e*)   a trust established for charitable purposes only (see **17.5** 'Exempt organisations');

(*f*)   (from 6 April 2000) an approved athletic or amateur games or sports body within *s 235* (see **17.2** 'Exempt organisations');

(*g*)   (from 6 April 2000) a designated broker receiving the distribution as income or gains of a special portfolio investment account (see **16.32** 'Exempt income and special savings schemes');

(*h*)   a qualifying fund manager within *s 784A* (see **2.24** 'Allowances, credits and rates') receiving the distribution in respect of assets held in an approved retirement fund or an approved minimum retirement fund;

(*i*)   a qualifying savings manager within *s 848B* (see **16.33** 'Exempt income and special savings schemes') receiving the distribution in respect of assets held in a special savings incentive account; or

(*j*)   a person entitled to Sch F exemption in respect of the distribution under *s 189(2)*, *s 189A(2) or (3)(b)* or *s 192(2)* (see **16.19**, **16.18**, **16.26** 'Exempt income and special savings schemes' respectively);

(*k*)   from 3 February 2005, a PRSA administrator (see **2.23**) receiving the distribution as income in respect of PRSA assets;

(*l*)   from 3 February 2005, a unit trust, the unit holders of which are exempt from capital gains tax on disposal of the units;

provided in each case that the recipient has made the appropriate declaration in writing under *Sch 2A* to the person from whom the distribution is received. As regards (*d*), (*g*), (*h*), (*i*) or (*j*), the recipient is for this purpose treated as beneficially entitled to the distribution. As regards (*a*), from 6 April 2001, no written declaration is required where the company making the distribution is a 51 per cent subsidiary of the recipient company. [*TCA 1997, ss 172B(8), 172C, Sch 2A; FA 1999, s 27(a)(c); FA 2000, s 30(1)(c), (2)(b); FA 2001, s 43; FA 2005, s 47*]

Non-resident persons. The requirement does not apply to a distribution to a '*qualifying non-resident person*', ie where the person beneficially entitled to the distribution is:

(*a*)   a person (other than a company), neither resident nor ordinarily resident in RI, who is resident for tax purposes in a '*relevant territory*', ie another EU Member State or a territory with which double tax arrangements are in force under *s 826* (see **15.2** 'Double tax relief – income and capital gains') or, from 1 July 2005, to a company resident in Switzerland holding at least 25 per cent voting control of the RI tax paying company [*FA 2005, s 51*]; or

(*b*)   a company not resident in RI where either (i) the company is controlled (as specially defined) by a person or persons resident for tax purposes in a relevant territory and not themselves controlled by a person or persons not so resident, or (ii) the principal class of shares of the company (or of another company of which it is a 75 per cent subsidiary within *ss 412–418*, see **12.15** 'Corporation tax', or (from 6 April 2000) of each of two or more companies which together wholly own (as defined) the company) is substantially and regularly traded on one or more recognised stock exchanges in relevant territories (or other stock exchange approved for the purpose), or (iii) (from 6 April 2000) the company is resident for tax purposes in a relevant territory (by virtue of the law of that territory) but is not controlled (as specially defined) by an RI-resident person or persons. This exemption has been extended to include cases where the parent company trades only on the Irish Stock Exchange [*FA 2007, s 38*];

provided in either case that the recipient has made the appropriate declaration in writing (accompanied by a current certificate) under *Sch 2A* to the person from whom the distribution is received.

For distributions in the first year of the scheme (ie before 6 April 2000) simplified requirements apply. The exemption applies where the person beneficially entitled to the distribution is:

(i)   a person whose address in the share register is in a relevant territory;

(ii)   a company within (*b*) above which has given the appropriate certificate under *Sch 2A* to the person from whom the distribution is received; or

(iii)   an RI-resident financial intermediary which has advised the company that the distribution is to be received for the benefit of a person meeting conditions broadly similar to (i) or (ii) above or of a further intermediary meeting similar conditions.

[*TCA 1997, s 172D, Sch 2A; FA 1999, s 27(a)(c); FA 2000, s 30(1)(d), (2)(a)(c)(d)*]

Qualifying intermediaries. The requirement does not apply to distributions made through one or more 'qualifying intermediaries' for the benefit of a person beneficially entitled to the distribution who is within the excluded or non-resident person exemptions referred to above in relation to the distribution. A '*qualifying intermediary*' is a person who is RI-resident or resident for tax purposes in a relevant territory (as above) who has entered into the requisite agreement with the Revenue Commissioners and has received the appropriate written authorisation (which has not expired or been revoked). Broadly only persons holding (or wholly owned by persons holding) a banking licence in an EU Member State or a relevant territory, members of a recognised stock exchange in an EU Member State or a relevant territory, and other persons considered suitable by the Revenue Commissioners may be accepted as qualifying intermediaries. A list of qualifying intermediaries is maintained by the Revenue Commissioners, who may supply the name and address of any qualifying intermediary to any person. [*TCA 1997, s 172E; FA 1999, s 27(a); FA 2000, s 30(1)(e)*]

Detailed obligations are imposed on qualifying intermediaries, requiring them to maintain and update separate exempt and liable fund records and to notify the distributing company (or any interposed qualifying intermediary) accordingly. For recipients to be included in the exempt fund the intermediary must have received from the non-liable person or interposed intermediary the appropriate declaration or certificate or notification referred to above (subject to special rules in the case of certain depositary banks in relation to American depositary receipts). A return (usually to be made by electronic means) may be required by written notice to be made to the Revenue Commissioners giving details of all relevant distributions received from distributing companies and payments representing such distributions received from intermediaries, and of all persons to whom such distributions or payments have been given, identifying in particular non-liable persons from whom the appropriate declaration or certificate has been received (and again subject to special rules in relation to American depositary receipts). [*TCA 1997, s 172F; FA 1999, s 27(a); FA 2000, s 30(1)(f)*]

Authorised withholding agent. The requirement does not apply to a distribution to an authorised withholding agent for the benefit of another person beneficially entitled to the distribution. To be an authorised withholding agent in relation to relevant distributions a person must:

(1)   be RI-resident or, if not so resident, both be resident for tax purposes in a relevant territory (as above) and carry on through an RI branch or agency a trade consisting of or including the receipt of relevant distributions on behalf of others;

(2)   have entered into the requisite agreement with the Revenue Commissioners; and

(3)   have received the appropriate written authorisation (which has not expired or been revoked).

Broadly only persons holding (or wholly owned by persons holding) a banking licence in an EU Member State or a relevant territory, members of a recognised stock exchange in an EU Member State or a relevant territory, and other persons considered suitable by the Revenue Commissioners may be accepted as authorised withholding agents. A list of authorised withholding agents is maintained by the Revenue Commissioners, who may supply the name and address of any such agent to any person. [*TCA 1997, s 172G; FA 1999, s 27(a); FA 2000, s 30(1)(g)*]

An authorised withholding agent is required to give written notice to each company from which it is to receive relevant distributions that it is such an agent in relation to those distributions. It must then in effect stand in the shoes of the distributing company in relation to the operation of these provisions, ie it must apply the withholding provisions to the onward distribution as if it were the relevant distribution from which it derives. [*TCA 1997, s 172H; FA 1999, s 27(a)*]

Statement to be given to recipients of relevant distributions. The company making a relevant distribution (or the authorised withholding agent treated as making it) must, at the time of making the distribution (or onward distribution), give to the recipient a written statement showing the name and address of the payer (and of the company making the distribution if different) and of the person to whom it is made, the date and amount of the distribution and the amount of the withholding tax (if any). The information may be included with the normal dividend information required by *s 152*, and the penalty for non-compliance with the requirements of that section apply equally to the statements required by these provisions. The information will generally be included on the dividend counterfoil. There is now provision for the electronic transmission of dividend statements to all shareholders. This provision applies in relevant distributions and declarations after the passing of the Act. [*TCA 1997, s 172I; FA 1999, s 27(a)*; *FA 2010, s 29*]

Credit for, or repayment of, the withholding tax. A person within the charge to income tax for a year of assessment who has borne dividend withholding tax in relation to a distribution in that year to which he was beneficially entitled may claim to have that tax set against his liability to income tax for that year, any excess being repayable. A person not within the charge to income tax for a year of assessment may similarly claim a refund of dividend withholding tax suffered. A person who falls within the exempt categories (see above) in relation to a relevant distribution, or who would have done so if the appropriate declaration had not been required, may similarly claim a refund of any withholding tax borne in relation to the distribution. The legislation has been amended to ensure that the general four-year time limit that applies to other tax repayments also applies to claims for repayments of DWT. [*FA 2007, s 38*] All claims must be accompanied by the written statement referred to above (ie normally the dividend counterfoil), and the Revenue Commissioners may also require production of such other evidence as they consider necessary that the claimant is entitled to the set-off or refund. [*TCA 1997, s 172J; FA 1999, s 27(a)*]

Accounting for dividend withholding tax. Any company making any relevant distributions in any month, and any authorised withholding agent treated as making any such distributions, is required to make a return (usually by electronic means) to the Collector-General within 14 days of the end of the month containing details of:

(*a*)   the name and tax reference number of the company making the relevant distributions;

(*b*)   (if relevant) the name of the authorised withholding agent;

(*c*)   the name and address of each person to whom a relevant distribution was made or treated as made during the month;

(*d*)   the date and amount of the relevant distribution to each such person;

(*e*)   the amount (if any) of dividend withholding tax deducted in relation to the relevant distribution or, in the case of stock dividends or other non-cash distributions, the amount required to be accounted for to the Collector-General as if it were dividend withholding tax in respect of the distribution (see above);

(*f*)   the aggregate of amounts within (E) relating to the month to which the return refers; and

(*g*)   (from 6 April 2000) where the distribution is excluded from these provisions by virtue of its being made out of exempt income or profits or disregarded income within *ss 140, 141* or *142* (see above), which of those sections is in point.

The dividend withholding tax to be returned as above is due at the time by which the return is to be made, and is to be paid by the person from whom the return is required to the Collector-General without assessment (although it may be assessed if not paid in full by the due date). There are provisions for assessment in cases where the inspector is dissatisfied with a return, or considers that a return should have been made, for interest on late or unpaid tax, and for the necessary adjustments where an item is incorrectly included in a return, subject to the usual appeal arrangements.

The Revenue Commissioners have appropriate powers of inspection to audit returns by companies or authorised withholding agents (see *s 904I; FA 2002, s 132(c)*).

[*TCA 1997, s 172K; FA 1999, s 27(a); FA 2000, s 30(1)(h); FA 2002, s 129(1)(a)*]

Stapled stock arrangements (ie agreements, arrangements or understandings, whenever made, under which a person to whom a distribution is made by a non-RI resident company has, directly or indirectly, exercised a right (which has not been revoked) to receive distributions from the non-resident company instead of receiving relevant distributions from an RI-resident company (the 'resident company')). Where, on or after 6 April 1999, a non-resident company makes distributions to persons under a stapled stock arrangement, the resident company is required, within 14 days of the end of each month in which such distributions are made, to make a return (usually by electronic means) giving details of the name and address of both the resident company and the non-resident company and of each person to whom such a distribution was made in the month, and of the date and amount of such distributions to each such person. [*TCA 1997, s 172L; FA 1999, s 27(a)*]

Market claims. With effect from 10 February 2000 (giving statutory force to administrative arrangements in operation before that date), where a relevant distribution by an RI-resident company has been made to the wrong person (eg through a delay in updating a share register) and tax was not withheld on the making of the distribution, obligations to deduct and account for tax similar to those described above are imposed on the broker or other intermediary settling the claim. An annual return is required of all such payments in a year of assessment by 15 February (for 1999/2000 and 2000/01 only, 21 May) following the end of the year. [*TCA 1997, s 172LA; FA 2000, s 30(1)(i); FA 2001, Sch 2 para 11*]

Summary. For a summary of the scheme, see Revenue Tax Briefing Issue 41 pp 24–27.

14 Double Tax Relief – Capital Transfers

Cross-references. For double tax relief on income tax, capital gains tax and corporation tax, see **15** 'Double tax relief – income and capital gains'.

14.1 A Convention between UK and RI to avoid double taxation over capital transfer tax (UK) and gift tax and inheritance tax (capital acquisitions tax – RI) was signed on 7 December 1977. It will also apply to any identical or substantially similar taxes imposed by either state in addition to or in place of these taxes. [*SI 279/78, art 2*] Due to the differences between the provisions concerning the persons liable for CAT and CTT, the relief given under this Convention attaches not to the persons who pay tax but to the property subject to the charge. Note also that 'settlement' is defined by reference to the UK legislation (see **14.4** below) and that the 'grossing-up' on UK lifetime gifts is taken into account for DTR purposes. *Finance Act 2008* amends *CATCA 2003, s 106* which provides for the making of arrangements for relief from double taxation. The amendment secures the position of the existing Irish/UK Double Taxation Treaty that came into effect in 1978,

    Commencement. [*SI 279/78, art 14*] The Convention entered into force on 2 October 1978 upon an Exchange of Notes and thereupon took effect retrospectively to the date of the introduction of each of the taxes. These dates are:

RI   –   gift tax – 28 February 1974
                inheritance tax – 1 April 1975
UK   –   capital transfer tax not on death – 27 March 1974
                capital transfer tax on a death – 13 March 1975

SCHEME FOR ELIMINATING DOUBLE TAXATION

14.2 In general each state retains the right to levy tax according to its own laws. [*SI 279/78, art 5(1)*] In cases where double taxation would occur, the rules provide for one State to allow as a credit against its own charge to tax any tax imposed by the other state. [*SI 279/78, art 8*] This is worked out as follows:

(*a*)   where one state taxes property which is situated in the other state, the state where the property is *not* situated must allow a credit for tax payable in the other state on the same event (ie death, gift, etc);

(*b*)   where both states impose tax on the same event and the property is situated in a third state, it is the state which has *subsidiary taxing rights* (see below) which must allow credit for the tax charged by the other state. [*SI 279/78, art 8(1)(2)*]

Computation. The property on which tax is charged is to be treated as reduced by any deductions (eg for debts, charges) allowed by the tax law of the state imposing the tax. [*SI 279/78, art 7*] The tax chargeable by a contracting State is to be reduced by any amount allowed as a credit in respect of tax levied on the same property by any non-contracting state. [*SI 279/78, art 8(4)(a)*]

The credit is only available in RI if the gift/inheritance bears its own tax. If the tax is payable out of the residue then the credit is available against tax in the UK on the residue. A lifetime gift liable to UK tax payable by the transferor is, for RI credit purposes, treated as reduced by the amount of the UK tax (ie the 'grossing-up' is taken into account). [*SI 279/78, art 8(3)*]

Claim for credit or repayment of tax must be made within six years of the event giving rise to the charge. [*SI 279/78, art 9*]

PLACE WHERE PROPERTY IS SITUATED

14.3 The place where property is situated is to be determined initially by each state under its own law. If this results in a disagreement then the question is to be determined solely according to the law of the state with *subsidiary taxing rights* (or, if there is no such state, by agreement). [*SI 279/78, art 6*]

SUBSIDIARY TAXING RIGHTS

14.4 The state with subsidiary taxing rights is the state which must allow a credit for tax charged by the other state, where the property is situated in a third state. (In effect, the other contracting state is regarded as having the 'primary' taxing rights.) Identifying the state with subsidiary taxing rights greatly depends on determining fiscal domicile.

Fiscal domicile. The domicile of a person (individual, company or body of persons) is initially determined according to the law of domicile or tax law of each contracting state. [*SI 279/78, art 4(1)*] If this results in the person being domiciled in both states, the question is determined by reference, successively, to permanent home, personal and economic ties, habitual abode and nationality. In default, the question is to be settled by agreement between the RI and UK revenue authorities. [*SI 279/78, art 4(2)*]

Subsidiary taxing rights. Except for settlements, the state with subsidiary taxing rights will be the state where, under the rules in *art 4(2)* above, the disponer or transferor is *not* domiciled. [*SI 279/78, art 5(2)(a)*] In relation to property comprised in a settlement (as defined by UK law – *UK Finance Act 1975, Sch 5 para 1(2)*) the state with subsidiary taxing rights is determined as follows. [*SI 279/78, art 5(2)(b)*]

Proper law of settlement when made	*Domicile of settlor at that time under SI 279/78, art 4(1)*	*State*
RI	UK	UK
Not RI*	UK*	RI
Not RI	Both–domicile falling to be determined by *SI 279/78, art 4(2)*	State of non-domicile under *SI 279/78, art 4(2)*

* Property becoming liable to RI tax due to a later change, in proper law or settlor's domicile, to the RI jurisdiction.

OTHER PROVISIONS

14.5 A contracting state may not discriminate by imposing more onerous tax on property owned by nationals of the other state, nor on the permanent establishment of an enterprise of the other state, nor on enterprises whose capital is controlled by residents of the other state. (This does not entitle the nationals of the other state to parity of personal allowances, reliefs and reductions.) [*SI 279/78, art 10*].

Complaints that the Convention is not being complied with may be made direct to the revenue authority of either state, and problems are to be resolved by agreement between the UK and RI revenue authorities. [*SI 279/78, art 11*] Information to be exchanged between revenue authorities not only for DTR purposes but also for purposes of domestic tax, such information to be treated as confidential. [*SI 279/78, art 12*]

Diplomatic and consular officials. The Convention does not affect the international fiscal privileges of such persons. [*SI 279/78, art 13*]

TERMINATION

14.6 The Convention may be terminated from the beginning of any calendar year after 1980 by either state giving at least six months' prior notice. [*SI 279/78, art 15*]

15 Double Tax Relief – Income and Capital Gains

Cross references. See also **14** 'Double tax relief – capital transfers'. See **31** 'Sch D, Case III' for foreign income etc. See Tolley's Income Tax, Tolley's Corporation Tax and Tolley's Capital Gains Tax for further details of taxation in UK.

15.1 Where the same income is liable to be taxed in both RI and another country, relief may be available:

(*a*)   under the terms of a double tax agreement between RI and that other country – see generally **15.2** below and see **15.3** *et seq.* for agreements with the UK;

(*b*)   under the unilateral double tax relief provisions contained in RI tax legislation – see **15.15** below.

For the calculation of double tax relief, see Revenue Tax Briefing Issue 13 pp 3–5, Issue 15 p 9.

There are a number of provisions in the Taxes Acts that grant preferential treatment for payments to and from treaty countries. These typically deal with granting exemption from Irish tax on payments by Irish companies to non-resident recipients of dividends and interest and favourable tax treatments of such payments when received by Irish companies from foreign sources. There is also capital gains tax exemption for gains from disposals of foreign company shares. The requirement is that there be a tax treaty in force with the relevant foreign country. There can be a delay in bringing the treaties into force because of ratification procedures in either country. Given the possibility of delay, the treaty requirement is being relaxed to mere signing of the treaty, ie once a treaty has been signed with the country, companies dealing with that country can avail of these domestic provisions.

DOUBLE TAX AGREEMENTS

[*TCA 1997, ss 826, 832–835, Schs 24, 25; FA 1998, s 60; FA 1999, s 67*]

15.2 The Republic of Ireland has agreements with the following countries (statutory instrument numbers in round brackets).

	In force*
Albania (16/2011)	Not yet in force
Australia (406/83)	1984
Austria (250/67 and 29/88)	1964 (protocol 1974/76)
Bahrain	2010
Belarus	2010
Belgium (66/73)	1973
Bosnia & Herzegovina	Not yet in force
Bulgaria (372/00)	2002/03

Canada (773/04)	2006
Chile (815/2005)	2009
China (373/00)	2001
Croatia (574/02)	2004
Cyprus (79/70)	1962
Czech (321/95)	1997
Denmark (286/93)	1994
Estonia (496/98)	1999
Finland (289/93)	1990
France (162/70)	1966
Germany (212/62)	1959
Georgia (18/2010)	2011
	In force *
Greece (774/04)	2005
Hong Kong (17/2011)	2012
Hungary (301/95)	1997
Iceland (775/04)	2005
India (521/01)	2002
Israel (323/95)	1996
Italy (64/73)	1967
Japan (259/74)	1974
Korea (290/91)	1992
Kuwait (21/2011)	Not yet in force
Latvia (504/97)	1999
Lithuania (503/97)	1999
Luxembourg (65/73)	1968
Macedonia (463/2008)	2010
Malaysia (495/98)	2000
Malta (502/2008)	2010
Mexico (497/98)	1999
Moldova (19/2010)	2011
Montenegro (18/20110	Not yet in force
Morocco (19/2011)	Not yet in force
Netherlands (22/70)	1965
New Zealand (30/88)	1989
Norway (80/70)	2002 (previously 1967)
Pakistan (260/74)	1968
Poland (322/95)	1996
Portugal (102/94)	1995
Romania (427/99)	2001
Russia (428/94)	1996
Serbia	2010

Singapore (34/2011)	Not yet in effect
Slovak Republic (426/99)	2000
Slovenia (573/02)	2003
South Africa (478/97)	1998
Spain (308/94)	1995
Sweden (348/87 and 398/93)	1988/89 (protocol 1994)
Switzerland (240/67 and 76/84)	1965 (protocol 1974/76)
Turkey (501/2008)	2011
UAE (20/2011)	Not yet in effect
United Kingdom (319/76, 209/95 and 494/98)	1976
United States of America (477/97 and 425/99)	1998 (protocol 1 September 2000)
Vietnam (435/2008)	2009
Zambia (130/73)	1967

(*a*)   A new agreement with Vietnam (SI 453/2008), which was signed on 10 March 2008, came into force on 24 December 2008 and is effective since 1 January 2009.

(*b*)   New agreements with Macedonia (SI 463/2008) and Malta (SI 502/2008), which were signed on 14 April 2008 and 14 November 2008 respectively came into force on 12 January 2009 and 15 January 2009, respectively. Both treaties came into effect on 1 January 2010.

(*c*)   New agreements with Turkey (SI 501/2008) and Georgia were signed on 24 October 2008 and 20 November 2008 respectively.

(*d*)   Legal procedures to bring the new agreement with Turkey into force were completed by Ireland in December 2008: the legal procedures have not yet been completed by Turkey and so the Treaty is not in force.

(*e*)   Negotiations for new agreements with the following countries are at various stages: Argentina, Armenia, Egypt, Kuwait, Morocco, Singapore, Tunisia, and Ukraine.

(*f*)   Negotiations are at various stages for the revision of existing agreements with Cyprus, France, Germany, Italy, Korea and Pakistan.

Part 1 is amended by adding six countries to the list of countries with which the State has entered into a Double Taxation Agreement. These countries are Bahrain, Belarus, Bosnia & Herzegovina, Georgia, Moldova, and Serbia. *[FA 2010]*

Part 3 is amended by adding eight countries/territories to the list of countries/ territories in *Pt 3* with which the State has entered into a Tax Information Exchange Agreement. These countries/territories are Anguilla, Bermuda, the Cayman Islands, Gibraltar, Guernsey, Jersey, Liechtenstein, and the Turks and Caicos Islands. All of these exchanges of information were commenced in early 2010. *[FA 2010]*

The addition of these 14 countries/territories to *Sch 24A* is the final step in the legislative and ratification procedure which will ensure that these Agreements will have the force of law. This section will have effect from the date of the passing of the Act.

In addition there is an Air Transport Agreement with the USSR (349/87).

New treaties with Argentina, Egypt, Kuwait, Malta, Morocco, Singapore, Tunisia, Turkey and Ukraine are being negotiated and the Cyprus, France and Italy treaties are in the process of renegotiation.

*The date of entry into force is 6 April in the year for income tax and capital gains tax before 2002, otherwise 1 January.

Various dates for entry into force, see **15.3 below.

Note: Arrangements relating to corporation profits tax (abolished from 6 April 1976) are adopted and preserved for the purpose of corporation tax. [*TCA 1997, s 827*]

ARRANGEMENTS WITH UK

15.3 A revised double tax agreement between UK and RI came into effect on 23 December 1976. It consists of a Convention signed on 2 June 1976 and Protocols signed on 7 November 1994 and 4 November 1998. The agreement is broadly based on the 1963 OECD model treaty and applies in respect of RI income tax, corporation tax and capital gains tax, and in respect of UK income tax, corporation tax, petroleum revenue tax and capital gains tax. It will apply to subsequent taxes of a similar nature. [*SI 319/76, art 2*]

The statutory instruments concerned (with their UK equivalent in brackets) are as follows: Convention 1976/319 (1976/2151) and Protocols 1995/209 (1995/764) and 1998/494 (1998/3151).

ARRANGEMENTS UNDER 1976 AGREEMENT

15.4 Special meaning of residence ('fiscal domicile'). For DTR purposes a person cannot be resident in both UK and RI. The residence of an *individual* is first determined under normal tax rules relating to abode, domicile, etc. If this results in him being technically resident in both states the question is decided by reference successively to permanent home, personal and economic ties, habitual abode, and nationality, and if necessary is decided by agreement between the states. A *company or body of persons* is deemed to be resident where its place of effective management is situated. [*SI 319/76, art 4*] See **38.78** 'Tax cases'.

15.5 Enterprises. *Permanent establishment* of an enterprise carried on by a person resident in UK or RI means a fixed place of business where the business of the enterprise is wholly or partly carried on, including a place of management, office, factory, etc. Certain fixed places of business are excluded (eg if used for advertising or storage). Carrying on business in State A through a broker or other agent of independent status will not cause a State B enterprise to have permanent establishment in State A. [*SI 319/76, Arts 3(1), 5; SI 494/98*] An article in Revenue Tax Briefing Issue 26 pp 11–14 sets out the criteria and guidelines applied in establishing the existence of a permanent establishment.

Business profits of a State A enterprise are taxable only in State A, unless the enterprise has a permanent establishment in State B in which case the profits attributable to the permanent establishment may be taxed in State B. Rules are laid down for identifying the profits of a permanent establishment. These provisions do not affect specific legislation in either state relating to non-resident life assurance companies. [*SI 319/76, art 8*]

15.6 Taxable in state of source. Certain kinds of profits or gains are taxable in the state in which the source of the profits or gains is situated. If the taxpayer is resident in the state which is not the state of source (see above for residence), the tax paid in the state of source is allowed as a credit against the tax on the same profits or gains in the state of residence. [*SI 319/76, art 21*] The kinds of profits or gains to which these arrangements apply are the following:

(*a*)   Income from immovable property, including income from agriculture and forestry. 'Immovable property' is as defined by the law of the state where it is situated, and further includes livestock and equipment used for agriculture or forestry, and other rights and property; [*SI 319/76, art 7*]

(*b*)   Business profits of a UK or RI enterprise which has a permanent establishment in the state of source, to the extent that these profits are attributable to that permanent establishment. Rules apply for identifying the profits of a permanent establishment; [*SI 319/76, art 8*]

(*c*)   Dividends, interest and royalties connected with the business done by such a permanent establishment in the state of source; [*SI 319/76, Arts 11, 12(3), 13(3); SI 494/98*]

(*d*)   Capital gains arising from sale of, or of assets forming part of, such a permanent establishment; [*SI 319/76, art 14(3); SI 494/98*]

(*e*)   Capital gains derived from immovable property or from shares (other than shares quoted on a Stock Exchange) deriving their value, or the greater part of their value, directly or indirectly from immovable property. Since 6 April 1999 (1 January 1999 for corporation tax), the reference to shares quoted on a Stock Exchange is replaced by a reference to shares substantially and regularly traded on a Stock Exchange, and the provision is extended to gains on interests in partnerships or trusts as well as shares; [*SI 319/76, art 14(1)(2); SI 494/98*]

(*f*)   Salaries, wages and remuneration of employees, and director's fees, if:

  (i)   the employee/director is present in the state of source (ie where the employment/directorship is exercised) for more than 183 days in the fiscal year, or

  (ii)   the employer/company is a resident of the state of source or has a permanent establishment there from which the remuneration is paid,

  [*SI 319/76, art 15*]

  If neither condition is fulfilled, see **15.8**(*c*) below;

(*g*)   Income of public entertainers and athletes; [*SI 319/76, art 16*]

(*h*)   Profits from operation of ships or aircraft as regards voyages confined solely to state of source; [*SI 319/76, art 9*]

15.7 Taxable only in the state of source. Before 6 April 1999, remuneration in respect of governmental functions and pensions paid by central or local government (see **38.76** 'Tax cases') are taxable in the state of source and exempt in the state of residence (if different), *unless either*:

(*a*)   the remuneration or pension relates to services which were rendered in connection with a trade or business; or

(*b*)   the recipient is a *national* of the other state and not a dual UK/RI national.

Since 6 April 1999, such remuneration continues to be taxable only in the state of source *unless* the services are rendered in the other state and the individual is a resident of the other state (not having become so solely for the purpose of rendering the services concerned) and a national of the other state, in which case it is taxable only in the other state. Such pensions similarly continue to be taxable only in the state of source unless the individual is resident in, and a national of, the other state, in which case they are taxable only in the other state. Similar treatment also applies to remuneration and pensions funded by central or local government from certain employments in educational institutions. [*SI 319/76, art 18; SI 494/98*]

If these conditions are not met the usual rules apply (see **15.6**(*f*) and **15.8**(*c*) for remuneration, and **15.8**(*d*) for pensions).

15.8 Taxable only in the state of residence. The following kinds of profits or gains are taxable only in the state of residence:

(*a*)   interest and royalties, except where the rule in **15.6**(*c*) applies; [*SI 319/76, Arts 12, 13*]

(*b*)   capital gains not covered by the rules in **15.6**(*d*) or (*e*), except:

   (i)   for any part taxable in the state of residence on the remittance basis but not remitted, and

   (ii)   from 6 April 1999, where the person chargeable was resident in the other state during the previous three years;

   [*SI 319/76, art 14; SI 494/98*]

(*c*)   salaries, wages and other remuneration and director's fees, if:

   (i)   the employee/director is present in the state of source (ie where the employment/directorship is exercised) for 183 days or less in the fiscal year, and

   (ii)   the employer/company is not a resident of the state of source and does not have a permanent establishment there from which the salary etc was paid;

   [*SI 319/76, art 15*]

(*d*)   pensions and annuities, other than government and local authority pensions falling within **15.7** above; [*SI 319/76, art 17*]

(*e*)   profits and capital gains derived from operation of ships or aircraft except where the rules in **15.6**(*d*) or (*h*) above apply; [*SI 319/76, Arts 9, 14(4); SI 494/98*]

(*f*)   other income not expressly mentioned, except trust income (see **15.10** below) and, from 6 April 1999, income of deceased estates and certain income in respect of property or rights connected with a permanent establishment in the other state through which business is carried on (the latter being dealt with under *SI 319/76, art 8*, see **15.5** above). [*SI 319/76, art 20; SI 494/98*]

15.9 Dividends. There are different rules depending on whether the dividend (meaning any distribution under RI or UK tax law, as appropriate) carries a tax credit. Where, as applied in each state before 6 April 1999, the dividend would carry a tax credit if the recipient were resident in the same state as the company issuing the dividend (called 'the state of source' below), but in fact the recipient is resident in the other state, the following rules apply:

(*a*)   The dividend is taxable in the state of the recipient's residence;

(*b*)   The dividend is also taxable in the state of source. However, a tax credit is allowed to the recipient in the same way as if he were resident in the state of source, provided he is beneficially entitled to the dividend. This includes the right to obtain repayment of any excess of the tax credit;

(*c*)   If the recipient is a company which alone or together with any associated companies controls directly or indirectly ten per cent of the voting power in the distributing company, the dividend is exempt from tax in the state of source; however, no tax credit is allowed.

SI 319/76, Art 11(1) provides for the situation where the dividend would not entitle a resident of the state of source to a tax credit (ie for all RI company dividends after 5 April 1999). In these circumstances, there is 'withholding tax' in the state of source up to the following maximum:

(i)   generally, 15 per cent of the gross amount of the dividend; or

(ii)   if the recipient is a company which controls directly or indirectly at least ten per cent of the voting power in the distributing company, five per cent of the gross amount of the dividend.

The above rules do not apply:

(*a*)   where the dividend is connected with the business of a permanent establishment in the state of source (see **15.6**(*c*) above);

(*b*)   to a recipient who holds ten per cent or more of the class of shares to which the dividend attaches, as regards any dividend which can only have been paid out of profits earned in a period ending twelve months before the recipient's holding reached ten per cent. This disqualification will not apply if the recipient can show that he acquired the shares for *bona fide* commercial reasons;

(*c*)   to a recipient who is exempt from tax in one state in such circumstances that if he were resident in, and exempt in, the other state his exemption in the first state would be limited or removed. [*SI 319/76, art 11; SI 494/98*]

Where a dividend suffers withholding tax in the state of source the tax thus paid will be allowed as a credit against the recipient's tax liability in his state of residence, to the extent that the overall rate of tax in the state of source does not exceed the overall rate in the state of residence. There is no credit for tax on the profits of the distributing company out of which the dividend is made except where the recipient is a company which controls directly or indirectly ten per cent of the voting power in the distributing company. [*SI 319/76, art 21*]

New amendments have been made to the pooling of foreign tax relief. In certain cases, where an Irish company receives a foreign dividend, the Irish tax on the dividend may be reduced by the foreign tax suffered in relation to that dividend. If there is an excess amount of foreign tax that cannot be set off in this way, the surplus may be pooled and offset against liability on other foreign dividends received by the company. These pooling arrangements are amended such that in the future they will apply separately to dividends that are taxable at the 25 per cent rate and no dividends that are taxable at the 12.5 per cent rate. Any surplus of foreign tax arising on dividends taxable at the 12.5 per cent rate will not be offset against tax on dividends taxable at the 25 per cent rate. There is not a similar restriction in the case of dividends taxable at the 25 per cent rate. These rules apply to dividends received on or after 31 January 2008. [*FA 2008, s 21B*]

15.10 Trust income. The Convention does not specify how trust income is to be treated. It will continue to be dealt with by agreement between the Revenue authorities of UK and RI according to the nature of the income concerned.

15.11 Charities, superannuation schemes, and pension businesses of insurance companies. The above Convention rules do not apply and the following *reciprocal exemption* applies to such a body resident in one state in respect of:

(*a*)   dividends received from a company resident in the other state;

(*b*)   income from immovable property in the other state; and

(*c*)   capital gains taxable in the other state.

Where the Revenue authorities of the first-mentioned state certify that such dividends, income or gains are not taxable in that state by virtue of an exemption for such a body, then there is a reciprocal exemption from tax in the other state on the dividends, income or gains. [*SI 319/76, Arts 11, 14A; SIs 1976/319, 494/98*]

15.12 Pension Scheme Contributions. Tax relief may be given in one state where an employee sent temporarily to work in that state pays contributions to an approved pension scheme in the other state. Any employer contributions will not be treated as taxable income of the employee, and the employer will obtain a deduction for such contributions. This applies from 6 April 1994 in respect of income tax, from 1 April 1994 in respect of corporation tax. [*SI 319/76, art 17A; SI 209/95*]

15.13 Other provisions. A resident of one state is entitled to the same personal allowances in the other state as a national of the other state not residing there. [*SI 319/76, art 22*] Non-discrimination by one state against nationals of the other state. [*SI 319/76, art 23*] Allegations that an assessment does not comply with the Convention are to be presented to the state of residence. Difficulties are to be resolved by agreement between the Revenue authorities. [*SI 319/76, art 24*] Exchange of information between the Revenue authorities not only for purposes of DTR but also for purposes of domestic tax. [*SI 319/76, art 25*] A number of anti-avoidance provisions apply. [*SI 319/76, Arts 10, 11(5) (as originally enacted), 12(4)(5), 13(4), 20(3); SI 494/98*]

EXAMPLE OF RELIEF UNDER 1976 AGREEMENT

15.14 For year of assessment 2006, an RI resident, who is married with two children under 11 and who spends 90 days of the year in the UK as director of a UK company, has the following income:

	RI Sources €	UK Sources £
Directorship of RI company	42,000	–
Directorship of UK company	–	3,000
Rents from RI property	2,000	–
Rents from UK property	–	1,800
Other RI income	1,000	–
Dividends from UK companies (including tax credit of £20)	–	200
	€45,000	£5,000

As UK income arises by reference to a 5 April year end, the above UK income is the time apportioned income from the tax years ending 5 April 2006 and 2007.

UK tax liability

The income from UK sources above is all liable to UK income tax as follows:

Directorship (see **15.6**(*f*))	3,000		
Rents (see **15.6**(*a*))	1,800		
	4,800	(say)	798
Dividends (see **15.9** above)			20
	Tax liability		£818

Effective rate of tax is:

$$\frac{818 \times 100}{5,000} - 16.36\%$$

Notes (i) The liability (at the special rate of 10%) on the dividends is met in full by the tax credit.

(ii) In some circumstances, a claim may be made for personal allowances (see Tolley's Income Tax under Non-residents and other Overseas Matters) but such a claim is usually only advantageous where the RI effective rate is lower than the UK effective rate.

RI tax liability

The income from all sources is liable to RI income tax as follows:

RI sources	45,000
UK sources (converted from sterling, say)	8,000
Taxable Income	€53,000
Tax on €53,000 at 20%/42%	13,240
less personal tax credit	3,260
Tax liability	€9,980

Effective rate of tax is:

Notes　　(i)　　As only the net UK dividend (gross dividend less tax credit) is liable to RI income tax no double tax relief applies to this income.

$$\frac{9.980 \times 100}{53,000} = 18.83\%$$

Double taxation relief at lower effective rate (ie 16.36 per cent) is given against RI tax liability. Since the lower rate is the UK tax rate, the entire UK liability is deductible.

PROVISIONS FOR UNILATERAL RELIEF

15.15 Overseas dividends etc derived from tax relieved income. Dividends or interest arising from the investment of RI profits which were exempted under exported goods relief or Shannon Airport relief in a territory with which there is no double tax agreement may be granted such relief as is just (with the same restrictions as in (A) and (B) above). [*TCA 1997, s 830; FA 1998, Sch 3 para 9*]

Corporation tax unilateral relief. Since 1 April 1998, relief from corporation tax in respect of profits represented by dividends is given in respect of tax payable under the law of any territory with which no relevant double tax arrangements are in force (see **15.2** above) by credit against corporation tax. Subject to certain exclusions, relief may be obtained for both direct tax on the dividend and underlying tax on profits represented by the dividend. There are special provisions for dividends paid to an RI-resident company by a related company resident outside RI (by reference, broadly, to 25 per cent voting control (to reduce to five per cent control by ministerial order)). For accounting periods ending after 14 February 2001, these provisions apply to a branch or agency in RI of a company resident in another EU member state (or, from 1 January 2002, in an EEA state with which double tax arrangements are in force) as if the branch or agency were an RI-resident company (but not so as to give relief for tax suffered in the state in which the company is resident). Since 2 February 2004, provision is made for the 'pooling' of foreign tax credits. Since 1 January 2002, there are special provisions for unilateral relief for withholding tax suffered in countries with which no double tax arrangements are in force on interest forming part of a company's trading income. [*Sch 24 Pt 2; FA 1998, s 60; FA 1999, s 81; FA 2000, s 71; FA 2001, s 41; FA 2002, ss 38, 57; FA 2004, s 31*]

Capital gains tax unilateral relief. Unilateral credit relief in respect of capital gains in certain countries has been provided for. The countries concerned are:

Belgium, Cyprus, France, Germany, Italy, Japan, Luxembourg, the Netherlands, Pakistan and Zambia. In these cases Ireland has a tax treaty that pre-dates the introduction of capital gains in the state. Where a person, whether an individual or a company, who is chargeable to tax in the State in respect of a capital gain, suffers tax on the gain in any other country concerned, the foreign tax will be credited against Irish capital gains tax on the gain. [*FA 2007, s 36*]

16 Exempt Income and Special Savings Schemes

Cross-references. See also **12.12** 'Corporation tax'; **18.4** 'Farming'; **19.3** 'Government and other public loans'; **29.2** 'Sch C'; **34.10** 'Sch E'.

16.116.1 Child benefit under the *Social Welfare Acts* is exempt from income tax. [*TCA 1997, s 194*]

CHILDCARE SERVICES RELIEF

16.2 Since 1 January 2006 certain payments received for the provision of childminding services are exempt from income tax. The exemption applies where the gross payments do not exceed €10,000 (before any deductions for expenses etc) to the childminder (or in aggregate where more than one childminder operate from the same premises). The gross payments threshold has been increased from €10,000 to €15,000. [*FA 2007, s 15*] Where payments exceed this sum, the full amount is taxable. The services must be provided in the childminder's own home to not more than three children that are not the children of the childminder or ordinarily living in the home. The claimant must notify the appropriate person recognised by the Health Services Executive that child minding services are being provided. Notification must be made by the return filing date for the tax year of claim. The exemption must be claimed each year by the return filing date for the tax year of claim and must include evidence that the appropriate notification has been made. The exemption does not affect entitlement to mortgage interest relief, to capital gains tax exemption on the sale of a principal private residence or to entitlement to the home carer's tax credit. [*FA 2006, s 13*]

16.3 Certain **employment grants** under *Údarás na Gaeltachta Act 1979, Industrial Development Act 1986, ss 21(5)(a), 25* or *Industrial Development Act 1993, s 12* or (after 5 April 1996) *Shannon Free Airport Development Company Limited (Amendment) Act 1970, ss 3, 4* [*TCA 1997, ss 223–225; FA 1999, s 38*] and **employment grants and recruitment subsidies** made to an employer under certain other schemes [*TCA 1997, s 226*] are disregarded for tax purposes. This previously applied to payments made by the Minister for Labour under the **Employment Incentive Scheme**, the **Employment Maintenance Scheme**, the **Enterprise Allowance Scheme** or the **Enterprise Scheme**; or under the **Enterprise Scheme** or the **Employment Subsidy Scheme** of An Foras Áiseanna Saothair; or out of the **Employer's Temporary Subvention Fund**; or under the **Employers' Employment Contribution Scheme**; or under the **Market Development Fund** of An Bord Tráchtála; or by the **Industrial Development Authority** under *Industrial Development (No 2) Act 1981, s 2*. [*FA 1976, s 25; FA 1979, s 27; FA 1981, s 18; FA 1982, s 18 as originally enacted; FA 1988, s 22; FA 1993, s 38; FA 1997, Sch 9 Pt II*]

16.4 Employment compensation. Since 4 February 2004 certain payments made to an employee or former employee by his employer or former employer are exempt from income tax and are not reckoned in computing total income for the purposes of the Income Tax Acts. The payments may be in one of two forms:

(i)   Payments made under employment legislation and in accordance with a recommendation, decision or determination of a 'relevant authority'. A 'relevant authority' is any one of the following:

    (*a*)   a rights commissioner,

    (*b*)   the Director of Equality Investigations,

    (*c*)   the Employment Appeals Tribunal,

    (*d*)   the Labour Court,

    (*e*)   the Circuit Court,

    (*f*)   the High Court.

A settlement arrived at under a mediation process provided for in the legislation is treated as a recommendation, decision or determination of a relevant authority;

(ii)   Payments made on foot of a written agreement between unconnected parties and without reference to a relevant authority provided that the claim would have been a bona fide claim on which a recommendation, decision or determination would have been made if referred to that authority (other than the Circuit or High Courts) and the payment does not exceed the maximum award that could be made by the relevant authority for that claim. (Effectively this limits settlements to the equivalent of two years' pay.) The employer must satisfy certain conditions regarding the maintenance of certain documents relating to the claim and the provision of access for the Revenue Commissioners to those documents if required.

Payments made in respect of earnings, changes in functions or procedures of employment or termination of employment are specifically excluded from the exemption.

    [*TCA 1997, s 192A; FA 2004, s 7*]

16.5 Gaeltacht Areas. Since 1 January 2004, payments received by qualified persons living in Gaeltacht areas under an Irish language student scheme (Scéim na bhFoghlaimeoirí Gaeilge) are disregarded for all purposes of the Income Tax Acts. Prior to the enactment of this provision the Revenue Commissioners operated a concession for many years under which such households were subject to tax on ten per cent of this income. [*TCA 1997, s 216B; FA 2004, s 12*]

16.6 Haemophilia HIV Trust. Income consisting of payments made by the trustees of the Trust for a beneficiary are disregarded for all income tax purposes. [*TCA 1997, s 190*]

16.7 Hepatitis C compensation payments. Income consisting of compensation payments by the Hepatitis C Compensation Tribunal (or under similar awards by the courts) is disregarded for income and capital gains tax purposes **from 1 January 2004** and for income tax purposes prior to that date. Tribunal payments are treated as if they were for personal injury damages (see **16.19** below). [*TCA 1997, s 191; FA 1998, s 9; FA 2004, s 17*]

16.8 Interest is exempt from income tax:

(i)   On securities used for payment of income tax [*TCA 1997, s 199*];

(ii)   On bonus payable to an individual under an instalment savings scheme (as under *FA 1970, s 53*) [*TCA 1997, s 197*];

(iii)   (from 6 April 2000) where it is paid to a non-RI resident company or a person not ordinarily resident in RI by:

(*a*)   a company in the course of 'relevant trading operations' within *ss 445, 446* (see **12.18** 'Corporation tax'), or

(*b*)   a 'specified collective investment undertaking' within *s 734* (see **12.22** 'Corporation tax'),

or where it is paid by a company or a collective investment undertaking (see **12.22** 'Corporation tax') in the ordinary course of a trade or business to a company which is non-RI resident and is regarded as resident in a '*relevant territory*', ie another EU Member State or a non-EU territory with which double tax arrangements have been made. Definitions of 'relevant territory' and 'arrangements' have been extended to cover arrangements that will have the force of law in addition to those that have the force of law. [*FA 2010, s 36*] A company is so regarded:

(1)   where double tax arrangements have been made, if the company is regarded as resident in that territory for corporation tax (or similar) purposes under those arrangements, or

(2)   otherwise, if under the law of that territory the company is resident for corporation tax (or similar) purposes in that territory.

Interest in respect of quoted Eurobonds to which *s 64(2)* applies, paid by a company to any person on or after 30 March 2001 is similarly exempt from income tax if the person is non-RI resident and is regarded as resident in a relevant territory (these conditions being interpreted in relation to persons as they are above in relation to companies). The exemption has been amended such that relief from Irish tax will only apply where the interest is liable to tax in the relevant territory. There will be no exemption where the recipient company would not have been taxed. [*FA 2010, s 36*] Since 22 March 2002, the exemption extends to interest paid on asset covered securities within *Asset Covered Securities Act 2001, s 2*.

Interest paid by a company holding or managing financial assets provided for in *s 110* is exempt from income tax from 6 February 2003 if the interest is regarded as paid out of the assets of the company and the recipient is non-RI resident and is regarded as resident in a relevant territory. [*FA 2003, s 48*] The definition of financial asset is extended to include; greenhouse gas emissions and contracts for insurance and reinsurance. The definition of qualifying asset is also extended to include the holding by a securitisation company of an interest in a financial asset through a partnership will now be treated as a qualifying company; [*TCA 1997, s 198; FA 2000, s 34; FA 2001, s 36; FA 2008, s 36*]

(iv) (since 6 April 1999) on certified contractual savings schemes ('SAYE' schemes) linked to approved savings-related share option schemes (see **34.8** 'Sch E'), terminal bonuses under SAYE schemes being similarly exempt. SAYE schemes may be offered by any 'qualifying savings institution' (see *s 519C(1)*), and must be certified by the Revenue Commissioners as qualifying for exemption. [*TCA 1997, s 519C, Sch 12B; FA 1999, s 68*]

Before 6 April 2000, (iii) above was replaced by a single exemption for interest paid to persons not ordinarily resident in RI by a company in the course of relevant trading operations. [*TCA 1997, s 198 as originally enacted; FA 1998, s 54; FA 1999, s 85(a)*]

16.9 Investment bonds etc (under *Central Fund Act 1965*). The premium on redemption is exempt from income tax and corporation tax except where it is part of trading profits. The relief does not apply to Agricultural Commodities Intervention Bills issued by the Minister for Agriculture, or to Exchequer Bills and other securities issued at a discount by the Minister for Finance, or to strips of securities (see **31.5** 'Sch D, Case III'). Any profit or gain on sale or redemption of such a security is, however, exempt from income and corporation taxes where the owner is non-RI ordinarily resident (except in the case of corporation tax chargeable on the income of an RI branch or agency of a non-resident company). [*TCA 1997, ss 45, 46, 48*]

16.10 RI securities. Certain government and other securities may be issued exempt from RI taxation so long as the beneficial owner is not ordinarily resident in RI (although the exemption does not apply to certain holdings of financial concerns) [*TCA 1997, ss 43, 49*] and the interest on certain securities issued to and continuously held by foreign-controlled companies may be exempt from corporation tax. [*TCA 1997, s 44*]

Finance Act 2010, s 31 amends the provisions in relation to Government Securities. *Section 42* is amended such that the exemption from tax in respect of accumulated interest payable in respect of Savings Certificates is extended to include similar products issued by Governments of other EU countries. *Sections 43, 45, 48* and *49* are amended so that all non-resident individuals will qualify for the exemption from tax.

16.11 Judges' expenses. An annual allowance paid to a judge of the District Court, the Circuit Court, the High Court or the Supreme Court under *Courts of Justice Act 1953, s 5(2)(c)*, in full settlement of necessary expenses as a judge not otherwise reimbursed out of moneys provided by the Oireachtas, is disregarded for all income tax purposes (and accordingly no Sch E deduction is allowed for such expenses). [*TCA 1997, s 196*]

16.12 Lotteries. Profits of lotteries licensed under *Gaming and Lotteries Act 1956* are exempt from tax under Sch D. [*TCA 1997, s 216*]

16.13 Military pay, pensions, etc. The following are exempt from tax: wound and disability pensions and related gratuities under *Army Pensions Acts 1923–80*, etc; military gratuities and demobilisation pay to officers of National or Defence Forces; deferred pay and gratuities under *Defence Act 1954*; gratuities for services with the Defence Forces; and certain pensions, etc payable to veterans of the War of Independence (or their widows or dependants). [*TCA 1997, ss 204, 205*]

16.14 National lottery profits are exempt from corporation tax in the hands of a company licensed by the Minister for Finance to hold the National lottery. [*TCA 1997, s 220*]

16.15 Patent royalties. Certain income arising to RI residents from patents devised etc in RI is exempt from income tax and corporation tax. Relief for individuals other than the deviser (or joint deviser) of the patent was abolished for income arising after 5 April 1994. Relief on patent income and distributions made by companies relating to the patent income is abolished as of 24 November 2010. The provisions of *Finance Act 2011, s 26* are such that income from a qualifying patent paid on or after 24 November 2010 is not exempt from tax. Also, the abolition of the exemption applies to distributions made by a company out of formerly exempt patent royalty income on or after 24 November 2010. *[FA 2011, s 26]*

The income attracting relief is any royalty or other sum paid in respect of the user of the invention to which the patent relates, where it is paid either:

(*a*)   by an unconnected person (see *s 10*) and not under any arrangement a main purpose of which was to circumvent any such connection;

(*b*)   for the purposes of activities treated as the manufacture of goods under the manufacturing companies relief if that relief continued to apply (or which would be so treated if carried on in RI by a company), other than financial services in the Custom House Docks Area and certificated Shannon Airport activities other than the repair or maintenance of aircraft (see **12.18** 'Corporation tax'); or

(*c*)   for use etc of the invention by the State under *Patents Act 1972, s 77* or by a foreign government under corresponding legislation.

The relief has been amended. The first amendment broadens the scope of a qualifying patent to include a patent for which the research, planning, processing, experimenting, testing, devising, designing, developing or similar activity is carried out within an EEA State. Previously such activities had to be substantially carried out in this State. The second amendment restricts the maximum relief available to €5,000,000 for a company for any calendar year. Where one of more persons are connected with the company, the amount of the relief available is restricted in aggregate to €5,000,000. The company and persons so connected may by notice in writing specify the allocation of the relief between the company and the connected person provided that notice is given before the due date for filing the company's corporation tax return. If no notice is given the Revenue will apportion the relief based on the relative amounts received by the company and each connected person. [*FA 2007, s 45*]

As regards (*b*), relief is restricted, for sums paid after 22 April 1996, to those which would have been paid on an arm's length basis.

From 2006 exemption may be restricted, see **2.45** 'Limitation on Income Tax Relief for High Earners'.

[*TCA 1997, s 234; FA 1973, s 34; FA 1992, s 19; FA 1994, s 28; FA 1996, s 32; FA 2006, s 17*]

See also **12.10** 'Corporation tax' as regards certain distributions arising from such royalties.

For an article setting out these provisions, see Revenue Tax Briefing Issue 38 pp 18–20 and Issue 53 p16.

16.16 Payments to Foster Parents. Since 2005, payments made to foster parents by the Health Services Executive in respect of the care of foster children are exempt from income tax. Certain discretionary payments made by the Executive to foster parents in relation to a child between the ages of 18 and 21 or who is permanently incapacitated (and was so before the age of 21) or is in full-time education (and instruction commenced before the age of 21) are also exempt. The exemption is extended to corresponding payments received from another EU Member State. [*TCA 1997, s 192B; FA 2005, s 11*]

16.17 Pay restructuring. A payment made by a 'qualifying company' to an employee in receipt of emoluments is exempt from tax up to a 'specified amount' where the payment is made under a 'relevant agreement' to which the employee is a party. Payments made to (or in respect of) the same person in respect of the same employment (or in respect of different employments with the same or an 'associated' qualifying company) are treated as a single aggregate payment for these purposes, and where the constituent payments are treated as income of different years of assessment, the exemption applies to payments treated as income of earlier years before later. Otherwise, the exemption applies to payments made earlier in a year before those made later. Companies are '*associated*' for this purpose if, on the date of the payment, one is under the control either of the other or of a third person who controls or is under the control of the other ('control' being specially and widely defined for the purpose).

Relief is withdrawn where, during the 'relevant period', certification is revoked, or the company fails to meet its reporting obligations (see below), or pay is increased beyond the permitted limits (see below). Withdrawal is by assessment under Sch D, Case IV for the year of assessment for which the relief was granted.

A '*qualifying company*' is a company certified for the purpose by the Minister for Enterprise and Employment, in accordance with laid down guidelines and on advice from the Labour Relations Commission. No certificate may be given after 31 December 2003. The Minister must be satisfied that the company is confronted with a substantial adverse change to its competitive environment which will determine its current or continued viability, to accommodate which and maintain its viability it must enter into a 'relevant agreement' with its 'qualifying employees'. The agreement must be designed solely to address that change and must reasonably be expected to address it. The Minister may direct the form of application by a company for certification. The certificate may specify such conditions as the Minster considers appropriate, and in the event of failure to comply with any such condition during the 'relevant period' the Minister may, by written notice to the company, revoke the certificate. The company must bear any costs incurred by the Labour Relations Commission in relation to its application.

A '*relevant agreement*' is a collective agreement, covering more than 50 per cent of the company's employees in receipt of emoluments (or more than 75 per cent of a *bona fide* class or classes of such employees comprising at least 25 per cent of all such employees), which is registered with the Labour Relations Commission and which provides, *inter alia*, for a substantial reduction in those emoluments (other than non-pecuniary emoluments) throughout the 'relevant period', and for a lump sum payment in compensation. The reduction must be at least ten per cent of the average annual emoluments in the two years preceding the date of registration of the agreement. Pay may be increased during the 'relevant period' provided that the increase is determined by reference to the reduced emoluments (plus previous increases) and is either part of a contractual incremental scale in place at least one year before the agreement was registered or is provided for under Partnership 2000 for Inclusion, Employment and Competitiveness or a successor agreement.

The qualifying company must, within one month (or such longer period as the Labour Relations Commission may allow) of each of the first five anniversaries of the registration of the agreement, confirm to the Commission in a specified form that all the terms of the agreement, so far as still relevant, continue to be in force.

The '*relevant period*' is the period of five years commencing with the date the relevant agreement was registered with the Labour Relations Commission.

The '*specified amount*' for agreements approved before 21 July 1999 is €7,620/£6,000 plus €255/£200 for each complete year of service (maximum 20 years) up to the date of registration of the relevant agreement. For agreements approved on or after that date, a higher limit applies where the reduction in emoluments exceeds 15 per cent. Where the reduction exceeds 15 per cent but does not exceed 20 per cent, the limit is €7,620/£6,000 plus €635/£500 for each complete year of service (maximum 20 years) up to the date of registration of the agreement. Where it exceeds 20 per cent, the limit is €10,160/£8,000 plus €765/£600 for each complete year of service (maximum 20 years) up to the date of registration of the agreement.

Compensation for loss of office, etc. Where, during the relevant period, an employee who has obtained relief as above receives from the qualifying company a payment (not within these provisions) chargeable under *s 123* (on retirement or removal from office, see **34.12** 'Sch E'), any relief from such charge under *s 201(5)* or *Sch 3* is reduced by the amount of the relief under these provisions. *ss 201, 480* and *Sch 3* do not apply to payments within these provisions.

[*TCA 1997, s 202; FA 1998, s 10; FA 2000, s 18; FA 2001, Sch 2 para 12*]

16.18 Permanently incapacitated individuals: special trusts. Income arising to the trustees of a 'qualifying trust', in respect of 'trust funds', which would otherwise be chargeable under Sch C **(29)**, Sch D, Case III **(31)**, Case IV **(32)** (by virtue of *s 59*, see **2.4** 'Allowances and rates', or *s 745*, see **32.13** 'Sch D, Case IV') or Case V **(33)** or Sch

F (**35**), is exempt from income tax and is disregarded in computing total income. Since 1 January 2004, chargeable gains accruing to the trust are exempt from capital gains tax. Exemption similarly applies to income and chargeable gains of the individual which is greater than 50 per cent of the total income and chargeable gains of the individual to or in respect of whom it arises, and which either

(*a*)   consists of payments made by the trustees to or in respect of an 'incapacitated individual' who is a subject of the trust; or

(*b*)   arises to such an individual from the investment of such payments, or of income or gains derived therefrom, and would otherwise be chargeable as above.

Prior to 1 January 2004, exemption applied only to income and only where the income from the trust was the sole or main income of the individual.

A '*qualifying trust*' is a trust established by deed in respect of which it is shown to the satisfaction of the inspector (or, on appeal, the Appeal Commissioners) that:

(i)   the trust is established exclusively for the benefit of one or more specified 'incapacitated individuals' for whose benefit subscriptions have been raised by public appeal (and in the case of which either total subscriptions do not exceed €381,000/£300,000 or not more than 30 per cent of subscriptions at specified times have been contributed by any one person);

(ii)   the trust requires the '*trust funds*' (ie those public subscriptions and money or other property derived from them) to be applied for the benefit of the specified individual(s), at the discretion of the trustees, and, in the event of the death of the specified individual(s), for charitable purposes or in favour of charitable trusts; and

(iii)   none of the trustees is 'connected' (within *s 10*) with any of the specified individuals.

An '*incapacitated individual*' is an individual permanently and totally mentally or physically incapacitated from being able to maintain himself or herself.

The requirement to make returns (see **28.1**) of such income applies notwithstanding the exemptions.

[*TCA 1997, s 189A; FA 1999, s 12; FA 2004, s 17*]

See also **7.5**(*v*) 'Capital acquisitions tax', and Revenue Tax Briefing Issue 38 pp 7, 8.

16.19 Personal injuries. Income and gains arising from the investment of damages paid pursuant to an order made by the Personal Injuries Assessment Board or following institution of a civil action, in respect of personal injury is exempt. This exemption is extended to certain income from offshore funds which is chargeable to tax under Case IV. [*FA 2007, s 11*] The injury must have given rise to mental or physical infirmity by reason of which the injured person is permanently and totally incapacitated from maintaining himself, and the income and gains combined must represent more than 50 per cent of the total income and chargeable gains of the injured person for the year of assessment. [*TCA 1997, s 189; FA 1999, s 13(a); FA 2004 ss 6, 17*] Prior to 1 January 2004, the exemption applied to income only and applied where that income was the sole or main income of the injured person. The Revenue accept that compensation in respect of a degenerative condition which will lead to such incapacity is within these provisions (see Revenue Tax Briefing Issue 44 p 28). See also Revenue Tax Briefing Issue 44 p 29 as regards reinvestment of proceeds of disposal of assets acquired out of compensation payments and assets acquired partly out of compensation payments and partly by borrowings. The requirement to make returns (see **28.1**) of such income and gains applies notwithstanding the exemptions.

16.20 Redundancy payments under *Redundancy Payments Act 1967* are exempt from income tax under Sch E. [*TCA 1997, s 203*]

16.21 Rent-a-room relief. For 2001 onwards, a limited exemption applies where an individual's sole or main residence is in RI, and sums otherwise chargeable under Sch D, Case IV or V are received in respect of residential use of a room or rooms in that dwelling (including sums for related incidental supplies of meals, cleaning and laundry services, etc). Provided that the aggregate of all such sums arising in a year of assessment does not exceed a specified limit (no deduction being made for expenses or any other matter), the profits or gains (or losses) of the year of assessment in respect of those sums are treated as nil. Where a charge would otherwise arise under Sch D, Case V, any wear and tear allowance under *s 284* (see **33.2** 'Sch D, Case V') which would be granted if claimed is deemed to have been granted (ie notional allowances are written off for the year).

The individual may, however, elect for the above provisions not to apply for a year of assessment, by written notice to the inspector on or before the specified return date for the year of assessment (see **28.11** 'Returns'), such an election having effect only for the year of assessment for which it is made.

The *'specified limit'* is **£4,440** for 2001, **€7,620** thereafter. The limit has been increased to €10,000. [*FA 2008, s 11*] The limit is, however, divided by the number of individuals to whom sums arise in respect of one residence, where there is more than one such individual.

The exemption no longer applies where a child pays rent to a parent. This was introduced as Revenue became aware of misuse of the scheme. [*FA 2007, s 14*]

The exemption no longer applies in relation to circumstances where the person in receipt of the income is an office holder, or employee of the person making the payment. [*FA 2010, s 12*]

This exemption does not affect the requirements for the making of income tax returns, or interest or capital gains tax reliefs (see **20.3**(*a*) 'Interest payable', **9.7**(*h*) 'Capital gains tax').

[*TCA 1997, s 216A; FA 2001, s 32*]

16.22 Residential Institutions Redress payments. Income consisting of an award by the Residential Institutions Redress Board is disregarded for the purposes of any income tax assessment. Any payment by the Board is treated as if it were for personal injury damages (see **16.19** below). [*Residential Institutions Redress Act 2002, s 22*]

16.2316.23 Scholarship income and bursaries etc are exempt although a benefit-in-kind charge may arise on other persons in certain circumstances (eg on parents in respect of a scholarship to their child under employer-sponsored schemes) unless certain other requirements are met. [*TCA 1997, s 193; Sch 32 para 2*]

16.24 State Employees – Foreign Services Allowance. Since 1 January 2005, allowances or emoluments certified by the Minister for Finance and paid to a member of the civil service, the permanent defence forces or An Garda Síochána, in compensation for additional living expenses arising from living outside RI are exempt from income tax. Foreign service allowances of certain agencies working in the overseas offices of those agencies are entitled to be paid in an equivalent manner to a member of the civil service, the permanent defence forces or An Garda Síochána. [*TCA 1997, s 196A; FA 2005, s 12; FA 2007, s 8*]

16.25 Stud fees. See **30.1** 'Sch D, Cases I and II'.

16.26 Thalidomide children. Payments received from the German foundation and from the Minister for Health are exempt, as is income derived from investing such payments. **Since 1 January 2004**, capital gains arising from assets acquired with any payment or from income arising from such payment are exempt from capital gains tax [*TCA 1997, s 192; FA 1999, s 13(b); FA 2004, s 17*]

16.27 Writers, composers, painters and sculptors resident, or ordinarily resident and domiciled, in RI, and not resident elsewhere, may claim exemption from tax on all earnings from works of cultural or artistic merit. *Finance Act 2011, s 17* introduces an upper limit of €40,000 per annum to the income tax exemption. The limit applies for the tax year 2011 and subsequent years. The Revenue Commissioners may not determine that a work meets these criteria unless it complies with guidelines (which are available free of charge from the Revenue Commissioners) drawn up by the Arts Council and the Minister for Arts, Heritage, Gaeltacht and the Islands with the consent of the Minister for Finance. See **38.242**, **38.243** 'Tax cases'.

The exemption operates for the year of assessment in which the claim (if accepted) is first made and subsequent years of assessment. An appeal procedure is available where the Revenue Commissioners fail to make a determination in relation to a work or works within six months of the claim to relief being made in respect of that work or works. From 2007, exemption in any one year may be limited, see **2.45** 'Limitation on Income Tax Relief for High Earners'. [*TCA 1997, s 195; FA 1969, s 2; FA 1994, s 14; FA 1996, s 14; FA 2006, s 17, FA 2010, FA 2011, s 17*]

For a general article on this relief, see Revenue Tax Briefing Issue 42 pp 17–19.

16.28 Miscellaneous concessions. It is understood that the following are, by concession, not normally charged to tax:

(i)   Meal vouchers to the value of 20 cent (15p) per day supplied to employees;

(ii)   Payments to foster parents under *Health Act 1953, s 55*;

(iii)   Long service awards at a cost not exceeding €20 (£15) per year of service to a maximum of 20 years, provided that no similar award has been received in the previous ten years (see Revenue Tax Briefing Issue 39 p 19);

(iv)   Continuing sick benefit during a period of absence from work under a taxpayer's own insurance policy, unless the benefit has continued for at least twelve months prior to commencement of the year of assessment;

(v)   Suggestion schemes. Certain payments under formally constituted schemes are exempted. See Revenue Tax Briefing Issue 32 pp 28, 29. This concession is withdrawn from 1 January 2004;

(vi)   Training courses. Certain expenses paid or reimbursed by employers are exempted, and a deduction similarly allowed for expenditure by employees not so reimbursed.

The inspector concerned should be consulted for the detailed conditions for exemption.

SPECIAL SAVINGS SCHEMES

16.29 Four savings schemes or investment products in effect offer the investor a special tax rate of ten per cent, 15 per cent or 20 per cent on an investment up to a maximum of €63,500/£50,000 (€95,250/£75,000 in certain cases). (See **16.30** below as regards restrictions where more than one type of investment is acquired and the application of the €95,250/£75,000 limit.) The four types of scheme are:

(*a*)   special savings accounts opened before 6 April 2001, under which interest is received under deduction of 20 per cent tax, no further liability arising on the depositor. See **13.9** 'Deduction of tax at source';

(*b*)   special investment policies with life assurance companies, underlying funds of which are subject to a special corporation tax rate of 20 per cent, but with special rules for the determination of taxable profits. Restrictions on fund investments apply similar to those in relation to schemes within (*c*) below. See generally **12.16** 'Corporation tax';

(*c*)   special investment schemes, under which special investment units may be purchased in authorised unit trusts, the income and gains arising to the scheme being taxable at a special rate of 20 per cent. See **16.31** below;

(*d*)   special portfolio investment accounts, under which income and gains of investments held in such accounts with designated stockbrokers are taxable at 20 per cent, to be accounted for by the stockbroker. See **16.32** below.

In addition, a new type of 'special savings incentive account', which may be commenced between 1 May 2001 and 30 April 2002, attracts a tax credit, payable into the account, equivalent to basic rate tax on the amount of subscriptions to the account which, if the account is held for the full five-year term, is not clawed back. See **16.33** below.

16.30 Restrictions on investments under schemes within 16.29 above. An individual may normally have only one of the four types of investment described at **16.29** above. However, provided he does not have a joint interest in any such investment, he may have both a special savings account within **16.29**(*a*) and one of the three types of investment within **16.29**(*b*), (*c*) or (*d*), but a limit of €31,750/£25,000 (rather than €63,500/

£50,000) must be applied to one of those investments. Alternatively, if the individual has only one investment, whether joint or not, the limit is increased to €95,250/£75,000. Married couples who have only joint investments may have two or three investments, including at least one within **16.29**(*a*) above and at least one within **16.29**(*b*), (*c*) or (*d*) above, or they may have four investments, two from each category, but limits of €31,750/£25,000 (rather than €63,500/£50,000) must then be applied to both of the accounts in one of those categories.

Any other restriction on investments by reference to the €63,500/£50,000 limit applies by reference to the €31,750/£25,000 limit where applicable. [*TCA 1997, s 839; FA 1999, s 66*]

16.31 Special investment schemes. A '*special investment scheme*' is an authorised unit trust scheme meeting the following conditions:

(*a*) the beneficial interests in the scheme assets must be divided into 'special investment units'; and

(*b*) the proportion of the aggregate consideration (calculated as under *ss 547, 580*) given for scheme shares which must relate to 'qualifying shares' and to 'specified qualifying shares' is:

(i) at any time before 1 February 1994, 40 per cent and 6 per cent respectively,

(ii) at any time in the year ending 31 January 1995, 45 per cent and 9 per cent respectively,

(iii) at any time in the year ending 31 January 1996, 50 per cent and ten per cent respectively,

(iv) at any time after 31 January 1996 and before 31 December 2000, 55 per cent and ten per cent respectively,

this requirement being abolished thereafter.

'*Qualifying shares*' are ordinary shares in RI-resident companies, or companies listed on the Irish Stock Exchange or dealt in on the smaller companies or unlisted securities markets of that Exchange, other than shares in investment companies or UCITS or whose value approximates to the market value of the company's assets. '*Specified qualifying shares*' are qualifying shares in companies with market capitalisation (at the time of the acquisition of the shares) of less than €255 million/£200 million (£100 million before 6 April 1998).

'*Special investment units*' are units so designated which are sold to an individual **before 1 January 2001** by the management company or trustee of the scheme, and in respect of which the following conditions are met:

(*a*) The aggregate investment by an individual in such units (jointly or otherwise) must not exceed €63,500/£50,000, and before 1 January 2001 the market value of his units could not exceed £50,000 on the fifth anniversary of his first scheme investment. Disposals of units are identified with acquisitions on a last in, first out basis for these purposes;

(*b*) Units must not be sold to or owned by an individual under full age;

(c)   Units must only be sold to individuals who are beneficially entitled to all amounts payable in respect of those units, and to whom all such amounts are to be paid;

(d)   Units may only be jointly owned by married couples to whom the units were sold as such;

(e)   Except in the case of married couples' jointly-owned units, units may not be held in more than one scheme, and married couples may only jointly hold units in a maximum of two schemes. Married couples with jointly-owned units may not also hold units on their own account;

(f)   A signed declaration must be made, in prescribed form and containing such information and undertakings as the Revenue Commissioners may reasonably require, to the management company or trustee in writing by the individual to whom units are sold, to the effect that the conditions in (B)–(E) are satisfied in relation to those units. The declaration must contain the full name and address of the person beneficially entitled to the units, and an undertaking to notify the management company or trustee if any of conditions (B)–(E) subsequently ceases to be satisfied. It must also contain such other information as the Revenue Commissioners may reasonably require.

As regards (a), (b), (d) and (e), ownership must be beneficial ownership. Declarations under (f) are to be retained and made available to the inspector as required.

A special investment scheme is not treated as a collective investment scheme (see **12.22** 'Corporation tax') (except in relation to certain stamp duty and VAT requirements). Income and gains arising to the scheme and accruing for the benefit of unitholders give rise to no liability on the unitholders, and within the scheme are chargeable to income tax and capital gains tax at a special rate of 20 per cent, before reduction by any other credit or relief. Distributions from RI-resident companies are generally chargeable, the tax credit (prior to abolition) being available for set off against the scheme's tax liabilities, any excess being repaid. This does not apply, however, to distributions in respect of eligible shares in qualifying companies under the business expansion scheme (see **21.2** 'Investment in corporate trades'), which are exempt from charge, any tax credit being ignored. Chargeable gains in respect of such eligible shares are also exempted (without prejudice to the relief of allowable losses). Otherwise, for the purposes of determining the scheme chargeable gains, assets are treated as disposed of and reacquired at market value on each 31 December (for 2000/01 and earlier years, 5 April). Indexation does not apply, nor does the exemption of government securities. (Special rules apply for shares disposed of within four weeks of acquisition.) Any net allowable capital losses in a year are treated as reducing chargeable income for that year, any excess being carried forward as a loss of the following year or, where the scheme ceases **from 1 January 2003**, unused capital losses carried forward may be deducted from chargeable gains accruing in the three years of assessment preceding the year of cessation, with the later years of assessment being relieved first. Where securities are disposed of in one year of assessment, and interest is receivable by the scheme in respect of the securities in the following year of assessment, the acquisition cost of the securities in the CGT computation is reduced by the amount of the interest accruing after the disposal (calculated as under *Sch 21*), and that amount is carried forward to the following year of assessment as a loss on the disposal.

The 'DIRT' scheme (see **13.9** 'Deduction of tax at source') applies to deposits made by the scheme trustees or managers.

Payments made to holders of units by the managing company or trustees by reason of rights as unitholders are disregarded for income tax purposes, and no chargeable gain arises on the disposal of units. [*TCA 1997, ss 737, 839(5); FA 1998, s 53; FA 1999, s 63; FA 2000, s 57(a), Sch 2; FA 2001, s 73, Sch 2 para 40; FA 2003, s 50*]

16.32 Special portfolio investment accounts. A '*special portfolio investment account*' is an account, designated as such, opened **before 6 April 2001** in which a 'relevant investment' is held and in respect of which the following conditions are met:

(a) The account must not be opened by or held in the name of an individual under full age;

(b) The account must be opened by and held in the name of the individual beneficially entitled to the income and gains in respect of the relevant investments therein;

(c) The account may not be a joint account, except in the case of an account opened and held as such by a married couple;

(d) Only one account may be held by an individual. Married couples may jointly hold two such accounts. Married couples with jointly-held accounts may not also hold accounts of their own;

(e) A signed declaration must be made, in prescribed form and containing such information and undertakings as the Revenue Commissioners may reasonably require, to the 'designated broker' in writing by the individual to whom interest is payable in respect of the relevant investment(s), to the effect that the conditions in (a)–(d) are satisfied in relation to the account. The declaration must contain the full name and address of that individual, and an undertaking to notify the designated broker if any of the conditions in (a)–(d) subsequently ceases to be satisfied. It must also contain such other information as the Revenue Commissioners may reasonably require;

(f) Each account and the related assets must be kept separately from all other accounts;

(g) The aggregate investment in an account must not exceed €63,500/£50,000, and before 6 April 2001 the market value of the investments could not exceed £50,000 on the fifth anniversary of the first investment;

(h) The investment requirements described at **16.31**(b) above apply also to such accounts.

For the purposes of (g) above, disposals are, where necessary, identified with later acquisitions before earlier.

A '*relevant investment*' is an investment in 'qualifying shares' and 'specified qualifying shares' which must be fully paid-up and acquired at market value, in addition to which certain government and other securities may be held. '*Qualifying shares*' are ordinary shares in companies listed on the Irish Stock Exchange or quoted on the

Developing Companies or Exploration Securities Markets of the Exchange, other than shares in investment companies or UCITS or whose value approximates to the market value of the company's assets. '*Specified qualifying shares*' are qualifying shares in companies with market capitalisation (at the time of acquisition of the shares) of less than €255 million/£200 million. A '*designated broker*' is a dealing member firm of the Irish Stock Exchange (or a member firm of a stock exchange elsewhere in the EU trading in RI through a branch or agency) which has notified the Revenue Commissioners of its intention to accept deposits from individuals for the purpose of acquiring relevant investments.

The provisions relating to special savings accounts (see **13.9** 'Deduction of tax at source') apply equally to special portfolio investment accounts, with certain modifications. The designated broker is deemed to have made a payment on the last day of each year of assessment of the aggregate income and gains arising from the relevant investments held in the account, and is required to account for tax equivalent to 20 per cent (or ten per cent) of that payment by 31 October following the end of the year of assessment (1 November in relation to 2000/01 and earlier years). No other tax liability arises on the account holder. The calculation of the income and gains is on broadly the same basis as applies in relation to special investment schemes (see **16.31** above), including the exemption of business expansion scheme investments. Additionally, the small chargeable gains exemption does not apply. A net loss is carried forward to set against income and gains of the following and future years. No other relief is available for such losses, except that where an account is closed on or after 1 January 2002, any unrelieved loss is treated as an allowable loss accruing to the account holder at the date of closure. [*TCA 1997, s 838; FA 1993, s 14; FA 1995, s 11(2); FA 1996, s 37; FA 1997, s 31; FA 1998, s 53; FA 1999, s 65; FA 2000, Sch 2; FA 2001, ss 56, 241, Sch 2 para 46; FA 2002, s 50*]

16.33 Special savings incentive accounts. A special savings incentive account is a scheme of investment commenced between 1 May 2001 and 30 April 2002 inclusive by an RI-resident individual aged 18 or over with a registered 'qualifying savings manager' (as defined, see *ss 848B(1), 848R*, and see also *SI 176/01, regs 3, 4*) in respect of which the following conditions are satisfied:

(*a*)   Apart from the associated tax credit (see below), only the individual (or spouse) may subscribe to the account, and such subscriptions must not be funded by borrowing or by deferral of repayment of borrowings;

(*b*)   Subscriptions (disregarding any withdrawals) may not exceed €254/£200 in any one month, and in the first twelve months must be of a monthly amount of at least €12.50/£10 which is agreed with the manager on commencement of the account;

(*c*)   The subscriptions (and tax credits) must be used by the manager only to acquire 'qualifying assets' held and managed by the manager, which are beneficially owned by the individual but may not be assigned or otherwise pledged as security for a loan;

(*d*)   The individual must, on commencing the account, make a signed declaration under *s 848F* to the manager containing specified information, and including an undertaking to inform the manager if the declaration ceases to be materially correct. In particular, the declaration includes a statement that the account holder is the beneficial owner of the assets in the account and has not commenced any other special savings incentive account;

(*e*) The manager must notify the individual if he or she ceases to be a registered qualifying savings manager, and accounts must be transferable in that event or between registered qualifying savings managers at the request of the individual (for which see *s 848N*). See *SI 176/01, regs 11, 12*;

(*f*) The manager must take reasonable measures to confirm the individual's PPS Number included in the declaration referred to in (*d*) above (and must retain for inspection copies of all material used to establish its correctness), and to ensure that the terms under which the account is commenced are and continue to be complied with. See *SI 176/01, reg 6* and the Guidance Notes published in accordance with those regulations.

The manager is required to notify the Revenue if he or she has reasonable grounds to suspect that the above terms are not being complied with in relation to a particular account. The manager is now also obliged to, when required by Revenue, make a return to them in electronic format which sets out, in relation to all SSIAs managed by them, whatever details Revenue may specify. [*FA 2007, s 32*]

'*Qualifying assets*' are deposit accounts (as broadly defined, including certain deposits with European credit institutions), shares (as under *Credit Union Act 1997, s 2(1)*), units in investment undertakings or units or shares in European UCITSs (see **12.22** 'Corporation tax'), certain life assurance policies, company shares on the official list of a recognised stock exchange (or to be so listed within 30 days of their allocation or allotment under a public offer) and government securities. They may only be acquired at arm's length out of money held in the account, and may not be purchased from the account holder or any connected person (within *s 10*). They must not be 'connected' with any other asset or liability of the account holder or a connected person, ie the terms on which either asset or the liability is acquired and held must not differ from those on which it would have been acquired and held in the absence of the other.

Income and chargeable gains arising in respect of qualifying assets held in the account are exempt from income tax and capital gains tax, although any tax return by the individual for the year of commencement of the account must include notification of that commencement. Deposit interest is not within the DIRT scheme (see **13.9** 'Deduction of tax at source'), and this applies also to dividends on credit union shares held in a special share account (see **13.9** 'Deduction of tax at source') within a special savings incentive account.

As regards (*e*) above, on a transfer all account assets must be transferred to a single transferee manager, and the account holder must make the appropriate declaration under *s 848O* to the new manager (in broadly similar terms to the declaration required under (*d*) above on commencement of the account). The transferor manager is also required to give to the transferee a notice containing specified information in relation to the account and a declaration as to fulfilment of his or her obligations.

Tax credit. For the first five years from commencement of a special savings incentive account, the account holder is treated as having been credited with tax at 20 per cent on the amount of subscriptions to the account grossed up at that rate (ie a €200 subscription gives rise to a €50 tax credit). The Revenue Commissioners will then (on the basis of a proper monthly return by the manager, see below) pay to the manager the amount of the tax credit, which is beneficially owned by the individual and must immediately be credited to the account. Subscriptions in the month in which the fifth anniversary of the commencement of the account falls, and any subsequent subscriptions, do not attract the tax credit. The Revenue Commissioners have appropriate powers of inspection to audit returns by qualifying savings managers (see s 904H; FA 2001, s 22(3)).

Termination of account. A special savings incentive account matures five years after the end of the month in which a subscription was first made where the account holder has made the appropriate declaration (see s 848I) to the qualifying savings manager or, if earlier, on the day of the account holder's death. The declaration under s 848I has to be made in the period of three months ending five years after the end of the month in which it commenced. An account is treated as ceasing at any time before it matures at which any of the conditions at (a)–(f) above cease to be met or at which the account holder is neither resident nor ordinarily resident in RI (and see SI 176/01, reg 10). Where an account either matures or ceases, it thereupon ceases to be a special savings incentive account, and the account assets (net of any tax liabilities as below) are treated for capital gains tax purposes (where relevant) as having been acquired at that time at their then market value or, in the case of life assurance policies, as having been commenced at that time with premiums having been paid equal in amount to the market value of the policy at that time.

Taxation of gains. A liability to income tax at 23 per cent arises on the manager of an account where a gain arises on the account's being treated as maturing or ceasing or on a withdrawal being made from the account. See below for the quantification of the gain in each case. The tax may be paid out of the account funds (any shortfall being a debt due to the manager from the account holder). It is payable without assessment at the time by which the monthly return in which it has to be included (see below) must be made, and may be assessed if not paid on or before that date. The Revenue have powers to raise estimated assessments where they are not satisfied with a return, and there are provisions for interest, appeals, collection, etc.

Gain on maturity. A gain is treated as accruing on an account on the day on which the account is treated as maturing. The gain is equal in amount to the aggregate market value of the account assets at that time *less* the amounts subscribed (including tax credits), so far as not previously withdrawn. Withdrawals of account assets (at market value, where appropriate, and before any deduction in respect of any related tax liability, see below) are for this purpose treated as withdrawals of subscriptions up to the full amount of the subscriptions made since commencement (and not previously treated as withdrawn).

Gain on cessation. A gain is treated as accruing on an account on the day on which the account is treated as ceasing. The gain is equal in amount to the aggregate market value of the account assets at that time.

Gain on withdrawal. A gain is treated as accruing where a withdrawal is made from an account before it is treated as maturing or ceasing (as above). The gain is equal in amount to the cash withdrawn and (where appropriate) the then market value of any other assets withdrawn.

Income post-maturity or cessation. Any income accruing on an account which has not been taken into account on maturity, cessation or withdrawal is, when received, treated as cash withdrawn from the account before it is treated as maturing or ceasing, the qualifying savings manager being liable (as above) to tax on the gain thereby arising.

Pensions Investment Credit. A new provision was introduced to encourage those on lower incomes to invest some or all of their SSIA funds into a pension product on maturity. This section provides for a claw-back of tax credits where a person availing of the credit invests in a pension product and withdraws the funds within one year. Where the withdrawal takes place before 10 April 2007, the pension investor will be assessed to income tax by the Revenue Commissioners in such an amount which ensures that the appropriate amount of tax credits are recovered. Where withdrawal takes place after 10 April 2007, the pension administrator is required to deduct the clawback amount from any payment being made. The amount of the clawback will be in the same proportion to the amount withdrawn as the total tax credits bear to the aggregate of the total tax credits and the amount of the SSIA funds invested in the pension product.

Returns. A qualifying savings manager is required to make both monthly and annual returns in relation to all special savings incentive accounts managed by him or her.

Monthly returns (including nil returns) are required within 15 days of the end of every month, giving details of all tax credits and liabilities in relation to accounts managed during that month, and accompanied by a declaration in specified form that, to the best of the manager's knowledge and belief, the details given are correct.

Annual returns (including nil returns) are required by 28 February following each year of assessment, containing specified information in relation to all accounts managed during that year, and accompanied by a declaration in specified form that, to the best of the manager's knowledge and belief, the accounts continue to meet the relevant conditions and that the information given in the return is correct.

See *SI 176/01, regs 7–9, 13, 14.*

Regulations. The Revenue have wide-ranging powers to make regulations for the purpose of the administration of special savings incentive accounts. See *SI 176/01.*

Penalties of €1,900/£1,500 and/or six months imprisonment may be imposed for the making of false declarations under these provisions. [*TCA 1997, ss 848B–848U; FA 2001, s 33; FA 2002, ss 49, 129(1)(a); FA 2006, s 41*]

For a general article on the new scheme, see Revenue Tax Briefing Issue 43 pp 25, 26.

17 Exempt Organisations

The following organisations etc, are specifically exempt from tax as indicated.

17.1 Agricultural societies. Profits of shows, etc, applied to the purposes of the society are exempt from income tax. [*TCA 1997, s 215*] See **38.226** 'Tax cases'.

17.2 Athletic or amateur games or sports: promotional bodies. Exempt from income tax or corporation tax on income applied to promotion. [*TCA 1997, s 235*] The conditions for exemption were tightened by *FA 1984, s 9*, which enables the Revenue Commissioners (subject to the usual appeal rights) to deny exemption where they are satisfied that the body was not established, or no longer exists, solely for the promotion of athletic or amateur games or sports, or was, wholly or partly, established to secure a tax advantage. Bodies exempt before 6 April 1984 continue to qualify, but relief may be withdrawn after 5 April 1984 from any body failing to meet the above conditions. See **2.32** 'Allowances, credits and rates' for the treatment of donations to approved sports bodies. See generally Revenue Tax Briefing Issue 44 p 20. See also **38.228** 'Tax cases'. Since 1 January 2003, a capital gain of any body within *s 235* or established by statute principally for the promotion of games or sport and any company wholly owned by such a body, where the gain is applied solely for that purpose, is not a chargeable gain. [*FA 2003, s 72*] Since 2 February 2006, the gain is exempt only if the entire proceeds giving rise to the gain are applied solely for the promotion of games or sport. Where only part of the proceeds are applied, the exemption applies to the appropriate part of the gain. [*FA 2006, s 74*]

17.3 Bord Gáis Éireann is exempt from corporation tax for accounting periods beginning before 25 March 1999. [*TCA 1997, s 220; FA 1999, s 77*]

17.4 An Bord Pinsean is exempt from corporation tax. [*TCA 1997, s 220*]

17.5 Charities (including hospitals, public schools, almshouses, ecclesiastical bodies) are exempt on income and gains applied to charitable purposes. This includes any profits from a trade of farming, and profits of any other trade where the work is mainly carried on by the beneficiaries of the charity. Gifts for maintenance of graves, memorials etc within certain limits are treated as gifts for charitable purposes. [*TCA 1997, ss 207, 208, 609; Charities Act 1961, s 50*] It is understood that, by concession, trading profits from occasional bazaars, jumble sales, gymkhanas, etc organised to raise funds for charity are generally exempted from liability to tax.
See **38.53–38.56** 'Tax cases'.
 Donations to Third World charities. For 2000/01 and earlier years, where a 'qualifying donation' is made to a 'designated charity', it is treated in the hands of the charity as an annual payment received under deduction of tax at the standard rate (see **2.5** 'Allowances, credits and rates') for the year in which the donation was made. The

charity may claim repayment of the notional tax deducted in the normal way (but restricted, where the donor has not paid all the tax referred to in the 'appropriate certificate' (see below), to the amount of that tax which has been paid).

A *'qualifying donation'* is a donation by an RI-resident individual who has given an 'appropriate certificate' to the charity in relation to the donation, and has paid the tax referred to in the certificate (and is not entitled to claim a repayment of any part of that tax). The donation must be a sum or sums of money totalling not less than £200 in the year of assessment of payment, and must neither be subject to a condition as to repayment nor give rise to a benefit for the donor or a connected person (within *s 10*). It must not be related to the acquisition of property by the charity from the donor (or a connected person) other than by way of gift.

There is an overall limit of £750 on qualifying donations by an individual in a year of assessment.

A *'designated charity'* is a charity designated for these purposes by the Minister for Foreign Affairs, who is required to maintain a list of designated bodies, to be published from time to time in the *Iris Oifigiúil*. A number of references to the requirement that qualifying educational bodies must be established in the State are being removed as a result of representations by the EU Commission. [*FA 2007*] The Irish Heritage Trust has been included as an eligible charity and has been removed from *Sch 26A*. [*FA 2008*] See also Revenue Tax Briefing Issue 44 Supplement p 19. The conditions for designation are set out in *s 848(2)*, broadly requiring the sole object of the charity to be relief and development in countries in Part 1 of the OECD List of Aid Recipients. Notice of withdrawal of designation must be published in the *Iris Oifigiúil* within one month, and is effective from the start of the year of assessment in which such notice is given.

An *'appropriate certificate'* is a certificate in prescribed form containing the donor's Revenue and Social Insurance Number, and a statement by the donor to the effect that the donation satisfies the above requirements, and that the donor has paid or will pay income tax of an amount equal to tax at the standard rate on the grossed-up amount of the donation, being neither tax the donor may charge against any other person or deduct, satisfy or retain out of any payments the donor is liable to make to any other person, nor tax deducted under the DIRT scheme (see **13.9** 'Deduction of tax at source').

For gifts after 5 April 2001, see **2.30** 'Allowances, credits and rates' and **12.9** 'Corporation tax'.

[*TCA 1997, ss 848, 848A(13); FA 2001, s 45(1); FA 2005, s 38*]

17.6 The Commission for Electricity Regulation is exempt from corporation tax. [*TCA 1997, s 220; FA 2000, s 84*]

17.7 The Courts Service is a body listed in *Sch 4* (see **17.26** below) from 2006 and is exempt from capital gains tax from 2 February 2006. [*FA 2006, ss 69, 74*]

17.8 Credit unions registered under *Credit Union Act 1997* are exempt from corporation tax. The earlier exemption of credit unions registered under the *Industrial and Provident Societies Acts* is accordingly repealed. [*TCA 1997, ss 212, 219A; FA 1998, s 58*] Since 6 April 1999, share or loan interest paid by a credit union is interest payable under deduction of tax and chargeable under Case III of Sch D, and is *not* a distribution (so that dividend withholding tax (see **13.12** 'Deduction of tax at source') does not apply). Since 1 January 2002, however, credit unions are brought within the DIRT scheme, subject to special conditions (see **13.9** 'Deduction of tax at source'). [*TCA 1997, s 700(1)(1A); FA 2000, s 32; FA 2001, s 57(1)(b)*]

17.9 Dublin Docklands Development Authority or any wholly-owned subsidiary is exempt from corporation tax and capital gains tax. [*TCA 1997, ss 220, 610, Sch 15 Pt I, Sch 32 para 3; FA 1988, s 42; FA 1997, s 49; FA 2001, s 79*]

17.10 European Economic Interest Groupings (EEIGs) within *EEC Directive No 2137/85* and *SI 191/89* are not within the charge to income tax, corporation tax or capital gains tax. Any assessment required to be made in respect of profits or gains arising to the EEIG is made on (and losses allowed to) members of the EEIG. The income tax and capital gains tax provisions relating to partnerships apply generally, with appropriate modification, to the activities of an EEIG, as if members of the EEIG were partners therein. [*TCA 1997, s 1014*]

17.11 Friendly societies. Unregistered societies with income not exceeding €205/£160 pa and registered societies not assuring to any person a gross sum in excess of €1,270/ £1,000 or €70/£52 pa annuity are exempt under Schs C, D and F.

A registered society must also:

(i)   be established solely for purposes under *Friendly Societies Act 1896, s 8(1)* and not for securing a tax advantage; and

(ii)   since establishment, have engaged solely in activities for those purposes and not in trading activities (other than insurance re members).

The society may appeal against a determination that it does not satisfy these conditions. [*TCA 1997, s 211*]

17.12 The Great Book of Ireland Trust. Income arising to the trustees from sales of The Great Book of Ireland is disregarded for all tax purposes, as are payments made by the trustees to Clashganna Mills Trust Ltd or Poetry Ireland Ltd. [*TCA 1997, s 210*]

17.13 Harbour authorities within RI are exempt under Sch D on profits arising from maintaining normal port facilities. Harbour companies established under *Harbours Act 1996, s 7*, and other companies controlling harbours and carrying on similar trading activities, are similarly exempt until 31 December 1998, with two-thirds of such profits being exempt for 1999 and one-third for 2000, profits being fully taxable thereafter. [*TCA 1997, s 229*]

See *s 842, Sch 26* as regards continuity of capital allowances and capital gains treatment where a harbour authority is replaced by a port company under *Harbours Act 1996*.

17.14 The Housing Finance Agency is exempt from corporation tax on trading income arising from the making of loans and advances under *Housing Finance Agency Act*

1981, s 5 and on income otherwise chargeable under Sch D, Case III (**31**). [*TCA 1997, s 218*]

17.15 Horse Ireland Limited (formerly the **Irish Horseracing Authority**), **Irish Thoroughbred Marketing Ltd** and **Tote Ireland Ltd** are exempt from corporation tax on profits, and gains on disposals are not chargeable gains. [*TCA 1997, ss 220, 610, Sch 15 Pt I*]

17.16 Investor Compensation Company Ltd is exempt from corporation tax on profits arising in any accounting period ending after 9 September 1998. [*TCA 1997, s 219B; FA 1999, s 76(1)(a)*]

17.17 The Irish Auditing and Accounting Supervisory Authority is a body listed in *Sch 4* (see 17.24 below) from 2006 and is exempt from capital gains tax since 2 February 2006. [*FA 2006, ss 69, 74*]

17.18 Local authorities, Health Service Executive (formerly health boards), agriculture committees and vocational education committees in respect of income tax (other than the requirement to deduct basic rate tax from certain interest payments, see **13.9** 'Deduction of tax at source') [*TCA 1997, s 214; FA 2005, Sch 6 (1)(c)*] and capital gains tax (see **9.7**(*k*) 'Capital gains tax'). See also **12.1** 'Corporation tax'.

17.19 National Co-operative Farm Relief Services Ltd. See **12.12** 'Corporation tax'.

17.20 National Treasury Management Agency profits are exempt from corporation tax and gains are not chargeable gains. [*TCA 1997, ss 230, 610, Sch 15 Pt I*]

17.21 National Pension Reserve Fund Commission profits are exempt from corporation tax and gains are not chargeable gains (see **9.7**(*k*) 'Capital gains tax'). [*TCA 1997, ss 230A, 610, Sch 15 Pt I; National Pensions Reserve Fund Act 2000, s 30(b)*]

17.22 National Development Finance Agency profits are exempt from corporation tax and gains are not chargeable gains. [*TCA 1997, ss 230AB, 610, Sch 15 Pt I; FA 2003, s 43*]

17.23 Nítrigin Éireann Teoranta is exempt from corporation tax on any income (otherwise chargeable under Sch D, Case I) arising in any accounting period ending before 1 January 2000 from the supply of gas (purchased from Bord Gáis Éireann) under contract to Irish Fertilizer Industries Ltd. [*TCA 1997, s 217*]

17.244 Non-commercial state-sponsored bodies (as listed in *Sch 4*, which is subject to amendment by order of the Minister for Finance). Income of such bodies which would otherwise be chargeable under Sch D, Case III, IV or V (ie *excluding* trade or professional income) is disregarded for all purposes of the *Tax Acts*, except the liability to deduct and account for tax on interest payments under the Deposit Interest Retention

Tax scheme (see **13.9** 'Deduction of tax at source') (and such a body is not treated as a company within the corporation tax charge for the purposes of the exception from treatment of a deposit as a 'relevant deposit' detailed at **13.9**(vii), nor as a person to whom the repayment provisions of *s 267* under the scheme apply). The exemption applies from the date of incorporation or establishment of the body, but no repayment may be made of income or corporation tax paid by such a body. [*TCA 1997, ss 227; FA 2003, s 64; FA 2004, s 40*; *FA 2006 s 69*]

17.25 Securitisation (Proceeds of Certain Mortgages) Act 1995, s 4(1) 'designated bodies' are exempt from income, corporation and capital gains taxes, and securities issued by such bodies carry similar exemptions. [*TCA 1997, ss 228*]

17.26 Superannuation funds and occupational pension schemes (see *ss 770–782, Sch 23*) approved by the Revenue Commissioners are exempt from tax on investment income. Investment includes dealing in financial futures or traded options (including on a non-RI exchange). There is a charge to tax at the standard rate (currently 20 per cent, see **2.5** 'Allowances, credits and rates') (before 5 December 2001, at a fixed 25 per cent rate) on refunds of employee contributions. [*TCA 1997, ss 774, 780; FA 1972, s 21; FA 1992, s 6; FA 2002, s 10; FA 2003, s 14; FA 2004, s 16; FA 2005, s 21; Social Welfare and Pensions Act 2005, s 36*]

17.27 Takeover Panel. The body designated under *Irish Takeover Panel Act 1997, s 3* is exempt from corporation tax on income. [*TCA 1997, s 219*]

17.28 Trade unions. Registered unions which are precluded by statute or rules from assuring to any person a gross sum exceeding €10,160/£8,000 or annuity exceeding €2,540/£2000 pa are exempt under Schs C, D and F on investment income applied solely to provident benefits or the education, training or retraining of members or their dependent children. Since 2 February 2006, all chargeable gains are exempt to the extent that the proceeds are applied solely for registered trade union activities. Since 1 January 2003, all chargeable gains are exempt where the gain is applied solely for registered trade union activities. Prior to that date the exemption was more limited. [*TCA 1997, ss 213, 610; FA 2000, s 74; FA 2003, s 72*; *FA 2006, s 74*]

17.29 Trust schemes approved by the Revenue Commissioners for providing retirement annuities to individuals etc in particular occupations are exempt from income tax on investment income. [*TCA 1997, ss 784(4), 785(5)(6)*]

17.30 United Nations Organisation or Council of Europe. For 2000/01 and earlier years, certain bodies having consultative status with these organisations may claim the same exemptions as charities [*TCA 1997, s 209*], but with the additional benefit that deeds of covenant to them for three years or longer will be recognised for tax purposes. [*TCA 1997, ss 792(1)(b)(iii), 848A(13); FA 2001, s 45(1)*] For donations after 5 April 2001, see **2.30** 'Allowances, credits and rates' and **12.9** 'Corporation tax'.

17.31 Tourism Ireland Limited is one of the bodies to which **17.24** above applies. It is also exempt from capital gains tax. [*FA 2003, s 72*]

17.32 A Personal Retirement Savings Account ('PRSA') is exempt from income tax on investment income held for the purposes of the PRSA. [*TCA 1997, s 787I*] See **2.23**.

17.33 Institute of Public Health in Ireland Limited and Private Residential Tenancies Board. These two bodies have been added to the list under *Sch 4*. *Schedule 4* lists the non-commercial State sponsored bodies who having exemption from tax in respect of non-trading income which would otherwise be chargeable to income tax or corporation tax. The exemption is granted with effect from 1 October 2002 for the Institute of Public Health in Ireland Limited and 1 September 2004 for the Private Residential Tenancies Board. [*TCA 1997, Sch 4; F(No 2) A 2008, s 36*]

18 Farming

[*TCA 1997, Pt 23*] **Cross-reference.** See also **33.3** 'Sch D, Case V' – property income as regards leasing of farm land.

18.1 Profits from farming in RI are assessable under Sch D, Case I as a single trade (whether carried on solely or in partnership). This does not, however, prevent the commencement and cessation basis (see **30.5** 'Sch D, Cases I and II') applying where a partnership trade is set up or ceases. [*TCA 1997, s 655(1)(2)*] See **17.5** 'Exempt organisations' as regards farming carried on by charities. See **38.221** 'Tax cases' as regards 'farming'.

INDIVIDUALS – BASIS OF ASSESSMENT

18.2 Individuals are assessed under Sch D, Case I. The normal accounts basis applies (see **30.3** 'Sch D, Cases I and II'), *except that* a 'full-time farmer' may elect (in writing, within 30 days of the date of the notice of assessment for the year) to be charged by reference to an average figure (see below), provided that he was charged to tax under Sch D, Case I on the current year basis in respect of farming profits in each of the two preceding years of assessment. [*TCA 1997, s 657(4)*]

An individual carrying on 'farming' in a year of assessment is a *'full-time farmer'* unless he, or his spouse living with him, carried on at any time during the year of assessment, solely or in partnership, another trade or profession (but excluding provision of accommodation in farm buildings by wife as ancillary activity in farm trade), or was a director controlling, directly or indirectly, more than 25 per cent of the ordinary share capital of a trading company. *'Farming'* means farming land in RI, other than market garden land (see **30.1**(ii) 'Sch D, Cases I and II'), 'occupied' wholly or mainly for the purposes of husbandry, and *'occupation'* of land means having the use thereof or the right to graze livestock thereon. [*TCA 1997, ss 654, 657(1)–(3)*]

The *'average figure'* for a year of assessment is arrived at by taking a 'fair and just' average of the profits or losses of the three years ending on the normal accounting date in the year of assessment concerned or, if there is no normal accounting date, on the last day of the year of assessment. Any necessary aggregation of profits and losses in those three years is made. Where an overall loss results, one-third of that loss will be allowable in the normal way for the year of assessment concerned, except that, for 2001, only 74 per cent of that amount is allowable, the balance of 26 per cent being carried forward under *s 382* (see **22.2**(*b*) 'Losses'). Losses so aggregated may not be relieved in any other way.

If there is a twelve-month period of account ending between 1 January 2002 and 5 April 2002 inclusive, those accounts are for these purposes treated as made up to a date in the year of assessment 2001 as well as in 2002. For 2001 only, the three-year average figure arrived at is reduced by 26 per cent.

An election, once made, continues in force for all subsequent years until withdrawn, except that it does not apply to years in which the individual is not a full-time farmer (see above). The election may be withdrawn for a year of assessment and subsequent years (in the return required under *s 951* (see **28.11** 'Returns')) provided that in each of the three preceding years of assessment the averaging basis was applied. The election is in any event deemed to have been (validly) withdrawn for any year in which the individual is not a full-time farmer, and for subsequent years.

Following such a withdrawal election (whether actual or deemed), the assessment for each of the first two of the last three years assessed on the averaging basis is increased to the amount of the profits assessed for the last such year, if either or both of them would otherwise have been less than that figure. Where any of those three years is the short tax year 2001, an adjustment is made to take account of the lower profits assessed for that year. Where 2001 is the final averaged year, the previous two years may be increased to 135 per cent of the profits assessed for 2001, and where it is one of the first two of those three years, the profits assessed for 2001 may be increased to 74 per cent of the profits of the final year.

Capital allowances and charges continue to be given or made as if the profits were assessed on the normal basis, and the cessation provisions under Sch D, Case I (see **30.5** 'Sch D, Cases I and II') will have effect, where appropriate, notwithstanding any election under these provisions.

The normal rules regarding computation of profits, delivery of returns, etc apply where assessments are raised on the averaging basis. [*TCA 1997, s 657(5)–(12); FA 2001, s 78(2)(c), Sch 2 para 37*]

A farmer who is in receipt of payments under the EU single payment scheme and FEOGA scheme during 2005 and who has not made an election under *s 657* (discussed above) may elect to have these payments averaged over three years for income tax purposes. If the trade is discontinued within the three years, the remainder of the payments are taxed in the year of discontinuance. The election must be made on or before 31 October 2006 and cannot be revoked. [*TCA 1997, s 657A; FA 2005, s 29*]

COMPANIES

18.3 Companies are liable to corporation tax (**12**) on all farming profits.

COMPULSORY DISPOSAL

18.4 A special relief may be claimed where cattle forming part of trading stock of a farming business are all compulsorily disposed of after 5 April 1993 under any statute relating to the eradication or control of livestock diseases (including all cattle required to be disposed of under a brucellosis eradication scheme), and there is an excess of amounts received as a result of that disposal over the value of the stock at the beginning of the accounting period of the disposal. This relief is extended to include situations where part of a livestock herd is disposed under any disease eradication scheme. [*FA 2008, s 33*] For disposals from 21 February 2001, the farmer may elect (by the specified return date for the period of the disposal, see **28.11** 'Returns') to have the excess treated as arising in four equal instalments, either in the accounting period of the disposal and the following three accounting periods, or in the four accounting periods following that of the disposal, but any part of the excess which would arise after a permanent discontinuance is brought into charge under Sch D, Case IV for the period of discontinuance. For disposals prior to 21 February 2001, the deferral period was two years.

Since 6 December 2000, this election is extended to the compulsory disposal of animals and poultry within *Diseases of Animals Act 1966, Sch 1 Pts I and II* for which compensation is paid by the Minister for Agriculture, Food and Rural Development.

Where, not later than the end of the period over which the excess is treated as arising (as above), expenditure of not less than the amount received as a result of the compulsory disposal is incurred (or, for disposals from 21 February 2001, is intended to be incurred) on replacement of the cattle, stock relief (see **18.9** below) at a special rate of 100 per cent may be claimed in respect of the amount of the excess brought in in each period. Where, however, such replacement expenditure is less than the amount so received, the relief is correspondingly reduced. For disposals from 21 February 2001, this applies to the aggregate deduction over the spreading period, the reduction being made, as far as possible, in a later rather than an earlier accounting period. For earlier disposals, the reduction is applied equally over the spreading period.

Special provision is made as regards instalments treated as arising in an accounting period of one year ending after 31 December 2001 and before 6 April 2002 on which the assessments for both 2001 and 2002 are computed. Any such instalment is split 74:26 between those years. Similar provision is made in relation to the 100 per cent relief for replacement stock. [*TCA 1997, s 668; FA 2001, s 49; FA 2002, s 29*] See also Revenue Tax Briefing Issue 50 pp 3, 4.

CAPITAL ALLOWANCES

18.5 A farm buildings allowance may be claimed for capital expenditure (net of grants etc) incurred on farm buildings (after 5 April 1971 and excluding buildings or parts of buildings used as dwellings), fences etc and (after 31 March 1989) roadways, holding yards, drains and land reclamation. The allowances are made during a writing-down period of seven years beginning with the chargeable period in which the expenditure is incurred, at the rate of 15 per cent per annum for the first six years and ten per cent per annum for the last year. Prior to 27 January 1994, the normal annual allowance was ten per cent, but accelerated allowances could be claimed up to 31 March 1992. In respect of expenditure incurred after 31 March 1991 and before 1 April 1992, the maximum accelerated allowance was 25 per cent (whether claimed in one or more than one chargeable periods). Between 1 April 1989 and 31 March 1991 inclusive, the maximum allowance was 50 per cent, and between 6 April 1982 and 31 March 1989 inclusive, 30 per cent. There was a special accelerated allowance of up to 50 per cent (in one or more chargeable periods) for expenditure between 1 April 1991 and 31 March 1993 inclusive on farmyard pollution control works in respect of which grant-aid has been paid under the Farm Improvement Programme or the Scheme of Investment Aid for the Control of Farmyard Pollution (and see now below). For expenditure incurred before 6 April 1982, farmhouses and cottages also qualified for capital allowances, but allowances were restricted to one-third of the expenditure in the case of farmhouses. Where an individual is not chargeable to income tax for a year of assessment, any annual allowances which would otherwise have been claimable are deemed to have been made and not carried forward. Where property is transferred, any allowances remaining for subsequent years continue to be claimable by the transferee. [*TCA 1997, s 658, Sch 32 para 23; FA 1974, s 22; FA 1980, s 27; FA 1982, s 16; FA 1983, s 15; FA 1988, s 52(1); FA 1989, s 15; FA 1990, s 77; FA 1991, s 25; FA 1993, s 34(2); FA 1994, s 23*]

An initial allowance of 20 per cent was also claimable on such expenditure incurred between 6 April 1974 and 5 April 1980. [*FA 1974, s 22(2)(a); FA 1980, s 27*]

Free depreciation could be claimed for capital expenditure incurred after 5 April 1977 and before 1 April 1989 on constructing fences, roadways, holding yards, or drains, or in land reclamation. [*TCA 1997, Sch 32 para 23; FA 1977, s 14; FA 1988, s 52(2)*]

Capital allowances on machinery and plant. In determining wear and tear allowances and balancing allowances and charges, the appropriate wear and tear allowances are deemed to have been made to the farmer for any years in which he did not farm, or was not taxable under Sch D, Case I, or was charged on the notional basis, or during which the machinery or plant was not used for farming purposes. [*TCA 1997, s 660*] See **8.6** 'Capital allowances'.

See under **8.3** 'Capital allowances' for basis periods in which expenditure is incurred.

Farm pollution control allowances. Special allowances may be claimed for capital expenditure incurred after 5 April 1997 and before 1 January 2009 on the construction of farm buildings (other than dwellings) or structures within the *s 659* Table (see below). This scheme has been extended for a further two years to 31 December 2010. [*F(No 2)A 2008, s 17*] A farm nutrient management plan must have been drawn up for the farmer in respect of farm land occupied by the farmer, by an agency or planner approved for the purpose by the Department of Agriculture, Food and Forestry, in accordance with the appropriate guidelines or scheme, and the buildings, etc must be constructed in accordance with the plan and be certified by the agency or planner as necessary to reduce or eliminate farming pollution. Expenditure including expenditure within these provisions is apportioned as may be just, but expenditure met directly or indirectly by the State or by any other person is excluded, as is expenditure which has attracted an industrial buildings allowance (see **8.5** 'Capital allowances') or farm buildings allowance (see above). Only expenditure properly attributable to work actually carried out in the qualifying period (as above) is treated as incurred in that period.

Subject to certain EU regulations, allowances for such expenditure are given in taxing the farming trade over a period of three years (seven years for expenditure incurred before 1 January 2005 and eight years for expenditure incurred before 6 April 2000), beginning with the chargeable period in which the expenditure is incurred. For expenditure incurred from 1 January 2005, subject to the election referred to below, the allowance is 331/3 per cent for each of the three years. For expenditure incurred after 5 April 2000 and before 1 January 2005, subject to the election, the allowance is 15 per cent of the expenditure in the first six years of the writing-down period and ten per cent in the seventh. Where the (irrevocable) election is made (on or before the specified return date for the chargeable period, see **28.11** 'Returns'), allowances may be given for up to 50 per cent of the expenditure (maximum allowance €50,000 from 2006, €31,750/£25,000 previously) in any year of the writing-down period, the balance of the expenditure being allowed as to 331/3 per cent in each of the three years (15 per cent in the first six years and ten per cent in the seventh for expenditure incurred from 6 April 2000 to 31 December 2004). For expenditure incurred before 6 April 2000, the allowance is 50 per cent of the expenditure in the first year (maximum allowance €19,050/£15,000 from 6 April 1998, previously €12,700/£10,000), the balance being relieved at a flat 15 per cent in each of the next six years and ten per cent in the seventh. Ineffective allowances are carried forward to the next and subsequent years.

On a transfer of the farm land in question (or part), the remaining allowances (or so much of them as is properly referable to the part transferred) for chargeable periods following that of the transfer are given to the transferee.

Buildings and structures within the Table are:

(*a*) waste storage facilities including slurry tanks;

(*b*) soiled water tanks;

(*c*) effluent tanks;

(*d*) tank fences and covers;

(*e*) dungsteads and manure pits;

(*f*) yard drains for storm and soiled water removal;

(*g*) walled silos, silage bases and silo aprons;

(*h*) housing for cattle, including drystock accommodation, byres, loose houses, slatted houses, sloped floor houses and kennels, roofed feed or exercise yards where such houses or structures eliminate soiled water; and

(*i*) housing for sheep and unroofed wintering structures for sheep and sheep dipping tanks.

Claims for farm pollution control allowances are made in the annual statement of farming profits or gains and determined by the inspector, subject to appeal to the Appeal Commissioners. [*TCA 1997, s 659; FA 1998, s 38; FA 2000, s 60; FA 2001, Sch 2 para 38; FA 2004, s 21; FA 2005, s 30; FA 2006, s 19*]

LOSSES

18.6 Relief for losses (see **22.2** 'Losses') will **not** be given in the following ways:

(*a*) By carry-forward of a loss incurred in a year of assessment for which the farmer was not chargeable to tax in respect of his farming profits; [*TCA 1997, s 661*]

(*b*) By set-off against other income, or profits of another trade, unless it is shown that, for the year of loss, the trade was being carried on on a commercial basis and with a view to profit. Nor will relief be given if a loss was incurred in each of the three previous years of assessment unless the activities in the year are carried on so as to justify a reasonable expectation of profits in the future and the activities in the three previous years could not reasonably have been expected to become profitable until after the year under review. These restrictions also apply to losses in market gardening but do not apply (i) where the trade is part of, and ancillary to, a larger undertaking, or (ii) where the trade commenced during the previous three years (ignoring changes where a person is carrying on the trade before and after the change). [*TCA 1997, ss 662, 663*]

TRADING STOCK

18.7 For stock relief, see **18.9** below.

Valuation. The normal basis of valuation of trading stock applies (ie lower of cost or market value). The Revenue will, however, accept that, for valuation purposes, the cost of trading stock may be taken as a percentage of the market value at a given date as follows:

(*a*)   cattle bred on the farm or purchased as immature stock: 60 per cent;

(*b*)   sheep and pigs bred on the farm or purchased as immature stock: 75 per cent;

(*c*)   harvested crops: 75 per cent.

Discontinued trade. Where, on a discontinuance, trading stock is transferred between farmers other than by sale or for valuable consideration, the transfer will normally be assumed to be at market value under *s 89(2)(b)* (see **30.31** 'Sch D, Cases I and II'). They may, however, jointly elect (in writing, before the specified return date for the period of the transfer under *s 950*, see **28.11** 'Returns') for the closing value of the stock in the transferor's discontinuance accounts to be the value taken in the transferee's accounts. [*TCA 1997, s 656*]

PAYMENT AND INTEREST

18.8 Farmers pay the tax on their farming profits at the same time as others chargeable under Sch D, Case I or II. See **25.1** 'Payment of tax'. See also **25.3** 'Payment of tax' as regards interest on unpaid tax.

STOCK RELIEF

18.9 No deduction under the provisions described below may be made in computing trading income for a company accounting period ending **after 31 December 2006** or, for a person other than a company, for a year of assessment **after 2006**, subject to EU State Aid rules. *Finance Act 2007* extended the reliefs under *ss 666 and 667A* by introducing *s 667B* which provides that the relief continues to apply for a further two years from 31 December 2006 to 31 December 2008; *Finance (No 2) Act 2008, s 18* extended the reliefs under *ss 666 and 667B* for a further two years to 31 December 2010; *Finance Act 2011, s 25* has extended the reliefs for a further two years to 31 December 2012; subject to this, where a person carries on a farming trade in respect of which he is chargeable under Sch D, Case I, he is entitled to a deduction from trading income for any accounting period of **25 per cent** (increased to **100 per cent** in certain cases, see below) of any '*increase in stock value*' (ie the value of opening stock *minus* the value of closing stock) over the period. For 2000/01 and earlier years, the person had to be resident in RI (and not resident elsewhere). Similar relief applies to farming trades carried on by partnerships. The deduction must be claimed by the specified return date for the period under *s 950* (see **28.11** 'Returns').

No relief is given for an accounting period which ends by virtue of the person ceasing to trade, or to be RI-resident, or to be within the Sch D, Case I charge.

The amount of the deduction may not exceed the Sch D, Case I trading income (disregarding the deduction itself). In the case of a company, trading income is for this purpose calculated after loss reliefs under *ss 396, 397* (see **12.17** 'Corporation tax') and capital allowances and balancing charges (see **12.9** 'Corporation tax'), and where a deduction is allowed for an accounting period, losses and capital allowances for earlier periods may not be carried forward to later periods, and no terminal losses may be carried back to earlier periods. In the case of a person other than a company, where a deduction is allowed for a year of assessment, there is similarly a prohibition on the carry forward of earlier losses or capital allowances and on the carry-back of terminal losses.

The increased **100 per cent** deduction referred to above applies to 'qualifying farmers'. A '*qualifying farmer*' is an individual:

(A)   who, in the year 2004 or any subsequent year of assessment, first qualifies for grant aid under the Scheme of Installation Aid for Young Farmers operated by the Department of Agriculture, Food and Forestry; or

(B)   who first becomes chargeable under Sch D, Case I in respect of farming profits in the year of assessment 2004 or a subsequent year, who is aged under 35 at the commencement of that first year of assessment, and who, at any time in that first year of assessment satisfies one of the following conditions:

(i)   is the holder of a qualification included in the Table to *s 667A* (or certified by Teagasc (The Agricultural and Food Development Authority) as corresponding to such a qualification or deemed by the National Qualifications Authority of Ireland to be of at least the same standard) and also (in certain cases) a certificate issued by Teagasc of satisfactory attendance of more than 100 hours at a course in either or both of horticulture or agriculture and attendance of more than 80 hours at a course of farm management training; or (in certain other cases) a certificate issued by the Further Education and Training Awards Council of satisfactory attendance at a Teagasc approved course of more than 80 hours of farm management,

(ii)   has achieved the required standard for entry into the third year of a full-time course of three years or more in any discipline (as confirmed by that institution) and holds a certificate issued by the Further Education and Training Awards Council of satisfactory attendance at a Teagasc approved course of more than 100 hours in either or both of horticulture or agriculture and attendance of more than 80 hours at a course of farm management training,

    (iii)   is the holder of a letter from Teagasc confirming satisfactory completion of an approved training course for persons with restricted learning capacity,

    (iv)   is the holder, prior to 1 January 2004, of a qualification set out in the Table to *s 667*, or equivalent as certified by Teagasc and satisfies certain further conditions as set out in *s 667A(7)*.

The list of courses required to comply with the educational conditions for the young trained farmer's relief has been extended in line with the list for Young Trained Farmer's Relief for the purposes of stamp duty. *Finance Act 2010, s 13* amends the Table so that Bachelor of Agricultural Science – Agri-Environmental Science awarded by University College Dublin is included in the list of qualifications. Provision is also made to ensure that any person who prior to 31 March 2008 fulfils the education requirements in place prior to the changes will continue to satisfy the educational requirements. Where the individual first becomes a 'qualifying farmer' in the year 2004, the 100 per cent relief is available for that year and for each of the three succeeding years of assessment. This is to be extended by ministerial order to individuals becoming qualifying farmers during 2005 and 2006 [*TCA 1997, s 667A; FA 2004, s 13; FA 2005, s 31*].

    Prior to 1 January 2004, the definition of *'qualifying farmer'* was an individual:

(A)   who, in the year 1993/94 or any subsequent year of assessment, first qualifies for grant aid under the Scheme of Installation Aid for Young Farmers operated by the Department of Agriculture, Food and Forestry; or

(B)   who first becomes chargeable under Sch D, Case I in respect of farming profits in a year of assessment after 1992/93, who is aged under 35 at the commencement of that first year of assessment, and who, at any time in that first year of assessment, either:

    (i)   holds a qualification included in the Table to *s 667* (or certified by Teagasc (The Agricultural and Food Development Authority) as corresponding to such a qualification) and also (in certain cases) a certificate issued by Teagasc of satisfactory attendance of more than 80 hours at a course of farm management training,

    (ii)   has satisfactorily attended any full-time course of at least two years' duration at a third-level institution, and holds a certificate issued by Teagasc of satisfactory attendance of more than 180 hours at a course of agriculture and/or horticulture training, or

    (iii)   having been born before 1 January 1968, holds a certificate issued by Teagasc of satisfactory attendance of more than 180 hours at a course of agriculture and/or horticulture training. (This condition is deleted with effect from 1 January 2004.)

The 100 per cent relief (as above) is available for 1995/96 to 1998/99 inclusive to individuals who became qualifying farmers before 6 April 1996, for 1996/97 to 1999/2000 for those who became qualifying farmers after 5 April 1996 and before 6 April 1997, for 1997/98 to 2000/01 for those who became qualifying farmers after 5 April 1997 and before 6 April 1998, for 1998/99 to 2001 for those who became qualifying farmers after 5 April 1998 and before 6 April 1999, for 1999/2000 to 2002 for those who became qualifying farmers after 5 April 1999 and before 6 April 2000, for 2000/01 to 2003 for those who became qualifying farmers after 5 April 2000 and before 6 April 2001, and (subject to EU State Aid rules) for 2001 to 2004 for those who become qualifying farmers after 5 April 2001 and before 1 January 2002, for 2002 to 2005 for those who become qualifying farmers after 31 December 2001 and before 31 December 2002, for 2003 to 2006 for those who become qualifying farmers after 31 December 2002 and before 1 January 2004, for 2004 to 2007 for those who become qualifying farmers after 31 December 2003 and before 1 January 2005 and (subject to Ministerial Order) for 2005 to 2008 for those who become qualifying farmers in the period from 1 January 2005 to 31 December 2006.

See also **18.4** above.

'*Accounting period*' for these purposes, for a person other than a company, is a period of twelve months ending on the date to which the accounts are usually made up (or otherwise it is a period of twelve months as determined by the Revenue Commissioners). Where the beginning or end of an accounting period does not coincide with accounting dates, there will be no opening (or closing) stock to use in ascertaining any increase in value. In these cases a 'reference period' will extend back to the beginning, or forward to the end, of the period of account which bridges the beginning or end of the accounting period. In any other case the reference period will begin or end with the date of an accounting period. Where a reference period applies, the increase or decrease in stock values and the trading profits are apportioned (in months and fractions of months) to the accounting period.

'*Trading stock*' is as defined in *s 89* (see **30.31** 'Sch D, Cases I and II') but excludes any stock to the extent that any payments on account have been received (for which see **38.138** 'Tax cases'). However, transfers between farmers other than for valuable consideration may, if they jointly so elect (in writing, before the specified return date (see **28.11** 'Returns') for the chargeable period of the transfer) be at book value at the date of discontinuance (see **18.7** above). A person commencing to trade at the beginning of an accounting period for which relief is claimed without opening stock taken over from a previous business will have an opening stock value attributed to it by the inspector who 'shall have regard to all the relevant circumstances of the case' particularly the movements in costs of stock items and changes in volume of trade during the period. There is a right to appeal against the inspector's decision. The inspector may also (subject to appeal) treat opening or closing stock as having such value as appears 'reasonable and just' where stock is acquired or disposed of otherwise than in the normal conduct of the trade. Where the basis of calculation for opening and ending stock differs, the opening stock will be amended to conform.

[*TCA 1997, ss 665–669; FA 1998, s 39; FA 1999, ss 54, 55; FA 2001, ss 46–48; FA 2003, ss 18, 19; FA 2004, s 13; FA 2005, ss 31; 32*]

MILK QUOTAS

18.10 Since 6 April 2000, a new scheme of capital allowances is introduced for qualifying expenditure incurred on or after that date for the purchase of milk quota (as defined). *Finance Act 2007* made a minor amendment to the interpretation of *s 669A*. The amendment relates to the definition of 'qualifying expenditure' and ensures that the relief currently provided for in respect of the milk quotas purchased under the Milk Quota Restructuring Scheme will continue to be available under the new Milk Quota Trading System. These may only be given in taxing a trade of farming and apply to quota purchased either:

(*a*)   after 31 March 2000 under a Milk Quota Restructuring Scheme; or

(*b*)   either:

    (i)   before 1 April 2000 by a lessee from an unconnected (within *s 10*) lessor where the lease agreement complies with EU regulations and was entered into before 13 October 1999 and ends after 30 March 2000, or

    (ii)   on or after 1 April 2000, being any milk quota not within (*a*).

Where (*b*) applies, qualifying expenditure is in certain cases adjusted to the maximum price set by the Minister for Agriculture, Food and Rural Development. Allowances are given for qualifying expenditure on a straight-line basis over seven years, and the normal balancing adjustment provisions apply on a subsequent sale or disposal or on the quota coming to an end or ceasing altogether to be used. [*TCA 1997, ss 669A–669F; FA 2000, s 61; FA 2001, ss 26, 27; FA 2002, s 30*]

Finance Act 2008 amended *s 657* which deals with the averaging of farm incomes by ensuring that the commencement of the Milk Production Partnership will not give rise to a tax clawback in respect of an earlier trade of farming. [*TCA 1997, s 657*]

19 Government and Other Public Loans

See also **29** 'Sch C'.

19.1 The Minister for Finance may direct that interest on securities already issued or to be issued should be payable gross, but the recipient is then assessable under Sch D, Case III. [*TCA 1997, s 36*] This treatment is extended to debentures, etc, and other securities of the Agricultural Credit Corporation (for securities issued before 28 February 2002), Bord na Móna, Electricity Supply Board and Iarnród Éireann, Aer Lingus, Aer Rianta or Aerlínte Éireann, eircom and Irish Telecommunications Investments plc (for securities issued before 15 February 2001), Radio Telefís Éireann, and Bord Gáis Éireann. [*TCA 1997, s 37; FA 2001, s 241*] Also certain securities issued outside Ireland by local authorities, provided they are not held by persons domiciled or ordinarily resident in RI (or, for securities acquired after 15 May 1992, by or through a branch or agency through which a financial concern carries on business in RI) [*TCA 1997, s 50*], securities of certain European bodies [*TCA 1997, s 39*], stocks issued under *Local Government Act 1946, s 87* [*TCA 1997, Sch 32 para 1(1)*], stock etc of the International Bank for Reconstruction and Development [*TCA 1997, s 40*], and securities issued by bodies designated under *Securitisation (Proceeds of Certain Mortgages) Act 1995*. [*TCA 1997, s 41*] Other than in the case of local authority securities issued outside RI, the terms of issue may include complete exemption (capital and interest) of beneficial owners not domiciled nor ordinarily resident in RI, or income tax exemption of such owners domiciled but not ordinarily resident (except that, for securities acquired after 15 May 1992 and held by or for a branch or agency through which a financial concern carries on business in RI, neither exemption applies). [*TCA 1997, s 49, Sch 32 para 1(2)*]

Exemption similarly applies to securities guaranteed by a Minister of State or issued by a company formed by the National Development Finance Agency (in these cases the paying company may deduct from Sch D, Case I profits the amount of interest so paid gross). [*TCA 1997, s 38; FA 2003, s 40*]

See **16.9** 'Exempt income and special savings schemes' as regards securities issued at a discount.

19.2 Government securities may also be issued exempt from RI taxation so long as in the beneficial ownership of persons not ordinarily resident there (although the exemption does not apply to securities acquired after 29 January 1992 and held by or for a branch or agency through which a financial concern carries on business in RI). [*TCA 1997, ss 43, 44*]

19.3 Accumulated interest on Irish National Savings Certificates is exempt [*TCA 1997, s 42*], but not interest on UK Government Stocks paid tax-free or on UK National Savings Certificates.

20 Interest Payable

DEDUCTION OF TAX

20.1 Interest is payable without deduction of tax, except where paid:

(*a*) by a company (otherwise than in a fiduciary or representative capacity or to an investment undertaking within *s 739B* (see **12.22** 'Corporation Tax') or where the provisions of *ss 267G–267K* apply (see **13.4** 'Deduction of tax at source'));

(*b*) to a person whose usual place of abode is outside RI; or

(*c*) by certain deposit-takers (see **13.9** 'Deduction of tax at source').

But (*a*) and (*b*) do not apply and no tax is deductible from interest paid:

(i) to or by a bank (or, from 30 March 2001, a building society) carrying on a bona fide banking business in RI or (for accounting periods ending from 3 February 2005) in a member state of the EU (but see below);

(ii) in the State to a securitisation company which is a qualifying company within the meaning of *s 110* (see **12.22** 'Corporation tax');

(iii) by a company at (ii) to a person resident in a double tax treaty country except, where the recipient is a company, where the interest is paid in connection with a trade or business carried on in RI by the company through a branch or agency;

(iv) by a company authorised by the Revenue Commissioners to make payments gross;

(v) on certain State-owned company securities;

(vi) by industrial and provident societies to RI residents;

(vii) by a close company which is a distribution under *s 437* (excess interest to certain directors);

(viii) to a person within (*b*) above by a company in the course of operations covered by a certificate relating to certain financial services or Shannon airport operations (see **12.18** 'Corporation tax') or by a 'specified collective investment undertaking' within *s 734* (see **12.22** 'Corporation tax');

(ix) from 6 April 1999 (and where (i)–(viii) do not apply), in the ordinary course of a trade or business by a company or collective investment undertaking (defined broadly as in **12.22** 'Corporation tax') to a company resident in another EU Member State, or in another territory with which double tax arrangements are in force (see **15.2** 'Double tax relief – income and capital gains'), *provided that* it is not paid in connection with a trade or business carried on in RI by the recipient company through a branch or agency. Since 10 February 2000, the recipient company is required to be resident in the non-RI state or territory, for the purposes of any tax corresponding to income or corporation tax, under the law of the State or territory, and from 30 March 2001 the exception is extended to payments by all collective funds; or

(x)   from 25 March 2002, by a company to another company if and so long as the other company is within *s 246(5)* (ie broadly a financial services company which complies with certain notification requirements);

(xi)   from 13 June 2003, on wholesale debt instruments of €500,000 (or equivalent if denominated in another currency other that US dollars) or US$500,000 or more held in a recognised clearing system, paid by or through a non-resident (not being an RI branch or agency) or wholesale debt instruments paid by or through an RI resident or branch and (i) held in a recognised clearing system, or (ii) the person beneficially entitled to the interest is RI-resident and has provided a tax reference number, or (iii) the person beneficially entitled is not RI-resident and has made a declaration to that effect.

Finance (No 2) Act 2008 amends *s 198* to extend the exemption for non-residents from income tax in respect of interest received from Irish resident persons where the company or person receiving the interest is a tax resident of another EU State or a country with which Ireland has entered into a double tax treaty. The amendment extends this exemption to interest payments on the wholesale debt instruments to which *s 246A* applies. The exemption is also extended to discounts on securities which were issued in the course of a trade or business by a company or investment undertaking where the company or person receiving the discount is a tax resident of another EU State or country with which Ireland has a double tax treaty.

[*TCA 1997, s 246A; FA 2003, s 49; FA 2006, s 47; SI 245/03; F(No 2)A 2008, s 25*]

See, however, **20.3**(*a*) below as regards certain mortgage interest payments.

As regards (vi) above, relief from deduction continues to apply to interest paid on securities redeemable within 15 years of issue, notwithstanding the expiry of the financial services and Shannon airport certificates.

[*TCA 1997, s 246; FA 1999, s 39; FA 2000, s 66; FA 2001, s 37; FA 2002, s 19; FA 2005, s 49; FA 2006, ss 46, 47*]

All interest paid by the National Treasury Management Agency and the National Development Finance Agency (see **17.20** and **17.24** 'Exempt organisations') is paid without deduction of tax. [*TCA 1997, s 230(2); FA 2003, s 43*]

There are special provisions for interest on quoted Eurobonds. [*TCA 1997, s 64*]

Any agreement providing for payment of interest less tax shall be construed as requiring payment of the gross amount. [*TCA 1997, s 255*]

Section 246 does not apply to interest paid under *SI 388/02 European Communities (Late Payment in Commercial Transactions) Regulations 2002*. See Revenue Tax Briefing Issue 52 p 25.

BUSINESS INTEREST

20.2 Where interest paid under deduction of tax is incurred for business purposes, it is deductible from profits assessable under Sch D, Cases I and II and under Case V (rental income). [*TCA 1997, ss 81(2)(l), 97(2)(e), 1088(1)*] See also **20.3**(*c*)(i) below. See **12.9** 'Corporation tax' as regards yearly interest paid by companies.

PERSONAL INTEREST RELIEF

20.3

(a) Interest on '**qualifying loans**' from a bank, stockbroker or discount house carrying on business in RI, or being yearly interest charged to tax under Sch D, attracts relief. For **2000/01 onwards**, relief is given by reference to the lesser of:

(I) the amount of interest actually paid; and

(II) either:

(a) €**5,080/£4,000** in the case of a married person whose spouse's income is treated as his or her own (see **23.1** 'Married persons') or a widow(er), or

(b) €**2,540/£2,000** in the case of any other individual.

The amounts in (II)(a) and (b) are increased to €8,000 and €4,000 respectively for the first seven years of assessment for which relief falls to be given to an individual in respect of a qualifying loan, provided that the first year of assessment is 1997/98 or later. Any resultant additional relief in the case of a married person is given equally to each spouse. [*FA 2003, s 9*]

For 2002, the amounts at (ll)(a) and (b) were €**6,350/£5,000** and €**3,175/£2,500** respectively for the first five years of assessment for which relief fell to be given to the individual in respect of a qualifying loan.

For 2001 only, the figures £4,000, £2,000, £5,000 and £2,500 above are replaced by £2,960, £1,480, £3,700 and £1,850 respectively.

The ceilings for **2007** were increased as follows:

(a) €**6,000** in the case of a married person whose spouse's income is treated as his or her own (see **23.1** 'Married persons') or a widow(er),

(b) €**3,000** in the case of any other individual,

(c) €**16,000** in the case of a married or widowed person who is a qualifying first time buyer, or

(d) €**8,000** in the case of a single person who is a qualifying first time buyer.

The ceilings were again increased for qualifying first time buyers in **2008** as follows:

(a) €**20,000** in the case of a married or widowed person who is a qualifying first time buyer, or

(b) €**10,000** in the case of a single person who is a qualifying first time buyer.

All limits apply to the aggregate of interest allowed under these provisions and certain annual payments paid abroad and set against income from abroad.

For 2009, *Finance (No 2) Act 2008, s 14* increased the rate at which mortgage interest relief is granted to first time buyers on relievable interest for the first five years of their mortgage and retains the 20 per cent interest rate for years six and seven. From 1 January 2009 the relief due to first time buyers will be as follows:

(*a*)   25 per cent for years 1 and 2;

(*b*)   22.5 per cent for years 3,4 and 5; and

(*c*)   20 per cent for years 6 and 7.

The rate of mortgage interest relief for non first time buyers is reduced from 20 per cent to 15 per cent.

Finance Act 2010, s 6 amends the provisions relating to mortgage interest relief under *s 244*. The amendments are such that tax relief on qualifying mortgage interest paid will continue to be available at current levels for the tax years 2010 through to 2017 in respect of interest on qualifying home loans taken out on or after 1 January 2004 and on or before 31 December 2011.

The section also inserts into *s 244* transitional measures that will be available in the tax years 2012 to 2017 inclusive and in respect of interest paid in those tax years on qualifying home loans taken out during 2012. The rate at which tax relief will be available will be 15 per cent for first-time buyers and 10 per cent for non first time buyers. The ceiling of qualifying interest for all these qualifying loans will be €6,000 for married or widowed persons and €3,000 for others. Loans taken out after 1 January 2013 will not qualify for mortgage interest relief and mortgage interest relief will be abolished in its entirety for the tax year 2018 and onwards.

For 1997/98 and subsequent years relief is restricted to the standard rate of income tax, and (from 2002 subject to relief by deduction of tax in certain cases, see below) is given by a reduction in income tax liability. [*TCA 1997, s 244; ITA 1967, s 496; FA 2000, s 17; FA 2001, Sch 2 para 13*]

A *qualifying loan* is a loan, or replacement for a loan, used by an individual solely for the purchase, repair, development or improvement of a building (or part) and grounds situated in RI, Northern Ireland or Great Britain, being the sole or main residence of the individual, his former or separated spouse, or a dependent relative other than a child (in the latter case, provided that the occupation is rent-free). It does not, however, include a loan used to defray payment to a spouse (unless separated) for the purchase of property, or (where the payment is excessive) any payment to a person connected with the borrower (as defined by *s 10*), and a loan is not a qualifying loan if the property purchased (or a superior interest in it) was disposed of by the purchaser or spouse after 25 March 1982. [*TCA 1997, s 244(1)(a)(4)*] It is understood that, for these purposes, temporary absences of up to one year are in practice ignored, as, generally, are periods of absence of up to four years during which a person is required to move home by reason of his employment (and successive such periods separated by a minimum of three months of occupation).

Payment of interest under deduction of tax. For 2002 onwards, special rules apply where an individual whose sole or main residence is situated in RI qualifies for interest relief (as above) in respect of a qualifying loan from a 'qualifying lender' (see *s 244A(3)*) which is secured by the mortgage of the freehold or leasehold estate or interest in the residence. Relief is obtained by deduction of standard rate tax from the qualifying interest, the lender recovering the tax deducted from the Revenue Commissioners (subject to regulations). There is no clawback of relief where it exceeds the individual's income tax liability. [*TCA 1997, s 244A; FA 2001, s 23*] The Revenue Commissioners have appropriate powers of inspection to audit repayment claims by qualifying lenders. [*TCA 1997, s 904F; FA 2001, s 22(3)*] They may also require qualifying lenders to furnish them with details of all borrowers in 2001 who are prospectively within the deduction scheme, for the purpose of facilitating such relief. [*FA 2001, s 24*]

For the detailed regulations, see *SI 558/01*.

For articles on the rules, guidelines and procedures regarding interest relief on home loans, see Revenue Tax Briefing Issue 34 pp 9–16, Issue 37 p 6.

Personal representatives of a deceased person, and trustees of a settlement under a will, generally continue to receive relief for interest on a loan which was a qualifying loan at the time of the deceased's death, as long as the property continues to be occupied by his widow, former or separated spouse or dependent relative (other than a child). [*TCA 1997, s 244(6)*]

Preferential loans. See **34.3** 'Sch E' for the charge to tax of notional interest on certain loans;

(*b*)   **Bridging loans.** On a move from one 'only or main residence' to another, the previous 'only or main residence' continues to be treated as such for a period of twelve months from acquisition of the new residence, provided that all appropriate steps are taken to dispose of the previous residence. Also, where an only or main residence is sold and replaced by means of a loan used only for that purpose, the interest *for the first twelve months* on that loan (including any subsequent loan wholly or partly replacing it) is eligible for relief up to the limits in (*a*) above (apportioned on a time basis if the twelve months extends over two tax years) *in addition to any other interest* paid during that time. [*TCA 1997, ss 244(5), 245*]

(*c*)   **Loan for purchasing ordinary shares in, or making a loan to, certain companies.** Since 8 December 2005, two alternative forms of relief are available for interest payable on such a loan, or a loan to repay an eligible loan, where the company concerned is a trading company (or a company whose business is holding stocks, shares or securities of a trading company). *Finance Act 2011, s 11* provides for this relief to be phased out for existing qualifying loans and abolished for loans taken out on or after 7 December 2010. For existing qualifying loans, the interest is restricted to 75% for interest paid in the tax year 2011, 50% for interest paid in the tax year 2012 and 25% for interest paid in the tax year 2013, with the relief abolished completely for the tax year 2014. The reliefs only apply if the loan is applied in the purchase, etc on or within a reasonable time after it is made and without previously being applied for some other purpose, and if there has been no recovery of capital (as defined, and from 6 February 2003, may occur during the period of two years prior to the loan being made). If any capital has been recovered, including any connected consideration, without reducing the loan, the relief for interest is reduced proportionately. It is understood that, in practice, relief will continue to be available where shares in the company are exchanged for shares in another close company as a result of a company reorganisation, provided that relief would have been available for investment in that other company. Since 2 February 2006, anti-avoidance measures are introduced in respect of loans to or for the benefit of connected companies [*FA 2006, s 65*]. Prior to 8 December 2005, relief applied also to a property company or holding company of a property company. Relief continues to apply to loans taken out before that date but from that date a replacement loan for shares in a property company must not exceed the outstanding loan balance or balance of the term of the loan that it replaces if relief is to be available. From 2007, the quantum of relief available to a high income earning individual in any one year may be restricted, see **2.45** 'Limitation on Income Tax Relief for High Earners' [*TCA 1997, ss 247(2), 248(1), 249; FA 2003, s 46; FA 2006 s 9, 17*]:

(i)   there is unrestricted relief if (A) the investor (borrower) has a material interest in the company (more than five per cent control) when the interest is paid, and (B) during the period of the loan, if the investor is a *company*, at least one of its directors is also a director of the company concerned or a connected company or, if an *individual*, his main work was the management or conduct of the company or a connected company, [*TCA 1997, ss 247(3), 248(2)*]

(ii)   an *individual* is entitled to unrestricted relief on such loans relating to a *private* company if, during the period of the loan, he was (A) if the company is a trading or property company, an employee (full-time or part-time) or director (full-time or part-time), or (B) if a holding company, a full-time employee or full-time director. He will not be eligible if the company or any person connected with it had made any loan or advance to him (or any connected person) except in the ordinary course of a business (as defined).

Public company. Similar relief applies, up to a maximum of €3,050/£2,400 (for 2001 only, £1,776), to eligible loans relating to a public company. The individual must be a full-time employee or full-time director and the relief only applies in relation to a public 'holding company' if it is resident in RI.

Full-time employee/director. An individual qualifies if he is required to devote substantially the whole of his time to the service, as employee or director, of the company concerned or a company which is a 90 per cent subsidiary of the company concerned. [*TCA 1997, s 250; FA 2001, Sch 2 para 14*]

Relief for individuals under (i) or (ii) above is phased out after 5 April 1992 where the company concerned is a '*quoted company*', ie a company whose shares are listed on a stock exchange or dealt in on certain other markets (extended, from 6 April 1997, to quotation on any stock exchange unlisted securities market), on a 'specified date'. The '*specified date*' is the later of:

(A)   the first day of the second year of assessment next after that in which the company became a quoted company, and

(B)   (i)   if the loan was applied before 6 April 1989, 6 April 1992,

        (ii)   if the loan was applied during 1989/90, 6 April 1993,

        (iii)   if the loan was applied after 5 April 1990, 6 April 1994.

Relief is restricted to 70 per cent of that otherwise available for the year of assessment starting on the specified date, to 40 per cent in the following year of assessment, and is abolished thereafter. However, no relief at all is given for interest on a loan applied after 28 January 1992 at a time when the company concerned is a quoted company. [*TCA 1997, s 252; FA 2001, Sch 2 para 15*]

For loans applied after 23 April 1992, relief to individuals under (i) and (ii) above is also denied unless the loan in question is applied for *bona fide* commercial purposes and not as part of a scheme or arrangement a main purpose of which is the avoidance of tax. [*TCA 1997, s 248(3)*]

Residential premises restriction. Relief for a chargeable period is reduced by the amount of any interest accruing **before 1 January 2002** (treating interest as accruing from day to day) and attributable to any part of a loan (or replacement for a loan) applied after 6 May 1998 directly or indirectly in the purchase, improvement or repair of premises which, at any time in the chargeable period, are '*rented residential premises*', ie any building or part used or suitable for use as a dwelling, and any outoffice, yard, garden or other land appurtenant to or usually enjoyed with that building or part, in respect of which any person is entitled to a rent or receipt from any easements. **Since 6 February 2003**, the restriction applies to interest accruing from that date on borrowings used to purchase residential premises from a spouse. [*TCA 1997, s 248A; F(No 2)A 1998, s 2; FA 2002, s 17(b); FA 2003, s 16(1)(b)*]

Investment property restriction. **Since 19 March 2003**, interest relief is restricted where the borrowings are used to invest in or lend to a company and used by the company on or after 1 January 2003 directly or indirectly to purchase a property to which the capital allowances restrictions of *s 409E* would apply if the property was purchased directly by the borrower or used by the company in paying off a loan to purchase such a property. Since **20 February 2004**, this restriction is extended to include borrowings used to acquire shares in a company deriving at least 75 per cent of its rental income from such a property. Relief is restricted to the individual's return from the company for the year comprising interest and/or distributions received by the individual from the company in the year and arising from the borrowed money. [*TCA 1997, s 250A; FA 2004, s 22*] **Business expansion scheme and film investment shares.** Relief is not available to individuals under the above provisions where a claim for relief under *Pt 16* or predecessor provisions (see **21.2–21.13** 'Investment in corporate trades') is made in respect of the amount subscribed for the shares for whose purchase the loan was made and the shares were issued after 19 April 1990, or where a claim for relief is made under *s 481* or predecessor provisions (investment in films, see

12.23 'Corporation tax') in respect of the amount subscribed for the shares for whose purchase the loan was made and the shares were issued after 5 May 1993; [*TCA 1997, s 251*]

(*d*)   **Loans for purchasing a share of, or making a loan to, a partnership** (or in replacing a prior eligible loan). Unrestricted relief is given to an individual on interest on such a loan provided that he personally acted in the conduct of the partnership trade between purchase or loan and payment of the interest and has recovered no part of the capital. If any capital has been recovered (including any connected consideration) the relief for interest will be reduced proportionately. From 2007, the quantum of relief available to a high income earning individual in any one year may be restricted, see **2.45** 'Limitation on Income Tax Relief for High Earners' [*TCA 1997, s 253; FA 2006, s 17*]. The Revenue have indicated that their practical requirements are that:

(i)   the borrowings must be introduced into the partnership by way either of loan or of contribution of capital,

(ii)   the money must be used wholly and exclusively for the purposes of the trade or profession, and

(iii) any recovery of capital must be used to repay the loan, if relief is not to be restricted.

However, in respect of loans received before 1 December 1985, interest relief will continue to be available concessionally where the strict conditions are not met, provided that:

(*aa*)   no relief would otherwise be available,

(*bb*)   the borrowings were individually identified so as to show the lender, the principal outstanding and the terms of repayment,

(*cc*)   the purpose for which the moneys were borrowed was stated (not necessary where total borrowings did not exceed about £10,000),

(*dd*)   there was no departure from or variation of the terms of the original loan, so as to extend the borrowing indefinitely, and

(*ee*)   there is, in the Revenue's view, no abuse of the concessional relief.

It is understood that, in practice, relief will continue to be available where the partnership is incorporated into a close company, provided that relief would have been available under (*c*) above for investment in that company.

Residential premises restriction. Relief for a chargeable period is reduced by the amount of any interest accruing **before 1 January 2002** (treating interest as accruing from day to day) and attributable to any part of a loan (or replacement for a loan) applied after 6 May 1998 directly or indirectly in the purchase, improvement or repair of premises which, at any time in the chargeable period, are '*rented residential premises*', ie any building or part used or suitable for use as a dwelling, and any outoffice, yard, garden or other land appurtenant to or usually enjoyed with that building or part, in respect of which any person is entitled to a rent or receipt from any easements. **Since 6 February 2003**, the restriction applies to interest accruing from that date on borrowings used to purchase a residential premises from a spouse. [*TCA 1997, s 248A; F(No 2)A 1998, s 2; FA 2002, s 17(b); FA 2003, s 16(1)(a)*]

Investment property restriction. Since 19 March 2003, interest relief is restricted where the borrowings are used to purchase a share in or make a loan to a partnership and used by the partnership to purchase a property to which the capital allowances restrictions of *s 409E* would apply if the property was purchased directly by the borrower (see **8.1** 'Capital allowances'). This will be provided for in *FA 2004*. [Statement of the Minister for Finance, 19 March 2003];

(*e*) **Loans for replacement of business capital.** Interest on loans to replace business capital withdrawn within the five years preceding the date of the loan will not be regarded as business interest. [*TCA 1997, s 254*]

EU SAVINGS DIRECTIVE

20.4 RI has incorporated into law the provisions of *Council Directive 2003/48/EC (3 June 2003) as amended* on Taxation of Savings Income in the Form of Interest Payments and Related Matters. Broadly, these provisions require 'paying agents' to obtain the name and address and country of residence of their customers who are individuals. For individuals opening accounts on or after 1 January 2004, a tax identification number or date and place of birth must also be obtained. The paying agent is required to maintain this information for five years from the date of cessation of the relationship and, from 31 March 2006, for five years from the date of payment of any interest. Since 1 July 2005, the paying agent is required to return to the Revenue details of interest paid by it within three months of the end of the tax year. For the year 2005, returns relate to interest payments made in the period from 1 July 2005 to 31 December 2005. From 2006, returns relate to payments of interest made in the tax year. Revenue are required to pass this information to the equivalent authority in the state of residence of the recipient within six months of the year end. A paying agent is any person paying interest in the course of a business or profession being carried on in RI. Interest is widely defined to include dividends or distributions paid in respect of building society shares or credit union shares, returns on a security, prizes paid on securities such as prize bonds and certain income and gains arising in respect of UCITS. Penalties will apply for failure to file returns or co-operate with the Revenue in auditing information. For a transitional period, Luxembourg, Austria and Belgium will continue to operate withholding tax. During that period, approximately 75 per cent of tax withheld in a particular year will be paid to the Revenue in the country of residence of the recipient of the interest within six months of the year end. RI recipients may seek exemption from the withholding tax by obtaining a certificate of residence status from the Revenue and furnishing this to the interest payer. Alternatively, RI recipients may seek a credit for withholding tax against their RI tax liability with any excess being refunded by the Revenue provided that a statement of interest received and tax withheld is obtained from the paying agent and submitted to the Revenue with a full tax return. The EU has entered into agreements with Andorra, Liechtenstein, Monaco, San Marino and the Swiss Confederation under which those countries will introduce measures equivalent to the Savings Directive. The

Finance Act 2005 amendments put on a statutory footing the exchange of information provisions of those agreements. Since 31 March 2006 penalties apply for non-compliance with any regulations made under the provisions. [*TCA 1997, ss 898B–898R; FA 2004, s 90, Sch 4; FA 2005, s 144; FA 2006, s 124; SI 286/05; SI 317/05*]

SHARI'A LAW

General

20.5 The term Islamic finance describes any financing arrangement that is compliant with the principles of Shari'a law. Specifically, there are sets of strict rules that forbid the making or receiving of interest payments. *Section 35 of Finance Act 2010* is designed to extend the tax treatment applicable to conventional finance transactions to Shari'a products which are the same in substance as the conventional products. It does this by inserting a new *Pt 8A*.

The new Part deals with the taxation of 'Specified Finance Transactions' and essentially treats the return on any product defined as a 'specified finance transaction' as interest for the purpose of the Tax Acts. The transactions covered by the legislation are:

(i)   *Credit Transactions*

These are essentially credit sales, loans or mortgages which are structured to comply with Shari'a principles. The customer either (1) retains the asset (this corresponds to a credit sale and is dealt with in paragraph (a) of the definition of 'credit transaction') or (2) raises funds by selling the asset immediately for cash (this corresponds to a conventional loan and is dealt with in paragraph (b) of the definition of 'credit transaction'). The new legislation provides that the difference between the amount paid for the asset by the financial institution and the amount paid for the asset by the borrower (ie the financial institution's profit on the sale) which is referred to as a 'credit return' will be treated in the same way as interest for the purposes of the Tax Acts.

The legislation also deals with the situation where an asset is acquired jointly by a financial institution and a customer on terms on which the customer promises to acquire the financial institution's share in the asset over an agreed period of time. The asset is generally rented to the customer for an amount equal to the economic return on investment and which is similar to the interest payable in a conventional transaction. The new legislation provides that the excess of the amounts paid to the financial institution (including any amount paid for the use of the asset) over the amount paid by the institution for the asset (ie the credit return) will be treated as interest for tax purposes.

(ii)   *Deposit Transaction*

This covers bank deposits that do not pay interest but provide for a return to the depositor in another way. So as to obviate the need to pay interest, the transactions are structured as quasi partnership arrangements whereby an investor provides money to a financial institution in return for a share in the profits (or losses) generated by the institution from the use of the money. The new provisions treat this profit share return (ie the deposit return) as if it were interest payable on a conventional bank deposit.

(iii)   *Investment transaction*

This refers to the purchase of securities and is similar to the Shari'a product known as 'sukuk'. A sukuk transaction is similar to a structured finance arrangement. Unlike a conventional structured finance transaction, an investor in a sukuk holds a share in the asset underlying the arrangement and which is managed by the sukuk issuer.'

There is no entitlement to interest on the sukuk, instead the investor shares in the profits and losses derived from the exploitation of the underlying assets by the sukuk issuer. This "investment return' can either take the form of a premium, a periodic payment or a combination of both. The new legislation treats this return as interest for tax purposes.

21 Investment in Corporate Trades

Cross-reference. See also **12.23** 'Corporation tax' as regards investment in film production companies, for which relief is (from 6 April 1993) available to both individual and corporate investors.

21.1 The relief for investment in corporate trades (frequently referred to as the Business Expansion Scheme) was introduced by *FA 1984*, and these provisions are dealt with at **21.2–21.13** below. The relief was extended by *FA 1986* to investment in research and development companies, but the extended relief ceased for shares issued after 5 April 1991. Following *FA 1993* and *FA 1995*, certain research and development activities are now treated as within the main relief.

The *Finance Act 2011, s 33* has introduced a new income tax relief for investment in corporate trades. This new relief will replace the business expansion scheme. The new relief is subject to a Ministerial Order and until such time, the current reliefs (Seed Capital Scheme and Business Expansion Scheme) under *TCA 1997, Pt 16* still apply. Please see **21.14** below.

BUSINESS EXPANSION SCHEME

21.2 Conditions for relief. A 'qualifying individual' who subscribes for 'eligible shares' in a 'qualifying company' which are issued on or before 31 December 2006 (or 31 December 2004, where certain conditions are satisfied) [*Finance Act 2007* extended the period for this relief for a further seven years until 31 December 2013], may claim income tax relief on his investment, provided that:

(i)   the purpose of the issue is to raise money for a 'qualifying trade' carried on by the company (or by certain subsidiaries of the company, see **21.11** below) or which it intends to carry on and in fact commences within two years of the issue (three years if the company spends at least 80 per cent of the money subscribed for the issue on research and development work connected with, and undertaken with a view to the carrying on of, the trade); and

(ii)   the money was used, is being used or is intended to be used:

(*a*)   with a view to creating or maintaining employment in the company or, in the case of advance factory building construction and leasing (see **21.6**(*d*) below), in either or both a company contracted to construct the building and a company leasing it, and

(*b*)   for the purpose of enabling the company to undertake or enlarge 'qualifying trade' operations; to carry out research and development; to acquire technological information and data; to develop new or existing products or services, provide new products or services; to identify new markets and develop new and existing markets for its products and services; or to increase its turnover.

Certification. In the case of advance factory building construction and leasing (see **21.6**(*d*) below):

(*a*)   relief is dependent on certification by an appropriate industrial development agency as to the status and location of the building; and

(*b*)   as regards (i) above, the trade is deemed to have commenced on commencement of construction of the building.

In the case of qualifying trading operations consisting of research and development within **21.6**(*e*) below, relief is dependent on certification by an appropriate industrial development agency that operations have commenced and that the operations have the potential to lead to the commencement of trading operations within **21.6**(i) (manufacturing), (ii) (certain services) or (*c*) (plant cultivation), and, as regards (i) above, the trade is deemed to have commenced on the date of issue of the certificate.

In the case of horticultural qualifying trading operations within **21.6**(*g*) below, relief is dependent on certification by the Minister for Agriculture, Food and Forestry that the construction, improvement or repair of the greenhouse(s) in which the cultivation takes place, or the installation or improvement of the irrigation or heating facilities, may be eligible for grant aid.

In the case of qualifying trading operations consisting of Custom House Docks Area financial services operations within **21.6**(*j*) below), relief is dependent on certification by the committee appointed for the purpose by the Minister for Finance that it is satisfied that they will contribute to the development of the exchange facility, and that a reasonable level of sustainable employment will result. Certification is limited to subscriptions not exceeding €2,539,476.16/£2,000,000 in total (the limit per company being €127,000/£100,000, see **21.8** below).

In the case of qualifying trading operations consisting of production, etc of qualifying recordings within **21.6**(*i*) below), relief is dependent on certification by the Minister for Arts, Culture and the Gaeltacht that the recording, etc may be treated as a qualifying recording. The certification may impose conditions as to the maximum amount of money to be raised by the issue of eligible shares in relation to a qualifying recording. Recycling companies which have had grant or financial assistance being made available to them by an industrial development agency have been included in the scheme. The Scheme will also apply to internationally traded services companies approved for employment grant aid instead of the current position where they are admitted to the scheme only where the grant has been paid [*FA 2007, s 19*]. Recycling companies which have received written confirmation from such an agency or board verifying that it has submitted a business proposal to it and that the activities of the company are qualifying environmental services shall also be included [*FA 2008*].

[*TCA 1997, ss 489(1)(2)(7)(15), 496(5)(7)(8), Sch 10 para 1; FA 1999, s 16(b); FA 2001, s 12(a); FA 2002, s 16(a)(iii); FA 2004, s 18, 19; FA 2005, s 27; FA 2007, s 19*]

Relief is allowed only when the company (or subsidiary) has carried on the trade for four months (or in the case of a 'relevant investment' (see **21.7** below), has commenced to carry on the relevant trading operations). In the case of qualifying trading operations consisting of research and development within **21.6**(*e*) below, the trade is deemed to have commenced on the date of issue of the appropriate certificate, and in the case of advance factory building within **21.6**(*d*) below it is deemed to have commenced on the commencement of construction. If, before the trade has been carried on for four months, the company (or subsidiary) is dissolved or wound up for *bona fide* commercial reasons, and not as part of a scheme the main purpose (or one such purpose) of which was tax avoidance, relief will nevertheless be available. [*TCA 1997, s 489(7)(8)(11)*]

Relief is also available where shares are subscribed for by a nominee for the individual claiming relief, including the managers of an investment fund designated by the Revenue Commissioners for this purpose. In the case of designated funds, the final date for the issuing of eligible shares is extended from 4 February 2004 to 31 December 2004 where certain conditions are satisfied. The Revenue Commissioners have wide powers to designate funds for this purpose, and to withdraw such designation (withdrawal being effective for subscriptions by the fund after the date of publication of the notice of withdrawal in *Iris Oifigiúil*). Specifically they must so designate a fund if, but only if, it is established under irrevocable trusts for the sole purpose of enabling 'qualifying individuals' to invest in 'eligible shares' of a 'qualifying company', and the terms of those trusts satisfy certain conditions as to the manner in which shares are purchased, dividends distributed, and moneys held, as to fund charges, and prohibiting connections between fund managers or trustees and the companies for whose shares the fund subscribes. The fund must close before the first investment is made, and annual audited accounts must be submitted to the Revenue Commissioners. Shares must be held by the fund for five years before they can be transferred into the name of a participant in the fund. [*TCA 1997, s 508; FA 2004, s 18, 19*]

21.3 A '*qualifying individual*' must subscribe for the shares on his own behalf, and must not, at any time in that period, be 'connected with' the issuing company (or a subsidiary of that company). He is so '*connected with*' any company:

(i)   of which he is a partner, director or employee, or of a partner company of which he is a director or employee, *except that* as a director or employee he is only 'connected with' a company if he (or a partnership of which he is a member) receives (or is entitled to receive) from that company (or from a company which is a partner of that company), during the five years following the issue, a payment other than by way of:

(*a*)   payment or reimbursement of allowable expenditure under Sch E,

(*b*)   interest at a commercial rate on money lent,

(*c*)   dividends, etc representing a normal return on investment,

(*d*)   payment for supply of goods at no more than market value, or

(*e*)   any reasonable and necessary remuneration for services rendered which is chargeable under Sch D, Case I or II (other than secretarial or managerial services, or those rendered by the company itself) or which is emoluments of the directorship or employment;

(ii)   of which an associate (as defined by *s 433(3)* but excluding a relative of the participator) meets any of the conditions at (i);

(iii)   if he directly or indirectly possesses or is entitled to acquire:

(*a*)   more than 30 per cent of its voting power, its issued ordinary share capital, or its loan capital and issued share capital together (loan capital including any debt incurred by the company for money borrowed, for capital assets acquired, for any right to income created in its favour, or for insufficient consideration, but excluding a debt incurred by overdrawing a bank account in the ordinary course of the bank's business). The threshold has been increased from €317,500 to €500,000 [*FA 2007, s 19*] – any individual below these new limits will not be considered a 'connected person' for the company in question], or

(b)   rights entitling him to more than 30 per cent of its assets available for distribution to the company's equity holders (as defined in *ss 413, 415*); or

(iv)   of which he has control (as defined in *s 11*);

and in applying (iii) and (iv), rights and powers of his associates (as in (ii) above) are attributed to him. A person is treated as entitled to acquire anything he is entitled to acquire at a future date or will at a future date be entitled to acquire.

An individual is not connected with a company by reason only of (iii) or (iv) above:

(A)   if, throughout the 'relevant period', the aggregate of all amounts subscribed for the issued share capital and loan capital of the company does not exceed €150,000 [*FA 2007, s 19*]; or

(B)   in the case of a 'specified individual' (see **21.7** below), by virtue only of a 'relevant investment' in respect of which relief has been given for the period prior to issue of the shares (see **21.7** below).

Relief given as a result of (A) or (B) above is not withdrawn by reason only that the individual subsequently becomes connected with the company under (iii) or (iv) above.

Relief is also denied where a person is 'connected with' (as above) a subsidiary of the issuing company (see **21.11** below) if it is a subsidiary during the 'relevant period', whether or not it becomes a subsidiary before, during or after the year of assessment in respect of which the individual claims relief and whether or not it is a subsidiary during the time that the circumstances in (i) to (iv) above exist; or where a person has at any time in the 'relevant period' had control (see (iv) above) of a company which has since that time, and before the end of the 'relevant period', become a subsidiary of the issuing company; or where a person directly or indirectly possesses or is entitled to acquire (as above) any loan capital (see (iii)(*a*) above) of such a subsidiary.

'*Relevant period*' in this context means the period from the date of incorporation of the company (or, if later, two years before the shares were issued) to five years after the issue of the shares.

Relief is denied where reciprocal arrangements are made aimed at circumventing this provision.

[*TCA 1997, ss 488(1), 493, Sch 10 para 2; FA 1984, s 18; FA 1994, s 16(1)(b)*]

21.4 A '*qualifying company*' must be incorporated in RI or in the European Economic Area (prior to 5 February 2004, incorporated in RI only). It must be resident in RI or in the European Economic Area and carrying on business in RI through a branch or agency (prior to 5 February 2004, resident only in RI). From 5 February 2004 to 31 December 2004, it must be a small- or medium-sized enterprise. Since 1 January 2005, it must be a micro-, small- or medium-sized enterprise. The company's shares, etc cannot be listed in the official list of a stock exchange or quoted on an unlisted securities market other than the Developing Companies Market. References to Developing Companies Market have been deleted and replaced any such reference with 'the Irish Enterprise Exchange'. [*FA 2007, s 19*] A company quoted on the Developing Companies Market may also be quoted on a similar exchange in another EU Member State or States, provided that it is quoted on the former market before or at the same time as it is first quoted on any of the latter. Its business must consist wholly of either:

(*a*)   carrying on one or more 'qualifying trades' wholly or mainly in RI; or

(*b*)   holding shares or securities of, or making loans to, 'qualifying subsidiaries' (see **21.11** below), with or without the carrying on of one or more 'qualifying trades' wholly or mainly in RI. Since 1 May 1998, it may alternatively consist of both the holding of shares or securities in, or making loans to, Exchange Axess Limited and the carrying on in limited partnership with that company of trading activities within **21.6**(*i*) below. A company satisfying this requirement before 1 January 2003 will continue to be a qualifying company where the limited partnership has since ceased. Although a winding-up or dissolution in the 'relevant period' generally prevents a company meeting these conditions, they are deemed met if the winding-up or dissolution is for *bona fide* commercial reasons and not part of a scheme the main purpose (or one such purpose) of which is tax avoidance, provided that any net assets are distributed to its members before the end of the 'relevant period' or (if later) the end of three years from commencement of winding-up.

Since 5 February 2004, a company is not a qualifying company if it is regarded as a firm in difficulty for the purposes of the Community Guidelines on State Aid for rescuing and restructuring firms in difficulty.
[*TCA 1997, ss 488(1), 495(2)(3)(a)(7)(8); FA 1999, s 16(a); FA 2000, s 19; FA 2003, s 15; FA 2005, s 27*]
As regards (*b*) above, money raised for a subsidiary's qualifying trade must be used only to acquire eligible shares in the subsidiary. [*TCA 1997, s 495(3)(b)*]

A company carrying on qualifying tourism activities (see **21.6**(*a*) below) which is seeking qualification must satisfy the Revenue Commissioners that it has had approved by The National Tourism Development Authority (previously, Bord Fáilte Éireann) a three year development and marketing plan designed to attract foreign tourists. Similarly, from 2 June 1995, a company carrying on a trade of the cultivation of horticultural produce (see **21.6**(*g*) below) must have had approved by the Minister for Agriculture, Food and Forestry a three-year development and marketing plan to increase exports or replace imports, and from 15 May 1996 a company whose trade consists of the production, etc of qualifying recordings must exist solely for the purpose of the production, etc of such recordings of a single new artist in relation to which the appropriate certificate has been given (see **21.6**(*j*) below).

'*Relevant period*' in this context means the period from the date of issue of the shares to three years after that date, or, if later, three years after the 'qualifying trade' was commenced following issue of the shares.

The company must also not at any time in the relevant period either:

(i)   have share capital which includes any issued shares not fully paid up;

(ii)   control another company (other than a 'qualifying subsidiary' (see **21.11** below)) or be controlled by another company (control in either case being as defined in *s 432(2)–(6)*, and being considered with or without persons connected with the company as defined in *s 10*);

(iii)   be a 51 per cent subsidiary (see **12.15** 'Corporation tax') of another company or itself have a 51 per cent subsidiary (other than a 'qualifying subsidiary', see **21.11** below); or

(iv)   be capable of falling within (ii) and (iii) by virtue of any arrangements.

A company in which a 'relevant investment' is made by a 'specified individual' (being that individual's first such investment in that company) (for shares issued before 2 June 1995, a 'relevant company') (see **21.7** below) is not a qualifying company if any transactions in the relevant period with another company were not at arm's length, and that other company was the immediate former employer of the individual concerned (or controlled or was controlled by a company which was the immediate former employer).

There is an additional exclusion if an individual who has acquired a 'controlling interest' in the company's trade, or in the trade of any subsidiary of the company, also has or has had such an interest in another trade concerned with similar goods or services, or serving a similar market, at any time in the period from two years before to three years after the later of the date of issue of the shares and the date the company or subsidiary commenced the trade.

In the case of a trade carried on by a company, a person has a '*controlling interest*' if he controls (within the definition of *s 432(2)–(6)*) the company; or if the company is close and he is a director of the company and the owner of or able to control more than 30 per cent of its ordinary share capital; or if at least half the trade could be regarded as belonging to him under *s 400(2)*. In any other case it is obtained by his being entitled to at least half of the assets used for, or income arising from, the trade. In either case, the rights and powers of any person's 'associates' are attributed to the person ('associate' being as defined in *s 433(3)*).

[*TCA 1997, ss 488(1), 495(4)–(6)(9)–(14)*; *FA 1984, s 15*; *FA 1995, s 17(1)(e)*; *FA 2006, s 127, Sch 2*]

A company claiming enhanced relief for certain research and development expenditure is excluded from being a qualifying company. See **12.9** 'Corporation tax'.

21.5 '*Eligible shares*' means new ordinary shares which, for five years after issue, carry no present or future preferential rights to dividends or assets (on a winding-up) or to be redeemed. [*TCA 1997, s 488(1)*] Certain shares carrying an assured return (see **12.10** 'Corporation tax') are excluded from relief. [*TCA 1997, s 489(14)(e)*]

21.6 A '*qualifying trade*' must be conducted on a commercial basis and with a view to the realisation of profits and must, throughout the 'relevant period' (as defined in **21.4** above) consist wholly or mainly of either or both of:

(i)   the manufacture of goods as defined for the purposes of the manufacturing companies' relief (see **12.18** 'Corporation tax'), subject to the exclusions referred to below; or

(ii)   the rendering of services (other than certain financial services, see **12.18**(viii) 'Corporation tax') in the course of a service industry in respect of which an employment grant has been made by Forbairt or the Industrial Development Agency (Ireland) under *Industrial Development Act 1993, s 12(2)* (previously by the Industrial Development Authority under *Industrial Development Act 1986, s 25*), or shares in the company were purchased or taken by either of those bodies under *Industrial Development Act 1986, s 31*, or in respect of which certain grants or other financial assistance have been made available by the Shannon Free Airport Development Co Ltd, Údarás na Gaeltachta or (for shares issued after 5 April 2001) a County Enterprise Board;

and, in the case of (i), in the period to 31 December 2002, the company must have claimed and be entitled to manufacturing companies' relief (or would have claimed and been entitled but for an insufficiency of profits). The time limit for investment in renewable energy projects has been increased from 31 December 2006 to 31 December 2011. This extension is subject to clearance by the European Commission from a State Aid perspective. [*FA 2007, s 51*] As regards (ii) since 5 February 2004, software development services for which grant aid approval has been issued but has not yet been paid will be a 'qualifying trade' as respects subscriptions for shares made from 4 February 2004 [*FA 2004, s 18 (2)(d)*]. See also **21.7** below for the extension of 'qualifying trades' in the case of certain 'relevant investments'.

Trades brought within the manufacturing companies' relief by virtue of **12.18**(vi)–(ix), (xiv)–(xvii) 'Corporation tax' are excluded from (i) above (and film production (see **12.23** 'Corporation tax') is in any event excluded). The scheme is, however, extended to include:

(*a*)   subject to certain restrictions, defined tourist traffic undertakings;

(*b*)   the sale of export goods by Trading Houses which qualify for the ten per cent rate of corporation tax under *s 443(12)* (see **12.18** 'Corporation tax');

(*c*)   cultivating plants by the process of micro-propagation or plant cloning;

(*d*)   the construction or leasing of an '*advance factory building*', ie a factory building within *Industrial Development Act 1986, s 2(1)* promoted by a local community group for local development and employment creation and undertaken without any prior leasing commitment;

(*e*)   research and development or other similar activity preliminary to the carrying on of trading operations within (i), (ii) or (*d*) above;

(*f*)   the cultivation of mushrooms within RI;

(*g*)   the cultivation of horticultural produce;

(*h*)   certain commercial research and development activities;

(*i*)   the production, publication, marketing and promotion of qualifying musical recording(s) by a new artist; and (*j*)   certain financial services operations on an exchange facility in the Custom House Docks Area (not being 'relevant investments', see **21.7** below);

(*k*)   trading operations carried on the coal, steel and shipbuilding sectors are excluded in respect of shares issued from 5 February 2004.

Certification by the appropriate Minister, agency, etc is required as regards (*d*), (*e*), (*g*), (*i*) and (*j*) above (see **21.2** above), and may impose financial limits in the case of (*i*).

Financial services carried on in the Custom House Docks site and brought within the manufacturing companies relief by *s 446* (see **12.18** 'Corporation tax') are also excluded from (ii) above (but see (*j*) above, and also see **21.7** below as regards certain 'relevant investments').

Leasing of machinery or plant or of land or buildings (other than within (*d*) above), and financing and refinancing activities, are not qualifying trading operations.

A trade of which only a part qualifies under this definition is treated as qualifying provided that at least 75 per cent of its turnover in the relevant period is from the qualifying part.

Adventures in the nature of trade are excluded.

[*TCA 1997, ss 488(1)(4), 496; FA 1984, s 16; FA 1987, s 11; FA 1990, s 41(2)(3); FA 1991, s 15(1)(e); FA 1994, s 48(3); FA 2001, s 12(c); FA 2003, s 15(c); FA 2005, s 27*]

21.7 Method of giving relief. Relief is given on the amount subscribed (subject to certain limits, see **21.8** below) as a deduction, in the year of assessment of the share issue, from the total income of the individual subscribing for the shares, as if the relief were a personal allowance. An investor in a 'designated fund' (see **21.2** above) may instead claim relief for the year of assessment of his investment in the fund, provided the eligible shares are issued in the following year of assessment. Exceptionally, for shares issued in the period from 1 January 2004 to 4 February 2004, relief may be claimed as if the shares had been issued in 2003 rather than 2004. Similarly, for shares issued in January 2002, relief may be claimed as if the shares had been issued in 2001 rather than 2002. For funds invested by a designated fund in the period from 1 January 2004 to 4 February 2004 relief may be claimed by the investor for 2003 rather than 2004 provided that the shares are issued by 31 December 2004. [*TCA 1997, s 489(3)(4)(4A); FA 2002, s 16(a); FA 2004, s 18*]

A 'specified individual' may, however, elect, in relation to a 'relevant investment' made by him, for relief to be given instead for any one of the six years of assessment immediately prior to the year of issue of the shares (the preceding five years for shares issued before 1 January 2002). Relief in respect of a second 'relevant investment' in the same company, made within either of the two years of assessment immediately following that in which the first such investment was made, may similarly, by election, be referred back to any of the six (five) years preceding the first investment. In either case, relief unused in that year may be carried forward (see **21.8** below) so as to obtain relief in nominated subsequent years before that in which the shares were issued, any relief still unused being carried forward to the year of issue of the shares. The limits at **21.8** below apply, so that relief to a maximum of €158,750/£125,000 in respect of any one 'relevant investment' may be obtained immediately provided that the general conditions are met. Where any amount raised by a designated fund between 1 January

2007 and 31 January 2007 is invested in qualifying companies on or before 31 December 2007, the individual investor who has subscribed to the fund will have the option of claiming relief on their investment for either the 2006 or 2007 tax year. This also applies in the case of direct investment where the shares are issued by 31 January 2007. [*FA 2007, s 19*]

The time limit for the carrying forward of unused relief under the scheme is extended to 31 December 2013. [*FA 2007, s 19*]

An election for relief to be referred back as above may be made by an individual in respect of a maximum of two 'relevant investments'.

A '*specified individual*' is a qualifying individual who:

(i) in each of the three years of assessment preceding the year of assessment immediately before that in which the individual makes his first or only 'relevant investment', was not chargeable to tax otherwise than under Sch E or (in respect of an employment outside RI) Sch D, Case III in respect of income in excess of the lesser of his income chargeable under Sch E or (as aforesaid) Sch D, Case III and €19,050/£15,000 (for 2001 only, £11,100), increasing to €25,000 and €18,500 respectively for relevant investments made from 5 February 2004. (Where the 'relevant investment' is in a company set up to trade as an exchange facility established in the Custom House Docks Area, this condition need not be satisfied.);

(ii) throughout the period beginning with the date of issue of the shares and ending two years later (or, if later, ending two years after the date on which the company began to carry on 'relevant trading operations') possesses at least 15 per cent of the issued ordinary share capital of the company in which the 'relevant investment' is made; and

(iii) at the date of subscription for the shares comprised in the relevant investment (the last subscription where there is more than one), and in the preceding twelve months, does not possess and has not possessed, directly or indirectly, and is not and was not entitled to acquire, more than 15 per cent of the issued ordinary share capital, or the loan capital and issued share capital, or the voting power of any other company other than a company which, during the five years ending on the date of that subscription (or last subscription):

(A) was not entitled to any assets other than cash on hands, or a sum on deposit not exceeding €130/£100,

(B) did not carry on a trade, profession, business or other activity including the making of investments, and

(C) did not pay charges within *s 243* (see **12.9** 'Corporation tax').

As regards (ii) above, a failure by reason of the company's being wound up or dissolved before the end of the period concerned is disregarded provided that the winding up or dissolution is for *bona fide* commercial reasons and not part of a scheme or arrangement a main purpose of which was the avoidance of tax.

As regards (iii) above, there is an exception for an individual owning more than 15 per cent of only one other company where the company is a trading company (other than in land or financial services) with an annual turnover not exceeding £100,000/€127,000.

A '*relevant investment*' is the amount (or aggregate amounts) subscribed in a year of assessment by the specified individual for eligible shares in a qualifying company carrying on (or intending to carry on) 'relevant trading operations'; '*relevant employment*' is employment by the company in which the relevant investment is made, as a full-time employee or director (within *s 250*, see **20.3**(*c*)(ii) 'Interest payable'), throughout the period of twelve months beginning with the date of issue of the shares (or, if later, with the date of commencement of the employment); and '*relevant trading operations*' are defined in *s 497* broadly as qualifying trading operations (see **21.6** above) (other than those within **21.6**(*d*) above) certified by The National Tourism Development Authority (previously Bord Fáilte Éireann), An Bord Iascaigh Mhara or An Bord Tráchtála, or by an industrial development agency, or by the Minister for Agriculture, Food and Forestry, the Minister for the Marine or the Minister for Arts, Culture and the Gaeltacht, or by a County Enterprise Board to be a new venture which, having regard to its potential for the creation of additional sustainable employment, and the desirability of minimising the displacement of existing employment, may be eligible for grant aid (or, in the case of certain trading operations, within guidelines agreed to by the Minister for Finance). For the latter purposes, the category of 'qualifying trade' described at **21.6**(ii) above is extended to include the rendering of certain services for which either an appropriate grant or financial assistance would have been available from the appropriate authority but for its having been made by some other person, or certain feasibility study grants have been provided by an industrial development agency or County Enterprise Board, and, notwithstanding the exclusion referred to at **21.6**(ii), until 31 December 2004 only certain financial services operations on an exchange facility in the Custom House Docks Area. [*TCA 1997, ss 488(1), 489(5), 494, 496(2)(a)(iv)(v), 497; FA 1984, ss 11(1), 12, 14A, 16A; FA 1993, s 25; FA 1994, s 16; FA 1995, s 17; FA 1996, s 24; FA 1997, s 9; FA 2001, Sch 2 para 26; FA 2002, s 16(a)(ii); FA 2003, s 15; FA 2004, s 18; FA 2006, s 127, Sch 2*]

21.8 Limits on relief. Except in the case of investments through 'designated funds' (see **21.2** above), relief is restricted to investments of not less than €250/£200 (for 2001 only, £148) by any one person in any one company in a year of assessment. In all cases there is an upper limit on investments by an individual in a year (whether in one or more companies) in respect of which relief may be given of €31,750/£25,000 (for 2001 only, £18,500). The relief has been increased to €150,00 in the case of individuals and €2,000,000 in the case of companies. [*FA 2007, s 19*]. Where relief in any year of assessment is limited, either because of insufficiency of income or because of the €31,750 (€150,000 [*FA 2007*]), etc maximum, the unrelieved investment may be carried forward for relief in succeeding years up to and including 2006. Relief carried forward is given in priority to current relief, earlier years being relieved first. [*TCA 1997, s 490; FA 1984, s 13; FA 1993, s 25(c); FA 1999, s 16(c); FA 2001, s 12(b), Sch 2 para 25; FA 2002, s 16(b); FA 2004, s 18(1)(b)*]

See also **21.12** below as regards married persons.

Restriction of relief for shares issued on or after 3 December 1997

In relation to shares issued after 11 April 1989, there is an additional restriction (subject to transitional provisions) on the amount which may be raised by a company and attract relief. This limits relief to the amount by which sums raised by all previous issues of eligible shares by the qualifying company fell short of £1,000,000 (£100,000 in the case of qualifying trading operations within **21.6**(*i*) above), disregarding sums raised which did not attract relief under these provisions. The sums in respect of which relief is available are apportioned where there is more than one individual entitled to relief in respect of the issue in question. [*TCA 1997, s 491; FA 1984, s 13A; FA 1991, s 15(1); FA 1993, s 25(d)*]

The additional restriction on the amount which may be raised by a company and attract relief is revised (subject to transitional provisions) for eligible shares issued on or after 3 December 1997. For shares issued on or after 1 January 2002, relief is limited to the amount by which:

(i)   where 21.6(*j*) applies, €127,000;

(ii)   where 21.6(*d*) applies, €1,270,000; or

(iii)   in all other cases (including 'relevant investments', see **21.7** above), €1,000,000 for shares issued from 1 January 2004 (previously €750,000);

exceeds all amounts raised by previous issues of eligible shares (other than those which did not attract relief under these provisions). For shares issued from 5 February 2004, no more than €750,000 may be raised in any six-month period.

For shares issued after 2 December 1997 but before 1 January 2002, the limitation is to the amount by which:

(*a*)   where **21.6**(*j*) applies, €127,000/£100,000;

(*b*)   in the case of a 'relevant investment' (see **21.7** above), €635,000/£500,000;

(*c*)   where **21.6**(*d*) applies, €1,270,000/£1,000,000; or

(*d*)   in all other cases, €317,500/£250,000;

(*e*)   €150,000 from 1 January 2007 to 31 December 2013 [*FA 2007, s19*];

exceeds all amounts raised by previous issues of eligible shares (other than those which did not attract relief under these provisions), but excluding (where (*a*) above applies) the first €508,000/£400,000, or where (*d*) above applies the first €317,500/£250,000, of amounts raised by way of 'relevant investments' (see **21.7** above).

For these purposes a share issue raising amounts consisting partly of relevant investments and partly of other amounts is treated as two separate issues, that relating to the relevant investments being treated as having been made on the day before the date of the actual share issue.

Where there are 'associated companies' (as above), the restriction is extended to apply by reference to issues of eligible shares by all such companies before or on the same date as the issue in question (other than issues on the same day by the issuing company itself), subject to the same exclusions as regards relevant investments.

The sums in respect of which relief is available are apportioned where there is more than one individual entitled to relief in respect of the issue in question. [*TCA 1997, s 491; FA 1998, s 34(a); FA 2002, s 16(c); FA 2004, s 18; FA 2005, s 27*]

Under the *transitional provisions* referred to above, the earlier provisions (as above) continue to apply to shares issued up to (variously) 5 April 1998 or 30 September 1998 in certain cases where proposals to issue eligible shares were well advanced before 3 December 1997. [*FA 1998, s 35*]

21.9 Claims for relief. A claim for relief in respect of any shares issued by a company in a year of assessment must be made not earlier than the date on which relief becomes allowable (see **21.2** above), and must be made within two years of the end of that year of assessment (or, if later, within two years of the end of the initial four months' trading giving rise to eligibility for relief, see **21.2** above). The time limit by which a claim must be made is extended by three months in limited circumstances. [*F(No 2)A 2008, s 26*] It must be accompanied by a certificate (form RICT 3) issued by the company stating that the conditions for relief, in respect of the company and the trade, are satisfied in relation to those shares. Before issuing such a certificate, the company must supply to the inspector a statement that those conditions were fulfilled from the beginning of the '*relevant period*' (as defined in **21.4** above), and such statement must contain such information as the Revenue Commissioners may reasonably require, and be in such form as they may direct, and must contain a declaration that it is correct to the best of the company's knowledge and belief. A certificate may not be issued without the inspector's authority (form RICT 2), nor where a notice under *s 505(2)* (see **21.13** below) has been given to the inspector. If such a certificate is issued or statement made fraudulently or negligently, or the certificate should not have been issued (see above), the company is liable to a fine of up to €630/£500 (€1,265/£1,000 in the case of fraud). The provisions are suitably modified where relief is claimed in respect of shares held by a 'designated fund' (see **21.2** above). From 2007, the quantum of relief available to a high earning individual in any one year may be limited, see **2.45** 'Limitation on Income Tax Relief for High Earners' [*FA 2006, s 17*]. For the purpose of calculating interest on overdue tax (see **25.3** 'Payment of tax'), tax charged by an assessment is regarded as due and payable notwithstanding that relief is subsequently given on a claim under these provisions, but is regarded as paid on the date on which a claim is made which results in relief being granted, unless it was either in fact paid earlier or not due and payable until later. Interest is not refunded in consequence of any subsequent discharge or repayment of tax giving effect to relief under these provisions. [*TCA 1997, ss 503, 508(5)–(7)*]. The taxpayer has a right of appeal in relation to the determination made by the Revenue Commissioners regarding the extent of tax relief allowable to them in any given tax year [*FA 2007, s 19*].

21.10 Restriction or withdrawal of relief. Relief allowed in the 'relevant period' (as defined in **21.3** or **21.4** above as appropriate) may be withdrawn if on any subsequent event it appears that the claimant was not entitled to relief. [*TCA 1997, s 489(9)*] See **21.6** above as regards withdrawal of relief in respect of 'relevant investments' where 'relevant employment' is not commenced within a certain time.

Disposal of shares. Where an individual disposes of, or of interest in or right over, shares, on the purchase of which relief was obtained, before the end of the 'relevant period' (as in **21.3** above), then:

(*a*)   if the disposal is not at arm's length, all relief is withdrawn;

(*b*)   otherwise, relief is withdrawn to the extent of the amount or value of consideration received.

Sales out of a holding of ordinary shares of any class in a company on only part of which relief has been obtained are treated as being of shares on which relief has been obtained rather than others. Where a holding includes shares attracting relief but issued at different times, shares issued earlier are deemed disposed of before those issued later. For this purpose, shares are treated as being of the same class only if they would be so treated if dealt in on an RI stock exchange.

There are provisions to prevent a double or triple tax charge arising under these provisions, the relief for employee share subscriptions (see **34.5** 'Sch E') and the Approved Profit-Sharing Schemes provisions (see **34.7** 'Sch E').

Where, on a capital reorganisation, new shares or debentures are allotted (without payment) in proportion to a holding of shares which have attracted relief, and are treated for capital gains tax as being the same asset (see **9.15** 'Capital gains tax'), the disposal of the new shares or debentures is treated as a disposal of shares which have attracted relief.

Relief is lost where the individual otherwise entitled to relief directly or indirectly enters into an option arrangement or an agreement, within the relevant period, either binding the individual to dispose of the shares, or requiring another person to acquire them, other than at market value at the time of the disposal/acquisition. [*TCA 1997, s 498; FA 1998, s 34(b)*]

See, however, **21.12** below as regards transactions between married persons.

Value received from company. Entitlement to relief in respect of shares issued by a company is reduced by the amount of any 'value received' from the company (including any company which, during the 'relevant period' (as in **21.3** above), is a subsidiary of that company, whether it becomes a subsidiary before or after the individual receives any value from it) during the relevant period.

An individual '*receives value*' from a company if it:

(i)   repays, redeems or repurchases any part of his holding of its share capital or securities, or makes any payment to him for the cancellation of rights;

(ii)   repays any debt owed to him other than an 'ordinary trade debt' (ie one incurred for normal trade supply of goods on normal trade credit terms (not in any event exceeding six months)) incurred by the company, or any other debt incurred by the company on or after the earliest date on which he subscribed for the shares which are the subject of relief and otherwise than in consideration of the extinguishment of a debt incurred before that date but with effect from 5 February 2004 , any loan made by a '*specified individual*' (see **21.7** above) to the company that is converted to eligible shares within one year of the making of the loan and meets certain audit certification requirements is not to be treated as the receipt of value from the company;

(iii) pays him for the cancellation of any debt owed to him other than such a debt as is mentioned in the exceptions in (ii) above or a debt in respect of such a payment as is mentioned in **21.3**(i)(*d*) or (*e*) above;

(iv)   releases or waives any liability of his to the company (which it is deemed to have done if payment of the liability is twelve months or more overdue) or discharges or undertakes to discharge any liability of his to a third person;

(v)   makes a loan or advance to him (defined as including the incurring by him of any debt either to the company (other than an 'ordinary trade debt', see (ii) above) or to a third person but assigned to the company);

(vi)   provides a benefit or facility for him;

(vii)   transfers an asset to him for no consideration or for consideration less than market value, or acquires an asset from him for consideration exceeding market value;

(viii)   makes any other payment to him except one either falling within **21.3**(i)(*a*) to (*e*) above or in discharge of an 'ordinary trade debt' (see (ii) above); or

(ix)   is wound up or dissolved in circumstances such that the company does not thereby cease to be a 'qualifying company' (see **21.4** above), and he thereby receives any payment or asset in respect of ordinary shares held by him.

The amount of the value received by an individual is that paid to or receivable by him from the company; or the amount of his liability extinguished or discharged; or the difference between the market value of the asset and the consideration (if any) given for it; or the net cost to the company of providing the benefit. In the case of value received within (i), (ii) or (iii) above, the market value of the shares, securities or debt in question is substituted if greater than the amount receivable.

An individual also '*receives value*' from the company if any person 'connected with' the company (as defined in **21.3** above) purchases any shares or securities of the company from him, or pays him for giving up any right in relation to such shares or securities. The value received is the amount receivable, or, if greater, the market value of the shares, etc.

All payments or transfers, direct or indirect, to, or to the order of, or for the benefit of, an individual or an 'associate' (as defined in **21.3**(ii) above) of his are brought within these provisions, as are payments, etc made by any person 'connected with' the company (as defined in *s 10*).

Relief is, where appropriate, withdrawn or withheld in respect of shares issued earlier before shares issued later. [*TCA 1997, s 499, Sch 10 para 3(1)*; *FA 2004, s 18*]

Value received other than by claimant. Relief is also reduced where, in the 'relevant period' (as in **21.3** above), the issuing company (including a subsidiary at any time in the relevant period) repays, redeems or repurchases any of its share capital belonging to any member other than (i) the individual, or (ii) another individual whose relief is thereby reduced (see above), or pays such a member for cancellation of his rights to its share capital. The reduction is the amount receivable by the member or, if greater, the nominal value of the share capital in question (with relief being restricted in proportion to the relief otherwise available where two or more individuals are involved). This restriction of relief does not apply in relation to the redemption on a date fixed before 26 January 1984 of any share capital, nor in relation to the redemption, within twelve months of issue, of any shares issued after 5 April 1984 to comply with *Companies (Amendment) Act 1983, s 6* (public company not to do business unless certain requirements as to share capital complied with). Relief is reduced in respect of shares issued earlier rather than shares issued later where relevant.

Where, in the 'relevant period' (as in **21.3** above), a member of the issuing company receives, or is entitled to receive, any 'value' from the company, then in applying the percentage limits referred to at **21.3**(iii)(*a*) above, the following amounts are treated as reduced:

(i) the amount of the company's issued ordinary share capital;

(ii) the amount of that capital 'relevant' to the provisions in question; and

(iii) the amount at (i) not included in (ii).

The reduction in (ii) and (iii) is in each case the same proportion of the total amount as the 'value' received by the member(s) entitled to the shares comprising the amount bears to the sum subscribed for those shares. The reduced amount at (i) is the sum of those at (ii) and (iii).

The capital '*relevant*' to a provision is those shares whose proportion of the total issued ordinary share capital is in each case compared with the appropriate percentage of that capital.

A member receives '*value*' from the company for this purpose where any payments, etc are made to him which, if made to an individual, would fall within (iv) to (viii) inclusive above, excluding those within (viii) made for full consideration. The amount of value received is as defined above. [*TCA 1997, s 501, Sch 10 para 3(1)(2)*]

Replacement capital. An individual is not entitled to relief in respect of shares issued by a company where, at any time in the 'relevant period' (as in **21.3** above), the company (or a subsidiary) begins to carry on a business (or part) previously carried on at any such time otherwise than by the company or a subsidiary, or acquires the whole or greater part of the assets used for a business so carried on, and the individual is a person who, or one of the group of persons who together, either:

(i) owned more than a half share (ownership and, if appropriate, respective shares being determined as under *s 400(1)(a)(b)(2)(3)*) at any such time in the business previously carried on, and also own or owned at any such time such a share in the business carried on by the company (or by a subsidiary); or

(ii) control (as in *s 432(2)–(6)*), or at any such time have controlled, the company, and also, at any such time, controlled another company which previously carried on the trade.

For these purposes, the interests, rights and powers of a person's 'associates' (as in *s 433*, but excluding a relative of a participator) are attributed to that person.

An individual is similarly not entitled to relief in respect of shares in a company which, at any time in the relevant period, comes to acquire all the issued share capital of another company, and where the individual is the person who, or one of the persons who together, control or have at any such time controlled the company and who also, at any such time, controlled the other company. [*TCA 1997, s 500*]

Assessments for withdrawing relief are made under Sch D, Case IV for the year of assessment for which relief was given, and, if the event giving rise to the withdrawal occurred after the date of claim, may be made at any time within four years (ten years for claims relating to 2002 and prior years, provided the claim is made by 31 December

2004 (*FA 2003, s 17; SI 508/03*)) after the end of the year of assessment in which the event occurs, without prejudice to the extension of the time limits in cases of fraud or neglect (see **6.2** 'Assessments to income tax'). No assessment may be made by reason of any event occurring after the death of the person to whom the shares were issued.

See also **21.12** below as regards assessments on married persons.

Where a person has made an arm's length disposal of all the ordinary shares issued to him by a company in respect of which relief has been given, no assessment may be made in respect of those shares by reason of any subsequent event unless he is at the time of that event 'connected with' the company (as defined in **21.3** above).

The date from which interest runs on overdue tax (see **25.3** 'Payment of tax') under these provisions is the date on which the event took place which gave rise to the withdrawal of relief, except that, where relief is withdrawn under the anti-avoidance provisions (see **21.13** below), it is the date on which relief was granted unless the relief was given under PAYE, in which case it is 5 April in the year of assessment in which relief was so given. [*TCA 1997, s 504*]

21.11 Subsidiary companies. The existence of certain subsidiaries does not prevent the parent being a 'qualifying company' (see **21.4** above), and a 'qualifying trade' (see **21.6** above) being carried on by the subsidiary may enable shares issued by the parent to attract relief under these provisions. The necessary modifications to the provisions apply where such a subsidiary exists.

The conditions imposed on any such subsidiary are that, until the end of the 'relevant period' (as in **21.4** above):

(i)   the subsidiary is a 51 per cent subsidiary (see **12.15** 'Corporation tax') of the qualifying company;

(ii)   no other person has control (as defined in *s 11*); and

(iii)   no arrangements exist whereby (i) or (ii) could cease to be satisfied;

and that the company either:

(*a*)   itself satisfies all the conditions for being a qualifying company as regards residence and purpose, and is an unquoted company and not wholly or partly a holding company (see **21.4** above); or

(*b*)   exists solely for the purpose of carrying on a trade consisting solely of any or all of:

    (i)   purchasing goods or materials for use by the qualifying company or its subsidiaries,

    (ii)   sale of goods or materials produced by the qualifying company or its subsidiaries, or

    (iii)   rendering services to or on behalf of the qualifying company or its subsidiaries.

The winding-up or dissolution, in the relevant period, of the subsidiary or of the qualifying company does not prevent the above conditions being met, provided that the winding-up, etc meets the conditions applied in relation to qualifying companies (see **21.4** above). [*TCA 1997, s 507, Sch 10 para 1*]

21.12 Married persons. The relief available under these provisions for subscriptions by a wife whose income is, by election, treated as that of her husband is available only against her total income, ie no excess of relief over total income may be set against her husband's total income. [*TCA 1997, s 489(3)*]

Limits on relief. The €630/£500 and €31,750/£25,000 limits (or 2001 equivalents) for investments attracting relief in a year of assessment (see **21.8** above) apply to the aggregate of the investments by a husband and wife where the wife's income is, by election, treated as that of her husband. Where in such a case a husband and wife are separately assessed, the relief is allocated to each in the proportion in which they subscribed for shares giving rise to relief. [*TCA 1997, ss 490(1), 1024(2)(a)(xi); FA 2001, Sch 2 para 25*]

Disposal of shares. For the purposes of *s 498* (see **21.10** above), a disposal of shares which have been the subject of relief under these provisions from one spouse to another is ignored where the wife is treated as living with her husband (see **23.1** 'Married persons') at the time of the disposal. Where, following such a transfer *inter vivos*, the shares are subsequently disposed of to a third person, the disposal is taken into account for the purposes of *s 498*, any consequent assessment being raised on the transferee spouse (by reference to the inter-spouse transaction) if the wife is, at the time of that subsequent disposal, no longer treated as living with her husband. [*TCA 1997, s 498(2)*]

Assessments for withdrawing relief. Where relief was obtained in respect of shares subscribed for by a spouse at a time when the wife's income was, by election, treated as that of her husband, and a subsequent withdrawal of relief falls to be made on a disposal of those shares at a time when the wife's income is no longer so treated, the assessment withdrawing relief is raised on the person making the disposal by reference to the actual reduction of tax flowing from the relief, regardless of any allocation of that relief. [*TCA 1997, s 504(2)*]

Capital gains tax. On a disposal between spouses of shares in respect of which relief has been obtained, the restriction of allowable expenditure by reference to the excess of cost of subscription over consideration on disposal (or the relief obtained if less) (see **21.13** below) does not apply, ie the transfer continues to be treated as giving rise to neither gain nor loss. [*TCA 1997, ss 489(12), 506(1)*]

21.13 Miscellaneous. The following general provisions apply in relation to the business expansion scheme.

Anti-avoidance. Relief otherwise due to an individual is denied where shares are issued other than for *bona fide* commercial reasons or as part of a scheme the main purpose, or one such purpose, of which was tax avoidance. [*TCA 1997, s 502*]

Capital gains tax considerations. On a disposal (other than between spouses, see **21.12** above) of shares in respect of which relief has been given and not withdrawn, the allowable expenditure for capital gains tax purposes is determined without regard to that relief, except that where the expenditure exceeds the consideration (ie a loss), the expenditure is reduced by the lesser of (*a*) the amount of the relief and (*b*) the excess.

Any question of whether or not a disposal is of shares in respect of which relief has been given and not withdrawn, and as to which of such shares issued at different times a disposal relates, is determined as at **21.10** above.

Where only part of a holding of ordinary shares in a company has attracted relief, and there has been a reorganisation of share capital within *s 584*, the new holding of shares is treated as two new holdings, one identified with shares attracting relief, the other with the remainder of the shares originally held. [*TCA 1997, ss 489(12), 506*]

Information. Certain events leading to withdrawal of relief must be notified to the inspector within 60 days by either the individual who received the relief, the issuing company, or any person 'connected with' that company (as defined in *s 10*) having knowledge of the matter. The inspector may require such a notice, and other relevant information, where he has reason to believe notice should have been given.

The inspector also has wide powers to require information in other cases where relief may be withdrawn, restricted or not due. The requirements of secrecy do not prevent his obtaining such information as he requires. [*TCA 1997, s 505, Sch 10 para 4*]

INCOME TAX RELIEF FOR INVESTMENT IN CORPORATE TRADES

21.14 The *Finance Act 2011, s 33* introduces a new relief for investment in corporate trades. The relief amends *TCA 1997*, by replacing *Pt 16*, which deals with the Business Expansion and Seed Capital Schemes. It will introduce a new incentive for investment in corporate trades called the Employment and Investment Incentive and Seed Capital Scheme. Introduction of the new incentive, which will require European Commission approval, will be subject to a Commencement Order from the Minister for Finance.

The current provisions will remain in place until such time as that Commencement Order gives effect to the new provisions. The section retains many of the provisions already present in the pre-existing *Pt 16*.

The lifetime limit which a company may raise is €10 million with the annual limit capped at €2.5 million. Relief will be available for investments up to 31 December 2013. The holding period for a shareholder is now three years instead of the previous five years. The method of granting the relief has also been amended with tax relief at 30% in the year of investment and a further 11% three years later provided the company meets certain requirements in relation to employment and R&D.

A summarised list of the most significant changes is as follows:

- The qualifying trades limitations have been removed and the scheme is available to the majority of small and medium-sized trading companies. The scheme is now open to trades generally.

- The certification requirements for the majority of qualifying companies have been simplified.

- It will be easier for companies carrying on green energy activities (ie activities undertaken with a view to producing energy from renewable sources) to qualify.

- The lifetime company investment limit has been increased from €2 million to €10 million.

- The annual amount that can be raised by companies has been increased from €1.5 million to €2.5 million.

- The period for which shares need to be held has been reduced from five years to three years.

- The maximum rate of tax relief for subscriptions for eligible shares has been reduced from 41 per cent to 30 per cent, in recognition of the reduced holding period.

- A further 11 per cent of tax relief may be available at the end of the holding period provided the company concerned has increased its number of employees since the investment was made, or the company has increased its expenditure on research and development.

The only significant change to the Seed Capital Scheme is that it too will be simplified, by removing the limitation on qualifying trades.

22 Losses

[*TCA 1997, Pt 12, Sch 32 para 15*] **Cross-reference.** See **12.17** 'Corporation tax' for losses by companies.

22.1 Losses are computed as for profits [*TCA 1997, s 381(4)*] and may be created or augmented by capital allowances, so far as they exceed balancing charges. [*TCA 1997, ss 392, 393*] Assessments under *s 238* (interest, annual payments etc not payable out of taxed profits) are treated, conditionally, as losses, but not interest paid re patent rights; nor rents payable to non-residents; nor interest from which tax was deducted by virtue of *s 246(2)* (see **20.1** 'Interest payable'). [*TCA 1997, s 390*]

22.2 Relief for losses may be claimed:

(*a*)   By **set-off** against other income in same year of assessment, first against income of the same kind (ie earned or unearned) as that to which the loss relates, then against the individual's other income, then spouse's earned/unearned income, and finally spouse's other income, except that a spouse's losses may only be set against the other spouse's income if, by election, the wife's income is treated as the husband's for income tax purposes. See **38.224** 'Tax cases' as regards 'income'; [*TCA 1997, s 381*]

(*b*)   By **carry-forward** (if not relieved under (*a*) above) against subsequent profits of the same trade without time limit; [*TCA 1997, s 382*]

(*c*)   By carry-back of a **terminal loss** arising on discontinuance (either permanent or notional) under *s 69* (changes of proprietorship). Any loss (as computed) incurred in the twelve months preceding the date of cessation can be set against profits (as computed) assessed for the three years preceding the year of cessation, using latest years first. The computed loss involves splitting of accounts and of relevant capital allowances (excluding those brought forward). The computed profit is reduced by capital allowances as above, any payments or losses deductible for tax purposes by an individual, any dividends paid by a company. (But if such payments are deducted from profits, a corresponding amount is deducted from the terminal loss applicable against earlier years, except where are payments made wholly for purposes of the trade.) On notional succession, the continuing partner has no claim for his share of losses. [*TCA 1997, ss 385–388*]

Finance Act 2009, s 6 brought in new provisions in relation to dealing in development land, specifically dealing with losses in relation to the special 20 per cent rate that existed until 1 January 2009. The section also inserts a new *s 644AA* which introduces new rules for the treatment of certain trading losses arising from a trade of dealing in residential development land where if profits had been earned the profits would have qualified for the 20 per cent incentive rate of income tax.

Under normal income tax rules, a loss sustained in a trade may be set sideways against the person's other income in the year in which the loss arises or may be carried forward for set-off against the income from the trade in subsequent tax years. In the case of losses sustained in a trade of dealing in residential development land, this could lead to a mismatch in that such losses (sustained in a trade in which if profits had been made would have been taxed at 20 per cent) could be set against the person's other income taxable at the higher 41 per cent rate. The new section provides that such losses must first be converted into a tax credit, valued at 20 per cent of the loss, and then allows the tax credit to be set sideways in the year the loss is sustained against tax payable on the person's other income. Any unused part of the tax credit may be carried forward and set-off against tax on the income from the trade in subsequent years. Where dealing in residential development land is part of a larger trade, any carried forward tax credit may be set against tax on the income from the larger trade.

As respects a claim for the sideways set-off of losses arising in a trade of dealing in residential development land against a property developer's other income, the new rules apply where such a claim had not been made to and received by Revenue before 7 April 2009.

As respects the carry forward of such losses within the trade, the new rules apply unless the carry forward claim by the property developer was made to and received by Revenue before that date. For the purposes of the new rules, where a trade comprises partly of dealing in residential development land and partly of other activities the new section requires each part to be treated as a separate trade.

Finally, where a claim for terminal loss relief (ie on the permanent cessation of a trade) had not been made to and received by Revenue before 7 April 2009, the new section restricts the relief so that any part of the terminal loss that relates to a loss sustained, before 1 January 2009, in a trade of dealing in residential development land is 'ring-fenced' and can only be set against income arising in that trade, or in that part of a trade, in prior years.

From 2007, the quantum of loss relief available to a high earning individual in any one year may be limited, see **2.45** 'Limitation on Income Tax Relief for High Earners'.[*FA 2006, s 17*]

The above reliefs do not apply to any loss incurred from the sale of stallion services (from which the income is exempt, see **30.1** 'Sch D, Cases I and II'). [*TCA 1997, s 381(2)*] There are restrictions for certain farming and market gardening losses (see **18.6** 'Farming') and for losses arising in certain electricity, petroleum, film and music trades (see **22.6** below).

22.3 Losses under Sch D, Case IV or V may be set off against profits of that Case of the same year or carried forward indefinitely against subsequent profits assessed under that Case. [*TCA 1997, ss 383, 384*] *Finance Act 2010, s 14* provides for clarification of the order of priority of set off for Case V Losses and capital allowances. The section amends *s 384* and expressly provides that Case V capital allowances arising in a year are to be deducted in priority to Case V Losses that are brought forward from a previous year. See **32.3** 'Sch D, Case IV' and **33.7** 'Sch D, Case V'. From 2007, the quantum of relief available to a high earning individual in any one year may be limited, see **2.45** 'Limitation on Income Tax Relief for High Earners'. [*FA 2006, s 17*]

22.4 Expenditure on approved buildings in RI, or on ornamental gardens or grounds occupied or enjoyed with such buildings, incurred by the owner or occupier in respect of their repair, maintenance or restoration, may be treated as if it were a loss, sustained in the year of assessment (accounting period in the case of a company) in which it was incurred, in a separate trade carried on by that person. It may thus be relieved as under **22.2**(*a*) above, or, in the case of a company, as under **12.17** 'Corporation tax'. The ringfencing provisions of *ss 396A, 420A* (see **12.17**, **12.15** 'Corporation tax') are disregarded in relation to such a loss. Expenditure is reduced for this purpose by any payment received related to the work done, and by any part attracting relief under any other taxing provision. Only expenditure properly attributable to work carried out in a chargeable period is treated as incurred in that period.

Relief also applies to expenditure by the owner or occupier on the maintenance or restoration of approved gardens.

An unrelieved loss (as above) in respect of expenditure in the chargeable period (other than expenditure on approved gardens) may be carried forward for relief in either of the next two chargeable periods (earliest first), relief originating in an earlier chargeable period being relieved in priority to that of a later period.

There is additionally relief on aggregate expenditure in relation to an approved building of up to €6,350/£5,000 (for 2001 only, £3,700) in a chargeable period on:

(*a*) the repair, maintenance or restoration of objects or collections of intrinsic national, scientific, historical or aesthetic interest in the approved building, subject to broadly similar approval and access requirements as apply to the building under (i) and (ii) above;

(*b*) the installation, maintenance or replacement of a security alarm system in the building; and

(*c*) public liability insurance for the building;

and similar additional relief applies to approved gardens.

Approved buildings are those determined, on application by the owner or occupier:

(i) by the Minister for Arts, Culture and the Gaeltacht to be intrinsically of scientific, historical, architectural or aesthetic interest; and

(ii) by the Revenue Commissioners to afford *reasonable access* to the public or to be in use as a 'tourist accommodation facility' for at least six months in any calendar year (including at least four between 1 May and 30 September).

A '*tourist accommodation facility*' must be either in the register of guest houses kept by the National Tourism Development Authority (previously, Bord Fáilte Éireann) or in the list published by the National Tourism Development Authority under *Tourist Traffic Act 1957, s 9*.

Relief may not apply for any chargeable period before that in which such application is made.

Approved gardens are similarly defined, with an additional qualifying category of horticultural interest.

Reasonable access requires:

(*a*)   access to the whole or a substantial part of the building at the same time;

(*b*)   access at reasonable times for at least four hours on at least 60 days in any year, including at least 40 days in the period 1 May to 30 September, subject to temporary closure for repairs, etc; and

(*c*)   access at reasonable cost (if any).

As regards (*b*) above, with immediate effect for approvals after 23 March 2000, and with effect for chargeable periods beginning after 30 September 2000 for earlier approvals, at least 10 of the 40 days between 1 May and 30 September must be Saturdays or Sundays. With effect from 1 January 2005, details of access must be publicised annually and a notice relating to access details must be conspicuously displayed at or near the entrance to the building on the days on which access is available to the public.

Evidence has to be produced that details of opening dates and times, or of periods of use as a tourist accommodation facility, have been supplied for publication to Bord Fáilte Éireann by 1 January (1 November for 2002 onwards and for accounting periods beginning after 31 December 2001) both in the chargeable period and in previous chargeable periods (up to a maximum of five) beginning with the chargeable period in which the building was first approved for relief. Similarly for such periods, evidence that a tourist accommodation facility was included in the appropriate register or list (as above) must be provided.

There is provision for withdrawal of approval, with consequential adjustments, and for powers of inspection by representatives of the approving authority. A change from satisfying the 'reasonable access' requirement to being in use as a 'tourist accommodation facility', or *vice versa*, does not give rise to a withdrawal of approval, the revised approval being in effect treated as given at the time of the original approval.

Claims are made to the Revenue Commissioners in such form as they may prescribe.

Passive investors. Relief for losses under these provisions may be restricted where ownership of the interest giving rise to the right to claim the relief is transferred to an individual and at the time of the transfer (or within the following five years) the building is an approved building. The restriction applies if there are arrangements of any sort at the time of the transfer enabling the transferor (or a connected person within *s 10*) to determine how qualifying expenditure is to be incurred, or to participate in the tax benefits accruing to the transferee, or to re-acquire the interest, or if the transfer was made for the sole or main purpose of facilitating a claim. On a claim by the transferee to relief under *s 381* (see **22.2(*a*)** above) in respect of qualifying expenditure on the approved building, the relief is limited to €31,750 for any year of assessment. Any excess over that figure may be carried forward (as described above in cases of insufficient income). The restriction does *not*, however, apply where:

(1)   the qualifying expenditure was incurred before 5 December 2001;

(2)   in relation to qualifying expenditure incurred after 4 December 2001 and before 31 December 2003, the determinations relating to the building by the Minister and the Revenue Commissioners (as in (i) and (ii) above) were made before 5 December 2001;

(3)   in relation to qualifying expenditure incurred before 31 December 2001, the Revenue Commissioners had, before 5 December 2001, indicated in writing that proposals made were broadly acceptable to them as regards a recommendation under (ii) above, and the Department of Arts, Heritage, Gaeltacht and the Islands had similarly before that date indicated in writing that following a visit they would, if required, recommend that a determination be made under (i) above; or

(4)   in relation to qualifying expenditure incurred before 31 December 2003, a determination had before 5 December 2001 been made under (i) above, and the transferee had undertaken to gift, directly or indirectly, to the transferor, being a charity authorised as such by the Revenue Commissioners, the full value of the relief under the claim, and does so.

[*TCA 1997, ss 482, 409C; FA 1982, s 19; FA 1994, s 18; FA 1997, s 17; FA 1998, s 33; FA 2000, s 49; FA 2001, Sch 2 para 24; FA 2002, ss 14, 42, FA 2005, s 28*]

Loss relief under *s 381* to owners of significant buildings and gardens who are passive investors has been abolished with effect from the tax year 2010. [*FA 2010, s 20*] Transitional arrangements exist for the years 2010 and 2011 in respect of works that were carried out on or before 4 February 2010 and such work that begins after that date but was under written contract on or before that date. From 2007, the quantum of relief available to a high earning individual in any one year may be limited, see **2.45** 'Limitation on Income Tax Relief for High Earners' [*FA 2006, s 17*]

See **34.3** 'Sch E – emoluments' as regards exemption from treatment as a benefit of certain loans of art objects on display in approved buildings or gardens.

LIMITED PARTNERSHIPS

22.5 Where an **individual** 'limited partner' sustains a loss or incurs capital expenditure in the partnership trade, or pays interest by reason of his participation therein, relief may be restricted.

A *'limited partner'* is a partner carrying on a trade:

(*a*)   as a limited partner in a limited partnership registered under the *Limited Partnerships Act 1907*;

(*b*)   as a general partner in a partnership, but who is not entitled to take part in the management of the trade, and who is entitled to have his liability for debts or obligations incurred for trade purposes discharged or reimbursed by some other person, in whole or beyond a certain limit;

(*c*)   who, under the law of any territory outside RI, is not entitled to take part in the management of the trade, and is not liable beyond a certain limit for debts or obligations incurred for trade purposes; or

(*d*)   (after 28 February 2000) as a general partner the greater part of whose working time is not spent on the day-to-day management or conduct of the trade. (Since 28 February 1998 to 28 February 2000, this applied only where the trade activities include producing, distributing or holding (or holding an interest in) films or video tapes, or exploring for or exploiting oil or gas resources.)

In relation to contributions made after 10 April 1994, a general partner is treated as within (*b*) above where, in connection with a contribution to the partnership trade, either:

(1)   there exists any agreement, arrangement, scheme or understanding under which the partner is required to cease to be a partner before he is entitled to receive back from the partnership the full amount of his contribution; or

(2)   by virtue of any such agreement, etc, a creditor's entitlement to recover any debt of the partner or partnership from the partner is in any way limited or restricted.

As respects a contribution made after 23 April 1992, any loss, etc sustained by, or allowance for expenditure made to, a limited partner in respect of a trade as above for a year of assessment may be relieved under the '*specified provisions*' only against profits of the same trade, and no relief is available for the excess of the loss etc over his 'contribution' to the trade at the end of the year of assessment (or at the time he ceased to carry on the trade if he did so during that year of assessment). Where (*d*) above applies, the requirement that relief be given only against profits of the same trade does not apply to losses or allowances arising before 1 March 2000 (28 February 1998 where (*d*) applied from that date). For contributions before 24 April 1992, relief is available in full against profits of the same trade, but relief is not available against other income for the excess of the loss etc over his contribution (as above). In relation to trades of managing and letting holiday cottages, where construction work was contracted for and commenced before 24 April 1992 and completed before 6 April 1993, these changes apply from 1 September 1992 instead of 24 April 1992.

If relief has been allowed under any of the 'specified provisions' (see below) for an earlier year of assessment (ignoring years before 1985/86) at any time during which the individual carried on the trade as a limited partner, the loss, etc or allowance for the year of assessment is restricted by the excess of the sum of the loss, etc or allowance for that year and the earlier amounts relieved over the 'contribution'.

The restrictions do not apply to individual general partners brought within (*d*) above from 29 February 2000 in relation to losses, etc derived from '*excepted expenditure*', ie expenditure within *s 409A* (see **8.1** 'Capital allowances'), or which would be within that section but for certain transitional provisions, or expenditure which would be within *s 409B* (see **8.1** 'Capital allowances') but for certain transitional provisions or the exclusion from that section of buildings (other than holiday camps) in certain areas. They similarly do not apply to such individual partners, as a transitional measure, where they carry on any of the following trades and the losses, etc are derived from the trade:

(I)   trades consisting wholly of leasing machinery or plant to a qualifying company within *s 486B* (investment in renewable energy generation, see **12.9** 'Corporation tax'), where the expenditure was incurred on provision of the machinery or plant under an obligation entered into between lessor and lessee before 1 March 2001;

(II)   trades in which capital allowances are available in respect of whitefish fishing boats under *s 284(3A)* (see **8.6** 'Capital allowances'), but only for interest on loans taken out before 4 September 2000, allowances for expenditure incurred before that date, and losses for 2001 and earlier years of assessment (except to the extent that they arise from allowances under *s 284(3A)*);

(III) trades in which a double rent allowance is due under various renewal schemes (see **30.24** 'Sch D, Cases I and II') in respect of premises occupied for the purposes of the trade, provided that the individual concerned became a partner and made a contribution to the trade before 29 February 2000, and the lease giving rise to the double allowance was granted to or acquired by the partnership before that date. The exclusion does not, however, apply to losses, etc of a year of assessment for which a double rent allowance is not due or any year of assessment after such a year, and in relation to premises in qualifying resort areas they cease to be available in any event after 2004.

The '*specified provisions*' are:

(i) *section 305* (relief of certain excess capital allowances against general income);

(ii) *section 381* (relief of losses against general income, see **22.2**(*a*) above); and

(iii) *sections 245–255* (relief for certain interest payments, see **20.3**(*a*) 'Interest payable').

The partner's '*contribution*' to the trade at any time is the aggregate of:

(A) capital contributed and not subsequently, directly or indirectly, withdrawn or received back from the partnership or from a person connected (within *s 10*) with the partnership (other than anything, in relation to expenditure for the trade, which the partner is or may be entitled to withdraw or receive at any time he carries on the trade as a limited partner, or which he is or may be entitled to require another person to reimburse to him); and

(B) any profits or gains of the trade to which he is entitled but which he has not received in money or money's worth.

In determining whether or not relief is obtained under a relevant provision as respects a contribution made after 23 April 1992, any relief which would not have been obtained but for a contribution made after that date is treated as obtained as respects such a contribution.

A partner is treated as receiving back an amount contributed to the partnership if he received that amount or value for the sale of his interest (or part) in the partnership; if the partnership (or a person connected with it within *s 10*) repays that amount of a loan or advance from him; or if he receives that amount of value for assigning any debt due to him from the partnership (or from a person connected with it, as above).

Similar provisions apply where a company which is a limited partner sustains a loss or incurs capital expenditure in the partnership trade, or where it or any other company pays a charge by reason of its participation in the trade. The '*specified provisions*' under which relief is restricted are:

(*aa*) *section 243* (relief for charges on income, see **12.9** 'Corporation tax');

(*bb*) *section 308(4)* (relief for certain capital allowances against profits generally, see **12.9** 'Corporation tax');

(*cc*) *section 396(2)* (relief for trading losses against profits generally, see **12.17** 'Corporation tax'); and

(*dd*) *section 420(1)(2)(6)* (group relief, see **12.15** 'Corporation tax').

[*TCA 1997, s 1013; FA 2000, s 70; FA 2001, Sch 2 para 55; FA 2005, s 37*]
　　See also **38.134** 'Tax cases'.

PASSIVE TRADERS

22.6 Trade losses arising to individuals who are not primarily engaged in the day-to-day management or conduct of certain trades are ring-fenced to the trade and cannot be set against other income. The trades concerned are (i) the generation of electricity; (ii) trading operations which are petroleum activities; (iii) the development or production of films, film projects, film properties or music properties; (iv) the acquisition of rights to participate in the revenues of film properties or music properties; and (v) the production, distribution or holding of an interest in either or both a film negative and its associated soundtrack, a film tape or a film disc, an audio tape or audio disc or a film property produced by electronic means or a music property produced by electronic means. The restriction applies from 2002 for the generation of electricity and from 2003 for the activities in (ii)–(v). [*TCA 1997, s 409D; FA 2003, s 12*]

23 Married Persons

Cross-references. See Allowances, credits and rates at **2.4** for the rate bands applicable to married persons having a single income or two incomes, at **2.9** for the single allowance applicable to married persons on election and at **2.11** for the married allowance plus the additional allowance for the year of marriage.

23.1 Where a wife is 'living with her husband' (see below), income tax is assessed, charged and recovered on the income of each as if they were not married. [*TCA 1997, s 1016(1)*] A husband and wife may, however, jointly elect for both incomes to be deemed to be the husband's for income tax purposes, and assessable on him (unless separate assessment has been claimed – see **23.2** below). He will then be entitled to married allowance. Such an election may be made at any time during the year of assessment for which election is made, and will continue to have effect until withdrawn by either spouse. An election will in any case be deemed to have been made for any year unless one spouse has, during the year or previously, given notice that he or she wishes to be assessed as a single person. [*TCA 1997, ss 1017, 1018*] The effect of the election is that the wife is not a chargeable person (see **38.91** 'Tax cases'). No election under *s 1018* may be made (or be deemed to have been made) where the wife's income is not assessable and chargeable to tax in RI (see **38.90** 'Tax cases'). Any overdue tax which is attributable to the wife's income may be collected direct from her, and a husband may disclaim liability for unpaid tax attributable to his deceased wife's income (so that it becomes payable out of her estate). For assessments made on or after 10 February 2000, this applies equally to collection of tax attributable to the husband's income from him, and the wife may similarly disclaim liability. [*TCA 1997, s 1022; FA 2000, s 29*]

For the year of marriage husband and wife are taxed as if unmarried throughout the year. However, where the tax paid and payable by both for that year exceeds that which would have been paid and payable had they been married throughout the year, they may jointly claim (in writing) a repayment of one-twelfth (for 2001 only, one-ninth) of that excess for each income tax month or part month in the year during which they were married. The repayment is allocated in proportion to the tax paid and payable in the year by each spouse. [*TCA 1997, s 1020; FA 2001, Sch 2 para 57*]

A married woman is treated as '*living with her husband*' unless they are (*a*) separated under a Court Order or separation deed, or (*b*) in fact separated in circumstances where permanent separation is likely. [*TCA 1997, s 1015(2)*]

The *Status of Children Act 1987, s 3* applies in that:

(*a*)   relationships between persons are to be determined without regard to whether the parents of any person are or have been married to each other, unless the contrary intention appears; and

(*b*)   an adopted person shall, for the purposes of (*a*), be deemed from the date of the adoption to be the child of the adopter or adopters, and not the child of any other person or persons.
[*TCA 1997, s 8*]

Assessment on either spouse. Where an election under *s 1018* (see above) has been (or is deemed to have been) made, the husband and wife may jointly elect for the wife, rather than the husband, to be assessed under *s 1017* in respect of both their incomes. This will also apply without election in certain cases where the year of marriage is after 1992/93, the election under *s 1018* is deemed to have been made but has not in fact been made, and the inspector considers that the wife's income exceeds that of the husband. In either case, the income of both husband and wife is deemed to be that of the wife, and the wife is assessed and charged in respect of both incomes. All other relevant provisions of the *Taxes Acts* specified to apply to the husband then apply to the wife (including entitlement to the married allowance, see **2.11** 'Allowances, credits and rates'). A joint election by the spouses under these provisions must be made before 1 April in the first year of assessment to which it is to apply (6 July in relation to 2001 and earlier years), and continues to apply for subsequent years until withdrawn by joint notice given before 1 April (6 July in relation to 2001 and earlier years) in the first year for which it is withdrawn. [*TCA 1997, s 1019; FA 2001, Sch 2 para 56*]

Where this provision applies other than as a result of an election by the spouses, it continues to apply, whether or not the wife's income exceeds that of the husband, unless and until the spouses either elect under *s 1018* for *s 1017* to apply in relation to the husband, or apply for separate assessment (see **23.2** below). Where a notice under *s 1018(4)(a)* or an application under *s 1023* for separate assessment (see **23.2** below) is withdrawn, and but for the original notice or election the wife would have been assessed and charged on both spouses' incomes for the year of withdrawal, then unless an election has actually been made under *s 1018(1)* for joint assessment on the husband, the wife will, for the year of withdrawal and subsequent years, be assessed and charged on the joint income. [*TCA 1997, s 1019(4)*]

Where either husband or wife is assessed on their joint income and separate assessment under *s 1023* (see **23.2** below) does not apply, any repayment of tax is allocated to husband and wife in proportion to the tax deducted or paid on their respective total incomes (subject to a *de minimis* limit of £20/€25 in respect of a repayment to the spouse who is not assessed and charged under *s 1017*). The inspector may, however, allocate a repayment on a just and reasonable basis where he is satisfied that it arises (or arises in greater part) by reason of an allowance or relief attributable to one spouse only. [*TCA 1997, s 1021; FA 2000, Sch 2*]

23.2 Separate assessment to income tax may be claimed by either spouse within the six months before 1 April in the year of assessment (6 July in relation to 2001 and earlier years), or the following 1 April (6 July) if the year of assessment is the year of marriage, and will be effective for that year and subsequent years until withdrawn (in writing before 1 April/6 July). The total tax liability is unaffected. [*TCA 1997, s 1023; FA 2000, Sch 1 para 6; FA 2001, Sch 2 para 58*]

If separate assessment is claimed, certain basic allowances are divided between the spouses half and half. These are the married allowance, child allowance for own or adopted children, age allowance and blind person's allowance. Other allowances are, in general, divided in proportion to the amount of payments, etc. The special deduction for PAYE taxpayers is divided in proportion to the respective emoluments giving rise to the deduction. The amount of taxable income in the standard and higher rate bands is that applicable where both incomes are deemed to be those of the husband, and is divided equally. Any amount of unused allowance, or of unused tax rate band, is carried over to the other spouse (although special rules apply in respect of the standard rate band for 2000/01 onwards).

Any reduction of income tax due to marginal age exemption or marginal low income exemption (see **2.7**, **2.8** 'Allowances, credits and rates') is apportioned between spouses in proportion to the income tax payable by each but for such exemption.

[*TCA 1997, s 1024; FA 1998, ss 14(1)(d), 16(c), 17(c); FA 1999, ss 47(2)(b), 70(2)(b); FA 2000, ss 3(b), 21(2), Sch 1 para 7; FA 2001, ss 11(1)(c), 23(b)*]

23.3 Maintenance payments as specified below, which are made by one party to a marriage for the benefit of the other, are payable without deduction of tax, but are deductible in computing total income of the payer (see **2.1** 'Allowances, credits and rates') and are chargeable under Sch D, Case IV (**32**) on the other party. Payments for the maintenance of a child are also made without deduction of tax, but are not deductible from the payer's total income and are not treated as the child's income. For child allowance purposes (see **2.17** 'Allowances, credits and rates'), the payment is treated as spent by the payer (and only by the payer) on maintaining the child, regardless of whether it was in fact paid to the other party to the marriage.

For any year of assessment in which such a maintenance payment has been made, and in which the parties to the marriage are separated (but the marriage is neither annulled nor dissolved but both RI-resident, they may jointly elect for the wife's income to be treated as that of her husband as under *s 1017* (see **23.1** above). The maintenance payments are then ignored in calculating total income, and separate assessment (see **23.2** above) applied to determine respective liabilities.

For these purposes a *maintenance payment* is a legally enforceable periodical payment (or part) made under or pursuant to a maintenance arrangement (ie a court order, etc giving rise to a legally enforceable obligation and made or done in consideration or consequence of the dissolution or annulment of a marriage or the legal separation of the partners) at a time when the wife is not living with the husband. It must be made for the benefit of the other party to the marriage or of the payer's child (including any child in respect of which he had previously been entitled to child allowance (see **2.17** 'Allowances, credits and rates')).

Maintenance arrangements made before 8 June 1983 are excluded until either the arrangement is varied or replaced, or both parties to the marriage jointly elect (in writing) for their inclusion, whereupon any future such payments are included.

[*TCA 1997, ss 1025, 1026; FA 1983, s 4; FA 1997, s 5; FA 2000, Sch 1 para 8*]

24 Mines

See generally *TCA 1997, Pt 24, Ch 1.*

COAL MINES

24.1 Marginal Coal Mine Allowance. The Minister for Finance, after consultation with the Minister for the Marine and Natural Resources, may direct that the tax chargeable on the profits of a marginal coal mine for any particular year of assessment or accounting period is to be reduced to an amount (including nil) as specified by him. [*TCA 1997, s 671*]

MINE DEVELOPMENT ALLOWANCE

24.2 An annual allowance is given for capital expenditure incurred in searching for, discovering, testing or winning access (by underground or surface working) to minerals, including works likely to have little value when the operation ceases, but not the cost of acquiring the site or the minerals.

The allowance is calculated to spread the difference between the cost and the residual value over the estimated life of the deposits (up to 20 years). The allowance must be claimed within 24 months of the end of the year of assessment. Balancing allowances and charges are made on cessation or sale. [*TCA 1997, s 670*]

With effect from accounting periods ending after 3 February 2004, the tax treatment of short-term finance leases by a company lessor may follow the accounting treatment. Where such a claim is made, no annual allowance is available. See **8.7** 'Capital allowances'. [*TCA 1997, s 80A; FA 2004, s 35*]

'NON-BEDDED' MINERAL MINES

24.3 The following provisions apply to mines being worked for the purpose of obtaining 'non-bedded' minerals (as specified in the Table to *s 672*). [*TCA 1997, s 672*]

24.4 Marginal mine allowance is applicable as in **24.1** above. [*TCA 1997, s 682*]

24.5 Groups of companies. Exploration expenditure by one member of a group of companies may, by election, be deemed the expenditure of another member (whether or not in existence at the time of the expenditure). [*TCA 1997, s 675*]

24.6 Capital allowances apply for income tax and corporation tax as follows:

(*a*)   *exploration investment allowance* of 20 per cent on expenditure incurred after 5 April 1974;

(*b*)   *plant and machinery* (other than cars, lorries etc):

(i)   investment allowance of 20 per cent on new assets purchased after 5 April 1974,

(ii)   wear and tear allowances without regard to (i);

(*c*)   *mineral depletion allowance* is given under *s 670* (see **24.2** above) on capital expenditure in *acquiring*, after 31 March 1974, any entitlement to work deposits of minerals (provided they are actually worked).

With effect from accounting periods ending after 3 February 2004, the tax treatment of short-term finance leases by a company lessor may follow the accounting treatment. Where such a claim is made, no annual allowance is available.

The *Finance Act 2011, s 27* has abolished, with effect from 1 January 2011, the 20 per cent investment allowance in respect of mineral exploration expenditure provided for under *TCA 1997, s 677* and the 20 per cent allowance for capital expenditure on new machinery and plant provided for under *TCA 1997, s 678* for the purposes of a trade of working a qualifying mine. *[FA 2011, s 27]*

See **8.7** 'Capital allowances'. [*TCA 1997, s 80A, ss 677–680; FA 1998, s 40; FA 2004, s 35*]

24.7 Mine rehabilitation expenditure. Net rehabilitation expenditure incurred after the cessation of the working of a qualifying mine is allowable as a deduction, and where the trade of working the mine also ceased it is treated as incurred on the date of cessation. A compulsory contribution to a mine rehabilitation fund will generally attract relief over the estimated life of the mine (with a restriction on cumulative allowances at any given time to the total payments into the fund up to that time). Payments by the fundholder are treated as taxable income in the hands of the recipient, with actual rehabilitation costs being allowable (as above). [*TCA 1997, s 681; FA 1998, s 41*]

24.8 Sale of a scheduled mining asset (including a licence to work) for a capital sum is taxable (less any original purchase price) under Sch D, Case IV for the year of assessment (or accounting period of a company) in which received. Tax is deductible from a payment to a non-resident. An individual may elect, within 24 months after end of the year of assessment in which the sum is received, for it to be treated as six annual receipts. [*TCA 1997, s 683*]

25 Payment of Tax

Cross-references. See also **7.12** 'Capital acquisitions tax'; **9.5** 'Capital gains tax'; **12.6** 'Corporation tax'; **13.9** 'Deduction of tax at source'; **26.11** 'Residential property tax'; and **39.10** 'Value-added tax'.

INCOME TAX

25.1 Income tax is payable:

(*a*)　　except where the self-assessment provisions apply, on profits or gains of any trade or profession assessed under Sch D, and on any other income except as (*b*) below, on **31 October** in the year of assessment (1 November for 2000/01 and earlier years) or within one month following the date of assessment, if later. [*TCA 1997, s 960; FA 2001, Sch 2 para 52*]

　　　　See **28.11** 'Returns' as regards payments of preliminary tax under self-assessment procedures;

(*b*)　　On income charged under Sch E where deduction at source is applied, by deduction from emoluments as and when paid. [*TCA 1997, ss 985, 986; FA 2001, Sch 1 para 1(t)*] See **34.7** 'Sch E' for the PAYE system.

Finance Act 2011, s 79 provides that tax can be paid to Revenue by credit card, debit card or any other method or methods of payment which is or are approved by Revenue. The section authorises Revenue to make regulations relating to these payment methods.

　　Finance Act 2011 introduces a new *TCA 1997, s 960Q* which places sanctions on persons who either make a false claim for a tax credit or tax allowance, or knowingly or carelessly assist another person to make a false claim for a tax credit or tax allowance. A person guilty of either of the foregoing offences will be liable to a penalty of €3,000. Any person who benefited from a false claim for a tax credit or allowance will be obliged to repay that tax to the Revenue Commissioners, along with interest from the date the person benefited from the claim to the date of repayment of tax to the Revenue Commissioners.

　　[*TCA 1997, s 960, FA 2011, s 21*]

COLLECTION

25.2 Tax is collected by the Collector-General and his officers with rights of distraint and court proceedings. For procedure see *ss 961–972* (as amended). For priority in bankruptcy and liquidation see *Companies Act 1963, ss 98, 285* and *ss 974, 982, 994, 995, 1000*. Tax deducted from sub-contractors in the construction industry may be set against tax liabilities, see **13.8** 'Deduction of tax at source'.

　　Provisions relating to the collection and recovery of taxes across all the various Acts have been steamlined and simplified and replaced with an integrated collection and recovery regime across all the various tax heads. Currently, the collection and recovery provisions relating to income tax are applied for the purposes of the legislation relating to, for example, value added tax, stamp duty and gift tax and inheritance tax. [*F(No 2)A 2008, s 94 and Sch 4*]

The new provisions make certain changes to the existing provisions in that they will extend the recovery of tax by sheriff/county registrar to excise duties and will enable the Collector-General to institute bankruptcy proceedings to recover stamp duties and excise duties. In addition the offset provisions are being amended by the inclusion of an anti-avoidance provision in the case of an assignment of a right of a repayment between 'connected persons'.

PAYE and VAT payments in default may be collected from the holder of a fixed charge (created after 27 May 1986) over the book debts of the defaulting company, up to the amount received by the holder of the charge from the company, in payment of debts due to the holder, after notification by the Revenue Commissioners of the liability of the holder under this provision. The amount for which the holder of the charge may be liable is further restricted where the existence or creation of the charge has been notified to the Revenue Commissioners. [*TCA 1997, s 1001*]

Attachment of third-party debts to tax defaulters, other than wages and salaries and amounts in dispute, may be made. This extends to VAT and other Government levies. For procedure see *s 1002* (as amended).

Finance Act 2011 introduces a change to *TCA 1997, s 1002* where previously wages and salaries owed to an employee by an employer were not considered debts for the purposes the section. Wages and salaries now due to an employee will be a debt due to the employee for the purposes of *TCA 1997, s 1002* .

The Revenue Commissioners now have the power to issue a Notice of Attachment to an employer, requiring the employer to pay over to the Revenue Commissioners monies owed to an employee. This money will be deducted from the net salary or wages of the employee over a specified period of time and paid to the Revenue Commissioners.

The section also gives powers to the Revenue Commissioners to inspect the books and records of the employer with severe penalties for failure to comply with the requirements of the Revenue Commissioners when inspecting such records. [*FA 2011, s 74*]

For the meeting of tax liabilities by the donation to certain national institutions of cultural items whose export would diminish (or whose import would enhance) the accumulated cultural heritage of RI, see *s 1003* (as amended). This section has been further amended to remove the minimum value limit of €50,000 in respect of any one item for collections consisting wholly of manuscript or archival material. In order to qualify such collections are required to have been in existence for at least 30 years and each item must have been part of the collection for that period also. [*FA 2008, s 131*] For the meeting of tax liabilities by the donation of heritage property (including buildings, gardens and contents) to the Irish Heritage Trust, see *s 1003A*, inserted by *FA 2006, s 122* which became effective on 6 October 2006 (*SI 520/2006*). *Finance (No 2) Act 2008* reduced this relief from 100 per cent of the market value of the heritage items or heritage property to 80 per cent of the market value. The restriction applies on or after 1 January 2009. [*F(No 2)A 2008, s 87*]

Section 1003A is amended to extend the tax relief to donations of heritage property (houses and gardens) to the Office of Public Works (OPW). Such properties must meet stringent criteria in relation to heritage value, as under the existing scheme. The relief available is restricted to 80 per cent of the market value of the properties donated. In addition, the €6 million overall annual limit on the value of such properties that can be donated under the existing scheme is retained. The explicit approval of the Minister for Finance will be required before any individual property can be accepted by the OPW under the scheme. The acceptance of a donation will be subject to whatever conditions the Minister may decide to apply in each case. [*FA 2010, s 28*]

A special provision was included in the *Finance Act 2008* to extend the period until the end of 2008 for the acquisition by the Irish Heritage Trust of a particular collection of paintings and furniture which is to be displayed in Fota House in County Cork. To facilitate this the annual limit of the value of heritage property that may be donated in any one tax year was increased from €6,000,000 to €8,000,000 for the 2008 tax year only.

INTEREST ON UNPAID TAXES

25.3 Interest, without deduction of tax, is payable from the due date for payment of any income tax or corporation tax. The rate is 0.0219 per cent per day or part of day from 7 April 2009. The applicable rate was 0.0273 per cent per day or part of a day from 1 April 2005 to 30 June 2009 and 0.0322 per cent per day or part from 1 April 1998 to 31 March 2005 (2 per cent per month or part if the liability arises before 1 September 2002 and is settled before 1 April 2005). It is recoverable under the same powers as income tax, etc. [*TCA 1997, ss 953, 1080; FA 1998, s 133(1)(6); FA 2001, s 236(b); FA 2002, s 129(1)(d)(f); FA 2005, s 145*] See *s 921* regarding composite charge and *s 1080(1)(b)* re interest on assessments under appeal. Interest on tax undercharged because of fraud or neglect runs from the date when the tax would have been payable but for that fraud or neglect, and is charged at a higher rate of 2 per cent per month or part month for liabilities arising prior to 1 January 2005. [*TCA 1997, s 1082; FA 2005, s 145*] Interest on PAYE not paid over by an employer is at 0.0322 per cent per day or part (before 1 September 2002, at 1 per cent per month or part with a minimum amount of £5). [*TCA 1997, s 991(1); FA 1998, s 133(1)(6); FA 2002, s 129(1)(e)*] For interest on tax deducted from sub-contractors in the construction industry and not paid over, see **13.8** 'Deduction of tax at source'.

Interest on unpaid wealth tax or capital acquisitions tax is not deductible for IT or CT. [*TCA 1997, s 1089(2)*]

For interest on overpaid tax, see **28.11** 'Returns'.

SURCHARGE FOR LATE SUBMISSION OF RETURNS

25.4 Delivery of certain returns of income after a 'specified date' will result in a surcharge being added to any income, corporation or capital gains tax due for the year of assessment or accounting period in respect of income, profits or chargeable gains which are, or would be, contained in the return and on, or by reference to, which the tax would have been chargeable. The surcharge need not be separately assessed, and if the related assessment does not include the surcharge, all the provisions regarding collection and recovery of tax and interest on unpaid tax, etc apply as if the assessment were increased by the amount of the surcharge. Any tax deducted and not repaid (other than PAYE deductions relating to a director or spouse), or tax credit (prior to their abolition) or set-off available, is taken into account before the surcharge is calculated.

The surcharge is five per cent (maximum **€12,695/£10,000**) where the return is delivered within two months of the 'specified date', otherwise **ten per cent** (maximum **€63,485/£50,000**).

Returns to which the surcharge applies are those which the person is required by the inspector to deliver under:

(*a*)   *section 877* (profits or gains);

(*b*)   *section 878* (returns for incapacitated persons and non-residents);

(*c*)   *section 879* (sources of income);

(*d*)   *section 880* (sources and amounts of partnership income);

(*e*)   *section 881* (married women);

(*f*)   *section 884* (return of company profits);

(*g*)   *section 888(2)(a)* (details of terms and provisions of leases and payments made);

(*h*)   *section 888(2)(d)* (return by agent of payments arising from premises);

(*i*)   *section 895(6)* (foreign bank accounts, see **28.4** 'Returns');

(*j*)   *section 951* (self-assessment returns, see **28.11** 'Returns'); and

(*k*)   *section 1023* (total incomes of husband and wife);

and include the extension of any of those provisions to capital gains tax. A return for a year of assessment is a return requiring details of income of that year of assessment.

The surcharge will also apply (from a date to be appointed) for failure to file electronically when required to do so by the Revenue – see **28.14** 'Electronic filing of tax returns'.

The '*specified date*' is 31 October in the year following the year of assessment (31 January for 2000/01 and prior years), and the last day of the nine-month period (or the 21st day of the 9th month if earlier for accounting periods ending **from 1 January 2003)** commencing on the day after the end of the accounting period. In either case, the last day of the six-month period commencing on the day after the person concerned was required by notice to deliver the return is substituted if later. For the first year of assessment of a new business, it is instead the specified date which applies for the second year of assessment, provided that neither the taxpayer nor (unless the spouse is assessed as a single person under *s 1016*) the spouse of the taxpayer was at any time in that first year carrying on a trade, etc commenced in an earlier year.

Incorrect returns delivered on or before the specified date are deemed to have been delivered after that date unless the error is remedied on or before that date (or unless, where neither fraud nor negligence is involved, the error is corrected without unreasonable delay). Since 1 January 2004, failure to provide the relevant information relating to an exemption, allowance, deduction, credit or other relief specified in the form to be information to which the subsection applies, is treated as the filing of an incorrect return if the matter is not remedied promptly from the time at which the omission comes to the notice of, or is drawn to the attention of, the taxpayer. In these circumstances the return is deemed to be filed within two months of the filing date (unless it is actually filed later). A surcharge imposed for this reason must be included in the assessment. The provision enables appeals against its application. [*TCA 1997, s 1084(1)(b); FA 2004, s 86*] If the inspector serves notice requiring the production of accounts, books, etc under *s 900* by reason of his dissatisfaction with any statement of profits or gains from a trade or profession contained in a return delivered on or before the specified date, the return is treated as delivered after that date unless the inspector's requirements are met within the time specified in the notice.

[*TCA 1997, s 1084; FA 1986, s 48; FA 1995, s 30; FA 2000, Sch 2; FA 2003, s 42; FA 2004, s 86*]

Late returns – Statement of Practice. Returns received within seven days of the filing date will normally be accepted as being made on time (although this will not apply to taxpayers or practitioners who abuse the procedure and regularly make returns within the seven-day period of grace). Similarly occasional late filing by a taxpayer up to four weeks after the filing date will be accepted without penalty provided that the correct amount (if any) of preliminary tax was paid on time and that there are reasonable grounds to believe that the default represents an uncharacteristic slip by an otherwise complying taxpayer. In the latter case, a note should be attached to the late return outlining why it is considered that the relief should apply. (Statement of Practice SP–GEN/1/93, April 1993.)

TAX AND DUTIES CIVIL PENALTIES REGIME

25.5 The *Finance (No 2) Act 2008, s 98* and *Sch 5* introduced provisions that relate to tax and duty civil penalties. The new provisions introduce a number of new provisions relating to the civil penalty regime and make a number of miscellaneous amendments to the tax and duty codes. The Revenue Commissioners indicated that it was necessary to make the changes to the old civil penalty regime as it may have contravened *Art 6 of the European Convention of Human Rights*. The new penalties legislation is effective for any penalties unpaid at the date of the passing of the Finance Act (ie 24 December 2008) The provisions are as follows:

Legislation has been implemented to give effect to the conclusion in the Law Reform Commission's Report 'A Fiscal Prosecutor and a Revenue Court'. Having regard to the provisions of the European Convention on Human Rights, a person should be given an opportunity to have an independent tribunal examine whether that person is liable to a civil penalty for contravention of tax or duty legislation.

Section 1077B has been inserted to give effect to this conclusion. The new provision applies to penalties arising under all taxes and duties (except customs) administered by the Revenue Commissioners. The provision also applies to both tax-geared penalties (that is, where the penalty is a percentage of the tax evaded) and fixed penalties (that is, where the penalty is set out in, or fixed by, the provision imposing it). The new section provides that, in future, where Revenue and a taxpayer are unable to agree settlement terms, a civil penalty will not be sought by Revenue against the wishes of a person unless a court has determined that the person concerned has actually contravened the provision in question and that a penalty is, in fact, due under that provision.

Section 1077C is inserted and provides that where a person is found by a court to be liable to pay a penalty, that penalty may be collected and recovered in the same way as tax is collected and recovered.

Section 1077D is to be inserted to place on a statutory footing the practice of the Revenue Commissioners as respects the recovery of penalties from the estate of a person after death. Penalties will only be recovered from an estate where the person either agreed in writing to pay the penalties or a court has determined, before the person's death, that the person was liable to the penalties.

The various tax codes have been amended so as to place on a statutory basis the current practice of the Revenue Commissioners as respects the level of tax-geared penalties sought in settlements arising out of Revenue audits and investigations.

A range of fixed penalties have been brought up to date and standardised and the amounts of such penalties (which have not been increased in many years) are to be increased. A number of consequential amendments have also been made to various provisions of the tax and duty codes as a consequence of this new legislation.

26 Residential Property Tax

26.1 Residential property tax (RPT) was introduced by *FA 1983, ss 95–116* with effect on and from 5 April 1983 as an annual tax on individuals owning and occupying residential property. It **was abolished after 5 April 1996.** See, however, **26.2** below as regards continuation of the requirement for a clearance certificate in certain cases. Provisions relating to repayment of tax and interest on repayments are contained in *FA 2003, s 155*. For the constitutionality of RPT, see **38.98** 'Tax cases'.

A new **anti-speculative property tax** was introduced as a short-term measure by *F(No 2)A 2000*, but was repealed by *FA 2001, s 230* without having ever come into effect. See, however, *Stamp Duties Consolidation Act 1997, ss 92A, 92B and Sch 1* as amended by *F(No 2)A 2000, Pt I and Sch* and *FA 2001, s 208* as regards increased stamp duties on residential property, with reliefs for first-time purchasers and other owner-occupiers.

RPT CLEARANCE ON SALE – LIABILITY OF PURCHASER

26.2 Special provisions for the recovery of unpaid RPT apply in relation to sales of residential property under contracts made after 31 July 1993. Where the consideration exceeds the market value exemption limit of €1,140,000 (€1,000,000 for sales from 5 April 2003 to 4 April 2004 inclusive, €436,000 for sales from 5 April 2002 to 4 April 2003 inclusive, £342,000 for sales from 5 April 2001 to 4 April 2002 inclusive, £300,000 for sales from 5 April 2000 to 4 April 2001 inclusive, £200,000 for sales from 5 April 1999 to 4 April 2000 inclusive, £138,000 from 5 April 1998 to 4 April 1999 inclusive, £115,000 from 5 April 1997 to 4 April 1998 inclusive, and £101,000 from 5 April 1996 to 4 April 1997 inclusive), the person by or through whom the consideration is paid (the *'purchaser'*) must deduct a 'specified amount' from the consideration unless the vendor has obtained a clearance certificate from the Revenue Commissioners (see below). The purchaser must forthwith deliver a return on the appropriate form to the Revenue Commissioners, accompanied by payment of the amount deducted (subject to a penalty of up to £1,000/€1,265 for failure to comply). On proof of such payment the purchaser is treated as having discharged his liability to pay the 'specified amount' to the vendor. Any amount deducted which is not accounted for is recoverable from the purchaser in the same way as RPT. There are provisions for an estimated amount to be recovered from the purchaser where, in the opinion of the Revenue Commissioners (and subject to appeal), the purchaser has failed to meet his obligation in full.

It should be noted that the requirement for a clearance certificate continues despite the abolition of RPT after 5 April 1996. However, for sales completed after 10 February 2000, the requirement for a clearance certificate is removed where the property was previously acquired after 5 April 1996 by a *bona fide* purchaser for full consideration.

Finance Act 2007, s 118 abolished the requirement for a clearance certificate for residential property tax for sales of residential property completed on or after 1 February 2007.

The '*specified amount*' is one and one-half per cent of the difference between the purchase consideration and the relevant exemption limit (as above) multiplied by the number of 5 Aprils (after 4 April 1983) on which the property has been in the ownership of the vendor, up to a maximum of five.

The vendor may, before the date of the contract for sale, apply (on the appropriate form) to the Revenue Commissioners for a certificate that there is no outstanding RPT on the property in question, and if such a certificate is issued, no deduction is required to be made by the purchaser.

There are provisions dealing with sales involving more than one vendor and for cases in which a vendor holds the property as trustee. Also, where a property is transferred between spouses (after 16 June 1993), any outstanding RPT liability of the transferor remains as a first charge on the property for a period of twelve years, unless the property is subsequently transferred for full consideration which does not exceed the market value exemption limit (as above) on the 5 April immediately preceding that later transfer.

[*FA 1983, s 110A; FA 1993, ss 107, 108; FA 1997, s 132; FA 1999, s 198; FA 2000, ss 134, 135; FA 2003, s 154*]

27 Residents and Non-Residents

Cross-reference. For non-resident companies, see **12.19** 'Corporation tax' and for company residence see **11.3** 'Companies'.

Revenue leaflets. See generally RES 1 (Going to Work Abroad?) and RES 2 (Coming to Live in Ireland?).

RESIDENTIAL STATUS

27.1 A person resident in RI for a year of assessment is normally chargeable to RI tax on all his income whether arising inside or outside RI, subject to any double tax agreements which may apply. Subject to any double tax agreement which provides for a single 'fiscal domicile' (see **27.2** below), a person will be treated as resident in RI in accordance with the following.

Residence. An individual is treated as resident in RI for a year of assessment only if either:

(*a*)   more than 183 days (for 2001 only, 135 days) are spent in RI during that year; or

(*b*)   more than 280 days (for 2001 and 2002 only, 244 days) are spent in RI in that and the preceding year of assessment.

A day at the end of which the individual is present in RI is counted as a day spent in RI for this purpose. The *Finance (No 2) Act 2008, s 15* amends *s 819* to provide that, in determining the number of days spent in the State for tax residence purposes, an individual shall be present in the State for a day if he or she is present at any time during that day. A year during which not more than 30 days (for 2001 only, 22 days) are spent in RI will, notwithstanding (*b*) above, not be a year of residence.

An individual may elect to be treated as resident for a year, provided that the Revenue Commissioners are satisfied that he or she is in RI with the intention, and in such circumstances, that he or she will be resident for the following year of assessment.

These provisions do not apply for 1994/95, but commence for 1995/96, where the individual:

(i)   was RI-resident in 1991/92 but not in 1992/93 or 1993/94;

(ii)   was RI-resident in 1992/93 but not in 1993/94;

(iii) was RI-resident in 1993/94 but, apart from the above provisions, would not be so for 1994/95; or

(iv)   left RI in 1992/93 or 1993/94 for the purpose of commencing a period of ordinary residence outside RI, and did not recommence RI ordinary residence before 6 April 1994.

Any officer of the Revenue Commissioners is entitled to make a determination regarding the residence of individuals. [*TCA 1997, s 819; FA 1994, s 158; FA 2001, Sch 2 para 42; FA 2008, s 135*]

Split year residence. For the purposes of a charge to tax on employment income, where, during a year of assessment (the *'relevant year'*) an individual who has not been

429

resident in RI for the preceding year of assessment satisfies the Revenue Commissioners that he or she is in RI with the intention, and in such circumstances, that he or she will be resident for the following year of assessment, and the individual would otherwise be resident for the relevant year, he or she is resident in that year only from the date of arrival in RI. Similarly where a resident individual leaving RI other than for a temporary purpose satisfies the Revenue Commissioners that he or she will not be resident in the following year of assessment, residence will cease in the relevant year from the day after the date of departure from RI. The relevant year in either case is in effect split into separate years of assessment of residence and non-residence for these purposes. [*TCA 1997, s 822*]

Individuals non-resident but ordinarily resident in RI are treated as resident for the purposes of taxation under Sch C or Sch D (other than in respect of employment income from employment the duties of which are performed wholly outside RI (disregarding incidental RI duties) and income from a trade or profession carried on wholly outside RI). Other foreign income not exceeding €3,810/£3,000 (for 2001 only, £2,220) in any year of assessment is also excluded. [*TCA 1997, s 821; FA 2001, Sch 2 para 43*]

Ordinary residence. An individual is ordinarily resident in RI for a year of assessment where he or she has been resident in RI for each of the three preceding years. Ordinary residence only ceases after three consecutive years of non-residence in RI. [*TCA 1997, s 820*]

Personal allowances of citizens, subjects or nationals of EU Member States. Non-RI resident citizens, etc of Member States are entitled to personal allowances proportionate to the amount of their income which is subject to RI tax. If such a non-resident is a resident of another Member State, the entitlement will be increased to 100 per cent where at least 75 per cent of total income is subject to RI tax. [*TCA 1997, s 1032*] See also **27.5** below.

Appeals on any question where an individual is required to satisfy the Revenue Commissioners under the above provisions must be made within two months of the date on which notice of the adverse decision is given, and lies to the Appeal Commissioners in the same way as an appeal against an assessment. [*TCA 1997, s 824*]

For **company residence**, see **11.3** 'Companies'. RI resident companies pay corporation tax (**12**) on their profits and gains wherever arising.

EXEMPTIONS

27.2 'Fiscal domicile' under double tax agreement. A double tax agreement may provide that although a person is resident in RI under the rules above he is to be regarded as resident only in the other State and not in RI (eg conventions based on the OECD model – see **14** 'Double tax relief – capital transfers' and **15** 'Double tax relief – income and capital gains' for agreements with the UK). It is understood that, in practice, an individual transferring his permanent residence from the UK will normally be given full personal allowances for the year of transfer, and any earnings from non-RI employments ceasing before the date of transfer will be ignored in computing RI tax liability for that year.

Individuals who give property to the State on leaving RI after 31 August 1974, and who become resident in another State for tax purposes, are not regarded as ordinarily resident thereafter, nor will return visits to RI to advise on administration of the property render the person resident or ordinarily resident, provided the visits total

182 days or less in the year of assessment (for 2001 only, 135 days). This applies to income tax, capital acquisitions tax, capital gains tax, and wealth tax. This modification ceased to have effect as of 4 February 2010. [*TCA 1997, s 825; FA 2001, Sch 2 para 44, FA 2010, s 151*]

RELIEFS FOR INCOME EARNED OUTSIDE IRELAND

27.3 Deduction of emoluments for qualifying days out of RI prior to 31 December 2003. A special relief may be claimed by RI-residents in relation to emoluments from:

(A)　an office of director of a company carrying on a trade or profession which is within the charge to corporation tax (or would be if it were RI-resident); and

(B)　an employment which is not with any statutory body and the emoluments from which are paid otherwise than out of State revenue.

Provided that the duties of the office or employment are performed wholly or partly outside RI, and that in any year of assessment the number of 'qualifying days' in that year (or in a 'relevant period' in relation to that year) is at least 90 (for the year of assessment 2001 itself, 67), then a deduction is allowed from the assessable emoluments. A '*qualifying day*' is a day of absence from RI for the purpose of performing the duties of an office or employment, which is one of at least 11 (before 29 February 2000, 14) consecutive such days (including the day of departure) which are substantially devoted to the performance of such duties. A day may only be counted once. Before 26 January 2000, the individual had only to be absent from RI at the end of a day for it to qualify, but with effect from that date, only days throughout which the individual was absent from RI qualify. **No day after 31 December 2003 is a qualifying day**. A '*relevant period*' is a continuous period of twelve months part of which coincides with the year of assessment in question, and no part of which is comprised in any other relevant period.

The deduction is the proportion of all income, profits or gains from an office, employment or pension (including income, etc from offices or employments the duties of which are performed in RI) represented by the fraction:

$$\frac{D}{365}$$

where D is the number of 'qualifying days' in the year of assessment concerned. For 2001 only, the denominator is 270 instead of 365.

For 2000/01 onwards, the maximum deduction available to any individual under these provisions for a year of assessment is £25,000 for 2000/01, £18,500 for 2001, €31,750 thereafter, and for 1999/2000 the £25,000 limit applies to any deduction(s) in respect of income, profits or gains accruing or paid on or after 29 February 2000.

The relief does not apply to offices or employments the emoluments from which are taxed on the remittance basis (see **31.2** 'Sch D, Case III'), or where the split year residence basis (see **27.1** above) applies. Relief is also denied where the emoluments are UK employment income, or income from employment exercised in the UK, except that, from 6 April 1998, this does not apply to seafarers where, in any period of at least 11 (before 29 February 2000, 14) consecutive days in which a 'qualifying individual' is absent from RI for the purpose of performing duties of a 'qualifying employment' (those terms being as defined for the seafarer allowance, see **2.14** 'Allowances, credits and rates'), the ship on which those duties are performed in that period visits both a UK port and a port outside both RI and the UK.

With effect from 1999/2000 onwards (and for 1998/99 in relation to income etc accruing after 10 March 1999), the provisions are revised to exclude earnings consisting of benefits in kind, severance payments, payments for restrictive covenants or rights to acquire shares or other assets and to take into account any deduction from earnings in respect of pension scheme or retirement annuity contributions. It is also made clear that separate calculations are required where there is more than one foreign employment in a year (although qualifying days from different employments may be amalgamated in satisfying the 90 qualifying day test).

[*TCA 1997, s 823; FA 1994, s 154; FA 1995, s 170; FA 1998, s 14(1)(c); FA 1999, s 21; FA 2000, s 47; FA 2001, s 31*]

For an article on these provisions, with a number of examples, see Revenue Tax Briefing Issue 40 pp 11, 12.

Reduction in tax on income from qualifying employments. Since **6 April 1998,** an RI-resident individual in receipt of income, profits or gains from a 'qualifying employment', the duties of which are performed wholly outside RI (disregarding incidental duties in RI) in a territory or territories with which double tax arrangements are in force (see **15** 'Double tax relief – income and capital gains'), may claim a reduction in tax on his or her total income to a 'specified amount'. The full amount of the income, profits or gains from the employment must be subject to tax (without relief or exemption) in the territory in which the employment is held or in the territory or territories in which the duties are performed, and the foreign tax must have been paid and not repaid or entitled to be repaid. The individual must also be present in RI at the end of at least one day in any week during which he or she is absent from RI for the purpose of performing duties of the employment.

Where relief is so claimed for a year of assessment, the individual is not entitled to a credit for the foreign tax paid on the income, etc from a 'qualifying employment' in the year.

No relief is available where the income, etc from the employment is taxable on the remittance basis (see **31.2** 'Sch D, Case III'), or where the split year residence rules of *s 822* (see **27.1** above) apply, or for income etc paid to a proprietary director (within *s 472*, see **2.13** 'Allowances, credits and rates') of the paying company or his or her spouse. Relief is similarly denied where the income, etc is the subject of a relief claim under *s 472B* (see **2.14** 'Allowances, credits and rates') or *s 823* (as above).

A '*qualifying employment*' is an office or employment held outside RI in a territory with which double tax arrangements are in force (see **15** 'Double tax relief – income and capital gains') for a continuous period of at least 13 weeks (for 2001 only, 10 weeks), but excluding any office or employment with a board, authority, etc established in RI by or under statute, or the emoluments of which are paid out of RI State revenue.

The '*specified amount*' is determined by the formula:

where   A is the tax otherwise chargeable on the individual for the year of assessment (other than in respect of tax retained out of charges paid), after taking account of any reductions of tax but before credit for foreign tax on any income, etc of the year;

B is the total income for the year excluding the income, etc from the qualifying employment; and

C is the total income for the year.

$$\frac{A \times B}{C}$$

For these purposes the income, etc from a qualifying employment does *not* include amounts paid in respect of expenses incurred wholly, exclusively and necessarily in the performance of duties of the employment.

[*TCA 1997, s 825A; FA 1998, s 13; FA 2001, Sch 2 para 45*]

Finance Act 2010, s 10 amends *s 825B* which provides an incentive for foreign employees to undertake an assignment in Ireland. The incentive currently applies to employees who are nationals of, and who are employees of companies, in countries that are not party to the European Economic Area Agreement but with which Ireland have a double tax agreement. The scheme is extended under *FA 2010, s 10* to include EU and EEA nationals who come to live and work here on or after 1 January 2010.

Finance Act 2010, s 11 amends *s 825A* to bring the meaning of a day in line with the meaning of a day for tax residence purposes. An individual will be deemed to be resident in the State for a day if he or she is present here at any time during the day.

[*TCA 1997, ss 825A, 825B; FA 1998, s 13; FA 2001, Sch 2 para 45*; *FA 2010, s 10* and *s 11*]

Seafarer allowance. See **2.14** 'Allowances, credits and rates'.

DOMICILE AND NATIONALITY

27.4 Domicile is quite distinct from residence or nationality. An individual can only have one domicile and, broadly speaking, it is the *legal system* in which he has, or is presumed to have, his permanent home (ie a person cannot be domiciled in the United Kingdom, he must be domiciled in England and Wales, or Scotland or Northern Ireland, etc). A child acquires a 'domicile of origin' from his parents (usually father) and retains this domicile unless as an adult he acquires a 'domicile of choice'. Domicile is a very technical legal matter but occasionally arises in tax law, see eg **31.2**(i) 'Sch D, Case III' and **38.94–38.96** 'Tax cases'.

Nationality denotes the sovereign State to which the person belongs. Citizenship of Ireland is governed by the *Irish Nationality and Citizenship Act 1956* and occasionally arises in tax law, see eg **27.5**(*a*) below.

Finance Act 2010 has introduced a new levy where an individual is Irish domiciled and an Irish citizen. The new provisions in relation to the 'domicile levy' are under *Pt 18C*. The levy is charged on such an individual as follows:

(a)   whose worldwide income exceeds €1,000,000;

(b)   whose Irish-located property is greater than €5,000,000; and

(c)   whose liability to Irish income tax was less than €200,000.

The amount of the levy is €200,000. Irish income tax paid by an individual will be allowed as a credit against the domicile levy. The tax is payable on a self-assessment basis on or before 31 October in the year following the valuation date (ie 31 December every year).

The new *Pt 18C* contains provisions dealing with appeals relating to the value of land or buildings, the making and amending of assessments by Revenue and the right of Revenue to make enquiries and make assessments. In addition, it applies the provisions of *Pt 40, Ch 1, Pt 40, Ch 1* and *s 1080*, which relate to appeals, penalties and interest on overdue tax respectively to the domicile levy.

The levy applies in respect of the tax year 2010 and subsequent years. [*FA 2010, s 150*]

NON-RESIDENTS

27.5 Subject to any double tax agreement which may apply, non-residents are taxable on income derived from RI, under the normal Schedules (but see **19.1**, **19.2** 'Government and other public loans' for certain exemptions), and to capital gains tax in respect of RI-situated assets and certain assets disposed of during temporary non-residence (see **9.2** 'Capital gains tax'). It is, however, understood that, by concession, such liability will not be pursued, except by set-off in a relief claim, where a non-resident who is not assessable in the name of an agent receives interest without deduction of tax, unless the interest is under the management and control of a branch in RI.

In addition, non-residents:

(*a*)   are not eligible for personal allowances (see **2** 'Allowances, credits and rates'), with the following exceptions:

   (i)   a citizen of Ireland,

   (ii)   a person previously resident in RI but compelled to live elsewhere on account of his health or the health of a member of his family,

   (iii)   a national etc, of a State in respect of which an exemption order under *Aliens Act 1935, s 10* applies (includes UK subjects) or of an EU Member State,

(iv)   a person who was before 6 April 1935 entitled to relief under *FA 1920, s 24* (under which certain non-UK residents were entitled to tax allowances, eg through being British subjects, residents of Channel Islands or Isle of Man, or in Crown service overseas),

   and in these cases the non-resident is entitled to a proportion of the personal allowances to which he would be entitled (if resident) equal to the proportion the amount of his income taxable in RI bears to his total income from all sources [*TCA 1997, s 1032(2)*] (but see **27.1** above as regards certain EU citizens entitled to full allowances); and

(*b*)   may be assessed in the name of a trustee, agent, etc, as though resident in RI and in actual receipt of the income or gains. Exceptions are provided for certain financial trades (see *s 1035A* and Revenue Guidance Note – Investment Management Services), transactions through brokers, etc. *Section 1035A* has been amended to ensure that the exemption under this section is wide enough to apply to UCITS formed under the law of a Member State other than Ireland and that uses a management company authorised under Irish regulations. The issue arises at this stage because of changes made to the UCITS Directives that facilitate the management in one EU Member State of a UCITS formed under the law of another Member State. [*FA 2010, s 32*] There is a deemed agency if a resident appears to be making less than a normal profit in his business dealings with a non-resident. In certain circumstances, assessment may be made on a percentage of the turnover of the agent etc. There is special provision for a non-resident manufacturer assessed on the sale through an RI agent of goods manufactured by him. [*TCA 1997, ss 1034–1040, 1043; FA 2003, s 51*]

FINANCE (NO 2) ACT 2008

27.6 The *Finance (No 2) Act 2008* provided for the repayment of tax where a non-domiciled individual is in receipt of emoluments in the State. The new basis offers an alternative system which will allow a refund of tax to be claimed in certain circumstances. PAYE must be operated at the outset, however. The proposal does not have unlimited use and only non-Irish domiciles assigned from companies with countries with which there is a DTA will benefit.

In addition to restrictions imposed on the employer's country of incorporation, additional limitations apply in respect of the employees in question which are designed to ensure that employment arrangements cannot be restructured in order to fall within the proposed regime.

Where all conditions are satisfied, an employee may make a claim on their tax return for the appropriate year for their taxable income to be determined based on the higher of:

(*a*)   the actual amount attributable to Irish duties that was remitted in that year; or

(*b*)   €100,000 plus 50% of the balance attributable to Irish duties.

Anti-avoidance provisions apply when income for a particular tax year is remitted in a later year. Employers and assignees affected by the proposals will need to monitor and track assignees' employment income per year of assessment in order to manage the anti-avoidance provisions.

28 Returns

Cross-references. For capital gains, see **9.4** 'Capital gains tax'. For companies, see **12.5** 'Corporation tax'. See **10.5** 'Claims' regarding error or mistake in return. For penalties for late returns, see **25.4** 'Payment of tax'. See also **13.9** 'Deduction of tax at source'.

28.1 Subject to the self-assessment provisions detailed at **28.11** below, returns must be made when required by a notice given to the taxpayer by an inspector. [*TCA 1997, s 877; FA 2000, Sch 2*] Service of notice by post is sufficient. [*TCA 1997, s 869; FA 1999, s 22*] Requirements for individuals are provided in *s 879* and for employers regarding employees in *ss 897, 897A*. Any person who does not receive a notice but who is chargeable to tax must inform the inspector within one year after the end of the year of assessment. [*TCA 1997, s 876*] If a taxpayer informs the inspector, within 21 days of receiving his own return, that his wife is in receipt of an income, or if the inspector otherwise decides, the inspector may require the wife to render a separate return of her income. [*TCA 1997, s 881*]

If the inspector is not satisfied with a person's return of income or gains, he may require that person (and his spouse if she is living with him) to deliver a statement of his assets and liabilities at the date of the notice. Further supporting evidence and statements may be required.

The statement must include:

(i)   in the case of an individual, unless the return was made in a representative capacity or as trustee, all the assets to which he is beneficially entitled and all the liabilities for which he is liable;

(ii)   in the case of a person making a return in a representative capacity, all the assets to which the owner of the income or gains concerned is beneficially entitled, and in relation to which that person acts in a representative capacity, and all the liabilities for which the owner of the income or gains concerned is liable;

(iii) in the case of a trustee returning trust income or gains, all the assets and liabilities comprised in the trust.

In relation to (i), assets of an unmarried child under 18 are included where either they were previously disposed of by the individual or the consideration for their acquisition by the child was directly or indirectly provided by the individual.

The return must include full details of each asset or interest, including its location and date of acquisition, all expenditure incurred in respect of it and all insurance policies in respect of it, with further information in the case of a non-arm's length acquisition. The usual declaration as to completeness and correctness may be required under oath. [*TCA 1997, s 909; FA 1999, s 207*]

The Revenue Commissioners have wide powers to obtain information relevant to the liability of a taxpayer from financial institutions and to apply to the Courts to obtain relevant information from financial institutions (and, since 25 March 2004, their offshore subsidiaries) in any case where there are reasonable grounds for suspecting that any taxpayer may have failed, or may fail, to comply with any requirement under the *Taxes Acts*, or that a revenue offence (see **28.2** below) has been, is being or is about to be committed, and that such failure or offence is likely to have led, or to lead, to serious prejudice to proper assessment or collection of tax. This power has been extended to allow the Revenue Commissioners to apply to the Appeal Commissioners for consent to issue a notice to obtain information from 'third parties' in relation to a class of persons rather than an individual. [*FA 2010, s 153*] The definition of financial institution has been expanded to include financial institutions authorised in another Member State operating in Ireland under a passport arrangement. [*F(No 2)A 2008, s 92*] *Pt 38* has been amended in several ways, Certain returns required to be made and information required to be given can now be in electronic format. This includes any information from Government Departments, returns by stockbrokers, auctioneers etc. A further amendment is to ensure that the *Post Office Savings Bank Act 1861, s 4* (which restricts the disclosure of information relating to deposits) will not prohibit the disclosure to Revenue of certain information in relation to payments made by financial institutions. [*FA 2008, s 133*] These powers extend to information required to enable the Revenue to comply with exchange of information provisions as provided in a double taxation agreement or exchange of information agreement. Since 25 March 2005, Revenue can access information of a life assurance company relating to a class or classes of policies and their policyholders where a Revenue Commissioner is satisfied that there are circumstances suggesting that such class or classes of policies have been used as an investment vehicle for untaxed funds. This information can be used only to seek a High Court order for wider access to information held by the life assurance company in relation to that class or those classes of policy and their policyholders. The Revenue are empowered to apply to a judge of the District Court for a search warrant. A further amendment has been introduced in respect of situations where the necessity to apply for a search warrant would be inappropriate (eg when seeking information from an unrelated third party). This amendment introduces a power to apply to a judge of the District Court for an order requiring the person named therein to supply specified information to the Revenue Commissioners, when they are carrying out an investigation with a view to initiating criminal proceedings. The Revenue Commissioners are also entitled to question suspects in Garda custody, who have been arrested and detained by the Gardaí in respect of certain Revenue offences. This power is limited to offences under the Customs Act and to serious extraction type frauds relating to Relevant Contracts Tax and VAT. [*TCA 1997, ss 902B, 906A–908B; FA 1999, s 207; FA 2000, s 68(1)(c); FA 2002, s 132(e); FA 2003, s 38; FA 2004, ss 87, 88; FA 2005, s 140; FA 2007, s 124*] See **38.233** 'Tax cases' for an unsuccessful application under an earlier version of these provisions. See also Statement of Practice SP–GEN/1/99, May 1999 for the Revenue approach to use of these powers. A new Revenue power introduced allows an authorised officer from the Revenue Commissioners question a suspect held in Garda custody where the individual was arrested and detained for Revenue offences. The offences concerned are serious indictable offences under Revenue law which are 'arrestable offences' within the meaning of the *Criminal Law Act 1997, s 2*. [*FA 2008, s 134*]

28.2 Penalties may be exacted for failure to make returns or for making incorrect or incomplete returns (including accounts) fraudulently or negligently etc or assisting in making incorrect returns etc. Increased penalties may be imposed on bodies of persons and personally on the secretary of such bodies. Serious tax offences in relation to returns may be punishable on conviction on indictment by a fine of up to €12,695/£10,000 and/ or five years' imprisonment. [*TCA 1997, ss 1052–1079; FA 2003, ss 160, 162; FA 2004, s 86; FA 2005, s 141, 142*] Since 28 March 2003, it is an offence to falsify, conceal or destroy material relevant to, or that might be relevant to, an investigation into an offence punishable by conviction on indictment by a fine of up to €127,000 and/or five years imprisonment. [*TCA 1997, ss 1078A, 1078B, 1078C,* introduced by *FA 2003, s 161*] Since 25 March 2005, the offence of 'facilitating' tax and duty evasion is introduced and extends to any person who is reckless in relation to facilitating tax and duty evasion. See Revenue Tax Briefing Issues 36 and 49 as regards Revenue approach to penalties and in particular their mitigation. See also **1.8** 'Administration and general' as regards publication of names of tax defaulters and **38.230–38.232** 'Tax cases'.

28.3 Accounts, books etc. An inspector may demand accounts and inspection of books and records relevant to a person's tax liability or (to enable compliance with an exchange of information agreement) a foreign tax liability. [*TCA 1997, s 900; FA 1999, s 207; FA 2003, s 38*] See **30.8** 'Sch D, Cases I and II' for obligation of taxpayer to keep books and records. See **38.235** 'Tax cases'.

The Revenue Commissioners are concerned with the use of computer software to alter records contained in electronic point-of-sale devices. *Finance Act 2011, s 75* introduces two specific offences:

(*a*) either to knowingly or wilfully use such software for the purpose of tax evasion; or

(*b*) to provide or make available such software to another for the purpose of tax evasion.

The penalties for persons found guilty of this offence are very severe and can be as high as a fine of €126,970 and/or a term of imprisonment of up to five years.

28.4 Banks (including Post Office Savings Banks) **and financial institutions** may be required to give particulars of interest paid exceeding **€65/£50** in any year received or retained in RI (and such returns may be required without notice, see **28.13** below). Such payments may be excluded from the return if the recipient serves notice on the payer that the person beneficially entitled to the interest is not resident in RI. If the payer is not satisfied that the recipient was resident (or ordinarily resident) outside RI at the date of payment, the recipient must provide an affidavit stating his name and address and country of residence (or ordinary residence), and, if appropriate, those of the person beneficially entitled to the interest. If the payer is so satisfied, but the person beneficially entitled to the interest is not the recipient and is resident (or ordinarily resident) in RI, the recipient must state, in a notice to the payer, the name and address of the beneficial owner. The payer must retain the notice and accompanying affidavit(s) for six years. If so requested by the Revenue Commissioners, the payer must confirm whether or not such a notice has been served by a named person from a specified address, and furnish the Revenue Commissioners with the relevant notice and affidavit(s). These provisions do not apply to interest paid or credited by credit unions (within *Credit Union Act 1997*). [*TCA 1997, s 891; ITA 1967, s 175; FA 1995, s 168; FA 1998, s 131*] Nor do they apply to payments of interest on 'relevant deposits', see **13.9** 'Deduction of tax at source'. See also **20.4** 'Interest payable' on the implementation of the EU Directive on Taxation of Savings Income and reporting obligations for paying agents.

Returns are similarly required of **interest paid without deduction of tax to non-RI resident companies** after 5 April 1999 under *s 246(3)(h)* (see **20.1**(vii) 'Interest payable'). *s 891* (above) does not apply where this provision applies. [*TCA 1997, s 891A; FA 1999, s 40*]

Returns must be filed by a person by or through whom certain payments in respect of wholesale debt instruments are paid without deduction of tax. [*TCA 1997, s 246A; FA 2003, s 49; SI 245/03*]

Since 31 March 2006, Revenue may, with the consent of the Minister for Finance, make regulations regarding information to be returned by assurance companies, collective funds and financial institutions. [*TCA 1997, s 891B; FA 2006, s 125*]

Foreign deposit accounts. Any person carrying on an RI business in the course of which he acts as an intermediary in connection with the opening of foreign deposit accounts by or on behalf of RI residents is required to make a return giving full details (which he must take reasonable care to confirm) in relation to all RI residents for whom he has so acted in a chargeable period (year of assessment or accounting period as appropriate), and the account holders are obliged to supply such details to him. The return must be made by 31 October following the year of assessment (31 January in relation to 2000/01 and earlier years), or nine months after the end of the accounting period, as appropriate. Penalties of up to €2,535/£2,000 apply to both the intermediary and the account holder in relation to failures to comply with the above requirements. Also, an RI resident opening a foreign deposit account is required to provide the inspector with full details in a return as under *s 951* (see **28.11** below), and any failure falls within the surcharge provisions of *s 1084* (see **25.4** 'Payment of tax'). [*TCA 1997, s 895; FA 2001, Sch 2 para 50*] See also Statement of Practice SP–IT/1/92 and **28.13** below. For chargeable periods commencing before 15 February 2001, *s 895* is applied *mutatis mutandis* in relation to certain life assurance policies and deferred annuity contracts with foreign insurers by *s 594* (see **9.7**(*g*) 'Capital gains tax') and in relation to material interests in offshore funds (see **32.8** 'Sch D, Case IV'), other than certain undertakings for collective investment (for which see **12.22** 'Corporation tax'), by *s 896*. For chargeable periods commencing on or after 15 February 2001, *s 896* is revised by *FA 2001, s 232* to refer to intermediaries acting in respect of offshore products (as defined) generally. See Revenue Tax Briefing Issue 49 pp 18–20.

28.5 Customers, business contacts etc. The Revenue Commissioners have wide powers to obtain from third parties (other than financial institutions, see **28.1** above) any books, records, documents and other information which may be relevant to enquiries into the liabilities (including (for the purposes of compliance with an exchange of information agreement) foreign tax liabilities) of a named taxpayer. Persons carrying on a profession are not required to disclose information or professional advice of a confidential nature relating to clients, and need only produce such information as is material to a liability in relation to the client. Applications may be made to the Courts in relation to failures likely to lead or to have led to serious prejudice to the proper assessment and collection of tax. [*TCA 1997, ss 902, 902A; FA 1999, s 207; FA 2003, s 38*] See Statement of Practice SP–GEN/1/99, May 1999 for the Revenue approach to use of these powers.

28.6 Nominee holders. Any registered holder of securities (as widely defined) may be required to furnish the inspector with the name and address of the beneficial owner of any such securities which he does not himself beneficially own, and with details of the holding concerned and of the date of registration. [*TCA 1997, ss 892, 899*] Such returns may be required without notice (see **28.13** below).

28.7 Partnerships. The senior partner is responsible, when required by notice, for making a return of all partnership income and any other statements required, and for producing accounts, books etc. [*TCA 1997, s 880; FA 2001, Sch 2 para 48*] See also **28.11** below.

28.8 Payments exceeding €635/£500 pa to any RI resident. Returns may by specific notice be required from any trader (including a body of persons carrying on a non-trading activity) of such payments made either to non-employees for services rendered or in respect of copyright (but not for any tax year more than three years before date of notice). [*TCA 1997, ss 889, 899*] Such returns may be required without notice (see **28.13** below).

28.9 Rating authorities must provide information concerning rates and rateable valuations when required by notice from an inspector. [*TCA 1997, s 898*]

28.10 Representatives of incapacitated persons and non-residents are held responsible for returns. [*TCA 1997, ss 878, 1045, 1046*] So also are personal representatives of deceased persons [*TCA 1997, s 1048(3)*] and other persons in receipt of income of others in excess of €635/£500. [*TCA 1997, ss 890, 899*] A return under *s 890* may be required without notice (see **28.13** below).

SELF-ASSESSMENT

[*TCA 1997, ss 950–959 as amended*]

28.11 *Sections 950–959* require 'chargeable persons' to make returns, without notice, of income tax, corporation tax and capital gains tax, and payment of 'preliminary tax'.

The '*chargeable persons*' concerned are all persons chargeable to income or corporation or capital gains tax for the chargeable period, other, as respects income tax, than those all of whose income is dealt with under PAYE (or by restriction of PAYE credits, etc), or who are exempted by an inspector by notice, or who are chargeable only by reason of being required to account for tax deducted from annual payments. Since

2005, Revenue are empowered to take into account the extent of non-PAYE income before deduction of losses, capital allowances etc in deciding if this income should be taken into account in determining whether or not an individual is a 'chargeable person'. [*FA 2005, s 14*] A return under *s 1023(5)* by one spouse satisfies the obligations of both spouses in this respect. Returns may be made by an agent, and will be accepted as duly authorised unless the contrary is proved. The exclusion of those whose income is dealt with under PAYE does not apply to directors (or their spouses) of companies other than companies which, during the year of assessment and the two preceding years, were not entitled to any assets other than cash not exceeding €130/£100, did not carry on any trade, business or other activity (including investment), and did not pay any charges. See also Statement of Practice SP–IT/1/93, April 1993 as regards the exclusion in practice of certain non-proprietary directors. For chargeable periods commencing **from 1 January 2004**, persons in receipt of exempt income, profits or gains from stallion fees, commercial woodlands and stud greyhound service fees are chargeable persons for the purposes of filing a return. See **30.1** 'Sch D, Case I and II'. [*FA 2003, s 35*]

The return is required to be made by 31 October in the year of assessment following that for which the return is required (31 January for returns for 2000/01 and earlier years), or by the last day of the period of nine months following the end of an accounting period (or the day three months after the commencement of winding-up in certain cases). For accounting periods ending **from 1 January 2003** the due date is the 21st day of the month, if earlier. The return must contain broadly the information required by a notice under *ss 877* or *879* or *884* as appropriate. The precedent partner in a partnership is required to make the appropriate return which would be required by a notice under *s 880*. The normal provisions relating to incorrect returns apply as if the return had been made under notice, and the late submission surcharge (see **25.4** 'Payment of tax') applies. The filing and payment date was extended by concession from 31 October 2003 to 21 November 2003 for 2002 returns and payments (including 2003 preliminary tax and capital gains tax) filed and paid electronically. Extensions to 18 November 2004, 17 November 2005 and 16 November 2006 apply in respect of 2003, 2004 and 2005 returns and payments filed electronically.

Under *s 1085*, various claims by companies to loss reliefs (including group relief and relief for manufacturing losses on a value basis), capital allowances, ACT set-off and ACT surrender (see **12.9**, **12.15**, **12.17**, **12.26** 'Corporation tax') are restricted where a return is not made, or is treated as not made, by the required date. (See **28.14** below for requirement to file electronically). Where the return is made within two months after that date, loss relief and capital allowance claims are restricted to 75 per cent of the maximum claim (maximum restriction €31,740/£25,000 in relation to each such claim), and ACT surrender claims and claims for ACT set-off are restricted to 75 per cent of the maximum claim (maximum restriction €12,695/£10,000). Otherwise, loss relief and capital allowance claims are restricted to 50 per cent of the maximum claim (maximum restriction €158,715/£125,000 in relation to each such claim), and claims for ACT set-off and ACT surrender claims are restricted to 50 per cent of the maximum claim (maximum restriction €63,485/£50,000). For chargeable periods commencing from 1 January 2004, failure to provide the relevant information relating to an exemption, allowance, deduction, credit or other relief specified in the form, being information to which the subsection applies, is treated as the filing of an incorrect return if the matter is not remedied without unreasonable delay from the time at which the omission comes to the notice of, or is drawn to the attention of the taxpayer. In these circumstances the return is deemed to be filed within two months of the filing date (unless it is actually filed later). [*TCA 1997, s 1084(1)(b); FA 2004, s 86*]

The '*preliminary tax*' for a chargeable period is the amount which, in the opinion of the chargeable person, is likely to be assessable for that period, and it is payable on or before 31 October in the year of assessment for income tax (1 November for 2000/01 and earlier years), or on or before 1 November next following the year of assessment for capital gains tax for 2000/01 and earlier years (no preliminary capital gains tax being required for 2001 onwards). For corporation tax, it is payable within six months of the end of the accounting period (or by the 28th day of the month (or such earlier day as may be specified by order, eg by 20 December 2001 for accounting periods ending in the period 21 June to 30 June 2001) where it would otherwise be payable later in the month) for accounting periods ending before 1 January 2002, and by not later than 31 days before the end of the accounting period (or by the 21st day of that month if earlier) for accounting periods ending after 31 December 2005. For accounting periods ending in the transitional period 1 January 2002 to 31 December 2005, preliminary tax is paid in two instalments, the first within six months of the end of the accounting period and the second within one month before the end of the accounting period, the due date for the first instalment being not later than the 28th of the month for accounting periods ending on or before 2 July 2003 (although not before 28 June 2002) and not later than the 21st of the month thereafter, and the due date for the second instalment being not later than the 28th of the month for accounting periods ending before 1 January 2003 and not later than the 21st of the month thereafter, the required ratio being in effect 4:1 for those ending in 2002, 3:2 in 2003, 2:3 in 2004 and 1:4 in 2005. New provisions have been introduced to ease the burden of Preliminary tax compliance for companies. The changes introduced are as follows:

(*a*)   Small companies are permitted to calculate their preliminary tax payments based on 100 per cent of the previous tax liability if their tax liability for the prior period did not exceed a certain threshold. The threshold is increased from €50,000 to €150,000. The threshold has subsequently been increased to €200,000; [*FA 2008, s 47*]

(*b*)   New companies which do not expect their tax liability to exceed €150,000 in their first year are no longer obliged to pay preliminary tax in that first year. [*FA 2007, s 47*] The threshold has been increased to €200,000. [*FA 2008, s 47*]

The *Finance (No 2) Act 2008* provides for the payment of preliminary tax by large companies in two instalments, The first instalment will be payable in the 6th month of the accounting period (ie 21 June for a company with calendar year accounts) and the amount payable will be **50 per cent** of the corporation tax liability for the preceding accounting period or **45 per cent** of the corporation tax liability for the current accounting period (ie 21 November for a company with calendar accounts) and the amount payable will bring the total preliminary tax paid to **90 per cent** of the corporation tax liability for the current accounting period. The revised arrangements apply generally where the accounting period is more than seven months in length (for shorter accounting periods, preliminary tax of **90 per cent** of tax liability is payable in one instalment as before). [*Finance (No 2) Act 2008, s 38*]

The section also makes a number of consequential amendments to the preliminary tax provisions including (i) the facility which enables companies to make a top-up payment of preliminary tax where capital gains or certain gains on financial instruments arise after payment of preliminary tax and (ii) the facility which enables a group company to surrender excess preliminary tax paid to another group company in certain circumstances.

The section also ensures that income tax deducted on relevant payments made by companies is paid in accordance with corporation tax rules.

The revised preliminary tax rules take effect for accounting periods commencing on or after 14 October 2008. In relation to capital gains tax, the payment date for disposals made in the period 1 January to 30 November of a year of assessment will be 15 December, while the payment date for disposals made in December will be the following 31 January. The revised dates apply to disposals made in 2009 and subsequent years. [*F(No 2) A 2008, s 34*]

Section 249 is also amended to ensure that income tax due on certain payments made by resident companies (eg certain interest and royalty payments and employer paid medical insurance premiums) is paid in accordance with the corporation tax rules. *s 249(3)* is amended to provide that the due date for making a return of income tax on relevant payments is not later than the 21st day of the 9th month after the end of the accounting period – the same date as applies for corporation tax returns. *s 239(5)* is amended to bring the due dates for payment of income tax on relevant payments into line with those applying to corporation tax. The amendment brings the legislation into line with current Revenue practice. [*F (No 2) A 2008, s 39*]

The transitional rule which related to preliminary tax for the first three accounting periods in respect of which a company applied International Financial Reporting Standards (IFRS) or equivalent Irish Generally Accepted Accounting Practice (GAAP) to gains and losses from financial instruments, was made permanent. The rule provides that the amount of preliminary tax to be paid one month before the month end of the accounting period does not have to take account of unrealised gains or losses on financial instruments that arise from movements in the fair value of those instruments in the last two months of the accounting period; the company makes a top-up payment one month after the end of the accounting period, to bring the amount of preliminary tax up to 90 per cent of the final liability for that accounting period. [*FA 2008, s 47*]

Preliminary tax is treated as a payment on account of the liability assessed for the period. No preliminary tax is payable where an assessment has been received for the chargeable period on or before the due date for payment.

Preliminary income tax may be paid by direct debit where appropriate arrangements are made with the Collector-General, and when so paid it is treated as having been paid by the due date. For 2001 onwards, the tax due will generally be collected on the ninth day of the month in three equal monthly instalments in the first year to which such arrangements apply (eg in October, November and December) and in eight monthly instalments in subsequent years (eg in May through December), although the Collector-General has wide discretionary powers to vary the timing and amount of payments.

Previously, the tax was generally collected in equal monthly instalments on the ninth day of each month in the calendar year in which the due date fell (for 1999/2000 and 2000/01, in the tax year itself). For the administrative arrangements for payment by direct debit, see Statement of Practice CG/1/99, February 1999, replacing CG/1/96, April 1996.

For 2000/01 and earlier years, where there is default in the payment of preliminary income or corporation tax, or where, at any time prior to the due date for payment, the inspector considers it appropriate, he may issue a notice of the amount of preliminary tax he considers ought to be paid for the period (except that no such notice may be issued after the chargeable person has delivered a return (as above) for the period). That amount is then payable by the due date unless, on or before the date by which the return for the period is due, the chargeable person either makes a payment of preliminary tax in the normal way or notifies the Collector that he considers no liability will arise for the period. However, where the return for the period is not made by the due date, and the amount of preliminary tax notified by the inspector (increased by any surcharge for late submission, see **25.4** 'Payment of tax') exceeds any preliminary tax paid (again including any surcharge), the excess continues to be payable. The inspector may at any time he considers it appropriate reduce (including to nil) the amount specified in a notice. A notice ceases to have effect on and from the date on which an assessment is made for the period unless enforcement action has at that time been taken for recovery of the tax notified. Preliminary tax so notified is collectible as if it were assessed tax in respect of which no appeal was outstanding.

Since 1 November 2003 interest is payable in limited circumstances and is at a rate of 0.011 per cent per day or such other rate as may be set by order (see **1.15** 'Interest on repayments'). Previously, preliminary tax in excess of liability for a period was repaid, and carried interest (without deduction of tax) at 0.0161 per cent per day or part (before 1 September 2002, at 0.5 per cent per month or part), subject to a €10/£10 *de minimis* limit, unless it arose from a relief under *s 438(4)* (see **12.7** 'Corporation tax') or *s 286A* (see **8.6**(*b*) 'Capital allowances'). These provisions continue to apply to preliminary tax payments made before 1 November 2003, provided the return for the relevant year is lodged with the Collector General on or before 31 October 2004. [*FA 2003, s 17; SI 508/03*]

New provisions have been introduced to reduce the interest exposure of large companies in a group that do not meet their 90 per cent preliminary tax obligation. The provision allows a group company which has exceeded its 90 per cent preliminary tax obligation to allocate the overpayment to another member of the group which has not met its preliminary tax obligation. To avail of this relief :

(*a*) the companies have to be members of the same group;

(*b*) both companies have to be 'large' companies;

(*c*) both companies have to give notice jointly to the Revenue Commissioners; and

(*d*) the claimant company must have paid 100 per cent of its tax liability on or before its tax return due date. [*FA 2007, s 47*]

Assessments. Where the inspector is satisfied that the preliminary tax paid meets the assessable liability for the period, he may elect not to make an assessment for the period, and must notify his decision to the chargeable person, who may, provided that he has made a return for the period, nonetheless require the making of an assessment. The giving of such notice by the inspector does not, however, prevent the inspector subsequently making an assessment for the period concerned. An assessment may not be made before the date by which a return is required for the period unless the return has already been made. Otherwise, provisions broadly similar in effect to the general assessment provisions apply to the making of an assessment under these provisions, and the inspector has the necessary powers (subject to appeal) to make enquiries and amend assessments. There is a time limit on the making or amending of assessments of four years (six years prior to 1 January 2005) from the end of the chargeable period in which a return is delivered provided that the return makes full and true disclosure of all material facts. [*FA 2003, s 1; SI 508/03*] Subject to appeal, this does not, however, prevent the making of an assessment to give effect to determination of an appeal, to take account of events occurring after delivery of the return, to correct a computational error or an error of fact, or where income is assessed on a current year basis. Provided that points subject to genuine doubt as to the application of law are drawn to the inspector's attention in the return, they do not prevent a full and true disclosure.

Nothing in the above prevents an inspector making a capital gains tax assessment under *ss 977(3), 978(2)(3)* (assessments on third parties), *s 980(5)(6)* (disposals over €500,000 of land, minerals, goodwill etc) or *s 1042* (non-residents), and the tax under such an assessment is due and payable under the appropriate provision, notwithstanding the self-assessment arrangements.

Appeals. There is no appeal against a notice of preliminary tax (for 2000/01 and earlier years), or against items in an assessment based on accepted particulars either contained in the return for the period or agreed with the chargeable person. Appeal, on specified grounds, may be made against assessments raised in cases of failure to deliver, or unsatisfactory, returns only when the return is delivered and an amount of tax has been paid on foot of the assessment at least equal to the liability if the assessment were based on that return. Similar rights of appeal apply in respect of amended assessments.

Payment. See above as regards preliminary tax. Where an assessment is made before the date for payment of preliminary tax, it is due on or before that date. Where an assessment is made on or after that date and the requirements for preliminary tax have been satisfied, the balance payable is due:

(i)   for income tax for 2001 onwards, and capital gains tax for 2001 and 2002 on or before 31 October in the next following year of assessment;

(ii)   for capital gains tax for 2003 onwards, on or before 31 October in the tax year for gains realised before 1 October in the year and 31 January following the tax year for gains realised in the period from 1 October to 31 December;

(iii)   for income tax for 1995/96 to 2000/01 inclusive, by 30 April in the next but one year of assessment;

(iv)   for income tax for earlier years of assessment (see *FA 1988, s 18; FA 1995, s 31*), by the specified return date for the year of assessment (ie 31 January following that year) or, if later, within one month of the date of the assessment;

(v)   for capital gains tax for 2000/01 and earlier years, by 31 January following the year of assessment, or within one month of the date of the assessment, if that is later;

(vi)   for an accounting period of a company, on the return filing date for accounting periods ending from 1 January 2003 and within one month of the date of assessment for earlier periods;

(vii)   for income tax for 2001 onwards and capital gains tax for 2002, where a return delivered by 31 October contains full and accurate disclosure of all material facts but an assessment is required to correct eg a computational error, then provided that the excess of the final liability over the amount paid by 31 October is not more than the greater of £500/€635 and five per cent of the tax payable for the year (or £2,500/€3,175 if less), the extra tax is due and payable by 31 December (ie a two-month margin of error is allowed).

Where, however, any of (i) to (vi) above apply and either:

(*a*)   the chargeable person has defaulted in payment of preliminary tax for the period;

(*b*)   the preliminary tax was not paid by the date of its becoming due and payable; or

(*c*)   the preliminary tax paid was less than, or less than the lower of, as the case may be:

other than in the case of corporation tax liabilities:

(i)   90 per cent of the tax payable for the period or, for capital gains tax for 1998/99 to 2000/01 inclusive, the whole of the tax payable for the period,

(ii)   in the case of income tax liabilities, 100 per cent of the tax payable for the immediately preceding chargeable period (74 per cent for chargeable period 2001, 135 per cent for 2002 to take account of the short year of assessment 2001) subject to certain adjustments for additional tax payable for that period and for reliefs for investment in corporate trades (**21**) and for investment in films (see **12.23** 'Corporation tax'). Where (v) above applies to allow a margin of error in payment of additional tax for the preceding chargeable period, a similar margin of error is allowed in relation to the increased preliminary tax required based on the liability for that period, and

(iii)   in the case of income tax liabilities for a year of assessment in relation to which arrangements have been made to pay the preliminary tax by direct debit (see above), 105 per cent of the income tax payable for the preceding year of assessment but one (78 per cent for chargeable period 2001, 142 per cent for 2003), subject to the same adjustments as in (ii) above, unless the income tax payable, or taken as payable (see below), for that year was nil; or

in the case of corporation tax liabilities:

(i)   for accounting periods ending before 1 January 2002, 90 per cent of the tax payable for the period;

(ii)   for accounting periods ending after 31 December 2005, 90 per cent of the tax payable for the period (with a saving where any shortfall arises from chargeable gains arising in the accounting period but after the due date for payment of preliminary tax (ie broadly in the last 31 days of the accounting period) and provided that the difference is made up within one month of the end of the accounting period), or, in the case of a company whose profits for the preceding chargeable period were less than €50,000 (reduced *pro rata* for accounting periods of less than 12 months), and if less, 100 per cent of the corporation tax liability for that preceding accounting period (adjusted for any difference in length between the two periods);

(iii)   for accounting periods ending in the due date change transitional period 1 January 2002 to 31 December 2005, as in (ii) above but with an additional requirement that, broadly, the required payment is split between the pre- and post-transitional period due dates in the ratio 4:1 for accounting periods ending in 2002, 3:2 in 2003, 2:3 in 2004 and 1:4 in 2005;

the tax payable is treated as having become due and payable on the due date(s) for payment of the preliminary tax for the period, split, where (*c*)(iii) applies in the case of corporation tax liabilities, in the ratio referred to in that subparagraph between the two instalment dates. Additional tax due following amendment of an assessment is treated as due and payable as if it were charged under the original assessment, unless the assessment was made after a full and accurate return had been delivered or the assessment had previously been amended following such delivery, in which case the additional tax is treated as having become due and payable not later than one month from the making of the amendment. On determination of an appeal, any excess of the tax found to be payable over the amount paid on foot of the assessment is treated as due and payable as if charged by the original assessment unless:

(I)   that excess does not exceed ten per cent of the tax payable; and

(II)   the payment date under the original assessment was not determined under (*a*), (*b*) or (*c*) above;

in which case the excess is treated as due and payable within one month from the date of determination of the appeal.

As regards (*b*)(ii) and (iii) above, for a year in which the person concerned was not a chargeable person, the income tax payable is taken as nil. However, there are special provisions preventing married couples exploiting their ability to alternate periods of chargeability, in effect requiring their joint liability to be taken into account for these purposes.

For 2001 and subsequent chargeable periods, where the profits of the preceding chargeable period are increased under the 'corresponding period' rules on a change of accounting date (see **30.3** 'Sch D, Cases I and II'), any additional tax thereby payable without an amended assessment is due and payable by 31 October following the later chargeable period (ie twelve months after the normal due date for the chargeable period in respect of which the additional tax arises). The additional tax payable for the preceding chargeable period is disregarded in determining the preliminary tax required for the chargeable period. Where the additional tax for the preceding chargeable period was payable by virtue of an amended assessment, it is similarly treated as having been due and payable by 31 October following the chargeable period itself.

The capital gains tax postponement provisions of *s 579(4)(b)* (beneficiary of non-resident trust) and instalment provisions of *s 981* (hardship) are not affected by the above self-assessment provisions as regards due dates for payment.

Commencements and cessations. The Revenue Commissioners' Statement of Practice SP–IT/2/91 sets out the practice to be adopted in paying preliminary tax and filing returns in cases of commencement and cessation.

For the year of assessment in which a taxpayer commences to be a chargeable person, the tax payable for the preceding year is taken to be nil, so that no interest charge can arise by virtue of preliminary tax not being paid for the first year of assessment. The full liability for that year will, however, have to be paid within one month of the assessment for the year being received, otherwise an interest charge will arise. Preliminary tax for the second and subsequent years of assessment must be accounted for in the usual way. The Revenue Commissioners consider that taxpayers should, in their own best interests, pay their best estimate of the preliminary tax for the first year of assessment, to avoid cash flow problems arising from having to pay preliminary tax for the second and third years of assessment, the full liability for the first year of assessment and the balance of liability for the second year of assessment within the period from 30 (or 1) November in the second year of assessment to 30 (or 1) November in the third year of assessment.

A taxpayer already a chargeable person but commencing a new source of income must account for preliminary tax in the usual way.

As regards returns for the year of assessment in which a Sch D, Case I or II source commences, if the first year's accounts are not completed by the filing date (see above), the return should show 'Source commenced on (date). Estimated profit (€)'. The accounts should, at the latest, be submitted with the return for the second year of assessment. Estimated figures are not acceptable for other sources of income commencing in the year of assessment.

For the year of assessment in which a taxpayer ceases to be a chargeable person, preliminary tax must be accounted for in the usual way.

Returns for the final year must show the actual figures to the date of cessation. Any penultimate year revision under Sch D, Case I or II should not be overlooked.

See **7.10** 'Capital acquisitions tax' as regards self-assessment of that tax.

28.12 A Statement of Practice was issued by the Revenue Commissioners in September 1988 specifying the documents required to be enclosed with the various types of return. These are as follows, although specific circumstances may of course require further documentation.

Type of income	*Documentation*
Trade/profession	Accounts and computations (including losses, capital allowances and balancing charges).
Investment income	Schedules by category as per return of income received and tax credits. Dividend counterfoils etc to be submitted only at inspector's request.
Rental income	Statement of gross receipts and expenses for each let premises, with computation of assessable profit (or allowable loss).
Salary, wages, fees etc	P60.

Allowances, deductions	Details of interest, VHI, retirement contributions etc paid (certificates only on request). RICT forms and F45s should be attached (unless already submitted).
Capital gains	Computation of chargeable gains/allowable losses.
Other matters	Details of expressions of doubt, special features etc where relevant.

Accounts should not be sent to inspectors in advance of returns (on eg form CT1) as they will not be dealt with until the return is received.

RETURNS REQUIRED WITHOUT NOTICE

28.13 In addition to those required under the self-assessment system (see **28.11** above), returns of certain information etc may, under *s 894*, be required to be made without notice. These are the returns under:

(*a*)   *s 888(2)(d)(e)* (by managing and collecting agents of premises and bodies paying rent subsidies, etc, see **33.10** 'Sch D, Case V');

(*b*)   *s 889* (fees, commissions etc, see **28.8** above);

(*c*)   *s 890* (income received on behalf of others, see **28.10** above);

(*d*)   *s 891* (interest paid or credited without deduction of tax, see **28.4** above);

(*e*)   *s 891A* (interest paid to non-RI resident companies, see **28.4** above);

(*f*)   *s 892* (by nominee holders of securities, see **28.7** above);

(*g*)   *s 893* (by certain intermediaries in relation to collective investment undertakings, see **12.22** 'Corporation tax' – abolished for chargeable periods commencing after 14 February 2001).

Any person having information or making, crediting or receiving payments within any of those provisions must make such a return as would be required if a notice were issued under the provision. The return must be made by 31 October following the year of assessment (in relation to 2000/01 and earlier years, 31 January following the year) where the chargeable period to which the payment etc relates is a year of assessment, or nine months after the end of the accounting period where it is an accounting period of a company.

Returns without notice under a particular provision are not required from any person who would be excluded from making a return under the provision. The inspector may give written notice excluding any person from the requirement to make returns without notice, or limiting the information to be included therein.

The validity of a notice under any of the provisions at (*a*)–(*g*) above is not affected by the requirement to make a return without notice, and the issue of such a notice does not remove the obligation to make a return without notice.

The penalty provisions of *ss 1052, 1054* (see **28.2** above) apply in cases of failure to deliver a return without notice as required under these provisions. [*TCA 1997, ss 894, 899; FA 2001, Sch 2 para 49; FA 2003, s 158*]

See also *ss 895, 896* at **28.4** above as regards certain returns by intermediaries.

See also **1.12** 'Administration and general' as regards certain reportable offences and **28.4** above as regards returns relating to foreign deposit accounts.

Statement of Practice. The Revenue Commissioners have issued a Statement of Practice (SP–IT/1/92) clarifying the extent to which information has to be reported automatically. The Statement also sets out the matters to be included in returns in each category, and the person(s) on whom the obligation to make the return falls, and deals with various procedural matters. See also Revenue Tax Briefing No 62.

ELECTRONIC FILING OF TAX RETURNS

28.14 For the legal framework for making electronic tax returns, see *ss 917D–917K*, introduced by *FA 1999, s 209* and amended by *FA 2001, s 235*. In outline, for transmission of an electronic return to satisfy the obligation to make a return, the following conditions must be satisfied:

(*a*) the person making the transmission must be approved by the Revenue Commissioners for the purpose;

(*b*) the transmission must comply with procedures and processes laid down by the Revenue Commissioners;

(*c*) the transmission must incorporate the digital signature or (from 25 March 2005) electronic identifier of the person making the transmission or an authorised person; and

(*d*) receipt of the transmission must have been acknowledged by the Revenue system.

See *SI 289/00, SI 112/01, SI 441/01, SI 522/01*.

From a date to be appointed, the Revenue will be empowered to make regulations requiring specific groups of taxpayers to file returns or pay tax by electronic means and to provide for the repayment of tax by electronic means. Failure to comply will result in penalties and the surcharge provisions of *ss 1084* and *1085* will apply. Provision is made for the exclusion of persons who could not reasonably be expected to have the capacity to make returns or pay tax by electronic means. [*TCA 1997, s 917EA; FA 2003, s 164; FA 2005, s 22*]

The *Finance (No 2) Act 2008* provides for an extension to return filing and payment deadlines where returns and payments are made electronically vie the Revenue Online Service (ROS). A number of amendments are made to the *TCA 1997* and the *Value-Added Tax Act 1972* to extend and align the existing deadlines for Corporation Tax, Relevant Contracts Tax and Value-Added Tax. With effect from 1 January 2009, where returns and payments are made electronically, the return filing and payments deadlines for these taxes will be the 23rd of a month. This has the effect of extending filing and payment deadlines by two days for Corporation Tax, four days for VAT and nine days for RCT. A similar extension to the 23rd of a month is also being made in relation to PAYE and PRSI by way of an amendment to the PAYE Regulations.

TAX AND DUTIES CIVIL PENALTIES REGIME

28.15 *The Finance (No 2) Act 2008, s 98 and Sch 5* introduced provisions that relate to tax and duty civil penalties. These introduce a number of new provisions relating to the civil penalty regime and make a number of miscellaneous amendments to the tax and duty codes. The Revenue Commissioners indicated that it was necessary to make the changes to the old civil penalty regime as it may have contravened Article 6 of the European Convention of Human Rights. The new penalties legislation is effective for any penalties unpaid at the date of the passing of the Finance Act (ie 24 December 2008). The provisions are as follows:

Legislation has been implemented to give effect to the conclusion in the Law Reform Commission's Report A Fiscal Prosecutor and a Revenue Court. Having regard to the provisions of the European Convention on Human Rights, a person should be given an opportunity to have an independent tribunal examine whether that person is liable to a civil penalty for contravention of tax or duty legislation.

Section 1077B has been inserted to give effect to this conclusion. The new provision applies to penalties arising under all taxes and duties (except customs) administered by the Revenue Commissioners. The provision also applies to both tax-geared penalties (that is, where the penalty is a percentage of the tax evaded) and fixed penalties (that is, where the penalty is set out in, or fixed by, the provision imposing it). The new section provides that, in future, where Revenue and a taxpayer are unable to agree settlement terms, a civil penalty will not be sought by Revenue against the wishes of a person unless a court has determined that the person concerned has actually contravened the provision in question and that a penalty is, in fact, due under that provision.

Section 1077C is inserted and provides that where a person is found by a court to be liable to pay a penalty, that penalty may be collected and recovered in the same way as tax is collected and recovered.

Section 1077D is inserted to place on a statutory footing the practice of the Revenue Commissioners as respects the recovery of penalties from the estate of a person after death. Penalties will only be recovered from an estate where the person either agreed in writing to pay the penalties or a court has determined, before the person's death, that the person was liable to the penalties.

The various tax codes have been amended so as to place on a statutory basis the current practice of the Revenue Commissioners as respects the level of tax-geared penalties sought in settlements arising out of Revenue audits and investigations.

A range of fixed penalties have been brought up to date and standardised and the amounts of such penalties (which have not been increased in many years) are to be increased. A number of consequential amendments have also been made to various provisions of the tax and duty codes as a consequence of this new legislation.

29 Schedule C – Paying Agents

Cross-reference. See also **19** 'Government and other public loans'.

29.1 Sch C applies to paying agents (bankers and others) who are entrusted with the payment in RI of interest, annuities, dividends etc, out of public revenue. They must deduct tax at the standard rate (which is then charged on them under Sch C) and pay the net amount to the persons entitled to the interest etc. Since 25 March 2005, a banker is not a paying agent by virtue only of clearing a cheque or arranging for a cheque to be cleared. Since 31 March 2006, certain payments to collective investment funds that are subject to the gross roll-up regime (see **12.22** Corporation Tax) are excluded from the tax deduction requirement. [*TCA 1997, ss 17, 32, 33, Sch 2; FA 2005, s 4; FA 2006, s 46*]

29.2 Dividends on securities of foreign territories beneficially owned by non-residents are exempt. [*TCA 1997, s 35*].

29.3 The collection or realisation of coupons is charged under this Schedule [*TCA 1997, s 17(1)*] and see *s 812* (as amended) where the right to interest from securities is sold but not the securities themselves, and *s 51* where funding bonds are issued in respect of interest.

30 Schedule D, Cases I and II – Profits of Trades, Professions etc

30.1 Tax is charged under **Sch D, Case I** on the profits or gains of trades of all kinds carried on in RI or by RI residents elsewhere [*TCA 1997, s 18*] including:

(i) mines, quarries, gravel pits, sand pits, ironworks, gasworks, canals, railways and the rights of markets, fairs and tolls etc [*TCA 1997, ss 18(2), 56*];

(ii) market gardens (ie nurseries and gardens in RI used for the sale of produce other than hops). [*TCA 1997, ss 654, 655(3)*];

(iii) cattle dealers and milk sellers occupying farmland insufficient for the keeping of cattle on it. [*TCA 1997, s 53*] The word 'cattle' in this context refers only to bovine animals, and does not include sheep or pigs (see **38.165** 'Tax cases');

(iv) exploration or exploitation activities on the continental shelf. [*TCA 1997, s 13*]

Profits from the occupation of commercial woodlands, except where assessable under Sch D, Case V, and stallion and greyhound fees are exempt from tax. Since 1 August 2008, the exemption on stallion and greyhound stud fees is removed. [*FA 2006, s 22*]

With effect from 1 August 2008, stallions are to be treated as stock in trade and income or gains arising from stallion stud fees or from the sale of stallions will be subject to taxation. The normal expenses for the upkeep of stallions will be allowed against tax and a deduction in respect of the purchase cost of a stallion will be provided over 4 years at 25 per cent per annum. Stallions purchased on the open market after 31 July 2008 are to be valued, for the purposes of the four year deduction, at their purchase price. In cases where stallions are standing at stud prior to the termination date of the exemption or where stallions transfer to stud from racing or training or are bred on farm or held as stock in trade, the cost of the stallion for the purposes of the four year deduction will be the prevailing market value of the stallion as of 1 August 2008 or the date the stallion first stands at stud, as appropriate. The section also provides that the Revenue Commissioners may consult with any person they see fit in determining the market value of a stallion. This taxation treatment will also apply to syndicated owners of stallions. However, in cases where the syndicate member is not wholly or mainly engaged in farming the costs and losses arising from the ownership of the stallion will be offset solely against profits and gains from horse-breeding.

Finally, any additional tax paid in respect of exempt stallion stud fee income under the provisions introduced by *Finance Act 2006, s 17* may be carried forward as a credit against income tax for future years. In these circumstances, the entitlement to carry forward any relief denied resulting from the operation of s 17 as a deduction against future income will not be available. [*FA 2007, s 26*]

For tax years and chargeable periods commencing **from 1 January 2004**, details of the profits, gains and losses must be included in the tax return, see **28.11** 'Returns'. For limitations on the exemption from 2007, see **2.45** 'Limitation on Income Tax Relief for High Earners' [*FA 2003, s 35; FA 2006, s 17*]

The exemption of stallion and greyhound stud fees is generally restricted to stallions or greyhounds and services within RI, except that it is extended to part-owners of stallions and greyhounds kept outside RI who acquired and hold their part-ownership for the purposes of servicing mares or bitches owned or part-owned by them in the course of an RI breeding trade. [*TCA 1997, ss 231–233*] Certain restrictions may apply to distributions out of such exempt profits, see **12.10** 'Corporation tax'.

For the distinction between employment and self-employment, see **38.129–38.133** 'Tax cases' and, for the report of the Employment Status Group, Revenue Tax Briefing Issue 43 pp 3–8.

Trades carried on abroad are charged under Sch D, Case III (**31**).

See Revenue guidance note 'Guidance on Revenue Opinions on classification of activities as trading' regarding submissions on whether or not an activity constitutes trading.

30.2 Tax is charged under **Sch D, Case II** in respect of any profession not contained in any other Schedule. [*TCA 1997, s 18(2)*]

BASIS OF ASSESSMENT

30.3 Except in the case of new or discontinued businesses (as to which see **30.4**, **30.5** below), the assessment is on the full amount of the profits (as adjusted) of the year of assessment (but see **18.2** 'Farming' for an alternative basis for full-time farmers). Where only one set of accounts is made up to any date in a year of assessment, and is for a period of one year, the profits or gains of that year are taken as those of the year of assessment. However, where:

(*a*)   the only account made up to a date in a year of assessment is not for a period of one year; or

(*b*)   accounts are made up to more than one such date;

the assessment is based on the profits or gains of the twelve months to the date of the accounts in (*a*) or to the last of the dates in (*b*) or, in cases not within (*a*) or (*b*), on the actual profits of the year of assessment. If the profits of the corresponding period of twelve months (including, with effect from 2003, the profits of the second tax year of trading) before the basis period for the year of assessment exceed the amount assessed in the year preceding the year of assessment, the assessment for that preceding year is to be based on the profits of the corresponding period.

Since 1 January 2006, any uplift in value of work-in-progress in the accounts of service providers arising from the application of the guidance note issued by the Urgent Issues Task Force of the Accounting Standards Board regarding Application Note G of Financial Reporting Standard 5 is taxed over a period of five years. [*FA 2006, s 56*]

To accommodate the short year of assessment 2001 (which runs from 6 April 2001 to 31 December 2001), these rules are modified as follows:

(i)   Where the profits of a period of twelve months are taken as the profits of the year of assessment 2001, the assessment is based on 74 per cent of those profits;

(ii) Where accounts are made up for a period of twelve months ending in the period 1 January 2002 to 5 April 2002 (so that no period of account ends in the year of assessment 2001), those accounts are treated as having been made up for a twelve-month period ending in 2001 as well as in 2002 (so that 74 per cent of the profits of that period are assessable for 2001 and (assuming the following account does not end before 1 January 2003) 100 per cent of those profits are assessable in 2002). The corresponding period in 2000/01 is then the immediately preceding twelve months;

(iii) Where 2001 is assessed on the actual profits of the year of assessment, and the profits assessed for 2000/01 are less than the actual profits of that year of assessment, the assessment for 2000/01 is adjusted to the actual profits of that year of assessment;

(iv) Where 2002 is assessed on the profits of a twelve-month period of account ending in that year, and the profits assessed for 2001 are less than 74 per cent of the profits of the corresponding period in relation to 2001, the assessment for 2001 is adjusted to 74 per cent of the profits of that corresponding period. For this purpose, if the twelve months immediately preceding the basis period for 2002 end in the period 1 January 2001 to 5 April 2001, they are nonetheless treated as the corresponding period in relation to 2001;

(v) Where 2002 is assessed on the actual profits of the year of assessment, and the profits assessed for 2001 are less than the actual profits of that year of assessment, the assessment for 2001 is adjusted to the actual profits of that year of assessment.

[*TCA 1997, s 65; FA 2001, Sch 2 para 2; FA 2003, s 11*]

See Revenue Tax Briefing Issue 45 pp 15–18 for an article on the special 2001 rules, including a number of examples.

Apportionments etc are to be made by reference to months and fractions of months. [*TCA 1997, s 107*]

See also under **8** 'Capital allowances' and **22** 'Losses'.

NEW BUSINESSES

30.4 First tax year. On actual profits (as adjusted for tax purposes) from date of commencement to the following 31 December (5 April for 2000/01 and prior years). [*TCA 1997, s 66(1)*]

Second tax year. Where there is only one account made up to a date in the second tax year and that account is for a period of one year, on the profits of that year. Otherwise:

(*a*) if the only account made up to a date in that year is for a period other than one year, or if more than one account is made up to a date in that year, and the commencement was at least one year before the account date (or the last such account date), the assessment is on profits of one year ending on that date (or on the last such date);

(*b*) in any other case, the assessment is on profits of the second tax year itself. (But see **30.3** above relating to assessments for corresponding twelve-month periods.)

Where the short tax year 2001 is the second tax year, and the basis period for the year is a period of twelve months, the assessment is based on 74 per cent of the profits of that twelve-month period.

[*TCA 1997, s 66(2)(3A)(3B); FA 1998, s 8; FA 2001, Sch 2 para 3; FA 2003, s 11*]

Third tax year. On profits of accounts for the third year, with right to claim reduction of assessment by any amount by which the profits assessed for the second tax year exceed the actual profits of that year. Claim must be made with the return required under *s 951* (see **28.11** 'Returns'). If, after reducing the assessment for the third year to nil, a balance of that excess remains, the balance may be carried forward as a trade loss and utilised in subsequent years of assessment. [*TCA 1997, s 66(3)(3B)(3C); FA 2001, s 78(2)(a), Sch 2 para 3*]

Short-lived businesses. A special relief is available for businesses permanently discontinued within their third year of assessment of operation, and in the case of which the aggregate profits which would otherwise be assessed exceed the aggregate profits arising over the whole period of operation. Any person chargeable to tax on those profits may give notice by 31 October (31 January for 2000/01 and prior years) following the year of assessment of cessation (ie the normal return date, see **28.11** 'Returns') requiring the assessment for the penultimate year of assessment to be reduced to the actual profits arising in that year. [*TCA 1997, s 68*]

BUSINESSES PERMANENTLY DISCONTINUED

30.5 See **30.4** above as regards short-lived businesses.

The assessment for the final year is on the actual profits from the first day of the final tax year to the date of discontinuance. The Revenue have the right to increase the assessment for the previous year to the actual profits for that year. [*TCA 1997, s 67(1)(a); FA 2001, Sch 2 para 4*]

Discontinuance applies on the death of an owner, although in practice, where a wife succeeds to the trade of her deceased husband, the cessation provisions are not normally applied (see Revenue Tax Briefing Issue 9 p 3). [*TCA 1997, s 67(2)*] Also a change in ownership, including a transfer to or from a partnership (but see **30.6** below), is cessation of old business and commencement of new. [*TCA 1997, s 69*] See also **38.164** 'Tax cases'.

Post-cessation receipts are usually assessable (but under Case IV). See *ss 91–95* for provisions, including debts written off and subsequently realised, and a change from the 'conventional basis' to the 'earnings basis' in computing earnings on cessation.

PARTNERSHIPS

30.6 Each partner is individually assessed on his share of adjusted profits, including partnership salary, interest on capital etc. Assessments will be adjusted in opening and final years as in **30.4** and **30.5** above for the partner joining or leaving the partnership but assessments on other partners will be unaffected. The partnership business as a whole is not treated as having ceased unless the business actually terminated, or all partners retire except one so that it becomes a sole proprietorship, or completely different partners take over from all retiring partners.

The senior partner must make a return showing apportionments between partners and capital allowances claimed by him for division in the same ratio as profit sharing, including allowances brought forward from earlier years, even though partners are different. Similarly with balancing allowances and charges. If all partners agree hardship is caused by this treatment, they may request re-apportionment. A partner's share of accumulated losses is lost when he leaves the partnership. [*TCA 1997, ss 880, 1007, 1008, 1010; FA 2001, Sch 2 para 48*]

Limited partnerships. See **22.5** 'Losses' as regards restriction of relief.

ASSESSABLE PROFITS, ALLOWABLE DEDUCTIONS ETC

See also **8** 'Capital allowances', **22** 'Losses' and **38.99–38.165** 'Tax cases'. Headings below after **30.7** are in alphabetical order.

30.7	General	**30.21**	Pension schemes
30.8	Books and records	**30.22**	Pre-trading expenditure
30.9	Car running expenses	**30.23**	Redundancy payments
30.10	Entertainment expenses	**30.24**	Rent – double allowance for certain premises
30.11	Farming	**30.25**	Scientific research expenditure
30.12	Finance leasing	**30.26**	Share schemes
30.13	Gifts of money	**30.27**	Shares, securities etc
30.14	Illegal trading	**30.28**	Staff recruitment and covenants
30.15	Industrial and provident societies	**30.29**	Trade and professional association subscriptions
30.16	Keyman etc insurance	**30.30**	Trade marks
30.17	'Know-how'	**30.31**	Trading stock
30.18	Land transactions	**30.32**	Unemployed – double allowance for emoluments
30.19	Mining activities	**30.33**	Universities
30.20	Patents		

GENERAL

30.7 Provisions as to assessable and non-assessable income, allowable and non-allowable deductions are generally similar to those for purposes of UK income tax. Unless otherwise provided in the Tax Acts no sum is deductible in computing profits or gains unless expended wholly and exclusively for the purposes of the trade or profession. Prohibitions include capital expenditure or withdrawals, sums recoverable under contracts of insurance or indemnity, annuity or other annual payments and patent royalties. [*TCA 1997, s 81*] *Section 81* is amended by *Finance (No 2) Act 2008, s 23.* This section is now extended to prohibit a deduction in computing the amount of profits or gains to be charged to tax of any amount paid or payable under a contract to a connected person as compensation for a transfer pricing adjustment in another jurisdiction, The appropriate (correlative) adjustments to Irish tax liabilities can only be obtained under the Double Tax Agreement or EU Arbitration Convention mechanisms. For relevant case law, see **38.99–38.165** 'Tax cases'. For an article on provisions for expenditure, see Revenue Tax Briefing Issue 41 pp 14, 15.

Professional accounts. The Revenue Commissioners have issued a Statement of Practice (SP–IT/2/92) setting out the basis on which professional accounts may be drawn up for tax purposes. Except in the case of barristers (for whom special arrangements apply), the 'earnings basis' (see *s 91(5)*) is considered to be the strict legal basis, but certain 'conventional' bases, including a cash basis and anything between a full earnings basis and a simple cash basis, may be acceptable (except in the first three years following commencement). The basic requirements that must be demonstrated for a conventional basis to be acceptable are that:

(*a*)   profits will not, taking one year with another, differ materially from those determined on the earnings basis;

(*b*)   bills are issued at regular and frequent intervals; and

(*c*)   precise details of the basis used appear as a note to the accounts.

Debtors and creditors must normally be included, but work-in-progress need be included only where its exclusion would materially affect the annual taxable profits. Specific debt provisions are acceptable, including a proportion of long-standing small debts justifiable by reference to previous experience.

Public private partnership (PPP). For an article on the deductibility of bid/tender costs and the tax treatment of surplus land (or cash) introduced by the public body, see Revenue Tax Briefing Issue 39 pp 7–9.

BOOKS AND RECORDS

30.8 Every person carrying on, on his own or another's behalf, any trade, profession, etc, assessable under Sch D must maintain proper books and records as specified relating to that trade, etc, and retain them for six years subject to a penalty up to €1,520/£1,200. [*TCA 1997, s 886*] Authorised officers of the Revenue have power of entry to inspect such books etc, subject to a penalty up to €1,265/£1,000, but this power does not extend to documents relating to clients of professional persons. [*TCA 1997, s 905; FA 1999, s 207; FA 2002, s 132(d)*]

Any individual carrying on a business (the precedent partner in the case of a partnership) must ensure that any invoice, credit note, debit note, receipt, account, statement of account, voucher or estimate relating to an amount of €7/£5 or more issued in the course of the business bears one of his 'tax reference numbers', ie his PPS (previously RSI) number, or any reference number issued by the inspector, or his VAT registration number. If he has no tax reference number, he must state his full name and address. [*TCA 1997, s 885; FA 2001, Sch 1 para 1(q)*]

See also **1.9** 'Administration and general' as regards electronic data processing and **28** 'Returns'.

CAR RUNNING EXPENSES

30.9 The reduction in allowable car running expenses for cars costing in excess of a set sum is **abolished** for expenditure incurred in an accounting period ending after 31 December 2001 or in a basis period ending after that date for 2002 or a later year of assessment. Prior to 1 January 2002, expenses incurred for business purposes (including any deduction claimed from emoluments, see **34.3** 'Sch E', or as an expense of management under *CTA 1976, s 15*) in respect of a car costing more than £17,000 are reduced by the proportion by which the excess of the cost of the car over that limit bears to the cost of the car. New provisions have been introduced linking the availability of capital allowances and leasing expenses to the carbon emission levels of cars and will come into effect in respect of cars purchased or leased on or after 1 July 2008. Please see below for details of these new provisions. [*FA 2008, s 31*] There is a proportionate reduction for periods of less than one year. The £17,000 limit applies to expenses incurred in an accounting period ending after 31 December 2000 and before 1 January 2002, or in a basis period ending after 31 December 2000 for 2000/01 or 2001. Previously the limit was £16,500 for expenses incurred before 1 January 2001, £16,000 before 1 December 1999, £15,500 before 2 December 1998, £15,000 before 3 December 1997, £14,000 before 23 January 1997, £13,000 before 9 February 1995 and £10,000 before 27 January 1994, and the reduction was one-third of the amount by which the cost of the car exceeded that limit unless the taxpayer elected for the expenses to be reduced instead by the proportion by which the excess of the cost of the car over that limit bears to the cost of the car (as now applies without election as above). [*TCA 1997, s 376; FA 1976, s 32; FA 1992, s 21(2); FA 1994, s 21(2); FA 1998, s 29(b); FA 1999, s 53(b); FA 2000, s 35(b); FA 2001, s 61; FA 2002, s 28*]

The allowable cost of leasing a car of retail price over a specified limit is also (and continues to be) restricted to the proportion of that cost that the limit bears to the retail price. The specified limit has been increased to €24,000 for the tax year 2007 and for corporation tax, for accounting periods ending on or after 1 January 2007. [*FA 2007, s 21*] The specified limit is €23,000 for expenditure incurred in an accounting period ending after 31 December 2005 or in a basis period ending after that date. The limit was €22,000 for expenditure incurred in an accounting period ending after 31 December 2001 and before 1 January 2006 or in a basis period ending between those dates. For earlier periods, the specified limit was the same as that applicable to the car running expenses deduction (as above). The increases from £16,000 to £16,500, from £15,500 to £16,000, from £15,000 to £15,500, from £14,000 to £15,000, from £13,000 to £14,000 and from £10,000 to £13,000 applied only to new cars registered on or after 1 December 1999, 2 December 1998, 3 December 1997, 23 January 1997, 9 February 1995 and 27 January 1994 respectively. For secondhand cars as at each of these dates, the limit remained at £10,000, being increased to £17,000 at the same time as the increase to that figure for new cars. For all dates on which an increase applied other than 23 January 1997, 3 December 1997, 2 December 1998 and 1 December 1999, the increase did not apply in relation to expenditure incurred in the twelve months following each of those dates under a contract entered into before the date. [*TCA 1997, ss 373, 377; FA 1998, s 29(a); FA 1999, s 53(a); FA 2000, s 35(a); FA 2001, s 61(1)(a); FA 2002, s 28*]

The Euro equivalents of the amounts referred to above, so far as relevant are:

£17,000	€21,585.55
£16,500	€20,950.68
£16,000	€20,315.81
£15,500	€19,680.94
£15,000	€19,046.07
£14,000	€17,776.33

New provisions relating to Carbon Emissions: the new provisions cater for three broad categories of business car: those whose carbon dioxide emissions are up to 155g/km, those between 156 and 190g/km and those above 190g/km. Any balancing allowances or balancing charges which may arise on a subsequent disposal of business cars will be computed on a proportional basis to ensure the appropriate amount of relief is given.

The degree to which car leasing expenses will be deductible under the revised scheme also depends on the carbon dioxide emissions of the vehicle.

The new *Pt 11C* comprises six sections and is, in many respects, a restatement of the existing *Pt 11*, modified to take account of the new conditions.

Section 380K sets out the definitions used in *Pt 11C*, including the emissions limits for each of the taxation categories.

Section 380L provides for the modified levels of capital allowances which will apply to cars in different emissions categories. The section also provides for a proportionate balancing allowance or charge in the event that the vehicle is subsequently disposed of.

Section 380M provides for the deductibility of expenditure incurred on the leasing of such vehicles. The rate at which these leasing charges are allowed closely mirrors the capital allowances regime set out in *s 380L*.

Section 380N addresses the situation where a hire purchase agreement ends without the potential purchaser becoming owner of the vehicle. A re-categorisation of payments previously made into leasing payments, suitably apportioned, is then made.

Section 380O provides for circumstances where the lessee or hirer of a vehicle becomes the owner. An aggregation of all payments is made before being apportioned into capital and leasing payments modified to account for the new rules.

Section 380P excludes the provisions of this Part for vehicles acquired for short term hire (taxis etc.) and also for vehicles acquired for testing. [*FA 2008, s 31 – The details at the impacts are set out in the Summary of the 2008 Budget Measures (p B9).]*

ENTERTAINMENT EXPENSES

30.10 Such expenses (including the provision of accommodation, food, drink or any other form of hospitality, and the provision of gifts) are not deductible in computing profits or gains, or as management expenses. Similarly, no allowance is available in respect of assets used for business entertainment. Entertainment of *bona fide* staff members is excluded from the prohibition unless only incidental to its provision for others. The cost of any business entertainment may be determined by the inspector, subject to the usual right of appeal. [*TCA 1997, s 840*] It is understood that, by concession, expenditure on certain small gifts to charities of a local nature, and subscriptions to local trade associations, made for trade purposes are not regarded as within the exclusion under *s 840*.

These provisions apply equally to the reimbursement to an employee of entertainment expenses incurred on the employer's behalf by the employee.

FARMING

30.11 Profits from farming in RI are chargeable under Sch D, Case I. See under **18** 'Farming'.

FINANCE LEASING

30.12 A finance lease is a lease which transfers substantially all the risks and rewards of ownership of an asset to the lessee. For the Revenue's views on the tax treatment applicable to finance leases of assets used for the purposes of a trade or profession, see Revenue Tax Briefing Issue 24 pp 16–20, Issue 25 pp 1–3.

GIFTS OF MONEY

30.13 Gifts of money accepted by the Minister for Finance for public purposes are allowable as a deduction from total income if made by an individual, or as a loss in a separate trade (and disregarding certain 'ringfencing' provisions) if made by a company. [*TCA 1997, s 483; FA 2002, s 56*] See also **2.30** 'Allowances, credits and rates' and **12.9** 'Corporation tax' as regards gifts for education in the Arts.

ILLEGAL TRADING

30.14 See under **32.4** 'Sch D, Case IV' and also **38.149–38.151** 'Tax cases'.

INDUSTRIAL AND PROVIDENT SOCIETIES

[*TCA 1997, ss 698–701*]

30.15 See under **12.22** 'Corporation tax'.

KEYMAN ETC INSURANCE

30.16 In general, premiums paid under policies insuring against loss of profit upon certain contingencies are admissible deductions, and all sums received under such policies are trading receipts when received. Although strictly allowability of premiums and taxation of benefits are separate issues, it will usually be the case that both are either within or outside the scope of taxation of the trade (although a benefit will not be treated as non-chargeable simply because no claim is made for relief on the premium).

A policy taken out by an employer covering such contingencies as sickness, accident or death of an employee (which includes a director) will be treated as within the taxation of the trade where:

(*a*)   the sole relationship is that of employer and employee;

(*b*)   the employee has no substantial proprietary interest in the business (broadly 15 per cent of ordinary share capital);

(*c*)   the insurance is intended to meet loss of profit resulting from the loss of the employee's services as distinct from loss of goodwill or other capital loss; and

(*d*)   in the case of insurance against death, the policy is short-term covering only a specified number of years (broadly not more than five years or a longer term not extending beyond the employee's likely period of service).

The policy must have no surrender value and no investment content, and relate only to the adverse effect of the contingencies on the employer's business (ie not matters such as debts which would become repayable on the contingency). Benefits must not be payable other than to the employer.

The taxation consequences of a policy not meeting these conditions will be determined under the general principle stated at the start of this section.

(Revenue Tax Briefing Issue 11 p 3).

'KNOW-HOW'

30.17 Expenditure on acquiring know-how for use in a trade (but not the cost of know-how purchased together with the trade) is an allowable deduction under Case I. Three changes have been made to the *s 768*:

(*a*)   the prohibition on a deduction where 'know-how' is bought as part of a trade that is being acquired will operate by providing that relief will not be permitted under the section in cases where one company buys the 'non-know-how' assets of the trade;

(*b*)   tax relief for expenditure on 'know-how' will only be available where it is bought for *bona fide* commercial reasons and not as part of a tax avoidance scheme;

(*c*)   the Revenue Commissioners are entitled to consult experts to assist them in the evaluation of claims in respect of expenditure on 'know-how'.

Finance (No 2) Act 2008, s 30 relaxed this restriction such that a deduction for know-how is still available in these circumstances subject to certain limitations.

In particular, the following restrictions apply:

(*a*)   the deduction is only available for set off against profits of the trade of the person claiming the deduction;

(*b*)   the company claiming the deduction can never acquire the trade or part of the trade where the know-how was used;

(*c*)   excess know-how deduction not utilised in the current year must be carried forward for use in subsequent accounting periods and cannot be set against other income or group relieved; and (*d*)   no tax deduction is available to any connected company for royalties paid to the company claiming the know-how deduction.

Where relief is claimed for know-how and it is subsequently found not to have been due, a claw back of the relief takes place by way of an assessment under Case IV of Sch D. Such as assessment would give rise to a tax charge at **25 per cent** so is penal in the context of a tax deduction being claimed at **12.5 per cent**. [*TCA 1997, s 768; FA 2008, s 40*]

LAND TRANSACTIONS

30.18 See under **3.9** 'Anti-avoidance'.

MINING ACTIVITIES

30.19 See under **24** 'Mines'.

PATENTS

30.2030.20 Capital expenditure incurred by a trader or individual deriving income therefrom on the purchase of patent rights is allowed by equal annual instalments over 17 years, the remainder of the first 17 years of life of the patent, or the period for which the rights are acquired, whichever is less. Balancing allowances or charges are made when the patent lapses or is sold with suitable adjustment for part sale. Any capital sum received is assessable under Sch D, Case IV (after deducting the capital cost where purchased) but spread equally over the year of receipt and five succeeding years (or charged for the year of receipt if the taxpayer so elects within one year thereafter or, within the same period, the taxpayer may apply to be charged for some other period). [*TCA 1997, ss 754–762*]

With effect from accounting periods ending after 3 February 2004, a company lessor may claim to have the tax treatment of the income from the short-term leasing of assets computed on the basis of normal accounting practice – the lease interest income only is taxable and no claim to capital allowances arises. Where such a claim is made, no annual allowance is available. See **8.7** 'Capital allowances'. [*TCA 1997, s 80A; FA 2004, s 35*]

PENSION SCHEMES

30.21 The costs of setting up, or amending, and contributions paid to, approved schemes are allowed, subject to spreading in certain cases. Relief for an accounting period or basis period is restricted or eliminated by any excess brought forward of relief given for earlier periods over the relief which would have been available had relief for those periods been restricted to the contributions actually paid. [*TCA 1997, ss 84, 774, 775, Sch 32 para 26; FA 2003, s 14; FA 2005, s 21*]

PRE-TRADING EXPENDITURE

30.22 Special reliefs apply for the set up and commencement of trades:

(*a*)   expenditure incurred for trade purposes in the three years before commencement which would be allowable as a Case I deduction if incurred after commencement, but which is not so allowable apart from these provisions, is treated as having been incurred on commencement;

(*b*)   trade charges (see **12.9** 'Corporation tax') paid by companies at any time prior to commencement are treated as paid on commencement, so far as not otherwise deductible;

(*c*)   where an individual has been assessed under *s 238* (see **13.1** 'Deduction of tax at source') in respect of an annuity or other annual payment made wholly and exclusively for the purposes of a trade commenced after the payment was made, the amount assessed is treated under *s 390* (see **22.1** 'Losses') as a trade loss arising on commencement.

Expenditure allowed under (*a*) above is not available for relief under *s 381* (against other income, see **22.2**(*a*) 'Losses') or *ss 396(2), 420, 455(3)* or *456* (against other profits or gains, see **12.17** 'Corporation tax', or by group relief, see **12.15** 'Corporation tax').

Where these provisions apply, no other relief may be given for the expenditure or payment concerned. Identical rules apply under Sch D, Case II to professions set up and commenced after 21 January 1997.

[*TCA 1997, ss 82, 243(3), 390(2)*]

REDUNDANCY PAYMENTS

30.23 Lump sum payments made under *Redundancy Payments Act 1967* are deductible and corresponding rebates are assessable. [*TCA 1997, s 109*]

RENT – DOUBLE ALLOWANCE FOR CERTAIN PREMISES

30.24 Urban renewal: lease granted in qualifying period. Where a deduction is allowed for rent under a 'qualifying lease' in respect of 'qualifying premises' occupied for trade or professional purposes, a further deduction is allowed, for the first ten years for which rent is payable in relation to any qualifying lease of those premises, equal in amount to the deduction in respect of the rent. The relief is restricted where such a deduction is claimed in relation to a 'qualifying lease' of 'qualifying premises' created out of an interest held by a person, and that person or a connected person (within *s 10*) takes a qualifying lease in respect of other qualifying premises, which he occupies for the purposes of his trade or profession, and which would otherwise attract a further deduction as above. A further deduction will then only be available in respect of the other premises if that person can show that the lease was not undertaken for the sole or main benefit of obtaining such a reduction. The relief is not available as respects a 'qualifying lease' granted after 20 April 1997 where the rent is payable to a connected person (within *s 10*).

A '*qualifying lease*' is a lease of 'qualifying premises' granted in the 'qualifying period' or within one year thereafter on *bona fide* commercial terms by a lessor to a person not connected (within *s 10*) with the lessor or with any other person entitled to a rent in respect of the premises. A 'finance lease' as defined in *s 345(8)(b)* (broadly a lease at the inception of which the aggregate of the present discounted value of the minimum payments under the lease and any initial payment amounts in value to 90 per cent or more of the arm's length net value of the premises, or a lease which in all the circumstances provides for the lessee all the risks and benefits of ownership of the premises other than legal title thereto) is not a qualifying lease for these purposes. A lease of premises within an 'enterprise area' (see below) ceases, however, to be a 'qualifying lease' from 6 April 1999 where the lease was granted after 30 July 1999 for areas within **8.10**(*a*) 'Capital allowances', after 30 December 1999 for areas within **8.10**(*b*) 'Capital allowances', and irrespective of the date of grant for areas within **8.10**(*c*) 'Capital allowances'.

'*Qualifying premises*' means premises in an 'enterprise area' within **8.10**(*a*), (*b*) or (*c*) 'Capital allowances', or a qualifying multi-storey car park, for which capital allowances are available by virtue of *s 343* or *s 344* (see **8.10** 'Capital allowances'), or premises in an area designated for this purpose by the Minister for Finance (which designation may specify a shorter qualifying period within that referred to above) consisting of either:

(i)   an industrial building or structure for construction or refurbishment expenditure on which, in the qualifying period, capital allowances are available by virtue of *s 341* or *s 342* (see **8.10** 'Capital allowances'); or

(ii)   an hotel on which all entitlement to industrial buildings initial or annual allowances has been irrevocably disclaimed (see *s 345(5)(6)*) in relation to construction or refurbishment expenditure in the qualifying period;

and which is let on *bona fide* arm's length commercial terms. In the case of refurbishment expenditure, there is a further condition that the expenditure is at least ten per cent of the market value of the premises (excluding land) immediately before the expenditure was incurred.

The '*qualifying period*' is:

(*a*)   in relation to premises in enterprise areas within **8.10**(*a*) 'Capital allowances', the period from 1 August 1994 to 31 July 1997 inclusive (extended to **31 July 1998** where the relevant local authority has certified (before 1 October 1997) that at least 15 per cent of the total cost had been incurred before 31 July 1997, and further extended to **31 December 1998** in certain cases involving delays outside the direct control of the person incurring the expenditure);

(*b*)   in relation to premises in enterprise areas within **8.10**(*b*) 'Capital allowances', the period from 1 July 1997 to **31 December 1999** inclusive;

(*c*)   in relation to premises in enterprise areas within **8.10**(*c*) 'Capital allowances', the period from 1 August 1994 to **31 December 1999** inclusive; or

(*d*)   in relation to qualifying multi-storey car parks, the period from 1 August 1994 to **31 July 1997** inclusive (extended to **30 September 1998** where at least 15 per cent of the total construction expenditure was certified before 30 September 1998 by the relevant local authority (under the relevant guidelines) to have been incurred before 1 July 1998).

There is provision against double relief where relief is given under these provisions.

[*TCA 1997, ss 339, 340, 344(1), 345, 350A, Sch 7; FA 1998, s 24; FA 2000, s 42*]

See below as regards leases on premises in the Temple Bar or Custom House Docks Areas of Dublin, and as regards earlier leases in certain other areas. Where further deductions continue to apply in relation to rent under such earlier leases, the above provisions do not apply. [*FA 1986, s 45(2); FA 1994, s 35(1)(d)(iii)*] See also **2.27** 'Allowances, credits and rates', **8.10** 'Capital allowances' and **33.11** 'Sch D, Case V'.

Lease granted before 1 August 1994 or in relation to premises in the **Temple Bar** or **Custom House Docks Areas** of Dublin. Where a deduction is allowed for rent under a 'qualifying lease' in respect of 'qualifying premises' occupied for trade or professional purposes, payable in the ten-year period commencing on the day on which rent is first payable in respect of those premises under the 'qualifying lease', a further deduction is allowed equal in amount to the deduction in respect of rent. This relief is restricted where such a deduction is claimed in relation to the 'qualifying premises' in which a person holds an interest, and that person takes a 'qualifying lease' in respect of other 'qualifying premises', which he occupies for the purposes of his trade or profession, and which would otherwise attract a further reduction as above. Relief will then only be available in respect of the other premises if that person can show that the lease was not undertaken for the sole or main benefit of obtaining a further deduction under these provisions. The restriction is extended, as regards rent payable under leases entered into after 5 May 1993, to refer to both the claimant and persons connected with him within *s 10*. Relief is not available as respects a 'qualifying lease' granted after 20 April 1997 where the rent is payable to a connected person within *s 10*.

As respects 'qualifying leases' entered into after 17 April 1991, the double allowance is by reference to rent paid *for* a rental period rather than that paid *in* a rental period, and where in a period or periods preceding the commencement of a 'qualifying lease' rent was payable by the same person (or a person connected with him within *s 10*) in relation to the same premises under a 'qualifying lease', double allowances are due only for the first ten years of the aggregate of such periods. As respects qualifying leases entered into after 10 April 1994, this applies to confine double allowances in respect of any one qualifying premises to a maximum of ten years, regardless of whether or not the claimants (if more than one) are connected.

The aggregate reduction in tax liability of an individual from the original reduction in respect of the rent and from the further reduction under these provisions may not exceed the amount of the rent giving rise to the allowances.

'*Qualifying premises*' means an 'industrial building or structure' (see **8.5** 'Capital allowances'), or premises treated as such under *FA 1986, s 42* (see **8.10** 'Capital allowances'), which is on a site wholly within certain designated areas of Dublin, Athlone, Castlebar, Cork, Dundalk, Kilkenny, Letterkenny, Limerick, Sligo, Tralee, Tullamore, Wexford, Waterford or Galway (see *FA 1986, Sch 4 Pts II–VII* and *SIs 1988, Nos 92, 287, 314*) and which is let on *bona fide* arm's length commercial terms. It also includes such a building in the Temple Bar Area (see *Sch 6*), whether or not it is an industrial building or structure, provided that it was in existence on 1 January 1991 or constructed in the period 6 April 1991 to 5 April 1998 and is approved by Temple Bar Renewal Ltd.

After 23 April 1992, only industrial buildings or structures in respect of which capital expenditure incurred in the 'qualifying period' attracts industrial buildings allowances satisfy the conditions for industrial buildings or structures to be qualifying premises. As regards rent payable under a lease entered into after 5 May 1993, where the capital expenditure is incurred on refurbishment of the premises, there is a further requirement that the refurbishment expenditure is at least ten per cent of the market value of the premises (excluding land) immediately before the expenditure was incurred.

A *'qualifying lease'* is a lease of such premises granted in, or (except as below) within two years of the end of, the 'qualifying period' on *bona fide* commercial terms by a lessor to a person not connected (within *s 10*) with the lessor or with any other person entitled to a rent in respect of the premises. (In relation to premises in the Temple Bar Area, the lease must have been granted before 31 December 1999.) A 'finance lease' as defined (broadly a lease at the inception of which the aggregate of the discounted present value of the minimum payments under the lease and any initial payment amounts in value to 90 per cent or more of the arm's length net value of the premises, or a lease which in all the circumstances provides for the lessee all the risks and benefits of ownership of the premises other than legal title thereto) is not a qualifying lease for these purposes.

The *'qualifying period'* is:

(i)   in relation to premises in the Custom House Docks Area of Dublin (as specified in *Sch 5* or as extended by order of the Minister for Finance under *s 322(2)*, see *SI 466/99/*), the period of eleven years ending on **24 January 1999**;

(ii)   in relation to premises in the Temple Bar Area, the period commencing on 6 April 1991 and ending on **5 April 1999** (31 December 1999 in certain cases where substantial expenditure had been incurred by 5 April 1999); or

(iii)   in relation to premises in other designated areas, the period commencing on 23 October 1985 and ending on **31 July 1994**.

No relief is available in respect of rent payable under a qualifying lease for any part of a rental period after 31 December 2008. Relief is similarly denied for rent payable for any part of a rental period between 3 December 1998 and 31 December 2003 unless either:

(*a*)   (in the case of a qualifying premises within the Custom House Docks Area by virtue of a ministerial order under *s 322(2)*) a written agreement or contract to secure the development of the building or structure comprising the qualifying premises, or in which those premises is located, was entered into in the qualifying period but by 2 December 1998 with the Dublin Docks Development Authority; or

(*b*)   (in the case of any other qualifying premises) such a written agreement or contract was entered into in the qualifying period but by 2 December 1998, and the development was wholly or mainly completed before 1 January 2000.

Relief is similarly denied for rent payable between 1 January 2004 and 31 December 2008 in respect of qualifying premises to which (*a*) or (*b*) above applies, *except* in the case of qualifying premises within (*b*) above the construction or refurbishment of which either was completed before 1 April 1998, or was commenced before that date and the premises occupied under a qualifying lease before 9 February 1999. [*ss 322, 324, 330, 333, Sch 5, Sch 6, Sch 32 para 13; FA 1986, ss 41, 45, Sch 4 as amended; Urban Renewal Act 1998, s 20(1)(a)(2); FA 1999, ss 42, 43; FA 2000, ss 37, 39*]

See also **2.27** 'Allowances, credits and rates', **8.10** 'Capital allowances' and **33.4**, **33.5** 'Sch D, Case V'.

Qualifying resort areas. Where a deduction is allowed for rent under a 'qualifying lease' in respect of 'qualifying premises' occupied for trade or professional purposes, a further deduction may be claimed, for the first ten years for which rent is payable in relation to any 'qualifying lease' of those premises, equal in amount to the deduction in respect of the rent. The relief is restricted where such a deduction is claimed in relation to a 'qualifying lease' of 'qualifying premises' created out of an interest held by a person, and that person or a connected person (within *s 10*) takes a 'qualifying lease' in respect of other 'qualifying premises', which he occupies for the purposes of his trade or profession, and which would otherwise attract a further deduction as above. A further deduction will then only be available in respect of the other premises if that person can show that the lease was not undertaken for the sole or main benefit of obtaining such a deduction. The further deduction is not available as respects a 'qualifying lease' granted after 20 April 1997 where the rent is payable to a connected person within *s 10*.

A '*qualifying lease*' is a lease of 'qualifying premises' granted in the period **1 July 1995 to 30 June 1998** inclusive (the '*qualifying period*') on *bona fide* commercial terms by a lessor to a person not connected (within *s 10*) with the lessor or with any other person entitled to a rent in respect of the premises. A 'finance lease' as defined in *s 354(5)(b)* (broadly a lease at the inception of which the aggregate of the present discounted value of the minimum payments under the lease and any initial payment amounts in value to 90 per cent or more of the arm's length net value of the premises, or a lease which in all the circumstances provides for the lessee all the risks and benefits of ownership of the premises other than legal title thereto) is not a qualifying lease for these purposes.

The qualifying period is extended to **30 June 1999** where at least 15 per cent of the total expenditure is certified on or before 30 September 1998 by the relevant local authority (under the relevant guidelines) to have been incurred before 1 July 1998, and to **31 December 1999** where at least 50 per cent is so certified on or before 30 September 1999 to have been incurred before 1 July 1999.

'*Qualifying premises*' means a building or structure the site of which is wholly within a '*qualifying resort area*' ie a part of Achill, Arklow, Ballybunion, Bettystown, Bundoran, Clogherhead, Clonakilty, Courtown, Enniscrone, Kilkee, Lahinch, Laytown, Mosney, Salthill, Tramore, Westport or Youghal described in *Sch 8*, let on *bona fide* arm's length commercial terms, in respect of capital expenditure on the construction or refurbishment of which capital allowances fall or will fall to be made under *s 352* or *s 353* (see **8.11** 'Capital allowances'), being either:

(*a*)   an industrial building or structure consisting of a hotel, holiday camp or registered holiday cottage (see **8.5**(ii) 'Capital allowances'); or (*b*)   a building or structure which is not an industrial building or structure, and which is in use for the purposes of the operation of one or more 'qualifying tourism facilities'.

Registered holiday cottages within (*a*) above and registered holiday apartments and other listed self-catering accommodation within (*b*) above are, however, excluded unless the person incurring the expenditure elects by written notice to disclaim all industrial buildings allowances (see **8.11** 'Capital allowances') in respect of the construction or refurbishment expenditure. Such an election, which is irrevocable, must be included in the return required for the first year of assessment or accounting period (see **28.11** 'Returns') for which such an allowance would otherwise fall to be made. A copy of the election must be furnished to any person to whom a qualifying lease of the premises is granted, who must include a copy in his return for the year of assessment or accounting period in which rent is first payable under the lease. Where such an election is made, then on any event on which a balancing allowance or charge (see **8.5**(*c*) 'Capital allowances') is to be brought into account in respect of the premises, the residue of expenditure is nil, and the special provisions regarding buildings bought unused (see **8.5** 'Capital allowances') do not apply as regards any purchaser of the relevant interest in the premises. Also, as regards registered holiday apartments and other listed self-catering accommodation within (*b*) above, where an industrial buildings allowance falls to be made in respect of acquisition, construction or refurbishment expenditure, any loss which would not have arisen but for the allowance may not be relieved against other income (see **22.2**(*a*) 'Losses', **12.17**(*a*) 'Corporation tax'), and the allowances may not themselves be claimed against other income. These restrictions do not, however, apply to a holiday cottage, etc where either:

(*a*)   before 5 April 1996, a binding contract for the acquisition or construction was entered into, or an application for planning permission for the construction received by the relevant authority, or a written opinion issued by the Revenue Commissioners that an allowance for the expenditure would not be restricted by virtue of *s 408* (see **8.5** 'Capital allowances'); or

(*b*)   before 5 April 1996, expenditure was incurred on the acquisition of the land on which the construction or refurbishment is to take place by the person who incurred the construction or refurbishment expenditure, or a binding written contract entered into for its acquisition, and it can be proved to the satisfaction of the Revenue Commissioners that a detailed plan had been prepared, and detailed discussions with the planning authority had taken place (supported by an affidavit by the authority), after 7 February 1995 and before 5 April 1996.

[*TCA 1997, ss 351, 354, 355, Sch 8; FA 1998, s 27; FA 1999, s 45*]

See also **8.11** 'Capital allowances', **33.12** 'Sch D, Case V'.

SCIENTIFIC RESEARCH EXPENDITURE

30.25 Expenditure on scientific research (as defined) is allowed as an expense if non-capital. Balancing allowances and charges arise on cessation of use. Allowances must be claimed within 24 months of the end of year of assessment. [*TCA 1997, ss 763–765*] See also **30.33** below and **38.154** 'Tax cases'.

SHARE SCHEMES

30.26

(*a*)   **Approved profit-sharing schemes.** Any sum expended by a company in establishing an approved profit-sharing scheme (see **34.6** 'Sch E') is an allowable deduction (or a management expense, see **12.9** 'Corporation tax'), provided that the trustees acquired no shares prior to approval being given. Where approval is given more than nine months after the end of the accounting period in which the sum is expended, it is treated as expended in the accounting period in which approval is given; [*TCA 1997, s 518*]

(*b*)   **Qualifying employee share ownership trusts.** Any sum expended by a company in establishing a qualifying employee share ownership trust within *Sch 12* is an allowable deduction (or a management expense, see **12.9** 'Corporation tax'). Where the trust is established more than nine months after the end of the accounting period in which the sum is expended, it is treated as expended in the accounting period in which the trust is established.

Relief is similarly available for contributions to the trust provided that:

(i)   the trust is a qualifying trust at the time the contribution is made,

(ii)   at that time the company (or a company it controls (within *s 432*, see **12.7** 'Corporation tax')) has employees eligible to benefit under the trust, and

(iii) the sum is expended by the trustees for a 'qualifying purpose' or purposes before the expiry of nine months after the end of the accounting period in which the contribution was made (or within such further time as the Revenue Commissioners may allow).

'*Qualifying purposes*' are the acquisition of shares in the company or of certain 'specified securities', the repayment of sums borrowed and payment of interest on such sums, the payment of sums to beneficiaries under the trust, the meeting of expenses and, from 6 April 2001, the payment of any sum or the transfer of securities to the personal representatives of a 'deceased beneficiary' under the trust.

A '*deceased beneficiary*' for these purposes is a person who, on the date of their death, would, had such shares, etc been available, have been eligible to have shares, etc appropriated to them under an *Sch 11* approved profit sharing scheme (see **34.6** 'Sch E') and who was a beneficiary under the terms of an approved employee share ownership trust the trust deed of which provided for the transfer of securities to the trustees of that approved profit sharing scheme and for the payment of sums, and the transfer of securities, to the personal representatives of deceased beneficiaries.

The trustees are for these purposes treated as expending sums in the order in which they are received.

The trustees of a qualifying trust are not chargeable to income tax on dividends to the extent that the income from them is expended for a qualifying purpose within the period required by the trust deed. They are not, however, entitled to set-off or payment of tax credits under *s 136* (prior to their abolition see **12.24** 'Corporation tax') in respect of dividends.

Where securities are transferred to an approved profit-sharing scheme (as under (*a*) above) or, from 6 April 2001, to the personal representatives of a deceased beneficiary (as above) under the trust, no chargeable gain arises.

For trusts approved on or after 25 March 1999, where securities are sold on the open market, any gain is not a chargeable gain to the extent that the sale proceeds are used to repay trust borrowings, to pay interest on such borrowings or, from 6 April 2001, to pay a sum to the personal representatives of a deceased beneficiary (as above) under the trust. Since 16 April 2001, this is extended to sums received on the redemption of securities.

Since 6 April 2001, the payment of any sum out of the proceeds of sale of securities, or the transfer of any securities, by the trustees to the personal representatives of a deceased beneficiary (as above) under the trust is exempt from any charge to income tax.

The above reliefs cease to apply from the date on which the Revenue Commissioners withdraw approval of the trust as a qualifying trust.

Special provisions apply from 12 December 2000 to trusts established by ICC Bank plc or a successor to a trustee savings bank, extended from 16 April 2001 to ACC Bank plc and a company which acquired control of the Irish National Petroleum Corporation Ltd.

Since 3 February 2005, certain payments made to members of qualifying trusts with an associated approved profit sharing scheme are treated as distributions and subject to dividend withholding tax; [*TCA 1997, s 130, 519, Sch 12; FA 1998, s 36; FA 1999, s 69; FA 2000, s 26, Sch 2; FA 2001, ss 13, 16(b), 17; FA 2002, s 13(1)(c)(e)(2); FA 2004, s 15; FA 2005, s 18*]

(*c*) **Approved savings-related share option schemes.** Any sum expended after 5 April 1999 by a company in establishing an approved savings-related share option scheme (see **34.8** 'Sch E') is an allowable deduction (or a management expense, see **12.9** 'Corporation tax'), provided that no rights are granted under the scheme before approval is given. This does *not* include expenses incurred after 5 April 2000 to enable a trust or company set up for the purpose to acquire and hold scheme shares. Where approval is given more than nine months after the end of the accounting period in which the sum is expended, it is treated as expended in the accounting period in which approval is given; [*TCA 1997, s 519B; FA 1999, s 68(a); FA 2000, s 51*]

(*d*) **Approved share option schemes.** Any sum expended by a company in establishing an approved share option scheme within *Sch 12C* (see **34.9** 'Sch E') is an allowable deduction (or a management expense, see **12.9** 'Corporation tax'), provided that no rights are granted under the scheme before approval is given (except insofar as certain rights granted after 14 February 2001 under schemes approved on or before 31 December 2001 are treated as granted under approved schemes, see **34.9** 'Sch E'). This does *not* include expenses incurred to enable a trust or company set up for the purpose to acquire and hold scheme shares. Where approval is obtained more than nine months after the end of the accounting period in which a sum is expended, it is treated as expended in the accounting period in which approval is given; [*TCA 1997, s 519D(6); FA 2001, s 15(a)*]

(*e*) **Other employee benefit schemes.** Since 3 February 2005, a deduction in respect of employee benefits is allowed in an accounting period where the full amount of the benefit is paid out to the employee during the accounting period or within nine months of the end of the period. Any sum not paid out in that time is carried forward for deduction in the following period to the extent that employee contributions are paid out in that period. This provision does not apply to approved share schemes, pension schemes or accident benefit schemes. The meaning of an employee benefit contribution has been expanded such that any action which results in assets being held, or able to be used under the terms of an employee benefit scheme, or in an increase in the value of such assets, is within the meaning of an employee benefit contribution, and consequently covered by the provisions of *s 81A* [*TCA 1997, s 81A; FA 2005, s 17; FA 2008, s 25*]

SHARES, SECURITIES ETC

30.27

(*a*) **'Bond Washing'** transactions where income is received from securities bought and sold within six months or from securities held for over one month and either the purchase or the sale was not at current market price or an agreement regarding the sale was made at, or before, the purchase. [*TCA 1997, s 748*] If the transaction is by a share dealer (other than *bona fide* discount house in RI or a recognised dealer member of a stock exchange in RI) then the purchase price used for computing profit or loss for tax purposes is reduced by an 'appropriate amount' of income. This reduction is not required in respect of:

(i) overseas securities purchased **on or after 1 January 2003**, where (i) the interest payable on all overseas securities is included in the trading account of the dealer, and (ii) the dealer elects to waive any entitlement to tax credits due on the securities (whether under a double tax agreement or otherwise). The election must be made in the tax return of the dealer. A separate election must be made for each chargeable period, and

(ii) securities purchased **on or after 1 January 2003** that are exempt from capital gains tax under *s 607* (see **9.7(*f*)** 'Capital gains tax') where the interest is taxable as trading income.

[*TCA 1997, s 749; FA 2003, s 31*]

For traders other than share dealers, the 'appropriate amount', and tax thereon, is ignored in any loss repayment claim. [*TCA 1997, s 751*] Any exemption entitlement to a person shall not extend to the 'appropriate amount' of the income. [*TCA 1997, s 750*] The 'appropriate amount' is the pre-acquisition portion of the dividend, interest etc calculated from the last 'ex-div' day. It is the net dividend etc after deduction of tax for purposes of *s 749* and gross dividend etc for *ss 750* and *751*; [*TCA 1997, Sch 21*]

(*b*)   **'Dividend Stripping'** transactions. Where a person carrying on a trade of dealing in shares etc holds ten per cent or more of the issued shares of one class (other than fixed rate preference shares) acquired within ten years of receiving a dividend or distribution on them which is wholly or partly paid out of pre-acquisition profits, then such part of the net dividend etc paid out of pre-acquisition profits is treated as a trading receipt which had not borne tax. [*TCA 1997, s 752(3)*] An exemption entitlement to a person shall not extend to such receipts out of pre-acquisition profits [*TCA 1997, s 752(4)*] and a person not dealing in shares etc may not claim repayment for loss relief against the gross amount of such dividends. [*TCA 1997, s 753*] Provisions include persons acting in concert etc and see *Sch 22* for determination of pre-acquisition profits;

(*c*)   **Exchanges of shares, etc.** Since 11 February 1999, where shares held as trading stock of dealers in securities are exchanged in circumstances such that, were they held other than as trading stock, the new shares would be treated as the same asset as the original shares, with no disposal of the original shares, for capital gains tax purposes (company reorganisations, etc, see **9.15** 'Capital gains tax'), the exchange will be similarly treated for the purposes of any Sch D, Case I computation. Where any additional consideration is received for the exchange, this treatment does not apply to a corresponding proportion of the original shares (by reference to market value of the new holding at the time of the exchange). These provisions are subject to *s 751B* (see below). [*TCA 1997, s 751A; FA 1999, s 59*]

Irish Government bonds. Special provisions apply to exchanges of Irish Government bonds in the period 11 February 1999 to 31 December 1999 inclusive under the Exchange Programme initiated by the National Treasury Management Agency. Where the holder so elects (within two years after the end of the chargeable period in which the exchange takes place), tax is deferred broadly as follows:

(i)   for *dealers in securities*, the increased tax which (apart from these provisions) would be chargeable in the chargeable period of the exchange by virtue of the exchange, less tax so chargeable on any interest accrued up to the time of the exchange, is deferred to the chargeable period in which the new bonds are disposed of,

(ii)   for any other holder, any capital gains tax which (apart from these provisions) would be chargeable in respect of the exchange (after relief for any allowable losses), is deferred to the chargeable period in which the new bonds are disposed of;

[*TCA 1997, s 751B; FA 1999, s 59*]

(*d*)   **Stocklending and repo transactions.** See Revenue Tax Briefing Issue 36 pp 20, 21, Issue 43 p 14.

See also **3.6** 'Anti-avoidance legislation'.

STAFF RECRUITMENT AND COVENANTS

30.28 The cost (net of grants etc) of recruiting and training staff (all or the majority of whom are RI citizens) prior to setting up a manufacturing business is allowed equally over the first three years of assessment in the same way as capital allowances (**8**). [*TCA 1997, s 769*]

See **34.12** 'Sch E' as regards allowance of certain payments, etc for restrictive covenants by employees.

TRADE AND PROFESSIONAL ASSOCIATION SUBSCRIPTIONS

30.29 Trade and professional associations may enter into arrangements with the Revenue, under which entrance fees, subscriptions etc paid to an association are a deductible trading expense to the payer, and non-capital payments by the association to members are taxable trade receipts. The association is taxable on the surplus of such receipts over expenditure, as well as on investment income etc. Contributions by members towards capital expenditure of the association are excluded from the arrangements.

For a short article on such arrangements, see Revenue Tax Briefing Issue 29 pp 13, 14.

TRADE MARKS

30.30 Costs of registration or renewal are allowed. [*TCA 1997, s 86*]

TRADING STOCK

30.31 Trading stock is defined as property of any description, whether real or personal, which is either:

(*a*)   property such as is sold in the ordinary course of trade or would be so sold if it were mature, or if its manufacture, preparation or construction were complete; or

(*b*)   materials used in the manufacture etc of property in (*a*) above.

On the discontinuance of a trade (other than by reason of the death of a single individual who carried it on) trading stock on hand is valued either (i) at amount realised on sale (or value of consideration) if transferred to a person carrying on (or intending to carry on) a trade in RI and who can deduct the cost as an expense for tax purposes (subject, from 6 December 2000, to the exclusion of certain financial assets and to the 'connected persons' provisions below), or (ii) in any other case, at open market value at the date of discontinuance. Since 6 December 2000, where (i) applies and the transferor and transferee are 'connected' (as specially and widely defined, see *s 89(1)(b)(ii)*), the arm's length consideration is substituted. If, however, the arm's length consideration is greater than both the book value immediately prior to the discontinuance and the actual transfer price, the transferor and transferee may jointly elect for the greater of the latter two figures to be taken as the value instead. Such an election, signed by both parties, must be included in the transferor's return for the chargeable period of the discontinuance. [*TCA 1997, s 89; FA 2001, s 42*] See **18.9** 'Farming' for certain special provisions for farmers. See also **38.161** 'Tax cases'.

UNEMPLOYED – DOUBLE ALLOWANCE FOR EMOLUMENTS

[*TCA 1997, s 88A; FA 1998, s 16*]

30.32 A double deduction may be claimed for 'emoluments' paid to a 'qualifying individual' in respect of a 'qualifying employment' (and for the related PRSI employer's contribution) for the 36 months following commencement of the employment. No extra deduction is available where either the employer or the employee receives (or has received) in respect of an employment any grant or subsidy funded wholly or mainly, directly or indirectly, by the State or by a statutory board or public or local authority (other than in relation to certain activities, programmes and courses for the unemployed). For the meaning of 'emoluments', 'qualifying individual' and 'qualifying employment', see **2.13** 'Allowances, credits and rates'.

UNIVERSITIES

30.33 Payments before 6 April 2001 to RI Universities for the purpose of research or teaching industrial relations, marketing or any other subject approved by the Minister for Finance, are allowable. Relief is also granted for payments to the National College of RI, an institution comprising the Dublin Institute of Technology or a college established under *Regional Technical Colleges Act 1992, s 3*. For years of assessment 2000/01 onwards or for accounting periods ending on or after 6 April 2001, the relief is extended to sums paid to a body of persons or trust established in RI for the sole purpose of granting aid to any of the above bodies to enable them to undertake research in, or teach, an approved subject. [*TCA 1997, ss 767, 848A(13); FA 2000, s 22; FA 2001, s 45(1)*] See also **30.25** above. For payments after 5 April 2001, see **2.30** 'Allowances, credits and rates' and **12.9** 'Corporation tax'.

31 Schedule D, Case III – Interest Receivable and Overseas Income

31.1 Tax is charged under Sch D, Case III on:

(*a*)   interest, annuities and other annual payments (but excluding certain bank and other deposit interest receivable under deduction of tax (see **13.10**) and any amounts chargeable under Sch D, Case V);

(*b*)   discounts;

(*c*)   profits on securities bearing interest payable out of public revenue and not chargeable under Sch C;

(*d*)   interest paid without deduction of tax on securities issued under authority of the Minister for Finance or deemed to be such;

(*e*)   income from foreign securities and not charged under Sch C; and

(*f*)   income from foreign possessions, which include trades wholly carried on and controlled abroad and offices, employments and pensions (excluding certain overseas pensions etc for past services analogous to RI old age pensions etc) with benefits in kind taxable to the same extent as if arising in RI, see **34.3** 'Sch E'.

[*TCA 1997, ss 18(2), 57, 200; FA 1998, s 18; FA 2005, s 20*]

See **38.167–38.174, 38.221** 'Tax cases' for relevant case law.

ASSESSMENTS

31.2 All profits assessable under Case III are treated as a single source. Adjustments are not made therefore in respect of each item which is new or ceases, but only when all Case III sources are new, or when they all cease. [*TCA 1997, s 70(1)*] See **38.167** 'Tax cases'.

Assessment is on actual income arising in the year of assessment, including the year in which a source ceases. [*TCA 1997, s 70(2)*]

Foreign securities and possessions are normally assessable on the full income arising, whether remitted or not. But in the case of persons not domiciled in RI, or RI citizens not ordinarily resident there, the remittance basis still applies to income from such sources (other than sources in Great Britain or Northern Ireland). *Finance Act 2010, s 9* provides that the remittance basis only applies to individuals who are not domiciled in the State and will no longer be available to individuals who are non-ordinarily resident here. From 2006, the remittance basis does not apply to income from an office or employment to the extent to which that income is attributable to the performance in RI of that office or employment. [*FA 2006, s 15*] Any income arising abroad and not remitted is subject to the same deductions and allowances (including interest relief) as if it had been so received. [*TCA 1997, ss 70, 71, 73*] Also, interest on money borrowed to purchase, improve or repair property abroad is deductible from the rents received in the same way as for RI rents (see **33.2** 'Sch D, Case V'), except that the residential premises restriction which applies in RI from 23 April 1998 applies to overseas property from 7 May 1998. [*TCA 1997, s 71(4)(4A); F(No 2)A 1998, s 1(2)*] See **31.4** below for double taxation relief and **27.1** 'Residents and non-residents'.

There are anti-avoidance provisions relating to the use of loans repayable out of foreign income to avoid tax on remittances. [*TCA 1997, s 72*]

See also **38.225** 'Tax cases'.

Unremittable income. Where a taxpayer satisfies Revenue Commissioners that, owing to legislation or executive action in country of origin, income arising in that country cannot be remitted, tax thereon may be held in abeyance until, in their opinion, that income becomes remittable. There is a right of appeal to Appeal Commissioners within 21 days of notification of the Revenue Commissioners' decision. [*TCA 1997, s 1004*]

DOMICILE AND RESIDENCE

31.3 As regards income derived from RI or UK sources the question of domicile or ordinary residence normally makes no difference, but see **29** 'Sch C' and **19** 'Government and other public loans'.

As regards income derived from sources outside those countries (viz., in the Dominions or abroad) the question is of importance.

Persons who are not domiciled in RI, and RI citizens not ordinarily resident there, deriving income from sources outside RI and Great Britain and N Ireland, are assessable to RI tax on that income on the basis of remittance to the Republic, and not on the whole income arising. But see *s 72* for treating as constructive remittances foreign income set against loans enjoyed in RI.

DOUBLE TAXATION RELIEF

31.4 Income from UK (see also **15.3** et seq. 'Double tax relief – income and capital gains'). While the Convention is in force the Tax Acts are modified by *s 73*.

STRIPS OF SECURITIES

31.5 When a unit of a 'security' (within *s 815(1)*, see **3.6** 'Anti-avoidance legislation') is 'stripped' (ie where the holder creates obligations ('strips') to pay interest and principal separate from other such obligations), the security is deemed to have been disposed of at market value at that time. The holder is deemed to have acquired each strip for a proportion of the 'opening value' of the unit at that time corresponding to the proportion which the market value of the strip at that time represents of the total market value of all the strips of the unit. Each strip is then deemed to be a non-interest bearing security, any profits or gains on whose disposal or redemption are chargeable to tax under Sch D, Case III (unless chargeable under Case I, see below).

The '*opening value*' of a unit of a security is its market value if held by a dealer as trading stock, otherwise the lower of that market value and the nominal value (ie the value by reference to which interest is expressed to be payable or, if there is no such value, the price paid on issue).

Where a person other than a dealer in securities acquires a strip of an exempt security within *s 607* (see **9.7**(*f*) 'Capital gains tax') (other than by creation of the strip), the strip is deemed to be acquired for the lesser of:

(*a*)   the amount bearing the same proportion to the nominal value (as above) of the unit from which the strip was created as the market value of the strip at the time of issue of the security would have borne to the total market value of all the strips of the unit had the unit been stripped at that time; and

(*b*)   the amount paid for acquisition of the strip.

All strips held by companies on the last day of an accounting period, or by other holders on the last day of a year of assessment, are deemed to be disposed of and re-acquired at market value on that day. The amount included in the charge under Sch D, Case III for that chargeable period is then the aggregate net gains for the period less any unrelieved aggregate net losses from such deemed disposals brought forward from earlier periods.

When strips are reconstituted into a unit of a security, each strip is deemed to have been sold at market value at that time, and the unit to have been acquired for the aggregate of such market values of all the constituent strips. [*TCA 1997, s 55; FA 2001, Sch 2 para 1*]

For the powers of the Minister for Finance to authorise strips of Government securities, see *FA 1997, s 161*.

32 Schedule D, Case IV – Miscellaneous Income

32.1 Tax is charged under Sch D, Case IV in respect of any annual profits or gains not falling under any other case of Sch D and not charged by virtue of any other Schedule. [*TCA 1997, s 18(2)*] Particular items specified as chargeable under Case IV are stated below or under the appropriate headings elsewhere in this book, and can be traced through the index. See **38.175–38.179** 'Tax cases' for relevant case law.

32.2 Assessment is on the profits in the year of assessment or on the average of such period, not being greater than one year, as the inspector directs. [*TCA 1997, s 74*]

32.3 Losses may be set off against Case IV profits of the same year or carried forward indefinitely against subsequent profits assessed under that Case. [*TCA 1997, s 383*]

32.4 Illegal and unknown sources of income. Assessments may be made charging to tax under Sch D, Case IV as 'miscellaneous income' profits or gains from sources not known to the inspector, or which arose (or may have arisen) wholly or partly from an illegal source or activity. The unknown or illegal nature of the source the subject of such an assessment is to be disregarded in determining liability, and neither that nature nor the general description of the source as 'miscellaneous income' is by itself ground for discharge of the assessment on appeal. [*TCA 1997, s 58*] For the position prior to the introduction of this provision by *FA 1983*, see **38.149–38.151** 'Tax cases'.

OFFSHORE FUNDS

[*TCA 1997, ss 740–747A, SCHS 19, 20*]

32.5 Introduction. After 5 April 1990, 'offshore income gains' arising on disposals of certain interests in 'offshore funds' which are not considered to distribute sufficient income are charged to income tax or corporation tax under Sch D, Case IV rather than to capital gains tax. Broadly, the capital gains tax regime applies to any part of such a gain accruing before 6 April 1990, but the whole of the gain arising thereafter (without indexation) is taxed as income. Special provisions apply to funds which operate 'equalisation arrangements'. See also **32.15** below as regards special rate where capital gains tax still applies to offshore fund disposals.

DISPOSALS WITHIN OFFSHORE FUND PROVISIONS

32.6 Disposal of material interests in non-qualifying offshore funds. The offshore fund rules apply to a disposal by any person of an asset if, at the time of the disposal, the asset constitutes either:

(a)   a 'material interest' in an 'offshore fund' (see **32.8** below) which is or has at any 'material time' been a 'non-qualifying offshore fund' (see **32.9** below); or

(b)   an interest in an RI-resident company or in a unit trust scheme which has RI-resident trustees, provided that at a 'material time' after 31 December 1990 the company or unit trust scheme was a 'non-qualifying offshore fund' and the asset constituted a 'material interest' in that fund (and for this purpose the provisions of *s 584(3)* equating original shares with a new holding on a reorganisation apply).

[*TCA 1997, s 741(1)*]

A '*material time*' is any time on or after 6 April 1990 or, if the asset was acquired after that date, the earliest date on which any 'relevant consideration' was given for the acquisition of the asset. '*Relevant consideration*' is that given by or on behalf of the person making the disposal or a predecessor in title which would be taken into account in determining any gain or loss on disposal under the *Capital Gains Tax Acts*. [*TCA 1997, s 741(7)*]

With some modifications, a disposal occurs for offshore fund purposes if there would be a disposal under the *Capital Gains Tax Acts*. Death is an occasion of charge, as the deceased is deemed to have made a disposal at market value, immediately before his death, of any asset which was or had at any time been a 'material interest' in a 'non-qualifying offshore fund'. In addition, *s 586(1)* will not apply, and there will therefore be a disposal at market value, if an exchange or arrangement is effected under *ss 586, 587* in such a way that securities, etc in a company, which is or was at a material time a 'non-qualifying offshore fund', are exchanged for assets, etc which do not constitute interests in such a fund. [*TCA 1997, s 741(2)–(6)*]

32.7 Offshore funds operating equalisation arrangements. There are specific provisions to enable funds operating 'equalisation arrangements' to satisfy the 'distribution test' (see **32.10** below) which the nature of such funds might otherwise preclude. As a corollary, provision is also made to ensure that the 'accrued income' paid to outgoing investors as part of their capital payments is treated as income for tax purposes when the fund qualifies as a distributor.

For these purposes, an 'offshore fund' operates '*equalisation arrangements*' where the first distribution paid to a person acquiring a 'material interest' by way of 'initial purchase' includes a payment which is a return of capital (debited to the fund's 'equalisation account') determined by reference to the income which had accrued to the fund in the period before that person's acquisition. An acquisition is by way of '*initial purchase*' if it is by way of direct purchase from the fund's managers in their capacity as such or by way of subscription for or allotment of new shares, etc.

'*Accrued income*' *chargeable to income tax – application of offshore fund rules.* A disposal is one to which the offshore fund provisions apply (subject to the exception detailed below) if it is a disposal by any person of a 'material interest' in an 'offshore fund' operating equalisation arrangements where:

(a)   the disposal proceeds are not a trading receipt; and

(*b*)   the fund is not, and has not at any material time (see **32.6** above) been, a 'non-qualifying offshore fund' (see **32.9** below)

(ie the provisions apply also to distributing funds (see **32.10** below) with equalisation arrangements).

Capital gains tax rules for disposals apply as they do for other offshore fund disposals (see **32.6** above) with some variations. Death is not treated as a disposal in this context. In addition, *s 584(3)* (reorganisations, etc) (including that paragraph as applied by *s 586* or *s 733* (exchange of securities) but not by *s 585* (conversion of securities)) does not apply, and there is a disposal at market value in such circumstances.

Exception. The offshore fund legislation does not apply as indicated above to a disposal where the fund's income for the period preceding the disposal is of such a nature that the part relating to the interest in question is in any event chargeable under Sch D, Case III (**31**) on the person disposing of the interest (or would be so chargeable if residence/domicile/situation of asset requirements were met). [*TCA 1997, ss 741(2)(3), 742*]

MATERIAL INTERESTS IN OFFSHORE FUNDS

32.8 An '*offshore fund*' is:

(*a*)   a company resident outside RI;

(*b*)   a unit trust scheme which has non-RI resident trustees; or

(*c*)   any other arrangements taking effect under overseas law which create rights in the nature of co-ownership under that law;

in which any person has a 'material interest'. [*TCA 1997, s 743(1)*]. Finance Act 2007 sought to remove any uncertainty around the tax treatment of foreign investment structures. The amendment provides that the gross roll-up regime which was available to offshore funds in EU/EEC and OECD countries will not apply to foreign entities unless they are either:

(*a*)   an undertaking for collective investment formed under the law of an offshore state, similar in all material respects to an Investment Limited Partnership, and that holds a certificate of authorisation from the relevant foreign authority;

(*b*)   a regulated fund authorised under the UCITS directive (as amended);

(*c*)   a company formed under the law of an offshore state, similar in all material respects to an authorised investment company within the meaning of *CA 1990, Pt XIII* and that holds an authorisation issued by the authorities of that state providing for the orderly regulation of such companies; or

(*d*)   a unit trust scheme the trustees of which are not resident in the State which is similar in all material respects to an authorised unit trust scheme within the meaning of the Unit Trust Act 1990 and that holds an authorisation issued by the authorities of that offshore state.

A '*material interest*' is one which, when acquired, could reasonably be expected to be realisable (by any means, either in money or in asset form) within seven years, for an amount reasonably approximate to its proportionate share of the market value of the fund's assets. For these purposes, an interest in an offshore fund which at any time is worth substantially more than its proportionate share of the fund's underlying assets is not to be regarded as so realisable. [*TCA 1997, s 743(2)–(4)*]

Exceptions. The following are not material interests:

(i)   interests in respect of loans, etc made in the ordinary course of banking business;

(ii)   rights under insurance policies;

(iii)   shares in a company resident outside RI where:

(*a*)   the shares are held by a company and the holding is necessary or desirable for the maintenance and development of a trade carried on by the company or by an associated company (within *s 743(7)*),

(*b*)   the shares confer at least ten per cent of the voting rights and, on a winding-up, a right to at least ten per cent of the assets after discharge of all prior liabilities,

(*c*)   the shares are held by not more than ten persons and all confer both voting rights and a right to assets on a winding-up, and

(*d*)   at the time of acquisition of the shares the company could reasonably expect to realise its interest for market value within seven years only by virtue of an arrangement requiring the company's fellow participators to purchase its shares and/or provisions of either the overseas company's constitution or an agreement between the participators regarding that company's winding-up;

(iv)   interests in companies resident outside RI at any time when the holder is entitled to have the company wound up and to receive in that event, in the same capacity, more than 50 per cent of the assets after discharging all prior liabilities.

[*TCA 1997, s 743(5)–(8)*]

'*Market value*' for the purposes of the offshore funds legislation is determined according to capital gains tax rules with the necessary modification of *s 548(5)* (market value in relation to rights in unit trust schemes) where appropriate. [*TCA 1997, s 743(9)*]

The gross roll-up regime is grandfathered for investors who have invested in EC/EEC and OECD offshore funds prior to 20 February 2007, provided their interest in those funds would not have qualified as a personal portfolio investment undertaking ('PPIU') had the fund been regulated. Broadly, where an investor or a person connected with an investor has influence over the assets that are put into a regulated fund, the fund may be regarded as a PPIU (see *s 40*). The **20 per cent/23 per cent** tax rates will, therefore, continue to apply for interests held in such retail funds where an investor has a purely passive interest.

Existing investors in unregulated funds which previously qualified for the gross roll-up regime will suffer marginal tax rates on income distributions on or after 20 February 2007 where the interest in the fund would qualify as a PPIU if the fund were regulated. Capital gains from such funds would be taxed at **20 per cent**. Investors who invest in unregulated EC/EEC or OECD offshore funds on or after 20 February 2007 will also be subject to this tax treatment.

The PPIU provisions which provide for a **43 per cent** tax rate on income distributions and disposals in certain specified circumstances will only apply to regulated funds that qualify for the gross roll-up regime. The **43 per cent** tax rate will apply from 20 February 2007 to any income distributions or capital gains arising from that date in respect of an interest in a fund which qualifies as a PPIU. [*FA 2007, s 39*]

See also **28.4** 'Returns'.

NON-QUALIFYING OFFSHORE FUNDS

32.9 An offshore fund is a '*non-qualifying offshore fund*' except during an 'account period' in respect of which it is certified by the Revenue Commissioners as a distributing fund pursuing a 'full distribution policy' (see **32.10** below). For these purposes, an '*account period*' begins on 6 April 1990 (or, if later, when the fund begins to carry on its activities) and on the ending of an account period without the fund ceasing to carry on its activities, and ends on the fund's accounting date (or on the ending of a period for which it does not make up accounts) or, if earlier, twelve months from the beginning of the period or on the fund's ceasing to carry on its activities. In addition, if the fund is a company resident outside RI, an '*account period*' ends when it ceases to be so, and if the fund is a unit trust scheme with non-RI resident trustees, it ends when those trustees become RI resident. [*TCA 1997, s 744(1)(2)(8)–(10)*]

Conditions for certification. Subject to the modification of conditions for certification in certain cases noted below, an offshore fund is not to be certified as a 'distributing fund' for any account period if, at any time in that period:

(*a*) more than five per cent by value of the fund's assets consists of interests in other offshore funds (but see below);

(*b*) more than ten per cent by value of the fund's assets consists of interests in a single company. For this purpose:

  (i) the value of an interest in a single company is determined as at the most recent occasion (in that or an earlier account period) on which the fund acquired an interest in that company for money or money's worth. However, an occasion is disregarded if it is one on which *s 584* (equation of original shares and new holding) applied, including that section as applied by *s 585* or *s 586* (reorganisations, conversions of securities, etc), and on which no consideration was given for the interest other than the interest in the original holding, and

  (ii) an interest is disregarded, except for determining the total value of the fund's assets, if it consists of a current or deposit account provided in the normal course of its banking business by a company whose business it is to provide such account facilities in any currency for members of the public and bodies corporate;

(*c*) the fund's assets include more than ten per cent of the issued share capital, or any class of it, in any company; or

(*d*) there is more than one class of material interests (see **32.7** above) in the fund and, were each class and the assets represented by it in a separate offshore fund, each such separate fund would not pursue a 'full distribution policy'. For this purpose, interests held solely by persons involved in the management of the fund's assets are disregarded if they carry no right or expectation to participate in profits and no right to anything other than the return of the price paid on winding-up or redemption.

Where, however, the Revenue Commissioners are satisfied that an apparent failure to comply with any of (*a*)–(*c*) above occurred inadvertently and was remedied without unreasonable delay, that failure may be disregarded.

[*TCA 1997, s 744(3)–(7), Sch 19 para 14*]

Modifications of conditions for certification. The conditions for certification in (*a*)–(*d*) above are modified in certain cases, as follows:

(A) *Investments in second tier funds.* If an offshore fund (a 'primary fund') would fail to meet the conditions in (*a*)–(*c*) above because of investments in another offshore fund (referred to below as a 'second tier fund') which could itself be certified as a qualifying distributing fund (without any modification of the conditions in (*a*)–(*c*)), then the primary fund's interests in the second tier fund are left out of account, except for determining the total value of the primary fund's assets, in establishing whether the primary fund is prevented by (*a*)–(*c*) above from being certified as a distributing fund. In addition, where the above applies, if at any time in a primary fund's account period that fund's assets include an interest in another offshore fund or in any company, and the qualifying second tier fund's assets also include an interest in that other fund or company, then the primary fund's interest is aggregated with its proportionate share of the second tier fund's interest in determining whether the primary fund is within the limits in (*a*)–(*c*) above. Its share of the second tier fund's interest is the proportion which the average value during its account period of its own holding of interests in the second tier fund bears to the average value during the period of all interests in the second tier fund; [*TCA 1997, Sch 19 paras 6, 7, 9*]

(B) *Investments in trading companies.* Where the assets of an offshore fund include an interest in a company whose business is wholly the carrying on of trade(s), the limit in (*b*) above of ten per cent of a fund's assets invested in a single company is increased to 20 per cent, and the ten per cent limit in (*c*) above on the proportion of a class of share in any company is increased to allow holdings of up to 50 per cent. For these purposes companies are excluded if their business consists to any extent of banking or moneylending or of dealing, including dealing by way of futures contracts or traded options, in commodities, currency, securities, debts or other assets of a financial nature; [*TCA 1997, Sch 19 para 10*]

(C) *Wholly-owned subsidiaries.* Where an offshore fund has a 'wholly-owned subsidiary' company, the receipts, expenditure, assets and liabilities of the fund and the subsidiary are aggregated so that the fund and the subsidiary are treated as one for the purposes of determining whether the fund is within the limits in (*a*)–(*d*) above. In the same way, the interest of the fund in the subsidiary, and any distributions or other payments between the fund and the subsidiary, are left out of account. A '*wholly-owned subsidiary*' is one owned either directly and beneficially by the fund, or directly by the trustees of the fund for the benefit of the fund, or, in a case within **32.8**(*c*) above, in some other corresponding manner. Where the subsidiary has only one class of issued share capital, ownership of at least 95 per cent of that capital by the offshore fund constitutes the subsidiary a wholly-owned subsidiary for this purpose, and only a corresponding proportion of the subsidiary's receipts, expenditure, assets and liabilities are then aggregated with those of the offshore fund; [*TCA 1997, Sch 19 para 11*]

(D)   *Subsidiary dealing and management companies.* The investment restriction in (*c*) above does not apply to so much of an offshore fund's assets as consists of share capital of a company which is either:

(1)   a wholly-owned subsidiary of the fund (as defined in (C) above) whose sole function is dealing in material interests in the offshore fund for management and administrative purposes and which is not entitled to any distribution from the fund, or

(2)   a subsidiary management company of the fund whose sole function is to provide the fund, or other funds with an interest in the company, with advisory services or administrative, management and related property-holding services on arm's length commercial terms. For the purposes of determining whether a company is a subsidiary management company of a fund, that company and any wholly-owned subsidiary companies it may itself have are regarded as a single entity; [*TCA 1997, Sch 19 para 12*]

(E)   *Disregard of certain investments.* Certain holdings which would otherwise fall within the restriction at (*c*) above are not taken into account for the purposes of that restriction. This applies where no more than five per cent of the value of the offshore fund's assets consists of such holdings and of interests in other non-qualifying offshore funds. [*TCA 1997, Sch 19 para 13*]

THE DISTRIBUTION TEST

32.10 An offshore fund pursues a '*full distribution policy*' with respect to an account period if:

(*a*)   a distribution is made for that account period or for some other period falling wholly or partly within that period;

(*b*)   subject to the modifications specified below, the distribution represents at least 85 per cent of the fund's income and is not less than 85 per cent of its 'Irish equivalent profits' for that period;

(*c*)   the distribution is made during, or within six months after the end of, the account period; and

(*d*)   the distribution is in a form such that any part of it received in RI by an RI resident which is not part of the profits of a trade, etc is chargeable under Sch D, Case III.

These conditions may equally be satisfied by any two or more distributions taken together. [*TCA 1997, Sch 19 para 1(1)*]

The conditions in (*a*)–(*d*) above are subject to modification in certain cases (see **32.11** below).

A fund is treated as pursuing a full distribution policy for any account period in which there is no income and no 'Irish equivalent profits', but it will not be so treated for any account period for which no accounts are prepared. [*TCA 1997, Sch 19 para 1(2)(3)*]

'*Irish equivalent profits*' of an offshore fund are the total profits, excluding chargeable gains, on which, after allowing for any deductions available, corporation tax would be chargeable, assuming that:

(i)   the offshore fund is an RI resident company in the account period in question;

(ii)   the account period is an accounting period of that company; and

(iii)   any dividends or distributions from RI resident companies are included.

The effect of (i) above is that certain sums received without deduction of or charge to tax on account of the fund's actual resident status are nevertheless brought into account.

The deductions referred to above include a deduction equal to that allowed against a fund's income where legal restrictions prevent distribution (see above), a deduction equal to any foreign capital tax allowed as a deduction in determining the fund's income for the account period in question, and a deduction equal to any income tax paid (by deduction or otherwise) by, and not repaid to, the fund in respect of income of the account period. [*TCA 1997, Sch 19 para 5*]

Legal restrictions on distributions. Where in an account period an offshore fund is subject to restrictions imposed by the law of any territory on making distributions by reason of an excess of losses over profits as computed according to the law in question, a deduction is allowed from the fund's income of any amount which cannot be distributed but which would otherwise form part of the fund's income for that account period. [*TCA 1997, Sch 19 para 1(6)*]

Apportionment of income and distributions between account periods. Where a period for which accounts are made up, or for which a distribution is made, covers the whole or part of two or more account periods of the fund, the income or distribution is apportioned on a time basis according to the number of days in each period. A distribution made out of specified income but not for a specified period is attributed to the account period in which the income arose. Where no period or income is specified, a distribution is treated as made for the last account period ending before the distribution. If the distribution made, or treated as made, for an account period exceeds the income of that period, the excess is reallocated to previous periods, to later periods before earlier ones, until exhausted, unless the distribution was apportioned on a time basis as above, in which case the excess is first reapportioned on a just and reasonable basis to the other account period(s). [*TCA 1997, Sch 19 para 1(4)(5)*]

MODIFICATIONS OF DISTRIBUTION TEST

32.11 The basic rules of the distribution test in **32.10**(*a*)–(*d*) above are modified in the following circumstances:

(*a*)   **Funds operating equalisation arrangements.** Where an offshore fund operates such arrangements (see **32.7** above) throughout an account period, an amount equal to any 'accrued income' which is part of the consideration for certain disposals in that period is treated as a distribution for the purposes of the distribution test. This applies to a disposal:

(i)   which is a disposal of a material interest in the fund either to the fund or to the fund managers in their capacity as such, and

(ii)   which is one to which the offshore fund rules apply (whether or not by virtue of their application to disposals from distributing funds with equalisation arrangements), or which is one to which the rules would apply if the provisions regarding the non-application of *s 584(3)* applied generally and not only for the purpose of determining whether a disposal from a distribution fund with equalisation arrangements is brought within the rules (see **32.7** above), and

(iii)   which is not a disposal within the *exception* referred to at **32.7** above (where the income of the fund is, or would be, chargeable to tax under Sch D, Case III in any event).

The '*accrued income*' is that part of the consideration which would be credited to the fund's equalisation account if the interest were resold to another person by way of initial purchase (see **32.7** above) on the same day. However, there are provisions to ensure that this accrued income figure is reduced where the interest disposed of was acquired by way of initial purchase (by any person) after the beginning of the account period by reference to which the accrued income is calculated. In addition, where an offshore commodity dealing fund (and see (*c*) below) operates equalisation and there is a disposal within (i)–(iii) above, one-half of the accrued income representing commodity profits is left out of account in determining what part of the disposal consideration represents accrued income.

For the purposes of the distribution test, the distribution which the fund is treated as making on a disposal is treated as being paid to the person disposing of his interest, in the income form required by **32.10**(*d*) above, out of the income of the fund for the account period of the disposal. Where a distribution is made to the managers (in their capacity as such) of a fund operating equalisation arrangements, it is disregarded for the purposes of the distribution test except to the extent that it relates to that part of the period for which the distribution is made during which the managers (in that capacity) held that interest. [*TCA 1997, Sch 19 paras 2, 4(4)*]

(*b*)   **Funds with income taxable under Sch D, Case III.** Where sums forming part of the income of an offshore fund within **32.8**(*b*) or (*c*) above are chargeable to tax under Sch D, Case III on the holders of interests in the funds (or would be so chargeable were the necessary residence, etc rules met), any such sums which are not actually part of a distribution complying with the part of the distribution test in **32.10**(*c*) and (*d*) above are treated as distributions which do so comply made out of the income of which they are part and paid to the holders of the interests in question; [*TCA 1997, Sch 19 para 3*]

(*c*) **Funds with commodity dealing income.** Where an offshore fund's income includes 'commodity dealing' profits, one-half of those profits is left out of account in determining the fund's income and Irish equivalent profits for the purposes of the distribution test in **32.10**(*b*) above. '*Commodities*' are defined as tangible assets dealt with on a commodity exchange, excluding currency, securities, debts or other financial assets. '*Dealing*' includes dealing by way of futures contracts and traded options. Where the fund's income includes both commodity dealing profits and other income, its expenditure is apportioned on a just and reasonable basis and the non-commodity dealing business is treated as carried on by a separate company when determining what expenditure, if any, is deductible under *s 83* (management expenses) in computing Irish equivalent profits. See also (*a*) above for position where a commodity dealing fund operates equalisation arrangements; [*TCA 1997, Sch 19 para 4*]

(*d*) **Wholly-owned commodity dealing subsidiaries.** In a situation within **32.9**(C) above, the fund and the subsidiary dealing company are similarly treated as a single entity for the purposes of the distribution test; [*TCA 1997, Sch 19 para 11*]

(*e*) **Investments in second tier funds.** In a situation within **32.9**(A) above, the Irish equivalent profits of the primary fund for the period are increased by its 'share' of the 'excess income' (if any) of the second tier fund in determining whether not less than 85 per cent of the primary fund's Irish equivalent profits are distributed. The '*excess income*' of the second tier fund is the amount by which its Irish equivalent profits exceed its distributions. There are provisions for apportioning excess income between periods on a time basis when the account periods of the primary and second tier funds do not coincide. The primary fund's '*share*' of the excess income is the proportion which the average value during its account period of its own holding of interests in the second tier fund bears to the average value of all interests in that fund. [*TCA 1997, Sch 19 paras 6, 8, 9*]

CERTIFICATION PROCEDURE

32.12 Fund requesting certification. Application for certification as a distributing fund for an account period must be made within six months of the end of that period. The application must be accompanied by a copy of the fund's accounts covering or including the account period for which certification is sought, and the Revenue Commissioners must be furnished with such information as they may reasonably require for that purpose. If they are satisfied that nothing in *TCA 1997, s 744(2)(3)* (see **32.9** above) prevents certification, the fund will be certified as a distributing fund for that period. Certification may be withdrawn retrospectively if it subsequently appears to the Revenue Commissioners that the accounts or information supplied do not fully and accurately disclose all the relevant facts and considerations.

An appeal may be made to the Appeal Commissioners against a refusal or withdrawal of certification within 30 days of the date of the relevant notice. The normal income tax appeal provisions apply generally to any such appeal. [*TCA 1997, Sch 19 paras 15, 16*]

Investor requesting certification. No appeal may be brought against an assessment (see **32.13** below) on the grounds that a fund should have been certified as a distributing fund in respect of an account period. However, where a fund does not apply for certification, an investor who is assessed to tax for which he would not be liable if the fund were certified may by notice in writing require the Revenue Commissioners to take action with a view to determining whether the fund should be so certified. If more than one such request is received, the Revenue Commissioners are taken to have complied with each if they comply with one.

Broadly, the procedure is as follows:

(i)   The Revenue Commissioners invite the fund to apply for certification. The time limit for application (see above) is then extended, if necessary, to 90 days from the date of the Board's invitation;

(ii) If the fund does not then apply for certification, the Revenue Commissioners must determine the question as if such application had been made, having regard to any accounts or information provided by the investor;

(iii) If, after the Revenue Commissioners have determined that the fund should not be certified, other accounts or information are provided which were not previously available, the Revenue Commissioners must reconsider their determination;

(iv) The Revenue Commissioners must notify the investor who requested them to take action of their decision;

(v)   The Revenue Commissioners have wide powers enabling them to disclose to interested parties information regarding their, or the Appeal Commissioners', decisions or details of any notice given to a fund regarding a lack of full and accurate disclosure of information (see above).

[*TCA 1997, Sch 19 paras 17–20*]

CHARGE TO INCOME OR CORPORATION TAX ON OFFSHORE INCOME GAIN

32.13 Where a disposal to which the offshore fund rules apply gives rise to an 'offshore income gain' (see **32.14** below), then (subject to below) that gain is treated for all purposes as income assessable under Sch D, Case IV arising to the investor at the time of the disposal.

The following provisions have effect in relation to income tax or corporation tax on offshore income gains as they have in relation to capital gains tax:

(*a*)   *ss 29, 30* (persons chargeable) except that:

(i)   in the case of non-residents carrying on a trade in RI through a branch or agency, the requirement that assets be situated in RI does not apply, and

(ii)   in the case of individuals resident and ordinarily resident but not domiciled in RI, *s 29(4)(5)* have effect as they do in respect of gains from assets situated outside RI;

(*b*)   *s 25(2)(b)* (gains accruing to non-resident companies carrying on a trade in RI through a branch or agency).

Charitable exemption applies similarly to that for capital gains tax (see **9.7(***l***)** 'Capital gains tax').

Where a disposal to which the offshore fund rules apply is one of settled property, any offshore income gain will escape the Sch D, Case IV charge provided that the general administration of the trust is ordinarily carried on outside RI and a majority of the trustees is not resident or ordinarily resident in RI. [*TCA 1997, s 745*]

See, however, **32.15** below as to offshore funds in certain offshore States.

COMPUTATION OF OFFSHORE INCOME GAIN

32.14 The computation of the gain depends upon whether the disposal is of an interest in a non-qualifying fund or of an interest involving an equalisation element.

Disposals of interests in non-qualifying funds. A '*material disposal*' (ie one to which the offshore fund rules apply otherwise than by virtue of the provisions regarding distributing funds operating equalisation arrangements (see **32.7** above and further below)), gives rise to an '*offshore income gain*', ie a gain of an amount equal to the 'unindexed gain' or, if less, the 'post-6 April 1990 gain'.

Subject to the modification to the capital gains tax rules mentioned in **32.6** above and to the exceptions detailed below, the '*unindexed gain*' is the gain calculated under capital gains tax rules without indexation allowance and without regard to any income tax or corporation tax charge arising under the offshore fund rules. The exceptions are as follows:

(*a*)   if the material disposal forms part of a transfer to which *s 600* (rollover relief on transfer of business to company) applies, the unindexed gain is computed without any deduction falling to be made under that section in computing a chargeable gain;

(*b*)   where the computation of the unindexed gain would otherwise produce a loss, the unindexed gain is treated as nil, so that no loss can arise on a material disposal.

[*TCA 1997, Sch 20 paras 1–3, 5*]

Post-6 April 1990 gains. A person making a material disposal who acquired, or is treated as having acquired, his interest in the offshore fund before 6 April 1990, is treated as having disposed of and immediately reacquired his interest at market value on that date. The offshore income gain from 6 April 1990 to the date of disposal is then calculated in the ordinary way. If the person making the material disposal acquired his interest after 5 April 1990 by way of a deemed no gain/no loss disposal (other than by virtue of the indexation provisions of *s 556(4)*), the previous owner's acquisition of the interest is treated as his acquisition of it, and this provision may continue to apply to earlier owners where they in turn acquired the interest after 5 April 1990. [*TCA 1997, Sch 20 para 4*]

Disposals involving an equalisation element. A disposal to which the offshore fund rules apply by virtue of the provisions relating to distributing funds operating equalisation arrangements (see **32.7** above) (a *'disposal involving an equalisation element'*) gives rise to an offshore income gain of an amount equal, subject to below, to the 'equalisation element' relevant to the asset disposed of. [*TCA 1997, Sch 20 para 6(1)(3)*]

The *'equalisation element'* is the amount which would be credited to the fund's equalisation account in respect of accrued income if, on the date of the disposal, the asset disposed of were acquired by another person by way of 'initial purchase' (see **32.7** above). However, where the person making the disposal acquired the asset in question after the beginning of the account period by reference to which the accrued income is calculated, or at or before the beginning of that period where that period straddles 6 April 1990, there are provisions to ensure that the equalisation element is reduced to exclude any part which accrued prior to either 6 April 1990 or the investor's period of ownership. Where any of the accrued income represents commodity dealing profits (see **32.11**(*c*) above) one-half of that income is left out of account in determining the equalisation element. [*TCA 1997, Sch 20 para 6(2)(4)–(6)*]

Part I gains. Where the offshore income gain as computed above would exceed the 'Part I gain', the offshore income gain is reduced to the lower figure. If there is no 'Part I gain', there can be no offshore income gain. The *'Part I gain'* is, broadly, the amount which would be the offshore income gain on the disposal if it were a material disposal within the rules in *Sch 20 paras 1–5* described above, as modified by certain consequential amendments. [*TCA 1997, Sch 20 paras 7, 8*]

MISCELLANEOUS

32.15 Offshore income gains accruing to persons resident or domiciled abroad. There are consequential provisions made in connection with gains accruing to certain non-resident investors in offshore funds, which modify, for the purposes of the offshore funds legislation, provisions relating to:

(*a*)   gains of non-resident settlements under *ss 579, 579A* (see **9.17** 'Capital gains tax');

(*b*)   chargeable gains accruing to certain non-resident companies under *s 590* (see **9.17** 'Capital gains tax'); and

(*c*)   avoidance of tax by the transfer of assets abroad under *ss 806, 807* (see **3.8** 'Anti-avoidance legislation').

To the extent that an offshore income gain is treated by virtue of (*a*) or (*b*) above as having accrued to any person resident or ordinarily resident in RI, that gain is not deemed to be the income of any individual under *ss 806* or *807* or any provision of *Pt 31* (settlements).

Finance Act 2010, s 31 inserts a new *Pt 27, Ch 5*. This sets out the tax treatment of a relevant UCITS. It ensures that an investment undertaking formed under the law of a Member State other than Ireland will not be liable to tax in Ireland by reason only of having a management company that is authorised under Irish law. A relevant UCITS is defined as an undertaking for collective investment in transferable securities that is subject to the EU UCITS Directive, formed under the laws of an EU Member State other than Ireland, whose management company is authorised as a management company under Irish regulations, and which would not be liable to tax in Ireland if its management company were not authorised under Irish regulations.

The section provides that a relevant UCITS is not chargeable to tax in Ireland in respect of its relevant profits. It also provides that unit holders in a relevant UCITS are to be treated in the same manner as unit holders in an offshore fund. [*TCA 1997, s 746, Pt 27 Ch 5; FA 1999, s 58; FA 2010, s 31*]

Capital gains tax rate. Where there is a disposal of a 'material interest' in an 'offshore fund' (see **32.8** above), which is not, and has not at any 'material time' (see **32.6** above) been, a 'non-qualifying offshore fund' (see **32.9** above), the rate of tax on any chargeable gain arising is **40 per cent**, notwithstanding the general reduction in the rate of capital gains tax from 3 December 1997 (see **9.3** 'Capital gains tax'). This applies equally to a disposal of an interest in an RI-resident company or unit trust scheme which, at a material time after 31 December 1990, was an offshore fund other than a non-qualifying offshore fund, where the interest constituted a material interest in that fund. [*TCA 1997, s 747A; FA 1998, s 66*]

Deduction of offshore income gain in determining capital gain. There are provisions to prevent a double charge to tax when a disposal gives rise to both an offshore income gain and a chargeable gain for capital gains tax purposes.

Where an offshore income gain arises on a 'material disposal' within **32.14** above, the gain is deducted from the sum which would otherwise constitute the amount or value of the consideration in the calculation of the capital gain arising on the disposal under the *Capital Gains Tax Acts*, although the offshore income gain is not to be taken into account in calculating the fraction under *s 557* (part disposals).

Where the *Capital Gains Tax Acts* disposal forms part of a transfer within *s 600* (rollover relief on transfer of business to company) then, in determining the amount of the deduction from the gain on the old assets, the offshore income gain is deducted from the value of the consideration received in exchange for the business.

Where an exchange of shares or securities constitutes a disposal of an interest in an offshore fund (see **32.6**, **32.7** above), the amount of any offshore income gain to which the disposal gives rise is treated as consideration for the new holding.

Where the offshore fund provisions apply to a disposal of an interest in a fund operating equalisation arrangements (see **32.7** above) and the disposal:

(*a*)   is not to the fund or to its managers in their capacity as such;

(*b*)   gives rise to an offshore income gain in accordance with **32.14** above; and

(*c*)   is followed subsequently by a distribution to either the person who made the disposal or to a person connected with him (within *s 10*) and that distribution is referable to the asset disposed of;

then the subsequent distribution (or distributions) is (are) reduced by the amount of the offshore income gain. [*TCA 1997, s 747*]

Offshore funds in certain offshore States. With effect from 1 January 2001, a special regime applies to RI residents holding an interest in an offshore fund which either (*a*) being a company, is resident in another EU Member State, an EEA State or a State which is an OECD member with which RI has a double tax treaty, or (*b*) being a unit trust scheme, the trustees are so resident, or (*c*) being arrangements within *s 743(1)* (see **32.8**(*c*) above), those arrangements take effect by virtue of the law of such a State. An RI resident acquiring such an interest is deemed to be a chargeable person within self-assessment (see **28.11** 'Returns') and must make, and include details of the acquisition in, a tax return. Broadly, the provisions assimilate the tax treatment of holders of such interests to that applicable to investors in domestic funds. Since 3 February 2005, losses on disposal of units are not relievable for tax purposes. [*TCA 1997, ss 747B–747F; FA 2001, s 72; FA 2002, s 46; FA 2003, s 55; FA 2004, s 30; FA 2005, s 43*]

33 Schedule D, Case V – Property Income

33.1 Tax is charged under Sch D, Case V in respect of rent for any premises in RI and receipts for any easement (not falling under *s 104*, see **33.7** below) which are deemed to arise from a single source. The basis of assessment is as for Sch D, Case III (**31**) [*TCA 1997, s 75*].

See **38.147** 'Tax cases' regarding rental income falling within Sch D, Case I. See **16.21** 'Exempt income and special savings schemes' for rent-a-room relief.

33.2 Computation is on the aggregate of gross rents receivable *less* (i) any rent payable in respect of the premises by the lessor; (ii) any rates borne by him; (iii) (except as below) interest on borrowed money used to purchase, improve or repair the premises; (iv) the cost to the lessor of goods or services (other than maintenance and repairs) which he is bound by the lease to provide and for which no separate consideration is receivable; and (v) the cost to him of maintenance, repairs, insurance and management. [*TCA 1997, s 97*] But (i) or (iii) (the rent payable or interest on borrowed moneys to purchase, improve or repair premises) will not be an allowable deduction to the lessor *for any period prior to the first occupation by a lessee* (as to which see **38.180** 'Tax cases'). [*TCA 1997, s 105*] See **33.8** below.

Industrial buildings allowances are claimable against income [*TCA 1997, s 278*] but may be ring-fenced in certain circumstances – see **8.1** 'Capital allowances'. Machinery and plant wear and tear allowances (see **8.6** 'Capital allowances') may also be available in relation to *bona fide* commercial furnished lettings. [*TCA 1997, ss 284(7), 406; FA 2001, s 62(1)(b)*]

Accountancy fees incurred for preparing a rent account are an allowable deduction, but a limit of ten per cent of gross rents is imposed on any deduction for landlord's salary for managing premises in the case of rental companies. Mortgage protection plan premiums are treated by the Revenue Commissioners as a cost of managing the premises. For these and other aspects of management expenses, see Revenue Tax Briefing Issue 25 p 11 and Issue 53 p 16.

There are anti-avoidance measures relating to the sale by an individual of the right to receive rental income in consideration of payment of a capital sum. The capital sum is subject to income tax at the marginal rate in the year of receipt or entitlement to receipt and any profit or gain arising from the right to receive rent is taxable in the hands of the recipient as rent under Sch D, Case V. These measures are effective for capital sums received **on or after 6 February 2003**. [*FA 2003, s 36*]

Restriction on relief for interest. As regards (iii) above, **from 2006** (in the case of companies, accounting periods commencing on or after 1 January 2006) no interest relief is available unless the claimant can show that the registration requirements of the *Residential Tenancies Act 2004, Pt 7* have been complied with in respect of all tenancies relating to the premises for the chargeable period. For this purpose, written confirmation from the Private Residential Tenancies Board to the claimant confirming the registration of the tenancy is acceptable as evidence of compliance with the registration requirement. [*FA 2006, s 11*] Subject to the exceptions referred to below, for interest accruing **before 1 January 2002** (treating interest as accruing from day to day), no deduction is available for interest on money employed after 22 April 1998 in the purchase, improvement or repair of premises which, at any time in the tax year, are '*residential premises*' (ie any building or part used or suitable for use as a dwelling and any outoffice, yard, garden or other land appurtenant to or usually enjoyed with that building or part). A just and reasonable apportionment is made where only a part of the premises consists of residential premises. The restriction does not, however, apply:

(*a*)   to interest on money employed on or before 31 March 1999 in the purchase of residential premises under a contract evidenced in writing before 23 April 1998;

(*b*)   to interest on money employed in the improvement or repair of residential premises in respect of which, on 23 April 1998 or during the previous twelve months, any person was entitled to a rent or receipts from any easements, where the person chargeable either had an estate or interest in the premises on that day or is or would be entitled by virtue of (*a*) above to a deduction under (iii) above for interest on borrowed money employed in their purchase;

(*c*)   where the premises consist of a holiday cottage to which *s 352* applies, or a registered holiday apartment or other listed self-catering accommodation within *s 353*, or of qualifying premises within *ss 356, 357* or *358* (qualifying resort areas, see **8.11** 'Capital allowances', **33.12** 'Sch D, Case V');

(*d*)   where the premises (not being within (*c*) above) are within a qualifying rural area (see **8.12** 'Capital allowances');

(*e*)   where the premises (not being within (*c*) or (*d*) above) consist of a holiday cottage, holiday apartment or other self-catering accommodation, either registered under *Tourist Traffic Act 1939, Pt III* or specified in a list under *Tourist Traffic Act 1957, s 9*, in respect of which an application for planning permission for development was received by a planning authority before 23 April 1998, and was granted subject to a condition (in force during the tax year) that the premises may not be used by any person for residential use in excess of two consecutive calendar months at any one time; or

(*f*)   where (i) the premises were converted into multiple residential units before 1 October 1964, (ii) they were acquired under a contract evidenced in writing after 4 January 2001 and the number of residential units is not subsequently reduced by more than 50 per cent (and there are at least three such units throughout the year of assessment in question), and (iii) certain conditions as to the proportion of units let for social housing are satisfied. (In support of (i), the Revenue will accept a sworn affidavit from the previous owner of the property, produced by the vendor's solicitor on conveyance, confirming that the property was in fact so converted (see Revenue Tax Briefing Issue 45 p 19).)

For these purposes, borrowed money employed after 22 April 1998 on the construction of a building (or part) for use, or suitable for use, as a dwelling, on land in which the person chargeable had an estate or interest, together with any borrowed money which that person employed in the acquisition of the land, is deemed to be borrowed money employed in the purchase of residential premises. Where this applies, (*a*) above applies only where:

(A)   the money was employed on or before 31 March 1999;

(B)   the person chargeable had, before 23 April 1998, an estate or interest in land (or a contract evidenced in writing to acquire such an estate or interest); and

(C)   in respect of any building (or part) for use, or suitable for use, as a dwelling to be constructed on that land, the person chargeable had either entered into a contract evidenced in writing before 23 April 1998 for the construction of that building (or part) or, if no such contract exists, satisfies the Revenue Commissioners that the foundations were laid in their entirety before that date.

Where any premises are, at any time after 22 April 1998, the sole or main residence of a person chargeable in respect of those premises, no deduction under (iii) above is allowed for any interest payable for any year or part year commencing after the date on which the premises cease to be the sole or main residence of that person.

These restrictions **cease to apply from 1 January 2002**, but **since 6 February 2003** the restrictions apply to interest accruing from that date on borrowings used to purchase a residential premises from a spouse.

There is a further restriction on interest on borrowed money used to purchase, improve or repair a rented premises, which can be deducted in computing the amount of taxable rental income as introduced in *FA 2009*. Where the borrowed money is used to purchase, improve or repair a residential premises, only 75 per cent of the interest on the borrowings can now be deducted instead of the normal 100 per cent. [*FA 2009, s 5*]

[*TCA 1997, s 97(2A)–(2G)*; *F(No 2)A 1998, s 1(1)*; *FA 1999, s 31*; *FA 2001, s 34*; *FA 2002, s 17(a)*; *FA 2003, s 16*]

33.3 Farm land. A deduction may be allowed from the total income of a 'qualifying lessor' of 'farm land'. Where total income includes profits or gains chargeable under Sch D, Case V, and in computing the amount of those profits or gains a surplus arising from rent from any farm land let under a 'qualifying lease' has been taken into account, a deduction is allowed to the lessor of the lesser of:

(*a*)   the 'specified amount' in relation to the surplus; and

(*b*)   the amount of the profits or gains chargeable under Sch D, Case V.

The deduction is treated as if it were a personal allowance.

A *'qualifying lessor'* is an individual aged 40 or more (prior to 1 January 2004, 55 or more), or permanently incapacitated by reason of physical or mental infirmity from carrying on a trade of farming, who has not, after 30 January 1985, leased the farm land in question (with or without others) from a connected person (within *s 10*) (with or without others) on other than arm's length terms.

'Farm land' is land in RI occupied wholly or mainly for husbandry, including a building (other than a dwelling) on the land used for farming that land.

A *'qualifying lease'* is a lease of farm land in (or evidenced in) writing, for a definite term of five years or more, made on an arm's length basis between qualifying lessor(s) and 'qualifying lessee(s)'.

A '*qualifying lessee*' is an individual not connected (see above) with the qualifying lessor (or with any of the qualifying lessors), who uses the leased farm land for a trade of farming he carries on solely or in partnership.

The *specified amount* in relation to a surplus is the amount of that surplus (or aggregate amount of such surpluses), limited to:

(i)   from 1 January 2007, €15,000 for leases for a definite term of seven years or more and €12,000 for leases between seven and ten years and €20,000 for leases in excess of ten years;

(ii)   from 1 January 2006, €15,000 for leases for a definite term of seven years or more and €12,000 for all other leases;

(iii)   from 1 January 2004 to 31 December 2005, €10,000 for leases for a definite term of seven years or more and €7,500 for all other leases;

(iv)   €7,618.43/£6,000 for leases for a definite term of seven years or more under contracts made between 23 January 1996 and 31 December 2003 (€5,078.95/ £4,000) for such leases under contracts made after 29 January 1991 and before 23 January 1996);

(v)   €5,078.95/£4,000 for leasing contracts taken out after 22 January 1996 not within (ii) above (€3,809.21/£3,000) for such contracts taken out after 29 January 1991 and before 23 January 1996);

(vi)   €3,555.27/£2,800 for leasing contracts taken out between 20 January 1987 and 31 December 1987; and

(vii) €2,539.48/£2,000 in any other case;

subject to an overall limit for a qualifying lessor of €15,000 (€12,000), €10,000 (€7,500), €7,618.43 (€5,078.95), €5,078.95 (€3,809.21), €3,555.27 or €2,539.48 as appropriate.

The specified amount is proportionately reduced when the rent(s) taken into account are less than the rent(s) receivable for a full year.

Where a wife's income is, by election, treated as that of her husband, the deduction under these provisions is determined separately in relation to each spouse's income.

Since 1 January 2005, payments under the EU Single Payment Scheme operated by the Department of Agriculture under Council Regulation (EC) No 1782/2003 of 29 September 2003 are treated as rent from farm land. There are provisions for apportionment by the inspector where a qualifying lease relates partly to farm land and partly to any other goods, property or services, so that only the part of the surplus properly attributable to the farm land attracts relief. His decision is subject to review by the Appeal Commissioners or Circuit Court on appeal. The inspector has power to require the lessor to furnish such information as the inspector considers necessary. [*TCA 1997, s 664; FA 2004, s 14; FA 2006, s 12*]

33.4 Residential premises. In computing rental income, a deduction may be allowed for certain expenditure incurred between 29 January 1981 and 31 March 1987 inclusive or between 27 January 1988 and 31 March 1992 inclusive (the '*qualifying periods*') on the construction of premises for rent. The deduction is allowed for the period in which the premises are first let under a 'qualifying lease'.

The qualifying period was extended to 31 July 1992 where expenditure was incurred on the construction of qualifying premises the foundations of which were completed before 29 January 1992.

To qualify, the premises must consist of a building or part of a building (together with any outhouses, gardens, etc):

(i) used solely as a dwelling;

(ii) of floor area not less than 30 sq metres or more than 90 sq metres (75 sq metres for expenditure incurred before 1 April 1984) in the case of a self-contained flat or maisonette in a building of two or more storeys (but restricted to 75 sq metres in relation to expenditure before 1 April 1987 unless it contains three or more rooms designed and constructed as, and suitable for use as, bedrooms); or of not less than 35 sq metres or more than 125 sq metres in any other case;

(iii) in respect of which, if it is not a new house (within *Housing (Miscellaneous Provisions) Act 1979, s 4*), there is in force a 'certificate of reasonable cost', granted by the Minister of the Environment and Local Government, in which the construction cost specified is not less than that actually incurred; or, in the case of a new house provided for sale in respect of which a claim was made before 23 May 1984, a 'certificate of reasonable value', as defined in the *Housing (Miscellaneous Provisions) Act 1979, s 18*, in which the amount stated to be the reasonable value of the house is not less than the net price paid for the house;

(iv) first let (without having previously been used) in its entirety under a 'qualifying lease' and continuing to be so let throughout the ten years following the first letting (ignoring reasonable temporary void periods between lettings);

(v) open to inspection by persons authorised in writing by the Minister of the Environment and Local Government at all reasonable times; and

(vi) complying with such conditions as to construction standards and services as the Minister may lay down under the *Housing (Miscellaneous Provisions) Act 1979, s 4*.

Premises occupied by a person 'connected with' (as defined by *s 10*) the person claiming the deduction do not qualify unless the terms of the lease are such as might have been expected to result from arm's length negotiations.

A *'qualifying lease'* is one granted in consideration of rent payments falling within Sch D, Case V, with any premium not exceeding ten per cent of the 'relevant cost' of the premises. Specifically excluded, however, are leases under the terms of which anyone can at any time directly or indirectly acquire an interest in the premises at less than market value.

'Relevant cost' is the aggregate of expenditure on both land and construction (with any necessary apportionment of expenditure on larger projects, see below).

In relation to expenditure incurred after 31 March 1984 and before 1 April 1987, the deduction allowed in any chargeable period (year of assessment for income tax, accounting period for corporation tax) in respect of qualifying premises is restricted to the amount of rent from those premises. See below as regards the necessary apportionments. Unallowed expenditure is carried forward to the next and subsequent chargeable periods as if incurred in such periods, but subject to the same overall restriction on allowance to gross rent.

The **allowable expenditure** is that incurred in the 'qualifying period' on the construction of the premises, which includes that incurred on the development of the land (including gardens, access, etc) such as costs of demolition, groundworks, landscaping, walls and mains supplies, and any other buildings for use by the occupants of the premises. Where, however, a premium or like sum is payable directly or indirectly to the lessor or to any person 'connected with' him (as defined by *s 10*), and all or part of it is not treated as rent under Sch D, Case V, the allowable expenditure is reduced by the amount of the premium, etc not treated as rent, or, where any part of the construction cost falls outside the 'qualifying period', to the same proportion of the premium, etc as the allowable expenditure bears to the whole construction cost. Such a reduction for a period straddling 31 March 1984 is allocated to the part falling on or before and the part falling after that date in proportion to expenditure treated as incurred in each part.

Any question of whether (or how much) expenditure was actually incurred in the 'qualifying period' (or in the part thereof falling after 31 March 1984) on construction work or land development is to be determined by the inspector, subject to review on appeal to the Appeal Commissioners or Circuit Court. Where qualifying premises form part of a building or consist of a building which is part only of a larger development, any necessary apportionment of cost is similarly determined, both for this purpose and in determining 'relevant cost' (see above).

Any allowance given under these provisions is treated as rent received by the person to whom the allowance was given if the **premises cease to qualify**, or if ownership of the interest in the lease passes to any other person, within ten years after the first letting. If ownership of the interest passes but the premises continue to qualify, the new owner of the interest is entitled to the same deduction as was granted to the original lessor, but ignoring any reduction in respect of a premium, etc (see above), and limited to the '*relevant price*' paid by the new owner. This is the same proportion of the total price paid by him as the allowable construction expenditure by the original lessor bore to the 'relevant cost' of the premises, see above. For the purposes of restriction of relief (see above) in respect of expenditure actually incurred on qualifying premises in a period straddling 31 March 1984, but partly on or before and partly after that date, the deduction granted to the new lessor is treated as incurred on or before and after that date in proportion to the actual expenditure incurred in each part.

In practice, where the interest passes on death to the spouse of the owner of the interest (and the spouse was not the assessable spouse for the year of death), an offset is permitted of the deduction due to the surviving spouse against the amount assessable on the deceased spouse in the year of death (see Revenue Tax Briefing Issue 23 pp 15, 16).

Where premises on which expenditure was incurred in the 'qualifying period' are sold unused, the buyer (or, if the premises are sold unused more than once, the last such buyer) is treated as having in that period incurred construction expenditure equal to:

(i)   if the original expenditure was incurred as a trading expense by a builder, the lesser of the 'relevant price' (see above) paid to the builder and that paid on the last sale unused;

(ii)   in any other case, the lesser of the allowable expenditure actually incurred on construction of the premises and the 'relevant price' on the last sale unused.

Expenditure is apportioned, where necessary, as for the new lessor of qualifying premises in the preceding paragraph.

Expenditure on **conversion** into two or more dwellings of a building, not in use as a dwelling or in use as a single dwelling prior to the conversion, will similarly qualify for relief as if the expenditure had been incurred on the construction of the premises, with necessary modifications to the scheme of relief. Planning permission must have been obtained. The restriction of relief to the amount of the rent arising from the premises in a chargeable period applies to conversion expenditure incurred after 26 January 1988 and before 1 April 1992 as it applies generally to earlier expenditure (but see below as to certain urban renewal reliefs). [*TCA 1997, Sch 32 para 14; FA 1981, ss 23, 24; FA 1983, ss 29, 30; FA 1984, s 37; FA 1988, s 27; FA 1991, s 56; FA 1992, s 34(a)(ii)*]

For expenditure incurred between 1 April 1985 and 31 March 1987 inclusive or between 27 January 1988 and 31 March 1992 inclusive (and not met directly or indirectly by the State or any statutory body or public or local authority), relief is further extended to:

(*a*)   expenditure on the conversion into a dwelling of a building not previously in use as a dwelling; and

(*b*)   expenditure in the course of a conversion on 'refurbishment' (see **33.5** below), but excluding expenditure attributable to any part of the building which, on completion of the conversion, is not a dwelling (with any necessary apportionment of overall expenditure being made on the basis of floor area), or which otherwise attracts relief under any other provision of the *Tax Acts*.

The extended reliefs applicable to expenditure on urban renewal (see below) apply equally for these purposes. 'Refurbishment' is defined slightly differently in relation to buildings in the Temple Bar Area, to require that the work be in character with the existing building, and for this purpose all conversion work is treated as refurbishment.

[*TCA 1997, Sch 32 para 14; FA 1985, s 22; FA 1988, s 29; FA 1991, ss 56(2), 58; FA 1992, s 34(c); FA 1993, s 32(c)*]

Urban renewal. The above reliefs are extended in the case of qualifying premises on a site wholly within the Custom House Docks Area (as designated in *Sch 5* or by subsequent order, see *SI 466/99*) to include expenditure incurred in the period 25 January 1988 to **31 December 1999** inclusive. The reliefs are also extended in the other areas designated by *FA 1986, Sch 4 Pts III–VII* (or by subsequent order under *FA 1987, s 27*) to include expenditure incurred up to 31 July 1994 (and where at least 15 per cent of the total construction expenditure on qualifying premises was certified before 24 February 1994 by the relevant local authority (under the relevant guidelines) to have been incurred before 26 January 1994, further such expenditure incurred between 1 August and 31 December 1994 inclusive is treated as having been incurred in the qualifying period), and in the Temple Bar Area (see *Sch 6*) to include expenditure on buildings approved by Temple Bar Renewal Ltd incurred up to **5 April 1999** (31 December 1999 in certain cases where substantial expenditure had been incurred by 5 April 1999). In relation to expenditure on conversions (as above), the restriction of allowances to the amount of rent arising from the premises in a chargeable period does not apply to expenditure in any of the above areas after 29 January 1991. For expenditure incurred after 25 January 1994 on the conversion of flats and maisonettes in the Custom House Docks and Temple Bar Areas, the maximum permissible floor area is increased from 90 to 125 square metres, and from 12 April 1995 this applies also to construction expenditure. From 2007, the quantum of relief available to a high income earning individual may be limited in any one year, see **2.45** 'Limitation on Investment Relief' [*TCA 1997, ss 322, 325, 326, 329, 330, 334, 335, 338, 372AU, Sch 32 para 14; FA 1986, ss 41, 43, Sch 4; FA 1987, s 27; FA 1991, ss 56, 58; FA 1992, ss 29(a), 34(a)(c); FA 1993, s 32(a); SI 314/88; FA 1994, ss 36, 37(b)(d); FA 1995, ss 32(1)(a), 33, 34(1)(a)(c)(2); Urban Renewal Act 1998, s 20(1)(a)(2); FA 1999, ss 42, 43; SI 465/ 99; FA 2002, s 24(3), Sch 2 para 1*]. See also **33.11** below and **2.27** 'Allowances, credits and rates', **8.10** 'Capital allowances' and **30.24** 'Sch D, Cases I and II'.

33.5 Refurbishment of residential premises. The provisions described at **33.4** above apply *mutatis mutandis* to expenditure incurred between 1 April 1985 and 31 March 1987 inclusive or between 27 January 1988 and 31 March 1992 inclusive on the 'refurbishment' of a building in which, prior to that refurbishment, there are two or more dwellings and which, after refurbishment, contains two or more dwellings. They do not, however, apply to expenditure attributable to any part of the building which, after the refurbishment, is not a dwelling (with any necessary apportionment of overall expenditure being made on the basis of floor area). Relief is given as if the refurbishment expenditure was expenditure on the construction of the building.

'*Refurbishment*' means either or both of:

(*a*) the carrying out of works of construction, reconstruction, repair or renewal; and

(*b*) the provision or improvement of water, sewerage or heating facilities;

provided that the Minister for the Environment and Local Government grants a certificate of reasonable cost certifying that the work was necessary to ensure the suitability as a dwelling of any house in the building. It is not relevant whether or not the number of dwellings in the building, or the shape or size of any such dwelling, is altered in the course of the refurbishment.

Relief is *not* available unless any required planning permission is obtained, and is also denied where the expenditure is met directly or indirectly by the State or by any statutory board or public or local authority, or is otherwise relieved under any other provision of the *Tax Acts*.

Specific variations to the provisions described at **33.4** above include the following:

(i) The reference to a premium, etc in the definition of 'qualifying lease' is to a premium, etc payable after completion of refurbishment, or payable before completion in connection with the refurbishment. Market value is substituted for 'relevant cost' in the definition;

(ii) References to the first letting of the premises are to the letting on completion of the refurbishment or, if not then let, to the first subsequent letting;

(iii)   References to the 'relevant price' are to the net price paid on sale or, if only a proportion of the refurbishment expenditure falls to be treated as having been incurred in the qualifying period, that proportion of the net price paid on sale;

(iv)   The restriction of relief to the amount of the rent arising from the premises in a chargeable period applies to refurbishment expenditure incurred after 26 January 1988 and before 1 April 1992 as it applies generally to earlier expenditure (but see below as to certain urban renewal reliefs).

The extended urban renewal reliefs detailed at **33.4** above apply equally for these purposes. In the Temple Bar Area, a slightly different definition of 'refurbishment' applies, requiring the work to be in character with the building.

From 2007, the quantum of the above reliefs available to a high income earning individual may be limited in any one year, see **2.45** 'Limitation on Investment Relief'.

[*TCA 1997, ss 322, 327–329, 330, 336–338, 372AU, Sch 32 para 14*; *FA 1985, s 21*; *FA 1988, s 28*; *FA 1991, s 57*; *FA 1992, s 34(b)*; *FA 1993, s 32(b)*; *FA 1994, s 37(c)(d)*; *FA 1995, s 34(1)(a)(d)*; *Urban Renewal Act 1998, s 20(1)(a)(2)*, *FA 1999, ss 42, 43*; *SI 465/99*; *FA 2002, s 24(3), Sch 2 para 1*]

33.6 Premiums etc payable under the terms of a lease not exceeding 50 years (including cost of works so required to be borne by the lessee) are treated as additional rent then due equal to the premium reduced by one-fiftieth for each complete year (other than the first) comprised in the lease. Where a premium is payable other than to the lessor, the assessment is under Sch D, Case IV on the recipient. Sums received for waiver, surrender, assignment at undervalue, etc are included. Sums so taxable on the recipient are treated as rent paid by the payer. [*TCA 1997, ss 98, 102, 103*] For assignments of short leases and sales with terms of reconveyance, see *ss 99, 100*.

Where a premium is payable by instalments, the tax chargeable may be paid by agreed instalments over a period not exceeding eight years before the last of the premium instalments is payable if the Revenue Commissioners are satisfied that undue hardship would otherwise be caused. [*TCA 1997, s 98(8)*]

'Premium' includes any like sum, whether payable to the immediate or a superior lessor or to a person connected with either of them. [*TCA 1997, s 96(1)*]

The duration of a lease is determined by provisions under *s 96(2)*.

Provision is made for both lessors and lessees (and any other affected person) to take part in appeal proceedings to determine the taxable amount of any premium. [*TCA 1997, s 947*]

For a case involving a sale and lease-back avoidance scheme, see **38.115** 'Tax cases'.

Reverse premiums. A '*reverse premium*' is a payment or other benefit received **on or after 7 June 2001** by way of inducement in connection with a '*relevant transaction*' (ie a transaction under which a person is granted an estate or interest in, or a right in or over, land) being entered into by the person receiving the payment etc (or a connected person within *s 10*). For tax purposes, a reverse premium is regarded as a receipt of a revenue nature. Where a relevant transaction is entered into by a person receiving a reverse premium for the purposes of a trade or profession carried on (or to be carried on) by that person, the amount or value of the reverse premium is to be taken into account as a trade or professional receipt by that person under Sch D, Case I or II. Otherwise (and subject to the special treatment in the case of assurance companies, see below), the amount or value of the premium is treated as if it were an amount of rent.

Where two or more parties to the '*relevant arrangements*' (ie the relevant transaction and any arrangements entered into in connection with it at any time) are connected (within *s 10*) and the terms of those arrangements are not such as would reasonably have been expected at arm's length, the full amount or value of the reverse premium is treated as accruing in the chargeable period in which the relevant transaction is entered into or, where appropriate, the first chargeable period of the trade or profession which the recipient subsequently begins to carry on and for the purposes of which the relevant transaction was entered into. Otherwise, it is understood that a reverse premium is chargeable in accordance with the accepted principles of commercial accounting, ie by spreading over the period of the lease or, if shorter, to the first rent review.

Special provisions apply where the reverse premium is received by an assurance company carrying on life business (see **12.16** 'Corporation tax').

The above provisions do not, however, apply where the recipient is an individual and the property in question is, or will be, occupied by him or her as their only or main residence. Nor do they apply to the extent that the payment or benefit is consideration for the first leg of a *bona fide* commercial sale and lease-back arrangement (as defined) or is (apart from the current provisions) taken into account as a trade or professional receipt under Sch D, Case I or II. [*TCA 1997, s 98A; FA 2002, s 18*]

33.7 Mining etc rents. Rents and payments for easements, where the leased premises or easements are used or employed for mining etc assessable under Case I (see **30.1** 'Sch D, Cases I and II'), are subject to deduction of tax at source (**13**) under *s 237* or *s 238* and are not allowable as deductions from trading profits, and (so far as not otherwise chargeable) are charged with tax under Sch D, Case IV. The same applies to other annual payments, royalties, tolls etc in respect of any premises. [*TCA 1997, s 104*]

33.8 Losses and deficiencies. Rent irrecoverable, or voluntarily forgone by reason of hardship, is a subject of adjustment of the assessment (with further revision if later recovered) [*TCA 1997, s 101*]. Profits and losses in a year are aggregated, and net losses on letting may be carried forward against future profits under Sch D, Case V. [*TCA 1997, ss 97(1), 384*] *Finance Act 2010, s 15* provides for clarification of the order of priority of set off for Case V Losses and capital allowances. The section amends *s 384* and expressly provides that Case V capital allowances arising in a year are to be deducted in priority to Case V Losses that are brought forward from a previous year. Where rent receivable under a lease does not cover the admissible expenses borne by the lessor, he is neither chargeable under Case V, nor eligible for loss relief under *s 384*. [*TCA 1997, s 75(4)*] See also **33.2** above.

33.9 Non-residents. Tax under *s 238* is deductible at source from rental payments, etc, made (whether in or out of RI) to a non-resident, the latter being entitled to claim repayment of any tax so suffered in excess of his liability as under Case V. [*TCA 1997, s 1041*] See generally an article in Revenue Tax Briefing Issue 42 p 35.

33.10 Returns. For the purposes of obtaining particulars of profits or gains chargeable to tax by virtue of *ss 96–106* (see **33.1**, **33.6**, **33.7** above), the inspector may by written notice require lessors, lessees and occupiers of premises to provide specified information in relation to leases and payments thereunder. Managing and collecting agents for premises, and certain public bodies making payments in the nature of, or for the purpose of, rent or rent subsidy in relation to premises, may also be required to deliver details of the premises and the owner(s) thereof, and of the rents and other payments arising, and of other specified particulars (and such returns may be required without notice, see **28.13** 'Returns'). The on persons in receipt of rental income as an agent for other persons to report the details of this income on request by the Revenue Commissioners. This provision has been extended to include income from all property wherever situated. [*FA 2008, s 136*]

URBAN RENEWAL – RESIDENTIAL ACCOMMODATION

33.11 Construction expenditure. In computing rental income, a deduction may be claimed for certain construction expenditure attributable to work carried out between 1 August 1994 and 31 July 1997 inclusive (the *'qualifying period'*) on 'qualifying premises' for rent. The deduction is allowed for the period in which the premises are first let under a 'qualifying lease'.

The qualifying period may be extended to 31 July 1998 where the relevant local authority certified (before 1 October 1997) that at least 15 per cent of the total cost had been incurred before 31 July 1997. This may be further extended to 31 December 1998 in certain cases involving delays outside the direct control of the person incurring the expenditure, and to 30 April 1999 in certain cases where substantial expenditure had been incurred by 31 December 1998.

'Qualifying premises' means a house (which includes any building or part of a building suitable for use as a dwelling, and land or outbuildings appurtenant thereto or usually enjoyed therewith) used solely as a dwelling:

(*a*)   the site of which is wholly within an area designated for the purpose by the Minister for Finance, which designation may specify a shorter period within the qualifying period referred to above;

(*b*)   of floor area not less than 30 sq metres or more than 125 sq metres (90 sq metres as regards expenditure incurred before 12 April 1995) in the case of a self-contained flat or maisonette in a building of two or more storeys, or of not less than 35 sq metres or more than 125 sq metres in any other case;

(*c*)   first let (without having previously been used) in its entirety under a 'qualifying lease' and continuing to be so let throughout the ten years following that first letting (ignoring reasonable temporary void periods between lettings);

(*d*)   in respect of which, if it is not a new house (within *Housing (Miscellaneous Provisions) Act 1979, s 4*), there is in force a certificate of reasonable cost, granted by the Minister for the Environment and Local Government, in which the construction cost specified is not less than that actually incurred;

(e) complying with such conditions as to construction standards and service provision as the Minister may lay down under *Housing (Miscellaneous Provisions) Act 1979*;

(f) open to inspection by persons authorised in writing by the Minister at all reasonable times; and

(g) which (or the development of which it is part) must comply with guidelines issued by the Minister, in furtherance of *Urban Renewal Act 1986* objectives, concerning:

(i) design, construction and refurbishment of the houses,

(ii) total floor area and dimensions of rooms,

(iii) provisions of ancillary facilities, and

(iv) the 'balance' between the houses, the development and the location.

A house occupied by a person connected (within *s 10*) with the person claiming the deduction is excluded unless the lease is on arm's length terms.

A '*qualifying lease*' of a house is a lease the consideration for the grant of which consists of periodic payments of rent within Sch D, Case V, with or without the payment of a premium not exceeding ten per cent of the 'relevant cost' of the house. There is, however, an exclusion for leases under the terms of which anyone can at any time directly or indirectly acquire an interest in the house at less than market value. The '*relevant cost*' of the house is the aggregate of expenditure on the land and construction of the house (with any necessary apportionment of expenditure on whole buildings or on larger developments).

The expenditure for which a deduction is allowable is that incurred on the construction of the house, including expenditure on the development of the land (including gardens, access, etc), in particular demolition, groundworks, landscaping, walls, mains supplies and outhouses, etc for use by the occupants of the house. Where, however, a premium or like sum is payable directly or indirectly to the lessor or to any person connected (within *s 10*) with him, and all or any part of it is not treated as rent under Sch D, Case V, the expenditure for which a deduction is allowed is reduced by the amount of the premium, etc not treated as rent or, where any part of the construction cost falls outside the qualifying period, to the same proportion of that amount as the expenditure for which a deduction is allowable bears to the whole construction cost.

Expenditure met directly or indirectly by the State, a statutory board or a public or local authority is excluded.

Where qualifying premises form part of a building or consist of a building which is part of a larger development, any necessary apportionment of cost is made.

If the house ceases to be qualifying premises, or if the lessor disposes of his interest, within ten years after the first letting under a qualifying lease, any deduction under these provisions is treated as rent received by the person to whom the deduction was allowed. If the lessor disposes of his interest but the house continues to be qualifying premises, the new owner of the interest is entitled to the same deduction as was granted to the original lessor, but ignoring any reduction in respect of a premium, etc (see above), and limited to the '*relevant price*' paid by the new owner, ie the same proportion of the total price paid by him as the expenditure for which a deduction was allowable to the original lessor bore to the relevant cost (as above) of the house.

Where a house on which construction expenditure was incurred in the qualifying period is sold unused, the buyer (or, if the premises are sold unused more than once, the last such buyer) is treated as having in that period incurred construction expenditure equal to:

(i) if the original expenditure was incurred as a trading expense by a builder, the lesser of the relevant price (as above) paid to the builder and that paid on the last sale unused;

(ii) in any other case, the lesser of the construction expenditure actually incurred on the house and the relevant price (as above) on the last sale unused.

An appeal lies to the Appeal Commissioners on any question arising under these provisions as it would in relation to an assessment to tax.

For capital gains tax purposes, a deduction under these provisions is treated as if it were a capital allowance, and any rent treated as received as above as a balancing charge.

There is provision against double relief where relief is given under these provisions.

Finance Act 2011, s 24 has made a number of changes to *s 23* type relief. The summarised changes are as follows: for chargeable periods on or after the date to be specified by order of the Minister for Finance it is proposed that such reliefs will be restricted to income from that property itself. In addition, after a 10-year holding period, any unused relief will be lost. If the property is sold within this period or on or after the relevant day the new owner will not get *s 23* relief and the seller continues to be subject to a claw back of relief already given which would be in the form of additional rental income subject to tax at marginal income tax rates in the case of an individual investor. Where any properties, to which the relief applies are not let under a qualifying lease by six months after the relevant day, the holding period will commence on that day. This will have the effect of shortening the period over which the relief can be claimed.

From 2007, the quantum of relief available to a high earning individual in any one year may be limited, see **2.45** 'Limitation on Investment Relief'.

[*TCA 1997, ss 339, 340, 346, 350, 350A, 372AU; FA 1998, s 24(1); FA 1999, s 44(a)(b); FA 2002, s 24(3), Sch 2 para 1*]

See **33.4, 33.5** above as regards earlier reliefs, which continue in certain areas.

Conversion expenditure. The provisions described above in relation to construction expenditure apply *mutatis mutandis* to certain 'conversion expenditure' attributable to work carried out between 1 August 1994 and 31 July 1997 inclusive (the *'qualifying period'*) on 'qualifying premises' for rent, provided that planning permission has been granted for the conversion under the relevant Acts. The deduction is similarly allowed for the period in which the premises are first let under a 'qualifying lease'.

The qualifying period may be extended to 31 July 1998 where the relevant local authority certified (before 1 October 1997) that at least 15 per cent of the total cost had been incurred before 31 July 1997. This may be further extended to 31 December 1998 in certain cases involving delays outside the direct control of the person incurring the expenditure, and to 30 April 1999 in certain cases where substantial expenditure had been incurred by 31 December 1998.

'Conversion expenditure' is expenditure incurred:

(*a*) on the conversion into a house of a building, not previously in use as a dwelling, the site of which is wholly within a designated area, or which fronts onto a designated street, etc (or part); or

(*b*) on the conversion into two or more houses of a building, not previously in use as a dwelling or in use as a single dwelling, the site of which is wholly within a designated area, or which fronts onto a designated street;

including expenditure on the carrying out of works of construction, reconstruction, repair or renewal, and on the provision or improvement of water, sewerage or heating facilities, in relation to the building and any outoffice appurtenant thereto or usually enjoyed therewith, but excluding expenditure attributable to any part of the building which (after the conversion) is not a house (any necessary apportionment being on a floor area basis), or otherwise attracting tax relief. Conversion expenditure also includes expenditure on development of the land on which the building is situated (as for construction expenditure, see above).

Designated areas and streets, etc are those designated for the purpose by the Minister for Finance, which designation may specify a shorter period within the qualifying period referred to above.

'Qualifying premises' and *'qualifying lease'* are defined broadly as in relation to construction expenditure, except that premises fronting onto designated streets, etc are included (see above), the maximum permitted floor area in the case of a self-contained flat or maisonette in a building of two or more storeys is 125 sq metres (instead of 90), and references to the relevant cost of the house are references to the market value of the house after conversion (apportioned on a floor area basis where necessary).

There is provision against double relief where relief is given under these provisions.

From 2007, the quantum of relief available to a high earning individual in any one year may be limited, see **2.45** 'Limitation on Investment Relief'.

[*TCA 1997, ss 339, 340, 347, 350, 350A, 372AU*; *FA 1998, s 24(1)*; *FA 1999, s 44(a)(b)*; *FA 2002, s 24(3), Sch 2 para 1*]

See below as regards earlier reliefs, which continue in certain areas.

Refurbishment expenditure. The provisions described above in relation to construction expenditure also apply *mutatis mutandis* to certain 'refurbishment expenditure' attributable to work carried out between 1 August 1994 and 31 July 1997 inclusive (the *'qualifying period'*) on 'qualifying premises' for rent, provided that any necessary planning permission has been granted for the 'refurbishment' under the relevant Acts. The deduction is similarly allowed for the period in which the premises are first let under a 'qualifying lease'.

The qualifying period may be extended to 31 July 1998 where the relevant local authority certified (before 1 October 1997) that at least 15 per cent of the total cost had been incurred before 31 July 1997. This may be further extended to 31 December 1998 in certain cases involving delays outside the direct control of the person incurring the expenditure, and to 30 April 1999 in certain cases where substantial expenditure had been incurred by 31 December 1998.

'Refurbishment expenditure' means expenditure on the 'refurbishment' of a building wholly within a designated area, or fronting on a designated street, etc, in which (both

before and after the refurbishment) there are two or more houses, other than expenditure attributable to a part which, on completion of the work, is not a house (any necessary apportionment of general expenditure being on a floor area basis). Expenditure otherwise attracting tax relief is excluded.

Designated areas and streets, etc are those designated for the purpose by the Minister for Finance, which designation may specify a shorter period within the qualifying period referred to above.

'*Refurbishment*' of a building means either or both of:

(*a*)   the carrying out of any works of construction, reconstruction, repair or renewal; and

(*b*)   the provision or improvement of water, sewerage or heating facilities;

certified by the Minister for the Environment and Local Government, in a certificate of reasonable cost relating to any house contained in the building, as necessary to ensure the suitability as a dwelling of any house in the building, regardless of whether or not the number of houses in the building, or the shape or size of any such house, is altered in the course of the refurbishment.

'*Qualifying premises*' and '*qualifying lease*' are defined broadly as in relation to construction expenditure, except that premises fronting onto designated streets, etc are included (see above), the maximum permitted floor area in the case of a self-contained flat or maisonette in a building of two or more storeys is 125 sq metres (instead of 90), and references to the relevant cost of the house are references to the market value of the house after refurbishment (apportioned on a floor area basis where necessary). The ten-year period referred to in (*c*) above commences on the completion of the refurbishment if that is earlier than the date of first letting.

There is provision against double relief where relief is given under these provisions.

From 2007, the quantum of relief available to a high earning individual in any one year may be limited, see **2.45** 'Limitation on Investment Relief'. [*TCA 1997, ss 339, 340, 348, 350, 350A, 372AU; FA 1998, s 24(1); FA 1999, s 44(a)(b); FA 2002, s 24(3), Sch 2 para 1*]

Integrated area plans and 'living over the shop' scheme. Provisions similar to those described above in relation to construction, conversion or refurbishment expenditure also apply to qualifying premises in 'qualifying areas' for leases granted between **1 August 1998 and 31 December 2002** inclusive (extended to 31 December 2006 where the relevant local authority or company authorised by that authority certifies (before 1 October 2003, on application made before 1 August 2003) that at least 15 per cent of the total cost had been incurred before 1 July 2003), except that in each case relief is restricted to cases where the floor area is at least 38 sq metres and not more than 125 sq metres. The period is extended to 31 July 2008 provided that the conditions relating to the extension to 31 December 2006 are satisfied and at least 15 per cent of the construction or refurbishment cost is incurred by 31 December 2006. For expenditure incurred during 2007, relief is restricted to 75 per cent of expenditure incurred. For expenditure incurred in the period from 1 January 2008 to 31 July 2008, relief is restricted to 50 per cent of expenditure incurred. A '*qualifying area*' is an area, within an area to which an Integrated Area Plan (within *Urban Renewal Act 1998, Pt II*) applies (or is treated as applying), which is so designated for one or more of construction, conversion or refurbishment by order of the Minister for Finance (now a 'qualifying urban area'), and the construction, conversion or refurbishment must be certified by the local authority concerned (or company authorised by such authority) as being consistent with the objectives of the Plan. Each designation order must specify a qualifying period within that referred to above. The Minister has power to amend or revoke any order. Where part of a building is outside of a qualifying area, relief is determined by floor area apportionment.

These provisions are extended under the 'Living over the Shop Scheme' to expenditure on the conversion, refurbishment or 'necessary construction' of qualifying premises consisting of a house fronting on to a 'qualifying street' (or comprised in a building (or part) which does so) incurred between **6 April 2001 and 31 December 2004** inclusive (or in any shorter period within that period which may be specified in the order designating a particular street as a 'qualifying street', see below). The period is extended to **31 December 2006** where a valid application for full planning permission has been made and acknowledged as received by 31 December 2004 (or 10 March 2002 in the case of permission sought under the *Local Government (Planning and Development) Regulations 1994*) or, where planning permission is not required, a detailed plan of the construction or refurbishment work is prepared, a binding written contract relating to that work is in existence and work to the value of five per cent of the development costs has been carried out by 31 December 2004. The period in which expenditure must be incurred is extended to **31 July 2008** provided that the conditions relating to the 31 December 2006 extension have been satisfied and at least 15 per cent of the construction or refurbishment cost is incurred by 31 December 2006. For expenditure incurred during 2007, relief is restricted to 75 per cent of expenditure incurred. For expenditure incurred in the period from 1 January 2008 to 31 July 2008, relief is restricted to 50 per cent of expenditure incurred. The house must be comprised in the upper floor(s) of an 'existing' or 'replacement building' the ground floor of which is in use for commercial purposes (or is temporarily vacant but subsequently so used), and the allowance is dependant on the corporation of the borough in whose area the house is situated certifying in writing that the conversion, refurbishment or construction is consistent with the aims, objectives and criteria for the Scheme as outlined in circular UR 43A of 13 September 2000 (as amended). For these purposes the following definitions apply. A *'qualifying street'* (within *s 372BA*) is a street (or part) in the county borough of Cork, Dublin, Galway, Limerick or Waterford which is so designated by order by the Minister for Finance. 'Street' for this purpose includes a road, square, quay or lane. An *'existing building'* is a building which existed on 13 September 2000, and *'necessary construction'* in relation to such a building means construction of either (*a*) an extension which increases the floor area by not more than 30 per cent and which is necessary to facilitate access or to provide essential facilities, or (*b*) an additional storey or storeys necessary for the restoration or enhancement of the streetscape, or (*c*) a *'replacement building'*, ie a building or structure (or part) constructed to replace an existing building where either (i) a demolition notice or order on the existing building (or part) was given or made after 12 September 2000 and before 31 March 2001 and the replacement building is consistent with the character and size of the existing building, or (ii) demolition of the existing building (being a single storey building) was required for structural reasons to facilitate the construction of an additional storey or storeys necessary for the restoration or enhancement of the streetscape.

From 2007, the quantum of relief available to a high earning individual in any one year may be limited, see **2.45** 'Limitation on Investment Relief'.

[*TCA 1997, ss 372A, 372B, 372BA, 372F–372H, 372J, 372K, 372AK–372AP, 372AS, 372AT, 372AV; FA 1998, s 76; Urban Renewal Act 1998, s 11; FA 2000, s 44; FA 2001, s 60; FA 2002, ss 23(1)(b)(c), 24, 25, Sch 2 paras 1, 2; FA 2003, ss 26, 27(1), 30; FA 2004, s 26; FA 2006, ss 11, 25; SI 642/04*]

See also **2.27** 'Allowances, credits and rates', **8.10** 'Capital allowances' and, as regards integrated area plans, **30.24** 'Sch D, Cases I and II'.

Town renewal schemes. Provisions similar to those described above in relation to construction, conversion or refurbishment expenditure also apply to qualifying premises in 'qualifying areas' for leases granted between **1 April 2000** and **31 December 2004** inclusive, except that in each case relief is restricted to cases where the floor area is not less than 38 sq metres or more than 125 sq metres (for expenditure incurred after 5 April 2001, 150 sq metres), and in certain cases a 'certificate of compliance' granted by the Minister may be required instead of a certificate of reasonable cost. The qualifying period is extended to **31 December 2006** where a valid application for full planning permission has been made and acknowledged as received by 31 December 2004 (or 10 March 2002 in the case of permission sought under the *Local Government (Planning and Development) Regulations 1994*) or, where planning permission is not required, a detailed plan of the construction or refurbishment work is prepared, a binding written contract relating to that work is in existence and work to the value of five per cent of the development costs has been carried out by 31 December 2004. The period in which expenditure must be incurred is extended to **31 July 2008** provided that the conditions relating to the 31 December 2006 extension have been satisfied and at least 15 per cent of the construction or refurbishment cost is incurred by 31 December 2006. For expenditure incurred during 2007, relief is restricted to 75 per cent of expenditure incurred. For expenditure incurred in the period from 1 January 2008 to 31 July 2008, relief is restricted to 50 per cent of expenditure incurred. A '*qualifying area*' is an area, within an area to which a Town Renewal Plan (under the relevant legislation) relates (or is treated as relating), which is so designated by order by the Minister for Finance (now a 'qualifying town area'), and such an order may designate different classes of premises for relief. Each designation order must specify a qualifying period within that referred to above. In relation to refurbishment expenditure, relief is extended to include expenditure on certain work on the facade of a building, and on buildings in which, either before or after the refurbishment, there is only one house. The Minister is empowered to amend or revoke a designation order. Where part of a building is outside a qualifying area, relief is determined by floor area apportionment. **From 2007**, the quantum of relief available to a high earning individual in any one year may be limited, see **2.45** 'Limitation on Investment Relief'. [*TCA 1997, ss 372AA, 372AB, 372AE–372AG, 372AI, 372AJ, 372AK–372AP, 372AS, 372AT, 372AV; FA 2000, s 89; FA 2001, s 80; FA 2002, ss 24, 25, Sch 2 para 1; FA 2003, ss 26, 30; FA 2004, s 26; FA 2006, ss 11, 25*] See also **2.27** 'Allowances, credits and rates', **8.10** 'Capital allowances'.

For an article on Town Renewal Relief, including a list of towns recommended for designation, see Revenue Tax Briefing Issue 42 pp 24–27.

Park and ride facilities. Provisions similar to those described above in relation to construction expenditure apply to expenditure in a '*qualifying period*' **1 July 1999 to 31 December 2004** inclusive on the construction of '*qualifying premises*', defined as above (in relation to construction expenditure) except that the requirement in (*a*) is that the site of the house is wholly within the site of a 'qualifying park and ride facility' (see **8.10** 'Capital allowances'), and that the house is certified as complying with the relevant guidelines relating to such facilities, the requirement in (*b*) is that the total floor area is not less than 38 sq metres and not more than 125 sq metres, and (*g*) does not apply. The qualifying period is extended to **31 December 2006** where a valid application for full planning permission has been made and acknowledged as received by 31 December 2004 (or 10 March 2002 in the case of permission sought under the *Local Government (Planning and Development) Regulations 1994*) or, where planning permission is not required, a detailed plan of the construction or refurbishment work is prepared, a binding written contract relating to that work is in existence and work to the value of five per cent of the development costs has been carried out by 31 December 2004. A person is entitled to a deduction for capital expenditure under this provision only insofar as that expenditure, when aggregated with:

(i)   other expenditure, incurred at the same park and ride facility, in respect of which a deduction would, disregarding this restriction, be made under this provision; and

(ii)   expenditure, incurred at the same park and ride facility, in respect of which there is provision for a deduction under *s 372Y* or *s 372AR* (owner occupiers, see **2.27** 'Allowances, credits and rates');

does not exceed one-quarter of the total expenditure incurred at that facility for which a deduction or allowance may be made under this provision, or *s 372V* or *s 372W* (see **8.10** 'Capital allowances'), or *s 372Y* or *s 372AR* (see **2.27** 'Allowances, credits and rates'), disregarding this restriction and the similar restrictions applicable under *s 372W* and *s 372Y* or *s 372AR*. The local authority must have issued a certificate that it is satisfied that this requirement has been met. The period in which expenditure must be incurred is extended to **31 July 2008** provided that the conditions relating to the 31 December 2006 extension have been satisfied and at least 15 per cent of the construction or refurbishment cost is incurred by 31 December 2006. For expenditure incurred during 2007, relief is restricted to 75 per cent of expenditure incurred. For expenditure incurred in the period from 1 January 2008 to 31 July 2008, relief is restricted to 50 per cent of expenditure incurred.

From 2007, the quantum of relief available to a high earning individual in any one year may be limited, see **2.45** 'Limitation on Investment Relief'.

[*TCA 1997, ss 372U, 372X, 372Z, 372AK–372AP, 372AS, 372AT, 372AV; FA 1999, s 70(1); FA 2002, ss 23(1)(e), 24, Sch 2 paras 1, 2; FA 2003, s 26; FA 2004, s 26; FA 2006, ss 11, 25*]

See also **2.27** 'Allowances, credits and rates', **8.10** 'Capital allowances'.

Earlier reliefs. See **33.4**, **33.5** above as regards construction, conversion and refurbishment expenditure on houses in the Temple Bar or Custom House Docks Areas of Dublin, and as regards earlier reliefs for expenditure in certain other areas. See also **2.27** 'Allowances, credits and rates', **8.10** 'Capital allowances' and **30.24** 'Sch D, Cases I and II'.

QUALIFYING RESORT AREAS – RESIDENTIAL ACCOMMODATION

33.12 The provisions described at **33.11** above apply also to construction, conversion and refurbishment expenditure incurred in a '*qualifying period*' **1 July 1995 to 30 June 1998** inclusive on a dwelling the site of which is wholly within a '*qualifying resort area*', ie a part of Achill, Arklow, Ballybunion, Bettystown, Bundoran, Clogherhead, Clonakilty, Courtown, Enniscrone, Kilkee, Lahinch, Laytown, Mosney, Salthill, Tramore, Westport or Youghal described in *Sch 8*, with the difference that the requirement (see **33.11**(*g*) above) that for a house to be qualifying premises it must comply with Ministerial guidelines is replaced by a requirement that:

(*a*)   throughout the period of ten years beginning with the first letting under a qualifying lease (or, in the case of refurbishment expenditure, and if later, the date of completion of the refurbishment), the house is used primarily for letting to and occupation by tourists, with or without prior arrangement;

(*b*)   during that period, the house is not let or leased to, or occupied by, any person for more than two consecutive months at any one time or for more than six months in any year; and

(*c*)   a register of lessees of the house is maintained, containing particulars of the name, address and nationality of each lessee during that period, and of the dates of their arrival and departure.

The definition of qualifying lease is correspondingly framed to remove the references to lease premiums (while allowing for single rental payments), and the reduction of the allowable deduction where a premium or like sum is payable is not applicable.

The qualifying period is extended to **30 June 1999** where at least 15 per cent of the total expenditure is certified on or before 30 September 1998 by the relevant local authority (under the relevant guidelines) to have been incurred before 1 July 1998, and to **31 December 1999** where at least 50 per cent is so certified on or before 30 September 1999 to have been incurred before 1 July 1999.

[*TCA 1997, ss 351, 356–359, 372AU, Sch 8*; *FA 1998, s 27*; *FA 1999, s 45*; *FA 2002, s 24(3), Sch 2 para 1*]

See also **2.43** 'Limitation on Investment Relief', **8.11** 'Capital allowances', **30.24** 'Sch D, Cases I and II'.

DESIGNATED ISLANDS – RESIDENTIAL ACCOMMODATION

33.13 The provisions described at **33.11** above apply also to construction, conversion and refurbishment expenditure incurred in a '*qualifying period*' **1 August 1996 to 31 July 1999** inclusive on a dwelling the site of which is on a '*designated island*', ie (in Cork) Bere, Clear, Dursey, Hare, Long, Sherkin and Whiddy; (in Donegal) Arranmore, Inishbofin, Inishfree and Tory; (in Galway) Inisbofin, Inisheer, Inishmaan and

Inishmore; (in Limerick) Foynes; (in Mayo) Claggan, Clare, Inishbiggle, Inishcottle, Inishlyre and Inishturk; (in Sligo) Coney, with the differences that:

(*a*)   the requirement (see **33.11**(*g*) above) that for a house to be a qualifying premises it must comply with Ministerial guidelines does not apply;

(*b*)   a 'qualifying lease' must be of at least twelve months' duration;

(*c*)   there is an additional requirement that the house is used, throughout the period of any qualifying lease, as the sole or main residence of the lessee; and

(*d*)   refurbishment expenditure may be incurred on a building in which there is only one house.

The qualifying period was extended to 31 December 1999 where the relevant local authority has certified (before 1 November 1999) that at least 15 per cent of the total cost had been incurred before 1 August 1999.

    [*TCA 1997, ss 360–363, 365, 372AU; FA 1999, s 46; FA 2000, s 43; FA 2002, s 24(3), Sch 2 para 1*]

    See also **2.27** 'Allowances, credits and rates'.

QUALIFYING RURAL AREAS – RESIDENTIAL ACCOMMODATION

33.14 The provisions described at **33.11** above apply also to construction, conversion and refurbishment expenditure, incurred in a '*qualifying period*' which commenced on **1 June 1998** and ended on **31 December 2004,** on a dwelling the site of which was wholly within a '*qualifying rural area*', ie an area of Cavan, Leitrim, Longford, Roscommon or Sligo specified in *Sch 8A* as inserted by *FA 1998, s 77(b)*, but with the following differences:

(*a*)   the qualifying lease must in all cases be of at least three months' duration (twelve months before 6 April 1999);

(*b*)   the floor area of the dwelling must in all cases be at least 38 sq metres and not more than 175 sq metres (for expenditure incurred before 6 April 2001, 140 sq metres in the case of construction expenditure, 150 sq metres in the case of conversion or refurbishment expenditure, and in all cases 125 sq metres before 6 April 1999);

(*c*)   there is in all cases a further exclusion from being qualifying premises of any house which is not, throughout the period of the qualifying lease, used as the sole or main residence of the lessee;

(*d*)   the requirements as to meeting certain *Urban Renewal Act 1986* objectives (see **33.11**(*g*) above) do not apply;

(*e*)   in relation to refurbishment expenditure, the building on which the expenditure is incurred may contain one (rather than two) or more houses before and after the refurbishment.

The qualifying period is extended to **31 December 2006** where a valid application for full planning permission has been made and acknowledged as received by 31 December 2004 (or 10 March 2002 in the case of permission sought under the *Local Government (Planning and Development) Regulations 1994*) or, where planning permission is not required, a detailed plan of the construction or refurbishment work is prepared, a binding written contract relating to that work is in existence and work to the value of five per cent of the development costs has been carried out by 31 December 2004. The period in which expenditure must be incurred is extended to **31 July 2008** provided that the conditions relating to the 31 December 2006 extension have been satisfied and at least 15 per cent of the construction or refurbishment cost is incurred by 31 December 2006. For expenditure incurred during 2007, relief is restricted to 75 per cent of expenditure incurred. For expenditure incurred in the period from 1 January 2008 to 31 July 2008, relief is restricted to 50 per cent of expenditure incurred.

Finance Act 2011, s 24 has made a number of changes to *s 23* type relief. The summarised changes are as follows: for chargeable periods on or after the date to be specified by order of the Minister for Finance it is proposed that such reliefs will be restricted to income from that property itself. In addition, after a 10-year holding period, any unused relief will be lost. If the property is sold within this period or on or after the relevant day the new owner will not get *s 23* relief and the seller continues to be subject to a claw back of relief already given which would be in the form of additional rental income subject to tax at marginal income tax rates in the case of an individual investor. Where any properties, to which the relief applies are not let under a qualifying lease by 6 months after the relevant day, the holding period will commence on that day. This will have the effect of shortening the period over which the relief can be claimed.

From 2007, the quantum of relief available to a high earning individual in any one year may be limited, see **2.45** 'Limitation on Investment Relief'.

[*TCA 1997, ss 372L, 372P–372R, 372T, 372AK–372AP, 372AS, 372AT, 372AV; FA 1998, s 77; F(No 2)A 1998, s 4; FA 1999, s 47(1)(c)(d)(e); FA 2000, s 45; FA 2001, s 59; FA 2002, ss 23(1)(d), 24, Sch 2 para 1; FA 2004, s 26; FA 2006, ss 11, 25; SI 642/ 04*]

See also **8.12** 'Capital allowances'.

RESIDENTIAL ACCOMMODATION FOR STUDENTS

33.15 The provisions described at **33.11** above apply also to construction, conversion and refurbishment expenditure, incurred in a '*qualifying period*' **1 April 1999 to 31 March 2003** inclusive, on a dwelling which, throughout the 'relevant period', is used for letting to and occupation by students under a 'qualifying lease' in accordance with guidelines issued by the Minister for Education and Science (which are in place of the guidelines specified in **33.11**(*g*) above), and the site of which is wholly within a '*qualifying student accommodation area*', ie a 'qualifying area' as specified in those guidelines. The qualifying period is extended to **31 December 2004** where the relevant local authority or company authorised by that authority certifies (before 1 October 2003, on application made before 1 August 2003) that at least 15 per cent of the total cost had been incurred before 1 July 2003. The qualifying period is extended to **31 December 2006** where:

(*a*)   a valid application for full planning permission in accordance with the *Planning and Development Regulations 2001 to 2003* is received by a planning authority by 31 December 2004 and acknowledged as received by that date;

(*b*) a valid application for full planning permission in accordance with the *Local Government (Planning and Development) Regulations 1994* is received by a planning authority by 10 March 2002 and acknowledged in accordance with the applicable regulations; or

(*c*) where planning permission is not required, a detailed plan of the construction or refurbishment work is prepared, a binding written contract relating to that work is in existence and work to the value of five per cent of the development costs is carried out by 31 December 2004.

The period in which expenditure must be incurred is extended to 31 July 2008 provided that the conditions relating to the 31 December 2006 extension are satisfied and at least 15 per cent of the construction or refurbishment cost is incurred by 31 December 2006. For expenditure incurred during 2007, relief is restricted to 75 per cent of expenditure incurred. For expenditure incurred in the period from 1 January 2008 to 31 July 2008, relief is restricted to 50 per cent of expenditure incurred.

The guidelines may *inter alia* include provisions relating to such matters as design, ancillary facilities and amenities, terms and conditions of leases, and the students and educational institutions for whom the accommodation is provided. They may also specify the requirements as to floor area (in place of those described in **33.11** above). The '*relevant period*' is the period of ten years beginning with the first letting under a qualifying lease (or, in the case of refurbishment expenditure, and if later, the date of completion of the refurbishment). For expenditure incurred after 4 December 2001 on the purchase of a dwelling from a builder, the provision treating the purchaser as having incurred eligible expenditure equal to the purchase cost where the building is bought unused is extended to cases where the purchase is within one year after the commencement of use subsequent to the incurring of the expenditure by the builder. Unless a binding written contract exists before that date, expenditure incurred **from 18 July 2002** is subject to anti-avoidance measures requiring that only the person who has incurred the expenditure (the investor) can receive rent from the building; any borrowings by the investor must be from a financial institution and the investor must be personally responsible for interest and repayments of capital with no arrangement existing whereby any other person agrees to be responsible for the investor's loan obligations. Only bona fide management fees reflecting services provided and amounting to not more than 15 per cent of the gross rent receivable by the investor are deductible. (See Revenue Explanatory Note on the operation of the provisions of the Taxes Consolidation Act 1997 in relation to the Student Accommodation Scheme). The requirements relating to receipt of rent and management fees will not apply where the Revenue have given a written opinion before 6 February 2003 that the lease between the investor and an educational institution (or a subsidiary) would be a qualifying lease.

Finance Act 2011, s 24 has made a number of changes to *s 23* type relief. The summarised changes are as follows: for chargeable periods on or after the date to be specified by order of the Minister for Finance it is proposed that such reliefs will be restricted to income from that property itself. In addition, after a 10-year holding period, any unused relief will be lost. If the property is sold within this period or on or after the relevant day the new owner will not get *s 23* relief and the seller continues to be subject to a claw back of relief already given which would be in the form of additional rental income subject to tax at marginal income tax rates in the case of an individual investor. Where any properties, to which the relief applies are not let under a qualifying lease by 6 months after the relevant day, the holding period will commence on that day. This will have the effect of shortening the period over which the relief can be claimed.

From 2007, the quantum of relief available to a high earning individual in any one year may be limited, see **2.45** 'Limitation on Investment Relief'. [*TCA 1997, ss 380A–380F, 372AK–372AP, 372AS, 372AT, 372AV; FA 1999, s 50; FA 2002, s 24, Sch 2 para 1; FA 2003, ss 26, 32; FA 2004, s 26; FA 2006, ss 11, 25*]

RENTED RESIDENTIAL ACCOMMODATION

33.16 The provisions described at **33.11** above apply with certain modifications to expenditure incurred **after 5 April 2001** and before 1 August 2008 on the refurbishment of all rented residential property, ie without the requirement to be in a designated area or to front on a designated street and for a certificate of reasonable cost, and with no limitations on floor area. There is, however, an exclusion for houses in relation to which the lessor has not complied with the regulations as to standards and registration of rented houses and rent books. The allowances for such expenditure, which are not available if any of the reliefs in *ss 322–372AJ* (renewal reliefs, see **33.4, 33.5, 33.11– 33.14** above) or *ss 380A–380F* (student accommodation, see **33.15** above) are available in respect of the property, are at the rate of **15 per cent pa** (up to the total amount of the expenditure). They are given for the chargeable period in which the expenditure was incurred (or, if the property was not let under a qualifying lease during that period, the chargeable period of the first such letting after the expenditure was incurred) and for subsequent chargeable periods in which the property continues to be qualifying premises. For expenditure incurred in 2007, only 75 per cent of that expenditure is relieved. For expenditure incurred in the period from 1 January 2008 to 31 July 2008, only 50 per cent of that expenditure is relieved.

The definition of 'refurbishment' for this purpose is widened to include work carried out to comply with the *Housing (Standards for Rented Houses) Regulations 1993 (SI 147/93)*, but excludes work on the development of land. The premises may also consist of only one house both before and after the refurbishment.

Finance Act 2011, s 24 has made a number of changes to *s 23* type relief. The summarised changes are as follows: for chargeable periods on or after the date to be specified by order of the Minister for Finance it is proposed that such reliefs will be restricted to income from that property itself. In addition, after a 10-year holding period, any unused relief will be lost. If the property is sold within this period or on or after the relevant day the new owner will not get *s 23* relief and the seller continues to be subject to a claw back of relief already given which would be in the form of additional rental income subject to tax at marginal income tax rates in the case of an individual investor. Where any properties, to which the relief applies are not let under a qualifying lease by six months after the relevant day, the holding period will commence on that day. This will have the effect of shortening the period over which the relief can be claimed.

From 2007, the quantum of relief available to a high earning individual in any one year may be limited, see **2.45** 'Limitation on Investment Relief'. [*TCA 1997, ss 380G–380J, 372AK–372AP, 372AS, 372AT, 372AV; FA 2001, s 63; FA 2002, s 24, Sch 2 para 1; FA 2006, ss 11, 25*]

34 Schedule E – Emoluments

34.1 Tax is charged under Sch E on the emoluments of offices and employments including salaries, fees, wages, perquisites, profits, or gains, or the amount of annuity pension or stipend. [*TCA 1997, ss 19, 112*] Benefits received under an approved permanent health benefit scheme are taxable. [*TCA 1997, s 125(3)*] Special arrangements apply in relation to perquisites consisting of medical and long-term care insurance premiums (which are paid under deduction of standard rate tax, see **2.22**(*a*)(*d*) 'Allowances, credits and rates'), to ensure that the employee receives standard rate relief only and that the employer receives relief for the gross premium. [*TCA 1997, s 112A; FA 2001, s 21*] See Revenue Tax Briefing Issue 43 p 24. For a general article on the taxation of fringe benefits, see Revenue Tax Briefing Issue 40 pp 23–26.

For the distinction between employment and self-employment, see **38.129–38.133** 'Tax cases' and, for the report of the Employment Status Group, Revenue Tax Briefing Issue 43 pp 3–8.

Pensions to former employees or their dependants are assessable even though voluntary or capable of being discontinued. [*TCA 1997, s 790*] Also widows', orphans' and old-age pensions under the *Social Welfare Acts*, but not death grants. [*TCA 1997, s 126(2)*]

See **38.181–38.190** 'Tax cases' for case law regarding scope of Sch E.

Foreign employments are charged under Sch D, Case III (**31**).

See **27.3** 'Residents and non-residents' as regards special relief for certain income earned outside RI.

Finance Act 2011, s 16, provides that airline crew are subject to Sch E under the PAYE system where the aircraft is operated by an enterprise having its effective management in the State. The aircraft in question must at least partly operate in the State. Therefore where the aircraft does not take off or land in the State, the airline crew will not be effected by these new provisions. Further clarification will be required on the operation of this section.

34.2 The basis of charge is the actual emoluments of the year of assessment under the Pay As You Earn system, except where the inspector notifies the employer that deduction of tax by him is impracticable. Such notice may be cancelled by further notice if changing circumstances so warrant. Emoluments of an office or employment for a year in which the office, etc is not held are treated as emoluments of the last year in which it was held or, if it has never before been held, of the first year in which it is held. See also **38.191** 'Tax cases'. [*TCA 1997, ss 112, 984*]

Unpaid remuneration which has been allowed as a business deduction under Sch D will be deemed to have been paid as an emolument (on the last day of the period of account in which it accrued or, if that period is longer than twelve months, on each 31 December (for 2000/01 and earlier years, 5 April) in the period; or on the date the employment ceased, if earlier) subject to PAYE for which the employer is accountable, *unless* (i) such emoluments are included in the Sch D assessment on the professional practice etc of the recipient or (ii) payment is actually made within six months of the date payment is deemed to have been made as above, or, if later, eighteen months from the first day of a period of account which is for longer than one year. [*TCA 1997, s 996; FA 2001, Sch 2 para 54*]

DIRECTORS AND EMPLOYEES

34.3 Directors, and employees receiving €1,905/£1,500 pa or more (for 2001 only, £1,110 pa or more), are chargeable on all expenses, provision of accommodation, entertainment, services (including domestic), benefits or facilities whatsoever ('benefits in kind'), paid in respect of them by their employer (or by certain other persons) and not refunded, but relief may be claimed under *s 114* (see below). Exceptions apply to accommodation, supplies or services provided in the employer's premises and used solely in performing duties, costs of meals in canteens in which meals are provided for staff generally, the cost of providing death or retirement benefits (except contributions to PRSAs, see **2.22** 'Allowances, credits and rates'), the cost of acquisition or production of assets remaining the property of the employer (but assessable benefit arises on the use of the asset by the employee and if the asset is transferred to him), and provision of certain art objects (see below). Since 6 April 1999 there is also an exception for provision of an annual or monthly public bus or train pass (for which see Revenue Tax Briefing Issue 41 p 22), (extended from 1 January 2004 to include LUAS services and from 1 January 2005 to include ferry services within the State) and for provision of any form of child minding service or supervised activity to care for children of directors or employees, either in premises made available solely by the employer or in other premises where the employer is wholly or partly responsible for financing and managing the provision (and in either case the premises must comply with the requirements of *article 9, 10 or 11 of the Child Care (Pre-School Services) Regulations 1996 (SI 398/ 96)*). Since 6 April 2001, the childcare exception is extended to certain capital expenditure on the construction or refurbishment of premises in relation to which the employer is not otherwise involved in the provision of childcare services. *Finance Act 2011, s 7* has removed the exception for the provision of childcare services from the benefit in kind legislation. The provision of childcare facilities by the employer will be taxable as a benefit in kind from 1 January 2011 and subsequent years. Since 2005, the cost to a company of providing personal security assets and services to its directors or employees is excluded from the benefit in kind provisions subject to certain conditions being met. This exemption does not extend to modes of transport. [*TCA 1997, s 118A; FA 2005 s 10*] By concession, a benefit to the value of €250 or less per annum (€100 prior to 1 January 2005) to an employee is ignored. **Since 1 January 2004**, business use and private use are defined for the purposes of the legislation. Business use is the use of an asset in the performance of the duties of the employee's office or employment. Private use is defined as the use of an asset other than for business use. **Since 1 January 2004**, the following are not benefits in kind:

(*a*)   provision of mobile telephones, computer equipment and home high-speed internet connections where the benefit is provided by the employer for business use and any private use is incidental;

(*b*)   payment of subscriptions to professional bodies where membership is necessary for the performance of the duties of the office or employment or facilitates the acquisition of knowledge necessary for or directly related to those duties or prospective duties (up to 31 December 2010). The payment of subscriptions to professional bodies is now taxable as a benefit in kind as of from 1 January 2011;

(*c*)   private use of a company van where the following conditions are satisfied:

    (i)   it is necessary in the performance of work duties,

    (ii)   the employee is required to keep the van at his private residence when not in use,

    (iii)   other than travel to and from work, private use of the van is prohibited,

    (iv)   the employee spends at least 80 per cent of his time away from the work premises.

[*TCA 1997, ss 116–120A; FA 1999, ss 33, 34; FA 2001, s 25, Sch 2 para 7; FA 2004, s 8; FA 2005, ss 7, 8; FA 2011, s 7*]

Finance (No 2) Act 2008, s 7 amended *Pt 5, Ch 3 (ss 118 and 118B)*. It provides for an exemption from the general benefit in kind charge in respect of the first €1,000 expended by employers in the provision of bicycles and any associated safety equipment to their employees or directors, provided the bicycles and bicycle safety equipment in question are used for travelling to and from work or between work places. The exemption can only be availed of once in every five year period by an employee or director. Salary sacrifice arrangements can be operated in respect of the exemption but must be completed over a period not exceeding 12 months. The section applies to expenses incurred by an employer in the provision of bicycles or associated safety equipment on or after 1 January 2009.

Since 1 January 2004, the employer is required to account to the Revenue for any tax due in respect of taxable benefits in kind (excluding shares (from 25 March 2004, only shares in the employer company or its holding company) and contributions to PRSAs (see **2.22** 'Allowances, credits and rates')), and to recoup this tax from the employee by deduction from payments due to the employee. See 'payment of tax' below.

Benefits in kind are subject to PAYE, PRSI and levies, **since 1 January 2004**. (See Employer's Guide to operating PAYE and PRSI for certain benefits at www.revenue.ie/pdf/bikguide.pdf.) [*FA 2003, s 6*]

Preferential loans. Also treated as an emolument of a director or employee (as above) is the benefit (calculated as below) of certain preferential loans. The loans concerned are those:

(i)   made directly or indirectly by the employer (or future employer (or, **since 4 February 2004**, former employer)) of the recipient or his spouse, or by any person connected (as defined by *s 10*) with the employer, other than in the normal course of domestic, family or personal relationships; and

(ii)   at no interest or at a rate of interest less than the 'specified rate'.

For this purpose, 'loans' include replacement loans, loans taken over from the original lender, and the arranging, guaranteeing or in any way facilitating a loan or the continuation of a loan.

A loan is not a preferential loan if the rate of interest is at least that charged on similar arm's length loans made in the course of the employer's trade to non-employees.

Finance Act 2010, s 4 amends *s 122* such that loans which no longer qualify for relief under *s 244* are charged to tax under *s 122*.

The *'specified rate'* from **2009** is **5 per cent** for home loans and the rate for all other loans has been reduced to **12.5 per cent.** The reduction to **12.5 per cent** in respect of all other loans is effective from 1 January 2009. The *'specified rate'* for **2008** is **5.5 per cent** for home loans and **13 per cent** (12.5 per cent post 1 January 2009) for all other loans. The *'specified rate'* for **2007** was **4.5 per cent** for home loans and **12 per cent** for all other loans. The *'specified rate'* for 2004 onwards is **3.5 per cent** where the interest is (or would if any were payable be) 'qualifying interest' (see **20.3**(*a*) 'Interest payable') or certain other interest payable to non-residents, 11 per cent in any other case (both rates being subject to variation by regulations by the Minister for Finance), or, if the employer makes fixed term, fixed interest house purchase loans as part of his trade, the rate normally charged by him on such loans at arm's length (other than to employees) at the time the preferential loan was made (if less than **3.5 per cent** or that rate as varied). For 2003 the figures were **4.5 per cent** and **11 per cent** respectively, for 2002 they were five per cent and **12 per cent** respectively, for 2001 they were **6 per cent** and **12 per cent** respectively, for 2000/01 they were **4 per cent** and **ten per cent** respectively, for 1999/2000 they were **6 per cent** and **ten per cent** respectively, and for 1995/96 to 1998/99 inclusive they were **7 per cent** and **11 per cent** respectively.

The sum charged as an emolument of a year of assessment is the difference between the aggregate amount of interest payable in the year (if any) and interest at the specified rate on the outstanding loan(s). With effect from 1st January 2011, the taxable benefit in kind will only be reduced by the interest paid by the employee as opposed to the interest payable under the terms of the loan agreement. *[FA 2011, s 7]*

A similar charge arises in any year of assessment in which such a loan, or any interest payable on such a loan, is released or written off, in whole or part. The charge is on the amount so released or written off in the year.

Any amount charged under these provisions in respect of preferential interest rates or the release or writing off of interest is treated as interest paid in the year of assessment of the charge, eligible for relief subject to the usual conditions (see **20.3** 'Interest payable'). It is not treated as emoluments for the purposes of employee allowance (see **2.13** 'Allowances, credits and rates').

Since 2005, the provision is extended to include employees in receipt of emoluments taxable under Case III of Sch D.

Notification. The employer may be required by the inspector to give details of preferential loans as above.

[*TCA 1997, s 122; FA 1982, s 8; FA 1989, s 6; FA 1992, s 9; FA 1994, s 9; FA 1995, s 9; FA 1999, s 10; FA 2000, s 15; FA 2001, s 5; FA 2002, s 8; FA 2003, s 4; FA 2004, s 10; FA 2005, s 9*]

Notional loans, etc relating to shares. Subject to the profit-sharing scheme provisions of *Pt 17, Ch 1* (see **34.6** below), the preferential loan provisions (above) also apply to certain notional interest-free loans. These arise where shares (which includes securities and interests in shares or securities) are acquired at an under-value by an employee or director (or a connected person), defined as under the preferential loan provisions, in pursuance of a right or opportunity available by reason of the employment. The notional loan is of an amount initially equal to so much of the under-value (ie market value on acquisition less any consideration given in money or money's worth) as is not otherwise chargeable as an emolument, and is reduced by any subsequent payment(s). Where the shares were acquired before 4 March 1998, the loan is treated as having been made on that day in an amount equal to the amount of the loan outstanding on that day.

The notional loan remains outstanding until either:

(i)   it is made good by subsequent payments;

(ii)   (where the shares were not fully paid-up on acquisition) any outstanding or contingent obligation to pay for them is released, transferred or adjusted so as no longer to bind the employee or director (or any connected person);

(iii)   the shares are surrendered or otherwise disposed of so that neither the employee or director nor any connected person retains a beneficial interest in them; or

(iv)   the employee or director dies.

Where (ii) or (iii) above applies on or after 4 March 1998, the preferential loan provisions apply as if the outstanding balance of the notional loan had been released or written off, and, if the employment has then terminated, as if it had not. No charge arises, however, by reference to any disposal effected after the death of the employee or director.

Where shares acquired as above (but whether or not at under-value) are subsequently disposed of (as under (iii) above) on or after 4 March 1998 for a consideration in excess of their then market value, the outstanding amount of the excess is treated as emoluments from the employment for the year of the disposal. [*TCA 1997, s 122A; FA 1998, s 15*]

The charges under *s 122A* in respect of a notional loan and the deemed write-off of a notional loan do not apply to shares acquired by directors or employees under approved profit-sharing schemes (see **34.6** below) or approved share option schemes (see **34.8** below). This does *not*, however, apply to the charge where shares are disposed of at an overvalue. (Revenue Tax Briefing Issue 32 p 6).

Cars provided by employer – position since 1 January 2004. The 'cash equivalent' of the benefit of a car provided by an employer for use by *any* employee, *less* any amounts which the employee is required to, and does, make good to the employer, is treated as an emolument of his employment for the year of assessment, unless there is no *private use* in the year *and* such use is prohibited. Where the employer is an individual, cars provided in the normal course of his domestic, family or personal relationships are excluded. A car provided for the employee's spouse, children and their spouses, parents, servants, dependants or guests is treated as provided for the employee's use. Vans are treated somewhat differently (see below) and motorbikes are excluded from the definition of 'car'.

Finance (No 2) Act 2008, s 6 has introduced a new carbon emissions based system of calculation of the benefit in kind (BIK) in respect of company cars provided for employees. The effective date will be determined by Ministerial Order. As of 1 March 2011, the Ministerial Order has yet to be signed. The scheme is structured on the seven-bands adopted for Vehicle Registration Tax (VRT). Cars in the lowest bands of carbon emissions remain at the current BIK charge, and higher charges apply for vehicles with higher emission levels, Existing vehicles retain the current method of calculation of benefit in kind. References in the existing legislation are being changed from miles to kilometres and the special provisions introduced for the short 2001 tax year are now being deleted.

Private use is use other than *business use*, meaning travel in the car which the employee is necessarily obliged to do in the performance of the duties of the employment.

The '*cash equivalent*' of the benefit is 30 per cent of the car's original market value, ie its price, including VAT and duty, in an open market retail sale immediately before its first registration (in practice, its list price, subject to any discount obtained and normally available in respect of a single retail sale). The cash equivalent is not reduced where the employer bears no part of the cost of fuel for private use, insurance, repair or vehicle excise duty. Where business mileage exceeds 15,000 miles, the cash equivalent of the benefit will be reduced from 30 per cent of the original market value of the car to the percentage set out in the table below. Time apportionment will apply where the car is available to the employee for only part of the year.

Business mileage		Percentage of original market value
Lower limit miles	Upper limit miles	
15,000	20,000	24
20,000	25,000	18
25,000	30,000	12
Over 30,000		6

NOTE: Thresholds below are subject to a Ministerial Order.

Annual Business Kilometre Thresholds		
A, B & C OMV%	D & E OMV%	F & G OMV%
24,000 or less	30%	35%	40%
24,001 to 32,000	24%	28%	32%
32,001 to 40,000	18%	21%	24%
40,001 to 48,000	12%	14%	16%
48,001 and over	6%	7%	8%

[*FA 2003, s 6(1)(b)*]

An employee whose business mileage exceeds 5,000 miles in a year of assessment and who spends 70 per cent or more of his or her time in the year performing duties of the employment away from the employer's place of business, may, provided that an average of at least 20 hours per week is spent performing those duties, elect for a **20 per cent** reduction in the cash equivalent. When requested (in writing), a 'relevant log book' relating to the year of assessment must be furnished to the inspector within 30 days, failing which the relief is not available. A '*relevant log book*' is a daily record of business use of the car(s) concerned, containing details of distances travelled, the nature and location of business transacted and the amount of time spent away from the employer's place of business, certified by the employer as being, to the best of his knowledge and belief, true and accurate. The log book must be retained for six years after the year of assessment (unless written authorisation for a shorter period is given by the inspector). The usual rights of appeal against an inspector's decision apply.

The provision to an employee of a van for private use is taxable at five per cent of the original market value of the van. Time apportionment applies where the van is only available to the employee for part of the year. A van is defined as a mechanically propelled vehicle constructed or designed solely or mainly for the carriage of goods, has a roofed area to the rear of the driver's seat, has no side windows or seating fitted in that roofed area and has a gross vehicle weight of no more than 3,500 kilograms. No reduction is available for business mileage. No benefit in kind arises where a van is necessary for the employment duties of the employee, the employee is required to bring it home after work but is otherwise prohibited from using it for private purposes and the employee is required to work away from his employer's premises for at least 80 per cent of his work time. [*TCA 1997, s 121A; FA 2003, s 6(1)(c); FA 2004, s 8*]

Position to 31 December 2003. Vans and motorbikes are treated as cars. The 'cash equivalent' of the benefit of a car is taxed as above but is reduced, where the employer bears no part of the cost in the year of:

(i)   fuel for private use by the employee, by 4.5 per cent of that value;

(ii)   insuring the car, by 3 per cent of that value;

(iii)   repairing and servicing the car, by 3 per cent of that value; and

(iv)   vehicle excise duty, by 1 per cent of that value.

Where the car is made available to the employee for part only of the year of assessment, the cash equivalent for the year is correspondingly reduced. This may also apply to periods during which the employee is working outside RI (see Revenue Tax Briefing Issue 22 p 8).

For 2001 only, the cash equivalent is 74 per cent of the amount so determined.

The cash equivalent determined as above is further reduced if business mileage in the year exceeds 15,000 miles (for 2001 only, 11,100 miles). The maximum reduction is 75 per cent, which applies where business mileage exceeds 30,000 miles in the year (for 2001 only, 22,200 miles). The reduction where business mileage exceeds 15,000 (11,100) miles and is less than 30,001 (22,201) miles is as follows:

Business mileage	Percentage reduction
15,001–16,000	2.5%
16,001–17,000	5%
17,001–18,000	10%
18,001–19,000	15%

Business mileage	Percentage reduction
19,001–20,000	20%
20,001–21,000	25%
21,001–22,000	30%
22,001–23,000	35%
23,001–24,000	40%
24,001–25,000	45%
25,001–26,000	50%
26,001–27,000	55%
27,001–28,000	60%
28,001–29,000	65%
29,001–30,000	70%

For 2001 only, the mileage bands are reduced by 26 per cent.

An employee whose business mileage exceeds 5,000 miles in a year of assessment (for 2001 only, 3,700 miles), and who spends 70 per cent or more of his or her time in the year performing duties of the employment away from the employer's place of business, may, provided that an average of at least 20 hours per week was spent performing those duties, elect for a **20 per cent** reduction in the cash equivalent. Where business mileage exceeds 15,000 (for 2001 only, 11,100 miles), this is instead of the tapering relief (as above). The requirements relating to maintenance and production of a log book are as set out above.

Car pools. Cars (and vans from 1 January 2004) included in a pool for use by employees of one or more employers are treated as not being available for private use. A 'pool' car must be available in the year to, and used by, more than one employee, and not ordinarily used exclusively by one of them; any private use must be incidental; and it must not normally be kept overnight at or near any employee's residence (other than on the employer's premises). Claims to 'pool' treatment may be made by any employee (or by the employer on behalf of all of them), and the inspector's decision is appealable (within two months of its being notified) as though it were an assessment. A decision on appeal applies to all employees concerned, whether or not they took part in the appeal.

Notification. The **employee** must notify particulars of the car (or van, from 1 January 2004), its original market value, and business and private mileages in a year of assessment to the inspector within thirty days of the end of the year, failing which (or if the inspector is not satisfied with the particulars supplied) the figures applicable for the year will be such as are determined by the inspector 'to the best of his judgment'. In the absence of sufficient evidence to the contrary, private mileage of any person's company car(s) will be taken as 5,000 miles (for 2001 only, 3,700 miles). The usual rights of appeal against an assessment based on such figures apply. The **employer** may also be required to give notice of the particulars.

Estimates of liability for a year of assessment may be made before the end of the year by the inspector in the usual way for the purposes of PAYE or Sch E assessment.

But see 'payment of tax' below relating to the taxing of benefits in kind from 1 January 2004.

Connected persons. Cars made available, and costs borne, by persons connected with (as defined by *s 10*) the employer are treated as made available, or borne, by the employer.

[*TCA 1997, s 121; FA 1982, s 4; FA 1992, s 8; FA 2001, Sch 2 para 8*]

See **38.189** 'Tax cases' for an unsuccessful challenge to the constitutionality of the above car benefit provisions.

Parking levy in urban areas. *Finance (No 2) Act 2008, s 2* introduced a parking levy, which applies where an employer provides car parking facilities for employees. The section provides that the areas to which a levy will apply and the date from which the levy will apply will be designated by order of the Minister for Finance. As at 1 March 2011 no Ministerial Order has been signed to bring the parking levy into operation. The levy applies where an employee has an entitlement to use a parking space and such space is provided directly or indirectly by his or her employer. In general, the levy applies to private cars and will not apply to disabled drivers or employees of the emergency services in the context of responding to an emergency situation. Occasional permission to park for not more that 10 days a year is excluded as is occasional use by a retired person. The charge for a full year is €200 where an employee has an ongoing entitlement to use a parking space. Where parking spaces are shared by employees, the levy is reduced to €100 where the ratio of employees to parking spaces is two to one or more. Reductions to the levy are also provided for to take account of job sharing, maternity leave and certain shift work.

Employers are required to deduct the levy from employees' net wages or salary and to remit the levy to Revenue at the same time as they remit income tax deducted under the PAYE system.

Use of private car in employment. Reimbursement of allowable motoring expenses may be effected by way of flat-rate travel allowances based on the Civil Service rates. See Revenue leaflet IT51 'Employees' Motoring Expenses', Revenue Tax Briefing Issue 44 Supplement p 36, Issue 46 p 22 and Issue 59 Supplement p 35 and Circulars 6/2005 and 17/2006 issued by the Department of Finance.

Premises or other assets. These are taxed based on the value of the asset provided. In the case of premises, the value of the benefit is the value of the market rent obtainable on the basis that the landlord bears the cost of repairs, insurance etc. Revenue practice is to take 8 per cent of the market value of the premises as the value of the benefit to the employee. Since 1 January 2004, the value of a benefit arising from other assets is computed based on five per cent of the market value of the asset. Prior to that date there was no statutory basis for computing the value of such benefit. Since 1 January 2005, the value of a benefit arising from the use of land is computed in the same way as premises. [*TCA 1997, s 119; FA 2003, s 6(1)(a); FA 2005, s 7*]

Loans of art objects owned by a company to a director or employee are, on a claim by the director etc, exempt from any benefit-in-kind charge or treatment as a distribution (see **12.7** 'Corporation tax') provided that the object is kept in an approved building or an approved garden (see **22.4** 'Losses') owned or occupied by the director etc. An '*art object*' is a work of art or scientific collection determined by the Minister for Arts,

Culture and the Gaeltacht to be intrinsically of significant national, scientific, historical or aesthetic interest, and determined by the Revenue Commissioners to be an object to which reasonable public access and viewing facilities are afforded (for which see the requirements applied to approved buildings under **22.4** 'Losses') at the same dates and times as apply to the building or garden in which the object is kept. A Revenue Commissioners' determination may be revoked for the year of assessment in which such access and viewing facilities cease to be provided and for subsequent years of assessment. There are provisions for inspection of the art object at any reasonable time by certain authorised persons, obstruction of or interference with whom may lead to a fine of up to €630/£500. This exemption applies for 1994/95 and subsequent years, but may be backdated to years of assessment 1982/83 onwards where the building or garden in which the object was kept was an approved building or garden (see **22.4** 'Losses') and the Revenue Commissioners are satisfied that reasonable public access and viewing facilities were provided in relation to the object.

The capital gains tax exemption of works of art loaned for public display (see **9.7**(*v*) 'Capital gains tax') does not apply to an object which is an 'art object' for these purposes.

[*TCA 1997, s 236; FA 1994, s 19(7)*]

Expenses. It is understood that various concessions are operated to exempt from tax certain expenses paid or reimbursed by employers, or to allow a deduction from emoluments for expenses incurred by directors or employees. Broadly these fall into the following categories.

(*a*)   travelling, etc expenses:

    (i)   of a director of two or more companies between the places at which his duties are carried out,

    (ii)   paid to an unremunerated director of a company not managed with a view to dividends,

    (iii)   of a director who holds the position as part of a professional practice, provided that no claim is made to a deduction under Sch D,

    (iv)   of a wife accompanying a director or employee whose health is so precarious as to prohibit unaccompanied foreign travel,

    (v)   during public transport disruption caused by industrial action, or

    (vi)   home leave travel expenses (once a year) for expatriate employees working in RI,

    (vii)   of an employee travelling to attend an emergency at the normal place of work outside normal working hours (see Revenue eBrief 6/2006);

(*b*)   removal, etc expenses where an employee has to change residence in order to take up a new employment or to transfer within an employer's organisation;

(*c*)   provision of home-to-work transport for severely disabled employees;

(*d*)   certain travelling expenses between RI and overseas for non-domiciled employees of non-resident concerns;

(*e*)   certain expenses of external training courses.

As regards (*b*) above, the Revenue Commissioners' Statement of Practice SP–IT/1/91 extends the concession to similar payments made to or for an employee taking up employment with a new employer (and see Revenue Tax Briefing Issue 31 p 9 for an update on the Statement of Practice).

Various arrangements are acceptable to the Revenue for the reimbursement of employees' subsistence expenses.

Flat rate expenses deductions have been agreed for certain categories of employee. For a full list, see Revenue Tax Briefing Issue 44 Supplement pp 31–33.

Subsistence payments. Flat-rate payments re-imbursing allowable expenditure may be made at Civil Service rates. See Revenue leaflet IT54 'Employees' Subsistence Expenses' and Revenue Tax Briefing Issue 40 p 9, Issue 44 Supplement pp 36, 37, Issue 46 p 22, Issue 49 Supplement pp 36, 37, July 2003 Supplement pp 35, 36 and Issue 61 and Circular 18/2006 issued by the Department of Finance. See also Revenue leaflet IT51 'Employees' Motoring Expenses' for rates applicable from 1 January 2003 to 1 July 2005.

Entertainment expenses incurred by an employee on the employer's behalf and reimbursed to the employee are, in practice, not assessed on the employee, but are disallowed to the employer (see **30.10** 'Sch D, Cases I and II').

Awards relating to passing an examination, or acquiring a qualification, relevant to the employment are not assessable provided the award can reasonably be regarded as reimbursement of study and examination expenses (see Revenue Tax Briefing Issue 39 p 19).

Pension contributions and contributions to Personal Retirement Savings Accounts of up to a specified percentage of remuneration for a year of assessment may be deducted as an expense incurred in that year. For contributions made from 4 December 2002, this is subject to a maximum remuneration of €254,000 per annum. For 2002 onwards, the specified percentage is 20 per cent for those aged 30 but under 40, 25 per cent for those aged 40 but under 50 and 30 per cent for those aged 50 or over (the age being determined at any time during the year of assessment), otherwise 15 per cent. Previously it was 15 per cent in all cases. Since 6 February 2003, where an election is made before the due date for tax filing in the year, any contribution made in that year (other than contributions paid under any net pay arrangement) before the due date may be treated as paid in the previous tax year. Provision is made for the carry-forward of unrelieved contributions. [*TCA 1997, ss 774(7), 787B; FA 2002, s 10(1)(a)(ii), (2); FA 2003, s 14)*]

Returns. Directors and their spouses are generally required to make returns of their income under the self-assessment system. [*TCA 1997, s 950(1)*] See **28.11** 'Returns'.

Payment of Tax. With effect **from 1 January 2004**, the employer is required to deduct from the employee the tax due by the employee in respect of the benefit, based on a best estimate of the amount of income likely to be chargeable to tax. Where the employer is unable to deduct sufficient from the employee to meet the tax payment, the employer is required to pay the tax due and recover the shortfall from the employee. Where the employee does not reimburse the employer by the tax year end (extended, by concession, to 31 March following that year end), the amount outstanding at that time is to be treated as an emolument chargeable to income tax in the same way in the following tax year. Any tax paid by the employer is treated as tax paid by the employee. Benefits in kind in the form of shares (restricted, from 25 March 2004 to shares in the employer company or its parent) and contributions by companies to Personal Retirement Savings Accounts are excluded from this provision. **Since 25 March 2004**, an employer may make an arrangement with the Revenue Commissioners to account directly for tax in respect of benefits to employees rather than through the PAYE system where the benefits in kind are minor or irregular. Where such an arrangement is made, the benefit does not form part of the total income of the employee and no credit for or repayment of tax is due in respect of the benefit. Written application for such an arrangement must be received by the Revenue Commissioners in the year of assessment to which it relates and any tax due on foot of the arrangement must be paid within 46 days of the year end – otherwise the arrangement is disregarded and the PAYE provisions are applied in full to the benefits. [*TCA 1997, ss 985A and 985B; FA 2003, s 6(1)(d); FA 2004, s 9*]

SHARE, ETC OPTIONS

[*TCA 1997, ss 128, 128A, 128D; FA 2000, s 27; FA 2001, Sch 1 para 1(c), Sch 2 para 9; FA 2002, s 11; FA 2003, ss 7, 8; FA 2005, s 16, FA 2009, s 12; FA 2010, s 17*]

34.4 Where a person realises a gain by exercising, assigning or releasing (which includes agreeing to a restriction on the right to exercise) a right to acquire shares in a company, being a right he obtained after 5 April 1986 as a past, present or prospective director or employee of that or any other company, he is chargeable under Sch E for the year in which the gain is realised on the difference between:

(i)   the market value (as under *s 548*) at the time the gain is realised of the shares or other assets (or, in the case of an assignment or release, the consideration received for the assignment or release); and

(ii)   the consideration, if any, (apart from services in the office or employment) which he gave for the grant of the right, plus, in the case of the exercise of a right, the consideration, if any, for acquisition of the shares or other assets;

with just apportionment by the inspector of any entire consideration given, or given in part, for grant of the right.

The market value of share awards on or after 1 January 2011 will be subject to PAYE at their marginal rate, to employee PRSI at 4% and to the new Universal Social Charge at 7%. Employer PRSI of 10.75% will also be due.

The employer is obliged to withhold PAYE, PRSI and the USC on such awards on or after 1 January 2011. The effective combined withholding rate will be 52% (41% PAYE, 4% PRSI and 7% USC) for most employees. *[FA 2011, s 10]*

A person acquires a right as a director or employee for this purpose if it is granted to him, or to another person who assigns it to him, by reason of his office or employment, unless his emoluments are assessable on the remittance basis under *s 71(3)* (see **34.2** above and **31.2** 'Sch D, Case III'). **Since a date to be appointed**, rights acquired at a time when a person is not RI tax resident are taxable in the same way. In this instance, the RI tax is proportionate to the period of employment exercised in RI. A statement of practice on the application of this new provision is awaited.

If a right can be exercised more than seven years after being obtained, tax liability can arise at the time the right is obtained, as well as on its exercise, and for this purpose the value of the right is to be taken as not less than the market value at the time the right is obtained of the assets over which the right is granted (or exchange assets) less the least possible consideration for which the assets may be acquired. Any tax charged on receipt of the right is then deducted from any tax chargeable on its exercise. Otherwise, no liability arises under any other provision on receipt of the right where tax may become chargeable under these provisions on its exercise.

There are provisions preventing avoidance by the grant or assignment of the right to a third party, by its assignment, in whole or part, for another right, or by entering into joint arrangements with another person or persons having rights within these provisions. Payment of tax chargeable in respect of rights exercised from 6 April 2000 to 28 March 2003 to acquire shares in a company, may by election be deferred for up to seven years or until the shares are sold. An election must be made by the return filing date in the year following the tax year in which the rights are exercised. **Since 28 March 2003**, deferral of tax arising on the exercise of rights to acquire shares has been abolished.

Special provisions apply in respect of options exercised before 6 February 2003 where the market value or sale proceeds of the shares is less than the tax arising on exercise of the right. Payment of the income tax liability, whether currently due or deferred, may, by election, be reduced to a payment on account equal to the market value or sale proceeds of the shares. Special arrangements apply regarding the date for valuation of market value and date of payment of tax. To avail of the relief, an election must be submitted before 1 June 2003 in a form prescribed by the Revenue. Late elections may be admitted where the delay is due to absence, illness or other reasonable cause. In all cases, the balance of income tax outstanding falls due for payment if any shares are sold by the individual (or his spouse, if jointly assessed, or following transfer of the shares to his spouse after 25 February 2003). A payment equal to the lesser of the aggregate unpaid tax and aggregate net gains is payable by 31 October in the year following the year of disposal of the shares. Any amount of tax paid prior to 6 February 2003 in excess of the market value is not repayable. The relief is not available where neither tax due in respect of the exercise of rights to acquire shares that are not eligible for the relief has not been paid nor payment arrangements agreed with the Collector General. Where the provisions are not satisfied, any amount of tax chargeable which is unpaid remains payable as if the relief did not apply. Unpaid tax will not be pursued after death and will be discharged by the Revenue.

Since 6 April 2000 to 29 June 2003, where a charge arose under these provisions for a year of assessment, the person in receipt of the option was a chargeable person under self-assessment unless either the gain was dealt with by restriction of allowances or tax credits under PAYE or the person has been exempted from making a return by notice given by the inspector under *s 951(6)* (see **28.11** 'Returns'). For options exercised, assigned or released on or after 30 June 2003, the tax payable cannot be collected under PAYE. [*TCA 1997, s 128B; FA 2003, s 8*]

Finance (No 2) Act 2008, s 10 amends *s 128* which deals with the tax treatment of directors and employees of companies who are granted rights to acquire shares or other assets. It is an anti-avoidance provision aimed at preventing abuse when rights are exchanged. The section details various situations whereby the section takes effect including, *inter alia*, where the right was granted to another person by reason of the person's office or employment, connected persons, transactions otherwise than by means of a bargain at arm's length. It is effective from 20 November 2008. *Finance (No 2) Act 2008, s 12* introduces a new *s 128D* which provides for the calculation of the charge to income tax on the acquisition of restricted shares. *Finance Act 2010, s 17* provides that the trust in which the shares are held, must be established in the State or in another EEA State and that the trustees must also be resident in the State or in another EEA State. The section further provides that it is the amount of income chargeable to tax on the acquisition of the shares that is reduced and not the amount of income tax payable.

Where a gain is realised by the exercise of a right to acquire shares on or after 30 June 2003, the gain is taxable at the higher rate of income tax for the year in which the right is exercised. Tax is payable within 30 days after the exercise of the right without assessment. Each payment of tax must be accompanied by a return detailing the gains, the tax due and other details, including a declaration that the return is complete. Application may be made to the Revenue for the standard tax rate to apply where appropriate. Details of the gains must be included in the return of income.

For capital gains tax purposes, any gain chargeable under these provisions on the exercise of a right is treated as consideration given for the shares or other assets acquired on the exercise. Where an election to reduce the tax payment to market value or sale proceeds is made, the difference between the acquisition cost and market value at the date of disposal is not an allowable loss until such time as the tax liability has been paid in full. [*TCA 1997, s 128A(4B)* introduced by *FA 2003, s 7*]

Any person who either:

(*a*)   grants a right to which these provisions may apply;

(*b*)   allots any shares or transfers any assets in pursuance of such a right;

(*c*)   gives consideration for the assignment or release, in whole or part, of such a right; or

(*d*)   receives written notice of the assignment of such a right;

must notify the inspector in writing (eg on form SO2) by 31 March following the end of the year of assessment (for 2000/01 and 2001, 30 June, before 6 April 2000, within 30 days after the end of that year). Since 6 April 2000, this applies equally to rights granted by non-RI resident persons to employees or directors of RI-resident companies (on which the responsibility to notify then falls) or, from 25 March 2002, to employees or directors of non-resident companies carrying on business in RI through a branch or agency in which the director or employee is employed (in which case the responsibility falls on the company's RI representative). There are penalty provisions for failure to comply. *Finance (No 2) Act 2008, s 11* has included *s 128C(15)* to the list of provisions to which *s 29* applies. This provides for penalties where employers fail to make returns of information in respect of the award of convertible securities and where the fraudulently or negligently make incorrect returns. This is effective from the date of the passing of the Act. *Section 897B* has been inserted by *Finance Act 2010, s 18* which provides that it is mandatory for employers to file returns of information to the Revenue

Commissioners regarding shares and other securities awarded to directors and employees. *Schedule 27* has also been amended to provide for penalties where employers fail to make required returns of information and where the fraudulently or negligently make incorrect returns.

See generally Revenue Tax Briefing Issue 31 pp 14–16, Issue 35 p 18, Issue 36 p 16, Issue 40 pp 27, 28, Issue 41 p 28, Issue 52 pp 26–31, Issue 53 p17 and Revenue leaflet CG16 'Relevant tax on a Share Option'.

RELIEF FOR NEW SHARE SUBSCRIPTION

[*TCA 1997, s 479; FA 1986, s 12; FA 1993, s 26; FA 1996, s 12; FA 1998, s 11, FA 2011, s 10*]

34.5 Prior to 8 December 2010, an 'eligible employee' subscribing for 'eligible shares' in a 'qualifying company' is entitled to deduct the amount of his subscription from his total income as if it were a personal allowance, subject to maximum relief of **€6,350/ £5,000** in total (ie in all years of assessment). Relief is **not** available under these provisions where an entitlement to relief under *s 489* (see **21.2** 'Investment in corporate trades') arises in respect of shares subscribed for. *Finance Act 2011, s 10* has abolished this relief in respect of shares subscribed for on or after 8 December 2010.

An '*eligible employee*' is a director or employee of the 'qualifying company' or, if the 'qualifying company' is a holding company, of a '75 per cent subsidiary' of the 'qualifying company'.

A '*qualifying company*' is a company incorporated and resident in RI, and not resident elsewhere, which is either a trading company (ie its business consists wholly or mainly of carrying on trade(s) wholly or mainly in RI) or a holding company (ie its business consists wholly or mainly of holding shares or securities of '75 per cent subsidiaries' which are trading companies).

A '*75 per cent subsidiary*' is defined as for membership of a group of companies (see **12.15** 'Corporation tax').

'*Eligible shares*' are fully paid up new shares forming part of the ordinary share capital of the qualifying company, issued to, and acquired by, an eligible employee at not less than market value. They must at no time in the three years following issue (five years before 12 February 1998) carry any preferential rights, present or future, to dividends or assets in a winding up or to redemption, and they must not be subject to any restrictions which do not attach to all shares of the same class. If there is more than one class of ordinary shares in the qualifying company, the majority of issued shares of the same class as the eligible shares must not be eligible shares, and must not be held by persons who acquired them in pursuance of a right or opportunity made available to them as directors or employees of the qualifying company or of any of its 75 per cent subsidiaries.

Withdrawal of relief. Relief is withdrawn if, within three years of acquisition (five years before 12 February 1998), the shares, or an interest in or right over them, are disposed of, or the eligible employee receives money or money's worth, not constituting taxable income in his hands, in respect of the shares. Before 12 February 1998, only 75 per cent of the relief is withdrawn if the disposal, etc occurs after the fourth anniversary of the issue. Shares are identified for this purpose in the same way as detailed under 'Disposal of shares' in relation to the Business Expansion Scheme at **21.10** 'Investment in corporate trades'. There are, however, provisions (effective from 12 February 1998) to prevent a double or triple tax charge arising under these provisions, the Business Expansion Scheme and the Approved Profit-Sharing Schemes provisions (see **34.7** below).

Where, on a capital reorganisation, a 'new holding' is brought into existence which, for capital gains tax purposes (see **9.15** 'Capital gains tax'), is treated as being the same asset as eligible shares acquired under the current provisions, then it is so treated for the purposes of current provisions. The reorganisation does not give rise to a disposal of the eligible shares to the extent that the consideration consists of the new holding.

For **capital gains tax** purposes, on any disposal of eligible shares, any amount in respect of which relief has been given and not withdrawn under the current provisions is excluded from allowable expenditure in computing the chargeable gain.

Anti-avoidance. There is a general prohibition on relief unless shares are subscribed for and issued for *bona fide* commercial reasons and not as part of a scheme the main purpose, or one such purpose, of which is the avoidance of tax.

APPROVED PROFIT-SHARING SCHEMES

34.6 These provisions allow directors and employees of companies to receive shares in those companies free of income tax under certain conditions. *Finance Act 2011, s 10* allows shares appropriated to employees under Revenue approved profit sharing schemes to continue to be exempt from income tax but will be subject to PRSI and the universal social charge introduced in *Finance Act 2011*. This change is effective from 1 January 2011. For relief for the costs of establishing such schemes, see **30.26** 'Sch D, Cases I and II'.

Provided that the scheme is approved by the Revenue Commissioners, a company will provide funds to RI-resident trustees who will purchase certain defined shares (see below) and appropriate such shares to eligible employees (see below) up to a limit of €12,700/£10,000 (for 2001 only, £7,400) market value to any one individual in any year of assessment. The €12,700/£10,000 (or lower 2001) limit is increased to a once-off €38,100/£30,000 in respect of appropriations of certain shares transferred to the scheme from a qualifying employee share ownership trust (see below) where, at each time in the five years commencing with the date of establishment of the trust, 50 per cent of the shares were pledged as security for borrowings (the five years and 50 per cent being subject to reduction by the Minister for Finance by order), and at the time of the transfer a period of at least ten years had elapsed beginning with the date the trust was established and ending with all the shares pledged as security becoming unpledged. The Revenue Commissioners now allow for a loan period of less than ten years on a case-by-case basis, where, for example, an ESOT has sufficient income from dividends to pay off such loans earlier than expected. [*FA 2008, s 14*]

An employee etc to whom shares are appropriated (a '*participant*') must contract not to assign, charge or dispose of his beneficial interest in the shares within a 'period of retention' (see below); to permit the trustees to retain his shares throughout that period;

to pay to the trustees a sum equal to income tax at the standard rate on the 'appropriate percentage' of the 'locked-in value' (see **34.7** below) should he direct them to transfer the shares to him before the *'release date'* (ie the third) anniversary of their appropriation to him); and not to direct them to dispose of his shares before the release date other than by sale for the best consideration obtainable. The participant may, however, at any time direct the trustees to accept, in respect of his shares, certain share exchanges or other offers made to all holders of the same class of shares. Where shares appropriated to a participant are replaced by a new holding following a company reconstruction under *s 584* (other than certain bonus issues following repayment of share capital), the new holding is broadly treated in the same way as the original shares would have been.

Any assignment, etc of his interest within the 'period of retention' renders the participant ineligible for tax relief (and to a charge to tax as at the time the shares were appropriated to him). Alterations to the scheme must be approved, and approval may be withdrawn if the Revenue Commissioners cease to be satisfied with the conditions. Appeal may be made to the Appeal Commissioners within thirty days of the notification of any decision of the Revenue Commissioners.

'Period of retention' begins on the date the shares are appropriated to the participant and ends two years later or, if earlier, on cessation of employment due to injury, disability or redundancy, on death or on reaching pensionable age for social security purposes.

Employee share ownership trust shares. Subject to the condition below, where shares are transferred by a qualifying employee share ownership trust (see **30.26**(*b*) 'Sch D, Cases I and II') to an approved scheme, and subsequently appropriated within the above rules to a participant, the period of retention ends on the day following that on which the shares were appropriated, and that day is also the release date. The condition is that the employee share ownership trust had held the shares for at least the period of three years immediately before the transfer to the approved scheme, and that the participant was a beneficiary under that trust throughout that three-year period. For shares appropriated on or after 25 March 1999:

(*a*)   this three-year holding period requirement is reduced to two years (and where the holding period is less than two years the period of retention ends two years after the start of the holding period), and where the holding period is less than three years, the release date is similarly in effect three years after the start of the holding period; and

(*b*)   where the shares were transferred to the scheme after the first day on which they could have been so transferred in accordance with the terms, etc of the qualifying employee share ownership trust, the appropriation is deemed, for capital gains tax purposes, to have taken place on the day following the first day on which they could have been so transferred.

Since 16 April 2001 the provisions are recast to provide that the holding period requirement is satisfied by combining the periods the shares were held in both the employee share ownership trust and the profit-sharing scheme.

[*TCA 1997, ss 509–511A, 515, Sch 11 Pt 2; FA 1982, ss 52(7), 56(1)(2), Sch 3 para 1(4); FA 1992, s 17; FA 1995, s 16; FA 1997, s 50; FA 1998, s 36(1)(a); FA 1999, s 69; FA 2000, s 24; FA 2001, Sch 2 para 27, 60; FA 2002, s 13(1)(b)(2)*]

Contributory and 'salary forgone' schemes. Schemes which are part-funded by salary forgone or by employee contributions may be approved on a concessional basis. See Revenue Tax Briefing Issue 20 p 3, Issue 46 p 34.

Scheme shares. These must be ordinary shares of:

(i)   the company concerned;

(ii)   a company controlling the company concerned;

(iii)   a company (or its controlling company) which is a member of a consortium owning the company concerned or a company controlling the company concerned, and which itself owns at least three-twentieths of the ordinary shares of the company so owned;

(iv)   (from 16 April 2001) a company which issued the shares to the trustees of an employee share ownership trust (see **30.26** 'Sch D, Cases I and II') in an exchange within *s 586* (see **9.15** 'Capital gains tax'), the shares being subsequently transferred to the trustees of an approved scheme (including shares issued to the trustees of the employee share ownership trust on a reorganisation or reduction of share capital within *s 584* (see **9.15** 'Capital gains tax') after the exchange which represent the shares issued in the exchange or the 'specified securities' (see below) issued in the exchange referred to in the definition of such securities);

and they must be either:

(*a*)   quoted shares;

(*b*)   shares in a company not controlled by another company; or

(*c*)   shares in a company controlled by a quoted company (other than a company which is, or would if RI-resident be, a close company).

They must be fully paid up and not redeemable. They must not be subject to any restriction differing from that attaching to other shares of the same class, except for certain restrictions imposed under the company's articles of association requiring director or employee shares to be disposed of. Where there is more than one class of shares, the majority of the class of shares appropriated under the scheme must be held by persons who are not directors or employees who received special rights of acquisition, or trustees for such persons, or, where the shares are within (*c*) but not within (*a*) above, companies which control the company whose shares are in question or of which that company is an associated company.

Since 16 April 2001, relief is extended to '*specified securities*', ie securities (other than ordinary shares) transferred to the scheme trustees by the trustees of an employee share ownership trust (see **30.26**(*b*) 'Sch D, Cases I and II') to whom they had been issued on an exchange within *s 586* (see **9.15** 'Capital gains tax') (including securities representing those securities which were issued as a result of a subsequent reorganisation or redemption of share capital within *s 584* (see **9.15** 'Capital gains tax')), and similar securities acquired using dividends received in respect of the securities. If the company which issued the securities on the exchange is a company limited by shares (within *Companies Act 1963, s 5*), the employee share ownership trustees must, as a result of the exchange, have acquired at least the same proportion of the company's ordinary share capital as they held before the exchange. For such securities, the conditions described above in relation to shares are replaced by a requirement that the specified securities be issued by a company not under the control of any company (unless it has quoted shares and is not (or if RI-resident would not be) a close company). The only restrictions to which they may be subject are certain restrictions imposed by the company's articles of association which require disposal of all specified securities held in certain circumstances, and restrictions which attach to all specified securities of the same class.

'*Control*' and '*associated company*' are as defined in *s 432*.

[*TCA 1997, s 509(1), Sch 11 Pts 1, 3; FA 2002, s 13(1)(a)(c)(2)*]

Persons eligible for inclusion in the scheme on similar terms must include all full-time employees or directors who are chargeable to tax under Sch E and who have been employees or directors throughout a qualifying period which may not exceed three years (five years for schemes approved before 25 March 1999). The requirement for employees (but not directors) to be full-time ceases to apply for schemes approved on or after 10 May 1997. Also eligible are individuals who were employees or directors in the eighteen months prior to the appropriation of shares to them (and for schemes approved on or after 25 March 1999, the eighteen month restriction on an individual's eligibility does not apply where the shares to be appropriated were transferred to the scheme by the trustees of a qualifying employee share ownership trust (see above) of which, at the time of the appropriation or within the preceding 30 days, the participant was a beneficiary). A person is not eligible if, in the same year of assessment, shares have been appropriated to him under another approved scheme by the company or group or consortium concerned (except, from 23 March 2000, in the case of certain company reconstructions or amalgamations or, from 12 December 2000, in the case of a scheme established by ICC Bank plc or a successor to a trustee savings bank), or if within the previous twelve months he had a material interest (ie 15 per cent of the ordinary shares) in such a company, being a company which was a close company, or which would have been close were it RI-resident or were its shares not quoted. There are provisions to prevent schemes being set up so as to discourage any description of employees from participating, or to confer benefits wholly or mainly on directors or higher-paid employees, or, where the grantor is a member of a group of companies (consisting of a company and any company it controls or (from 30 March 2001) with which it is associated (as specially defined)) favouring directors or more highly-paid employees in the group (and subject to special provisions in the case of ICC Bank plc or successors to trustee savings banks). [*TCA 1997, Sch 11 paras 4, 12–14; FA 1998, s 36; FA 1999, s 69(1)(c); FA 2000, s 25; FA 2001, ss 16(a), 17*]

Information. The Revenue Commissioners may by notice in writing require any person, within not less than thirty days, to furnish them with such information as they think necessary for the purposes of determining either whether scheme approval should be given or withdrawn, or the liability to tax of a participant. [*TCA 1997, s 510(7)*]

Finance (No 2) Act 2008, s 9 introduced an amendment to *Sch 11 and 12* which deal with approved profit sharing schemes and employee share ownership trusts, respectively. The amendment allows the Revenue Commissioners to withdraw approval for these schemes where companies fail to make the required returns of information. A further amendment was made to *Sch 11 Pt 2*. The amendment is an anti-avoidance amendment and takes effect from 4 February 2010. As of from this date, the Revenue Commissioners will not approve a scheme unless they are satisfied that there are no arrangements in place that provide for loans to be made to employees eligible to participate in the scheme. *Schedule 11 Pt 3* has been amended such that shares appropriated to employees on or after 4 February 2010 cannot be shares in certain service companies. [*FA 2010, s 19*]

34.7 Charge to tax. There is no charge to income tax on an eligible employee when the shares are appropriated to him. On disposal by the trustees before the release date (see **34.6** above) or, if earlier, the participant's death, tax is chargeable on the participant under Sch E for the year of assessment in which the disposal takes place on the 'appropriate percentage' of the 'locked-in value'. A disposal by the participant of his beneficial interest in the shares (other than on his insolvency or otherwise by operation of law) is deemed to give rise to a disposal of the shares by the trustees for a consideration equal to that obtained by the participant for his interest.

The '*appropriate percentage*' of the locked-in value depends on the date of disposal, as follows.

before third anniversary of appropriation	100%
on or after third anniversary	No charge

If the participant ceases employment with the company because of injury, disability, redundancy or reaching pensionable age for social security purposes before the third (or fifth) anniversary, the appropriate percentage is 50 per cent.

'*Locked-in value*' of shares is their market value when appropriated to the participant (or on any earlier date(s) agreed in writing between the trustees and the Revenue Commissioners) as reduced by any capital receipt charged to income tax under these provisions (see below), or the disposal proceeds if less. Disposal proceeds may be taken as market value of the shares if the disposal is to the participant, or otherwise in a bargain not at arm's length, or is a deemed disposal following the participant's disposal of his beneficial interest (see above). Disposal proceeds are reduced by any payment previously made to the trustees for a rights issue, but payments consisting of proceeds from a disposal of other rights are ignored. Disposals are allocated to appropriations on a 'first in, first out' basis.

[*TCA 1997, ss 510(2)(4), 511(3), 512*]

Any **excess or unauthorised shares** (ie shares appropriated in excess of the limits referred to in **34.6** above, or to an ineligible person) not previously disposed of are treated as disposed of by the trustees at market value immediately before the release date (see **34.6** above) or, if earlier, the participant's death. Any disposal is treated as being of authorised shares in priority to excess or unauthorised shares. [*TCA 1997, s 515; FA 2001, Sch 2 para 27*]

Capital receipts are charged as if they were consideration for a disposal (see above) for the year in which the trustees or the participant became entitled to them. Excluded, however, are receipts which are (*a*) taxable income in the hands of the recipient, or (*b*) proceeds of disposal of scheme shares, or (*c*) new shares issued in a company reconstruction under *s 584* (other than certain bonus issues following repayment of share capital), or (*d*) proceeds of rights used to exercise other rights. Capital receipts of £10/€13 or less, and those arising after the death of the participant, are not charged. Where a capital receipt exceeds the locked-in value of the shares to which it is referable immediately before the receipt arose, that value is substituted for the amount of the receipt in determining the charge. [*TCA 1997, ss 513, 514*]

If, on the participant's direction, the shares are transferred to him before the release date (see **34.6** above), the **trustees are assessable** to income tax under Sch D, Case IV on an amount equal to the appropriate percentage (see above) of the locked-in value (see above) at the time of the direction. Credit is given to the participant for the tax so paid. [*TCA 1997, s 516*]

Capital gains tax is chargeable on disposal of the shares by the participant, without deduction for any amount determined for purposes of charging income tax under the above provisions. For this purpose, a participant is treated as absolutely entitled to his shares as against the trustees. No capital gains tax is chargeable on the trustees if they appropriate shares to participants within eighteen months of acquisition (shares acquired earlier being taken to be appropriated before shares of the same class acquired later). [*TCA 1997, ss 509(3)(a), 510(5)(6)(b)*]

The **company** making payments to the trustee under the scheme **may deduct** them in computing profits (or as management expenses) if (*a*) they are necessary to meet reasonable administration costs of the trustees, or (*b*) they are applied by the trustees in acquiring shares within nine months, or such longer period as the Revenue Commissioners may allow, of the end of the period of account in which the company charges them as an expense. There is an overall limit on the amount deductible of the amount of the trading income (after adjustment for losses, capital allowances, balancing charges and stock relief) or, in the case of an investment company, the income less other management expenses. For this purpose, sums are treated as applied by the trustees in the order in which they are received. The amount deductible is also limited to what the Revenue Commissioners consider 'reasonable' in the circumstances. [*TCA 1997, s 517*] See **30.26**(*a*) 'Sch D, Cases I and II' as regards deduction of scheme establishment costs.

Dividends received on shares by the trustees are not liable to the additional rate charge (see **36.1** 'Settlements') if the shares are appropriated within eighteen months of acquisition (shares acquired earlier being taken as being appropriated before shares of the same class acquired later). [*TCA 1997, s 510(6)(a)*]

Returns. There is an automatic annual return requirement of information from the trustees of Approved Profit Sharing Schemes, Employee Share Ownership Trusts, Approved Savings-Related Share Option Schemes and Approved Share Option Schemes. Submission of the information is required by 31 March every year in respect of the previous calendar year. [*FA 2008*]

SAVINGS-RELATED SHARE OPTION SCHEMES

34.8 With effect **from 6 April 1999**, a company may establish a scheme for its directors and employees to obtain options to acquire shares in itself or another company without any charge to tax on the receipt of the options or on any increase in value of the shares between the date of the option being granted and the date on which it is exercised. The relief, other than on receipt of the option, is withdrawn where an option is exercised within three years of being obtained in the circumstances described at (*j*) or (*l*) below.

Where, after 5 April 2000, an individual acquires shares under an approved scheme from a trust or company set up to acquire and hold scheme shares, no chargeable gain or allowable loss accrues to the trust or company on that disposal, the individual nevertheless being treated as acquiring the shares for a consideration equal to the amount paid for them.

The scheme must be linked to an approved certified contractual savings scheme (see **16.8**(iv) 'Exempt income and special savings schemes'), on which interest and bonuses are exempt from tax, to provide the funds for the acquisition of the shares when the option is exercised. Monthly contributions to all such schemes must not be permitted to exceed £250/€500, and the minimum monthly contribution set for any scheme must not exceed £10/€12. The limits may be altered by the Minister for Finance, as may the specifications of the associated savings scheme. The requirements for approval of the share option scheme and its participants etc are stated below. [*TCA 1997, s 519A; Sch 12A para 25; FA 1999, s 68; FA 2000, s 51; FA 2008*]

See **30.26**(*c*) 'Sch D, Cases I and II' as regards deduction available to the company for expenses in setting up the scheme.

Approval of a scheme is by the Revenue Commissioners (on application in writing by the company which has established the scheme ('the grantor'), and accompanied by such particulars and supported by such evidence as the Revenue Commissioners may require) and is given if the following conditions are satisfied. 'Control' for these purposes is as under *s 432*.

(*a*)   The directors and employees may obtain rights to acquire 'scheme shares', see below;

(*b*)   The scheme shares are to be paid for out of savings (and interest) with a contractual savings scheme (SAYE) (under *s 519C*) which is certified by the Revenue Commissioners for this purpose;

(*c*)   Rights under the scheme must not (save as permitted under (*d*) to (*n*) below) be exercisable before the 'bonus date' ie the date on which the SAYE repayments fall due. For this purpose, the repayments may be taken as including, or as not including, a bonus, and the decision on this must be taken when options under the scheme are acquired. Where repayments are taken as including the maximum bonus, the time when the repayments fall due is the earliest date on which the maximum bonus is payable. In any other case, it is the earliest date on which a bonus is payable;

(*d*)   If a participant dies before the bonus date, the rights must be exercised, if at all, within twelve months after his death. If he dies within six months after the bonus date, the rights may be exercised within twelve months after the bonus date;

(*e*)   If a participant ceases to hold the office or employment which makes him eligible for the scheme (and does not hold any office or employment in the grantor or any 'associated company' of the grantor or any company of which the grantor has control) because of injury, disability, redundancy or retiring on reaching a 'specified age', his rights must be exercised, if at all, within six months of his so ceasing. If he so ceases for any other reason within three years of obtaining the rights, they cannot be exercised at all (except as under (*l*) below). If he so ceases for any other reason more than three years after obtaining the rights, the scheme must provide either for forfeiture of the rights or for their exercise within six months of his so ceasing. The *'specified age'* is, from 6 April 2000, an age, not less than 60 and not more than the pensionable age within *Social Welfare (Consolidation) Act 1993, s 2*, which must be set for the purposes of the scheme. Previously it was the pensionable age (as above);

(*f*)   A participant continuing in employment after reaching the specified age may exercise his rights under the scheme within six months;

(*g*)   Rights under the scheme must not be transferable or capable of being exercised later than six months after the bonus date (except as under (*d*) above);

(*h*)   The participant's contribution under the SAYE contract must secure, as nearly as may be, repayment equal to the amount required for purchase of the shares in the option acquired;

(*i*)   The price at which scheme shares may be acquired under the option must be stated when the option is obtained and not be manifestly less than 75 per cent of the market value of shares of the same class at that time or, if the Revenue Commissioners and the grantor so agree in writing, at some earlier time. The scheme may provide for such variation of the stated price as may be necessary to take account of any variation in the share capital of which the scheme shares form part.

The scheme *may* also include the following provisions.

(*j*)   If a person obtains control of the company whose shares are scheme shares as a result of making a general offer to acquire the whole of its issued share capital or all the shares of the same class as the scheme shares, rights under the scheme to acquire shares may be exercised within six months of that person obtaining control. Rights under the scheme may also be exercised at any time when a person is bound or entitled to acquire shares in the company under *Companies Act 1963, s 204* (power to acquire shares of dissenting shareholders). Where the court sanctions a compromise or arrangement with creditors and members under *Companies Act 1963, s 201*, or if the company passes a resolution for voluntary winding-up, rights under the scheme to acquire shares may be exercised within six months of the sanction being given or the resolution passed. If these rights are exercised within three years of their being obtained, then the exemption from tax on exercise as above will not apply;

(*k*)   If any other company (the 'acquiring company') (i) obtains control of the company whose shares are scheme shares as a result of making a general offer to acquire the whole of its issued share capital or all the shares of the same class as the scheme shares, or (ii) obtains control of such a company in pursuance of a compromise or arrangement with creditors and members sanctioned by the court under *Companies Act 1963, s 201*, or (iii) becomes bound or entitled to acquire shares in the company under *Companies Act 1963, s 204*, then the scheme may provide for the rights to acquire scheme shares to be exchanged for rights to acquire shares in the acquiring company, or in another company falling within (i) below in relation to the acquiring company, which are equivalent, as regards value and conditions, to the rights under the existing scheme. The new rights are then treated as having been granted at the time the original rights were granted. The exchange must take place within six months of the company taking unconditional control, or of the court sanctioning the compromise or arrangement, or within the period during which the acquiring company remains bound or entitled to acquire the shares;

(*l*) Where a person ceases to hold the office or employment giving rise to eligibility under the scheme (and does not hold any office or employment in the grantor or any 'associated company' of the grantor or any company of which the grantor has control) by reason only that it is in a subsidiary of which the grantor ceases to have control, or that it relates to a business (or part) which is transferred to a person other than a subsidiary or 'associated company', the rights under the scheme may be exercised within six months of the change. If rights are so exercised within three years of their being obtained, then the exemption from tax on exercise as above will not apply;

(*m*) The scheme may extend to other companies of which the company concerned has control and is then a 'group scheme' with 'participating companies';

(*n*) If at the bonus date, rights under a scheme are held by a person who is then employed by a company which is not a participating company (see (*m*) above) but which is an 'associated company' of the grantor, or is under the control of the grantor (with or without others acting in concert), the rights may be exercised within six months of that date. If rights are so exercised within three years of their being obtained, then the exemption from tax on exercise as above will not apply.

[*TCA 1997, Sch 12A paras 1, 2, 10, 16–26; FA 2000, s 51*]

The Revenue Commissioners may not approve a scheme if it appears to them that there are features which are neither essential nor reasonably incidental to its purpose of providing share options for employees and directors, or which have or would have the effect of discouraging any eligible persons from participating. Where the company establishing the scheme is a member of a group of companies (consisting of a company and any company it controls or (from 30 March 2001) with which it is associated (as specially defined)), the scheme must not in effect be restricted wholly or mainly to directors or the more highly-paid employees in the group. If, after approval, any of the above conditions cease to be satisfied or required information is not provided, approval is withdrawn, but existing rights to tax-free exercise of options remain. If an unapproved alteration is made to the scheme, the approval ceases from the date of the alteration. There is a right of appeal within thirty days of notification of the Revenue

Commissioners' decision to withhold or withdraw approval of a scheme or of an alteration to a scheme. [*TCA 1997, Sch 12A paras 3–5; FA 2001, s 16(c)*] In relation to similar UK provisions, in *CIR v Burton Group plc Ch D 1990, 63 TC 191* an appeal against an Inland Revenue refusal to approve an alteration imposing performance conditions was upheld, and a similar decision was reached in *CIR v Reed International plc and cross-appeal CA 1995, 67 TC 552*, where the amendment removed a contingency on which options would be exercisable and would be required to be exercised within a specified period. This did not amount to the acquisition of a new and different right to acquire scheme shares.

'**Scheme shares**' must:

(i)   form part of the ordinary share capital of the grantor; or of a company which has control of the grantor; or of a company which either is, or has control of, a company which is a member of a consortium (as defined) owning either the grantor or a company which controls the grantor (and which beneficially owns at least 15 per cent of the ordinary share capital of the company so owned);

(ii)   be (*a*) quoted on a recognised stock exchange or (*b*) shares in a company not under the control of another company or (*c*) shares in a company under the control of a company whose shares are quoted on a recognised stock exchange (other than a company which is, or would if RI-resident be, a close company);

(iii)   be fully paid and not redeemable and not subject to any restrictions (as defined but excluding any provisions similar in purpose and effect to those of the Model Code set out in the Listing Rules of the Irish Stock Exchange) other than restrictions which attach to all shares of the same class. Certain restrictions connected with cessation of employment may apply to scheme shares without applying to all shares of the same class. These permit the articles of association to impose a restriction requiring all shares held by directors or employees to be disposed of on cessation of the employment, and all shares acquired by persons who are not directors or employees, but which were acquired in pursuance of rights or interests obtained by directors or employees, to be disposed of immediately they are so acquired. The required disposal must be by sale for money on specified terms, and the articles must also provide that any person disposing of shares of the same class (however acquired) may be required to sell them on the same terms; and

(iv)   except where the scheme shares are in a company whose ordinary share capital is all one class, the majority of shares of the same class must be held by persons other than (*a*) shareholders who acquired their shares as directors or employees of that or any other company and not in pursuance of an offer to the public, (*b*) trustees for such shareholders, and (*c*) where shares are within (ii)(*c*) above and not within (ii)(*a*) above, companies which control the company whose shares are in question or of which that company is an 'associated company'.

[*TCA 1997, Sch 12A paras 11–15*]

Persons eligible to participate must include every person who:

(A)   is an employee or a full-time director (see **20.3**(*c*)(ii) 'Interest payable') of the grantor or, in the case of a group scheme, a participating company;

(B)   has been such an employee or director at all times during a qualifying period, which must not exceed three years; and

(C)   is chargeable to tax in respect of his office or employment under Sch E.

The above persons must be able to obtain and exercise rights on similar terms, but there may be variation of rights between participants according to their remuneration, length of service or similar factors. A person must **not** be eligible if he, and/or certain associates of his, has, or at any time within the preceding twelve months has had, a material interest (broadly more than 15 per cent of ordinary share capital) in a close company (within the meaning of *s 430*, see **12.7** 'Corporation tax') which is a company whose shares may be obtained under the scheme or that company's holding company or a member of a consortium owning such a company. For this purpose 'close company' includes a non-resident company which would otherwise be close and a company which would be close except for its stock exchange quotation. [*TCA 1997, Sch 12A paras 8, 9, 27*]

Information. The Revenue Commissioners may by notice in writing require any person to provide (in not less than thirty days) such information as they think necessary, and as the person to whom the notice is addressed has or can reasonably provide, for the performance of their functions under these provisions. [*TCA 1997, Sch 12A para 6; FA 1999, s 68(b)*]

'Associated company'. For the above purposes, a company is an '*associated company*' of another at a given time, if at that time (or, except in (*e*) or (*l*) above, at any time in the previous twelve months), one of the two has control of the other, or both are under the control of the same person or persons. [*TCA 1997, Sch 12A para 1(1); FA 1999, s 68(b)*]

Summary. For a summary of these provisions, see Revenue Tax Briefing Issue 42 pp 30–34.

APPROVED SHARE OPTION SCHEMES

34.9 *Finance Act 2011, s 10* has removed the exemption from tax on approved share option schemes in respect of share option schemes that are granted and/or exercised after 24 November 2010. With effect **from 6 April 2001 up to 24 November 2010**, a company may obtain approval as below for a scheme for its directors and employees to obtain options to acquire shares in itself or another company without any charge to tax on receipt of the options. Provided that the shares acquired on exercise of an option, or any replacement shares, are not disposed of within three years of the option being obtained, there is also no charge to tax on any increase in value of the shares between the date of grant of the option and its exercise, and the shares are deemed to have been acquired for a consideration of the amount paid for their acquisition. Options acquired after 14 February 2001 but prior to approval of a scheme are treated as having been acquired under an approved scheme, provided that the scheme was approved on or before 31 December 2001 and that, at both the time the option was obtained and (if it was exercised before approval was granted) the time it was exercised, the scheme would have been capable of approval had these provisions been in force on 15 February 2001.

Where the shares are acquired by the director or employee from a trust or company set up to acquire and hold scheme shares, no chargeable gain or allowable loss accrues to the trust or company on that disposal. This does not alter the deemed base cost of the shares to the employee or director (as above).

[*TCA 1997, s 519D; FA 2001, s 15(a)*]

See **30.26**(*d*) 'Sch D, Cases I and II' as regards deduction available to the company for expenses in setting up the scheme.

Approval of a scheme is by the Revenue Commissioners (on application in writing by the company which has established the scheme ('the grantor'), and accompanied by such particulars and supported by such evidence as the Revenue Commissioners may require) and is given if the following conditions are satisfied. 'Control' for these purposes is as under *s 432*, and a company is a member of a consortium owning another company if it is one of not more than five companies between them beneficially owning at least 75 per cent of the other company's ordinary share capital and each owning at least five per cent of that capital.

(*a*)   The directors and employees may obtain rights to acquire 'scheme shares' (see below);

(*b*)   The scheme may not permit the transfer of scheme rights, but may provide that, if the participant dies before exercising them, they may be exercised up to a year after the date of death (and the loss of exemption on exercise within three years does not then apply);

(*c*)   The price at which scheme shares may be acquired under the option must be stated when the option is acquired and must not be less than the market value of shares of the same class at that time or, if the Revenue Commissioners and the grantor so agree in writing, at some earlier time. The scheme *may* provide for such variation of the stated price as may be necessary to take account of any variation of the share capital of which the scheme shares form part;

The scheme *may* also include the following provisions:

(*d*)   If any other company (the 'acquiring company') (i) obtains control of the company whose shares are scheme shares as a result of making a general offer to acquire the whole of its issued share capital or all the shares of the same class as the scheme shares, or (ii) obtains control of such a company in pursuance of a compromise or arrangement with creditors and members sanctioned by the court under *Companies Act 1963, s 201*, or (iii) becomes bound or entitled to acquire shares in the company under *Companies Act 1963, s 204* (power to acquire shares of dissenting shareholders), then the scheme may provide for the rights to acquire scheme shares to be exchanged for rights to acquire shares in the acquiring company, or in another company falling within (i) below in relation to the acquiring company, which are equivalent, as regards value and condition, to the rights under the existing scheme. The new rights are then treated as having been granted at the time the original rights were granted. The exchange must take place within six months of the company taking unconditional control, or of the court sanctioning the compromise or arrangement, or within the period during which the acquiring company remains bound or entitled to acquire the shares;

(*e*)　　The scheme may extend to other companies of which the grantor has control, and is then a 'group scheme' with 'participating' companies.

[*TCA 1997, Sch 12C paras 1, 2, 7, 17–19; FA 2001, s 15(b)*]

The Revenue Commissioners may not approve a scheme if it appears to them that there are features which are neither essential nor reasonably incidental to its purpose of providing share options for employees and full-time directors (ie those required to devote substantially the whole of their time to the service of the company), or which have or would have the effect of discouraging any eligible persons from participating. Where the grantor is a member of a group of companies (consisting of a company and any companies it controls or with which it is associated (as specially defined)), the scheme must not in effect be restricted wholly or mainly to directors or the more highly-paid employees in the group. If, after approval, any of the above conditions cease to be satisfied or required information is not provided, approval may be withdrawn, but existing rights to tax-free exercise of options remain. If an unapproved alteration is made to the scheme, approval ceases from the date of the alteration. There is a right of appeal within 30 days of notification of the Revenue Commissioners' decision to withhold or withdraw approval of a scheme or of an alteration to a scheme. [*TCA 1997, Sch 12C paras 3–5; FA 2001, s 15(b)*] In relation to similar UK provisions, in *CIR v Burton Group plc Ch D 1990, 63 TC 191* an appeal against an Inland Revenue refusal to approve an alteration imposing performance conditions was upheld, and a similar decision was reached in *CIR v Reed International plc and cross-appeal CA 1995, 67 TC 552*, where the amendment removed a contingency on which options would be exercisable and would be required to be exercised within a specified period. This did not amount to the acquisition of a new and different right to acquire scheme shares.

'**Scheme shares**' must:

(i)　　form part of the ordinary share capital of the grantor; or of a company which has control of the grantor; or of a company which either is or has control of a company which is a member of a consortium owning either the grantor or a company which controls the grantor and which beneficially owns at least 15 per cent of the ordinary share capital of the company so owned;

(ii)　　be (*a*) quoted on a recognised stock exchange or (*b*) shares in a company which is not under the control of another company or (*c*) shares in a company controlled by a company whose shares are quoted on a recognised stock exchange (other than a company which is, or would if RI-resident be, a close company);

(iii)　　be fully paid-up and not redeemable and not subject to any restrictions (as defined but excluding any provisions similar in purpose and effect to those of the Model Code set out in the Listing Rules of the Irish Stock Exchange) other than restrictions which attach to all shares of the same class. Certain restrictions connected with cessation of employment may apply to scheme shares without applying to all shares of the same class. These permit the articles of association to impose a restriction requiring all shares held by directors or employees to be disposed of on cessation of the employment, and all shares acquired by persons who are not directors or employees, but which were acquired in pursuance of rights or interests obtained by directors or employees, to be disposed of immediately they are so acquired. The required disposal must be by sale for money on specified terms, and the articles must also provide that any person disposing of shares of the same class (however acquired) may be required to sell them on the same terms; and

(iv)   except where the scheme shares are in a company whose ordinary share capital is all of one class, the majority of shares of the same class must be held by persons other than (*a*) shareholders who acquired their shares as directors or employees of that or any other company and not in pursuance of an offer to the public, (*b*) trustees for such shareholders, and (*c*) where shares are within (ii)(*c*) above but not within (ii)(*a*) above, companies which control the company whose shares are in question or of which that company is an 'associated company' (within *s 432*).

[*TCA 1997, Sch 12C paras 11–16; FA 2001, s 15(b)*]

Persons eligible to participate must include every person who:

(A)   is an employee or full-time director of the grantor or, in the case of a group scheme, a participating company;

(B)   has been such an employee or director at all times during a qualifying period (which must not exceed three years); and

(C)   is chargeable to tax in respect of the office or employment under Sch E.

Subject to the 'key employee or director' provision referred to below, they must be able to obtain and exercise rights under the scheme on similar terms, but there may be variation of rights between participants according to their remuneration, length of service or similar factors or because of approaching normal retirement. A person must **not** be eligible if he or she, and/or certain associates, has, or at any time within the preceding twelve months has had, a material interest (broadly more than 15 per cent of ordinary share capital) in a close company (within *s 430*, see **12.7** 'Corporation tax') being a company whose shares may be obtained under the scheme or such a company's holding company or a member of a consortium owning such a company. For this purpose, 'close company' includes a non-resident company which would otherwise be close and a company which would be close but for being quoted on a stock exchange.

A '*key employee or director*' is one whose specialist skills, qualifications and relevant experience are certified by the company to the Revenue Commissioners to be vital to its success. Such individuals may be granted options which do not meet the 'similar terms' requirement described above, provided that, in any year of assessment, they do not also acquire options which do meet those terms and that not more than 30 per cent in total of the shares in respect of which options have been granted are within this exception.

[*TCA 1997, Sch 12C paras 7–10, 21; FA 2001, s 15(b)*]

Information. The Revenue Commissioners may by notice in writing require any person to provide (in not less than 30 days) such information as they think necessary, and as the person to whom the notice is addressed has or can reasonably provide, for the performance of their functions under these provisions. In particular they may request a certificate from the auditor of the grantor as to certain aspects of eligibility. [*TCA 1997, Sch 12C para 20; FA 2001, s 15(b)*]

EXPENSES

34.10 Expenses *wholly, exclusively and necessarily* incurred in performance of duties may be claimed [*TCA 1997, s 114*], including wear and tear (but not initial allowances) of cars, machinery etc. [*TCA 1997, s 301(1)*] For many trades, flat rate allowances have been agreed under *s 115* with the trade union concerned, but this does not debar a claim being made instead for the expenses actually incurred. Business entertainment expenditure is not an allowable expense (see also **30.10** 'Sch D, Cases I and II') [*TCA 1997, s 840*] but it is understood that, in practice, where entertainment expenses incurred by an employee on the employer's behalf are reimbursed by the employer, the expenses are disallowed to the employer and are not brought into charge on the employee under *s 117* (see **34.3** above). See generally **38.195–38.199** 'Tax cases' for relevant case law. See also **34.3** above as regards concessional relief available in respect of certain expenses incurred by directors and employees.

PAYE SYSTEM

34.11 Under the PAYE system the employer deducts tax on any payment of emoluments in accordance with Regulations designed to equate cumulative allowances and reliefs and to apply them, weekly or monthly, to cumulative gross pay. There have been amendments introduced to the enabling provisions for the PAYE regulations. The Revenue Commissioners are empowered to amend the PAYE regulations, thereby ensuring that existing practices and procedures are supported by relevant enabling provisions and regulations. There are provisions for operation of tax deduction cards, accounting by employer to Revenue, and recovery from employer, inspection of wages sheets and other records, penalties, etc. There is also a *de minimis* limit for operation of PAYE (which is substantially higher in the case of an individual with one domestic employee). Provisions also apply for charge of interest on deductions from pay not handed over on due dates, for estimation and recovery of tax, including interest, not paid over or under-remitted, and for priority in bankruptcy, liquidation, etc. Since 2005, an individual having a material interest in a company (broadly, having 15 per cent control either directly or with others) receives no credit for PAYE deducted by the company unless there is documentary evidence to show that the PAYE has been remitted to Revenue. Where there is a shortfall in PAYE due by the company, any PAYE paid is applied first against the liabilities of those not having a material interest in the company and is then pro-rated amongst those with a material interest in proportion to their emoluments. In certain circumstances a person who holds a fixed charge on the book debts of a company may become liable to discharge the company's liability to PAYE and PRSI. The extent of such liability can be determined by the person providing to Revenue a copy of all the papers lodged with the Companies Registration Office in relation to the fixed charge. There is now a straightforward section stating the exact details required by the Revenue in relation to the fixed charge. [*FA 2007, s 120*] Since 31 March 2006, specific provision is made to ensure the operation of PAYE where the employer is non-resident, payment is made by an intermediary, employment is not exercised wholly in RI or employees work for a person who is not their employer. [*TCA 1997, ss 903, 983–995,*

1000; FA 1999, ss 24, 25; FA 2001, s 237, Sch 2 para 53; FA 2002, s 129(1)(e); FA 2003, s 157; FA 2005, s 13; FA 2006, s 16] See **25.2** 'Payment of tax' as regards collection of certain payments in default.

The consolidated PAYE regulations are contained in *SI 559/01 as amended*.

No formal Sch E assessments are made except where the taxpayer within four years (five years for tax years 2002 and previous) so requires, or payments in the year refer to other years, or liability to tax at the higher rates exists. Since 25 March 2005, a statement of liability sent to an employee may be treated as an assessment if the Inspector so directs and notifies the employee. All the provisions of the Income Tax Acts relating to appeals against assessments and collection and recovery of tax then apply to the statement. [*TCA 1997, s 997; FA 2003, s 17; SI 508/03; FA 2005, s 26*]

See **38.192** 'Tax cases' regarding allowance in assessment for PAYE deducted.

For more detailed coverage of the PAYE (and PRSI) system, see **Bloomsbury's Tax Guide** or **Judge Irish Income Tax**.

RETIREMENT, COMPENSATION ETC.

34.12 Payments by the employer for the provision of retirement benefits under schemes etc are generally assessable under Sch E unless under:

(i)   a statutory superannuation scheme;

(ii)   certain Government schemes; or

(iii)   an approved scheme (as defined).

[*TCA 1997, ss 770, 777, 778*]

See also **2.22**, **2.23** 'Allowances, credits and rates'.

Payments received on retirement or loss of office are chargeable to tax under Sch E unless they:

(*a*)   result from the death or disability of, or injury to, the holder of the office or employment;

(*b*)   consist of payments for restrictive covenants liable to tax at higher rates (see below);

(*c*)   arise from schemes, the premiums for which were chargeable on the holder of the office or employment;

(*d*)   are paid under such a scheme as is mentioned under (i)–(iii) above;

(*e*)   arise in part from foreign service comprising:

    (i)   three-quarters of the whole period of service,

    (ii)   (where service exceeds ten years) the last ten years, or

    (iii)   (where service exceeds 20 years) half of the period of service including ten of the last 20 years, or (*f*)   do not exceed the appropriate limit (see below) (with provisions to prevent the splitting of payments to take advantage of this exemption). Only the excess over the exemption limit is chargeable in appropriate cases.

An additional new exemption was introduced in respect of redundancies of up to €5,000 for each eligible employee, who has more than two year's full time continuous service, where an employer bears the cost of retraining workers as part of a redundancy package. The retraining must be designed to improve skills or knowledge used in obtaining employment or setting up a business and the course completed within six months of the employee being made redundant. The exemption will not apply to spouses or dependants of the employer, and the employees must avail of the retraining rather than receive cash. [*FA 2008, s 22*]

As regards (*a*) above, see **38.237, 38.238** 'Tax cases'.

(*d*) above does not apply to certain allowances paid to members of the Oireachtas and certain public servants, and such allowances (other than certain lump sum elements) are taxable under PAYE (see **34.11** above). It also does not apply to benefits under statutory schemes established or amended on or after 10 May 1997 which are paid in connection with redundancy or abolition of office, or to facilitate greater efficiency or economy within the employing body, unless they are normal retirement benefits under the scheme (whether or not enhanced or paid early).

The *appropriate limit* referred to at (*f*) above is the greater of the 'basic exemption' and the Standard Capital Superannuation Benefit, the latter being calculated by deducting the 'relevant capital sum' from one-fifteenth of the product of the average annual remuneration of the last three years of service (or the whole period of service if less than three years) and the number of complete years of service. If the claimant has not previously (for 2002 onwards, in the previous ten years of assessment) made a claim for exemption or reduction of liability under this provision, and the 'relevant capital sum' received or receivable in respect of the office or employment is less than €10,000 (before 2002, less than €5,080/£4,000), the appropriate limit is increased by the shortfall below that amount.

The '*basic exemption*' is €10,160/£8,000 plus €765/£600 for each complete year of service (£6,000 and £500 respectively for payments made before 1 December 1998).

The '*relevant capital sum*' is the aggregate of all non-chargeable lump sums received and the value of all non-chargeable lump sums receivable (including any which may be received by exercise of an option or right to commute a pension, whether or not such option or right is exercised, unless the option or right has been irrevocably surrendered under scheme rules) under a scheme within (i)–(iii) above.

Finance Act 2011, s 8 has introduced a cap on the relief to which an individual is entitled on ex-gratia payments. As of from 1 January 2011, an individual is entitled to tax relief on an ex-gratia payment subject to a maximum lifetime sum of €200,000. Any payments from 1 January 2011 (including payments received prior to 1 January 2011) that an individual received are included in computing the €200,000 maximum. Any payments received for the purposes of retraining subject to the maximum of €5,000 are not included in this limit. Also not included are payments made on account of the death of an employee or injury or disability of the holder of an office or employment.

The tax liability on such a payment is computed by treating the payment as additional income of the year of assessment of retirement, etc. An amount calculated by the following formula is substituted, however, where a reduced liability would result.

where   P is the lump sum payment less the exempt amount;

T is the claimant's total tax liability on income for the previous three years (five years for payments made prior to 1 January 2005) of assessment (before any double tax relief);

I is the claimant's total taxable income of the previous five years of assessment.

$$P \times \frac{T}{I}$$

[*TCA 1997, ss 123, 124, 201, Sch 3; ITA 1967, Sch 3 para 4(b); FA 1993, s 8(b)(ii); FA 1999, s 14; FA 2002, s 15; FA 2005, s 19, FA 2011, s 8*]

Since 25 March 2005, where the exemption is claimed and the payment is on account of death, injury or disability, the person making the payment must report to Revenue within 46 days of the end of the year of assessment in which the payment is made, the name, address, personal public service number and the amount of the payment and the basis on which the payment is not chargeable to tax (including, where the payment is on account of injury or disability, the extent of that injury or disability). [*TCA 1997, s 201A; FA 2005, s 19*]

Sums received on reorganisation as compensation for actual or possible reduction of future remuneration, change of duties or place of employment are charged under Sch E but the income tax thereon is limited to three times the tax on one-third thereof. [*TCA 1997, s 480*]

Payments etc received in respect of certain restrictive covenants entered into by a person who holds, has held or is about to hold an office or employment are treated as remuneration from the office or employment (if they would not otherwise be so treated) and subject to PAYE where appropriate. A corresponding deduction may be available to the payer as a trading deduction or as a management expense. [*TCA 1997, s 127*]

For service involving career breaks, job-sharing or movement within a group of companies, see Revenue Tax Briefing Issue 36 p 13. See also **16.17** 'Exempt income and special savings schemes' as regards interaction of the above provisions with the provisions for exemption of certain lump sums in respect of pay restructuring agreements.

FINANCE (NO 2) ACT 2008

34.13 The *Finance (No 2) Act 2008* provides for the repayment of tax where a non-domiciled individual is in receipt of emoluments in the State. The new basis offers an alternative system which will allow a refund of tax to be claimed in certain circumstances. PAYE must be operated at the outset, however. The proposal does not have unlimited use and only non-Irish domiciles assigned from companies with countries with which there is a DTA will benefit.

In addition to restrictions imposed on the employer's country of incorporation, additional limitations apply in respect of the employees in question which are designed to ensure that employment arrangements cannot be restructured in order to fall within the proposed regime.

Where all conditions are satisfied, an employee may make a claim on their tax return for the appropriate year for their taxable income to be determined based on the higher of:

(*a*)   the actual amount attributable to Irish duties that was remitted in that year; or

(*b*)   €100,000 plus 50 per cent of the balance attributable to Irish duties.

Anti-avoidance provisions apply when income for a particular tax year is remitted in a later year. Employers and assignees affected by the proposals will need to monitor and track assignees' employment income per year of assessment in order to manage the anti-avoidance provisions.

35 35 Schedule F – Distributions

Cross-references. See also 'Corporation tax' at **12.10** for distribution and **13.12** 'Deduction of tax at source' for dividend withholding tax.

35.1 Schedule F applies to all dividends and other distributions in the year of assessment made by a company resident in RI, unless specially excluded from income tax. All such distributions are deemed to be income however they fall to be dealt with in the hands of the recipient. No distribution chargeable under Sch F is chargeable under any other income tax provision. [*TCA 1997, s 20; FA 2000, Sch 2*]

35.2 Tax credits are abolished for distributions made after 5 April 1999. [*TCA 1997, s 136(1); FA 1998, Sch 5 para 1*] See now **13.12** 'Deduction of tax at source' as regards dividend withholding tax which applies after that date.

[*TCA 1997, s 4(1), 136; CTA 1976, ss 83, 88; FA 1978, s 28; FA 1983, s 28; FA 1988, s 31, Sch 2; FA 1990, s 36, Sch 1; FA 1992, s 38; FA 1994, s 27; FA 1995, ss 39, 45, Sch 2; FA 1997, s 37, Sch 2; FA 1998, s 61, Sch 5 para 1; FA 2000, Sch 2*]

36 Settlements

[*TCA 1997, ss 791–798, 805*]

Cross-reference. See also 7 'Capital acquisitions tax'.

36.1 Trustees of settlements are taxed (at the standard rate) in their representative capacities under the Schedule appropriate to the income received. In addition a surcharge of 20 per cent is assessed on income of *accumulation* and *discretionary* trusts unless it is (i) distributed as income during the year of assessment or within eighteen months thereafter, or (ii) before being distributed, treated as the income of the settlor or any other person, or (iii) income of a charity or of an occupational pension scheme, or (iv) less than the trustees' expenses for the year which are properly chargeable to income (including the annual discretionary trust charge (see **7.14** 'Capital acquisitions tax') but not capital gains tax (**9**), see Revenue Tax Briefing Issue 33 p 19).

The surcharge is chargeable for the year of assessment in which ends the period of 18 months beginning immediately after the end of the year of assessment in which the income arose. [*TCA 1997, s 805*]

Beneficiaries receive income from settlements which is treated as net of standard rate of income tax (but any surcharge suffered by the trustee is ignored).

Income deemed to be that of settlor or disponer. In such a case (see below) the income is deemed to be the 'top slice' of the settlor's or disponer's income. The settlor/disponer is entitled to reclaim the amount of tax paid by him from the trustees (and must repay to the trustees any excess tax recouped). [*TCA 1997, ss 793, 797*]

DISPOSITIONS OF INCOME

36.2 See **38.200–38.206** 'Tax cases' regarding existence of settlement.

In the following cases, income disposed of (by trust, covenant, agreement or arrangement) is deemed nonetheless to be income of the disponer and of nobody else.

(*a*) *Revocable dispositions*, ie subject to a power of revocation exercisable, without the consent of anyone except spouse, by the disponer or his spouse so that beneficial enjoyment of the income could revert to him; [*TCA 1997, s 791*]

(*b*) *Dispositions of income not made for valuable and sufficient consideration*, except where the disposition absolutely divests the disponer of the income-producing capital, and except for the exempt deeds of covenant below. [*TCA 1997, s 792*]

Deeds of covenant. Since **6 April 1996** (or, in certain cases involving hardship, **6 April 2000** (see *Sch 32 para 27; FA 1998, s 7*)), income under such a disposition is *not* deemed to be that of the disponer, who is not taxable thereon, where:

(A) for payments before 6 April 2001, the period for which it is payable can exceed three years and the beneficiary is:

(i)   an RI university or college, where the covenant is for the purpose of promoting research,

(ii)   an RI university, college or school, where the covenant is for the purpose of assisting the teaching of natural sciences, or a fund making grants to such institutions for such purposes,

(iii)   a human rights body having consultative status with UNO or the Council of Europe; or

(B) the period for which it is payable can exceed six years and the beneficiary is an individual who is either:

(i)   aged 65 years or over, or

(ii)   permanently mentally or physically incapacitated (but see **36.3** below as regards incapacitated persons aged under 18 and unmarried).

As regards (A) above, for payments after 5 April 2001 see **Ch 2** 'Allowances, credits and rates' and **12.9** 'Corporation tax'.

Where, however, such a disposition or dispositions (other than within (B)(ii)) is or are made by an individual, the exemption does not apply (and the settlor, if living, is accordingly taxable) to the extent that the income for a year of assessment under such dispositions amounts in aggregate to more than five per cent of the settlor's total income for the year (the aggregate payments within the five per cent limit being apportioned, where necessary, in proportion to the beneficiaries' entitlements).

[*TCA 1997, ss 792, 848A(13); ITA 1967, s 439; FA 1995, s 13; FA 2001, s 45(1)*]

See also **38.204**, **38.205** 'Tax cases'.

Except for (A) above, covenants in favour of charities are *not* relieved of income tax.

SETTLEMENTS ON CHILDREN, ETC

36.3 Income paid under a settlement to a child, under 18 and unmarried, of the settlor is deemed to be income of the settlor if he is taxable as an RI resident. 'Settlement' is widely defined and includes the transfer of a business or admission of child into partnership. Income is deemed to be paid in cases of future or contingent interests or discretionary trusts and where it is not allocated. Since 6 April 1995 (and in respect of payments before that date under settlements made after 7 February 1995), this is extended to all settlements on persons under 18 and unmarried unless, not being a child of the settlor, such a person is permanently mentally or physically incapacitated. [*TCA 1997, ss 794, 795, 798; ITA 1967, s 443; FA 1995, s 12(1)(2)*]

The exception is income accumulated under a trust (contained in an 'irrevocable instrument' as defined) of property, and payments out of such property or accumulated income. [*TCA 1997, ss 794(5), 796*]

DELIVERY OF INFORMATION BY THIRD PARTIES

36.4 The *Finance (No 2) Act 2008* inserted *s 896A*. The section provides for delivery of information by a third party where that party is concerned with the making of a trust and the settlor is resident in the State but the trustees are not resident in the State. In addition, the section provides that an authorised office of the Revenue Commissioners may, by notice in writing, request a party to a settlement to provide details of the settlement. [*F(No 2) A 2008, s 93*]

ANTI-AVOIDANCE

36.5 *Finance Act 2011, s 29* has introduced further anti-avoidance legislation in respect of close companies. A new *s 436A* has been included in the *TCA 1997* and is designed to counter attempts to extract funds from close companies on a tax-free basis through the use of settlements.

The section inserted *TCA 1997, s 436A*, which provides that amounts settled by a close company on or after 21 January 2011 in connection with *relevant* settlements will be treated as a distribution to the trustees of the settlement. The section also contains a provision to ensure that where on or after 21 January 2011 an individual who is or was a member of a close company, or a relative of such an individual, receives an amount in money or money's worth out of assets comprised in a relevant settlement, the amount received (net of any consideration given) will be treated as annual profits or gains of the individual, or relative, chargeable to income tax under Case IV of Sch D in the year of assessment in which it is received.

37 Social Welfare System

37.1 The RI Social Welfare system is broadly similar to the social security system in the UK. There are four basic kinds of benefit schemes:

(*a*)   *Social Insurance*, funded in part by contributions from insured persons and their employers and by self-employed contributors, and providing certain benefits such as unemployment benefit, disability benefit and retirement pension, some subject to contribution conditions. A separate scheme ('wet time' insurance) applies for building labourers who lose working time due to bad weather;

(*b*)   *Occupational Injuries Benefits*, with no contribution conditions, available to insured persons injured at work;

(*c*)   *Social Assistance*, distinct from the insurance benefits and paid directly out of State funds on the basis of a means test, providing such benefits as unemployment assistance, allowance for deserted wives and non-contributory old age pension;

(*d*)   *Miscellaneous Benefits*, notably children's allowances but also including free travel for disabled persons, footwear for children and certain supplementary allowances.

Only aspects of the Social Welfare system which affect tax and PAYE deductions are discussed below.

SOCIAL INSURANCE CONTRIBUTIONS

37.2 Compulsory insurance. Almost all kinds of employees over the age of 16 and under 66 must be insured and periodic contributions must therefore be paid in respect of their employment. The main exceptions are persons employed by their spouses or employed under oral contracts at home or on a farm by prescribed relatives. Part of the total contribution is paid by the employee (usually by deduction by the employer under the PAYE system) and the other part by the employer.

   Pay-related social insurance ('PRSI') employee contributions are calculated as a percentage of the contributor's earnings accountable for tax purposes (currently four per cent), with any amount of earnings over an annual limit (**€40,420** from 1 January 2003) being ignored. The first €127 pw of earnings (€26 pw for contributors paying Class B, C and D contributions) are ignored in calculating the PRSI payable. No contributions are payable where earnings are less than €287 in any given week. Eleven contribution Classes are laid down, according to the kind of employment, and the percentages for the employer's and employee's contributions are laid down for each class (with variations within each class depending on level of earnings and whether the employee has a medical card or is a woman in receipt of certain benefits). There is no annual limit for employer's contribution. Since 1 January 2004, PRSI will also apply to benefits in kind (see **34.3** 'Sch E – Emoluments').

Self-employed contributions are calculated as a percentage of reckonable emoluments or income as follows:

From **6 April 2001**   **3%** of reckonable emoluments or income

subject to a minimum of €253. No contribution is payable where the aggregate of reckonable emoluments and reckonable income before deducting capital allowances or pension scheme contributions is below €3,174.

A person availing of the childcare services relief provided under *s 216C* (see **16.2** Exempt Income and Special Savings Schemes) is liable for a social insurance contribution of €253 per annum. [*Social Welfare Law Reform and Pensions Act 2006*]

The annual contribution is €157 where no return is required by the tax authorities.

Earnings in excess of the annual PRSI limit referred to above were ignored up to 5 April 2001, but the ceiling is abolished thereafter. Provisions are laid down regarding persons exempted from making contributions.

[*Social Welfare Act 1988, s 10*]

Voluntary contributions. A person under age 66 who ceases to be employed or self-employed, after at least 156 weeks in insurable employment or insurable self-employment throughout which contributions were paid, may elect to pay voluntary contributions to maintain their insurance record. Voluntary contributions are also a percentage of the contributor's reckonable income, ignoring any excess over the annual PRSI limit referred to above, subject to an annual minimum and maximum. The percentage payable is 6.6 per cent where contributions previously paid provide insurance for old age contributory pension purposes, otherwise 2.6 per cent. Voluntary contributions by a person previously self-employed who ceases self-employment are limited to €253.

Intermittent unemployment insurance contributions payable by building labourers over 16 and their employers under the *Insurance (Intermittent Unemployment) Acts 1942–1978* are paid in a different way, by affixing stamps in a book. Benefits are taxable.

FÁS apprenticeship levy. Since 6 April 1996 to 5 April 2000, employers in certain industries were liable to pay an additional 0.25 per cent apprenticeship training levy for each employee. The industries concerned are construction, printing and paper, motor and engineering (mechanical and electrical but not electronic). The levy is abolished from 6 April 2000, to be replaced by a new National Training Fund levy of 0.7 per cent payable by all Class A and Class H employers. There is a corresponding reduction in the employer's PRSI contribution rates, so that there is no overall increase in the employer's costs.

Youth employment and income levies and health contributions. See **Ch 41**.

SOCIAL INSURANCE BENEFITS

37.3 Below is a list of available social insurance benefits (excluding occupational injuries benefit) with notes of whether there are contribution conditions and whether they are taxable.

Benefit	Contributions Conditions	Taxable under PAYE s 126]
Unemployment benefit	Yes	Yes**
Pre-retirement benefit	Yes	No
Disability benefit	Yes	Yes**
Maternity benefit	Yes	No
Pay-related benefit	No	Yes**
(Payable with any of the above and with injury benefit in **37.4** below on claims made before 21 July 1994)		
Invalidity pension	Yes	No*
Contributory survivor's pension	Yes	Yes
Contributory orphan's allowance	Yes	Yes
Deserted wife's benefit	Yes	No*
Deserted wife's allowance	No	No
Retirement pension	Yes	Yes
Contributory old age pension	Yes	Yes
Death grant	Yes	No
Treatment benefits	Yes	No
Intermittent unemployment ('wet time') benefit	No	No

*Taxable under Sch E, but in practice only taxed where the period of payment is one year or more.

**Exclusive of child dependant allowances and of the first €13/£10 pw of unemployment benefit, and exclusive of disability and/or injury benefit for the first 36 days incapacity for work. [*TCA 1997, s 126; FA 1992, s 15; SI 19/94; FA 1995, s 10(1); FA 1997, s 4(1)*] However, for 1995/96 to 2006 inclusive all unemployment benefit of persons employed in short-time employment is non-taxable. [*TCA 1997, s 126(8); FA 1995, s 10(2); FA 1996, s 4; FA 1997, s 4(2); FA 1998, s 6; FA 1999, s 11; FA 2000, s 16; FA 2001, s 6; FA 2002, s 7; FA 2003, s 5; FA 2005, s 5*]

OCCUPATIONAL INJURIES BENEFITS

37.4 These benefits are available to insured employees who are injured in the course of their employment or who contract prescribed occupational diseases. There are no contribution conditions.

Benefit		*Taxable under PAYE*
Injury benefit		Yes
Disablement benefit (after initial period)		No, (but taxable under Sch E)*
Free medical care		No
Death benefits:	widow's pension	No, (but taxable under Sch E)
	dependent widower's pension	No, (but taxable under Sch E)
	orphan's pension	No, (but taxable under Sch E)
	dependent parent's pension	No, (but taxable under Sch E)
	funeral grant	No

*The taxability of disablement benefit is currently the subject of an appeal to the High Court.

SOCIAL ASSISTANCE BENEFITS

37.5 The following means-tested benefits are available for persons who do not meet contribution conditions in **37.3** above: Unemployment assistance; Non-contributory widow's pension; Non-contributory orphan's pension; Social assistance allowances for deserted wives and prisoners' wives; One parent allowance; Non-contributory old age pension; and Blind person's pension.

OTHER BENEFITS

37.6 There are a number of other miscellaneous benefits, most notably child benefit. These are not taxable.

38 Tax Cases

38.1 This chapter gives brief summaries of reported (and some unreported) RI tax cases relevant to current legislation. See **1.2** 'Administration and general' as regards UK Court decisions. Where comparable current provisions have replaced those at issue in a case, the current statutory reference is quoted.

An alphabetical list of the cases summarised below, under the names of the parties, is appended to the end of this chapter.

ASSESSMENTS AND APPEALS PROCEDURES

38.2 Discovery. A company carrying on the business of quarrying and of manufacturing concrete blocks and cement pipes deducted in its accounts the estimated value of the sand and gravel extracted from its own land used in its manufacturing. The deduction was not queried by the revenue authorities until 1966/67 when, on appeal, the Circuit Court Judge held the deduction was not permissible. The company acquiesced in this decision but appealed against additional assessments for 1961/62 to 1965/66, withdrawing the deduction, which the inspector then made. The assessments were upheld, rejecting the contention that there had been no 'discovery'. *W Ltd v Wilson* TL 110; II ITR 627.

38.3 Discovery. In the case, the substantive issue in which is dealt with at **38.115** below, a preliminary point was whether an additional assessment could be raised following a change of view by the inspector, where the original assessment had been the subject of an appeal which had been settled by agreement with the inspector. Held, under *s 933(3)(b)* the assessment or amended assessment in these circumstances has 'the same force and effect' as an assessment in respect of which no appeal had been made, and since it was not contested that an unappealed assessment which becomes final and conclusive can be the subject of an additional assessment under *s 924(1)*, the position could not be different in this case. The *Hammond Lane Metal Co Ltd v O'Culacháin* IV ITR 197.

38.4 Appeal adjourned for agreement of figures – whether a determination. A Special Commissioner heard an appeal against an estimated Case I assessment for 1935/36. A relevant point was whether the trade had ceased in that year and he decided that it had, adjourning the appeal for agreement of the figures. New facts came to the knowledge of the inspector and at a subsequent hearing the Commissioner decided he was not satisfied that the trade had ceased in 1935/36. The taxpayer's application for a *certiorari* to quash the second decision was refused. There had been no determination of the appeal. *The State (PJ Whelan) v Smidic* 2 ITC 188; I ITR 571; [1938] IR 626.

38.5 Res judicata – equitable estoppel. A company appealed against its excess profits duty assessment for the year to 27 March 1915, objecting to its 'pre-war standard' by reference to which its excess profits liable to the duty were ascertained. After litigation, the appeal was determined by the Court of Appeal. Errors were discovered in the calculation of the standard, and in the assessment for the three years to March 1920 the Revenue used an amended standard. The company appealed, contending that the standard fixed for the year to March 1915 was binding for subsequent periods. Held, the Revenue was free to correct the calculation of the standard. The matter was not *res judicata* nor was the Revenue estopped on grounds of equity. *Bolands Ltd v CIR* 1 ITC 42; I ITR 34; 4 ATC 526.

38.6 Res judicata – decision purporting to govern subsequent assessments. The appeal was against an assessment for 1952/53. Included in the assessment was a bad debt recovery in the basis period, to the extent to which, with previous recoveries, it exceeded a doubtful debt allowance made in the 1940/41 assessment. The 1940/41 assessment was determined on appeal by a Circuit Court Judge who said in deciding the matter that any recoveries would not be assessable. In the 1952/53 appeal, the Circuit Court Judge decided he was bound by the decision of his predecessor. His decision was reversed by the High Court, applying *Smidic*, **38.4** above. The jurisdiction of the Circuit Court Judge in the 1940/41 appeal was limited to the determination of the appeal before him. *Bourke v P Lyster & Sons Ltd* 3 ITC 247; II ITR 374.

38.7 1. Residence. 2. Appeals – evidence of documents. The taxpayer appealed against assessments under Sch D, Case III on interest and income from securities and possessions, on the grounds that (i) he was, as regards one year, not resident in RI, having spent a total of twelve months in the Isle of Man, including most of the year in question, and (ii) he had assigned his interest in the securities, etc to his son by a document executed under seal in the Isle of Man. The document was in the possession of the son in Africa, and the taxpayer had taken no steps to make it available. Held, the taxpayer was resident in RI throughout, and secondary evidence of the terms of any document should not be admitted where the original was in existence. *Hewson v Kealy* 2 ITC 286; II ITR 15.

38.8 Case stated – questions of law. When a court has before it a case stated by a judge, the following principles apply in deciding whether a particular decision was correct in law (the same principles apply in relation to cases stated by appeal commissioners):

(*a*)   findings of primary fact by the judge should not be disturbed unless there is no evidence to support them;

(*b*)   inferences from primary facts are mixed questions of fact and law;

(*c*)   if the judge's conclusions show that he has adopted a wrong view of the law, they should be set aside;

(*d*)   if his conclusions are not based on an incorrect view of the law, they should not be set aside unless the inferences which he drew were ones which no reasonable judge could draw;

(*e*)   some evidence will point to one conclusion, other evidence to the opposite: these are essentially matters of degree and the judge's conclusions should not be disturbed (even if the Court does not agree with them, for [the Court is] not retrying the case) unless they are such that a reasonable judge could not have arrived at them or they are based on a mistaken view of the law.

O'Culacháin v McMullan Brothers Ltd V ITR 200. See generally **4.1** 'Appeals'. For another issue in this case, see **38.35** below.

38.9 Whether point of law involved. The Commissioners were upheld in refusing to state a Case, following their confirmation of an estimated assessment, on the ground that no point of law was involved. *R v Special Commissioners (ex parte Stein)* 1 ITC 71; I ITR 62. (*Note.* Later UK cases suggest that, in most such confirmations, it would be a question of law as to whether there was evidence for the decision insofar as it was one of fact.)

38.10 Whether point of law involved – evidence to be reviewed. In a capital gains tax case, the only issue for decision by the Circuit Court Judge had been the value of land at 6 April 1974. The appellant contended that no point of law was involved, so that the decision must stand. Held, it was necessary to have regard to the whole of the Case Stated, including the summaries of the evidence of both parties, the findings of the judge as to what evidence he accepted and what he rejected and the expert opinions on values. Unless the conclusions from the primary facts were ones that no reasonable Commissioner or Circuit Judge could draw, the decision could not be set aside. There was evidence here to support the valuation arrived at. *McMahon v Murphy* IV ITR 125.

38.11 Retirement of Commissioner after Case demanded. In an appeal, the Stated Case was signed by one of the two Special Commissioners who heard it, the other having since retired. The High Court required the retired Commissioner to sign the Case, before proceeding with the hearing. *O'Dwyer v Irish Exporters and Importers Ltd* 2 ITC 251; I ITR 629; [1943] IR 176. (For another issue in this case, see **38.118** below).

38.12 Appeal-stated case – 'immediate' expression of dissatisfaction. On an appeal being decided in favour of the Revenue, the appellant company's representative failed verbally to express dissatisfaction with the decision under *s 941*. Written dissatisfaction was expressed to the Court on the following morning, with a request that a case be stated for the opinion of the High Court. The request was refused on the grounds that dissatisfaction had not been expressed 'immediately after the determination' of the appeal and that the Court had no discretion in the matter. Held, the requirement for 'immediate' expression of dissatisfaction should not be construed so strictly as to involve its expression at the conclusion of the hearing, and that the requirement was in any event directory and not mandatory. As the Circuit Court's decision had been in accordance with what had been understood to be correct practice, there were no grounds for an order of *mandamus*, but the proper course was for a case to be stated in the normal way. *Multiprint Label Systems Ltd v Neylon* III ITR 159; [1984] ILRM 545.

38.13 Respondent's notification of Stated Case. It came to the notice of the Judge that a copy of the Stated Case had not been sent to the respondent until a fortnight after the appellant had transmitted it to the High Court. The Judge, albeit 'with some regret', ordered the case to be struck out of the list, as the requirement of *s 941(5)* had not been complied with. *A & B v Davis* 2 ITC 350; II ITR 60.

38.14 Interest on tax paid pending appeal. Following the decision at **38.154** below, the question arose as to the calculation of interest under *s 941(9)* where too much tax has been paid in accordance with a Commissioners' or lower Court decision. It was held that the rate under the *Courts Act* should be applied. *Texaco (Ireland) Ltd v Murphy* [1992] ILRM 304.

38.15 Application for mandamus. The taxpayer claimed a repayment of tax under *ITA 1967, s 154*. The Special Commissioners refused the relief, whereupon the taxpayer applied for *mandamus* to them to repay the tax, on the ground that they had misconstrued the law. Held, the Commissioners had been acting in a judicial and not an executive capacity and *mandamus* did not lie to compel them to alter their decision, even if they had misconstrued the law. *R v Special Commissioners (re Spain)* 1 ITC 227; I ITR 221; [1934] IR 27.

38.16 Application for mandamus. The company, which was incorporated on 3 August 1983 and manufactured rainwear, applied for a tax clearance certificate which was required in connection with a government contract. The Collector General refused to issue the certificate on the grounds that two of the directors had also been directors of J Meek & Co (Ireland) Ltd, which had carried on a similar business, employed many of the same staff, and had gone into liquidation in July 1983 owing arrears of £126,414 plus interest in respect of PAYE/PRSI. Melbarien Enterprises Ltd had always discharged its liabilities for PAYE, PRSI and VAT promptly. Held that the Collector General was bound to act judicially and was not entitled to take into account the liabilities of a separate company and the order of *mandamus* should issue to the respondents to consider and deal with the application of the tax clearance certificate according to law. *Melbarien Enterprises Ltd v Revenue Commissioners* (19 April 1985, unreported), HC.

38.17 Application for judicial review, certiorari and mandamus. The taxpayer companies, who were linked, were engaged in the commercial exploitation of a hot car wash system. A complex sequence of transactions involved the payment of substantial advance royalties to Pandion by two other companies, who then granted similar sub-licences to Ospreycare. Ospreycare subcontracted manufacture to OSD Ltd. The taxpayer companies sought what they termed as 'advance rulings' from the Revenue Commissioners, without disclosing the full facts of transactions already entered into. Relief was sought, respectively, under *s 234* for income from a qualifying patent, and under *s 243* for payments in respect of patents, and letters confirming the availability of relief in given circumstances were received by the representative of the companies from the Revenue Commissioners. Subsequent claims for relief and vacation of an assessment based on the actual transactions were, respectively, partially allowed and denied by the

Inspector of Taxes concerned. The Judge observed, *inter alia*, that the Revenue Commissioners were not agents for the Inspector, and that the sequence of transactions did not form a tax avoidance scheme under the principles of the UK case *Furniss v Dawson* 55 TC 324. The Judge did not allow the claims for *certiorari* and *mandamus* by Ospreycare relating to corporation tax assessments for the calendar year 1984, or a declaration giving that company the benefit of certain 'advance rulings'. A declaration was made, however, relating to a claim by Pandion, resulting in a repayment of tax to that company of £290,824 with interest. *Pandion Haliaetus Ltd, Ospreycare Ltd and Osprey Systems Design Ltd v Revenue Commissioners* III ITR 670.

38.18 Reopening of settled appeal by Circuit Judge. Some three years after entering in the tax appeal book his decision on an appeal against a partnership assessment, the presiding Circuit Judge re-entered the appeal, heard further submissions by the taxpayers and reduced the assessment. In granting an absolute order of *certiorari* directing the Circuit Judge to quash the later order, the High Court found that the Circuit Judge had no jurisdiction to act as he had done, any claims for hardship following final and conclusive determination of the appeal falling to be dealt with by the Revenue Commissioners. In *re McGahon* (8 February 1982, unreported), HC.

38.19 Legality of proceedings. The Revenue Commissioners had instituted proceedings against two companies for the recovery of customs duties and taxes totalling £1,982,280. It was claimed that the companies carried on business in such a manner as to defraud the Revenue Commissioners and an additional charge relating to the illegal export of large sums of RI currency had been dropped. In addition to the Plenary Summons in the High Court, assessments were served on the two companies for income tax, corporation tax and VAT totalling £1,926,726 (this excludes customs duties of £55,000), relating to the same matter. Appeals were made and the companies obtained a Conditional Order of Prohibition preventing the Appeal Commissioners hearing the appeals on the grounds that, *inter alia*, the State could not use both the courts and taxing administration to obtain the same amount of tax, which they disputed. The two companies now sought to have the Conditional Order of Prohibition made absolute, but this was refused by the Court. The Judge held that, although the sums claimed may be identical, the two procedures are separate and distinct. By placing the issue before the High Court, the Revenue did not waive their right to have the same issues decided under the tax code. The Appeal Commissioners were not seeking to exercise a judicial power and function, but to determine the tax payable. The application by the two companies therefore failed. *The State (Calcul International Ltd and Solatrex International Ltd) v Appeal Commissioners and Revenue Commissioners* III ITR 577.

38.20 Whether estimated assessments and other matters constitutional. The appellant, who was unrepresented, presented a wide-ranging challenge to the constitutionality of several sections of the *Taxes Acts*. He had not submitted returns or accounts for the four years to 5 April 1985, and estimated assessments were issued, becoming final and conclusive. Subsequently distraint orders were issued for the unpaid taxes under *s 962(2)*, bringing the total, with costs, to £33,057. The Supreme Court upheld the High Court decision that an incorrect trade description on an assessment and the signature of a subordinate did not make either of the documents invalid, that the authentication of documents and the making of assessments were administrative and not judicial functions and that the taxpayer's constitutional right of access to the courts had not been infringed because he retained the right to apply to the inspector under *s 933(7)* to re-open the assessments, providing outstanding returns were submitted and tax and interest currently assessed and charged paid. *Deighan v The State (Hearne and others)* III ITR 533.

38.21 Interest on overpaid tax. Following the decision at **38.130** below, the taxpayer claimed interest under *FA 1976, s 30* on the tax overpaid. For certain of the years concerned, the assessments issued and appealed against pursuant to the earlier appeal showed no further tax due (as the full liability had been deducted under PAYE), and for the remainder no assessment had been issued by agreement with the taxpayer's agents pending further progress of the appeal. *FA 1976, s 30* required interest to be paid only where the tax in question had been charged by assessment. The taxpayer's claim was allowed. In relation to the nil assessments, the tax charged should have been the total specified as being due and payable, and not the net amount unpaid at the date of the assessment. As regards the years for which no assessment was issued, the taxpayer was entitled to rely on the agreement that there was no need for formal assessment and appeals for the years in question. *Mooney v O'Coindealbháin* IV ITR 62.

38.22 In a further case resting on similar facts, in which the taxpayer claimed interest on the tax repaid in the absence of formal assessments, the Supreme Court declined to give a decision in the particular case without further detailed information. However, the judge indicated that, the Revenue Commissioners having come to be in possession of the taxpayer's money by mistakenly assigning him to an incorrect category, they were obliged to refund the resulting overpayment, and 'simple justice would seem to require that they should pay interest but at a rate to be decided by the trial judge and not at the deluxe rate specified in [*FA 1976, s 30*] on the money that they held on a form of constructive trust for the taxpayer'. *O'Rourke v Revenue Commissioners* V ITR 321. The High Court accordingly awarded simple interest at the rates ruling under *Courts Act 1981, s 22(1) (unreported, 18 December 1996), HC*.

38.23 Tax repayment pending appeal. An overpayment of tax resulting from a determination by the Appeal Commissioners must be refunded to the taxpayer pending the outcome of a case stated to the High Court and any appeal therefrom to the Supreme Court. *Robert Harris v JJ Quigley and Liam Irwin* (unreported, 1 December 2005), SC, *Irwin v Grimes* [2008] IEHC 86

38.24 Entitlement of Revenue Commissioners to refuse to be cross examined. This case related to a VAT assessment raised on the plaintiff company. The Plaintiff maintained that the assessment was raised without the tax inspector having 'reason to believe' that there was a VAT liability which is a prerequisite in raising an assessment. The Appeal Commissioners held in favour of the Revenue Commissioners upholding the VAT assessment. Judicial review proceedings were brought by the Plaintiff on the basis that they should have been entitled to cross examine the tax inspector to establish 'reason to believe'. The High Court refused the application stating that the refusal to allow the tax inspector to be cross examined was within jurisdiction. *Menolly Homes Limited v Appeals Commissioners and Another* [2010] IHEC 49.

38.25 Revenue Commissioner's entitlement to set off refunds of tax due to a taxpayer against other tax liabilities of that taxpayer. This case related to a VAT refund that was due to the Plaintiff company which the Revenue Commissioners off set against a tax liability of the Plaintiff under another tax head. The Court held that the Revenue Commissioners are entitled to set off tax refund against other tax liabilities in this manner under *s 1006A. Kanwell Developments Ltd v The Revenue Commissioners* [2008] IEHC 380.

38.26 Entitlement of a taxpayer to take proceedings against the Revenue Commissioners under an assumed alias. The Court heard this preliminary application prior to the substantive hearing. The Court held that the taxpayer was not entitled to assume an alias in taking the proceedings. *Doe & Anor v Revenue Commissioners* [2008] IEHC 5.

38.27 Entitlement of appeal an interim determination by the Appeal Commissioners. The applicant in this case, Mr Brendan O'Rourke ('Mr O'Rourke') is seeking, among other reliefs, a declaration that he has a right of appeal against the Appeal Commissioners' ruling in relation to **tax** assessments pending the hearing of other grounds of appeal. The proceedings concerned the issue of whether Mr O'Rourke was entitled to appeal to the Circuit Court a decision by the Appeal Commissioners on a preliminary issue while there are ongoing appeals in respect of which the Appeal Commissioners have made no determination. The Court decided that tax appeals are a creature of statute and the jurisdiction and general powers of the Appeal Commissioners are conferred by statute. An analysis of the provisions governing those appeals confirms that in respect of any individual assessment there is a single appeal, which appeal is determined (and can only be determined) by the Appeal Commissioners. The Court decided that the legislative intention favours the efficient administration of **tax** appeals; there should be a single right of appeal at the end of the hearing before the Appeals Commissioners. For the reasons as outlined by the Appeal Commissioners, there is only one appeal, though there maybe a number of grounds of appeal. *O'Rourke v The Appeal Commissioners* [2010] IEHC 264.

CAPITAL ACQUISITIONS TAX

38.28 *CATA 1976, s 2 para 9* – **whether a business – whether niece worked 'substantially full-time'.** B, a man of advancing years, owned a farm which he let as grazing land under an agreement whereby the landowner was responsible for herding and for the reporting of eventualities. The appellant, his niece, visited the farm every day to herd the cattle and examine the fences, and looked after the management of the farm and buildings. Apart from her household duties, the management of B's lands was her prime concern, and she did work of lasting value for his benefit. Held, relief was due under *CATA 1976, s 2 para 9*, whereby the rates of tax appropriate to a transaction between parent and child applied to the gift of the farm to the appellant. 'Substantially full-time' could be construed to imply 'continued presence ... on a day-to-day basis whereby ... labour (including expertise) is put at the disposal of the disponer whereby material benefit is conferred, or is attempted to be conferred, on the disponer's business', and the attention given to B's lands was sufficient to indicate that a farming business was being carried on. It was not essential to show that the niece or nephew had taken over the entire running of the business. *A E v Revenue Commissioners, Circuit Court (SE Circuit)* V ITR 686; [1984] ILRM 301. See **7.4** 'Capital acquisitions tax'.

38.29 Share valuation – *CATA 1976, s 17*. A tax avoidance scheme involved the restructuring of a company's share capital so that on a liquidation the greater part of the distribution would accrue in respect of preference shares rather than the ordinary shares which formed part of the estate in question. There was, however, provision for the preference shares to be redeemed at par by special resolution, and the ordinary shareholders retained voting control. The High Court judge, affirming the decision of the Appeal Commissioners, held that the market value of the ordinary shares (on which the CAT assessment would be based) was the low figure to be obtained on a liquidation, by virtue of *CATA 1976, s 17* (as it applied before 24 February 1993, see **7.8** 'Capital acquisitions tax'). The Supreme Court upheld this decision. *Revenue Commissioners v Henry Young* V ITR 294.

38.30 Whether one per cent charge imposed on certain discretionary trusts applied to an estate in the course of administration – *FA 1986, s 103(1) (now s 20(1) CATCA 2003)*. By her will dated 21 January 1988, JHI appointed 3 individuals to be executors and trustees. She devised and bequeathed all her property to her trustees upon trust for sale. She directed her trustees to stand possessed of the Trust Fund, which was comprised of the proceeds of sale and unsold and unconverted property, upon such trust for the benefit of the beneficiaries, as defined, or any one or more of them exclusive of the other or others in such shares or proportions and subject to such terms, limitations and provisions as the trustees should from time to time by deed or deeds revocable or irrevocable executed before the Vesting Day, as defined, but without infringing the rule against perpetuities, appoint. The testatrix died on 16 September 1993. By assent in writing dated 28 October 1997, the executors assented to the vesting of cash and securities in themselves as trustees of the trusts of the will of the testatrix. By deeds of appointment dated 28 October 1997 and 19 February 1998, the trustees appointed the trust funds to certain named beneficiaries. On the execution of the latter deed, the discretionary trust created by the will of the testator was effectively wound up. The trustees accounted to Revenue for the initial three per cent charge imposed by *FA 1984, s 106(1)*, which became due on 28 October 1997 when the administration of the estate was completed, but claimed they were not liable for the one per cent charge in respect of the period prior to the completion of the administration of the estate. The High Court judge affirmed the decision of the Appeal Commissioners and the Circuit Court that the trustees were not liable for the one per cent charge for the chargeable dates 5 April 1995, 5 April 1996 and 5 April 1997. *Revenue Commissioners v Executors and Trustees of the Jeannie Hammett Irvine Will Trust* HC, 2006.

38.31 See also **38.206** below.

CAPITAL ALLOWANCES

38.32 Plant and machinery – poultry house. The company carried on the business of egg production and incurred expenditure on a deep pit poultry house and equipment. The raised cedarwood poultry house contained tiered stacks of cages, under which ran a deep concrete pit for cleaning purposes. The house was specially designed to provide a controlled environment. The High Court upheld the Circuit Judge's finding that the building was plant within *ss 284, 285* (see **8.6**(*b*) 'Capital allowances') and so attracted 100 per cent wear and tear allowances. *O'Srianáin v Lakeview Ltd* TL 125; III ITR 219.

38.33 Plant and machinery – law books. A barrister incurred expenditure on certain law books, consisting mainly of a complete set of Irish and English Law Reports. Held, the books must be regarded as plant within *ss 284, 285* (see **8.6**(*b*) 'Capital allowances') and so attracted 100 per cent wear and tear allowances. *Breathnach v McCann* TL 121; III ITR 113.

38.34 Plant and machinery – suspended ceiling in supermarket. The company, which carries on business throughout RI through supermarkets and stores, had installed a suspended ceiling in the selling area of one of its stores. Other companies within the group had installed similar standard type suspended ceilings. The company contended that the ceiling qualified as plant under *ss 284, 285* for the purpose of capital allowances. Held, that the suspended ceiling was part of the setting in which the goods were sold and did not constitute plant. *Dunnes Stores (Oakville) Ltd v Cronin* IV ITR 68.

38.35 Plant and machinery – filling station canopies. The taxpayers claimed capital allowances under *s 284* as plant on canopies erected over the pump areas of their filling stations. Their claim was allowed by the Circuit Judge, and that decision was affirmed in the High Court. Relying in particular on a *dictum* of Lord Hailsham in the UK case *Cole Bros Ltd v Phillips* 55 TC 188, the function of the canopies – the provision of an attractive setting for the sale of the taxpayers' products, the advertisement and promotion of those products, the creation of an overall impression of efficiency and financial solidarity in relation to the business of selling petrol, and the attraction of customers to stop and purchase those products – was performed in the actual carrying out of the trade, so that they were part of the means by which the trade was carried on in the appropriately prepared setting. The decision was upheld in the Supreme Court. *O'Culacháin v McMullan Bros Ltd* V ITR 200. For another issue in this case, see **38.8** above.

38.36 Plant and machinery – refurbishment of grandstand. In the case the facts of which are outlined at **38.103** below, it was held in the High Court, following *McMullan Bros Ltd* (**38.35** above), that the grandstand in question was part of the means of attracting people to visit the racecourse, and hence part of the means by which the trade was carried on. The net expenditure on items (*a*) and (*e*) therefore constituted expenditure on plant, for which capital allowances were available. The expenditure on the existing and new bar areas (items (*b*) and (*d*)) did not constitute expenditure on plant. The decision was upheld in the Supreme Court. *O'Grady v Roscommon Race Committee* V ITR 317.

38.37 Plant and machinery – investment allowances. The appellant carried on a trade of plant hire contractor, and incurred expenditure of £100,000 on provision of a crane for use in that trade, the greater part of such use being in 'designated areas' for the purposes of *FA 1971, s 22*. He claimed an investment allowance on the ground that *FA 1971, s 22(1)* required only that the machinery or plant be provided for use in a designated area, without the use of the word 'exclusively'. The inspector contended that as the subsection did not use the word 'substantially' either, no allowance was due. In the High Court it was held that the inspector's view was to be preferred, but this decision was overturned by the Supreme Court, where Finlay CJ considered that the statute was ambiguous, and that the clear intention of the legislature was that an allowance should be available in such cases. In the High Court, Murphy J also expressed the view that in any event the use of the words 'provided' in *sub-s (1)* and 'provision' in *sub-s (2)* made it clear that the expenditure must result in the asset being provided both for trade purposes and for use in a designated area, and that this condition could not be met by a plant hire contractor, as the use in the designated area was provided by the payment of a hire charge by the customer, not by the contractor's expenditure. This ground was not pursued in the Supreme Court. *McNally v O'Maoldhomhniagh* IV ITR 22. See **8.6**(*c*) 'Capital allowances'.

38.38 Plant and machinery – film production. A company entered into a complex film investment agreement the effect of which was that the £910,000 production cost was met by payment of £217,000 out of the company's own resources and £693,000 out of a loan to the company from RTE, the producers of the film, repayable out of defined profits from distribution. The Circuit Court judge's decision that the company was trading was upheld, but his finding that only the £217,000 attracted capital allowances was overturned. His decision was affected by the benefit of hindsight as to the commercial failure of the film. The £910,000 was paid for the provision of plant and attracted capital allowances in full. *Airspace Investments Ltd v Moore* V ITR 3.

38.39 Industrial buildings allowance: building within a complex: computer housing. The appellant company had erected a complex of buildings in a number of stages, including factory premises and a separate building housing a computer, showrooms and offices. Held:

(i)   the building was an 'industrial building' to the extent that it housed the computer, as the computer was principally used for industrial rather than clerical purposes;

(ii)   in determining whether expenditure on non-qualifying parts was one-tenth or less of the whole (see **8.5** 'Capital allowances'), it was expenditure on the whole complex which had to be considered, not just that on the separate building. *O'Conaill v Waterford Glass Ltd* (1982) TL 122; IV ITR 187.

38.40 Industrial buildings allowance: bonded transit sheds. The company, which engaged in business as shipping agents, stevedores, customs clearance agents etc, stored goods and cargo such as newsprint in bonded transit sheds for short periods. The sheds were used merely as a clearing house for goods unloaded from ships. Industrial buildings allowance under *s 271* was claimed in respect of a dock undertaking. The Judge held that the company was not carrying on a business as storekeeper or warehouse-man and the transit sheds qualified as industrial buildings and structures in use for the purposes of a dock undertaking within the meaning of *s 268(1)(b)*. *Patrick Monahan (Drogheda) Ltd v O'Connell* III ITR 661.

38.41 Industrial and provident societies – ITA 1967, s 220(5). In a case turning on the interpretation of *ITA 1967, s 220(5)* it was held that (i) all capital allowances, not just those under *ITA 1967, Part XVI*, were to be diminished under this provision, and (ii) the words 'capital allowances' were to be construed in accordance with the definition of 'capital allowance' in the interpretation section (*ITA 1967, s 218*). *Irish Agricultural Wholesale Society Ltd v McDermot* (1977) TL 112.

CAPITAL GAINS TAX

38.42 Abandonment of an option for consideration – whether within *s 540(4)* – application of *s 535(2)(a)*. The taxpayer and his wife each granted to the other an option over valuable shares for substantial consideration, a small further amount being payable in each case on exercise. The shares were then sold to a company, subject to those options, for similarly small amounts, whereupon the company offered to pay each spouse a sum slightly more than the payment made on grant of the option for its abandonment. The offers were accepted, and the company subsequently sold on the shares to an industrial and provident society owned by the taxpayer and his wife for full value. A capital gains tax assessment was raised on the basis that a chargeable gain arose in each case on the receipt of the capital sum in return for the abandonment of the option. The taxpayer contended that the transactions fell within *s 540(4)*, which provides that the abandonment of an option shall not constitute a disposal. The Revenue Commissioners contended that *s 540(4)* did not apply to the abandonment of an option for consideration, and that if that were not so *s 535(2)(a)*, which (subject to the exceptions in the *Act*) deems the obtaining of a capital sum derived from an asset to be a disposal of that asset, applied notwithstanding *s 540(4)*. The Circuit Court Judge found in favour of the taxpayer (reversing the Appeal Commissioners' decision), but in the High Court the taxpayer lost on both counts. On the ordinary meaning of the words, and looking at the substance of the transaction, the 'abandonment' of an option does not include agreeing not to exercise the option in return for payment. On the second point, where *s 540(4)* did apply so that the abandonment was excluded from being a disposal, it did not operate to exempt a capital sum received in respect thereof from the liability clearly arising under *s 535(2)(a)*. In the Supreme Court, the High Court decision was upheld on the interpretation of 'abandonment', although the decision on the second point was doubted. *Kearns v Dilleen* V ITR 514. See generally **9.6**, **9.15** 'Capital gains tax'.

38.43 Bargain at Arm's Length. The respondent entered into an agreement with George Wimpey plc ('Wimpeys') to establish and operate a joint venture coastal quarry. Wimpey's paid Stg£1m for 50 per cent of the share capital in the respondent's company that owned the quarry site. The respondent entered into a non-competition agreement with Wimpeys in consideration of Stg£2m. The share transfer agreement was initially stamped based on a consideration of Stg£1m but, following negotiations with the Revenue regarding capital gains tax, was ultimately stamped based on a consideration of Stg£3m. It was agreed that a payment for non-competition is not subject to capital gains tax, not being a gain realised on the disposal of an asset. The Revenue argued that while the share purchase and non-competition agreements combined constituted a bargain at arm's length, each element was not a bargain. As such, the entire Stg£3m consideration should be subject to capital gains tax. It was held, inter alia, that in the absence of fraud or sham or other vitiating circumstances, documents must be taken on their face. The appeal was disallowed. *O'Connell (Inspector of Taxes) v Fleming* (unreported, 22 March 2002), HC.

38.44 Compulsory acquisition – adjustment of compensation for capital gains tax liability. An award for compulsory acquisition of land was made with an addendum that an additional award would be made if the compensation was subject to capital gains tax. After the capital gains tax liability had been established, a further award was made by way of special case stated for the opinion of the High Court. Held, the *Acquisition of Land (Assessment of Compensation) Act 1919, s 2* makes no provision for compensation to be adjusted because of claims made subsequent to the initial award. The further award was therefore disallowed. *Re Heron* III ITR 298.

38.45 Disposals of land, etc – clearance under *s 980(8)*. The company, which was ordinarily resident in RI, had applied for *mandamus* following the refusal by the Revenue of a clearance certificate under *s 980(8)* (deduction of capital gains tax from proceeds of certain disposals) in relation to a property sale. The case was remitted to the inspector with an order directing him to consider the matter in accordance with the law. The issue of a clearance certificate was mandatory if the conditions laid down in *s 980(8)* were met, and a wide-ranging investigation into transactions with other companies concerning the property sold was not within the inspector's powers. There was no doubt that, prior to the sale, the company owned the land in question. *Financial Indemnity Co (Ireland) Ltd v O'Ceallaigh* III ITR 124. (See **9.5** 'Capital gains tax'.)

38.46 Disposal of land by mortgagee – no clearance certificate – repayment of tax deducted by purchaser. In a case where the mortgagee was treated under *s 537(2)* (see **9.4** 'Capital gains tax') as having disposed of property as nominee for the mortgagor for the purpose of enforcing its security, and no clearance certificate had been obtained to enable the purchase price to be paid without the 15 per cent deduction under *s 980(4)* (see **9.5** 'Capital gains tax'), the mortgagee sought repayment by the Revenue Commissioners of the 15 per cent deducted. Held, the 15 per cent deduction had been properly made and paid over to the Revenue Commissioners on account of the mortgagor's liability. The mortgagee's only remedy was to seek reimbursement from the mortgagor. *Bank of Ireland Finance Ltd v Revenue Commissioners* IV ITR 217.

38.47 Loan with conversion rights – whether 'debt on a security' – *s 541(1)(a)*. A cash sum advanced subject to rights of conversion into ordinary shares of a company was held to constitute a 'debt on a security', so that the ensuing loss was an allowable loss for CGT purposes. The loan complete with its rights and entitlements had the necessary element of marketability and potential increase in value to distinguish it from a simple debt. *Mooney v McSweeney* V ITR 163. See **9.7**(*n*) 'Capital gains tax'.

38.48 The taxpayer had advanced a cash loan to a company subject to rights of conversion into ordinary shares at a pre-determined price. The company subsequently went into liquidation, and the taxpayer claimed relief for the loss on the loan against other gains. The Revenue Commissioners refused relief on the grounds that the loan was no more than a debt, but the Circuit Court judge granted the relief, holding that it was necessary to look to the time of the agreement for the loan, and that the agreement gave the taxpayer an incorporeal property in the company. *N v Inspector of Taxes* (unreported, 4 May 1995), Circuit Court. See **9.7**(*n*) 'Capital gains tax'.

38.49 The taxpayer disposed of shares in a company for consideration consisting of interest-bearing loan notes redeemable on 30 days' notice between specified dates. The loan notes were not transferable or assignable except on the death of the note holder. Held, following *Mooney v McSweeney*, **38.47** above, the loan notes were not a 'debt on a security' and were therefore excluded from charge to capital gains tax on disposal by *s 541. O'Connell v Keleghan* (unreported, 16 May 2001), SC. See **9.7**(*n*) 'Capital gains tax'. (For another issue in this case, see **38.182** below.)

38.50 Replacement of business assets – 'rollover relief'. The taxpayer and his wife purchased a farm in 1975, and then emigrated to Canada. During their absence the farm was let on conacre, and shortly after return in 1978 it was sold. Another holding of land was then purchased. They had never lived in or worked the original farm. It was claimed that land was deemed to be occupied by the taxpayer and his wife by virtue of *FA 1974, s 17*, and that relief under *s 597* in respect of replacement of business assets was due. Held, reversing the decision of the Circuit Court, that the income tax deeming provisions did not apply to *s 597*, and that 'rollover relief' applies only to a person carrying on a trade, in this instance the conacre tenant. *O'Coindealbháin v Price* IV ITR 1. See **9.7**(*s*) 'Capital gains tax'.

38.51 Time of disposal – conditional contract. A contract for the sale of land included a condition that the contract was subject to the obtaining by the purchaser of planning permission for the property within four months. Planning permission was ultimately obtained more than 16 months later. The vendor argued that the contract had lapsed on the grounds that the condition was a condition precedent. Held that a condition providing that a contract is subject to planning permission is a condition subsequent. *O'Connor v Coady* (unreported, 12 November 2003), HC. Revenue have since issued a statement to the effect that, for capital gains tax purposes, the time of disposal in a conditional contract continues to be the time when the condition is satisfied.

38.52 Capital gains tax covered under Irish Italian Double Tax Agreement. This case involved the disposal of shares and a scheme for the avoidance of CGT. The Court held that capital gains tax does come within the ambit of s 2.4 of the Convention signed between Ireland and Italy on 11 June 1971. The Court also held that the test for whether an individual is resident in the State for a day for the purposes of *s 819* is whether the individual was present in the State at the end of the day. *Kinsella v Revenue Commissioners* [2007] IEHC 250.

It should be noted that from 1 January 2009, the test to determine whether an individual is present in the State is changed and an individual will be deemed to be resident on a day where they were present in the State at any time during the day.

CHARITIES

38.53 The Pharmaceutical Society of Ireland, formed by statute to hold examinations for persons desiring to be pharmaceutical chemists and to form a register of them if approved, was held not to be charitable. Its activities of conducting schools and examinations were held to be trading. *Pharmaceutical Society of Ireland v CIR* 2 ITC 157; I ITR 542; 17 ATC 587.

38.54 Trading by charity. A hospital established for the relief of the sick poor also admitted paying patients for treatment in an Annexe. The hospital and the Annexe were administered as one undertaking. Held, that the treatment of the private patients was severable from the charitable activities and amounted to carrying on a trade. *Davis v Superioress, Mater Misericordiae Hospital Dublin* 2 ITC 1; I ITR 387; [1933] IR 480, 503.

38.55 Trading by charity. The appellant charity was bequeathed an estate including a small retail business, which it carried on, employing for this purpose a disabled man who, if not so employed, would have been a beneficiary of the charity. It claimed exemption under *s 208* for the profits of the business on the ground that the employee running it should be regarded as a beneficiary of the charity. Held, the employee was not a beneficiary and relief was therefore not due. *Beirne v St Vincent de Paul Society (Wexford Conference)* 1 ITC 413; I ITR 383.

38.56 Foreign charity active in Ireland – whether entitled to exemption under *ss 207, 208*. A religious order established for charitable purposes only ran an old people's home in RI. The operation was, however, merely a branch of an Institute registered in the USA which controlled all major financial and property matters. It was held that the requirement that a body of persons or trust be 'established for charitable purposes only' required it to be so established in RI. However, in the High Court the Judge upheld the grant of exemption to the charity on the basis that it was established in RI, expressing the opinion that '... a foreign charity with no activities base (for want of a better expression) in RI is not entitled to an exemption but a foreign charity which does have such a base is entitled to it in respect of funds applied towards the RI charitable activities'. *Revenue Commissioners v Sisters of Charity of the Incarnate Word* [1998] ITR 65. See generally **17.5** 'Exempt organisations'.

CONSTRUCTION INDUSTRY SUB-CONTRACTORS

38.57 Haulage contractors. A firm of sand and gravel merchants entered into arrangements with lorry owners under which the lorry owners purchased materials from a company under the same control and operating from the same premises as the merchants, and undertook to sell the materials to the merchants and to deliver them as directed, receiving only the sale proceeds (which varied according to the distance of travel to delivery) net of the cost of purchase owed to the supplier. It was held that the lorry owners' activities under these arrangements did not constitute 'the haulage for hire of materials', so that *s 531* did not require tax to be deducted from payments to them. *O'Grady v Laragan Quarries Ltd* IV ITR 269. See **13.8** 'Deduction of tax at source'.

CORPORATION TAX

38.58 Close company – advertising agency – whether 'service company' within *s 441.* The company carried out market research and prepared creative proposals for customers. If these were accepted, the company would then carry out further work, depending on what was required. The High Court upheld the Circuit Judge's finding that the company was not carrying on a profession, nor was it providing professional services. It was thus not liable to surcharge under *s 441* (see **12.7** 'Corporation tax'). *Mac Giolla Mhaith v Brian Cronin & Associates Ltd* TL 124; III ITR 211.

38.59 Export sales relief – deposit interest. The company moved its residence from RI to Holland in 1975. It continued to carry on a manufacturing business in RI through its Dublin branch, and dividends were paid tax-free (due to export sales relief) into a Swiss bank account. Interest accrued on the account, and some withdrawals were used by the RI branch. The point at issue was whether the RI branch was liable to corporation tax on the interest under *s 25(2)*. Held, that the Dublin branch had no control over the funds in the Swiss bank account, and that the income therefrom was not chargeable to corporation tax. *Murphy v Data Products (Dublin) Ltd* IV ITR 12.

38.60 Franked investment income – date of receipt. An interim dividend payable to the parent company was declared at a Board meeting of the paying company shortly before its year end, and was to be settled through the inter-company account. That account was not written up until some time after the year end. The recipient company wished to claim relief under *s 157* (see **12.13** 'Corporation tax') for its accounting period coinciding with that of the subsidiary. It was agreed that a dividend may be paid by set-off in an inter-company account, and that an interim dividend is not received until paid. It was held that the dividend was received on the date of the subsidiary company's Board meeting at which it was declared. *Murphy v The Borden Co Ltd* III ITR 559.

38.61 Group of companies – insolvency – appropriation of tax payments by members to meet other group companies' liabilities. See *Frederick Inns Ltd*, **38.244** below.

38.62 Management expenses. An investment company incurred expenditure in looking at potential takeovers, including audit and evaluation work, investigation costs and tax advice. The Circuit Court judge's decision that the costs were not management expenses within *s 83* (see **12.9** 'Corporation tax'), being in the category of capital expenditure, was upheld in the High Court and the Supreme Court. *Hibernian Insurance Co Ltd v MacUimis* [2000] ITR 75.

38.63 Manufacturing companies relief: 'manufacture'. The appellant company imported green unripened bananas into RI. They were then ripened by subjection to ethylene gas in specially constructed ripening rooms in a process taking from four to twelve days and requiring constant skilled control and testing. It claimed manufacturing companies relief (see **12.18** 'Corporation tax') on the basis that the ripening process constituted manufacturing within the State within *CTA 1976, s 54.* Held, the relief was due. 'Manufacture' was not defined in the statute and, although it must be construed strictly, it was necessary to look to the scheme and purpose as disclosed by the statute. The relief was manifestly aimed at increasing employment in RI and promoting exports, both achieved by the operation in question. It was then a matter of degree as to whether the process was within the statutory provision. The bananas represented a commercially different product and the process fell within the definition. *Charles McCann Ltd v O'Culacháin* III ITR 304; [1986] IR 196. (*Note.* Similar wording applies to the revised manufacturing companies' relief introduced by *FA 1980*, see **12.18** 'Corporation tax' and **38.65** below.)

38.64 A company offering banana ripening services to fellow group members was held not to be entitled to the manufacturing companies relief. The exclusion from the definition of 'goods' of those resulting 'from a process which consists primarily of ... applying methods of ... maturation or other similar treatment to any foodstuffs' (now contained in *s 443(6)(a)(ii)*), introduced following the decision in *Charles McCann Ltd* (**38.63** above), overrode the provision in (what is now) *s 443(21)* that the rendering of services by a trade to another person, involving the application of a manufacturing process to goods belonging to that person, was to be regarded as the manufacture of goods. *O'Connell v Fyffes Banana Processing Limited* (unreported, 24 July 2000), SC.

38.65 Manufacturing companies relief was claimed under *s 448(2)* (see **12.18** 'Corporation tax') in respect of a company which purchased milk from farmers and resold it after pasteurising and packaging it to make it legally saleable. It was held that the degree of change brought about by the company's activities was sufficient to amount to a manufacturing process, resulting in a commercially different product from the raw milk. Relief was therefore allowed. *Cronin v Strand Dairy Ltd* III ITR 441.

38.66 The production of J Cloths and nappy liners from bales of fabric was held to be a manufacturing process within *FA 1980, s 42*. The cutting folding and packaging of the material by machine did not bring about any change in the raw material, but the utility, quality and worth of the new product were enhanced by, and could not be dissociated from, the process carried out. See, however, **12.18** 'Corporation tax' as regards the changes introduced by FA 1990, s 41. *O'Laochdha v Johnson and Johnson (Ireland) Ltd* IV ITR 361.

38.67 A company, as part of its trade, 'conditioned' wort purchased from a brewery company. This involves the storing of bottles of wort at a constant temperature of 58 to 60 degrees Fahrenheit for 14 days, during which an irreversible chemical reaction takes place, and is absolutely essential to produce a commercially saleable product. Conditioning was carried out in three insulated and thermostatically controlled conditioning rooms, and was regularly monitored by the brewery company. After such treatment, the bottles are stored for a further 14 days before delivery to retailers. The High Court upheld the Circuit Judge's decision that the conditioning was an integral part of the manufacturing process and not ancillary, and constituted a manufacturing process for the purposes of the relief. *Hussey v M J Gleeson & Co Ltd* IV ITR 533.

38.68 The company carried on the business of producing day old chicks. This involves an elaborate hatching out process of the eggs from the laying hens through a number of stages in 'settler' machines in specially heated and humidified rooms. At 19 days, eggs containing chicks are moved to a hatching room. Finally, the chicks are packed in purpose built containers for despatch in batches of 3,500 females and 450 males for use as breeding stock. The Circuit Court Judge considered himself constrained by the *Charles McCann Ltd* and *Strand Dairy Ltd* decisions (**38.63, 38.65** above) to hold that manufacturing relief was due, and his decision was upheld in the High Court by Keane J. *Kelly v Cobh Straffan IR Ltd* IV ITR 526. (Keane J, however, doubted his own decision in *Brosnan v Leeside Nurseries Ltd* in the Supreme Court, see **38.69** below.)

38.69 A company engaged in the import and cultivation of chrysanthemums was held not to qualify for the manufacturing companies relief, overturning the Circuit Court judge's decision. Whilst 'cultivation' and 'manufacture' are not mutually exclusive in the sense that a manufacturing process can be applied to cultivated goods, an alteration in goods achieved by cultivation cannot be said to have been brought about by a manufacturing process. *Brosnan v Leeside Nurseries Ltd* V ITR 21.

38.70 Manufacturing companies relief: income from sale of 'goods'. The advertising revenue of a newspaper publisher was held to be within the relief. It was accepted that newspapers were 'goods' for these purposes, and since the advertising revenue could not arise without the newspaper sales, it arose in respect of those sales. *McGurrin v Champion Publications Ltd* IV ITR 466. See now **12.18**(xvii) 'Corporation tax'.

38.71 Manufacturing companies relief: 'manufactured within the State'. The company claimed manufacturing relief under *s 448(2)* in connection with the production of advertising materials by means of TV commercials etc. The company carried out the filming, but printing of the film took place in the UK. There was no manufacturing work force or plant in RI. Held that the activities of the company were that of a service industry and not a manufacturing company. *O'Culacháin v Hunter Advertising Ltd* IV ITR 35.

38.72 Manufacturing companies relief: FA 1990, s 41: retrospective relief. Following the decision in **38.71** above, *FA 1990, s 41* retrospectively allowed relief for film production. However, *s 448(6)* imposes a condition that relief must be claimed before the assessment for the relevant period has become final and conclusive. The assessments under appeal had become final and conclusive before the passing of *FA 1990*. The taxpayer company claimed that *s 448(6)* is merely a procedural section and should not over-ride the clear intention of the subsequent legislation in *FA 1990*. The appeal failed in the light of the clear wording of the relevant provisions. *Saatchi and Saatchi Advertising Ltd v McGarry* V ITR 376. See **12.18**(xi) 'Corporation tax'.

38.73 Small companies rate: associated companies. The limits on profits below which a reduced rate of corporation tax applied under *CTA 1976, s 28* are reduced where a company has associated companies within *s 432* (see **12.22** 'Corporation tax'). The appellant company, resident and trading in RI, was under common control with a company resident and trading in Northern Ireland. Held, the scheme of the *Corporation Tax Acts* brings all companies within the charge with an exemption for non-resident companies. The reference to associated companies in *CTA 1976, s 28* must therefore be interpreted as including all companies under common control, wherever incorporated. *Bairead v Maxwells of Donegal Ltd* TL *134; III ITR 430*.

38.74 Loss relief – changes of trade and ownership – *s 401*. The respondent company had ceased pig slaughtering and the manufacture of meat products, and subsequently acted as a distribution centre for the company which had acquired its share capital. Its intention to recommence the former activities was established. The case concerned claims for the allowance of losses incurred before the change of ownership. Held, confirming the Circuit Court decision, that:

(*a*)   there was no permanent cessation of trade;

(*b*)   there was no major change in the nature or conduct of the trade within the meaning of *s 401(2)(a)*; and

(*c*)   it was not established that the time of the change in ownership of the company was after the scale of the company's activities had become small or negligible and before any considerable revival of the trade, within *s 401(2)(b)*, so that the company was entitled to the loss reliefs claimed. *Cronin v Lunham Brothers Ltd* III ITR 363; [1986] ILRM 415. (See **12.17** 'Corporation tax'.)

DEDUCTION OF TAX AT SOURCE

38.75 Professional fees – credit for tax withheld. The amendment made to *FA 1987, s 19* by *FA 1990, s 26*, which gave credit for tax withheld from payments received in one period against the tax liability for the following period, was held to be unconstitutional and invalid. The effect on property rights was out of proportion to the objective the amendment was designed to achieve. *Daly v Revenue Commissioners, Ireland and the Attorney General* V ITR 213. See **13.11** 'Deduction of tax at source'.

DOUBLE TAXATION

38.76 Government employment. A staff nurse, a national of both RI and the UK, was resident in RI and employed by the Western Health and Social Services Board in Northern Ireland. A claim for relief under *Article 18(2) of the Double Taxation Relief (Taxes on Income and Capital Gains) (UK) Order 1976 (SI 319/76)* was refused on the grounds that: (i) the term 'local authority' in that *Article* must be interpreted under UK law, and did not include the Health Board; and (ii) the performance of nursing services for the Health Board were not 'services rendered in discharge of functions of a governmental nature'. *Travers v Ó'Síocháin* V ITR 54. See **15.7** 'Double tax relief – income and capital gains'.

38.77 Interest paid to non-resident parent company. Under *Article 12 of the Irish/Japanese Double Taxation Relief Order 1974 (SI 259/74)*, interest paid to a Japanese parent company may be subject to withholding tax not exceeding ten per cent. *s 130(2)(d)(iv)*, however, normally requires such interest to be treated as a distribution, not subject to withholding tax. The Revenue contention that the *Order* overrules *s 130* was rejected. The *Order* merely imposes a ceiling of ten per cent on the tax which may be levied in RI in these circumstances. It does not impose an obligation to levy any such form of taxation. *Murphy v Asahi Synthetic Fibres (Ireland) Ltd* III ITR 246.

38.78 Agreement with UK – fiscal domicile of settlement. A settlement was created in December 1981. One of the two trustees was resident in RI, the other in the UK. Following a reconstruction of the share capital of a UK trading company in which the settlor had held a majority of the shares, he renounced a letter of allotment and transferred the shares covered by the letter to the trustees. They sold the shares in January 1982. The UK Revenue issued a CGT assessment on the trustees, who appealed, claiming relief under *Article 4 of the Ireland/UK* agreement. They contended that the place of effective management of the settlement was in RI, so that the only liability was to RI CGT. The Special Commissioner upheld the UK Revenue contention that the place of effective management was not in RI, and that under the relevant UK provision (the predecessor to *Taxation of Chargeable Gains Act 1992, s 69(1)*) the trustees were to be treated as UK resident. On the evidence, the settlement was effectively managed from the UK, the RI trustee being 'a trustee in name rather than in reality'. The fact that the trustees had operated a bank account in RI was not conclusive. *Wensleydale's Settlement Trustees v CIR* [1996] STC (SSCD) 241.

FARM TAX

38.79 De facto repeal of Farm Tax Act 1985 – whether enforceable for earlier years. The *Farm Tax Act 1985* was brought into effect on 6 October 1986, but in the 1987 Budget speech, the Minister for Finance stated that it was to be repealed and that tax for 1987 would not be collected. No repealing legislation was, however, introduced. The applicant was assessed to farm tax for 1986, and sought to prohibit the continuance of proceedings for collection of the tax on the ground *inter alia* that, in the circumstances, it would be improper to enforce the *Act*. His application was upheld in the High Court and the Supreme Court. The failure to introduce amending provisions meant that the legislation had been interfered with unlawfully, and in that event it ceased to be enforceable not only for the future but for the past also. *Purcell v Attorney General and the Minister for the Environment* V ITR 288.

LIQUIDATIONS

38.80 Preferential claims in liquidation. The State claimed preferential payment, in respect of a company in the hands of the Receiver, of income tax for one year of assessment (year ended 5 April 1946) and of corporation profits tax for a different year (year ended 31 March 1945). Held that under the terms of the *1908 Companies (Consolidation) Act* the State's rights extended to one year's assessment in respect of each tax assessed separately and distinctly. *Attorney General v Irish Steel Ltd and Crowley* 2 ITC 402; II ITR 108.

38.81 Tax on deposit interest in voluntary liquidation: whether a charge within Companies Act 1963, s 281. The liquidator sought a determination as to whether corporation tax on deposit interest earned in the course of a voluntary liquidation is a preferential charge within the meaning of *Companies Act 1963, s 281.* The Judge held that the answer to the question was in the affirmative and the decision was affirmed in the Supreme Court. *Re A Noyek & Sons Ltd, Burns v Hearne* III ITR 523. Note that the liability to pay over corporation tax differs, depending on whether the liquidation is voluntary or compulsory. See also judgments in the cases of *Donnelly* **38.83**, *Hibernian Transport* **38.84** and *Wayte (Holdings)* **38.85** below.

38.82 Scheme of arrangement with creditors: Revenue priority. The company obtained agreement to a scheme of arrangement at a meeting of all its creditors, at which no distinction was made as to status or quality of the various claims, and at which the Revenue Commissioners were outvoted. Held, the approval of the Revenue Commissioners, as a separate category (having a preferential claim in liquidation in respect of part of their claim), should have been sought at a separate meeting before the scheme was put to the ordinary creditors. *Re Donmac Agricultural Ltd* HC, 1981.

38.83 Expenses of liquidation – whether tax on realisation of assets a 'necessary disbursement'. In a case brought against a liquidator in respect of corporation tax liability on disposal of certain assets, it was held that the tax payable was neither an expense of the realisation nor a 'necessary disbursement' of the liquidation. The liability was therefore governed as to priority in the liquidation by the specific provisions. *Revenue Commissioners v Donnelly* [1983] ILRM 329. See now **9.4** 'Capital gains tax' as regards *FA 1983, s 56* provisions. See also **38.84** below.

38.84 Deposit interest in liquidation: liability: whether a 'necessary disbursement': status of Revenue claim. In a case where substantial deposit interest had been earned on money in the hands of the Official Liquidator, it was held that:

(i)   such interest is liable to income tax, corporation profits tax or corporation tax as appropriate;

(ii)   the tax thereon is not a 'necessary disbursement' of the liquidation, following *Revenue Commissioners v Donnelly* (see **38.83** above);

(iii)   the Revenue Commissioners' claim in relation to the tax thereon is not preferential; and

(iv)   the Revenue Commissioners' claim does not rank as an unsecured debt in the winding-up (but see now *s 571*).

In the matter of Hibernian Transport Companies Ltd and Others III ITR 120; [1984] ILRM 583.

38.85 Deposit interest in receivership: liability to tax. A receiver, appointed by a debenture-holder, deposited monies with the Agricultural Credit Corporation in his name as 'receiver' of the company. The Revenue claimed that the receiver was liable to pay corporation tax on the interest earned. The Judge held that *s 76* does not incorporate the provisions of *s 52* into the corporation tax code, and that *companies* only, and not their officers, are assessable to corporation tax. Re *Wayte (Holdings) Ltd (In Receivership), Burns v Hearne* III ITR 553. See also judgments in the cases of *Donnelly* **38.83**, *Hibernian Transport* **38.84** and *Noyek* **38.81** above.

38.86 Surcharge on undistributed income of close company. The Revenue sought to impose the 20 per cent surcharge under *s 440(1)* on a close investment company in liquidation. The company referred to *s 434(2)* which gives a company a period of 18 months after the end of an accounting period in which to make distributions, and claimed that *s 130(1)* unfairly penalised a company in liquidation by reducing to six months following the penultimate period the time within which a dividend deductible from the amount subject to the surcharge might be paid and reducing to nil the period following the ultimate period within which such a payment could be made. Held that there were no manifestly unfair circumstances in this case, and that the Appeal Commissioner was correct in holding that *s 130(1)* did not prevent the application of *s 440(1)* in this case. *Rahinstown Estate Company (in Liquidation) v Hughes* III ITR 517.

38.87 Appropriation of tax payments to earlier years. The Collector General contended that an existing arrangement with the taxpayer entitled him to appropriate payments made for current liabilities against arrears of other group companies. The fact that a new managing director of the company was unaware of the arrangement did not alter the position. The contention of the Collector General was upheld. *Re Metal Products Ltd (In Receivership), Uniacke v The Collector General* HC, January 1988.

MARRIED PERSONS

38.88 Aggregation of income. Prior to the amending legislation in *FA 1980*, the plaintiffs sought and obtained a declaration that the provisions of *ITA 1967, ss 192–198* inclusive as then enacted (providing for the aggregation of the wife's income with that of her husband for income tax purposes) were repugnant to the Constitution. In a subsidiary judgment, it was held that the provisions in question were void *ab initio*, but that only those taxpayers who had previously challenged through the Courts the constitutionality of the provisions in relation to specific assessments were entitled to seek repayment of tax deducted under such assessments. *Francis and Mary Murphy v Attorney General* V ITR 613; [1994] ITR 53; [1982] IR 241.

38.89 Following the *Murphy* case (**38.88** above), *FA 1980, s 21* was enacted to prevent assessments made after 25 June 1980 for 1979/80 or earlier years resulting in a lower liability than would have arisen under the old aggregation rules. In the High Court, this section was held to be unconstitutional and invalid, following the *Murphy* decision. *Bernard and Ann Muckley v Attorney General and Revenue Commissioners* III ITR 188.

38.90 Assessment of husband on non-resident wife's income. On a claim for the married allowance and double rate bands, the taxpayer's wife's income was not capable of being assessed and charged to tax in RI (by virtue of her non-residence). It was held that no election for joint assessment under *s 1017* (whether actual or deemed) could be made. *Fennessy v McConnellogue* V ITR 129. See **23.1** 'Married persons'.

38.91 Application of *TCA 1997, s 194* – whether wife a 'chargeable person'. In proceedings relating to goods distrained to satisfy an income tax liability, it was held that, where *s 194* applies (see **23.1** 'Married persons'), the wife is not a 'chargeable person' for income tax purposes, regardless of whether she was actually entitled to or in receipt of income. *Gilligan v Revenue Commissioners and Others* V ITR 424.

RESIDENCE, ORDINARY RESIDENCE AND DOMICILE

(See also *Hewson v Kealy* **38.7** above.)

38.92 Company registered in RI and abroad. A company registered in both RI and the USA merchanted linen goods. Most of its sales were in the USA where its only director resided, but the goods were warehoused in Belfast. The company was held to be resident in RI and liable under Case I on the whole of its profits. *Hood (John) & Co Ltd v Magee* KB(I) (1918) 7 TC 327.

38.93 Jurisdiction of Courts in relation to determination of domicile. In an income tax case, the High Court reversed a decision by the Special Commissioners that the taxpayer had not given up his domicile of origin. The Supreme Court held that domicile is a question of fact and the Commissioners' decision, if one of fact, could not be reviewed by the Courts. However, in this case the Special Commissioners had approached the question as one of law and had misconstrued the law. The case was remitted to them to determine the question of domicile as one of fact. *Earl of Iveagh v Revenue Commissioners* 1 ITC 316; I ITR 259; [1930] IR 431.

38.94 Domicile and ordinary residence. The appellant was born in 1870 in Ireland, his father having been born in Italy and having owned residences both in Ireland and in England. The appellant had lived altogether in England up to 1892, when he inherited the English residence and certain entailed property in Ireland. From 1892 to 1922 he resided, whenever not outside the British Isles, at one or other of those properties, neither being regarded as his chief home. His five children were born in Ireland. The property in Ireland was kept permanently ready for his occupation, and from 1922 to the date of the appeal he visited it with his family every year, spending 165 days there in 1923/24, 182 days in 1924/25 and 170 days between 6 April 1925 and 11 December 1925. He also had an interest in an Irish colliery throughout, either as sole proprietor or as director and chief shareholder of the successor owning company. He was admittedly resident in Ireland for 1923/24, 1924/25 and 1925/26. He claimed that he had elected that his domicile should be in England, and had abandoned his former RI domicile, although stating that he had not abandoned all intention of returning to his home in RI. In the course of the High Court hearing, it was admitted that he was ordinarily resident in RI, and the Court held that he was also domiciled in RI, having failed to discharge the onus of proof in regard to the claimed domicile change. *Prior-Wandesforde v Revenue Commissioners* 1 ITC 248; I ITR 249.

38.95 Domicile of choice – whether abandoned. A woman born of RI domiciled parents had acquired an English domicile of choice. She commenced residence in what had previously been a holiday home in RI when, following the death of her husband, she was obliged to vacate her previous home (a company flat) in England. Since 1982, whilst continuing to reside in RI, she had sought a property in England, with the intention of returning to live in England. In 1993 she had purchased a property in London which was still undergoing refurbishment. The Circuit Court judge, hearing her appeal against assessments founded on her having been RI-domiciled since 1982, found that she had acquired an RI domicile of choice in 1982. It was held in the High Court that the correct question was not whether she had acquired an RI domicile of choice but whether she had abandoned her English domicile of choice, thus reviving her RI domicile of origin. There was insufficient evidence to support the Revenue contention that the English domicile had been abandoned. *Clair Proes v Revenue Commissioners* V ITR 481.

38.96 Domicile of choice – acquisition and retention. The plaintiff's brother, whose domicile at death was in question, had an RI domicile of origin and was an RI citizen.

He took up residence in France from 1949 until his death in 1984, and on the facts he was held to have acquired a French domicile of choice. Although there was evidence that he had, in 1983, formed an intention to abandon his French domicile, that intention was ineffective in law as he had not in fact changed his residence at the time of his death. He therefore died domiciled in France. *Rowan v Rowan* III ITR 572.

38.97 Domicile of choice – acquisition – abandonment. The taxpayer, of RI domicile of origin, was born in London and had spent most of his working life in Scotland, with regular annual visits of a month or two to RI. He had inherited the family property in RI, and, on its destruction by fire, had acquired other property in RI. For the last 32 years of his life he lived in RI, with regular visits to Scotland, mainly in connection with his declining business interests. He owned, but not for his own personal use, property in Scotland. In his will he declared that he had acquired and retained a Scottish domicile of choice. Held, the RI domicile of origin had never been replaced by a domicile of choice. The acquisition of a domicile of choice requires the establishment of an intention to reside in the chosen country for an indefinite time, and the actions of the taxpayer had not shown any such intention, having always indicated that the taxpayer contemplated that he might return to RI. Even if he had acquired a Scottish domicile of choice, there was clear evidence that in the last 32 years of his life he had resolved to make his permanent home in RI, and hence to abandon his domicile of choice. *Revenue Commissioners v Shaw and Talbot-Crosbie* [1982] ILRM 433.

RESIDENTIAL PROPERTY TAX

38.98 Whether tax unconstitutional. The appellants in two separate proceedings sought to obtain a declaration that the residential property tax introduced by *FA 1983, ss 95–116* was unconstitutional. The cases referred specifically to the method of determining market value and to the income exemption limit (particularly the aggregation of the income of all persons normally residing in the property), and on the direction of the judge, consideration of the appeals was confined to the facts of each case. Both appeals were dismissed, but with a rider that the decisions need not preclude another appellant bringing a similar case on different facts. *Madigan v Attorney General; Gallagher v Attorney General* III ITR 127; [1986] ILRM 136.

SCHEDULE D, CASES I AND II – EXPENDITURE

38.99 The cost of rebuilding business premises destroyed in the RI rebellion of 1916 (less an *ex gratia* Government grant) and of adapting temporary premises, was held to be capital and not an admissible deduction for excess profits duty. *Fitzgerald v CIR* 1 ITC 100; I ITR 91; [1926] IR 182, 585.

38.100 Improvement of sanitation. A company carried on business as woollen manufacturers. Following the installation of a new water and sewerage scheme in the locality of its mill, and in compliance with Orders made by the local authority, it replaced the earthen privies at its mill, housed in various sheds detached from the mill building, by water closets in a concrete structure attached to the mill building. Held, reversing the High Court decision, that the expenditure was capital or on improvements, and not allowable. *Vale v Martin Mahony & Bros Ltd* 2 ITC 331; II ITR 32; [1947] IR 30, 41.

38.101 Replacement of weighbridge building. For the purposes of its trade as leather manufacturers, a company had a weighbridge in its factory premises, comprising the weighbridge with a ramp in the open next to a small building, separate from the main factory building, housing the weighbridge machinery and also providing some workshop and storage accommodation. Following severe storm damage, the building was demolished and replaced by a smaller building, housing only the weighbridge machinery, and no improvement on the old. Held, affirming the Special Commissioners' decision, that the cost of demolishing and replacing the building was allowable. No new capital was brought into existence and the replacement was of a small part of the factory premises as a whole which were the 'entirety'. (A new building was also erected for workshop and storage accommodation, but the cost of this was charged to capital and not claimed as allowable.) *Hodgkins v Plunder & Pollak (Ireland) Ltd* 3 ITC 135; II ITR 267; [1957] IR 58.

38.102 Rebuilding of premises. A company carried on business from a 300-year-old building. It was in very bad condition and the company was advised that it was not feasible to put it in a state of good repair. It was therefore demolished except for the rear wall and part of a side wall and replaced by a modern two storey shop at a total cost of £6,509 of which the architect allocated £4,919 to 'repairs'. The company claimed to deduct the £4,919. On appeal, the Circuit Judge allowed £1,276. The High Court disallowed the whole. The expenditure brought into being new premises and was capital, applying Viscount Cave's test in *Atherton* 10 TC 155, (a UK case). *Curtin v M Ltd* 3 ITC 227; II ITR 360; [1960] IR 97.

38.103 Refurbishment of grandstand. The taxpayers promoted and organised horse races at a racecourse. Extensive works were carried out on the public grandstand. These included:

(*a*)   widening of the steps on the lower terrace (with a consequent 40 per cent increase in the standing area);

(*b*)   extending the existing bar;

(*c*)   replacing wet and crumbling walls;

(*d*)   construction of a new reserve bar; and

(*e*)   replacement of the existing roof and supports.

It was held that net expenditure on item (*c*) was an allowable repair, but that items (*a*) and (*e*) constituted renewals and improvements to the grandstand (which was the 'entirety' to be considered in this case) and were not allowable deductions. Items (*b*) and (*d*) were clearly capital improvements and not deductible. *O'Grady v Roscommon Race Committee* V ITR 317. As regards capital allowances for the disallowed expenditure, see **38.35** above.

38.104 Quarry – cost of removal of top soil. A company worked a limestone quarry, using the limestone mainly to produce limestone flour. To ensure the purity of this product, the top soil had to be removed before blasting the limestone from the side of the quarry. Held, reversing the decision of the Special Commissioner, that the cost of removing the top soil was allowable. It was part of the cost of manufacture of the marketable product. *Milverton Quarries Ltd v Revenue Commissioners* 3 ITC 279; II ITR 382; [1960] IR 224.

38.105 Technical information, etc in return for sum payable in instalments. In 1958 an RI company s Ltd decided to expand its business in plumbers' brassware and for this purpose agreed to pay W, a leading English firm in the business, 'the capital sum of £15,000', payable in instalments over some six years, in return for the supply by W for ten years of technical information and an exclusive licence in RI in any patents it held. Thereafter S's turnover increased substantially and, in the event, it did not call on W for advice after 1963, although its liabilities under the agreement continued. Its payments under the agreement were held to be capital and not deductible in computing its profits. *S Ltd v O'Sullivan* TL 108; II ITR 602.

38.106 Exclusivity payments by petrol company. The appellant, a petrol company, entered into exclusivity agreements with retailers under which it paid lump sums and, in addition, undertook to reimburse the retailer in respect of sums expended on decoration, re-siting and maintenance of pumps, and other works. The lump sums were calculated by reference to estimated gallonage, although retailers were not aware of this fact. Initially, agreements were for one to three years, but ultimately, they were made for periods of up to ten years or more. The Supreme Court held, by a four-to-one majority, that payments where the agreement was for ten years or less were of a revenue nature and allowable, and, by a three-to-two majority, that there was no ground for according a different treatment to payments where the agreement was for longer than ten years. *Dolan v AB Co Ltd* TL 109; II ITR 515.

38.107 Expenses of action relating to liability assumed by company on its formation. With a view to forming a company to take it over, persons contracted with a builder for the construction of a cinema. The cinema was completed and opened for business in November 1947 and a company was registered on 3 January 1948, taking over all the assets and liabilities of the cinema business on the same day. At that time, the balance due to the builder had not been settled. The matter reached the High Court, which awarded the builder £650 with costs, which the company duly paid. The company admitted the £650 to be capital but claimed to deduct its legal expenses of £903 in connection with the court action. The expenses were held to be capital, made in relation to a capital liability and solely referable to the capital structure of the company. *Casey v AB Ltd* TL 104; II ITR 500; [1965] IR 668.

38.108 Expenses of formation of holding company. In order to avoid certain consequences of a new system of quotas which might adversely affect the business of three companies in the bacon trade, their shareholders agreed to set up a new holding company, exchanging their shares for shares in the new company. They agreed that the expenses of forming the company should be shared between two of the companies, of which the taxpayer company was one and claimed its share of the expenses as a deduction in computing its profits. Held, the expenses were capital and disallowable. *Per* two of the three judges who heard the case, the expenses were also disallowable as not having been incurred wholly or exclusively for the purposes of the trade; the third expressed no opinion on this. *Kealy v O'Mara (Limerick) Ltd* 2 ITC 265; I ITR 642; [1942] IR 616.

38.109 Interest on loan applied to redeem share capital. Interest on a loan applied by a company to redeem preference shares issued to finance the purchase of additional premises was held to have been laid out to enable the company to carry on and earn profits in the trade. The company was entitled to redeem the preference shares, and the purpose of the loan was to fill the ensuing gap in the financing of the trade. The interest was thus laid out wholly and exclusively for the purposes of the trade and an allowable deduction in computing profits of the trade. *MacAonghusa v Ringmahon Company* (unreported, 29 May 2001), SC. (The High Court judgment ([1999] ITR 81) contains a wide-ranging review of the authorities on the 'wholly and exclusively' requirement.)

38.110 Payment to settle action alleging infringement of rights by construction of factory. A manufacturing company decided to move to another site and to build a new factory there for the purpose. It received all the requisite planning approvals, but while the factory was under construction, tenants of adjacent houses commenced proceedings against it, alleging the factory would infringe their rights to light and air. The company's legal advisers considered the claim unsustainable but advised compromise if possible. In the event the company settled the action, paying the tenants £225 as compensation and £75 for costs, and claimed these amounts as deductions in computing its profits. Its claim was upheld. The expenditure was wholly and exclusively for the purposes of its trade and, applying a *dictum* of Lawrence L J in *Southern v Borax Consolidated Ltd* (a UK case reported at 23 TC 597), paid to defend its assets and not capital. *Davis v X Ltd* 2 ITC 320; II ITR 45.

38.111 Settlement of action for nuisance. A company manufacturing building materials secured the settlement of an action for nuisance and the withdrawal of planning objections by purchasing the complainant's adjacent property, a payment of £8,000, the delivery of building materials to the complainant and payment of costs. The company accepted that the property purchase was capital expenditure, but sought to claim the remaining expenditure as a deduction from profits. The Judge held, noting the different circumstances from *Davis v X Ltd* 2 ITC 320 (see **38.110** above), that the remaining expenditure was capital. *Insulation Products Ltd v Inspector of Taxes* [1984] ILRM 610.

38.112 Costs of promoting private Bills. A gas undertaking was carried on by a committee constituted by a private Act. On modernisation of the works, a number of the employees became redundant and the committee promoted a private Bill (eventually passed) to enable it to pay pensions to its former employees. The Special Commissioners allowed the cost of promoting the Bill and their decision was upheld as one of fact, there not having been a palpable error of law. *McGarry v Limerick Gas Committee* 1 ITC 405; I ITR 375; [1932] IR 125.

38.113 Payments towards statutory sinking fund. Under a private Act of Parliament, a company issued debenture stock to finance its carrying out a Government contract and was required to set aside part of its receipts to establish a sinking fund to repay the debentures. The sums so set aside were held not to be deductible, following *Mersey Docks & Harbour Board v Lucas* (a UK case reported at 2 TC 25). *City of Dublin Steam Packet Co v O'Brien* KB (I) 6 TC 101.

38.114 Woodlands – initial planting of new acreage. The taxpayer, who had elected for Sch D treatment of his woodlands, had cleared 84 acres of waste land preparatory to the planting of young trees, it being accepted that the clearance expenditure was a capital expense. The case concerned whether or not the cost of purchase and planting of the new trees was a revenue expense and it was held to be capital, affirming the High Court decision. *Wilson-Wright v Connolly* (unreported, 20 December 1976), SC. The judgment distinguished between the cost of the original planting which was regarded as a capital expense and replanting which was regarded as a revenue expense.

38.115 Lease premium – avoidance scheme. In a relatively straightforward sale and lease-back scheme exploiting the provisions of *ss 98* and *102*, the inspector's attempt to deny a deduction for the full amount of the premium paid on a lease, where the lessor had validly elected to be taxed on instalments as they arose, was rejected. The legislative provisions were unequivocal and the scheme operated by the company was fully tax effective. *The Hammond Lane Metal Co Ltd v O'Culacháin* IV ITR 105. See **33.6** 'Sch D, Case V'. For a preliminary issue in this case, see **38.3** above.

SCHEDULE D, CASES I AND II – RECEIPTS

38.116 Compulsory sales of requisitioned goods. The appellant company, being brewers, held large stocks of barley for manufacturing purposes. The barley was not normally sold or traded. Under wartime regulations, the stocks were requisitioned, being thereafter sold as directed to millers at a set price plus commission. The profit on these transactions was assessed as arising from the trade. The Court of Appeal, in a majority decision, held, following the UK case *Glenboig Union Fireclay Co Ltd v CIR* 12 TC 427, that the receipts were in respect of the taking by compulsion of a capital asset and were not trade profits. *Arthur Guinness, Son and Co Ltd v CIR* C/A 1923, 1 ITC 1; I ITR 1; [1923] 2 IR 186.

38.117 Compensation for detention of ships during coal strike. A gas company owned two ships to carry coal to its works. They were compulsorily detained in England during the 1920 coal strike. The company received compensation from the UK Government in 1924. It was treated as a trading receipt in its 1925/26 assessment (based on its 1924 profits) and the assessment was upheld. *Alliance & Dublin Consumers' Gas Co v McWilliams* 1 ITC 199; I ITR 207; [1928] IR 1. (*Note*. The date the compensation should be brought into account was not an issue.)

38.118 Cancellation of agreement to supply cattle to subsidiary. In a case in which the facts are special and complex, a decision by the Commissioners that compensation paid by the Minister of Agriculture to a company, on his ceasing to supply cattle to a subsidiary of the company (formed pursuant to an agreement with the Minister), was not a trading receipt, was upheld as one of fact for which there was evidence. *O'Dwyer v Irish Exporters and Importers Ltd* 2 ITC 251; I ITR 629; [1943] IR 176. (For another issue in this case see **38.11** above.)

38.119 Merchant bank: sale of investment. The appellant company, a merchant bank, had a wholly-owned subsidiary investment holding company (TT), which in April 1967 acquired the two issued shares in Hummingbird Ltd, a property investment company, which subsequently made substantial capital profits on certain land investments (see **38.136** below) transferred to it by the appellant company in December 1967. In April 1976, the appellant company, which was experiencing trading difficulties, purchased the two shares in Hummingbird Ltd from TT for £2, and wound up the company, the liquidator paying over £675,000 to the appellant company. Held, reversing the Appeal Commissioners' decision, that the £675,000 was not part of the appellant company's trading profits. All the evidence suggested that the property from which the profits derived was acquired as a long-term investment, and the sale of the Hummingbird Ltd shares to the appellant company by TT could not be regarded as a normal trading transaction. The fact that the realised proceeds were used to defray trading losses was not sufficient to characterise the proceeds as trading profits. *Guinness and Mahon Ltd v Browne* TL 133; III ITR 373.

38.120 Investment sales by company formed to provide credit for farmers, etc. A company was established by statute to give credit to persons engaged in agriculture and facilitate borrowing by farmers on the security of their farms. It was accepted as carrying on a banking business for the purposes of *ITA 1918, s 36* (similar to *ITA 1967, s 496*). It was assessed on the footing that its profits less losses on the realisation of its investments were part of its trading profits. In the two relevant years, there were respectively ten and six sales, mostly of Government securities. On appeal, the Commissioners found that the gains or losses were in an operation of business in carrying out a scheme of profit making, and part of the trading receipts. Held, the Commissioners had not misdirected themselves in law and their decision was one of fact for which there was evidence. *Agricultural Credit Corporation Ltd v Vale* 2 ITC 46; I ITR 474; [1935] IR 681.

38.121 Training grant – whether capital or revenue receipt. A training grant under *Industrial Development Act 1969, s 39* was held to be taxable as a revenue receipt. The moneys were paid with the object of relieving the company's wage bill, and did not affect the company's capital position. *Jacob International Ltd Inc v O'Cleirigh* TL 128; III ITR 165; [1985] ILRM 651.

38.122 Ex gratia payment by government on recommendation of 1926 Irish Grants Committee. In 1926 the UK Government set up an Irish Grants Committee to consider claims from British subjects who had suffered hardship or loss because of their support of the Government before the partition. A taxpayer carrying on business in RI claimed an award of £29,469 for losses sustained or profits lost and £11,437 for loss of goodwill. The Government, on the recommendation of the Committee, made an *ex gratia* payment of £14,000 in two instalments in the two years to 31 January 1930. The taxpayer was assessed on the footing that the instalments were trading receipts of the years in which received. Held, the payments were not trading receipts. *Robinson (trading as James Pim & Son) v Dolan* 2 ITC 25; I ITR 427; [1935] IR 509.

38.123 Recovery under insurance against loss of profits. A baker's premises were destroyed by fire in May 1942. He was able to continue trading in temporary premises but with reduced turnover and a rise in working costs. He was insured against this for one year, the premiums having been allowed in computing his profits. After negotiation, he received £1,300 in November 1944 under the policy, having incurred professional expenses of £130 in settling his claim. Held, the £1,300 less the £130 was a trading receipt and should be brought into account as at May 1943. *Corr v Larkin* 3 ITC 13; II ITR 164; [1949] IR 399.

38.124 Gift to professional jockey. The owner of the winner of the 1921 Irish Derby gave the winning jockey a present of £400. The evidence was that owners sometimes make presents to winning jockeys but this was the only present received by this jockey in the relevant period. Held, confirming the decision of the Commissioners, that the £400 was an assessable receipt of his vocation. *Wing v O'Connell* I ITR 155; [1927] IR 84. (*Note.* In the report the £400 is sometimes referred to as an 'emolument' or 'remuneration'. Under the law in force at the time, Sch D, Case II covered employments as well as professions and vocations. The assessment was under Sch D, Case II and it is thought that the jockey would have been so assessed under present-day legislation).

38.125 Debt recoveries following death of trader – trade continued by executor. A trader died and the executor continued to carry on the business on behalf of the residuary legatees. It was held that recoveries by the executor of debts allowed as bad in periods before the death could not be brought into the assessments for periods after the death. *CD v O'Sullivan* 2 ITC 422; II ITR 140; [1949] IR 264. (But see now *s 87*.)

SCHEDULE D, CASES I AND II – TRADE, BUSINESS, ETC

38.126 Services supplied without charge – notional receipt. The appellant company had six subsidiaries and one associated company and operated as a holding company, although it had also been accepted by the Revenue as carrying on a trade of managing and financing the subsidiaries. The appellant company's expenses had previously been charged out to the subsidiaries, but in the two accounting periods in question substantial expenses were incurred and not charged out, thus creating losses. Also in those accounting periods the appellant company received dividends, net of tax credits at 30 per cent, from two of the subsidiaries, and the sum of the dividends received and associated tax credits exceeded the trading loss for each period. The appellant company sought to treat this franked investment income as profits against which its trading losses could be set under *s 157* (see **12.13** 'Corporation tax'). The Appeal Commissioner held that the appellant company's accounts for each period should be adjusted to include notional income in respect of the services provided, and concluded that the appropriate amount to be included was ten per cent of the income of the paying companies. Held, the decision that a notional amount in respect of services provided should be included in the appellant company's accounts was correct, but there was no evidence to support the basis of computation of the amount made by the Appeal Commissioner. The case was remitted to the Appeal Commissioner to be decided on the basis of its being a bona fide transaction in the ordinary course of business. *Belville Holdings Ltd v Cronin* TL 131; III ITR 340.

38.127 Meaning of 'trade, business' etc. The appellant company, which had previously traded by steam vessels out of Dublin, had, by 1920, sold all its boats, but continued to receive a substantial investment income and to make an annual payment of £3,000 under an earlier agreement relating to its previous passenger trade. It appealed against assessments for accounting periods following the sale of its boats, on the ground that it was not carrying on 'any trade or business or any undertaking of a similar character, including the holding of investments', within the charge to Corporation Profits Tax under *FA 1920, s 52(2)(a)*. Citing in particular the 'various and elaborate operations ... directed towards the general benefit ... of the company and its shareholders' and the 'repetition of acts' represented by the making of the annual payments, the Court held that the company was carrying on a 'trade or business or undertaking of a similar character'. *City of Dublin Steampacket Co Ltd v Revenue Commissioners* 1 ITC 118; [1926] IR 436. The same conclusion was reached on a later appeal regarding the company's income following its being put into liquidation. *City of Dublin Steampacket Co Ltd (in Liquidation) v Revenue Commissioners* 1 ITC 285; I ITR 318; [1930] IR 217.

38.128 Meaning of 'trade, business', etc. The appellant company, founded to make and maintain a railway line, had, under various acts and agreements, passed all the powers and privileges with regard to the line to a working company, and was at the time in question entitled only to a rent of £30,000 pa (with an entitlement to profit share which had not in fact been activated). All remaining receipts and expenditure related to investments or to the running of the company itself. A similar contention by the company to that in *City of Dublin Steampacket Co Ltd v Revenue Commissioners* (**38.127** above) was again rejected by the Court. *CIR v Dublin and Kingstown Railway Co* 1 ITC 131; I ITR 119; [1930] IR 317.

38.129 Employment or self-employment – insurance agent. In a case in which it was held that the defendant was self-employed, the distinction between a contract of service and a contract for services was examined. The test was defined as 'Is the person who has engaged himself to perform these services performing them as a person in business on his own account?'. The nature and degree of control exercised by the employer was only one relevant consideration, others being eg whether the person performing the services provides his own equipment, or has his own helpers, what degree of financial risk he takes, what degree of responsibility for investment and management he has, and whether and how far he has an opportunity for profiting from sound management in the performance of his task. *McDermott v Loy* TL 118; III ITR 43.

38.130 Employment or self-employment – Employment Office manager. In a case in which the facts were unusual, it was held that the appellant, who was required to provide premises, staff, etc under a written contract with the Minister for Social Welfare, was engaged under a contract for services and was therefore self-employed. The judgment contains a useful summary of the factors to be considered in distinguishing between a contract for services and one of service, and their application to a written contract. *O'Coindealbháin v Mooney* IV ITR 45. (See also **38.21** above for a case concerning interest on overpaid tax consequent upon this decision.)

38.131 Employment or self-employment – fishing crew. The taxpayer was the skipper of a fishing vessel. No contract of service existed for crew members, who were normally re-engaged weekly by custom. Crew members were remunerated by means of a share of the proceeds of sale on an agreed basis, but did not share in losses. The Court had to determine whether an employer-employee relationship existed, and, if so, whether the taxpayer was guilty of failure to submit PAYE and PRSI returns. The Judge held that the skipper and crew members were partners in a joint adventure renewed each Monday morning. *Director of Public Prosecutions v McLoughlin* III ITR 467. (See also *Minister for Social Welfare v Griffiths* (unreported, 14 *February 1992), HC*, where a similar decision was reached in relation to social welfare legislation.)

38.132 Employment or self-employment – journalists. In the winding-up of a newspaper company, certain persons who had worked for the newspaper applied to be treated as employees and hence as preferential creditors. All had been dealt with for tax purposes under Sch D. The liquidator applied to the Court for a ruling as to whether they were employees for this purpose. Held, in the case of a sub-editor working two shifts a week and a regular columnist, that the contracts under which they worked were contracts of service, so that they were entitled to be treated as employees. In the case of another regular contributor, it was held that she was a freelancer who secured commissions in advance, and that she was not employed under a contract of service. *In re Sunday Tribune Ltd (in liquidation)* [1998] ITR 177.

38.133 See also *Louth v Minister for Social Welfare* IV ITR 391, *Henry Denny & Sons (Ireland) Ltd v Minister for Social Welfare* V ITR 238 and *ESB v The Minister for Social Community and Family Affairs* (unreported, 21 February 2006), HC as regards a deepsea docker, a supermarket food demonstrator and meter readers respectively, each held to be employed under contracts of service. (Social welfare cases.)

38.134 Limited partner – share of losses – avoidance scheme. The taxpayer was one of seven limited partners in a partnership, five of whom were also directors of the sole general partner, Southern Metropole Hotels Co Ltd ('the company'). Registration of the limited partnership was not in accordance with the *Limited Partnerships Act 1907*, but the finding of fact by the Appeal Commissioners was that the trade was carried on in partnership. Each limited partner contributed £50 as capital in the partnership. The company entered into a five-year agreement with the partnership whereby the company lent money to the partnership, which the partnership used to buy plant and machinery. This was then let to the company at ten per cent of cost per annum, the partnership being responsible for wear and tear. In the first year the partnership borrowed £30,000, its leasing income was £222 and the amount claimed for wear and tear under *s 298* was £13,000. The taxpayer's claim to relief for his share of the losses (against his personal income), which was allowed by the Appeal Commissioners, was challenged by the Revenue on the grounds that the agreement had no commercial reality and was contrived entirely for its tax advantage. Held, the scheme was not of so extreme a character as to be regarded as having no commercial reality, and it could be regarded as a trading transaction qualifying for the relief sought. *McCarthaigh v Daly* TL 127; III ITR 253; [1986] ILRM 116. See now **22.5** 'Losses' as regards anti-avoidance legislation.

38.135 Sale of undeveloped land purchased for development – whether within Sch D, Case I. A company was set up to purchase, develop and sell land. The owners had previously built houses for sale on land not owned by them. After land had been purchased by the company, the owners had a disagreement and decided not to proceed with development. The land was accordingly sold. Held, upholding an appeal against an assessment under Sch D, Case I, the transaction was an isolated one by a company which had not commenced any trade and which did not buy the land with the intention of selling it undeveloped. There was no evidence of an adventure in the nature of trade. *Spa Ltd v O'hArgain* (unreported, 1974), HC.

38.136 Sale of land during development – whether within Sch D, Case I. The appellant company acquired land on which it commenced development with a view to letting. The property was sold during development, and the Revenue assessed the profits under Sch D, Case I, following *s 640*. Held, that *s 640* did not apply, as the entire interest was sold, and that the Appeal Commissioners finding that there was no adventure in the nature of trade should stand. *Mara v Hummingbird Ltd* TL 114; II ITR 667.

38.137 Farmland rezoned for development – whether sale within Sch D, Case I. A land development company acquired farmland unsuitable for development, which it let to a participator until it commenced farming on the land on its own account. A subsequent rezoning rendered the land suitable for development, and the land was transferred to the parent company. Held, there was evidence that the farmland was purchased without any intention to develop the land as building land, but that the company commenced to trade in the land at the time that, following the rezoning, it decided to exploit the land as development land. *O'hArgain v Beechpark Estates Ltd* TL 116; III ITR 9.

38.138 Purchase and resale of whiskey in bond. A publican had for many years bought considerable quantities of whiskey in bond from a distillery company. Apart from a small amount used in his public house, he resold it to the distillery after four or five years at varying terms, but generally at cost plus an amount for 'interest'. He was free to sell the whiskey to others but did not do so. On appeal, the Commissioners found that the transactions constituted the carrying on of a business for excess profits duty purposes and their decision was upheld. *Representatives of P J McCall, dec'd v CIR* 1 ITC 31; I ITR 28; 4 ATC 522.

38.139 Statutory body to operate insurance scheme. The appellant was a Board set up by statute to carry into effect a scheme for the compulsory insurance of livestock shipped to Britain. The shippers paid levies to the Board to form a Fund out of which were to be met claims under the scheme, the Board's expenses and 'no other moneys'. The Board appealed against Case I assessments on its surpluses. It was conceded for the Board that it was carrying on a trade, but it was contended that its receipts were earmarked to meet its expenses and claims on it, and that the relevant Act did not contemplate that it was a profit-making business. Held, applying, inter alia, *Mersey Docks and Harbour Board v Lucas* (a UK case reported at 1 TC 385), and dismissing the appeal, that the provision in the Act as to the application of its receipts did not preclude assessment of its surpluses. (Whether there should be any provision for its unexpired risks was not an issue before the court.) *The Exported Live Stock (Insurance) Board v Carroll* 3 ITC 67; II ITR 211; [1951] IR 286.

38.140 Changes in trade leading to new trade. A partnership trading as retail fuel merchants acquired interests in coal-bearing land and commenced the production of coal, retaining some of their old customers but thereafter supplying the coal produced mainly to wholesalers and to certain large public concerns. Held that a new trade was set up when coal production commenced. *O'Loan v M J Noone & Co* 2 ITC 430; II ITR 147; [1949] IR 171.

38.141 Bookmaker – profits from sweepstakes on English races – whether trading receipts. A bookmaker whose activities included the purchase of Irish Hospitals Sweepstakes tickets relating to races run in both RI and England contended that the profits from tickets relating to English races were from private gambling, and not subject to tax, as he did not attend meetings and could not influence the odds. Held, the profits were correctly assessed under Sch D, Case I. Distinguishing the UK case *Graham v Green* 9 TC 309, the existence of a bookmaking business was sufficient to require the inclusion of all such profits as trading income. *HH v Forbes* TL 113; II ITR 614.

38.142 Banking company – Government securities – whether trade under Sch D, Case I. The respondent company was a subsidiary of a joint stock bank and engaged in hire-purchase, credit finance and leasing. In order to meet minimum liquidity requirements, Government stocks were purchased and held to maturity, but the company did not otherwise deal in stocks and shares although it had power to do so. The Revenue sought to tax realised gains, treated by the company as exempt capital gains, of £213,375 in 1977 and £922,300 in 1978 as arising from a trade of dealing in securities assessable under Sch D, Case I. Held, reversing the decisions in the lower courts, that the realised gains were part of the company's trading profits and chargeable to corporation tax. *Browne v Bank of Ireland Finance Ltd* III ITR 644.

SCHEDULE D, CASES I AND II – MISCELLANEOUS

38.143 Current cost accounting – whether acceptable for tax purposes. The High Court upheld the decision of the Appeal Commissioners that accounts for tax purposes are to be prepared on the historical cost accounting convention, and that the current cost accounting convention was not applicable. *Carroll Industries plc and P J Carroll and Co Ltd v O'Culacháin* IV ITR 135.

38.144 Stallion fees. The appellant company owned a stallion, and mares were brought for service and kept on the farm for about four months, their keep being paid for. Held, that the profits from stallion fees did not accrue from the occupation of farm lands, charged under Sch B, but from a trade assessable under Sch D. *Cloghran Stud Farm v Birch* 2 ITC 65; I ITR 495; [1936] IR 1.

38.145 Land transaction – application of *s 641*. A company in liquidation sold to a director its interest in a lease it had previously acquired from another director at a rent of IR£2,500 without fine or premium. It contended that, under *s 641*, the profit on disposal of the lease fell to be computed by reference to a deemed acquisition cost based on the capitalised value of the rent. Held, the profit was to be computed on ordinary principles of commercial accounting. *s 641(2)(b)* did not require a value to be substituted for cost overriding such principles. The assessment must be made on a calculation of the difference between the amount (if any) expended on acquisition of the lease and the amount expended on its disposal, with any appropriate and permissible deductions and additions. *Cronin v Cork and County Property Co Ltd* III ITR 198.

38.146 A similar decision was reached in another case where a company acquired a lease of land from a fellow subsidiary and the fee simple, with a declaration of merger, from the parent company, and claimed a deduction in its trading accounts based on the market value of the rent reserved in the lease. *O'Connlain v Belvedere Estates Ltd* III ITR 271.

38.147 Whether rental income falls within Sch D, Case I. The taxpayer let unfurnished a shop and a number of flats, with no provision of services. She negotiated the lettings and supervised the properties herself. Held, that the letting did not amount to the carrying on of a trade. (The substantive issue was the taxpayer's entitlement to earned income relief.) *Pairceir v E M* TL 107; II ITR 596.

38.148 Grass-cutting rights on military land – whether profits assessable under Sch D, Case I. A company obtained grass-cutting rights over Government land 'subject to military use of the land'. Assessments for the years 1962/63 to 1969/70 inclusive under Sch D, Case I on profits from processing the cuttings into grass meal were upheld. The company's contention that the assessments should have been under Sch B up to 1968/69, and that the profits were exempt for 1969/70 under *FA 1969, s 18*, were rejected on the grounds that the predominant use of the land was military, and that for the purposes of Sch B and *FA 1969, s 18* there could only be one occupier, here the Government. *O'Conaill v Z Ltd* TL 111; II ITR 636; [1982] ILRM 451.

38.149 Illegal trading. A turf commission agent was assessed on his profits from promoting for charity two large sweepstakes. Under the law then in force, the carrying on of the sweepstakes was a criminal offence, although they were extensively advertised and the State took no steps against them. The Supreme Court reversing the decision of the High Court, held the profits were not assessable. Unless expressly authorised, the Revenue cannot tax profits from activities declared by the State to be unlawful. *Hayes v Duggan* 1 ITC 269; I ITR 195; [1929] IR 406, 413. See now **32.4** 'Sch D, Case IV'.

38.150 The appellant's trade consisted of the placing of automatic slot machines in public houses, shops and clubs. In a previous appeal, which had not proceeded to the High Court because of a technicality, the Circuit Judge had determined that the trade was illegal. Held that (i) it was not open to the taxpayer, in support of his appeal, to prove that the trade was illegal, but that (ii) where, as in this case, the Revenue knew the trade was illegal when the assessments were made, the assessments were invalid, following *Hayes v Duggan* (**38.145** above). *Collins v Mulvey* 3 ITC 151; II ITR 291; [1956] IR 233. See now **32.4** 'Sch D, Case IV'.

38.151 The taxpayers set up an enterprise called Investment International to carry on a chain letter scheme. In the absence of accounts, the inspector raised estimated assessments, against which appeals were made on the grounds that the scheme was illegal. Held, the scheme was illegal and, following *Hayes v Duggan* (**38.149** above), the profits could not be assessed. *McMahon v Howard and Patwell* HC,1985. See now **32.4** 'Sch D, Case IV'.

38.152 Tickets issued by shipping company paid for in advance abroad. To facilitate the emigration of RI citizens to America, a UK shipping company whose activities included carrying on business in RI through an RI branch office, and with agents in America, operated a scheme under which someone in America, eg a relative of a would-be emigrant, could purchase a 'Prepaid Certificate' in America which entitled the would-be emigrant to a ticket from the company's RI agents for the journey to America. If the would-be emigrant did not take up a ticket, the American purchaser of the Certificate was refunded his money, less a cancellation fee. The Supreme Court held that the passenger's ticket was not issued under an RI contract and hence, applying a *dictum* of Cave L C in *Maclaine v Eccott*, 10 TC 481 (a UK case), there was no liability to RI tax on the profit from the issue of the ticket. *Cunard Steamship Co Ltd v Herlihy* 1 ITC 373; I ITR 330; [1931] IR 287, 307.

38.153 Trade managed abroad – no control from RI. The trustees of a will gave an Australian company power of attorney to manage a sheep-farming business in Australia forming part of the estate. Yearly and quarterly accounts were sent to the trustees and the profits regularly remitted to them less a percentage which they directed to be carried to reserve. The trustees and beneficiaries, all of whom resided in RI or the UK, did not interfere in any way in the management of the business. The trustees were assessed under Case I on the profits. Held, reversing the decision of the Commissioners, there was no liability under Case I. *Trustees of Ferguson (dec'd) v Donovan* 1 ITC 214; I ITR 183; [1929] IR 489.

38.154 Scientific research expenditure – exploration. A claim for relief under *s 765* (as expenditure on scientific research) in respect of expenditure on exploring and drilling for oil was allowed. The clear wording of the proviso to *s 765(1)* granted allowances for such expenditure, and the further provisions of *s 670*, relating to the situation where exploration work proved fruitful, were not relevant. *Texaco Ireland Ltd v Murphy* IV ITR 91; [1992] ILRM 304. See **30.24** 'Sch D, Cases I and II'. For a subsequent decision relating to interest on tax paid pending appeal, see **38.14** above.

38.155 Stock relief – payments on account. A company engaged in the production of prefabricated type houses and buildings normally required a 15 per cent deposit on execution of a contract for supply of a building. The High Court, reversing the Circuit Judge's finding, held that the deposits represented payments on account in respect of trading stock, and hence fell to reduce the amount on which stock relief was available under *FA 1975, s 31* (see now **18.8** 'Farming'). *O'Laoghaire v Avonree Buildings Ltd* TL 119; [1984] ILRM 196. See also **30.29** 'Sch D, Cases I and II'.

38.156 Stock relief – company with several trades. A company carried on a number of different activities. If all the activities were taken together, stock relief under *FA 1975, s 31(1)(9)* was not due, but the company claimed the relief for the two individual trades of millers and hardware. The Judge held, reversing the finding of the Circuit Court, that a company may be held to carry on different trades for the purposes of tax, whether or not the different activities were taken on separately, and that it was a question of fact for the Circuit Court Judge to decide whether the company was carrying on a number of separate trades. On the facts, the judge held that two of the activities (milling and the licensed trade) were separate trades and remitted the case to the Appeal Commissioner for a decision on the other activities (including hardware). *Re P McElligott & Sons Ltd* [1985] ILRM 210.

38.157 Stock relief – whether company engaged in manufacturing trade. A company imported components for agricultural machinery, purchased local materials, assembled the machines and then sold them to farmers and agricultural contractors. Approximately 25 per cent of the company's goods were sold direct to farmers, 20 per cent direct to dealers and 55 per cent to farmers with the dealer acting as an intermediary. The company claimed stock relief under *FA 1975, s 31*, either on the basis of carrying on a manufacturing trade, or on the sale of plant and machinery to farmers. In the High Court it was held, confirming the decision of the Circuit Court, that the company's operations were assembly and not manufacture, and that the intervention of an intermediary denied the character of direct sales to farmers for a substantial part of the turnover, but the Supreme Court reversed the decision, finding that the company's operations did amount to manufacture (and accordingly making no finding on the second point). Applying the tests referred to in *McCann Ltd v O'Culacháin* (**38.63** above), an ordinary adequately informed person would attribute the word 'manufacture' to the process carried on by the company. *Irish Agricultural Machinery Ltd v O'Culacháin* III ITR 611; [1990] IR 535.

38.158 Exchange losses. In 1947 an American corporation, with a world-wide trade, commenced trading through an RI branch. Separate accounts were made up for the branch to 31 December and, immediately after the end of each year, the RI auditors were told the cost in dollars of goods sent to the branch from America in the year, with their sterling equivalent at the year end rate, and similarly as regards the proportion of the corporation's head office, etc expenses charged out to the branch. The aggregate amounts so notified for the two years to 31 December 1948 were $24,300 (sterling equivalent £6,075). The $24,300 was not remitted to America. In the branch accounts the £6,075 was charged to profits, allowed as a deduction in arriving at its profits for tax and shown in the Balance Sheet as the balance of a 'Home Office Current Account'. Sterling was devalued on 19 September 1949, and in the 1949 accounts the £6,075 was revalued at the 19 September rate, thus increasing it by £2,603. The company's claim to deduct this £2,603 in computing its 1949 profits was refused. The deductions in the 1947 and 1948 computations concluded the matter. *Revenue Commissioners v L & Co* 3 ITC 205; II ITR 281. See now **12.8** 'Corporation tax'.

38.159 The taxpayer company incurred considerable currency exchange losses in relation to a borrowing, repayable on demand but intended to be repaid over five years, for the purchase of business premises. The Circuit Court judge held that the losses were deductible for tax purposes, and in the High Court and Supreme Court his decision was upheld. The test for deductibility was whether the loan was a means of fluctuating and temporary accommodation, and this was a question of fact rather than law, on which the Circuit Court judge had been entitled to come to the decision he did. *Beauchamp v F W Woolworth plc* 61 TC 542 considered and distinguished. *Brosnan v Mutual Enterprises Ltd* V ITR 138. See now **12.8** 'Corporation tax'.

38.160 Statutory reduction of capital in company – whether consequent fall in value of bank's investments allowable. A bank held stocks in a railway; it was common ground that any profit or loss on the realisation of these stocks should be brought into the computation of its profits. The stocks were reduced by the *Irish Railways Act 1933*, holders receiving new stock certificates in place of the old. The bank's claim to deduct the consequent fall in the market value of its investments in the railway company was refused. There had been no realisation or conversion of an investment. *Davis v Hibernian Bank Ltd* 2 ITC 111; I ITR 503.

38.161 Whether unsold investments may be valued as stock-in-trade. The appellant was a company which dealt in stocks and shares, any profits or losses on its sales entering into its trading profits for assessment. It was assessed on the basis that its unsold investments should be brought in at their cost. The company claimed that, as dealt with in its accounts, they should be brought in at cost or market value if lower. The High Court upheld the assessments, applying *Davis v Hibernian Bank Ltd*, see **38.160** above, and finding no precedent, or evidence of usual accountancy practice, to support the company's contention. *A B Ltd v Mac Giolla Riogh* 3 ITC 301; II ITR 419.

38.162 Sale of investments earmarked for reserve fund. Under a private Act of Parliament a gas company was empowered, but not obliged, to set up a dividend equalisation fund. In fact it did so, earmarking investments to form the fund. A deduction for the loss on realising some of the investments was refused as one not connected with, or arising out of, its trade (*s 81(2)*); the Act did not impose a duty on the company to create the fund. *Alliance & Dublin Consumers' Gas Co v Davis* 1 ITC 114; I ITR 104; [1926] IR 372.

38.163 Accounts made up for both six and twelve-monthly periods. In an excess corporation profits tax case, a company had, in addition to normal twelve-month accounts, produced six-month accounts at the half and full-year stages. The appeal turned on whether the provisions of *FA 1920, s 54* applied so that, accounts having been produced for periods less than twelve months, it fell to the Revenue Commissioners to determine the accounting periods for taxation purposes. Held that the fact that twelve-month accounts had been made up precluded the operation of the section to impose liability by reference to any shorter or longer period. *Revenue Commissioners v R Hilliard and Sons Ltd* 2 ITC 410; II ITR 130. (*Note.* The provisions of *s 27* now impose different requirements for the determination of accounting periods.)

38.164 Flour miller and baker – flour milling partly discontinued – whether trade ceased. A company carried on business as flour millers (at two mills) and bread bakers, about half of the flour it milled being used at its bakeries. After making losses, the mills were closed in August 1922, but one was re-opened in April 1923, mainly to supply the bakeries. The Special Commissioners' decision that it had carried on a single trade throughout was upheld as one of fact for which there was evidence. *Boland's Ltd v Davis* 1 ITC 91; I ITR 86.

38.165 'Occupation by a dealer in cattle' – scope of 'cattle'. In a case involving liability under *s 53*, it was held that the reference in that section to '... occupation by a dealer in cattle ...' referred only to occupation by a dealer in bovine animals, and not by a dealer in sheep or pigs. *De Brun v Kiernan* TL 117; III ITR 19; [1982] ILRM 13.

38.166 Classification of Royalty Income. This case related to whether income generated from an invention fell within the definition of royalty income under *s 141(5)(d)*. The Court held that the term 'radical innovation' should be given its ordinary meaning and that the reasonable man test applies in determining whether something should be considered to be a radical innovation. The *Revenue Commissioners v Wen-Plast (Research and Development) Limited* [2007] IEHC 66.

SCHEDULE D, CASE III

38.167 Computation of income from different sources treated as one source. The taxpayer had for several years been in receipt of UK interest and dividends, and in the year in question commenced trading in the UK as an insurance underwriter. He was assessed on the preceding year basis in respect of the interest, etc and on the Sch D, Case I commencement basis in respect of the underwriting profits, the sum of the amounts so calculated being assessed under Sch D, Case III. He appealed on the ground that *s 70(1)* directed that all income under Case III be treated as arising from one source, so that the preceding year basis must be applied to all his income assessable under that Case. Held, upholding the appeal, that the clear direction of *s 70(1)* took precedence over the provisions of *s 73* for an alternative basis of assessment in respect of certain UK possessions. *O'Conaill v R* 3 ITC 167; II ITR 304; [1956] IR 97.

38.168 Interest received assessable without deduction for interest paid. The appellant County Council was held to be liable under Sch D, Case III on bank interest received with no allowance for interest paid (in full to the Commissioners of Public Works and others) by various Rural District Councils and Boards of Guardians of Poor Law Unions within the County. *Phillips v Limerick County Council* 1 ITC 96; I ITR 66; [1925] 2 IR 139.

38.169 Interest arising on unsecured loan stock. It was found that the loan stock was a speciality debt and that the physical location of the stock determined the source of the interest payable on it *PV Murtagh (Inspector of Taxes) v Mr Samuel Rusk* (unreported, 11 October 2005), HC.

38.170 Bank interest arising during liquidation. Interest credited to a deposit account, into which the liquidator of a company had paid receipts from disposing of the assets, was held to have been properly assessed under Case III. *Irish Provident Assurance Co Ltd (in Liquidation) v Kavanagh* 1 ITC 52; I ITR 46; [1930] IR 231; 4 ATC 115.

38.171 Voluntary pension from overseas employment. The taxpayer's wife had been managing director of an English family company carrying on business in England. Following her resignation (and eventually becoming resident in RI), the company, under a series of resolutions, made annual payments to her of varying amounts. Held, the payments were correctly assessed as foreign possessions under Sch D, Case III, since they fell within *s 790* as voluntary pensions. Certain exceptional payments were excluded. *McHugh v A* 3 ITC 257; II ITR 393; [1958] IR 142.

38.172 Foreign pensions. The taxpayer, resident in RI at the relevant time, was in receipt of a UK National Insurance Retirement Pension in respect of both his own contributions and those of his wife, based partly on voluntary contributions made while resident in RI. He appealed against assessments on the pension payments under Sch D, Case III, on the ground (inter alia) that there was no related foreign possession as required under that case, since the payments arose from no legal document and were subject to restrictions. Held, the pensions were correctly assessed as arising from foreign possessions. *Forbes v Dundon* 3 ITC 365; II ITR 491; [1964] IR 447.

38.173 Foreign pension – assignment to company. On 4 April 1961, C assigned his UK pension to C Ltd, a private company, for £2,805. He did not notify his former employer of the assignment, but continued to receive the pension, handing over the cheques to C Ltd. He claimed that there was a cessation for Sch D, Case III in 1960/61, so that the assessments for that and the following year should be on the actual rather than the preceding year basis. The Appeal Commissioner took the view that there had been a valid equitable assignment of C's pension to C Ltd on 4 April 1961, and that C's subsequent receipt of the pension had been as trustee for C Ltd. His decision was upheld in the High Court. *Cronin v C* TL 106; II ITR 592.

38.174 Advance payment of rent – whether a premium. The taxpayer company, resident in RI, let premises in the UK to a UK company for seven years from 6 April 1950. The rent was expressed to be £625 per annum payable as to £3,000 in advance on signature of the lease and as to the balance by seven annual payments of £196 8s 6d commencing on 5 April 1951. The £3,000 was held to be income arising from overseas possessions for the purposes of Sch D, Case III, rejecting the contention that it was a premium or fine and capital. *O'Sullivan v P Ltd* 3 ITC 355; II ITR 464.

SCHEDULE D, CASE IV

38.175 River Conservancy Board surplus. The receipts of a statutory river conservancy board comprised mainly rates but included also receipts from fishing licences, fines and bank interest. In the relevant years its receipts exceeded its expenses, and it was assessed under Case VI (now Case IV) on the proportion of this surplus which its receipts other than rates bore to its total receipts. Its appeal against the assessments was allowed. It was a rating authority empowered to levy rates to cover its expenditure. If, by faulty estimation, the rates it levied exceeded its expenditure less its 'other receipts', the overall excess was available to reduce future rates and was not liable to income tax. *Moville District of Conservators v Ua Clothasaigh* 3 ITC 1; II ITR 154; [1950] IR 301.

38.176 Statutory body for registration of veterinary surgeons. A statutory body whose functions included the maintenance of a register of veterinary surgeons was assessed under Case VI (now Case IV) on the excess of its receipts (registration fees and proceeds of sales of register) over its expenditure. Its appeal against the assessment was allowed. Its activities were not analogous to carrying on a trade and, applying a *dictum* of Lord Dunedin in *Leeming v Jones*, a UK case (reported at 15 TC 333), its surplus was not income. *The Veterinary Council v Corr* 3 ITC 59; II ITR 204; [1953] IR 12.

38.177 Statutory body – whether levies received liable to tax. The Racing Board is a statutory body with two sources of income, the operation of the totalisator (agreed to be within Sch D, Case I) and a levy on on-course betting (the subject of the appeal). It was held that the levy was not liable to tax. While a public body may be liable to tax on moneys received for services provided for the public, there can be no basis for taxing the receipts from pure taxation as constituting something analogous to a trade. The Board is enabled to raise funds by a levy on bookmakers to whom it supplies no direct service, and to apply the moneys so raised for public purposes. *The Racing Board v O'Culacháin* IV ITR 73.

38.178 Ex gratia payment for services. The taxpayer, general manager of Y Ltd, gave advice and assistance to X Ltd (with the permission of Y Ltd). There was no agreement that he would be remunerated for his services. X Ltd was then dissolved by statute and a new company Z Ltd was set up, with the taxpayer as its general manager. Shortly before its dissolution X Ltd made an *ex gratia* payment to the taxpayer which was assessed on him under Case VI (now Case IV). His appeal against the assessment was allowed; the payment to him was a personal testimonial. *McGarry v EF* 3 ITC 103; II ITR 261; [1954] IR 64. (*Note.* An alternative contention for the Revenue that the payment was an emolument of an office or employment held by the taxpayer under X Ltd was not pursued.)

38.179 Fees received after discontinuance. A barrister, who had been assessed on a receipts basis, arranged for fees due prior to his appointment to the bench to be paid to a company in which he had no interest though the entire shareholding was held by his two sons and a son-in-law. Following the decision in *Dolan v K* (see **38.187** below) the Judge held that the fact that the income was not received directly by the taxpayer did not exempt it from being assessed on him as fees received after discontinuance under *s 91*. *O'Coindealbháin v Gannon* III ITR 484; [1986] IR *154*.

SCHEDULE D, CASE V

38.180 Letting fees and legal expenses were incurred by a company in securing tenants for a building it had constructed and which it intended to let. Held, such fees and expenses were costs of management of the premises constituting an expense of the transactions under which the rents were received. They were thus allowable under *s 97(2)(d)*. *GH Ltd v Browne; Stephen Court Ltd v Browne* TL 120; III ITR 95; V ITR 680; [1984] ILRM 23*1*.

SCHEDULE E AND PAYE – GENERAL

38.181 Voluntary payment on retirement. The president of a college retired after 31 years' service and the governing body granted him, in addition to his maximum pension, etc entitlements, an additional sum of £1,000 'on account of a great number of services unrewarded, as expressed in a labour of lengthened overtime work during the past seven or more years, and the limited statutory pension to which he is entitled'. The Special Commissioners dismissed an assessment on the £1,000, holding it was a personal gift. Their decision was upheld as one of fact for which there was evidence. *Mulvey v Coffey* 2 ITC 239; I ITR 618; [1942] IR 277.

38.182 Payment as inducement to take up employment. As part of a company share sale, a substantial shareholder (K) entered into a service agreement with the purchaser. In a side letter signed by K, it was expressly recognised that £250,000 of the sale price of K's shares was paid as an inducement to enter into the service agreement, and was repayable if K failed to comply with the terms of the agreement. Although K continued in employment with another subsidiary of the purchaser, he never took up employment under the agreement, but no money was in fact repaid. It was held that the £250,000 was a taxable emolument within Sch E. It had to be inferred that the purchasers were satisfied to accept K's continued service with the other subsidiary as compliance with the terms of the agreement. The UK case *Shilton v Wilmshurst* 64 TC 78 discussed and applied. *O'Connell v Keleghan* (unreported, 16 May 2001), SC. (See **38.49** above for another issue in this case.)

38.183 Emoluments not in cash – when taxable. The case at **38.182** was referred back to the High Court to determine the year of assessment of the emolument. The period of service was to commence in January 1990 and cease in June 1991. The loan note was non-transferrable and redeemable in November 1991 although not actually redeemed until February 1993. It was held (1) that although the monies were not paid until February 1993, based on the provisions of *s 110* the appropriate year of assessment was 1991/92, being the last year in which the office or employment was held, and (2) based on the UK case of *Abbott v Philbin* 39 TC 82, the test to be applied is whether the loan note is something that by its nature is capable of being converted to money. The respondent could not see any return on the loan note until November 1991 at the earliest as he could not have raised any money on foot of it or sold it prior to that date. Therefore, the appropriate year of assessment was 1991/92. *O'Connell v Keleghan* (unreported, 25 July 2002), HC.

38.184 Payments under will to manage properties – whether remuneration. Under his father's will, a taxpayer received ten per cent of certain rents 'so long as (he) continues to manage and look after' the property. He was assessed on the amounts received as remuneration from an employment. Held, the payments were conditional gifts under the will and did not arise from an employment. *O'Reilly v Casey* 2 ITC 220; I ITR 601; [1942] IR 378.

38.185 Children's contributory pension – whether income of widow to whom payable. Under the *Garda Síochána Pensions Order 1981 (SI 199/81)* a children's contributory pension may be payable with the widow's pension (and in certain cases separately therefrom) for the benefit of the children. Held, the children's pension is the beneficial property of the children in respect of whom it is payable, and is thus not assessable as the personal income of the widow to whom it is payable. *O'Coindealbháin v O'Carroll* IV ITR 221.

38.186 Increase in widow's pension in respect of dependent children – whether income of widow to whom payable. Following *O'Coindealbháin v O'Carroll*, **38.185** above, it was held that the dependent child addition to a widow's contributory pension was assessable on the widow. *Ó'Síocháin v Neenan* V ITR 472.

38.187 Professed nun employed as school teacher. A professed nun employed as a school teacher, but bound by Constitutions of her Order to hand over her earnings to the Order, was held to have been correctly assessed under Sch E on the earnings. *Dolan v K* 2 ITC 280; I ITR 656; [1944] IR 470.

38.188 Director resident overseas – Sch E. The appellant, resident abroad throughout the relevant period, was a director of a company incorporated, and carrying on trade, in RI, although managed, controlled and resident in France. None of the duties of his office were carried on in RI. Held, the office was nevertheless 'within RI' and emoluments therefrom thus taxable under the Sch E provisions. *Tipping v Jeancard* 2 ITC 360; II ITR 68; [1948] IR 233.

38.189 Benefits in kind – company cars. A challenge to the constitutionality of the charge on the benefit of private use of a company car under *s 121* was unsuccessful. *Browne and Others v Revenue Commissioners* IV ITR 323. See **34.3** 'Sch E'.

38.190 Rent of house occupied by employee paid by employer. A company arranged with the Midleton Urban District Council that the Council would provide houses to be let to the company's employees. An employee of the company occupied one of the houses, the company paying the rent for him. He was required by the terms of his employment to live in Midleton but not in any particular house, whether or not provided by the Council. Sch E assessments on him, in which the rent paid for him was treated as part of his emoluments, were upheld, applying *Hartland v Diggines*, a UK case (10 TC 247). *Connolly v McNamara* 3 ITC 341; II ITR 452.

38.191 Emoluments received after year in which earned. A taxpayer was employed as part-time solicitor by a Harbour Board, his remuneration to be his taxed costs, billed half-yearly. In the event, the employment lasted only from December 1924 to May 1925 and he presented two Bills of Costs in July 1925, covering the whole period of employment and including profit costs of £422 referable to the work done in 1924/25. Held in his appeal against his Sch E assessment for 1924/25, that the £422 was assessable for that year as the amount earned in that year, rejecting the argument that the assessment could not include an amount not received in that year. *MacKeown v Roe* 1 ITC 206; I ITR 214; [1928] IR 195.

38.192 Remuneration assessed under Sch E; tax accounted for under PAYE when remuneration paid in subsequent year. A Sch E assessment for 1962/63 had been made in November 1964 on the taxpayer, a company director, bringing out tax due of £591. The remuneration assessed included a bonus not paid until December 1964, when tax of £646 was accounted for under PAYE. In proceedings taken by the Revenue to recover the tax of £591 with interest, it was held that the assessment had been correctly made. *Bedford v Hannon* TL 105; II ITR 588.

38.193 PAYE – emoluments paid on behalf of employer – liability of payer to account for income tax and PRSI contributions. The defendants, who carried on business in partnership, formed a limited company to provide overseas consultancy services. There was some confusion between the affairs of the two entities, but for the period in question the wages of the limited company's employees were paid by the partnership, on the understanding that the partnership would be reimbursed. The Collector General sought payment from the partnership of income tax (under PAYE) and PRSI contributions in respect of the employees concerned. Judgment was given against the defendants in relation to the income tax (and interest thereon), as the words 'employer' and 'employee' in the relevant regulations (*SI 28/60*) were defined as meaning 'any person paying emoluments' and 'any person in receipt of emoluments', so that the partnership, in paying the wages, was obliged to make the appropriate deductions and account for the sums so deducted. As regards the PRSI contributions, there were no such extended definitions in the relevant legislation, so that there was sufficient substance in the defence that the partnership was merely acting as paymaster, and making periodical loans of the amounts paid to persons in reality employed by the limited company, for that part of the claim to be remitted for plenary hearing. *Hearne v J A Kenny & Partners* IV ITR 113.

38.194 PAYE regulations – defamation – whether procedure unconstitutional. The Revenue had issued an enforcement notice in respect of unpaid PAYE against the plaintiff, a practising solicitor. He sought a declaration that the operation of certain sections of *ITA 1967* was unconstitutional and claimed damages on the basis that the enforcement notice had been incorrectly issued, as he had paid the tax concerned. The Judge awarded damages totalling £10,500 for defamation following the publication of the enforcement notice, but held that no issues as to the infringement of constitutional rights arose. *Kennedy v Hearne and others* III ITR 590.

SCHEDULE E – EXPENDITURE

38.195 General expenses. In each of two cases, an engineer claimed a deduction from his emoluments assessable under Sch E in respect of the cost of:

(i)   subscriptions to professional associations;

(ii)   renewals of books and journals;

(iii)   protective clothing;

(iv)   replacing equipment;

(v)   entertainment of builders and business callers; and

(vi)   travelling expenses not reimbursed by the employer;

and in one case:

(vii)   home telephone; and

(viii)   proportion of maid's wages.

Held, only items (iii) and (iv) were properly allowable, as the remaining items were not 'exclusively' incurred in performance of the duties of the respective offices as required by *s 114*. *O'Broin v Mac Giolla Meidhre; O'Broin v Pigott* 3 ITC 235; II ITR 366; [1957] 159 IR 98.

38.1966 The taxpayer, an officer in the Defence Forces, claimed as a deduction from emoluments taxable under Sch E:

(i)   room rent in the Officers' Mess;

(ii)   extra cost of messing;

(iii)   travelling expenses between home and quarters; and

(iv)   gratuities to batman.

Held, the gratuities to batman were not wholly, exclusively and necessarily incurred in the performance of his duties, particularly as there was no legal obligation to pay them, and so failed the test under *s 114*. The remaining expenses had already been dismissed on similar grounds by the Circuit Judge. *Kelly v H* 3 ITC 351; II ITR 460; [1964] IR 488.

38.197 Director's travelling expenses. A director of five companies incurred travelling expenses in carrying out his duties, the major part of which was reimbursed to him. There was evidence that the balance would have been reimbursed had he so requested. He claimed the balance as a deduction from his emoluments. Held, no allowance was due, as there was no proof that he was obliged to defray the expenses out of his emoluments. *MacDaibhéid v Carroll* TL 115; III ITR 1.

38.198 Doctor's travelling expenses. A doctor employed part-time as a senior house officer in a general hospital claimed a deduction from her emoluments in respect of travelling expenses between her home and the hospital following her being called to the hospital by telephone. She attended the hospital on weekday mornings, but was required always to be available on call when not on duty (or to arrange for a replacement). She could have to give advice and instructions by telephone before returning to the hospital, and considered herself medically responsible for the patient even before her arrival at the hospital. Held, following the UK case of *Pook v Owen* 45 TC 571, in the very peculiar and exceptional circumstances, the expenses were allowable. As contended for the taxpayer, it was an essential feature of the employment to provide advice over the telephone, and the duties commenced from the time at which she was first contacted by the hospital. *FG v O'Coindealbháin* HC, 1985.

38.199 Travelling expenses between home and place of employment. The taxpayer, a schoolteacher, claimed a deduction from his emoluments taxable under Sch E in respect of the costs of a pony and trap used to convey him between home and school, a distance of some five miles. He claimed that he could not obtain a suitable residence nearer the school, and that his physical condition did not permit him to walk or cycle the journey. Held, the expenditure was neither 'wholly and exclusively' nor 'necessarily' incurred in the performance of his duties, and was thus prohibited as a deduction. *Phillips v Keane* 1 ITC 69; I ITR 64; [1925] 2 IR 48.

SETTLEMENTS

38.200 Existence of trust: outgoings of residence provided for. Under the terms of a will, a taxpayer was entitled to the use and occupation of Slane Castle, and to receive a sum not exceeding £3,500 per annum for its maintenance and upkeep other than repairs. Taking one year with another she spent this amount on this maintenance and upkeep. Held, reversing the Special Commissioners' decision, that the £3,500 per annum received by her was impressed in her hands with a trust under which it was to be expended on the property, and was not part of her income for super-tax purposes. *Conyngham (Marchioness) v Revenue Commissioners* 1 ITC 259; I ITR 231.

38.201 Whether Partnership Deed, etc a settlement. On 29 March 1944 a taxpayer carrying on a business as cafe proprietor entered into a Deed of Partnership with three of his sons, hitherto full-time employees in the business, and his mother-in-law, aged 80, who took no part in the business. The Deed gave him extensive powers which conferred upon him a commanding position in the partnership and the conduct of its business. On 3 April 1944 the mother-in-law by Deed irrevocably assigned her interest in the partnership to the taxpayer in trust for his other four children. The partnership assessments for 1944/45 and 1945/46, at the beginning of which all seven children were unmarried minors, were on the footing that the whole of the income was income of the father. On appeal, the Special Commissioner found that the partnership was a *bona fide* commercial transaction; that the two Deeds were separate and not part of a scheme; and that the partnership income should be treated as income of the persons entitled to it under the two Deeds. His decision was upheld by a majority of the Supreme Court, reversing the decision of the High Court. The Revenue relied on *FA 1922, s 20(1)(a)* (similar to *s 791*) as regards the income of the children who became partners; and on *FA 1937, s 2* (similar to *s 794 et seq.*) as regards the income of all seven. Although the father's dominating position might enable him effectively to terminate the partnership, that would not enable him to obtain the beneficial ownership of income treated as that of the other partners by virtue of *ITA 1918, s 20* (similar to *ITA 1967, s 26*). The Deed of Partnership in itself was not a settlement and the Commissioner's finding that the two Deeds were not an arrangement was one of fact and conclusive. *O'Dwyer v Cafolla & Co* 2 ITC 374; II ITR 82; [1949] IR 210.

38.202 Whether Deed of Appointment a settlement. The appeal related to income under a settlement appointed, pursuant to a power in the settlement, to a minor unmarried daughter of the settlor, and the issue was whether the Deed of Appointment was a settlement for the purposes of the relevant legislation (similar to *s 791 et seq.*). It was held that the appointment was a settlement. *E G v Mac Shamhrain* 3 ITC 217; II ITR 352; [1958] IR 288.

38.203 *TCA 1997, s 791* – **settlement income deemed income of settlor.** In a case in which the facts are special, it was held (by a majority decision) that income arising in a settlement, which was to be applied to certain charitable and religious purposes for as long as the settlor was a member of a religious Order, was income of the settlor under the predecessor of *s 791. Hughes v Smyth* 1 ITC 418; I ITR 411.

38.204 Religious order – right to income under deed of covenant. Three members of a religious order entered into a deed of covenant under which they covenanted to pay sums to their Prior for the benefit of each of 17 other members of the order. Individual members of the order subscribed to a vow of poverty and did not hold individual bank accounts, but in this instance the money was held by the Prior as a trustee for each beneficiary, and they could use the covenant income for their own purposes. It was contended that tax deducted from the covenant income should be repaid to the beneficiaries, as *s 792(1)(b)(iv)* had been complied with. Held, that the money had been applied for the benefit of the beneficiaries, and the covenants were valid for tax purposes. *Revenue Commissioners v HI* TL 126; III ITR 242.

38.205 Deeds of covenant – whether payments applicable for the benefit of named children – whether *s 187* applicable. Payments were made under deeds of covenant to an RI-based charity in favour of named children in third world countries. The payments were applied mainly in providing schools attended by the named children and by others. It was held (i) that the payments were 'applicable for the benefit of a named relevant individual', and hence within *s 792(1)(b)(v)* (see **36.2** 'Settlements'), and (ii) that the benefit of the low income exemption in *s 187* (see **2.8** 'Allowances and rates') is available to non-residents, and hence to the charity as trustee. *Action Aid Ltd v Revenue Commissioners* V ITR 392.

38.206 Capital acquisitions tax – discretionary settlement. A discretionary trust entitled the taxpayer to income from trust property at age 21, and she would become absolutely entitled to the property at age 35. A power of appointment was exercised in her favour before she reached the age of 35. The taxpayer claimed she had a defeasible absolute interest from age 21 (before capital acquisitions tax was imposed) and that no benefit was received by her on appointment (in 1978), so that no CAT liability arose. Held, the interest received at age 21 was a limited interest, and the appointment in 1978 resulted in her receipt of a further interest, bringing a liability to CAT. *Revenue Commissioners v Jacob* (unreported, 11 December *1984), SC.* See **7.2**, **7.15** 'Capital acquisitions tax'.

VALUE-ADDED TAX

38.207 Meaning of 'installation of fixtures'. The appellant, whose trade was the erection of television aerials, sought a determination that his work entailed the 'installation of fixtures' within the meaning of *VATA 1972, s 10(8)* and was, as such, liable to VAT at the then lower rate of three per cent (now designated as activities within the *VATA 1972, Sixth Schedule* – see **39.9** 'Value-added tax'). Held, having regard to the substantial work involved in securing them to premises and their purpose that television aerials were fixtures. *John Maye v Revenue Commissioners* III ITR 332; [1986] *ILRM 377.*

38.208 Whether interest payable on VAT refunds. In the first motion the Judge granted judgment in the sum of £15,887.84 with costs in respect of interest on late payments of PAYE and PRSI. As part of their defence the company had cross-claimed for interest on £354,389.30, this sum being late refunds of VAT due to the linked plaintiff company of the second motion. The Judge refused this claim as the two cases involved different companies. There is no provision in *VATA 1972* for payment of interest on refunds due to taxpayers, no matter what the delay is by the Revenue, and the Judge pointed out that under *VATA 1972, s 20(1)* a claim for a refund had to be 'shown to the satisfaction of the Revenue Commissioners' and an enforceable right might not arise until this was done. However, he accepted that there was an arguable case which should be put down for Plenary Hearing. *Hearne v North Kerry Milk Products Ltd; Kerry Cooperative Creameries Ltd v Revenue Commissioners* (unreported, 25 June 1985), HC. (*Note:* The Plenary Hearing was not set down by the plaintiffs and the issue remains open. The proceedings in the second motion had the effect of producing a quick refund. In *Navan Carpets v O'Culacháin* (see **38.224** below) the Court did use its discretion under *Courts Act 1981, s 22* to award interest on a repayment of corporation tax.). In *Bank of Ireland Trust Services Limited (formerly Erin Executor and Trustee Company Limited) (as trustee of Irish Pension Fund Property Unit Trust) v Revenue Commissioners* (unreported, 29 November 2002), HC it was held that the VAT repayments under appeal qualified for payment of interest in the same manner as Income tax – the Revenue argument that Income tax and VAT operated differently was rejected.

38.209 Charge card company – whether exempt supplier. The appellant company sought judicial review of the Revenue Commissioners' decision that its activities were exempt under Sch 1 to the *VAT (Exempted Activities) (No 1) Order 1985 (SI 430/85)*. It contended that the services it supplied were akin to debt factoring, and that they did not involve the 'reimbursement' of the trader (as specified in the *Order*). It was held, refusing the judicial review sought, that in the context of the three mutually dependent agreements involved in a transaction, the word 'payment' is to be substituted for the word 'reimbursement' in interpreting the Order. *Diners Club Ltd v Revenue Commissioners* III ITR 680. See **39.6**(*c*) 'Value-added tax'.

38.210 Place of supply of services. A Dublin firm of solicitors acted for defendants in the RI courts under instructions from various Lloyd's syndicates whose establishments were in London. VAT was charged on the services on the basis that they were supplied in RI to the defendants for whom they acted, but it was contended for the solicitors that the services were supplied to the Lloyd's syndicates and were thus not chargeable to VAT. Held, the primary commercial transaction was with the Lloyd's syndicates, so that the services were not chargeable to VAT. *Bourke v Bradley* IV ITR 117. See now *FA 1989, s 54* and **39.7** 'Value-added tax'.

38.211 Property let under leases exceeding ten years – deduction of input tax on expenses. The taxpayer company claimed credit for input tax on overheads, administration, maintenance, development and management of property let on leases exceeding ten years. Notwithstanding the self-supply charge under *VATA 1972, ss 3(1)(f), 4(4)* (see **39.7** 'Value-added tax'), it was held that the input tax was deductible. *Erin Executor and Trustee Co Ltd (as Trustee of the Irish Pension Fund Property Unit Trust) v Revenue Commissioners* V ITR 76.

38.212 Retail schemes – treatment of excise duty. Under Retail Scheme 3, output VAT for a period is estimated by apportioning receipts by reference to the purchases for resale over a certain period. In relation to dutiable goods, excise duty may in certain circumstances be paid separately from the purchase price of the goods. It was held that the duty, although not itself subject to VAT, must be included in the computation as a purchase giving rise to a retail sale at the rate applicable to the dutiable goods. *D H Burke & Son Ltd v Revenue Commissioners and Others* V ITR 418.

38.213 Revenue Rule of Thumb. The plaintiff was seeking specific performance of a contract for sale of a property. The contract for the sale provided that in addition to the purchase price the purchaser would pay the vendor VAT if exigible. In determining whether or not VAT should be charged on the disposal of a property, the Revenue adopts a rule of thumb in determining if property has been developed for VAT purposes, and does not consider property to have been developed for VAT purposes where the cost of the development work does not exceed ten per cent, subject to a maximum of €100,000, of the amount on which VAT would be chargeable on the disposal ('the ten per cent rule'). The court held that a rule of thumb applied by the Revenue, which provides that the Revenue will not seek to recover VAT on the disposal of an interest in property to which the rule is applied, is of no legal significance, as VAT is a statutory tax. The court further held that where the disposal of a property is liable to VAT, the VAT is exigible notwithstanding the availability of the Revenue rule of thumb. *Forbes v Tobin* HC 2001/30.

38.214 Taxable Person. The respondent sought to recover VAT incurred on expenditure relating to the proposed development and leasing of a football stadium. The proposed project was abandoned and the repayment claims were rejected by the inspector who was of the view that the respondent was not a taxable person within the meaning of *Article 4, Sixth Council Directive 77/388/EEC.* The Appeal Commissioner found in favour of the respondent. The case was referred to the High Court which also found in favour of the respondent *Brendan Crawford, Inspector of Taxes v Centime Ltd* (unreported, 21 October 2005), HC.

38.215 Transfer of a business. The respondent claimed repayment of an input tax credit in respect of certain purchases which he claimed were not in connection with the transfer of a business which had previously been carried on in the premises concerned but which had ceased at the time of the purchase, so that *VATA 1972, s 3(5)(b)(iii)* did not apply. The Appeal Commissioners finding in favour of the respondent was upheld. *O'Shea v Colle Parkview Ltd* (unreported, 25 May 2000), HC.

38.216 Transfer of a business. The respondent sought to recover the VAT paid on the acquisition of a number of shops. The repayment claim was rejected by the inspector who was of the view that the transaction was not liable to VAT under the provisions of *VATA 1972, s 3(5)(b)(iii)*. The Appeal Commissioner found in favour of the respondent. The case was referred to the High Court which also found in favour of the respondent. The appellant pursued an appeal to the Supreme Court which upheld the decision of the Appeal Commissioners ie s *(3)(5)(b)(iii)* did not apply. *O'Culacháin v Stylo Barratt Shoes Ltd* (unreported, 31 March 2004), SC.

38.217 Supply of a package of services. The respondent supplied cable TV and radio services and argued that the fee received for connecting and reconnecting a customer to their cable TV for the purpose of receiving communication signals was in respect of a distinct supply of connection/reconnection services (liable to VAT at 13.5 per cent) and was not an inseparable part of the supply of the TV cable service (liable to VAT at 21 per cent). The Appeal Commissioners agreed with the respondent ie that the supply of connection/reconnection services was a separate service liable to VAT at 13.5 per cent. The High Court and Supreme Court upheld this decision. *Cablelink Ltd v MacCarthaigh (DA)* (unreported, 15 May 2003), SC.

MISCELLANEOUS

38.218 Anti-avoidance – transfer of assets abroad – information powers – *s 808(6)*. The plaintiffs sought a declaration that, under *s 808(6)*, they were excluded from the requirement under that section to provide certain information to the Revenue, on the ground that the transactions concerned were 'ordinary banking transactions carried out in the ordinary course of a banking business'. Two types of transaction were involved: Type A, under which a client would request a personal advance from a Dublin bank on security of a letter of hypothecation of funds on deposit with a sterling area bank; and Type B, under which a client would approach a Dublin bank with a cheque or other negotiable instrument and request that the funds be transferred on deposit with a sterling area bank. He would then separately request a loan on security of a letter of hypothecation over the funds in question. Held that Type A transactions were in the ordinary course of the banking business, and covered by the exclusion, but that Type B transactions were not. *Royal Trust Co (Ireland) Ltd and Whelan v Revenue Commissioners* [1982] ILRM 459. See **3.8** 'Anti-avoidance legislation'.

38.219 In another case involving *s 808(6)*, a notice dated 24 August 1974 was served on the plaintiffs requesting them to furnish within 40 days particulars of transactions entered into by any of their individual clients relating to ten named countries (eg Channel Islands, Cayman Islands etc) over a six-year period. The transactions specified included the formation or acquisition of companies or partnerships, the creation of settlements and the transfer of assets to settlements, and the notice also requested the names of others to whom clients were introduced for the purpose of any of the specified transactions. Held, the notice was not *ultra vires* the section on the grounds that it requested information relating to transactions before 6 April 1974, the date of implementation of the charging section; neither was it invalid either because it sought information substantially beyond that required for the purposes of the section or because of the high cost of compliance. The plaintiffs had not established that the notice was unduly burdensome and oppressive. *Warnock and Others (practising as Stokes Kennedy Crowley and Company) v Revenue Commissioners* III ITR 356. See **3.8** 'Anti-avoidance legislation'.

38.220 Tax avoidance scheme – application of 'Ramsay' principle in RI. The appellants entered into a complicated tax avoidance scheme of pre-ordained steps, the purpose of which was to obtain relief for an allowable loss in excess of £1 million under *s 589(4)*. No actual loss of this amount was made, although the transactions entered into were real as distinct from sham. The Appeal Commissioners took the view that the doctrine of 'fiscal nullity' developed by the UK cases of *W T Ramsay Ltd v CIR* 54 TC 101 and *Furniss v Dawson* 55 TC 324 applied. Held, that the legislature in RI has not enacted a general prohibition of tax avoidance schemes, and it is for the Oireachtas to determine such a prohibition. Accordingly the scheme succeeded. *P and J McGrath v McDermott* III ITR 683; [1988] IR 258. See now **3.1** 'Anti-avoidance legislation'.

38.221 Following *McGrath* (**38.221** above), a tax avoidance scheme (now closed off by *s 242* (see **3.10** 'Anti-avoidance legislation')), involving the payment of a capital sum by a subsidiary for an annuity geared to the profits of the parent company granting the annuity, nevertheless failed. The payment for the annuity was allowed as a charge on income, and, following actuarial evidence, the Circuit Court judge held that the greater part of the annuity was a capital receipt, and his decision was upheld in the High Court. However, the decision was reversed in the Supreme Court, where it was held that the annuity was not a return of capital and was taxable in full under Sch D, Case III (**31**). *McCabe v South City and County Investment Co Ltd* V ITR 107.

38.222 Assessability of transactions in basis period for year for which legislation introduced. A builder appealed against his 1935/36 assessment, based on his profits of the year 1934. *FA 1935* imposing income tax for 1935/36, included a provision which, in effect, included in builders' profits fines, etc received, and the capitalised value of ground rents created, on their disposals of houses built (thus overruling an RI court decision and bringing RI law in step with UK law as interpreted in *CIR v John Emery & Sons* 20 TC 213). The assessment included fines and the value of ground rents relating to houses disposed of in 1934. The assessment was upheld, rejecting the contention for the taxpayer that the legislation did not apply to transactions before 6 April 1935. *Connolly v Birch* 2 ITC 201; I ITR 583; [1939] IR 534.

38.223 Personal representatives – liability in respect of estate income. The respondents claimed that income received by them as executors of an estate was not assessable on them, as the *Succession Act 1965, s 10(3)* indicated that personal representatives were no longer 'receiving or entitled to the income' within *s 52*. It was held that *s 52* is a re-enactment of *Administration of Estates Act 1959, s 7* and does not alter the legal position that, until administration is completed, the income of an estate is the income of the personal representatives. *Moloney v Allied Irish Banks Ltd* III ITR 477.

38.224 Order of deduction of reliefs. The appellant company was entitled to relief for 1975/76 (i) under *s 248* in respect of interest £277,661, and (ii) under *ITA 1967, s 307* in respect of trading losses £246,022. The company's only income was a dividend of £500,000 received from a subsidiary under deduction of tax £175,000. Under (i), relief was agreed to be due on £253,978 (ie on income £500,000 less trading losses £246,022), giving rise to a repayment of £88,892.30. As regards (ii), it was agreed that £229,552 of the £500,000 dividend was to be left out of account, leaving £270,448. The inspector considered that relief was only available on the residue of £16,470 after deducting the interest charge under (i), whilst the taxpayer considered the full £246,022 could be relieved against the gross income before deduction of the interest charge. Held, income in *ITA 1967, s 307* means gross income and not income after deduction of charges. An Order was subsequently made for payment of interest on foot of the repayment of tax as found to be due, under *Courts Act 1981, s 22*. *Navan Carpets Ltd v O'Culacháin* III ITR 403.

38.225 Compulsory sale of dollar balances to State. Under wartime emergency powers, a taxpayer was compelled to sell to the Minister of Finance dollars to her credit in a New York bank representing US income collected on her behalf by the bank. The Minister credited the sterling equivalent to her credit in an RI bank. It was held that there had been a remittance to RI of the US income. *O'Sullivan v O'Connor* 2 ITC 352; II ITR 61; 26 ATC 463.

38.226 Agricultural societies. A committee which managed annual races was held not to be established for the promotion of livestock breeding, and so not an 'agricultural society' exempt from income tax under *s 215*. *Trustees of Ward Union Hunt Races v Hughes* 2 ITC 152; I ITR 538.

38.227 Farming – whether large scale piggery qualifies. A partnership carried on a large scale piggery on a nine acre holding of land, of which the sixteen pig houses occupied three acres. Six thousand pigs could be accommodated, and the annual output of twenty-four thousand pigs was sold to a bacon factory of which three of the partners were directors. Apart from sick pigs, all the animals were kept in the pig houses. The partnership claimed to be carrying on farming and so to be within *FA 1969, s 18* and *FA 1974, s 13* (see **18** 'Farming'). Held, the use of the land for the purposes of rearing and fattening pigs and generally attending to their health and welfare was farming the land. *Knockhall Piggeries and Others v Kerrane* III ITR 319; [1985] ILRM 655.

38.228 Promoting athletic or amateur games or sports – *s 235* exemption. The appellants, a solicitor and an accountant, formed and funded a club with themselves as trustees '... for the sole purpose of promoting athletic or amateur games or sports ...', and claimed exemption under *s 235* for income from the funds provided on the ground that they were a body of persons established for those purposes. The only members other than themselves were four people, being members of their families or employees, and most of the income was donated at the trustees' discretion to financing members' sporting activities. Held, upholding the High Court decision and reversing that of the Appeal Commissioner, that a body of persons for this purpose means an appreciable number of persons, not merely two, united by some common tie, and that the two trustees did not qualify. Their appeal was dismissed. *Revenue Commissioners v O'Reilly and McGilligan* III ITR 28; [1984] ILRM 406. See now *s 235* (**17.2** 'Exempt organisations').

38.229 The making of investments. A company formed to acquire, *inter alia*, a large family estate in land with a view to its management and development, and a life interest in land in England, was held not to be 'a company whose business consists mainly in the making of investments, and the principal part of whose income is derived therefrom' for management expenses purposes, as required by *CTA 1976, s 15(6)*. *Howth Estate Co v Davis* 2 ITC 74; [1936] ILTR 79. This case was followed in another case involving a family estate company, in which part of the estate was sold, the proceeds being invested in Stock Exchange securities. In the relevant year, however, the bulk of the company's income was rental income from the estate, the income for this purpose being the actual rental income rather than the amounts of the Sch A or B assessments. *Casey v Monteagle Estate Co* 3 ITC 313; II ITR 429; [1962] IR 406.

38.230 Penalties under *ITA 1967, s 500* – whether constitutional. Following failure by the plaintiff to deliver returns required by notice under *ITA 1967, s 172*, the inspector sued the plaintiff claiming a penalty of £500 under *ITA 1967, s 500* in respect of each of the years in question. The plaintiff claimed that the relevant provisions were unconstitutional, the point at issue being whether the penalties were criminal in character and not civil penalties recoverable as a liquidated sum in the civil courts. The Supreme Court upheld the High Court decision that the requirement to pay a penalty into the Central Fund is not indicative of a criminal offence and is not repugnant to the Constitution. *McLoughlin and Tuite v Revenue Commissioners and Attorney General* III ITR 387.

38.231 Penalty – criminal or civil proceeding. A prosecution had been taken out against the taxpayer for the recovery of a penalty for failure to make a return under *s 986*. The Court was asked to decide whether the recovery of the penalty was a criminal or civil proceeding. The Judge held that the recovery of a penalty under *s 987* is not a criminal proceeding. *Director of Public Prosecutions v Downes* Circuit Court *III ITR 641*. See also *McLoughlin and Tuite* at **38.230** above.

38.232 Penalties awarded while assessments open. In a case turning on legislation similar to that now contained in *s 1052*, a taxpayer failed to make a return. Estimated assessments were made on him against which he appealed, but before the appeals had been determined, penalties were awarded against him for his failure to make his return. The Supreme Court held that the action for penalties should not have been brought before the assessments had become final and it failed accordingly. *AG for Irish Free State v White* 38 TC 666.

38.233 Returns – bank accounts – Order sought under *s 908*. An application, seeking an Order to direct a bank to furnish to the inspector full particulars of all accounts maintained by the taxpayer, was refused. A condition precedent to the granting of such an Order is that the taxpayer has been duly required by an inspector to deliver a statement of the profits or gains arising to him from any trade or profession (ie under *s 877*) or a return of income (ie under *s 879*). The inspector's request for accounts under *s 900* did not satisfy this condition. *J B O'C v P C D and a bank* III ITR 153. See **28.1** 'Returns'.

38.234 Following the case at **38.233** above, it was held in another case that *s 879(4)* (which deems a return to have been required by notice if it has in fact been delivered in prescribed form) applies for the purpose of meeting the condition in relation to a *s 908* application. The requirement that the inspector must have 'reasonable grounds' for making the application was clearly met in this case. *Re FA 1983, s 18 and re G O'C and A O'C* V ITR 346.

38.235 Power under *s 900(2)(a)* to call for documents in support of returns. The taxpayer's accountants, engaged to produce accounts for tax purposes, refused to produce to the inspector the nominal ledger they had drawn up from the taxpayer's primary records and from discussions with the taxpayer, on the grounds that they were the property of the accountants and subject to professional privilege. Held in the Supreme Court, confirming the High Court decision, that the inspector was entitled to demand such evidence in support of the accounts, and that in the circumstances the determination of the taxpayer's profits at the figure stated in the accounts could not stand. *Quigley v Burke* V ITR 265.

38.236 Damages – adjustment for tax. A director was awarded damages for breach of contract, including an element for loss of future earnings which exceeded the limit of exemption of such payments under *s 201*. Held, following *BTC v Gourley* ([1955] 3 All E R 796) that the first £3,000 of the award, which was tax-free, should be reduced by an allowance for the tax which would have been payable on it as earnings. *Glover v BLN Ltd* [1973] IR 432.

38.237 Redundancy payments to disabled employees. On the closure of a plant, a redundancy package was agreed for all affected employees, no distinction being made between disabled and other employees, and disregarding the fact that the jobs of certain employees would in fact continue. However, the company furnished the inspector with a list of 49 employees (including the appellants) the termination of whose employment was stated to be by reason of disability, and provided medical certificates. It was held that the payments to disabled employees whose jobs were not continuing were not within the exemption of *s 201(2)(a)*, which required the payment to be made 'on account of' the disability. The payments here were made because of redundancy. The payments to disabled employees whose jobs were continuing were, however, within the exemption. *Cahill v Harding and Others* IV ITR 233. See **34.12** 'Sch E'.

38.238 Ex gratia payment on ill-health retirement. A senior employee aged 60 was advised to retire on grounds of ill-health and did so. The employer agreed to his early retirement and made an *ex gratia* payment to him of £325,000. Held the payment fell within the exemption of *s 201(2)(a)*. There was a clear finding of fact by the Appeal Commissioner that the payment was made because of early retirement due to ill-health, rather than because of retirement at a time when the taxpayer was in ill-health. *Cahill v Harding*, **38.237** above, applied. *O'Shea v Mulqueen* V ITR 134. See **34.12** 'Sch E'.

38.239 Ex gratia payment – tax exemption limit. The taxpayer was made redundant in May 1981 and received a lump sum *ex gratia* payment, a statutory redundancy payment, and a refund of pension contributions. The matter in dispute was whether the refund of pension contributions net of tax was a 'relevant capital sum' for the purposes of *ss 3 para 1*, thereby reducing the maximum exemption against the *ex gratia* payment to £6,000. The Appeal Commissioners held that a refund of pension contributions is not a lump sum and that *s 780(6)* totally excludes its treatment as income for any other purposes of the *Income Tax Acts*. The effect of this decision was that the higher exemption limit of £10,000 was due against the *ex gratia* payment. *JK v O'Coindealbháin*, Appeal Commissioners June 1986.

38.240 Interest on debts out of Funds in Court. In a case in which the facts are complex, the substantive decision was that the Courts are not bound to deduct tax under *ss 237* and *238* when paying interest on debts out of Funds in Court, and that the practice of the Courts to provide retrospectively at final allocation for payment of income tax in respect of income accruing to Funds in Court, even though no formal assessment has been made, should not be upset. *Re Colclough dec'd., Colclough and Others v Colclough and Robb* TL 103; II ITR 332; [1965] IR 668. (*Note*. Although subsequent legislation limits the application of this decision, it still has relevance to eg interest payable to non-residents and to the practice of the Courts generally.)

38.241 Annuity 'free of tax': whether annuitant entitled to retain refund of tax. The annuitant was able to reclaim from the Revenue Commissioners tax paid by trustees in respect of a payment by way of annuity 'free of income tax'. Held, the annuitant was under no liability to account to the trustees for the tax refunded to her. In *re Swan decd, Hibernian Bank Ltd v Munro and Others* V ITR 565; [1945] IR 216.

38.242 Income tax – exemption of earnings under *s 195*. The appellant, a distinguished journalist, claimed that newspaper articles written by him were original and creative works within the meaning of *s 195*, and therefore exempt from tax. He had previously been granted exemption in respect of earnings from his book 'Death of an Irish Town' (which had first appeared as a series of newspaper articles) and all subsequent newspaper articles until 1974/75. The Judge held, confirming the decision of the Circuit Court, that the newspaper articles concerned did not come within the exemption tests of *s 195*. *Healy v Inspector of Taxes* III ITR 496.

38.243 The appellant, a primary school principal and teacher, wrote a series of four original books, intended primarily for the education of children, entitled 'Pathways to History'. He claimed exemption under *s 195*. The Appeal Commissioner reversed the Revenue Commissioners' refusal of exemption, and the High Court upheld that decision. The Appeal Commissioner had heard evidence on which he had come to the decision that, essentially as a matter of fact, the works were 'original' and 'creative' as those words were used in *s 195*, and there was ample justification for that decision. *Revenue Commissioners v O'Loinsigh* V ITR 98. See **16.27** 'Exempt income and special savings schemes'.

38.244 Appropriation of tax payments between separate companies in a group. In a case in which a number of companies in a group were insolvent, with substantial amounts of tax outstanding, the Revenue Commissioners negotiated with the companies as a group for a payment on account of tax liabilities to be made out of the proceeds of sale of properties by certain members of the group. These payments, when received, were appropriated to meet the tax liabilities of group members in the proportion that each member's liability bore to the total tax liabilities of the group. It was held that any contribution by a company to the payment on account of group tax liabilities other than its own tax liability was *ultra vires*, and that the Revenue Commissioners were obliged to repay to each of the contributing companies the difference. In *re Frederick Inns Ltd (in liquidation) and Others* IV ITR 247.

The following is an alphabetical list of all the tax cases summarised above. Each case is listed under the names of both parties except where the Revenue Commissioners, etc are a party, when only the taxpayer's name is listed.

39 Value-Added Tax

General note. This chapter provides a summary of the wide-ranging and complex provisions relating to value-added tax and of the applicable European law. For more detailed coverage, see **Bloomsbury Professional's Tax Guide and VAT Acts 2011.** The VATA 1972 has been consolidated in to a new VAT Consolidation Act 2010. The 'VAT ACTS 2011' by Pat Kennedy considers the new VAT Consolidated Act and cross references all the sections from the VATA 1972 to the new consolidated acts. For further analysis of the new consolidated Act, it is recommended that readers refer to this text.

Headings in this section are:

39.1 Value-Added Tax is charged under the *Value-Added Tax Act 1972 (VATA)* and came into force on 1 November 1972, replacing turnover tax and wholesale tax. This chapter deals with VAT law *from 1 March 1976* onwards, contained in the *VATA 1972* as amended by subsequent *Finance Acts* and the *VAT(A)A 1978* (see below). Further detailed provisions are made in regulations and orders.

The *Value-Added Tax (Amendment) Act 1978 (VAT(A)A)* was passed on 20 December 1978 and took effect on 1 March 1979 by Ministerial order. It implemented the requirements of the *EEC Sixth Directive on VAT (17 May 1977)*.

Administration. VAT is administered by the Revenue Commissioners (VAT), Dublin Castle Dublin 2, and is collected by the Collector-General, Sarsfield House,

Francis Street, Limerick, who deals with returns, payment etc. Statements of Practice (mostly in the form of Information Leaflets) are listed on the Revenue's website (www.revenue.ie), which also contains an extensive listing showing the rate applicable to over 2,500 goods and services, which is regularly updated with classification decisions. See also the regular articles and reports in the Revenue Tax Briefing. All forms and leaflets may be obtained from the Revenue Forms and Leaflets Service on (01) 8780100 or by e-mail at forms@revenue.ie.

SCHEME OF TAX

39.239.2 VAT is a tax borne indirectly by the consumer of goods and services. It taxes the 'value added' at each stage in the chain of transactions leading to the non-trading or exempt consumer. The tax is charged on supplies by taxable persons ie traders (and on imports, see **39.19**–**39.25** below) who must then account to the Revenue Commissioners for this amount. [*VATA 1972, s 19(2)*]. As regards supplies *received by* a taxable person for business purposes, he may claim repayment of any 'deductible tax' which he himself has paid over to his supplier under an invoice. VAT exempt businesses, non-trading entities and consumers generally cannot reclaim any VAT incurred, but there are exceptions to this rule.

VAT is charged on any supply in RI of taxable goods or taxable services by a taxable person in the course of his business. [*VATA 1972, s 2*]. *Imported goods* are charged to VAT on their *value* and the tax operates like a customs duty (see **39.19** below). Special arrangements apply to imports from EU Member States (see **39.20** *et seq.* below). *Supplies* of taxable goods and taxable services are charged on the *total consideration* (net of VAT) to which the taxable person making the supply becomes entitled (see **39.10** below).

Cash receipts basis. A taxable person may opt to account for VAT on the basis of cash actually received if most of his business consists of sales to non-registered persons or his turnover is less than €1,000,000/£500,000 pa [*FA 2007, s 87*] (see **39.11** below).

RATES

[*VATA 1972, ss 11(1), 15(1); FA 1990, ss 98, 102; FA 1991, s 80; FA 1992, s 173(1)(2); FA 1995, s 128; FA 1996, s 92; FA 1997, s 103(a); FA 1998, s 110; FA 1999, s 127; FA 2000, s 111; FA 2001, s 187; FA 2002, s 103; FA 2003, s 119; FA 2004, s 59, FA 2005, s 103; FA 2009; FA 2010, s 121; F(No.2)A 2011, s 3.* See also **38.213** 'Tax cases'].

39.339.3 From 1 March 1993 onwards, the rates are:

General	21%	From 1 January 2010
General	21.5%	From 1 December 2008
		(1 March 2003 until 30 November 2008)
General	21%	(from 1 January 2001 to 28 February 2002 only, **20%**)
Second Schedule	0%	
Third Schedule	10%	

Sixth Schedule	13.5%	(from 1 March 1991 to 31 December 2002, 12.5%)
	9%	Reduced rate applying to certain services and goods from 1 July 2011 until 31 December 2013
Eighth Schedule	13.5%	(from 1 July 1995 to 31 December 2002, 12.5%)
	2.5%	(from 1 March 1993 to 29 February 1996)
Livestock (including	2.8%	(from 1 March 1996 to 28 February 1997)
horses), live greyhounds	3.3%	(from 1 March 1997 to 28 February 1998)
and the hire of horses	3.6%	(from 1 March 1998 to 28 February 1999)
	4.0%	(from 1 March 1999 to 29 February 2000)
	4.2%	(from 1 March 2000 to 31 December 2000)
	4.3%	(from 1 January 2001 to 31 December 2003)
	4.4%	(from 1 January 2004 to 31 December 2004)
	4.8%	(from 1 January 2005)

SCHEDULED GOODS AND SERVICES

[*VATA 1972, Schs 1–8 as amended*].

39.4 *Finance Act 2010* makes a number of amendments to the Schedules of the VAT Act. The amendments replace the First, Second and Sixth Schedules to the VAT Act and renames the other Schedules of the VAT Act. The amendments involve renumbering, reordering and some simplification of the wording, in preparation for the consolidation of the VAT Act. There are also a small number of substantive changes. These include a clarification of the VAT exemption for professional medical care (which brings the Irish legislation more in line with the VAT Directive), an amendment in relation to the exemption for public postal services (to provide that individually negotiated contracts are not exempt, which is in line with a 2009 Judgement in the European Court of Justice) and a new provision providing VAT exemption for certain Islamic financial products that are comparable to non-Islamic financial products that qualify for an exemption from VAT — provisions in relation to Islamic finance are also contained in Part 1 of the Bill. [*FA 2010, s 124* and *125*]

First Schedule (Exempted Activities) – see **39.6** below.

Second Schedule (Zero-rated) includes: children's clothing (not fur skin) and footwear (not for skating or swimming) for average size child aged under eleven and sold on basis of size or age; food and drink for humans (there has been clarification that the supply of drinkable products made from fruit and vegetables are taxable at the standard rate of VAT – [*FA 2007, s 94*])(but *excluding* dutiable beverages, manufactured beverages other than tea, coffee, cocoa, etc, ice creams, etc, sweets, biscuits and chocolates, etc, crisps and nuts, etc, and bakery products other than bread, and see also *VATA 1972, Sixth Schedule* below); it has been clarified that the supply of tea and coffee in non-drinkable form is zero rated but the supply of same in drinkable form is not [*F(No 2)A 2008, s 76*]; human oral medicines; food and oral medicines for animals other than pets; medical equipment and appliances (other than artificial teeth and corrective spectacles and contact lenses); candles (other than certain ornamental ones); certain fertilisers; food-producing seeds, etc; goods supplied for transport out of the EU or to a taxable person elsewhere in the EU or within the customs-free airport, or by one taxable person within the customs-free airport to another in the customs-free airport or in a free port, or by one taxable person in a free port to another, and certain supplies to travellers outside RI (including repayment procurement services); agency and certain other services connected with the export of goods; supply, hiring or repair, etc of certain sea-going ships and (from 1 May 2001) equipment therein and of international commercial aircraft and of equipment incorporated or used in such aircraft and goods supplied for fuelling or provisioning such ships and aircraft); work on imported goods intended for export; supply of gold to the Central Bank of Ireland; most printed books (including bound volumes of music), booklets and atlases, but excluding newspapers, catalogues, stationery, albums, diaries etc (see Statement of Practice VAT/10/94); sanitary towels and tampons; certain services provided by the RNLI or by the Commissioner of Irish Lights. Also included are the supply of qualifying goods and services to, or the intra-Community acquisition or importation of qualifying goods by, an authorised person (excluding certain self-supplies, see **39.7** below) within *VATA 1972, s 13A* (introduced by *FA 1993, s 90*). This applies to most supplies etc to or by persons most of whose turnover is dispatched or transported outside RI (and who are duly authorised for this purpose by the Revenue Commissioners). See also **39.21** below as regards zero-rating of certain intra-community transactions. Certain transport services included in charges for imported goods, and certain navigation services by the Irish Aviation authority, are also included.

Third Schedule (ten per cent) is generally abolished after 28 February 1993. It is retained in relation to the following supplies under contracts entered into or arrangements made before 25 February 1993: a domestic dwelling supplied under a contract made with a private individual; and the letting of immovable goods (other than in the course of provision of certain sporting facilities) by a hotel etc or in holiday accommodation, campsites, etc, and the short-term hire of motor vehicles, at charges fixed at the time of the agreement for the supply.

Fourth Schedule (Services taxed where received). The word 'agents' has been substituted with 'intermediaries'. [*FA 2007, s 95*] Advertising services; services (not connected with land) of consultants, engineers, lawyers, accountants, data-processors, and information-providers; provision of staff; banking, financial and insurance services; financial fund management functions [*FA 2004, s 65(b)*]; certain non-competition agreements; transfers and assignments of copyrights, patents, trade marks, etc; hiring out of movable goods other than means of transport; and (from 1 July 1997) telecommunications services (as defined in *FA 1997, s 96(c)*). Radio and television broadcasting services, electronically supplied services (as described in *FA 2003, s 113*); agency services when procuring any of the above services; the provision of access to, and of transport or transmission through, natural gas and electricity distribution systems and the provision of other directly linked services [*FA 2004 s 65(a)*] effective from 1 January 2005; See also Information Leaflet No 1/05.

Fifth Schedule (Farming, etc): Part I lists agricultural production activities ('Annex A' activities); Part II lists agricultural services ('Annex B' services).

Sixth Schedule (13.5 per cent) includes: coal, peat and other solid fuels; electricity supply; gas for heating or lighting (excluding welding, cutting and lighter fuels and motor vehicle gas); most heating oils; agricultural services of field work, reaping, mowing, threshing, baling, harvesting, sowing, planting, disinfecting and ensilage of agricultural products, destruction of weeds and pests, dusting and spraying of crops and land, and lopping and tree felling and similar forestry services, and of stock minding and rearing and farm relief and advisory services (excluding management and accountancy services); certain goods and services supplied in connection with the repair and maintenance of agricultural machinery; prepared food and drink otherwise within *VATA 1972, Second Schedule* (see above) supplied by vending machine or in staff canteens, restaurants, hotels or other catering establishments; ice creams, etc, sweets, biscuits and chocolates, etc, crisps and nuts, etc and bakery products other than bread (all excluded from *VATA 1972, Second Schedule*), and non-alcoholic fruit juices, supplied with meals in staff canteens, etc; hot take-away food and drink and other food and drink supplied with it (excluding drink otherwise excluded from *VATA 1972, Second Schedule*); (amended from 25 March 2005), the sale of food and drink which has been heated and is above the ambient air temperature when provided to the customer, is liable to VAT at 13.5 per cent when purchased at a take-away outlet, supermarket, garage or other outlet; promotion of and admission to cinema performances; live entertainment supplied in connection with the supply of meals and drink; certain funfairs; waste disposal services; admissions to certain exhibitions of a kind normally held in museums or art galleries (not within **39.6(***t***)** below). *Finance (No 2) Act 2011, s 3* provides for a second reduced VAT rate of 9%, in respect of certain goods and services, for the period 1 July 2011 to 31 December 2013. Thereafter the rate will revert to the rate of 13.5% currently applying to goods and services taxed at the reduced rate. The amendment provides that the 9% rate will apply mainly to restaurant and catering services, hotel and holiday accommodation, admissions to cinemas, theatres, certain musical performances, museums and art gallery exhibitions, fairgrounds or amusement park services, the use of sporting facilities, hairdressing services, printed matter such as brochures, maps, programmes, leaflets, catalogues, magazines and newspapers. Professional services supplied by veterinary surgeons, and services of a kind supplied by veterinary surgeons are included, as is the provision of sports facilities other than by non-profit-making organisations (see **39.6(***j***)** below). Also included are immovable goods (ie land); services consisting of the development of and work on immovable goods (including the installation of fixtures), so long as the value of any *movable* goods supplied therewith does not exceed two-thirds of the total consideration, and routine cleaning of immovable goods; newspapers and periodicals (at least fortnightly) dealing mainly with current affairs (see Statement of Practice VAT/10/94) (amended, from 1 May 1998, to include all newspapers and periodicals, and brochures, catalogues, maps, sheet music etc, and stationery, diaries, albums etc); letting of immovable goods (other than in the course of provision of certain sporting facilities) by a hotel etc or in holiday accommodation, campsites, etc; provision of holiday accommodation; tour guide services; short-term hire of passenger vehicles and boats (under 15 tons) or of sports or pleasure craft or caravans, tents etc; certain works of art and important literary manuscripts and antique furniture, silver, glass or porcelain; repair and maintenance of most movable goods and alteration of most used movable goods; services (other than *VATA 1972, First Schedule* health services) consisting of care of the human body, including health studios etc; professional services supplied by jockeys; certain supplies of photographic, cinematographic and video software and related services; driving instruction not within **39.6**(*d*) below; certain cakes, biscuits etc not included in *VATA 1972, Second Schedule*. Concrete ready to pour and certain concrete blocks are included unless within the auction or margin schemes, see **39.7** below. Greyhound food supplied in bulk is included, and works of art, etc within the auction or margin schemes (see **39.7** below) are excluded (and see *VATA 1972, Eighth Schedule* below). Certain member-owned and public golf club green fees in excess of €25,500 pa are included, as are, from 1 September 1997, nursery or garden centre stock consisting of live plants, bulbs, etc (not being Second Schedule food-producing seeds, etc) and cut flowers and ornamental foliage (not artificial or dried) (for which see Statement of Practice SP–VAT 1/97). Since 1 May 1998, live poultry and ostriches are added, as, from 1 July 1998, are animal insemination services and livestock semen.

Seventh Schedule (21.5%) was introduced by *FA 2010*. This Schedule lists the activities that are within the scope of VAT when undertaken by a State or public bodies. This amendment transposes *Council Directive 2006/112/EC of 28 November 2006 Annex I* on the common system of value-added tax. [*FA 2010, s 129*]

Eighth Schedule (13.5 per cent) was introduced in implementation of the margin and auction schemes (see **39.7** below). It applies to a specific list of art, antiques and collectors' items which under certain circumstances are liable to VAT at the Eighth Schedule rate but, when supplied under the margin or auction schemes, are liable at the general rate on the appropriate margin.

CHARGE ON SUPPLIES WITHIN THE STATE

39.5 Except as below, VAT is only chargeable on supplies of goods and services in RI (and on imports of goods into RI). The definitions of the place of supply mean that the following are chargeable to RI VAT:

(*a*) supply of goods located in RI at the moment of supply or the transport of which begins in RI (see **39.19** for exports);

(*b*) supply of services by a person whose establishment (ie fixed place of business) or, if he has no establishment anywhere, whose usual place of residence is in RI (excluding, from 25 March 1999, the hiring of means of transport for use outside the EU);

(*c*) supply of RI land and buildings and any associated services supplied by estate agents, architects or on-site supervisors;

(*d*) receipt for business purposes of *VATA 1972, Fourth Schedule* services (see **39.4** above) (not within (*g*) below) by a person whose establishment (or, if none, usual place of residence) is in RI, unless, broadly, he also has an establishment in another State and the services are most directly for use in that establishment; or by an RI department of State, local authority or statutory body where supply is by person with no establishment in the EU, or with an establishment in another

Member State such that VAT is not payable in that State (and see Information Leaflet No 1/05);

(*e*)   supply of transport taking place in RI;

(*f*)   physical performance in RI of: valuation of work on movable goods; artistic, entertainment, sporting or scientific, etc, services; handling etc of goods for transport;

(*g*)   services consisting of the hiring out of movable goods by a person established outside the EU and not in the EU where the goods are, or are to be, effectively used in RI;

(*h*)   supplies consisting of the supply and installation or assembly of goods in RI where the customer is a business, a Department of State, a local authority or a body governed by Statute or a person carrying on an exempt activity within the *VATA 1972, First Schedule* and the supplier is not established in RI. Since 28 March 2003, these supplies are taxed in a manner similar to *VATA 1972, Fourth Schedule* services. ie the customer, not the supplier is the person liable to account for the VAT;

(*i*)   electronic services supplied from outside the EU by a person only established outside the EU and received, otherwise than for business purposes, by a person whose usual place of residence is RI.

The place of supply rule in respect of Fourth Schedule Services received from abroad by a department of State, a local authority or a body established by statute in the State is amended so that the services should be taxed in the country where they are supplied. Intermediary services not relating to Fourth Schedule Services will now be taxed in the place where the underlying transaction is taxed. [*FA 2007, s 77*]

These rules may be added to by Order.

[*VATA 1972, ss 3(6), 5; VAT(A)A 1978, s 5; FA 1985, s 42; FA 1986, s 81; FA 1990, s 100; FA 1992, ss 167(c), 169; FA 1999, s 121; FA 2001, s 183: FA 2003, ss 118, 131*].

Special rules apply in relation to supplies within the EEC. See **39.20** *et seq.* below.

EXEMPTED ACTIVITIES

39.6 No VAT is chargeable in respect of any exempted activity. [*VATA 1972, s 6*]. Persons carrying on such an activity are not taxable persons, unless they can and do waive the exemption. The exempt activities are listed in the *VATA 1972, First Schedule* of the *VATA* as amended (the list may be added to by Order).

Finance Act 2011, s 60 makes a number of minor amendments to the First Schedule. The exemption for betting has been extended to cover commissions earned by remote betting intermediaries. The exemption for cultural services has been extended to include supplies of cultural services by public bodies. Prior to 1 July 2010 these services were outside the scope of VAT and this provision confirms that notwithstanding the changes to VAT treatment of public bodies from 1 July 2010 the provision of these services will not become subject to VAT. The exemption for public postal services has also been updated to confirm that public postal services that are provided as part of a universal service (as that term is defined by EU law) will be exempt when provided by an Post or other Designated bodies.

Effect of exemption is that although a person is not liable to account for VAT on his own supplies he suffers VAT, in the same way as a non-trading consumer, on any taxable supplies *received by him* in the course of the activity. He generally cannot claim any deduction of tax under **39.12** below. However, depending on the nature of the activities undertaken it is possible to deduct VAT in respect of certain activities carried out abroad.

Waiver of the exemption is available in the case of (*g*) below (although in the latter case see **39.7** below as regards anti-avoidance provisions in relation to which the waiver does not apply). It means that a person must account for tax on supplies by him and can claim deduction of tax on supplies received. It also means that the person can pass onto his business customers the right to claim such deduction. Waiver must apply to *all* the person's supplies (limited waiver is allowed in specific circumstances) and continues in effect until cancellation by the taxpayer. The right to waive exemption from VAT is removed in respect of short term letting or newly acquired or developed residential property, There are various provisions regarding the types of lettings excluded from the waiver and also the criteria for determining when a property is considered to be acquired or developed. [*FA 2007, s 78*] Waiver is claimed by notifying the Collector-General and may involve clawback of input deduction. [*VATA 1972, s 7; FA 1991, s 78; FA 1997, s 100; FA 2002, s 100; FA 2003, s 117; SI 63/79, reg 4; SI 228/98; SI 504/03*].

Exempted activities are:

(*a*) Professional services, comprising:

    (i) medical services not within (*a*)(iii) below, except such services supplied in the course of a business of selling goods,

    (ii) professional services of a dental or optical nature, and

    (iii) dental technician services and dentures, etc;

(*b*) Insurance services and related agency services;

(*c*) Financial services, ie banking and money lending services, shares and securities dealing, credit and charge card schemes, underwriting services, credit guarantee, unit trust and collective and special investment scheme management, and related agency services (excluding certain share and security management and safekeeping services and the services of loss adjusters). See also **38.209** 'Tax cases';

(*d*) School and university education (and, from 1 May 1997, all children's or young people's education), and vocational training provided by recognised establishments and similar bodies, including heavy goods vehicle driving instruction;

(*e*) Hospital and medical care provided by a hospital, nursing home, etc;

(*f*) Catering services for hospital patients and school pupils;

(*g*) Letting land, but not by an hotel etc, nor machinery, etc let separately from land, nor provision of parking facilities, nor hire of safes, nor provision of sports facilities (but see (*j*) below);

(*h*) Services for the protection or care of children and young persons provided either otherwise than for profit or (from 1 May 1997) by persons regulated under *Child*

Care Act 1991, Pt VII; supplies given free to members (except for any membership subscription) by non-profit-making bodies of a political, religious, philanthropic etc nature; supplies closely related to welfare and social security made by non-profit-making bodies;

(*i*) Sports etc facilities provided by a non-profit-making body; promotion of and admissions to sporting events (but not promotion of facilities by persons other than non-profit-making organisations, see *VATA 1972, Sixth Schedule*). Exemption does not apply to member-owned, and State- or local authority-owned, golf clubs to the extent that their non-member green fees exceed €27,500 pa (€25,500/£20,000 pa prior to 1 May 2006). See also Statements of Practice SP–VAT 4/92 and 1/95;

(*j*) Passenger transport or accommodation, and related agency services;

(*k*) Supplies of goods used in the course of a business which were charged to VAT on being acquired but without the VAT being deductible (see **39.10** below);

(*l*) Funeral undertaking;

(*m*) Broadcasting (excluding advertising);

(*n*) The acceptance of off-course bets, or on-course bets on horse or greyhound races, and, from 25 March 2002, of off-course totalisator bets, and the issue of lottery tickets;

(*o*) Agency services connected with collection of insurance premiums;

(*p*) Blood bank services and similar services relating to human organs and human milk;

(*q*) Promotion of or admission to most live performances (but not dances or where simultaneous provision of food or drink facilities);

(*r*) Certain services and closely linked goods supplied by recognised cultural bodies;

(*s*) Services supplied by certain independent groups of persons to members;

(*t*) Public postal services;

(*u*) (Since 1 January 2000) certain supplies relating to investment gold.

(v) Homecare services when provided by natural or legal persons duly recognised by the Health Care Executive under the *Health Act 1970, s 61A*.

[*VATA Sch 1; VAT(A)A 1978, s 24; FA 1980, s 82; FA 1982, s 87; FA 1985, s 49; FA 1986, s 89; FA 1987, s 45; FA 1989, s 61; FA 1990, s 106; FA 1991, s 85; FA 1992, s 194; FA 1993, s 94; FA 1994, s 99; FA 1995, s 139; FA 1997, s 110; FA 1999, s 138; FA 2000, s 122; FA 2001, s 199; FA 2002, s 110; FA 2005, s 112; FA 2006, ss 100, 101; FA 2007, s 93*].

The supply of **racehorse training services** is taxable at the *VATA 1972, Third Schedule* rate. In general, the Revenue Commissioners are prepared to regard ten per cent of the gross fees charged as being appropriate to training only, the remaining 90 per cent being for the keep and care of the horses and still considered an agricultural service for which the farmer may or may not elect to register and charge VAT. However, liability arises on the whole of the gross fees where either a taxable activity other than farming or racehorse training is carried on the turnover from which exceeds the exemption limit (see **39.3** above), or a farmer elects to register for VAT (see **39.17** below).

SUPPLIES OF TAXABLE GOODS AND TAXABLE SERVICES

39.7 Taxable goods and taxable services are goods and services the supply of which is not an exempted activity. [*VATA 1972, s 1(1); FA 1992, s 165(a)(viii)(ix)*].

Goods means all movable and immovable objects, new or used, but does not include things in action or money. It includes land and buildings (see below). The provision of electricity, gas or any form of power, heat, refrigeration or ventilation is a supply of goods. [*VATA 1972, s 1(1); VAT(A)A 1978, s 4(c); FA 1996, s 88(b)*]. *Finance (No 2) Act 2008* deletes para (b) from sub-s (1C) to ensure that the whole section applies only to supplies of immovable goods.

Supply in relation to goods means transfer of ownership by agreement, handing over goods under a hire-purchase agreement (although hire purchase services are exempt), handing over goods manufactured or derived from other goods of the customer, compulsory acquisition, and certain self-supplies. Certain contract work is, however, treated as a supply of services (although the rate is that applicable to a supply of the finished goods). It is confirmed that the handing over of goods under a hire-purchase agreement is a supply of goods and that the transfer of ownership at the end of the hire purchase agreement is not a supply of goods. The supply of repossessed goods by the finance house is also a taxable supply. [*FA 2007, s 76*] A self-supply arises where business goods, on the purchase, import etc of which the person is entitled to a tax deduction, or which were acquired VAT-free on the transfer of a business, are appropriated to a non-business use or disposed of free of charge. Self-supply also occurs where goods are applied for business purposes in circumstances where a full deduction of input tax is not available. Such self-supplies are deemed to have been made for consideration in the course of the business, except gifts of industrial samples or gifts costing no more than €20 each to the donor. Disposals by eg receivers and liquidators of goods forming part of the assets of a taxable person's business (including 'immovable goods' – see below) are deemed to be supplies by the taxable person. Where ownership of goods is transferred as security for a loan or debt or in connection with a transfer of a business, the transfer of goods is outside the charge to VAT. Similarly the sale of goods repossessed under hire purchase agreements is from 25 March 1999 not treated as a supply of goods where the customer was not entitled to deduct VAT on the original transaction, and a similar rule applies from 30 March 2001 to goods acquired by insurers in a claim settlement. Where agreements amongst a chain of buyers and sellers are fulfilled by delivery by the first seller to the last buyer, the delivery is treated as a simultaneous delivery by each seller. The supply by auction, or through an agent, of livestock (including live horses) or live greyhounds, and the supply by auction of vegetables, fruit, flowers, poultry, eggs or fish, have previously been treated as the simultaneous supply to and by the auctioneer or agent. A special auction scheme covers secondhand movable goods apart from the aforementioned. It allows the auctioneer effectively to act as principal and account for VAT on the margin. A similar scheme applies to dealers, allowing VAT to be accounted for on the dealer's margin. *VATA 1972, s 10A* has been amended to change the rules for the taxation of second-hand means of transport and agricultural machinery for the special schemes under *VATA 1972, ss 12B* and *12C* to the margin scheme under *VATA 1972, s 10A*. [*FA 2010, s 119*] Special rules apply in both cases as to the status of the supplier of the goods, in particular in relation to imported goods. [*VATA 1972, ss 3, 10A, 10B; VAT(A)A 1978, s 4; FA 1982, s 75; FA 1983, s 78; FA 1990, s 99; FA 1992, s 167; FA 1995, ss 119, 120, 126–128, 141; FA 1996, ss 89, 91, 92(b); FA 1998, s 105; FA 1999, ss 120(b), 125, 126; FA 1998, s 105; FA 1999, s 120(b); FA 2001, ss 182, 185, 186; FA 2003, s 120; SI 63/79, reg 31; SI 363/95; FA 2010, s 119*]. For the special rules applying to the supply of alcohol products, see *VATA 1972, s 3B*, introduced by *FA 1993, s 84*.

Where goods are sold under retention of title, but entitlement is in effect granted to the purchaser, a supply may in practice be treated as having taken place provided that the purchaser and vendor treat the transaction in the same manner.

Services are not separately defined but *supply* of services is widely defined as the performance or omission of any act or the tolerance of any situation, other than a supply of goods. Where consideration is received in respect of services without there being any legal entitlement, the services are nonetheless treated as supplied for that consideration. Where the services of a barrister or solicitor are paid for under a policy of insurance, the services are nonetheless deemed to be supplied to the person indemnified under that policy. See also **38.210** 'Tax cases' for earlier position. Supply of food for immediate human consumption by vending machine, cafe, restaurant etc is deemed to be supply of services. Special EU-wide provisions apply to telecommunications services. Transfer of goodwill or intangible business assets in connection with transfer of a business is outside the charge to VAT. Special provisions apply to services supplied through an agent. A self-supply of services occurs when a person supplies himself, his family, his staff or his business with services which would be taxable if supplied to anyone else (only self-supplies of catering services are at present taxable, see *SI 63/79, reg 24*). Certain imported services not giving rise to liability in the source country are treated as supplies by the importer, unless the tax would be wholly deductible as input tax. [*VATA 1972, ss 3(1A), 5; VAT(A)A 1978, ss 4, 5; FA 1982, s 76; FA 1986, s 81; FA 1989, s 54; FA 1992, s 169; FA 1995, s 123; FA 1996, s 90; FA 1997, s 99; FA 1998, s 107; FA 2000, s 108; FA 2001, s 183; SI 363/95*].

See also **39.20** *et seq.* below as regards transactions between EU Member States.

For the special scheme introduced from 1 January 2000 for the VAT treatment of investment gold, see *VATA 1972, s 6A* introduced by *FA 1999, s 122* (as amended by *FA 2000, s 109*) and *SI 439–441/99*.

Land and buildings are termed 'immovable goods'. See **39.28 for new VAT rules on land and buildings which apply as of 1 July 2008.** The following relates to the supply of immoveable goods prior to 1 July 2008. With certain exceptions, a supply of immovable goods only occurs where a person disposes of or creates an interest in land which has been developed since 1 November 1972, and for which he was entitled to claim a VAT input deduction in respect of the acquisition or development of the land. 'Development' is defined in *VATA 1972, s 1*. Generally, no VAT charge arises if the person owned the land on 1 November 1972 and it has not been developed between then and the date of disposal, or where there was no right to claim deductible tax. 'Interest in land' means any estate or interest for a period of at least ten years or one capable of being extended by the tenant to a term of ten years or more, but not a mortgage. [*VATA 1972, s 4; FA 1997, s 98; FA 1998, s 106*]. Subject to approval by the Revenue

Commissioners, where tax is chargeable in respect of the letting of immovable goods, there is provision for the lessor and lessee jointly to apply for the tax to be payable by the lessee by way of an accounting mechanism in the lessee's VAT return. [*VATA 1972, s 4A; FA 1994, s 93; SI 184/95*]. See Revenue Tax Briefing Issue 40 p 31 as regards applications under *VATA 1972, s 4A*.

A number of provisions are included in *VATA 1972, s 4* (with ancillary provisions elsewhere) aimed at preventing avoidance of VAT on the letting of immovable property to VAT-exempt companies. In this regard, with effect from 25 March 2002 the VAT value of certain disposals of immovable goods, other than freehold interests, must exceed the VAT exclusive cost of acquisition of the interest and development of the property unless the Revenue are satisfied that the VAT value of the interest being disposed of has fallen because of an unforeseen change in market conditions. If the disposal of the interest in property fails this test it is treated as a VAT exempt letting for which a person cannot waive exemption and the person disposing of the interest will suffer an irrecoverable VAT cost. [*VATA 1972, s 4(3A); FA 2002, s 99; FA 2003, s 114*].

Where a property is used for vatable purposes and then used for a VAT exempt purpose an irrecoverable VAT cost may be suffered if the property has been used for vatable purposes for less than 20 years. Also, the subsequent sale of the property could be liable to VAT at which time there may be an entitlement to an additional VAT input credit. [*FA 2005, s 100 (b) (3)(ab)*].

The disposal of a freehold interest in property with sitting tenants is only liable to VAT if the property has been developed for or on behalf of the landlord. [*VATA 1972, s 4(9); FA 2005, s 100(d)(9)(a)*].

TAXABLE PERSONS

39.8 The following are taxable persons and liable to VAT. A taxable person must, within 30 days of becoming a taxable person, supply particulars to the Revenue Commissioners, who keep a register of taxable persons to each of whom a registration number is issued [*VATA 1972, s 9; VAT(A)A 1978, s 7; FA 1992, s 171; SI 30/93*]:

(*a*) Any person who otherwise than as an employee of another person engages in the supply in RI of taxable goods or taxable services (subject to the exemptions below);

(*b*) In the particular event only, a person who disposes of an interest in land in connection with the disposal or development of the same land by a taxable person;

(*c*) Any person receiving *VATA 1972, Fourth Schedule* services in RI (see **39.5**(*d*) above);

(*d*) So far as specified by Order, the State and local authorities. State and public bodies are brought within the scope of VAT as of from 1 July 2010 where they provide services outside their regulatory function or if they engage in any activity listed in *VATA 1972, Sch 7* or where there is likely to be distortion of competition [*FA 2010, s 117*];

(*e*)   Any person engaging in intra-community acquisitions of goods (see **39.20** below).

[*VATA 1972, ss 4(5), 8; VAT(A)A 1978, s 6; FA 1986, s 82; FA 1992, s 170(2); FA 1995, ss 122, 124; FA 2001, s 184*].

Similar requirements are imposed in respect of certain liquidators, receivers, etc whose disposals are treated as supplies by a taxable person (see **39.7** above). [*FA 1983, s 80*].

Group registration. Certain interlinked business activities may be treated as carried on by one of the persons carrying on those activities. Special provisions apply in relation to certain intra-group transactions in land. A VAT group is to be considered a 'single taxable person'. [*VATA 1972, s 8(8); FA 1991, s 79; FA 2002, s 101(c); FA 2006, s 95(b); SI 63/79, reg 5; FA 2007, s 79*].

The licensee of **licensed premises on which dances are held** (or the company whose nominee he is) is deemed to be the promoter of such dances, and to have received the admission money (less tax) and any proceeds in connection with the dances. [*VATA 1972, s 8(3C); FA 1992, s 170(1)(b)*]. Information Leaflet No 20/2001 states that, where the dances being promoted are for the benefit of non-profit making organisations, no liability will arise on the admission charge. See also *SI 63/79, reg 20*.

In the case of **persons not established in RI** who supply **cultural, artistic, entertainment, etc services** in RI, any person (unless acting in a private capacity) who receives the services is the taxable person in relation to that supply and has to account for the tax accordingly. Any promoter, agent, etc who (again unless acting in a private capacity) commissions or procures the services is treated for this purpose as the person receiving the services. This normally applies from 25 March 2002, but may be deferred to 1 March 2003 in certain cases involving Arts Council funding. [*VATA 1972, s 8(1)(2)(aa); FA 2002, s 101(a)(b)(i)*].

A person not established in the EU who supplies electronic services to private consumers in RI must account for the VAT due in RI and is only entitled to recover RI VAT incurred under the provisions of the Thirteenth VAT Directive. Usually, a non-EU supplier would have to register for VAT in each Member State in which he makes such supplies. However, with effect from 1 July 2003 he can opt to account in one Member State for the VAT due in each Member State in respect of supplies of electronic services to private consumers. Where he opts to account in RI for the VAT due in respect of the specific supplies within the EU he must submit quarterly VAT returns which should identify the amount of VAT due for each Member State of consumption. He should also keep full and true records of all transactions covered by the scheme and make them available, on request, to each Member State. [*FA 2003, s 116*].

Mobile traders, etc. With effect from 25 March 2002, any person (the 'premises provider') who owns, occupies or controls premises in RI and who, in the course of business, allows a person (a 'mobile trader') not established in RI to supply goods in the course of business on those premises for less than seven consecutive days must, at least 14 days before those supplies commence, provide full details to the Revenue Commissioners. The period of occupation for which the services are supplied has been extended from seven days to twenty eight days *[FA 2011, s 56]*. Failure to do so may render the premises provider jointly and severally liable to be treated as the taxable person in relation to the mobile trader's supplies. Similar rules apply where the premises provider allows a non-RI established promoter to supply cultural, artistic or entertainment, etc services (as above) on the land. [*VATA 1972, s 8(2)(d); FA 2002, s 101(b)(ii), FA 2011, s 56*].

Natural Gas/Electricity. Certain recipients of supplies of natural gas or electricity are deemed to be taxable persons and are liable to account for VAT on the receipt of those supplies when they are supplied to them by a person not established in the State [*FA 2004, ss 58(b)*].

Exemptions. A person is not a taxable person, and therefore not required to register, unless he elects to be a taxable person, if:

(i)   he is a farmer (see **39.17** below) for whose supply in any continuous twelve-month period of:

     (*a*)   agricultural (other than insemination, stock-minding and stock-rearing) services the total consideration has not exceeded, and is not likely to exceed, €27,500 (€25,500 prior to 1 May 2006),

     (*b*)   (from 1 July 1998) livestock (from 25 March 1999, bovine) semen the total consideration has not exceeded, and is not likely to exceed, €55,000 (€51,000 prior to 1 May 2006) (disregarding supplies to farmers licensed as artificial insemination centres or to taxable persons under the control of the farmer),

     (*c*)   nursery or garden stock or cut flowers or ornamental foliage within Sixth Schedule (see **39.4** above), other than wholesale supply, the total consideration has not exceeded, and is not likely to exceed, €55,000 (€51,000 prior to 1 May 2006),

     (*d*)   any combination of services and goods within (*a*), (*b*) or (*c*) above the total consideration has not exceeded, and is not likely to exceed, €27,500 (€25,500 prior to 1 May 2006), or

     (*e*)   goods within (*b*) and (*c*) above the total consideration has not exceeded, and is not likely to exceed, €55,000 (€51,000 prior to 1 May 2006);

(ii)   the total consideration for his supplies of taxable goods and services has not exceeded, and is unlikely to exceed, a given limit of €27,500 (€25,500 prior to 1 May 2006) in any continuous twelve-month period;

(iii)   as (ii) above, with higher limit, if 90 per cent of receipts are derived from supplies of taxable goods (excluding goods chargeable at the 21 per cent rate produced wholly or mainly from zero-rated materials). The limit is €55,000 (€51,000 prior to 1 May 2006) in any continuous twelve-month period; or

(iv)   he (1) carries on a sea fishing business and his supplies of taxable goods or services consist exclusively of supplies, in the course of the business, of unprocessed fish to taxable persons or non-taxable overseas buyers, or (2) his taxable supplies are as in (1) together with supplies of either or both of machinery, equipment, etc used in the business, and of other supplies the consideration for which has not exceeded that which would cause the limit under either (ii) or (iii) above to be breached if there were no other supplies.

See also **39.24** below as regards 'distance selling' within the EU.

These exemptions do not apply in relation to services within (*c*) above. Where a person who is a taxable person by virtue of the receipt of such services is a farmer (or would be so but for the provision of racehorse training services, see **39.17**(ii)(*b*) below) or fisherman (see (i) (iv) above), he is (unless he otherwise elects) a taxable person only in respect of the receipt of such services and intra-Community acquisitions of goods (see **39.20** below) and (where relevant) the provision of racehorse training services. See also **39.21** below.

For the purposes of (ii) and (iii) above (and (i) above where supplies within (i)(*a*), (i)(*b*) or (i)(*c*) are made), the consideration received by certain linked persons must be aggregated in determining whether the relevant limits are exceeded. This applies where a person exercises control (see *VATA, s 8(3B)*) over one or more other persons and supplies of the same type of goods or services are made by any two or more of those persons (whether or not including the person exercising control).

The registration limits above do not apply to foreign traders who are not established in RI and who make taxable supplies in RI. They are obliged to register for VAT irrespective of the level of their RI supplies. [*SI 413/92, reg 7*].

See also **39.6** above and **39.17** below as regards provision of racehorse training services.

[*VATA 1972, s 8(3); VAT(A)A 1978, s 6; FA 1980, s 81; F(No 2)A 1981, s 11; FA 1982, s 77(a); FA 1983, s 79; FA 1984, s 86; FA 1989, s 55; FA 1992, s 170(1)(a), (2)(e); FA 1993, s 85; FA 1994, s 94; FA 1997, s 101; FA 1998, s 108; FA 1999, s 123*].

A person who is a taxable person as a result of an election that the above exemption shall not apply may (subject to conditions) apply for the cancellation of the election. Other taxable persons may be treated as not being taxable persons if the Revenue Commissioners are satisfied that they would not be taxable persons unless they elected to be so. Special provisions apply from 23 March 2000 to cancellation of registration in relation to *VATA 1972, Sixth Schedule* services consisting of the letting of immovable goods by a hotel, etc or in holiday accommodation, campsites, etc (see **39.4** above and *SI 253/00*). [*VATA 1972, s 8(5)–(6); FA 1992, s 170(2)(f); FA 1993, s 85(e); FA 2000, s 110; SI 63/79, reg 3*].

By concession, landlords who undertake to provide insurance, cleaning, security services, etc, otherwise than by means of their own labour or resources, to VAT registered lessees, may apply to be registered for VAT and, also by concession, transmit the deduction for VAT charged on such goods and services to those lessees. Landlords already registered may similarly apply to avail themselves of this concession.

See also **39.20** *et seq.* below as regards persons engaging in intra-community acquisitions of goods.

AMOUNT TAXABLE

39.9 VAT is charged on the total consideration receivable from the transaction (excluding the amount of VAT itself) except as follows. *Open market price* (exclusive of VAT) applies where all or part of the consideration is not in money and where, for a non-business reason, the consideration is nil or is less than the open market price. Special arrangements apply in relation to hire purchase transactions. *Cost of provision* by the relevant person applies to self-supplies of goods or services, and statutory seizure. Goods subject to excise duty (other than certain alcohol products) but supplied before payment of duty to an unregistered person are chargeable on the consideration plus the duty payable had it become due at the time of supply. Consideration given for a stamp, coupon, voucher or token exchangeable for a specified amount of goods or services (other, from 1 May 1998, than telecommunications services) is disregarded except to the extent that the consideration exceeds that amount. The time of supply of telephone cards has been amended so that it is the same for VAT purposes as any other voucher which can be redeemed for a specific value. This means that when a coupon, stamp, telephone card, token or voucher is sold for consideration, this consideration is disregarded for VAT purposes unless any part of this consideration exceeds the value of that coupon, stamp, etc (referred to as the 'redeemable value'). VAT is accountable later, on the supply of services or goods sold in exchange for the voucher.

A new subsection provides that a coupon, stamp, telephone card, etc. sold to another person or a series of persons in the course of business are liable to VAT on the sale of the coupon, etc. and not when the coupon, etc. is exchanged for goods or services. [*FA 2010, s 118*] This does not apply to supplies of such stamps, etc to or by intermediaries in the course of their business. Regulations deal with valuation of goods supplied in return for trading stamps, coupons etc not so disregarded, of 'simultaneous supplies' to and by auctioneers, agents etc and of immovable goods (see **39.7** above). Provisions have been included relating to special schemes in respect of auctioneers. Where an auctioneer sells goods on behalf of a finance house which the finance house repossessed and which was the subject of a failed hire purchase agreement, the sale is subject to VAT. A new *VATA 1972, s 10B* has been inserted into which provides that subsequent supply of goods that were acquired by auction is a taxable unless the goods are motor vehicles for which no deductibility was allowed or are goods used solely in the course of an exempted activity. [*VATA 1972, ss 10, 10A, 10B; VAT(A)A 1978, s 8; FA 1982, s 78; FA 1992, s 172; FA 1993, s 86; FA 1994, s 95; FA 1995, ss 125–127; FA 1997, s 102; FA 1998, s 109; FA 2001, ss 185, 186; FA 2002, s 102; SI 63/79, regs 19, 32, 33; FA 2010, s 120*] See **39.7** above as regards anti-avoidance provisions relating to letting of immovable property. See also Information Leaflet 3/2001.

Net receipts. When income tax is deducted at source from the consideration receivable in the case of construction industry sub-contractors and certain fees for professional services (see **13.8**, **13.11** 'Deduction of tax at source'), VAT is charged on the *gross* amount before such deduction of tax. [*FA 1987, s 39*].

Livestock (which includes horses) are charged in full at a substantive rate of 4.8 per cent from 1 January 2005, (4.4 per cent from 1 January 2004 to 31 December 2004, 4.3 per cent from 1 January 2001 to 31 December 2003, 4.2 per cent from 1 March to 31 December 2000, 4.0 per cent from 1 March 1999 to 29 February 2000, 3.6 per cent from 1 March 1998 to 28 February 1999, 3.3 per cent from 1 March 1997 to 28 February 1998, 2.8 per cent from 1 March 1996 to 28 February 1997). Live greyhounds and the hire of horses are also within these charging provisions. See **39.19** below for imports. [*VATA 1972, s 11(1); FA 1985, s 43; FA 1987, s 39; FA 1990, ss 98, 102(c); FA 1992, s*

173; FA 1996, s 92(a); FA 1997, s 103(a); FA 1998, s 110; FA 1999, s 127; FA 2000, s 111; FA 2001, s 187(b); FA 2004, s 59; FA 2005, s 103]

Racehorse training services. See **39.6** above, **39.17** below.

Mixed supplies. Prior to *FA 2006* the so called 'package rule' applied to goods and services attracting different VAT rates (including exemption) when supplied as a package for a single price. Essentially the package was treated as liable to VAT at the rate applying to the item in the package attracting the highest rate of VAT. With effect from a date to be set by ministerial order, detailed rules concerning the treatment of 'composite', 'multiple', 'individual' and 'ancillary' supplies for the purposes of determining the taxable amounts will apply. [*VATA 1972, ss 10(8), 11; VAT(A)A 1978, ss 8, 9; FA 2006, s 97*]

Fourth Schedule services are taxed on the consideration paid for them by the recipient. [*VATA 1972, s 10(5); VAT(A)A 1978, s 8*].

INVOICES AND RECORDS

39.10 An invoice must be issued by a taxable person whenever he supplies goods or services to a person engaged in taxable or VAT-exempt supplies; a department of state, local authority or body established by Statute; or he supplies goods to a person other than an individual in another Member State or under the distance selling arrangements, see **39.24** below, in such circumstances that VAT is chargeable. An invoice must also be issued by a flat-rate farmer who supplies agricultural produce or services or (after 31 August 1999) second-hand agricultural machinery (see **39.17** below). The form of invoices, time for issue, etc are prescribed by regulations. When goods are handed over at the end of a hire purchase agreement there is no longer an obligation for an invoice to be furnished at that time. Also where a finance company receives a credit note in respect of the return of goods which had been under a hire purchase contract, they are no longer obliged to issue the final user a document corresponding to this credit note. [*FA 2007, s 90*] Special rules apply where there is a subsequent increase or deduction in the consideration or where tax is invoiced at a rate higher than should have applied. Since 1 July 1996, special arrangements apply to supplies of goods under hire-purchase type arrangements, involving the issue of the invoice to the finance company, which issues appropriate documentation to the customer. Provision is made for these requirements to be met where electronic data processing systems are employed. Since 1 January 2004, special provisions will apply to self-billing by VAT registered customers and the outsourcing of the issue of invoices and retention of invoices. Since 25 March 2004 where a supplier in RI supplies goods or services to a customer in another Member State of the EU in a situation where the customer is liable for the VAT under the EU Sixth Directive, then that supplier must issue a VAT invoice. See Information Leaflet No 1/2006 January 2006. [*VATA 1972, s 17; VAT(A)A 1978, s 15; FA 1986, s 86; FA 1990, s 105; FA 1992, s 180; FA 1993, s 91; FA 1995, s 132; FA 1996, s 97; FA 1999, s 134; FA 2000, s 115; FA 2001, s 193; FA 2003, s 122. See also SIs 230, 269, 275, 276/92; SIs 488, 489/98; SI 443/99; SI 504/02; FA 2004, s 63*]

Every taxable person must keep full records of all transactions affecting his VAT liability. Any non-taxable person who, in the course of business, supplies goods or services must keep all invoices issued to him in respect of goods and services supplied to him for the purposes of his business. In each case the documents, together with suitable receipts, accounts, books etc, must be kept for six years. A new provision is introduced to cater for the taxable treatment of a taxable person who claims a deduction for VAT in respect of qualifying accommodation for conferences. The taxable person must retain full and true records in relation to the attendance at qualifying conferences. [*FA 2007, s 89*] Since 28 March 2003, records relating to property transactions must be kept for the VAT life of the property plus six years and records relating to waiver of exemption must be kept for the duration of the waiver plus six years [*VATA 1972, s 16; FA 1992, s 179; FA 1999, s 133; FA 2003, s 121; SI 63/79, reg 9*]. Authorised offices of the Revenue Commissioners have powers of entry, search, inspection and removal of records, etc as respects VAT liability or entitlement to repayment, and may require details of customers and suppliers and of gifts, inducement payments, etc in connection with supplies to customers. [*VATA 1972, s 18; FA 1979, s 48; FA 1982, s 85; FA 1984, s 89; FA 1992, s 181; FA 1995, s 133*]. See *SI 439/99* as regards records of transactions in gold.

CASH RECEIPTS BASIS

39.11 Instead of the usual sales (or invoice) basis, a taxable person may, subject to regulations, be authorised to determine the tax due during any taxable period on the basis of cash actually received during the taxable period if either:

(i)   90 per cent of the consideration on which he is chargeable to VAT comes from supplies of taxable goods or taxable services to *non-registered persons* (ie in most cases, if he is a retailer selling almost entirely direct to the public); or

(ii)   the total consideration he is entitled to receive from taxable supplies has not exceeded, and is not likely to exceed, €635,000 in any continuous period of twelve months. The Minister for Finance has the right to increase this limit by order.

The Revenue Commissioners have powers to cancel or limit any such authorisation. The cash receipts basis is not in any event available in respect of imported goods (whether from within the EU or not).

[*VATA 1972, s 14; VAT(A)A 1978, s 13; FA 1982, s 83; FA 1992, s 177; FA 1994, s 97; SI 259/94; FA 1995, s 131; SI 316/97*].

Detailed rules are contained in *SI 306/92* (as amended), with certain transactions deemed to result in cash receipts, etc. An eligible person wishing to opt for the cash receipts basis can do so either initially on his VAT registration form or by applying to his inspector of taxes.

See also Statements of Practice SP–VAT 2/92, April 1992 and SP–VAT 16/92, October 1992.

Schemes for retailers. A number of schemes are approved by the Revenue Commissioners for the computation of VAT where a retailer sells many kinds of goods chargeable at different rates (see VAT leaflet No 1). See **38.212** 'Tax cases'.

DEDUCTIBLE TAX

39.12 From his liability to VAT for his supplies of goods and services in a taxable period, a taxable person may deduct the total amount of VAT charged to him in that period:

(*a*)   on supplies, *for which invoices were issued*, to him by other taxable persons and by flat-rate farmers; and

(*b*)   on goods imported by him (but see **39.20** *et seq.* below as regards imports from EU countries), on *VATA 1972, Fourth Schedule* services received by him, on certain self-supplies and on certain business services.

Special arrangements apply in relation to the auction and margin schemes (see **39.7** above) and supplies by flat-rate farmers (see **39.17** below). Certain documents issued by finance companies (see **39.10** above) are accepted instead of invoices.

A new provision has been introduced which provides for the deduction of VAT incurred in providing qualified accommodation to persons attending qualifying conferences as delegates. Delegate means a taxable person or their agent attending conferences in the furtherance of business. Qualifying accommodation means accommodation provided to a delegate for the period commencing no earlier than the night before the qualifying conference begins and ceasing on the night a qualifying conference ends, A qualifying conference means a conference or meeting in the course of furtherance of business and must have a minimum of 50 delegates. The conference organiser may be obliged to provide information in relation to the location of the conference, the nature of the conference, and the delegates attending the conference occurring on or after 1 July 2007. [*FA 2007, s 83*]

Where *VATA 1972, s 4A* applies in relation to the lessee of immovable goods (see **39.7** above), a deduction is allowed in respect of the tax for which the lessee is liable.

There is an additional requirement that the goods and services are used by the taxable person for the purposes of his taxable supplies or of certain overseas activities. This replaces the prohibition on deduction at (iv) below which applied before that date.

A farmer or fisherman who is a taxable person only in respect of intra-Community acquisitions of goods and certain services received from abroad (and, in certain cases, the provision of racehorse training services) (see **39.8** above, **39.21**(*b*) below) is not entitled to such a deduction (except in relation to racehorse training services, where applicable).

Where a taxable person's deductible tax exceeds his VAT liability for his supplies in a taxable period, the excess is generally refunded to him. This will occur eg if his supplies are of zero-rated goods.

A special scheme permits second-hand car dealers to claim a deduction for residual VAT included in the purchase price of dealing stock (for which see *SI 201/96* and Revenue Tax Briefing Issue 36 pp 25, 26), and from 1 September 1999 a special scheme similarly applies for agricultural machinery (see *SI 443/99*).

Special anti-avoidance rules apply from 30 March 2001 to property transferred in connection with the transfer of a business.

No deduction is allowed on the following supplies received:

(i)   non-taxable supplies of food and drink, accommodation, or personal services, to self, agents or employees;

(ii)   entertainment expenses for self, agents or employees;

(iii) purchase or hiring of motor vehicles (except as trading stock or by driving schools) or purchase of petrol (except as trading stock);

(iv)   expenditure on provision of food, drink, accommodation or other entertainment services as part of a taxable advertising service.

(i) above includes expenditure on, or on the fitting out of, a building to provide such accommodation, and (ii) above similarly includes expenditure on, or on the fitting out of, a building or facility to provide such entertainment.

Apportionment of input tax. Input tax is apportioned where it relates partly to taxable supplies, and partly to other supplies or activities. The allowable proportion is determined by reference to the extent the inputs are used in making taxable supplies in the context of the taxable person's full range of activities. See *SI 63/79, regs 16, 34, SI 2000/254* Revenue Guide to Apportionment of Input Tax (October 2001) and Revenue Tax Briefing Issue 46 p 31.

[*VATA 1972, ss 12–12D; VAT(A)A 1978, s 10; FA 1982, s 80; FA 1986, s 84; FA 1987, s 41; FA 1991, s 81; FA 1992, s 174; FA 1993, s 88; FA 1994, s 96; FA 1995, ss 129, 130; FA 1996, s 93; FA 1997, s 104; FA 1998, s 111; FA 1999, ss 128, 130, 131; FA 2000, s 112; FA 2001, ss 188–191; FA 2002, s 104; FA 2003, s 120; SI 63/79, reg 22*].

RETURNS

39.13 *Taxable period* means a period of two months beginning on the first day of January, March, May, July, September or November. [*VATA 1972, s 1(1); FA 1973, s 90*].

VAT becomes 'due' (as distinct from payable) on the issue of the invoice (or expiry of the time for issue of the invoice), or at the time of delivery or rendering, or (in cash trading) on receipt of the cash. The latest time at which the tax can become due is the receipt of the total consideration. For certain intra-community transactions, the due date is the 15th day of the month following the transaction, or on earlier issue of an invoice by the supplier. [*VATA 1972, s 19(1)(1A)(2)(2A); FA 1992, s 182(a)(b); FA 1997, s 107(a); FA 2002, s 106(a)*]. See *SI 413/92, regs 8, 12* as regards foreign currency, and Information Leaflet No 7/01 on postponed accounting on intra-Community transactions.

A return must normally be furnished to the Collector-General *within nine days after* the tenth day of the month immediately following each taxable period. The return must state the amount of tax which became due in the taxable period and the amount (if any) of deductible tax. The return must be accompanied by a remittance of the balance of the tax payable, net of any advance payment (see below). Special rules apply in relation to certain intra-community transactions involving motor vehicles and other new means of transport and to certain supplies of excisable goods. There is provision, from 25 March 2002, for returns to be made by a person acting under the authority of a taxable person. [*VATA 1972, s 19(3)–(5); FA 1973, s 82; VAT(A)A 1978, s 16; FA 1992 s 182(c); FA*

1993, s 92; FA 1997, s 107(b); FA 2002, s 106(b); SI 247/93]. Similar provisions apply to liquidators, receivers, etc whose disposals are treated as supplies by a taxable person (see **39.7** above), and who must issue a statement to the taxable person on making such a return. *[FA 1983, s 84]*. The Collector-General may authorise a taxable person to submit returns for longer periods containing up to six consecutive taxable periods (which may, in certain cases, be aligned with the commercial accounting period), subject to such conditions as he considers proper and, if he so requires, to a payment on account at the normal due dates and, from 30 March 2001, to special direct debit arrangements. Authorisation may be withdrawn in various circumstances, and will be if the taxable person so requests. The preferential status of the Revenue Commissioners in a liquidation or bankruptcy is preserved. Special rules apply to a non-EU established person who opts to account for VAT in RI in respect of the supplies of electronic services to private consumers in the EU. *[VATA 1972, s 19(3)(aa); FA 1989, s 58; FA 1995, s 134; FA 2001, s 194; FA 2003, s 116; SI 294/96]*.

Provision is made, with effect from 25 March 2002, for letters of expression of doubt as to the correct application of VAT law to accompany returns, and for the consequences thereof, including cases where the Revenue Commissioners do not accept the expression of doubt as genuine. *[VATA 1972, s 19B; FA 2002, s 107]*.

If no return is furnished, the inspector, or other officer authorised by the Commissioners, may estimate the amount payable and serve notice on the taxable person for payment of that amount. A reduced estimate may be substituted where the original estimate was excessive. The inspector may also serve notice for an assessed amount of tax where he has reason to believe that the amount of tax paid by the taxable person was less than his true liability or that he was given a greater refund than was properly due to him, although where an appeal is made against such an assessment, interest under *VATA 1972, s 21* (see **39.14** below) may be avoided by the payment with the appeal of at least 80 per cent of the final liability and the payment of the balance within one month of determination of the appeal. The estimate or assessment must be made within four years for periods ending after 1 May 2003 (six years for periods ending between 1 May 1998 and 1 May 2003 and ten years for periods ending before 1 May 1998) except in cases involving fraud or neglect. *[VATA 1972, ss 22, 23, 30; VAT(A)A 1978, s 17; FA 1985, s 47; FA 1992, s 185; FA 1995, s 136; FA 1998, s 115; FA 1999, s 136; FA 2000, ss 117, 118; FA 2001, s 196; SI 63/79, reg 13; SI 277/92; SI 295/ 00; SI 512/03]*.

Advance payment. On 1 December 1993 and annually thereafter until 1 December 1995, an advance payment was required of one-twelfth of the total net tax due for the 'relevant period', provided that the total net tax due for that period exceeded £1,000,000 (£300,000 on 1 December 1993 only). The '*relevant period*' was the year ending on 30 June immediately preceding the 1 December in question (or where the person concerned became a taxable person during that year, the part of that year during which he was a taxable person). There were provisions for a late payment surcharge at the rate of 0.25 per cent per day. This provision was **abolished** with effect from 7 November 1996. *[VATA 1972, s 19(6); FA 1993, s 92(c); FA 1997, ss 107(c), 114; SI 303/93; SI 345/93; SI 342/94]*.

PAYMENT AND REFUND

39.14 The time for payment of the tax 'payable' for a taxable period (ie the amount by which the VAT chargeable on his supplies exceeds his deductible tax) is the same as for the return. Liquidators, receivers, etc making a return (see **39.13** above) may deduct the sums accounted for from proceeds of the related disposals.

Refund of tax is be due if the taxable person's deductible tax exceeds his VAT liability on his supplies. Refund is made after receipt of the return, and claims must generally be made within four years (six years for claims relating to taxable periods before 1 May 2003 for claims submitted before 1 January 2005). Refund may, however, be deferred where the business activities of the taxable person are closely interlinked with those of one or more other persons who are in arrears with returns or payments, and security may be required before repayment is made where the Revenue Commissioners consider it necessary. Tax overpaid may be repaid unless the repayment would unjustly enrich the claimant (eg if the claimant had charged VAT at too high a rate and those overcharged could not be reimbursed). [*VATA 1972, s 20; FA 1986, s 87; FA 1989, s 59; FA 1991, s 83; FA 1992, s 184; FA 1995, s 135; FA 1998, s 114; FA 2000, s 116; FA 2003, s 124; SI 63/79, reg 17; SI 512/03*]. See *SI 38/95* as regards refunds on certain medical apparatus purchased through voluntary donations, *SI 98/96* and *SI 305/99* as regards refunds on touring coaches of exempt coach operators, *SI 334/96* as regards refunds to diplomatic personnel and *SI 441/99* as regards refunds relating to gold transactions. A refund may be increased by the amount of any advance payment made in the period (see **39.13** above) or consist of the excess of any advance payment over the net tax due for the period. [*VATA 1972, ss 19(3), 20(1); FA 1993, ss 92(a), 93; FA 1997, s 108*].

Two amendments are made to *VATA 1972, s 20(5)* which deals with unjust enrichment. In principle unjust enrichment can occur in circumstances where a trader who originally overpaid tax to Revenue because of an error in law gets a windfall gain if that tax is repaid. Such a windfall gain could be considered to be unjust where the cost of the overpaid tax was not actually borne by the trader but was passed on to customers in the price the trader charged for goods and services.

Paragraph (a) provides that Revenue must make a refund of an overpaid amount unless they determine that the refund would result in the unjust enrichment of the claimant.

Paragraph (b) provides that a claim for refund of an overpaid amount must set out full details of the case and the claimant must furnish any relevant documentation requested by Revenue. It also specifies what factors Revenue will have regard to in its determination as to whether or not unjust enrichment arises, including any factors that the claimant brings to their attention. Revenue may request all reasonable information and shall refund so much of the overpaid amount as would not unjustly enrich the claimant. [*F(No 2)A 2008, s 73*]

Security. The Revenue Commissioners may serve notice on any taxable person requiring him to give security, as a condition of his supplying taxable goods or services, for the payment of any tax which is or may become due. An appeal may be made against the requirement within 21 days of the date of service of the notice. [*VATA 1972, s 23A; FA 1992, s 186*].

Interest at 0.0322 per cent per day or part thereof (1 per cent per month or part thereof before 1 September 2002) is charged on unpaid tax payable by virtue of a return or an estimated liability notice, and (from 1 September 2002) on refunds arising from over-claims for deductible input tax. Special provisions apply in the case of direct debit arrangements (see **39.13** above). Since 1 November 2003, interest is paid at the rate of 0.011 per cent per day in the case of an overpayment of tax as a result of a mistaken assumption of Revenue. The interest is calculated from the date of payment of the tax in the case of an overpayment of tax or, in the case of any other refundable amount, the 19th day of the month following the month in which the person would have been entitled to receive the refund, but where a VAT return was due the interest will be calculated from the date the return was received. Where the refund is not due to the mistaken assumption of the Revenue, interest is only payable from six months after the claim for refund is received. [*VATA 1972, s 21; FA 1978, s 46; FA 1998, s 133(3)(6); FA 2001, s 195; FA 2002, s 108; FA 2003, ss 124, 125; SI 512/03*].

APPEALS AND PROCEEDINGS

39.15 On application, the Revenue Commissioners may determine (subject to appeal) into which *Schedule*, if any, particular goods fall and whether a particular activity is an exempted activity. [*VATA 1972, s 11(1B); FA 1973, s 80(d)*]. A new provision allows a right of appeal to a person aggrieved by a determination made by the Revenue Commissioners in respect of the value of an open market supply. [*FA 2007, s 91*]

Recovery of tax and **appeals** are in general governed by similar provisions as for income tax, see **4** 'Appeals' and **25.2, 25.3** 'Payment of tax'. The requirement to pay tax on a determination of the Appeal Commissioners prior to the appeal being reheard by a judge of the Circuit Court no longer exists. [*VATA 1972, ss 24, 25; FA 1983, s 85; FA 1988, s 73; FA 1991, s 84; FA 1992, s 187; FA 1995, s 137; FA 1997, s 109; FA 1998, s 134(2); FA 2000, s 119; FA 2002, s 109; FA 2005, s 108; FA 2007, s 91; FA 2010, s 128*]

Penalties are laid down for failure to comply with various provisions, for making fraudulent returns, etc Provision is made for the recovery of such penalties, generally within six years. Inclusion of penalty of €4,000 where there's a failure to comply with the notice issued to furnish records relating to transactions in the transitional period under the special schemes for second hand means of transport and agricultural machinery.

Additional penalties have been introduced by the *Finance Act 2011, s 58*. There is a raft of new penalty provisions to ensure that penalties will apply, *inter alia*, for:

(*a*)   failure to submit a VIES return for services;

(*b*)   failure to create a Capital Good Scheme Record;

(*c*)   failure to issue a Capital Goods Scheme record where required;

(*d*)   failure to provide necessary documentation on the assignment or surrender of a legacy lease; and (*e*)   failure to notify Revenue if you cease to be a qualifying person for the purposes of having a VAT 13B authorisation.

[*VATA 1972, ss 26–31; FA 1973, ss 83, 84; FA 1976, s 57; VAT(A)A 1978, ss 18–20; FA 1982, s 86; FA 1984, s 90; FA 1992, s 188–191; FA 1994, s 98; FA 2000, s 120; FA 2001, s 197; FA 2005, s109, s110, FA 2010, s 58*].

Regulations may be made by the Revenue Commissioners on a large number of matters. [*VATA 1972, s 32; FA 1973, s 85; FA 1976, s 58; VAT(A)A 1978, s 21; FA 1984, s 91; FA 1985, s 48; FA 1986, s 88; FA 1989, s 60; FA 1992, s 192; FA 1995, s 138; FA 1999, s 137; FA 2000, s 121; FA 2003, s 130; FA 2005 s 111*].

PERSONS RESPONSIBLE

39.16 The secretary or any other officer acting as secretary for the time being of a *body of persons* is answerable, in addition to the body itself, for the compliance of the body with VAT law. [*VATA 1972, s 33*].

Agents etc. Before 1 January 2002, the Revenue Commissioners could have served notice on any person who acts on behalf of a taxable person not established in RI in relation to supplies of goods or services, or allows such supplies by a taxable person to be made on land owned, occupied or controlled by him, deeming him, from the date of service of the notice, to have made such supplies in the course of business. This provision is abolished from 1 January 2002. [*VATA 1972, s 37; FA 1992, s 193; FA 2001, s 198*].

See also **25.2** 'Payment of tax' as regards collection of certain payments in default.

FARMERS AND FISHERMEN

39.17 *Farmer* means a person who engages in at least one 'Annex A activity' in the *VATA 1972, Fifth Schedule* and whose sales consist exclusively of either:

(*a*)   supplies of agricultural produce (other than live greyhounds) and/or of 'Annex B service'; or

(*b*)   supplies as in (*a*) above and of one or more of:

   (i)   supplies of machinery, plant or equipment used in farming,

   (ii)   racehorse training services the total consideration for which has not exceeded, and is unlikely to exceed, €25,500 in any continuous period of twelve months, and

   (iii)   supplies other than those mentioned in (*a*) or in (i) or (ii) above, the total consideration for which has not exceeded that which would cause the limit referred to in either **39.8**(ii) or **39.8**(iii) above to be breached if there were no other supplies.

Where a person would be a farmer under this definition but for exceeding the limit in (*b*)(ii) above, he is a taxable person only in respect of the supply of racehorse training services and any intra-Community acquisitions of goods and certain services received from abroad. See further **39.6**, **39.8** above, **39.21**(*b*) below.

[*VATA, s 8(3A)(9); FA 1982, s 77(b)(c); FA 1983, s 79; FA 1989, s 55(b)(c); FA 1990, s 101; FA 1994, s 94(c)(d)*].

See **39.8** above as regards exemption of certain farmers from treatment as taxable persons. A farmer, or a person who would be a farmer but for the provision of racehorse training services (see above), who is not a taxable person (or is only taxable in respect of intra-Community acquisitions of goods and certain overseas services, see above) is a 'flat-rate farmer' and is entitled to levy a flat-rate addition on his supplies (see below). [*VATA 1972, s 12A; VAT(A)A 1978, s 11; FA 1982, s 81(1)(b); FA 1993, s 89(b)*].

Flat-rate addition on supplies. A flat-rate addition of **5.2 per cent** from 1 January 2007 (**4.8 per cent** from 1 January 2005, **4.4 per cent** from 1 January 2004 to 31 December 2004, **4.3 per cent** from 1 January 2001 to 31 December 2003, **4.2 per cent** from 1 March to 31 December 2000, **4.0 per cent** from 1 March 1999 to 29 February 2000, **3.6 per cent** from 1 March 1998 to 28 February 1999) of the agreed consideration is recoverable by the purchaser on supplies by a flat-rate farmer of agricultural produce or services. This does not apply to payments of agrimonetary compensation by Co-ops to flat-rate farmers. The person supplied can treat the addition as deductible tax, if an invoice is issued. It is the responsibility of the purchaser to prepare the invoice and to give the farmer a copy; if this is not done the farmer is not obliged to issue the invoice. Special rules apply to a subsequent increase or reduction in the consideration. [*VATA 1972, ss 12A, 13(3)(c), 17; VAT(A)A 1978, ss 11, 15; FA 1990, s 103; FA 1992, ss 175, 176(a), 180(c); FA 1996, s 94; FA 1997, s 105; FA 1998, s 112; FA 1999, s 129; FA 2000, s 113; FA 2001, s 189; FA 2004, s 61; FA 2005, s 105*]. The flat-rate addition is regarded as compensation for the inability of a flat-rate farmer (being not a taxable person) to deduct VAT suffered on his purchases.

Flat-rate farmers are similarly required to issue invoices in relation to certain supplies after 31 August 1999 of second-hand agricultural machinery. [*VATA 1972, s 12C; FA 1999, ss 131, 134; FA 2000, s 114; SI 443/99*].

See also Information Leaflet No 12/2001.

Fishermen. Fresh water fishing and fish farming are both 'Annex A activities' so that a person carrying on either of these activities will be a 'farmer' unless his turnover from non-fishing or non-fish-farming activities exceeds the limit referred to in (*b*)(iii) above. If he chooses not to be taxable, such a person will be entitled to the flat-rate addition, like any flat-rate farmer. A *sea fisherman* is not a taxable person (unless he elects) unless his turnover from sales to non-taxable persons (excluding non-taxable overseas buyers) exceeds the limit referred to in **39.8**(iv) above. There is no flat-rate addition for sea fishermen. Instead, seafishing vessels exceeding a gross tonnage of 15 tons are *zero-rated*, as are modifications, repairs and maintenance to such vessels, and fishing boats of 15 tons or less (and repairs etc to them), and fishing nets and other equipment, and marine diesel used in a registered seafishing vessel carry a right to *repayment* of VAT suffered (see **39.18** below). [*VATA 1972, ss 8(3)(9), 12A, 13; VAT(A)A 1978, ss 6, 11, 12; F(No 2)A 1981, s 11; FA 1983, s 79; FA 1989, s 55(a)(c); FA 1994, s 94(b)(d); SI 63/79, reg 29*].

See also **39.20** *et seq.* below as regards persons engaging in intra-Community acquisitions of goods.

RELIEF BY REPAYMENT

39.18 VAT borne by a non-taxable person may be repaid in certain cases specified in the *VAT Regulations 1979* and subsequent *Orders* (see eg *SI 353/94*). [*VATA 1972, s 13; VAT(A)A 1978, s 12; FA 1982, s 82; FA 1985, s 45; FA 1987, s 43; FA 1989, s 92; FA 1992, s 176; FA 1998, s 113; FA 2002, s 105*] See also Information Leaflet No 18/2001. The main transactions in which the person supplied (who suffers VAT as part of the consideration paid) will be entitled to repayment by the Revenue Commissioners are:

(*a*)   construction etc of farm buildings, and works of land reclamation or drainage, as regards costs incurred by a flat-rate farmer;

(*b*)   supply, modification, repair or maintenance to a fishing boat not exceeding 15 tons gross tonnage, in circumstances which qualify for State financial assistance, and supply of fishing nets and other equipment and marine diesel used in a registered sea-fishing vessel;

(*c*)   purchase of radios by an institution for the blind;

(*d*)   purchase of importation, or adaptation, of a car for a disabled driver or passenger;

(*e*)   purchase of a caravan etc for use as a residence (provided it is rateable);

(*f*)   supply of goods and services within RI for the purposes of his business to a person trading only outside RI (if a non-exempt trade), or in RI only where the recipient is treated as the taxable person (see **39.8** above), where the tax would be deductible if the business were carried on in RI (but excluding means of transport for hire out for use in RI);

(*g*)   medical equipment purchased by a hospital, university, etc, laboratory (repayment of excess over *VATA 1972, Third Schedule* rate only).

(*h*)   20 per cent of the tax charged to that accountable person in respect of the purchase, hiring, intra-Community acquisition or importation of a qualifying vehicle (within the meaning assigned by paragraph (c)), where that vehicle is used primarily for business purposes, being at least 60 per cent of the use to which that vehicle is put, and where that accountable person subsequently disposes of that vehicle the tax deducted by that person in accordance with this subsection shall be treated as if it was not deductible by that person for the purposes of paragraph (xxiv)(c) of the First Schedule [*F(No 2)A 2008, s 73*].

IMPORTS AND EXPORTS

39.19 The following applies only to transactions with **non-EU countries**. See **39.20** *et seq.* below as regards intra-community transactions.

Imported goods are chargeable to VAT at the appropriate rate (see **39.3** above) on their *value* and the tax is administered in the same way as a customs duty. Imports of exempt and zero-rated goods are both exempt. Where the import is from another Member State, the importer must provide certain information before zero-rating is allowed. [*VATA 1972, ss 11(1), 15; VAT(A)A 1978, s 14; FA 1990, s 104; FA 1991, s 82; FA 1992, s 178; FA 1996, s 96; SI 363/95; FA 2010, s 125*]

VAT is collected at the point of importation. [*FA 1982, s 84*]. See also *VAT (Imported Goods) Regulations 1982 (SI 279/82)*. The Revenue Commissioners may, under regulations, repay tax chargeable on imports in certain cases (see *VATA 1972, s 15(5A) inserted by FA 1992, s 178(c)* and **39.18**(*f*) above).

Imports of Fourth Schedule services are chargeable, see **39.5** above. Imports of other services are not chargeable.

Services connected with imports and exports are exempt, see **39.4** above.

Goods exported by the supplier are zero-rated as are goods transported to the Shannon customs-free airport.

Certain goods and services supplied to exporters are zero-rated, see **39.4** above.

Retail export scheme. Relief from VAT may be obtained on goods purchased in RI by non-EU visitors. Conditions required to be complied with to avail of zero-rating have been strengthened, If the conditions are not complied with the supply of goods is no longer eligible for zero rating. The supply of services refunding agent relating to the supply of those goods is no longer eligible for zero rating. [*FA 2010, s 123*] See Information Leaflet (April 1998). [*VATA 1972, s 13; VAT(A) s 12; FA 1992, s 176; FA 1997, s 106; FA 1998, s 113; FA 1999, s 132; SI 34/98; FA 2010, s 123*]

SUPPLIES BETWEEN EU MEMBER STATES

39.20 Since 1 January 1993, a new system replaced that previously applicable to imports and exports (see **39.19** above) in the case of 'intra-Community acquisitions of goods' and 'intra-Community transport of goods'. This includes most supplies of goods and certain supplies of transport services, with special arrangements relating to 'new means of transport' and distance selling (including mail order). The existing arrangements continue to apply to imports and exports from and to countries outside the EU, either directly or through another Member State or states where VAT has not been chargeable, and to supplies of services other than the transport services referred to above.

An '*intra-Community acquisition of goods*' is the acquisition of goods despatched or transferred from one Member State to another as the result of a supply by a person in one Member State to a person in another. Except in the case of 'new means of transport', they must also be supplied by a person registered (or obliged to be registered) for VAT (or by a person carrying on an exempted activity) in one Member State to a person in another Member State other than an individual who is not a taxable person. Goods which have been subject to VAT under the margin or auction schemes (see **39.7** above) are excluded. [*VATA 1972, s 3A(1)(1A); FA 1992, s 168; FA 1993, s 83; FA 1995, s 121; FA 1997, s 97*].

The '*intra-Community transport of goods*' is the transport of goods which actually starts in one Member State and actually ends in another. [*VATA 1972, s 5(6)(h); FA 1992, s 169(b)*].

'*New means of transport*' means land vehicles of cylinder capacity exceeding 48cc or power exceeding 7.2kW, sea craft of any type (including hovercraft) exceeding 7.5m in length, and aircraft with a take-off weight exceeding 1,550kg, intended for the transport of persons or goods, supplied either within three months of entering into service (six months in the case of land vehicles) or with usage not exceeding 6,000km, 100hrs sailing or 40hrs flying time respectively. Sea vessels and aircraft within the *VATA 1972, Second Schedule* (see **39.4** above) are excluded. [*VATA 1972, s 1; FA 1992, s 165(a)(vi); FA 1994, s 91*].

An outline of the effect of these changes is contained in **39.21** *et seq.* below. These and the very large number of detailed amendments to *VATA 1972* to give effect to the changes are (together with other general provisions) contained in *FA 1992, ss 165–195*. See also *SI 413/92, SI 54/93* and *SI 448/94*.

39.21 Intra-community acquisition of goods (other than new means of transport, see **39.22** below). The liabilities in respect of such transactions depend on the status of supplier and purchaser.

(*a*)   *Purchase by taxable person in one Member State from taxable person in another Member State.* The supply is zero-rated in the Member State of the supplier. The supply is taxable in the Member State of the purchaser at the rate applicable in that State, the tax being payable by the purchaser through the normal VAT return. The tax will normally be simultaneously deductible (subject to the usual rules as to deductibility). [*VATA 1972, ss 2(1A), 3A(2), 8(1A)(2B), 10(5A), 19(1A), Sch 2 para (i); FA 1992, ss 166, 168, 170, 172(g), 182(a), 195(2)(a)*]. See also Statement of Practice SP–VAT 8/92, October 1992 and Information Leaflet No 26/2001;

(*b*)   *Purchase by a person not registered for VAT in one Member State from taxable person in another Member State.* VAT is payable in the Member State of the supplier at the rate applicable there. The transaction is not taxable in the Member State of the purchaser. In the case of RI purchasers:

    (i)   persons who make supplies in the course or furtherance of business, but who come within the small turnover exemptions from registration (see **39.8** above) are not required to register and account for VAT on their acquisitions unless they exceed the acquisitions threshold of €41,000 in any continuous period of twelve months. If the small turnover exemption thresholds are exceeded they are required to register for VAT (and accordingly fall within (*a*) above). The registration thresholds have been increased to €35,000 in the case of services and €70,000 in the case of goods [*FA 2007, s 79*],

    (ii)   non-taxable entities and exempt businesses are similarly required to register if the €41,000 limit is exceeded (and see Information Leaflets No 11/2001 and No 13/2001) The limit does not apply if these parties also received *VATA 1972, Fourth Schedule* services in the same year,

    (iii)   private individuals are not subject to any limitation but are only liable in respect of new means of transport. See also **39.24** below as regards direct selling (eg by mail order),

    (iv)   farmers and fishermen (see **39.17** above) who would be exempt from registration (see **39.8**(i)(iv) above) but for intra-Community acquisitions of goods or the receipt of certain services from abroad (see **39.8**(*c*) above) are, unless they otherwise elect, taxable persons only in respect of such acquisitions and services. Similarly a person who would be a farmer but for the provision of racehorse training services (see **39.17**(ii)(*b*) above) and who is a taxable person by virtue of intra-Community acquisitions of goods or the receipt of certain services from abroad (see **39.8**(*c*)) is, unless he otherwise elects, a taxable person only in respect of racehorse training services and such acquisitions and overseas services.

[*VATA 1972, ss 2(1A), 8(1A)(3), 19(1A); FA 1992, ss 166, 170, 182(a); FA 1993, s 85; FA 1994, s 94(a)*].

A purchase from a non-registered person in another Member State is not an intra-Community acquisition of goods and gives rise to no VAT liabilities.

39.22 New means of transport. The intra-Community acquisition of new means of transport is, regardless of the status of the purchaser, zero-rated in the Member State of the supplier, and taxable at the applicable rate in the Member State of final delivery. There are special arrangements for payment of the tax by a purchaser who is a private individual (see *SI 412/92*) or a trader not entitled to a deduction for the tax, and for repayment of the tax where the vehicle etc is subsequently re-exported. [*VATA 1972, ss 2(1A), 8(1A)(2B), 13(3A), 19(1A)(4), Sch 2 para (i); FA 1992, ss 166, 170, 176(b), 182(a)(c), 195(2)(a); FA 1993, s 92(b); FA 1999, s 135; SI 413/92, reg 7; SI 248/93*].

39.23 Intra-Community transport of goods (and related ancillary and agency services) supplied to a person registered for VAT are taxable in the Member State which registered that person, who must account for the tax, and who will normally obtain a simultaneous deduction (subject to the usual rules as to deductibility).

Such supplies to a non-registered person are taxable in the Member State in which the transport of the goods actually started (or in the Member State in which the services are physically performed in the case of ancillary and associated agency services). New provisions have been included to cater for the accession to the EU of the Republic of Bulgaria and Romania.

[*VATA 1972, ss 5(3A), 6; FA 1992, s 169; FA 2001, s 183(a)*].

See also Information Leaflet No 16/2002 regarding transport services.

39.24 Distance selling (including mail order), where goods (other than new means of transport, see **39.22** above) are despatched by a supplier in one Member State to a non-registered person in another Member State, gives rise to VAT liability in the Member State of the supplier (see **39.21** above) *unless* the total consideration for such supplies by a supplier to a particular Member State (excluding dutiable goods) exceeds, or is likely to exceed, €35,000. Where the limit is exceeded, liability arises in the Member State where the goods are delivered, and the supplier is required to make arrangements for registration in that Member State and for accounting for the tax on such supplies.

[*VATA 1972, ss 2(1A), 3(6), 8(1A)(2B), 19(1A); FA 1992, ss 166, 167(c), 170, 182(a); FA 1999, s 120(c); SI 413/92, regs 5, 10*].

See also Information Leaflet No 8/2001.

39.25 Miscellaneous. See also:

(a)   *VATA 1972, ss 3(1)(g), 10(4B), 12(1)(a)(iib) as inserted by FA 1992, ss 167(a)(iii), 172(f), 174(a) and amended by FA 1993, s 82, FA 1994, s 92, FA 1999, ss 120(a), 124 and SI 413/92, reg 5* as regards certain transfers between branches of a business operating in different Member States and transfers of 'new means of transport' (see **39.20** above);

(b)   *VATA 1972, s 3A(4) inserted by FA 1992, s 168* as regards goods supplied to a non-taxable person in RI from outside the EU but liable to tax on importation into another Member State;

(c)   *VATA 1972, s 3B inserted by FA 1993, s 84 and SI 413/92, reg 14* as regards supplies of alcohol products (and see Statement of Practice SP–VAT 3/93, July 1993);

(d)   *VATA 1972, ss 12A(1), 13(3)(c) inserted by FA 1992, ss 175(2), 176(a)* as regards repayment of flat rate addition (see **39.18** above) on intra-Community transactions;

(e)   *VATA 1972, s 13A inserted by FA 1993, s 90 and amended by FA 1996, s 95 and FA 2001, s 192* which, in conjunction with *para (via) of Sch 2 inserted by FA 1993, s 95(b)*, zero-rates certain supplies to, and intra-Community acquisitions and importations by, persons whose output is mainly transported or dispatched from RI (and see Information Leaflet No 21/2001);

(f)   *VATA 1972, s 19A inserted by FA 1992, s 183* as regards returns of intra-Community supplies;

(g)   *SI 413/92, regs 5–7* regarding 'triangulation' (ie transactions involving more than two countries);

(h)   *SIs 196, 197/99* and Statement of Practice SP–VAT 1/99, June 1999 regarding the abolition of duty-free sales on intra-Community journeys.

TRAVEL AGENT'S MARGIN SCHEME

39.26 *Finance (No 2) Act 2008* produced significant changes for the Irish Travel industry. A Tour Operator Margin Scheme (TOMS) will be introduced with effect from 1 January 2010.

The aim of this scheme is to ensure that Irish tour operators only have to register and account for VAT in Ireland. The scheme will require the tour operator to account for VAT @ 21.5 per cent **(21% as of from 1 January 2010)** on the margin it makes from its tour operating activities. Although the tour operator will only have to account for VAT on its margin it will not be entitled to recover VAT on goods or services bought in for direct onward sale to the traveller. Tour operators will still be able to recover VAT incurred on general overhead expenses.

Finance Act 2010 inserts a new subsection to *VATA 1972, s 17* to which ensures that an accountable person's entitlement to deduct VAT incurred on accommodation at qualifying conferences will not be restricted by the operation of the travel agent's margin scheme. [*FA 2010, s 127*]

Irish tour operators that are not already VAT-registered will be required to register when the scheme comes in.

The introduction of the scheme is to bring Ireland in line with the rest of the EU.

Finance (No 2) Act 2008 inserted *VATA 1972, s 10C* to provide for a travel agent's margin scheme which came into effect on 1 January 2010. The new section transposes into Irish law the travel agent's margin scheme as provided for in *Council Directive 2006/112/EC, Arts 306-310*. The travel agent's margin scheme applies to tour operators and travel agents, acting as principals, whose supplies consist of services such as transport, accommodation etc. which they have bought-in from third parties for onward supply to travellers.

The supply of such services as a travel package is treated as a single supply. The amount on which tax is payable is the profit margin realised by the travel agent on the supply of the travel package. Travel agents will have no entitlement to deduct input VAT incurred on those bought-in services but will be entitled to deduct VAT incurred on their overheads, subject to the normal rules.

Sub-s (1) contains definitions of the key elements of the scheme. These definitions cover 'bought-in services', 'margin scheme services', 'travel agent', 'travel agent's margin' and 'travel agent's margin scheme'.

Sub-s (2) provides that margin scheme services supplied by a travel agent to a traveller are treated for VAT purposes as a single supply.

Sub-s (3) provides the rule for determining the place of supply of margin scheme services.

Sub-s (4) provides that the travel agent's margin scheme applies to services supplied in the State by a travel agent.

Sub-s (5) provides that the profit margin exclusive of tax is the amount on which tax is chargeable.

Sub-s (6) provides that a travel agent may not deduct input VAT in respect of bought-in services.

Sub-s (7) provides for the apportionment of the consideration payable for a supply which covers both margin scheme services and other goods or services.

Sub-s (8) provides that the travel agent's services are treated as intermediary services (for the purpose of zero-rating them) if the bought-in services (eg hotel services) are availed of by the traveller outside the Community.

Sub-s (9) deals with the apportionment of the travel agent's margin for a travel package that includes travel both inside and outside the Community.

Sub-s (10) provides that the travel agent must account for VAT due on margin scheme services in the normal VAT return.

Sub-s (11) provides for Revenue Commissioners' regulations which will cover, in particular, provisions for simplified accounting arrangements.

Finance (No 2) Act 2008, s 74 provided that the Revenue Commissioners may make regulations relating to the operation of the travel agent's margin scheme.

VATA 1972, First Schedule is amended to remove the exemption for agency services in the arrangement of passenger transport or accommodation with effect from 1 January 2010.

VAT CHANGES – FINANCE ACT 2008

39.27 The *Finance Act 2008* introduced a plethora of changes to the existing VAT code. The changes were primarily in relation to VAT on property but other changes were also introduced to bring the VAT legislation in line with terminology and definitions of EU Directive 2006/112/EC. The changes are being dealt with in a separate section rather than amending the existing text of the chapter. There are also transitional measures introduced for property transactions that occur prior to 1 July 2008 that fall between the old rules and the new rules, for example leases that have been entered into with time left to run as at 1 July 2008.

VAT ON PROPERTY – NEW RULES (POST 1 JULY 2008)

Old System – VATA 1972, s 4A

39.28 *VATA 1972, s 4A* is the legislative reference for the old rules on supplies of immoveable property. **(See 39.7 above)** In general, the system in relation VAT on property transactions up to 1 July 2008 was to tax the supply of a property if it had been developed since 1972 and if the supplier had an entitlement to a deduction for the VAT incurred on acquisition or development of the property. The effect of this was twofold. It applied VAT to new residential property as such properties pass to a consumer; these properties then fall out of the VAT net. In the case of commercial properties however, where the use was for a taxable business, the trader was obliged to charge VAT indefinitely on any sale. This contrasts with the position for properties that are subject to a long lease where the freehold reversion falls out of the VAT net. This led to difficulties in ascertaining the taxable status of a property particularly in relation to older properties that may have been subject to a number of transactions and where records may not be readily available.

Leases of ten years or longer in duration were treated as a supply of goods and taxed upfront.

The basis for calculating the VAT charge (the capitalised value of the lease) and the anti-avoidance legislation that underpins it were regarded as complex. Short-term leases (less than ten years) were treated as an exempt supply of a service. However, a taxpayer was entitled to waive the exemption on such leases and to choose to charge VAT on the rents. The landlord was then entitled to deduct the VAT costs on the acquisition or development of the property.

Transitional Measures VATA 1972, s 4C

There are a number of transitional measures which are intended to provide a smooth shift from the pre-1 July 2008 rules to the new rules so as to minimise any adverse effects on taxpayers. The transitional rules are contained within *VATA 1972, s 4C* and apply to a number of categories of transactions:

(*a*)   Supplies of properties that are over twenty years old and have not been made 'new' by refurbishment or adaptation for materially altered use will have no VAT liability attached to them;

(b)   The supply of properties less than twenty years old will be subject to the new rules – if the property is considered new, the supply will be taxable; otherwise, a CGS adjustment will apply unless the parties exercise the option to tax the supply;

(c)   A change of use of commercial properties less than twenty years old will be subject to a CGS adjustment;

(d)   VAT incurred by a tenant (prior to the introduction of the new system) on the capitalised value of a long lease (that is a lease of ten years or more) will be subject to the rules of the CGS where the VAT was incurred within the last twenty years;

(e)   Where a waiver of exemption applies in relation to a short-term letting the landlord will, subject to conditions, be given a number of options, that will entail either cancelling the waiver of exemption using the current rules or continuing to tax the rents until the lease expires. An amendment has been made by *F(No 2)A 2008* to ensure that the landlord cannot avoid the liability imposed under *VATA 1972, 7B(3)* simply by being part of the VAT group with the tenant. Any further lettings will be fully subject to the new rules.

Finance Act 2010, s 115 amends *VATA 1972, s 4C* which relates to the transitional measures in relation to the supplies of immoveable property. The amendment provides that the capital goods scheme will apply to transitional properties in certain circumstances. Transitional properties are properties that are subject to the VAT on property rules that applied prior to 1 July 2008 (see **39.7** above) and are disposed of, or are let, on or after 1 July 2008 under the new rules.

New Rules – VATA 1972, s 4B

The new provisions relate to the sales and letting of property. Sales of completed property can be divided into two categories – sales of new and old property. Completed property is property which can be used for the purposes for which it was designed.

New Property

The sale (supply) of a completed property which is:

(a)   A new freehold or a freehold equivalent (eg a leasehold of 99 years or greater); and

(b)   Which is developed and sold (supplied) in the course or furtherance of a business, is subject to VAT. [*VATA 1972, s 4B*]

A new property is defined as:

(i)   The first supply of a completed property within five years of its completion of development is subject to VAT;

(ii)   Any subsequent supply of a property that occurs within five years of its completion is subject to VAT if it takes place within two years of occupation and if a prior sale was subject to VAT and took place between unconnected parties. [*VATA 1972, s 4B(2)*]

Old Property

Sales of 'old' property (for example a building sold six years after completion) are exempt from VAT. Where a sale is an exempt sale, and the property is sold within its VAT life, there is an adjustment under the capital goods scheme. Where the sale of property is exempt from VAT the seller and purchaser can exercise a joint option to tax the sale. [*VATA 1972, s 4B(5)*] In such circumstances, the purchaser accounts for VAT on the sale on a reverse charge basis. Development does not include minor development. Minor development is work that does not materially alter the use of the property and which is less than 25 per cent of the consideration for the sale of the property.

Letting of Property

The letting of property is exempt from VAT, but the landlord may opt to tax a letting. The option under the new regime applies on a letting by letting basis and is not a general option applicable to all lettings. Under the old regime, a landlord could not opt to charge tax on a letting by letting basis. A waiver of exemption meant landlords had to charge. VAT on rent on all properties let on a short lease. The landlord may now opt (or not opt) to tax each letting separately. Where such an option is exercised in respect of a property, the rental payments will be subject to the standard rate of VAT. The option can be exercised either by entering a written agreement with the tenant to tax the rent or by issuing a notice to the tenant.

VATA 1972, s 4B deals with supplies of property. *Finance Act 2010, s 114* amends this section. The amendments clarify the 'joint option for taxation' provision and provide for a joint option for the taxation of the sale of a property where there is a 'forced sale'. This latter change will apply in the case of forced sales by examiners, receivers, liquidators and other bodies such as finance companies.

The option is not available where the landlord and the tenant are connected. However, this restriction does not apply where the tenant is entitled to deduct at least 90 per cent of the VAT chargeable. In addition, no option is allowed if the property is occupied by any party connected to the landlord irrespective of the tenant's entitlement to VAT recovery or whether the lessor and lessee are unconnected. The option does not apply where the property is occupied for residential purposes.

Capital Goods Scheme

The Capital Goods Scheme (CGS) is a mechanism for regulating deductibility over the 'VAT-life' of a capital good. For VAT purposes a capital good is a developed property. The scheme operates by ensuring that the deductibility for a property reflects the use to which the property is put over the VAT-life (adjustment period) of the property. The CGS is provided for in *VATA 1972, s 12E*. A feature of the scheme is a number of definitions, such as, initial interval, adjustment period, etc. These definitions reflect the various component parts of the scheme.

The VAT incurred on the acquisition or development of a property is deductible in accordance with the normal rules relating to deductibility. A person who is engaged in fully taxable economic activities is entitled to deduct all of the VAT charged on the acquisition or development of a property to be used in the business. A person who is engaged in partly taxable and partly exempt economic activities is only entitled to deduct the percentage of VAT charged that corresponds to the percentage of taxable use. It is important to note that the entitlement to deduct VAT is determined by *VATA 1972, s 12* and is independent of the CGS. The CGS is a mechanism for adjusting deductibility, not in determining entitlement to deductibility.

At the end of the first twelve months following completion (or acquisition, where the property is acquired following completion), the taxpayer must review the amount of VAT deducted on the acquisition or development of the property. If the proportion of taxable use of a property during that twelve month period differs from the proportion of the VAT deducted on the acquisition or development of that property, then an adjustment is required. If too much VAT has been deducted, the taxpayer must pay back the excess. If too little VAT has been deducted initially, the taxpayer is entitled to claim the deficiency as an input credit.

This adjusted amount deductible for the first twelve months is the benchmark figure for comparison purposes under the scheme for the remainder of the VAT-life of the property. The scheme requires an annual review, over the VAT-life of the property by the owner of the property, of the use to which a property is put (in terms of taxable or exempt use). Where there is a change in the proportion of use for taxable purposes for any year in comparison with the use during the initial 12 months, an adjustment of a proportion of the VAT deductibility will be required.

The annual adjustments will reflect the difference between the use in the initial twelve months and the use in the year being reviewed. Ultimately, the proportion of VAT deducted following all annual adjustments will reflect the actual use of the property over the adjustment period or VAT-life of the property. The VAT-life of a property is made up of twenty intervals. In the case of a refurbishment the VAT-life is ten intervals. Except in relation to the second CGS interval, a CGS interval is twelve months.

Under *VATA 1972, s 12E(1)* the scheme applies to developed immovable goods (properties) on the acquisition or development of which VAT has been charged to a 'taxable person', ie a person that is engaging in an economic activity. Under *VATA 1972, s 12E(3)* properties acquired or developed after 1 July 2008, it is provided that in most cases each capital good will have a VAT-life or adjustment period of twenty intervals. It is during this period that adjustments are required to be made. Once the period has elapsed, there are no further obligations under the scheme

A review must be carried out at the end of the first interval of twelve months, [*VATA 1972, s 12E(4)*] At the end of this period the owner must examine the use to which the property was put during that twelve months. Where the percentage of taxable use during the first year differs from the percentage of the VAT deducted by the owner on the acquisition or development of the property, then an adjustment is required. If the percentage of taxable use for the initial interval is less than the percentage of the VAT deducted on the acquisition or development of the property, VAT is payable by the owner. If the percentage of taxable use for the initial interval is greater than the percentage of the VAT deducted on the acquisition or development of the property, then the owner is entitled to additional deductible VAT. This review must be carried out at the second and subsequent intervals. [*VATA 1972, s 12E(5)*]

Where a tenant has a leasehold interest in a completed property and carries out development work on that property then the tenant 'creates' a capital good. The tenant is regarded as the owner of this capital good. This development is a refurbishment and the adjustment period is ten years. All of the obligations in relation to the initial, second and subsequent intervals above arise for the tenant in relation to the development work carried out. Any change in use must be adjusted for over the adjustment period, which is ten intervals. [*VATA 1972, s 12E(8)*]

Each owner of a capital good is required to keep a record of the capital good. [*VATA 1972, s 12E(12)*]. The record must contain the following information about the property:

(*a*)   The amount of VAT charged in relation to the owner's acquisition or development of the property

(*b*)   The amount of the VAT charged that was deducted initially

(*c*)   The date on which the adjustment period begins

(*d*)   The number of intervals in the adjustment period.

(*e*)   The Initial Interval proportion of deductible use

(*f*)   The total reviewed deductible amount

(*g*)   The proportion of deductible use for each interval

(*h*)   Details of any adjustments under the scheme

(*i*)   Details of any sale of the property

Failure to create and maintain a capital good record for each capital good is liable to a penalty in accordance with *VATA 1972, s 26*.

VAT CONSOLIDATION ACT 2010

39.29 The *Value-Added Tax Consolidation Act 2010* was signed into law on Tuesday 23 November 2010. The Act is Number 31 of 2010. The corresponding provisions in the VATA 1972 have been repealed.

Finance Act 2011, s 61 provides for the inclusion of a schedule of miscellaneous amendments to the *Value-Added Tax Consolidation Act 2010*. This Act was enacted in November 2010 and consolidated the then law relating to VAT. The consolidation process revealed a number of minor errors, eg cross-references, ambiguities, inconsistencies, etc, in the existing law. The correction of these errors was not possible in a Consolidation Bill, as it would have invalidated the Bill as a Consolidation measure. In keeping with commitments made in the debates on the Bill, the opportunity is now being taken to correct the errors.

The Bloomsbury Professional's publication 'VAT ACTS 2011' by Pat Kennedy considers the new VAT Consolidated Act and cross references all the sections from the *VATA 1972* to the new consolidated acts. For further analysis of the new consolidated Act, it is recommended that readers refer to this text.

40 Wealth Tax

40.1 Wealth tax (WT) was introduced by the *Wealth Tax Act 1975 (WTA)* **and suspended, pending abolition, by** *FA 1978, s 38*. For details, see 1983/84 or earlier editions of this book.

41 Health Contributions and Universal Social Charge

41.1 Health contributions under the *Health Contributions Act 1979* are generally payable, where the person is over the age of 16, at **two per cent** of assessable income less superannuation contributions and capital allowances. No contribution is payable where income is less than €22,880 for 2006. The exemption has been increased to €26,000 for 2009 and 2010. There is a deduction for any health contribution paid as part of pay-related social insurance contributions deducted under PAYE. Since 1 January 2004, levies apply to benefits in kind (see **34.3** 'Sch E – emoluments').

PRSI & HEALTH CONTRIBUTIONS - SELF-EMPLOYED

Class S (Self-Employed)

Tax Year 2009

Self Employed Income chargeable as below:	Total
3% PRSI and 3.333% Health Contribution on all income up to €75,036	6.333%
3% PRSI and 4% Health Contribution on all income from €75,036 to €100,100	7%
3% PRSI and 4.167% Health Contribution on all income over €100,100	7.167%

Tax Year 2010

Self Employed Income chargeable as below:	Total
3% PRSI and 4% Health Contribution on all income up to €75,036	7%
3% PRSI and 5% Health Contribution on all income over €75,036	8%

PRSI & Health Contributions - Employers/Employees

Class A (Normal rate at which contributions are made)

Tax Year 2009 (applicable from 1 January 2009 to 30 April 2009)

Employee's Income chargeable as below:	Total	Employer's rate
Earnings up to €52,000 to PRSI @ 4% plus a Health Contribution of 2%	6%	10.75%
Earnings from €52,000 to €100,100 to a Health Contribution of 2%	2%	10.75%
Earnings over €100,100 (€1,925 per week, €3,850 per fortnight and €8,342 per month) to a Health Contribution of 2.5%	2.5%	10.75%

Tax Year 2009 (applicable from 1 May 2009 to 31 December 2009)

Employee's Income chargeable as below:	Total	Employer's rate
Earnings up to €75,036 to PRSI @ 4% plus a Health Contribution of 4%	8%	10.75%
Earnings over €75,036 (€1,443 per week, €2,886 per fortnight and €6,253 per month) to a Health Contribution of 5%	5%	10.75%

Tax Year 2010

Employee's Income chargeable as below:	Total	Employer's rate
Earnings up to €75,036 to PRSI @ 4% plus a Health Contribution of 4%	8%	10.75%
Earnings over €75,036 (€1,443 per week, €2,886 per fortnight and €6,253 per month) to a Health Contribution of 5%	5%	10.75%

Employees are exempt from PRSI on the first €127 per week or €26 per week for employees on a modified PRSI rate. Employees earning €352 or less per week in 2009 or 2010 are exempt from PRSI and Health Contribution. However, where earnings exceed €352 per week in 2009 or 2010, the employee's PRSI Free Allowance remains at €127 per week or €26 per week for employees on a modified PRSI rate. Employees earning €500 or less per week in 2009 or 2010 are exempt from Health Contribution.

UNIVERSAL SOCIAL CHARGE

41.2 The *Finance Act 2011, s 3* has introduced a new Universal Social Charge effective as of 1 January 2011. This Universal Social Charge replaces the income levy and the health levy. The Universal Social Charge will be applied on an individualised basis, a charge of 2 per cent on income up to and including €10,036, a charge of 4 per cent for income in excess of €10,036 but not greater than €16,016 and a charge of 7 per cent thereafter. The charge will apply to all income in a similar manner to the Tax Acts, but including certain income which is statutorily exempt from income tax. The charge will be applied before granting relief for pension contributions. There will be an age-related exemption to the 7 per cent rate for persons aged over 70 years.

An exemption threshold of €4,004 will apply so as to exclude those on very low incomes. Where this threshold is exceeded, the Universal Social Charge will be payable on all income.

Rate	Employed	Self Employed
0%	14,004	4,004
2%	10,036	10,036
4%	10,037–16,016	10,037–16,016
7%	Over 16,016	16,017–100,000
10%		Over 100,000

The increased rate of 10% for self employed individuals doesn't apply where that individual is over 70 years of age and has a medical card. The increased rate of 10% to self employed individuals and the reduced rate to medical card holders will not apply after the year 2015.

The USC will apply to gains from profit sharing schemes, approved saving related schemes and approved share option schemes. There will be a deduction allowable for trading losses and capital allowances where the individual is actively involved in the trade. The USC will apply before a deduction for certain capital allowances and also certain donations. Maintenance payments to separated spouses will still be available as a deduction in certain circumstances.

The tax free element of ex-gratia payments, employment income to which the remittance basis applies to and PAYE income paid under an exclusion order to individuals resident in a tax treaty country are all outside the USC charge.

Irish and EU deposit interest together with gains from certain investment undertakings are exempt from the USC. A special USC rate of 45% will apply to certain bonus payments made to employees of certain financial institutions covered by the Bank Guarantee Scheme.

The apparent saving for an employee has been eroded by the removal of the ceiling for PRSI. The net effect for employees and self employed individuals is set out in the table below.

Combined PRSI/Income Levy &Health Levy versus PRSI/USC

41.3

Earnings	2010 Employee	2011 Employee	2010 Self Employed	2011 Self Employed
<€75,036	10%	11%	9%	11%
>€75,036	9%	11%	12%	11%
>€100,000	9%	11%	12%	14%
>€174,980	11%	11%	14%	14%

42 Stamp Duty

42.1 Stamp duty is a tax has been in existence for some 300 years. There were a number of consolidating statutes in *SA 1804*, *SA 1870* and *SA 1891* and these formed the core legislative provisions in relation to stamp duty. Subsequent more recent legislation heavily amended stamp duty law, resulting in the *Stamp Duties Consolidation Act, 1999* (*SDCA 1999*). While the *SDCA 1999* amends and consolidates the law, the opportunity was not taken to update and re-examine the taxation of stamp duty. Therefore the *SDCA 1999* merely served to consolidate established principles but did not attempt to extend or simplify stamp duty. *Finance Act 1991* replaced the mandatory nature of stamp duty with voluntary stamp duty where the imposition is now on the person connected with the document to return tax. Stamp duty differs from most other taxes in that it applies to instruments and not transactions as with all of the other capital taxes.

BASIS OF CHARGE

42.2 The main charging provision for stamp duty is *SDCA 1999, s 2(1)* of which states:

'2(1) Any instrument which:

    (a) is specified in Schedule 1, and

    (b) is executed in the State or, wherever executed, relates to any property situated in the State or any matter or thing done or to be done in the State, shall be chargeable with stamp duty.'

SDCA 1999, s 2(1)(b). To fall within the basic charging provision there must be a chargeable instrument listed in *SDCA 1999, Sch 1* and that instrument must fall within the provisions of *SDCA 1999, s 2(1)(b)* outlined above. To be chargeable to stamp duty an instrument must be one of those listed in *SDCA 1999, Sch 1* which sets out categories of instruments which are within the charge to stamp duty and their applicable rate of duty. The rules dictating which head of charge a document is chargeable under are determined either because the document is listed under a particular head in *SDCA 1999, Sch 1*, it is deemed to be a particular type of document by legislation, or held to be so treated under case law.

SDCA 1999, s 1(1). As mentioned in the introduction above, stamp duty is a mandatory tax since 1991. *SDCA 1999, s 1(1)* lists the categories of accountable persons, being the persons liable for the payment of stamp duty on an instrument. Any unpaid stamp duty (and any surcharges and/or penalties) is a debt due by the accountable person to the Minister for Finance for the benefit of the Central Fund. The debt may be recovered by legal action at the instance of the Attorney General, the Minister for Finance or the Revenue Commissioners. In addition, the Revenue Commissioners may raise an assessment for stamp duty payable even if the document is not actually presented for stamping.

RATES

42.3 The rate of stamp duty applicable to an instrument depends on a number of factors. The first of these is whether the document is transferring residential property or non-residential property. Different rates apply to the two types of property. As the name suggests, residential property is exactly that and non-residential property is all other forms of property such as; goodwill, sites. Residential property is sub-divided into first time buyer rates and full rates. Transfers of shares are stampable at a rate of **1 per cent**.

Stamp duty is levied at the appropriate rate on the consideration passing for the transfer. *SDCA 1999, s 44* provides that duty is levied on the market value of the property conveyed on any instrument where the consideration cannot be ascertained, provided that such instrument would have been liable to duty had the consideration been ascertainable. *Finance Act 2010, s 136* contains an anti-avoidance provision in relation to the avoidance of stamp duty through a contrived creation and use of a debt as consideration. The amendment provides that a debt, where paid by a person other than the transferee, is to be included for stamp duty purposes as consideration for the conveyance of the property.

Finance Act 2011, s 63 has abolished a number of property reliefs as of from 8 December 2010.

The rates applicable to property are as follows:

The new stamp duty rates applicable to the purchase of all residential properties on or after 8 December 2010 are as follows:

Aggregate Consideration	*First Time Buyer*	*Full Purchaser*
First €1,000,000	1%	1%
Balance	2%	2%

New Rates were introduced in 2008 for residential property for non-first time buyers (investors and owner occupiers):

Consideration	*Rate*
First €125,000	Nil
Next €875,000	7%
Excess over €1,000,000	9%

New Rates were introduced on 31 March 2007 to 8 December 2010 for residential property for first time buyers:

A full exemption from stamp duty was introduced in respect of the purchase of residential property by a qualifying first time buyer.

For instruments executed on or after 2 December 2004 and before 31 March 2007:

Aggregate Consideration	*First Time Buyer*	*Full Rate*
Up to €127,000	Exempt	Exempt
€127,000–190,500	Exempt	3%
€190,501–254,000	Exempt	4%
€254,001–317,500	Exempt	5%

€317,501–381,000	3%	6%
€381,001–635,000	6%	7.5%
Over €635,000	9%	9%

NON-RESIDENTIAL PROPERTY

For instruments executed on or after 15 October 2008:

Aggregate Consideration	*Rate of Duty*
Not exceeding €10,000	*Exempt
€10,001–€20,000	1%
€20,001–€30,000	2%
€30,001–€40,000	3%
€40,001–€70,000	4%
€70,001–€80,000	5%
Over €80,000	6%

Non-residential property executed on or after 1 January 2001

Aggregate Consideration	*Rate of Duty*
Not exceeding €10,000	*Exempt
€10,001–€20,000	1%
€20,001–€30,000	2%
€30,001–€40,000	3%
€40,001–€70,000	4%
€70,001–€80,000	5%
€80,001–€100,000	6%
€100,001–€120,000	7%
€120,001–€150,000	8%
Over €150,000	9%

Changeover to euro 1 January 2002

Residential Property only

Aggregate Consideration	*First Time Buyer*	*Full Rate*
Up to €127,000	Exempt	Exempt
€127,000–190,500	Exempt	3%
€190,501–254,000	3%	4%
€254,001–317,500	3.75%	5%
€317,501–381,000	4.5%	6%
€381,001–635,000	7.5%	7.5%
Over €635,000	9%	9%

Non-Residential Property Only

Aggregate Consideration	Rate of Duty
Up to €6,350	Exempt
€6,351–12,700	1%
€12,701–19,050	2%
€19,051–31,750	3%
€31,751–63,500	4%
€63,501–76,200	5%
Over €76,200	6%

6 December 2001

Residential Property Only

Aggregate Consideration	First Time Buyer	Full Rate
Up to £100,000	Exempt	Exempt
£100,001–150,000	Exempt	3%
£150,001–200,000	3%	4%
£200,001–250,000	3.75%	5%
£250,001–300,000	4.5%	6%
£300,001–500,000	7.5%	7.5%
Over £500,000	9%	9%

27 January 2001

Residential Property Only

	First Time Buyer	Owner/Occupier	Investor(New)	Investor(2nd)
Up to £100,000	Nil	Nil	3%	9%
£100,001–150,000	Nil	3%	3%	9%
£150,001–200,000	3%	4%	4%	9%
£200,001–250,000	3.75%	5%	5%	9%
£250,001–300,000	4.5%	6%	6%	9%
£300,001–500,000	7.5%	7.5%	7.5%	9%
Over £500,000	9%	9%	9%	9%

15 June 2000

Residential Property Only

	First Time Buyer	Owner Occupier	Investor
Up to £100,000	Nil	Nil	9%
£100,001–150,000	Nil	3%	9%
£150,001–200,000	3%	4%	9%
£200,001–250,000	3.75%	5%	9%
£250,001–300,000	4.5%	6%	9%

| £300,001–500,000 | 7.5% | 7.5% | 9% |
| Over £500,000 | 9% | 9% | 9% |

23 April 1998

Residential Property Only

Up to £60,000	Nil
£60,001–100,000	3%
£100,001–170,000	4%
£170,001–250,000	5%
£250,001–500,000	7%
Over £500,000	9%

23 January 1997

Up to £5,000	Nil
£5,001–10,000	£1.00 per £100 or part thereof
£10,001–15,000	£2.00 per £100 or part thereof
£15,001–25,000	£3.00 per £100 or part thereof
£25,001–50,000	£4.00 per £100 or part thereof
£50,001–60,000	£5.00 per £100 or part thereof
Over £60,000	£6.00 per £100 or part thereof

Transition period: Contract dated prior to 23.01.1997 subsequent deed dated on or before 30.04.1997

Residential Property Only

£150,001–160,000	£7 per £100 or part thereof
£160,001–170,000	£8 per £100 or part thereof
Over £170,000	£9 per £100 or part thereof

1 September 1990

Up to £5,000	Nil
£5,001–10,000	£1.00 per £100 or part thereof
£10,001–15,000	£2.00 per £100 or part thereof
£15,001–25,000	£3.00 per £100 or part thereof
£25,001–50,000	£4.00 per £100 or part thereof
£50,001–60,000	£5.00 per £100 or part thereof
Over £60,000	£6.00 per £100 or part thereof

A separate head of charge covering conveyances or transfers on sale of certain policies of insurance and policies of life insurance was created in 1992

28 January 1988

Up to £1,000	Nil
£1,001–2,000	25p per £50 or part thereof
£2,001–6,000	50p per £50 or part thereof
£6,001–7,500	See list aside*
£7,501–10,000	£1.00 per £50 or part thereof
£10,001–20,000	£1.50 per £50 or part thereof

£20,001–50,000	£2.00 per £50 or part thereof
£50,001–60,000	£2.50 per £50 or part thereof
Over £60,000	£3.00 per £50 or part thereof

14 May 1975

Up to £1,000	Nil
£1,001–2,000	25p per £50 or part thereof
£2,001–6,000	50p per £50 or part thereof
£6,001–7,500	(see list aside)
£7,501–10,000	£1.00 per £50 or part thereof
£10,001–20,000	£1.50 per £50 or part thereof
£20,001–50,000	£2.00 per £50 or part thereof
Over £50,000	£3.00 per £50 or part thereof

17.07.1982
½ rate introduced for relatives where consideration exceeds £1,000

4 August 1973

1949 –16.07.1982
1% for relatives where consideration exceeds £6,000

*List of scale rates 04.08.1973–01.08.1990

Up to £1,000	Nil		
£1,001–2,000	25p per £50 or part thereof	£6,001–6,250	£70
£2,001–6,000	50p per £50 or part thereof	£6,251–6.500	£80
£6,001–7,500	(*see scale rate list aside)	£6,501–6,750	£90
£7,501–10,000	£1.00 per £50 or part thereof	£6,751–7,000	£100
£10,001–50,000	£1.50 per £50 or part thereof	£7,001–7,250	£110
Over £50,000	£2.50 per £50 or part thereof	£7,251–7,500	£120

7 May 1969

Scale rate (0.5% to 2%) up to £2,500
1% for relatives (grant houses exempt)
2% up to £6,000
3% up to £50,000
Reduced scale rate under £500

1 August 1951

Scale rate (0.5% approx) to £500
1% for grant approved and relatives
Scale rate (1% to 3%) up to £1,000

1 December 1947

Scale rate (0.5% approx) to £500
1% for grant approved and relatives
Scale rate (1% to 3%) up to £1,000

29 April 1910

Scale rate (0.5% approx) to £500

1 January 1892

Scale rate (0.5% approx) to £300

ADMINISTRATION, RETURNS AND ASSESSMENT

42.4 Stamp duty is a tax on documents. The accountable person is the person who must return the tax. The accountable person varies depending on the class of instrument in the transaction. [*SDCA 1999, s 1*]

Accountable person

Instrument Heading	Accountable Person
(1)	(2)
Conveyance or transfer on sale of any stocks or marketable securities	Purchaser or transferee
Conveyance or transfer on sale of any property other than stocks or marketable securities or a policy of insurance or a policy of life insurance	Purchaser or transferee
Duplicate or counterpart of any instrument chargeable with any duty	The person listed as accountable for the original
Lease	The lessee
Voluntary disposition inter vivos under *SDCA 1999, s 30* or *SDCA 1999, s 54*	All the parties to the instrument
Any other instrument not specified above table	All the parties to the instrument

Timing of Payment. Stamp duty is payable within 30 days of the first execution of the instrument unless it is submitted for adjudication within the first execution of the instrument whereby the instrument must be stamped in accordance with the assessment of the Revenue Commissioners within 14 days of the issue of the Notice of Assessment. [*SDCA 1999, s 2(3)(b)*] When an instrument is presented for stamping, it must set out all factors which affecting the liability of the instrument. This can also be contained in an adjoining letter in circumstances where it is inappropriate to include same in the actual instrument. Where an instrument qualifies for an exemption is does not need to be presented for stamping once the correct transaction certificate has been inserted in the document. Certain reliefs require the document to be submitted for adjudication. (See below).

SDCA 1999, s 14 is amended to facilitate the introduction of the e-stamping (see below) by providing for an incentive to encourage the presentation to Revenue of instruments executed before the enactment of the Bill in respect of which stamp duty chargeable has not been paid within the prescribed period of 30 days. Provided such instruments are presented to the Revenue for stamping before the expiration of the period of 56 days commencing on the enactment of the Bill, together with the stamp duty chargeable on such instruments and appropriate interest, a penalty will not be applied to such instruments. The measure is intended, in anticipation of the introduction of e-stamping, to facilitate the smooth transition to e-stamping. [*F(No 2)A 2008, s 80*]

E-Stamping. *SDCA 1999* is amended to allow for the introduction of the e-stamping of instruments for stamp duty purposes. In recent years, Revenue has developed an on-line system (ROS) to facilitate the submission of returns and the payment of taxes on line. Revenue us currently engaged in a major strategic development that will see the introduction of a self service e-stamping system. That system will allow a full 24/7 self service on-line process where the user can file, pay and receive an instant stamp without Revenue requiring to see the instrument in up to 90 per cent of cases. The amendments make technical, definitional and other necessary changes to the stamp duty legislation in advance of the implementation of the e-stamping system. Finally, the section will be the subject of a Commencement Order. It is thought that the Commencement Order will coincide with the finalisation of Regulations governing the e-stamping system. [*F(No 2)A 2008, s 81*]

Adjudication. Adjudication is a procedure whereby the Revenue Commissioners give an opinion on whether a document is assessable to stamp duty and in the event that it is assess the liability attaching to same. [*SDCA 1999, s 20*] A person may opt to submit a document for adjudication and this is where there are complications with the document. There are certain situations in which adjudication is obligatory. The main categories include, inter alia:

(*a*) Conveyances, leases or intervivos transfers which operate as a voluntary conveyance [*SDCA 1999, s 30*];

(*b*) Conveyances of transfers in contemplation of a sale [*SDCA 1999, s 33(3)*]. *SDCA 1999, s 34*[was amended to include schemes involving the exchange of property and applies to instruments executed on or after 20 November 2008 [*F(No 2)A 2008, s 82*];

(*c*) Conveyances availing of sub-sale relief [*SDCA 1999, s 46(6)*];

(*d*) Transfers between associated companies [*SDCA 1999, s 79*];

(*e*) Transfers of property availing of Reconstruction and Amalgamation Relief [*SDCA 1999, s 80*];

(*f*) Transfers to Young Trained Farmers Relief [*SDCA 1999, s 81*];

(*g*) Transfers availing of Farm Consolidation Relief [*SDCA 1999, s 81C*];

(*h*) Transfers of a Site to a Child [*SDCA 1999, s 83A*];

(*i*) Conveyances or transfers or leases to charities for charitable purposes [*SDCA 1999, s 82(1)*];

(*j*) Transfers availing of Consanguinity Relief [*SDCA 1999, Sch 1 para 1*];

(*k*) Where the Revenue Commissioners so require [*SDCA 1999, s 20*].

Transaction certificates. Certificates are used in instruments in two situations; either to avail of a lower rate of stamp duty or where an exemption from stamp duty is to be claimed. Where the correct certificate has not been included, the document may be liable to the maximum rate of stamp duty. The furnishing of an incorrect certificate is a Revenue Office. See Revenue Leaflet SD10A which outlines the certificates to be included in certain instruments.

Appeals. An accountable person who is dissatisfied with an assessment of stamp duty made by the Revenue Commissioners is entitled to appeal against such assessment to the Appeal Commissioners where [*SDCA 1999, s 21(2)*] the instrument was executed on or after 23 May 1994. An appeal may only be lodged following payment of the duty in accordance with the assessment. [*SDCA 1999, s 21*] Where an accountable person is disputing the Revenue Commissioners' valuation of land for the purpose of an assessment the matter must be referred to the Land Values Reference Committee. The provisions of *Pt 1* apply to appeals on assessments of stamp duty to the Appeal Commissioners save to the extent modified by *SDCA 199, s 21*. Notice of intention to appeal must be given in writing to the Revenue Commissioners within 30 days after the date of the assessment.

The determination of the Appeal Commissioners is final and conclusive unless:

(*a*)   the matter is required by the accountable person to be reheard by a judge of the Circuit Court. In such a case the accountable person must give notice in writing to the Revenue Commissioners within ten days after the determination of the Appeals Commissioners. At or before the time of the rehearing, the Revenue Commissioners are required to transmit to the Circuit Court judge the prescribed form in which the Appeal Commissioners' determination of the appeal is recorded.

(*b*)   an appeal is taken by way of case stated on a point of law by the accountable person or the Revenue Commissioners to the High Court from the Appeal Commissioners' determination or the Circuit Court judge's decision on a rehearing. Where either the accountable person or the Revenue Commissioners is dissatisfied with a determination of the Appeals Commissioners on a point of law, he or it must immediately after the determination declare his or its dissatisfaction to the Appeal Commissioners and, having declared such dissatisfaction, must within 21 days after the Appeal Commissioners' determination send a notice in writing to the Clerk of the Appeal Commissioners requiring the Appeal Commissioners to state and sign a case for the opinion of the High Court.

SHARES

42.5 A sale of shares in an Irish registered company for a cash consideration will be chargeable to stamp duty under the 'Conveyance or Transfer on sale of any stocks or marketable securities' head of charge and be liable to duty at the rate of 1 per cent of the consideration. 'Stocks and marketable securities' are defined in *SDCA 199, s 1* and both are widely defined. The acquisition of stock or marketable securities of a company registered outside the State is exempt from Irish stamp duty unless it relates to:

(*a*)   any immovable property situated in Ireland or any right over or interest in such property; or (*b*)   any stocks or marketable securities of a company which is registered in Ireland (except a company which is an investment undertaking within the meaning of *s 739B*). [*SDCA 1999, s 88*]

The accountable person for stamp duty in relation to the transfer of shares is the purchaser. [*SDCA 1999, s 2*] Usually a sale of shares will be executed using two documents. The share purchase agreement transfers the beneficial interest in the shares and the stock transfer form transfers the legal interest. It is the stock transfer form that is the chargeable document for the purposes of stamp duty. There is a requirement for company law purposes that the purchaser's name must be entered onto the share register and the stock transfer forms are required to do this. As such, stock transfer forms are always executed in relation to the sales of shares in an Irish company.

CONTRACTS TREATED AS CONVEYANCES ON SALE

42.6 The definition for conveyance on sale is extremely wide. However, certain instruments fall outside the scope of the definition. One of the limitations of the definition is that where an instrument does not actually transfer title to the property, it is not a conveyance. The other limitation is that the transfer has to be 'on sale'. Case law and legislation have extended the scope by introducing *SDCA 1999, s 31* which brings certain contracts or agreements within the charge to stamp duty. [*SDCA 1999, s 31*] *SDCA 1999, s 31* is a general provision that deems contracts or agreements for the sale of property to be conveyances on sale (unless they are specifically exempted). The contracts exposed to stamp duty under this section are any written contracts or agreements for the sale of:

(*a*)   any equitable estate or interest in any property (with no exceptions). This is usually referred to as the first limb; or

(*b*)   any estate or interest in any property, except the following:

   (i)   immovable property situate in the State,

   (ii)   property locally situate out of the State,

   (iii)   goods, wares or merchandise,

   (iv)   stock or marketable securities, not including share warrants issued under *CA 1963, s 88*,

   (v)   any ship or vessel or aircraft or any part interest in such property.

This is usually referred to as the second limb.

Any such contract shall be charged with *ad valorem* duty as if it was an actual conveyance on sale of the interest in the property contracted to be sold. The charge to duty under (*a*) applies to the equitable interest only. It is important to note that the charge to duty under (*b*) refers to the legal title of property. The exceptions to the charge under (*b*) are inserted to prevent a double charge to duty arising.

Where a purchaser has paid *ad valorem* duty and then enters into a contract or agreement for sale of the acquired beneficial interest before having obtained a conveyance or transfer of the property and the consideration for the sale is in excess of the consideration for the purchase, the stamp duty is paid at the *ad valorem* rate on the excess consideration [*SDCA 1999, s 31(2)*]. If the consideration is not in excess of the original consideration then it is charged with a fixed duty.

Where *ad valorem* stamp duty has been paid at contract stage and a conveyance or transfer is then made to the purchaser or subpurchaser, the conveyance or transfer shall not be chargeable with any duty and upon application to the Revenue Commissioners they can either:

(*a*)   denote the payment of *ad valorem* duty upon the conveyance or transfer; or

(*b*)   transfer the *ad valorem* duty to the conveyance or transfer upon the production of the original contract or agreement duly stamped. [*SDCA 1999, s 31(3)*]

The accountable person for duty under these provisions is the purchaser [*SDCA 1999, s 31(4)*]. A contract or agreement for the sale of a number of assets in consideration of a single payment may have to be apportioned amongst the various assets for stamp duty purposes. The stamps branch provide a Form ST22 upon which apportionment should be carried out.

DEEMED CONVEYANCES ON SALE

42.7 The concept of conveyance on sale has been extended in the legislation to bring within the charge to stamp duty certain instruments referred to as 'deemed conveyances on sale'. There are currently eleven deemed conveyances on sale in the SDCA and all are dealt with in separate sections. In brief the list of 'deemed conveyances on sale' is as follows:

Instruments that are not conveyances:

1.   certain contracts to be chargeable as conveyances on sale [*SDCA 1999, s 31*];

2.   resting in contract [*SDCA 1999, s 31A*];

3.   licence agreements [*SDCA 1999, s 31B*];

4.   agreements in connection with, or in contemplation of, sale [*SDCA 1999, s 34*];

5.   certain contracts for sale of leasehold interests to be chargeable as conveyances on sale [*SDCA 1999, s 36*];

6.   deeds of enlargement [*SDCA 1999, s 35*];

7.   surrender and merger of leasehold interest [*SDCA 1999, s 67*];

Instruments that are not sales:

8.   conveyance or transfer in contemplation of sale [*SDCA 1999, s 33*];

9.   voluntary dispositions inter vivos chargeable as conveyances or transfers on sale [*SDCA 1999, s 30*];

10.   sale of an annuity or right not before in existence [*SDCA 1999, s 32*];

11.   partitions or divisions [*SDCA 1999, s 38*];

12.   exchanges [*SDCA 1999, s 37*];

13.   calculation of ad valorem duty on stock and securities [*SDCA 1999, s 40*];

14.   how conveyance in consideration of debt, etc., to be charged [*SDCA 1999, s 41*].

42.8 The charge to duty under the lease head arises on the creation of a lease, and in certain circumstances on executing an agreement for the creation of a lease, of lands, tenements or heritable subjects. The duty is charged on the rent payable under the lease and any premium payable, and the rate of duty is ascertained by reference to the term created by the lease.

Premium. The rate of stamp duty applicable to the premium is calculated by reference to the consideration passing and not to the term of the lease whether definite or indefinite. Any consideration (other than the rent) consisting of money, stock or security moving either to the lessor or to any other person. The rate will be determined based on whether the property transferring is residential or non-residential property. As outlined above.

Rent. The rate of duty payable on the rent is ascertained by reference to the term of years granted or deemed to be granted by the lease. Stamp duty is charged on the average annual rent payable under the lease. The date of creation of the lease may differ from the commencement date. If the date of creation of the lease is subsequent to the commencement date then the expired period of the lease is taken into account in calculating the term, then stamp duty is chargeable on the lease as of the date of creation. Duty is chargeable under three terms:

(*a*)   where the term does not exceed 35 years or is indefinite (1 per cent);

(*b*)   if the term exceeds 35 years but does not exceed 100 years (6 per cent); and

(*c*)   if the term exceeds 100 years (12 per cent).

There is an exemption for residential leases for a term less than one year where the rent under the lease is less than €30,000.

The transfer of an existing lease is chargeable under the conveyance on sale head of charge.

PROPERTY

42.9 *Finance Act 2011* has implemented the changes to the stamp duty property regime as announced in the Budget on 7 December 2010.

The Act has abolished the following stamp duty reliefs:

(*a*)   transfer of a site to a child;

(*b*)   owner occupier relief;

(*c*)   first time buyer relief (except in relation to houses purchased for incapacitated persons in certain limited circumstances);

(*d*)   consanguinity relief on the transfer of residential property,

There are transitional measures where a first time buyer had signed a contract for the purchase of a residential property in advance of 8 December, first time buyer's relief will continue to apply on the purchase provided the deed of transfer is signed before 1 July 2011.

The new stamp duty rates applicable to the purchase of all residential properties are as follows:

Aggregate Consideration	First Time Buyer	Full Purchaser
First €1,000,000	1%	1%
Balance	2%	2%

[*FA 2011, s 66*]

The previous exemption from stamp duty on transfers of residential property valued under €127,000 is abolished. The section also incorporates transitional arrangements where a purchaser had entered into a binding contract before Budget day and executes the instrument before 1 July 2011. In this situation, the changes will not result in an increase in the amount of stamp duty payable.

Residential Property. Prior to 8 December 2010, there werea number of reliefs available from stamp duty in respect of residential property. The applicability of the reliefs depended on whether a purchaser is an owner occupier, a first time buyer or an investor. If an individual qualified as a first time buyer, they automatically qualified as an owner occupier as the conditions for a first time buyer encompass the conditions for an owner occupier. An owner occupier does not have to be a first time buyer. The definitions are as follows:

First time buyer. A first time buyer is a person who has not, either jointly or individually, purchased or built a residential house or apartment and where the property purchased is occupied by the purchaser, or a person on his behalf, as his/her only or principal place of residence and where no rent, other than rent obtained under rent a room arrangements, is derived from the property for a period of two years from the date of the purchase. Prior to 5 December 2007, the period where no rent could be obtained was five years. Under the Finance Act 2008, this period has been reduced from five years to two years for deeds executed on or after the 5 December 2007. For instruments executed before 5 December 2007, to the extent that a dwelling house or apartment is rented out on or after 5 December 2007, it will not involve a clawback of the relief where this occurs in the third, fourth or fifth year of ownership.

The Revenue have granted concessionary relief where a parent is acting as a co-mortgagor as follows:

> Revenue is prepared to accept that a child, who is a first time buyer, will not be precluded from claiming first time buyer relief where a parent acts as a co-mortgagor in the following circumstances:
>
> (*a*)   the transfer of the house is taken in the name of the child.
>
> (*b*)   it is the intention of both the child and the parent that the parent is not to take a beneficial interest in the house.
>
> (*c*)   the parent has been joined into the mortgage solely at the request of the lending institution for the purpose of providing additional security for the monies being advanced for the purchase.
>
> (*d*)   it is not intended that the parent will be contributing to the repayment of the mortgage in the normal course.

Where the four conditions set out above are satisfied, Revenue will treat the parent as effectively acting in the role of guarantor for the loan. Where the purchase monies are being provided by someone who is not a first time buyer they should be unconditionally gifted to the first time buyer.

Deemed first time buyers. There are two particular situations where a person is deemed to be a first time buyer.

(*a*)   The trustees of a trust (to which *s 189A* applies), whose trust funds are raised by public subscriptions for the benefit of permanently incapacitated persons, in respect of the first house(s) bought after the establishment of the trust, for occupation by the beneficiary or if more than one, each of the beneficiaries.

(*b*)   A spouse to a marriage the subject of a decree of judicial separation, a deed of separation, a decree of divorce or a decree of nullity in the case of the first acquisition of a house by the spouse following the separation or divorce provided that the spouse had, in relation to the former marital home:

    (i)   not retained an interest in that home;

    (ii)   immediately prior to the date of the decree of deed of separation is not beneficially entitled to an interest in a house other than the marital home;

    (iii)   there is no longer a strict requirement that the former spouse still occupies the family home prior to the claimant spouse acquiring a new property.

(*c*)   Where two or more persons have acquired a property jointly and qualified as first-time purchasers and subsequently one of them buys out the other person's share in the house, the purchaser buying out the interest will be treated as a first time purchaser.

Owner Occupier. An owner occupier as a person who purchases a house which is to be occupied by the purchaser, or a person on his behalf, as his only or principal place of residence and no rent, other than rent under the rent-a-room scheme, is derived from the property for a period of five years from the date of the purchase.

Investor. An investor includes any person who does not qualify as a first-time purchaser or an owner occupier. For example, a person who purchases a second home or a holiday property is regarded as an investor, even if the property is not rented. This is because the property is not occupied as a principal private residence.

Rent a Room Relief. Under this scheme there is no clawback of the first time buyer relief where rent is received by the person in occupation of the house, on or after 6 April 2001, for the letting of furnished accommodation in **part** of the house. Provided that the purchaser continues to occupy the house as his or her PPR for the relevant period, a clawback of stamp duty will not arise even where the rent received is in excess of the annual threshold which applies for income tax purposes. This threshold has been increased from €7,620 to €10,000 for the tax year 2008 and beyond.

Owner occupier reliefs:

(*a*)   This relief is for owner occupiers of new properties. There is a stamp duty exemption for new houses or apartments that have a qualifying floor area certificate that the property is under 125 sq metres. [*SDCA 1999, s 91A*] (*b*)   This is an owner occupier relief for new houses or apartments that exceed the floor area of 125 sq metres. [*SDCA 1999, s 92*]

The relief is as follows:

In respect of a site and construction contract the larger of:

(i)   the site cost

or

(ii)   25 per cent of the total cost of the site and construction

Where the purchase is of a conveyance of a completed new house or apartment 25 per cent of the total cost. [*SDCA 1999, s 92(1)(a)(iii)*] The stamp duty rate is applied to this 25 per cent cost.

First Time Buyer Relief

There is a complete exemption from stamp duty for first time buyers in respect of any purchase of residential dwelling. [SDCA 1999, s 92]

Prior to *FA 2007* the relief for first time buyers operated as follows:

Reduced stamp duty rates to applied to the purchase of both new and second-hand properties. The reduced rate was applied after the application of either *SDCA 1999, s 91A* or *92*. This relief does not apply even where a person has bought a property in a fiduciary or nominee capacity. [*SDCA 1999, s 92B(1)(b)(ii)*]

Clawback of Reliefs. A person who has availed of any of the reliefs above must remain an owner occupier that does not derive rent (except Rent-a-Room Relief) from the property. The clawback period was reduced from five years to two years by *FA 2008*. The Revenue must be notified within 6 months of the date of the receipt of the rent. The clawback consists of the amount of stamp duty that would have been payable should the reliefs not apply less the duty (if any) that was paid.

Commercial Property. Commercial property does not have any reliefs attaching to same and is liable to stamp duty at the non-residential property rates. This means that any property which is not residential that is transferred for consideration exceeding €150,000 will be liable to stamp duty at a rate of 9 per cent. The rates were amended under *Finance (No 2) Act 2008, s 87*. The new rates applicable to non residential property in respect of instruments executed on or after 15th October 2008.

Aggregate consideration	Rate
Not exceeding €10.000	Exempt
€10,001–€20,000	1%
€20,001–€30,0000	2%
€30,001–€40,000	3%
€40,001–€70,000	4%
€70,001–€80,000	5%
Over €80,000	6%

There are special rules relating to commercial property that is transferred together with a contract for the completion of the construction of the property on the site. There are two rules for calculating stamp duty on commercial contracts where there are contracts both for the site and the building works. The treatment depends on whether the contracts are regarded as interlocked or whether they are entirely separate. Where the commercial property is already fully or at least substantially completed and regardless of whether they are interlocked or not, stamp duty is calculated on the total purchase consideration at the relevant commercial property rate. However, where the property is not substantially complete at the time of the purchase, stamp duty may be assessed on a lesser amount depending on the circumstances. Where the contracts are not regarded as interlocked and no substantial development has been completed, stamp duty will only be chargeable on the value of the site together with the value of the works completed at the date of the transfer. [*SDCA 1999, s 29*]

Sub-sale relief. Sub-sale relief applies where there is contract for the sale of land and before a conveyance in respect of that contract is taken, another contract is entered into for the sale of the land. So 'A' contracts to sell land to 'B' and before 'B' takes a conveyance of the land, 'B' contracts to sell the land to 'C'. The conveyance will move from 'A' to 'C' and 'C' will be the only party to pay stamp duty. The chargeable consideration will be the consideration under the contract from 'B' to 'C'. The relief operates to only charge to stamp duty the conveyance from the original vendor and the final purchaser. The relief can apply to a chain of sub-sales and also to partial sub-sales. The amount of consideration stampable is the amount passing under the final contract regardless of whether it is less or more than the original contact for sale. [*SDCA 1999, s 46*]

EXEMPTIONS AND RELIEFS

42.10

(*a*)   **Local Authority housing** which is conveyed, transferred or leased by the Local Authority under the provisions of the *Housing Acts 1966–1992* is relieved in full. [*SDCA 1999, s 93*]

(*b*)   **Industrial and provident society housing** which is conveyed, transferred or leased to a member or to a member and spouse by the society registered under the relevant Acts, is relieved in full. [*SDCA 1999, s 93*]

(*c*)   **Charities**. Any conveyance, transfer or lease of land made by or to a body established for charitable purposes in Ireland or Northern Ireland shall be relieved from duty [*SDCA 1999, s 82*], except where the charity executes a deed of enlargement [*SDCA 1999, s 35(2)*]. The relief must be claimed and the instrument stamped with a denoting stamp that it is not liable to duty in accordance with [*SDCA 1999, s 82(2)*].

(*d*)   **Consanguinity relief.** Relief is available where a conveyance effects a transfer between two people who are related by way of blood. The relief is available for both conveyance on sale and voluntary disposition. Such transactions are liable for half the duty that would have been payable under the relevant head of charge [*SDCA 1999, Sch 1 para (15)*]. The parties must be connected in one of the following ways:

lineal descendant, parent, grandparent, step parent, husband or wife, brother or sister of a parent or brother or sister, or lineal descendant of a parent, husband or wife or brother or sister (foster child is now included in the definition of child).

Finance Act 2011, s 63 has abolished this relief in relation to residential property transactions in respect of transactions on or after 8th December 2010.

(*e*)   **Transfer of a Site to a Child.** *Finance Act 2011, s 63* has abolished this relief in respect of transactions on or after 8 December 2010.The transfer or lease of a site not exceeding €500,000 from a parent to a child shall be exempt in full from stamp duty, provided the site is to be used for the construction of the child's principal private dwelling. Prior to *FA 2008* the threshold was €254,000. The definition of a child will include foster children. The site shall be no bigger than 1 acre excluding the area on which the dwelling house is constructed. [*FA 2007*] There is a limit of one site for each child and the usual clawback provisions are expected to operate. The requirement is that the child built a dwelling house to be occupied as its sole or main residence not that the house be the child's first residence. It should be noted that there is a corresponding relief from CGT for transferring a site to a child but no corresponding relief from CAT. [*SDCA 1999, s 83A*]

(*f*)   **Liquidations.** The transfer of property on liquidation by distribution in specie is not liable to stamp duty.

(*g*)   **Transfers between associated companies.** *Any transfer or conveyance between associated companies is exempt from ad valorem duty,* provided that certain conditions are met. [*SDCA 1999, s 79*] The relief applies to the conveyance on sale head, the conveyance or transfer on sale of stocks or marketable securities or the conveyance or transfer on sale of a policy of insurance, or life insurance, where the risk is located in the state, which transfers the beneficial interest in property between associated companies. The relief reduces the ad valorem stamp duty to 0 per cent on the instrument for instruments exempted after 8 February 1995. Prior to this the reduced rate was two per cent. In order to qualify for relief, the following three conditions must be satisfied:

(*a*)   the instrument must be chargeable under either the conveyance on sale head, the conveyance or transfer on sale of stocks or marketable securities or the conveyance or transfer on sale of a policy of insurance, or life insurance, where the risk is located in the state;

(*b*)   the beneficial interest must be transferred; and

(*c*)   the transfer must take place between associated companies.

Associated for the purposes of this section means that at the time of the execution of the instrument the transferor and transferee must be associated to each other to the extent that:

(i)   one body corporate was the beneficial owner of not less than 90 per cent of the ordinary share capital of the other body corporate, or a third body corporate was the beneficial owner of not less than 90 per cent of the ordinary share capital of both the transferor and the transferee, and

(ii) one body corporate is beneficially entitled to not less than *90 per cent of any profits available for distribution* (being profits available for distribution as defined in *s 414*) to the shareholders of the other body corporate, or a third body corporate is beneficially entitled to not less than 90 per cent of any profits available for distribution to the shareholders of the transferor and the transferee, and

(iii) one body corporate is beneficially entitled to not less than *90 per cent of any assets of the other body corporate available for distribution* (being assets available for distribution as defined in *s 415*) to its shareholders on a winding-up, or a third body corporate is beneficially entitled to not less than 90 per cent of any assets available for distribution to the shareholders of the transferor and the transferee on a winding-up.

(*h*) **Reconstruction and Amalgamation relief.** Any instrument effecting a reconstruction or amalgamation are exempt provided that certain conditions are met. To qualify, the following conditions have to be satisfied:

The Revenue Commissioners have to be satisfied that the scheme is a bona fide reconstruction of any company or companies or an amalgamation of any companies which qualifies with certain other conditions. [*SDCA 1999, s 80(2)*] To qualify for the relief a company with limited liability must be registered (meaning incorporated) or since 30 July 1965 the company must be established by an Act of the Oireachtas or its nominal share capital has been increased. [*SDCA 1999, s 80(2)(a)*] A transferee company must be:

(*a*) a limited liability company incorporated with a view to carrying out the reconstruction or amalgamation, which must be reflected in the objects of the memorandum of association of the company [*SDCA 1999, s 80(6)*]; or

(*b*) a limited liability company that has increased its capital with a view to carrying out the reconstruction or amalgamation which must be effected by way of resolution of the company stating the purpose of the increase [*SDCA 1999, s 80(6)*]. The increase in the share capital relates to an increase in the nominal share capital or the issue of the unissued share capital; or

(*c*) a company established by Act of the Oireachtas which is effected by Act or other authority, or a company established by Act of the Oireachtas after 1965 which has an increase in its capital with the view to acquiring the undertaking or shares of an existing company, for the purposes of reconstruction or amalgamation.

The reconstruction and amalgamation carried out under paras (*a*) to (*c*) above must result in the acquisition of either:

(i) the undertaking of an existing company; or

(ii) not less than 90 per cent of the issued share capital of an existing company.

Consideration for the acquisition, discounting any transfer to or discharged by, the transferee company of liabilities of the existing company, cannot be less than 90 per cent of the issue of shares in the transferee company where:

(*a*) an undertaking has to be acquired if shares are to be issued to the existing company or to the holders of shares in the existing company; or

(*b*) shares are to be issued to the holders of shares in the existing company in exchange for the shares held by them in the existing company. [*SDCA 1999, s 80(2)(c)(i) and (ii)*]

(*i*) **Young Trained Farmers relief.** Full relief from stamp duty is provided on the transfer of land to young trained farmers who meet certain conditions and where the instrument is executed on or after 25 March 2004. [*SDCA 1999, s 81A*] This section applies for instruments executed before the passing of *FA 2007* and contains transitional arrangements (see *sub-s (13)*) which enable the educational qualifications held before 25 March 2004, for the purposes of relief under *SDCA 1999, s 81*, to be treated as educational qualifications for the purposes of *SDCA 1999, s 81A*. The list of qualifying agricultural training courses has been amended to include the Degree in Agri-Environmental Sciences in University College Dublin. [*FA 2010, s 141*] A new section [*SDCA 1999, s 81AA*] has been included for transfers after this date. This relief was extended further to 31 December 2008 by *FA 2006*. This relief has again been extended under *F(No 2)A 2008* to 31 December 2010. *SDCA 1999, s 81A* includes new education criteria and a simplified refunds procedure. The relief applies to transfers by sale or by way of gift (ie does not extend to leases). A power to revoke the transfer whether it be contained in the instrument conveying or transferring the land itself or otherwise, will disqualify the young trained farmer from the relief. Further transitional arrangements are contained in *SDCA 1999 s 81A* and they enable the educational qualifications held before the passing of *FA 2007*. The time limit within which a young trained farmer can complete their education has been extended from three to four years. [*FA 2007*] Instruments in respect of which relief is sought must be adjudicated. Further detailed information on the required educational requirements and the relief in general are contained in the Revenue Leaflet SD 2A. A qualified young farmer must be under 35 years at the date of the execution of the instrument.

(*j*) **Commercial woodlands.** Where a conveyance or lease of land occurs consisting of trees that are managed on a commercial basis with a view to the realisation of profits, then the value of such trees contained in the conveyance or lease is exempt from duty provided that the instrument contains a certificate to the effect that the trees are growing on a substantial part of the land conveyed or leased. [*SDCA 1999, s 95*] The land remains liable to duty.

(*k*) **Petroleum and mineral licences and leases.** Any licence or lease granted under *Petroleum and Other Minerals Development Act 1960 ss 8, 9, 13 or 19* or transfer of all or any interest therein is exempt from duty. [*SDCA 1999, s 104*]

(*l*) **Surrender of a Lease.** A lease made in consideration for the surrender or abandonment of an existing lease is exempt. [*SDCA 1999, s 52(1)*].

(*m*) **Mere Conveyance.** A mere conveyance other than one relating to any immovable property situate within the State, or right or interest therein, or stock or share of a company registered in the State shall be exempt from duty (*SDCA 1999, Sch 1*).

(*n*) Letters of Allotment. Any instrument which renounces or releases any letter of allotment to shares in an unquoted company shall be liable to duty as if it were an instrument renouncing or releasing any letter of allotment to share in a quoted company pursuant to *SDCA 1999, Sch 1*. [*Sch 1 (SDCA 1999, s 63)*]

(*o*) **Financial Services Agreements.** The following instruments are exempt from duty provided that they do not relate to any immovable property or stocks or shares situate within the State or any rights or interests therein:

(i) a debt factoring agreement undertaken in the ordinary course of business. Such an agreement is defined as the transfer, or agreement to transfer, a debt or part thereof. [*SDCA 1999, s 90(1)*] Where the debt is secured over immovable property situate within the State, for example, a debt factoring agreement made by a builder, then the exemption is lost. Debt factoring agreements include discounting of invoices;

(ii) a swap agreement, such as interest or currency swaps are exempt from duty. A swap agreement is one where the parties agree to exchange either the payment or repayment of monies in respect of which the parties have rights and obligations. [*SDCA 1999, s 90(1)*];

(iii) a forward agreement is an agreement to buy or sell commodities, currency, money payable or receivable, stocks or marketable securities at a specified future date where the price, exchange rate, interest or share value is fixed or determinable at the time of execution of the agreement. Also covered are agreements which alter the parties rights by reference to certain movements in a specified stock exchange index or indices. [*SDCA 1999, s 90(1)*];

(iv) a financial futures agreement, which is the forward agreement outlined above and which is currently dealt with and quoted on a recognised stock exchange or futures stock exchange is exempt;

(v) an option agreement is an agreement conferring a future right at one party's discretion to buy or sell, to or from another party, stocks and securities, commodities or currency, the right to receive or the liability to pay sums depending on the movements of a stock exchange index or indices, or to borrow or lend money at a rate of interest that is determined at the time of execution. Such agreement is exempt. [*SDCA 1999, s 90(1)*]

(*p*) **Loan Capital.** Any issue or transfer of loan capital of a company or body corporate, is exempt from stamp duty. [*SDCA 1999, s 85*] The definition of loan capital includes debenture stock, bonds or funded debt or any capital raised which has the form of borrowed money. [*SDCA 1999, s 85(1)*] The exemption for loan capital has been amended to remove the requirement that the loan capital is redeemable in 30 years and provides that the exemption will not apply if the transfer is linked wholly or partly and directly or indirectly to an equity index. [*FA 2008*]

(*q*)   **Abolished Heads of Charge.** The following heads of charge have been amended to abolish the fixed duty of €12.50 and the requirement for a certificate to be included in the instrument in the absence of the fixed duty being paid [*FA 2007*]:

   (i)   'Conveyance or Transfer of any kind not already described in the First Schedule',

   (ii)   'Exchange – instruments effecting',

   (iii)   'Release or Renunciation of any property, or of any right or interest in any property, and

   (iv)   'Surrender of any property, or of any right or interest in any property'.

(*r*)   **Wills.** Testamentary instruments are exempt from stamp duty. [*SDCA 1999, s 113(c)*]

(*s*)   **Mortgages.** Instruments chargeable under the mortgage, bond, covenant debenture head where the amount secured is less than €254,000 are exempt from duty. [*SDCA 1999, s 58*] The 'Mortgage Head of Charge' has been abolished in respect of instruments executed on or after 7 December 2006. [*FA 2007*]

(*t*)   **Dublin Docklands Authority.** Stamp duty is exempt on any instrument whereby any land, easement, wayleave, water right or any other right is acquired by Dublin Docklands Development Authority [*SDCA 1999, s 99*].

(*u*)   **Intellectual Property.** Stamp duty is not chargeable on the sale, transfer, or other disposition of intellectual property as defined under *SDCA 1999, s 101*. This section provides an unexhaustive list of intellectual property that falls within this exemption. All goodwill associated with the intellectual property is also exempted under the section. [*SDCA 1999, s 101*]

(*v*)   **Assignment of Housing Authority Mortgages.** Stamp duty is not chargeable where a housing authority transfers, sells or assigns its mortgages to a designated body. [*SDCA 1999, s 105*] The transfer of such securities by a designated body is also exempt. An exemption from stamp duty has been introduced for transactions by housing authorities and the Affordable Homes Partnership. Stamp duty shall not be chargeable on any instrument giving effect to the conveyance, transfer or lease of a house, building or land to a housing authority. The section applies to instruments entered into on or after 1 April 2011. *[FA 2011, s 64]*

(*w*)   **Memorandum and Articles of Association.** With effect from 15 May 1996 there is no longer a requirement to have the memorandum and articles of association stamped as if it were a deed *CA 1963, s 7 and 14* as amended by *FA 1996, s 112*).

(*x*)   **Farm consolidation relief.** *Finance Act 2007* introduced a new relief for instruments executed between 1 July 2007 and 30 June 2009 on the purchase of land effected for the purpose of consolidation. [*SDCA 1999, s 81C*] The relief has been extended for another two years until 30 June 2011 by *F(No 2)A 2008*. The relief has been extended to include purchases and sales of land within 18 months of each other irrespective of the order in which the purchase or sale takes place. [*FA 2008*] There are many conditions attaching to the relief including the requirement for a consolidation certificate from Teagasc.

(*y*) **Greenhouse gas emissions**. *Finance Act 2008* introduced a new exemption from stamp duty on the sale, transfer or other disposition of greenhouse gas emissions allowances.

(*z*) **De Minimis duty.** There is an exemption from the 1 per cent stamp duty on share transfer forms where the duty involved is less than €10. [*F(No 2)A 2008, s 80*]

(*zz*) **Unit Funds.** Exemption under SDCA 1999, s 88B(2) from stamp duty where a domestic fund issues units directly to a foreign fund. Transfers of assets within certain unit trusts are not subject to stamp duty under SDCA 1999, s 88E. *[FA 2010, s 138]*

LEVIES

42.11 Some duties are imposed as a matter of policy by specific statutory regulations. There is little to connect them and each is dealt with individually. They appear to be more a tax levy than a charge to stamp duty. However, as the levy is charged on a document that has to be produced and on which the duty payable is stamped, these charges are technical instances of stamp duty.

A levy of €2.50 per annum is imposed on cash cards that enable the holder to withdraw cash from ATMs. The rate for a card with a Laser facility, but no ATM facility, is €2.50 per annum. A card which has both an ATM and Laser facility combined now attracts duty of €5 per annum. Cash card accounts are those maintained by banks or financial institutions through which cash transactions undertaken by a cash card will be processed. The duty only applies on those accounts where the holder has an address within the State. The rates applicable are those imposed by the *F(No 2)A 2008*.

The Act also provides that the preliminary duty in respect of ATM, Debit and Combined Cards due on 15 December 2008 in respect of the year 2008 will be based on 40 per cent of the liability for such cards for the year 2007. The preliminary duty for the year 2009 and subsequent years will remain at 80 per cent of the liability for the previous year. [*F(No 2)A 2008, s 85*]

The duty on Bills of Exchange is increased from €0.30 to €0.50 for Bills drawn on or after 15 October 2008. In the case of cheques, the increase applies to cheques supplied by financial institutions to customers on or after 15 October 2008. [*F(No 2A 2008, s 86*]

Stamp duty is levied on certain life assurance policies under *SDCA 1999, s 124B*. This section has been amended to exclude pensions and reinsurance premiums. The due date for payment of the levy by insurance provider has also been brought forward. [*FA 2010, s 139*]

The levy imposed on health insurers has been increased. The increased levy applies to all renewals and new contracts entered into on or after 1 January 2010. The increases are as follows:

(*a*)　Persons under the age of 18 – €55

(*b*)   Persons over the age of 10 – €185

[*FA 2010, s 140*]

The due dates for payment of the Health Insurance Levy have been brought forward. The increased levy applies to all renewals and new contracts entered into from 1 January 2011, at the rate of €66 for each insured person aged less than 18 years and €205 for each insured person aged 18 years or over. *[FA 2011, s 65]*

Pension Levy

42.12 *Finance (No 2) Act 2011, s 4* inserts a new *Stamp Duties Consolidation Act 1999, s 125B* which imposes an annual stamp duty of 0.6% on the market value of assets under management in pension schemes approved by the Revenue Commissioners under Irish tax legislation. The schemes affected are Retirement Benefit Schemes (ie, Occupational Pension Schemes), Retirement Annuity Contracts and Personal Retirement Savings Accounts (other than what are known as vested PRSAs). The value of the assets subject to the levy in respect of each year, is the market value of the assets on the date of publication of the Finance (No 2) Bill 2011 (ie 19 May 2011) in respect of the year 2011 and on 1 January in each of the years 2012, 2013 and 2014 or, where scheme accounts are prepared, on the last date of the accounting period ending in the 12 month period preceding those valuation dates. The levy will apply for a period of four years (2011 to 2014) and is payable twice yearly at the rate of 0.3% on each due date.

Chargeable persons will be required to deliver a statement on each payment date setting out the chargeable amount and the stamp duty payable. The levy will not apply to the assets of occupational pension schemes in respect of employees whose employment is or was wholly exercised outside the State. In other words, the levy will not apply to the extent that a scheme is intended to provide retirement benefits outside the State. In addition, it will not apply where the trustees of a scheme have passed a resolution to wind-up the scheme and where the business in respect of which the scheme was established is insolvent.

Provision is made to allow pension scheme trustees or administrators the option of adjusting the benefits payable under a pension scheme, on foot of payment of the duty. The chargeable persons for the levy are trustees of pension schemes and the insurers and administrators having the management of the assets of pension schemes.

FINANCE ACT 2007, s 110

42.13 The *Finance Act 2007, s 110* introduced legislation to counteract schemes where there was perceived abuse in relation to the structuring of transactions to avoid a charge to stamp duty. The legislation is targeted at transactions specifically in relation to the development of land.. The legislation is subject to a Ministerial Order which has yet to be made but remain an ongoing threat as the provisions could be potentially be signed in at any stage. This section was repealed in its entirety by *FA(No 2)A 2008, s 81* and reinstated with the same charging provisions, but subject to certain exemptions being made to those charging provisions. The exemptions relate to certain transactions involving public private partnership arrangements and certain incentive schemes for capital allowances purposes. [*FA (No 2)A 2008, s 81*] It is important to note that the new section is still subject to a Commencement Order. The Minister has refused to clarify whether the provisions are intended to be retrospective. The changes relate to development land and specifically aim to close off mechanisms that developers have been using to avoid a charge to stamp duty. The amendments provide the following:

(*a*)   Any contract or agreement in respect of the sale of land or an interest in land that is entered into and more than 25 per cent of the total consideration has passed under that agreement, will itself become stampable where no conveyance or transfer of the land is presented for stamping within 30 days of the first such time [undefined] at which a conveyance or transfer, (made in conformity with the contract or agreement and executed by the parties) should have been taken – (effectively closing off 'resting on contract');

(*b*)   Where the holder of land in the State enters an agreement with another person whereby that person or a nominee is entitled to enter the land to carry out the development of the land and receives a payment amounting to greater than 25 per cent of the market value of the land, then within 30 days the agreement will become chargeable to stamp duty – (effectively closing off 'licence schemes'); and

(*c*)   An agreement for lease or a lease exceeding a term of 35 years and where 25 per cent or more of the consideration has been paid, will be charged with the same duty as it were an actual lease made for the term and consideration set out in the agreement.

These new rules are subject to the passing of a Ministerial Order and it is important to note that the proposed changes do not come into effect immediately but 'on such day or days as the Minister for Finance may ... appoint'. The Minister may, by Ministerial Order, appoint different days for the different provisions.

43 Finance Act 2011 – Summary of Provisions

(Enacted 6 February 2011)

TAXATION MATTERS

43.1

s 1   **Interpretation.**

s 2   **Income Tax Levy.** *TCA 1997, Pt 18A*. Abolition of the Income Levy as of 1st January 2011 and for subsequent years of assessment. See **2.2** 'Income Tax Levy'.

s 3   **Universal Social Charge.** Introduction of a new universal charge in place of the income levy and the health levy. See **2.2** 'Income Tax Levy' and **41.2** 'Health Contributions and Universal Social Charge'.

s 4   **Amendment to *TCA 1997, s 15* (Rate of Charge).** See **2.5** 'Allowances, Credits and Rates for Income Tax'.

s 5   **Amendment of *TCA 1997, s 188* (Age Exemption Limit).** The age exemption limit was reduced for both single and married persons. See **2.9** 'Age Exemption'.

s 6   **Personal Tax Credits.** Various credits were reduced for 2011 and subsequent years. Amendments to the treatment of certain qualifying health expenses for tax relief purposes. See **2.9**, **2.12**, **2.13**, **2.14**, **2.15**, **2.19**, **2.21**, **2.22**, **2.23**. 'Allowances, credits and rates'.

s 7   **Benefit in Kind.** The exception for the provision of childcare services by an employer and the payment of subscription fees as taxable benefits in kind has been removed. See **34.3** – 'Directors and Employees'.

s 8   **Ex-Gratia Lump Sum Payments.** Amendment to *TCA 1997, s 201*. See **34.12** 'Allowances, Credits and Rates'.

s 9   **Amendment to *TCA 1997, s 470B* (age-related tax credit for health insurance).** Increase in the age related credit and abolishing of the credit for individuals over the age of 50. See **2.23** 'Health Expenses'.

s 10   **Employment related Share Schemes.** Amendments to both approved profit sharing schemes and share option schemes and abolition of relief on new shares purchased on issue. See **35.5**, **35.6** and **35.9** 'Schedule E – Emoluments'.

s 11   **Amendment to *TCA 1997, s 248*.** Relief for interest on borrowings by an individual to acquire shares in or lend to a trading company is phased out and abolished for loans made after 7 December 2010. See **20.3** 'Interest Payable'.

s 12   **Trade Union Subscriptions.** Abolishment of tax relief for trade union subscriptions for the tax year 2011 and subsequent tax years. See **2.29**. 'Allowances, Credits and Rates'.

s 13   **Relief for energy efficiency expenditure on premises in the State.** Relief from income tax at the standard rate for an individual who is not the landlord of a residential premises in the State. See **2.44** 'Allowances, Credits and Rates for Income Tax'

s 14   **Rent Relief.** Amendment to *TCA 1997, s 473* Rent relief abolished for leases entered into on or after 7 December 2010 with a seven-year phasing out of the relief for existing leases. See amendment to list of qualifications under this section. See **18.9** 'Farming'.

s 15   **Relief for third level education fees.** Amendment to *TCA 1997, s 473A*. Reduction in the credit available. See **2.34** 'Allowances, Credits and Rates for Income Tax'.

s 16   **Taxation of airline crew.** Amendment to *TCA 1997, Pt 5 Ch 5*. Employment income for airline crew is taxable under Schedule E where the airline for which they are employees has its effective management in the State. See **34.1** 'Schedule E and Emoluments'.

s 17   **Artist's Exemption.** Amendment to *TCA 1997, s 195*. Relief on works of artistic merit is now capped at €40,000 for the year 2011 and subsequent years. See **16.27** 'Exempt Income and Special Savings Schemes'.

s 18   **Amendment to *TCA 1997, Sch 13*.** Updates the list of bodies obliged to operate professional services withholding tax.

s 19   **Retirement benefits.** Changes are made to the tax treatment of pension products and approved retirement funds. See **2.24** and **2.25** 'Allowances, Credits and Rates'.

s 20   **Amendment of *TCA 1997, s 531*** (payments to subcontractors in certain industries). Makes administrative changes to the scheme of Relevant Contracts Tax. See **13.8** 'Deduction of Tax at Source'.

s 21   **Anti-avoidance.** False claims for tax credits or reliefs. New *TCA 1997, s 960Q* which imposes sanctions on a taxpayer for falsely claiming reliefs or credits. Penalty introduced of €3,000. See **215.1** 'Payment of Tax'.

s 22   **Cesser of Financial Resolutions.** Deals with various cessers of financial resolutions in the Taxes Acts as of from the passing of the Finance Act 2011 (6 February 2011).

s 23   **Accelerated Capital Allowances.** Restrictions introduced for type of income accelerated allowances may be set against and the period for which unused losses can be carried forward. See **8.5** and **8.12** 'Capital Allowances'.

s 24   **Section 23 Relief.** Amendment to *TCA 1997, s 372AP*. There were a number of restrictions imposed on Section 23 type relief properties. The provisions are subject to a Ministerial Order. See **33.11**, **33.14**, **33.15** and **33.16** 'Property Income – Case V'.

s 25   **Farm Stock Relief.** Amendment of *TCA 1997, s 666*. Relief has been extended to 31 December 2012. See **18.9** 'Farming'.

s 26   **Patent Relief s.** *TCA 1997, ss 141 and 234*. Termination of relief for qualifying patent income and distributions from a company relating to patent income. See **16.15** 'Exempt Income and Special Savings Schemes'.

s 27   **Amendment to capital allowances for mining activities.** Abolition of investment relief and capital allowances at a rate of 20% of new plant and machinery. See **8.7** 'Capital Allowances' and **24.6** 'Mining'.

s 28 **Amendment to *TCA 1997, s 817*.** Anti-avoidance provisions on the disposal of shares in a close company. Amendments to certain provisions. See **3.2** 'Anti-avoidance Legislation'.

s 29 **Close Companies.** Additional anti-avoidance provision introduced in relation to settlements by a close company. See **12.7** – 'Corporation Tax' and **36.5** 'Settlements'.

s 30 **Deposit Interest Retention Tax.** Increase in rate by two per cent. See **13.9** 'Deduction of Tax at Source'.

s 31 **Assets of overseas life assurance companies.** Increase in the tax rate on of tax applying to life assurance policies and investment funds by 2 percentage points. See **12.16** 'corporation tax'.

s 32 **Film Investment Relief.** *TCA 1997, s 481* – Relief extended to 31 December 2015. See **12.23** 'Corporation Tax'.

s 33 **Investment in Corporate Trade.** *TCA 1997, Pt 16*. Introduction of a new income tax relief for investment in corporate trades. See **21.14** 'Investment in Corporate Trades'.

s 34 **New start up Companies Relief.** The relief for start up companies has been extended to 31 December 2011. The relief has also been connected to employer's PRSI in an effort to encourage employment. See **12.28** 'Corporation Tax'.

s 35 **Foreign tax credit.** Amendment to ensure that trade charges cannot increase the amount of foreign tax credit. See **12.9** and **12.18** 'Corporation Tax'.

s 36 **Amendment to *TCA 1997, s 840*.** Ability of a deduction for interest on borrowings to purchase assets from a group company has been restricted. See 12.5 'Corporation Tax'.

s 37 **Interest on Borrowings.** *TCA 1997, s 247*. Amendment to interest on borrowings on loans applied in lending to or acquiring shares in other companies. See **12.9** 'Corporation Tax'.

s 38 **Energy Efficient Equipment – capital allowances.** The scheme for accelerated capital allowances has been extended to 31 December 2014. See **8.17** 'Capital Allowances'.

s 39 **National Co-operative Farm Relief Services.** Amendment to remove the availability of the relief after 1 January 2011. See **12.12** 'Corporation Tax'.

s 40 **Securitisation of assets.** *TCA 1997, s 110*. Extension to the definition of qualifying assets which can be acquired by a s 110 company to include (a) commodities and (b) plant and machinery which is subject to lease and (c) an extension of the application of the section to additional carbon offsets. See **12.22** 'Corporation Tax'.

s 41 **Research and Development.** Amendment to *TCA 1997, s 766*. See **12.9** 'Corporation Tax'.

s 55 **Value-added tax: interpretation.**

s 56 **Value-added tax: amendment of *VATA 1972 s 17*.** Mobile Traders. Increase of the period of occupation for reporting requirements from 7 days to 28 days. See **39.8** 'Value Added Tax'.

s 57   **Value-added tax: amendment of *VATA 1972, s 95*.** Transitional arrangements relating to deductibility for housing and burial plots sold by public authorities. Applies to sales on or after 1 July 2010.

s 58   **Value-added tax: amendment of *VATA 1972, s 115*.** Introduces new penalty regimes for various administration areas. See **39.15** 'Value Added Tax.

s 59   **Value-added tax: amendment of *VATA 1972*.** Amends sections 16, 59, 66 and 87 of the VAT Consolidation Act 2010 to extend the VAT reverse charge mechanism to the scrap metal sector.amendment to forced sale situations.

s 60   **Value-added tax: amendment of *VATA 1972*.** Various amendments to exempt bodies under the First Schedule. . See **39.6** 'Value Added Tax'.

s 61   **Amendment to *VATCA 2010*.** See **39.39** 'Value Added Tax'.

s 62   **Stamp duty: interpretation.**

s 63   **Abolishment of Property Reliefs.** *SDCA 1999*. A number of property based reliefs have been abolished under this section as of from 8 December 2010. See.**41.10** 'Stamp Duty'.

s 64   **Amendment to *SDCA 1999, s 106B*.** Introduction of an exemption from stamp duty on all property transactions by housing authorities and the Affordable Homes Partnership in respect of transactions on or after 1 April 2011. See **42.10** 'Stamp Duty'.

s 65   **Health Insurance Levy.** Amends *SDCA 1999, s 125A*. Increases the health insurance levy and takes effect on or after 1 January 2011. See **42.11** 'Stamp Duty'.

s 66   **Amendment to *SDCA 1999, s 106B*.** Introduction of new rates of stamp duty in respect of residential property only. See **42.9** 'Stamp Duty'.

s 67   **Capital acquisitions tax: interpretation.**

s 68   **Capital acquisitions tax: amendment of *CATCA 2003, ss 89(4)(a)(i), 102A(2)(c) and 104(3)*.** Certain reliefs affected. Agricultural relief, business property relief and CAT/CGT set off. See generally **Ch 7** 'Capital acquisitions tax'.

s 69   **Capital acquisitions tax: amendment of *CATCA 2003*.** Tax-free thresholds. See **7.4** 'Capital acquisitions tax'.

s 70   **Capital acquisitions tax: amendment of *CATCA 2003*.** Payment and return date brought forward. See **7.12** 'Capital acquisitions tax'.

s 71   **Interpretation (*TCA 1997*).** 'Interpretation'.

s 72   **Anti-Avoidance.** New provisions included in relation to disclosure obligations. See **3.1** 'Anti-Avoidance.

s 73   **Anti-Avoidance.** New start date for the provisions in relation to disclosure obligations. See **3.1** 'Anti-Avoidance.

s 74   **Amendment to *TCA 1997, s 1002*.** Attachment of debt to an employee. See **25.2** 'Payment of Tax'.

s 75 **Amendment of *TCA 1997, s 1078*.** Amendment which makes the destruction of computerised records an offence. See **28.3** 'Returns'.

s 76 **Amendment of *TCA 1997*.** Amendments to the tax defaulter publication list. See **1.8** 'Administration and General'.

s 77 **Amendment of *TCA 1997*.** Introduction of legislation protecting taxpayer confidentiality. See **1.18** 'Administration and General'.

s 78 **Collector-General.** Amendment to ensure that the Collector General doesn't have to issue physical receipts for tax paid.

s 79 **Miscellaneous amendments to *TCA 1997, s 960E*.** Allows tax to be paid in various different ways. See **25.1** 'Payment of Tax'.

s 80 **Miscellaneous amendments to *TCA 1997, s 25A*.** Government arrangements with government of other territories in relation to tax. See generally **Ch 15** 'Double Tax Relief'.

s 81 **Miscellaneous technical amendments.**

s 82 **Capital Services Redemption Account.** Fixes a new annuity for 30 years in respect of the estimated borrowing in 2011 for Voted Capital Services in relation to the Capital Services Redemption Account. It also amends the 2010 annuity in the light of the actual amount of capital borrowing in 2010.

s 83 **Care and management of taxes and duties.**

s 84 **Short title, construction and commencement.**

OTHER MATTERS

ss 42–54 **Customs and Excise.**

ss 77–111 **Solid Fuel Carbon Tax.**

44 Finance (No 2) Act 2011 – Summary of Provisions

(Enacted 22 June 2011)

TAXATION MATTERS – FINANCE ACT (NO 2) 2011

44.1

s 1   **Research and Development.** Amendment to TCA 1997, s 766B (limitation of tax credits to be paid under TCA 1997, s 766 or s 766A). See **12.9** 'Corporation Tax'

s 2   **Air travel Tax.** Amends Finance (No 2) Act 2008, s 55 to empower the Minister for Finance to appoint, by order, a day on or after where passenger departures would not be subject to tax.

s 3   **Amendment to the VAT Rate** provides for a second reduced VAT rate of 9%, in respect of certain goods and services, for the period 1 July 2011 to 31 December 2013. Thereafter the rate will revert to the rate of 13.5% currently applying to goods and services in VATCA 2010, Sch 3. See **39.3** and **39.4** 'Value-Added Tax'.

s 4   **Introduction of Pension Scheme Levy.** See **42.11** 'Stamp Duty' and **2.26** 'Allowances, Credits and Rates'.

s 5   **Care and management of taxes and duties.**.

s 6   **Short title, construction and commencement.**

Table of Cases

P

Q

R

Table of Statutory References

T

Index

This index is referenced to paragraph numbers. The entries printed in bold capitals are main subject headings in the text. Abbreviations used are:

ACT	= Advance corporation tax	DTR	= Double tax relief
CAT	= Capital acquisitions tax	IT	= Income tax
CGT	= Capital gains tax	RPT	= Residential property tax
CPT	= Corporation profits tax	UK	= United Kingdom
CT	= Corporation tax	VAT	= Value-added tax